T0314163

Microeconomic Foundations II

Microeconomic Foundations II

Imperfect Competition, Information, and Strategic Interaction

David M. Kreps

PRINCETON UNIVERSITY PRESS | PRINCETON AND OXFORD

Copyright © 2023 by Princeton University Press

Princeton University Press is committed to the protection of copyright and
the intellectual property our authors entrust to us. Copyright promotes the
progress and integrity of knowledge. Thank you for supporting free speech
and the global exchange of ideas by purchasing an authorized edition of this
book. If you wish to reproduce or distribute any part of it in any form, please
obtain permission.

Requests for permission to reproduce material from this
work should be sent to permissions@press.princeton.edu

Published by Princeton University Press,
41 William Street, Princeton, New Jersey 08540
99 Banbury Road, Oxford OX2 6JX
press.princeton.edu

All rights reserved

ISBN 978-0-691-25014-4
ISBN (e-book) 978-0-691-25013-7
British Library Cataloging-in-Publication Data is available

Editorial: Joe Jackson, Josh Drake, and Whitney Rauenhorst
Production Editorial: Mark Bellis
Production: Danielle Amatucci
Publicity: Kate Hensley
Copyeditor: Cyd Westmoreland

This book has been composed in Helvetica, Palatino, and Computer Modern
typefaces.

The publisher would like to acknowledge the author of this volume for providing the print-ready files from which this book was published. This book
has been composed using TeXtures, an implementation of Donald Knuth's TeX.
Figures were drawn using Adobe Illustrator. The author thanks Westchester
Publishing Services for technical assistance.

Printed on acid-free paper. ∞

Printed in the United States of America

10 9 8 7 6 5 4 3 2 1

In memory of Hugo F. Sonnenschein

Contents

Preface

This is the second volume of what I hope will someday be a three-volume introduction to the foundations of microeconomics, intended as a textbook for first-year graduate students.

It is common for the Preface to explain the author's purpose and philosophy in writing the book that follows. In this case, however, I have elected to put this sort of material in the first chapter in this volume, Chapter 17. All readers are urged to read Chapter 17 before diving into the "meat" of the book. For this Preface, I say, very simply, that the purpose of this volume is to provide a first-year graduate student in economics with a basic understanding of the models and methods that have dominated microeconomic theory since the 1970s.

For instructors who may be contemplating adopting this volume, a few further words of warning and then advice seem appropriate. (For students: It won't hurt for you to read these warnings and words of advice.)

First, my writing style—to which the adjective "chatty" seems to be irrevocably attached—is intentional. This is a textbook, not a reference book. It is intended to be read, not to be used to look up results. Instructors are, of course, charged with constructing an in-class narrative for their students. I do not intend to displace your narrative with my own, but instead to provide a second perspective. For students starting in a Ph.D. program in economics that will lead to a career as an economist, microeconomics is one of the most important foundations of their study, research, and eventual career. Hearing different perspectives on the subject is surely a worthwhile investment. At the Stanford Graduate School of Business, generations of students have been blessed to have this material taught to them by my colleague Robert Wilson. He sees many things differently from how I see them, and I am pleased to have offered this material as a "second opinion." I hope it serves a similar purpose for you.

Second, it will quickly become apparent that I have very strong opinions about what theory can tell you and what it cannot. I offer my own opinions freely and without apology. There are classic papers that I cover about which I ask the leading question: It may be beautiful theory, but is it good economics? And, then, my answer is a clear: I don't think so. (You'll have to read the book to see which classics get this back of the hand from me. And so as not to offend various colleagues too greatly: Progress is the product of many different types of accomplishment. Progress can come from understanding why a beautiful piece of theory is flawed in terms of what it teaches us about the real world.) If my opinions about specific pieces offend you, let your students know it, and let them know why I'm wrong.

Third and perhaps most important: I set out to create one volume for each of the ten-week, twenty-session academic quarters of Stanford University. Volume I comes close; I taught it in ten weeks with reasonable success, typically omitting only one chapter (aggregation). With a few exceptions, Volume I was designed to be one session per chapter; a few chapters took two sessions.

In this volume, there are fewer chapters, but they are generally longer. With the possible exception of Chapter 18, this is a two-session-per-chapter book. Because there are fewer chapters, I still believe that twenty sessions should be sufficient to cover the text. Put it this way: The text portion of Volume I is 436 pages long. At 486 pages, the text portion of this volume is not that much longer. This volume contains significantly more figures. And the ratio of chat to math in this volume is higher than in Volume I. Students who come from a math background may decide, therefore, that this book more difficult, but, I hope and expect, the median student will feel otherwise.

However: As part of your course, you may be obligated to spend a considerable amount of time on the appendices, which is where noncooperative game theory happens. My attitude toward noncooperative game theory—it is a method of analysis and not, in itself, economics—is made clear in Chapter 17. But my understanding is that, in many institutions, it is considered part of the curriculum to teach students the game theory needed for the topics covered here. If that applies to you, even a fifteen-week, thirty-session course is likely to be very tight. You will need to make some choices.

And for students or individuals who are using this volume for self-study: The topics covered in this volume are very dense with nuance. There is rarely a single "story," but a number of stories that compete for attention. Chapter 17 discusses this at greater length. But, for now, understand that the "story" of each chapter is not as linear or straightforward as in Volume I. Most if not all chapters take up variations and extensions of the chapter's basic ideas. You must be patient, and being patient means that reading any chapter in one go is less than optimal. In most chapters, I try to give a relatively simple initial story; that's plenty for your first session. Understand the basic story, think about it, and then move on to the variations. In Chapter 17, I describe this volume as a collection of *études*. Following that analogy, most chapters open with a simple set of "finger exercises," which are then made increasingly complicated. When you have a firm grasp on the basic story of a chapter, then you can move on to see how it is made more complex. (That said, a few chapters—Chapter 26 on Mechanism Design in particular—consist of one difficult exercise after another.)

I am free with opinions in both the chapters and the appendices. Some of those opinions are controversial among economists. In particular, your instructor may think that I'm wrong. You should hear all sides, and then make up you own mind.

And, I say it several times in Chapter 17, but I repeat it here: You can't learn this stuff by reading it only. You must *do* it, which means doing the problems at the end of each chapter, excluding Chapter 17. Try the problems—I'll give the unrealistic advice that you should try *all* of them—and...

The *Online Supplement*

... if you get stuck trying to solve one, or if you are just curious about the answer to any problem, the solutions to all the problems can be found in an *Online Supplement*, which is available (for free) on the internet at press.princeton.edu/online-supplement/microfoundations-II.

The *Online Supplement* contains more than solutions to the problems.

- For each chapter, there is an overview and an annotated outline of the contents of the chapter. I suspect that many readers will find it helpful, before starting a chapter, to go to the *Online Supplement* and read the overview and annotated outline, to learn what the chapter is about and how it is organized.

- For a few chapters, there is "bonus coverage" of models and topics that didn't make it into the main text.

- You will also find some "bonus coverage" that goes beyond what is in the book. For instance, a file called "Supplement to Appendix 12 & 13" provides some ideas about off-path beliefs and sequential rationality that differ from the mainstream theory of such things. As I write this, I hope to add some chapters that cover topics not covered in the book itself.

- Ocassionally, some Excel spreadsheets are present, for you to download and with which you can explore ideas presented in the text.

- And, finally: My experience both reading and writing books of this length and complexity is that typographical errors and, occasionally, worse errors, make it past editing. The *Online Supplement* contains an item called *Errata*, which lists all typos (and worse errors) that are discovered after publication. Prior to reading any chapter, I strongly advise that you consult the *Errata*, to fix errors that have been found. I hope to keep the list of *Errata* current, so if you find any error not listed there, please email me at kreps@stanford.edu.

I urge you to find the *Online Supplement* and read the file "Read Me First" before tackling the book.

Conventions

Notational conventions carry over from Volume I: In each chapter, propositions, definitions, lemmas, and so forth are numbered sequentially. That is, if the first such item in Chapter 20 is a definition, it is Definition 20.1; if the second such item in Chapter 20 is a proposition, it is Proposition 20.2. Figures in a chapter are also numbered sequentially, but in a different list. So the first figure in Chapter 20 is Figure 20.1. Problems are numbered sequentially in still another list, equations in still another list, and tables in yet another.

The use of third-person singular pronouns in books such as this has become an exercise in political correctness. I use *she*, *her*, and *hers* when only one actor is involved; the second actor is *he*, *him*, and *his*. Adhering to the demands of political correctness , when there are two actors and a logical status ordering, *she* has higher status, as in: *she is the employer, he is the employee.* With a tip of the hat to Robert Aumann, in many places, she is Alice and he is Bob.

Having paid my dues to political correctness as outlined in the previous paragraph, the dollar is the standard currency in this book.

Acknowledgments

I am blessed with many generous colleagues, who have been of enormous help as I was writing this volume. I was a participant in the development of some of these ideas, but (in my estimation) I began with considerable expertise in perhaps 30% of what is covered in the text, with some knowledge of another 30%, and as a complete ignoramus on the remaining 40%. (My percentage of knowledge concerning the appendices was somewhat better.) So, if nothing else, writing this book has been very educational for me. When I was lost or confused or just unsure what to do, I sent out emails, and my wonderful colleagues responded with advice, suggestions, and always good grace.

I would point, in particular, to Andy Skrzypacz and Joel Sobel as two colleagues whose generosity in this regard was...simply unbelievable. In addition, and with heartfelt gratitude, I acknowledge the generous help of Dilip Abreu, Mohammad Akbapour, Pierpaolo Battigalli, Jeremy Bulow, Vince Crawford, Eddie Dekel, Yossi Feinberg, Drew Fudenberg, Robert Gibbons, Jerry Green, Ted Groves, Faruk Gul, John Hatfield, Bengt Holmstrom, Paul Klemperer, Jonathan Levin, Eric Maskin, Steve Matthews, Paul Milgrom, Roger Myerson, John Nachbar, Michael Ostrovsky, David Pearce, Phil Reny, John Roberts, Al Roth, Ariel Rubinstein, Ken Shotts, Marciano Siniscalchi, Ennio Stacchetti, Takuo Sugaya, and Robert Wilson. My apologies to individuals whose names I have inadvertently omitted. I also thank students at the Stanford Graduate School of Business who offered helpful comments and corrections; Bharat Chandar stands out in this regard.

The financial support of the Chi-fu Huang and Marina Chen Charitable Trust is gratefully acknowledged.

Many individuals at Princeton University Press contributed enormously in the preparation of this volume, not the least by dealing with a stubborn and opinionated author. In particular, I thank Senior Editor Joe Jackson, Editorial Director Eric Crahan, Assistant Editor Josh Drake, Editorial Assistant Whitney Rauerhorst, Associate Managing Editor Mark Bellis, Design Project Manager Wanda España, and especially copyeditor Cyd Westmoreland (among many others at PUP). Technical assistance from Westchester Publishing Services was extremely helpful. And, at Stanford, Barbara McCarthy and her team at Visual Services provided crucial advice and assistance in preparing my formated TeX files for publication.

In the course of my career, I have hero-worshipped two individuals for their intellect and also their humanity. Volume I was dedicated to the first of these, Kenneth J. Arrow. It is any honor and pleasure to be able to dedicate Volume II to the memory of my other professional hero, Hugo F. Sonnenschein.

Microeconomic Foundations II

Chapter Seventeen

Introduction to Volume II: Not a Symphony, but Ètudes

Readers of Volume I, *Choice and Competitive Markets*, may expect that this second volume will be similar in form and content. If you have such expectations, set them aside: This volume is utterly different from Volume I, and my first task is to explain why and what you should expect instead.

Volume I concerned (1) the basic models of choice by individual economic agents (consumers and firms), (2) more specifically, the utility-maximizing and profit-maximizing choices of those agents in *competitive* market environments, environments in which they have no influence over prices, and (3) how those choices are reconciled in a *general equilibrium*.

Three characteristics of the models of Volume I are noteworthy:

- To the extent that more than one economic agent is explicitly involved, agents collectively affect the opportunities of other agents only through market prices, and all agents act as if prices are unresponsive to what they themselves do. Therefore, given prices, no agent is (directly) concerned with the actions of any other agent.[1] Economic opportunities for each agent are limited to price-mediated, competitive markets.

- No agent has information about states of nature that another agent lacks. Agents are well informed.

- Each agent is fully capable of making optimal choices, given her objectives and the opportunities that circumstances present to her. Agents are cognizant of all relevant uncertainty, even if they lack information that others possess, and they anticipate accurately what will transpire in every possible future contingency. In a word, agents are *hyper-rational*.

Roughly speaking, in this volume, subtitled *Imperfect Competition, Information, and Strategic Interaction*, we study economic choices and interactions where the first two of these characteristics fail to hold. But in the models discussed in this volume, the third characteristic is maintained.

Volume I concludes with General Equilibrium Theory, in which (virtually) everything that came before comes together in one grand framework. In a sense, Volume I is like a symphony in which early movements provide themes, all of

---

[1] There are a few minor exceptions, particularly in the discussion of externalities and Lindahl equilibria in Chapter 15.

which are blended together in a grand final movement.[2]

No such grand synthesis is presented in this volume. Economic theorists have created more or less "general equilibrium models" in which many of the issues studied in this volume are unified. However, in my opinion, none of those unified theories captures everything of importance. Instead, I contend that economic models with imperfect competition, private information, and strategic interaction are best employed to model and analyze specific economic contexts and, in so doing, to gain insight into real-world contexts. The terms *partial equilibrium* or *small-world model* are appropriate: A particular relatively isolated piece of the economic environment is identified, modeled, and analyzed, so that (one hopes) insight is gained into that piece of the environment.

Franklin Fisher (1989), in his cri de cœur "Games Economists Play: A Noncooperative View," distinguishes between *generalizing theory* and *exemplifying theory*. Quoting him (p.117), "Generalizing theory proceeds from wide assumptions to inevitable consequences. It speaks in terms of what must happen, given the background circumstances." Fisher's first example of generalizing theory is General Equilibrium and the First and Second Theorems of Welfare Economics. In contrast (and again quoting from p.117), "Exemplifying theory does not tell us what *must* happen. Rather it tells us what *can* happen. In a good exemplifying-theory paper, the model is stripped bare, with specializing assumptions made so that one can concentrate on the phenomena at issue."

I prefer the term *exemplifying modeling* to Fisher's *exemplifying theory*. And I think that Fisher credits the generality of General Equilibrium too much: How "general," in the sense of being general conditions of real-life economic systems, are the assumptions that all markets are perfectly competitive, or all actors have access to the same information, or (in the sense of Chapter 16 in Volume I) all actors have perfect contingent foresight concerning future equilibrium prices? But setting those quibbles aside, I agree wholeheartedly with Fisher on this distinction. Theories in microeconomics that involve imperfect competition, private information, and strategic interaction are exemplifying: They employ models simple enough to provide insight into what *might* take place in a specific context.

This leads to Fisher's complaint about exemplifying theory: Such models settle nothing, because their conclusions derive from their assumptions and, just as much, from what the model builder leaves *out* of the model. Models can be shaped and tweaked to get virtually any conclusion the model builder desires; skeptics use the term *reverse engineering* to describe the practice of beginning with a desired conclusion and then creating a model from which that conclusion emerges.

So, how are the fruits of exemplifying modeling to be judged? Two types of tests can be employed. The first involves the intuitive appeal of the model: Do the assumptions on which the model was built make sense? Does the logic that leads from assumptions to conclusions seem sensible? What does the model ignore? And there is the possibility of empirical testing: Which predictions can be made, and are

---

[2]   Experts in classical music will observe that I am stretching things in this analogy, for which I apologize.

those predictions falsified when investigated in a sufficiently rich and varied set of circumstances?

What's in this volume? Tools of this trade

As a practicing economist and, in particular, as a practicing microeconomist, the odds are good that you will engage in exemplifying modeling. To help understand a particular economic phenomenon of interest, you may create and analyze a structured model of it. And even if you aren't directly in the model–creation business, you will need to understand such models. Because interesting economic phenomena often involve imperfect competition, private information, and (dynamic) strategic interactions, the models with which you must deal will probably possess some of these features. To define these terms:

- Agents do not necessarily take prices (when there are prices) as given. Agents may set prices, either unilaterally or as the result of a process of interaction with others. As far as price-and-market-mediated interactions go, this is *imperfect competition.*

- Agents may possess *information* that others lack. This can be information about the underlying state of nature, and it can be information about actions taken by themselves or others.

- When a specific agent's actions affect directly the choices and/or outcomes available to other agents—so that agents are concerned with what other specific agents do—we have a situation with *strategic interaction.* And when we add the modifier *dynamic*, we add the idea that agents may act and react to the actions taken by other agents. Indeed, in some cases, the economic essence is that agents interact repeatedly, with opportunities to react to the earlier actions of others.

Over the years, economists have developed paradigmatic models of these features, such as Akerlof's (1970) market for lemons, Spence's (1974) model of job-market signaling, and Green and Porter's (1984) model of collusion with imperfect price information. It is unlikely that one of these paradigmatic models will fit perfectly the context you are trying to understand, but these paradigms provide the techniques and basic ideas you will use in building your own model (or that are used to build a model that you wish to understand).

This describes the basic nature of Volume II: It is a book of *ètudes*, models on which you learn and practice the techniques that go into the construction of models fitted to the specific contexts and phenomena in which you will be interested.

The organization of these ètudes creates a dilemma. On one hand, the different models can be organized contextually: We might have, say, a chapter on oligopoly, which would include models from the classic work of Cournot and Bertrand, through to Green and Porter's model of collusion in repeated interactions with noisy prices. A separate chapter on auctions would deal with private-values and then common-value auctions.

Alternatively, we could organize the models based on the underlying mode of analysis. Start with models of static, one-shot interactions, with no private information, including the classic models of oligopoly. Move on to, say, models in which one party acts and a second (or several) others respond, such as von Stackelberg competition or the classic principal–agent model. At some point, models of dynamic interactions with an infinite horizon are considered, and simple models of oligopolistic collusion are provided. At another point, private information is explored, and (say) models of entry deterrence are discussed.

The problem with the first method is that virtually any contextual topic, covered completely, requires the full gamut of techniques, from basic static interactions to complex, multi-period interactions with private information that is strategically revealed and/or hidden. The problem with the second method is that the discussion will jump from contextual topic to contextual topic. Neither option is attractive.

In this volume, I present things in a hybrid fashion. The first five chapters gradually introduce the tools of modeling and analysis: Chapter 18 looks at situations that can be modeled with straightforward strategic-form games, in which the participants are assumed to act once, simultaneously and independently. Chapter 19 concerns situations modeled by simple action–reaction games: One party "sets the rules," and the other parties respond. Chapter 20 introduces incomplete information and beliefs-based equilibria. And Chapters 21 and 22 introduce the complexities of dynamics.

However, these chapters are written contextually. Chapter 18 concerns the classic models of oligopolistic competition—those of Cournot and Bertrand. Chapter 19 concerns moral hazard and the basic principal–agent model. Chapter 20 is about adverse selection, screening, and signaling. Chapter 21 introduces dynamics in the context of the Coase Conjecture; and Chapter 22 concerns repeated play, reciprocity, and reputation. The final four chapters are then contextual: Bilateral bargaining in Chapter 23, auctions in Chapter 24, matching markets in Chapter 25, and mechanism design in Chapter 26.

By organizing things in this fashion, I have tried to make this a book about economics, where game theory is the main tool of analysis, and more complex tools are introduced one by one. It is a text on economics using game theory, not game theory illustrated by economics.

"Foundations" has a double meaning

The title of these volumes begins with *Microeconomic Foundations*. One meaning of "foundations" is that the topics covered are the building blocks out of which economists study microeconomic phenomena (and also some macroeconomic phenomena, when the macroeconomics has "microfoundations"). But, there is a second meaning: In selecting models and contexts to discuss, I favor the "classics," papers and books such as Akerlof's (1970) "The Market for 'Lemons'," Spence's (1974) "Market Signaling," Green and Porter's (1984)"Noncooperative Collusion under Imperfect Price Information," and Rubinstein's (1982) "Perfect Equilibrium in a Bargaining Model." As warranted by expositional ease, I simplify in places, and I modify details. But I strongly believe that your education as an economist should include knowledge of the seminal work on each subject.

There has been and continues to be a deluge of extensions, amendments, qual-ifications, and improvements to the classics, and in places, I provide some "next steps." My selection is based on my perception of whether the methods employed serve a pedagogical function and on personal familiarity. Personal familiarity in-troduces a "home bias" in what is selected, for which I apologize.

However, this volume is not intended to be up to date or to cover all important work on any topic. Any specific topic covered in this volume can be—and often is—the basis of a full course that covers subsequent work. If you plan to work on any of these topics, you have a lot of reading to do to get up to date. What this volume tries to do—all I think a first textbook can do—is to provide you with a foundation (third meaning?) for your subsequent reading. So, in terms of up to date: Only a handful of papers that I cover are relatively recent, where my definition of "relatively recent" stretches to include any paper published in the current century.

This volume is limited in another way. Entire contextual topics are omitted; examples are networks, search, asset pricing with private infomation, and corporate finance. The ètudes presented in this volume are intended to strengthen your skills while covering some, but not all, important contextual areas. With your skills strengthened, you should (I hope) be able to absorb and then contribute to the literatures in contextual areas that are not covered here.

The bottom line is that this is a textbook of ètudes, not a reference book on the topics covered. It is, perhaps, a bit more than "Introductory (Finger) Exercises for the Economist," but it should be approached in the spirit of such books.

Assertions and proofs

In Volume I, I aimed to prove rigorously nearly every assertion. There were a few notable exceptions, and in places I only sketched the proof (often asking you to supply the missing steps as a problem, with the solution available online). That is no longer my objective in Volume II. Instead, my obective is to expose you to a variety of different models of economic phenomena and, to achieve the desired breadth, in places I tell you what is proved in the original source and send you to that source to see how the proof goes.

This approach comes with a warning: Journal articles are often not self-contained; they rely on previous work. Notation is not always consistent from article to article (or from this volume to the article I discuss). A skill you must develop is "reading backward"; I will cite a result from Article X and send you there to see the proof. Article X will use different notation from mine, and the proof there will rely on a result from Article Y, with still different notation. Volume I aimed to be self-contained, to spare you from having to make your way through this sort of maze. In this volume, to get the full picture, reading backward is sometimes required.

Noncooperative game theory

With few exceptions, the language of modeling and analysis in this volume is noncooperative game theory. This language isn't necessary, but it is reasonably well suited to formulating and then analyzing models of *some* economic phenomena that are of interest. And this way of doing business has become standard in the literature.

That said, this is *not* a textbook on noncooperative game theory, any more than Volume I was a textbook on real and convex analysis. To make your way through Volume I requires at least a good working knowledge of real and convex analysis; in precisely similar fashion, to make your way through this volume requires a good working knowledge of noncooperative game theory. In Volume I, the bare mathematical necessities were provided in a series of appendices; in similar fashion, appendices in this volume provide a review (blended with some strong opinions) of what you need to know about noncooperative game theory.

Game theory is *not* economics. It is a useful mathematical (abstract) language for building and studying models in economic contexts, as well as for building and studying models in at least some parts of political science, sociology, and social psychology. (I am told that it also can be fruitfully employed in various branches of the biological sciences and computer science, although I know little about this.) Game theory is useful because it has considerable virtues in deductive rigor, in understanding which assumptions lead to which conclusions, and in communicating ideas. But it has some very significant weaknesses. Perhaps its two greatest weaknesses are:

1. It relies on hyperrationality of economic agents. This is not new; in Chapter 16 (in Volume I), when we considered adaptations of general equilibrium to economies with time and uncertainty, the relevant equilibrium concept was an Equilibrium of Plans, Prices, and Price Expectations (EPPPE). In an EPPPE, consumers not only are assumed to know and react to prices of goods and securities being sold today; they are assumed to make their immediate consumption and security-purchase decisions based on accurate expectations about future equilibrium prices (contingent on states of nature). This, we observed, is asking a lot of the agents in the model. And, in some of the models discussed in this volume, we ask even more.

2. Game theory, as applied in the models encountered in this volume, begins with the specification of a game: a set of players; rules for how they can interact; and payoffs they receive, depending on how they interact. It is assumed that the game is *common knowledge* among the players: They know the rules; they believe that their rivals know the rules; they believe that their rivals believe that they know the rules; and so forth. The introduction of so-called *games of incomplete information* loosens this modeling straitjacket to some extent. But, to keep the models tractable (amenable to analysis), this loosening barely begins to reflect the confusion and ambiguity of real-life interactions.

In 1990, when the methods of noncooperative game theory were at the height of economic fashion, I gave a series of lectures on what I saw as the strengths and weaknesses of this mode of modeling and analysis as a tool of economics (Kreps 1990b). I'd say things a bit differently today: Given what has happened in the intervening years, I'm more skeptical about how these methods have been used.

One thing is worth saying right away: One cannot run an empirical test of "game theory." Game theory cannot be falsified empirically, any more than convex analysis can be. What can and should be tested to the extent possible—and what are certainly amenable to falsification—are the predictions that are derived from the contextual models discussed in this volume, models built with the language of noncooperative theory.

And, since empirical tests of applications of game theory are not always available or easy, practicitioners—that means you—must employ common sense. Go back to the first paragraph in this section, and the italicized *some* in the penultimate sentence. Not every economic phenomenon of interest is amenable to game-theoretic analysis, and not every game-theoretic model of some phenomenon passes the test of being sensible or capturing the most important aspects at work in the real world. As game theory is enlisted in this volume to model specific phenomena, it is essential that you ask and answer the subjective question: Does this model and analysis provide valuable insight into the phenomena? (In some cases, with models that are justifiably regarded as landmarks in the literature, I provide my own, negative opinion.) When and if you enlist these methods in your own research, answering this question—and being able to explain to others what those insights are—is even more important.

Concerning the appendices

In Volume I, the appendices succinctly outline the basic results in real and convex analysis that the text requires. A similar plan for this volume would mean appendices that outline basic concepts from and results in noncooperative game theory. Such appendices are provided, but they are longer and far more conversational than the appendices in Volume I. Controversies about the meaning of Berge's Theorem or the Separating Hyperplane Theorems may exist, but if they do, they surely aren't important to economists. But how one thinks about the application of game theory in economic modeling—when and why is it appropriate and/or useful in generating economic insight—is controversial; in the text but also in the appendices, I often wax philosophical on such issues. And, to be clear, the commentary that I provide is, in places, controversial among economists. Since I had personal involvement in the development of some of these concepts, I am certainly biased. You should seek out other perspectives to correct for my biases and to make up your own mind on these questions.

In particular, I present game theory as a tool for modeling and analyzing economic interactions. In so doing, I interpret game-theoretic concepts and constructs from what might be called an "intuitionist" perspective. Those parts of the game-theory literature that pursue foundational issues about game-theoretic concepts and constructs—in particular, what is known as *epistemic game theory*—might in contrast be said to take a "formalist" perspective. I do not mean to denigrate work that takes a more formalist perspective and, indeed, I suggest in the appendices sources that pursue these perspectives. But, for a textbook intended for first-year graduate students in economics, or even economics students who are taking a deeper look at the applications of game theory to economic issues, I believe the "intuitionist" perspective is appropriate. To put it plainly: Game theory, to be a fruitful tool of economic analysis, must support and not replace economic intuition. If you stipulate this view of the role game theory should play in economic analysis, I contend that the "intuitionist" perspective is the appropriate perspective to take.

Because the appendices are more than a collection of definitions and propositions in noncooperative game theory, readers who have not taken a course in game theory may conclude that the appendices can substitute for a full course on the subject. Instructors may conclude that they can use the appendices to "review" game theory as part of a course they teach, where "review" is very broadly interpreted. If one wants a nodding acquaintance with game-theoretic techniques, this may be so. However, the appendices are insufficient for anything approaching mastery of the material they cover. Game theory is a mathematical discipline, and to understand deeply any branch of mathematics, one needs to *do* the math, not just read about it. This requires problem sets, which the appendices do not contain. There are many excellent textbooks in game theory, and you will get more out of the economics in this volume if you consume one of them, preferably in a structured course or organized reading group on the subject, complete with working on the problems provided.

The craft of model building and analysis

A book of ètudes for, say, the piano, is intended primarily to promote the technique of performing or playing the piano, not to instruct the user in music composition. In this sense, the analogy between a book of piano ètudes and this volume breaks down. It is true (and I've emphasized here) that the point of this volume is for you to learn and practice the techniques of analysis that are nowadays applied in microeconomics. But as a practicing economist, you must both compose—build the model—and then perform, that is, provide a reasoned analysis of your model. I hope this volume helps you both to build and then analyze models. In this respect, what you read here provides examples of how this has been done by others. But reading about models and their analysis is insufficient; both are crafts that you learn best by doing. At the end of each chapter (after this one) are problems. Many have you complete proofs or arguments that are left undone in the text. Others—fewer perhaps—require you to construct variations on models in the text. In an ideal world, you would do them all. In the real world, you will get much more out of this volume if you do your fair share of these problems.

And, as you do the problems, please note: Solutions for all the problems in this volume are available in the *Online Supplement*, available online at the URL press.princeton.edu/online-supplement/microfoundations-II.

Chapter Eighteen

Cournot and Bertrand

Markets with a small number of sellers are quite common. Modeling the actions of those sellers—how they set prices and/or quantities, how they act and react to one another—has long challenged economists. Antoine Augustin Cournot, in 1838, and then Joseph Bertrand, in 1883, proposed simple equilibrium models in which the sellers act once, simultaneously and independently; models that come to very different (equilibrium) conclusions. These are early game-theoretic models in economics—perhaps the earliest—appearing long before game theory was formalized.

I doubt that there are many economic theorists today who view these two models as realistic on their own.[1] However, they are often used as parts of theoretical models that explore important issues; Chapter 22 provides examples. And, because they are so simple, they are a good place to begin to develop models of imperfect competition. Moreover, modeled as games, they present the simplest sort of equilibrium: Nash equilibrium in strategic-form games, and so they get us started with game-theoretic methods. So in this (relatively short) chapter, we begin with the basic Cournot and Bertrand models and then look at some variations.

18.1. Basic Cournot

Imagine that there are N suppliers of some perishable commodity. Because the good is a commodity, consumers are as happy with the product produced by one supplier as they are with product from any other. Because the good is perishable, it must be sold (and, presumably, consumed) within a short time following production. Imagine as well that production is done in distinct and remote locations, where each supplier n decides, on her own, an amount $x_n \geq 0$ to produce and

---

[1] That said, I was privileged to attend a seminar at which Franklin Fisher presented to a room full of theorists his 1989 paper "Games economists play" (see the discussion in Chapter 17). To illustrate the silly practices that ensue from the application of noncooperative game theory, Fisher described how a distinguished economist—whom, he said, he would not identify so as not to cause embarrassment—called upon to provide expert testimony on the welfare implications of a merger proposal, computed the levels of consumer surplus in the 3- and 4-firm Cournot equilibria, with the difference being this expert's estimate of the welfare costs if the merger were allowed to proceed. Later, Kenneth Arrow admitted to being that economist and convinced most people in the room that it wasn't that unreasonable a thing to do. Now, the audience was a room filled largely with theorists, but still, Arrow was quite convincing.

This is not to say that Arrow took the Cournot model seriously as theory. But faced with a practical question, he believed that this was the best answer he could give. And, indeed, while I doubt many economic theorists take the model seriously as theory, more practical-minded Industrial Organization (IO) economists do enlist the model, because (in their judgement) it is the best one can do as part of an exemplifying model.

bring to a central marketplace. Imagine that each supplier turns up on "market day," bearing the amount of output she chose to produce. And imagine that the price at which the goods can be sold is given by market clearing for a demand function $D : (0, \infty) \to [0, \infty)$, whose argument is the price p that clears the market and whose range gives the quantity X that is consumed. Assume that D is strictly decreasing where it is strictly positive and is continuous everywhere. That is, given the levels x_n, the equilibrium price is the price $p(x_1, \ldots, x_n)$ that solves

$$D\big(p(x_1, x_2, \ldots, x_N)\big) = x_1 + x_2 + \ldots + x_N.$$

(What if $\lim_{p \to 0} D(p)$ is finite? What if $\lim_{p \to \infty} D(p) > 0$? These technicalities must be dealt with, but for now, just go with the spirit of the model.) Of course, this means that two vectors of production levels $(x_1, \ldots, x_N)$ and $(x'_1, \ldots, x'_N)$ such that $x_1 + \ldots + x_N = x'_1 + \ldots + x'_N$ give the same price.

Is there any real-world situation that comes close to matching this imagined market situation? Probably the closest are local agricultural markets in rural districts for perishable foodstuffs. Farmers have some control over how much produce to bring on market day to the market town. At least for some foodstuffs, perishability is reasonable. The assumption that the goods are a commodity is not, as anyone who has watched buyers pick through, say, a bin of tomatoes, can attest. The assumption that suppliers (farmers) have complete ability to choose how much they bring to market is questionable. The assumption that a single price that clears the market given the amounts supplied is also questionable; unsold (perishable) goods at the end of the market day are often sold at distressed prices (although the goods that remain are often themselves of distressed quality, having been rejected by shoppers during the day).

So, at best, this imagined market is very much a simplification and idealization of anything real. And, to study what happens in this imagined market, still more assumptions are needed: How do suppliers decide on their levels of production x_n? Assume that each supplier n has a (continuous, strictly increasing) total-cost function $\mathbf{TC}_n(x)$ and a conjectured total quantity $X_{\neg n}$ that the other suppliers will supply. Supplier n (therefore) chooses x_n to maximize

$$P\big(x_n + X_{\neg n}\big)x_n - \mathbf{TC}(x_n),$$

taking $X_{\neg n}$ as given, where P is the inverse demand function, that is, the function that associates to each total quantity X the price $P(X) = p$ that satisfies $D(p) = X$.[2]

---

[2]   Is this function P well defined? Is it possible that for two prices p and p', $p \neq p'$, $D(p) = D(p') = X$, in which case, the definition of $P(X)$ is unclear? Yes, this can happen, but since we've assumed that D is strictly decreasing where it is strictly positive, this can only happen for $X = 0$. This and other technicalities will be discussed in Section 18.2. For now, continue to go with the spirit of the model.

A simple parameterization

Suppose that $N = 2$, $D(p) = A - p$ for $0 < p < A$ and $D(p) = 0$ for $p \geq A$, for a strictly positive constant A. Define $P : [0, \infty) \to [0, \infty)$ by $P(X) = A - X$ for $0 \leq X < A$ and $P(X) = 0$ for $X \geq A$. Both D and P are linear and strictly decreasing where they are strictly positive, namely on the set $(0, A)$. Assume that, for each firm, $\mathbf{TC}(x_n) = kx_n$, for $0 < k < A$; each supplier has (the same) constant and strictly positive marginal cost.

Think of the situation as a strategic-form game. The players are the two suppliers. Each has strategy set $\mathcal{X}_n = [0, \infty)$, where the strategy of each is the quantity x_n they bring to market. For each strategy profile (x_1, x_2), the corresponding price is

$$P(x_1, x_2) := \begin{cases} A - x_1 - x_2, & \text{if } x_1 + x_2 \leq A, \text{ and} \\ 0, & \text{if } x_1 + x_2 > A, \end{cases}$$

so the payoff function for firm n is $v_n(x_n, x_{\neg n}) = P(x_1, x_2)x_n - kx_n$, for $n = 1, 2$.[3]

It is straightforward to compute, for each value x_2, the best response x_1 by the first firm to x_2. Denoting this best response $x_1^*(x_2)$, it is

$$x_1^*(x_2) = \begin{cases} 0, & \text{if } A - x_2 \leq k, \text{ and} \\ [A - x_2 - k]/2, & \text{if } A - x_2 > k. \end{cases}$$

The best-response function for the second firm is symmetric, and the condition for the profile (x_1, x_2) to be a Nash equilibrium is that $x_1 = x_1^*(x_2)$, and simultaneously, $x_2 = x_2^*(x_1)$. That is, (assuming that $A > k$), the equilibrium quantities x_1^e and x_2^e must simultaneously satisfy

$$x_1^e = \frac{A - x_2^e - k}{2} \quad \text{and} \quad x_2^e = \frac{A - x_1^e - k}{2}, \tag{18.1}$$

which has the unique solution $x_1^e = x_2^e = [A - k]/3$, giving a price $p^e = P(x_1^e, x_2^e) = [A + 2k]/3$. For readers who remember their intermediate microeconomics, compare this to the monopoly price (if the two firms merged and set their total quantity to maximize the sum of their profits) of $[A + k]/2$, and compare it to the "perfect competition" outcome, at which the price is k (and quantities assigned between the two firms are indeterminate, as long as the total production level is $A - k$).

Since the simultaneous equations (18.1) have a unique solution, this is the unique pure-strategy Nash equilibrium for this game.[4] And there are no mixed-strategy equilibria, although the argument showing this is given on the next page.

---

[3] I use the terms *payoff* and *profit* to mean the same thing throughout this chapter. Therefore, insofar as a firm faces any uncertainty about its net profit, it is risk neutral in units of net profit. In this chapter, this modeling choice is not controversial, at least by the dictates of the "profit-maximizing-firm-model." However, please see the subsection *Modeling considerations* in Appendix 9, pages 489–90, for a general discussion of payoffs in game-theory-based models.

[4] In the literature, you may find the modifiers "Nash," "Cournot," and even "Cournot–Nash" attached to this equilibrium. See the Bibliographic Notes for more on this terminological mess.

However, uniqueness comes with a small caveat, which hides a headache that will reappear when we try to generalize from this simple parameterization. Suppose that $\mathbf{TC}(x_n) \equiv 0$; that is, the constant marginal cost k is 0. Then there is another pure-strategy Nash equilibrium: $x_1 = x_2 = A$. Of course, the price is then $A - 2A$, except that $P(X) = 0$ if $X > A$. So it really implies that the price is 0. Both firms make a lot of stuff, "sell" what they make for 0, and have costs of 0. This is a Nash equilibrium, because unilaterally making less won't help; as long as (say) supplier 1 makes A (or more—it is also a Nash equilibrium for both suppliers to produce any $x_n \geq A$), the price will be 0, and the profits of the second supplier are 0, no matter what the second supplier chooses to produce.

The headache arises because of the kink in the inverse-demand function P at $X = A$. Kinks may do all sorts of inconvenient things in more general parameterizations to an individual supplier's marginal-revenue function, fixing the total supply from its rivals; see the example in Section 18.2 depicted in Figure 18.1.

However, in this simple setting, as long as $k > 0$, the problem goes away: If the equilibrium price is 0—that is, if we reach the kink—both suppliers want to cut back on their production simply to save on total cost. In this simple parameterization, there is indeed a unique pure-strategy equilibrium.

Even more can be said about this game: It is dominance solvable. Since $x_2 \geq 0$, any choice of $x_1 > (A-k)/2$ is strictly dominated for the first supplier by $(A-k)/2$, and similarly for the second supplier. I assert that this is so, and indeed it is. But I haven't proved this assertion; that is left for you to do in Problem 18.1. (And please note that this requires that $k > 0$.)

But then, if we know (by strict dominance) that the second supplier will produce some quantity x_2 between 0 and $(A - k)/2$, for the first supplier, any amount less than $(A - k)/4$ is strictly dominated by producing $(A - k)/4$. (I'm assuming you are doing the simple math to verify that my assertions are true.) Since the same is true for the second supplier, after a second round of iterated strict dominance, each supplier is left with production levels between $(A - k)/4$ and $(A - k)/2$. But if the second supplier is sure to produce at least $(A - k)/4$, then $3(A - k)/8$ for the first supplier strictly dominates any larger quantity. And so forth; after countably many iterations, the only strategies left undominated for each are the quantities $(A-k)/3$. This, we've already confirmed, constitutes a Nash equilibrium.[5] Moreover, this shows that there can be no mixed-strategy equilibria: Any other pure strategy played with positive probability in a mixed-strategy equilibrium can be eliminated by iterated strict dominance.

And still more: Imagine the following "dynamic learning" model. The market in question meets every week, with the weeks numbered 1, 2, 3, ... In week 1, both suppliers bring to market some quantities x_1^1 and x_2^1, both between 0 and $A - k$. In week 2, supplier n, believing that her rival will persist with x_{-n}^1, brings her best response to this; that is, $x_n^2 = x_n^*(x_{-n}^1)$. And so forth. I assert (and you are asked to prove in Problem 18.2) that $\lim_{t \to \infty} x_n^t = (A - k)/3$. That is, if the two suppliers

---

[5] If you haven't read Appendix 9 and are wondering why I bothered to say that these two remaining strategies constitute a Nash equilibrium, do read Appendix 9.

anticipate in each period that their rival will repeat what he did in the previous period, their production levels will converge to the Cournot quantities.

Three or more oligopolists

Suppose that $N \geq 3$, but that the rest of the parameterization of the previous subsection is maintained:

$$D(p) = \begin{cases} A - p, & 0 < p \leq A, \\ 0, & p \geq A, \end{cases} \quad \text{and} \quad \mathbf{TC}_n(x_n) = kx_n, \text{ for } n = 1, \ldots, N,$$

for strictly positive constants A and k such that $A > k$. Still thinking of the situation as a strategic-form game, a (pure-strategy) Nash equilibrium is a strategy profile $(x_1^e, \ldots, x_N^e)$ where each n is choosing a best response to the choices of her rivals, which is

$$x_n^e = \frac{A - X_{\neg n}^e - k}{2}, \quad \text{where} \quad X_{\neg n}^e = \sum_{n' \neq n} x_{n'}^e.$$

If we look for a symmetric solution (where each x_n is some x^e), this gives us the equation

$$2x^e = A - (N - 1)x^e - k, \quad \text{which gives} \quad x^e = \frac{A - k}{N + 1}.$$

And, in this Nash equilibrium, the price that results is $p^e = (A + Nk)/(N + 1)$. As N rises, the equilibrium price approaches the competitive market price.

This is, in fact, the unique pure-strategy Nash equilibrium for this situation, viewed as a strategic-form game, although the argument that this is so must await developments in Section 18.2.

Note, however, that with $N \geq 3$, dominance solvability no longer works.[6] The first step in dominance solvability was to observe that strategies $x_n > (A - k)/2$ are strictly dominated by $(A - k)/2$. That still holds true. But the next step was to say that, since the other supplier will not supply more than $(A - k)/2$, supplying any less than $(A - k)/4$ is dominated by supplying $(A - k)/4$. And, for $N \geq 3$, that is no longer true. If two other suppliers each supply $(A - k)/2$, then any supply by a third supplier causes price to fall below the marginal cost of k, and that third supplier is best off supplying 0. There is no strict dominance beyond the first step.

And the neat dynamics story no longer works. Suppose $N = 3$ (or more), and all three begin supplying $(A - k)/2$. Then each, assuming her rivals will continue, optimally supplies 0. But if all three supply 0, then each, assuming this will continue, go back to $(A-k)/2$. One might hope that if all suppliers begin within

---

[6] For $N = 2$, the mixed-strategy equilibria were eliminated via dominance solvability, so that argument is not available for $N \geq 3$. I am fairly certain that there can be no mixed-strategy equilibria for $N \geq 3$, but, if so, I offer no proof here.

some neighborhood of the Nash equilibrium quantities, the process will converge. But suppose $N = 3$ and each begins with $(A - k + \epsilon)/4$. The best response of each is

$$\frac{A - k - 2(A - k + \epsilon)/4}{2} = \frac{A - k - \epsilon}{4},$$

which, since we didn't specify a sign for ϵ, engenders the original three quantities.[7]

18.2. Cournot "In General"

As noted in the introduction to this chapter, most economists fail to take the Cournot model very seriously as theory per se. It is used in applied work or as an element in a model of broader scope: For instance, in a model of entry deterrence, the post-entry "outcome," if there is entry, is modeled as a Nash equilibrium of the Cournot game. But concern with the "general theory" of the Cournot model is limited. Nonetheless, as a finger exercise in finding Nash equilibria of strategic-form games, it may be helpful to look at specifications more general than the linear model of Section 18.1.

Suppose we have N suppliers, each with her own total-cost function $\mathbf{TC}_n(x_n)$. Rather than work with the market demand function, it is more convenient to work directly with an inverse demand function $P(X)$, which associates to each total quantity X the price $P(X)$ that will clear the market. To ensure the existence of a Nash equilibrium, some limitations must be placed on the total-cost functions and inverse demand:

Assumptions 18.1.

a. *Inverse demand is defined for total quantities $X \in (0, \infty)$, with range $[0, \infty)$. It is continuous everywhere, is strictly decreasing where it is strictly positive, and is strictly positive for some level of supply. It satisfies $\sup_{X \in (0,\infty)} X \cdot P(X) < \infty$ and $\lim_{X \to 0} X \cdot P(X) = 0$.*

b. *Each total-cost function $\mathbf{TC}_n : [0, \infty) \to [0, \infty)$ is continuous, satisfies $\mathbf{TC}_n(0) = 0$, is strictly increasing, and satisfies $\mathbf{TC}_n(x_n) \geq k_n x_n$ for a strictly positive scalar k_n.*

The assumptions on total-cost functions are straightforward. That $\mathbf{TC}_n(0) = 0$ is without any loss of generality; a strictly positive fixed cost ($\mathbf{TC}_n(0) > 0$) has no bearing on what follows, as long as total costs are continuous at 0.[8] However, the assumption that $\mathbf{TC}_n(x_n) \geq k_n x_n$ for some $k_n > 0$—in words (and loosely),

---

[7] Perhaps one gets almost-sure convergence if the system is perturbed "randomly," but before we engage in such explorations, we might want to investigate how general this simple model is.

[8] That is, the intermediate-microeconomics story that fixed costs can be avoided by producing 0 is not permitted. However, if we married Cournot competition with fixed costs that can be avoided by producing 0, or with sunk costs of entry, we would get some interesting stories about entry into and exit from oligopolies, which leads to interesting stories about entry deterrence. Some of this is discussed in Chapter 22.

supplier n's marginal cost is never less than some strictly positive amount—plays a role in what follows.

The assumptions on inverse demand are also straightforward, except for one part. The assumption that inverse demand is strictly decreasing where it is strictly positive and continuous is standard enough for this sort of partial equilibrium analysis. That $\sup X \cdot P(X) < \infty$ is fairly innocuous; roughly put, if total wealth in the economy is finite, then there should be a finite upper bound on how much is spent on this one good. But the assumption $\lim_{X \to 0} X \cdot P(X) = 0$ doesn't work if, for instance, demand comes from a collection of consumers with Cobb–Douglas utility functions and who, therefore, wish to spend a fixed fraction of their income on each good.

While we work here with inverse demand for expositional convenience, what do these assumptions say about the "corresponding" demand function D? The assumption $X \cdot P(X)$ is bounded in X immediately implies that $\lim_{X \to \infty} P(X) = 0$, and the assumption that P is continuous on its entire domain means that for all small enough $p > 0$,[9] there is some X such that $P(X) = p$. But, for large X, the two possibilities are $P(X) > 0$ for all $X > 0$ and $P(X) = 0$ for all $X \geq \overline{X}$, for some $\overline{X} < \infty$. (Once $P(X)$ hits 0, it cannot become strictly positive again, since it is continuous everywhere and strictly decreasing where it is strictly positive; apply the intermediate-value theorem to derive a contradiction.) In the first case, for all small p, D defined as the inverse of P is well-defined and strictly positive; in the latter case, we conventionally define $D(0) = \overline{X}$. At the other end of the interval, where $X \to 0$, the two possibilities are $\lim_{X \to 0} P(X) = \infty$ and $\lim_{X \to 0} P(X) < \infty$. In the former case, D defined as the inverse of P is well defined for all large values of p. In the latter case, writing $\overline{p}$ for $\lim_{X \to 0} P(X)$, we conventionally define $D(p) = 0$ for all $p \geq \overline{p}$. And, with these definitions, D defined as the "inverse" of P (scare quotes because the two conventions are at work) shares the "same" properties as P: continuous everywhere and strictly decreasing where it is strictly positive. Of course, the "linear" case of Section 18.1 corresponds to the case where $\overline{p} = \overline{X} = A$.

Now think of the situation as a game among the N suppliers, where the strategy set for each supplier is the quantity $x_n \in [0, \infty)$ that she chooses to bring to the market, and payoff functions are defined by

$$v_n(x_1, x_2, \ldots, x_N) = x_n P(x_1 + \ldots + x_n) - \mathbf{TC}_n(x_n),$$

and $v_n(x_1, \ldots, x_N) = 0$ if $x_1 + \ldots + x_N = 0$. (We need this last line because P's domain is $(0, \infty)$; that is, P is not defined at 0.)

Proposition 18.2. *If Assumptions 18.1 hold, then a Nash equilibrium for this game exists.*

---

[9] Since P is not identically 0, there is some X^0 such that $P(X^0) > 0$, and "small enough" p includes all $p \in (0, P(X^0)]$.

Proof. Apply Glicksberg's Existence Theorem, which is given in Appendix 9 as Proposition A9.11. To apply Glicksberg's Theorem, the strategy sets for each player must be compact—that certainly isn't true, at least, not yet—and the payoff functions must be continuous in the full array of all player's strategies.

For compactness, Assumptions 18.1 are enlisted. Let $\overline{R} := \sup_X X\,P(X)$ and, for supplier n, let $\overline{x}_n = \overline{R}/k_n$. If supplier n chooses to produce more than $\overline{x}_n$, her total cost will more than exceed any revenues she might take in. Hence, producing $x_n = 0$ stictly dominates producing more than $\overline{x}_n$. It follows immediately that if we find a Nash equilibrium where we limit each n to producing a quantity in the compact set $[0, \overline{x}_n]$, this strategy profile will be an equilibrium for the game without this restriction. So we will apply Glicksberg's Theorem to the game with suppliers' strategy sets meeting this restriction.

And, concerning continuity: The only place where there is an issue is if we have a sequence (in ℓ) of strategy profiles $(x_1^\ell, \dots, x_N^\ell)$ approaching $(0, \dots, 0)$. But if $(x_1^\ell, \dots, x_N^\ell) \to (0, \dots, 0)$, then $x_1^\ell + \dots + x_N^\ell \to 0$, so the total revenues split among the suppliers approaches 0 (from $\lim_{X \to 0} X\,P(X) = 0$). Their total costs all approach 0 as well, which gives the required continuity.

Glicksberg applies; a Nash equilibrium exists.   ∎

However, Glicksberg only guarantees the existence of a Nash equilibrium in mixed strategies and, at that, in mixed strategies that can involve Borel probability distributions on the various pure strategy sets. One would like to know: Does a Nash equilibrium in pure strategies exist? If so, is it unique? What about mixed-strategy equilibria? I can give partial answers to these questions. However, the answers are only partial, because of the possibility of "kinks" in inverse demand.

Consider the following example: There are two suppliers, each of whom has constant marginal cost of 1. Inverse demand is given by

$$P(X) = \begin{cases} 10 - 9X, & 0 \le X \le 90/91, \\ 10/9 - X/81, & 90/91 \le X \le 90, \text{ and} \\ 0, & X \ge 90. \end{cases}$$

Figure 18.1 depicts this inverse-demand function, albeit not to scale.

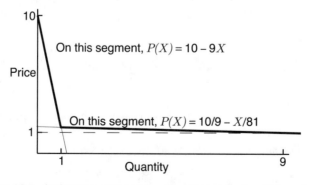

Figure 18.1. An inverse-demand function that gives two Cournot equilibria

I assert that, in this model, $x_1 = x_2 = 1/3$ is a Nash equilibrium, as is $x_1 = x_2 = 3$. These are the two Nash equilibria for the two "linear" portions of inverse demand; that is, $x_1 = x_2 = 1/3$ is the unique Cournot equilibrium if $P(X) = 10 - 9X$, and $x_1 = x_2 = 3$ is the unique Nash equilibrium if $P(X) = 10/9 - X/81$. Hence, with the given kinked inverse-demand function, these are both Nash equilibria if, given (say) supplier 1 is following one or the other, supplier 2 does not wish to "move" to the other segment of the inverse-demand function.

If supplier 1 is producing $x_1 = 3$, supplier 2 cannot get onto the steeper part of inverse demand, so $x_2 = 3$ is clearly supplier 2's best response. The slightly harder case is if supplier 1 chooses $x_1 = 1/3$. But then, by producing $1/3$, supplier 2 causes price to be 4, for a net profit of $(4 - 1)(1/3) = 1$. And, for any quantity x_2 that moves to the flatter portion of inverse demand, price must be strictly less than $10/9$, so profit margin per unit sold is strictly less than $1/9$, while any quantity greater than 9 causes price to fall below the marginal cost of 1. So, by moving to the flatter portion of inverse demand, supplier 2 must make strictly less than 1.

This example is, admittedly, extreme. But it highlights the problem with "kinked" inverse demand, where the scare quotes are there because, even if you smoothed over the kink in the example (so that P is continuously differentiable), the problem remains. In general, in an N-firm model, suppose supplier n believes its rivals will supply $X_{\neg n}$ in total. Supplier n then faces the problem of choosing x_n to maximize

$$x_n P(X_{\neg n} + x_n) - \mathbf{TC}_n(x_n).$$

Assuming both P and $\mathbf{TC}$ are differentiable (P where it is strictly positive), the first-order condition for an interior (strictly positive) maximum is

$$P(X_{\neg n} + x_n) + x_n P'(X_{\neg n} + x_n) = \mathbf{TC}'_n(x_n).$$

You probably recognize that this equation is the marginal-revenue-equals-marginal-cost rule from intermediate micro, except that marginal revenue for supplier n, the left-hand side of the equation, is for an inverse-demand function "shifted" on account of the (fixed, in the mind of supplier n) quantity $X_{\neg n}$. If we make the usual assumptions (for intermediate micro, not real life) that marginal cost is nondecreasing, and if marginal revenue is strictly decreasing (for x_n such that $P(x_n + X_{\neg n}) > 0$), we'll have a single intersection. So, suppose we add the following assumptions:

Assumptions 18.3. *In addition to Assumptions 18.1, assume:*

a. *For each n, $\mathbf{TC}_n$ is continuously differentiable and convex on its domain $[0, \infty)$. (Assumption 18.1(b) implies $\mathbf{TC}'_n(0) > 0$.)*

b. *$P(X)$ is continuously differentiable where it is strictly positive, with strictly negative derivative.*

c. For all $X \geq 0$, $x \rightarrow P(x + X) + xP'(x + X)$ is strictly decreasing, where $P(x + X)$ is strictly positive.

Then, at least, we'd know that supplier n's optimal choice of x_n given $X_{\neg n}$ is unique and is given by the first-order conditions; albeit if the constraint $x_n \geq 0$ binds—which is if $\mathbf{TC}'_n(0) \geq P(X_{\neg n})$—then n's optimal choice is $x_n = 0$.

Assumption 18.3(c) fails in the example: Marginal-revenue functions, even shifted, jump discontinuously upward at the kink. The discontinuous jump upward can be fixed by smoothing out the kink (which also makes P differentiable). But, smoothing out the kink doesn't change the fact that (shifted) marginal revenue is increasing over a range of quantities.

I don't know whether Assumptions 18.3 are sufficient to guarantee a unique pure-strategy Nash equilibrium; I doubt it. So, let us replace Assumption 18.3(c) with something stronger:

Assumption 18.3(c′). $P'(X)$ is nonincreasing where $P(X) > 0$.

In other words, inverse demand P is concave where it is positive.

There's nothing to be done about the behavior of marginal revenue once (if) we get to a scale of total output such that price reaches 0. Marginal revenue will be 0 after that scale is reached, so if marginal revenue is ever negative before then (and, it more or less must be; do you see why?), there will be a discontinuous jump upward. However, that isn't too big a worry, as long as marginal cost is strictly positive; given $X_{\neg n}$, supplier n is not going to choose an x_n that drives price to 0.

And, for $x_n + X_{\neg n}$ such that $P(x_n + X_{\neg n})$ is strictly positive, Assumption 18.3(c′) implies Assumption 18.3(c): $x_n \rightarrow P(x_n + X_{\neg n})$ is strictly decreasing and P' is negative and nonincreasing, hence, $x_n \rightarrow P(x_n + X_{\neg n}) + x_nP'(x_n + X_{\neg n})$ is strictly decreasing.

Lemma 18.4. *If Assumptions 18.1 and 18.3(a), (b), and (c′) hold, then $\lim_{X \rightarrow 0} P(X) < \infty$. Accordingly, the case of $X = 0$ requires no special handling; we can define $P(0) :=$ $\lim_{X \rightarrow 0} P(X)$ and proceed normally.*

Proof. This is trivial. Since P is nonincreasing, $\lim_{X \rightarrow 0} P(X)$ exists, but (in general) might be infinite. However, Assumption 18.3(c′) implies that P is concave where it is strictly positive, so if X^0 is any strictly positive supply level with $P(X^0) > 0$, for all $X < X^0$, $P(X) \leq P(X^0) + P'(X^0)(X - X^0)$, which establishes the upper bound $P(X^0) - P'(X^0)X^0$ on $P(X)$ for $X < X^0$. ∎

Although it is not relevant to what follows, observe that Assumption 18.3(c′) also implies that, for some $\overline{X}$, $P(\overline{X}) = 0$.

Proposition 18.5. *Suppose Assumptions 18.1 and 18.3(a), (b), and (c′) hold. Then the Cournot game has a unique pure-strategy Nash equilibrium.*

Note, in particular, that Assumptions 18.3(b) and (c′) hold for linear inverse demand. So, with linear inverse demand, there is a unique pure-strategy Nash equilibrium for any number of suppliers who have (possibly) different total-cost functions, as long as those total-cost functions satisfy the relevant parts of Assumptions 18.1 and 18.3.

I leave the proof of this proposition as Problem 18.5; if you get stuck, see the *Online Supplement*. But, allow me to give you a head start and outline the proof; it involves a cute construction.

It may seem natural to work with the best-response functions for each supplier, which are

$$\hat{x}_n(X_{\neg n}) := \arg \max\nolimits_{x_n \geq 0} \{P(x_n + X_{\neg n})x_n - \mathbf{TC}_n(x_n)\}.$$

(The "arg max" means the value of $x_n \geq 0$ that maximizes the term inside the brackets.) We know that, for interior solutions, the first-order conditions are

$$\hat{x}_n(X_{\neg n}) \text{ is the unique solution to } P(x_n + X_{\neg n}) + x_n P'(x_n + X_{\neg n}) = \mathbf{TC}'_n(x_n).$$

However, these best-response functions are not as convenient as the function $x_n^*(X)$ defined as: the quantity supplied by supplier n, given that the total supply, including $x_n^*(X)$, is X. To prove Proposition 18.5 (at least, using the method of proof I suggest), you must supply a characterization of this "function"; indeed, you must prove that it is a function; that is, for a total supply X, there is only a single quantity $x_n^*(X)$ that is consistent with n optimizing against $X_{\neg n} = X - x_n^*(X)$. (Assumption 18.3(c′) is the key.) And, then, the definition of a Cournot equilibrium becomes simple: It is a fixed point of the equation

$$\sum_{n=1}^{N} x_n^*(X) = X.$$

Show that this equation has a unique fixed point, and you are done.

18.3. Basic Bertrand

In contrast to Cournot's conception of quantity-based oligopolistic competition, Bertrand (1883) proposes price-based competition. The suppliers of the good in question—still a commodity—simultaneously and independently declare the price they will charge for the good. Buyers hear all these price declarations and head for whichever supplier declares the lowest price. In case of ties for lowest price declaration, buyers split themselves equally between the low-price suppliers.

In the (unlikely) case that we want to take this model seriously, a few details need specification. First, you might worry that a supplier, after learning that the price she quoted is not the least, might quickly revise her price. That introduces interesting dynamics into the story, which we are not (yet) in a position to discuss. (Chapter 22 discusses this possibility.) So you must think of suppliers who are unable to modify their original price declarations. Second, the equal-allocation-of-customers-in-case-of-ties story needs some rationale. Perhaps sales take place on a given day, but prices are declared a few days in advance, and in case of ties, buyers choose randomly among the low-price suppliers; you can then rely on the strong law of large numbers to get roughly equal customers at each low-price supplier. And one might worry about capacity or stock-out constraints or suppliers who have no wish to fulfill all the demand that they face. In the basic model, a supplier is both able and obligated to meet all demand that shows up at her door. The obligation may make sense; the ability is somewhat more problematic, and you might want to think of this as a "make to order" business, where suppliers book orders, then provide the goods (and buyers are willing to wait for the time it takes to have their orders filled).

As with Cournot, we can think of this situation as a strategic-form game in which each supplier is a player, and each supplier's strategy set is the set of all prices $[0, \infty)$. But from a mathematical perspective, it is not a very pleasant game, because the payoff functions are discontinuous. If, say, there are two suppliers, both of whom have constant and identical marginal cost k, and if the (continuous, nonincreasing) market demand function is D, firm 1's payoff function is

$$v_1(p_1, p_2) = \begin{cases} 0, & \text{if } p_1 > p_2, \\ D(p_1)[p_1 - k]/2, & \text{if } p_1 = p_2, \text{ and} \\ D(p_1)[p_1 - k], & \text{if } p_1 < p_2, \end{cases}$$

and similarly for supplier 2. Not only is firm 1's payoff discontinuous in p_1 for fixed p_2; it has a discontinuity of a very unpleasant sort: At $p_1 = p_2$, it is neither upper nor lower semi-continuous.

Despite these unpleasant payoff functions, the more-or-less unique Nash equilibrium of this game is easily described under certain conditions.

Proposition 18.6. *Suppose that*

a. *there are $N \geq 2$ prospective suppliers,*

b. *each of whom has a linear total-cost function $\mathbf{TC}_n(x_n) = k_n x_n$,*

c. *if $k^* = min\{k_n; n = 1, \ldots, n\}$, at least 2 of the suppliers have $k_n = k^*$, and*

d. *market demnd D is continuous, nonincreasing, and satisfies $D(k^*) > 0$.*

Then in any (pure-strategy) Nash equilibrium of the game, at least 2 suppliers with $k_n = k^*$ quote the price $p_n = k^*$, suppliers with $k_n > k^*$ quote some price strictly greater than k^*, and (as long as two suppliers with $k_n = k^*$ quote k^*), other suppliers with $k_n = k^*$ quote a price greater or equal to k^*.[10] And in any Nash equilibrium (under these conditions), every supplier has payoff = profit equal to 0.

---

[10] If $D(k^*) = 0$, then in equilibrium, suppliers can all quote any price at which $D(p) = 0$; no units of the good change hands.

The reason I said this equilibrium is "more-or-less" unique enters here: Suppliers with $k_n > k^*$ can quote any price strictly greater than k^*. But the outcome doesn't change: The market price is k^*, with demand $D(k^*)$ equally split among those suppliers with $k_n = k^*$ who quote $p = k^*$.

You've probably heard this story before. Or, rather, you've seen simple arguments that in a Nash equilibrium of the Bertrand-competition model, suppliers charge their marginal cost and so make 0 profit. Notwithstanding those simple arguments, a full proof, while easy, is not short:

Proof. Suppose the strategy profile $(p_1, \ldots, p_N)$ is a Nash equilibrium. Let $p^* = \min\{p_n; n = 1, \ldots, N\}$, and let $N^* = \{n : p_n = p^*\}$. If $p^* > k^*$ and N^* does not contain one of the suppliers for which $k_n = k^*$, then that supplier has payoff (or profit) 0. By changing her price announcement to, say, $k^* + \epsilon$ for some ϵ small enough so that $D(k^* + \epsilon) > 0$ and $k^* + \epsilon < p^*$, she gets demand $D(k^* + \epsilon)$ all to herself, making ϵ per unit sold, for a strictly positive payoff.

And if $p^* > k^*$ and N^* contains all the suppliers n for which $k_n = k^*$: If $D(p^*) = 0$, all the suppliers have 0 payoff, and one of the suppliers for which $k_n = k^*$, by following the strategy outlined in the last paragraph, can change her announcement and receive positive payoff. While if $D(p^*) > 0$, each of the suppliers for which $k_n = k^*$ has payoff $D(p^*)(p^* - k^*)/m$, where $m \geq 2$. Any one of them, by charging $p = p^* - \epsilon$ (where ϵ is small enough so that $p^* - \epsilon > k^*$, and $p^* - k^* - \epsilon > (p^* - k^*)/m$) captures the entire market and makes $D(p^* - \epsilon)(p^* - \epsilon - k^*)$, which is a larger payoff than she was receiving in the alleged equilibrium.

Next, rule out $p^* < k^*$. Since $D(k^*) > 0$, so is $D(p^*)$, and some supplier (suppose she is supplier n) is facing positive demand at a price less than her constant marginal cost. Her payoff is strictly negative. If, instead, she charges $p = k_n$, she will do no worse than 0 payoff.

We conclude that, in an equilibrium, p^* must equal k^*.

If a supplier with $k_n > k^*$ quotes p^*, she gets some demand at a price below her marginal cost and receives a strictly negative payoff. She can instead quote a price above p^*, getting no demand and making 0 profit. So, in equilibrium, any supplier for whom $k_n > k^* = p^*$ must charge a price above p^*.

As for the suppliers with $k_n = k^*$: At least one of them must be quoting p^* (since p^* is the minimum, and it can't be coming from a supplier with $k_n > k^*$). Any of them who quotes $p^* = k^*$ gets positive demand, but still receives payoff 0; any who quotes $p_n > p^*$ gets payoff 0. If only one of them quotes p^*, and if the second lowest quote is, say, p', the one quoting p^*, by quoting $p^* + \epsilon$ (where ϵ is small enough so that $D(p^* + \epsilon) > 0$ and $p^* + \epsilon < p'$) will get demand $D(p^* + \epsilon)$ at a price above her marginal cost, making strictly positive profit. So two of the n for whom $k_n = k^*$ must be quoting $p_n = k_n = p^*$.

And we still are not done: We've eliminated all possibilities except for strategy profiles as described in the proposition, but are those strategy profiles equilibria? They are, and I'll let you finish the proof: First show that every supplier receives 0 payoff. Then show that no supplier, by changing her price, can receive a strictly positive payoff. (Although I'm leaving it to you to finish the proof, I'll still put in an endproof mark.)   ∎

The proposition doesn't put many restrictions on market demand (assuming the good in question is a commodity; that is, not differentiated by supplier), but it is very restrictive in terms of the suppliers' total-cost functions. For instance, what if all suppliers have linear total-cost functions, but only one supplier has the minimum marginal cost? Or what if suppliers have total-cost functions with rising marginal costs? Both of these variations are covered (to some extent) in the problems (Problems 18.5 and 18.6); if you work through the problems (or read the solutions in the *Online Supplement*), they'll indicate just how delicate the Bertrand model is as currently formulated.

Capacity constraints (and orders refused)

Consider the possibility that the suppliers of the good in question face capacity constraints. To keep things simple, suppose:

- $N = 2$;

- demand is linear where it is strictly positive, $D(p) = M(A - p)$ for $M > 0$; and

- the two suppliers have linear total costs $\mathbf{TC}_n(x_n) = k_n x_n$, where each $k_n < A$, up to a capacity constraint c_n for each.

(Why $M(A - p)$ and not simply $A - p$? The parameter M will represent the scale of the market. Keep reading.)

The meaning of a capacity constraint is that, if, after prices are announced, demand shows up at one supplier or the other that exceeds that supplier's capacity, purchasers in excess of the supplier's capacity are denied the good.

So, to make it very concrete, suppose $M = 100{,}000$, $A = 20$, $k_1 = 1$, $k_2 = 5$, and $c_1 = c_2 = 1$ million. To complete the model, we need to specify payoff functions $v_n(p_1, p_2)$ for $n = 1, 2$. And it is not completely obvious how to do this.

Suppose, for instance, that $p_1 = 5$, and $p_2 = 10$. Of course, then demand for $100{,}000(20 - 5) = 1.5$ million units arrives at supplier 1's store. But this supplier can only serve 1 million, and so $v_1(5, 10) = 1$ million $\times$ ($\$5 - \$1$) = $\$6$ million, where I'm using dollars as the currency for expositional clarity. The question is, what happens to supplier 2? Her payoff is $X \times (\$10 - \$5)$, where X is the amount of demand she faces, presumably composed of demand that went first to supplier 1 and came away empty handed. But how large is X? Demand for 500,000 units went unsatisfied by supplier 1, but perhaps some of the unsatisfied demand is from buyers who are willing to buy at $5 per unit but not at $10. *Which "segment" of demand did supplier 1 satisfy, and which segment was denied?* Until we can answer that question, we can't specify X.

And there is no single right answer. It depends on the nature of the market one is trying to model. To show why, consider two different stories. In each story, we think of the demand side as consisting of 2 million possible customers, each of whom will purchase either 1 unit of the good or none. Each has a reservation price for the 1 unit: One of the 2 million has reservation price $20. One has reservation price $19.99999. One has reservation price $19.99998. And so forth, down to the 2 millionth prospective purchaser, whose reservation price is $0.000001. And, in the usual fashion of this sort of reservation-price model, a prospective buyer purchases his one unit if he can buy for a price equal to his reservation price or less. Now for the two stories:

Story 1. The good is a service. Suppose the good in question is a service, where the important feature of a service is that it cannot be resold. Suppose that the 1.5 million customers willing to purchase at $5 per unit queue up at supplier 1's facility in more or less random order. Each has a two-third's chance of being served, which means (by invocation of the strong law of large numbers) a representative sample of one-third of this population goes away unsatisfied. That's 500,000 unsatisfied customers. But only (approximately) two-thirds of those have reservation prices above the $10 price charged by supplier 2 and so are willing to go to supplier 2 and pay $10 for the service. So, in this story, $X = 333,333$.

But is it reasonable to suppose that a random selection of the 1.5 million whose reservation price is $5 or above come away unsatisfied? If, for instance, supplier 1 takes all orders and then only fills two-thirds of them at random, then yes, this may be a reasonable supposition. However, prospective buyers might be able to influence their odds of getting their one unit of service by, say, queuing up very early. Who has the greatest incentive to do this? A buyer whose reservation price is between $20 and $10 gains $5 by being able to purchase from supplier 1 rather than supplier 2. A buyer whose reservation price r is $10 or less gains $r - 5$ by being able to purchase from supplier 1; this buyer nets 0 if her demand is not filled, since she does not buy from supplier 2. If $r \leq \$10$, then $r - \$5 \leq \$5$ (don't look for some mystery here); the high-reservation-price buyers have greater incentive to get a unit from supplier 1, and if they can take steps to increase their odds, they are (presumably) more likely to to so. In which case, $X = 333,333$ may be an overestimate.

Story 2. The good is a physical good that can be resold, and a competitive "aftermarket" market for the good is created and functions efficiently. Imagine that this story starts out the same way as Story 1, with a random one-third selection of the 1.5 million with reservation prices $5 and above queuing up at supplier 1, with 500,000 being turned away. Two-thirds of those 500,000, or 333,333, move to to supplier 2. The remaining 166,667 who were turned away have values between 5 and 10, so they (presumably?) go empty handed, unwilling to pay $10 to supplier 2.

However, this may not be the end of the story. Take a handful of those with values around $9 (say). Among the 1 million customers who did get an item from firm 1 are some with values in the neighborhood of $6. At this point, imagine that a resale market springs up; think of eBay or Craig's list. An individual with a unit of the good that is worth $6 to himself would surely be willing to resell to an individual for whom the good is worth $9. And, if we assume this aftermarket reaches an efficient outcome, the price in the secondary market will settle around $8.67: There are 1,333,333 units "in circulation," and the marginal buyer for the

1,333,333th unit has a reservation price around $8.67.

But this aftermarket adds two complications. First, if it were the case that the aftermarket price of the good is $8.67, and if individuals in the economy realize this, a prospective buyer with a reservation price above $10 would be better off purchasing his one unit in the aftermarket than from the second supplier. Suppose—and this may strain credibility—that an efficient and competitive aftermarket will be created after suppliers 1 and 2 have done their business, all prospective buyers know this, and all can anticipate the aftermarket equilibrium price. I contend that the aftermarket equilibrium price *must be* $10. If it were more than $10, then buyers with reservation prices in excess of $10 would buy from the second seller, so total supply (including supply of the good bought for own use) would be more than 1 million units. And the competitive price in the aftermarket, with that much total supply, is less than $10. However, if the price is less than $10, then no buyer with a reservation price in excess of $10 would buy from the second supplier, so total supply would be the 1 million coming from the first supplier, which gives an equilibrium aftermarket price of $10 exactly. And a $10 aftermarket price does give an equilibrium: Buyers with reservation prices less than $10 who are lucky enough to get a unit from the first supplier sell their units in the aftermarket (for $10) to those buyers with reservation prices at $10 and above who were unlucky with the first supplier.

Which then brings on the second complication. Someone utterly uninterested in consuming this particular good—call this person a *scalper*—would (depending on the personal costs of doing so) queue up at supplier 1's facility, hoping to purchase for $5 a unit that can then be sold in the aftermarket for $10. It isn't clear how much of supplier 1's capacity of 1 million will go to consumers with reservation prices above $10, how much will go to prospective consumers with reservation prices below $10, and how much will go to scalpers. But, in the aftermarket, those 1 million units will wind up in the hands of the 1 million consumers with reservation prices $10 and above. The demography of buyers from supplier 1 is important if we wish to identify who pays how much (ultimately) for their unit and who makes a $5 speculative profit by getting a unit from the first supplier and reselling it. But if all we want to know (to finish the model of price competition between the two sellers) is X, the quantity sold by the second supplier (if she quotes $10, supplier 1 quotes $p < \$10$, and supplier 1 has capacity for 1 million units), then X equals 0.

So which is it? Is $X = 333,333$ or 0? Or is it something else? Note that this question doesn't arise (with Bertrand-style competition) if the two duopolists announce the same price. Any unsatisfied demand from one supplier is happy to go to the other; anyone left unsatisfied at both (because the sum of the suppliers' capacities is less than demand at the price they both name) has nowhere else to go. And, if one of the two contemplates naming a price less than the price named by her rival, we know how much demand she faces, namely all of it (at the lower price she names). It is the level of demand reaching the higher-price duopolist that is problematic. And, of course, to verify that some (say, equal price) strategy profile is an equilibrium, we must be able to show that neither duopolist wishes to *raise* her price, which means we must be able to answer the question: If she raises her price, how much demand will she face as a function of the price she chooses?

In the basic model of Bertrand competition, the assumption that total costs are linear (no fixed costs and constant marginal costs) is very helpful: In equilibrium, no supplier will ever quote a price below her marginal cost (unless, in equilibrium, someone else is quoting a lower price—see Problem 18.6), and so a supplier is (perhaps weakly) happy to serve any demand that appears at her door. But to model Bertrand-style competition among oligopolists with rising marginal costs, you may need to confront these questions. Suppose, for instance, we have a duopoly in which the duopolists have rising marginal costs. Suppose we want to verify that the two of them quoting the same price p is an equilibrium. To do so requires evaluating the payoff to the first supplier if she deviates from p. If she charges a price $p' < p$, then (presumably) she faces much more demand, and her marginal cost of serving some of it may exceed the price she named. Is she required to serve all of it? Or can she refuse demands that would be unprofitable to fulfill? In contrast, suppose she deviates to a price $p' > p$. Must her rival serve all the demand that the rival now faces? Or can her rival turn away demand? And if her rival can turn away demand, how much of that demand shows up at her door? Very different answers to the question "What are the Bertrand equilibria when suppliers have rising marginal costs?" are obtained, depending on what answers to these questions are assumed. Roughly speaking, the answers are *too many* if all demand must be served and, perhaps, *not enough*, if demand can be turned away. To get a taste of this, see Problem 18.7.

Why bother you with these stories? I do so to make the following general point: It is relatively easy to write down a specific strategic-form game and assert that it is a model of a specific real-life situation. But does the model capture what is important in the real-life situation you are trying to understand? (In this context, is the good a service; will an after-market spring up?) Unless and until you confront the real-life situation in greater detail, you don't know that you have the right model.

18.4. Differentiated Goods

The discontinuity in demand that is present in Bertrand competition is, of course, unrealistic. If one supplier of a good charges a few cents less than another supplier, do we really believe that all customers will abandon the second for the first? For a variety of reasons, while the good in question may have appearance of a commodity, there may be (even) slight differences in the good that lead some demand at supplier 2, even if her price is a bit greater than the price quoted by supplier 1.

One simple way to investigate how this might work (and to compare Bertrand competition with Cournot competition) is to write down "differentiated" demand functions. In a linear model, we have

$$D_n(p_n, p_{\neg n}) = A_n - a_n p_n + b_n p_{\neg n}; \quad n = 1, 2, \tag{18.2}$$

where we assume that the A_n and a_n are positive. The sign of b_n depends on the relationship between the two goods: If b_1 is positive, then a rise in the price of good 2 increases demand for good 1; roughly speaking, good 1 is a substitute for good 2. Negative b_n, in contrast, would be the case where the goods are complements.

Suppose the two duopolists have linear total-cost functions, with marginal costs k_n. With this simple linear-demand-constant-marginal-cost parameterization, each duopolist's problem is maximization of a concave objective function, so the first-order conditions for optimality (the optimal response of duopolist n to the price set by $\neg n$) are sufficient for the unique optimal response:

$$p_n^*(p_{\neg n}) := \frac{A_n + b_n p_{-n} + a_n k_n}{2a_n}.$$

And the unique Bertrand-Nash equilibrium is the profile $(\hat{p}_1, \hat{p}_2)$ for which $p_n^*(\hat{p}_{\neg n}) = \hat{p}_n$ for $n = 1, 2$. To simplify the algebra, let $C_n = A_n + a_n k_n$; then the solution of these two simultaneous linear equations is

$$p_n = \frac{2a_{\neg n} C_n + b_n C_{\neg n}}{4a_n a_{\neg n} - b_n b_{\neg n}}.$$

(This solution requires that $4a_1 a_2 > b_1 b_2$. We'll assume more momentarily.)

We can "invert" the two demand functions given by equations (18.2) to find the corresponding inverse demand functions. Sparing you the algebra, these are

$$P_n(x_n, x_{\neg n}) = \frac{a_{\neg n} A_n + b_n A_{\neg n}}{a_1 a_2 - b_1 b_2} - \frac{a_{\neg n}}{a_1 a_2 - b_1 b_2} x_n - \frac{b_n}{a_1 a_2 - b_1 b_2} x_{\neg n}, \quad n = 1, 2 \quad (18.2')$$

where, to be able to invert equations (18.2), we require $a_1 a_2 \neq b_1 b_2$; in fact, assume that $a_1 a_2 > b_1 b_2$, $a_1 > 0$, and $a_2 > 0$, so $4a_1 a_2 > b_1 b_2$ follows.

Of course, now that we have the system of inverse-demand functions, we can investigate what happens if, instead of Bertrand or price competition, we think of the duopolists as engaging in quantity competition. That is, we imagine that they simultaneously and independently choose quantities x_1 and x_2, prices are set to clear markets (that is, equations (18.2') are used to give prices), and payoffs are, in the usual fashion, the profits each earns. What is the Cournot-Nash equilibrium in this case? Let

$$\mathcal{A}_n = \frac{a_{\neg n} A_n + b_n A_{\neg n}}{a_1 a_2 - b_1 b_2} \,, \; \mathcal{C}_n = \mathcal{A}_n - k_n \,, \alpha_n = \frac{a_{\neg n}}{a_1 a_2 - b_1 b_2} \,, \text{ and } \beta_n = \frac{b_n}{a_1 a_2 - b_1 b_2} \,.$$

Then, again sparing you the algebra, the Cournot-Nash equilibrium has the quantity supplied by supplier n as

$$x_n = \frac{2\alpha_{\neg n} \mathcal{C}_n - \beta_n \mathcal{C}_{\neg n}}{4\alpha_1 \alpha_2 - \beta_1 \beta_2}.$$

How do the two equilibria compare? Grinding through the algebra is possible, but there is an easier way. Take the case where $b_n > 0$ for both n, and follow along in Figure 18.2. This is a typical picture of "price competition" when the goods are substitutes (that is, the $b_n > 0$). To be very concrete, this figure is drawn for $A_1 = 15, a_1 = 2, b_1 = 1, k_1 = 1, A_2 = 10, a_2 = 4, b_2 = 2$, and $k_2 = 1$. For these values, the Bertrand equilibrium prices are $p_1 = 5$ and $p_2 = 3$.

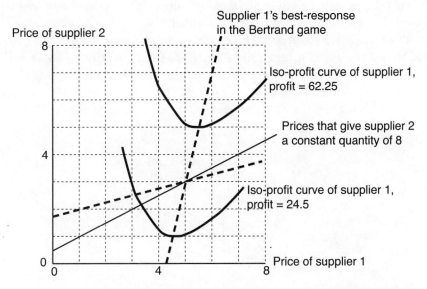

Figure 18.2. Comparing Cournot and Bertrand with differentiated goods (see the text for explanation)

The dashed lines in the figure are the two best-response functions for Bertrand competition: $p_n^*(p_{\neg n}) = (A_n - b_n p_{\neg n} + a_n k_n)/(2a_n)$. Of course, they intersect at the Bertrand equilibrium prices. The "curves" are iso-profit curves for supplier 1; that is, for a constant k, the locus of pairs (p_1, p_2) such that $k = (A_1 - a_1 p_1 + b_1 p_2) \times (p_1 - k_1)$. I've supplied the supplier-1 iso-profit curves for profit levels 62.25 and 24.5. Note that supplier 1's profit is greater for larger values of p_2, since $b_1 > 0$. Note also that these iso-profit curves bottom out along the line $(p_1^*(p_2), p_2)$. This result is another "of course." In Bertrand compeitition, supplier 1 regards p_2 as fixed and chooses p_1 to make her profit as large as she can, which means (see the figure) that she pushes to the highest indifference curve that she can reach, along the line $p_2 = $ constant.

Finally, consider the solid line, which gives the price pairs (p_1, p_2) that provide supplier 2 with a constant quantity of 8. In general, lines of this sort have the form $K = A_2 - a_2 p_2 + b_2 p_1$, or $p_2 = (A_2 - K + b_2 p_1)/(a_2)$. The important thing to note is that, because $b_2 > 0$, this line is upward sloping.

Now for the part of the argument that will take some thought. Suppose the two suppliers are engaged in Cournot competition. That is, supplier 1 chooses her quantity taking as fixed the quantity of supplier 2. That is to say, supplier 1 is choosing a *price*-quantity pair off the demand function she faces, taking x_2 as fixed.

We can model her maximization problem in terms of the price she selects, as long as she maximizes holding fixed x_2. So, if she regards supplier 2 as coming to market with $x_2 = 8$, she will choose the price p_1 that maximizes her profit—moves her to the highest iso-profit curve—consistent with $x_2 = 8$. *Given the shape of her iso-profit curves and the fact that the line of price pairs that give supplier 2 a constant level of output, this price level will be to the right of her best-response curve, for all levels of x_2.*

Figure 18.3 provides a magnified look at Figure 18.2, with two iso-profit curves for suppler 1 drawn in. The lower of the two is supplier 1's optimal response to a choice of $p_2 = 3$ by supplier 2 in Bertrand competition. Since supplier 1 takes p_2 as fixed, this highest iso-profit curve is tangent to the horizontal line $p_2 = 3$. But if there is Cournot competition, and if supplier 2 has a fixed quantity $x_2 = 8$, supplier 1 is choosing her best price-quantity combination off the (positively) sloped line *prices that give supplier 2 a constant quantity of 8*. The optimal iso-profit curve for supplier 1 is a bit higher; the corresponding price supplier 1 charges is higher as well.

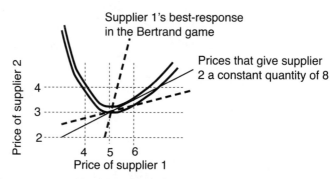

Figure 18.3. Cournot competition gives higher prices than Bertrand competition

What is the "best price response to supplier 2 choosing x_1 curve," algebraically? If supplier 2 is fixed at x_2, supplier 1's problem, in terms of prices, is to

$$\text{Maximize } (A_1 - a_1 p_1 + b_1 p_2)(p_1 - k_1), \quad \text{subject to } p_2 = \frac{A_2 - x_2 + b_2 p_1}{a_2}.$$

Substitute the constraint into the objective function, as supplier 1's problem is to maximize

$$\left(A_1 - a_1 p_1 + b_1 \frac{A_2 - x_2 + b_2 p_1}{a_2} \right) \times \left(p_1 - k_1 \right). \tag{18.3}$$

And here is the economic inutition. If supplier 2 is fixing x_2, then as supplier 1 raises her price, supplier 2, to maintain quantity x_2, raises her price. When the goods are substitutes, that's a good thing for supplier 1; the marginal impact on her profit of raising her price is larger than if supplier 2 has fixed her price. (You see that algebraically by looking at the coefficient on p_1 in the first parentheses: Instead of a_1, it becomes $a_1 + b_1 b_2 / a_2$.)

Please note: If you maximize the expression in (18.3) in p_1, you'll have $p_1^*(x_2)$; the best price for supplier 1 to charge, if supplier 2 has fixed her supply at x_2. If you want to plot this best-response function on Figures 18.2 or 18.3, you still have work to do. Fix a level of x_2, and you have p_1, but then you must find the corresponding level of p_2. That is, parametrically vary x_2, finding $p_1^*(x_2)$ and then solve $x_2 = A_2 - a_2 p_2 + b_2 p_1^*(x_2)$, and you can go back to the picture. And if you do all the algebra involved (it is not difficult, but it is tiresome), you will find that if (p_1, p_2) lies on this "best response to various x_2 surface," $p_1 > p_1^*(p_2)$. But the pictures should convince you of that.

And then, finally: The "best p_1 responses to fixed quantities x_2" lies to the right of $p_1^*(p_2)$. By an entirely symmetric argument, the "best p_2 responses to fixed quantities x_1" lies above $p_2^*(p_1)$. So where they meet, which is the price pair of the Cournot equilibrium, is necessarily to the right of $p_1^*(p_2)$ and above $p_2^*(p_1)$, which means the "northeast" quadrant formed by the two dashed lines in Figure 18.3: The Cournot equilibrium prices are both larger than the Bertrand equilibrium prices.

That's the story if the goods are substitutes. What is your guess as to the story if the goods are complements? Take a guess, and then proceed to Problem 18.8; you'll find the answer in the *Online Supplement* (if you have problems working it out on your own.)

The nice thing about looking at Bertrand and/or Cournot in the case of differentiated commodities is that you can deal with rising marginal costs and suppliers with different total-cost functions. But it is, I think, a bit of a "cheat" simply to assume a demand system such as equations (18.2). It would be preferable to have a story about what makes the goods differentiated. Perhaps the most common of these stories is the story of "travel costs"; the two suppliers sell identical goods, but they are located in different places, and prospective buyers take into account the cost of travel when deciding whether to purchase and from whom. These stories at their most basic are quite simple, but they can quickly become complex: Problem 18.9 allow you to explore a simple formulation that is easy to "solve" and then one, a bit more complex, that is very difficult to analyze.

Bibliographic Notes

The two (very) classic works that form the backbone of this chapter are Cournot (1838) and Bertrand (1883). Nathaniel T. Bacon (1897) published a translation of Cournot's book into English that has been digitized and can be found on the internet. Bertrand's article is a critical review of Cournot's book, in which he proposed that if firms competed in prices instead of quantities, then the equilibrium price would equal the marginal cost of production. This argument was subsequently formalized in Edgeworth (1889), which is available in Edgeworth's *Collected Papers* (1925).

Until the rise of noncooperative game theory in economics, one spoke of Cournot equilibrium and Bertrand equilibrium as two different equilibrium concepts of the same model. Nowadays, when it is fashionable to use game-theoretic language, it is more common to speak in terms of Nash equilibria of the Cournot (quantity-setting) and Bertrand (price-setting) models. I try to be consistent and use the current language, although in Section 18.4, concerning on differentiated goods, since direct comparisons are being made, I used "Cournot-Nash equilibrium" as shorthand for "Nash equilibrium of the Cournot game" and, similarly, Bertrand-Nash equilibrium.

Problems

■ 18.1. Consider the basic Cournot model of a duopoly with linear demand $D(p) = A - p$ and (identical) constant marginal cost $0 < k \leq A$ for both firms (Section 18.1). I was fast and somewhat loose in determining the best-response function of each firm and in asserting that there was a unique Nash equilibrium to the game. And I gave almost no details when I asserted that the game was dominance solvable with iterated strict dominance. Supply all the missing details, noting where things fall apart if $k = 0$.

■ 18.2. For the basic Cournot model of a duopoly with linear demand $A - p$ and identical constant marginal cost k, with $k < A$, suppose x_1^1 and x_2^1 are chosen arbitrarily from $[0, \infty)$, and then x_1^t and x_2^t are recursively defined for $t = 2, 3, \ldots$, by $x_n^t = x_n^*(x_{\neg n}^{t-1})$. Show that $\lim_{t \to \infty} x_n^t = (A - k)/3$ for $n = 1, 2$.

■ 18.3. Assume Assumptions 18.1 and 18.3(a), (b), and (c'). Prove Proposition 18.5.

a. As a warm up, consider the function $\hat{x}_n(X_{\neg n})$, which gives supplier n's best response if his rivals are producing $X_{\neg n}$ in total. Show that

$$\hat{x}_n(X_{\neg n}) = \begin{cases} 0, & \text{if } \mathbf{TC}'_n(0) \geq P(X), \text{ and} \\ \text{is the solution to } P(x_n + X_{\neg n}) + x_n P'(x_n + X_{\neg n}) = \mathbf{TC}'_n(x_n), \\ \qquad \text{otherwise.} \end{cases}$$

Show that it is well-defined (in the second case, there is a unique solution). Just for fun, show that it is nonincreasing in $X_{\neg n}$.

b. Define $x_n^*(X)$ as in the discussion following the statement of the proposition; that is, $x_n^*(X)$ is the amount supplied by supplier n consistent with total supply being X. Show that

$$x_n^*(X) = \begin{cases} 0, & \text{if } \mathbf{TC}'_n(0) \geq P(X), \text{ and} \\ \text{is the solution to } P(X) + x_n P'(X) = \mathbf{TC}'_n(x_n), \\ \qquad \text{otherwise.} \end{cases}$$

Show that this is well-defined (for each X, there is a unique solution), and show that it is strictly decreasing in X. (What does it mean if $x_n^*(X) > X$?)

c. Show that there is a unique solution to $\sum_n x_n^*(X) = X$, which completes the proof.

■ 18.4. Suppose $N = 2$, both firms have total-cost function $\mathbf{TC}_n(x_n) = 40x_n$, and inverse demand is given by

$$P(x) = \begin{cases} 100 - x, & \text{for } x \leq 40.05, \\ 79.95 - x/2, & \text{for } x \geq 40.2, \end{cases}$$

and, for $40.05 < x < 40.2$, inverse demand is chosen so that the transition between these two linear segments is smooth (continuously differentiable). (If you extend the two line segments to the value $x = 40.1$, they meet at $p = 59.9$, so this smooth transition is feasible while maintaining strictly decreasing demand.)   •

a. Suppose we search for a Cournot equilibrium where the total quantity supplied by the two firms is 40. Using the rule from Problem 18.3(b) for computing $x_n^*(X)$, verify that $x_n^*(40) = 20$. So, in the spirit of that analysis, $x_1 = x_2 = 20$ is a candidate for a Cournot equilibrium.

b. If each supplier provides 20, what is the profit earned by each supplier?

c. Suppose supplier 2 supplies 20, and supplier 1 chooses to supply 25 instead of 20. What is the profit of supplier 1? Given that supplier 2 supplies 20, what quantity supplied by supplier 1 maximizes the profit of supplier 1?

d. How do you explain what is happening here?

■ 18.5. Consider the simple Bertrand (price-competition) model (commodity item being supplied by N firms), where market demand is given by $D(p)$, for nonincreasing and continuous D. Suppose all $N \geq 2$ suppliers have linear total-cost functions $\mathbf{TC}_n(x_n) = k_n x_n$, where $k_1 < k_2 \leq k_3 \leq \ldots \leq k_N$. Suppose that $D(k_1) > 0$. Are there circumstances in which this model admits a Nash equilibrium? Are there circumstances in which it does not? The answer to both questions is Yes, and the real question is: Can you develop a theory that explains when this model has (or doesn't have) a Nash equilibrium? To keep this problem from becoming a huge mess, restrict attention to pure-strategy Nash equilibria only.

■ 18.6. This problem concerns Bertrand competition for suppliers with capacity constraints.

a. Suppose demand is given by $D(p)$. Suppose that there are two suppliers who engage in Bertrand (price) competition, and that supplier 1 names a price $p_1 > p_2$. Of course, in the spirit of Bertrand competition, demand level $D(p_2)$ shows up at supplier 2, while no one (for the time being) shows up at supplier 1. But suppose supplier 2 has capacity $c_2 < D(p_2)$, so can only serve c_2 of the demand that arrives. Per each of the two stories in the subsection *Capacity constraints* (page 23) concerning what happens to unsatisfied demand, how much demand then arrives at supplier 1? (Here are the formulas: What you must do is justify

them: In story 1, demand at supplier 1 is $[(D(p_2) - c_2)/D(p_2)]D(p_1)$, while in
story, it is 0 if $c_2 \geq D(p_1)$ and $D(p_1) - c_2$ otherwise.)

b. Suppose demand is given by $D(p) = A - p$. Suppose there are two suppliers
   who engage in Bertrand (price) competition, both with linear total-cost functions $\mathbf{TC}_n(x_n) = kx_n$ for $k < A$. Each supplier has a capacity equal to the
   Cournot-equilibrium quantity $(A-k)/3$, and the two engage in Bertrand (price)
   competition. Is it an equilibrium for each supplier to set a price of $(A + 2k)/3$
   (which is the Cournot-equilibrium price)? Answer this question twice: First,
   answer it for story 1 about what happens if $p_1 > p_2$. Then answer it for story 2.

■ 18.7. Consider the simple Bertrand model, with only two suppliers, facing linear
demand $D(p) = 10 - p$, where each has total-cost function $\mathbf{TC}_n(x_n) = x_n^2/2$. That
is, marginal cost is rising, given by $\mathbf{MC}_n(x_n) = x_n$. Because the two are identical,
it is somewhat natural to look for equilibria where the two name the same price p.

a. Suppose the "rules" are that, after prices (p_1, p_2) are named, each supplier must
   serve all demand that she faces at the price she named. What prices p are
   equilibrium prices in the sense that $(p_1, p_2) = (p, p)$ is an equilibrium profile?

b. Suppose (p_1, p_2) is the profile of prices named by the two, with $p_1 < p_2$. Suppose
   that supplier 1, faced with demand $10 - p_1$, is allowed to serve as much of
   this demand as she feels is profitable for her, and that if she chooses to serve
   $x_1 < 10 - p_1$, the demand facing supplier 2 is $10 - x_1 - p_2$. (This, essentially, is in
   accord with second story on page 23.) If $p_1 > p_2$, symmetric rules apply. What
   prices p are equilibrium prices in the sense that $(p_1, p_2) = (p, p)$ is an equilibrium
   profile?

■ 18.8. For the linear demand model with differentiated commodities in Section 18.4,
how do the Bertrand-equilibrium and the Cournot-equilibrium prices compare, if
$b_n < 0$ for $n = 1, 2$? (To be clear, b_n is the constant in the demand function D_n as
in the specification of demand given at the very bottom of page 25.)

■ 18.9. *A relatively easy "travel-cost" model and one a degree more complex.* A common way to generate "product differentiation" with otherwise identical goods is
by using travel costs. The suppliers of the good are found at different locations,
and buyers, who are scattered in space, take into account their travel costs when
deciding whether to buy at all and, if so, from which supplier. Part a gives a version of this story that is relatively easy to solve, although it is only relatively easy;
a complete solution still takes energy and ingenuity. Part b complicates the story,
making it much more difficult.

a. Suppose there are two suppliers of the good in question, who are located at
   opposite ends of a line segment. Along the line segment (between them) are
   located prospective buyers. To be concrete, suppose there is a uniform distribution of consumers arrayed on the interval $[0, 1]$, where the consumer who
   lives at location $t \in [0, 1]$ will be called consumer t. Because the two suppliers

are located at opposite ends of this interval, I'll refer to them as supplier 0 and supplier 1, rather than 1 and 2, where the index refers to the suppliers' location.

The total-cost function of each supplier is $\mathbf{TC}_n(x_n) = x_n$. That is, the suppliers have no fixed costs and constant marginal costs of 1.

Each consumer chooses to purchase either 1 unit of the good or none. To keep things simple, suppose that each consumer has the same reservation "utility" r for the good, measured in dollars. But in contemplating whether to buy from supplier 0, from supplier 1, or not at all, consumer t takes into account the costs of going to either supplier. The cost of going to supplier 0 for consumer t is ct for $c > 0$; his cost of going to supplier 1 is $c(1 - t)$. (In other words, cost of travel is c times the distance required in one direction.) Hence, if supplier 0 is charging price p_0 and supplier 1 is charging p_1, consumer t compares $p_0 + ct$, $p_1 + c(1 - t)$, and r. If r is the least of these, consumer t does not purchase the good. If $p_0 + ct$ is least, consumer t buys his one unit from supplier 0. If $p_1 + c(1 - t)$ is least, he buys from supplier 1.

To be clear about what this means, note first that for any p_0 and p_1, if consumer t chooses to buy from supplier 0, so do all consumers at locations $t' < t$, and if consumer t chooses to buy from supplier 1, so do all consumers at locations $t' > t$. Hence, given p_0 and p_1, there are values t_0 and t_1, $t_0 \leq t_1$, such that consumers from 0 to t_0 buy from supplier 0, consumers from t_1 to 1 buy from supplier 1, and consumers from t_0 to t_1 do not buy. In such a case, the demand facing supplier 0 is t_0, and supplier 0's profit is $t_0 \times (p_0 - 1)$, while the demand facing supplier 1 is $1 - t_1$, so her profit is $(1 - t_1) \times (p_1 - 1)$. Since the "marginal consumers"—the consumers sitting at t_0 and t_1—are "infinitessimal" in terms of their individual demand, it doesn't matter to the suppliers' profits which supplier these marginal consumers choose.

Assume that $r > 1$. That is, the marginal cost of supplying to any consumer is strictly less than the consumers' reservation values. (If $r \leq 1$, the only possible equilibria involve no sales at all or, in the case $r = 1$, sales to the two endpoint consumers, which is the same as no sales at all in terms of profits and consumer surplus.)

. What are the Bertrand equilibria in this case? (I'm not ruling out the possibility that there are multiple equilibria, and in fact, in some cases, there are.) By a Bertrand equilibrium, I mean Nash equilibrium of the game, where the two suppliers simultaneously and independently post prices p_0 and p_1, consumers see those prices, and arrange their demand accordingly. Start with the case that r is "large," where I leave it to you to decipher what I mean by "large." If you are able to do that, consider the case of general values of $r > 1$.

Finally (for part a), what problem do you encounter if you try to compare the Bertrand equilibrium with a Cournot-competition equilibrium? (My solution in the *Online Supplement* wimps out on this final piece of part a.)

b. Now suppose that the same geometry and travel costs apply, but each consumer t considers purchasing a variable amount of the good, if he buys any at all. Specifically, suppose each consumer has utility function for the good, gross of travel costs, $Ax - x^2/2 + m$, where m is the money the consumer has left over from his purchases. Assume m is "large," so each consumer t contemplates three courses of action: (1) Don't go to either store, and don't purchase any of the good, for net utility 0. (2) Go to supplier 0 and purchase $A - p_0$ units of the good, where p_0 is the supplier 0's price, for a net utility $(A - p_0)^2/2 - ct$. (3) Go to supplier 1 and purchase $A - p_1$ units of the good, for a net utility of $(A - p_1)^2/2 - c(1 - t)$. Consumer t, after evaluating these three possible courses of action, carries out whichever gives him the highest net utility.

Go far enough into the analysis of this problem so that you can explain why this elaboration on the story in part a makes the problem much more complex. (The *Online Appendix* completely wimps out on part b.)

■ 18.10. *The free-rider problem.* Imagine a collection of N individuals who contribute jointly to some project. The range of possible contributions by individual n is $[0, A]$ for some (large) finite A. Individual n's payoff is a function of the profile of contributions $(x_1, x_2, \ldots, x_N)$ made by all N individuals: For each n, there is a strictly increasing, concave, and continuously differentiable function $u_n : R_+^N \to R$, and n's payoff from $(x_1, x_2, \ldots, x_N)$ is $u_n((x_1, x_2, \ldots, x_N)) - x_n$. (That is, x_n measures the "personal disutility" to n of making the contribution x_n, but while larger x_n is "distasteful" for n, it does improve the gross payoff (gross of this disutility term) to all N individuals.

Assume that for all $x = (x_1, \ldots, x_N) \in [0, A]^N$ such that $x_n = A$, $\partial u^n/\partial x_n\big|_x < 1$. That is, the net marginal payoff to individual n of increasing her contribution, when she is making a maximal contribution, is negative.

a.   Recalling Chapter 8 from Volume 1, how do you find the Pareto-efficient levels of contribution in this situation?

b.   Suppose we view this situation as a strategic-form game, where the N individuals simultaneously and independently choose their contribution levels. What can you say about the existence of Nash equilibria of this game? Are these equilibria efficient?

■ 18.11. *A Tiebout-equilibrium game.* Suppose we have nine individuals, each with their own taste for a particular local public good. Individual n, for $n = 1, \ldots, 9$, has utility function $nx - m$, where x is either 1 or 0, depending on whether the individual lives in a location in which the public good is provided or not. The strategies available to each player are to choose to live in location A or B. Location A provides the public good (assuming anyone chooses to live in A), while location B does not. But the public good must be paid for: If N individuals show up at location A, each pays $15.1/N$ in taxes to finance this public good, so the payoff to player n, if she chooses A, is $n - 15.1/N$. (The payoff from choosing location B is 0.)

Find all the pure-strategy Nash equilibria of this game. Then produce one mixed-strategy equilibrium.

Chapter Nineteen

Moral Hazard and Incentives

In Volume I, the notion that market prices can be attached to "goods" is never questioned or challenged. A "good" is a well-defined and understood thing, measured in well-defined and understood units, and, once the units of account or currency are established, a price per unit is has a clear meaning. Real life is not so simple. For one thing, even if the good is something as tangible as pippen apples, measured in kilos, and the price is \$2.99 per kilo, apples come in a variety of quality levels. Is the price \$2.99 for a random kilo of apples, or \$2.99 for a hand-picked kilo? This isn't a major issue if the buyer of apples can discern reasonably well the quality of the apples she picks out of the bin. But in some instances, the quality of the "good" is hard for the buyer to discern or guarantee.

This is particularly germane when the commodity is a service of some sort, provided by the seller. The service provider could be an employee of a firm or an independent contractor hired by a firm. She could be your barber or your doctor. Unlike many consumption goods and inputs to the production process, service providers have some discretion concerning what they provide. How hard will they exert themselves? How will they allocate their time among different productive tasks? How much care will they take in providing whatever service they provide?

This begs the question: How should the "units" of such services be measured? In many cases—perhaps a majority of cases involving employees—the unit is time on the job. Perhaps the employee is a wage earner, paid by the hour. For other employees, such as your instructor if you are reading this as a student, the employee is paid an annual (or 9-month) salary, with salary reviews every year. But, there are cases in which piece-rate pay is employed: A employee who bands armatures is paid a set amount for each armature he or she bands; in an on-line executive education program in which I have taught, I am paid a fixed amount for each "live" (video) session, plus a different amount per participant-student who takes the course. And there are hybrid cases; for instance, professional soccer players are paid an annual salary, agreed to in advance, supplemented with performance bonuses based on ex post measures of performance.

Several issues are involved in these different systems, but the focus in this chapter is on an employee's or contractor's discretion concerning what he does and how well he does it, and how his choices are affected by the manner in which he is compensated. In the classic language of the insurance industry, the exchange involves a *moral hazard*: Alice hires Bob on an hourly basis, based on a promise by Bob to work hard and in Alice's best interests. But Bob's promise may go unfulfilled. So Alice, to align Bob's interests with her own, provides Bob with incentives to work hard and in her interests. This could involve some form of piece-rate pay, or a performance bonus based on a review of what Bob did for her, or prospects of promotion or a raise in pay rate. Or it may be that Bob is hardworking—it isn't a matter of Bob exerting himself—but Alice worries that Bob will spend his time and energy on a mix of tasks that match his tastes and interests, rather than tasks that are most valuable for her. So she structures his compensation to align his interests with her own.

The combination of moral hazard and incentives is not limited to employment. In a business-to-business (B2B) contract, Alice Industries purchases goods or services from Bob Builders, Incorporated, where Bob, Inc. has some discretion concerning the quality of the goods and/or services it provides. Alice hires Bob Builders as primary contractor for her home-renovation project, worrying how long it will take and how well the work will be done; Bob Builders, in turn, hires Carol Electric to do the electrical work, with similar concerns. When Alice, a venture capitalist, invests in entrepreneur Bob, she worries that Bob will not exert himself to make the venture a success. Bondholders worry that management of a firm will take actions that favor equity holders; equity holders worry that top management will feather their personal nests at the expense of equity holders. And, in the context of casualty insurance, Bob (either an individual or a firm) may purchase fire insurance from Alice Casualty. The odds of a fire at Bob's house or place of business depend on how careful Bob is about clearing brush from around the structure or about properly storing flammable materials. Once insured, Bob's incentive to clear brush or carefully store oily rags is diminished; Alice Casualty, in consequence, constructs the terms of Bob's insurance to give him greater incentive to do these things.

Hidden action versus moral hazard

Economists prefer to avoid value judgments in their professional capacity.[1] Hence, in the economics literature, alternatives to the value-laden term *moral hazard* are sought. Many economists take the position that Bob, responding in a fashion that is personally optimal for himself given the circumstances in which he finds himself, is not acting immorally. If Bob misbehaves, the fault is Alice's for not structuring Bob's incentives properly. (This generally doesn't extend to breaking the law; and Bob breaking a promise that he gave freely is gray-area behavior.) So, in place of *moral hazard*, the term *hidden action* is used: Bob takes actions that are consequential to Alice but are hidden from her.

This term doesn't quite capture the full dimensions of the general issue. There are cases in which Bob's actions are not hidden from Alice, but still, Bob's actions are *uncontractible*:[2] Alice cannot craft a legally enforceable arrangement that prevents

---

[1] A more accurate statement is that they like to *pretend* that they avoid value judgments. Notwithstanding any such pretense, the fundamental structure of orthodox economics is based on some fairly controversial value judgments.

[2] Economists have a penchant for abusing the English language, turning nouns—Alice signed a *contract* with Bob—into verbs—Alice *contracted* with Bob—and then manufacturing adjectival forms for the new verbs. According to dictionaries, manifolds are contractible, while diseases are contractable, so economists have a choice between "ible" and "able." I took a quick survey of colleagues: A majority, but not a strong majority, voted for "ible."

Bob from certain actions, whether she observes them or not.[3] Bottom line: When you see the terms *moral hazard* and *hidden action*, they both connote imperfectly the collection of issues and models that are explored in this chapter.

The structure of this chapter

The general subject of moral hazard (or hidden action) and incentives has spawned a huge literature. As with most contextual topics in this volume, lengthy books have been written on the subject. For a textbook, choices of what to cover and in what depth must be made:

1. This chapter deals primarily with the context that goes by such names as *the principal–agent* problem and *agency theory*, in which Principal Alice employs Agent Bob (or, in places, several agents). Other contexts are slighted in the expectation that you'll be able to export the analyses given here to those contexts.

2. The first part of the chapter—Sections 19.1 through 19.4—deals with what might called the "classic" principal–agent model, in which Principal Alice, with an unrealistic amount of knowledge about Agent Bob and the circumstances of the prospective job, designs an optimal-for-herself scheme that is offered to Bob on a take-it-or-leave-it basis. This part of the chapter deals in such issues as existence proofs and somewhat general characterizations of the "optimal" contract.

3. Modeling the principal–agent relationship is a good deal simpler if the principal restricts herself to relatively simple incentive contracts. Section 19.5 studies a particular parametric model in which the principal only considers linear incentive schemes; then this model is used to explore multitasking and comparative performance evaluation.

4. In Section 19.6, a rationale for restricting consideration to linear incentive schemes is provided.

5. Throughout the chapter, the agent's risk aversion drives the principal–agent problem. While this is true of much of the literature, problems of moral hazard and incentives can arise even when both the agent and principal are risk neutral. Section 19.7 wraps up by indicating how this can happen.

---

[3] For now, I speak of "legally enforceable"; but this phrase is both too strong—if the agreement is broken, will the offended party incur the costs of invoking enforcement through the courts? (a topic for Volume III) and too weak: Chapter 21 shows how repeated interactions between the parties can render a jointly observed contingency into something on which a binding agreement can be conditioned, even if third-party enforcement is absent. And, in a society filled with strictly honorable individuals, a handshake agreement between the parties may suffice for contractibility (which is also Volume III material). I apologize for this use of a somewhat ugly and less than perfectly precise term, but the idea is important to this story. So I hope that it is clear enough.

19.1. A Very Simple Model

We begin with the very simplest version of the principal–agent problem.

Alice, the *principal*, employs Bob, her *agent*, to manage a venture for her. Bob chooses a level of effort to exert, which is either *take it easy*, denoted e (for easy), or *work hard*, denoted h. Alice does not observe Bob's effort choice or, at least, cannot employ an enforceable contract that specifies his effort choice; she instead observes the *outcome* v of Bob's effort, which for simplicity is either that the venture is a *rousing success* or a *moderate success*. Bob's level of effort affects the probability of a rousing success, with π_e being the probability of a rousing success if his effort level is e, and π_h being the probability of a rousing success if his effort level is h. The story, naturally, is that $\pi_h > \pi_e$. To keep from having to consider special cases, assume that $0 < \pi_e < \pi_h < 1$.

Alice induces Bob to take the job with a contingent contract. This contract specifies a payment to Bob of w_0 if the venture is moderate success and a payment of w_1 if it is a rousing success. Alice's gross payoff (gross of what she pays Bob) is v_1 if the venture is a rousing success and v_0 if it is a moderate success; her net payoffs are $v_1 - w_1$ and $v_0 - w_0$, respectively. Alice is risk neutral concerning her payoff, hence her expected net payoff (which is her objective function) is

$$\pi_h(v_1 - w_1) + (1 - \pi_h)(v_0 - w_0), \text{ if Bob chooses } h, \text{ and}$$
$$\pi_e(v_1 - w_1) + (1 - \pi_e)(v_0 - w_0), \text{ if he chooses } e.$$

Bob is risk averse and evaluates his choices based on the expected utility of his wage, less an amount of "disutility" related to his level of effort. Letting u be the utility function of his wage, and normalizing his disutility of effort to be 0 if he chooses e and $d > 0$ if he chooses h, his overall (expected) utility (which he seeks to maximize) is

$$\pi_h \, u(w_1) + (1 - \pi_h) \, u(w_0) - d, \text{ if he chooses } h, \text{ and}$$
$$\pi_e \, u(w_1) + (1 - \pi_e) \, u(w_0), \text{ if he chooses } e.$$

Bob takes the job only if it promises him expected utility of at least u_0, his so-called *reservation level* of utility. If Alice does not employ Bob, her expected payoff is 0.

Assumptions 19.1.

a. *Bob's utility function u is continuously differentiable, strictly increasing, and strictly concave.*

b. *The domain of the function u includes an open interval that contains the closed interval*

$$\left[u_0 - \frac{\pi_e d}{\pi_h - \pi_e}, \quad u_0 + \frac{(1 - \pi_e)d}{\pi_h - \pi_e} \right].$$

c. *Let w^b be the solution to $u(w^b) = u_0$. Then $\pi_e v_1 + (1 - \pi_e)v_0 > w^b$.*

Under these assumptions, the "answer" to Alice's problem is as follows:

"Proposition." *Let w^b be as in Assumption 19.1, and let w_0^* and w_1^* be values such that*

$$u(w_0^*) = u_0 - \frac{\pi_e d}{\pi_h - \pi_e} \quad and \quad u(w_1^*) = u_0 + \frac{(1 - \pi_e)d}{\pi_h - \pi_e}.$$

Let

$$V_e := \pi_e v_1 + (1 - \pi_e)v_0 - w^b \quad and \quad V_h := \pi_h(v_1 - w_1^*) + (1 - \pi_h)(v_0 - w_0^*).$$

If $V_e > V_h$, then Alice should offer Bob a flat wage of w^b, which he accepts, receiving a sure thing payment of w^b for a utility of u_0, he chooses e, and Alice's expected payoff is V_e. If $V_h > V_e$, then Alice should offer Bob the wage schedule of w_0^* if the project is a moderate success and w_1^* if it is a rousing success, which Bob accepts and under which he chooses h, for a net expected utility of u_0, and Alice's expected payoff is V_h. If $V_e = V_h$, Alice should follow either of those two plans—offer w^b no matter what the outcome is, or offer w_1^*, w_0^* —and Bob responds as detailed above, depending on which plan Alice offers.

Giving formal meaning to this "Proposition"

This result is introduced as the answer to Alice's problem, using vague terminology about what Alice "should" do. And it is given as a "Proposition," with scare quotes indicating that it employs vague terminology. So our first task is to formalize what these vague terms mean, and to give a precise and formal proposition that is susceptible of proof.

We formalize this situation as an extensive-form game: Alice moves first, setting the terms of the contract, namely, the values of w_1 and w_0, which may be equal. Bob, having seen Alice's terms, then chooses among three options: refuse the contract, in which case Bob's payoff is u_0 and Alice's is 0; accept the contract and supply effort level e; or accept the contract and supply effort level h. The payoffs, as a function of these actions, are: Alice's payoff is her expected net return; Bob's payoff is his expected net utility. (And, at this point, if you are unfamiliar with the notions of extensive-form games and subgame perfection, please consult Appendices 10 and 11.)

We might then go looking for Nash equilibria of this game, of which there are rather a lot. For instance, let $w^\dagger = \pi_e v_1 + (1 - \pi_e)v_0 - \delta$, for $\delta > 0$ small enough so that $w^\dagger > w^b$. (Assumption 19.1(c) guarantees that such a δ exists.) Suppose Bob's strategy is: If Alice offers any contract other than a flat wage of $w^\dagger$, he refuses the contract, leaving her a payoff of 0. If she offers a flat wage of $w^\dagger$, he accepts and provides effort level e, which provides Alice with an expected payoff of δ. Hence Alice's best response to this strategy is to offer the contract that Bob is "insisting" on; this constitutes a Nash equilibrium.

But this Nash equilibrium is based on threats by Bob that are not credible. That is, for the game we've formulated, suppose Alice offers Bob the wage schedule

$w_1 = w_0 = w^b + \epsilon$ for small $\epsilon > 0$. If Bob accepts this and chooses e, his expected utility is a bit more than u_0. Yet his strategy in the preceding paragraph is to turn this down, for a payoff of (only) u_0. If Alice gets to make her offer on a take-it-or-leave-it basis—no bargaining allowed—Bob's threat to turn down this offer is not credible. In the language of game theory, the Nash equilibrium of the previous paragraph is not subgame perfect. And that is how we formalize the "Proposition":

Proposition 19.2. *In any subgame-perfect Nash equilibrium of the game as formulated here, Alice's offer, Bob's response, and the resulting net payoffs to the two players, are all as specified in the "Proposition." That is, if $V_e > V_h$, Alice offers Bob the wage w^b regardless of outcome; he accepts and chooses e. If $V_h > V_e$, she offers him the wage package w_0^*, w_1^*; he accepts and chooses h. If $V_e = V_h$, she can randomize as she pleases between these two; he responds according to the offer made.*

This proposition does not describe in full a subgame-perfect equilibrium; it doesn't specify Bob's response to off-path offers by Alice. And it does not say that there is a unique subgame perfect equilibrium, because there are many of those: For some off-path offers by Alice, Bob may have more than one best response. He is constrained in the equilibrium in how he responds to Alice's on-path offer, but his (sequentially rational) responses to off-path offers that leave him indifferent are whatever he wishes.

Of course, Alice's on-path offer does leave Bob indifferent between possible responses. If $V_e > V_h$, her offer of w^b leaves him indifferent between rejecting the offer or accepting and choosing e; if $V_h > V_e$, her offer of w_0^*, w_1^* leaves him indifferent among all three of his responses. But in equilibrium, he *must* respond to the on-path offer as described. You might find it helpful at this point to consult the subsection "Where 'ties' have important consequences" in Appendix 11 (page 555). In the game formulation I've specified, w_1 and w_0 are continuous variables. If Alice offers Bob (w_0^*, w_1^*), so that Bob is indifferent between all three of his possible responses, Alice can force the response h that she desires by offering instead $(w_0, w_1 + \epsilon)$, for any (small) $\epsilon > 0$. Since she would want to "force" Bob with the smallest possible ϵ, a game-theoretic analysis requires that, along the path of play, he takes the action that she prefers whenever he is indifferent. Because if he didn't, she would not be choosing a best response to his strategy.

Why does Alice have all the bargaining power?

The proof of this proposition is coming, but there is a serious modeling question to be addressed first. Because the formal model has Alice making an offer to which Bob must respond, combined with the assumption that we look (only) for subgame-perfect equilibria, we've effectively given Alice all the bargaining power. She makes a take-it-or-leave-it, fait-accompli offer, and (in essence) covers her ears and refuses to hear any counteroffers from Bob. It is certainly legitimate to ask why we've fixed things in this fashion.

This is how the literature proceeds, but that is hardly a satisfactory explanation. And, as long as we think of this as a negotiation between one principal, Alice, and one agent, Bob, giving Alice all the bargaining power is hardly satisfactory. We expect the two to bargain, which is the topic of Chapter 23.

However, suppose we think of Alice as an employer, dealing with many employees, either simultaneously or sequentially. As discussed in Chapter 22, this can provide her with a relatively strong bargaining position vis-à-vis individual employees. But this raises other concerns. We analyze Alice versus Bob, assuming that Alice can tailor the offer she makes to Bob's specific characteristics, namely, his probabilities of having a rousing success as a function of his level of effort, his utility function u, his reservation level of utility u_0, and his personal disutility d of effort level h. If Alice's bargaining power stems from the fact that she deals with a variety of different employees, then (presumably) they differ in these characteristics; the question becomes: Can she tailor the deal she offers Bob to his characteristics, while tailoring the deals offered to Daniel, Edward, and Frank to their individual characteristics?[4] If not, then her best course of action may be to offer a menu of compensation schemes, letting her employees select among them (or reject them all).[5] To model such phenomena takes ideas from Chapter 20, so we leave this matter for now.

A different answer is that we are merely searching for an efficient arrangement, and one method for characterizing efficient arrangements is to maximize the payoff to one party subject to a greater-than-or-equal-to constraint on the payoff of the other party. Since u_0 is a (more or less) free parameter of the problem, we can interpret the program as the search for efficient arrangements between principal Alice and agent Bob.

Proof of Proposition 19.2

To prove Proposition 19.2, we solve two subproblems. What is the best that Alice can do for herself, if she sets a scheme (w_0, w_1) that motivates Bob to choose e? And then what is best for her, if her offer to Bob motivates him to choose h?

A change of variables simplifies the exposition. Rather than choosing a wage package (w_0, w_1), we work in terms of Bob's utilities from such a pair of wages. That is, we make Alice's choice be the utility-levels package (z_0, z_1), where $z_0 := u(w_0)$, the utility Bob will get from the wage he is offered in case the outcome is a moderate success, and $z_1 := u(w_1)$, his utility from the wage he receives if the outcome is a rousing success. To translate these utility levels into the corresponding dollar values for Alice's objective function, let ψ be the inverse function to u; that is, if $u(w) = z$, then $\psi(z) = w$. Note that ψ is strictly increasing, continuously differentiable, and strictly convex.

---

[4] For readers who know the terminology, the question is: Can she act as a first-degree "price-discriminating" monopsonist?

[5] In other words, she could engage in second- or third-degree "price discrimination."

Consider the following two minimization problems:

Problem e: Minimize $\pi_e \psi(z_1) + (1 - \pi_e)\psi(z_0)$, subject to

$$\pi_e z_1 + (1 - \pi_e)z_0 \geq u_0, \text{ and } \pi_e z_1 + (1 - \pi_e)z_0 \geq \pi_h z_1 + (1 - \pi_h)z_0 - d.$$

Problem h: Minimize $\pi_h \psi(z_1) + (1 - \pi_h)\psi(z_0)$, subject to

$$\pi_h z_1 + (1 - \pi_h)z_0 - d \geq u_0, \text{ and } \pi_h z_1 + (1 - \pi_h)z_0 - d \geq \pi_e z_1 + (1 - \pi_e)z_0.$$

Problem e captures the problem facing Alice if she wishes to devise a wage offer for Bob that minimizes what she must pay him to induce him to accept and to choose effort level e; the objective function is the expected amount he is paid (which she wishes to minimize); the first constraint says that he'd be happy to take this offer and supply effort level e rather than declining the offer; and the second constraint says that, having taken this offer, he (weakly) prefers effort level e to effort level h. Problem h has her minimizing what she must pay him to induce him to accept and to choose effort level h.

Note that, in both problems, we formulate the constraints with weak inequalities, following the observation that Alice can force the response she wants with an arbitrarily small variation in the variables. (This is obvious for Problem h; for Problem e, it is a tiny bit harder to show but is true.) And, note that we have Alice minimizing the wage she expects to pay to Bob, rather than maximizing her expected profit net of that wage. This is legitimate, because if she forces Bob's choice of action (which is what the constraints do), her gross expected profit is fixed, so maximizing her expected net profit is the same as minimizing the expectation of what she pays Bob.

Lemma 19.3. *The unique solution to Problem e is $z_1^* = z_2^* = u_0$. The unique solution to Problem h is $z_0^* = u_0 - \pi_e d/(\pi_h - \pi_e)$ and $z_1^* = u_0 + (1 - \pi_e)d/(\pi_h - \pi_e)$.*

Proof of the lemma. In both problems, the objective function is strictly convex, and the feasible set is convex. Hence, the solution must be unique. We need only argue that we do indeed have solutions to each problem.

The argument that $z_0^* = z_1^* = u_0$ is the solution for Problem e is simple, if you recall the final section of Chapter 8 in Volume I, concerning efficient risk sharing. If Bob is choosing e, Alice and Bob together "own" a venture whose possible values are v_1 and v_0, with probabilities π_e and $1 - \pi_e$, respectively. Efficient risk sharing, since Alice is risk neutral and Bob is risk averse, is for Alice to bear all the risk. That is, to share the risk efficiently, Alice must set $w_0 = w_1$ or, in terms of the formulation, $z_0 = z_1$. And this "flat wage" setting is entirely consistent with Bob choosing e: He won't choose h if his wage doesn't change with the outcome. To solve Alice's problem, all that remains is to find that flat wage that makes her as well off as possible, which is the lowest w consistent with Bob choosing to work at all. This, of course, is $w_0 = w_1 = w^b$, which gives $z_0^* = z_1^* = u_0$.

The argument for Problem h is a bit less obvious. The key is to note that the proposed solution z_0^*, z_1^* is precisely where the two constraints simultaneously bind.

(You can do the simple algebra to show that this is the proposed solution.) Why must both constraints bind? Of course, at any feasible solution, both constraints must hold, so consider a point z_0, z_1 where there is slack in the first constraint. Then lower z_0 a bit. This loosens the second constraint and improves the objective function. Hence, at the optimum, the first constraint must bind. As for the second constraint, rewrite it as $(\pi_h - \pi_e)(z_1 - z_0) \geq d$. If this constraint doesn't bind, lower z_1 by $(1 - \pi_h)\epsilon$ while raising z_0 by $\pi_h\epsilon$, for small ϵ. This has no impact on the first constraint, while the second constraint is still satisfied if ϵ is small. Since $z_1 > z_0$ (the second constraint is satisfied), strict convexity of ψ implies that $\psi'(z_1) > \psi'(z_0)$, and a quick application of Taylor's Theorem shows that this improves the objective function. This argument is a bit informal, because the first part assumes that, starting from the pair (z_0, z_1), we can lower z_0. What if z_0 is the lowest possible value of u? In this case, we would have $z_0 < z_0^*$, and either $z_1 \leq z_1^*$, in which case (z_0, z_1) fails the first constraint, or $z_1 > z_1^*$, in which case the second constraint is slack.

If you are not convinced by either of these somewhat loose arguments, recall that for these two problems, the first-order/complementary slackness (FO/CS) conditions are both necessary and sufficient for a solution. Then see Problem 19.1 and its solution in the *Online Supplement*.   ∎

I provide the somewhat informal proof here to emphasize the intuition: To induce Bob to choose h, $w_1 > w_0$ or, in terms of utilities, $z_1 > z_0$, is required. But Alice doesn't want to push z_1 and z_0 apart any farther than is required to meet the second constraint, as to do so means even less efficient risk sharing. And to induce Bob to take the job at all, his expected utility must be at least his reservation utility. But Alice doesn't want (at her optimal offer) to leave Bob with more utility than u_0, as to do so means paying him more, which means less for her. The solution for Alice, therefore, is at the intersection of these two constraints.

This proves the lemma. But, from here, the proof of the Proposition is clear. Alice will certainly wish to induce Bob to accept the contract; if he does not, her payoff is 0, and Assumption 19.1(c) ensures that, by offering a flat wage $w^b + \epsilon$ for small ϵ, his sequentially rational response is to accept and choose e, which means a strictly positive payoff for her. Hence, in any subgame-perfect equilibrium, her offer will induce him to accept. It might induce him to choose e, and it might induce him to choose h. But again relying on his response being sequentially rational, Alice maximizes her payoff from a response of e by solving Problem e, and she maximizes her payoff from a response of h by solving Problem h. (This of course, depends on the "indifferent Bob does what Alice wants" argument.) We know what the unique solutions to these two problems are; Proposition 19.2 simply states that Alice chooses whichever gives her the higher expected payoff.

The first-best solution (from Alice's perspective)

At the risk of over analyzing a pretty simple problem, compare the solution provided by Proposition 19.2 with the "first-best" solution, meaning the solution to Alice's wage-setting problem if she could contractually enforce Bob's choice of action, although she must satisfy the so-called participation constraint that his expected utility is at least u_0.

I believe that this is the first time in these volumes the term "first-best" has been encountered. It is far from the last: "First-best" is a term that economists, and this volume, frequently employ. It goes back to Volume I, Chapter 8, and it refers to efficient arrangements of the actions and affairs of the economic actors, efficient in the sense of Pareto efficiency, where all informational and strategic imperfections are dismissed from consideration. You can think, generally, about what would be possible if a benevolent, all-knowing, and all-powerful dictator were able enforceably to tell all the economic actors what they must do. In some applications, including this one, things are complicated by participation constraints—the economic actors have an inalienable right to "opt out"—in which case the actors' "opt-out" utilities must be met or exceeded by the benevolent dictator.

We could ask for the full set of Pareto-efficient outcomes, if Alice and Bob are subject to the dictates of this benevolent dictator, subject to participation constraints on both sides: Bob must be given expected utility of at least u_0: and Alice must have an expected payoff that is no less than 0. However, for this problem, since we have supposed that Alice has all the bargaining power, the "first-best" is the efficient arrangement that Alice would choose if *she* were the dictator, subject only to Bob's opt-out or participation constraint. That is, in this context, first-best means: Which Alice-dictated action by Bob, together with which wage-payment system, maximizes Alice's payoff, subject to Bob achieving his reservation net expected utility of u_0.

The analysis is simple: Assumption 19.1(c) implies that she wants him to choose either e or h. Once that is decided, efficient risk sharing is her remaining concern, which means giving Bob a constant wage:

- If her decision is to have him choose e, a flat wage of $w^\flat$ is sufficient to meet his participation constraint.

- And, if she decides to have him choose h, the wage $w^\sharp$ she must offer is the solution to $u(w^\sharp) = u_0 + d$; that is, $w^\sharp = \psi(u_0 + d)$.

Note that, as long as $\pi_h < 1$, z_1^* and z_0^*, the utility levels she must offer to get him to choose h (as cheaply as possible for her) if she can't fix his effort, satisfy

$$z_0^* = u_0 - \frac{\pi_e}{\pi_h - \pi_e}d < u_0 < u_0 + d < u_0 + \frac{1 - \pi_e}{\pi_h - \pi_e}d = z_1^*,$$

and so by monotonicity of ψ, $w_0^* < w^\flat < w^\sharp < w_1^*$. Moreover,

$$
\begin{aligned}
\pi_h w_1^* + (1 - \pi_h)w_0^* &= \pi_h \psi\left(u_0 + \frac{1 - \pi_e}{\pi_h - \pi_e}d\right) + (1 - \pi_h)\psi\left(u_0 - \frac{\pi_e}{\pi_h - \pi_e}d\right) \\
&\geq \psi\left(\pi_h\left[u_0 + \frac{1 - \pi_e}{\pi_h - \pi_e}d\right] + (1 - \pi_h)\left[u_0 - \frac{\pi_e}{\pi_h - \pi_e}d\right]\right) \\
&= \psi\left(u_0 + \frac{\pi_h(1 - \pi_e) - (1 - \pi_h)\pi_e}{\pi_h - \pi_e}d\right) = \psi(u_0 + d) = w^\sharp,
\end{aligned}
$$

where the inequality comes from Jensen's inequality, since ψ is convex. Or, in words, the expected wage that Alice pays Bob, if she wishes to induce him to work hard, is greater than the wage she would pay him if she could force him to work hard. In consequence of which:

Because Alice cannot force Bob to work hard, there are parameter values for which she will choose a wage schedule that has him choose effort level e, even though the first-best (efficient) level of effort is h. The fact that she cannot force his choice of effort can introduce an inefficiency into their interaction. (If you don't see why the italicized statement follows from the last multiline display, think harder about it.)

If Bob is also risk neutral, or even if only Bob is risk neutral

If both Bob and Alice are risk neutral, then any risk-sharing scheme is efficient. And if only Bob is risk neutral, then efficient risk sharing would imply that Alice should be left with a profit that is independent of the level of success of the venture. This can be achieved and, what is more, it can be achieved while implementing the first-best solution.

To keep the algebra to a minimum, assume that risk-neutral Bob has utility function $u(w) = w$. (If Bob's utility function is $aw + b$, then d can be rescaled to be measured in dollars of disutility, so this is without any real loss of generality.)

The expected "size" of the total pie if Bob chooses e is $\pi_e v_1 + (1 - \pi_e)v_0$. Alice must provide Bob with utility u_0, which is now u_0 dollars. So, the best she can do for herself, if he is to choose e, is $\pi_e v_1 + (1 - \pi_e)v_0 - u_0$. Similarly, if Bob chooses h, Alice must compensate him with $u_0 + d$ dollars, so the best she can do for herself is $\pi_h v_1 + (1 - \pi_h)v_0 - u_0 - d$. So, overall, if she can achieve these first-best outcomes, she'll choose to have Bob pick e if $\pi_e v_1 + (1 - \pi_e)v_0 \geq \pi_h v_1 + (1 - \pi_h)v_0 - d$, and she'll choose to have him pick h otherwise.

So, suppose $\pi_e v_1 + (1 - \pi_e)v_0 \geq \pi_h v_1 + (1 - \pi_h)v_0 - d$. Alice proposes to Bob that she'll pay him

$$w_0 = v_0 - [\pi_e v_1 + (1 - \pi_e)v_0 - u_0] \text{ in case of a moderate success, and}$$
$$w_1 = v_1 - [\pi_e v_1 + (1 - \pi_e)v_0 - u_0] \text{ in case of a rousing success.}$$

This leaves her with a sure-thing outcome of $\pi_e v_1 + (1 - \pi_e)v_0 - u_0$ in either case. And, as long as $\pi_e v_1 + (1 - \pi_e)v_0 \geq \pi_h v_1 + (1 - \pi_h)v_0 - d$, risk-neutral Bob, facing this wage scheme, will choose e.

Alternatively, if $\pi_e v_1 + (1 - \pi_e)v_0 < \pi_h v_1 + (1 - \pi_h)v_0 - d$, then Alice proposes to Bob that she'll pay him

$$w_0 = v_0 - [\pi_h v_1 + (1 - \pi_h)v_0 - u_0 - d] \text{ in case of a moderate success, and}$$
$$w_1 = v_1 - [\pi_h v_1 + (1 - \pi_h)v_0 - u_0 - d] \text{ in case of a rousing success.}$$

This leaves her with a sure-thing $\pi_h v_1 + (1 - \pi_h)v_0 - u_0 - d$ and, if $\pi_e v_1 + (1 - \pi_e)v_0 < \pi_h v_1 + (1 - \pi_h)v_0 - d$, then Bob, facing this wage scheme, will choose h.

In either case, what is happening here is straightforward. Because Bob is risk neutral, it is efficient to have him bear all the risk. So, essentially, Alice sells the rights to the profit stream from this venture to Bob for whichever of $\pi_e v_1 + (1 - \pi_e)v_0 - u_0$ and $\pi_h v_1 + (1 - \pi_h)v_0 - u_0 - d$ is greater.[6] Bob, now the residual claimant to the risky venture, of his own volition will choose whichever of e or h is more efficient; as residual claimant, he internalizes the cost to himself of choosing h instead of e.

This begs the question: If Bob is strictly risk averse, can Alice sell him the venture for a fixed amount, so that he internalizes the cost of choosing h or e? She can do so, but (except for one very special case) she won't be able to realize as much expected net profit as she gets as per Proposition 19.2. If she sells the venture for a fixed price, Bob is bearing all the risk. That is inefficient risk sharing: So that Bob is prepared to pay Alice's price—so that his expected utility is u_0—he won't be willing to pay what Alice gets per Proposition 19.2. (This loose argument is incomplete, and there is a very special case in which it is simply wrong. Problem 19.2 asks you to fix things.)

The fundamental trade-off

These special cases provide insight into the basic trade-off that Alice faces if Bob is not risk neutral and if Alice can't control Bob's choice of action.

Because the overall "returns" from this venture are uncertain, Alice's choice of w_1 and w_0 amounts to a scheme of risk sharing: The two wages are Bob's shares; $v_1 - w_1$ and $v_0 - w_0$ are Alice's shares. If Alice is risk neutral and Bob is risk averse, we know that efficient risk sharing entails Alice shouldering all the risk; that is, having $w_1 = w_0$. Any movement away from this equal-wage solution—presumably movement in the direction of having w_1 be larger than w_0—is inefficient and is increasingly inefficient the larger is $w_1 - w_0$.

But if $w_1 = w_0$, Bob has no incentive to exert himself by choosing h. If the first-best solution has Bob choosing e, this is not a problem: Alice can implement $w_1 = w_0 = w^b$ and, although she can't enforce Bob choosing e, he'll do so on his own. The problem arises if Alice would like to implement a scheme that causes Bob to choose h. To do this, to provide him with incentives to exert himself, she must have $w_1 > w_0$ and by a discrete amount, to cover his disutility of effort. The larger $w_1 - w_0$ is, the more incentive he will have to exert himself, but (the trade-off) the less efficient will be the resultant risk sharing.

If Alice can control Bob's level of effort, she doesn't need to trade off risk-sharing efficiency for effort incentives. If Bob is risk neutral, she doesn't need to worry about risk-sharing efficiency, and she can even shift all the risk onto Bob. (Indeed, if *she* were risk averse and he is risk neutral, she can, by shifting all the risk onto him, achieve the first best.)

But in the context of the original formulation, Alice may face a fundamental trade-off: She can induce Bob to exert himself, but doing so "costs" in terms of efficient risk sharing. In this ultra-simple version of such problems, her best policy

---

[6] We are assuming here that Alice, in selling the venture to Bob, still has all the bargaining power. In the context of selling him the business, this is an even more heroic assumption than it was previously.

is either to go for efficient risk sharing and resign herself to his choosing not to exert himself, or to sacrifice efficient risk sharing (but as little as it necessary), to induce him to work hard. In the next section, we'll see how well this basic insight works (or doesn't) in less simple formulations.

(And, to foreshadow future discussion: Do not conclude that this "fundamental trade-off" is the essence of the principal–agent problem or, more generally, problems of moral hazard and incentives. In Section 19.7, I'll argue that, while inefficient risk sharing is an important consideration, it isn't necessary for a moral-hazard-and-incentives problem to be present.)

Comparative statics

Bob's expected utility is being held to u_0 in all cases, so the only question of comparative statics we can ask is: How does Alice's expected payoff vary with changes in the various parameters of the model, namely, $v_1, v_0, u_0, \pi_e, \pi_h$, and d?

Proposition 19.4, begun. *Alice's expected payoff is strictly decreasing in u_0, is weakly decreasing in d, and weakly increasing in π_h, and is strictly increasing in both v_1 and v_0. In regions where Alice's best option involves inducing Bob to choose h, Alice's expected payoff is strictly decreasing in d and strictly increasing in π_h. The impact of increases in π_e depend on whether Bob is choosing e or h: For higher values of π_e, Bob chooses e, and Alice's expected payoff is strictly increasing in π_e; for sufficiently low values of π_e, so that Alice induces Bob to choose h, Alice's expected payoff is strictly decreasing in π_e.*

The proof is quite straightforward for u_0, v_1, and v_0, and it is relatively straightforward for the other parameters. But, for the sake of completeness, see Problem 19.3 and its solution in the *Online Supplement*. And, except for the result for π_e, these comparative statics results are (I think) fairly intuitive. The impact of π_e on Alice's expected net payoff, however, may require a bit of explanation: As π_e approaches π_h (recall: $\pi_e < \pi_h$ is required), Alice no longer wishes to "spend" what it would take to motivate h. And since she is allowing Bob to choose e for the unchanging wage w^b, she prefers higher π_e, which makes her gross—and therefore her net—expected payoff larger. However, for smaller values of π_e, it may be worthwhile for her to motivate h. (This may not happen, even if π_e approaches 0: If v_0 is close to v_1 and d is large, Alice might settle for v_0 even if π_e is very small.) And, in this region, higher π_e requires a larger gap between w_1^* and w_0^*, to motivate h, although here a bit of algebra is needed to show that this means lower expected net payoffs for Alice.

The one comparative static that is not entirely straightforward involves Bob's utility function u. It seems natural to suppose that Alice's expected payoff should be decreasing the more risk averse Bob is, but once we start shifting utility functions, the meaning of the parameters u_0 and d becomes a bit problematic, since they are expressed in utility terms. These difficulties can be overcome as follows:

Proposition 19.4, completed. *Compare Alice's expected payoff with two different Bobs, Bob1 and Bob2, where Bob1 is strictly more risk averse than Bob2. To make the comparison possible, write $\hat{u}$ for Bob1's utility function and $\check{u}$ for Bob2's utility function, and assume* *that $\hat{u}(w^\flat) = \check{u}(w^\flat) = u_0$, and $u(w^\sharp) - \check{u}(w^\sharp) = u_0 + d$. The, using hats and checks on top of V_e and V_h to denote those values for the two Bobs, we have $\hat{V}_e = \check{V}_e$ (of course), and $\hat{V}_h < \check{V}_h$.*

The interpretation of the conditions $\hat{u}(w^\flat) = \check{u}(w^\flat) = u_0$ and $\hat{u}(w^\sharp) = \check{u}(w^\sharp) = u_0 + d$ is that, in dollar terms, the two Bob's have the same reservation wages for both taking is easy and working hard. The proof is given in the *Online Supplement*, as part of the solution to Problem 19.3.

19.2. A Somewhat General Model

We are able to get nearly complete answers from the very simple model in Section 19.1, because the model has only two outcomes and two possible actions by Bob. As we generalize the model, the methods of Section 19.1 continue to apply, but the answers become much more complicated without some strong assumptions.[7]

Alice wishes to hire Bob to perform some service and, in pursuit of this objective, makes a wage offer to him. If he accepts Alice's offer, Bob chooses among a finite collection of *actions*, denoted $A = \{a_1, \ldots, a_N\}$. Alice's wage offer is contingent on a finite set of *contractible outcomes*, one and only one of which will be observed. The set of contractible outcomes is denoted $X = \{x_1, \ldots, x_M\}$, and the probability that outcome x_m occurs if Bob chooses action a_n is π_{mn}.

We again have the adjective *contractible*. To reiterate, these are outcomes that can be used to condition Bob's wage in an enforceable manner. It is reasonable to suppose that each of these outcomes is *observable* to both Alice and Bob. But observability by them is not necessarily enough; Alice's commitment to pay what she (contingently) promises must be credible. This credibility might arise through a third-party enforcement mechanism (Bob sues Alice if she reneges), or perhaps as per Chapter 22, credibility might derive from Alice's concern to maintain a reputation for fair dealing.[8]

The wage schedule that Alice proposes, therefore, is a function w with domain X. We assume that there is a range of *possible* wages W that Alice can propose, which is an interval of real numbers unbounded above. The range W might be all of R, it might be a closed interval $[\underline{w}, \infty)$, and it might be an open interval $(\underline{w}, \infty)$. We require that Bob's utility-of-wage function u has domain that contains W and is strictly increasing, strictly concave, and continuously differentiable.

For technical reasons, one case is ruled out: If W has the form $(\underline{w}, \infty)$ for finite $\underline{w}$, it must be that $\lim_{w \downarrow \underline{w}} u(w) = -\infty$. If instead $\lim_{w \downarrow \underline{w}} u(w)$ is finite, then $\underline{w}$ must be a feasible wage for Alice to offer.

As before, we model the situation as a game in which Alice first proposes a wage schedule $w : X \to W$, and Bob responds: He can reject Alice's offer, which

---

[7]   The model and analysis to follow are based on the seminal paper Grossman and Hart (1983). The presentation follows closely the presentation of these issues in Kreps (1990a.)

[8]   If this seems to be making much out of an otherwise obvious point, wait for Chapter 22, and more significantly in terms of real-life economic practice, a general discussion of transaction-cost economics in Volume III).

provides him utility u_0 and provides Alice with payoff 0; or he can accept the offer and choose an action $a_n \in A$, which provides Alice with expected payoff

$$V(a_n) := \hat{V}(a_n) - \sum_{m=1}^{M} \pi_{mn} w(x_m)$$

and provides Bob with expected payoff

$$\sum_{m=1}^{M} \pi_{mn} u\big(w(x_m)\big) - d_n,$$

for a vector $d = (d_1, \ldots, d_N)$ of Bob's *disutilities* from choosing the various actions and for his utility-of-wage function $u : W \to R$. For notational convenience, assume that $d_1 = 0$ and $d_n > 0$ for $n = 2, \ldots, N$; that is, action a_1 is the uniquely least-onerous action for Bob, and his utility function is normalized so that the disutility of action a_1 is 0. We further assume that for some $w^b \in W$, $u(w^b) = u_0$—that is, Alice is allowed to offer the wage function $w(x_m) \equiv w^b$, which leads Bob to choose to participate and to choose a_1—and that $w^b \geq 0$. (In words, Bob's outside option involves a certainty-equivalent greater or equal to a wage of \$0.) Finally, when we move to analysis, we look for subgame-perfect Nash equilibria of this game, where Bob learns Alice's wage offer and responds. And, in line with Assumption 19.1(c), we assume that $\hat{V}(a_1) - w^b > 0$; that is, Alice can profitably employ Bob by offering $w(x) \equiv w^b$.

- At this level of generality, the net expected benefit to Alice if Bob faces a wage scheme $\big(w(x_m)\big)_{x \in X}$ and chooses action a_n is the difference between her gross expected payoff $\hat{V}(a_n)$ and the expected wage she pays him, $\sum_{m=1}^{M} \pi_{mn} w(x_m)$. It is typical in models to assume that Alice's gross payoff depends (only) on x_m and can be written as $\sum_{m=1}^{M} \pi_{mn} \hat{v}(x_m)$; when we specialize to effort incentives in Section 19.3, we assume that this holds. But, for the time being, we allow her expected gross payoff to depend on the action a_n in ways that go beyond the influence this choice has on the probabilities π_{mn}.

- As in Section 19.1, Bob is strictly risk averse and Alice is risk neutral,[9] so that efficient risk sharing means loading all the risk onto Alice (i.e., providing Bob with a fixed wage). But for any fixed wage provided to Bob, he has no incentive to choose an action more onerous than action a_1. If, instead, Bob is risk neutral (and even if Alice is risk averse), one *may* be able to obtain the first-best solution by having Alice sell the opportunity to Bob for a fixed payment, following which Bob chooses the first-best action on his own. Note the italicized *may*: At this level of generality, this option may not be possible. Problem 19.4 provides conditions under which it is possible; Section 19.7 discusses a case in which, arguably, it is not.

---

[9] Since we have the general term $\hat{V}(a_n)$ as Alice's gross expected payoff if Bob chooses a_n, we could reinterpret $\hat{V}(a_n)$ as a gross certainty equivalent. But, importantly, Alice is risk neutral with regard to the (random) wage paid to Bob, so it is simplest to assume she is risk neutral altogether.

- In Section 19.3, we will assume that the actions a_m are linearly ordered and that $d_n < d_{n+1}$; with that assumption, the interpretation of the a_n as increasingly onerous levels of effort is natural. But, for now, the actions a_n come from an arbitrary set. For example, they might represent different allocations of a fixed amount of time between a collection of different "dimensions" of the job. (This interpretation will return in Section 19.5, when we discuss *multitasking*.)

- I've assumed that there is a single least-onerous action, which is labeled a_1, and that Bob's disutility from a_1 is $d_1 = 0$. If there is a tie for the least onerous action, fix one of those that provides the maximal gross benefit to Alice $\hat{V}(a)$, make that action a_1, and discard all the other actions that are tied for most onerous. You should have no problem, once we've done the analysis, to see that doing this is virtually without any loss of generality: If Alice is going to induce Bob to choose any of the tied-for-least-onerous actions—and maintaining the assumption that Bob, when indifferent among several actions, chooses the one that Alice prefers—she'll induce one that gives herself the highest gross benefit, and she is indifferent between any of those.[10]

Minimizing the cost of inducing a particular action: Formulation and existence

To find a subgame-perfect equilibrium outcome, we follow the scheme of Section 19.1. For each action choice a_n, we ask: What is the least expected-cost wage offer that Alice can propose that will induce Bob to accept and then choose action a_n?

As in Section 19.1, instead of wage levels as variables, we use the utilities that Bob attaches to each wage level. Let $Z := \{z \in R : z = u(w) \text{ for some } w \in W\}$. Please note: Z is an interval of real numbers, which is always open above, although it may either extend to $+\infty$ or may be bounded above by some $\bar{z}$ (that is not attained). On the left-hand side, Z can be unbounded below: It must be unbounded below if W is unbounded below or if W is open on its left-hand side; it is bounded below by some $\underline{z}$ if and only if W is closed on its left-hand side at $\underline{w}$. As in Section 19.1, we use $\psi : Z \to W$ to denote the inverse function of u; ψ is continuously differentiable, strictly convex, and strictly increasing.

For each action a_n, we look for solutions to

Alice's expected-cost-minimization problem, for inducing Bob to choose a_n:

$$\text{Minimize} \sum_{m=1}^{M} \pi_{mn}\psi(z_m) \text{ over } z = (z_1, \ldots, z_m) \in Z^M, \text{ subject to the constraints}$$

$$\sum_{m=1}^{M} \pi_{mn}z_m - d_n \geq u_0, \text{ and} \tag{19.1a}$$

$$\sum_{m=1}^{M} \pi_{mn}z_m - d_n \geq \sum_{m=1}^{M} \pi_{mn'}z_m - d_{n'} \text{ for } n' = 1, \ldots, N; n' \neq n. \tag{19.1b}$$

---

[10] While we assume that Bob is generous in this sense in our analysis, it is not as innocuous as in Section 19.1. In the simple model of Section 19.1, Alice can, at arbitrarily small cost, force the decision from Bob that she desires. Here, this is not necessarily true. See Problem 19.5.

The first constraint is called the *participation constraint*, which guarantees that Bob accepts the contract. The second set of constraints—one for each other action $n' \neq n$—consists of so-called *incentive constraints*: Bob (weakly) prefers a_n to $a_{n'}$. For later purposes of writing down FO/CS conditions, it is convenient to rewrite these constraints as

$$\sum_{m=1}^{M} \pi_{mn} z_m \geq u_0 + d_n, \text{ and} \tag{19.2a}$$

$$\sum_{m=1}^{M} (\pi_{mn} - \pi_{mn'}) z_m \geq d_n - d_{n'}, \text{ for } n' = 1, \ldots, N; n' \neq n. \tag{19.2b}$$

If $\pi_{mn} > 0$ for all m and n, each of these minimization problems has a strictly convex objective function, subject to linear constraints, ensuring that the feasible set is convex. Hence a solution, if one exists, is unique. But what if some $\pi_{mn} = 0$? And, are we assured that solutions exist?

The existence issue is real, in the following sense. It is possible that no vector $z \in Z^M$ satisfies all the constraints for some a_{n°; that is, the feasible set for inducing a_{n° may be empty. This could happen, for instance, if d_{n° is so large that $z_0 + d_{n^\circ}$ exceeds $u(w)$ for all $w \in W$.[11] And even if, say, $Z = R$, sets of other actions may "dominate" a particular action a_{n°.[12]

Suppose, though, that action a_{n° cannot be feasibly induced. Then a_{n° can be ignored in the problem of inducing any other action a_n; that is, the constraint (19.1b) that a_n must be at least as good as a_{n° is redundant and can be ignored. The reason is as follows: Suppose that, for the vector $z = (z_m)$ and action a_n, (19.1a) holds and (19.1b) holds for all $a_{n'} \neq a_n$ other than a_{n°. And suppose that (19.1b) fails for a_n and a_{n°. Then, because a_{n° is better at z than is a_n, and (19.1a) holds for z and a_n, (19.1a) must hold for a_{n° and z. And since, at z, a_n is better than all the other $a_{n'}$, a_{n° must be better than all the $a_{n'}$ by simple transitivity. Which means that z implements a_{n°, contradicting the hypothesis that a_{n° is infeasible.

Hence, any of the original actions that cannot be feasibly induced can be ignored altogether. Without loss of generality, we can assume that we are working with a set of actions, each of which can be induced. This, by itself, doesn't guarantee that a solution to Alice's problem exists: The set of vectors z satisfying all the constraints may be nonempty, but it certainly isn't compact. So, we must worry about existence. But, taking easy stuff first, what about contingencies x_m such that $\pi_{mn} = 0$?

Proposition 19.5.

a. *Concerning Alice's problem of implementing a_n at minimum expected cost: Suppose x_m is such that $\pi_{mn} = 0$. Then, if $z \in Z^M$ is a feasible vector (satisfies all the*

---

[11] Why wasn't this a problem in the two-by-two model of Section 19.1? There's a simple answer, but be sure you find it.

[12] Suppose $M = 2$ and $N = 3$; $\pi_{11} = 1/2$, $\pi_{12} = 1/3$, and $\pi_{13} = 1/4$; $d_1 = 0$ and $d_2 = 1$. For which values of d_3 is it impossible to find a feasible solution to the constraints that action a_2 is preferable to actions a_1 and a_3?

constraints) and if $z'_m \in Z$ is such that $z'_m < v_m$, then z'_m can be substituted for z_m, and the vector z so modified is still feasible. Moreover, suppose z is a solution to the expected-cost-minimization problem for inducing m, and $z'_m \in Z$ is such that $z'_m < z_m$. Then substituting z'_m for the original z_m remains a solution.

b. Suppose that Z is unbounded below. If, for two actions a_n and $a_{n'}$, $\pi_{mn} = 0$ while $\pi_{mn'} > 0$, then Alice can preclude Bob considering action $a_{n'}$ when trying to induce action a_n by setting z_m large-enough negative. In particular, suppose that, for action a_n and every $n' \neq n$, a contingency $x_{m(n')}$ exists with $\pi_{mn} = 0$ and $\pi_{m(n')n'} > 0$. Then Alice, by setting $z_m = u_0 + d_n$ for all m such that $\pi_{mn} \gtrless 0$ and z_m large enough negative for m such that $\pi_{mn} = 0$, can induce Bob to choose a_n at the first-best cost to her, $\psi(u_0 + d_n)$.

Proof. Consider how z_m for contingencies x_m such that $\pi_{mn} = 0$ affects the contraints. It is irrelevant to the participation constraint (19.1a). And it only affects constraints (19.1b) for n' such that $\pi_{mn'} > 0$ by lowering the right-hand side. So if z is feasible and we have such a z'_m, substituting z'_m for z_m only loosens constraints; feasibility is retained. And, since the value of z_m has no affect on the objective function, optimality is also retained.

Part b of the proof should be obvious, given part a. (See Problem 19.7 for an example and an extension.)   ∎

There is a bit of economic reality—some would say, unreality—buried in part b of Proposition 19.5. The modeling conceit that Z is unbounded below says that Alice can threaten Bob with contingent consequences so dire that they overwhelm any possible upside he has from taking a particular action. But, with the further modeling conceit that, for some actions a_n and contingencies x_m, $\pi_{mn} = 0$, such a threatened consequence in contingency x_m can be definitively ruled out by Bob choosing a_n. In real life, is the principal (Alice) able credibly to inflict on an agent (Bob) outcomes that are so dire? And can the agent dismiss those dire consequences entirely by choosing an available action? Both of these suppositions are unrealistic. But, in some contexts, perhaps "dire enough" and "nearly rule out" are enough to get something close to what such a model suggests. The latter parts of Problem 19.7 take you down this path.

Be that as it may, in the literature you will find analyses of problems of moral hazard and incentives that rely on these modeling conceits. You must decide how credible you find the conclusions of such analyses.

Moving on to existence of a solution: Suppose we could insert an upper bound on the wages that Alice can credibly promise, say, $\$10^{100}$. Then we get existence rather easily. If Z is bounded below, we're done: A lower bound on Z is only possible if the lower bound is attained, and an upper bound on wages means that the possible values of Z are drawn from a compact set. So, we only need to worry about a lack of compactness at the "bottom," which is if Z is unbounded below.

But, if Z is unbounded below, an upper bound on possible values of z_m combined with the participation constraint implies a lower bound on the values of z_m

for contingencies x_m such that $\pi_{mn} > 0$. This, in turn, implies an effective "lower bound" on the values of z_m for x_m such that $\pi_{mn} = 0$; a bit of algebra shows that if Z is unbounded below and the values of z_m for x_m such that $\pi_{mn} > 0$ are bounded, then there is a level of $z \in Z$ so small that, if assigned to x_n such that $\pi_{mn} = 0$, it guarantees that no $a_{n'}$ that gives positive probability to x_n will be chosen over a_n.

And, in my opinion, for this sort of exemplifying theory, it is entirely reasonable to assume that there is some huge but finite upper bound on wages that can credibly be offered.

But, more to show that we don't need such an assumption in this context than because it provides true economic insight, here is the result:

Proposition 19.6. *Concerning Alice's problem of implementing a_n at minimum expected cost: If it is feasible to induce Bob to choose a_n, a solution exists to the problem of doing so at minimum expected cost.*

This subsection concludes with the proof of this proposition. Should you bother with this proof? It is based on an interesting economic observation or, rather, an observation that is interesting *in theory*: If a sequence of wage vectors on contingencies with positive probability (under a_n) diverge, and if they all satisfy the participation constraint, then—*because Bob is strictly risk averse*—their expected cost to Alice must diverge to $+\infty$. If seeing why this is true is of interest to you, read on. If not, you probably won't lose anything by skipping ahead to the next subsection.

The proof begins with a lemma.

Lemma 19.7. *Suppose $\{z^k; k = 1, 2, \ldots\}$ is a sequence of vectors from Z^M such that each vector satisfies the participation constraint (19.1a) for action a_n. Suppose further that, letting*

$$\zeta^k := \max \{|z_m^k| : m = 1, \ldots, M \text{ such that } \pi_{mn} > 0\},$$

we have $\limsup_k \zeta^k = \infty$. Then $\limsup_k \sum_{m=1}^M \pi_{mn} \psi(z_m^k) = \infty$.

Proof of Lemma 19.7. Since both the participation constraint and the quantity $\sum_m \pi_{mn} \psi(z_m^k)$ are unaffected by the values of z_m^k for m such that $\pi_{mn} = 0$, for purposes of the proof of the lemma, we can assume that $\pi_{mn} > 0$ for all m. (This won't be true for the proof of the proposition itself.)

Either Z has a finite lower bound or is unbounded below. If Z has a finite lower bound, then the result is nearly immediate. Because then the only way that $\limsup_k \zeta^k = \infty$ is possible is if, along some subsequence k', $\lim_{k'} \max\{z_m^k\} = \infty$, and (since ψ is convex), along this same subsequence, Alice's expected wage payment must approach ∞. So, for the remainder of the proof, we assume Z is unbounded below.

Look along a subsequence k' such that $\lim_{k'} \zeta_0^k = \infty$ and, without loss of generality, relable indices in the subsequence to be $1, 2, 3, \ldots$. Let

$$\bar{\nu}^k := \max \left\{ z_m^k : m = 1, 2, \ldots, M \right\}, \quad \text{and} \quad \underline{\nu}^k := \min \left\{ z_m^k : m = 1, 2, \ldots, M \right\}.$$

Either $\lim_k \underline{\nu}^k = -\infty$ or not. If not, then along some (further) subsequence, $\lim_{k'} \underline{\nu}^{k'}$ is finite. And, since we are already looking along a subsequence for which $\lim_k \max\{|\bar{\nu}^k|, |\underline{\nu}^k|\} = \infty$, it must be that, along the subsequence k', $\lim_{k'} \nu^{k'} = \infty$. But then it follows trivially that, along this subsequence, Alice's expected wage payment goes to ∞ (remember, ψ is convex), which establishes the result of the lemma.

This leaves the case that $\lim_k \underline{\nu}^k = -\infty$, which we assume holds for the remainder of the proof. But since the sequence of wage vectors satisfies the participation constraint, to balance the wage payment with unboundedly large negative utility, which has probability bounded away from 0, the utility of some other wage payment must be going to ∞. That is, to satisfy the participation constraint, $\lim_k \underline{\nu}^k = -\infty$ implies $\lim_k \bar{\nu}^k = \infty$.

Temporarily, let $M_k^- := \{m : z_m^k \leq 0\}$, and $M_k^+ = \{m : z_m^k > 0\}$. We know that, far enough out in the sequence, both sets are nonempty. Let

$$\rho_k^- := \sum_{m \in M_k^-} \pi_{mn}, \quad \text{and} \quad \rho_k^+ := \sum_{m \in M_k^+} \pi_{mn}.$$

Write Alice's expected wage payment for the kth wage vector

$$\sum_m \pi_{mn} \psi(z_m^k) = \rho_k^- \sum_{m \in M_k^-} \frac{\pi_{mn}}{\rho_k^-} \psi(z_m^k) + \rho_k^+ \sum_{m \in M_k^+} \frac{\pi_{mn}}{\rho_k^+} \psi(z_m^k),$$

and apply the convexity of ψ to the convex combinations in each of two sums on the right-hand side to conclude that

$$\sum_m \pi_{mn} \psi(z_m^k) \geq \rho_k^- \, \psi\left(\sum_{m \in M_k^-} \frac{\pi_{mn}}{\rho_k^-} z_m^k \right) + \rho_k^+ \, \psi\left(\sum_{m \in M_k^+} \frac{\pi_{mn}}{\rho_k^+} z_m^k \right).$$

Using the short-hand notation

$$Z_k^- := \sum_{m \in M_k^-} \frac{\pi_{mn}}{\rho_k^-} z_m^k, \quad \text{and} \quad Z_k^+ := \sum_{m \in M_k^+} \frac{\pi_{mn}}{\rho_k^+} z_m^k,$$

this is

$$\sum_m \pi_{mn} \psi(z_m^k) \geq \rho_k^- \, \psi(Z_k^-) + \rho_k^+ \, \psi(Z_k^+).$$

And, of course, the participation constraint, which must hold for every k, is $\rho_k^- Z_k^- + \rho_k^+ Z_k^+ \geq u_0$, in these terms.

But because we know the largest value of z_m^k goes to ∞ in k, while all the terms in the sum making up Z_k^+ are nonnegative, we know that Z_k^+ must go to ∞ in k. And, similarly Z_k^- must go to $-\infty$ in k. Let $\underline{\delta} = \psi'(-1)$, and $\overline{\delta} = \psi'(1)$. We know that $0 < \delta^- < \delta^+$. Since ψ is strictly convex, we know that these values provide subgradients; that is,

$$\psi(z) - \psi(1) \geq \overline{\delta}(z - 1) \quad \text{and} \quad \psi(z) - \psi(-1) \geq \underline{\delta}(z + 1).$$

Use the first of these for Z_k^+ and the second for Z_k^- to get

$$\psi(Z_k^+) \geq \overline{\delta}(Z_k^+ - 1) + \psi(1), \quad \text{and} \quad \psi(Z_k^-) \geq \underline{\delta}(z + 1) + \psi(-1).$$

Hence

$$\sum_m \pi_{mn} \psi(z_m^k) \geq \rho_k^- \left[\underline{\delta}(Z_k^- + 1) + \psi(-1)\right] + \rho_k^+ \left[\overline{\delta}(Z_k^+ + 1) + \psi(1)\right].$$

The terms on the right-hand side $\rho_k^- [\underline{\delta} + \psi(-1)] + \rho_k^+[\overline{\delta} + \psi(1)]$ are certainly bounded in k, while what remains is

$$\rho_k^- \underline{\delta} Z_k^- + \rho_k^+ \overline{\delta} Z_k^+ = \underline{\delta}\left[\rho_k^- Z_k^- + \rho_k^+ Z_k^+\right] + (\overline{\delta} - \underline{\delta})\rho_k^+ Z_k^+.$$

The first term on the right-hand side is bounded below by $\underline{\delta} u_0$ (recall the participation constraint), while $(\overline{\delta} - \underline{\delta}) > 0$, ρ_k^+ is bounded below by the smallest π_{mn} (which is strictly positive), and $Z_k^+ \to \infty$. Done. ∎

If you've read all the way through this proof, it may as well be observed that it doesn't really take strict concavity of u = strict convexity of ψ. All that is needed is u is concave, so ψ is convex, and for at least two values of z, call them z^+ and z^-, with $z^+ > z^-$, a subgradient at z^+ has greater slope than does a subgradient at z^-. Or, in other words, u is not linear.

Proof of Proposition 19.6. With this lemma in hand, the proof of the proposition is relatively simple. Going back to Alice's minimization problem, let $\{z^k\}$ be a sequence in Z^M that approaches the infimal expected wage that Alice must pay. (We don't yet rule out that the limit of expected wages paid under z^k is $-\infty$, although that will soon be ruled out.) Note that each z^k in the sequence must satisfy all the constraints.

Look at the values assigned by z^k to contingencies m such that $\pi_{mn} > 0$. Let me write $\hat{z}^k$ for this projection of z^k onto those components only. Since we know that Alice can implement the action a_n, we know that the expected wages she pays under z^k (or $\hat{z}^k$, since these are the same) are bounded away from $+\infty$. The lemma then tells us that $\hat{z}^k$ must lie within a bounded set; if they did not (and since the participation constraint must be met by each), the expected wages they provide would have to diverge to $+\infty$. Hence, we can (looking along a subsequence as needed) find a vector $\hat{z}^*$ that is the limit of the $\hat{z}^k$. By continuity, $\hat{z}^*$ provides Alice with the infimal expected wages she can attain. And, by continuity, $\hat{z}^*$ satisfies the participation constraint. [13]

There remains the constraints (19.2b). Two cases: First, if Z is bounded below, we can take the original sequence z^k, and on components m such that $\pi_{mn} = 0$, replace each z_m^k with its original value or u_0, whichever is smaller. Thus modified, z^k continues to satisfy all the constraints, and now the components for which $\pi_{mn} = 0$ also live in a bounded set, so we can extract a limit point for all components and, by continuity, we are again done.

And if Z is unbounded below: Once you have the limit $\hat{z}^*$, for every action $a_{n'}$ such that there is some x_m with $\pi_{mn} = 0$ but $\pi_{mn'} > 0$, one can produce a z_m so large negative that, together with $\hat{z}^*$, the constraint (19.1b) for n and n' holds. Do this for each m and n', and then if for a given m, there is more than one n', take the least of all the large-negative values of z_m, and you have a full solution to Alice's problem.   ■

Subgame-perfect equilibria for the game

Solving Alice's expected-cost-minimization problem for each action a_n feeds into the larger problem of finding a subgame-perfect equilibrium for the game in which she proposes a wage schedule and Bob responds.

Recall that Alice's gross payoff if Bob chooses a_n is written $\hat{V}(a_n)$. Write $C(a_n)$ for the minimum expected wage payment she must make to induce a_n, and write w^n for an optimal wage payment in that problem. (Remember that there can be more than one solution in terms of the wage payment she proposes for contingencies x_m such that $\pi_{mn} = 0$.) If the list of actions $\{a_n\}$ includes actions for which there is no feasible solution to the expected-wage minimization problem, you can set $C(a_n) = \infty$. Or you can discard such actions from the model; it doesn't matter, as we have already discussed.

A subgame-perfect equilibrium is found as follows: Let $V(a_n) = \hat{V}(a_n) - C(a_n)$. Let n^* be the index of the action a_n that maximizes $V(a_n)$. Then Alice proposes w^{n^*}, Bob accepts, and Bob chooses action a_{n^*}; this provides the outcome of a subgame-perfect equilibrium and, moreover, this is among Alice's favorite subgame perfect equilibria. (For all off-path proposals that Alice might make, Bob responds in some sequentially rational fashion.)

But, I've been careful to say that this is *a* subgame-perfect equilibrium. There are several reasons for this use of the indefinite article:

1. As in Section 19.1, how Bob responds to off-path proposals that Alice might

---

[13] Although W is unbounded above, it is entirely possible that Z is bounded above, in which case, Z is open at the top. So you might worry that some components of $\hat{z}^*$ are "infeasible" in the sense that they equal the least upper bound of Z, which is not in Z. I'll leave it to you to deal with this possibility with a substantial hint: If this happens, what does it mean for the expected wage?

make may not be unique. So there are degrees of freedom in his off-path behavior.

In Section 19.1, we skated past this bit of nonuniqueness by saying that, while Bob's subgame-perfect strategy might not be unique, Alice's strategy was unique, and Bob's on-path response was unique. Hence, we had a unique subgame-perfect-equilibrium outcome. In this general context, we don't even have that.

2. As discussed, if for action a_{n*} there are contingencies x_m such that $\pi_{mn*} = 0$, Alice may have some degrees of freedom on the on-path wage she proposes for x_m. This will definitely be true if Z is unbounded below; it may or may not be true if Z has a finite lower bound. Since Alice's proposal at such contingencies x_m is part of the "outcome" of the game, we may lose uniqueness. But this isn't a huge concern: The payoffs of Alice and Bob are not affected by this lack of uniqueness, so we could hope that we have unique subgame-perfect-equilibrium payoffs.

3. But a serious problem remains that dashes even these modest hopes, which was foreshadowed by footnote 10. Suppose that Alice wishes to implement action a_{n*} and proposes w^{n^*}. It is entirely in the nature of solutions to her expected-cost-minimization problem that, at the schedule w^{n^*}, other actions, including perhaps refusing the deal altogether, will be equally attractive to Bob. In the simple model of Section 19.1, this was certainly true if she wished to implement action h. But, in Section 19.1, she can "force" Bob to choose h at arbitrarily small cost by slightly increasing the payoff from the good outcome. If, in equilibrium, Bob "intended" to choose e at the schedule that is optimal for h, she could resort to such a variation. Hence, in Section 19.1, the only subgame-perfect equilibrium *requires* Bob to choose the action that Alice desires.

   In the general formulation here, however, it is possible that Alice cannot at vanishingly small cost "force" the action she prefers. For an example, see Problem 19.5. Now, as long as Bob is willing, when indifferent, to take whichever action is best for Alice, the problem can be ignored. Then in a sense, the equilibrium that we've described gives *the* subgame-perfect equilibrium payoffs to Alice and Bob for a subgame-perfect equilibrium that Alice (weakly) prefers to any other subgame-perfect equilibrium. But in at least some cases, this result relies on compliant behavior on the part of Bob. There can be other subgame-perfect equilibria, with other payoffs, if Bob isn't such a compliant fellow.[14]

Berge's Theorem?

Assuming that Bob will, when indifferent, do whatever is best for Alice, we can think of Alice as facing a parametric optimization problem: She maximizes her (expected) payoff, maximizing over the choice of action a_n to induce and, for that action, minimizing the expected wages to pay Bob. Fix Bob's utility func-

---

[14] A way around this sort of nonuniqueness is to suppose (1) that wage offers must be in an integer number of pennies or dollars, and (2) the data of the model are "generic." Then, there won't be any ties. But that's not how the literature does things.

tion, the collection of contingencies $\{x_1, \ldots, x_M\}$, the list of Bob's possible actions $\{a_1, \ldots, a_N\}$, and the interval of feasible wages W (and corresponding feasible wage-utility levels Z). We still have a long list of numerical parameters: the gross payoffs as a function of Bob's choice of action, $\{\hat{V}(a_n); n = 1, \ldots, N\}$; Bob's reservation utility level u_0; the vector of disutilities $(d_n)_{n=1,\ldots,N}$; and the probability matrix $(\pi_{mn})_{m=1,\ldots,M;n=1,\ldots,N}$. Write γ for this list of parameters, and consider (1) the function that maps γ into Alice's optimal expected payoff, and (2) the correspondence that maps γ into Alice's optimal choices of action to induce and the corresponding wage offer she makes to induce the desired action. This isn't quite the setting of Berge's Theorem as applied in Volume·I, because of the discrete choice of action to induce. But still one might hope for a result along the lines of: *If we write $V^*(\gamma)$ for Alice's optimal expected payoff as a function of γ, then $\gamma \to V^*(\gamma)$ is continuous.*

No such luck. For at least two reasons, the function $\gamma \to V^*(\gamma)$ can admit discontinuities. It is possible to have a sequence $\{\gamma^k\}$ converging to a γ, where $\lim_k V^*(\gamma^k) > V^*(\gamma)$, and it is possible to have $\lim_k V^*(\gamma^k) < V^*(\gamma)$. If you miss this sort of analysis, which dominated Volume I, Problems 19.8, 19.9, and 19.10 will allow you to explore what can go wrong. (Even if you don't miss this sort of analysis, Problems 19.8 and 19.9 provide useful insights into the nature of solutions to Alice's problem in cases that may not seem extreme but, in fact, are extreme.)

Minimizing the cost of inducing a particular action: First-order, complementary-slackness conditions

Consider the (sub)problem of inducing Bob to choose action a_n at minimal expected cost to Alice. Because the problem has a convex objective function and a convex feasible set, any feasible solution to the first-order, complementary-slackness (FO/CS) conditions is necessarily a solution to the problem. And, if we assume that the constraint qualification is met, any solution to the problem must admit a solution to the FO/CS conditions. Pick the action a_n to be induced. Let λ be the multiplier on the participation constraint (19.1a) and, for $n' \neq n$, let $\mu_{n'}$ be the multiplier on the incentive constraint for n'. Then, *if we assume that there is no lower bound on Z, or if the lower bound on Z doesn't bind for any z_m,*[15] the FO/CS conditions are

$$\text{For } m = 1, \ldots, M, \quad \pi_{mn}\psi'(z_m) = \lambda\pi_{mn} + \sum_{n' \neq n} \mu_{n'}(\pi_{mn} - \pi_{mn'}), \quad \text{where}$$

$$\lambda\left(\sum_n \pi_{mn}z_m - u_0 + d_n\right) = 0, \quad \text{and} \quad \mu_{n'}\left(\sum_{m=1}^{M}(\pi_{mn} - \pi_{mn'})z_m - d_{n'} + d_n\right) = 0,$$

the latter for $n' \neq n$. And, of course, the multipliers must be nonnegative.

---

[15]   And if Z is bounded below and that constraint binds, how do the FO/CS conditions change? You are asked to supply the answer to this question in Problem 19.8. For the remainder of this section and the next, the text will assume that Z is unbounded below or that, in the solutions to Alice's expected-cost-minimization problems, the lower bound doesn't bind. In a few places, you are asked to think through how a binding lower bound on the z_m changes results.

Suppose $\pi_{mn} = 0$. Then the first-order (FO) condition reads $0 = \sum_{n' \neq n} \mu_{n'}(\pi_{mn} - \pi_{mn'})$. For n' such that $\pi_{mn'} = 0$, the n'th term in the summation is 0, but not for n' such that $\pi_{mn'} > 0$. For any such n', then, $\mu_{n'} = 0$ is required. This is entirely consistent with what we said before: For n' such that $\pi_{mn} = 0 < \pi_{mn'}$, Alice chooses z_m low enough so that Bob would never consider choosing n' over n. If there is no lower bound on Z or if the lower bound doesn't bind for z_m, then she can ensure that this constraint is slack. (If Z has a lower bound and the lower bound binds for such an m, how does this argument change?)

Now look at m such that $\pi_{mn} > 0$. In the FO condition, divide through by π_{mn} to get

$$\psi'(z_m) = \lambda + \sum_{n' \neq n} \mu_{n'}\left(1 - \frac{\pi_{mn'}}{\pi_{mn}}\right).$$

This expression provides an important economic insight: Let z^0 be the solution to $\psi'(z^0) = \lambda$, and let $w^0 = \psi(z^0)$. Then you can think of w^0 as a *base-level* wage paid by Alice to Bob. If $\pi_{mn'} > \pi_{mn}$—that is, if m is more likely if action $a_{n'}$ is taken than if a_n is taken, then the term $\mu_{n'}(1 - \pi_{mn'}/\pi_{mn})$ is negative; this term contributes a bit of a penalty to w^0. But if m is more likely under a_n than $a_{n'}$, the term $\mu_{n'}(1 - \pi_{mn'}/\pi_{mn}) > 0$ (assuming the constraint on $a_{n'}$ binds), and we get a bit of a bonus from w^0. Of course, this argument is a bit loose: Whether w_m is greater than or less than w^0 depends on a weighted sum of the terms $(1 - \pi_{mn'}/\pi_{mn})$, for n' whose corresponding constraints bind and where the weights are given by the multipliers. But the intuition is clear: *The wage w_m in contingency m is higher if, on balance, the observed m is more likely if the desired action n was taken, relative to (binding) alternative actions n'; it is lower if (on balance) contingency m is more likely under binding alternatives n' than it is under the desired action n.*

Holmstrom's Informativeness Principle

When would Alice wish to use a piece of information while creating a wage offer for Bob? When should she ignore a piece of information? Roughly speaking, the answer is: Any piece of information that sheds light on the relative likelihood that Bob took the action that Alice wishes to induce vis-à-vis another action that is binding in the solution to her problem may be useful. Any information that sheds no light on these relative likelihoods should not be employed.

This general idea is known as Holmstrom's (1979) Informativeness Principle. Holmstrom proposed this principle in the context of a *first-order-condition* analysis of the problem, which is discussed in Section 19.4. But this is a good place to describe the result.

Suppose the space of contractible contingencies X is actually the product of two spaces, $X = X^1 \times X^2$. Instead of having $X = \{x_1, \ldots, x_M\}$, we have $X = \{(x_m^1, x_k^2)_{m=1,\ldots,M; k=1,\ldots,K}\}$ where $X^1 = \{x_1^1, \ldots, x_M^1\}$, and $X^2 = \{x_1^2, \ldots, x_K^2\}$. Denote the probability of the outcome (x_m^1, x_k^2) if Bob takes action a_n by π_{mkn}. For marginal probabilities of x_m^1, write $\pi_{mn} = \sum_{k=1}^{K} \pi_{mkn}$.

Suppose Alice has been offering an expected wage-minimization wage offer for inducing action a_n, using *only* the contingency space X^1. That is, in considering the wage scheme that induces action a_n at least expected cost to her, she has been looking over the space W^{X^1}. It is suggested to her that she could also employ the information/contingencies in X^2—that is, she could offer a "richer" wage scheme from $W^{X^1 \times X^2}$—and she wonders whether there is any point in doing so. To keep the story simple, suppose Z is unbounded below, so the FO/CS conditions (necessary and sufficient for a solution) include, as before, the FO condition

$$\psi'(z_m) = \lambda + \sum_{n' \neq n} \mu_{n'} \left(1 - \frac{\pi_{mn'}}{\pi_{mn}} \right).$$

Now suppose that, for all n' that have $\mu_{n'} > 0$—in words, n' such that, at the wage scheme $z = (z_m)_{m=1,\dots,M}$, $a_{n'}$ gives the same net expected utility for Bob as does a_n—we have

$$\frac{\pi_{mkn'}}{\pi_{mkn}} = \frac{\pi_{mn'}}{\pi_{mn}} \quad \text{for all } k = 1, \dots, K,$$

then setting $z_{mk} = z_m$ for all k gives a solution to the FO/CS conditions, and hence is (still) a solution. There is no need for Alice to use the information/contingencies provided by x^2. Indeed, if we assume that the π_{mn} are all strictly positive, this is the unique solution: Employing the extra information in some nontrivial fashion (for binding m') will only make things worse. [16]

The "converse" result—that if there is some variation in k in the ratios $\pi_{mkn'}/\pi_{mkn}$, for n' that have $\mu_{n'} > 0$, then Alice will improve matters by using the extra information—is not so straightforward, because more than one n' may be binding. In general, the answer is a definitely indefinite: Using x^2 *might* help. But in two special cases, we can strengthen this to "using x^2 *will definitely* help":

1. Suppose $N = 2$, and Alice is trying to find the least-expected-cost way to induce a_2, the more onerous action. Then, continuing to employ her original scheme that employed x^1 only is definitely suboptimal; basing the wage on both x^1 and x^2 will lower her costs. This conclusion follows immediately from the FO/CS conditions; the conditions based on x^1 no longer hold for (x_m^1, x_k^2) such that $\pi_{mk1}/\pi_{mk2} \neq \pi_{m1}/\pi_{m2}$. (Put an X in the margin here. This case will return in Section 19.3.)

2. Suppose the information in x^2 shifts the likelihood ratios in a uniform direction. For instance, if there is some x_k^2 such that, for all x_m and some a_n and all $n' \neq n$, $\pi_{mkn'}/\pi_{mkn} > \pi_{mn'}/\pi_{mn}$, then employing x^2 (at least to the extent that the wage offer changes if x^2 is x_k^2) will save Alice some (expected) money. Again, the proof is immediate if you stare at the FO conditions for optimality.

---

[16]   However, see Problem 19.17.

19.3. Back to Effort Incentives

Now let us specialize the general model of Section 19.2 to the case of *effort incentives*. The actions a_1 through a_N represent the possible levels of effort that Bob can provide, with $d_1 = 0 < d_2 < \ldots < d_N$: Greater effort is more onerous for Bob. But greater effort results in better gross outcomes for Alice: $\hat{V}(a_1) < \hat{V}(a_2) < \ldots < \hat{V}(a_N)$.

Because the disutility of effort rises strictly with the index of the action—that is, $d_n < d_{n+1}$ for $n = 1, \ldots, N - 1$—we can identify the action with its level of disutility. (In the general formulation of Section 19.2, two distinct actions could have the same disutility. Not here.) So, in this section, we dispense with naming the actions a_n; that is, the nth action is named "the action that has disutility d_n," or just action d_n. Accordingly, we write $\hat{V}(d_n)$, and so forth.

In this section, we also identify contingencies x_m with the gross payoff to Alice in that contingency; that is, x_m is the contingency that "Alice's gross payoff is x_m." Hence, $\hat{V}(d_n) := \sum_{m=1}^{M} \pi_{mn} x_m$. (Hence, $x_m \in R$.) Think, for instance, of the situation in which Bob is a sales representative for Alice, and x_m is the (random) gross profit accruing to Alice from sales made by Bob. Then $w(x_m)$ can be thought of as the sales commission paid to Bob—or perhaps his base wage plus the sales commission—as determined by those gross profits.[17]

Assume that $x_m \neq x_{m'}$ for $m \neq m'$.[18] With this assumption, we renumber the contingencies so that $x_1 < x_2 < \ldots < x_M$.

Given these assumptions, conventions, and interpretations, further assumptions on the π_{mn} are required to ensure that $\sum_{m=1}^{M} \pi_{mn} x_m = \hat{V}(d_n) > \hat{V}(d_{n'}) = \sum_{m=1}^{M} \pi_{mn'} x_m$ if $n > n'$. The typical assumption is that, for $n > n'$, $\{\pi_{mn}\}$ is first-order stochastically greater than $\{\pi_{mn'}\}$:

Assumption 19.8. First-order stochastic dominance. *For all* $m = 1, \ldots, M$, *and* n *and* n' *such that* $n > n'$, $\sum_{m'=m}^{M} \pi_{m'n} \geq \sum_{m'=m}^{M} \pi_{m'n'}$, *with at least one strict inequality.*

While not necessary for $\hat{V}(d_n) > \hat{V}(d_{n'})$ if $n > n'$, this is sufficient. This is a standard result, proved using the discrete version of integration by parts. For $m = 2, \ldots, M$, write $\delta_m = x_m - x_{m-1} > 0$. Set $\delta_1 = x_1$. Then $x_m = \sum_{m'=1}^{m} \delta_{m'}$, and

$$\hat{V}(d_n) = \sum_{m=1}^{M} \pi_{mn} x_m = \sum_{m=1}^{M} \pi_{mn} \left[\sum_{m'=1}^{m} \delta_{m'} \right] = \sum_{m'=1}^{M} \delta_{m'} \left[\sum_{m=m'}^{M} \pi_{mn} \right].$$

---

[17] This story doesn't quite track many real-life applications: In many cases, the sales commission paid to a salesperson is based on the gross value of sales made, not the gross profit to the principal (Alice) that accrues from those sales. (Think it through: There is a "hidden information" problem that explains this.)

[18] This is not innocuous. If $x_m = x_{m'}$ for some $m \neq m'$, you might think that we could "join" these two contingencies into one. But that's not correct. (Why not?) And note that actual contractible contingencies can be "richer" than a scalar. For instance, suppose that Alice can condition Bob's bonus on both the level of sales he books and also the client to which the sales are made. The model can accommodate this, *as long as Alice's gross profits in each contractible contingency are different from one another.* (But see Assumption 19.8. Things are not so simple as this makes them seem.)

Suppose Assumption 19.8 holds. Choose $n > n'$. We must show that

$$\hat{V}(d_n) = \sum_{m'=1}^{M} \delta_{m'} \left[\sum_{m=m'}^{M} \pi_{mn} \right] > \sum_{m'=1}^{M} \delta_{m'} \left[\sum_{m=m'}^{M} \pi_{mn'} \right] = \hat{V}(d_{n'}).$$

Since $\sum_{m=1}^{M} \pi_{mn} = \sum_{m=1}^{M} \pi_{mn'} = 1$, the first terms (the terms for $m' = 1$) on the two sides of the required inequality are the same. Since $\delta_{m'} > 0$ for $m' = 2, \ldots, M$, the other terms on the left-hand side are greater than or equal to the corresponding terms on the right-hand side. And, for the terms for which there is a strict inequality in the bracketed expression as per Assumption 19.8, the left-hand term is strictly greater than the corresponding right-hand term, giving the desired result.

The first-best and second-best levels of effort

Let $V^{\sharp} = \max_{d_n} \{ \hat{V}(d_n) - \psi(u_0 + d_n) \}$. That is, $V^{\sharp}$ is the first-best level of expected payoff that Alice can obtain from Bob, where "first-best" means that she must meet his participation constraint but, having done so, she gets to pick how much effort he exerts. Let $d^{\sharp}$ be the first-best maximizing effort level for Alice to induce. Let V^* be her second-best expected payoff—"second-best" meaning, the best she can do if she isn't able to choose Bob's effort level, but instead must motivate him to choose any effort level larger than d_1—and let d^* be the level of effort that achieves this second best.

It is obvious that $V^* \leq V^{\sharp}$. And, excluding "special" cases, the inequality is strict unless $d^* = d_1$: The expected wage that she must pay to induce any $d \neq d_1$ is strictly greater than $\psi(u_0 + d)$, because she must compensate Bob for the risk he faces. (Suppose, though, that $N = M = 2$, $\pi_{11} > 0$, $\pi_{12} = 0$, and feasible utility levels are unbounded below. If $d^* = d_2$, what happens?)

But what about d^* versus $d^{\sharp}$? A seemingly intuitive conjecture is that, since providing Bob with incentives involves a "compromise" between efficient risk sharing and strong incentives, the compromise means that the second-best level of effort d^* will be (weakly) smaller than the first-best level, $d^{\sharp}$. But this is not true in general. Think of a case with three actions and multiple contingencies, where Z is unbounded below. Suppose that $\pi_{13} = 0$, while π_{11} and π_{12} are both strictly positive. Then, action d_3 can be implemented at its first-best cost. [19] With this as a starting point, you shouldn't have any problems creating a numerical example. (See the solution to Problem 19.11.) (And if you think this solution is a cheat because $\pi_{13} = 0$, see what happens if $\pi_{13} = \epsilon$ as $\epsilon \to 0$.)

Increasing wages for better performance?

Another seemingly intuitive conjecture in this context is that, when it comes to finding the optimal wages for Alice to pay, to induce the choice of any action/effort

---

[19] You should at this point say, "Of course." But, in case not: Alice threatens Bob with a horrible, terrible outcome, should contingency 1 occur. Taking actions d_1 or d_2 means risking that this horrible, terrible fate will befall him. Only action d_3 is safe.

level, the wage paid should be (weakly) increasing in the outcome. Although this may seem intuitive, it is not true, in general. Suppose $N = 2$ and $M = 3$. Suppose

$$\pi_{11} = 0.25, \pi_{21} = 0.25, \pi_{31} = 0.5,$$
$$\pi_{21} = 0.2, \pi_{22} = 0.1, \text{ and } \pi_{32} = 0.7.$$

Note that $\pi_{\cdot 2}$ does first-degree-stochastically dominate $\pi_{\cdot 1}$. Suppose $u(w) = \sqrt{w}$, $u_0 = 20$ (so $w^b = 400$), $d_2 = 5$, $x_1 = 0$, $x_2 = 1000$, and $x_3 = 10,000$. It is immediate that inducing a_1 will cost Alice 400 in wages, while her gross payoff is 5250, for a net of 4850. And you can verify that a solution to the FO/CS slackness conditions for inducing a_2 gives $w(x_1) = 400, w(x_2) = 0$, and $w(x_3) = 900$, for an expected wage payment of 710, against a gross payoff of 7100, for a net of 6390.

Why does this happen? Why is Bob paid less—paid 0, in fact—when the gross outcome is 1000, while if the gross outcome is 0, he is paid 400? The reason is apparent from the first-order conditions:[20]

$$\psi'(z_m) = \lambda + \mu_1 \left(1 - \frac{\pi_{m1}}{\pi_{m2}} \right). \tag{19.3}$$

Alice seeks to pay Bob more when the evidence is stronger that he chose action a_2, and, therefore, if we compare the "inverse likelihood ratios" π_{m1}/π_{m2} for $m = 1, 2, 3$, these ratios are, respectively, 1.25, 2.5, and 5/7. The best evidence that Bob chose a_2 is if $x_3 = 10,000$ is observed, the second-best evidence is if $x_1 = 0$ is observed, and the evidence that he chose a_1 is strongest when $x_2 = 1000$ is observed. Hence, to encourage Bob to choose a_2, he is paid the most at x_3, second most at x_1, and least at x_2.

The monotone-likelihood property

To avoid tedious discussion of special cases, assume for the remainder of this section that $\pi_{mn} > 0$ for all m and n. Also, assume that it is feasible to induce every action d_n.

Suppose there are only two actions ($N = 2$), and Z is unbounded below. Then the first-order condition for the wage offer that induces action d_2 is equation (19.3). A necessary and sufficient condition for wages to increase in m is therefore that π_{m1}/π_{m2} decreases in m. In fact, this works just as well if there is a lower bound on Z:

Proposition 19.9. *In the case $N = 2$, suppose the ratio π_{m2}/π_{m1} is increasing in m. Then, in the optimal wage offer for implementing d_2, $w(x_m)$ is (weakly) increasing in m.*

---

[20] Because Z in the case of $u(w) = \sqrt{w}$ is $[0, \infty)$, there is a further constraint, $w(z_m) \geq 0$, which binds in this case at x_2. So, if you are minded to prove that I've given you the true solution by providing the full FO/CS conditions—which is part of your assignment in Problem 19.8—you should find that you need another multiplier, the multiplier on the constraint $z_2 \geq 0$.

I leave the proof of this as part of Problem 19.12; the only issue is to deal with the case that Z is bounded below.

The antecedent property in Proposition 19.9, for general (finite) N, is:

Definition 19.10. *The matrix* $(\pi_{mn})_{m=1,\ldots,M;\ n=1,\ldots,N}$ *satisfies the* **monotone-likelihood property** *if, for all* n, n', m, m' *such that* $n > n'$ *and* $m > m'$,

$$\frac{\pi_{mn}}{\pi_{mn'}} \geq \frac{\pi_{m'n}}{\pi_{m'n'}}.$$

It satisfies the **strict monotone-likelihood property** *if all the inequalities are strict.*

The interpretation of this property is that, when comparing the relative likelihoods of actions d_n and $d_{n'}$ for $n > n'$, the larger the gross outcome is, the more likely it is that Bob chose d_n relative to his having chosen $d_{n'}$. In the literature, you may encounter the assertion that "this condition is natural." I don't believe so or, rather, I can think of lots of situations in which it is not natural; see Problem 19.9 (which will give you some concrete examples of this property and first-order stochastic dominance).

Proposition 19.11. *If* (π_{mn}) *satisfies the monotone-likelihood property, then* $\pi_{\cdot n}$ *is (weakly) stochastically increasing in* n. *If the monotone-likelihood property holds with at least one strict inequality for each* n *and* n', *then Assumption 19.8 holds.*

But as the example given on page 62 shows, the converse is certainly not true. This proposition is simple to prove.

If the monotone-likelihood property holds, and *if* we knew, in solving for the minimum expected wage to induce a_n, that no constraint of the form "a_n *is as good as* a_{n+k} *for* $k > 0$" binds, then we would know that the optimal solution would involve wages that are (weakly) increasing in the outcome: Taking for simplicity the case where Z is unbounded below, the FOC is

$$\text{For } m = 1, \ldots, M, \quad \pi_{mn}\psi'(z_m) = \lambda\pi_{mn} + \sum_{n' \leq n} \mu_{n'}(\pi_{mn} - \pi_{mn'}),$$

where the assumption about the binding constraints allows me to limit the summation to $n' \leq n$; for $n' > n$, since $\mu_{n'} = 0$ by complementary slackness. And, remembering that we are assuming that $\pi_{mn} > 0$ for all m and n, we can rewrite this as

$$\text{For } m = 1, \ldots, M, \quad \psi'(z_m) = \lambda + \sum_{n' < n} \mu_{n'}\left(1 - \frac{\pi_{mn'}}{\pi_{mn}}\right).$$

The multipliers are all nonnegative, and an increase in m decreases $\pi_{mn'}/\pi_{mn}$ for $n' < n$, which in turn means an increase in $\psi'(z_m)$, which means an increase in z_m, which means an increase in w_m. But, in general, we can't assume that, in seeking to induce d_n, constraints concerning d_n versus d_{n+k} for $k > 0$ don't bind.

The convexity-of-the-distribution-function property

What does it take to get the result that wages are increasing in the gross outcome? The following condition is the standard in the literature.

Definition 19.12. Convexity of the Distribution Function. *The matrix of probabilities* $(\pi_{mn}; m = 1, \ldots, M, \ n = 1, \ldots, N)$ *satisfies the* **convexity-of-the-distribution-function** *(CODF) property if, for n, n', and n'', all less than or equal to N satisfying $n > n' > n''$, and for $\beta \in (0,1)$ satisfying $d_{n'} = \beta d_n + (1 - \beta)d_{n''}$,*

$$\sum_{m'=m}^{M} \pi_{m'n'} \geq \beta \sum_{m'=m}^{M} \pi_{m'n} + (1 - \beta) \sum_{m'=m}^{M} \pi_{m'n''}, \quad \textit{for all } m = 1, \ldots, M.$$

(Since the term "distribution function" is commonly associated with $\sum_{m'=1}^{m} \pi_{m'n}$ for $m = 1, 2, \ldots, M$, convexity of this function is equivalent to concavity of the "anti-distribution function" $\sum_{m'=m}^{M} \pi_{m'n}$, which is how the property is defined.)

This is not the easiest condition to wrap one's head around, but a special case may help: Suppose the d_n are evenly spaced: $d_n = (n - 1)\delta$ for some $\delta > 0$. Write Π_{mn} for $\sum_{m'=m}^{M} \pi_{m'n}$; that is, Π_{mn} is the probability under action d_n of seeing an outcome x_m or greater. The even spacing of the d_n allows us to write $d_n = d_{n-1}/2 + d_{n+1}/2$, and, therefore, the CODF property is

$$\Pi_{mn} \geq \Pi_{mn-1}/2 + \Pi_{mn+1}/2, \quad \text{which implies} \quad \Pi_{mn} - \Pi_{mn-1} \geq \Pi_{mn+1} - \Pi_{mn}.$$

(It takes a bit of algebra to show that this is fully equivalent to the condition, but it is.) If we also assume first-order stochastic dominance, the idea is: More effort increases the probability of good outcomes—this is a consequence of first-order stochastic dominance—but at a decreasing (or, at least, a nonincreasing) rate.

The point of CODF is in the following result. Begin with the least onerous action, d_1. We know how Alice optimally (in terms of minimizing the expected wage required) induces d_0: She sets $w(x_m) \equiv w^\flat$. That simple case disposed of, consider the problem of inducing d_n, for $n > 1$, at the least expected cost. A simpler problem for Alice is the problem of inducing d_n at the least expected cost subject to the participation constraint and the constraint that d_n is more attractive to Bob than is d_{n-1}. Spelling this out, for $n > 1$, Alice is to solve

Alice's relaxed (expected-cost-of-inducing-d_n) problem:

$$\textit{Minimize} \sum_{m=1}^{M} \pi_{mn} \psi(z_m) \textit{ over } z = (z_1, \ldots, z_m) \in Z^M, \textit{ subject to the constraints}$$

$$\sum_{m=1}^{M} \pi_{mn} z_m - d_n \geq u_0, \textit{ and } \sum_{m=1}^{M} \pi_{mn} z_m - d_n \geq \sum_{m=1}^{M} \pi_{mn-1} z_m - d_{n-1}.$$

We call this Alice's relaxed problem, because a bunch of constraints in her "real" problem have been relaxed. Temporarily denote by $z^n = (z_m^n)_{m=1,\dots,M}$ the solution to Alice's relaxed problem—a solution exists because Proposition 19.6 applies—and write $w_m^n = \psi(z_m^n)$, so that w^n is the corresponding wage scheme.

Proposition 19.13. *Suppose that (π_{mn}) satisfies the monotone-likelihood and CODF properties. Then (for $n > 1$) the wage scheme w^n that solves her relaxed problem also satisfies all the constraints that Alice actually faces in minimizing the expected wage she must pay to induce Bob to choose d_n. That is, Bob, facing w^n, will choose d_n over **any** other $d_{n'}$. Moreover, w^n will be (weakly) increasing in m.*

The proof of this proposition begins with a lemma:

Lemma 19.14 *Suppose the wage scheme $w = (w_1,\dots,w_M)$ is nondecreasing in m. Let $z_m = u(w_m)$, so that Bob's net payoff (net of his disutility of effort) if he faces this wage scheme and chooses action d_n is*

$$U(d_n) := \sum_{m=1}^{M} \pi_{mn} z_m - d_n.$$

If (π_{mn}) satisfies the CODF property, then U is concave in d_n in the following sense: For $n < n' < n''$, if $d_{n'} = \beta d_n + (1-\beta)d_{n''}$, then $U(d_{n'}) \geq \beta U(d_n) + (1-\beta)U(d_{n''})$.

Note that this lemma is stated for *any* nondecreasing-in-m wage scheme—nothing is assumed or implied about the scheme optimizing anything—and it only requires the CODF property.

Proof of the lemma. We employ the discrete version of integration by parts:

$$U(d_n) = \sum_{m=1}^{M} \pi_{mn} z_m - d_n = z_1 + \sum_{m=2}^{M} \pi_{mn}\left[\sum_{m'=2}^{m}(z_{m'} - z_{m'-1})\right] - d_n$$

$$= z_1 + \sum_{m=2}^{M}(z_m - z_{m-1})\left[\sum_{m'=m}^{M} \pi_{m'n}\right] - d_n.$$

This is the sum of a constant and a nonnegatively weighted set of functions concave in d_n (that is, in n), less the identify function in d_n. Of course, it is concave in d_n. ∎

Proof of the proposition. It goes almost without saying that if the solution to Alice's relaxed problem satisfies all the constraints in her "real" problem, then the solution to her relaxed problem is also the solution to her real problem. So that's what we prove.

Continue to denote the solution to Alice's relaxed problem for inducing d_n by $w^n = (w_m^n)_{m=1,\dots,M}$, with corresponding utility levels $z^n = (z_m^n)_{m=1,\dots,M}$. Even though the relaxed problem didn't involve actions other than d_n and d_{n-1}, we can use z^n to define $U^n(d_{n'}) := \sum_m \pi_{mn'} z_m^n - d_{n'}$ for all the actions $d_{n'}$.

I assert that, in the solution to the relaxed problem, the constraint that d_n is at least as good as d_{n-1} must bind. That is, $U^n(d_n) = U^n(d_{n-1})$. The reason is that, if this constraint doesn't bind, then the solution to the relaxed problem would necessarily give a constant wage ($= \psi(u_0 + d_n)$), from the FO/CS conditions. (Don't pass this by until you understand why this assertion is true.) But at that wage scheme, d_{n-1} is strictly preferred by Bob to d_n, a contradiction.

And, from the monotone-likelihood property applied to the FO/CS conditions, the wage scheme w^n must be nondecreasing in m. So the lemma applies: U^n is concave in the d_n.

Take some $n' < n - 1$, if there are any, and write $d_{n-1} = \beta d_{n'} + (1 - \beta)d_n$ for $\beta \in (0, 1)$. Then $U^n(d_{n-1}) \geq \beta U^n(d_{n'}) + (1 - \beta)U^n(d_n)$. But since $\mathrm{U}^n(d_n) = U^n(d_{n-1})$, this inequality becomes $\beta U^n(d_n) \geq \beta U^n(d_{n'})$. Drop the β's to conclude $U^n(d_n) \geq U^n(d_n)$. That is, at this wage scheme w^n, d_n is at least as attractive as any $d_{n'}$ for $n' < n$.

And take some $n' > n$, if there are any, and write $d_n = \gamma d_{n-1} + (1-\gamma)d_{n'}$. Apply the concavity of U^n in $d_{n'}$ and the fact that $U^n(d_n) = U^n(d_{n-1})$ in similar fashion to conclude that $U^n(d_n) \geq U^n(d_{n'})$ for all $n' > n$. At the wage scheme w^n, d_n is at least as attractive as any $d_{n'}$ for $n' > n$. Now reread the first sentence of this proof, and we're done. ∎

This proposition is directly interesting for (at least) five reasons. The first four are:

1. If the two properties hold, we know that the optimal wage scheme is nonde-creasing in Alice's gross profit level x_m. One can go further and give conditions under which the optimal wage scheme is a convex or a concave function of x_m; see Grossman and Hart (1983) for such results.

2. If you ever need to "solve" a problem of this sort where you know that the two conditions hold, for each d_n you can solve its relaxed problem, which involves only the "d_n-is-at-least-as-good-as-d_{n-1}" constraint, rather than $N - 1$ such constraints. (Indeed, if $M = 2$, Section 19.1 points you to the quick solution of such problems—find where the two constraints both bind—at least, as long as a lower bound on Z doesn't get in the way.)

3. In this regard, one doesn't really need the monotone-likelihood condition in the following sense: As long as the solution to the relaxed problem produces a wage scheme w^n that is nondecreasing, the CODF property is all it takes to ensure that the solution to the relaxed problem is the solution to the real problem. (And be sure you understand this assertion, which may involve reviewing the proof.)

4. Go back to pages 59–60, the discussion of Holmstrom's Informativeness Principle. Note specifically the paragraph that I asked you to mark with an X. Can you see the implications of that remark in this context? (If not, think harder.)

19.4. A Continuum of Actions and the First-Order Approach

The fifth reason that Proposition 19.13 is of interest is because of its connection to the so-called *first-order approach*, which, historically, is how the early literature "solved" the principal–agent problem.

The general model of Section 19.2—hence its specialization to the case of effort incentives in this section—assumes a finite number M of contractible contingencies and a finite number N of possible effort levels. It might be desirable to allow for an infinite number of contingencies and/or an infinite number of effort levels.

The technology so far employed—finding for each effort level a_n the expected-cost-minimizing wage scheme for inducing that effort level and the corresponding optimal expected cost $V(a_n)$, and then using that together with the gross expected benefit to the principal $\hat{V}(a_n)$ to find the optimal effort level to induce—can be made to work with an infinite number of contractible contingences. It requires optimization over an infinite number of variables, which can be a bit challenging technically. But results analogous to necessity and sufficiency of the appropriately extended FO/CS conditions are available.

The more challenging case is where there are an infinite number of effort levels, as then the analogous program involves an infinite number of constraints. To be concrete, suppose that (1) there is a finite number M of contractible contingencies, as before, (2) we are in the context of effort incentives, so each action can be identified with its disutility of effort, and (3) Bob can choose his action/disutility d from a closed interval of the real line, $[\underline{d}, \overline{d}]$, assuming he takes the job. Let $\pi_m(d)$ be the probability of the mth outcome, if Bob chooses d. Now suppose we are looking for the expected-cost-minimizing wage scheme for implementing some specific action $d^o \in [\underline{d}, \overline{d}]$. For a fixed set of utilities $\{z_m\}$ that Bob receives, define $U : [\underline{d}, \overline{d}] \to R$ by

$$U(d) := \sum_{m=1}^{M} \pi_m(d) z_m - d$$

for Bob's expected net utility from choosing d. (Of course, U is parameterized by the set $\{z_m\}$; we would write $U(d; \{z_m\})$ if we wanted to be explicit about this dependence.) And then, if we are looking for a wage scheme that induces d^o, the constraints that must be satisfied are the participation constraint $U(d^o) \geq u_0$ and the "d^o-is-best" family of incentive constraints, or $U(d^o) \geq U(d)$ for all $d \in [\underline{d}, \overline{d}]$. If the functions π_m are differentiable, then $U(d)$ is differentiable, and the notion that $U(d^o) \geq U(d)$ for all d suggests that, at least locally, we are looking for a scheme of wages, hence z_m, for which $U'(d^o) = 0$, or

$$\sum_m \pi'_m(d^o) z_m - 1 = 0. \tag{19.4}$$

At least, if the left-hand side of (19.4) is not 0—I remind you, I should be writing $\pi'_m(d^o; \{z_m\})$—then a small change from d^o in one direction of the other gives a larger value of U, and so we are certainly violating the constraint that d^o is best.

However, suppose we know that $d \to U(d)$ is concave. Then the FOC (19.4) guarantees that d^o is a global maximizer. Therefore, the question is, if we define

Alice's expected-cost-minimization problem, based on the first-order approach:

$$Minimize \sum_{m=1}^{M} \pi_m(d^o)\psi(z_m), \ over \ (z_1, \ldots, z_M) \in Z^M, \ subject \ to$$

$$\sum_{m=1}^{M} \pi_m(d^o)z_m - d^o \geq u_0, \ and \ \sum_{m=1}^{M} \pi'_m(d^o)z_m - 1 = 0,$$

under what conditions are solutions $\{z_m^*\}$ guaranteed to give a concave-in-d function $\sum_{m=1}^{M} \pi_m(d)z_m^* - d$?

One might guess that the monotone-likelihood and CODF properties will be sufficient, and this is correct. But it takes a bit of work.

The monotone-likelihood property is defined just as before, since it (only) involves comparing two actions at a time for each of the m possible outcomes. And then we have following lemma:

Lemma 19.15 (Milgrom, 1981). *Assume that each function $d \to \pi_m(d)$ is continuously differentiable. Then, each π_m satisfies the monotone-likelihood property if and only if $\pi'_m(d)/\pi_m(d)$ is increasing in m for each m.*

Proof. $\pi'_m(d)/\pi_m(d) = d\ln(\pi_m(d))/dd$. So for $d > d'$,[21]

$$\int_{d'}^{d} \frac{\pi'_m(\delta)}{\pi_m(\delta)}d\delta = \ln(\pi_m(d)) - \ln(\pi_m(d')); \quad hence \quad \frac{\pi_m(d)}{\pi_m(d')} = \exp\left[\int_{d'}^{d} \frac{\pi'_m(\delta)}{\pi_m(\delta)}d\delta\right].$$

In the direction from $\pi'_m(d)/\pi_m(d)$ to $\pi_m(d)/\pi_m(d')$, the rest of the argument is trivial. In the other direction, you need to use continuity of the π'_m and π_m functions, but it isn't hard. ∎

Defining the CODF property involves only cosmetic changes.

Definition 19.12'. Convexity of the Distribution Function. *The family of probabilities $\{\pi(d); m = 1, \ldots, M, d \in [\underline{d}, \overline{d}]\}$ satisfies the convexity-of-the-distribution-function (CODF) property if, for d, d', and d'' satisfying $d' = \beta d + (1 - \beta)d''$ for $\beta \in [0, 1]$,*

$$\sum_{m'=m}^{M} \pi_{m'}(d') \geq \beta \sum_{m'=m}^{M} \pi_{m'}(d) + (1 - \beta) \sum_{m'=m}^{M} \pi_{m'}(d''), \ for \ all \ m = 1, \ldots, M.$$

---

[21] I apologize for the possibly confusing use of d', which is just a generic disutility level other than d, versus π'_m, which is the derivative of π_m.

Moreover, the analog to Lemma 19.14 holds· For any scheme of wages $\{w_m\}$ that is nondecreasing in m, the corresponding utility levels $\{z_m = u(z_m)\}$ are also nondecreasing in m. Hence, if the CODF condition holds, the function $U(d) = \sum_m \pi_m(d)z_m - d$ is a concave function. (The proof is virtually identical to the proof of Lemma 19.14.)

So, taking the optimization problem defined near the top of page 69, and using λ as the multiplier on the participation constraint and μ the multiplier on the first-order-condition (equality) constraint, we get as first-order conditions

$$\pi_m(d^o)\psi'(z_m) - \lambda\pi_m(d^o) - \mu\pi'_m(d^o) = 0, \quad \text{or} \quad \psi'(z_m) = \lambda + \mu\frac{\pi'_m(d^o)}{\pi_m(d^o)}.$$

If we know that the muliplier μ is nonnegative, then the monotone-likelihood condition, as rewritten equivalently in Lemma 19.15, would tell us that $\psi'(z_m)$ is increasing in m, and hence z_m is increasing in m, hence U is concave. We'd be done.

However, μ is the multiplier on an equality constraint, so it is, in theory, unsigned. Rogerson (1985) comes to the rescue:

Proposition 19.16 (Rogerson, 1985). *Assuming (i) each π_m is twice continuously differentiable, (ii) the monotone-likelihood property holds, and (iii) the CODF property holds, then the solution to the problem*

$$\textit{Minimize } \sum_{m=1}^{M} \pi_m(d^o)\psi(z_m), \textit{ over } (z_1, \ldots, z_M) \in Z^M, \textit{ subject to}$$

$$\sum_{m=1}^{M} \pi_m(d^o)z_m - d^o \geq u_0, \textit{ and } \sum_{m=1}^{M} \pi'_m(d^o)z_m - 1 \geq 0$$

is a solution to Alice's full problem and, moreover, at the solution, the second constraint is binding for all $d^o > \underline{d}$.

You should consult Rogerson (1985) for the detailed proof. But, to give the intuition: By relaxing the second contraint from an equality to an inequality constraint, we have a standard (for these volumes) convex constrained optimization (minimization) problem, for which the first-order conditions are necessary and sufficient and for which μ, the muliplier on on the first-order-condition constraint, is nonnegative. Hence, the z_m are nondecreasing, and, therefore, U is concave. But what if the second constraint doesn't bind? Then $U'(d^o) > 0$, and at the alleged cost-minimizing scheme, Bob wants to do more than d^o. Rogerson shows that this is impossible: It would mean that Bob is being over motivated and, by reducing the "spread" in his incentive scheme in the right way, you can increase Alice's expected payoff. See the paper for details.

To circle back to Proposition 19.13: When the set of actions is finite and assuming the two properties hold, one only needs the constraint that d_n is at least as good as d_{n-1} and, at the solution, one finds that this constraint binds. When the set of actions is an interval, there is no one-level-less-onerous action. But the first-order approach *in essence* is doing the same thing: It checks that d^o, the action to be induced, is a local maximum, which (under the two properties) makes d^o a global best action for Bob.

Applying the first-order approach: Success or failure only

Specialize to the case where Alice, the principal, offers employment to Bob, the agent, where

- there are only two contractible outcomes if Bob takes the job, x_f and x_s, where x_f is "failure" and x_s is success. Alice can offer Bob a (contingent) wage (w_f, w_s), where wages are drawn from some interval W of the real line;

- Bob, if he accepts Alice's offer, must choose his level of effort from a closed interval of possible effort levels, $[0, \overline{d}]$, where we sometimes write $\underline{d}$ for effort level 0, to emphasize that this is the lowest level of effort that Bob can choose;

- the probability of the success outcome, if Bob chooses effort level d, is $\pi(d)$, for a function $\pi : [0, \overline{d}] \rightarrow [0, 1]$ that is strictly concave, twice-continuously differentiable, and strictly increasing;

- Bob is an expected-utility-of-wage-less-disutility-of-effort maximizer; if he takes the contract (w_f, w_s), he chooses d to maximize $(1 - \pi(d))u(w_f) + \pi(d)u(w_s) - d$, where u is strictly increasing, strictly concave, and continuously differentiable (and ψ is the inverse of u);

- Bob will only accept the contract if his optimized expected utility (optimizing over d) is at least u_0; and

- Alice seeks to maximize her expected net profit, $\pi(d)(\hat{v}_s - w_s) - (1 - \pi(d))w_f$, where d is the optimized choice of effort level by Bob; that is, $\hat{v}_s$ is Alice's gross reward from a success, with her gross reward from a failure normalized to be 0.

Assume that:

- if $w^\flat = \psi(u_0)$, then $w^\flat \in W$ and, moreover, $\pi(\underline{d})\hat{v}_s > w^\flat$; and

- if we define

$$z_f^*(d) := u_0 + d - \frac{\pi(d)}{\pi'(d)}, \quad \text{and} \quad z_s^*(d) := u_0 + d + \frac{1 - \pi(d)}{\pi'(d)},$$

for $d \in [0, \overline{d}]$, then $\psi\big(z_f^*(\overline{d})\big)$ and $\psi\big(z_s^*(\overline{d})\big)$ are both in the interior of W.

Proposition 19.17. *In the setting outlined in the preceding bullet points, we look for subgame-perfect-equilibrium outcomes to the game where Alice makes a wage offer (w_f, w_s) and then Bob either accepts or rejects and, if he accepts, chooses an effort level. (If Bob rejects, Alice's payoff is 0.)*

a. *Both the monotone-likelihood and CODF properties hold, so use of the first-order approach is justified.*

b. $z_f^*(d)$ (and therefore $w_f^*(d)$) is nonincreasing in d.

c. $z_s^*(d)$ (and therefore $w_s^*(d)$) is nondecreasing in d.

d. The wage offer $(w_s, w_f) = (z_f^*(d), z_s^*(d))$ is the solution to Alice's subproblem of inducing Bob to take action $d > \underline{d}$ as cheaply as possible. Of course, if Alice chooses to induce the choice of $\underline{d}$, she offers $w_f = w_s = w^b$.

e. The function $C^*(d) := (1 - \pi(d))w_f^*(d) + \pi(d)w_s^*(d)$, the expected wage that Alice must pay Bob to induce the choice of d, is increasing in d.

f. The functions z_f^*, z_s^*, and C^* are continuous functions of d, except perhaps at $\underline{d}$. They are discontinuous at $\underline{d}$ if $\pi(\underline{d}) > 0$. If $\pi(\underline{d}) = 0$, $\lim_{d \downarrow \underline{d}} z_s^*(d) > z_s^*(\underline{d})$, but C^* and z_f^* are both continuous at $\underline{d}$.

About the proof: The assumption that π is *twice*-continuously differentiable is required to cite Proposition 19.16, and it also simplifies the proof in places. Because there are only two contingencies, strictly increasing π implies that the monotone-likelihood property holds, and (strict) concavity of π implies the CODF property. This gives part a.

The key step—the step where the first-order approach is applied—is the proof that $z_f^*(d)$ and $z_s^*(d)$ as defined are indeed the solution; that is, the key step is the proof of part d. It runs as follows: The two (ordered) contingencies are $x_f = x_1$ and $x_s = x_2$, with $\pi_1(d) = 1 - \pi(d)$ and $\pi_2(d) = \pi(d)$. Hence $\pi_1'(d) = -\pi_2'(d) = \pi'(d)$. So, for this special case, the general constraint that $\sum_m \pi_m'(d) z_m - 1 = 0$ specializes to

$$-\pi'(d)z_f + \pi'(d)z_s = 1, \quad \text{or} \quad z_s - z_f = \frac{1}{\pi'(d)}.$$

Plug this into the participation constraint, which must bind if the two values of z are interior to Z, and the formulas for z_s and z_f emerge.

The remainder of the proof is a slog through some calculus and a lot of algebra. If you are so minded, try to prove this on your own. If not, I include the proof in the *Online Supplement*.

An implication of the discontinuity of $C^*(d)$ at $\underline{d}$ is that, if $\pi(\underline{d}) > 0$, it is never optimal for Alice to induce "a bit more" than $\underline{d}$: Alice's net expected value of inducing d is $\pi(d)\hat{v}_s - C^*(d)$. The gross expected value, $\pi(d)\hat{v}_s$ is continuous in d, while $C^*(d)$ jumps up discontinuously at $\underline{d}$. So, if $\hat{v}_s$ is close to 0, Alice will settle for $\underline{d}$. But at some critical value of $\hat{v}_s$, far enough from 0, she is indifferent between inducing $\underline{d}$ or some $d > \underline{d}$, and for larger $\hat{v}_s$, she prefers to induce an effort level greater than $\underline{d}$.

In the context this model, let $d^*(\hat{v}_s)$ be the optimal level of d for Alice to induce as a function of the gross value to her of a success. In the event of a tie, define $d^*(\hat{v}_s)$ as the largest d that is optimal. And let $\hat{V}^*(\hat{v}_s) := \pi(d^*(\hat{v}_s))\hat{v}_s - C^*(d^*(\hat{v}_s))$. That is, $\hat{V}^*(\hat{v}_s)$ is Alice's net expected payoff as a function of $\hat{v}_s$ in the subgame-perfect equilibrium we've constructed. If there are ties for the best d, let $d^*(\hat{v}_s)$ be the largest of these. Then

Proposition 19.18. *Both $d^*(\hat{v}_s)$ and $\hat{\mathcal{V}}^*(\hat{v}_s)$ are nondecreasing in $\hat{v}_s$.*

Or, in words, the higher is the reward from a success, the no-lower are both the level of effort Alice chooses to induce and her overall net payoff.

Proof. That $\hat{\mathcal{V}}^*(\hat{v}_s)$ is nondecreasing in $\hat{v}_s$ is obvious. If we have two values, $\hat{v}_s$ and $\hat{v}'_s$ with $\hat{v}_s > \hat{v}'_s$, and if $d^*(\hat{v}'_s) = d'$, then Alice, with success having value $\hat{v}_s$, can induce d' at the same cost $C^*(d')$ as when success has value $\hat{v}'_s$; $C^*(d)$ for all d is constant in the value of success. And, $\pi(d')\hat{v}'_s \leq \pi(d')\hat{v}_s$; indeed, the inequality is strict if $\pi(d') > 0$. So using d' gives at least as much with $\hat{v}_s$ as with $\hat{v}'_s$, and in most cases more.

It takes a little more to show that $d^*(\hat{v}_s)$ is nondecreasing in $\hat{v}_s$. But it still is relatively easy. Again, choose values $\hat{v}_s$ and $\hat{v}'_s$ such that $\hat{v}_s > \hat{v}'_s$. Again let $d' = d^*(\hat{v}'_s)$. By the way we defined $d^*(\hat{v}_s)$, we know that

$$\text{for all } d < d', \quad \pi(d)\hat{v}'_s - C^*(d) \leq \pi(d')\hat{v}'_s - C^*(d').$$

And, because π is strictly increasing,

$$\text{for all } d < d', \quad \pi(d)(\hat{v}(s) - \hat{v}'(s)) < \pi(d')(\hat{v}(s) - \hat{v}'(s)).$$

Adding together the two inequalities, we have

$$\text{for all } d < d', \quad \pi(d)\hat{v}_s - C^*(d) \leq \pi(d')\hat{v}_s - C^*(d').$$

But this implies that $d^*(\hat{v}_s) \geq d'$. ∎

19.5. Linear Incentive Schemes

Critics of the classic principal–agent model—the model we have so far studied—begin their many objections with the observation that Alice is somehow endowed with knowledge that a real-life Alice would never possess. She knows precisely the probability distributions over contingencies resulting from each action choice by Bob, both as assessed by Bob and by herself, and they coincide. And she knows Bob's utility function, his level of disutility for every action, and his reservation level of utility. Hence, she is—in the model, but hardly in real life—able to tailor the wage scheme she offers to Bob to a remarkable, and remarkably unrealistic, degree. The optimal wage offer to Bob shifts dramatically with small changes in probabilities, because likelihood ratios drive the optimal scheme: If both π_{mn} and $\pi_{mn'}$ are small, the ratio $\pi_{mn'}/\pi_{mn}$ can change significantly with small (absolute) changes in either numerator or denominator. If Z is bounded,[22] things aren't so very delicate, as very tiny values of π_{mn} have little influence on Bob's behavior. But, still, Alice-in-these-models knows things that Alice-in-real-life probably does not.

Another objection begins with the idea that Alice, the principal, often deals with many agents or employees and, for reasons having to do with the psychology of motivation,[23] she must offer similar incentive schemes to her cohort of employees. This can lead to Alice offering her agents a menu of incentive schemes from which they select—this is Chapter 20 material—but the point is that incentives that are fine-tuned to each agent individually, even if possible, are impractical.

The long list of objections doesn't end here, but it's a start. And based on these two objections and others, critics go on to say, "No wonder that, in the real world, we see simple incentive schemes," the prototypical of these being how real-life salespeople (and others) are compensated: They are paid a base wage B and given a fraction b of the dollar value of the sales they make. This scheme, called *linear incentives*, has spawned two distinct threads in the literature.

The first of these threads simply assumes that principals like Alice restrict themselves to linear schemes for unmodeled but nonetheless valid reasons, then goes on to ask: Among linear incentive schemes, which is best? (The second thread, which tries to justify the restriction, is introduced in Section 19.6.)

The parametric model of Holmstrom and Milgrom (1991)

Holmstrom and Milgrom (1991) employ the following parametric model.

- Alice offers Bob a wage contract. If Bob accepts, he chooses an action a from a (for now) abstract set of actions A.

- Bob's choice of a generates an expected gross reward $\hat{V}(a)$ for Alice.

- Contractible information about Bob's choice of a is provided by a multivariate random variable x, the distribution of which is jointly Normal, with mean vector $\mu(a)$ and fixed variance–covariance matrix Σ.

- The contract offered by Alice is linear in x. Specifically, Bob's wage, if he acccepts Alice's offer, is $w(x) = B + bx$, for scalar B and vector b. Therefore, Bob's wage $w(x)$, if he chooses a, has Normal distribution with mean $B + b\mu(a)$ and variance $b\Sigma b$.

---

[22] A lower bound on Z may be natural, if payments to Bob must be nonnegative and $0 pay has finite utility. And, at least for some utility functions, such as constant-absolute-risk-aversion (CARA) functions, an upper bound on Z is automatic. However, as observed in Rabin and Thaler (2001), bounded-above utility functions (for computing expected utility) are intuitively pathological; risk aversion "ought to" vanish as wealth approaches infinity, which implies no upper bound. On the other hand, if the agent is (strictly) risk averse and the principal is risk neutral (or, even, less risk averse than the agent), unbounded-above utility functions are not that problematic: The principal won't exploit this feature of the agent's utility function by offering him huge rewards with small probabilities, because— see Lemma 19.7—doing so costs her in expected wages more than it helps in terms of inducing desirable behavior.

[23] To be discussed in Volume III, but, for now, look in the literature of social psychology for *social comparisons* and *equity theory*.

- If Bob accepts Alice's offer, he chooses a to maximize his expected utility of his wage less the (dollar denominated) disutility $d(a)$ of the action a, for a constant-absolute-risk-aversion (CARA) utility function, $u(z) = -e^{-\lambda z}$. That is, he picks a to maximize

$$\mathbf{E}\big[u\big(w(x) - d(a)\big)\big] = \mathbf{E}\big[- \exp\big(- \lambda(B + bx - d(a))\big)\big],$$

where λ is his coefficient of absolute risk aversion, exp(argument) means e^{argument}, and the expectation is over the random vector x, the distribution of which is determined by his choice of a. Bob accepts the contract if his maximized expected utility is at least $-e^{-\lambda w^b}$; that is, if his maximized certainty equivalent is at least w^b. Assume that $w^b \geq 0$.[24]

- Alice is risk neutral and chooses b and B to maximize her expected net payoff, $\hat{V}(a^*(B, b)) - [B + b\mu(a^*(B, b))]$, where the contract induces Bob to accept the offer, and $a^*(B, b)$ is his optimal choice of a, given the terms B and b.

This model is special in many different ways, beyond the idea that Alice is considering only linear contracts:

- Until this section, Bob's disutility of action choice a, $d(a)$, was measured in utility units, subtracted directly from his expected utility of wages. That is, $\sum_m \pi_{mn} u\big(w(x_m)\big) - d_n$ has expressed Bob's payoff. In this model, disutility is measured in dollars and goes inside the utility function; in the context of earlier models, we'd write $\sum_m \pi_{mn} u\big(w(x_m) - d_n\big)$. I'll have more to say about this change in Section 19.6.

- The assumptions of joint Normality of x and Bob having CARA utility make for very tractable analysis, because of the following mathematical fact: *Suppose W has a Normal distribution with mean μ and variance σ^2. Then the expectation of e^W is $e^{\mu+\sigma^2/2}$.*

  I offer no excuses for the Normality assumption except for tractability. But the CARA utility assumption is somewhat reasonable as an approximation, as long as this particular encounter with Alice doesn't have a huge impact on Bob's "permanent income": His coefficient of risk aversion in such cases is unlikely to change much in this one encounter. Assuming it doesn't change at all is, therefore, a reasonable approximation.[25]

- In real life, Bob's choice of action might be expected to shift the variance as well as the mean of x. This would happen if some actions he might take are riskier

---

[24] This assumption is not necessary; once you master this model, see what changes if $w^b < 0$ is allowed.

[25] But because the likelihood ratios of two Normally distributed variables with different means and the same variance diverge enormously in the tails, if Alice were not restricted to linear incentive schemes, she could asymptotically attain the first-best results by threatening Bob with hugely dire punishments for very low outcomes x. Restricting her to linear incentive schemes prevents this.

than others. If that is an important phenomenon in a context of interest, this model misses it (although it isn't that hard to accommodate).

What emerges if we make all these functional assumptions?

Proposition 19.19. *Suppose Alice offers Bob a contract where his compensation will be $B + bx$. Suppose that, when indifferent between two courses of action, Bob will take the action favored by Alice.*

a. *Given the data of the problem and the offer (B, b), Bob's choice of $a \in A$, if he accepts the contract, is to pick a to maximize $b\mu(a) - d(a)$. If more than one a achieves the maximum, he chooses the one with the lower $d(a)$. Write $a^*(b)$ for this optimizing choice. (If, for a given b, there are two maximizing values of a, call them $a^\sharp$ and $a^\flat$, and if $d(a^\sharp) = d(a^\flat)$, which implies that $\mu(a^\sharp) = \mu(a^\flat)$, then a^* for this b is defined to be whichever gives a higher value of $\hat{V}(a)$. And, if two values of a tie for this as well, $a^*(b)$ can be defined arbitrarily.)*

b. *Alice, if she decides to offer a contract with "slope term" b, chooses B as*

$$B = w^\flat - b\mu(a^*(b)) + d(a^*(b)) + \lambda\frac{b\Sigma b}{2},$$

where $b\Sigma b$ is to be understood as b as a row vector times the matrix Σ times b as a column vector. And her net expected payoff will be

$$\hat{V}(a^*(b)) - w^\flat - d(a^*(b)) - \lambda\frac{b\Sigma b}{2}. \tag{19.5}$$

She will choose b (and, hence, B) to maximize this expression.

Before giving the proof, note the formula (19.5) for Alice's net expected payoff. This assumes, of course, that she can predict how Bob will respond to her offer; in particular, she "knows" all the parameters in the model, and she can predict $a^*(b)$.[26] Given these very standard modeling conceits (for this literature), she gets the gross payoff from the action she chooses less: Bob's reservation wage $w^\flat$; the term $d(a^*(b))$, which compensates him for his dollar-valued disutility from the choice $a^*(b)$; and a final amount of compensation that must be paid to him for taking on the risk inherent in the compensation scheme.

It is also worth mentioning that the proposition as stated is sloppy. For one thing, it is evoking "subgame perfection plus" as an underlying solution concept, where the "plus" is the assumption that indifferent Bob will choose according to Alice's preferences. More significantly, in part a, it implicitly assumes that Bob's problem of maximizing $b\mu(a) - d(a)$, for whichever b Alice selects, has a solution. If A is finite,

---

[26] What about the objections to the classic principal–agent model with which this section began; that Alice lacks such precise information? The story is that even if her prediction is a bit off, it doesn't change the result that much, as long as she "pads" B enough to get Bob to agree to the contract. But this story, while true, is not being justified here.

this assumption is okay, but in specific applications, it could present problems. Nonetheless, I'll proceed with a proof, under the (now explicit) assumption that, for each b that Alice might contemplate, Bob's problem has a solution.

Proof. If Bob takes action a, his monetary compensation is $B + bx$, and his expected utility is

$$\mathbf{E}\big[-\exp\big(-\lambda(B + bx - d(a))\big)\big],$$

where $-\lambda(B + bx - d(a))$ has mean $-\lambda\big(B + b\mu(a) - d(a)\big)$ and variance $\lambda^2 b \Sigma b$. Apply the mathematical fact, and his expected utility is

$$-\exp\left(-\lambda(B + b\mu(a) - d(a)) + \lambda^2 \frac{b\Sigma b}{2}\right).$$

This makes his certainty equivalent equal to

$$\mathrm{CE}(a; B, b) = B + b\mu(a) - d(a) - \lambda\frac{b\Sigma b}{2}.$$

Given B and b and his decision to accept, Bob will choose $a \in A$ to maximize his certainty equivalent (which is the same as maximizing his expected utility). Note that B and $\lambda b \Sigma b/2$ are constants in Bob's certainty equivalent, so they don't affect his choice of a given B and b; he will choose a to maximize $b\mu(a) - d(a)$. So we can write his optimal choice of a, given he accepts the contract, as $a^*(b)$ (regarding $a \to \mu(a)$ and $a \to d(a)$ as fixed parameters of his problem), understanding that, for some b, more than one a may maximize $b\mu(a) - d(a)$.

The intuition here is simple: Since Bob has CARA utility, the base payment B has no affect on his preferences. And since Σ is independent of his choice, it plays no role in that choice. He is choosing the mean of his monetary reward less his disutility of effort and, of course, he wants that difference to be as large as possible.

While B and Σ do not affect Bob's choice of a once he accepts the contract, they do affect his certainty equivalent and, therefore, his decision whether to accept Alice's offer. Thus Σ affects Alice's choice of B. If she settles on a "slope term" b for the compensation scheme she offers, and if Bob, in consequence, will choose $a^*(b) \in A$ if he accepts, then to get him to accept—to meet his participation constraint—Alice must set B so that

$$B + b\mu(a^*(b)) - d(a^*(b)) - \lambda\frac{b\Sigma b}{2} \geq w^b.$$

By the usual argument and assumption that, if he is indifferent between two actions, he takes the one preferred by Alice, she will set B so that we get equality in the previous display, or

$$B = w^b - b\mu(a^*(b)) + d(a^*(b)) + \lambda\frac{b\Sigma b}{2}.$$

This makes her expected compensation

$$\hat{V}(a^*(b)) - B - b\mu(a^*(b)) = \hat{V}(a^*(b)) - \left[w^b - b\mu(a^*(b)) + d(a^*(b)) + \lambda\frac{b\Sigma b}{2} \right] - b\mu(a^*(b)),$$

which gives the formula in equation (19.5).

Concerning the parenthetical remark in part a of the proposition: Suppose that Alice settles on b^* for the maximizing slope term for herself, and suppose that, at b^*, there are multiple values of a that maximize $b\mu(a) - d(a)$. Specifically, suppose that $a^\sharp$ and a^b are both maximizers of $b^*\mu(a) - d(a)$. Suppose that $d(a^b) > d(a^\sharp)$, so that (per the proposition) $a^*(b^*) = a^\sharp$. In such a case, I assert, the equilibrium outcome automatically has Bob choosing $a^* = a^\sharp$: The B^* that accompanies a^* provides too little compensation for Bob to meet his participation constraint and then choose a^b.

However, if there are $a^\sharp$ and a^b, both maximizers for Bob at b^*, such that $d(a^\sharp) = d(a^b)$ and $\mu(a^\sharp) = \mu(a^b)$, this leaves open the possibility that $\hat{V}(a^\sharp) \neq \hat{V}(a^b)$. And then the rule for determining a^* is, whichever maximizer also maximizes $\hat{V}$. This is the plus in subgame-perfect-plus; Bob, wholly indifferent, will choose the better a from Alice's perspective.   ∎

One-dimensional effort incentives

Suppose we specialize this model to the case of one-dimensional effort incentives. Assume:

- The set $A = [0, \infty)$, and $d(a) = a$. That is, we identify the action with the dollar-denominated cost to Bob of that effort, where effort 0 costs him 0.[27]

- The contractible outcome x is one-dimensional. Given Bob chooses action/effort a, x is Normally distributed with mean $\mu(a)$ and variance σ^2. The function μ is twice continuously differentiable, strictly increasing, and strictly concave, and it satisfies $\mu(0) = 0$ $\mu'(0) > 1$, and $\lim_{a\to\infty} \mu'(a) < 1$. Alice's gross payoff is x, so $\hat{V}(a) = \mu(a)$.

To set a benchmark, first imagine that Alice could contractually fix Bob's choice of action. Then, on grounds of efficient risk sharing, she'd pay him a fixed wage of $w(a)$ that, to satisfy the participation constraint, must satisfy $-e^{-\lambda(w(a)-a)} \geq e^{-\lambda w^b}$. There is no reason for her to pay him any more, which means $w(a) = w^b + a$. Hence, if she fixes his choice of action at a, her expected net profit is $\mu(a) - w^b - a$, which she wishes to maximize. The FOC for an interior solution is $\mu'(a) - 1 = 0$; strict concavity of μ ensures a unique solution; and the solution is interior based on the assumptions that $\mu'(0) > 1$ and $\lim_{a\to\infty} \mu'(a) < 1$. Denote this first-best level of effort $a^\sharp$.

---

[27] In Sections 19.3 and 19.4, I dispensed with a and referred to "the action that has disutility d" simply as action d. In this section, I continue the use of a because, in subsequent developments, $d(a)$ will not be d.

Now to analyze Alice's real problem, where she picks B and b and Bob, if he accepts, chooses a.

Corollary 19.20.

a. If Bob accepts the contract with terms B and b, his choice of $a^*(b)$ is the solution to $\mu'(a) = 1/b$ if $\mu'(0) > 1/b$, and it is $a = 0$ if $\mu'(0) \leq 1/b$. (If $b > \lim_{a \to \infty} 1/\mu'(a)$, he chooses arbitrarily large a.)

b. Reframe Alice's decision as the decision which $a \in [0, \infty)$ to induce: She can induce him to choice any action a in the interval $[0, \lim_{a' \to \infty} 1/\mu'(a'))$; the unique b that will induce a from this interval is $b(a) := 1/\mu'(a)$.

c. Write $V(a)$ for Alice's net expected payoff if she induces action a. Then

$$V(a) = \begin{cases} \mu(a) - w^b - a - \dfrac{\lambda(b(a))^2 \sigma^2}{2} = \mu(a) - w^b - a - \dfrac{\lambda \sigma^2}{2(\mu'(a))^2} & \text{, if } a > 0, \text{ and} \\ \mu(0) - w^b & \text{, if } a = 0. \end{cases}$$

If $\mu'(0) < \infty$, $a \to V(a)$ is discontinuous at $a = 0$.[28] So, Alice's optimal choice of a is either $a = 0$ or the solution to the first-order condition

$$\mu'(a) - 1 + \lambda \sigma^2 \frac{\mu''(a)}{\mu'(a)^3} = 0.$$

In either case, she always chooses an effort level by Bob that is less than the first-best level $a^\sharp$.

Proof. Part a is immediate from Proposition 19.19(a). Given b, if Bob accepts, he wishes to maximize $b\mu(a) - d(a) = b\mu(a) - a$ in this specific parameterization. Since μ is strictly concave, the solution (if one exists) is unique. The first-order condition (FOC) for an interior solution is $b\mu'(a) = 1$, or $1/\mu'(a) = b$. If $b \in (1/\mu'(0), \lim_{a \to \infty} 1/\mu'(a))$, there is an interior solution to the FOC; if $b \leq 1/\mu'(0)$, the solution is clearly $a = 0$; if $b \geq \lim_{a \to \infty} 1/\mu'(a)$, then Bob wishes to choose a arbitrarily large.

That is, for every $a \in (0, \lim_{a \to \infty} 1/\mu'(a))$, there is a $b(a)$, namely, $1/\mu'(a)$, that will induce Bob to choose a, as long as Bob agrees to the contract. For $a = 0$, the contract $B = w^b$, and $b = 0$ does the trick.

Proposition 19.19 tells us how large B must be to induce Bob to agree to the contract, and it tells us that Alice's expected payoff is given by equation (19.5), which in this case specializes to

$$\mu(a^*(b)) - w^b - a^*(b) - \lambda \frac{b^2 \sigma^2}{2}. \tag{19.5'}$$

---

[28] But what if $\mu'(0) = \infty$?

Making a the driving variable, this is

$$\mu(a) - w^\flat - a - \lambda \frac{\sigma^2}{2\mu'(a)^2}. \tag{19.5''}$$

This immdiately implies everything in part c except for the final sentence. It is worth pausing, however, over the discontinuity in $V(a)$; this should remind you of Proposition 19.7(f) on page 72.

For the final sentence, since $\mu'(0) > 1$ is assumed, the first-best level of effort, $a^\sharp$, is strictly greater than 0. If the second-best level of effort (that is optimal for Alice) is $a = 0$, this is immediately less than $a^\sharp$. Suppose instead that Alice optimally chooses a that satisfies the first-order condition for an interior maximum:

$$\mu'(a) - 1 + \lambda\sigma^2 \frac{\mu''(a)}{\mu'(a)^3} = 0.$$

Because μ is strictly concave, μ'' is nonpositive. Hence, the first-order condition for Alice's optimal a is $\mu'(a) =$ something greater than or equal to 1. Since μ' is decreasing, this means that the solution to this first-order condition is less than $a^\sharp$, strictly so if μ'' is strictly negative.   ∎

An intuitive explanation the last part of the corollary is: The first-best action $a^\sharp$—the solution to $\mu'(a) = 1$—maximizes Alice's share of "total pie" that is produced, taking into account that she must compensate Bob by $w^\flat + a$. Increasing a beyond this point clearly lowers Alice's share: To compensate Bob for his efforts, she must pay him an incremental amount greater than what his additional effort produces in total and, *in addition*, it increases the risk on him, for which additional incremental compensation is required. Hence, increasing a above $a^\sharp$ makes no sense for Alice. But lowering a below $a^\sharp$ places less risk on Bob and lowers the risk-bearing compensation he must be offered. While $a < a^\sharp$ lowers the size of the total (expected) pie ($\mu(a)$) minus $w^\flat + a$ (because $\mu'(a) > 1$), the reduction in Bob's compensation for bearing risk suffices to make $a < a^\sharp$ best for Alice. [29]

We can go on from here to harvest some comparative-statics results. Just for the practice, Problem 19.14 asks you to do so, for the special case $\mu(a) = \gamma a^{1/2}$ for a strictly positive parameter γ.

Multitasking

Holmstrom and Milgrom (1991) propose the general model (the model of the proposition, not the simple version of the corollary) as a first step in deriving a number

---

[29] (1) Let me reiterate that, if $a^\sharp$ is close to zero, Bob's risk-sharing compensation, which is bounded away from zero for $a > 0$, may make $a = 0$ optimal for Alice. (2) I remind you that, for the general model of past sections, this doesn't generalize, because there are circumstances—not in this model but in general—where inducing a larger effort can be accomplished by *reducing* the risks Bob faces; see Problem 19.11.

of interesting "applied" conclusions. I sketch one of their applications here: their analysis of multitasking and its consequences for job design.

The term *multitasking* refers to the idea that a single agent—who will continue to be Bob—may have more than one task to perform for the principal, Alice. For instance, School Teacher Bob must devote time and energy teaching the basics to his students, so that they can pass the end-of-year tests. But at the same time, he should be inspiring students to learn. Although the terminology doesn't quite fit, the analysis also fits in cases where the agent performs a single task—think of a contractor building a house—for which there are several dimensions of the quality of performance (for example, how fast the house is built, but also the quality of the build). In either context, suppose there are good and accurate measures of how well the agent/teacher/contractor does in one task, for instance: How many students show grade-level proficiency in the year-end tests? How quickly is the job finished? And suppose measures of performance on the second task/dimension are less good or even nonexistent: How can accurate and contractible measures of the number and degree of inspired students be constructed? How well can the quality of a build be measured, in the timeframe relevant for paying the contractor? In such circumstances, the principal can give the agent powerful incentives to perform well on the measurable task/dimension. But should she do so? What is the impact on how well the agent does on the other, harder to measure task/dimension?

Issues of multitasking and incentives can be studied with the general form of the principal–agent problem from earlier sections. But important insights can be obtained in models where the principal restricts herself to linear incentive schemes.

Suppose, in particular,

- A is $[0, \infty)^2$, with $a \in A$ taking the form (a_1, a_2), representing the amount of effort that the agent provides in two different and relevant activities.

- The principal's gross reward function takes the form $\hat{V}((a_1, a_2)) = \gamma_1 \hat{V}_1(a_1) + \gamma_2 \hat{V}_2(a_2)$ for strictly concave, strictly increasing functions $\hat{V}_\ell$ and scalars γ_1 and γ_2. The scalars γ_1 and γ_2 are superfluous, but they allow commentary later on about what is the effect of Alice putting more weight on one or the other activity.

- The cost to the agent of the choice $a = (a_1, a_2)$ is a strictly increasing, strictly convex, and twice-continuously differentiable function $d : A \to R$, whose mixed second partial is (by convexity) strictly positive. That is, the marginal cost to the agent of increasing effort in activity 2, or $\partial d/\partial a_2$, is strictly increasing in the level of activity 1.

- Suppose that there is only one contractible outcome measure, x_1, and the distribution of x_1 depends only on a_1. (To fit the general model, x_1 is Normally distributed with a mean $\mu(a_1)$ and fixed variance σ^2, for μ strictly concave, strictly increasing, and twice-continuously differentiable.)

- The principal considers offering the agent a linear compensation scheme, of the form $B + bx_1$, for scalars B and b.

This stylized model fits the two stories: Activity 1 is teaching children the basics or finishing the house in good time, which responds positively to teacher/contractor efforts to teach to the test/finish construction. Activity 2 is inspiring students or building with quality, measurement of which is impossible in a timeframe relevant to compensating the teacher/contractor. The question is: Does the principal, Alice, wish to motivate the agent, Bob, to devote more time and effort to task 1 and, if so, how strongly?

Rather than grind through the algebra (read the paper!), here is Alice's conundrum. So that we are looking at interior solutions, suppose that, with no incentive terms, Bob will devote positive effort to both tasks; that is, there is an interior solution (a_1^b, a_2^b) to

$$\left.\frac{\partial d(a_1, a_2)}{\partial a_1}\right|_{(a_1^b, a_2^b)} = \left.\frac{\partial d(a_1, a_2)}{\partial a_2}\right|_{(a_1^b, a_2^b)} = 0. \qquad (19.6)$$

If we interpret w^b as Bob's reservation certainty equivalent for taking the job, Alice, to induce Bob to choose (a_1^b, a_2^b), optimally offers Bob $B = w^b + d(a_1^b, a_2^b)$. The interpretation is that Bob takes personal satisfaction in the choice (a_1^b, a_2^b) and, therefore, to get Bob to accept the job and make this choice, Alice can offer him a fixed wage.

Should Alice then induce $a_1 > a_1^b$ by offering Bob contract of the form $B + bx_1$ for $b > 0$? This might well be the thing to do, if she were concerned solely with a_1 and its impact on $\hat{V}_1(a_1)$. Indeed, if σ^2 is close to 0, Alice could induce (nearly) a "first-best" choice of a_1. But this is not her only concern. And, assuming differentiability and that the mixed-partial $\partial^2 d/\partial a_1 \partial a_2 > 0$, inducing $a_1 > a_1^b$ necessarily entails a choice of $a_2 < a_2^b$. So, in this story, as Alice contemplates how much incentive she should provide Bob concerning a_1, she must take into account that any increase in a_1 means a decrease in a_2 and so a loss in $\hat{V}_2(a_2)$ from $\hat{V}_2(a_2^b)$. Holmstrom and Milgrom interpret this: Although Alice may have available high-powered incentives concerning activity/aspect a_1 (true, say, if σ^2 is close to 0), her optimal solution may be to offer only relatively low-powered incentives. Indeed, and in theory (I know of no real-life cases), if the weight γ_2 on $\hat{V}_2$ is huge relative to γ_1, Alice may want to choose $b < 0$, to motivate Bob to *lower* a_1 from a_1^b, since this results in an increase in a_2.

The paper provides details (and a complete model), including analysis of cases where there are imperfect measures of both activities, but the first has much lower noise than the second. And the authors use their results to discuss the consequences for job design: Suppose a firm requires that employees address a long list of tasks and must decide how to bundle the tasks into jobs: Suppose there are four tasks, t_1 through t_4, and two "positions" in the firm, where each position is filled by employees who can attend to two of the four tasks. One job design bundles $\{t_1, t_2\}$ and $\{t_3, t_4\}$; another bundles $\{t_1, t_4\}$ and $\{t_2, t_3\}$. If, say, there are very accurate measures of performance of tasks t_1 and t_3, and poor or nonexistent measures of performance on tasks t_2 and t_4 then, from the perspective of providing strong incentives when one can, bundling t_1 and t_3, and providing high-powered incentives for the employee who must attend to those two, while bundling t_2 and t_4 and relying on softer incentives for employees whose job is to attend to those two, provides better incentive solutions than other bundles.

This paper is worth reading both for the specific insights it provides and as a wonderful example of how to use theory to inform real-world issues, using a "right-sized" and simple basic model creatively. I recommend it very strongly.

Relative performance and tournaments

The linear-incentive scheme model can be used as well to get insights into another topic in incentive theory, concerning relative-performance evaluation.

Holmstrom's Informativeness Principle is sometimes misinterpreted to draw the following wrong lesson: If Bob has no impact on the value of some random observable, then (risk-averse) Bob's compensation should never be a nontrivial function of this observable, as to do so only adds noise to his compensation.

We can easily see that this is wrong from the general Holmstrom–Milgrom model. Suppose that Bob undertakes only one activity—a is real-valued—and there are two contractible pieces of data on which his compensation could be based, x_1 and x_2. Suppose μ_1 is a strictly increasing function of a, while μ_2 is constant in a. Hence, we satisfy the premise of the wrong statement: Bob's choice of action has no impact on the value of x_2. But suppose that $x_1 = \mu_1(a) + \epsilon$ and $x_2 = \mu_2 + \epsilon$, where ϵ is a mean-zero random variable. Then Alice, observing $x = (x_1, x_2)$, can "invert" these data to learn $\mu_1(a)$ and, therefore, a:

$$\mu_1(a) = x_1 - x_2 + \mu_2.$$

Hence, by basing Bob's compensation on $x_1 - x_2$, Alice can disentangle what Bob has chosen, which allows her to attain the first-best.

This is an extreme example. But if the correlation between x_1 and x_2 is nonzero, there is useful information in x_2, useful for reducing the "uncertainty" Alice faces in trying to discern which value of a Bob has chosen. Holmstrom's Informativeness Principle is not about whether the agent affects some piece of information, but whether that information helps the principal discern (in a statistical sense) what the agent did.

This observation leads to the idea that if two or more agents are subject to common "noise," then discernment of the actions of any one can be improved—and so incentives can be improved—by looking at the outcomes of others. Begin with the following simple model. Suppose Alice employs two agents, Bob and Carol.

- Each performs a single task, choosing an action: a_{Bob} denotes Bob's choice, and a_{Carol} denotes Carol's. Possible actions for each are drawn from $[0, \infty)$.

- Each produces a gross profit contribution for Alice, denoted x_{Bob} and x_{Carol}, respectively. Bob's contribution x_{Bob} equals $\mu(a_{Bob}) + \epsilon_{Bob}$; Carol's is $x_{Carol} =$

$\mu(x_{\text{Carol}}) + \epsilon_{\text{Carol}}$, for a strictly increasing, strictly concave, continuously differentiable function $\mu : [0, \infty) \to R$, and joint mean-0 Normally distributed random variables ϵ_{Bob} and ϵ_{Carol}, both with variance 1 and with covariance 1/2 between them. For expositional purposes, assume $\mu(a) = a^{1/2}$. [30]

- Alice restricts herself to linear compensation schemes.

- Bob and Carol are both risk-averse expected-utility maximizers with same utility function $u(w, a) = -e^{-\lambda(w-a)}$; the choice of action a carries a dollar-valued disutility a.

Suppose Alice ignores the correlation, choosing to reward Bob based on x_{Bob} alone. She offers him a compensation scheme $B + bx_{\text{Bob}}$. Assuming he accepts this offer and chooses a_{Bob}, his certainty equivalent is $B + b\mu(a_{\text{Bob}}) - a_{\text{Bob}} - \lambda b^2/2 = B + ba_{\text{Bob}}^{1/2} - a_{\text{Bob}} - \lambda b^2/2$. His best choice of a_{Bob} is therefore the solution to

$$b\frac{1}{2a_{\text{Bob}}^{1/2}} = 1, \quad \text{or} \quad a_{\text{Bob}} = b^2/4,$$

$$\text{for a certainty equivalent} = B + \frac{b^2}{2} - \frac{b^2}{4} - \frac{\lambda b^2}{2} = B + b^2\left[\frac{1 - 2\lambda}{4}\right].$$

To get Bob to accept, Alice sets B so that

$$B + b^2\left[\frac{1 - 2\lambda}{4}\right] = w^\flat, \quad \text{or} \quad B = w^\flat - b^2\left[\frac{1 - 2\lambda}{4}\right].$$

And, therefore, Alice's net expected payoff if she picks the "slope" term b is

$$(1 - b)\mu(d_{\text{Bob}}) - B = (1 - b)\frac{b}{2} - w^\flat + b^2\left[\frac{1 - 2\lambda}{4}\right] = \frac{b}{2} - \frac{b^2}{4} - \frac{2\lambda b^2}{4} - w^\flat.$$

This is maximized at $b = 1/(1 + 2\lambda)$, at which Bob chooses $a_{\text{Bob}} = 1/(4(1 + 2\lambda)^2) = 1/(2 + 4\lambda)^2$, and Alice nets an expected $1/(4(1 + 2\lambda)) - w^\flat$.

Suppose instead that Alice offers Bob the wage scheme $B + bx_{\text{Bob}} - cx_{\text{Carol}}$ for scalars B, b, and c. Assuming $b, c > 0$, Bob gets more the better he does and the *worse* Carol does. Bob's certainty equivalent depends on both his choice of action a_{Bob} and Carol's, a_{Carol} (still assuming both accept): His wage $B + bx_{\text{Bob}} - cx_{\text{Carol}}$ is Normally distributed with mean $B + ba_{\text{Bob}}^{1/2} - ca_{\text{Carol}}^{1/2}$ and variance $b^2 - bc + c^2$, hence his certainty equivalent is

$$\text{CE} = B + ba_{\text{Bob}}^{1/2} - ca_{\text{Carol}}^{1/2} - \frac{\lambda(b^2 - bc + c^2)}{2} - a_{\text{Bob}}.$$

Bob, maximizing this over a_{Bob}, gets the same answer as before: He chooses $a_{\text{Bob}} = b^2/4$. And please note: Bob cares what Carol does, because it affects his payoff.

---

[30] This function μ has $\mu'(0) = \infty$. Why does that make life simpler?

However, in this model, his conjecture about a_{Carol} this doesn't change his choice of a_{Bob}.[31]

Suppose Alice makes a symmetric wage offer to Carol, so that Carol's choice is symmetrically $a_{\text{Carol}} = b^2/4$. Then Bob's CE is

$$\text{CE} = B + (b - c)\frac{b}{2} - \frac{\lambda(b^2 - bc + c^2)}{2} - \frac{b^2}{4},$$

from which we derive in the usual fashion the value of B: Alice sets B so that Bob and Carol both just receive their reservation certainty equivalent:

$$B+(b-c)\frac{b}{2} - \frac{\lambda(b^2 - bc + c^2)}{2} - \frac{b^2}{4} = w^b, \quad \text{and so} \quad B = w^b - (b-c)\frac{b}{2} + \frac{\lambda(b^2 - bc + c^2)}{2} + \frac{b^2}{4}.$$

The same B applies to Carol, and we can write down Alice's net payoff from her two agents as functions of b and c:

$$(1 - b + c)\big(\mu(a_{\text{Bob}}) + \mu(a_{\text{Carol}})\big) - 2B$$

$$= (1 - b + c)(b) - 2w^b + b(b - c) - \lambda(b^2 - bc + c^2) - \frac{b^2}{2}$$

$$= b - \lambda(b^2 - bc + c^2) - \frac{b^2}{2} - 2w^b.$$

Sparing you the simple algebra, Alice maximizes her net payoff by choosing

$$b = \frac{1}{1 + 3\lambda/2}, \quad c = \frac{b}{2} = \frac{1}{2 + 3\lambda}, \quad \text{and } B = \frac{3\lambda}{2(2 + 3\lambda)^2} + w^b, \text{ leading Bob and Carol}$$

to choose $a_{\text{Bob}} = a_{\text{Carol}} = \dfrac{1}{(3\lambda + 2)^2}$, providing net payoff $\dfrac{1}{2 + 3\lambda} - 2w^b$ for Alice.

These choices by Bob and Alice are greater than what each would choose if Alice didn't use this scheme of making their wages depend on the other's outcome, and Alice's net payoff is greater than twice what she would get from each individually if she didn't use this scheme.

Why? It isn't that Bob and Carol are made worse off by this "competition." It is in the nature of this model that Alice provides each with the certainty equivalent w^b. But this relative-evaluation scheme allows Alice to reduce the uncertainty facing Bob and Carol in their compensation, which means that less must be given them to compensate for their risk they assume, which means more for Alice. Plus, because they face less risk, in trading off incentives and inefficient risk sharing, Alice can

---

[31] A fine point here is that Bob's wage is Normally distributed *only if* he has a deterministic assessment concerning what Carol is doing. If, say, he assessed that Carol was mixing between two (or more) different values of a_{Carol}, his wage is a mixture of Normals, and the analysis gets much more difficult. But, happily, in this story Carol will optimize with a single value of a_{Carol} and, per a Nash-equilibrium-style analysis, Bob is presumed to know what that is.

"push" the incentive lever a bit harder, causing Bob and Carol to choose larger values of a, getting each closer to the first-best level of a.

Game theory and these models

It is worthwhile to digress briefly into the type of game-theoretic analysis being used here and, in particular, why the model with Bob *and* Carol is a step more complex in terms of the game-theoretic analysis than the previous models in which Alice deals only with Bob.

As noted from the start of this chapter, we're modeling these situations as extensive-form games in which Alice presents Bob with a fait accompli: "Bob, Here is the wage scheme I'm offering." Bob then responds. He can reject Alice's offer, but if he does not, the terms that she has named are the terms he faces. And we assume that, whatever Alice's offer is, Bob optimizes for himself, given the terms of that offer. In places I use fancy terminology such as "Bob's sequentially rational response." But, because Bob knows the terms Alice has offered, his information set is singleton; his beliefs are trivial. We are assuming (only) subgame perfection.[32]

Once we add Carol, the game-theoretic concept remains subgame perfection, but at one level of greater complexity. Bob and Carol, in the analysis presented, are playing a simultaneous-move game in the subgames, in which (implicitly) they are simultaneously choosing their effort levels. And we look for a Nash equilibrium between the two in these subgames. It is, in this specific model, a particularly simple Nash analysis, because both Bob and Carol have *(almost)* dominant strategy choices: Assuming each accepts, the optimal choices for each of their effort levels is independent of what they conjecture the other agent will do.

Why the parenthetical *almost*? Because the decision to accept Alice's offer depends on the prospective certainty equivalent each can obtain, and their CEs do depend on what the other agent is expected to do.

And, to be fully truthful, I haven't done a full analysis of the game that is implicit in the discussion. I assumed that Alice would make the same offers to Bob and to Carol, so *if* the game restricted Alice to identical offers, I've covered all bases. But, what if Alice can make different offers to Bob and Carol? It turns out that she (Alice) wouldn't want to do this, but I certainly haven't shown that. (So, consider this a challenge. You do it.)

The threat of collusion

While Bob's choice of effort (once he accepts) doesn't depend on what he believes Carol will do, Alice's choice of B depends on her beliefs about what each agent will do. And this leads to the following real-world consideration.

Suppose Alice, anticipating that Bob and Carol will individually optimize, proposes to each the optimal scheme from before:

$$B = \frac{3\lambda}{2(2+3\lambda)^2} + w^b, \quad b = \frac{1}{1+3\lambda/2}, \quad \text{and} \quad c = \frac{1}{2+3\lambda}. \tag{19.7}$$

---

[32] In most places, I use subgame-perfection-plus, the "plus" being the additional assumption on Bob's behavior that, when indifferent, he takes the action that Alice prefers.

Suppose Bob and Carol get together and... conspire?, collude?, cooperate?... choose the verb you like best...to jointly restrict their efforts. Much like two duopolists engaged in Cournot or Bertrand competition, who restrict output or raise prices jointly, Bob and Carol work together for their common good (and Alice's bad). Of course, each has an individual incentive to cheat on the deal; the Nash equilibrium in their simultaneous choice of action is what Alice has anticipated. But perhaps Bob and Carol can find a way to trust one another not to give in to their individual incentive to cheat on the deal; Chapter 22 discusses how this could happen.

What will they do? Given all the symmetry, they look for a common value a for their effort levels that makes each of their certainty equivalents as large as possible. The part of Bob's CE calculation that involves a_{Bob} and a_{Carol} is $ba_{Bob} - ca_{Carol}$ (and the symmetric term for Carol). So if they collude to choose a common a, they would do best to choose a that is appropriate for the "incentive term" $(b-c)a = a/(2+3\lambda)$. This, from earlier analysis, is $1/[4(2+3\lambda)^2]$. Which, of course, (or you could do the calculations, but because of strict concavity, we know) provides each with a CE in excess of w^b, as long as Alice bases her calculation of B on the mistaken conjecture that they would each choose d to be twice this level.

And this makes Alice strictly worse off than if she (Alice) reverted back to the solution $b = 1/(1 + 2\lambda)$ and $c = 0$ (and the appropriate B). By setting $c = 0$, she ensures that Bob and Carol have no incentive to collude: Each is literally on his or her own. You can do the algebra to show that this better than if Alice tries the values of B, b, and c in (19.7), and Bob and Carol collude. But we know that this is so, because: (1) If $c = 0$, the best $b = 1/(1 + 2\lambda)$, which elicits $a = 1/[4(1 + 2\lambda)^2]$ from each. Instead, under the compensation parameters in (19.7), the colluding pair are choosing $a = 1/[4(2 + 3\lambda)^2]$, which is even less effort. So (2) even if Alice set B at the "appropriate level" for $a = 1/[4(2 + 3\lambda)^2]$, she'd be doing worse than by fixing c at 0. And, still worse, (3) she is paying a B that is appropriate for $a = 2/[4(2 + 3\lambda)^2]$, which is greater still. She loses both by overpaying them in their fixed wage component for what effort they supply, while getting less effort from each than would be optimal, given that they will collude.

Designers of compensation systems that employ comparative performance evaluation know about this: It happens when the parties being compared can and do withhold effort as a joint enterprise, in situations where the employees being compared see that they have a common interest against management.

And, at the other end of the spectrum are situations where the parties being compared have the opposite "every employee for him- or herself" ethic and have the ability (through other possible activities) to harm the performance prospects of their peers.

'True" benchmarking

Return to the case in which agents (plural) do not collude but instead individually maximize. The term *benchmark compensation* is typically used when the compensation given an agent is tied directly the the difference between the agent's own outcome and a measure of the average outcome achieved by members of the bench mark group. That is, this involves wages for agent j of the form $B + b(x_j - \overline{x})$, where x_j is the measure of j's performance, and $\overline{x}$ is the "benchmark" performance. In the Bob and Carol story, we don't have this: $c = b/2$, not b. And it is clear why: Carol's performance reflects to some extent the "noise" in Bob's performance, but it has independent noise of its own. Alice wishes to use what she learns from x_{Carol} about Bob's choice a_{Bob}, but to put full weight on x_{Carol} is suboptimal, as it introduces into Bob's compensation a level of irrelevant, hence purely inefficient, uncertainty.

To get true benchmarking requires a story in which Alice compares how Bob has done to the average performance of a large number of Carols, large enough so that the idiosyncratic noise in the performance of each of the Carols is washed out by averaging. Here is a model:

Alice has many identical agents. One, on whom we focus, is Bob. And there are Carol1, Carol2, ..., Carol$J$. In this model, all $J + 1$ are identical: Each is offered a wage contract by Alice, which must be accepted or rejected. If accepted, each must choose a level of effort a: a_{Bob} for Bob and a_j for Carol$j$. As a result of these action choices, each generates a contribution to Alice's gross (of wages) profit x_{Bob} for Bob and x_j for Carol$j$. All these profits have a Normal distribution with mean $\mu(a_j)$ (where $j = \text{Bob}, 1, 2, \ldots, J$) and variance $\sigma^2 + \hat{\sigma}^2$. More specifically, $x_j = \mu(a_j) + \epsilon_j + \rho$, where $\{\rho, \epsilon_j; j = \text{Bob}, 1, \ldots, J\}$ is a collection of fully independent, mean-zero Normal variates, each ϵ_j has variance σ^2, and ρ, the common-to-all noise term, has variance $\hat{\sigma}^2$.

Alice, in designing the wage scheme for Bob, benchmarks his performance against the average performance $X_{\neg\text{Bob}} := (1/J) \sum_{j=1}^{J} x_j$, with Bob's compensation given by $B + b(x_{\text{Bob}} - X_{\neg\text{Bob}})$. The rationale for this scheme should be clear:

$$X_{\neg\text{Bob}} = \frac{1}{J} \left[\sum_{j=1}^{J} \mu(a_j) + \sum_{j=1}^{J} \epsilon_j + \sum_{j=1}^{J} \rho \right].$$

If Alice provides symmetrical wage schemes to all the Carols and if, as a consequence and per some symmetric Nash equilibrium in which each Carol chooses an action a, this is

$$X_{\neg\text{Bob}} = \mu(a) + \rho - \frac{1}{J} \sum_{j=1}^{J} \epsilon_j.$$

And, therefore, if Bob chooses a', the "incentive" term for him is

$$b \times (x_j - X_{\neg\text{Bob}}) = b \times \left[\left(\mu(a') + \epsilon_{\text{Bob}} + \rho \right) - \left(\mu(d) + \rho + \frac{1}{J} \sum_{j=1}^{J} \epsilon_j \right) \right].$$

The ρ's cancel out, and the term $(1/J)\sum_j \epsilon_j$ is Normal with mean 0 and variance σ^2/J. Now add the (by now, standard) assumptions about Bob's utility function being CARA, and we've transformed the problem to one in which his wage has a mean determined by his choice of effort and a variance of $\sigma^2 + \sigma^2/J$. Bob faces no risk in compensation because of ρ. And as J gets large, the "nothing-to-do-with-Bob" term $\left[\sum_{j=1}^{J} \epsilon_j\right]/J$ imposes vanishing compensation risk on Bob. This will redound to Alice's benefit in designing incentives for Bob..

This isn't the optimal scheme for Alice, for a finite J. If you wish, you can look for the optimal scheme of the form $B + bx_{\text{Bob}} - cX_{\neg\text{Bob}}$; you'll find that c is a bit less than b. But $c \to b$ as $J \to \infty$.

And there is another advantage in this for Alice. Especially if Bob and Carol work side-by-side, Alice must be concerned that they might collude. If they are not friendly, but each has the (unmodeled) opportunity to sabotage the other, it might be in their individual interests to do so. But, if Bob is benchmarked against a large number of Carols, (1) collusion is apt to get harder,[33] and (2) Bob sabotaging the efforts of a significant number of Carols is likely to be personally costly, while sabotaging just a few of many Carols won't generate much of a change in $X_{\neg\text{Bob}}$ and so won't be of much benefit to him.

Now, real life isn't so symmetric as is this model. In real-life applications of this idea, the principal faces an obvious trade-off: Benchmarking Bob against a large number of others has the positive effects we see in this model. But the larger the "comparison set," the more likely it becomes that some of the folks in the comparison set are quite different from Bob, and so introduce additional and extraneous noise. But the basic idea is there.

I'll leave "comparison-based compensation schemes" here, except to mention that in Problem 19.17, an entirely different story about such schemes is presented.

19.6. Linear Incentives? Holmstrom and Milgrom (1987)

I hope the previous section convinces you that incentive theory is much easier to do if you can restrict attention to linear incentive schemes. And rationale #1 for doing so is that this is what we see in a lot of cases in the real world.[34]

The second stream of literature on linear incentive schemes attempts to show why they make sense. One example of this stream of research Carroll (2015), based on the notion that there are many things the principal simply doesn't know—for instance, the range of actions that the agent might take—and the principal therefore looks for an incentive scheme that is *robust*, given her ignorance. I personally am a bit skeptical of how robustness is implemented in Caroll (2015), with a max-min criterion. So I'll leave this for you to explore on your own. But this is certainly a worthwhile direction of research.

---

[33] Why? At this point, I can only appeal to your intuition.

[34] I must point out that, having seen a number of real-world incentive schemes, I've seen a lot of schemes—mostly nonlinear—that are very dysfunctional, for a variety of reasons. See the last entry in the Bibliographic Remarks for some reading.

A different explanation is offered in the seminal work of this sort, Holmstrom and Milgrom (1987). Without going into all the details, and somewhat simplifying what they do, here is their model and its interpretation.

Begin with a variation on the general model of Section 19.2. Alice wishes to hire Bob to provide a service, which will result in one of a finite number M of contractible contingencies. For simplicity, identify each contingency x_m with Alice's gross payoff in that contingency. Alice offers Bob a wage scheme $w \in W^X$, where W is the set of feasible wages, and X is the set of M contingencies. Bob can either accept or reject the offer; if he accepts, he chooses an action a_n from an N-element set A, which determines a probability distribution $\pi(a_n)$ over the contingencies X; write π_{mn} for the probability of contingency m occuring if Bob chooses a_n. Bob seeks to maximize his expected utility, which is

$$\sum_m \pi_{mn} u\big(w(x_n) - d_n\big),$$

for a utility function u that has all the properties we've been assuming and for a vector of disutilities d_n, where d_n is the *dollar-valued* disutility associated with action a_n. Given the wage offer, Bob accepts if some action generates for himself a certainty equivalent wage of w^b or more, in which case he takes an action that maximizes his expected utility, resolving ties as Alice would prefer him to do.

And, just as before, Alice seeks a wage offer w that induces Bob to say "yes" and to take action a_n, to maximize her expected net payoff $\sum_m \pi_{mn}\big(x_m - w(x_m)\big)$.[35]

The change from the classic model of Section 19.2 is that, before, Bob's expected utility was $\sum_m \pi_{mn} u(w(x_m)) - d_n$. That is, the measure of disutility was in utility units, subtracted from Bob's expected utility of his wage. In this formulation, d_n is measured in "dollars"; it appears inside the utility function, subtracted from Bob's wage in each contingency. This is the formulation that we investigated in Section 19.5. But, unlike the developments in Section 19.5, Holmstrom and Milgrom allow Alice to choose any incentive scheme she wishes; she isn't limited to linear schemes. Hence, with this change in the formulation from Section 19.2, Holmstrom and Milgrom must go back and re-derive the sorts of results we derived in earlier sections.

This is not a trivial task. In the previous formulation, we used as decision variables $z_m = u\big(w(x_m)\big)$, so that Bob's expected utility from using an action $a_{n'}$ could be written as $\sum_m \pi_{mn'} z_m - d_{n'}$. Suppose that, in this formulation, we look at the problem of Alice trying to induce a_n at minimal cost, and we try to use decision variables $z_m^n = u\big(w(x_m) - d_n\big)$. This provides a relatively convenient objective function: $w(x_m) = \psi(z_m) + d_m$. But when it comes to the incentive constraints— that a_n is at least as good as $a_{n'}$—things aren't so pretty: if Bob contemplates $a_{n'}$, his expected utility is

$$\sum_m \pi_{mn'} u(w(x_m) - d_{n'}).$$

---

[35]   Holmstrom and Milgrom allow the principal to be risk averse. We'll stick to a risk-neutral Alice.

Since $z_m^n = u(w(x_m) - d_n)$ is $w(x_m) - d_n = \psi(z_m^n)$, or $w(x_m) = \psi(z_m^n) + d_n$, we can rewrite Bob's expected utility from choosing n' in terms of the decision variables z_{mn} as

$$\sum_m \pi_{mn'} \, u\big(\psi(z_m^n) + d_n - d_{n'}\big),$$

and the constraint that choice a_n is at least as good as choice $a_{n'}$ is a mess. Still, Holmstrom and Milgrom surmount these difficulties and, subject to some conditions, prove the existence of a solution to Alice's overall problem.[36] Denote the solution to this almost-the-classic principal–agent problem with notation n^* for the index of the action that Alice chooses to induce and w^* for wage payment for each of the M possible contingencies, where w^* induces a_{n^*} from Bob.

This is all by way of preparation for the model that is the focus of the paper. Imagine that Alice seeks to hire Bob to provide a service in each of L periods, denoted $\ell = 1, 2, \ldots, L$. Bob, if he accepts, must choose his effort level a^ℓ from the set A in each period ℓ; his choice a^ℓ generates an outcome x^ℓ in period ℓ, where the probability that $x^\ell = x_m$ if $a^\ell = a_n$ is π_{mn}, and where the outcome in each period is fully independent of the outcomes in other periods and the actions Bob chooses in other periods. Bob is paid only *after* period L, with a wage that depends on the full history of outcomes $x = (x^1, \ldots, x^L) \in X^L$, where x^ℓ is the outcome in period ℓ. Alice offers Bob a wage function $w : X^L \to W$ at the outset; Bob accepts or rejects; Bob then goes on, period by period, to choose a^ℓ. Bob's decision to accept is based on an expected-utility calculation: For his von Neumann-Morgenstern utility function u, he asks whether, by choosing his actions optimally, his expected utility of the utility function

$$u\left(w(x^1, \ldots, x^L) - \sum_{\ell=1}^L d^\ell \right)$$

gives him an ex ante certainty equivalent of at least $Lw^\flat$, where d^ℓ is the dollar-valued disutility of his choice of action a^ℓ. (Can he quit before the end of period L? If so, what is he paid? Assume for expositional ease that he cannot.)

Holmstrom and Milgrom then make a crucial "parametric" assumption: Bob's utility function $u(w)$ has constant absolute risk aversion; that is, $u(w) = -e^{-\lambda w}$ for $\lambda > 0$. I reiterate that this is not an outrageous assumption, as long as this is not a make-or-break economic situation for Bob. Be that as it may, this assumption is made.

---

[36] For readers who go on to consult the original paper, it may help to point out that for the set of "available actions" for Bob, the authors use the convex hull of $\{(\pi_{mn}); n = 1, \ldots, N\}$, relying on Bob's ability to randomize among the A_n to convexify the probabilities he can achieve. Of course, this has implications for the shape of the disutility functions, which become functions d on this convex hull of probabilities.

Consider the following two scenarios. Neither scenario is the Holmstrom and Milgrom model, but they set two benchmarks:

1. Suppose Alice makes her wage proposal w, and then Bob must respond by specifying how he will act in each period. That is, at the outset, he says something like, "In period 1, I'll choose action a^1, in period 2, a^2, ..., in period L, a^L," *and he is committed to carry out this plan.* Please note: This is *not* the first-best situation in which Alice writes a contract that (in an enforceable manner) specifies what Bob will do in each period. It is not a case in which Alice and Bob negotiate over which actions he will take. In this scenario, she offers a wage scheme $w \in W^{X^L}$, and she is done; Bob then freely chooses the sequence $(a^1, \ldots, a^L)$ that is best for himself given this wage offer. But he is committed to his ex ante choice of $(a^1, \ldots, a^L)$.

2. Just before period 1, Alice proposes a wage structure for that period only (an element of W^M), Bob accepts or rejects and, if he accepts, he chooses a^1. Regardless of what happened in period 1, just before period 2, Alice proposes a wage structure for that period, Bob accepts or rejects and, if he accepts, he chooses a^2. And so forth.

Scenario 1 is (except for the reformulation of the form of Bob's disutility term) the sort of thing outlined in Section 19.2, with a very complex set of actions for Bob, namely, A^L. One expects the sort of solution we had in Section 19.2, with contingency space X^L and an optimal wage scheme that is a complicated function whose domain is this contingency space. Scenario 2, in contrast, is just L separate and independent copies of the one-period model. Since Bob has constant absolute risk aversion, his utility function (essentially) doesn't change and, in each period, Alice would optimally propose the wage scheme that is optimal for her in a single period. Bob's overall compensation for the L periods would be a relatively simple *piece-rate*[37] scheme: If $w^*(x_m)$ is the one-period-model optimal wage in contingency x_m, Bob's overall compensation is given by the formula

$$\sum_{m=1}^{M} w^*(x_m) \times \#\{\ell : x^\ell = x_m\}, \tag{19.8}$$

where $\#\{\ell : x^\ell = x_m\}$ is shorthand for the number of periods in which $x_\ell = x_m$.

Holmstrom and Milgrom study an intermediate scenario: (1) Alice proposes a wage structure for all L periods, (2) as in scenario 1, Bob accepts or rejects this offer, but (3) as in scenario 2, Bob can adapt his effort choice in period ℓ to what has happened in previous periods.

And—the bottom line—the authors prove that among Alice's optimal wage schemes for their intermediate-scenario case is the wage scheme given by the For-

---

[37] The term *piece-rate* comes from a somewhat common compensation scheme in which, for each period's outcome x_m, there is associated *piece-rate payment* $w^*(x_m)$ on offer, and the employee's overall compensation is the sum of his piece-rate-based payments.

mula (19.8). (This is proved by an induction argument, inducting on L, the number of periods.)

Moreover, if $M = 2$, Formula (19.8) gives a linear wage scheme: Assume, for the case $M = 2$, that $x_2 > x_1$, and Alice (in the one-period model) optimally induces an action more onerous than the least onerous action, so that $w^*(x_1) < w^*(x_2)$. It takes a bit of algebra, but you can show that

$$w(x^1, \ldots, x^L) = w^*(x_1) \times \#\{\ell : x^\ell = x_1\} + w^*(x_2) \times \#\{\ell : x^\ell = x_2\}$$

$$= \left[Lx_1 \left(\frac{w^*(x_2) - w^*(x_1)}{x_2 - x_1} \right) - Lw^*(x_1) \right] + \left[\sum_\ell x^\ell \right] \times \frac{w^*(x_2) - w^*(x_1)}{x_2 - x_1}.$$

That is, for a base wage B equal to the first term in the square brackets on the right-hand side and an incentive term b equal to $(w^*(x_2) - w^*(x_1))/(x_2 - x_1)$, Bob's total compensation has the form $B + bX$, where $X = \sum_\ell x^\ell$ is the total gross payoff Bob generates for Alice over the L periods.

The interpretation that Holmstrom and Milgrom offer runs as follows: Suppose that Bob is a salesperson, and x^ℓ is the amount he sells in period ℓ. The L "periods" are days in a month or a quarter; Bob is paid at the end of the month or quarter according to his daily record of sales $(x^1, \ldots, x^L)$. Now imagine that the "optimal" scheme is nonlinear; suppose, for instance, that it calls for a substantial increase in Bob's quarterly pay if he sells more than $\$10,000,000$ in a given quarter, but not very much more if he does even better. Then, one can anticipate (and there is, at least, anecdotal, as well as more serious empirical evidence for) the following behavior by Salesperson Bob: If, near the end of a quarter, he is fairly far from $\$10,000,000$ in sales, he will slack off or, perhaps, arrange for sales that he will only book at the start of the next quarter. If, near the end, he has already recorded sales totaling $\$10,000,000$, he might engage in the same sort of gaming of the system. And if Bob is near but not quite at $\$10,000,000$ near the end of the quarter, he will push hard to get over this magic number, perhaps by expending extraordinary efforts in the short run or, worse, by booking less than desirable sales (say, to customers who are credit risks) or by engaging in mild bribery. In a word, because Salesperson Bob can track how he is doing over the quarter, and because he can adjust his behavior according to how he is doing, he can *game* an incentive scheme that has such things as hurdle levels or, for that matter, any nonlinearity.

In contrast, a linear incentive scheme subjects Bob to "constant incentive pressure." It doesn't matter how well he has done in the first two months of the quarter; his marginal incentive to make sales, given by b, is the same. Now, that isn't quite true for a general utility function u, because his evaluation of his compensation must be filtered through his utility function. But, with constant absolute risk aversion in the model, this "not quite true" becomes "absolutely true."

To connect the model's conclusion with this interpretation of their results, consider the following special case. Suppose Bob has two actions a_1 and a_2 (before we convexify), with a_2 more onerous than a_1, and in each period, there are two possible outcomes, $x_1 < x_2$, where a_2 gives higher probability of x_2 than does a_1. And suppose that, in the first-best world, where Alice and Bob can contractually specify Bob's action choice, Alice prefers to induce a_2. Then, in the limit, as $L \to \infty$, she can approach her first best in scenario 1 (where Bob must commit in advance to his effort choices in all L periods): She offers to pay Bob a bit more than $L(w^b + d_2)$, but only as long as the average number of "successes" in the L periods is close to the probability of success under a_2. If the average number of successes is sufficiently less than this probability—indicating that Bob did not commit to the choice of a_2 in all periods (or some randomization close to a_2 with probability 1), then Alice uses the fact that Z is unbounded below to threaten dire punishment. The point is: As L goes to ∞, Alice (and Bob) can trust to the law of large numbers to ensure (with probability very close to 1) that Bob gets close to the first-best payment $w^b + d_2$ in each period, as long as he commits to a_2 for most periods. Which, in scenario 1, permits Alice asymptotically to achieve the first-best outcome.

But this scheme won't work if Bob can dynamically adjust his action choice: If he has been having either a run of good luck (more x_2's than "expected"), he can slack off for a while. Or if he has had a run of really bad luck (so that the odds that he is "doomed" become significant), he may as well slack off.

To reiterate, the point of Holmstrom and Milgrom (1987) is to provide a rationale for the prevalence of linear incentive schemes. If you are willing (1) to accept that there must be a reason for them and (2) to proceed to study the consequences of the assumption that principals use linear incentives, which is what we did in Section 19.5, this explanation for linear incentive schemes is unnecessary. But, while challenging, this paper provides one solid story for why such schemes are prevalent: For agents who are continuously making effort choices, linear incentives provide constant incentive pressure; nonlinear schemes open up the possibility of "gaming" the scheme as the agent adapts his or her efforts to results so far achieved.[38]

19.7. Is Risk Aversion the Key to Agency Issues?

In Section 19.1, risk aversion on the part of the agent plays a crucial role in the story, in the following sense: If the agent Bob is risk neutral, Alice can achieve the first-best outcome by "selling the venture" to Bob. And, with that in mind, there is talk of the *fundamental trade-off* being more efficient risk sharing versus stronger incentives for Bob.

This may mislead you into believing that risk aversion on the part of the agent is necessary for there to be agency problems.[39] This is incorrect: Even if both Alice

---

[38] I reiterate that the paper does quite a lot more than I've sketched here. In particular, the authors also study a continuous-time model: Bob chooses effort over an interval of time, with observable-and-contractible contingencies being the path of a Brownian motion, where the effort choice affects the drift rate of the Brownian motion. Continuous-time models—especially those with Brownian motion—have been the focus of much study recently. But they can be controversial, and I leave it to a second-year course in microeconomic theory to discuss both their good and controversial aspects.

[39] We've already established that, strictly speaking, risk aversion on the part of the agent is not suffi-

and Bob are risk neutral, agency problems can arise.

This seems to run counter to the notion that, if Bob is risk neutral, Alice can "sell" the venture to Bob for a fixed price. New-owner-Bob then bears all the risk, which is efficient if he is risk neutral. And then, he fully internalizes the benefits from his effort choice. Therefore, he will, as owner-operator of the venture, choose the first-best level of effort.

This logic seems impeccable. But it depends on Alice being able to "sell" the venture to Bob. And, in some cases, this is impossible.

Multitasking

A simple illustrative example involving multitasking gives one reason for this. Suppose that Builder Bob is building a new house for Alice. The value of Bob's work to Alice depends on how long it takes Bob to complete the project—she is renting an apartment on a month-by-month basis while waiting—and it depends on the quality of the build. Alice can "sell" her rental costs to Bob by writing a contract in which he (effectively) pays her rent (in exchange for a fixed amount equal to the expected number of months times the monthly rent she is paying). This motivates him to finish quickly. But it also motivates him to cut corners when building, which lowers the quality of the build. And, while a warranty against defects in the build for some period of time can be considered, some cut corners will only be realized many years in the future, long after Builder Bob has fled the scene. The point is, there is no way for Alice to "sell" the risks of flaws in the construction to Bob. Therefore, she doesn't want him to bear all the risks of delay in completion, even if he is risk neutral; if he fully bears those risks, 5 years down the line, she may discover that the electrical wiring was not done so well, or there is some dry rot, because flashing was poorly installed.

Limited liability

A prominent institutional feature of real-world contracts is limited liability. Suppose Alice is a venture capitalist, and Bob is an entrepreneur. Instead of speaking of wages for Bob, think of VC-Alice proposing to Entrepreneur-Bob how "profits" will be shared in exchange for a capital infusion. The range of possible profit-sharing rules is limited by Bob's limited liability. So, in such cases, even if Bob is risk neutral (and I'm not asserting that entrepreneurs are naturally risk neutral), there can be an agency problem to solve. (See Problem 19.16.)

To put this in terms that track the models developed in this chapter, go back to the very general model of Section 19.2. Bob has N possible actions he might take, a_1 through a_N. There are M possible outcomes, x_1 to x_M, which (for simplicity) we assume are the possible gross (dollar) profits from the project. If Bob takes action a_n, π_{mn} is the probability that the gross profit is x_m.

---

cient: While admittedly extreme, if for every action other than the first-best action there is a contractible contingency that has zero probability under the first-best action and positive probability under other action, and if dire-enough punishments are available to the principal, the first-best action can be implemented at first-best cost to the principal.

Bob is risk neutral, and he suffers (dollar-denominated) disutility d_n if he chooses a_n. Hence, net of his disutility, the expected value to be split between Alice and Bob, if he takes action a_n, is

$$\sum_{m=1}^{M} \pi_{mn} x_m - d_n.$$

The first-best solution involves maximizing this value; let n^* be the index of first-best action.

For Bob to agree to the "deal" proposed by Alice, he requires an expected outcome of at least w^b. Therefore, for Alice to "sell the venture to Bob," she names the price

$$p = \sum_{m=1}^{M} \pi_{mn^*} x_m - d_{n^*} - w^b.$$

This leaves Bob, if he agrees to pay p and then chooses action a_n, with the uncertain payoff $x_m - p$. You can easily check that, if this is a feasible arrangement, and if Bob is risk neutral, he will then choose action a_{n^*}, giving him (precisely) net utility w^b.

The key here is the phrase *if this is feasible*. Suppose profit possibility $x_M = 0$. Bob's outcome if x_M happens is then $-p$. Bob's limited liability may then become an issue. If he promises to pay p to Alice after the dust settles, and x_M is the outcome, he declares bankruptcy. Or, if Alice demands payment upfront, and Bob doesn't have the required cash, he might borrow from some third party to pay Alice upfront, with the promise to repay the third party after the dust settles. With limited liability, if the outcome is x_M, the lender may be out of luck.

This is not to say that a scheme less extreme than "Alice sells the whole venture to Bob" may not give Bob sufficient incentive to pick the first-best action. However, even if Bob is risk neutral, there is an interesting and nontrivial agency problem here to be solved.

Joint production

Suppose Alice hires Bob and Carol, and the nature of their jobs is such that the gross (contractible) outcome depends on how much effort each provides. Even if both Bob and Carol are risk neutral, if Alice sells the venture to Bob, he must motivate Carol. Alice could try to get Bob and Carol to form a partnership to which she sells the venture, but that introduces a free-rider problem. This chapter has had nothing to say about how Alice should structure incentives for Bob and Carol in cases of so-called *interdependent production*. That is another topic to put on your reading list.

Bibliographic Notes

The issues discussed in this chapter are central to many issues in economics and have attracted enormous attention. So my list of references *should not* be deemed as authoritative, and I apologize to authors whose work I neglect but should have referenced.

The story developed in Sections 19.1 through 19.4—the classic principal–agent model—is the starting point for the literature on incentives to deal with issues of moral hazard. J. Mirrlees made many early and significant contributions to this theory, but his contributions were only published much later; the reference is to Mirrlees (1999), but his results were circulated in full form in 1975. Ross (1973), Holmstrom (1979), and Shavell (1979) are other early papers. I rely on the treatment found in Grossman and Hart (1983); Rogerson (1985) and Jewitt (1988) made further important contributions to the first-order approach.

I don't know who first formulated the linear incentives plus Normal signals plus CARA utility model, so I will call this "folk lore." But in terms of justifying linear incentives, the classic paper is Holmstrom and Milgrom (1987); a more recent and very different justification is offered by Carroll (2015).

The literature on multitasking begins with Holmstrom and Milgrom (1991).

The idea that it may be fruitful to base Bob's compensation on how Carol performs, if Carol's performance is correlated with Bob's, has many nearly simultaneous progenitors, among which are Baiman and Demski (1980), Green and Stokey (1983), Holmstrom (1982a,b), Lazear and Rosen (1981), Mookerjee (1984), and Nalebuff and Stiglitz (1983). In particular, Lazear–Rosen investigate so-called tournaments, in which the "best" performer wins a prize. The idea, briefly explored in this chapter, that Bob and Carol might collude is explored in Demski and Sappington (1984) and Moore, Ma, and Turnbull (1988).

Problem 19.17, which introduces a completely different rationale for "comparative-performance compensation," is taken (more or less) from Levin (2003) and MacLeod (2003).

This only begins to scratch the surface of papers about incentives and, in particular, the application of the basic theory to various contextual domains, including, for example, public finance and optimal taxation, a firm's interest in developing the human capital of its employees, incentives to obtain and use information, defense contracting, property and health insurance, and tax compliance and enforcement. There are also extensions to group-based incentives (and the resulting free-rider problem) and to situations in which agents work simultaneously for multiple principals. And, while the models in this chapter are all static, one-period models, important examples of incentives include the incentive to be promoted and to maintain a relationship. (The last topic will be touched on in Chapter 22.) Applications go so far as to see how the incentives provided by corporate tax considerations can significantly affect corporate form; see Scholes et al. (2014).

I mentioned at the end of Section 19.7 the possibility of production technologies for which contractible outcomes depend on the actions of more than one agent; so-called *interdependent* or *team production*. A classic article with which to start your reading is Holmstrom (1982b).

   With regard to the basic game-form of this chapter, in which Alice sets the terms, and Bob must accept those terms and respond: This basic extensive form, and the use of subgame perfection, is employed in any number of economic contexts. The first of these, which predates formal game theory, is Stackelberg equilibrium. Problem 19.18 provides a taste of this model.

   Finally, readers with "applied" interests in the economics of organization and microeconomic approaches to labor economics (or human resource management [HRM], or personnel economics) should take the theory of incentives as presented here with several jumbo-sized grains of salt. (This is undoubtedly an admonition that applies to all the chapters in this volume. But HRM is what I teach and write about when not doing economic theory, so I'm particularly sensitive when it comes to this topic.) Some more nuanced considerations will be presented in Volume III, if it ever appears. Meanwhile, and for a practitioner-level introduction to some of those nuances, see Kreps (2018).

Problems

■ 19.1 Give a more rigorous proof of Lemma 19.3 than is offered in the text, using the first-order, complementary-slackness conditions for Alice's two cost-minimization problems e and h from page 42.

■ 19.2 On page 46, I assert that, if Bob is risk averse, Alice cannot "sell Bob the venture" for a fixed amount and do as well as she can by employing him in the fashion of Proposition 19.2, except for one very special case. I give a loose argument for this; please tighten up my argument, while identifying that one very special case.

■ 19.3 Prove both the "begun" and "completed" portions of Proposition 19.4. The completed part is straightforward if you draw the right picture.

The next several questions concen the "general" model formulated in Section 19.2, with finitely many actions available to Bob and finitely many contractible contingencies for his wage payment.

■ 19.4. If Bob is risk neutral—assume his utility function is $u(w) = w$, so you don't need to bother rescaling u^0 or the d_n—then the first-best solution can be implemented by having Bob pay Alice a fixed amount, so he bears all the risk, leaving it to him to choose whichever action he desires. A proof of this is requested, but to make this assignment reasonable, the following pieces are added to the model.

   Suppose Alice's gross returns depend on a grand state of nature $\omega \in \Omega$, with $\hat{v}(\omega)$ the gross payoff in state ω. Assume Ω is finite. Suppose that, if Bob chooses action a_n, Alice and Bob share a probability assessment $\rho(\cdot|a_n)$ over Ω; that is, for each $\omega \in \Omega$, $\rho(\omega|a_n)$ is the probability that they jointly assess that the state of nature will be ω if Bob takes action a_n. Also suppose that the contractible contingencies x_1 through x_m represent a partition of Ω—that is, each x_m is an *event* within Ω—and (of course) that $\pi_{mn} = \sum_{\omega \in x_m} \rho(\omega | a_n)$. Finally, assume Alice is risk neutral, so that $\hat{V}(a_n) = \sum_\omega \hat{v}(\omega) \rho(\omega | a_n)$.

■ 19.5. Suppose there are two contractible states, x_1 and x_2, and three possible actions by Bob, a_1, a_2, and a_3, all of which are equally "distasteful" to Bob: $d_1 = d_2 = d_3 = 0$. Suppose $\hat{V}(a_1) = \hat{V}(a_2) = 10$, $\hat{V}(a_3) = 15$, and $w^b = 5$. Finally, suppose $p_{11} = 0.6, p_{12} = 0.4$, and $p_{13} = 0.45$. What does Alice want to have happen? And what problem do you have in claiming that her preferred outcome is the unique outcome of a subgame-perfect equilibrium?

■ 19.6. Provide answers to the questions raised in footnotes 11 and 12 (page 51), and also the question "(Why not?)" in footnote 18 (page 61).

■ 19.7. In the context of the model formulation of Section 19.2, the possibility that $\pi_{mn} = 0$ for some m and n means that, if Alice observes x_m, she knows that Bob did not choose a_n. To illustrate what impact this can have, suppose that there are four observable states, x_1 through x_4, and three possible choices of action by Bob, a_1 through a_3. Suppose the π_{mn} values are given by

$$\pi_{11} = 1/4, \quad \pi_{21} = 1/4, \quad \pi_{31} = 1/4, \quad \pi_{41} = 1/4,$$
$$\pi_{12} = 0, \quad \pi_{22} = 1/3, \quad \pi_{32} = 1/3, \quad \pi_{42} = 1/3,$$
$$\pi_{13} = 0, \quad \pi_{22} = 0, \quad \pi_{33} = 1/2, \quad \pi_{43} = 1/2.$$

Suppose that Bob's utility function u is defined for wages $w \in (0, \infty)$, that $\lim_{w \to 0} u(w) = -\infty$, and that $u_0 = 2$. (Suppose that Alice is constrained to pick a strictly positive wage for Bob; that is, she is constrained to wage schemes in which $w_m > 0$ for $m = 1, 2, 3$. Show that, in these circumstances, and regardless of the values of d_2, d_3 (for $d_3 > d_2 > d_1 = 0$) u_0, and the $\hat{V}(a_n)$, Alice can achieve the first-best arrangement; that is, the arrangement in which she bears all the risk and Bob chooses the action that Alice most desires if she can choose the effort level that Bob selects.

While the theoretical treatment of wage payments for contingencies with zero probability is fairly straightforward, some... interesting things can happen when probabilities are very small, because it is the relative probabilities (the likelihood ratios) that are important in designing incentives. The next two problems give you a taste of this. And Problem 19.10 continues the discussion of the possible failures of Berge's-Theorem logic from pages 57-8.

■ 19.8. Consider an example with $M = 3$ and $N = 2$. For very small ϵ, the probabilities are

$$\pi_{11} = 2\epsilon, \pi_{21} = 0.7 - \epsilon, \pi_{31} = 0.3 - \epsilon,$$
$$\pi_{12} = 2\epsilon^2, \pi_{22} = 0.4 - \epsilon, \pi_{32} = 0.6 - \epsilon.$$

Suppose $u_0 = 3$, $d_2 = 3$, and (of course) $d_1 = 0$. Also suppose $\hat{x}_1 = 0, \hat{x}_2 = 50$, and $\hat{x}_3 = 5000$. Suppose u is given by $u(w) = \ln(w)$.

a. What is the optimal wage contract for Alice to offer if $\epsilon = 0$? What is Alice's not expected payoff?

b. Suppose ϵ is very small but strictly positive. What happens?

c. This is an example where, for a sequence of parameter values γ^k converging to a vector of parameters γ, $\lim_k V^*(\gamma^k) > V^*(\gamma)$. In three words or less, why does the logic of Berge's Theorem fail in this example?

■ 19.9. In the chapter, we largely ignored the possibility of infinitely many contractible contingencies. Suppose that there are not only an infinite number, but in fact the set of possible contingencies X is all of R. And suppose that there are two actions: e and h. Under e, the distribution of x (the resulting contingency) is Normal with mean 5 and standard deviation 1. Under h, the distribution is Normal with mean 6 and standard deviation 1. Finally, suppose Z is unbounded below. What happens?

■ 19.10. Not to be too mysterious about things, the answer to the last bit of Problem 19.8(c) is "lack of compactness" (or, if you prefer, "lack of boundedness." So, to eliminate that problem, suppose that Z is compact: There are wage levels $\underline{w}$ and $\overline{w}$ such that wages less than $\underline{w}$ or greater than $\overline{w}$ are not credible. For $\underline{z} = u(\underline{w})$ and $\overline{z} = u(\overline{z})$, both of these finite, $Z = [\underline{z}, \overline{z}]$. Show that, with this assumption, if we write γ for the vector of all the parameters $\gamma = ((\pi_{mn}), u_0, (d_n), (\hat{V}_n))$ and we write $V^*(\gamma)$ for Alice's (optimal) payoff as a function of these parameters, $\gamma \to V^*(\gamma)$ is upper semi-continuous. But $\gamma \to V^*(\gamma)$ is, in general, not continuous. Why not?

■ 19.11. On page 62, the possibility is raised of a model with effort incentives in which Bob has three actions, d_1, d_2, and d_3, and in which Alice, faced with the problem of motivating Bob, will choose effort level $d^* = d_3$, while her first-best choice (she can choose his effort level) is d_2. (It can't be d_1, for reasons given in the text. To be clear, I'm assuming d_1 is least onerous and d_3 is most onerous.) Provide a numerical example in which d_3 is the second-best effort level, but d_2 is first-best.

■ 19.12. In the formal developments in Sections 19.2 and 19.3, I assumed that Z was unbounded below or that, at least, if Z had a lower bound, it wasn't binding in any of Alice's expected-cost-minimization problems.

a. How do the FO/CS conditions (given in the text on page 58) change if there is a lower bound on $z \in Z$ which may be binding?

b. Provide a solution to the FO/CS conditions for the example on page 63.

c. Prove Proposition 19.9 for the general case where Z can have a finite lower bound.

■ 19.13. In the context of the effort-incentive specialization of Section 19.3: Imagine that Bob is a sales representative for Alice, visiting a prospective client. Bob can exert no effort to make a sale, he can exert a bit of effort which will give good odds of a sales of moderate size but very little chance of a big sale, or he can, with even greater effort, try to make a big sale. In terms of the gross profit to Alice, suppose that no sale is worth 0 to her, a moderate sale is worth 10,000, and a big sale is worth 50,000. Number the three outcomes as: no sale is $m = 1$; a moderate sale is $m = 2$; and a big sale is $m = 3$. And assign no effort, a bit of effort, an greater effort, respectively, to $n = 1, 2,$ and 3. Suppose that

$$\pi_{11} = 0.8, \pi_{21} = 0.15, \text{ and } \pi_{31} = 0.05,$$
$$\pi_{12} = 0.3, \pi_{22} = 0.6, \text{ and } \pi_{32} = 0.1$$
$$\pi_{13} = 0.5 - p, \pi_{23} = p, \text{ and } \pi_{33} = 0.5.$$

For which values of p does this result in $\hat{V}(a_n)$ strictly increasing in n? For which values of p do the three distributions $(\pi_{\cdot n})$ satisfy first-order stochastic dominance? For which values of p does the monotone-likelihood property hold?

■ 19.14. Take the model discussed on pages 78 to 80, adding the assumption that the function μ takes on the particular form $\gamma a^{1/2}$ for scalar $\gamma > 0$. Assume (for reasons that will become apparent) that A, the set of feasible actions (or effort levels) for Bob, is $[0, \bar{a}]$, for $\bar{a} > \gamma^2/4$. Recall that other (fixed) parameters of the problem are: λ, Bob's coefficient of absolute risk aversion; σ^2, the variance of the outcome measure x; and w^b, Bob's reservation wage.

a. Suppose Alice could contractually fix Bob's level of effort. What contract does she offer (as a function of various parameters)? What is Bob's effort level? What is Alice's expected payoff?

b. Suppose Alice cannot contractually fix Bob's level of effort; he chooses whichever level of effort is best for him, given the wage offer of Alice. What is the best linear contract $w(x) = B + bx$ for Alice to offer? What is Bob's chosen level of effort at this contract? What is Alice's expected payoff?

c. Provide comparative statics for the solution to part b in the parameters λ, σ^2, w^b, and γ.

All the usual rules apply. Alice makes a take-it-or-leave-it offer—no bargaining—and an indifferent Bob will choose among his best options in the way Alice would prefer.

■ 19.15. When discussing the paper by Holmstrom and Milgrom (1987), concerning a rationale for linear incentive schemes, I noted that, for a general u, using as decision variables $z_m^n = u(w(x_m) - d_n)$ for the problem of motivating d_n at least cost would lead to an unpleasant formulation of the incentive constraints that d_n is at least as good as $d_{n'}$ for the other n'. But Holmstrom–Milgrom go on to assume that Bob has CARA utility. Why does this reduce the unpleasantness?

■ 19.16. Imagine an entrepreneur, Diane, who seeks venture-capital financing. If Diane can raise $1 million from a venture capitalist (VC), she will be able to pursue a venture that she has developed. Once embarked on this, she must choose between a less-risky and a more-risky strategy. The less-risky strategy will result in gross outcomes (not including the initial investment of $1 million) of $0 with probability 0.1, $5 million with probability 0.8, and $35 million with probability 0.1. The more-risky strategy will result in one of these three outcomes, but the probabilities are 0.65, 0.2, and 0.15, respectively. Diane is risk neutral.

In real life, Diane would shop her idea to several VCs, who might or might not agree with her assessments of the possible outcomes. In real life, she would negotiate with them, hoping that competition among them will get her the best possible deal. But, in keeping with the general game-theoretic methods of this chapter, assume instead that there is one venture capitalist (VC), who shares Diane's assessments about possible outcomes and who is also risk neutral. Diane will make a take-it-or-leave-it proposal to this VC, who will take accept Diane's offer if the offer provides a gross (of the initial $1 million) expected payback of $3 million or more. (Please note: In this story, it is Diane, who takes the eventual action, who also makes the proposal; the entity in the role of the "principal" is dealt with on a take-it-or-leave-it basis. So the story is structurally a bit different from the classic principal-agent model.)

The one complication is that Diane enjoys the benefits of limited liability: In any profit sharing plan she proposes, her (ex-post) share cannot be negative.

a. A common form of financial contract is a debt contract: A figure X is chosen, and Diane must pay to the VC X out of her profits, assuming she has X. If she has less, she pays whatever (positive) amount she has. Suppose, contrary to the basic story, that Diane can contractually commit to choosing one of her two options. What, from her perspective, is the best debt contract to offer?

b. But Diane cannot commit to her action choice. After she has signed an agreement with the VC and has the $1 million in funds, she chooses between the less- and more-risky strategies. And the VC knows this. How does a debt contract work in this case?

c. A second common form is an equity contract. In exchange for the start-up funds, Diane provides the VC with a percentage share in her gross profits. That is, a percentage α is chosen, and Diane must pay back to the VC α times her gross profits. How does an equity arrangement work in this simple story?

■ 19.17. *Another rationale for tying compensation to relative performance.* Section 19.5 tells one story about why the principal might wish to tie compensation for one agent to how that agent performs relative to other agents; viz., if the agents' measures of performance are correlated, how one agent does (in an equilibrium) can provide information about what effort choices other agents have made. Here is a second story.

a. Begin with the simple story from Section 19.1. Alice is the principal, Bob is the agent. If Bob accepts Alice's offer, then Bob chooses whether to work hard h or to take is easy e. Alice observes one of two possible outcomes: Bob's work is a rousing success, or only a moderate success. If Bob works hard, the chance that his work will be a rousing success is $\pi_h = 0.8$. If he takes it easy, the chance that his work will be a rousing success is $\pi_e = 0.2$. Alice begins by proposing a wage scheme (w_0, w_1), where w_1 is what Bob is paid if his work is a rousing success and w_0 is what he is paid for a moderate success. Alice is risk neutral; a rousing success is worth 100 to her, gross of the wages she pays Bob, while a moderate success is worth only 20. Bob is risk averse: He evaluates wage schemes according to the expected utility of the wage he receives, for utility function $u(w) = w^{1/2}$, subtracting from his expected utility a "disutility of effort" term which is 0 if he takes it easy and 3 if he works hard. He accepts Alice's offer if, given his own best choice of effort, he has an expected utility of at least 2.

What distinguishes this situation from Section 19.1 (and everything in this chapter) is that *Alice observes whether the job is a rousing success or not; Bob does not.* So, if Alice proposes to Bob the wage scheme (w_0, w_1), Bob chooses his effort level and, then, Alice tells him whether his efforts were a rousing success; in effect, Alice tells Bob whether she will pay him w_1 or w_0. Bob has no way of verifying whether Alice is being truthful of not.

If Alice sets $w_0 = w_1$, this is not a problem: Regardless of what she observes, she pays him this common wage. What is the optimal constant wage for Alice to offer Bob?

But suppose Alice wishes to induce Bob to work hard. In Section 19.1, she would offer a wage scheme with $w_1 > w_0$. Just for practice, what would be the full solution to this problem *if* Alice could be trusted always to tell the truth (or, if Bob could observe how well he did)?

If Alice cannot be trusted, and if $w_1 > w_0$, then, of course, Alice ex post (in any subgame perfect set of strategies) will report that Bob's efforts led only to a moderate success, so she owes him w_0 only. However, consider the following: Alice says to Bob, "I am going to pay w_1 regardless of my report. If I report to you that you achieved a rousing success, you will get all w_1. But if I report to you that you only achieved a moderate success, I will pay you only w_0, and I will (publicly, verifiably) burn $w_1 - w_0$." (If money-burning seems a bit outlandish to you, Alice could offer to donate $w_1 - w_0$ to some charity about which both she and Bob are completely indifferent.)

What happens?

b. Now suppose that there are, say, five Bobs, each identical to Bob in part a, *where the odds of achieving a rousing success (conditional on effort levels) are fully independent from one Bob to the next.* (Hence, the rationale for pay based on comparative success that drove the subsection *Relative performance and tournaments* on pages 83 to 89 is missing.) Consider Alice making the following sort of proposal to the Bobs: "I will pay each of you a base wage of B. In addition, I am creating a bonus pool of b dollars, which I promise to pay in its entirety to some subset of you. In particular, I will divide this equally among those of you who do achieve a rousing success."

What happens?

In the solution to this problem in the *Online Supplement*, after solving the specifics of this problem, I connect this model and its solution to real-world practices.

■ 19.18. *von Stackelberg duopoly.* Imagine two firms, labeled A and B, that produce products that are substitutes but not perfect substitutes. The inverse demand functions for their two goods are

$$p_A = a - x_A - bx_B, \quad \text{and} \quad p_B = a - x_B - bx_A$$

for a positive constant a and for $0 < b < 1$, with the same constants a and b appearing in both inverse demand functions. Each firm has a constant marginal cost of production c.

a. Suppose the competitive interaction between the firms is as follows. Firm A chooses its production quanity x_A, to which it is committed. Firm b observes this choice and then responds by choosing x_B. What is the subgame-perfect outcome?

b. Suppose instead that Firm A chooses the price p_A that it will charge, and then Firm B (knowing p_A) responds with a choice of p_B. What is the subgame perfect outcome?

c. Suppose $a = 10, b = 0.5$, and $c = 2$. Compute the two firms' quantities, prices, and profits for each of: The firms collude optimally (maximize the sum of their profits); they play Cournot (simultaneously name quantities); they play Bertrand (simultaneously name prices); the play as in part a above (called Cournot-von Stackelberg); and they play as in part b (called Bertrand-von Stackelberg).

Chapter Twenty

Private Information Part I: One-Shot Interactions

The subtitle of Volume II is "Imperfect Competition, Information, and Strategic Interaction." Chapter 18 and the models of Cournot and Bertrand introduced imperfect competition. Chapter 19, concerning moral hazard and incentives, introduced strategic interaction, albeit very simple strategic interaction. In this chapter, information—more precisely, private information—plays the starring role.

It is hardly surprising that, in many economic transactions, one party to the transaction begins in possession of information that the other party lacks. Chapter 19 concerned cases in which agent Bob knows, ex post, which action he took, while principal Alice must "guess" based on the results she observes. This chapter, in contrast, concerns cases in which Alice has information ex ante about how hard the job will be, information that Bob lacks. Or perhaps Bob has private information ex ante about his level of skill, information that Alice lacks. Or both.

In the competitive markets of Volume I, this didn't arise. The qualities and characteristics of the object being bought and sold were well known to all parties, and the "terms of trade" were, in equilibrium, determined by the equilibrium price. But, once we depart even a bit from that ideal situation, a host of issues arise. Private information crops up in all sorts of contexts; this chapter introduces the basic issues using four seminal contexts: Akerlof's (1970) market for lemons (used cars), Rothschild and Stiglitz' (1976) analysis of screening in insurance markets, Spence's (1974) model of signaling with education in job markets, and Crawford and Sobel's (1982) model and analysis of cheap talk. Other contexts in which private information is a crucial ingredient are discussed in later chapters.

One feature that recurs in models with private information is that, as actions by the parties reveal information to others, this affects what the others would like to do *subsequently*. And the prospect of those subsequent actions affects which actions are taken today. In this chapter, I sometimes draw attention to this feature in context, but I don't deal with it; all interactions are (essentially) one-shot interactions. Chapter 21 takes up private information and dynamics.

20.1. Adverse Selection: Akerlof's Market for Lemons

The seminal paper in the economics of information is Akerlof's (1970) "The market for lemons." To explain the euphemism: When a used car is purchased, the seller probably knows the quality of the car, but the buyer may be uncertain of its quality. A used car that turns out to be of low general quality is euphemistically called a *lemon*. A car that turns out to be of high quality, in contrast, is a *peach*.

Akerlof suggests the following model of a used-car market.[1] There are many used cars whose owners might be willing to sell, if the price is right. These cars differ in how much they are worth to their owners. Suppose that there are N used cars in total, and the distribution of values of the cars is (roughly) uniform from $2000 for the worst car to $6000 for the best. These are the values to the owners; there is as well a large number of prospective buyers, who value each individual car more than does the current owner. Specifically, a car that is worth q to its current owner is worth $q + 200$ to any of the many buyers. (Unlike a real used-car market, all these used cars are "identical" except for the value q.)

And—the key to the model—a current owner of a car knows its worth to herself and, therefore, what it would be worth to a buyer. Prospective buyers lack this information about each and every specific car; they are "risk neutral" in terms of their valuation, based on their rational conjectures about how much a car is worth.

The number of used cars N that might be sold is large, large enough so that we'll ignore the fact that it is an integer and (essentially) think of there being a continuum of such cars. But the number of prospective buyers large enough so that the market price of a car—the price the buyer pays a current (and soon to be previous) owner—is, by virtue of competition among the buyers, precisely the expected value of the car to the buyers.

Suppose there is no way for the owner of a good used car—that is, a peach, a car with a value q close to $6000—to prove to buyers that this is so. What then is the market equilibrium?

Assume (along with Akerlof, in his caricature market) that there is a market-clearing price p^* at which all used-car transactions take place. Start with the conjecture that $p^* = \$4200$, the average value of any car to a buyer. (The average car is worth $4000 to its current owner and is worth $200 more to buyers.) Then the owner of a car whose value q exceeds $4200 would not put her car on the market. The cars put on the market, if $p^* = \$4200$, would only be those for which $2000 \leq q \leq 4200$. The average value of a car from this population to a buyer is $(\$4200 + \$2000)/2 + \$200 = \$3300$. So perhaps $p^* = \$3300$.

But, if $p^* = \$3300$, the population of cars put up for sale would be those whose value q to their owners satisfies $2000 \leq q \leq 3300$, for an average value to buyers of $(\$3300 + \$2000)/2 + \$200 = \$2850$. So, if the market price is $3300, it should instead be $2850.

Where does this downward spiral end? The equilibrium condition is that the cars that are put up for sale are those whose value q to their owners satisfies $2000 \leq q \leq p^*$. These cars have an average value to their (initial) owners of $(2000 + p^*)/2$, so an average value to prospective buyers of $(2000 + p^*)/2 + 200$. An equilibrium in this market is achieved when

$$\frac{2000 + p^*}{2} + 200 = p^*, \quad \text{the solution to which is } p^* = \$2400.$$

---

[1] This is not quite the model in Akerlof's paper. See Problem 20.1 for variations.

Akerlof's model and its equilibrium can be depicted with a traditional supply-and-demand diagram, straight from intermediate microeconomics. The market price goes on the vertical axis and the quantity demanded or supplied goes on the horizontal axis. Supply is straightforward: If we write N for the total number of used cars, there is no supply for $p < \$2000$, supply N for $p > \$6000$, and linear supply for prices between \$2000 and \$6000, reflecting the assumed uniform distribution of q and the assumption that the owner of a car whose value to the owner is q will retain the car if the market price p is less than q and will sell the car if $p > q$.

Demand, however, is a bit complex. If the price is p, buyers reason that the cars being sold are those with values q (to their current owners) between \$2000 and p, for an average value of $(p + 2000)/2 + 200 = p/2 + 1200$ to buyers. So, if $p > \$2400$, the average car being sold is worth (on average) less than p, and there is no demand. At $p < \$2400$, the average care offered for sale is worth more than p to buyers, so every buyer wishes to buy a car. Letting K be the mass of prospective buyers, we get the demand function depicted in Figure 20.1(a), together with the supply function derived in the previous paragraph, and supply equals demand at $p^* = \$2400$, *assuming that $K > 0.1N$*. If $K < 0.1N$, then the picture is as in panel b of Figure 20.1, and $p^* < \$2400$; specifically, $p^* = \$(2000 + 4000K/N)$. Akerlof's conclusion that $p^* = \$2400$ is based on the premise of a "large enough" number of prospective buyers; I'll maintain his assumption in what follows.

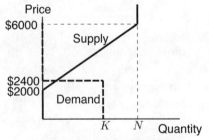

(a) Akerlof's equilibrium: If $K > 0.1N$, then supply equals demand at the equilibrium price of \$2400

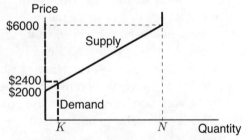

(b) But if K, the number of prospective buyers, is less than $0.1N$, where N is the total number of used cars that might be sold, then the equilibrium price is at a level less than \$2400

Figure 20.1. Supply equals demand in Akerlof's model. The key to Akerlof's model is demand. At prices $p > \$2400$, prospective buyers, anticipating which cars will be supplied, compute that the average car they might purchase is worth less than its price, so there is zero demand. Once prices fall below \$2400, the average car in the market is worth more than its price, so all K buyers wish to buy. If $K > 0.1N$, where $0.1N$ is the supply of cars at a price of \$2400, then competition among buyers pushes the equilibrium price to \$2400 (panel a). But if $K < 0.1N$, competition among sellers of lemons, wishing to sell their cars, pushes the price down to $\$(2000 + 4000K/N)$, as depicted in panel b.

The following observations are immediate.

- With a single price for all the used cars, owners whose cars are worth the least to them are the owners who sell. Assuming, as in the model, that the value to buyers is perfectly correlated with the value to sellers, the cars that are bought are from the "left hand" of the distribution of cars in terms of their value. The term *adverse selection* describes this situation, meaning a selection of cars whose distribution of quality is worse than the full distribution of car quality.

- There are potential "gains from trade" that are not realized. The owner of a peach values his car less than would a prospective buyer. But, being unable to prove that the car is a peach, the owner holds on to it. Despite the fact that buyers and sellers are price takers, the first theorem of welfare economics fails.

Of course, this is an extreme caricature. We can dress up the model in several ways to bring it a bit closer to reality. Some examples follow.

- Suppose some fraction α of the owners of used cars in the model will take any price for the cars because, for instance, they are moving away and taking their car with them is too difficult or expensive. This raises the equilibrium price of the cars in the market and means that more "gains from trade" are achieved. See Problem 20.2.

- Buyers are purchasing a good of uncertain quality. If they are risk averse (willing to pay less than the expected value of the car to themselves), this lowers the equilibrium price, reducing the number of cars that are sold. See Problem 20.3.

- Perhaps most significantly, owners of used cars may (and, in real life do) have some ability to demonstrate the quality of their cars. Suppose first of all that the seller of a used car whose value to herself is q, and whose value to any prospective buyer is $q + 200$, can costlessly show that this is so. Then the problem disappears: A car whose value is q to the seller and $q + 200$ to a prospective buyer will, because of competition among buyers, sell for $q + 200$.[2]

  One variation we can play on this is to assume that it costs the seller $k > 0$ to verify her car's value to prospective buyers. What happens then? (See Problem 20.4(a))

  Or, suppose a prospective buyer of a used car, by spending k, can ascertain its value. This is a more difficult situation to analyze; see Problem 20.4(b).

  Finally, suppose that buyers can have their car checked by a reputable firm, but the report issued by the reputable firm is only a noisy indicator of the quality of the car. Imagine, for instance, that if the car is worth q to its current owner, the reputable firm will issue a report that the car has "estimated value" $q^* = q + \epsilon$, where ϵ is some mean-zero random variable (whose distribution is independent of q). (Subjecting the car to this test multiple times doesn't provide a different draw of ϵ on each test, so there is no reason to have any car tested more than once. Also, in the story I've told, where no car can have $q > \$6000$, for a car

---

[2]   This requires that $K > N$; perhaps even a lot bigger.

of that value, either ϵ can't have mean zero or "estimated value" deserves the scare quotes that I've provided.) What if the cost of obtaining this report is a positive k? (Problem 20.5 provides an example of this situation. I urge readers to tackle this problem, once you feel that you've mastered the logic of the basic Akerlof model.)

It may occur to you that this analysis falls apart if the seller of a car worth q to herself can offer the car for sale on the following terms:

> My car is worth q to me, so it is worth $q + 200$ to any buyer. And I am willing to offer a guarantee that this is so, as follows: If you purchase my car (for, say, $q + 199$) and it turns out to be worth less than $q + 200$ to you, I will refund the entire purchase price, and you get to keep the car.

If such a money-back guarantee (plus, the buyer keeps the car!) were feasible, sellers would have no incentive to lie, and all cars would be sold for (roughly) what they are worth to buyers. So, what prevents this? There are at least two things: First, it may take time for the buyer to ascertain the quality of the car, and by the time he has done so, the seller may have absconded with the cash. And, second, even if the buyer can learn q quickly, to enforce this contract, it is necessary that a third party (the courts) can verify the value of q. That is to say (in the language of Chapter 19), the quality of the car may be uncontractible. Still, a partial guarantee may be feasible—the seller promises to pay for any necessary repairs in the first three months after purchase—which brings us to later topics in this chapter: screening and signaling.

20.2. Akerlof Meets Game Theory: One Seller

Akerlof's model is meant to describe the caricature of a competitive used-car market, which relies on the forces of competition among many buyers and many sellers to somehow find a market-equilibrium price. This is fine as far as it goes, but we can ask how things would turn out with "small numbers" of buyers and sellers, where buyers are uncertain about the quality of cars for sale. Suppose there is a single car, currently owned by Alice, the value of which is known to Alice but unknown to buyers, and a (reasonably) small number of prospective buyers. We address this situation with a noncooperative game-theoretic formulation and analysis.

Two or more buyers who bid for the car

The game-theory model that comes closest to Akerlof's competitive-market model, at least in spirit, has the following pieces.

- Alice, Bob, and Carol are the three players. Alice owns a used car, and Bob and Carol are prospective buyers.[3]

- Alice comes in many "types." (The language of a "type" of a player is established in Appendix 13. Please consult that appendix if this is new to you.) Specifically,

---

[3] We could have more than two prospective buyers but, in this formulation, two is enough.

her type is q, drawn from the interval $[2000, 6000]$, which is the value of her car to her if she doesn't sell it. Alice knows her type. Bob and Carol share a prior assessment concerning Alice's type, which is uniform on the interval $[2000, 6000]$.

- The sequence of moves is:
  1. Bob and Carol simultaneously and independently choose *bids* from $[0, 6500]$. For each buyer, this is the amount he or she is willing to pay. Denote these by p_{Bob} and p_{Carol}.
  2. Alice sees the bids of Bob and Carol and responds in one of three ways: she sells her car to Bob for p_{Bob}; she sells her car to Carol for p_{Carol}; she refuses to sell her car.

- Payoffs are:
  1. If Alice chooses to sell her car to Bob, her payoff is p_{Bob}, Bob's payoff is $q + 200 - p_{Bob}$, and Carol's payoff is 0.
  2. If Alice chooses to sell her car to Carol, her payoff is p_{Carol}, Bob's payoff is 0, and Carol's payoff is $q + 200 - p_{Carol}$.
  3. If Alice refuses to sell her car, her payoff is q, and Bob's payoff and Carol's payoff are both 0.

Proposition 20.1. *For the game just described, in one subgame-perfect equilibrium, $p_{Bob} = p_{Carol} = 2400$ (Bob and Carol each bid 2400), and Alice responds by selling her car to Bob if $q \leq 2400$ and rejecting both offers if $q > 2400$. Moreover, in every "subgame-perfect" equilibrium,*[4] *Bob and Carol each bid 2400, and Alice sells her car if $q < 2400$ and retains her car if $q > 2400$. Moreover, in every subgame-perfect equilibrium, including the one described in the first sentence, Bob and Carol each have an expected payoff of 0, and Alice's payoff (as a function of her type) is 2400 if her type $q \leq 2400$ and is q if $q \geq 2400$.*

Proof. The proof offered here is very pedantic, to illustrate the complexities of what is otherwise a simple set of ideas. And, following the proof, I delve into technical issues that arise in this sort of model. (Once the proof is done, I give you the option to skip the technical stuff.) Please bear with me.

To keep the proof simple, think of the extensive-form representation as follows: Bob and Carol simultaneously submit their bids; that is (say), Bob starts the game with a single-node information set, then Carol acts at a single information set that encompasses all of Bob's possible bids. Then Nature intervenes, selecting q at each node (p_{Bob}, p_{Carol}). And then at each single-node information set characterized by (q, p_{Bob}, p_{Carol}), Alice acts.[5]

---

[4] Why the scare quotes? In Appendix 11, subgame perfection is defined formally only for games with finitely many nodes; so my invocation of subgame-perfection is sloppy. In what follows, we look for Nash equilibria in which Alice's choice at every node (p_{Bob}, p_{Carol}, q) is a best choice for herself, given those three values. I'll continue to use the term "subgame-perfect" without the scare quotes; you can either mentally insert scare quotes or substitute for "subgame-perfect equilibrium" the phrase "a Nash equilibrium in the spirit of subgame perfection." (There is a second technical issue here; see the next footnote.)

[5] If Nature's choice of q comes before Bob or Carol submit their bids, then they are acting at infor-

Begin with the implications of subgame perfection: At each of Alice's single-node information sets, described by the triple (q, p_{Bob}, p_{Carol}), subgame-perfection implies that Alice will sell her car if $\max\{p_{Bob}, p_{Carol}\} > q$, refuse to sell if $\max\{p_{Bob}, p_{Carol}\} < q$, and do something if $\max\{p_{Bob}, p_{Carol}\} = q$. Go back to nature's nodes, one for each pair (p_{Bob}, p_{Carol}): The (expected) payoffs to Bob and Carol depend on to whom Alice sells the car, if and when she does (which is material if $p_{Bob} = p_{Carol}$). But we know that the *sum* of Bob's and Carol's (conditional expected) payoffs is

$$\frac{2000 + \max\{p_{Bob}, p_{Carol}\}}{2} + 200 - \max\{p_{Bob}, p_{Carol}\},$$

which is strictly positive if $\max\{p_{Bob}, p_{Carol}\} < 2400$, strictly negative if $\max\{p_{Bob}, p_{Carol}\} > 2400$, and precisely 0 if $\max\{p_{Bob}, p_{Carol}\} = 2400$.

With this, the first assertion of the proposition is clear: If Bob and Carol each bid 2400, and if Alice subsequently sells the car to Bob, Alice is choosing an on-path best response, while Bob and Carol each have a payoff of 0. If either Bob or Carol were to raise their bid, their payoff would be strictly negative. If either lowered their bid, their payoff would stay 0. Now, to fill in the equilibrium, we need to ensure that Alice chooses a subgame-perfect response at every triple (q, p_{Bob}, p_{Carol}), but that is easy to do: Have her (1) sell to Bob whenever $p_{Bob} \geq \max\{p_{Carol}, q\}$, (2) sell to Carol if $p_{Carol} > p_{Bob}$ and $p_{Carol} \geq q$, and (3) refuse to sell if $\max\{p_{Bob}, p_{Carol}\} < q$. The purported subgame-perfect equilibrium outcome is, in fact, the outcome of a subgame-perfect equilibrium.

Of course, there are other equilibria. Alice could instead always sell to Carol whenever $q \leq p_{Bob} = p_{Carol}$; this works just as well as always selling to Bob.

But, some care here is necessary. The proposition holds that in *all* subgame-perfect equilibria, Bob and Carol both bid 2400. In response to these on-path bids, if $q < 2400$, Alice doesn't care to whom she sells. However, in terms of constructing equilibria, it does matter to whom she sells. For instance, suppose Alice chooses to sell to Bob if $q \in [2000, 2200]$ and to Carol if $q \in (2200, 2400]$. Then Bob's payoff would be strictly negative and, since he can lower his bid (unilaterally) and get a payoff of 0, we wouldn't have an equilibrium. Alice's "selling strategy," in any equilibrium, must be arranged so that not only is the sum of Bob's and Carol's payoffs zero—an implication of subgame perfection—but each one must have a payoff of 0. Selling only to one or the other is but one way to do this. Another, for instance, is to sell to Bob if $q \in [2000, 2100] \cup (2300, 2400]$ and to sell to Carol if $q \in (2100, 2300]$. (It might seem that the most natural equilibrium response by Alice is to randomize 50-50 between selling to Bob or to Carol, if $q < 2400$, and this can be made to work. But see the discussion following the end of the proof.)

---

mation sets with "many" nodes, and so their actions are not roots of a proper subgame. Indeed, even if we delay Nature's choice until after Bob and Carol bid, but we put Bob's bid first, Carol's information set contains many nodes. However, a "subgame-perfect" Nash equilibrium is a Nash equilibrium with conditions added, and since Bob and Carol's actions "start" the game, we only need to verify that what they are doing is a best response to the strategies of their two fellow players.

As for the second assertion—that in any subgame perfect equilibrium, Bob and Carol both bid 2400—I'll provide the argument under the assumption that Bob and Carol each choose a pure strategy here; Problem 20.6 asks you to supply the argument if they consider mixed strategies (and see the *Online Supplement* for the full proof). First, suppose $\max\{p_{Bob}, p_{Carol}\} > 2400$. Then we know that the sum of Bob's and Carol's payoffs is strictly negative. So one or other is getting a strictly negative payoff. But in that case, whoever is getting a strictly negative payoff can unilaterally change his or her bid in a manner that gives a nonnegative payoff. Suppose that it is Bob who is getting a strictly negative payoff. Then we know that $p_{Bob} \geq p_{Carol}$. If $p_{Carol} < 2400$, then Bob can bid $p_{Carol} + \epsilon$ for small ϵ and have a positive payoff. If $p_{Carol} \geq 2400$, then Bob can bid 2399 and have a payoff of 0.

And suppose $\max\{p_{Bob}, p_{Carol}\} < 2400$. If $2400 > p_{Bob} > p_{Carol}$, then Carol's payoff is 0. But by bidding $(2400 + p_{Bob})/2$, Carol can raise her payoff to be strictly positive. A symmetric argument shows that $2000 > p_{Carol} > p_{Bob}$ cannot be part of an equilibrium. Which leaves $2400 > p_{Bob} = p_{Carol}$. We know that the sum of the two payoffs is strictly positive—let that sum be denoted by π—and, of course, one of the two must be getting a payoff $\leq \pi/2$. Whichever of the two that is—without loss of generality, suppose it is Bob—by raising p_{Bob} by a tiny amount ϵ, Bob is assured of getting the car with probability one. And it is clear that, for $\epsilon > 0$ but vanishingly small, this generates for Bob a payoff as close to π as he desires. Hence, again, we don't have an equilibrium.   ∎

The argument in the previous paragraph should seem familiar to you: It is, essentially, the argument for why Bertrand competition in the simplest model (two producers with constant and equal marginal costs) results in price equals marginal cost. Allowing Bob and Carol to have (pure) strategy spaces that are each an interval of real numbers is convenient for these purposes; if instead we limited Bob and Carol to bids that are multiples of one cent (and, for good measure, had instead of a uniform distribution of q over the interval $[2000, 6000]$, we supposed that $q \in \{2000.00, 2000.01, \ldots, 5999.99, 6000.00\}$, each with equal probability), the analogue to Proposition 20.1 would be . . . not quite so neat. Problem 20.7 asks you to analyze this finite-game case.

But having a continuum strategy space and a continuum state space (that is, $q \in [2000, 6000]$) comes at a cost in terms of technical matters. The rest of this subsection introduces those technical matters. If considerations of measurability make your head hurt, skip ahead to the next subsection; you won't miss any economic content. But if one is going to be rigorous about things, one must deal with these technical matters.

The technical issue concerns the set of feasible strategies for Alice, both pure and mixed. Think of this in terms of behavioral strategies. She has three choices at each of her information sets, where an information set for her describes her q and the two price offers. That is, she can base her decision on the information $(q, p_{Bob}, p_{Carol}) \in [2000, 6000] \times [0, 6500] \times [0, 6500]$. So, in the "spirit" of how extensive-form-game strategy sets are created, we might think of defining her set of possible pure strategies as the space of functions

$$S_{\text{Alice}} := \{\text{don't sell, sell to Bob, sell to Carol}\}^{[2000,6000] \times [0,6500] \times [0,6500]}.$$

If the collection of her information sets were finite or even countable, this is what we'd do. But $[2000, 6000] \times [0, 6500] \times [0, 6500]$ is uncountable. And one requirement of a game-theory model is that payoffs must be identified for each strategy profile. For, say, Bob, if he chooses p_{Bob}, Carol chooses p_{Carol}, and Alice chooses some s^o in the function space displayed, Bob's payoff can be computed in two steps. First, temporarily denote by $B_{s^o, p_{\text{Bob}}, p_{\text{Carol}}} : [2000, 6000] \to \{0, 1\}$ the function

$$B_{s^o, p_{\text{Bob}}, p_{\text{Carol}}}(q) = \begin{cases} 1, & \text{if } s^o(q, p_{\text{Bob}}, p_{\text{Carol}}) = \text{sell to Bob, and} \\ 0, & \text{if } s^o(q, p_{\text{Bob}}, p_{\text{Carol}}) = \text{sell to Carol or don't sell.} \end{cases}$$

Then Bob's payoff, if Alice plays strategy s^o, Bob chooses p_{Bob}, and Carol chooses p_{Carol}, is

$$\int_{q=2000}^{q=6000} (q + 200 - p_{\text{Bob}}) \cdot B_{s^o, p_{\text{Bob}}, p_{\text{Carol}}}(q) \frac{dq}{4000}.$$

To evaluate this integral, the function $B_{s^o, p_{\text{Bob}}, p_{\text{Carol}}}$ must be measurable, which in turn requires that Alice's strategy s^o must be measurable. Conclusion: For the pure-strategy set for Alice, we must restrict attention to *measurable* functions s^o from $[2000, 6000] \times [0, 6500] \times [0, 6500]$ to $\{$ don't sell, sell to Bob, sell to Carol $\}$.[6]

The problems multiply once we add in mixed strategies for Alice. Again, think in terms of behavioral mixing and, in particular, the "natural" behaviorally-mixed strategy in which, if $p_{\text{Bob}} = p_{\text{Carol}} = 2400$ and $q < 2400$, Alice flips a fair coin, so there is probability $1/2$ that she sells to Bob and $1/2$ that she sells to Carol. If we were to think in terms of this coin flip being done "independently" for different values of $q < 2400$, we'd have an uncountable collection of independent random variables, which presents further technical issues when it comes to evaluating payoffs for Bob and Carol: In essence, this randomization results almost surely in a nonmeasurable pure strategy. In this particular case, there are available fixes to this problem in the literature. But, in general, further care is required when it comes to defining mixed strategies for Alice.

The two seminal references on the technical issues are Aumann (1964) and Milgrom and Weber (1985). Aumann suggests that the space of mixed strategies for Alice in this situation be defined as the space of (measurable) functions on $\{$ don't sell, sell to Bob, sell to Carol $\}^{[2000,6000] \times [0,6500] \times [0,6500] \times [0,1]}$, with the interpretation that the fourth component u in $(q, p_{\text{Bob}}, p_{\text{Carol}}, u)$ is a uniform-on-$[0, 1]$ "randomizer."[7] Milgrom and Weber provide the concept of a *distributional strategy*, which is equivalent to Aumann's definition but more parsimonious (in that Aumann's definition

---

[6]   Because the integrand is bounded, measurability implies integrability.

[7]   It is with this definition that Aumann extends Kuhn's Theorem; see Sections A10.5 and A10.6.

allows for many "mixed strategies" that are strategically equivalent). These technical issues recur, for instance, in Chapters 23 and 24 on bilateral bargaining and auctions, respectively; they arise naturally when we imagine that players have private information about their types, where (for convenience) we model the support of the type distribution (in the assessment of other players) as an interval in R.[8] I do not mention these considerations subsequently, trusting that readers who are bothered by such things can, on their own, figure out how to deal with them.

What if there are, say, ten prospective buyers, who simultaneously and independently submits bids? The outcome is "essentially" the same, where "essentially" is added because, if two of these bidders submit bids of 2400, any others can submit bids less than 2400. All that is required is that, on path, at least two of the bidders bid 2400.[9]

Has this subsection been describing an *auction*? Yes, in a sense. Auctions, which are the subject of Chapter 24, can take many forms, and I wait until that chapter to deal with them in detail. But just to finish this subsection: We've described (more or less) a first-price, sealed-tender auction, with a common-value prize (the car is worth the same amount to every bidder), which is known to the seller but not to the bidders, and in which the seller sets a hidden *reserve price*; that is, Alice is allowed, *after* the bids come in, to declare that she is unwilling to sell to the highest bidder at the high bid.

One buyer, who makes a take-it-or-leave-it offer

What if there is only one prospective buyer, Bob? The rules are otherwise as before: Bob names the price p_{Bob} that he is willing to pay, and then Alice can sell at that price or refuse.

If, in the spirit of subgame perfection, we require Alice to sell if $q < p_{Bob}$ (and refuse if $q > p_{Bob}$), then we are allowing Bob to make a take-it-or-leave-it offer. And under these rules, the analysis is as follows

Bob, now a monopsonist, computes that, if he offers to buy for $p_{Bob} > 2400$, Alice will accept if $q < p_{Bob}$, and on average the car he buys, if she sells, will be worth $p_{Bob}/2 + 1200 < p_{Bob}$. So bids above \$2400 make no sense for him. And, if his bid p_{Bob} is less than \$2400, his payoff is

$$\int_{q=2000}^{q=p_{Bob}} (q + 200 - p_{Bob})\frac{dq}{4000} = \left(\frac{2000 + p_{Bob}}{2} + 200 - p_{Bob}\right) \times \left(\frac{p_{Bob} - 2000}{4000}\right)$$

$$= \left(\frac{2400 - p_{Bob}}{2}\right) \times \left(\frac{p_{Bob} - 2000}{4000}\right).$$

---

[8] Since I put nature's selection of q after Bob and Carol choose their bids p_{Bob} and p_{Carol}, and there are uncountably many such choices, it might seem that similar issues arise; after all, nature is certainly randomizing. If you think about it carefully, and if our sole objective is to be able to find expected payoffs for all three players given their choice of strategies, those issues don't arise. But, if we are using Aumann's fix for Alice, to preserve that each (p_{Bob}, p_{Carol}) is the root of a "proper" subgame, you would formally have to put nature's choice of u after Bob's and Carol's bids as well.

[9] Suppose there are, say, 100 bidders. Would it work to have them all randomize between submitting 2400 and 2399, each with probability $1/2$? It would not. Why not?

This is maximized at $p_{Bob} = 2200$.

It is perhaps worth pointing out that while this is the unique equilibrium in the spirit of subgame perfection, there are other Nash equilibria: Suppose Alice's strategy is to reject any offer less than \$2399 and to accept \$2399 or more. Bob's best response is to bid p_{Bob} = \$2399; this gives a Nash equilibrium, based on Alice's threat to reject p_{Bob} = \$2200, even if $q <$ \$2200. In fact, we can construct Nash equilibria in which, along the path of play, Bob bids any p_{Bob} in $[0, 2400]$, as long as Alice's strategy is to reject any bid other than the specified equilibrium bid.

Alice names her price

Suppose the extensive form is: Nature chooses q. Alice learns q. Alice names a price p—her *asking price*—at which she is willing to sell. (Assume that she is restricted to naming prices from $[2000, 6200]$.) Bob and Carol (or just Bob) indicate whether they are willing to buy at Alice's price and, if so, Alice must sell, although if both are willing to buy, Alice can choose to whom she sells.

To avoid having to repeat the caveat that, if both are willing to buy, Alice's subsequent "to-whom-do-I-sell" strategy must be equitable (cf. last paragraph on page 111), I suppose that Bob is the only buyer; Carol will re-enter at the end of this subsection.

In terms of game-theoretic analysis, this extensive form ratchets up the difficulties. Now, Bob must respond at information sets that contain a continuum of nodes. The "continuum" part presents technical issues, so suppose temporarily, for the sake of discussion, that Alice's type—the value of the car to her, or q—comes out of a finite but large set of values uniformly distributed over the interval $[2000, 6000]$. Suppose we look at a strategy for Alice in which her types *pool*, meaning that more than one type names the same price. To be very concrete, suppose that, if $q \in [2000, 2400]$, Alice names the price \$2400, and if $q \in (2400, 6000]$, she names the price \$6000. Bob, having heard one of those two prices, must draw the proper (equilibrium) inferences about q: Having heard \$2400, he infers that $q \in [2000, 2400]$; having heard \$6000, he infers that $q \in (2400, 6000]$. And, in an equilibrium, he responds in sequentially rational fashion, which is to agree to purchase for \$2400 and to say "no thank you" if Alice's named price is \$6000.

But to describe an equilibrium, we must deal with off-path beliefs by Bob: What if Alice names the price \$2200? What if she names \$4500? The point is that, with this formulation, we move from relatively simple "equilibria in the spirit of subgame perfection" (and, if q is drawn from a finite set, drop "in the spirit of") to sequentially rational behavior for Bob, given beliefs that he holds both on path and off. In other words, if you have consulted the appendices, we move from the relatively simple ideas of Appendix 11 to the significantly more complex ideas of Appendix 12, leavened by the notion of incomplete information in Appendix 13.

In this case, we can "fix" things for the equilibrium I've begun to describe: If Alice names a price p between \$2000 and \$2400, Bob believes that $q \in [2000, 2400]$, so his sequentially rational response is to say he is willing to buy. If Alice names a price $p \in (2400, 6000)$, he believes that $q \in [2000, p]$; he reasons that Alice would never choose a price in excess of q, and he is agnostic as to which price less than q motivated her to make this "mistake." With these beliefs, his sequentially rational response is to refuse to buy. The price 6000 is on-path; it does not come as a surprise to Bob, and he (correctly) infers that $q \in (2400, 6000]$; refusing to buy is (again) sequentially rational. And, if this describes Bob's beliefs and behavior, (one of) Alice's best response is to name the price \$2400 if $q \in [2000, 2400]$ and to name \$6000 if $q \in (2400, 6000]$. We have a...I'll use the term *sequential* equilibrium, although the adjective is unimportant; what matters is that Bob is now endowed with beliefs both on and off path, his on-path beliefs involve a correct application of Bayesian inference (given Alice's strategy), and his responses (both on-path and off) are sequentially rational, given those beliefs.

There are other, similar equilibria in this case, in which Bob "threatens with beliefs." For instance, suppose, if $q \in [2000, 2200]$, Alice names the price \$2200 and Bob accepts; if $q \in (2200, 6000]$, she names the price \$6000, and Bob refuses to buy. Alice's strategy, of course, determines Bob's on-path beliefs. And, to make this an equilibrium, we provide the following off-path beliefs by Bob: For any other price named by Alice, Bob holds the belief that $q = \$2000$, and (therefore) he accepts if she names a price less than \$2200 and rejects otherwise. Since Alice can sell her car for \$2200, she has no interest in naming a lower price; since any price above \$2200 means no sale, she may as well name \$6000. You can argue that Bob's off-path beliefs are...strange, but then, you are moving into the ideas of Appendix 14.

There is one final equilibrium that is worth mentioning. Suppose that Alice, in the equilibrium, with a car worth q, names a price $p = q + 200$. This is a *fully separating* equilibrium: Bob infers from her announcement the value of q, and so he is indifferent between purchasing the car or not. And, being indifferent, he randomizes between agreeing to purchase or not, with the probability that he purchases equal to $e^{(2200-p)/200}$, where p is the price she names. Bob is certainly behaving in sequentially rational fashion. But will this randomized strategy by Bob lead Alice to a truthful declaration of $p = q + 2000$? That is, if her car is worth, say, 4750, is naming a price $4750 + 200 = 4950$ a best response for her?

Let q be the value of the car to Alice. We can quickly rule out her naming a price $p < q$: Since Bob's response is to accept any price she names (at least, between \$2200 and \$6200) with positive probability, choosing $p < q$ means a positive probability of selling her car for less than it is worth to her.

This leaves the possibility of Alice submitting $p \neq q + 200$ for $p \in (q, 6200]$. If Alice attaches value q to the car and names any price $p = q' + 200$, her payoff is

$$\pi(p)p + (1 - \pi(p))q = q + \pi(p)p - \pi(p)q = q + \pi(p)(p - q) = q + e^{(2200-p)/200}(p - q)$$
$$= q + e^{(2000-q')/200}(200 + q' - q).$$

We must show that this is maximized at $q' = q$. So, write the right-hand side of the last display as $F(q'; q)$, and take its derivative in q':

$$\frac{\partial F(q'; q)}{\partial q'} = \frac{e^{(2000-q')/200}(q - q')}{200}.$$

(You can check my math.) This is 0 at $q' = q$, positive for $q' < q$, and negative for $q' > q$, so we have that $q' = q$ is the unique maximizer; it is uniquely optimal for Alice to be "truthful" and name $p + q + 200$.

Please note: This last equilibrium, in which Alice "fully reveals" her type q, works whatever is the distribution of q. The first equilibrium—call it the "Akerlof" equilibrium—depends to some extent on the distributional assumptions: It requires that the average q over the interval $q \in [2000, 2400]$ is 2200, so that a random car selected from that interval is worth \$2400 to the buyer.

And note that we can use the fully revealing equilibrium to bootstrap others: In particular, the equilibrium is constructed so that Bob purchases the car if $q = 2000$ with probability 1. If we scale the probabilities so that, if Alice asks for p, he buys the car with probability $\gamma e^{(2200-p)/200}$ for some $\gamma < 1$, we still have an equilibrium. (And this includes the equilibrium where he refuses to buy with probability 1 no matter what price she names.)

How do Alice and Bob fare in the Akerlof equilibrium versus the fully revealing equilibrium? Bob's payoff is 0 in both, so he is indifferent between them. For Alice, the comparison is more interesting. If $q > 2400$, she prefers the fully revealing equilibrium, as the Akerlof equilibrium gives her q for sure, while the second gives her $q + 200$ with probability $e^{(2000-q)/200}$ and q with complementary probability. But if $q \leq 2400$, the Akerlof equilibrium gives her a payoff of 2400 with probability one, while the other equilibrium gives her $q + 200$ with probability $e^{(2000-q)/200}$ and q with complementary probability. How do these compare? If you carry out the computations, you'll find that for $q < 2368.28$ (approximately), she prefers the Akerlof equilibrium, while for $q \geq$ this amount, she does better with the fully revealing equilibrium. And overall? If we average Alice's payoffs over all values of q (using the prior, uniform distribution on q), it turns out that the Akerlof equilibrium gives her an expected payoff of \$4020, or \$20 in excess of the average value to her of her car (distributed among her types very unevenly), while the other equilibrium gives her an average payoff that is a tiny bit less than \$4010.

So, we have many equilibria for the Alice-names-her-price game. Is there some basis on which we can select one? Since Alice is naming her price, one criterion might be: Which is best for her? But that doesn't really work, because different types of Alice have different preferences. I personally find the Akerlof equilibrium the more credible—perhaps because I find the complex randomization by Bob in the second equilibrium somewhat *incredible*. But that's only a personal opinion.

As a final comment, suppose we go back to more than one prospective buyer; now both Bob and Carol are interested in buying Alice's car, if the price Alice names is acceptable. As noted at the start of this subsection, if they both express interest, Alice must take care that her assignment rule (based on q) is equitable. As long as this care is taken , both the Akerlof equilibrium and fully revealing equilibrium can be sustained; the fully revealing equilibrium by having the indifferent-between-buying-and-not Bob and Carol buying with probabilities that present Alice with the right probability that one or the other (or both) will take the car off her hands.

Other mechanisms?

The discussion so far doesn't exhaust possible mechanisms or protocols or, to use game-theoretic language, extensive-forms, by which Alice's car might be sold. For instance, suppose Alice, Bob, and Carol (or, just Alice and Bob) simultaneously write down prices at which they are willing to transact. Alice writes down her asking price; Bob and Carol write down bids. If either bid is more than Alice's asking price, a deal is consummated at, say, the higher of the two bids. If Alice's ask is greater than either bid, Alice keeps the car. On technical grounds, this extensive-form game is easiest to analyze: Since all players move simultaneously—Alice, of course, with information about her type—the solution concept is simple Nash equilibrium. Chapter 24 begins with this caricature of a bargaining process, albeit not for this context, in which Alice knows q and Bob does not (or, Bob and Carol do not).

Or, perhaps there is some form of back-and-forth negotiation. Alice presents her asking price. Bob and/or Alice can accept this demand, or they can (simultaneously? sequentially?) present counter-offers, following which Alice can accept one of their offers or propose a counter to their (separate) counter-offers, and so forth. In such a game, Alice must take into account what inferences will be drawn by Bob and Carol from her (Alice's) first asking price, what will be their off-path beliefs (if she asks for an amount not part of the equilibrium strategy), and how these inferences and beliefs will affect any counter-offers they might make. Chapter 24 discusses back-and-forth negotiation as well, albeit with only Alice and Bob and, at first, without incomplete information.

Obvious questions to ask are: Of all possible mechanisms, which one(s) creates the largest surplus? Which one(s) produces the highest average profit for Alice, if we constrain Bob (or Bob and Carol) to an expected payoff of zero? Which one is best for a single buyer? These questions are answered in substantial generality in Samuelson (1984). But you must finish Chapter 26 before tackling that article.

Two levels of take-aways

This section and the previous one serve as a prelude to the rest of the chapter, on two levels.

Substantively—that is to say, focusing on the economics of the situation—the two sections present contrasting styles of modeling and analysis. In the classic Akerlof model, what might be termed a *reduced form* analysis is conducted. Akerlof defines what he thinks a single-price, competitive equilibrium entails, and then he shows what the equilibrium price must be, given the parameters of his model and his entailed conditions. He doesn't say how that equilibrium price will be accomplished; he just trusts that it will arise or, perhaps more accurately, he asserts that *if a single-price, competitive equilibrium comes about, this is what it must be.*

In this section, in contrast, a more *structural* approach is taken. We specify "rules" by which Alice and Bob, or Alice, Bob, and Carol interact, and then look for "reasonable" Nash equilibria given those rules, where "reasonable" means appealing to a refinement of Nash equilibrium, as is judged appropriate for the rules that are specified. This still involves a leap of faith: When more than one Nash-equilibrium candidate emerges, why is one or another of them our prediction? And, since the specification of "rules" change what seems possible, in taking the analysis back to the real world, we must decide which set of "rules" will best describe/predict what we see.

This chapter—more generally, this book—is agnostic as to which approach is better. (This reflects my own prejudices: Neither approach is better. They are complementary.) Going forward in this volume, when is suits the exposition, a "reduced form" analysis is presented. In other cases, a "structural," game-theoretic analysis is provided. Often they are compared and contrasted.

And technically: Different "rules" or extensive-forms involve different levels of complexity in terms of the game-theoretic analysis. For the remainder of this chapter, we study exchanges where the party or parties on one side of the transaction have private information that is material to the outcome for the other side. (That is, we don't take up two-sided incomplete information at all. That will come later in the volume, for instance, in Chapter 23.) And, we restrict attention to "one-shot interactions," where one of the two sides makes a proposal to which the other side responds. (Dynamic interactions are taken up in Chapters 21 and 22.)

With these limitations on what we do, the fundamental distinction in "rules" is then: Which side makes the proposal?

- If it is the uninformed side, then (when it comes to game-theoretic analysis) analysis in the spirit of subgame perfection is employed: The informed party, seeing what has been proposed and consulting her private information, is assumed to optimize, taking the terms of the proposal as fixed.

- But if the informed side moves first, we move from Appendix 11 to Appendix 12 and even Appendix 14: The respondent must make appropriate inferences from what is proposed. And the respondent is assumed to have off-path beliefs about the informed side's private information, if and when the proposal is unexpected, and is assumed to respond in sequentially rational fashion given those beliefs. That's Appendix 12 stuff. Furthermore, before the chapter ends, we'll invoke criteria from Appendix 14 concerning what are reasonable off-path beliefs, to try to pin down our predictions as to which is the "right" equilibrium.

So, if you haven't yet digested the concepts in Appendices 11 through 14, now would be the time.

20.3. Adverse Selection in Other Contexts

The phenomenon of adverse selection arises in many contexts besides the used-car market. To enrich the discussion to come, here are a few of them.

- *Adverse selection in voluntary retirement:* Some large American corporations, in the third quarter of the 20th century, offered their white-collar employees a guarantee of "lifetime employment": Short of malfeasance, derelection, or gross incompetence, the employee would not be fired until he or she reached the age of mandatory retirement. Although there was no legal status to this guaran tee, it was a powerful informal benefit that secured for the companies excellent employees overall. And, as long as retirement could be compelled at age 65, so-called "lifetime employment" (which, of course, was really guaranteed employment until age 65, or whatever age greater than 65 that the firm chose) could be sustained. But age-discrimination legislation made lifetime employment without any bound, unless the employee chose to retire. So firms became somewhat burdened with . . . very experienced employees. Moreover, changing market conditions for these corporations made reductions in force desirable.

So these firms, to encourage more experienced employees to retire and/or to execute a reduction in force, adopted generous "voluntary retirement programs," where employees were provided with incentive to pull the plug voluntarily, including severance pay tied to the employee's tenure with the organization. Perhaps needless to say, employees choosing to take advantage of these programs were those whose outside opportunities for gainful employment were best, which often meant those employees who were more valuable to the organization; thus the organization was left with an adverse selection of its "more experienced" employees.[10]

- *Adverse selection in financial markets:* When arranging financing for a new venture, an entrepreneur can try to arrange for debt or equity financing. If, as seems reasonable, the entrepreneur has information about the future prospects of her venture that outsiders lack, and if that information is relatively optimistic, then she will, on the margin, favor debt financing over equity. Hence, those new ventures that seek equity financing are an adverse selection out of the universe of all new ventures.[11]

  In similar fashion, if top managers of an ongoing concern, based on private information, have reason to believe that the market's valuation of their enterprise is lower than is warranted, they may seek to take the business private. If they have reason to believe that the market overvalues their enterprise, they may seek to liquidate their private holdings. On these grounds, publicly available shares in ongoing concerns may be an adverse selection of equity shares in all such concerns. (Insider-trading laws are intended to control such adverse selections.)

- *The Winner's Curse:* This refers to the idea that, in a class of auctions known

---

[10] At the same time, universities found themselves burdened by the tenure system, where an aging cohort of faculty members could not be compelled to "retire" and make room for new blood. In response, universities put in place programs to encourage voluntary retirement among senior faculty; as I understand it, a "carve out" in the law allowed institutions of higher education to offer *voluntary* retirement incentives based on an individual's age. At my own university, Stanford, the program was unimaginatively called the *Faculty Retirement Incentive Program*; anecdotally, this program has had similar adverse-selection effects, although my colleagues who have chosen not to retire would dispute this contention vigorously.

[11] This story is at least somewhat complicated by the notion that entrepreneurs may be "irrationally" optimistic about their own ventures. See the next bullet point concerning the winner's curse.

as common-value auctions, in which the "prize" being auctioned has the same ultimate value to all bidders—think of a mineral-rights auction in which the winning bidder gets the right to extract and sell oil or gas deposits from a particular tract of land, and where the chief uncertainty is the amount of oil and / or gas that will be found—and the bidders all have imperfect private information about the value of the prize. The winning bidder will tend to be among those bidders with the most optimistic information, hence is likely to be overly optimistic based on the totality of information. This is adverse selection in the sense that the winner of an auction is getting, as the prize, an "adverse selection" of all possible rights. (The Winner's Curse will be discussed further in Chapter 24.)

- *Life and health insurance:* Insurance companies write policies that pay death benefits to the estates of deceased individuals and that pay the medical bills of insured individuals. If we suppose that the individual seeking insurance has private information concerning his or her state of health, those in poor health are more likely than those in good health to seek insurance and to seek more insurance. Of course, other factors enter into the decision of whether and how much insurance to purchase, such as the individual's level of risk aversion and, in the case of life insurance (especially term life insurance) the level of the insuree's desire to protect his/her family from the loss of his/her earning power. But premium rates must reflect the notion that the insuree who is unhealthy is more likely to buy, and to buy more, insurance, and so those who are relatively healthy, upon seeing the cost of insurance, may forgo insurance altogether. Therefore, the insurance company faces an adverse selection of the entire population in its clientele. Indeed, the term *adverse selection* was first coined in the context of insurance.

    Note tht adverse selection in this context refers to insurees who have greater knowledge than does the insurance company about their underlying state of health. Issues of moral hazard can also intrude: An individual concerned with leaving something for his or her family may, upon purchasing a term insurance policy, be more willing to engage in skydiving or some other dangerous sport. In fact, in casualty insurance (fire insurance for commercial structures, for instance), moral hazard may be a greater concern on the part of the insurance company than adverse selection.

    The Affordable Care Act (colloquially known as Obamacare) illustrates this sort of adverse selection. Designed to provide (through subsidized private insurance companies, operating on state-administered exchanges) health-care insurance to the public, and to offer it at rates without regard to preexisting conditions, the original bill contained a mandate: Each adult must either have health insurance or pay a fine. Without such a mandate, premium rates that allowed insurance companies to come close to breaking even would induce younger and healthier individuals to forgo insurance. Remove such individuals and, more to the point, their premium payments from the "pool"—the adverse selection—and premium rates would have to be increased, which would drive

more relatively young and healthy individuals out, raising premium rates still
further. The young and healthy (or individuals rich enough to be willing to
self-insure) can still opt out of any health insurance, but the fine (1) pushes the
marginal individual to buy insurance and (2) provides funds to subsidize the
premia of those who do insure. (Or such was the theory; legal issues entangled
the mandate.)

20.4. A Toy Model of Adverse Selection in Insurance

Imagine a population of expected-utility-maximizing, risk-averse economic agents
who face the risk of sustaining a significant loss. To keep things simple, assume that
all these agents have CARA (constant absolute risk aversion) utility functions; that
is, utility functions of the form $-e^{-\lambda_i W_i}$, where the subscript i refers to the agent,
λ_i is her coefficient of absolute risk aversion, and W_i is her wealth. Assume that
each agent has a (small) probability π_i of, in any period, sustaining a significant loss
L (which, in this model, is the same for all agents). Assume that this probability is
independent of all other sources of uncertainty concerning the individual's wealth..
This, together with the CARA assumption, allow us to ignore the individual's other
sources of wealth and, in particular, her level of wealth (except for the chance of
this loss). Finally, suppose that the individual knows both her coefficient of risk
aversion and her own probability of sustaining the loss.[12]

An insurance company offers insurance against this loss. Suppose it offers full
insurance: For a premium p, the individual is paid L by the company if the loss
is sustained. The individual's decision whether to purchase this insurance then
involves a comparison of

$$-e^{-\lambda_i(-p)} = -e^{\lambda_i p} \quad \text{and} \quad (1-\pi_i)(-e^{-\lambda_i 0}) + \pi_i(-e^{-\lambda_i(-L)}) = \pi_i(1 - e^{\lambda_i L}) - 1.$$

The left-hand term is her (expected) utility if she buys the insurance; she pays the
premium but, should the loss occur, she is fully compensated. (Again, because
her utility is CARA, we can ignore her wealth level.) The right-hand term is her
expected utility if she goes without insurance; with probability $1 - \pi_i$, she has no
loss; with probability π_i, she loses L. She buys the insurance if the left-hand term
$-e^{\lambda_i p}$ is larger; she goes without if the right-hand term $\pi_i(1 - e^{\lambda_i L}) - 1$ is larger.
As is no doubt intuitive, the individual consumer is more inclined to buy if (1) she
is more risk averse and/or (2) her risks of a loss are greater.*

A numerical example will illustrate.[13] Suppose the population consists of 1100
individual agents. One hundred have coefficient of risk aversion equal to 0.0001,

---

[12] It may seem gratuitous to say that the individual knows her coefficient of risk aversion; this is
saying that she knows her own preferences, which seems noncontroversial. But, then, saying that she
knows her own *subjective* assessment of the probability of a loss should be equally noncontroversial; her
subjective probability assessments are, per Savage (1954), other aspects of her preferences. The more
substantial assumption here is that her subjective probability of a loss is "objective" in the sense that the
insurance company would accept her assessment, if they could force her to reveal that assessment.

[13] I'm going to throw out a bunch of numbers, all based on relatively simple calculations using Excel
spreadsheets. You can trust my numbers, but it might help your comprehension to replicate them.

one hundred have 0.00011, one hundred have 0.00012, and so forth, up to 0.0002. And 110 of them have $\pi_i = 0.01$, 110 have $\pi_i = 0.02$, and so forth, up to $\pi_i = 0.1$. Each of the $11 \times 10 = 110$ cells (one cell for each of the eleven coefficients of risk aversion and one of ten values for π_i) has 10 individuals. The size of the loss, L, is 5000.

The insurance company is a regulated monopoly, constrained to set the premium it charges to equal its average payout per policy. Since the average probability of loss is $(0.01 + \ldots + 0.1)/10 = 0.055$, if all 1100 customers purchased insurance, the average payout would be $5000 \times 0.55 = 275$. So, one imagines (if one is not very bright), the regulators should insist on a premium of $275. But, as I'm sure you anticipate, individuals with low risk of loss and/or those with lower coefficients of risk aversion will not buy. If you do the calculations for each of the 110 types, you get the purchase pattern shown in Figure 20.2(a). No one with $\pi_i \leq 0.03$ buys insurance, everyone with $\pi_i \geq 0.05$ does buy; for those folks with $\pi_i = 0.04$, they buy if their coefficient of risk aversion is 0.00013 or more.

But with this distribution of folks buying insurance, the average probability that the insurance company must pay out is 0.0712, so a "fair" premium is $356.08 (roughly). And, at this premium, no individual with $\pi_i = 0.04$ buys and, of those with $\pi_i = 0.05$, only individuals with $\lambda_i \geq 0.00015$ buy. (See panel b.) The average probability of payout becomes 0.07704, which makes the actuarially fair premium $385.25. A few more types with $\pi_i = 0.05$ won't buy at this price (panel c), and the average probability of payout becomes 0.07877, which raises the fair premium to $393.86, which causes some more types to forgo insurance (panel d), pushing the fair premium to $398.18 and there, finally, no further changes are recorded: Panel d is where the adverse selection vicious cycle reaches equilibrium.[14]

The story so far is that the insurance company is regulated. This feature was inserted into the story because insurance companies often are regulated. But we could alternatively suppose that the monopoly insurance firm can set any premium it chooses, with the objective of maximizing its expected profit (premia collected less expected payout on policies) per period. In this case, the insurance company

---

[14] Look at the situation in panel d, where the premium is $398.18. Among the customers who purchase insurance at that premium are those with coefficient of risk aversion 0.00002 and probability of loss 0.05. Among those who do not purchase are the 10 individuals with coefficient of risk aversion 0.00001 and risk of loss 0.06. In Akerlof's model, at any price, the worst cars are those offered for sale. Here, because of the confounding effect of differences in risk aversion, we have some "better" customers—better from the perspective of the insurance company—buying insurance, while some "worse" consumers do not. The insurance company faces an adverse selection of all prospective customers, but it is not "uniformly adverse." To take this back to, say, the Faculty Retirement Incentive Plan at Stanford University, colleagues of mine who chose not to retire, bristle when they read that this program causes an adverse selection in faculty members who choose not to retire. But "adverse selection" refers to the *population* of non-retirees, and not to each individual. The choice of whether to retire compounds a number of characteristics, including outside employment opportunities—leading to the adverse selection—but also, for instance, energy to continue to teach, which mitigates and perhaps even reverses the adverse-selection effect.

And, to add a technical point: In the Akerlof model, the "downward spiral" of adverse selection asymptotes to an equilibrium price of $2400; it doesn't get there in a finite number of steps. Here, the equilibrium premium is reached in a finite number (4) of steps, because of the discrete nature of the population of consumers.

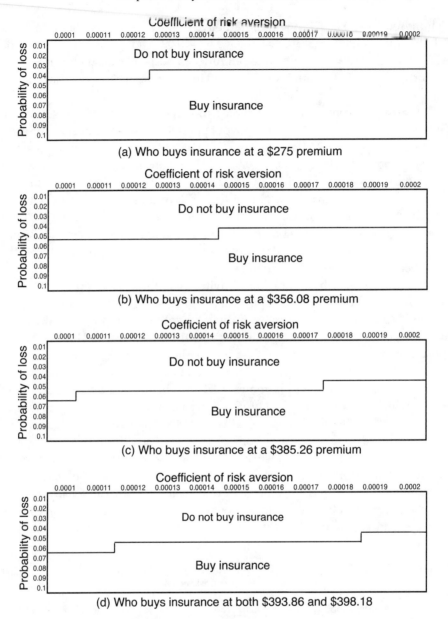

Figure 20.2. Which consumers buy insurance at various premium levels? (The size of the potential loss is $5000. See the text for explanation.)

sets a premium of $567.44 (roughly), for a profit of $32,557.74, insuring only 290 of the 1100 individuals in the population: all those with $\pi_i = 0.09$ and 0.1; those with $\pi_i = 0.8$ and $\lambda_i \geq 0.00015$; and the ten consumers with $\pi_i = 0.7$ and $\lambda_i = 0.0002$.

Adverse selection?

Is the term *adverse selection* appropriate in the case of the monopoly insurance company? To answer this question, suppose that there is no variation in the population about the risk of loss facing different consumers; they vary only in their level of risk aversion. Specifically, suppose there are twenty-one equal sized groups of consumers (for concreteness, 100 in each group) with the coefficients of risk aversion equal to $0.0001, 0.00011, \ldots, 0.00031$, and all consumers have a risk of loss of $\pi = 0.05$. Suppose the insurance company offers only full insurance. As it changes the premium it charges, it "loses" consumers whose level of risk aversion is such that they'd rather go without insurance than pay the premium: To get the least risk-averse consumers to buy insurance, the premium must be \$319.36 or less; to get all but the 100 least risk averse, the premium must be \$327.10 or less; and so forth, up to a premium of \$534.96, which only the most risk averse will pay. Taking into account the expected payout of $\$5000 \times 0.05 = \$250$ on each policy it writes, the company's profit-maximizing premium to set is \$381.45, at which level consumers with coefficients of risk aversion of 0.00017 and greater purchase.

Contrast this to a garden-variety monopolist from intermediate microeconomics.[15] To make the comparison as close as possible, imagine the monopolist sells a good for which each consumer has a prospective demand for one unit and one unit only—this is a not atypical situation if the good is a service—although different consumers have different reservation prices for the good. Suppose 100 of these consumers have a reservation price of \$534.96, another 100 have a reservation price of \$521.16, and so on, down to the last 100 (in a total population of 2100 consumers), whose reservation price is \$319.36. The marginal cost of supplying this service to a single consumer is \$250. Of course, I've just described the insurance market of the previous paragraph, and in the context of the theory of monopoly from intermediate microeconomics, the term *adverse selection* is unlikely to have surfaced.

So what about the original numerical example, where consumers vary both in their odds of a loss and their coefficients of risk aversion? Even in the case of a monopoly insurance company, the fact that, at the premium it chooses to charge, the selection of consumers who buy is an "adverse selection" of the whole population in terms of their risk of loss inclines economists to trot out the magic words *adverse selection*.

One way to make sense of this terminological mess is to focus on the monopoly's cost of providing the service. In the example where every consumer has the same risk of loss, 0.05, there is no variation in the risks faced by consumers; the marginal cost of servicing an additional client is a constant \$250. But in the case of the original two-dimensions-of-diversity example, the marginal costs of servicing additional clients *falls* as the number of clients increases, because the first clients to sign up (at the highest premium the insurance company contemplates) are among the most expensive. That is what justifies the term *adverse selection*.

---

[15] I assume that readers have taken an undergraduate-level course in microeconomics in which the simple theory of monopoly—remember "marginal cost = marginal revenue?"—was taught. If your memory of such things is faint, get a quick refresher. If you never had such exposure, get some. Might I go so far as to suggest Kreps (2019). And, either in that book or another (hopefully, one that is calculus based) at that level, read any material it may contain about price discrimination.

20.5. Screening as an Economic Concept

A two-item menu of insurance contracts

Go back to the story where the insurance firm is regulated and faces a population that has two dimensions of diversity: the individual's probability of sustaining a loss, and the individual's coefficient of risk aversion. Suppose the insurance company continues to offer full insurance for a premium of $398.18. But, in addition, it offers partial insurance: For a premium of $90.83, it will pay back $1000 if a client who purchases this insurance sustains the loss. Since this adds another option for customers without removing any option they had before, at worst it leaves each customer as well off as before. And, if anyone purchases this partial-insurance policy, they must be better off than before.

If you run the numbers, you'll find that 330 consumers purchase the partial-insurance policy, while 400 continue to purchase full insurance (370 consumers go without). The pattern of who buys which policy (and who goes without any insurance) is depicted in Figure 20.3(a).

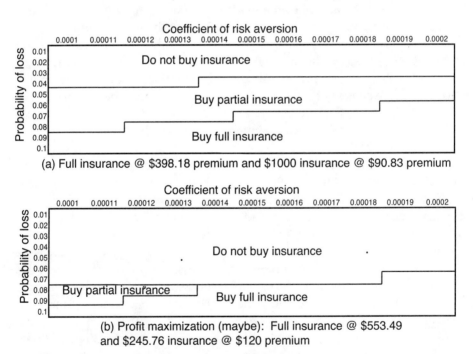

(a) Full insurance @ $398.18 premium and $1000 insurance @ $90.83 premium

(b) Profit maximization (maybe): Full insurance @ $553.49 and $245.76 insurance @ $120 premium

Figure 20.3. Two examples of full plus partial insurance. Panel a shows a pair of policies that nearly break even and, since the pair includes the "fair-odds" single full-insurance policy, a pair that can only raise consumers' expected utility. Panel b shows a pair of policies that, according to Solver, is the profit-maximizing pair (if one policy must be full insurance). But I am skeptical that Solver actually found the profit-maximizing pair.

Note that some individuals who had purchased full insurance when there was only one policy now prefer the partial insurance policy. This raises the odds that the insurance company must pay out on a randomly chosen full-insurance policy it writes; before the probability of a payout was 0.0796; now the probability is 0.0855. Hence, the insurance company is taking a loss on its full-insurance policies . But the probability of paying out on any of the partial insurance policies is 0.05484; a "fair" premium for this policy would be $54.84, and the company is charging $90.83. So the company is making an expected profit on these policies. And, overall, the regulators should be happy; the company's expected profit on the 730 policies it writes is $145.90, an overall average of about $0.20 per policy.

I invite you to build the spreadsheet that does the required calculations, to see what other "near break-even" policy combinations you can find. But if you do this, a word of warning: It is possible to find a pair of policies, one full insurance and other partial, which nearly breaks even. And then, if you *lower* the premium on the partial insurance policy—which certainly is good for consumers—it may raise the net profit of the company by attracting new consumers to the partial insurance policy. In a sense, we see this effect in this example: Start with the two policies in this example, except that the premium on the partial insurance contract is set at $145. No consumer buys partial insurance and, of course, the full-insurance policy breaks even. But lower the premium on partial insurance to, say, $142: Twenty consumers who were not purchasing insurance buy partial insurance, and 10 consumers switch from full to partial insurance, for a net expected profit to the company of $1477.[16] The discrete nature of this toy example causes discontinuities in the firm's profit function, as groups of ten customers at a time switch based on small differences between the three policies; these discontinuities explain in part some anomalous results you'll find if you play with this model. However, such things can happen in real life, and this is an important lesson for any regulators who are obsessed with making sure that insurance companies just break even: Their objective should be to maximize some weighted average of consumers' utilities.

And what about a profit-maximizing insurance company? Using an Excel spreadsheet, I asked the Solver add-in to maximize the firm's profit from two policies, one of which was constrained to be full insurance. The variables were the two premia and the payout on the partial insurance. Solver came back with an answer that, I found, was not really the maximizing combination. Starting from Solver's "solution," the most profitable pair I could find combines a $553.48 premium for full insurance and a $120 premium for a policy that pays $245.76 in case of loss; the firm's profit from this pair is $35,971.85. (See Figure 20.3(b) for which consumers purchase which policies.) But Solver doesn't handle discontinuities in the objective function very well; hence I am suspicious whether this or something close to it is really the optimum.

The term "screening" in economics

By offering consumers their choice between two policies, the insurance company— whether regulated or profit-maximizing—is engaged in *screening* customers. It

---

[16] Twenty policies sold fresh for $142 and ten switches give a net $280, but you must also calculate the expected payouts, which decrease by a total of $1197.

can't tell one customer from another in terms of the customer's tastes and preferences and—in this case—how much it will cost the firm to fulfill the contract in expectation—but by offering this choice, customers self-select in a way that (1) reveals some of that information and (2) can increase either or both total consumer welfare and profit to the firm.

If you look up the dictionary definition of "screen" (as a transitive verb) (in, say, the Merriam-Webster (online) Dictionary), you will find that this is a very flexible word, with five "main" definitional entries, three of which have two subdefinitions. The definition that comes closest to how the term is used here is

> *Definition 3b(1): to examine, usually methodically, in order to make a separation into different groups.*

This doesn't quite capture what is happening here. If pressed to amend the dictionary definition, I would try

> *3b(4): in economics, to offer a menu of choices to another party, so that the second party, by choosing from the menu, separates him/her/itself into one of several groups based on private **information** held by the second party.*

(This lengthy definition is good evidence that I would be a poor lexicographer.) You might wonder about the boldfaced term *information* in my definition. Most economists would accept that an individual's knowledge of her odds of sustaining a loss qualifies as private information. But I'm going further: The insurance company may know the distribution of coefficients of risk aversion in the population, or what fraction of the population prefers apples to oranges, but it doesn't know Joe's or Josephine's coefficient of risk aversion or preference between apples and oranges. If Joe and Josephine do know this—a virtual tautology in economic models, in which choices *reveal* individual preferences—then I count that as private information held by Joe and by Jo.

Screening, by this definition, is found nearly everywhere

If you have studied price discrimination,[17] you will have read about screening, although it is doubtful that the term "screening" was employed. Discrimination

---

[17] If you haven't studied price discrimination, here is an entirely superficial summary: A firm with market power can improve its profit if it can sell at a higher price to individuals with less elastic demand and at a lower price to individuals with more elastic demand. So, for instance, the local gourmet cheese shop gives seniors a 10% discount, not out of charity, but because seniors as a class have more elastic demand for gourmet cheese. The key here is the accounting identity that marginal revenue is price times $1 + 1/\nu$, where ν is the individual's/population's elasticity of demand. So, if seniors have more elastic demand—their ν is a "more negative" number than is the elasticity of demand for the population as a whole—for instance, the overall elasticity of demand for cheese is -3, but seniors as a group have an average elasticity of demand for choose of -5—their marginal revenue at any price is larger than the marginal revenue of the rest of the population. As long as the marginal costs of serving seniors is the same as for others, to equate marginal cost and marginal revenue, you lower the price to seniors.

Sustaining different prices for different groups of customers can be tricky, especially if the good is relatively easy to resell; if the discount for seniors were 50%, we might see senior citizens start a new career of buying gourmet cheese in bulk and reselling to nonseniors. For this reason, price discrimination is particularly prevalent in the realm of services: Grandpa may get a discount on his haircut at the local barber, a haircut that he can't "resell" to Junior. Discrimination by group membership—discounts for by group membership—discounts for seniors or college students—doesn't quite fit my definition, since this involves presenting different individuals with different prices; this is more in line with the first definition. But second- and third-degree price discrimination fits very nicely.

But we can go further. Apple offers its prospective customers a variety of personal computers and tablets, with each "type" (Mac Pro, iMac, Macbook Pro, Mac Mini, iPad, etc.) configured in a variety of ways. To say that any manufacturer who offers a "menu" of different products is engaged in "price discrimination" is probably unreasonable. But, per my definition, the manufacturer is screening. Indeed, taking this expanded definition to the point of terminological absurdity, a firm that offers customers as many widgets as the customer might desire at a single price per widget is offering a menu of choices; the quantity chosen by an individual customer reveals something about the individual's "private information" about his or her preferences. By (my) definition, this constitutes screening. Whether most economists would agree with this as a proper use of the term is questionable. ·

Put it this way: The main title of this chapter is "Private Information," and I include here a consumer's private information about her preferences, even when purchasing a commodity item. The term *screening* is typically used when the private information in question affects the uninformed party's valuation (ex post) of the deal: the buyer of a used car in Akerlof's market, where the seller knows things about the quality of the used car; the seller of insurance, where the purchaser has information about how much it will cost (in expectation) to fulfill the insurance contract; an employer hiring an employee, where the employee has private information about how productive she will be on the job. The term typically does not stretch to Apple Corporation selling different types of personal computers or Amazon selling appliances to customers who have private information about their preferences. However, the astute reader will recognize that, having snuck Amazon into this story, the case for calling this screening becomes stronger, insofar as Amazon can (and, it is alleged, does) use the information it gains selling stuff to customers today to modify the prices it offers the same customer tomorrow. But that takes us to topics that belong in Chapter 21, so I'll leave this thought hanging for now.

---

seniors, for college students, for individuals purchasing a subscription to a scholarly journal (relative to libraries, which usually pay much more)—is one form of price discrimination. Nonlinear prices (e.g., for electricity for your home) is another, and is referred to as second-degree price discrimination. And, in so-called third-degree price discrimination, the same "basic" good is sold with different terms and conditions (e.g., a seat on an airplane flying from NYC to Los Angeles on Saturday is cheaper than the same seat on Sunday, because business people, whose demand is inelastic—or, was, before COVID— are unlikely to want to fly on Saturday.) Most textbook treatments of price discrimination focus on "demand-side" rationales; concerning elasticities of demand by different groups. But, in some applications, price-discrimination is "cost" based (e.g., life-insurance policies for men have higher premia than the same policies for women, holding health status the same, because even holding health status the same, men as a group die sooner than women do, statistically).

20.6. Single Crossing

General results about screening when the "types" of the informed party are two- or more dimensional are difficult. But, if there is a single dimension of types along which types can be linearly ordered, and if the preferences of those types has a nice structure—so-called *single crossing*—then some interesting general results are available.

The (strict) single-crossing property

The concept of "single crossing" is employed in a variety of contexts in economic theory, with different but related definitions designed to fit the context. And, in a given context, the concept is formulated at different levels of abstraction. Here, I provide a simple and intuitive formulation designed to fit the context of screening.

Imagine a potential transaction between two "sides," buyers and sellers. The number of agents (they could be individual consumers or firms) on each side can be one, a few, or many. Individuals on one side have private information about their respective "types"; θ will denote a type, drawn from a set of possible types Θ. The set of types is linearly ordered; for expositional convenience, assume that $\Theta \subseteq R$, with $>$ ordering the types. Agents on the uninformed side of the transaction share a prior assessment π over the type of each informed agent; although it is irrelevant, you can assume that their assessments are that the types of the informed agents (if there are more than one) are independently and identically distributed.

A transaction, if it takes place, involves a single agent from each side. Each transaction involves two *terms of trade*, x and y. Every informed agent's preferences are strictly increasing in y and strictly decreasing in x, regardless of the agent's type.

Example 1. Used cars. The transaction involves the sale of a used car, where the sellers are the informed party, just as in Akerlof's model and the variations we explored. The price paid by the buyer to the seller is y; x will be the duration of a warranty provided by the seller to the buyer, under which the seller must affect repairs to the car as needed. (The seller prefers a higher sales price and to provide a less lengthy warranty.)

Example 2. Education as a signal. An uninformed company seeks to hire a prospective employee. The employee has private information about how valuable she will be to the company. The wage the company will pay the employee, if indeed she is hired, is y. The variable x is the amount of education the prospective employee chooses to undertake before employment, as a signal of her value. (The employee prefers a higher wage and less time spent in school.)

Example 3. Insurance. The transaction involves an uninformed insurance company providing insurance against loss by an informed consumer, who knows the probability that she will sustain the loss. The consumer's level of wealth after she pays the premium is y, while x measures the amount of risk she bears; specifically, x is the size of her possible loss L less the amount the company will pay back in the event of a loss. (The customer prefers a smaller premium (more wealth y after paying the premium) and more coverage (less exposure to loss x).)

One might quibble with this assumption in education-as-a-signal story—why is more education distasteful?—but that's the standard assumption in the literature. Otherwise, Assumption 20.1 fits with all three examples.

Assumption 20.1. *The set of conceivable terms of trade (x, y) for the transaction is an interval in R^2, namely, $\mathcal{T} = \{(x, y) : \underline{x} \leq x \leq \overline{x}, \underline{y} \leq y \leq \overline{y}\}$, where $\underline{x} < \overline{x}$ and $\underline{y} < \overline{y}$. For each type θ of informed party, type θ agents share preferences over the terms (x, y) (assuming the transaction takes place) that are complete, transitive, and continuous, and that are strictly decreasing in x and strictly increasing in y. (A type-θ agent's preferences over $\mathcal{T}$ are denoted by $\succeq_\theta$.)*

Proposition 20.2. *Fix a type θ and a point $(x, y) \in \mathcal{T}$. Fix any $x' \neq x$. Then one (and only one) of the following three statements is true: (a) $(x', \underline{y}') \succ_\theta (x, y)$; (b) $(x', \overline{y}') \prec_\theta (x, y)$; (c) there is a unique $y' \in [\underline{y}, \overline{y}]$ such that $(x, y) \sim_\theta (x', y')$. In case c, if $x' > x$, then $y' > y$; if $x' < x$, then $y' < y$. And if we write $y'(x')$ as the unique solution to $(x, y) \sim_\theta (x', y')$ for those x' for which case c holds (which is a closed subinterval of $[\underline{x}, \overline{x}]$ containing x), then $x' \to y'(x')$ is continuous.*

This is all very standard stuff, following the discussion in Section 2.4 in Volume I, so I will not bother with the (quite simple) proof. But, to draw the obvious picture, this proposition says that the preferences of a type-θ agent over $\mathcal{T}$ can be represented with an indifference-curve diagram, where preference increases in the northwest direction. Cases a and b allow for indifference curves to "run out" on the sides of the box $\mathcal{T}$. In applications, it is typical that these indifference curves are convex to the southeast corner,[18] which this can be shown to hold in specific examples. But for now, all we know is that each indifference curve describes a "continuous curve" that runs southwest to northeast. See Figure 20.4.

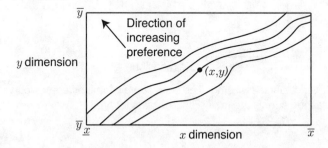

Figure 20.4. Indifference curves per Assumption 20.1

The single-crossing property concerns the relative "slopes" of indifference curves of different types of the informed party. In this context, think of higher types (bigger θ) as more desirable trading partners for the uninformed party: Higher θ indicates owners of better used cars; they are employees who will generate more profit for

---

[18] That is, sets $\{(x, y) \in \mathcal{T} : (x, y) \succeq_\theta (x', y')\}$ for $(x', y') \in \mathcal{T}$ are convex.

their employers; they have less risk of loss and, therefore, are better clients for insur-ance companies. So that the last example conforms, we identify θ as the probability of *no* loss.

The x and y variables have the following interpretation: The y variable repre-sents the financial outcome for the informed party: the price she receives for selling her car; the wage level of the employee; and, because in the insurance example the informed party is buying, not selling, the level of her wealth after she pays the premium for her insurance. The x variable is a way to indicate the "quality" of the transaction to the uninformed party: The owner of a good used car is more willing to offer a six-month warranty; a more productive worker shows this by choos-ing more education; a consumer who knows she is less prone to loss is willing to self-insure for a greater proportion of the risk she faces.

Single crossing refers to the incremental y that the informed party requires if she is to "do" more x. Specifically, from any point (x, y), the incremental amount h of the y variable that the informed party demands as compensation for increasing x to x' is smaller the higher is θ. Thus, if $\theta > \theta'$, the indifference curve for θ through any point (x, y) intersects the indifference curve for type θ' through the same point (x, y) only at (x, y), crossing from above to below. Formally:

Definition 20.3. Strict Single Crossing. *Preferences $\succeq_\theta$ for the different types $\theta \in \Theta$ have the **strict-single-crossing property** if: Suppose that types θ and θ' are such that $\theta > \theta'$. Suppose that (x, y) and (x', y') are such that $x' > x$, $y' > y$, and $(x', y') \sim_\theta (x, y)$. Then $(x', y') \prec_{\theta'} (x, y)$.*

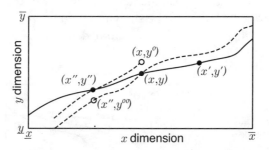

Figure 20.5. Strict single crossing. The solid curve is an indifference curve for type θ, and the dashed curves are indifference curves for type θ', where $\theta > \theta'$.

See Figure 20.5. Take an arbitrary point $(x, y) \in \mathcal{T}$ and two types θ and θ' with $\theta > \theta'$. I assert that Definition 20.3 implies that the θ indifference curve through (x, y) continues to the right everywhere below the θ' indifference curve through (x, y). The definition immediately implies this. Moreover, starting from (x, y) and moving to the left (less of both x and y), the θ indifference curve lies everywhere above the θ' indifference curve. This takes a simple argument: Take any point (x'', y'') to the left of (x, y) that lies on the θ indifference curve through (x, y). The definition implies that (x, y) lies strictly below the one point (x, y°) that lies on the

θ' indifference curve through (x'', y''). But by strict monotonicity, $(x, y^o) \succ_{\theta'} (x, y)$. So the point (x'', y^{oo}) on the θ' indifference curve through (x, y) must lie below the point (x'', y'').

Single-crossing (and more) in Example 3 (insurance)

For Examples 1 and 2 above (used cars and the job market, respectively), single-crossing is simply assumed to hold. But in the case of Example 2, insurance, one can show that it holds, under the following assumptions:

- The types are distinguished (only) by their probabilities of loss, $1 - \theta$. This is the probability that the consumer loses an amount of wealth L, common to all consumers.

- All consumers are expected-utility maximizers. All share a strictly concave, continuous, and twice-continuously differentiable utility function u applied to their final level of wealth, W. All consumers start with initial wealth level $W > L$.[19]

An insurance policy specifies the premium paid, P, and the amount the insurance company pays back in the event of a loss, I. But to conform with the notational conventions in the previous subsection, we work instead with the variables $y = W - P$ and $x = L - I$. That is, y is the amount of wealth left to the consumer if she does not sustain the loss (after buying the policy), x is the amount of risk she bears concerning the loss (so $x = 0$ is full insurance), and $y - x$ is her final wealth level if she does sustain the loss. Assume that premia must lie in the interval $[0, W]$, so that $y \in [0, W]$, and that I must lie in the interval $[0, L]$, so that $x \in [0, L]$. For some utility functions u, it is possible that $x - y$ lies outside the domain of u; I'll ignore this possibility. Then, working with the variables x and y, a type-θ consumer who purchases a policy (x, y) has expected utility

$$\theta u(y) + (1 - \theta)u(y - x);$$

recall that θ is the probability of *not* sustaining the loss. An indifference curve for a consumer of type θ is the set of points (x, y) such that $\theta u(y) + (1 - \theta)u(y - x) = k$ for k the expected-utility level along the indifference curve. To compare the relative slopes of indifference curves through a given point (x, y) for different values of θ, we can either implicitly differentiate in x (expressing y as a function of x) or in y (expressing x as a function of y) (and invoking the Implicit Function Theorem as we go). It is more convenient to treat x as a function of y; the implicit derivative $x'(y)$ is therefore a solution to

$$\theta u'(y) + (1 - \theta)u'(y - x(y))(1 - x'(y)) = 0,$$

---

[19] Assuming that all consumers are identical in these two respects is, of course, quite a stretch, as is the assumption that all face the same sized loss. So, this example is definitely in the category of exemplifying modeling.

and so we get

$$x'(y) = \frac{\theta u'(y) + (1-\theta)u'(y-x(y))}{(1-\theta)u'(y-x(y))} = 1 + \frac{\theta}{1-\theta}\frac{u'(y)}{u'(y-x(y))}.$$

It is immediate that $x'(y)$ at any point (x,y) is bigger, the bigger is θ, which means that (viewing the diagram with x on the horizontal axis), indifference curves for type $\theta > \theta'$ are less steep than those for type θ'. That is, the single-crossing property holds.

And, in fact, we can draw more conclusions. First, at the point $x = 0$, which represents full-insurance policies, $x'(y) = 1 + \theta/(1-\theta) = 1/(1-\theta)$, so $y'(x) = (1-\theta)$. The math may hide this economically intuitive point: At $x = 0$, or full insurance, a type-θ consumer values the first bit of risk she takes on as if she were risk neutral. That is, whatever y is, to compensate her for bearing a tiny bit δ of the risk, she requires $(1-\theta)\delta$ in lower premium.

And, $x'(y)$ decreases as y increases. To see this, note that $x'(y) \geq 1$, so $x(y)$ increases more quickly than y. Then, along the indifference curve, $y - x(y)$ is decreasing. And since u is strictly concave, u' is a decreasing function. Hence as y increases, $u'(y)$ decreases, and since $y - x(y)$ decreases, $u'(y - x(y))$ increases. The ratio of the two decreases, which says that $x'(y)$ decreases. To visualize the implications of this observation, recognize that if $x'(y)$ is decreasing, then $y'(x)$ is increasing. That is, indifference curves are convex to the southeast corner of $[0,L] \times [0,W]$. And, so, we have (for this case) the picture in Figure 20.6. Again, the math may hide simple economic intuition: The greater the share of the risk that the consumer bears, the more compensation she requires on the margin to maintain her expected utility.

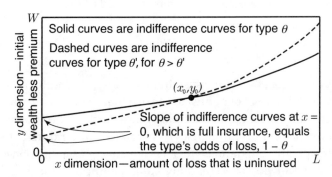

Figure 20.6. Indifference curves in the insurance example. In this example, indifference curves possess the strict single-crossing property, are convex to the southeast corner, and their slope at $x = 0$ (which is full insurance) equals the odds of loss for each type.

A final remark about these diagrams: The point $(x, y) = (L, W)$, which is the northeast corner, is the "no-insurance" point; $x = L$ means that the consumer is bearing all her risk, and $y = W$ means she is not paying a premium.

20.7. Insurance with Two Types

Suppose there are two types of consumer, high risk, with θ_H, and low risk, with θ_L, where $\theta_H < \theta_L$. (Remember, θ is the probability of *no* loss.) Suppose that there are many consumers of each type, who are expected utility-maximizers. As in Section 20.6, consumers have identical (risk-averse, smooth) utility functions, identical initial wealth W, and identical loss-possibility amount L. What will be the market outcome, assuming that insurance companies (or one company)—assumed to be risk neutral and to have no costs other than the expected payout on policies that they write[20]—are able to screen if they choose to do so? Throughout, assume that all policies on the market are known to all consumers, who choose among those policies the one that is best for themselves. The answer to this question depends on the "market structure" of insurance companies.

Some terminology and a preliminary result come first:

- A *separating equilibrium* is one in which no policy is purchased by both high-risk and low-risk types; there are policies for high-risk types and different policies for low-risk types. (This can include no insurance as a "policy.")

- A *pooling policy* is one that is purchased by both high-risk and low-risk types.

- In no equilibrium situation can there be more than one pooling policy: Suppose by way of contradiction that (x, y) and (x', y') are best options for both types. Then these two contracts must lie on a single high-risk type indifference curve and, simultaneously, on a single low-risk type indifference curve. But any two indifference curves, one for each type, intersect only once, by single crossing, giving a contradiction.

- Hence, a *pooling equilibrium* is one in which all consumers pool at a single policy. (This doesn't yet rule out a *hybrid* equilibrium, in which some of each type pool at a single contract, but some consumers of one type or the other or both also purchase a contract not chosen by the other type.)

Perfect competition: Rothschild and Stiglitz (1976)

Begin with the case of many competitive insurance companies, with free entry into and free exit out of the insurance business. A competitive-market equilibrium, then, is an array of contracts on offer by insurance companies, such that no company is taking a net expected loss (paying out more in expectation that the premia it charges), and no company could enter and offer a contract that would make a strictly positive profit. This is the case analyzed in the seminal paper on this topic, Rothschild and Stiglitz (1976).

The bottom line is that if there are relatively few low-risk consumers (relative to the number of high-risk consumers), a specific separating equilibrium ensues in which the high-risk types get full insurance and the low-risk types get a specific partial insurance policy. But if there are "too many" low-risk consumers relative to the number of high-risk consumers, there is no equilibrium at all.

---

[20] We could accommodate other costs, but to keep the argument simple, we make this assumption.

We reach this conclusion in several steps. The first few are straightforward.

- It is not an equilibrium for no insurance policies to be offered. Consider only the high-risk types for a moment. They are strictly risk averse. Insurance companies are risk neutral. So it is efficient in a social sense for the insurance companies to write full insurance ($x = 0$) insurance policies for the high-risk types. Moreover, the high-risk types are willing to pay more than their expected loss $(1 - \theta_H)L$ to avoid this loss. Hence, if no insurance policies were offered, an insurance company could enter and offer full insurance for a premium a bit greater than $(1 - \theta_H)L$, which all high-risk types would take. Low-risk types might buy this policy as well, if they are very risk averse and/or the insurance company sets the premium at not too much more than $(1 - \theta_H)L$, which would only decrease the overall expected payout on the policies written. Hence, the insurance company offering this policy is guaranteed a strictly positive profit.

- It is not an equilibrium for only the low-risk types to purchase insurance. The logic of the previous bullet point applies: A full-insurance policy with a premium a bit greater than $(1 - \theta_H)L$ will attract high-risk types if they are uninsured, and it will be profitable for the firm that offers this policy. If it attracts the low-risk types as well, all the better. (I'm not suggesting that the firm offering insurance to low-risk types would offer this, but that a new entrant would do so.)

- All active insurance policies (pairs (x, y) that are purchased by some consumer) must lie on a pair of indifference curves, one for each type. This is an immediate consequence of the assumption that all consumers have access to all contracts on offer, and each consumer chooses from among the best contracts for herself that are on offer. (Technically speaking, this requires as well an assumption that the set of policies on offer is compact, and we made that assumption explicitly in the middle of page 133.) For each type, call the indifference curve that contains all active policies for that type that type's active indifference curve. For low-risk types, if they do not purchase any insurance, their active indifference curve is the indifference curve through the point $(x = L, y = W)$, the "no-insurance" insurance policy.

- For each type, its active indifference curve must lie on or above the indifference curve through the "no-insurance" insurance policy, since not buying any policy is always an option for consumers.

- The two active indifference curves must intersect, although this doesn't rule out the intersection happening at the no-insurance point. (1) It is impossible that the high-risk active indifference curve lies everywhere below the low-risk active indifference curve; if this were so, high-risk consumers would choose whichever policy is offered to low-risk consumers. (2) And if the high-risk active indifference curve is everywhere above the low-risk active indifference curve, then low-risk consumers would choose a policy offered to high-risk consumers.

- The two active indifference curves can intersect in no more than a single policy by single-crossing. And all active policies for high-risk types must lie at or to the left of the intersection point along the high-risk active indifference curve, while all active policies for low-risk types must lie to at or to the right of the intersection point. If it were otherwise (e.g., a policy were offered along the low-risk indifference curve to the left of the intersection point, it would clearly be better for high-risk types than any policy on the indifference curve for them that is alleged to be their "active" indifference curve. Another way to put this is that, except for pooling, high-risk types get more coverage for higher premia; low-risk types get less coverage for smaller premia. See Figure 20.7.

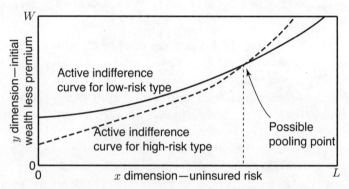

Figure 20.7. Active contracts must lie along the lower envelope of two indifference curves, one for each type. Moreover, contracts for the low-risk type must lie to the right of the intersection point and contracts for the high-risk type must lie to the left.

- In an equilibrium, every active insurance policy must earn zero profit for the company offering that contract. A quick argument is that, if some policy were earning a strictly positive profit, then a new entrant could copy that policy and also make a strictly positive profit. But this assumes that some consumers will do business with this new entrant. A stronger argument would be to show that, if some policy is earning a strictly positive profit, then a new entrant could put on the market a different policy that (1) is certain to attract customers (given that nothing else changes) and (2) will earn a strictly positive profit. And this stronger argument can be made. Follow along on Figure 20.8. The two indifference curves drawn there, one for each type, are the indifference curves identified in the previous step: These are the two indifference curves along one of which every active contract must lie.

    Suppose the point marked #1 is offered, is taken up by some low-risk types, and makes a strictly positive profit. Then a new firm could offer the point marked Alt #1, which offers the same payout and a slightly lower premium. This is not attractive to high-risk types (it lies below the active indifference curve for high-risk types), and it attracts all the low-risk types. (They prefer it to #1.) And, as long as it is close to #1—that is, as long as the reduction in premium is small enough—it still makes a strictly positive profit.

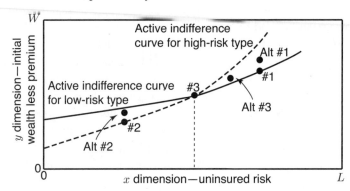

Figure 20.8. No active contract can earn strictly positive profit. (See text for details.)

Suppose the contract for high-risk types marked #2 earns a strictly positive profit. Then the contract marked Alt #2 will attract all the high-risk types but not low-risk types and, if it is close enough to #2, it will earn a strictly positive profit, which is inconsistent with equilibrium. (In this case, it is unimportant that it lies below the low-risk type indifference curve; if it attracts some low-risk customers, it becomes even more profitable.)

Finally, we have the potential pooling contract #3. Suppose it makes a strictly positive profit. Consider two cases. (1) Contract #3 is purchased only by high-risk types and makes a strictly positive profit. Then, by dropping the premium a small amount in the manner of Alt #2, a policy is created that is attractive to all high-risk types, and if the drop in premium is small enough, it will still make a positive profit from them. And it will also attract all low-risk types and make an even greater (strictly positive) profit from each of them. (2) Contract #3 is purchased by at least some low-risk types, and it makes a positive profit overall. Therefore, it makes a strictly positive profit from its low-risk types. We need an alternative policy that attracts only low-risk types, and a contract such as Alt #3 does that; it offers a lower premium and a lower payback, such that the contract lies between the two indifference curves. If the reductions in both premium and payback are small enough, it will continue to make a positive profit, *in this case in part because, by attracting only low-risk types, one eliminates the potentially unprofitable part of the population that may have been buying #3.*

Hence, no policy being offered can earn a strictly positive profit. And therefore, no policy can earn a strictly negative profit, for if a firm offered a policy earning a strictly negative profit, the firm's overall profit would be strictly negative—it can't make up its losses with some other policy—and the firm would exit, which means we are not at an equilibrium.

Let me sum up where we are. In an equilibrium, if one exists, there must be *at least* one policy for high-risk types. I'll say that there must be one *or more* policies for the low-risk types as well, although it could be that their only policy is the no-insurance policy (L, W). Each policy offered must earn precisely zero profit. The active policies must lie on the lower envelope of two active indifference curves, with the high-risk policies on the left of the intersection of the two indifference curves and the low-risk policies on the right.

- And we can eliminate the highlighted caveats "at least" and "or more" : Iso-profit "curves" for the insurance companies are straight lines.
  - To eliminate "or more": Suppose there are two active policies for the low-risk type, both lying along a single indifference curve, both earning zero profit. Consider the policy that is the 50-50 convex combination of the two. It also must earn zero profit, and (because of the shape of indifference curves) it must lie on a higher indifference curve for low-risk types than the original two. A company therefore can lower the convex combination policy's payout or raise its premium. It must be careful in doing this to stay above the original low-risk active indifference curve while remaining below the high-risk types active indifference curve; if you draw the picture, you'll see that both of these choices are possible. Hence this policy will not attract high-risk types, will be strictly preferred by the low-risk types to their two original policies, and will make strictly positive profit from them.
  - And to eliminate "at least": The argument for not having two (or more) active policies for high-risk types is simpler, since you don't have to worry about attracting low-risk types.

- It is not an equilibrium for the two types to pool at a single policy. Figure 20.8 and the policy marked #3 provides the picture. Suppose both types pooled at that point, making zero expected profit. Then the policy marked Alt #3, if it is close enough to #3 but between the two indifference curves (as shown) makes a strictly positive profit: For #3 to provide zero expected profit, it must be strictly profitable for the low-risk types. For this reason, and because Alt #3 is not attractive to high-risk types (who prefer #3) but is attractive to the low-risk types, it makes a strictly positive profit. Pooling is not an equilibrium.

So, if an equilibrium exists, it must consist of two policies, one for the high-risk types and a different one for the low-risk types, although we haven't ruled out that the policy for the low-risk types is no insurance at all.

- Now we add in the zero-profit condition. See Figure 20.9(a). It provides the two zero-(expected-)profit lines for the two types and locates a pair of policies on the respective zero-profit lines, one for the high-risk types (with a higher premium and more coverage) and one for the low-risk types (with a lower premium and lower coverage). Note that the zero-profit lines go through the no-insurance point, (L, W); an insurance policy that charges no premium and provides no coverage earns zero profit. Then, in panel b of this figure, I supply the respective indifference curves through these two contracts.

  Remember that the slopes of a type's iso-profit lines and the slope of their indifference curves at $x = 0$, or full insurance, are the same. And, as coverage diminishes and exposure increases—that is, as y increases—the slope of the indifference curve increases. You should check visually that panel b meets these conditions.

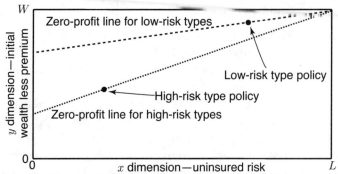

(a) The policies for each type must be on their respective zero-profit lines

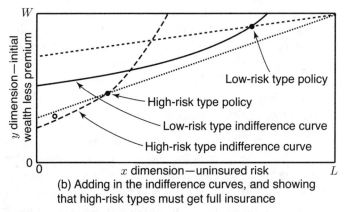

(b) Adding in the indifference curves, and showing
that high-risk types must get full insurance

Figure 20.9. The high-risk types must get full insurance in equilibrium. There are two policies, one for high-risk types and one for low-risk types, located on their respective zero-(expected-)profit lines. Given the slopes of indifference curves at full insurance, if the high-risk type doesn't get full insurance, there is room for a strictly positive profit policy to be added.

- But note that if the high-risk types are not getting full insurance, there must be a "gap" between the zero-profit line for the high-risk type and the high-risk types' indifference curve. This provides room for some firm to put in a strictly positive profit policy, in (say) the position of the open dot in panel b. This will happen whenever the high-risk types get less than full insurance. So they must, in any equilibrium, get full insurance.

- So we know that, in any equilibrium, the high-risk types get full insurance, and the low-risk types must get a policy along their zero-profit line, to the right of where the high-risk indifference curve hits the low-risk zero-profit line. The picture is Figure 20.10. Is this an equilibrium? In particular, can the low-risk policy lie strictly to the right of the intersection? The answer is no, once again. The open dot lies below the high-risk indifference curve, above the low-risk indifference curve, and below the low-risk zero-profit line. Hence it will attract all the low-risk consumers, none of the high-risk consumers, and lead to strictly positive profit.

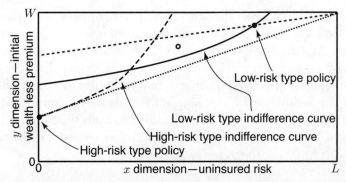

Figure 20.10. How about this case? Is it an equilibrium? There are two policies, one for high-risk types and one for low-risk types. The policy for the high-risk types gives the high-risk types full insurance at actuarially fair odds. And there is a zero-profit policy for the low-risk types, which is not attractive to the high-risk types. But it still isn't an equilibrium, as it is upset by the policy at the location of the open dot.

We are nearly done: *The only possibility for an equilibrium is that the high-risk consumers get full insurance at actuarially fair odds, and the low-risk types get a zero-profit policy that lies where their zero-profit line hits the high-risk indifference curve through the high-risk, full-insurance policy. See Figure 20.11.*

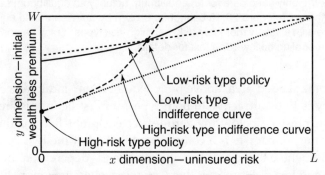

Figure 20.11. The only candidate for an equilibrium. There are two policies, one for high-risk types and one for low-risk types. The policy for the high-risk types gives that type full insurance at actuarially fair odds. And the low-risk contract lies at the intersection of the low-risk-zero-profit line and high-risk indifference curve through the high-risk contract.

Note that the high-risk types are indifferent between the two policies on offer, but for this to be an equilibrium, we require them to take the full-insurance option.

Might things—the shapes of indifference curves and the like—be such that the low-risk types are left with no insurance at all? The answer is: No. They always get a bit of insurance; I'll leave it to you to give the argument why. (Or see the solution to Problem 20.10.) But a more imporant question is: Is this arrangement an equilibrium? It is, we've argued, the only candidate for an equilibrium. But we haven't determined that it is one.

It is true that the high-risk types are doing as well as possible, If they are sep arated from the low-risk types. They are getting full insurance at actuarially fair odds for them. And the low-risk types can only be made better off, in a separating equilibrium, by a policy that will lose money for the company that offers it. So, as far as separating pairs of policies go, this seems an equilibrium situation.

But what if an insurance firm, looking at the situation in Figure 20.11, decided to look for a pooling policy that (1) is attractive to both types and (2) makes a strictly positive profit? See Figure 20.12 (in which I've moved the low-risk-type's indifference curve to make the figure easier to read).

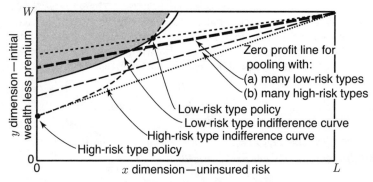

Figure 20.12. Is the only candidate for an equilibrium actually an equilibrium?. The candidate equilibrium in Figure 20.10 cannot be broken by any separating equilibrium. But if there are relatively more low-risk than high-risk types, it may be possible to break it with a pooling policy. (See text for details.)

First consider the shaded area, above both "equilibrium" indifference curves. If a pooling policy is to be attractive to both types, it must lie in this area. And to be profitable, it must lie below the zero-(expected-)profit line for the whole population. That line, of course, is a convex combination of the two zero-profit-for-a-type lines. But where that convex combination lands depends on the relative numbers of high- and low-risk types. If there are relatively more low-risk types, it is closer to the zero-profit line for low-risk types, as depicted by the line of heavy dashes. Or, it may be closer to the zero-profit line for high-risk types, if there are relatively more of them. As long as there are enough high-risk types to low-risk types, so the combined-type, zero-profit line doesn't intersect the shaded area, the only candidate for an equilibrium—shown in Figure 20.11—is an equilibrium. But with enough low-risk types, so the combined-type, zero-profit line passes into the shaded area, it is evident that a pooling policy exists that meets both conditions 1 and 2, breaking the array of policies in Figure 20.11. And, in this case, there is no equilibrium at all.

Oligopoly, sort of

The concept of perfect competition—in particular, perfect competition with free entry and exit—is that a firm, deciding whether to take a particular action, assumes that its action will have no influence on what other firms are doing. Firms enter when they believe that their actions will provide them with strictly positive profit, taking the current situation as otherwise fixed. No firm reasons that, "If I enter, or put this new product on the market, other firms will react." (And firms already in the market exit, or rearrange their offerings, under the same "no one else will react" hypothesis.) We can recast this idea in game-theoretic terms: A solution is the pure-strategy Nash equilibrium of a simultaneous-move game with more prospective entrants than demand can sustain. All players (firms) know the equilibrium strategies of their opponents, and with simultaneous moves, those strategies are fixed. An equilibrium is where every player, given the strategies of her rivals, is optimizing. So, an equilibrium in this spirit is a set of policies such that no inactive firm, assuming the equilibrium set of policies on offer, sees a strictly positive profit opportunity. Charles Wilson (1977) and John Riley (1979) propose variations on "perfect competition" in which firms have conjectures about rivals' reactions.

Wilson, in a concept he calls an *anticipatory equilibrium*, suggests that an array of insurance policies is an equilibrium if it is not possible to add a policy that (1) provides a strictly positive profit but (2) will not become strictly unprofitable (profit strictly less than zero) if policies from the original menu that become strictly unprofitable are withdrawn. Recall how we ruled out pooling policies in the previous subsection: An entrant can skim the low-risk types from a pooling contract, leaving the high-risk types with the pooling policy. But this action makes the formerly pooling policy unprofitable and, if it withdrawn, the newly proposed policy may find that it is bought by high-risk types, becoming strictly unprofitable itself. Hence, our previous argument for breaking pooling policies must (at least) be revisited. This allows for many equilibria, including equilibria in which a single pooling contract is offered. (Problem 20.11 asks you to present a diagrammatic example of this.)

In contrast, Riley defines what he calls a *reactive equilibrium*. In his definition, an array of insurance policies is an equilibrium if it is impossible to add a policy that (1) provides a strictly positive profit but (2) will not become strictly unprofitable if other firms, in response to the addition of this policy, are allowed to add still more policies. This doesn't impact our previous argument for breaking a pooling equilibrium: In that argument, a firm offers a policy that skims the low-risk types, leaving the high-risk types at the pooling contract. In response, if yet another policy is added, it could take from the first addition all its clientele, so that the first addition has zero profit. But the only way to make the first addition strictly unprofitable is to find a way to get high-risk types to buy it. And since the original pooling policy cannot (under Riley's rules) be taken away, the high-risk types will always stick with that policy or, perhaps, move to some further policy that is added as a reaction to the first addition. They will never change to first addition; the first addition is designed so that some status quo policy is preferred to it by the high-risk types.

However, Riley's concept kills the argument that broke the Rothschild–Stiglitz separating array with a pool: The pool works because it is attractive to both types. But any pool can be broken by yet another policy that skims its low-risk clients. So, with Riley's equilibrium concept, the surviving equilibrium *in all cases* is the

Rothschild–Stiglitz separating array: full insurance for the high-risk types at actu-arially fair odds, and partial insurance for the low-risk types, where their fair-odds line intersects the indifference curve for the high-risk types that passes through the high-risk types' fair-odds, full-insurance policy.

And for this reason, this "equilibrium" is called the Riley equilibrium.

What is one to make of these two variations?

- You can think of them simply as "reduced forms" for some unmodeled dynamic process of competition among firms.

- You can think of them as a form of *conjectural variations*, which explains the title of this subsection. Conjectural variations is a fairly old (and nowadays unfashionable) theory concerning the interactions of oligopolists. Given a status quo situation, each firm within an oligopoly has conjectures about how its rivals will react if it (the original firm) deviates from the status quo. Perhaps the most famous of these is the *kinked-demand* model: Take a Bertrand model, for differentiated goods with symmetric linear demand functions for goods that are substitutes, as in Section 18.4. An equilibrium status quo is a set of prices for which no firm wishes to change its price, if the firm conjectures:

  > If I raise my price, my rivals will shrug their collective shoulders and maintain the prices they are charging. But if I lower my price, to try to capture more market share, they will react by lowering the prices they charge by a commensurate amount.

  This conjecture about what will happen if a firm varies what it is doing implies that each firm thinks it faces a kinked-demand function, with more elastic demand for prices below its status-quo price, and less elastic demand for prices above its status-quo price. This provides for multiple equilibria. (If you've never seen the kinked-demand story worked out, Problem 20.12 will add to your general "cultural" knowledge.)

  Both the Wilson and the Riley stories can be thought of as invoking specific conjectural variations: Each firm says, "If I do this, rivals will do that." If doing "this" gives strictly positive profits, without running the risk of "that" rendering the original move strictly unprofitable, the original firm will do "this." And an equilibrium is where no such "this" exists.

- You can try to devise a dynamic, institutional story that justifies these equilibrium processes as reduced forms. For instance, imagine that this insurance indusry is regulated. The regulators in question believe that competition among the several firms will lead to "fair" prices for consumers. Instead: (1) The regulators are concerned with the ability of insurance companies to fulfill their obligations. If a new product enters the market that makes an old product unprofitable, the regulators allow the company offering the old product to withdraw it from the market. This gives the C. Wilson (1977) story. (2) The regulators insist that any product that is offered to the public cannot be withdrawn, even if a subsequent offering makes it unprofitable. So, companies are cautious not to offer products that will become unprofitable if competitors respond. This is the Riley (1979) story.

You must decide for yourself if either story is appealing, on any of these grounds.

Monopoly

Finally, suppose that there is a single monopoly insurance company. Following the classic analysis of Stiglitz (1977), I'll look at what an unregulated, unconstrained, (expected) profit-maximizing monopolist would do. The bottom line is depicted in Figure 20.13(a). The high-risk types get full insurance, and the low-risk types get partial insurance at a point where their indifference curve through the no-insurance point intersects the active high-risk indifference curve.

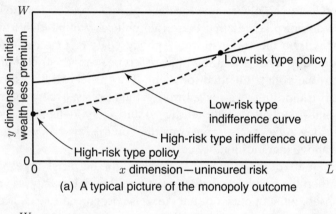

(a) A typical picture of the monopoly outcome

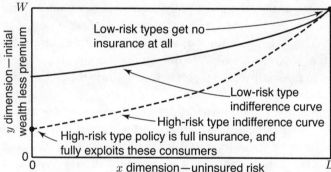

(b) If the relative number of high-risk types is large, they are
fully exploited, and the low-risk types get no insurance at all

Figure 20.13. The profit-maximizing monopoly insurance company. There are two policies, one for high-risk types and one for low-risk types. The policy for the high-risk types gives the high-risk types full insurance, and the low-risk contract lies at the intersection of the low-risk indifference curve through the no-insurance point and the high-risk indifference curve through the full-insurance policy they are provided. The exact locations of the two policies are determined by the relative number of high- and low-risk consumers. More high-risk consumers moves their full-insurance policy down. Typically, the low-risk types get some (partial) insurance, as in panel a. However, if there are enough high-risk types relative to the number of low-risk types, the high-risk types are fully exploited by the insurance company, and the low-risk consumers get no insurance, as in panel b.

Which two insurance contracts—what is the premium for the high-risk types' full insurance policy, and what are the corresponding terms for the low-risk types' partial insurance policy—are determined by the parameters of the model. But in particular, as the relative number of high-risk types rises, the premium for their full-insurance policy rises and the amount of insurance (and the corresponding premium) for the low-risk types decreases. If the relative numbers of high-risk types is large enough, the monopolist fully exploits the high-risk types, charging them a premium that makes them just indifferent between their full-insurance policy and no insurance at all, while the low-risk types are left with no insurance. This situation is depicted in Figure 20.13(b).

The argument for this bottom-line conclusion is straightforward. The monopolist is going to select two policies, one for the high-risk and one for the low-risk types, where we do not preclude that these two policies will be identical or that one or the other will be the "no-insurance" policy (L, W). One constraint that the insurance company faces is that the high-risk types cannot strictly prefer the low-risk policy to the policy intended for them. But this constraint is fully captured by the high-risk indifference curve through their policy. That is to say, if two policies for the high-risk types—call them (x, y) and (x', y')—lie on the same indifference curve, they generate the same constraint on the low-risk policy, namely that it cannot lie above that indifference curve.

So think, first of all, of the monopolist choosing the high-risk types' indifference curve, and then the policy on that curve. Once the high-risk types' indifference curve is chosen, which policy on that curve is chosen is a free choice for the monopoly: It doesn't impact the monopolist's other policy choice. And, on any indifference curve for the high-risk types, the most profitable policy is the full-insurance policy. This is because the slope of any high-risk indifference curve at full insurance is the slope of the iso-profit line for the monopolist, and indifference curves are convex to the southwest; I won't bother to draw the picture, but if it isn't obvious to you, please do draw it.

Hence, we know that the high-risk types get a full-insurance policy. As for the low-risk types, their policy cannot lie above the high-risk types' indifference curve, but it must lie on or above their indifference curve through the no-insurance point. Given the slope of the monopolist's iso-profit line for this type, we conclude that the best (most profitable) policy is where the low-risk types' indifference curve through the origin intersects the high-risk types' indifference curve through their full insurance policy. (Again, I leave it to you to draw the picture. This one is little bit harder, but still not very hard.)

So which two policies are chosen? Figure 20.13(a) indicates that the pair of policies is fixed by the premium charged the high-risk types. A higher premium moves the high-risk indifference curve through the full-insurance policy down and to the right, lowering both the amount of insurance and the premium for the low-risk types. So we have a classic trade-off for the monopolist. More profit from the high-risk types per policy means less profit per policy from the low-risk types. Obviously, other things held equal, relatively more high-risk types (relative to the number of low-risk types) moves the premium for the high-risk types up (moves their contract down in the picture); relatively fewer high-risk types moves the premium down (their "dot," up). And, if there are enough high-risk types, the monopolist gives up on the low-risk types entirely, fully exploiting the high-risk types.

Here are three final questions with answers, but without explanations; Problem 20.15 asks you to explain:

1. Is it ever possible that the monopolist takes an expected loss on high-risk types? (Answer: Yes.)

2. Is it ever possible that the monopolist takes an expected loss on low-risk types? (Answer: No.)

3. Is it ever possible that the high- and low-risk types are pooled at a single policy, assuming that both types are represented in the population? The answer is No, but this one is significantly harder to show than the first two. You must rule out pooling at full insurance.

This leaves one more possibility to investigate: Suppose insurance is supplied by a monopoly insurance company subject to regulation. See Problem 20.16.

Game-theoretic versions

In this section, all analysis was conducted without ever invoking game theory. (Well, not quite true. Can you find where?) It takes a bit of invention to give game-theoretic versions of C. Wilson and Riley, but for both the profit-maximizing monopoly and perfect competition, it can be done. Throughout, consumers reacted passively to the menus of offers put forward by insurance companies, by which I mean that they took those menus as given and made their best choices from what they were offered. So in a game-theory model, we don't need a large number of players in the role of the consumers. In fact, we can get by with just one, Alice, whose type is either high- or low-risk, with probabilities that match the proportions of high- and low-risk types in a multi-consumer model. And the monopoly story can be made into a game with one insurance company, call it Bob Assurance, Inc., who places a menu of offers in front of Alice and waits to see what happens.

(You might wonder: In the case where there is probability close to one that Alice is high-risk, Bob only offers one policy, the policy that will fully exploit her if she is high risk. What, then, if he offers that policy and she says, "No thanks"? He then knows she is low risk. But the same issue arises if he offers two policies, and she shows by taking partial insurance that she is low risk. The two could certainly recontract to the benefit of each. Except that, if high-risk Alice anticipates either of these scenarios, why buy the policy that Bob intends for her in his first menu? She'll get better terms by pretending to be low-risk. This is precisely the sort of question that will be addressed in Chapter 21, so I only mention it for now.)

As for the model of "perfect competition," how many insurance companies does it take in a game to replicate the results we obtained? It takes two. More are fine, but two—say Bob Assurance and Carol Casualty—suffice. The extensive form is that Bob and Carol simultaneously and independently offer menus of policies (premia

P and payout I amounts, which can be identified as points $(x, y) = (L - I, W - P)$), and then Alice, based on her type, makes a selection. Corresponding to the "equilibrium" identified by Rothschild and Stiglitz, if it is indeed an equilibrium, is where Bob and Carol both offer both the policies in Figure 20.11. Each has a payoff of 0, and neither can do better by deviating. Unless, of course, the probability that Alice is low-risk is sufficiently close to 1. Then there is no pure-strategy equilibrium.

What about mixed-strategy equilibria? I'll leave this for you to ponder.

More than two types?

Having explored the case of two types for approximately thirteen pages, and with two more full topics left to cover in this chapter, I won't push on the extension of this analysis to more than two types. If you are interested, references are supplied at the end of the chapter.

20.8. Signaling: Spence's Job Market

Roughly contemporaneous with the Rothschild and Stigliz (1976) analysis of screening in the context of competitive insurance markets, Spence (1974) provides the seminal analysis of *signaling* in a competitive market with private information. The distinction between screening and signaling is simple: Screening involves the uninformed side of the market proposing a menu of options to the privately informed side; the informed side then employs their private information to choose from the menu provided. In contrast, signaling has each agent from the informed side taking the initiative by taking some action that reveals (or hides) her private information, after which the two sides transact.

In the context of insurance, signaling would involve each consumer who faces a loss proposing a premium and level of insurance (or payout in case of a loss) to insurance companies, which would then either accept or reject the consumer's proposal. (Or, the consumer proposes that she will accept some specific deductible, and insurance companies then bid for her business by quoting premia they would charge her.) Roughly speaking, a consumer who proposes less coverage is revealing that she has a smaller chance of a loss (or, in a two-dimensional context, is less risk averse, or both). Spence (1974) studies a different context, namely, a labor market in which each informed party—now a prospective employee—has private information about her abilities and how much profit she will generate for any firm that employs her. She signals her ability by the amount of education she obtains before entering the labor force; more able workers get more education, and firms reward more education with higher wages. The obvious question is: Why don't less able prospective employees stay in school longer to get the higher wage? The reason is that education is personally distasteful, and it is relatively more distasteful for less able individuals. So, in a separating signaling equilibrium, more able types choose a level of education that is high enough so that less able individuals settle for wages appropriate for their (low-ability) type, rather than submit themselves to the (for them) very arduous educational process.

A competitive economy with two types

To flesh out the verbal story of the previous paragraph, consider the following formal model of a competitive labor market. To facilitate comparisons with the insurance-market model, the model has two types of employee and a continuum of education levels.

- There is a population of many prospective employees. Some, labeled type A, are more productive; some, labeled type B, are less productive. The type of any individual is private information to that individual. The proportion of all prospective employees who are type A is α.

- There are many employers who compete to hire these employees. Employers offer each prospective employee a wage, and the prospective employee accepts the highest offer she receives.

- Before presenting herself to employers and asking for wage offers, each prospective employee chooses an education level $e \in [0, \bar{e}]$. When the employee presents herself to employers, the education level she selected is known to all.

- The productivity of an employee—the amount of value she provides an employer—is $\gamma_X + \beta_X e$, where $X = A$ or B, $\gamma_A > \gamma_B > 0$, and $\beta_A \geq \beta_B \geq 0$. That is, more productive (type A) employees generate more value for their employers, and while education does not lessen value and may increase it, it increases (at any fixed level) the value of type As more than that of type Bs. (In his original model, Spence assumes that $\beta_A = \beta_B = 0$; that is, education does not enhance an employee's value to employers at all.)

- Employers, observing an employee with education level e, and having had experience with employees who presented that level of education, assess the probability $\pi(e)$ that the employee is type A and that, therefore, this employee, if hired, will be worth

$$w(e) := \pi(e)[\gamma_A + \beta_A e] + [1 - \pi(e)][\gamma_B + \beta_B e].$$

For each level of e, this assessment $\pi(e)$ is unanimously held. And since employers compete "Bertrand" style, we simply assume that, given these beliefs, the employee will receive wage $w(e)$.

- Employees, in equilibrium, know what assessments employers will hold as a function of their education level e; hence they know what wage they can expect to receive as a function of e. And they choose their education level to maximize their net utility:

$$w(e) - \rho_X e^2, \quad X = A \text{ or } B, \quad 0 < \rho_A < \rho_B.$$

That is, employees like more money and dislike education, with rising marginal distaste for education. Moreover, and the key to what is coming, type-B employees dislike education more than do type-A employees.

The single-crossing property holds, where the x-variable is education and the y-variable is the wage w that employees receive. A k-level indifference curve for type-X is the set of points such that $w - \rho_X e^2 = k$, or $w = k + \rho_X e^2$, so (letting a picture substitute for simple algebra) the picture is as shown in Figure 20.14(a): Indifference curves are half-parabolas with their bottoms at $e = x = 0$ and with steeper slope for type B than for type A.

If there were no private information—if the type of each prospective employee were discernible to all employers—the competitive-wage schedules, in which employees are paid their full value to their employers, would be the two dashed lines in Figure 20.14(b). And, were this the case, an efficient and competitive arrangement would have type A workers solve the problem

$$\text{Maximize } \gamma_A + \beta_A e - \rho_A e^2 \text{ in the variable } e,$$

which gives as maximum $e_A^* := \beta_A/(2\rho_A)$ and $w_A^* := \gamma_A + \beta_A e_A^* = \gamma_A + \beta_A^2/(2\rho_A)$, with symmetric formulas for type-B employees.

And, it could work out that this efficient and competitive outcome is acheived, even with private information, if the picture is as in Figure 20.14(c). This happens when type B's utility for the type-A deal, (e_A^*, w_A^*), is worse for type B than is the type B deal, (e_B^*, w_B^*). About this outcome:

- In Spence's original treatment, with $\beta_A = \beta_B = 0$, this can never happen. Why not? (See Problem 20.17.)

- We didn't discuss on the possibility of an efficient outcome in the case of the insurance market. Is there any possibility of an efficient outcome? Is an efficient and competitive outcome possible in that context? (Also Problem 20.17)

Spence is interested in the case where efficiency is impossible. As just mentioned, efficiency is impossible when $\beta_A = \beta_B = 0$ (education does not enhance employee value), but efficiency may also be impossible, even if the two values of β are strictly positive. All that is needed is that type B's prefer A's efficient deal to her own. See Figure 20.15. What happens then? How certain is it that, when a competitive and efficient arrangement is feasible, it will happen?

Signaling equilibria in "reduced form"

Thinking of a labor market with many prospective employees and many employers, we can ask: What constitutes a competitive-market equilibrium? Consider the following definition.

Definition 20.4. *A **competitive-market equilibrium** in the context of this model consists of*

a. *two finite, non-empty lists of education levels* $E_A = \{e_A^1, e_A^2, \ldots, e_A^a\}$ *and* $E_B = \{e_B^1, e_B^2, \ldots, e_B^b\}$,

b. *an assignment of each type-A individual to one element of E^A and each type-B to one element of E^B, where ϕ_A^k is the proportion of type As assigned to e_A^k, and ϕ_B^j is the proportion of type Bs assigned to e_B^j, and*

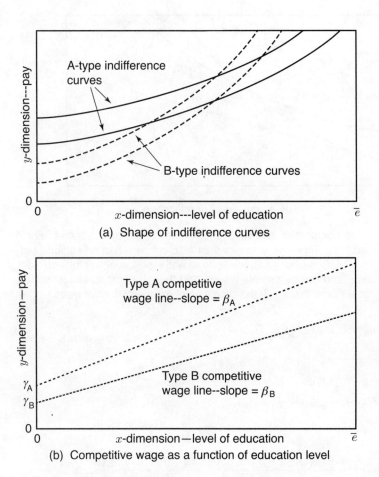

(a) Shape of indifference curves

(b) Competitive wage as a function of education level

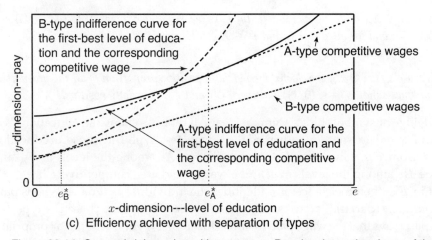

(c) Efficiency achieved with separation of types

Figure 20.14. Spence's job market with two types. Panel a shows the shape of the two types' indifference curves, panel b shows the "fair wage schedules for the two types," and panel c shows a situation in which the efficient outcome can be achieved.

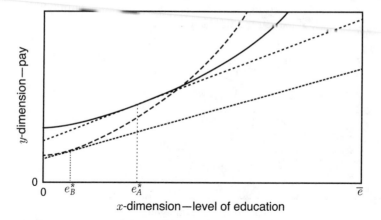

Figure 20.15. The competitive and efficient outcome cannot be sustained. For if type As are paid the competitive wage for their efficient choice of education level, e_A^*, the type Bs will choose that education level as well in preference to their efficient level of education (and commensurate wage), and then the competitive wage will have to take into account that e_A^* is the choice of all prospective employees.

c. *a wage schedule* $w : E_A \cup E_B \to R_+$,

such that

d. *if* $e \in E_A \setminus E_B$, *then* $w(e) = \gamma_A + \beta_A e$,

e. *if* $e \in E_B \setminus E_A$, *then* $w(e) = \gamma_B + \beta_B e$,

f. *if* $e \in E_A \cap E_B$, *then*

$$w(e) = \frac{\alpha \phi_A(e)(\gamma_A + \beta_A e) + (1 - \alpha)\phi_B(e)(\gamma_B + \beta_B e)}{\alpha \phi_A(e) + (1 - \alpha)\phi_B(e)}, \quad and$$

g. *for all* $e \in E_A$ *and* $e' \in E_A \cup E_B$, *type* As *weakly prefer* $(e, w(e))$ *to* $(e', w(e'))$ *and to* $(0, 0)$; *and for all* $e \in E_B$ *and* $e' \in E_A \cup E_B$, *type* Bs *weakly prefer* $(e, w(e))$ *to* $(e', w(e'))$ *and to* $(0, 0)$.

h. *Every* $e \in E_A \cup E_B$ *is selected by a strictly positive proportion of all the prospective employees; that is,* $\alpha \in (0, 1)$, *and every* ϕ_A^k *and* ϕ_B^j *is strictly positive.*

This deluge of symbols hides a simple idea. All type As choose an education level e from E_A and are subsequently paid the wage $w(e)$. Type Bs choose an education level e from E_B. Given the distribution of type As among the levels in E_A and of type Bs among the levels in E_B, the wages paid are "competitive": If $e \in E_A$ is not in E_B, then the choice of e identifies the individual as type A, who is paid appropriately (part d). Part e is similar for education levels only chosen by type Bs. And, part f says that the wage paid for any education level in $E_A \cup E_B$ is appropriate, given the average productivity of such an individual, based on equilibrium choices. Part g says that type As' choices are among the best (for them) on offer, and type Bs' choices are among the best for them. Finally, part h requires that the lists E_A

and E_B are not padded with choices that no employee takes. These are all real choices.

What this definition does not explain or consider is what wage a prospective employee, say, of type A, could expect to get from employers if she presented herself with an education level that is outside of the set $E_A \cup E_B$. For now—this will be the crux of Spence's model, so this is just "for now"—imagine that employers, having no experience with education levels outside the set $E_A \cup E_B$, simply refuse to deal with any employee who strays from "convention."

It does, however, assume that both E_A and E_B are nonempty; in equilibrium, every prospective employee finds employment at some "conventional" level of education. For now, this is an assumption; justification will come later.

The definition assumes that, in an equilibrium, there are only finitely many levels of education that are chosen. We can do better than that:

Proposition 20.5. *In a competitive-market equilibrium, there can be at most one education level in $E_A \cap E_B$. There can be at most two education levels in E_A. There can be at most two education levels in $E_B \setminus E_A$, although there can be two levels in $E_B \setminus E_A$ and, in addition, one in $E_A \cap E_B$. If $e_A \in E_A$ and $e_B \in E_B$, then $e_A \geq e_B$.*

Proof. All these assertions follow from simple pictures of the sort drawn in Figures 20.14 and 20.15. Begin with condition g: All the education levels and implied wage payment for type As must lie on a single type-A indifference curve, and similarly for type Bs. Single-crossing implies that there can be at most one pooling level of education $e \in E_A \cap E_B$, which is where the two indifference curves cross. Moreover, there can't be an education level e_A to the left of this intersection point, as it would then be strictly preferred by type Bs to contracts on their indifference curve, and (for the same reason) there can't be contracts $e \in E_B$ to the right of the intersection point.

It is worth observing that the two relevant indifference curves must intersect: If they didn't, one would be "above" the other, which would grossly violate condition g.

As for the sizes of E_A and E_B: Take E_A first. Type As' indifference curves are strictly convex. The "type-A competitive-wage line" is . . . a line. So it can only intersect the relevant type As' indifference curve in at most two places. And if both intersections occur to the right of where the two indifference curves meet, the point where the indifference curves meet carries a wage higher than the wage for type As only, so the pooling contract can't be part of the equilibrium.

As for the type Bs: Again, there can be at most two intersection points with their one equilibrium indifference curve and their competitive wage line. But even if both intersection points are to the left of the place where the two indifference curves meet, that meeting point will be above the line, which could be a part of an equilibrium.

I appreciate that I'm going through this "proof by picture" very quickly; you may need to draw the pictures to convince yourself that what I'm saying is true. Figure 20.16 gives you a head start.

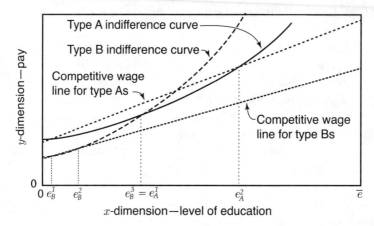

Figure 20.16. Proving Proposition 20.5. The type Bs can choose between three education levels, e_B^1, e_B^2, and e_B^3. The first two are chosen only by type Bs, so those two get the competitive wage for type Bs. Education level e_B^3 is also e_A^1, so it gets a wage that is a convex combination of the competitive wages for the two types. As the figure is drawn, it seems that a bit more than half of the employees presenting this wage level are type As, so the wage is a bit closer to the type-A competitive wage. And some type As take e_A^2, earning the competitive wage for that type alone.

A game-theoretic version of this model

To shed further light on this model, it helps to turn the model into a noncooperative game and think in terms of the different game-theoretic equilibrium concepts discussed in Appendices 10 (Nash), 11 (subgame perfect), 12 (with off-path beliefs and sequential rationality, leading to sequential equilibria), and 14 (with "intuitive" restrictions on off-path beliefs). Do not think that "shed light" equals "dispositively answer." After analyzing the general situation as a game, one still must decide (subjectively) whether game-theoretic equilibrium analysis is appropriate for even this caricature of a labor market.

- In the game-theory version of the Spence's job market, three players are enough. Alice is the prospective employee, who is either type A or type B. Bob and Carol represent firms that may seek to hire Alice after she chooses her level of education. Alice's type is private information to her; Bob and Carol share a subjective assessment that Alice is type A with probability α.

- The game is in extensive form. Alice chooses a level of education e from $[0, \bar{e}]$ as the first move. Bob and Carol observe Alice's choice, and simultaneously and independently bid for Alice's services by proposing wages w_{Bob} and w_{Carol} that they are willing pay her. They also have the option of saying "Sorry Alice, but I'm not interested in hiring you." Alice considers the two offers (assuming she gets two), and if one is higher than the other, she accepts it. If they are equal, she can choose either Bob or Carol to be her employer.

- Payoffs: For Alice, $\max\{w_{\text{Bob}}, w_{\text{Carol}}\} - \rho_X e^2$, where $X = A, B$ and refers to

Alice's type. (If both Bob and Carol pass on hiring Alice, her payoff is $-\rho_X e^2$.)
For Bob: If he does not hire Alice, 0. If he does, and if she is type X, $\gamma_X + \beta_X e - w_{\text{Bob}}$, for $X = A, B$. Carol's payoffs are symmetric with those of Bob.

This description of the extensive form contains a bit of a cheat. (Did you recognize it?) I said "Alice considers the two offers (assuming she gets two), and if one is higher than the other, she accepts it. If they are equal, she can choose either Bob or Carol to be her employer." That sounds like a choice made (in equilibrium) by Alice. An honest description of an extensive-form game would say instead, "Finally, Alice can choose to accept or reject any offers made, although she can only accept one offer." And then, we'd discuss in the analysis what would be equilibrium behavior for Alice in this position.[21]

On this point (although it may not seem to be on point, at first), consider the questions: Does this game (with Alice having the final choice) contain any proper subgames? Does subgame perfection add anything beyond simple Nash? (You must have the material in Appendices 10 and 11 front of mind for this discussion.)

- At the start of the game, nature chooses whether Alice is type A or B. If we depict this as a single node with nature moving, it is the root of a proper subgame; if we depict is as two initial nodes, technically, it is not. But in defining subgame perfection, we "fixed" this minor definitional glitch, by insisting that a subgame-perfect Nash equilibrium must first of all be Nash for the entire game. Either way, subgame perfection at this point adds nothing to simple Nash.

- Next comes Alice's choice of education at one of two information sets (her type). These are singleton-node information sets, but neither is the root of a proper subgame, because what follows for Bob and Carol are information sets that cross between the successors of these two nodes. So subgame perfection won't add anything here.

- Next are the bids of Bob and of Carol. Since they don't know Alice's type—they speculate about it, but they don't know it—no proper subgames can be found here. Again, subgame perfection adds nothing.

- And, finally, we come to Alice's decision. Alice knows everything that has happened: She knows her type, she knows which education level she chose, and she knows the two wage offers from Bob and Carol. So, from each of these single-node information sets to payoffs—a single step—does constitute a proper subgame. Subgame perfection at this stage adds: "Alice considers the two offers (assuming she gets two), and if one is higher than the other, she accepts it. If they are equal, she can choose either Bob or Carol to be her employer."

So, to bring this back to my cheat: I'm implicitly invoking subgame perfection at this final move. And, as long as I'm careful to restrict discussion to subgame-perfect

---

[21] I could formulate the extensive-form so that Alice must accept the higher of her two offers—it is the only move available to her—and if the two offers are equal, she must choose one or the other. This—designing the game so that desired behavior is a player's only option—is a cheat of a different sort, and one that reappears in Chapter 22.

Nash equilibria in what follows, my cheat is harmless.

Proposition 20.6. *Corresponding to every competitive-market equilibrium*

$$\{E_A, E_B, \{\phi_A^k; k = 1, \ldots, a\}, \{\phi_B^j; j = 1, \ldots, b\}, w\}$$

is a subgame-perfect Nash equilibrium of the extensive-form game in which

a. *Alice, if type A, behaviorally mixes over the choices of education level $e \in E_A$, choosing e_A^k with probability ϕ_A^k;*

b. *Alice, if type B, behaviorally mixes over the choices of education level $e \in E_B$, choosing e_B^j with probability ϕ_B^j;*

c. *Bob and Carol both bid $w(e)$ if Alice presents any education level $e \in E_A \cup E_B$;*

d. *Bob and Carol both say, "no thank you," if Alice presents an education level $e \notin E_A \cup E_B$; and*

e. *Alice accepts the highest offer she receives, if she receives any at all, choosing to work for Bob if she gets two identical offers (or otherwise picks one of the two).*

And, corresponding to every subgame-perfect Nash equilibrium outcome of the extensive-form game is a corresponding competitive-market equilibrium (with what I expect is the obvious translation).

The proof is entirely straightforward, except, perhaps, on one point. I assumed in the definition of a competitive-market equilibrium that both E_A and E_B are nonempty; there is at least one conventional education level for each type. Why does this happen "for free" in subgame-perfect equilibria?

The reason is buried in the extensive form. Alice of either type must choose an education level; she doesn't have an "opt out" option. So, in any strategy, there will be on-path education level choices by Alice, at least one if she is type A and at least one if she is type B. Observing those education levels is on-path for Bob and Carol, so, in any equilibrium, they must hold correct assessments (determined by Alice's strategy) concerning which type of Alice they face. And then Bertrand-style competition for Alice's services take over: In any equilibrium, they must offer Alice the competitive-market wage, given those equilibrium beliefs, and given Alice's strategy. Bob, for instance, can't say "no thank you" to any on-path education choice by Alice: If he did, Carol's better response to this would be to offer Alice a wage of $0.01, which Alice would be obligated to take, which would induce Bob to offer $0.02, and so forth. On-path choices of e by Alice must generate competitive-wage responses in a subgame-perfect equilibrium.

Sequentially rational wage offers for off-path education levels and sequential equilibria

However, off-path choices of education level in a subgame-perfect Nash equilibrium can generate the response "No thanks" from both Bob and Carol, because they are off-path. And that response by Bob and Carol keeps Alice from choosing them.

Suppose, though, that Alice presents herself for employment with off-path education level e. Bob and Carol are, essentially, looking at a situation where they know e but don't know Alice's type. (If we put Bob's choice of action—a wage offer or "no thanks"—first, his information set contains just two nodes. Carol's information set will contain many more, because she doesn't know what Bob has "done." But, her strategic problem is the same as his.)

In the spirit of sequential rationality, we imagine that Bob attaches beliefs to the two nodes in his information set: Given this unexpected education choice e, Alice is type A with probability $\pi(e)$. If he offers her a wage of $w(e; \pi) = \pi(e)(\gamma_A + \beta_A e) + (1 - \pi(e))(\gamma_B + \beta_B e) - \epsilon$ and it is accepted, he is ahead by ϵ in expectation. This conditionally weakly dominates saying "no thanks." At a minimum, he should offer $\gamma_B + \beta_B e - \epsilon$, which is what Alice is worth, if he believes that she must be type B. She can't possibly be worth less.

And, if we go all the way from subgame-perfection to sequential equilibrium, Bob and Carol must have the same off-path beliefs about Alice's type, from which point, in any sequential equilibrium, Bertrand competition between them pushes their wage offers all the way up to $w(e; \pi) = \pi(e)(\gamma_A + \beta_A e) + (1 - \pi(e))(\gamma_B + \beta_B e)$. We have:

Proposition 20.7. *In any sequential equilibrium of this game, Bob and Carol must submit identical bids in the face of any education choice by Alice (on- or off-path), and the least bid they can submit facing education level e is $\gamma_B + \beta_B e$.*

Corollary 20.8. *Recall that $e_B^* = \beta_B/(2\rho_B)$ is the first-best education level for type B Alice, which provides her with wage $\gamma_B + \beta_B^2/(2\rho_B)$ if she is known to be of type B. At this level of education and wage, her net utility is*

$$\gamma_B + \frac{\beta_B^2}{2\rho_B} - \rho_B \left(\frac{\beta_b}{2\rho_B} \right)^2 = \gamma_B + \frac{\beta_B^2}{4\rho_B}.$$

Hence, in any sequential equilibrium, type-B Alice must have a payoff of at least this much. And in any sequential equilibrium where, along the path of play, type-B Alice chooses an education level $e \in E_B \setminus E_A$ with positive probability—in words, she separates herself from type-A Alice with positive probability—that level must be e_B^* and e_B^* only. (We can construct a lower bound on the payoff for type-A Alice, as well, but it isn't as interesting.)

This corollary follows, because type-B Alice can always "defect" to the education choice e_B^* and is assured of this payoff. In a sequential equilibrium, she must do at least this well.

This lowers the number of possible equilibria. For instance, in the equilibrium depicted in Figure 20.16, although it is a bit hard to see, type-B Alice is sitting on an indifference curve lower than the one that the corollary guarantees. Hence, Figure 20.16 depicts an outcome that is not the outcome of a sequential equilibrium.

Still, there are a lot of possible equilibria. Indeed, there are a lot of possible equilibria even if we add to the requirement that we have sequential equilibrium a further requirement that the beliefs of Bob and Carol that Alice is type-A are a nondecreasing function of the (off-path) education level she presents.

Figure 20.17 provides a few examples. Panel a depicts a fully separating equilibrium in which type-B Alice chooses e_B^*, and type-A Alice chooses a very inefficient (for her) education level e_A. The very heavy line describes the wage function $e \to w(e)$, which, in this case, involves beliefs that satisfy the condition that the probability that Alice is type A is nondecreasing in the education level.

Panel b is a pure pooling equilibrium, where both types choose $e_{A\&B}$. This puts type-B Alice on a higher indifference curve than e_B^* would give her (if she separated at that level); it is a bit hard to see, but it puts Bob at on a lower indifference curve than he could attain in the first-best arrangement, which is also a sequential-equilibrium outcome. Because $e \to w(e)$ is flat over the interval $[e_{A\&B}, e_A^*]$, this wage offer does not meet the extra condition.

Panel c depicts an equilibrium where both types separate with positive probability and pool with positive probability. Although it isn't obvious, this equilibrium is consistent with the extra condition.

At this point, I hope the problem is clear: With only two types and uncountably many possible education levels, Proposition 20.5, adapted to the game-theoretic version of the problem, proves that most education choices will be off path. And, while it helps a bit to insist that off-path wage offers are derived from off-path beliefs and to insist that those beliefs are commonly held and even monotonic in e (in the sense above), this still gives a huge amount of freedom for choosing beliefs that support equilibria. Compare with screening: If the uninformed party sets the possible terms of trade, we do have to worry how the informed party would react to some off-path offer not in the equilibrium menu. Because the off-path offer comes from the uninformed party, the other side doesn't have "beliefs" to play with; each type of the informed party can simply and directly evaluate every offer in any menu. In contrast, with signaling, when an off-path signal is sent, the other (uninformed) side must wonder: Which type sent it? Hence, Rothschild and Stiglitz find at most one equilibrium, and maybe none. In contrast, Spence finds a multitude of possible equilibria. And it isn't the difference in context. It is relatively straightforward to adapt the Rothschild and Stiglitz (1976) analysis to Spence's job market and to adopt the Spence (1974) analysis to the insurance market of Rothschild and Stiglitz; see Problems 20.19 and 20.20

The intuitive criterion

The so-called *intuitive criterion* (Cho and Kreps 1987) "solves" the problem of too-many possible off-path beliefs. Or, rather, an analysis in the spirit of the intuitive criterion works: The formal intuitive criterion, discussed in Appendix 14, Section A14.5, is defined for signaling games, games with a single signal sender (like Alice) but only one receiver, unlike the situation here. And the formal definition, as well as its connection to strategic stability (Kohlberg and Mertens 1986, also discussed in Appendix 14) is limited to finite games. But the intuitive part of the intuitive criterion translates very easily to this context.

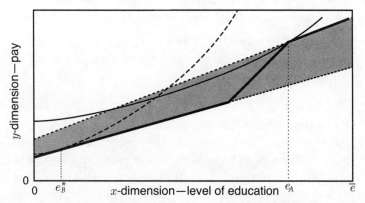

(a) A separating equilibrium that has type A choosing an inefficient level of education

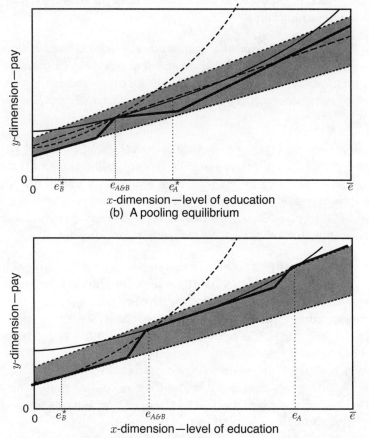

(b) A pooling equilibrium

(c) A mess: A mixed separating and pooling equilibrium for both types

Figure 20.17. Sequential equilibrium rules out some scenarios, but a lot of bad stuff can still occur. Sequential rationality (and common beliefs) means that wage offers, both on-path and off-path, must lie in the shaded regions. In each panel, the heavy zigzag is the wage function $w(e)$ that supports the outcome. See text for details.

Definition 20.9. *In the context of this game, an equilibrium is said to violate the intuitive criterion if there is an off-path education choice e such that*

a. *even if the off-path beliefs at e were that Alice is type A (in this context, the beliefs that provide the highest "reasonable" wage for education level e), type-B Alice would not choose e in preference to her equilibrium choices, and*

b. *if off-path beliefs at e were that Alice is type A, type-A Alice would defect to e.*

In other words, to sustain an equilibrium in which type-A Alice does not choose e, Bob and Carol must assess positive probability that e, were it chosen, would be chosen by type-B Alice, even though type-B Alice would never choose e in preference to her equilibrium payoff. The intuition here is that since type-B Alice would rather stick to the equilibrium than defect to e, even if type-A wages were offered at e, while type-A Alice would defect if Bob and Carol would interpret this as coming from type A, Bob and Carol should infer that e comes from type-A Alice, upsetting the equilibrium.

Proposition 20.10. *The only sequential equilibrium outcome that does not violate the intuitive criterion is the separating equilibrium in which type-B Alice chooses e_B^* (and is rewarded with wage w_B^*) and type-A Alice chooses the education level e, getting wage $\gamma_A + \beta_A e$, which maximizes her payoff subject to the condition that type-B Alice weakly prefers (e_B^*, w_B^*) to $(e, \gamma_A + \beta_A e)$.*

This is the Riley outcome: (1) If type-B Alice prefers (e_B^*, w_B^*) to (e_A^*, w_A^*), then the outcome is the competitive efficient outcome (Figure 20.18(a)). But (2) if type-B Alice strictly prefers (e_A^*, w_A^*) to (e_B^*, w_B^*), then type-A Alice picks the education level where type B's indifference curve intersects the competitive-wage line for type A (Figure 20.18(b)). That is, in case 2, type-A Alice chooses the smallest amount of education that keeps type-B Alice from mimicking her.

Proof. There are two steps in the proof. The first step is to prove that any equilibrium that involves pooling the two types violates the intuitive criterion. Follow along on Figure 20.19(a). Suppose we have a pool at the point marked $e_{A\&B}$. Follow the two type's indifference curves through this point up to where they hit the competitive-wage-for-type-A line. By single-crossing, the indifference curve for type-B hits first. And then, consider the education level labeled e. This must be an off-path education level, because if it were on-path, it must be from type A (all of type-B's other-than-$e_{A\&B}$ education choices fall below the one pooling point) and so lead to the wage-and-education point marked by the open dot. But this lies above A's indifference curve through $e_{A\&B}$, so it cannot be on-path.

   We can sustain that this education level is off path with beliefs by Bob and Carol that lead them to a wage offer along the heavier part of the dashed line at e. But these all involve positive probability of e coming from type B. And, per the intuitive criterion, since type B cannot do better with e than her equilibrium payoff, even if Bob and Carol assess probability one that it is type A, while type-A Alice can do better, it must be that Bob and Carol hold off-path beliefs that this comes

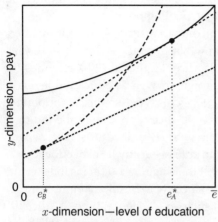

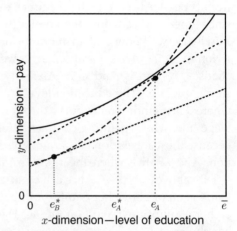

(a) When type Bs prefer their first-best contract to the first-best for type As

(b) When type Bs prefer type As' first-best contract to their own first-best

Figure 20.18. The two cases of the "Riley outcome," the only outcome in the signaling game that survives the intuitive criterion. In each case, we have separation, with type B getting her competitive-wage, efficient outcome, and type A getting the best deal she can, subject to separating from type B.

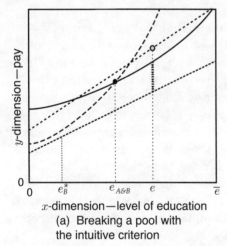

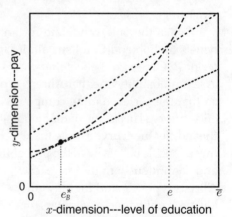

(a) Breaking a pool with the intuitive criterion

(b) In any equilibrium outcome that survives the intuitive criterion, type-A Alice must get her competitive-wage if she chooses an education level strictly to the left of e, as long as it improves on her equilibrium payoff.

Figure 20.19. Proving that the only equilibrium outcome that survives the intuitive criterion is the Riley outcome from Figure 20.17. Panel a shows why pooling is impossible. Panel b shows why, in a separating equilibrium, type-A Alice gets her competitive-efficient outcome, if this separates her from type-B Alice, and she gets the deal shown in Figure 20.17(b) if not. See text for details.

from type-A Alice. Which, of course, destroys the alleged equilibrium outcome, since type-A Alice would then prefer this to the pooling point.

Hence, we know that any equilibrium outcome that survives the intuitive criterion must involve separation. And we know that this means that type-B Alice chooses e_B^* and is paid w_B^*. As for type-A Alice, Figure 20.19(b) provides the simple picture. The education level e_B^* is shown, as well as education levels e, where Alice's indifference curve through (e_B^*, w_B^*) cuts type-A Alice's competitive wage line. The separating contract(s) for type-A Alice cannot be to the left of e, because those levels don't separate type A from type B, and we must have separation. And—here is where the intuitive criterion enters—at any level of education e' strictly above e, type-A Alice can be sure to get the wage $\gamma_A + \beta_A e'$ (as long as that value is on or above her equilibrium payoff), since type-B Alice cannot improve on her equilibrium payoff (at (e_B^*, w_B^*)) with such an e'. Hence, type-A Alice has her choice of $(e', \gamma_A + \beta_A e')$, for any $e' > e$. If $e_A^* > e$, then of course that's what she'll choose, which is Figure 20.18(a). And if $e_A^* \leq e$, then (because of the concave nature of indifference curves) type-A Alice's payoff declines the larger is her choice of education level, past e_A^*. Hence, no choice $e' > e$ is optimal; she'd do better with $(e' + e)/2$. This leaves as the only candidate for an equilibrium having type-A Alice choose e and, importantly, type-B Alice, who is indifferent between (e_B^*, w_B^*) and $(e, \gamma_A + \beta_A e)$, choose (e_B^*, w_B^*).[22] We must verify that this outcome is better for type-A Alice than the point (e_B^*, w_B^*), but that is an immediate consequence of strict single crossing.

This is the only candidate for an equilibrium, but is it one? What off-path beliefs by Bob and Carol sustain it (and do those beliefs violate the intuitive criterion)? One set of beliefs that works is: For off-path $e \in [0, e_B^*)$, Bob and Carol assess probability one that Alice is type B. For off-path $e \in (e_B^*, e)$, choose beliefs so that the corresponding competitive wages ride along type-B Alice's indifference curve. (This is one of many possible choices; just be sure to go no higher than the indifference curve.) Note that, because Alice's indifference curves are concave, these specific beliefs have the probability that Alice is type A rising monotonically and continuously until e is reached, at which point, they prescribe certainty that Alice is type A. And for off-path $e \in [e, \bar{e}]$, believe that any such off-path choice has probability one of coming from type-A Alice.[23] It is easy to verify that, with these specific off-path beliefs, we do have an equilibrium with no violations of the intuitive criterion.   ∎

---

[22] If this stipulation bothers you, imagine that there are only finitely many possible education levels. Then, except in the "coincidental" case that type-B Alice's indifference curve through her most preferred compeitive-wage-for-her education level hits the competitive-wage-for-type-A line at exactly one of the possible education levels, e_A^{**} would be the first feasible education level past the intersection point, and the intuitive criterion would apply to it directly.

[23] Remember, e may be on-path, if $e_A^* \leq e$, and it may be off-path, if $e_A^* > e$.

Many Alices and many insurance companies or employers or . . .

Does the game-theoretic analysis just completed, concerning a single prospective employee seeking wage offers, with two competing companies and using equilibrium concepts from game theory, shed light on labor markets with many prospective employees and many employers? While admitting my prejudice in the matter (I'm co-inventor of the intuitive criterion), I think so, but with a caveat: I have doubts about the relevance of signaling as opposed to screening for most labor markets.

To begin with the caveat: An insurance company, approached by a potential client who wishes to suggest a nonstandard sort of policy in terms of coverage, is likely to react with "I don't know what you are about, and I have no time to figure it out." Screening, rather than signaling, is the more appropriate way to envision the interaction. At the other end of this spectrum might be a private (non-dealership) sale of a used car. The uninformed buyer of a specific used car is much more likely to listen to representations of the owner of the car, such as, "This car is a peach, and to prove to you that it is, I'm willing to give you a three-month warranty on any hidden defects you may find." Or think of an entrepreneur who indicates to venture capitalists the quality of her venture by being willing to agree to onerous covenants in case the venture runs into cash-flow difficulties.

Spence chose labor markets and education as his context for investigating signaling, so that's what I've done here. But is signaling, rather than screening, appropriate? Labor markets, I think, can fall on either side. An employer of many blue-collar workers might treat high-school dropouts differently from high-school graduates, and those differently from candidates who complete a reputable trade school. A prospective employee who says, "I'm not just any drop-out. I finished three and one-half years of high school," is likely to be treated as just another dropout. At this level, screening by employers seems the more appropriate paradigm. In contrast, candidates for unique and specific positions in an organization typically have the opportunity to signal their quality. It may be fanciful, but imagine a young tenured professor at one department who wishes to move up to a more highly ranked department and, confident of her quality, tells prospective employers, "Wait on giving me tenure. I'm confident I'll re-earn it." Or think of a professional athlete whose agent tells teams, "My client is willing to give up guaranteed money for performance bonuses."[24]

All that said, in a context where signaling is deemed appropriate, I assert that larger numbers work in favor off-path belief restrictions like the intuitive criterion. In a specific labor market, there may be "standard practice" for these transactions. But with many informed types sending signals, if the standard terms can be upset by an offer that enlists the intuitive criterion, having more informed types increases the odds that one is likely to recognize this and, perhaps supported by an explanation of what she is doing and why,[25] upset the previous standard terms. And, then, this sort of "nonstandard" offer may spread by imitation, upsetting what was previously standard practice.

---

[24] In the case of performance bonuses, there is also an incentive story that can be told.

[25] See Section 20.9 on cheap talk

. . . more than two types

What if there are more than two types? Suppose there are three, types AA, A, and B, with type AA being better than type A in terms of productivity ($\gamma_{AA} > \gamma_A$ and $\beta_{AA} \geq \beta_A$) and less averse to education ($\rho_{AA} < \rho_A$). In the spirit of what we obtained with two types, consider as the sole reasonable equilibrium the following:

- Type B gets her competitive efficient deal, (e_B^*, w_B^*).

- If type B prefers (e_B^*, w_B^*) to (e_A^*, w_A^*), then type A gets (e_A^*, w_A^*). But if type B strictly prefers (e_A^*, w_A^*) to (e_B^*, w_B^*), type A gets the education level (and wage appropriate to that education level) found where the type-B indifference curve through (e_B^*, w_B^*) hits the competitive wage line for type A.

- And, then, we give type AA the best (for her) deal that we can, subject to the constraint that type A weakly prefers her "deal" (described in the previous bullet point) to the deal crafted for type AA.

Figure 20.20 provides a picture in which type B restricts what type A can have, and then type A restricts type AA.

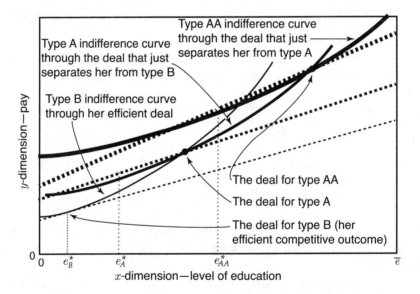

Figure 20.20. The second-best separating equilibrium. With three types, type B gets her efficient competitive deal, type A gets the best deal for her that separates her from type B, and type AA gets the best deal for her that separates her from type A. The three dashed lines are the three type-productivity lines, with heavier lines for more productive types.

This might be called the "second-best" separating arrangement; the first-best would be where each type gets her efficient and competitive deal; this is second-best because it recognizes the constraints imposed by the need to separate types. Note carefully, however, that a social planner would not necessarily see a need to separate types. If, for instance, the overall average productivity line coincides with (or is close to) the productivity line for type A, then it is pretty clear from the picture that types B and A would prefer to be part of a grand pool with type AA. But, type AA would not be happy with such an arrangement. Would the intuitive criterion permit her (type AA) to break out of such a pool? Yes. Does the intuitive criterion, applied in general to models with three or more types, give (only) this second-best separating equilibrium? In particular, does the intuitive criterion allow type A to break out of the pool shown in Figure 20.21?

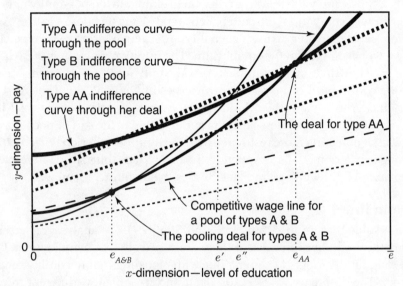

Figure 20.21. The intuitive criterion does not allow type A to separate from B.

It doesn't. Follow along on Figure 20.21. Suppose that the situation is such that B and A pool at the point $e_{A\&B}$, while AA gets separated at e_{AA}. A wage-offer function for off-path education choices that sustains this is:

- Up to $e_{A\&B}$, wages ride along the competitive wage line for type B, justified by off-path beliefs that any choice of education level below $e_{A\&B}$ must come from type B.

- Then, at $e_{A\&B}$, which is on path, beliefs are that it isn't type AA, but is the beliefs obtained from the prior by (only) ruling out type AA.

- From $e_{A\&B}$ to the point where A's indifference curve meets A's competitive wage line, which is education level e', beliefs mix between types B and A in proportions that give a wage that just rides along A's indifference curve. And from that point until e_{AA}, beliefs are that it must be type A, so wages ride along her competitive wage line.

- Then, at e_{AA}, we have the on-path belief that it must be type AA, and for all larger e, that belief is maintained.

Type A would like to break this pool. If she could choose an education level above $e_{A\&B}$ but below e' *and if this choice convinced the insurance companies that it could not* *be a type B who has chosen it, so that this education level would command a wage on or above type A's competitive wage line,* that would break the pool. But the intuitive criterion says that off-path choice e can only be ruled out as coming from type B if there is no conceivable way that B could benefit by its choice. And up to education level e'', if the insurance companies inferred that it must come from type AA, they would pay a wage that would make such a choice an equilibrium-value beater for B. (Note that type AA would also choose such an education level, if it led to this inference). So, to apply the intuitive criterion to eliminate the possibility of type B in the insurance companies' off-path beliefs, type A must choose $e > e''$. And at education levels e greater than e'', even if type A were inferred to by type A, she would be worse off than in the equilibrium. The intuitive criterion is of no help.

One can show that, with multiple types, the only intuitive-criterion-satisfying separating equilibrium is the one constructed as in Figure 20.20: The worst type gets its efficient deal, and then, inductively, each type gets the best deal it can while separating itself from less able types. But, to break the sort of pool shown in Figure 20.21, something more restrictive than the intuitive criterion is needed. That something is criterion D1—see Appendix 14, page 630ff—but, since I'm somewhat skeptical about D1, I won't go into details. See the literature, if you wish.

A bottom line

It is remarkable that, in the Rothschild and Stiglitz (1976) analysis of screening, no competitive equilibrium exists if there are relatively too many low-risk types. But, in roughly the identical context but with signaling, many equilibria can be produced. The difference isn't because insurance is somehow different from education; insurance can be modeled with signaling, and education with screening (Problems 20.19 and 20.20). And, this difference remains. So, what accounts for the difference?

Go back to the Rothschild–Stiglitz argument for why, when there are relatively many low-risk types, the Riley equilibrium is upset by a pooling contract. The insurance company that proposes this pooling contract can be sure how customers of each type will respond; their responses are fixed by "subgame perfection." The pooling contract is better for both types than their Riley-equilibrium contracts, so it is certain that they will accept in proportions that match the prior proportions.

But in a signaling model, the same "deviation" involves a customer proposing the off-path policy to insurance companies. Because the off-path policy is better for both types of customer than the two types' equilibrium outcomes, the insurance companies' off-path beliefs *might* match the prior proportions/probabilities of the two types. If this is so, then the separating equilibrium does indeed die. But— and this is the point—in a signaling model, when faced with an off-path proposal, the beliefs of the uninformed parties are not fixed. Criteria such as the intuitive criterion can and do restrict off-path beliefs. But no recognized criterion in the literature forces the insurance companies' beliefs faced with this off-path proposal. And with off-path beliefs, for instance, that the deviator is very likely to be high risk, the alleged equilibrium-breaking pooling contract doesn't break the equilibrium.

20.9. Cheap Talk

In signaling, the signal being sent is costly to the informed sender, and differentially so depending on the sender's type (or information). In screening, the different reactions by the informed party to the menu of options with which they are presented are based on differences in their "private information," which I've stretched to include differences in personal tastes. In both cases, it is not simply differences in what the informed parties know that distinguishes different types of informed party, but that acting on what they know affects different types differently.

But what about signals—and here I have in mind signals that literally are messages—that are costless for any sender to send? These are called *cheap-talk* messages, as in "talk is cheap." Is there any scope in economic contexts for useful cheap talk?

To keep the story as simple as possible, I limit discussion to the following interaction between Alice and Bob. Alice observes a state of nature $\theta \in \Theta$. She then sends a message m to Bob. Bob, on hearing m, takes an action $a \in A$, based on his prior π over Θ and the information contained in Alice's message. This ends the encounter: Alice's payoff is $U_{\text{Alice}}(a, \theta)$, and Bob's is $U_{\text{Bob}}(a, \theta)$. Because m does not appear in either player's payoff, the message is cheap talk.

What are the possible messages? In a formal model, what determines the set M from which a message m may be drawn? Think of this as being determined endogenously as part of an equilibrium: Alice and Bob, in a cheap-talk equilibrium, have established a vocabulary that each party understands.

It should be evident that, in some situations, mutually beneficial cheap talk can exist. To take the extreme case, suppose that Alice and Bob's interests are perfectly aligned: $U_{\text{Alice}} \equiv U_{\text{Bob}}$. Then, to the extent that Bob's (and Alice's) "best" choice of a depends on θ, Alice and Bob are better off if she can report to him which value of θ she observes.

And there are cases in which cheap talk has no role to play. For instance, suppose Alice and Bob have strictly opposing interests. Specifically, suppose that $U_{\text{Alice}}(\theta, a) + U_{\text{Bob}}(\theta, a) = \ell(\theta)$ for all $a \in A$. Then, one can show, in any cheap-talk equilibrium (a creature I have yet to define), Bob ignores whatever message m Alice might send. (I formalize this assertion in Proposition 20.12 later in this section; its proof can be found in the *Online Supplement*.)

The interesting cases are intermediate, where Alice's and Bob's interests are not perfectly aligned, but they do have some interest in common.

An example from Crawford and Sobel (1982)

The seminal paper on the theory of cheap talk is Crawford and Sobel (1982). They present a fairly general analysis of the problem, but also provide the following simple example, which illustrates the most important of their conclusions.

The state of nature θ is uniformly distributed on $[0, 1] = \Theta$. (This prior assessment is held in common by both Alice and Bob.) Bob's set of possible actions is $A = R$, and his utility function is $U_{\text{Bob}}(a, \theta) = -(a - \theta)^2$. Alice, in contrast, has $U_{\text{Alice}}(a, \theta) = -(a - \theta - c)^2$ for $c \neq 0$. So, given θ, Alice wants Bob to choose $\theta + c$, while Bob wants to choose θ.

Think of $c = 0.1$. With no cheap-talk from Alice, Bob will choose $a = 1/2$. So if θ is close to 0, Alice and Bob have a common interest in having Bob choose something between θ and $0.1 + \theta$. Their interests are not aligned perfectly, but Alice would rather have Bob choose θ (for θ close to 0) than $1/2$. So perhaps there is room for cheap talk. It can't be fully revealing and be believable: Suppose Alice says to Bob, "I'm going to tell you the value of θ precisely and honestly," and then reports $\theta = 0.2$. If Bob believed this, he would pick $a = 0.2$. But then Alice would make this report when $\theta = 0.1$.

Here is the definition of an equilibrium:

Definition 20.11. *A finite-vocabulary, pure-strategy, cheap-talk equilibrium con-sists of*

a. *A finite set M of messages*

b. *a reporting strategy for Alice, which is a (measurable) function μ from $\Theta \to M$, such that, for each $m \in M$, $\pi(\{\theta \in \Theta : \mu(\theta) = m\}) > 0$; and*

c. *a reaction strategy for Bob, which is a function α from $M \to A$;*

all such that

d. *Bob takes the correct inference from the m he hears and chooses a optimally from his perspective: $\alpha(m)$ maximizes $\mathbf{E}[U_{\text{Bob}}(a, \theta)|m]$, where $\mathbf{E}[\cdot|m]$ is the conditional expectation of θ given $\theta \in \{\theta' \in \Theta : \mu(\theta') = m\}$; and*

e. *for each θ, $\mu(\theta) = m = \arg \max_{m' \in M} U_{\text{Alice}}(\alpha(m'), \theta)$. That is, given how Bob will act, Alice wishes to report truthfully (to the extent that the vocabulary M permits this) what she has learned.*

In this definition, I use the general notation U_{Alice} and U_{Bob} for Alice's and Bob's utility functions, so that this definition will serve for more than this example. And, in part b, I assume that every message $m \in M$ is chosen with positive probability so that, as long as Alice's reporting strategy α is measurable, Bob has no problem forming conditional expectations.

For instance, in the example: Suppose $c = 0.1$, $M = \{\text{Big } \theta, \text{Small } \theta\}$ (or Big and Small), and Alice's strategy is

$$m(\theta) = \begin{cases} \text{"Small } \theta\text{"}, & \text{if } \theta \le 1/2, \text{ and} \\ \text{"Big } \theta\text{"}, & \text{if } \theta > 1/2. \end{cases}$$

If this is Alice's reporting strategy, Bob's optimal reaction strategy is to choose $a = 1/4$ if Alice reports Small and $a = 3/4$ if Alice reports Big. And, if that's how Bob will respond, then when (say) $\theta = 0.49$, Alice will net $-(0.25 - 0.49 - 0.1)^2 = -0.54^2$ by reporting Small and $-(0.75 - 0.49 - 0.1)^2 = -0.16^2$ by reporting Big. Big is the better response, but Small is what Alice is supposed to report. So, this isn't an equilibrium.

What is an equilibrium? Suppose Alice reports Small when $\theta \in [0, \theta^*]$ and Big when $\theta \in (\theta^*, 1]$. Bob's best response to this is to choose $\theta^*/2$ if Alice reports Small and $(1 + \theta^*)/2$ if she reports Big. Suppose the true state is θ. Alice's payoff is either $-(\theta^*/2 - \theta - 0.1)^2$ if she reports Small, or $-((1 + \theta^*)/2 - \theta - 0.1)^2$ if she reports Big. The better of the two for Alice depends on whether θ is closer to $\theta^*/2 - 0.1$ or to $(1 + \theta^*)/2 - 0.1 = \theta^*/2 + 0.4$. For low values of θ, she is closer to the former; for larger values of θ, she is closer to the latter, and she is just indifferent when she is midway between the two, which is at $\theta^*/2 + 0.15$. So for her to follow the rule, it must be that $\theta^*/2 + 0.15 = \theta^*$, or $\theta^* = 0.3$. This is an equilibrium; call it a *two-partition* equilibrium.

To be clear, Alice reports "Small θ" if $\theta < 0.3$ and "Big θ" if $\theta > 0.3$", and either one when $\theta = 0.3$. Bob responds with 0.15 when he hears "Small," with 0.65 when he hears "Big." And, with those responses, Alice's optimal reporting strategy is as specified.

There is at least one more equilibrium, namely, the "uninformative" equilibrium, in which Bob disregards anything that Alice might say; in the simplest formalization of this equilibrium, M is singleton. Can there be other, more informative equilibria? How about an equilibrium in which Alice reports Small if $\theta \in [0, \theta^*)$, Medium if $\theta \in [\theta^*, \theta^{**})$, and Large if $\theta \in [\theta^{**}, 1]$? If there is, because θ has a uniform distribution, Bob's reaction rule will be

$$\alpha(\text{message}) = \begin{cases} \theta^*/2, & \text{if the message is Small,} \\ (\theta^* + \theta^{**})/2, & \text{if the message is Medium, and} \\ (1 + \theta^{**})/2, & \text{if the message is Large.} \end{cases}$$

Is this an equilibrium? When is this an equilibrium? Go back to the case of a general c. The conditions for an equilibrium are that, when $\theta = \theta^*$, Alice is indifferent between reporting Small and Medium, and when $\theta = \theta^{**}$, Alice is indifferent between reporting Medium and Large. (The monotonicity in this problem implies that, if Alice is indifferent at the endpoints of the various intervals, then she optimally reports the truth within each interval. I'll leave it to you to provide the argument that this is so.)

- When $\theta = \theta^*$, Alice is indifferent between sending Small and sending Medium if θ^* is halfway between $\theta^*/2 - c$ and $(\theta^* + \theta^{**})/2 - c$, or $\theta^* = \theta^*/2 + \theta^{**}/4 - c$.

- When $\theta = \theta^{**}$, Alice is indifferent between sending Medium and sending Large if θ^{**} is halfway between $(\theta^* + \theta^{**})/2 - c$ and $(1 + \theta^{**})/2 - c$, or $\theta^{**} = \theta^*/4 + \theta^{**}/2 + 1/4 - c$.

So we have an equilibrium when θ^* and θ^{**} simultaneously satisfy

$$\theta^* = \frac{\theta^{**}}{2} - 2c \quad \text{and} \quad \theta^{**} = \frac{\theta^*}{2} + \frac{1}{2} - 2c.$$

The solution to these two simultaneous equations is

$$\theta^* = \frac{1}{3} - 4c, \quad \text{and} \quad \theta^{**} = \frac{2}{3} - 4c.$$

Hence, if $c = 0.1$, this cannot work; θ^* would have to be less than 0. But if, say, $c = 1/24$, we would have an equilibrium of this sort, with $\theta^* = 1/6$, and $\theta^{**} = 1/2$.

And when $c = 1/24$, we also have a two-partition equilibrium: You can easily verify that the two-partition equilibrium works for any $c < 1/4$, with $\theta^* = 1/2 - 2c$. And, as always, there is the completely uninformative one-message equilibrium.

For this example, we have the following results as the parameter c varies.

Proposition 20.12.

a. *Fixing c, every cheap-talk equilibrium (per Definition 20.11) is essentially a K-partition equilibrium for some integer K, meaning that there is a partition of the unit interval into cells $[0 = \theta_0, \theta_1), [\theta_1, \theta_2), \dots, [\theta_K - 1, 1 = \theta_K]$, such that, if θ is a member of the kth of these cells $[\theta_{k-1}, \theta_k)$ (closed on the right in the case $k = K$), Bob chooses $a = (\theta_{k-1} + \theta_k)/2$.*

b. *Fixing c, there is a finite integer $K(c)$ such that K-partition equilibria exist for $K = 1, 2, \dots, K(c)$. And, from the perspective of the ex ante expected utilities of Alice and Bob, equilibria with bigger K are Pareto-preferred to equilibria with smaller K.*

c. *As $c \to 0$, $K(c) \to \infty$.*

The only part of this proposition that requires explanation is the "essentially" in part a. Go back to the case $c = 1/24$ and the three-partition equilibrium: $[0, 1/6), [1/6, 1/2)$, and $[1/2, 1]$. Suppose Alice and Bob agree on four messages and their meanings:

$$\mu(\theta) = \begin{cases} \text{Small,} & \text{if } \theta \in [0, /16), \\ \text{Medium,} & \text{if } \theta \in [1/6, 1/2), \\ \text{Big\#1,} & \text{if } \theta \in [1/2, 5/8) \cup [7/8, 1], \text{ and} \\ \text{Big\#2,} & \text{if } \theta \in [5/8, 7/8). \end{cases}$$

The cheap-talk langugage has changed from the Small–Medium–Big vocabulary, but the outcome is the same, in terms of $\alpha(\mu(\theta))$. So, essentially, this is the same equilibrium.

Crawford and Sobel (1982) in all its glory

Crawford and Sobel (1982) provides a proof of Proposition 20.12, but in significantly greater generality. I won't provide details of the proof; read the paper, which is a true classic. Instead, I detail the nature of their setup.

Their setting is as laid out at the start of this section. Alice learns a state of nature θ and can send a cheap-talk message to Bob concerning the message. Then Bob chooses an action a, resulting in payoffs $U_{\text{Alice}}(a, \theta)$ and $U_{\text{Bob}}(a, \theta)$. The following assumptions are made:

- The sets Θ and A are both intervals of real numbers.

- The functions U_{Alice} and U_{Bob} are twice continuously differentiable.

- The functions U_{Alice} and U_{Bob} are strictly concave, so that for each θ, there are (unique) optimal actions $a^*(\theta)$ and $b^*(\theta)$ for Alice and Bob, respectively. (That is, given $\theta, a^*(\theta)$ is Alice's preferred choice of action—what she wants Bob to choose.)

- Both $\theta \to a^*(\theta)$ and $\theta \to b^*(\theta)$ are strictly increasing.

- For no θ does $a^*(\theta) = b^*(\theta)$.

It is easy to see that all these assumptions hold for the example provided above.

Given these assumptions, from the implicit function theorem, we know that a^* and b^* are continuous functions. Because $a^*(\theta) \neq b^*(\theta)$ for all θ, continuity of these functions implies (a) either $a^*(\theta) > b^*(\theta)$ for all θ, or $a^*(\theta) < b^*(\theta)$ for all θ. That is, the "bias" of Alice's preferred choice of action relative to Bob's is always in one direction. Moreover, $a^*(\theta) - b^*(\theta)$ is bounded away from zero: There is "minimum distance" between their preferred actions, which means that full revelation cannot be credible.

These assumptions suffice to prove generalizations of parts a and b: All cheap-talk equilibria are essentially partition equilibria. Fixing the model specification, there are K-cell partition equilibria up to some finite $\overline{K}$. And these equilibria are Pareto-ranked: Equilibria with bigger K are Pareto-better than equilibria with smaller K. Moreover, Crawford and Soel (1982) go on to derive generalizations of part c, after formulating what it means for Alice's and Bob's preferences to be "closer."

I reiterate: Please read this classic paper for the details, and also for an example of a wonderfully crafted theory paper.

A couple of (odd) results

While the general assumptions in Crawford and Sobel (1982) go far beyond the simple illustrative example, there are a lot of cheap-talk effects that their paper does not cover. For the balance of this subsection, assume that Θ and A are both finite sets.

Proposition 20.13. *Suppose* $U_{\text{Alice}}(a, \theta) + U_{\text{Bob}}(a, \theta) \equiv \ell(\theta)$ *—that is, the sum of Alice's and Bob's utilities are constant in a for each θ. Suppose that there is some action a^* that maximizes (over $a \in A$) $\sum_\theta \pi(\theta) U_{\text{Bob}}(a, \theta)$; that is, a^* is an optimal action for Bob if he has no information beyond his prior assessment. Define $U^*_{\text{Alice}}(\theta) := U_{\text{Alice}}(a^*, \theta)$, and $U^*_{\text{Bob}}(\theta) := U_{\text{Bob}}(a^*, \theta)$ (so $U^*_{\text{Alice}}(\theta) + U^*_{\text{Bob}}(\theta) = \ell(\theta)$). Then in every cheap-talk equilibrium, Alice's payoff in every state θ is $U^*_{\text{Alice}}(\theta)$, and Bob's payoff is $U^*_{\text{Bob}}(\theta)$. That is, every cheap talk equilibrium produces the same outcome, state by state, that the no-communication equilibrium produces.*

This is left for you to prove in Problem 20.21. While Definition 20.11 is given for pure-strategy equilibria only, see if you can prove this result for the (I hope obvious) generalization to mixed equilibria.

Roughly speaking, this says that when Alice's and Bob's interests are directly opposed, there is no scope for cheap talk. Conversely, if $U_{\text{Alice}} \equiv U_{\text{Bob}}$—if Alice's and Bob's interests coincide, the obvious (but not the only!) cheap-talk equilibrium has Alice revealing θ to Bob without guile. But suppose Alice's and Bob's interests only coincide some of the time. That is, for a subset of Θ, $U_{\text{Alice}}(\cdot, \theta) \equiv U_{\text{Bob}}(\cdot, \theta)$. For those θ for which this is true, is it (part of) a cheap-talk equilibrium for Alice to reveal those θ to Bob?

This need not be true, at least as stated. Suppose $\Theta = \{\theta_1, \theta_2\}$, $A = \{a_1, a_2\}$, and $\pi(\theta_1) = \pi(\theta_2) = 1/2$. Suppose U_{Alice} and U_{Bob} are as in Figure 20.22(a). Then, if Alice tells Bob when the state is θ_2, so that he can pick a_2, not telling him this leads him to infer that the state is θ_1, and he picks a_1. Alice nets 0 when the state is θ_1 and 5 when the state is θ_2, for an expected value of 2.5. But if, when the state is θ_1, she represents to Bob that the state is θ_2, and if he believes this, he'll choose a_2, which gives her 1 and 5, for an overall expected value of 3. Bob cannot believe that she will tell him the truth in states in which their interests align.

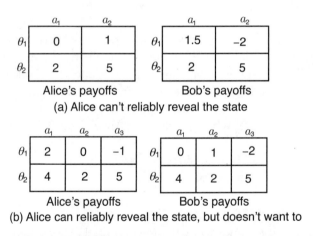

Figure 20.22. Two interesting cheap-talk examples

And, in the general model of Crawford and Sobel, more informative equilibria (defined by the number of partitions) are Pareto superior. But this is not a general result. Consider the data in Figure 20.22(b), where a third action for Bob has been added. Alice's and Bob's interests are perfectly aligned in state θ_2, and they both wish to avoid a_3 when the state is θ_1. So suppose Alice tells Bob the state. He'll choose a_2 in state θ_1 and a_3 in state θ_2, giving Alice an expected overall payoff of 2.5. And this is a cheap-talk equilibrium: Of course, Alice is happy with Bob's choice in state θ_2, and when the state is θ_1, she'd rather have him pick a_2 than a_3. However, a second cheap-talk equilibrium—one that is better for Alice in terms of her overall expected payoff, is to remain silent. Because then, Bob will pick a_1, netting for

Alice an expected payoff of 3, versus the 2.5 she gets in the "more informative" equilibrium. While these are purely made-up situations, without any discernible economic context attached, they do illustrate that cheap-talk—the costly revelation of private information—can be tricky.

Bibliographic Notes

The four truly seminal papers on topics discussed in this chapter are Akerlof (1970), Spence (1974), Rothschild and Stiglitz (1976), and Crawford and Sobel (1982). Wilson (1977) and Riley (1979) made very early and important contributions to the theory of screening. Stiglitz (1977) is the first analysis of monopoly pricing with screening in insurance markets of which I know. At roughly the same time that Crawford and Sobel wrote their paper, Green and Stokey (2007) wrote a discussion paper on cheap talk, which is also well worth studying. The differences between screening and signaling are explored in Stiglitz and Weiss (1990). The intuitive criterion and D1 applied to the Spence signaling model are first found in Cho and Kreps (1987) and Banks and Sobel (1987).

Beyond these papers is a vast literature on strategic information revelation, both in a one-time transaction and—the subject of Chapter 21—dynamically. It would take too many pages to list all the important papers, so I won't try. Instead, the final three problems in this chapter provide simple examples that illustrate three of my favorites.

Problems

The first five problems provide variations on Akerlof's market for lemons, as developed in Section 20.1. In all these problems, there are many sellers of used cars, and many more prospective buyers. The value of a used car to the seller is q, and the distribution of these valuations is uniform between \$2000 and \$6000, except in Problem 20.1(a). Because there are many more prospective buyers, the equilibrium price of any car is set by competition among the buyers.

Let me repeat from the text: Problem 20.5 is particularly worthwhile.

■ 20.1. In the text, I said that the value to a prospective buyer of a car that is worth q to the seller is $q+200$. This is *not* how the model works in Akerlof's classic paper, and in parts a and b, you will find specifications that Akerlof originally provided.

a. Suppose that there are only two possible values of cars to the owners, \$2000 and \$6000. Suppose that a car that is worth q to the owners is worth αq to buyers, for $\alpha > 1$. Suppose that, in the population of all used cars, $\pi \in (0, 1)$ is the proportion of cars that are worth \$2000 and $1 - \pi$ is the proportion that are worth \$6000. As a function of the parameters α and π, what is the equilibrium in the market?

b. Now go back to the specification that the distribution of values q is uniform from \$2000 to \$6000. But, as in part a, the value to a prospective owner of a used car whose value to the seller is q, is αq, for $\alpha > 1$. As a function of the parameter α, what is the equilibrium in the market?

■ 20.2. Suppose that, while the value of a used car to its current owner is q, distributed uniformly from \$2000 to \$6000, and the value to a prospective buyer is $q + 200$, a fraction $\rho < 1$ of owners of used cars *must* sell their cars at whatever price they can get. This fraction ρ is evenly distributed among all the values of q. As a function of ρ, what is the equilibrium in the market?

■ 20.3. Assume the precise formulation provided in the text, with one modification: Buyers are risk averse concerning the value of the car that they buy. To keep it simple, assume that all buyers are identically risk averse in the following sense: If the value $q + 200$ to a buyer is such that q has the density function $\phi(q)$, and if the buyer pays p for the car, the buyer's expected utility is

$$\int (q + 200 + 500 - p)^\gamma \phi(dq),$$

where the integral is over the range of cars for sale, and γ is a parameter of the model lying in the interval $(0, 1]$. (The value $\gamma = 1$ is risk neutrality; smaller γ is "more risk averse.") The equilibrium price p should be such that this expected utility (from purchasing a car) should equal 500^γ; that is, the price should be such that a buyer is indifferent between buying a car or not. As best you can, describe the equilibrium in the market as a function of γ. (In the solutions, I resort to numerical calculations for the values $\gamma = 0.1, 0.3, 0.5, 0.7,$ and 0.9.)

■ 20.4. In this problem, the value of a car that is worth q to a current owner and prospective seller is worth $q + 200$ to prospective buyers.

a. Suppose that, at a cost 50, the owner of a used car can purchase a "report" that accurately determines the value q of the car to the owner. This report is unimpeachable, and once purchased, can be shown to any prospective buyer. What is the nature of the market equilibrium in this case?

b. Part (a) assumes that the initial owner of the car, who knows its value, takes the initiative in generating the report. What if, instead, a propective buyer of a specific used car can, for a strictly positive cost, have the car inspected? Assume in this case that the results of this inspection provide the value q to the current owner (hence the value $q + 200$ to the buyer) and this report, while entirely trustworthy, is private to the prospective buyer who purchases it. Why is this scenario much more complicated than the scenario in part (a)? (I'm not asking you to find the market equilibrium in this case. Just see whether you can identify reasons that this situation is complicated.)

■ 20.5. Again in this problem, the value of a car that is worth q to a current owner and prospective seller is worth $q + 200$ to prospective buyers.

a. Suppose that each used car can be taken (for free in this part of the problem) by
    its owner to an "inspection station" that will issue a publicly available report or
    appraisal concerning the quality of the car. If a used car is worth q to its current
    owner (who knows this value), the "reported appraisal" is a random r that is
    $r = q + u$, where u is uniformly distributed between -500 and 500. Repeating
    the inspection doesn't change the report; if the car generates a report value of
    r on its first inspection, it generates the same report value on any subsequent
    inspections. However, the value of u for each car is independent of the value of
    u for all other cars. As in Problem 20.4(a), this reported appraisal is available
    to all prospective buyers. Once a car is appraised, the owner cannot hide the
    appraised value.

    Note that a car for which $q = 6000$ may generate a report value as large as
    6500; for cars whose q value is close enough to either 6000 or 2000, r *is not* the
    conditional expected value of the car.

    For simplicity, assume that all owners of used cars submit their cars to this
    inspection process. And, owners of used cars cannot hide from prospective
    buyers the value of the report r that their car generates.

    An equilibrium in this market is then, for each report r, a price $p(r)$ that the
    car sells for in the used-car market. (As in the base model, a car worth q to its
    owner is worth $q + 200$ to any buyer.)

    Find $p(r)$. And suppose owners of used cars can choose whether to get an
    appraisal (for free), but if they choose to have their car appraised, they cannot
    "hide" the results. Is it an equilibrium for all owners to get an appraisal?
    (The first question to answer is: What do you need that is not immediately
    computable, to verify it is an equilibrium?)

b. And what if the initial owner must pay, say, \$35 to receive this report? What if
    the price is \$50?

(Warning: My solution in the *Online Supplement* does not answer all questions. This
is a very challenging problem.)

∎ 20.6. Finish the proof of Proposition 20.1 by dealing with the possibility that Bob
or Carol might consider using a mixed strategy.

∎ 20.7. Suppose the basic game-theoretic model (pages 109-10) is changed so that
everything is finite: The value of the used car to Alice, q, is drawn from the
set $\{2000.00, 2000.01, \ 2000.02, \ldots, 5999.99, 6000.00\}$, with each of these 400,001
values equally likely. And Bob and Carol must choose their bids from the set
$\{2000.00, 2000.01, \ldots, 9999.99, \ 10{,}000.00\}$; that is, bids must be in multiples of one
cent. Is there a subgame-perfect equilibrium in which Bob and Carol both submit
the bid 2400.00? How about where they both submit the bid 2399.99?; 2399.98?;
2399.97; 2399.96?

The next two problems concern the "second" equilibrium for the game-theory model of Akerlof, in which Alice names her price, and Bob either purchases the car or not (beginning about halfway down page 116). Problem 20.8 is a simple exercise to ensure that you understand the equilibrium. Problem 20.9 provides a similar equilibrium in the context of income-tax compliance. (It is a caricature of the model in Reinganum and Wilde 1986.)

■ 20.8. Concerning the second equilibrium for the game-theory model in which Alice names her price and then Bob accepts or not, here are two alternative strategies for Bob. (Alice continues to name the price $p = q + 200$, whatever the value of q).

a. Suppose that we modify things so that, for some $\gamma < 1$, Bob accepts Alices offer with probability $\gamma e^{(2200-p)/200}$. Is this still an equilibrium?

b. And suppose that we instead modify Bob's strategy by "truncating" the range over which he accepts Alice's offer. If $p \leq 5200$, Bob (as before) buys with probability $e^{(2200-p)/200}$. But if $p > 5200$, Bob rejects Alice's offer with probability one. Is this still an equilibrium?

■ 20.9. Imagine that, in a particular society, each citizen has income that lies in the interval $[\underline{I}, \infty)$, where the marginal distribution for any citizen's income is given by the density function ϕ on this interval. Suppose that income taxes in this society are arranged as follows. Each citizen, having realized her income y, reports to the government an income level z and pays income tax αz for some $\alpha < 1$. Citizens can underreport their income to save on taxes and, in fact, in this society, everyone does so. The government can audit any citizen's tax return at a cost k and, if the government performs the audit, it learns the true value of y, in which case the audited citizen pays tax $\alpha y + \beta$, where $\beta > 0$ is a penalty for having been caught underreporting income. Can you construct an equilibrium in which the government, seeking to maximize its tax revenue, randomizes between auditing each citizen or not, and in which citizens all underreport their income?

Seven of the next eight problems are all relatively simple, but they are good for making sure you understand the basics of the screening and signaling models in the chapter. Problem 20.12 is also simple; it acquaints you with the kinked-demand model of conjectural variations in oligopoly, in case you haven't seen it before.

■ 20.10. In the Rothschild-Stiglitz model of a competitive insurance industry with two types, I asserted that the low-risk type is never left with no insurance at all, assuming there is an equilibrium. Why is that?

■ 20.11. Draw a picture that illustrates the possibility of a pooling equilibrium, if the equilibrium concept is C. Wilson's anticipatory equilibrium.

■ 20.12. *Kinked-demand:* Consider a symmetric two-firm oligopoly in differentiated goods, where each firm has constant marginal costs of 4 and no fixed cost and faces linear demand that takes the form $10 - p + q/2$, where p is one's own price and q is the price of the rival. As a warm-up, solve for the Bertrand equilibrium. Then, suppose each firm believes that, at a pair of equal prices $p^* = q^*$, if it (the firm) lower's its price, its rival will meet it. But if it raises its price, the other firm will stick to its price q^*. For which values of $p^* = q^*$ does this model of conjectural variations give an equilibrium?

■ 20.13. In the discussion of the analysis of the monopoly insurance company from Stiglitz (1977), I ask you to draw the pictures that support the two conclusions at the end of the third and fourth paragraphs on page 146. Do so.

■ 20.14. I asserted that, if there are enough high-risk types relative to the low-risk types, the monopoly insurance company chooses to fully exploit the high-risk types, pushing the low-risk types to no insurance at all. A precise statement is that, for some fraction ρ^* strictly less than one (depending on all the other data in the problem), if the fraction of high-risk types is anything greater than ρ^*, this outcome—full exploitation of the high-risk types and no insurance for the low-risk types—is profit maximizing. Prove this.

■ 20.15. Explain why the answers I give on page 147 to the three numbered assertions are correct.

■ 20.16. In the context of the two-type of consumer insurance model, suppose we have a monopoly provider of insurance that is subject to regulation. To keep matters simple, assume that the only revenues of the monopoly are the premia it collects and that its only costs are what it pays out on the policies it writes. The regulators insist that the company break even in expectation and that it offer at least one full-insurance policy. If they further insist that the company break even in expectation on every type of policy it writes, what can you say about the outcome?

■ 20.17. In the context of Spence's job market, Figure 20.14(c) shows a case in which, even if an employee's type is private information, an efficient outcome is possible. But, in the context of the insurance market example, this possibility never arose. Why not? And what happens in the Spence's original (1974) formulation, where $\beta_A = \beta_B = 0$?

■ 20.18. In the Spence model, suppose that there is a single monopsonist employer. To be concrete, think of there being one prospective employee, Alice, and one prospective employer, Bob. Alice learns her type, chooses an education level e, and reveals e to Bob; Bob offers her a wage w, and she either accepts his offer or declines it. (If she declines Bob's offer, her payoff is $0 less any disutility expended in getting the education level e.) Parameters are all as in the text. What will happen?

■ 20.19. Construct an analysis of signaling in the competitive insurance-market context of Rothschild and Stiglitz (1976). Assume that Alice is the informed party; she is either high- or low-risk with a given probability that she is low risk, in the minds of Bob and Carol, owners of two insurance companies.

■ 20.20 Construct an analysis of screening in the competitive labor-market context of Spence (1974). Employers Bob and Carol simultaneously offer Alice a menu of choices of the form, "If you get education e, I will pay you $w(e)$."

■ 20.21. Prove Proposition 20.13. If you can, prove it for mixed-strategy equilibria, although this requires that you generalize Definition 20.11 to include mixed equilibria.

The final three problems are caricatures of interesting (to me, at least) analyses of private information tackled in the literature. I stress that my versions of these analyses are caricatures of what happens in the papers: The analyses provided in the papers go far beyond the relatively simple answers to these problems.

Problem 20.22 is a fairly direct extension of ideas in the chapter but is still very important because it cleared up a lot of confusion in earlier literature concerning the phenomenon of entry-deterring limit pricing. It is taken from Milgrom and Roberts (1982a).

Problem 20.23 concerns the possibility that the informed party can *verifiably* reveal her information to the uninformed party; for instance, the owner of a peach of a used car can provide unimpeachable evidence to a buyer that her car is a peach. This (in many cases) leads to an "unraveling": In any pool of types that forms, if a type in the pool would get better treatment revealing her type than remaining in the pool, she reveals. But in part b, we consider the case in which the "informed" type may not be informed at all and, even if she is, she can conceal this fact by "keeping silent.". Dye (1988) is an excellent starting point in the literature for such considerations.

Problem 20.24 is a simple example taken from Kamenica and Gentzkow (2011). It is somewhat similar to the model of cheap talk, but with the sender able to commit a priori to the nature of the message she will send.

■ 20.22. Consider a monopoly firm, facing downward-sloping demand function $D(p) = 100,000(10 - p)$ in each of two periods. This firm has constant marginal cost c and fixed cost $F = 100,000$, so its profit-maximizing price is $(10 + c)/2$, netting a profit $100,000(10 - c)^2 - 100,000$. But this firm faces a problem: Another firm could enter the market in the second period, and if this other firm enters, it will produce an identical product and compete Bertrand style. So, if this second firm has constant marginal cost $c' = 5$ and fixed cost $F = 100,000$, the market price will be $\min\{c', c\}$, and if $c > c'$, the first firm's profit will be $-F$.

The problem is that the potential entrant doesn't know the value of c, the marginal costs for the incumbent monopoly. The potential entrant assesses that $c = 6$ with probability 0.8 and $c = 4$ with probability 0.2.

The sequence of events is: The incumbent monopoly firm charges a first-period price and reaps its profit in that period. Then the prospective entrant decides whether to enter. If it does, it incurs its fixed cost (you can think of this as a sunk cost of entry if you wish). If the entrant does not enter, the monopoly, still a monopoly, chooses its price and reaps its profit. If the entrant does enter, the (previously a) monopoly firm decides whether to remain or not. If it remains, it incurs its fixed cost and the two firms compete Bertrand style. If it departs, the second firm charges whatever price it wishes to charge.

Assume that the first firm, whichever is its marginal cost, understands that the second firm has marginal cost 5. So *if* the second firm enters, the first firm drops out if its (the first firm's) marginal cost is 6 but stays in if its marginal cost is 4.

The incumbent monopoly's payoff is the sum of its profits in the two periods. The prospective entrant's payoff is its profit (if any) in the second period. Both firms are risk neutral.

What price should the first firm charge in the first period?

Note: Assuming "Bertrand competition" if both the incumbent and the entrant are present in the second period calls for some delicacy in how you model things. This formulation makes the problem tractable if you make the right assumption about that situation, but it will take some care on your part.

■ 20.23. An entrepreneur (he) is seeking financing from a venture capitalist (she). To keep the problem simple, assume that the financing will be debt financing: That is, the VC will supply $10 million today, with repayment due in one year, at a negotiated interest rate r (so the payment due in one year will be $10(1+r)$ million). However, if the entrepreneur's venture fails, he will declare bankruptcy, and the VC will get nothing. (If the venture doesn't fail, the entrepreneur will be willing and able to pay the amount due, even if $r = 50\%$. Both the entrepreneur and the VC are risk neutral. The VC will agree to make the loan as long as her expected rate of return is at least 8%. Both the entrepreneur and the VC assess probability 0.9 that the venture will succeed, so that the VC will get an expected rate of return if r is set to that

$$0.9 \times \$10 \text{ million} \times (1+r) = 10 \times (1.08) \text{ million, which has solution} \quad r = 0.2.$$

The complicating feature here is that the entrepreneur may have private information about his chances of a successful venture, information that can be *verifiably communicated* if the entrepreneur chooses to do so, and the VC knows this. This information is such that, if it exists, it implies that the probability of a successful venture is π, uniformly distributed on $[0.8, 1.0]$.

a. Suppose the entrepreneur has this information, and the VC knows that he has it. What happens?

b. Suppose it is uncertain whether the entrepreneur has this information. With probability $1/2$, he has the information. With probability $1/2$, the entrepreneur is no better informed about the probability of success of the venture than is the VC. What happens? Does it matter if the entrepreneur is able verifiably to demonstrate to the VC that she does not have the information?

■ 20.24. (Taken directly from Kamenica and Gentzkow 2011.) Consider a judge deciding the guilt or innocence of an individual charged with a crime. The judge assesses probability 0.3 that the individual is guilty and 0.7 that the individual is innocent. She (the judge) wishes to come to the correct decision; her payoff is 1 if she convicts a guilty individual and 0 if the individual is innocent, and her payoff is 1 for acquiting an innocent individual and 0 for convicting a individual who is innocent.

The judge, absent any further information, will (of course) acquit the individual, for an expected payoff of 0.7. But before the judge renders a verdict, she will hear evidence from a prosecutor whose payoff is 1 if the individual is convicted and 0 if the individual is acquitted. The prosecutor, a wily individual, can produce any form of evidence he wishes, but he must report the results truthfully, and the judge must understand the nature of the evidence. By any form of evidence is meant: There are two outcomes—the defendent seems guility or he seems innocent—and the "nature of the evidence" is given by the likelihoods of the two outcomes (seems guilty or seems innocent), given the true state of nature (the defendent is guilty or is innocent). What will the prosecutor do?

Chapter Twenty-One

Private Information Part II: An Introduction to Dynamics

In the various models of Chapter 20, the actions of the informed party communicate information to the uninformed party. For instance, in the model of Akerlof's used-car market, where the market price is $2400, owners of used cars who value their cars at more than $2400 turn down offers. "Aha!" Bob concludes, "this used car must be worth at least $2400. Perhaps I should offer $2500" (although competition between Bob and Carol would probably push up a second round of offers). The problem with this argument is that the owner of a car worth, say, $2300, anticipating that Bob and Carol would draw this inference and offer more than $2400 if the initial offer is rejected, would not sell at $2400, which renders the inference attributed to Bob (and Carol) invalid.

Or, in the Spence signaling model, if the choice of a larger value of e involves actual time spent in school, then willingness to enroll in school for a larger e in a separating equilibrium tells employers that this is a high-value employee. Why not immediately offer an enrollee a wage appropriate for a high-value employee and allow the individual to skip the onerous schooling (insofar as it is not productive)?[1] In insurance, the choice by an individual of partial insurance instead of the full-insurance policy that is first-best for high-risk types indicates that the individual is a low-risk type. Why not use that information and renegotiate to a more efficient arrangement? Both in the Spence job market and the Rothschild and Stiglitz insurance market, the problem with this "logic" is the same: understanding what will happen subsequently, low-value types will mimic the initial education choice of high-value types; high-risk types will mimic low-risk types; they do so in both cases to get second offers that they prefer.

In Chapter 20, these issues are avoided by supposing that a second opportunity to transact does not exist. But is this reasonable for a useful model of real-world interactions? Perhaps sometimes the answer is Yes but, at least sometimes, the answer is No. And when the answer is No, the obvious question is, What then? The answer to this question, in turn, depends on whether the uninformed party can credibly commit not to use the information she obtains, begging the question, How (or, rather, when) can such a commitment be credible?

This chapter takes an extended look at what can happen in a relatively simple

---

[1] In the case of productive education, the problem doesn't arise if the low-value worker prefers her first-best arrangement (e_B^*, w_B^*) to the first-best arrangement for the high-value type, (e_A^*, w_A^*). But if the low-value type prefers (e_A^*, w_A^*) to (e_B^*, w_B^*), then a moment after the prospective employee passes e_B^* without taking a job, employers know she is high value and might try to offer her w_A^* if she completes e_A^*.

context—a monopolist selling a durable good—about which Coase (1972) conjectures that the monopolist, unable to resist the temptation to cut the price of the good once she makes some sales, in the end has no market power at all. Consumers who would otherwise buy at the monopoly price, if the monopolist could commit not to cut the price she charges, know that the monopolist must give in to this temptation. So they patiently wait for the inevitable price cut, refusing to buy at the initially posted price. Therefore, the monopolist winds up selling her good at (or near) marginal cost.

A short discussion of how the monopolist might credibly resist this temptation is supplied in this chapter. But, except for that short discussion, the issue of credible commitments is left for Chapter 22; this chapter is about what ensues if commitment is not possible.

For the most part, the chapter concerns a very simple formal model that is used to investigate the Coase conjecture. At the end of the chapter is a bit of chat about other contexts in which these problems arise. But, as the title of this chapter indicates, this is only an introduction to a huge literature that explores the issue of private information and its relevation in dynamic contexts.[2]

21.1. Analysis of the Coase Conjecture in the Textbook Model

Consider the following simple model from intermediate microeconomics. A single firm, the monopoly, produces a good at linear cost, with constant marginal cost 0,[3] for which demand is given by the linear inverse-demand function $P(x) = A - x$, where $A > 0$. If the monopolist (she) produces x units, her profit is $P(x)x = (A - x)x = Ax - x^2$, so she maximizes her profit by producing $A/2$ units, selling them at price $p = A/2$, for a profit of $A^2/4$.

The Coase conjecture concerns dynamic pricing of the good, so elaborate this textbook model as follows.

- The monopolist is able to produce the item instantly at constant marginal cost 0 whenever she wishes.

- A very large number of consumers are prospective buyers of this item; they are indexed by $i \in I$. Each prospective buyer wishes to purchase at most one of the items. Each prospective buyer obtains a constant flow of benefit from possessing the item, in the amount b_i per unit time. This value is private knowledge to the consumer.

---

[2] The private information in the context of a monopolist selling her wares is the valuation each consumer places on those wares. The decision by an individual consumer *not* to buy at a high price might reveal to the monopolist that this consumer places a lower value on the good. But then, *if* the monopolist will subsequently lower her price, savvy high-valuation consumers may mimic their low-valuation peers and refuse to buy at the initial, higher price.

[3] Having cost 0 instead of a constant marginal cost c, $A > c > 0$, simplifies the algebra. But everything that follows works for a strictly positive marginal cost, if you think of prices as the amount charged above marginal cost.

In the analysis to follow, I treat this very large number as a continuum of consumers. That is, $I = [0, A]$ for some market scale parameter $A > 0$.

- For the time being, there are two times at which the monopolist can sell the good, today ($t = 0$) and tomorrow ($t = 1$). At each of these two times, the monopolist is able to declare a price p_t at which she will sell the good to any willing buyer. (Please note that subsequent reference to the first period means $t = 0$; the first-period price is p_0.)

- Consumers discount the flow of benefits they derive from possessing the good with discount factor $\delta < 1$ per period. While the monopolist can only sell the good at times $t = 0$ or 1, purchasers enjoy the flow of services at the time t that they purchase the good and continue to enjoy the flow of services at times $t + 1, t + 2, \ldots$.

- Hence, a consumer who purchases the good at $t = 0$ has a (lifetime) payoff of $b_i/(1 - \delta) - p_0$ (consumers have payoffs that are quasi-linear in money). A consumer who purchases the good at $t = 1$ at price p_1 has a payoff of $\delta(b_i/(1 - \delta) - p_1)$.

- Let $B_i = b_i/(1 - \delta)$. As this model is analyzed, we will parametrically vary the discount factor δ, with the interpretation that, as $\delta \to 1$, the length in real time of a "period" goes to zero. For this interpretation to be valid, consumer i's parameter B_i (and not b_i) is held fixed, and the distribution of the parameters B_i is fixed, both as we vary δ. Hence, language such as "a type-B consumer" is used.

- The monopolist discounts the profit she makes at time t by the same δ^t.

The restriction to only two selling periods is temporary. In a few subsections, we will consider models with N time periods, $t = 0, 1, \ldots, N - 1$.

To finish specifying the model, the following questions must be answered.

- What is the distribution of the valuation parameters B_i? Throughout, assume that the Bs are uniformly distributed on $[0, A]$ with total mass A. That is, the "number" (actually, the measure) of consumers whose value of B lies in some interval $[\underline{B}, \overline{B}] \subseteq [0, A]$ is $\overline{B} - \underline{B}$. (This specification goes with the textbook assumption of a linear demand function: $D(p) = A - p$.)

- What is the level of sophistication of consumers? Specifically, in period 0, do they choose whether to buy or not by correctly anticipating p_1?

- What are the powers of commitment of the monopolist? Specifically, can she commit from the outset to the price p_1 she will charge at $t = 1$? Can she commit at the outset on a price p_1 that is contingent on the level of her sales at $t = 0$?

An Alice-and-Bob variation

A variation on this model has only two agents, Alice, who plays the role of the manufacturer, and Bob, the sole prospective customer. Bob's type B is uniformly distributed on $[0, A]$; Bob knows his type; Alice only knows the distribution of B.

In period 0, Alice offers Bob a unit of the good at the price p_0. Bob then either accepts or rejects this offer. If he accepts, the game ends, with payoffs $B - p_0$ for Bob and p_0 for Alice. If he rejects, Alice can make (after one unit of time elapses) a second offer p_1, which Bob accepts or rejects; rejection gives each a payoff of 0, while acceptance gives Alice δp_1 and Bob $\delta(B - p_1)$.

I'll use the "continuum of Bobs" story in what follows; the one-Bob variation is adopted by Sobel and Takahashi (1983). In most, *but not all*, respects the two models produce the same "answers"; see Problem 21.1.

Why *but not all*? See Problem 21.3.

Not Coase: Naive consumers and a well-informed monopolist

Begin with a specification of naive consumers: A type-B consumer will buy at $t = 0$ if $p_0 \leq B$. And assume that, while the monopolist, facing any particular consumer, doesn't know that consumer's value of B, she does know the full distribution of this parameter.

Suppose the monopolist sets price p_0 at time 0 and p_1 at time 1. (So I am assuming for the time being that the monopolist can commit to her second-period price.) The monopolist's profit is then $(A - p_0)p_0$ at $t = 0$ and, assuming $p_1 < p_0$, $(p_0 - p_1)p_1$ at $t = 1$, for total discounted profit

$$(A - p_0)p_0 + \delta(p_0 - p_1)p_1 = Ap_0 - p_0^2 + \delta p_1 p_0 - \delta p_1^2.$$

First-order conditions for an optimum are

$$A - 2p_0 + \delta p_1 = 0 \quad \text{and} \quad \delta p_0 - 2\delta p_1 = 0,$$

which has the easy solution $p_0^* = A/(2 - \delta/2)$ and $p_1^* = p_0^*/2 = A/\big(2(2 - \delta/2)\big)$.

I illustrate with $A = 10$. The classic monopoly solution is to set $p = 5$, for net profit $A^2/4 = 25$. In comparison, for $\delta = 0.8$, the solution to this model is $p_0^* = 6.25$ and $p_1^* = 3.125$, for a total (discounted) profit of 31.25. For $\delta = 0.99$, we get $p_0^* = 6.64$ and $p_1^* = 3.32$, for a total discounted profit of 33.22. As $\delta \to 1$ (interpreted as the period length approaching 0), p_0^* approaches $20/3$, p_1^* approaches $10/3$, and the monopolist's total profit approaches $100/3$. The monopolist does better than the classic model would suggest. Perhaps Coase has made a sign error!

Of course, he hasn't. Coase's point was that, if the monopolist cuts her price in the second period, savvy consumers would not buy in the first period. In this formulation, with naive consumers, the monopolist can take advantage of the naivete and engage in price discrimination, charging a high price for the (naive and high-valuation) consumers and then lowering her price to capture some of the "leftover" demand. Indeed, with such naive consumers and many periods, the monopolist would bring her price down starting from 10, all the way down to 0, engaging (in the limit, as the number of periods goes to infinity while the time between re-pricings goes to zero more quickly) in so-called first-degree price discrimination, where each consumer pays (nearly) his "reservation price," the monopolist pockets all the surplus, and the outcome is both efficient and very inequitable. Lesson: If you are going to be a monopolist, you should find a naive bunch of consumers to exploit.[4]

I assumed that the monopolist can commit to her second-period price. This assumption is unnecessary, as long as customers are naive. Whatever price she sets at time $t = 0$, all the consumers of type B such that with $B \geq p_0$ buy, so the remaining segment of demand is linear over the range 0 to p_0, for which the optimal price to set is $p_0/2$.

Also not Coase: Sophisticated consumers and a monopolist with powers of commitment

Since Coase's conjecture is based on the idea that consumers are savvy enough to anticipate the second-period price, let me move next to that situation, but assume that the monopolist continues to be able to commit to her second-period price p_1.

Suppose that a consumer of type B anticipates that the second-period price will be p_1. Assuming that $B > p_1$, this consumer, by waiting, will net $\delta(B - p_1)$. If he buys today, he nets $B - p_0$. So given p_0 and p_1, which types buy today? It is any type B such that $B \geq p_0$ and

$$B - p_0 \geq \delta(B - p_1) \quad \text{or} \quad B \geq \frac{p_0 - \delta p_1}{1 - \delta},$$

where I've assumed that if the two values are tied, the consumer buys today. Note that, if a type B wishes to buy at $t = 0$, so do all types $B' > B$.

There are three cases:

1. If $p_1 \geq p_0$ and $B \geq p_0$, the consumer buys today. Hence, if the monopolist chooses a price at $t = 0$ that is less or equal to the price she chooses tomorrow, her sales are $A - p_0$, and her profit is $(A - p_0)p_0$.

2. If $A \leq (p_0 - \delta p_1)/(1 - \delta)$, all consumers with $B > p_1$ buy tomorrow, giving the monopolist profit $\delta(A - p_1)p_1$.

---

[4] Not to be too flip about this, it is worth observing that, in real life, even with more savvy consumers, monopolists can and do use time to engage in price discrimination. The publisher of a novel charges a high price when the novel is first released, selling to readers who are impatient to read the very latest book. Then, as time passes, the price of the novel comes down—perhaps a paperback edition is released—to sell to readers who are less impatient. One sees similar price patterns in the marketing of consumer electronics. A different but related ploy is the institution of periodic sales: It used to be that white goods (sheets, bedding) went on sale every February. Consumers who could wait to stock up would wait for the sales, while consumers who needed new sheets and pillow cases in November would buy at the higher, regular prices. Since books are certainly durable, and consumer electronics and white goods are durable to at least some extent, the question is: Why doesn't Coase apply? Perhaps a better question is: Why aren't these examples counterexamples to Coase? The reason is that, in each case, the seller can somehow commit not to lower price too quickly, and so the seller can trade on the relative impatience of some prospective customers. Which begs the question: Why is the seller able to commit in these cases? The best (in my opinion) answer comes in Chapter 22. Keep reading.

3. If $p_1 < p_0$ and $A > (p_0 - \delta p_1)/(1 - \delta)$, then sales at $t = 0$ are $A - (p_0 - \delta p_1)/(1 - \delta)$, and sales at $t = 1$ are $(p_0 - \delta p_1)/(1 - \delta) - p_1 = (p_0 - p_1)/(1 - \delta)$, for total profit

$$\left[A - \frac{p_0 - \delta p_1}{1 - \delta} \right] p_0 + \delta \left[\frac{p_0 - p_1}{1 - \delta} \right] p_1 = A p_0 - \frac{p_0^2}{1 - \delta} + \frac{2\delta p_0 p_1}{1 - \delta} - \frac{\delta p_1^2}{1 - \delta}.$$

It is clear that Case 1 does better than Case 2 for the monopolist, so to find her optimal choices of p_0 and p_1, we must compare Case 1 with Case 3. To do so, let's maximize the Case-3 profit formula without the constraints. The profit function is strictly concave, because its Hessian matrix is negative definite (the on-diagonal terms are $-2/(1 - \delta)$ and $-2\delta/(1 - \delta)$, and the determinant is $4\delta/(1 - \delta)^2 - 4\delta^2/(1 - \delta)^2 > 0$), so the first-order conditions are necessary and sufficient for the optimum. And those first-order equations are

$$A - \frac{2p_0 - 2\delta p_1}{1 - \delta} = 0 \quad \text{and} \quad \frac{2\delta p_0 - 2\delta p_1}{1 - \delta} = 0.$$

Hence the optimum is $p_0 = p_1$, and $p_0 = A/2$, the same as Case 1.

Therefore, the solution for the monopolist is to "take the money and run." She sets $p_0 = A/2$, with a commitment to charge $p_1 = A/2$ (or anything higher), making monopoly profits at $t = 0$. Coase is wrong again. (But, of course, this isn't the situation he considered.)

The monopolist can commit to a pricing strategy, and, by so doing, foil sophisticated consumers

In the analysis just conducted, I assume that the monopolist can commit to the *price* p_1 she will charge in second period. But suppose she is able to do more than that. Suppose she can commit to a second-period *pricing strategy*, where the price she sets in the second period is contingent on the number of sales she records in the first period. Then she can do even better, even against sophisticated consumers, at least, under certain circumstances:

Suppose that I is finite (so I'm introducing a second variation, with many consumers but not a continuum of them). Suppose she knows that the distribution of the Bs is that precisely one consumer has $B = 0$, one has $B = A/(I-1)$, one has $B = 2A/(I-1), \ldots$, and one has $B = A$. (She doesn't know who is whom.) And suppose she is able credibly commit to the following:

> I am going to charge $p_0 = A/(2 - \delta/2)$. Since I is finite and I know the precise distribution of the Bs, I know that if all the type-Bs with $B > p_0$ buy, my sales will be precisely... [and here she inserts the number of sales she should make, if all types with $B > p_0$ buy, which I'll denote by] M.[5] And, if my first-period demand is M (or more), I will charge $p_1 = p_0/2$ in

---

[5] The formula for M is the integer part of $(I - 1)(1 - \delta/2)/(2 - \delta/2) - 1$. But don't worry about that; just realize that the monopolist can tell precisely how many items she will sell at that price, *if* every consumer with $B > p_0$ purchases.

the second period. But if my demand at $t = 0$ falls short of M, I am going to charge $p_1 = p_0$ again. (I'm stubborn that way.)

The point is that, with finitely many consumers, if any one of them with $B > p_0$ decides to wait for $t = 1$ to buy, sales at $t = 0$ will fall short of M, which means the price repeats, so there is no gain from waiting for any consumer with $B > p_0$. Hence, consumers with $B > p_0$ may as well purchase.

Indeed, if $I = 100$, if δ is close to 1, if the monopolist knows the full realized[6] distribution of the Bs, if she can reprice many times, and if she has the power to commit to this sort of *contingent* pricing strategy to which consumers respond in sequentially rational fashion, she can do even better than in the strategy just given: Let $\overline{B}$ be the type of consumer whose type is largest. She announces an initial price of $\overline{B} - \epsilon$ for some very small ϵ, with a commitment to hold to that price until the one consumer with $\overline{B}$ steps forward to buy; then (and only then) will she lower the price to "skim" off the second-high-B consumer, and so forth. (If there are, say, seven consumers whose B is $\overline{B}$, she commits to lower her price only after seven sales at the price $\overline{B} - \epsilon$ have been made.) If she can commit to this strategy, then a sequentially rational response by the consumers is to buy when it is their "turn," to get the little ϵ sooner rather than later. And, if the per-period discount factor δ is close to 1, she can almost (as $\delta \to 1$ and $\epsilon \to 0$) realize the first-degree-price-discrimination profit.

This sort of strategy is delicate: If there is a continuum of consumers, it doesn't work, because any single consumer (with $B > p_0$) can wait without affecting the measure of sales at $t = 0$. If we have Alice selling to just one Bob, it certainly doesn't work. So how about an intermediate case? Suppose there are I consumers for some finite I, and the monopolist believes that the family of reservation levels $\{B_i; i = 1, \ldots, I\}$ are independent and identically distributed. That is, unlike in the previous paragraph, the monopolist isn't certain about the realization of $(B_i)_{i \in I}$; she only knows its probability law. What then? (See Problem 21.2(c).)

Closer to Coase: Sophisticated consumers, a monopolist without the power to commit, and two periods

Coase's conjecture is based on sophisticated consumers, and also on an assumption that the monopolist cannot commit herself in this or any fashion. Or, putting it in terms of game theory, the monopolist can be expected to employ a sequentially rational pricing strategy at $t = 1$.[7]

---

[6] "Realized" here means she knows for certain that there is one consumer with a given value of B_i, a second with a second value, and so forth. This is different from when she knows the *probability* distribution of the vector $(B_i)_{i \in I}$; in those terms, knowing the "realized" distribution means her probability assessment about the vector of values attaches probability 1 to a single specific vector in R^I.

[7] Even in the model with a continuum of buyers, I've assumed (only) that the monopolist knows the volume of sales she makes, in which case her position as she sets out to choose p_1 is not the root of a proper subgame. So, technically, I can't say that we are looking for a subgame-perfect equilibrium. It wouldn't hurt to suppose that, as sales are recorded, the buyers "reveal" to the monopolist their types, in which case we could say something like "in the spirit of subgame perfection." And if that is more satisfactory to you, feel free. But, relative to the formal definitions in the appendices, "in the spirit of" is

This situation is analyzed in two steps:

- Suppose the monopolist sets the price at time $t = 0$ at p_0. Which customers will buy? What will p_1 be?

- And, once we answer that question: What is the optimal p_0 for the monopolist to set?

To answer the first question, suppose the monopolist sets price p_0 at $t = 0$. Based on this price, some subset of the consumers (perhaps the empty set) will purchase at $t = 0$. These are customers whose type B is such that

$$B - p_0 > \delta(B - p_1(p_0)), \quad \text{which is} \quad B > \frac{p_0 - \delta p_1(p_0)}{1 - \delta},$$

where $p_1(p_0)$ is the equilibrium price that the monopolist will charge at time 1. I write p_1 as a function of p_0 because in equilibrium, the higher is p_0, the fewer customers will buy at time 0, therefore the higher will be the price at time 1.

And, in fact, we can compute p_1 as a function of p_0: Note first of all that, if a customer of type B buys at time 0, so will any customer of type B' for $B' > B$. Hence, the customers who buy at time 0 will be a "segment" of high-valuation customers; the set will be $B \in [\hat{B}(p_0), A]$ (or $(\hat{B}(p_0), A]$) for some cutoff value $\hat{B}(p_0)$. (And, again, I warn you that for large enough p_0, it may be that no customers buy at time 0; all will wait for p_1.) The cutoff customer of type $\hat{B}(p_0)$ determines $p_1(p_0)$: *Because the monopolist will price in a sequentially rational fashion at time 1, and since this is the last time she gets to sell, she will set the monopoly price for the consumers who remain:*

$$p_1(p_0) = \frac{B(p_0)}{2}.$$

But, if this is $p_1(p_0)$, then the cutoff type $\hat{B}(p_0)$ must be indifferent between buying at $t = 0$ and $t = 1$. We have the equilibrium condition that

$$\hat{B}(p_0) - p_0 = \delta(\hat{B}(p_0) - p_1(p_0)).$$

Substitute $p_1(p_0) = \hat{B}(p_0)/2$, and we get

$$\hat{B}(p_0) - p_0 = \delta(\hat{B}(p_0) - B(p_0)/2) \quad \text{or} \quad \hat{B}(p_0) - p_0 = \delta\frac{\hat{B}(p_0)}{2} \quad \text{or} \quad \hat{B}(p_0) = \frac{p_0}{1 - \delta/2}.$$

And, since $p_1(p_0) = \hat{B}(p_0)/2$,

$$p_1(p_0) = \frac{p_0}{2 - \delta}.$$

---

more or less required, as this is a game with a continuum of players. And, of course, subgame perfection simply doesn't apply in the version with one Alice and one Bob.

The only caveat that must be added here is that, if p_0 and δ are such that $p_1(p_0)$, computed as just above, exceeds A, then the conclusion is that *no customer buys at time 0; they all wait for $t = 1$, when p_1 will equal $A/2$.*

If you want to try a numerical example, suppose $A = \$10$, and the monopolist tries $p_0 = 7$. What happens if $\delta = 0.5$? What if $\delta = 0.9$? Answers are given in the footnote; I suggest that you do the math before looking.[8]

Now we can go on to answer the second question. Writing the cutoff $\hat{B}$ and p_1 as functions of p_0 and the parameters A and δ, we have

$$\hat{B}(p_0; A, \delta) := \min\left\{A, \frac{p_0}{1 - \delta/2}\right\} \quad \text{and} \quad p_1(p_0; A, \delta) = \min\left\{\frac{A}{2}, \frac{p_0}{2 - \delta}\right\}.$$

The monopolist's profit in the first period is $\left(A - \hat{B}(p_0; A, \delta)\right)p_0$, and her (undiscounted) profit in the second period is $\hat{B}(p_0; A, \delta)^2/4$, so her full profit, as a function of the parameters A and δ and her choice of p_0, is

$$\pi(p_0; A, \delta) = \left[A - \min\left\{A, \frac{p_0}{1 - \delta/2}\right\}\right]p_0 + \frac{\delta}{4}\left(\min\left\{A, \frac{p_0}{1 - \delta/2}\right\}\right)^2.$$

Because of the minima, maximizing this in p_0 could be painful, but let me take a leap of faith: I'm going to maximize while ignoring the possibility that the optimal p_0 might be such that those two mins become relevant. That is, I maximize

$$\left[A - \frac{p_0}{1 - \delta/2}\right]p_0 + \frac{\delta}{4}\left(\frac{p_0}{1 - \delta/2}\right)^2.$$

This is quadratic in p_0 with a negative coefficient on the p_0^2 term (after you do a bit of algebra), so the first-order condition provides the maximum. The maximizing p_0 (again sparing you some algebra) is

$$p_0^* = \frac{(2 - \delta)^2}{2(4 - 3\delta)}A.$$

Since $(2 - \delta)^2 = 4 - 4\delta + \delta^2 < 4 - 3\delta$, $p_0^* < A/2$. And if $p_0^* < A/2$, the cutoff constraint doesn't bind:

$$B_0^* = \frac{2p_0^*}{(2 - \delta)} < \frac{2A}{2(2 - \delta)} = \frac{A}{2 - \delta} < A.$$

So, we have the answer:

$$p_0^* = \frac{(2 - \delta)^2}{2(4 - 3\delta)}A, \quad B_0^* = \frac{2 - \delta}{4 - 3\delta}A, \quad p_1^* = \frac{B_0^*}{2} = \frac{2 - \delta}{2(4 - 3\delta)}A, \quad \text{and} \quad \pi^* = \frac{(2 - \delta)^2}{4(4 - 3\delta)}A^2,$$

---

[8] If $\delta = 0.5$, $\hat{B} = \$9.33\ldots$, and $p_1 = \$4.66\ldots$. If $\delta = 0.9$, the formula for $\hat{B}$ gives $\$12.7272\ldots$; no customer buys at time 0, and $p_1 = \$5$.

values of δ

	0.50	0.60	0.70	0.80	0.90	0.95	0.99
p_0^*	4.50	4.45	4.45	4.50	4.65	4.79	4.95
cutoff	6.00	6.36	6.84	7.50	8.46	9.13	9.81
p_1^*	3.00	3.18	3.42	3.75	4.23	4.57	4.90
π^*	22.50	22.27	22.24	22.50	23.27	23.97	24.76

Table 21.1. Optimal price values and profit. For the model in which consumers are sophisticated, there are (only) two periods, and the monopolist has no commitment power, this gives optimal first- and second-period prices charged by the monopolist, as well as the "cutoff" value—the value of B at which the consumer is indifferent between buying in the first or the second period, and the optimal profit level. This table is for $A = 10$ and a variety of values of δ.

where B_0^* is the cutoff value at $t = 0$, and the derivation of π^* involves even more tedious algebra. Since the formulas are a bit murky, Table 21.1 provides values for the case $A = 10$ and a variety of values of δ.[9]

Unlike the monopolist facing naive consumers, this monopolist does not skim high-value customers with a high first-period price. If she were to try to do this—if she charged a relatively high first-period price—many high-value customers would sit and wait for the lower price to follow at $t = 1$. The math is simple: If she charges p_0 at $t = 0$, the cutoff value of B is $\min\{10, 2p_0/(2 - \delta)\}$. So, for instance, if $\delta = 0.9$, at any price above 5.5, *all* customers wait for the price (5) that she will charge in at $t = 1$. She can make some sales at $t = 0$ with a price below 5.5 (still in the case $\delta = 0.9$), but even at the classic monopoly price of 5, she only sells to customers whose $B \geq 10/1.1 = 9.0909$. Her optimal price at time 0, taking into account the foresight of customers, is only 4.65, and her total profit is 23.27.

This is less profit than a classic monopolist can get, but not much less. Indeed, we can supply a simple lower bound on her optimal profit: By charging (say) $p_0 = 10$ (or anything greater than $5(2 - \delta)$), she makes no sales at $t = 0$ and sets $p_1 = 5$, for a total profit of 25δ.

So, based on this model, Coase gets things somewhat right: The monopolist can't extract the classic monopoly profit. But his prediction that her monopoly profit "disappears" is not (yet) borne out. Indeed, as $\delta \to 1$, she realizes nearly the monopoly profit.

Nearly Coase: Sophisticated consumers; a monopolist without the power to commit; and (finitely) many periods

So far, we have sophisticated consumers and a monopolist without the power to commit. The next step is to add many periods.

The pattern for solving the N-period model can be established by considering $N = 3$. Fix δ throughout this discussion. Suppose that, at $t = 0$, the monopolist

---

[9]　If you examine the numbers in the table, you will see that p_0^* is not monotonic in δ. In particular, $p_0^* = (2 - \delta)^2 A/(2(4 - 3\delta))$ declines as δ rises from 0.5 to 2/3, and then it turns around and is increasing. This happens because, as δ increases, consumers are increasingly patient, but so is the monopolist. The behavior of π^* is similar for the same reason. If you wish to, see what happens if the monopolist has a discount factor δ, while the consumers' common discount factor is γ.

charges p_0^3—the superscript 3 denotes that this is a three-period model—and the cutoff value of the Bs who buy at $t = 0$ is B_0^3. Then, starting at $t = 1$, the situation is a two-period model where, instead of the Bs distributed uniformly from 0 to A, prospective customers are uniformly distributed from 0 to B_0^3. This depends, of course, on the idea that there is a cutoff value for the B—that all the consumers with $B \geq B_0^3$ buy at the price p_0^3, and none of those with $B < B_0^3$ do so—and it depends on the initial uniform distribution, so that if all consumers with $B \geq B_0^3$ are removed (because they have bought their one unit), what is left is uniform over the smaller range.

The point is that starting from time $t = 1$ in a three-period model is like starting from $t = 0$ in a two-period model, except the "scale" factor A is replaced by B_0^3. In the previous subsection, we saw what is optimal for the monopolist in a two-period model starting at an arbitrary scale—note that the price p_0^* that we computed is linear in A, and the profit π^* is scaled by A^2—and if the monopolist can be assumed to behave optimally from $t = 1$ "onward," our solution from the last subsection applies here with the scale reduced to B_0^3.

And this pattern can be applied inductively. Starting from $t = 0$ in a four-period model, suppose the optimal initial price is p_0^4 with cutoff B_0^4. Then, in a four-period model, from time $t = 1$, it is like a three-period model but with the "market scale" being B_0^4 instead of the initial A. If we have computed the solution for a three-period model, this tells us what happens in a four-period model beginning at time $t = 1$. And so forth.

Again, the keys are the uniform distribution of types, the "fact" (in equilibrium) that the segment of types who purchase at the first named price is all types above some cutoff value, and relevant variables scale according to the "consumers who are left," linearly so for prices and cutoffs, and by a factor of the square of the "remaining customers" for profit.

Define sequences $\{\alpha_n(\delta); n = 1, 2, \ldots\}$ and $\{\beta_n(\delta); n = 2, 3, \ldots\}$ recursively, starting with $\alpha_1(\delta) = 1/2$ and, for $n = 2, 3, \ldots$:

$$\alpha_n(\delta) := \frac{(1 - \delta + \delta\alpha_{n-1}(\delta))^2}{2 - 2\delta + \delta\alpha_{n-1}(\delta)} \quad \text{and} \quad \beta_n(\delta) := \frac{1 - \delta + \delta\alpha_{n-1}(\delta)}{2 - 2\delta + \delta\alpha_{n-1}(\delta)}.$$

Proposition 21.1.

a. *Fix δ. In the N-period model with sophisticated consumers and a monopolist who must re-optimize after each period, the optimal price for the monopolist to charge in period 0, denoted $p_0^N(\delta)$, is $\alpha_N(\delta)A$. This leads to a time $t = 0$ cutoff of $B_0^N(\delta) = \beta_N(\delta)A$; that is, consumers with $B > B_0^N(\delta)$ buy at time 0, while those with $B < B_0^N(\delta)$ wait. At time $t = 1$, the optimal price to charge is $p_1^N(\delta) = \alpha_{N-1}(\delta)B_1^N$, and the cutoff for types who buy at time $t = 1$ is $B_1^N(\delta) = \beta_{N-1}(\delta)B_0^N$. And so forth.*

b. *The monopolist's (net present value) of profit in the N-period model, denoted by $\pi_N(\delta)$, equals $\alpha_N(\delta)A^2/2$.*

c. *Prices decline: That is (suppressing the dependence on δ), $p_0^N > p_1^N > p_2^N > \ldots > p_{N-1}^N$: Although $\alpha_{N-1}(\delta) > \alpha_N(\delta)$, since $p_1^N = \alpha_{N-1}(\delta)B_0^N = \alpha_{N-1}(\delta)\beta_N(\delta)A$ and $\alpha_{N-1}(\delta)\beta_N(\delta) < \alpha_N(\delta)$, we have $p_0^N > p_1^N$, hence prices decline.*

d. *The limit as $N \to \infty$ of $\alpha_N(\delta)$, which I denote $\alpha_\infty(\delta)$, is*

$$\alpha_\infty(\delta) = \frac{\sqrt{1-\delta} - (1-\delta)}{\delta}.$$

Hence,

$$\lim_{N \to \infty} p_0^N = \frac{\sqrt{1-\delta} - (1-\delta)}{\delta} A \quad \text{and} \quad \lim_{N \to \infty} \pi_N = \frac{\sqrt{1-\delta} - (1-\delta)}{2\delta} A^2.$$

I will not prove this proposition here. It is a mess of algebra, with a bit of calculus thrown in; Problems 21.3 and 21.4 ask you to prove it in two steps. (So, if you wish, you can see the proofs in the *Online Supplement*.) The first step is to prove the following lemma:

Lemma 21.2.

a. *For $\delta \in (0, 1)$, define $\Phi_\delta : (0, 1) \to (0, 1)$ and $\Psi_\delta : (0, 1) \to (0, 1)$ by*

$$\Phi_\delta(\alpha) := \frac{(1 - \delta + \delta\alpha)^2}{2 - 2\delta + \delta\alpha} \quad \text{and} \quad \Psi_\delta(\alpha) := \frac{1 - \delta + \delta\alpha}{2 - 2\delta + \delta\alpha}.$$

Both Φ_δ and Ψ_δ are strictly increasing in α. The function Φ has a unique fixed point—that is, a value of α such that $\Phi_\delta(\alpha) = \alpha$—which is

$$\alpha_\infty(\delta) = \frac{\sqrt{1-\delta} - (1-\delta)}{\delta}.$$

For all δ, $\alpha_\infty(\delta) < 1/2$. For $\alpha > \alpha_\infty(\delta)$, $\Phi_\delta(\alpha) < \alpha$. And Φ_δ and Ψ_δ are both continuous.

b. *For $0 < \delta < 1$, the sequences $\{\alpha_n(\delta)\ n = 1, 2, \ldots\}$ and $\{\beta_n(\delta); n = 2, 3, \ldots\}$ are decreasing, with $\lim_{n \to \infty} \alpha_n(\delta) = \alpha_\infty(\delta)$.*

With this lemma and a lot of tedious algebra, you can prove the proposition.

If you do the required algebra, it may strike you as amazing that things just drop into place. It should be very clear that, with a linear specification of demand (that is, the Bs are uniformly distributed), there will be some sequence of constants $\{\alpha_N(\delta)\}$ such that p_0^N will be $\alpha_N(\delta)A$ and another sequence of constants—call this sequence $\{\gamma_N(\delta)\}$—such that $\pi_N = \gamma_N(\delta)A^2$. Whatever is the optimal pricing strategy for the monopolist if the initial scale of the market is A will be the optimal pricing strategy, when rescaled, if the initial scale of the market is A'. And profit is quadratic in the scale A because profit consists of the sum of prices (which scale linearly) times quantities (which also scale linearly). The existence of these two sequence of constants (and a third sequence $\{\beta_N(\delta)\}$ that gives cutoffs) should come as no surprise. But I have no intuition to offer as to why $\gamma_N(\delta) = \alpha_N(\delta)/2$; that part is a bit amazing.

Corollary 21.3. *Fixing δ and A, the monopolist's profit declines with N, the number of opportunities she has to reprice the good.*

Proof. The monopolist's profit, by Proposition 21.1(c), is $\pi_N(\delta) = \alpha_N(\delta)A^2/4$, and part b of the lemma establishes that the sequence $\{\alpha_N(\delta)\}$ is decreasing in N. ∎

What if we fix N and A and vary δ? Is δ closer to 1 better or worse for the monopolist? The answer is ambiguous: For small n, the monopolist can prefer δ closer to 1. However:

Corollary 21.4. *For any δ and δ' such that $1 > \delta > \delta'$, there exists an N such that, for all $n > N$, $\alpha_n(\delta) < \alpha_n(\delta')$. That is, for large enough n, the monopolist's profit is larger the further is δ from 1.*

Proof. Proposition 21.1(d) establishes that

$$\lim_n \alpha_n(\delta) = \alpha_\infty(\delta) = \frac{\sqrt{1-\delta} - (1-\delta)}{\delta}.$$

Simple algebra shows that if $1 > \delta > \delta'$, $\alpha_\infty(\delta) < \alpha_\infty(\delta')$. The lemma follows immediately. ∎

21.2. When Does the Coase Conjecture Hold?

Corollary 21.5. *Because*

$$\lim_{\delta \to 1} \frac{\sqrt{1-\delta} - 1 - \delta}{\delta} = 0,$$

we have $\lim_{\delta \to 1} \lim_{N \to \infty} \alpha_N(\delta) = 0$, and so, for any initial market size A,

$$\lim_{\delta \to 1} \lim_{N \to \infty} p_0^N(\delta) = 0 \quad and \quad \lim_{\delta \to 1} \lim_{N \to \infty} \pi^N(\delta) = 0.$$

The first assertion in the corollary is obvious—both terms in the numerator converge to zero, while the denominator converges to one—and then the rest of the corollary follows immediately from Proposition 21.1.

So, summing up, early subsections tell us that, in the context of this formal model, the Coase conjecture requires that

- consumers are sophisticated (anticipate future prices), and

- the monopolist cannot commit to future prices, but instead re-optimizes at each repricing event (she behaves in sequentially rational fashion).

Then, Corollary 21.5 would seem to say that,

- if there are many repricing events (N large) that are
- tightly packed (δ close to 1),

then, at least in the context of our model, the Coase Conjecture holds.

Except this seeming implication of the corollary is an overreach. The corollary concerns a double limit,[10] and double limits can be deceptive. This one certainty is, as we see from reversing the order of the two limits:

Proposition 21.6.

a. The monopolist's profit in the N-period model with discount factor δ satisfies $\pi_N(\delta) \geq \delta^N A^2/4$.

b. Hence, $\lim_{N \to \infty} \lim_{\delta \to 1} \pi^N(\delta) = A^2/4$.

Proof. Since $\pi^N(\delta) = \alpha_N(\delta)A^2/2$, for part a, it suffices to show that $\alpha_N(\delta) \geq \delta^N/2$. This is done by induction: For $N = 0$, $\alpha_0(\delta)$ was defined to be $1/2$, so we have the inequality for $N = 0$. Assume inductively that $\alpha_N(\delta) \geq \delta^N/2$. We have

$$\alpha_{N+1}(\delta) = \frac{(1 - \delta + \delta\alpha_N(\delta))^2}{2 - 2\delta + \delta\alpha_N(\delta)} \geq \frac{(1 - \delta + \delta\delta^N/2)^2}{2 - 2\delta + \delta\delta^N/2},$$

since on the left-hand side we are applying Φ_δ to $\alpha_N(\delta)$, while on the right-hand side we are applying it to $\delta^N/2$, and Φ_δ, by Lemma 21.2, is (strictly) increasing in its argument. Hence, we are done with the induction step if we show that

$$\frac{(1 - \delta + \delta\delta^N/2)^2}{2 - 2\delta + \delta\delta^N/2} = \frac{(1 - \delta + \delta^{N+1}/2)^2}{2 - 2\delta + \delta^{N+1}/2} \geq \frac{\delta^{N+1}}{2}.$$

Cross-multiply and expand the squared term: The required inequality is equivalent to

$$2\left(1 + \delta^2 + \frac{\delta^{2N+2}}{4} - 2\delta + 2\frac{\delta^{N+1}}{2} - 2\frac{\delta^{N+2}}{2}\right) \geq 2\delta^{N+1} - 2\delta^{N+2} + \frac{\delta^{2N+2}}{2},$$

and if you cancel out similar terms on the left- and right-hand sides, you get that $2(1 + \delta^2 - 2\delta) = 2(1 - \delta)^2$ must be nonnegative, which, of course, it is.

---

[10] I doubt many readers are new to double limits, but just in case: When I write $\lim_\delta \lim_N F(\delta, N)$, it means that for each δ you take the limit in N—call this $F(\delta, \infty)$—and only then do you take the limit in δ of $F(\delta, \infty)$.

As for part b, it is obvious that an upper bound on $\pi_N(\delta)$ is $A^2/4$. So, for fixed N, the inner limit $\lim_{\delta \to 1} \pi_N(\delta)$ satisfies

$$\frac{A^2}{4} \geq \pi_N(\delta) \geq \lim_{\delta \to 1} \delta^N \frac{A^2}{4} = \frac{A^2}{4}. \qquad \blacksquare$$

This proposition makes clear that conditions under which the Coase conjecture holds—at least, in the context of our model—are more than just "large N and δ close to 1." Large N and δ close to 1 are necessary, but those two conditions can hold (along with the other requirements), and the result can be anything from nearly zero profit to nearly monopoly profit. The double limit that "works"—the double limit in the corollary—says (essentially) that N must be going to infinity "faster" than δ is going to 1. The term "faster" here is vague; to make it precise, it helps to reframe the problem slightly.

Think of the monopolist being able initially to price the good at $t = 0$ and then reprice the good at times $h, 2h, 3h, \ldots, (N - 1)h$, for some (presumably) small h and large N. Besides the fixed parameter A (fixed as we take limits in h and N), we fix in addition a per-unit-of-time discount rate r, such that the δ that goes with a repricing period length h is e^{-rh}. Then, letting $T = (N - 1)h$, we have the interpretation that the monopolist will sell the good from time 0 to (just after) T, with the ability to name an initial price p_0 and, then, reprice the good $N - 1$ times, at $h = T/(N - 1)$, $2h = 2T/(N - 1)$, and so forth. Profits for the monopolist and benefits for consumers are discounted at *rate* r per unit time; that is, benefits/profits received at some time t are discounted back to time 0 by the factor $\delta(t) = e^{-rt}$.

With this reframing, for fixed parameters A and r and varying parameters h and N, we want to know, *What is the limit of the monopolist's profit if h is approaching 0 and N is approaching ∞?* Formally, we imagine that we have a sequence of pairs $\{(h_k, N_k); k = 1, 2, \ldots\}$ such that $h_k \to 0$ and $N_k \to \infty$. In words, we look along a sequence of models where the number of repricing opportunities the monopolist has goes to infinity, while the time between repricing opportunities goes to zero. Then, for such a sequence of paramenters, we ask for the limiting profit of the monopolist. I'll abbreviate $\pi_{N_k}(e^{-rh_k})$, the monopolist's profit for parameters h_k and N_k (and fixed A and r), as π_k. Then we have the following proposition.

Proposition 21.7. *Suppose $\lim_k h_k = 0$, $\lim_k N_k = \infty$, and $\lim_k h_k N_k$ exists, where limits of 0 and ∞ are allowed.*

a. *If $\lim_k h_k N_k = 0$, then $\lim_k \pi_k = A^2/4$.*

b. *If $\lim_k h_k N_k = T$ for some $0 < T < \infty$, then $\lim_k \pi_k = e^{-rT} A^2/4$.*

c. *If $\lim_k h_k N_k = \infty$, then $\lim_k \pi_k = 0$.*

Hence, in terms of this reframing, for the Coase conjecture to hold, h_k must be getting small, but N_k must be growing even faster, so much faster that the product $h_k N_k$ diverges to ∞.

(If $h_k N_k$ does not have a limit, then neither does π_k, although the proposition certainly applies to every convergent subsequence.)

Method of proof. Parts a and c are relatively direct, once we prove part b, so let us start there: We know that $\pi_k = \alpha_{N_k}(e^{-rh_k})A^2/2$, so this part of the proposition requires that we show that

$$\lim_k \alpha_{N_k}(e^{-rh_k}) = \frac{e^{-rT}}{2}, \quad \text{where } T = \lim_k h_k N_k.$$

You are asked to do this in Problem 21.5. This takes some technical skills: You take the difference equation for the $\alpha_N(\theta)$ and turn it into a differential equation. If you don't want to struggle with it, see the proof in the *Online Supplement*.

For part c, take a sequence $\{(h_k, N_k)\}$ such that $\lim_k h_k = 0$, $\lim_k N_k = \infty$, and $\lim_k h_k N_k \to \infty$. Take any $\epsilon > 0$, and let T be large enough so that $e^{-rT}A^2/4 < \epsilon$. Create a sequence $\{N'_k\}$ such that $\lim_k h_k N'_k = T$; for instance, let N'_k be the integer part of T/h_k. Of course, for large enough K, $N'_k < N_k$ for all $k \geq K$, so the monopolist's profit for h_k and N_k is less than her profit for h_k and N'_k; we know this from Corollary 21.3. Hence, the limit of monopolist's profit for h_k and N_k is less than the limit of her profit for h_k and N'_k, which by part b is $e^{-rT}A^2/4 < \epsilon$. Since $\epsilon > 0$ is arbitrary, we have part c.

And I leave part a to you: An "estimation" as in the previous paragraph is possible, or use Proposition 21.6, or see the next subsection.

Why is the Coase conjecture true? When it is true?
Interpreting Proposition 21.7

Proposition 21.7 tells us that, for the Coase conjecture to hold—that is, a durable-goods monopolist, who lacks the ability to commit, loses her monopoly power—it is insufficient that the monopolist has (a) many opportunities to reprice (b) that happen rapidly. For the conjecture to work—at least, in special case of our linear-demand model—it takes a "long" real-time horizon. The obvious question is: Why? We got to this conclusion with a mess of algebra and calculus, and it is a good thing that we used a formal model to refine Coase's conjecture. But is there economic intuition that goes beyond the algebra and calculus?

An intuitive explanation for why the Coase conjecture *fails* in cases a and b in Proposition 21.7 runs as follows: Suppose that the monopolist announces in period 0 that $p_0 \geq A$; "I'm not willing to sell anything this period." Of course, no consumer will buy; *whatever* they think she will do next period, waiting can't be worse than buying today. Then, in period 1, she announces $p_1 \geq A$, and similarly in every period, up to and including the next-to-last period. Then, in the final period, she sets the monopoly price of $A/2$. Viewed ex ante, this pricing policy generates for her the profit $e^{-rT}A^2/4$.

You might object that we do not allow the monopolist to commit to a pricing strategy. But the point of *no commitment* is that the monopolist can't credibly say: "This is what I plan to do," *and in so doing, change how customers will respond.* Or, put the other way around, commitment is about changing the behavior of customers, not having and carrying out a plan of action. This strategy requires no commitment, under this interpretation. If the monopolist announces $p_0 \geq A$, she makes no sales and no commitment about the future—none of the consumers will buy at this price, regardless of their beliefs about future prices—and similarly for every period up until the last one.

So, for a sequence of models $\{h_k, N_k\}$ with $h_k \to 0$, $N_k \to \infty$, and $h_k N_k \equiv T < \infty$, $e^{-rT} A^2/4$ is a lower bound on how much (ex ante) profit she can realize.

- Since we know that $\pi_N(\delta) = \alpha_N(\delta) A^2/2$ and $\alpha_N(\delta) \leq 1/2$, we know that $A^2/4$ is an upper bound on how much the monopolist can realize; this provides an immediate proof of Proposition 21.7(a), and it provides a simpler proof of Prosposition 21.6.

- What is more remarkable is that this lower bound on the monopolist's profit is tight for the limit of her profit in model k, as $k \to \infty$, in cases a and b. And, for case c, since her (optimal) profit approaches zero as $k \to \infty$, this "lower bound" for each finite k (that is, $e^{-rh_k N_k} A^2/4$) gives an asymptotically tight bound on her optimal profit, as $k \to \infty$.

This does not mean that, for large k, the optimal strategy for the monopolist is approximately this commitment strategy. All that we have shown is that this simple and implementable strategy provides the monopolist with close to her optimal profit. And consumers are very happy that this wait-until-the-last-period is not the monopolist's optimal stratgy. Suppose the monopolist were to say, "Since I can't do much better with the very complicated optimal strategy, I'll just use this wait-until-the-last-period strategy." The monopolist does nearly as well as in her optimal strategy. But consumers are much, much worse off.

A numerical example provides a sense of this. Suppose $T = 20$ years and $r = 0.1$ (a 10% per year rate of interest). Suppose the monopolist has 1000 equally spaced opportunities to reprice her good (or, roughly, new prices can be posted once a week). For a market of size $A = 10$, the wait-until-the-last-period strategy generates a profit for the monopolist of \$3.38 (approximately), while her optimal strategy improves this to \$4.023. But, for consumers, their (discounted) net surplus gain is \$1.69 with the wait-until-the-last-period strategy and \$43.97 if the monopolist uses her optimal strategy. To give more details about the optimal strategy, the monopolist starts with an initial price of \$0.80 and serves consumers with valuations of \$9.76 and above. (All these numbers are, of course, approximations.) Halfway through the first year (period 25), the price has fallen to \$0.47, and customers with valuations of \$5.68 and above have been served. At the one-year mark, the price is down to \$0.27, and customers with valuations \$3.07 have been served.[11]

---

[11] The spreadsheet giving all these calculations is provided in the *Online Supplement* as Spreadsheet21.3. An interesting exercise is to put in 7000 equally spaced oppoturnities to reprice; that is, roughly one per day. As long as $r = 0.1$ and $T = 20$ years, the monopolist's profit for "wait until the end" is still \$3.38. And, the consumers get a discounted net surplus gain of around \$1.69. But, the

This tells you why the Coase conjecture fails for sequences of models (h_k, N_k) for which $h_k N_k$ has a finite limit. But doesn't provide (economic) intuition for why the conjecture is correct when $h_k N_k \to \infty$. A reviewer of an early draft of this chapter challenged me to provide intuition, but I'm stumped: The standard intuition that is offered is that, if there is positive surplus to be gained by the monopolist in the future, she will benefit by "speeding up" the decline in prices to save on the discount, sacrificing tiny (or, more accurately, tin*ier*) profits to be earned in the current period. But, to be satisfactory, this explanation should work in case c and fail in the other two cases. I am unable explain this.

I make one suggestion: If one could give an intuitive explanation for why the wait-until-the-last-period strategy gives an asymptotically tight bound on the monopolist's optimal profit (as $h_k \to 0$, regardless of the behavior of N_k), *that* would explain everything. If someone comes up with a good argument (I'm the judge), it will be posted in the *Online Supplement*, with attribution, so go for it!

Infinitely many repricing periods from the outset

Suppose we eliminate the parameter N, assuming from the beginning that the monopolist has infinitely many opportunities to reprice the item. The remaining parameters are A, r, and h, the length of time over which the monopolist is committed to a particular price. The preceding analysis suggests that a "stationary"[12] equilibrium should emerge, and moreover, it should have a linear character: In any period n, before the monopolist names her price:

- the remaining consumers (those who didn't buy earlier) have valuations uniformly distributed on the interval $[0, B_n]$ for some B_n that is initialized at $B_0 = A$;

- the monopolist will set the price $p_n = \alpha B_n$ for some constant α; and

- a customer whose value is B will purchase the good the first time that B is greater than or equal to γ times the price p, for some constant γ.

The connections between these constants α and γ with the α_n and β_n are as follows. Think of n as being very, very large. At a point where the remaining consumers are those from 0 to B and there are n periods left to go, in the finite-horizon model, the monopolist sets the price at $\alpha_n B$. So, it is natural to think of $\alpha = \alpha_\infty$ (although, of course, we must prove that this works). And the new cutoff in the finite horizon model is $\beta_n B$. Here we are supposing that consumers buy if their valuation is above $\gamma p_n = \gamma(\alpha B)$, so the natural thing to hope for is that $\gamma \alpha = \lim_{n \to \infty} \beta_n$. Saving you the algebra, we have

$$\lim_{n \to \infty} \beta_n(\delta) = \frac{1 - \sqrt{1 - \delta}}{\delta}, \quad \text{from which} \quad \gamma = \frac{\sqrt{1 - \delta}}{1 - \delta}.$$

With that bit of foreshadowing, we can do some analysis.

---

numbers for the optimal strategy change, to \$3.48 or so for the monopolist and \$44.77 for consumers.

[12] Why the scare quotes? I'll explain in a bit.

Suppose the monopolist and the consumers act in this fashion, for arbitrarily given α and γ. For the moment, assume that $\alpha\gamma < 1$. The monopolist's value function in period n, $V(B_n; \alpha, \gamma)$, will satisfy the recursive equation (where $\delta = e^{-rh}$)

$$
\begin{aligned}
V(B_n; \alpha, \gamma) &= \alpha B_n(B_n - \gamma\alpha B_n) + \delta V(\gamma\alpha B_n; \alpha, \gamma) \\
&= \alpha(1 - \gamma\alpha)B_n^2 + \delta V(\gamma\alpha B_n; \alpha, \gamma) \\
&= \alpha(1 - \gamma\alpha)B_n^2 + \delta\left[\alpha(\gamma\alpha B_n)(\gamma\alpha B_n - \gamma\alpha(\gamma\alpha B_n)) + \delta V(\gamma\alpha(\gamma\alpha)B_n; \alpha, \gamma)\right] \\
&= \left[\alpha(1 - \gamma\alpha) + \delta(1 - \gamma\alpha)\alpha^3\gamma^2 + \delta^2(1 - \gamma\alpha)\gamma^4\alpha^5 + \ldots\right]B_n^2 \\
&= \frac{\alpha(1 - \gamma\alpha)}{1 - \delta\gamma^2\alpha^2}B_n^2,
\end{aligned}
$$

where I am recursively applying the recursive equation, and I get to drop the trailing term, because V is bounded and it is being multiplied by δ^k as $k \to \infty$. (In other words, I'm using value iteration for the value function of a specific policy by the monopolist, in the face of specific behavior by consumers, which is legitimate, because values are discounted and bounded.)

Conditions for α and γ to constitute an equilibrium begin with on-path optimality: (1) Given the monopolist's pricing strategy, the cutoff consumer at any stage n (the consumer whose value is $\gamma p_n = \gamma\alpha B_n$) is indifferent between buying in this period and waiting for price to come down to $p_{n+1} = \alpha B_{n+1} = \alpha(\gamma\alpha B_n)$, (2) For the given γ, the choice of α by the monopolist is optimal; it maximizes her value function.

We are guessing that

$$
\alpha = \frac{\sqrt{1 - \delta} - (1 - \delta)}{\delta} \quad \text{and} \quad \gamma = \frac{\sqrt{1 - \delta}}{1 - \delta}
$$

will work. *And, in fact, they do.* But despite my glib assertion that they do, there are complications.

Along the path of play, suppose we reach a time n when the remaining consumers—those who have yet to buy—constitute the set $[0, B_n]$. The monopolist is supposed to charge the price $p_n = \alpha B_n$. But, to verify that this is optimal for her (given the consumers' strategies), we need to show that charging a different price is no better. And, if she charges a different price, we must know: (1) How will consumers react? Will they (optimally) continue to adhere to the strategy given by the parameter γ, or will the monopolist's defection lead them to some other behavior? (2) What then happens in periods $n + 1$, $n + 2$, and so forth? The monopolist has taken play off the equilibrium path of play; we must specify her strategy once she defects (and then that of the consumers), if she defects. And, please note that the answer to the first questions—how the consumers react in the immediate period—depends on the answer to the second question, since the consumers are balancing "buy now" against "buy later."

Problem 21.7 asks you to show that my glib conclusion is correct, under the following answers to the these two sets of questions. The consumers, seeing a price $p'_n \neq \alpha B_n$, reason that, if the next period begins with a remaining cohort of consumers of the form $[0, B'_{n+1}]$—where the prime on B'_{n+1} indicates that this may be a different value than $B_{n+1} = \gamma \alpha B_n$ that would have resulted had the monopolist not defected—then the monopolist will revert to the α rule: She'll charge $\alpha B'_{n+1}$. Indeed, this choice fills out the monopolist's strategy from any point in the game tree in which the remaining set of consumers has the form $[0, B]$; in all such circumstances, on path or off, the monopolist charges αB. And, anticipating that this is how the monopolist will behave, the consumers decide whether or not to buy in this period based on this hypothesis, *which then justifies their working hypothesis that, next period, the remaining consumers will be a set of the form $[0, B'_{n+1}]$.* Concerning this:

- If you remember the concept of an *unimprovable* strategy from Volume I, Appendix 6, Section A6.4, and the result (Proposition A6.7) that, for well-behaved dynamic-programming problems, unimprovable strategies are optimal, you probably anticipate that the full proof shows that the monopolist's strategy, in the face of how the consumers behave, is unimprovable starting from any point where the remaining set of consumers is $[0, B]$. This implies that it is indeed optimal.

- However, the γ characterization of the consumers' strategies is not entirely accurate. This is how they behave if the monopolist adheres to the α rule. But if the monopolist deviates in period n, they also will deviate, although things return to "normal" starting in period $n + 1$, albeit starting with a new B.

- And, formally, carrying out this program is still inadequate, if one wants to claim that a proof has been given that there is an equilibrium with sequentially rational behavior for the game: Nothing has been said about what happens from positions in the game tree where the set of remaining consumers is not of the form $[0, B]$, for some B. However, if the goal is to verify that the on-path play works, we never reach such a point in the game tree, even if the monopolist defects somewhere along the line, since her assumed subsequent behavior leads consumers to act in a way that preserves this sort of "remaining consumers."[13]

- In the previous bullet point, I used the phrase "equilibrium with sequentially rational behavior" rather than "subgame perfect." This is a case where formal definitions given in game theory don't quite fit the needs of a model. One problem, of course, is the continuum of consumers. But suppose we could finesse that. There is still a problem in terms of what the monopolist knows

---

[13] We don't need to worry about consumers defecting, since there are a continuum of them, and one defection by a consumer changes nothing in terms of the game from the monopolist's perspective. If we had a large but finite number of consumers—more than one—and if the monopolist learns the identity of any consumer who purchases a good, things become very messy if a low-value consumer deviates and buys at a time when a higher-value consumer does not; indeed, I doubt that any one has ever dealt carefully with such a model.

at, say, period n. She presumably knows her level of sales in all prior periods. But unless we assume that, whenever a sale is made, that consumer's identity is revealed to the monopolist (and, indeed, to all the other consumers), each period is not the root of a proper subgame. [14]

- I promised an explanation for the scare quotes around "stationary." Stationarity as a concept in sequential decision theory refers to models with state variables. Here, at least for the relevant portion of the game tree, where play so far can be summarized by the set of consumers that have not yet purchased the good, we are looking (only) at "states" of the form $[0, B]$ for some B. And, stationarity in its standard form says that a strategy (presumably, the monopolist's strategy) is stationary (or time invariant) if every time a state recurs, the strategy prescribes the same action. Since, in this story, the only time a state recurs is if, in a given period, the monopolist makes no sales, "stationarity" in its standard form would allow her many degrees of freedom. But, what is meant in this context by stationarity is quite strong: Whatever the "state" $[0, B]$ is, her pricing rule is to charge αB. So, perhaps, to align with standard usage, one ought to call this strategy by the monopolist "super-stationary."

And with all this by way of commentary, Problem 21.7 asks you to prove my original glib assertion (and, as always, with the solution available in the *Online Supplement*).

So, what is the bottom line for this model with an infinite number of repricing periods from the start? With all the caveats listed above, we have a "stationary" equilibrium with sequentially rational behavior. For a given h (or δ), this equilibrium outcome is the limit of the finite-horizon equilibrium outcomes, as the number of repricing periods goes to ∞. And this equilibrium verifies the Coase conjecture: As $\delta \to 1$, which means as the time between repricings goes to zero, the initial price, and the monopolist's profit, both approach zero.

However, in this infinite-horizon model, other outcomes can be sustained as equilibrium outcomes; the infinite horizon "unhinges" the definite answer one derives for the finite-horizon models (in this case). I'll leave this for your further investigation; consult Gul, Sonnenschein, and Wilson (1986).

21.3. (How) Can the Monopolist Escape the Coase-Conjecture Trap?

It would probably come as something of a surprise to many durable-goods monopolists to learn that their inability to control their later actions leads them to price at

---

[14] If we worked instead with the Sobel–Takahashi (1983) formulation with Alice and Bob, we're in even worse shape, because Alice, having not made a sale up to period n, faces a lot of uncertainty about Bob's type. Which, again going back to the previous bullet point, has implications for "appropriate" beliefs by Alice starting from period n, given the history of prices she has charged and the fact that she has made no sale. Given her beliefs about Bob's optimal behavior in the face of the prices she has charged and the prices he expects her to charge, the "natural" beliefs for her to hold are that his type lies in a set of the form $[0, B]$, for some B that depends on the history of prices she quoted in the past. And, if this makes your head hurt, ignore this footnote.

marginal cost. Therefore, it is worth a page or so to sketch out some ways in which durable-good monopolists escape the Coase-conjecture trap.[15]

For one thing, if an appreciable fraction of the consumers are naive, things aren't so bad. See Problem 21.8.

If the item in question is a tangible durable asset, the monopolist could lease it, although this takes some institutional features that are, perhaps, not entirely standard. The basic idea is that, rather than selling the asset, in each period (a period being the length of time over which she cannot modify a sales' price for the item), she offers one-period leases. Recall that the one-period flow of benefits to a B_i-type customer is denoted b_i, where $b_i/(1 - \delta) = B_i$, or $b_i = (1 - \delta)B_i$. If B_i is uniformly distributed on $[0, A]$, then b_i is uniformly distributed on $[0, A(1 - \delta)]$, and the classic monopolist, employing such leases instead of sales, would set a one-period lease rate of $A(1 - \delta)/2$. And since the length of the lease is the length of time over which the monopolist must maintain her "price" or lease rate, in each period, this is the optimal lease-rate to set.

Of course, for tangible durable assets, prospective customers may want to guarantee ongoing availability of the asset, especially when employing the asset may involve sunk-cost investments by the customer. In theory, the monopolist solves this problem by offering an open-ended lease; the customer can renew the lease for as long as he wants, at the initial lease rate. Another potential problem is price discrimination; if the monpolist can offer different customers different per-period lease rates, then after the first period, she (the monopolist) has the incentive to go to prospective customers who did not lease in the first period and offer them leases, even open-ended leases, at a lower lease rate. And, if possible, perhaps in the first period, she would set a lease rate higher than $A(1 - \delta)/2$. But, if this were possible, the Coase problem reappears: Savvy customers, knowing that by waiting a few periods they can get a lower lease rate, will want to wait. So, perhaps, the monopolist, giving up on price discrimination, somehow guarantees all customers that they can get the best terms that she offers to any customer. Not in this context but another (discussed in Chapter 22), General Electric Corporation once employed such most-favored-customer guarantees; so this sort of contractual feature is not entirely fanciful.

It is worth observing at this point that Coase's seminal article was titled "Durability and monopoly." A monopolist providing a service, the demand for which recurs in every period, has no Coasian problem. (Which, of course, is just what this per-period lease idea accomplishes.)

Another method for avoiding the Coasian trap—in my opinion, probably the most empirically significant method—involves credibility borne out of reputation. Consider a monopolist who, over time, introduces a sequence of durable assets; think of Apple or Samsung introducing successive generations of smart phones. Customers for these items may look at the initial very high price and wonder, "Will

---

[15] It is worth noting that in Coase's (1972) seminal article, he states as obvious the basic conclusion of what has come to be known as his conjecture. Most of the article concerns ways a monopolist will avoid this trap, which include the lease idea that follows.

the price come down quickly? Should I wait?" Suppose that the manufacturer, early on, refuses to lower the price or, at least, to lower it quickly. This might engender a reputation that this is how the manufacturer prices her goods through time. And, the story goes, the manufacturer, pricing any particular generation of the good, can resist the temptation to lower the price more quickly because, were she to do this, she would lose the valuable reputation for not doing so (valuable in terms of subsequent generations of the product). This story is just as verbal and informal as was Coase's story, and you should be just as suspicious of it. Not to bury the lede too deeply, Chapter 22 develops formal models that confirm the logic that the manufacturer won't yield to temptation on any single generation of product in order to protect her reputation. But we'll be less successful in formally modeling how the manufacturer obtains this valuable reputation.

My bottom line on the Coase conjecture

As a piece of exemplifying theory, the Coase conjecture does well. Monopoly sellers of durable assets do face the problem of prospective customers waiting for prices to come down. The Coase conjecture takes this problem and announces an extreme consequence. While one needn't accept the extreme consequence as something akin to natural law, there are circumstances—fairly delicate circumstances—under which the extreme consequences are the logical outcome. But this is not natural law, and the delicacy of the required circumstances alerts us to what it takes and the many reasons, in the real world, we see durable-good monopolists selling their wares for significantly more than their marginal cost.

As a piece of theory, I think the value of Coase conjecture is in the problem it identifies, rather than the solution it offers to that problem. The problem is that, with sophisticated counterparties (they could be partners, rivals, customers, or suppliers), an inability to commit to do certain things and not do others in the future can have profound consequences for what one does today, as well as what counterparties do. This is a theme to which we will return repeatedly; the Coase conjecture, despite being both delicate and extreme, is the first hint that, when one models strategic interactions in economics, a narrow focus on today's interaction can miss—and miss badly—important economic phenomena.

21.4. Other Contexts

To follow up on that observation, go back to where this chapter began, with the paradigmatic models of Chapter 20: Akerlof's market for lemons; Rothschild–Stiglitz and screening in insurance markets; and Spence's model of job-market signaling. As observed in the introduction to this chapter, the conclusions of each of those static models are potentially at risk when placed in a dynamic context.

Various papers have placed those paradigmatic models in a more dynamic setting, to see what (if anything) survives. I don't believe that firm conclusions have emerged; indeed, different assumptions about who knows what and when can lead to dramatically different conclusions. In the *Online Supplement*, as some "bonus coverage," I sketch two analyses of dynamic job-market signaling through education, one by Nöldeke and Van Damme (1990) and another by Swinkels (1999) that make this point: Nöldeke and Van Damme conclude that the Riley equilibrium is the only reasonable outcome; Swinkels concludes that pooling is inevitable. Of course, the point is not that one or the other is correct; each is formally correct. Instead, it is that different contextual assumptions can and do lead to very different conclusions.

And, Problem 21.10 proposes a dynamic model of Akerlof's used car market due to Fuchs and Skrzypacz (2015), where delay in the timing of the (eventual) transaction becomes, in essence, the separating signal. This notion will be met again in Chapter 23, on bilateral bargaining.

The ratchet effect and the rat race

One strand—or rather, two strands—in the literature deserve mention here, because although they are economically significant, they are not explored in detail in this volume. These strands involve situations that mix Chapters 19 and 20.

Both phenomena concern situations, in the spirit of Chapter 19, where one party contracts with a second party (or parties) for several periods. The first party could be an employer hiring employees. In a B2B context, it could be one firm contracting with a second firm to provide a service or an input to the first firm's production process; you can think of Toyota contracting with a firm that manufactures seat assemblies for Toyota vehicles. It could be the government contracting with private firms, or government regulators regulating a private firm. To set language, I'll call the first party the principal (she) and the second party the agent (he).

The key to both phenomena is uncertainty on the part of the principal about how hard or costly it will be for the agent to accomplish the task or, alternatively (a distinction in interpretation without a formal difference) about how able the agent is. In some contexts, the agent has private information about this, as in Chapter 20; in other contexts, both parties are equally uncertain. But as time passes and early results are observed, the principal learns (imperfectly) about how hard or costly the task is for the agent, given his abilities.

Suppose that the agent, through dint of effort choice, can affect what the first party learns. Think, in general, that increased effort improves (stochastically) the observed results, leading the principal to infer that the task is easier or less costly or that the agent is naturally more able.

The multi-period nature of the situation now comes into play. Suppose there are only two periods in which the agent takes actions, where in each period, the principal structures incentives for the agent. Suppose that the principal cannot—or chooses not to—commit at the outset to the incentive structure to be imposed on the agent in the second period. Insofar as the "optimal" incentive structure imposed in the second period depends on what the principal learns about the difficulty or cost of the task, the agent, in the first period, chooses his level of effort *both* to get a good outcome for himself this period *and* to affect what the principal infers, which in turn affects the incentive structure that the agent will face in the second period.

The fundamental questions then are: Does this mean that the agent exerts more or less effort in the first period, on account of the impact his effort has on his second-period incentives? In view of this, how should incentives for the agent be structured?

And the answer is: It depends. Suppose the principal, if she learns that the task is easier or less expensive, imposes more onerous terms on the agent in the second period. Then in the first period the agent, on the margin, exerts less effort. This is called the *ratchet effect*; the first party uses early performance data to "ratchet up" the pressure on the second party. The agent, aware of this, exerts less effort in the first period, to make his life easier in the second period. And, perhaps, as a consequence, the principal should turn up the incentive pressure in the first period.

- For instance, a salesperson is rewarded based on how much better she does in period $t + 1$ than she did in period t. So, in period t, she has the incentive not to do so well that her rewards next period be based on a difficult-to-surpass performance this period. (Or, if she performs exceptionally well in period t, her incentives to move on to another job are increased.) (Why wasn't this a consideration in Holmstrom and Milgrom 1987? There is a simple answer, but be sure you know what it is.)

- Blue-collar workers, being paid on a piecerate that will be reset based on how productive they are in the current period, are motivated to restrict output in the current period to some extent and, in particular, to enforce social sanctions against so-called rate busters.

- If compensation to a supplier is based on observed cost in previous periods, and if observed cost is lower based both on the innate abilities of the supplier and the amount of effort the supplier exerts to effect immediate cost savings, and if the firm (or government) contracting with the supplier infers from lower observed cost today that the supplier is innately more able, so incentives tomorrow can be ratcheted up, the supplier today is motivated to put in less effort today.

Conversely, in some contexts, demonstrated innate ability today results in better terms tomorrow; say, a promotion or a contract renewal or expansion is in the offing if the employee/supplier is judged to be particularly able. Then the employee/supplier is motivated, on the margin, to "over-exert" today, to get the promotion or win the contract extension or renewal. This behavior is particularly prevalent where multiple employees are competing for a single promotion, or multiple suppliers are competing for a big contract extension; think of defense contractors building prototypes, where only one firm will get the big supply contract. Especially in such contest situations, the literature refers to this as a *rat race*.[16]

---

[16] Bengt Holmstrom, who wrote seminal papers concerning this issue in the context of employment and promotion, prefers *career concerns* to *rat race*. But *rat race* allows for alliteration.

Coming attractions: Credibility

In these contexts and others that are similar, the problem arises because the first party is unable to commit not to use information it obtains in early periods when setting the terms of trade in later periods. Multi-period contractual guarantees may be feasible, but often they are not. And, then, what is left (at least in the case of the ratchet effect) is a promise by the first party not to use the information gained to the detriment of the second party. "But," the game-theory-addicted analyst asks, "What about subgame perfection? How can such a promise be credible?"

This takes us back to the monopolist facing a Coase-conjecture problem. Coase's monopolist would like to "promise" prospective customers that she won't take advantage of information she gains based on sales she does (or doesn't) make, because "taking advantage" of that information is, in fact, to her detriment ex ante. In other contexts, one party wishes to threaten a counterparty that, if the counterparty takes a given action, the first party will take an action that hurts the counterparty, even though that action will also harm the first party, rendering the threat not credible.

So, to complement this chapter, with its focus on what happens if commitment is not available, Chapter 22 looks at models of how commitment—or credibility of promises and/or threats—can be achieved as an equilibrium phenomenon.

Bibliographic Notes

What has become known as the Coase conjecture appears in Coase (1972). Subsequent papers that addressed aspects of this include Stokey (1981), Bulow (1982), Kahn (1986), and Gul, Sonnenschein, and Wilson (1986). The one (prospective) buyer and one seller, game-theoretic version of the problem is often interpreted as a one-sided bargaining model, but the connections to the Coase conjecture are rather clear. (See the solution to Problem 21.1.) Papers focused on this model inclue Sobel and Takahashi (1983), and Fuchs and Skrzypacz (2013). Both of these papers provide (generalizations of) the basic recursion employed in this chapter. Fuchs and Skrzypacz provide the "continuous-time limit" for the case where Nh approaches a finite limit.

The three papers mentioned at the start of Section 21.5, which address Coase-conjecture issues in the context of Chapter 20, are Nöldecke and Van Damme (1990), Swinkels (1999), and Fuchs and Skrzypacz (2015).

The brief introduction to the rat race and the ratchet effect provided here is connected to a very sizeable literature. With apologies to the many authors whose papers I should cite but do not, a pair of very nice papers on these subjects are Holmstrom (1982) and Laffont and Tirole (1988).

It is common to identify Weiss (1983) as being (among?) the first to observe the commitment issue in the context of the Spence job-market model, if education takes time.

Problems

■ 21.1. Consider the Alice-and-Bob, one-seller-and-one-buyer version of the basic model: Alice can sell an indivisible good to Bob, whose reservation price is B. (The good has no value for Alice.) Bob knows his reservation price; Alice assesses that B is uniformly distributed on $[0, A]$. Alice quotes a price p_0 at time 0. If Bob purchases at time 0, the game ends; if not, Alice can quote a second price p_1 at time 1. If Bob buys at time 0 for price p_0, Alice's payoff is p_0, and Bob's payoff is $B - p_0$. If Bob buys at time 1 for price p_1, Alice's payoff is δp_1, and Bob's payoff is $\delta(B - p_1)$.

What is (are?) the sequential equilibrium of this game? In general, how does this game differ from the continuum-of-consumers model analyzed in the text?

■ 21.2. Let $\delta = 0.8$. Alice is the monopolist with marginal cost 0; there are 40 prospective customers, all named Bob, each of whom has B_i equal to either 10.5 or 6.5, each with probability $1/2$, independent of the values of other Bobs' reservation values. Suppose there are two time periods, $t = 0$ and $t = 1$, and that Alice must name integer prices.

a. Suppose the Bobs are naive; they buy at the first instance that the price is below their value of B_i. What should Alice do?

b. Suppose the Bobs are sophisticated; they anticipate correctly at time $t = 0$ what Alice will do at time $t = 1$. Suppose Alice does not have the ability to commit to her price at $t = 1$; she will charge whatever price is optimal for her from that point on. Which prices by Alice maximize her expected profit?

c. Suppose the Bobs are sophisticated, but Alice has the ability to commit to the prices she will charge. Moreover, she can make her commitment to p_1 contingent on her sales at $t = 0$ and, with that ability, she commits to the following: She will set $p_0 = 9$. If she sells 20 or more units at time $t = 0$, she will lower the price at time $t = 1$ to 6. But if she sells less than 20 units at time $t = 0$, she will refuse to sell any units at any price at $t = 1$. Assuming the 40 Bobs behave symmetrically and independently, how should they react to this strategy? Will this strategy be good for Alice, compared to charging $p_0 = 6$ and being done with it?

■ 21.3. (This problem illustrates a second reason that the Alice-and-Bob version of the problem is not identical with the many-consumers version; cf. pages 183-4 and 187.) Suppose that the monopolist faces a continuum of consumers of total mass 10, whose valuation parameters have the following distribution: With probability $1/2$, half of the consumers have $B_i = 10$, and half have $B_i = 5$; and with probability $1/2$, half have $B_i = 9$, and half have $B_i = 2$. To keep matters simple, assume that these consumers are naive; they will buy the first time the price is less than or equal to their valuation. (The seller has zero marginal cost. The common discount factor $\delta = 0.9$.) What should the monopolist do, if she can set a price p_0 at time $t = 0$ and a second price p_1 at time $t = 1$?

And why does the one-consumer, Alice-and-Bob version of the story give a different answer?

■ 21.4. Prove Lemma 21.2.

■ 21.5. Using Lemma 21.2 (or not, if you prefer), prove Proposition 21.1.

■ 21.6. Prove Proposition 21.7. Or, at least (and this is all I do in the *Online Supplement*), sketch out how the argument goes. (It is still a difficult assignment, unless you have had a very good course on turning difference equations into differential equations.)

■ 21.7. Support the glib assertion I made on page 199.

■ 21.8. Suppose in the basic model of the Coase conjecture, with two time periods ($t = 0, 1$), half the consumers are naive (will purchase at $t = 0$ if the price is below their valuation) and half are sophisticated (correctly anticipate p_1 and are prepared to wait if that is better for them). These consumers are evenly distributed: The total mass A of consumers has mass $A/2$ of naive consumers with B_is uniformly distributed between 0 and A; and mass $A/2$ of sophisticated consumers similarly distributed. What is the optimal pricing policy of the monopolist? The algebra becomes quite messy, so the solution I offer in the *Online Supplement* uses algebra to start, but then resorts to numerical optimization. I suggest you do the same, for the case $A = 10$ and $\delta = 0.9$.

■ 21.9. Throughout the discussion of the Coase conjecture in this chapter, we used the assumption that consumer valuations for the item are uniformly distributed over some interval $[0, A]$. Can anything be done to weaken this assumption?

If you consult papers in the literature, you will find that they deal with the more general assumption that the cumulative distribution of consumers takes the form $F(B) = \mu B^\nu$, for positive constants μ and ν, and for $B \in [0, A]$. That is, the total mass of consumers is of size μA^ν, and the mass of conumers whose valuation of the object lies within $[\underline{a}, \overline{a}] \subseteq [0, A]$ is $\mu[\overline{a}^\nu - \underline{a}^\nu]$. Why does this work?

■ 21.10. Go back to the basic Akerlof model from Chapter 20. Alice owns a used car worth q to her. Alice knows q. She will sell the car to either Bob or Carol, if the price is right. The value of the car to either Bob or Carol is $q + 200$. But, while Alice knows q, Bob and Carol do not. They share a prior assessment that q is uniformly distributed on the interval [\$2000, \$6000].

When the story was that Alice names her asking price for the car, two equilibria were described: In the first, Alice names the price $2400, if $q \in [\$2000, \$2400]$, and she names the price $6000, otherwise. Bob and Carol both express a willingness to buy in the first case, but not the second, and a deal is consummated (being careful about to whom the car is sold). In the second equilibrium, Alice names a price $q + 200$, and Bob and Carol express a willingness to buy with probability less than one, where the probabilities are set so that Alice is motivated to name $q + 200$ when the value of the car to her is q.

In the spirit of this chapter, in the first equilibrium, if Alice names the price $6000, Bob and Carol "know" that the value of q is between $2400 and $6000. So why don't they name a price (Akerlof might suggest $2800) at which they are willing to buy? This was ruled out by assuming that they had no such opportunity, and the idea that Alice would ask for, say, $2800 was ruled out by specifying off-path beliefs that would cause Bob and Carol to decline. Of course, if $q \in [\$2400, \$2800]$, and Alice accepted an offer of $2600, Alice with $q \in [\$2000, \$2400]$ would name $6000 and wait for the counter-offer.

And, in the second equilibrium, if Bob and Carol declined to buy, they still "know" the value of q. So, why not offer, say, $q + 100$? Of course, if this works, Alice in her first ask will ask for $6000 or something close, regardless of the value of q.

All of which is to say, Akerlof's story falls afoul of the sort of problems that beset Coase's monopolist. Dynamic considerations make the static equilibrium story suspect.

Fuchs and Skrzypacz (2015) propose the following dynamic version of Akerlof's story. Suppose that Bob and Carol adopt the strategy of offering to buy Alice's car with bids that increase linearly through time, starting with a bid of $2200 at time $t = 0$. At time t, both Bob and Carol bid $2200 + 200rt$, where r is the *discount rate*. That is, if the car is worth q to Alice, and if a deal is consummated at time t at a price p_t, Alice's payoff is

$$\int_0^t e^{-rs} \frac{q}{r} ds + e^{-rt} p = (1 - e^{-rt})q + e^{-rt}p,$$

and if Alice sells to, say, Bob, then Carol's payoff is 0, and Bob's is

$$\int_t^\infty e^{-rs} \left(\frac{q + 200}{r} \right) ds - e^{-rt} p = e^{-rt}(q + 200 - p).$$

(If Alice sells to Carol, Carol's and Bob's payoffs switch.)

Fuchs and Skrzypacz show that the strategies just described form a (dynamic) equilibrium in the "game" where Bob and Carol make bids for the car through time, until Alice sells it to one or the other. Because this game is played in continuous time, there are technical issues that arise; ignore those (or, better, read the paper). But:

a. Show that Alice's best response, if her car is worth q, is to wait until the time τ such that $2200 + 200r\tau = q + 200$ and then to sell; that is, it is better for q-type Alice to sell at time $\tau = (q - 2000)/(200r)$ than at any other time.

b. Show that neither Bob nor Carol wish to "speed things up" by bidding more than $2200 + 200rt$ at time t. This is much harder, because you must specify the continuation from such a "defection": If Alice sells, the game ends. But what if Alice turns down this early offer?

Chapter Twenty-Two

Credibility: Reciprocity and Reputation

Chapter 21 concerns situations in which, when private information is revealed, parties to whom it is revealed cannot restrain themselves from using the information, in some cases to their ex ante detriment. In such cases, they would like to promise their counterparties that they will not use the information or, more generally, to promise *how* they will and will not use the information. But such promises may lack credibility.

And credibility issues aren't only a matter of the revelation of private information. Toyota's use of long-term relational contracts with suppliers, a part of the Toyota Production System, has proved to be an innovation in vehicle (and other) manufacture as revolutionary as was Henry Ford's assembly line.[1] The idea, which has successfully spread to many other industries, is that Toyota, rather than vertically integrating, engages with suppliers—think of a firm that supplies Toyota with seat assemblies—to purchase from those suppliers over the long run, as long as the suppliers meet Toyota's rather stringent standards and play by Toyota's "rules." Toyota's benefits from this arrangement include enhanced focus on its core competences and the ability to enforce stringent standards on suppliers.[2] Both parties gain from economies of scale and scope; Toyota's seat suppliers are allowed to and do supply seat assemblies to other vehicle manufacturers. And a Toyota supplier's benefits include guaranteed steady work (as long as they meet Toyota's standards), the opportunity to learn from Toyota (a truly great manufacturing company), and an enhanced reputation as a Toyota supplier: "If they are good enough for Toyota," reasons other potential customers, "they must be very good."[3]

A key part of this relationship is investment by each side in the relationship. In particular, Toyota expects—as part of their "rules"—that suppliers make sunk-cost investments that enhance the efficiency of the relationship. But this leaves the supplier open to a *holdup* by Toyota. The concept is simple: Toyota pays suppliers for what they supply. For reasons that I leave for discussion later, in this particular case, Toyota names the price it is willing to pay on a take-it-or-leave-it basis. But, for the broader concept of a holdup, imagine that the price is a result of ongoing bilateral negotiation. At the outset, the sides agree on a price sufficiently high so that the

---

[1] The system is a package of complementary activities, including very lean work-in-process inventory (kanban), unwillingness to accept defects, production leveling, and continual improvement in design and methods (kaizen). The system, employed by other industries, has other names, such as World Class Manufacturing.

[2] Why can't Toyota hold a "seat assembly division" within Toyota to similar standards? That's a question for Volume III.

[3] If this story piques your interest, see Milgrom and Roberts (1993).

supplier can recoup the cost of the sunk-cost investments it has made through a price that is greater than its variable cost. But once the sunk-cost investments are made, Toyota is in a more powerful negotiating position: If Toyota demands to renegotiate the price it will pay, now aiming for a price that doesn't allow the supplier to recoup the cost of its sunk-cost investments, the supplier may feel pressured to agree, because the sunk costs are...sunk. Of course, the supplier can seek protection from being held up by long-term contractual guarantees provided prior to making the sunk-cost investments. But those investments extend over many generations of vehicles, with seat designs that, at the start of the relationship, are unknown to both parties. Contractual guarantees ex ante that are legally enforceable are somewhere between difficult and impossible. So, what protection against a holdup is effective? If it were credible, Toyota's *promise* not to hold up its suppliers would do. But what renders such a promise credible?

On the other side of the coin are threats that economic agents may wish to make to forestall certain actions by counterparties. The classic example in the economics literature is a multi-market monopoly—colloquially termed a *chain store*—which tells prospective entrants into one of its markets that, should they enter, a ruinous price war will ensue, even though the price war will be costly to the monopoly as well as the entrant. Or, returning to Toyota, Toyota may threaten a powerful supplier, if the supplier should attempt to use its powerful position to leverage a better deal, then Toyota will drop them as a supplier, even if this means (in the extreme) idling a production line until a replacement supplier can be found.

In what is perhaps the classic context of these issues, oligopolists will attempt to collude, to charge high prices in markets where they compete and to avoid competing in each other's "territory." Such attempts are typically based on a combination of promises—not to lower prices or invade another firm's territory—and threats, to respond vigorously with lower prices and competing invasions, should one of the firms in the collusive regime break their promise to behave. The issue with threats—just as with promises—is credibility. It might be sensible ex ante to issue these threats. But are they credible? Will the threats be carried out by one of the firms, once the firm is faced with a fait accompli of the behavior that the threats were meant to forestall?

Finally, we have norms of behavior in a society: Adherence to the norm benefits the collective as long as all members adhere. But suppose it is not in the private interest of any member to do so. Suppose, in fact, that adherence by others to the norm enhances each individual's prospective gain from taking advantage by norm-breaking behavior. What makes adherence credible?

In all these contexts, economists employ game-theoretic models of equilibria in repeated games—the stuff of Appendix 15—to understand how such promises and threats may be credible (or not). The basic formal constructions are provided in Appendix 15, which you should review (or, if this material is new to you, study) before reading this chapter. With the appendix as background, this chapter provides a selection of contextual applications to show how the abstract constructions of Appendix 15 are employed.

It is worth saying from the outset that the territory into which we are moving in this chapter intersects with territory that has been explored and studied by social psychologists and sociologists. I will touch on this briefly in the discussion of social norms, but for the most part, this chapter takes a strictly traditional economic perspective. In particular, agents have narrowly focused (one might say, selfish) objectives, which they pursue in an equilibrium. This is a useful perspective for many purposes, but it is only part of the story; a broader perspective will be offered in Volume III.

22.1. Oligopoly and Implicit Collusion

Consider an N-firm oligopoly in which firms engage in quantity competition for a single "commodity" good. That is, each firm n (simultaneously and independently) chooses a quantity x_n to supply to the market, which results in the equilibrium price $P(x_1 + \ldots + x_N)$, for a given inverse-demand function P.

To fix ideas, suppose that the N firms are identical, with constant marginal cost $c > 0$. Also suppose that the inverse-demand function is $P(X) = a - bX$, where a and b are strictly positive constants with $a > c$. Then the (unique) Cournot equilibrium has each firm supplying $x = (a-c)/(b(N+1))$. This gives an equilibrium price $= (a + Nc)/(N + 1)$ and profit $= (a - c)^2/((N + 1)^2 b)$ for each firm.

If, however, the firms were to form a cartel, in which each firm credibly committed to produce $1/N$ of the monopoly output $(a - c)/(2b)$, price would be the monopoly price $(a + c)/2$, and each firm would make profit $(a - c)^2/4Nb$.

Of course, this symmetric cartel solution is not a single-period quantity-competition equilibrium: If $N - 1$ of the firms are producing $(a - c)/(2Nb)$, the Nth firm optimally chooses to produce $(a - c)(N + 1)/(4Nb)$, which, for $N \geq 2$, is larger than $(a - c)/(2Nb)$ by the multiplicative factor $(N + 1)/2$.

However, now suppose that these N firms serve this market repeatedly and indefinitely, at dates $t = 0, 1, 2, \ldots$. In each period, each firm n chooses a quantity x_{nt} to supply to the market, resulting in market equilibrium price $p(t) = a - b(x_{1t} + \ldots + x_{Nt})$. Suppose that each firm seeks to maximize the discounted sum of its profits in the individual periods, all using the common per-period discount factor δ.

To finish the formulation, we must specify what each firm n knows about the past when choosing its time t quantity x_{nt}. For now, assume that firm n knows the history of all past prices $\{p(t'); t' < t\}$. Firm n also knows the history of its own past quantity choices. Therefore, a feasible (behavior) strategy for firm n can be made contingent on past prices and its own past quantity choices.

Suppose each firm promises and threatens all of its rivals with the following strategy:

> At time $t = 0$, I promise to produce $(a - c)/(2Nb)$. And I promise to continue to produce this amount in each subsequent period, as long as all past prices have been (at least) $(a + c)/2$. However, should any previous price be less than $(a + c)/2$, I will increase my production to $(a - c)/(b(N + 1))$, and I will continue with this level of production for the rest of time.

As a full strategy profile, do these strategies constitute a Nash equilibrium? Note first that, if all firms use these strategies, the equilibrium path is that all firms produce $(a - c)/(2Nb)$ in all periods. To check that we have an equilibrium, three numbers must be calculated:

- The per-period profit each firm makes when all firms produce $(a - c)/(2Nb)$. This number is easy: Total industry profit is the monopoly level of profit, or $(a - c)^2/(4b)$, and since the firms are symmetric and behaving symmetrically, each firm makes a $1/N$ share of the total, $(a - c)^2/(4bN)$.

- The per-period profit each firm makes if and when all firms resort to the producing the Cournot quantity $(a - c)/(b(N + 1))$. This is $(a - c)^2/((N + 1)^2 b)$.

- The optimal profit a firm can earn for one period if it optimally deviates from producing $(a - c)/(2Nb)$ while all its rivals are (still) producing that amount. Sparing you the algebra, this is $(N + 1)^2(a - c)^2/(16bN^2)$.

And, with these three numbers, no firm chooses to deviate from the equilibrium path (always produce $(a - c)/(2Nb)$) as long as

$$\left(\frac{1}{1 - \delta}\right)\frac{(a - c)^2}{4bN} \geq \frac{(N + 1)^2(a - c)^2}{16bN^2} + \delta\left(\frac{1}{1 - \delta}\right)\frac{(a - c)^2}{(N + 1)^2 b}.$$

The left-hand side is the present value (from any date onward, along the equilibrium path) of the on-path profit in this and each subsequent period; the right-hand side is the best a firm can do immediately by deviating plus the discounted present value of profit starting next period with Cournot-equilibrium profits forever after. Simplifying this inequality by removing similar terms gives the required condition:

$$\frac{1}{(1 - \delta)4N} \geq \frac{(N + 1)^2}{16N^2} + \frac{\delta}{(1 - \delta)(N + 1)^2}.$$

Multiply through by $(1 - \delta)$, and the required condition is

$$\frac{1}{4N} \geq (1 - \delta)\frac{(N + 1)^2}{16N^2} + \delta\frac{1}{(N + 1)^2}.$$

Fixing N, the term on the right-hand side is a convex combination of two terms, with weight δ on $1/(N + 1)^2$. So, if $1/4N$, the term on the left-hand side, is *strictly* greater than $1/(N + 1)^2$, then there is $\delta_0(N)$ close enough to 1 so that this inequality is satisfied (for this and all $\delta \geq \delta_0(N)$). And $1/(4N) > 1/(N + 1)^2$ for all $N \geq 2$, by straightforward algebra.

The algebra obscures some simple intuition. The inequality $1/(4N) > 1/(N+1)^2$ is the algebraic manifestation of the (obvious) fact that a $1/N$ share of the monopoly-price total profit is strictly greater than a $1/N$ share of the Cournot-equilibrium total profit, since the monopoly price generates a total profit strictly greater than the Cournot-equilibrium price (as long as there are at least two firms). Because the best any firm can do in terms of profit in a single period is bounded above (by the entire monopoly profit), a one-period deviation followed by a forever-after $1/N$ share of Cournot profits must be worse than a $1/N$ share of forever monopoly profits, if the weight on periods after this period approaches 1. That, very simply, is what is happening here.

Have I shown that this is a Nash equilibrium?

I expect that most economists, on reading the previous subsection, would answer, "Yes, he has," to the question: "Has Kreps shown that this is a Nash equilibrium?" But I'm among those who would answer, "Not really, not rigorously." So, to engage in what may be extreme fastidiousness, let me explain.[4]

To show that this is a Nash equilibrium, I must show that all deviations by firm n from its specified strategy are (weakly) unprofitable compared to sticking to that strategy, under the Nash hypothesis that the other players adhere faithfully to their part of the strategy profile.

And, given the specified strategies of the other players, player n faces a infinite-horizon, sequential-decision problem, the sort of problem analyzed in depth in Appendix 6 of Volume I. Moreover, those specified strategies allow us to think of n's problem as one in which, at every one of n's information sets, the "position" is one of two states:

State 1. So far, the observed prices have always been the monopoly price or more.

State 2. At some earlier date, the observed price was less than the monopoly price.

I can describe the position as being in one of these two states because, whichever state prevails, it fixes how n's rivals will behave going forward. That is, from any two information sets in the game tree belonging to firm n that are in the same state, the problems the firm faces going forward are identical.

Faced with this infinite-horizon, sequential-decision problem, the objective is to show that n's strategy is optimal in the sense of Appendix 6 of Volume I. This will prove that firm n's strategy is a best response to the strategies of its rivals from its first information set, in particular, confirming that we have a Nash equilibrium.

Firm n discounts its in-each-period profit with a discount factor $\delta < 1$. Its maximum in-each-period reward is bounded in absolute value (by $(a - c)^2/(4b)$, the full monopoly profit). So, its decision problem is fully convergent. We can show that its strategy solves its decision problem by showing that its strategy is unimprovable.

To show unimprovability, we first compute the firm's expected payoff beginning in either of the two states, if it follows the strategy.

- In the first state, where all prior prices have been at least the monopoly price, its strategy calls for it to produce $x_n = (a-c)/(2Nb)$. Doing so (and given the strategies of its rivals) gives the monopoly price, so the state remains. And a simple recursive formula tells us that the firm's expected payoff for the remainder of the

---

[4] The remainder of this subsection is very similar to the discussion of the same point in Appendix 15. If you carefully read that appendix, you can probably skip ahead. But I'll be brief.

game, starting from any point where the state is state 1, is $(a - c)^2 / (4bN(1 - \delta))$; that is, $(a - c)^2 / (4bN)$ per period.

- In the second state, where some prior price was less than the monopoly price, the firm is meant to supply its Cournot quantity. Its rivals all do the same, and a simple recursion tells us that its expected payoff for the remainder of the game for any position in which the second state prevails is the Cournot profit forever, or $(a - c)^2 / ((N + 1)^2 b(1 - \delta))$.

And to show unimprovability, recall that the drill is to show that the firm does not do strictly better by deviating from its strategy in a single period and then returning to the strategy. (Hence, the continuation values after a one-step deviation are as just computed.)

- In the first state, the firm can consider supplying more or less than its assigned quantity. Supplying less lowers its immediate profit (which takes a calculation I have not provided!) and keeps the process in the first state, so it does not give a one-step improvement. Supplying more will cause the state to move to the second state, because it will lead to a price less than the monopoly price. And the inequality we examined in the previous subsection shows that, even if firm n maximizes its immediate profit with such a deviation, for δ close enough to 1, this doesn't lead to a one-step improvement.

- And in the second state, nothing the firm does will change the state, so its continuation value is the same, whatever it does. It might as well optimize its current profit, which means producing the Cournot quantity this round. Or, put in contrapositive form, producing anything other the Cournot quantity will lower its immediate profit without changing its continuation value.

So, firm n's strategy is unimprovable from either state (given the strategies of the others). Hence it is optimal, hence we do have a Nash equilibrium.[5]

More than Nash? Is this equilibrium "perfect" in any sense?

And, more than that, we've shown that firm n's strategy is optimal from every point in the game tree where it has a choice to make, because every position is either state 1 or state 2. This is a measure of "perfection." It is incorrect to call this subgame perfection; even if we put firm n's choice node for each round t "first" in the game tree, unless firm n knows the quantity choices of its rivals at earlier times, its information set is rich with nodes. However, no matter what its beliefs are at its off-path information sets,[6] the strategies of its rivals going forward are fixed by the history of prices, so its strategy is sequentially rational for any beliefs. Regarding prices as *public signals* in the sense of pages 700 to 703, we have a *perfect*

---

[5] The level of fastidiousness provided here is not recommended when writing a paper for a journal, as it will likely elicit from referees or the editor the admonition to stop trying to pad the paper (or something stronger). And, it what follows, I revert to "sloppy" proofs. But behind each sloppy proof lies a careful proof of this sort.

[6] As long as the firm assigns positive probability only to nodes that are consistent with the prices it has seen.

public-signal equilibrium.

Note that, in terms of the various folk theorems of Appendix 15, this equilibrium corresponds in one sense but not in another to the equilibria of Proposition A15.1, the subgame-perfect folk theorem based on grim Nash punishment.[7] It is like Proposition A15.1 insofar as, if there is a deviation that leads to a lower-than-monopoly-level price, punishment consists of grim (Cournot) Nash punishment. But unless we assume that firms all observe one anothers' quantity choices, it fails to meet the assumption of Proposition A15.1 that each player observes the choices of her rivals at each date.

How general is this?

I've illustrated the basic idea with identical firms facing linear inverse demand and with constant marginal cost, employing identical strategies, leading to a symmetric and efficient (that is, monopoly-price) path of play. But the basic idea works for many variations:

- The firms can be asymmetric as to cost and have more general total-cost functions.

- The "equilibrium path" can involve asymmetric treatment of otherwise identical firms.

- The "equilibrium path" can provide a given firm profit levels that vary across periods.

- The "equilibrium path" can involve equilibrium prices that are less than or even more than the monopoly-profit price.

- The off-path "punishment mode" doesn't have to be *grim*. In particular, and depending on the discount factor δ and the "equilibrium path" payoffs to be sustained, a lengthy period spent playing a single-period equilibrium, after which collusion is reinstated, may suffice. ·

What is required is that there are:

1. an "equilibrium path" describing how each firm is supposed to behave, as long as all firms conform to this pattern of behavior, which is common knowledge among the firms;

2. a map from single-stage behavior to equilibrium prices that allows firms to tell when some one of their rivals has tried to "take advantage"; and

3. a static (one-period) Nash equilibrium profile of behavior for the firms;

all this such that

4. along the equilibrium path, at each time period, each firm's (discounted present value) of profit from conforming for the remainder of time is at least as large as the maximum profit the firm can earn by deviating in that time period plus

---

[7] If the use of "grim" here is mysterious to you, you should review Appendix 15.

the (discounted present value) of receiving the profit earned in the one-period equilibrium specified in point 3, for a long-enough period of time.

Bug or feature? Lots and lots of equilibrium outcomes

The above conditions mean that a lot of outcomes are possible equilibrium outcomes. Here is a picture: For a two-firm ($N = 2$) Cournot oligopoly, with $A = 10$, $b = 1$, $c = 4$, and $\delta = 0.95$, every point in the shaded region in Figure 22.1 is a possible equilibrium payoff vector for the two firms.

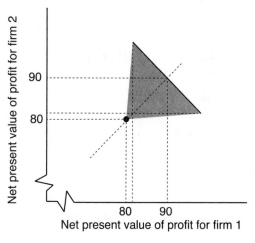

Figure 22.1. Possible equilibrium payoffs with grim Cournot punishment

Let me explain what is going on in this picture, because it isn't entirely straightforward. The straightforward parts are that, for the parameters given, the Cournot outcome generates payoffs of 4 apiece for the two firms, for a net-present value of 80 per firm. And the monopoly outcome generates a total profit of 9 per period, for a total net present value of 180. Split evenly, this is 90 per firm. There are asymmetric efficient equilibria; "efficiency" here refers to the two firms splitting the monopoly profit, so that the sum of their outputs must be the monopoly quantity 3; asymmetry refers to one firm producing more than 1.5 and the other correspondingly less. But to have an equilibrium, the firm producing less than 1.5 must be "content" with its inferior fate; it must not be better for it to take maximum advantage for one period and then revert to the symmetric Cournot outcome forever. This condition holds as long as the firm that produces more than 1.5 produces no more than 1.654 (approximately), which results in payoffs (in net present value terms) of 99.24 for the fortunate firm and 80.76 for the unfortunate firm. This is the extent of the solid line at the northeast boundary of the shaded region (with slope -1).

In the figure, all convex combinations of this line segment with the Cournot-outcome point (80, 80) are shaded. This isn't entirely straightforward. It is immediately okay *if* we enlist a theoretical conceit common to applications of various versions of the folk theorem,[8] namely, the existence of a *publicly observable random-*

---

[8]   As discussed in Appendix 16, there is a variety of results that fit under the general rubric of a folk

izing device. This is meant to be some, say, uniformly distributed random variable that the two firms both observe prior to play.[9] If such a coordinating device is available, the firms can use it to convexify the set of equilibrium payoffs: If I want as an equilibrium payoff a convex combination of the Cournot-outcome point and some point on the equilibrium-feasible efficient frontier, I have the firms observe this publicly observable randomizing device, and depending on the value, either proceed to the equilibrium that gives the feasible efficient point or to the grim Cournot equilibrium.

Is the shaded area the full extent of the feasible equilibrium payoffs? And what if there is no publicly available randomizing device? Suppose for now that we restrict attention to equilibrium payoffs based on the threat of grim play of the static, one-period Cournot equilibrium in case of defection. Even with this restriction, the answers to these two questions are delicate: As the payoffs get "closer" to the Cournot-equilibrium payoffs, the cost in future payoffs from defection decreases, but so does the amount that can be gained by one period of defection.

The exact extent of feasible-as-equilibria payoffs is theoretically of interest, but practically speaking, what is of greater importance is that there are so many equilibrium payoffs. One might argue that there is no reason for the firms to settle for an inefficient (for them) equilibrium, and one might argue that, in this toy example with symmetric firms, the symmetric equilibrium (the one identified exactly previously) is the "obvious" candidate.

But what if we suppose that the firms aren't precisely symmetric? Suppose, say, one firm has marginal cost 3 and the second has 2.9. Then it is quite unclear which equilibrium is "the answer" or, for that matter, whether there is a single, obvious answer. In the simple case of different but constant marginal costs, the efficient outcome is to have the firm with lower marginal costs do all the producing. If it can transfer profit to its rival, perhaps it should do so, since to earn the monopoly profit at its lower marginal cost, it needs the cooperation of its rival. But what is the right or fair amount to transfer? And, one might object, in any real-life context, anti-trust authorities would probably intervene in the case of such an arrangement.[10]

Indeed, in any real-life context and in the face of laws forbidding explicit collusion, how can firms come to an agreement? Recall item #1 on the list of requirements: "an 'equilibrium path' describing how each firm is supposed to behave, as long as all firms conform to this pattern of behavior, which is common knowledge among the firms." Is this really possible?

Implicit collusion—and even explicit collusion—does happen and has a long history. Adam Smith, in *The Wealth of Nations*, famously observed that "People of the same trade seldom meet together, even for merriment and diversion, but the conversation ends in a conspiracy against the publick, or in some contrivance to

---

theorem. No single result can claim to be *The* Folk Theorem. Therefore, I use "folk theorem(s)" or "a folk theorem."

[9] In many applications of this idea, such as in some parts of Appendix 15, the firms observe a fresh randomization in each period.

[10] Why only "would probably?" See Harrington and Skrzypacz (2011), discussed later this section.

raise prices."[11]

In some cases, the collusion is explicit and legal: Think of OPEC (the Organi-zation of Petroleum Exporting Countries) in its heyday (say, the 1970s and 1980s), when the oil ministers of the member nations would meet and set quotas for each country.[12]

Collusion is sometimes explicit, even if it is not legal: A very famous exam-ple involved the sale of large turbine generators in the United States in the 1950s by General Electric, Westinghouse, and Allis-Chalmers. The three firms used a technique called bid rigging, "sharing" the market by allowing one the three firms to win each job as it came along at a substantial profit, with the other two firms putting in noncompetitive bids. What makes this instance famous is not only the scale of the conspiracy but also the clever method that the three firms employed to determine which of them would win any particular job, while hiding what they were doing from the authorities: They creatively employed the lunar calendar.[13] More recent examples involved collusion in the sale of lysine (a chemical added to livestock feed), citric acid, and vitamins. In the cases of bid-rigging for large tur-bine generators and the pricing of lysine, explicit conversations were held among the conspirators, hence antitrust laws were broken. When the conspiracies were discovered, executives received prison sentences.

But it doesn't necessarily take explicit conversation to collude. In some cases, where one firm among the few is "dominant," the practice of price leadership can be observed, where the dominant firm sets a price that its rivals (to greater or lesser extent) follow, in fear that, if they undercut the dominant firm, they will be pun-ished. (Collusion in the sale large turbine generators, following the lunar-calendar conspiracy, moved on to this sort of practice; this will be discussed beginning on page 225.) Competing firms will sometimes segment the market, with each firm un-derstanding implicitly which segment—perhaps geography based, perhaps based on characteristics of the goods the firm sells—"belongs" to it, and which segments belong to its rivals, understanding as well that, should one firm "invade" another firm's segment, it will face competition in its own segment.

This discussion takes us away from "theory" and into institutional details, but it speaks to the question: Is the theoretical multiplicity of equilibrium outcomes a feature or a bug? My answer is that it is a feature, because it tells us that many things are possible: Even if each firm is maximizing its profit as it is theoretically meant to do, it may seem to be "cooperating" with rivals. And it is a feature, because trying to predict how this theory will work out in a particular context requires that the analyst dive into the institutional details of the situation, beginning with the psychological question: Do the participants seek an accommodation with one another, or is it a matter of "devil take the hindmost"?

---

[11] Smith (1776, Book I, Chapter X, Part II, page 152).

[12] OPEC faced two complications: There was a "competitive fringe" of countries outside OPEC, which would take advantage of OPEC restricting supply from its member nations. And members of OPEC would "cheat" on the quotas assigned; I'll say more about this on pages 224–5.

[13] This scheme for bid-rigging the sale of large-turbine generators was part of a larger conspiracy to fix prices in all manner of electrical equipment, involving other firms; for details, see Sultan (1974).

Price competition? Differentiated goods? Market segmentation?

The discussion so far has been premised on the assumptions that

1. firms compete in quantities; that is, each firm at each date t chooses a quantity to supply to the market; and

2. each firm learns the equilibrium price that prevails at date t before choosing its quantity for date $t + 1$.

These assumptions show that collusive equilibria are possible and that there may be a lot of them, but insofar as we are interested in understanding "price leadership" or "market segmentation" or "product differentiation and variety," richer models of the nature of competition are required. For price leadership, for instance, a model in which firms compete in terms of posted prices, Bertrand style, would seem more suitable. For market segmentation, some form of product differentiation and/or models of geographically separate markets, combined with a model of how firms compete (or not) is needed.

It isn't difficult to build such models: Simplifying quite a lot, the keys to any such model are: (1) the basis on which firms compete for sales, and (2) what each firm learns about its rivals' actions. The problems at the end of the chapter provide a few examples; the literature of Industrial Organization (research papers and textbooks) provides many more.

In all cases, collusion is almost always achieved by the dual promise and threat strategies of the simple model: Each firm promises to behave, as long as the other firms behave, but if some firm transgresses, each firm threatens to resort to period-by-period play of some single-period equilibrium, either forever (grimly), or for enough time so that no firm has an incentive to transgress.

This basic "design" for modeling collusion raises two questions:

1. What if firms can't be sure that some rival has transgressed?

2. Is grim play of some single-period equilibrium the strongest credible threat that firms can issue?

Non-Nash punishment?

Taking the second question first, Propositions A15.3 and A15.4 suggest that much stronger threats are credible in equilibrium, which widen the scope for collusion: The more severe the threat, the less tempted any firm is to take its maximal one-period advantage by deviating from its assigned "role."

In particular, these two propositions propose that a firm's minmax[14] value can be a credible threat against it: Transgress, and all of the firm's rivals will push the transgressor's payoff down to its minmax value. In the simple model of quantity competition among firms with a commodity good, the minmax value of each firm is, effectively, zero profit. This is so, because the rivals of a misbehaving firm can

---

[14] Roughly, the firm's minmax value is the worst payoff it can receive in a single period, if all of its rivals do their worst to it. For the precise definition and the use of minmax values in folk theorems, see Definition A15.2 on page 665 and the discussion that follows the definition.

threaten to flood the market, driving the price of the good below the misbehaving firm's marginal cost. This suggests that the space of feasible equilibrium payoffs is much larger than is depicted in Figure 22.1; in place of the Cournot-payoff threat point, the threat point is a zero-payoff for each firm.

This is so in theory, but note the following caveats:

1. Is it credible that a misbehaving firm will be punished by its rivals to this extent? Proposition A15.3 simply shrugs off this question, because it is only interested in Nash equilibrium outcomes. Proposition A15.4, however, says that minmax punishment is, under certain circumstances, credible, because it is part of a subgame-perfect Nash equilibrium.

2. Both Propositions A15.3 and A15.4 assume that the round-by-round choices of each player are observed by every other player. In a phrase, the propositions assume that deviators are identified, so non-deviators know who it is that must be punished. Perhaps this requirement holds in cases of firms competing for sales, but we didn't assume so, when we assumed that firms all learn (only) the equilibrium price that results from the choices of their rivals.

3. The construction of the off-path strategies in Proposition A15.4 is, to say the least, complex. Reversion to play of a single-period Nash (Cournot) equilibrium is perhaps more realistic.

4. Proposition A15.4 (and, for that matter, all results that bear the name "folk theorem") concern which payoffs can be sustained as $\delta \to 1$. As a practical matter, we'd like to know what is possible for a given $\delta < 1$. Punishment in the form of grim play of a single-period equilibrium makes the required computations feasible. More severe punishment is...not so amenable to analysis; see the discussion in Section A15.4 and, in particular, on page 661.

Noisy observables I: Price(s) observed (Green and Porter 1984)

The folk-theorem constructions are based on a threat: A deviator from the collusive scheme will be punished when and if it deviates. But what if firms involved in a collusive scheme can't be certain whether some rival has transgressed. What if a firm cannot tell, based on what it sees, whether there was a defection from equilibrium-path behavior? The standard terminology in the literature phrases this as: What if observables are *noisy*?

Green and Porter (1984) provide the seminal formal model. They model an oligopoly in which N identical, risk-neutral firms compete in quantities, as in the model provided above, but where the equilibrium price p_t in period t is a function P of the sum of quantities each firm supplies multiplied by a random variable θ_t, where the sequence $\{\theta_t\}$ is i.i.d. (the θ_t are jointly independent and identically distributed). That is, $p_t = \theta_t P(x_{1t} + \ldots + x_{Nt})$. Firms observe the price p_t at time t, but not the quantities supplied by their rivals nor the value of θ_t; you can think of θ_t as a shock to demand for the good. Hence, a low price could be the result of some member firm choosing a quantity larger than it "should," but it could also be the result of a small value of θ_t (i.e., low demand in the given period). If firms ignore instances where p_t is lower than expected, they encourage their rivals to deviate from their assigned quantities. If they take low values of p_t as an indication that some firm has deviated and, in consequence, they resort to grim play of the Cournot equilibrium, then it is only a matter of time before collusion will be irretrievably lost.[15]

Green and Porter propose the following as a (symmetric) equilibrium scheme: The three parameters of the scheme are a trigger price p^*, a punishment-period length T^*, and a quantity x^* smaller (and more profitable per firm, if each of the N firms supplies x^*) than is the (symmetric) Cournot profit per firm. At $t = 0$, each firm produces x^*. And they continue to do this as long as observed prices are above p^*. But at the first instance of a price $p_t \le p^*$, for the next T^* periods, firms all produce Cournot quantities, regardless of what is observed. (Note that "Cournot quantitites" must be computed with the impact of the θ_t in price taken into account. Assume that firms are risk neutral and that θ_t has expectation 1; then the "Cournot quantities" are what they would be if θ_t was deterministic and equal to 1.) After T^* periods of Cournot competition are done, firms revert to the *cooperative phase*, in which each firm produces x^*, and stay there until the next observation of a price less than or equal to p^*, which triggers another *punishment phase* of length T^*.

What does it take for this to be an equilibrium? If it is an equilibrium, each firm assumes that, during cooperative phases, its rivals all are conforming; that is, supplying x^*. Therefore, the firm can compute for every quantity x that it might supply the probability

$$\pi^*(x; x^*) := \text{Probability}\big(\theta_t P((N - 1)x^* + x) \le p^*\big).$$

Hence, in a cooperative phase, if the firm produces x, its expected net present value is the solution $V(x; x^*)$ to the recursive equation

$$V(x; x^*) = \mathbf{E}\big[\big(\theta P((N - 1)x^* + x) - c\big)x\big]$$
$$+ \delta\left[\big(1 - \pi^*(x; x^*)\big)V(x; x^*) + \pi^*(x; x^*)\left(\frac{1 - \delta^{T^*+1}}{1 - \delta}V' + \delta^{N^*}V(x; x^*)\right)\right],$$

where V' is the firm's expected profit in a period from the solution to Cournot competition, and $\mathbf{E}$ denotes expectation of the random variable θ (whose distribution is the distribution of the θ_t). The equilibrium condition is then that, for given p^*, T^* and x^*, $V(x; x^*)$ is maximized in x at $x = x^*$.

Will firms conform to these strategies during a punishment phase? Yes, they will. For the T^* periods of punishment, a firm can do no better than to produce the Cournot quantity in response to Cournot outputs by its rivals. And the firm can't, by deviating, hasten the return to cooperation; the strategies involve precisely T^* periods of punishment, without regard to what prices prevail in that period. This is not a particularly nice model to "solve" in closed form, even with specific

---

[15] Well, perhaps not. See Problems 22.7 and 22.8.

parametric assumptions about the function P and the distribution of the θ_t, and so I won't try to provide an example here. One might anticipate that increasing T^* and raising p^* will raise the corresponding r^*; punishment is more severe (lasts longer) and is more easily triggered, so firms are more cautious. But, at some point, it no longer is worth the effort to restrain one's output. In any case, a next step would be to find the "optimal" equilibrium of this sort from the perspective of the firms: Which values of p^*, T^*, and (corresponding) x^* give the largest value of $V(x^*; x^*)$?

Whatever the answer, please note: In most cases, punishment will be triggered eventually. (But see Problems 22.7 and 22.8.) And when this happens, *in equilibrium, every firm is "aware" that none of their rivals have caused it to happen. In equilibrium, in the cooperative phase, all firms are choosing x^* as their best choice.*[16] But to keep all the firms "honest," even though it is known by all that it is no one's fault, punishment for a while becomes necessary.

Is the scheme described by Green and Porter—described by some T^* and p^* and, in punishment phases, Cournot competition—the best in terms of overall profits of the colluding firms? In general, it is not. Abreu, Pearce, and Stachetti (1986) provide a methodology for finding the optimal cartel scheme in the case of identical firms whose choice of quantity is limited to a finite set and with a host of other assumptions. The optimal scheme they identify involves bouncing between cooperative and reward phases, but in place of p^* is a region of prices that triggers in any period what happens in the next period. Their answer is elegant, but getting there involves a lot of hard work.

Is there any real-life case that resembles this theoretical model? The story of OPEC in its powerful heyday comes close. Member countries would be allocated quotas (by mutual agreement) of crude oil to pump, which would raise the world spot price of crude oil.[17] This spot price would be the result of quantities pumped by member states of OPEC, the pumping activities of other countries outside of OPEC (the so-called competitive fringe), and shocks to demand (such as the weather). The problem—and here we diverge from the Green–Porter equilibrium model— was that member states could secretly exceed their quotas and "sneak" their excess output into the spot market, decreasing the spot price.

This led to the following cycle of events. The Oil Ministers of the member states would meet and agree to abide by quotas on how much each would extract. For a short time, member states would come close to obeying their quotas, which would of course cause non-member producers to increase their levels of output, to take advantage of the high prices. But then, slowly at first and then more rapidly, the spot price of crude would decline: Member states were probably cheating, but cheaters

---

[16] We can fancy-up the model still further by adding a random factor to production costs, so that firms sometimes find "cheating" irresistible. But doing so adds a significant level of complication to the model and, even so, it stretches the meaning of cheating. (For a caricature of this situation, see "A second example: Hidden information" in Appendix 15, pages 699-700, and the analysis of this example beginning on page 729.)

[17] Crude oil comes in many "grades," but the relative prices of the various grades are well-enough established that we can speak of a single world spot price of crude.

could never be adequately identified—there was a lot of finger pointing—and as the spot price began to decline with the inevitable punishment phase looming, every member state would cheat more and more, accelerating the decline in the spot price. Eventually, the Saudis, who were the enforcers of this cartel, would open the spigots, and the price of crude would collapse. And after punishment had gone on for a while, the member states would have their oil mininisters meet, reaffirm quotas, and begin the dance once again.

To be very pedantic, this was a case where competition was in terms of quantity, the (single) equilibrium price was observable to all, and quantities supplied could be hidden. This is similar to the Green–Porter model, but with a few differences.

Noisy observables II: Quantities observed (Skrzypacz and Hopenhayn 2004)

The notion that cartel members jointly observe a noisy market price and compete in Cournot fashion fits (roughly) the case of OPEC. However, in other market contexts, the model simply doesn't suit. Consider the case of General Electric and Westinghouse competing in the manufacture and sale of large turbine generators in the United States in the 1960s. This picks up from the story related briefly on page 220: GE, Westinghouse, and Allis-Chalmers had been caught in a clear conspiracy to rig bids in the 1950s, with executives given prison terms, and the firms were on guard about doing anything that looked like overt collusion. Prices of large turbine generators—machines sold to electric utilities that are used to turn mechanical energy into electiricty—collapsed in the resulting competition, which drove Allis-Chalmers from the market. In the early 1960s, then, it was a matter of two industrial giants sharing the market—entry barriers to overseas firms were high—with prices that were close to marginal cost.[18]

The competition, while not ruinous, was not desired by either firm; they wanted to collude to raise prices, but they had to avoid any whisper of overt conspiracy to accomplish this. The obvious question, then, is why didn't the logic of the folk theorem lead them to raise prices, each kept in check by the threat of a return to marginal-cost price competition?

The reason was that neither firm knew what prices its rival was "charging." A large utility—think of Consolidated Edison of New York (Con Ed)—having decided to buy a new generator, would announce that they were open to receive bids from any reputable supplier. GE would formulate a bid and present it to Con Ed in secret. Westinghouse would do the same. And then Con Ed would announce, "We are awarding the contract to... Westinghouse." GE wouldn't know what was in the bid that Westinghouse had proffered, and so they didn't know whether Westinghouse had submitted a low price or if it was some peculiarity of Con Ed and this particular generator that led Con Ed to give the job to Westinghouse. Complicating this was that the "values" to the two firms of a particular contract were different; but neither firm could be sure what the value of the contract was to

---

[18] I'm simplifying details. The fascinating story, with many of the details I'm omitting, is told in Porter (1980a).

its rival. The only information that was available to GE when Westinghouse was awarded the contract was that bare fact, as well as the terms of the offer it itself had proffered.

Here is a stylized model of this situation. Instead of calling the two firms GE and Westinghouse, call them A and B. In each period $t = 0, 1, \ldots$, a utility calls for bids for a generator.[19] The specifications for the generator change from period to period; the utility publishes the specs of the generator desired, so this is known to both A and B. The firms independently and privately proffer bids, denote them by b_{At} and b_{Bt}. And, then, the utility chooses between the two: Let θ_t be a noise term that applies in period t and is known to the utility but not to A or B (who know the distribution of θ_t): The contract is awarded to whichever of $b_{At} + \theta_t$ or b_{Bt} is smaller. This θ_t represents some "private value" of the utility for dealing with one of the two firms bidding; $\theta_t > 0$ means that the utility has private reasons for preferring to deal with B, with the size of θ_t measuring the size of these private reasons; and symmetrically if $\theta_t < 0$.

Finally, we assume that A and B have private valuations for being awarded the contract. Specifically, in each period t, there are random variables ϵ_{At} and ϵ_{Bt} such that, if A wins the contract with bid b_A, its net profit on the contract is $\epsilon_{At} + b_{At}$, while firm B nets 0; and vice versa if firm B is awarded the contract. Think of ϵ_{Xt} as a negative number, the cost to $X = A$ or B of fulfilling the contract.

Firms A and B have two shared concerns in this model and one conflicting concern: First, it is in their joint interest that the time t contract is awarded "efficiently" *to the extent possible*; that is, if $\epsilon_{At} > \epsilon_{Bt}$, it is "efficient" for firm A to be awarded the contract. Of course this concern is somewhat diminished if, say, $\epsilon_{At} > \epsilon_{Bt}$ 90% of the time; firm B aims to have some profit, some reasonable fraction of the time. To avoid this complication, suppose that the $\{\epsilon_{Xt}, X = A, B, t = 0, 1, \ldots\}$ are i.i.d., so that "efficiency" has each firm winning 50% of the time. And even then, because of the θ_t impact, the firms—even if they coordinated their bids—can't ensure that the utility will choose the lower bid. Hence it is appropriate to say "to the extent possible."

Their second shared concern is that they'd like to have their bids be large, so that their profit, when they win, is large. But, of course, their interests diverge concerning "market share": As long as the bids are profitable for the firms, each wishes to win as many of these contests as possible.[20]

---

[19] One can add a degree of more realism by modeling that the calls for bids from utilities come at random times, with the interarrival times being exponentially distributed. If the interarrival times are i.i.d. and independent of other sources of uncertainty in the model, this is just as complicated as the "one utility per time period" model, with the interorder discount factor being $\mathbf{E}[e^{-r\tau}]$, where τ is distributed according to the interarrival time random variable and r is the per-unit-time interest rate.. In fact, an even more realistic model would be that the distribution of the interarrival times "bunch": There are times where lots of utilities seek more generation capacity, because the general level of economic growth is heating up. But I'll ignore that additional complication.

[20] To give a sense of how much more complicated real life is than a caricature model: In the situation facing GE and Westinghouse, GE always had a cost advantage over Westinghouse. The cost of manufacture is driven by a firm's cumulative experience, and GE had about twice the cumulative experience of Westinghouse. However, GE wished to maintain its market share at around 67%, no less but no

If we look at the "game" at any single date t, this is a fairly standard first-price auction model. It is only fairly standard, because the θ_t interfere with the rule that (in this bidding-for-a-project application) the low bid will win. The theory of such auctions is very well developed and is the subject Chapter 24, but for now, I make the following "assumptions" that will, in Chapter 24, become propositions under standard assumptions. In the auction game between A and B at a single date t:

1. There is a unique symmetric Nash equilibrium in bidding strategies.

2. In this equilibrium, Firm X, for $X = A, B$, bids $f(\epsilon_{Xt})$, where f is a strictly decreasing function of ϵ_{Xt}. (Remember that this is a low-bid-wins competition.) Hence, if $\theta_t \equiv 0$ (with certainty), the winner of the auction would be whichever firm attaches a higher value to winning the auction.

So how can the firms collude to raise their bids? Suppose they could credibly agree that, at the conclusion of the auction at time t, the winner of the auction will pay the loser $k/2$ for some $k > 0$. This raises the relative cost of winning the auction by k (relative to losing the auction); the winner's marginal cost of fulfilling the contract increases by $k/2$, while the loser is compensated by $k/2$. This raises the equilibrium bid function f by precisely k. Here is the argument:

Without this change, the equilibrium bid function f satisfies, for each ϵ_{At}, that $f(\epsilon_{At})$ maximizes in b_{At} the quantity

$$(b_{At} + \epsilon_{At}) \times \text{Probability}\{b_{At} + \theta_t < f(\epsilon_{Bt})\},$$

where the expectation is over the values of θ_t and ϵ_{Bt}.[21] Suppose the scheme in the previous paragraph is put in place, and suppose firm B increases its bidding function by k; it bids $f^k(\epsilon_{Bt}) := f(\epsilon_{Bt}) + k$ when its private-value term is ϵ_{Bt}. Of course,

$$\text{Probability}\{b_{At} + \theta_t < f(\epsilon_{Bt})\} = \text{Probability}\{b_{At} + k + \theta_t < f(\epsilon_{Bt}) + k\}$$

for all b_{At}; I've just added k to both sides of the inequality. Therefore,

$$\text{Probability}\{b_{At} + \theta_t < f(\epsilon_{Bt})\} = \text{Probability}\{b_{At} + k + \theta_t < f^k(\epsilon_{Bt})\}.$$

Raising its bid by k—that is, bidding $f^k(\epsilon_{Ak}) = f(\epsilon_{Ak}) + k$—means that A wins precisely when it won before, in terms of two ϵ_{Xt} and θ_t.

What changes is the amount that A wins, if it wins the auction, *and also* what it wins if it loses the auction. If A wins the auction with these new bidding functions,

---

more, because it wanted Westinghouse to remain in the market, to forestall possible charges of predation and/or the entry of foreign manufacturers. Westinghouse, however, wanted to increase its overall market share. Westinghouse had less of a cost disadvantage in some classes of turbine generator, but the market in those generators was growing at a slower rate, so leaving those generators for Westinghouse was not a long-run, sustainable strategy.

[21] If ϵ_{At} is not independent of ϵ_{Bt}, we must make the probability conditional on ϵ_{At}.

the utility pays it k more than before. But A only keeps $k/2$ of that; it pays the other $k/2$ to B. And if it loses the auction, A is paid $k/2$ by B. *So, regardless of whether it wins the auction or loses, it gets $k/2$ more than it had before this scheme was implemented.* But if it is ahead by $k/2$ regardless of whether it wins or loses, this has no impact on its optimal choice of bid; bidding $f^k(\epsilon_{At})$ against the symmetric strategy for its rival is optimal.[22]

Of course, there are problems with this collusive scheme. The first and most important is that anti-trust authorities would look very much askance at this arrangement, if it were revealed. It must be done tacitly, and so the winning firm at time t must be willing to pay $k/2$ to its rival, without having (for instance) a legally enforceable contract drawn up between the two. *This is where the repeated-game nature of the model comes into play:* Suppose the firms agree (tacitly, please) to abide by this scheme as long as each winning firm makes the expected transfer of funds. But if either firm ever refuses to make the transfer payment, both firms resort to period-by-period play of the "Bertrand" bidding equilibrium. For each firm, abiding by the arrangement means a steady expected stream of $k/2$ more than they would get from period-by-period bidding equilibria. Breaking the deal means increasing the chances of winning the auction in any period by lowering the firm's bid and, if the firm does win, saving $k/2$, but at the cost of triggering punishment: As long as the per-period discount factor δ is close enough to one, abiding by the deal is clearly going to be superior.

A second problem—as much a problem of the model as of the equilibrium—is that the utility asking for bids is assumed to choose between the two bids it receives. It has preferences about whom it declares the winner, but if both bids are increased by some huge amount, the utility pays, or so the model assumes. In other words, in the model, this scheme "works" (all other problems aside) no matter how big is k. This is clearly unrealistic. For reasons we don't need to discuss here, having to do with how utilities are regulated, it is true that demand by utilities for capital equipment such as large turbine generators is very inelastic. But very inelastic demand does not mean completely inelastic: At least two factors constrain the increase of k. The utility could go to foreign producers (assuming they exist, which they do in real life) if k gets huge. Or the utility could simply delay its demand for an additional generator.

And a very large k is (more) likely to attract the attention of antitrust authorities.

Could such a scheme work in reality? Harrington and Skrzypacz (2011) observe that, in the case of some international cartels, something very much like this arrangement has been successfully employed, with the transfer payments being "disguised" in the form of sales of the item (a commodity such as industrial chemicals) at highly inflated prices from "losing" firms to firms that have won more than their "fair share" of contracts from downstream customers.

---

[22] While I assumed that A and B are symmetric, so we have a symmetric equilibrium, this was only for expositional ease. If you go back over the argument, assuming that A and B are not symmetric but have arrived pre-scheme at a bidding equilibrium, then with the scheme loaded on top, it remains an equilibrium for each to increase their old equilibrium bid functions by k, giving each $k/2$ more than before, each and every period.

I'll suppose, however, that this form of transfer payments won't work for Firms A and B, who are selling one-off items, such as large turbine generators. Certainly, this scheme would be dangerous for GE and Westinghouse, which are being closely monitored by the US antitrust authorities.

Skrzypacz and Hopenhayn (2004) suggest a scheme that is based on the same principle—if you raise the cost of winning a contract and simultaneously raise the benefit from losing, you will increase the equilibrium bid function—but that has a one-level better disguise. Suppose Firms A and B agree to the following: Each is initially endowed with some number of imaginary "chips," say, five apiece. These are not real, physical chips, but a notional quantity that management at both firms can monitor. Specifically, if in period t, firm A wins the contract, both firms decrease firm A's nominal endowment of chips by one and increase the endowment of Firm B. So, for instance, if Firm A wins the contract at $t = 0$ and $t = 1$, then going into $t = 2$, both firms know that firm A's supply of chips is 3 and firm B's is 7. If, at $t = 2$, Firm B wins, then Firm A's supply goes back to 4 and B's down to 6. And so forth.

And, if either firm runs out of chips, it must let its rival win the next auction (or two, or three). Enforcement of this rule is as in the k scheme: If a firm is out of chips and yet still wins a contract, the two firms resort to bare-knuckle grim play of the period-by-period Nash equilibrium. So, as long as these chips allow firms to collude with higher prices and δ is close enough to 1, this scheme is credibly self-enforcing.

Does the scheme allow for collusive higher prices? Does it provide "efficiency" in terms of which firm wins a particular auction? It isn't perfect, but it does improve matters to some extent. In equilibrium, chips have value, computed from the fact that they permit firms with chips to bid and compel firms without chips not to win. By solving the (quite complex) joint dynamic-programming/equilibrium problem, we can establish for each firm the incremental value to the firm of each chip, a value that increases the fewer chips the firm currently possesses. In formulating its bid at time t, assuming that the firm has at least one chip, it factors into its calculation that winning the bid increases its long-run costs by the incremental value of going from however many chips it currently possesses to one fewer, while losing the auction provides it with the incremental value of one more chip in its possession. In just the way that k increased the bids, the prospects of losing a chip by winning the auction and winning a chip by losing the auction causes the equilibrium bids to rise, although now the calculations of equilibrium bid functions become much more complex.

Skrypacz and Hopenhayn provide the calculation and some numerical examples, which you should consult if this scheme intrigues you.[23] But it is worth observing a trade-off in this scheme: As more chips are put into the system—if we endowed each firm with ten chips instead of five—the incremental values of chips fall, and so the collusive prices become lower. The "ideal" scheme for achieving

---

[23] The paper does more than this; in particular, it shows that "symmetric punishment" for defections cannot work in this context.

collusion is to give one chip to one of the firms and none to the other, so that (by the rules), they take turns winning successive auctions. Besides being a bit too obvious a form of collusion (obvious to anti-trust authorities), the one-chip regime (and more generally, a regime with only a relative handful of chips) has another problem: With a small numbers of chips, "efficiency" in terms of awarding the contract to the firm that values it most is somewhat lost, not only when one firm is out of chips, but when one firm has only one or two chips, whose incremental value is therefore very large, while the incremental gain to the other firm of losing this round is comparatively small.

To finish the story of GE and Westinghouse in the 1960s: Because of the real-life complications of their situation (see footnote 20 on page 226), and also because they had well-founded fears that the antitrust authorities in the United States were monitoring their actions, GE looked elsewhere for a solution. GE believed that collusion would be possible if, by some means, it could make public the bids it was making to utilities, and if they could convince Westinghouse to do likewise. But simply making bids public—that is, revealing bids to one's rival—would excite the interest of antitrust authorities. What GE did, then, was to find a way of making its bids public—in particular, to Westinghouse—with a scheme that was dressed up as "providing protection to our customers." Westinghouse, after a bit of time, copied GE's scheme and, with GE essentially taking the role of price leader, the two managed a very profitable implicit collusion for a decade or so. You can read about GE's scheme in Porter (1980b), and you can see how the Antitrust Division of the US Justice Department responded, after a decade of collusion, in Porter (1980c).

Some bottom lines on collusion, with and without noisy observables

The three pieces in a collusive scheme are: (a) the deal, or which parties get what and when while colluding; (b) the nature of "punishment," if and when it becomes necessary; and (c) the trigger for initiating punishment.

It helps on two grounds if the deal can be monitored perfectly. Then, at least in theory, punishment is something held over the heads of the colluders, never to be imposed. Hence, punishment can be severe, which helps enable collusion. And it makes implementation, once the scheme is understood by all concerned, relatively easy. The point of both the sidepayment scheme, where the winning bidder pays the loser $k/2$, and the "chips" arrangement, is to take an inherently noisy situation and, at least in terms of how collusion operates, to drive out the noise. Without going into details, the scheme employed by GE and Westinghouse during the 1960s came down to making their private bids public, again "clarifying" an otherwise noisy arrangement.

This takes us to what may well be the most common collusive scheme in real life: market segmentation. Roughly put, competitors in an industry divide the market into segments, with each segment the "property" of one (or a small number of accommodating) competitor(s). In such schemes, market segments are often based on geography or product characteristics. The point is that once segments are established and understood by all participants, the entry of a competitor into a segment that is the property of another competitor is the trigger for, at least, punishment of the offender. This punishment can take the form of a general price war, although segmentation can allow for more focused punishment; the offended party invades the segment of the offender or, in a form of "social" punishment, all industry participants invade the offender's segment. Even if the market cannot be perfectly segmented, segmentation of large chunks of it is still a valuable tool for oligopolists (of course, to the detriment of customers caught in one of the segments).

The Green–Porter model shows that if the noise cannot be driven out, punishment will be triggered, even if (per the equilibrium) no party is at fault. Such cases are more complex, because then colluders, knowing that there will be punishment periods, must be concerned (again, at least in theory) with how long punishment will last. Schemes where the noise is eliminated are much simpler, because then the threatened punishment can be as severe as possible, subject to the "credibility" constraint (namely that the parties involved, faced with a need to resort to punishment, can be counted on to carry it out).

The duration of punishment is only one design element; another element is what happens during a punishment phase. Easy designs, which we relied on exclusively in this discussion, involve reversion to some single-stage Nash equilibrium, either applied grimly (forever) or for some length of time. Both the minmax constructions of Appendix 14 and the analysis of Abreu, Pearce, and Stachetti show that punishments more effective than play of a stage-game Nash equilibrium can be implemented, although they are generally more complex. And, indeed, with identified deviators, one can imagine the threat of asymmetric punishment, where the deviator must "take its medicine" before being allowed back into profitable collusion.

Finally, there is the question of which (observable) outcomes trigger punishment: In all the constructions discussed, punishment is triggered by some publicly available information, be it a market price that is "too low" (or a failure to pay k or winning a bid when bereft of chips). The latter two triggers are particularly noteworthy, because they are "constructed" triggers; artifices constructed by the players that are useful *because* they are "public"; that is, where the participants to the scheme all (or both) understand when punishment has been triggered. Recent work by Sugaya (2023) considers much more complex collusive equilibria where players "punish" one another based on private information. Such equilibria work in theory; but it is easier to imagine real-lfe collusion based on public observables.

22.2. Entry Deterrence and Predation: The Chain-Store Paradox

Collusion concerns competitors in an industry finding ways to avoid fierce competition among themselves, so that all (except, of course, customers) benefit from higher prices. Entry deterrence, in contrast, is about firms in an industry impeding the entry of other firms, to preserve for themselves the profits they earn (again, to the likely detriment of customers).

The basic idea is simple. The incumbent firm or firms in the industry take steps that lead prospective entrants to assess that, if they enter, their post-entry profits will be insufficient to cover any costs of entry or will be below the level of profit the prospective entrant can achieve elsewhere.

One category of "things to do to deter entry" in the literature (and, one assumes, in real life) is to choose production technologies that will make the incumbent(s) fiercer competitors post entry. To fix ideas, imagine the industry has a single monopoly firm, facing market linear market demand $D(p) = A - p$, where p is price set by the monopoly. Applying the hoary principle that the monopolist should set marginal cost equal to marginal revenue (no Coase-conjecture problem in this story), if the monopolist has constant marginal cost c, it will choose $p = (A + c)/2$, realizing profit $(A - c)^2/4 - F$, where F is the firm's fixed costs (its total cost function is $\mathbf{TC}(x) = F + cx$).

Now suppose we move back to the moment at which this firm is choosing its technology, and suppose there is a trade-off it faces between its fixed cost F and marginal cost c. Specifically, it can have lower marginal costs if it is willing to take on higher fixed costs. Think of the trade-off as substitution in the production process between long-lived, fixed assets[24] and inputs to the production process that can be varied frictionlessly, depending on the quantity produced. Suppose that a function $F(c)$ captures these trade-offs, where F is decreasing in c. Assuming differentiability, a monopoly that is assured of being a monopoly would then choose c to maximize $(A - c)^2/4 - F(c)$, which has first-order condition

$$\frac{A - c}{2} = -F'(c).$$

If, however, the monopolist faces the prospect of entry sometime in the next several periods, a smaller value of c might forestall that entry: The post-entry variable profit of a firm in a two-firm market depends on the nature of competition. But in most models of competition—certainly in the case of quantity (Cournot) competition—the variable profit of one competitor is increasing in the marginal cost of its competitor. I won't carry out this toy model any further, but it should appeal to your intuition that the incumbent firm might choose a bigger fixed-cost, smaller marginal-cost technology than is optimal for a monopoly, if doing so increases the odds that it will remain a monopoly. (Problem 22.9 poses the issue as a sunk- versus marginal-cost trade-off, but otherwise gives a full example of this general idea.) Other concrete steps a monopoly might take to forestall entry into its markets include locking up suppliers of some essential input or forming long-term relationships with important customers.

A second story in the literature about entry deterrence takes a distinctly different approach: It assumes that prospective entrants are unaware of the production function of the incumbent firm and draw inferences about that technology from

---

[24] So F is the "rental" or "retirement" per-period cost of the chosen level of fixed-assets.

the production decisions of the incumbent firm, while the incumbent firm is a monopoly. Per this literature, this gives the incumbent firm, while it is a monopoly, the incentive to "misrepresent" its production technology (e.g., pretending that its marginal costs are lower than they actually are). Early papers of this sort suppose that prospective entrants make naive inferences, believing that the monopoly firm is charging a profit-maximizing price in periods when it is a monopoly. And the incumbent monopoly firm, knowing that prospective entrants make naive inferences, "pretends" to be more efficient—and therefore a more capable rival in the event of entry—by producing more and charging less than was "optimal" given its technology. Milgrom and Roberts (1982a) reanalyze this story assuming prospective entrants make rational (equilibrium) inferences, understanding that the monopoly firm is trying to deceive them; I recommended this paper in connection with Problem 20.22, and I repeat that recommendation here.

Predation, entry, and exit

Beyond these stories of concrete actions to deter entry are stories in which deterrence is more psychological in nature, based on an entrant's fear that, faced with entry, an angry incumbent will, even at great expense to itself, drive any entrant out of the market by *predation*. In economics, predation is defined as predatory price cutting, typically below marginal cost, to eliminate a rival. Think of a monopolist with constant marginal cost c, in a market in which demand in each period $t = 0, 1, \ldots$ is given by $D(p) = A - p$. Imagine that, as long as the monopolist is a monopolist and faces no entry, it sets a monopoly price of $p = (A + c)/2$, realizing per-period profit $(A - c)^2/4$, less a fixed cost F. Imagine the monopolist senses, at some time t, that a rival is contemplating entry into the monopolist's market. Suppose the prospective entrant shares the monopoly's cost function, except that entry invoves a further sunk cost C. And suppose that, should the entrant choose to enter and the monopoly choose to accommodate the entrant through restrained competition (as in Section 22.1), they will share profits for the rest of time that are more than sufficient to cover their fixed costs and, for the entrant, the sunk cost of entry.

What if the incumbent monopoly, to preserve its monopoly position, threatens to fight entry by charging a post-entry price of $p = c$ or even less? This will mean short-term losses for the monopoly (by at least the amount of its fixed cost), but it will also mean losses for its rival. If inflicting these losses on its rival drives the rival out of the market, it may be a worthwhile trade-off: short-term losses for a while, but then a bright future as a restored monopoly. Indeed, if the monopoly can convince the prospective entrant that it will behave in this fashion if the entrant does enter, then the entrant may rationally choose not to enter; the mere threat of predation suffices to keep the entrant out and, in such a case, costs the incumbent nothing.

Furthermore, suppose the monopoly, being an incumbent firm, has already sunk its sunk costs of entering the market. Suppose a prospective entrant has an identical cost structure, *which includes sunk costs of entry*. The monopoly can threaten that, if the entrant does enter, it will lower its price to a level that just breaks even in terms of fixed plus variable costs, which is a level that does not allow the entrant to amortize its entry costs. Perhaps this threat will keep the prospective entrant from becoming an actual entrant; this scenario can be turned into an Industrial Organization story about first-mover advantage.

The problem with these stories is it that they put the incumbent monopolist and the prospective entrant in symmetric positions *once the entrant has chosen to enter.* Is it credible that the incumbent, faced with a fait accompli of entry, will go to war? Isn't it more likely that the incumbent will accommodate itself to its new rival? If the monopoly could be sure that, by inflicting losses on an entrant, the entrant will leave in a reasonable amount of time, then the story could make sense: There is a rational trade-off of short-term lossess for greater long-term profit that might make the threat credible.

But once the entrant has entered, why is that the entrant will be the one to leave? One imagines that a war of attrition will break out, to see which firm gives in first. And, informally,[25] wars of attrition are won by the party with the greater resources to stay the course. Think of cases where an industrial or commercial giant—think of an Amazon or Alphabet—declares its intention to enter a market niche inhabited by a small and so-far successful start-up, causing the start-up to allow the giant to acquire it at what is, for the giant, a very good price. (Or in some cases, we might expect the small start-up to look for a more friendly "partner" with which to fight the unfriendly giant.)

The chain-store parable

The chain-store parable changes the story in ways that increase the "apparent" power of the incumbent monopoly relative to its prospective rivals. The incumbent monopolist—now a chain store—holds a monopoly position in a countable number of geographically separate regions, indexed $t = 0, 1, 2, \ldots$. In each region, there is a prospective entrant that must choose whether to challenge the monopolist in that region. The entrants move sequentially, at times $t = 0, 1, \ldots$; that is, the prospective entrant in region t decides whether to enter at time t.

- If the prospective entrant in region t doesn't enter, the chain store enjoys monopoly profit m (for monopoly) in that region, and the prospective entrant has payoff 0.

- However, if the region-t entrant decides to enter, then the chain store must decide whether to be accommodating and accept the entrant's presence in its market or to fight this entry.
  - If the chain store accomodates the entrant, then the chain store earns profit d (for duopoly) that is less than m but is still positive. And the entrant earns profit d', which is positive.
  - But if the chain store fights entry, then both the entrant and the chain store lose money. For convenience, I'll assume that the chain store's profit, if it decides to fight, is 0. As for the entrant, it does worse than if it had decided not to enter; its payoff is some negative amount a.

---

[25] Formal models of wars of attrition will be provided in Chapter 23.

We could conceivably add detail to what it means for the chain store to fight, but, as this is just a parable, let us assume that, if the region-t market entrant decides to enter, the chain store simply decides whether to accommodate or to fight. This gives us the simple extensive-form game model of the situation in each region depicted in Figure 22.2.

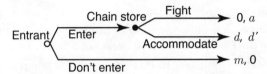

Figure 22.2. The chain-store parable stage game. (The payoffs for the chain store are given first. The values are arranged so that $m > d > 0$, and $d' > 0 > a$.)

Each entrant's payoff from the full game is its payoff in its one encounter with the chain store. The chain store's payoff is the discounted sum of its profits in all of its regions, discounted with discount factor δ.

If you reviewed Appendix 15, you will recognize the stage-game depicted in Figure 22.2 as a version of the threat game: The chain store wishes to threaten each entrant with a fight in the event of entry; if that threat keeps the entrant out, the chain store will reap monopoly profit m. However, the entrant in a given region, looking only at Figure 22.2, reasons that once it enters, if it enters, the chain store is faced with fighting and profit 0, or accommodating for profit $d > 0$; accommodation is better. The threat to fight is not credible.

And, indeed, one subgame-perfect equilibrium for the infinitely repeated game, with the chain store facing each prospective entrant in turn, is that every entrant enters, and the chain store accommodates each entry.

However, there is another subgame-perfect equilibrium for the infinitely repeated game, if δ is close enough to 1. The strategy profile of this alternate equilibrium is:

- Each entrant examines the history of all past encounters between "earlier" entrants and the chain store. If the chain store fought every time it faced entry, it stands to reason that it will do so again, so the entrant stays out. However, if in any early encounter, the chain store faced entry and accommodated the (earlier) entrant, then the chain store has shown weakness. So enter. (What about the very first entrant? The formal strategy is for every prospective entrant to stay out *unless* the chain store accommodated some earlier entrant. Since the first entrant sees no such earlier instance, it stays out.)

- As for the chain store in each period t: If it faces entry and if it has fought each and every entry it faced in the past, then fight this time. But if it faces entry and, in some past encounter, it accommodated entry, then it accommodates this entry as well. (And in the first period, its strategy is to fight if the first entrant enters.)

The strategies of the entrants are clearly best responses to the strategy of the chain store: The chain store will fight if it has always fought in the past, so entry is ill advised. But if it ever previously accommodated entry, then it will accommodate entry this time, so entry is best. For the chain store: If and when (if we are in a part of the game tree in which) the chain store accommodated some previous entry, it can expect entry in every subsequent encounter. It can do nothing to erase the blot on its reputation caused by its previous accommodation, so it is best to accommodate each entry it subsequently faces.

The one situation in which the optimality of these strategies requires a calculation is where, at some time t, (1) the current entrant has entered, and (2) the chain store has fought all previous entries. In this situation, the chain store can fight, in which case it gets 0 immediately and ensures (per their strategies) that all future entrants will stay out, for a net present value payoff of $\delta m/(1 - \delta)$; the discount factor δ out in front is because the chain store only starts getting m each period next time. Alternatively, the chain store can accommodate this entry, in which case it will face entry and accommodate in every future encounter, for a net present value of $d/(1 - \delta)$. The chain store's better immediate action, given it follows its strategy, is to fight as long as

$$\delta \frac{m}{1 - \delta} \geq \frac{d}{1 - \delta}, \quad \text{which is} \quad \delta \geq \frac{d}{m}.$$

Hence, if this inequality holds, the chain store's strategy is unimprovable, which implies optimality, and we have a subgame-perfect equilibrium.

As discussed in Appendix 15, this is an example of an *instrumental reputation*: The chain store carries a reputation for being willing to fight if it has always fought in the past, but if it ever accommodates an entry, it loses completely and forever its reputation. And this reputation is instumental: The chain store keeps this reputation at short-run cost, because it provides long-run benefits. The story might be more satisfactory if, occasionally, the chain store had to fight an entrant. But that is easy to add to the model: Suppose that in a handful of these markets, conditions are arranged so that the entrant's outcome if it enters and is fought is better than if it doesn't enter at all. That is, in terms of Figure 22.2, we have a few entrants for which $0 < a < d'$. Those entrants will choose to enter even if they are sure the chain store will fight. And, as long as there aren't too many of them, the chain store will fight them, to maintain its reputation for fighting and so to discourage most entrants, for whom $a < 0 < d'$, from entering. (This elaboration on the model is spelled out in Problem 22.10 as well as in Appendix 15.)

I stress that this "reputation" is the product of a bootstrap. *It is valuable because it keeps entrants out.* And it keeps future entrants out, because its value induces the chain store to protect it by fighting: *It keeps entrants out because it is valuable.* Another, just-as-good-in-theory, subgame-perfect equilibrium has every entrant enter and the chain store always accommodate. This isn't quite some folk theorem, because the model has a sequence of "short-lived" entrants. But the multiplicity of equilibria produced by folk theorems is present as well in this model.

So why one equilibrium and not the other? It may appeal to your intuition that, with one powerful and long-lived chain store facing a sequence of entrants, each of which can operate only in one market, the chain store ought to be able to choose the equilibrium it prefers. And it certainly prefers the equilibrium in which it has this powerful reputation. But, that said, we might expect a story about how the chain store, early on, built this powerful reputation. No such story is offered here; at best, this is story about how the chain store, if it found that it had this reputation, might protect it as an equilibrium phenomenon.

The paradox

Selten (1978) points out the following problem with the equilibrium in which the entrants all stay out. Suppose the chain store encounters a prospective entrant in a fixed finite number of regions at a corresponding fixed finite number $T + 1$ of times, $t = 0, 1, \ldots, T$. In region T, the chain store has no reputation to protect—this is the final encounter with a prospective entrant—so subgame perfection implies that it will accommodate entry by the region-T prospective entrant, if the region-T prospective entrant chooses to enter. The region-T prospective entrant realizes that this is so, and so in any subgame-perfect equilibrium, *regardless of how the chain store acted in the past*, the region-T entrant enters. But, then, in region $T - 1$, the actions of the chain store will not affect what happens in region T, so the chain store will accommodate entry in any subgame-perfect equilibrium, and so the region-$T - 1$ prospective entrant is sure to enter, regardless of history. And so forth. The reputation construction unravels from the end, and every prospective entrant enters to be met with accommodation.

Or, in the language of credibility, the threat to fight the final entrant is not credible, rendering not credible the threat to fight the next-to-last entrants, and so forth.[26]

Selten regards this as a paradox, because experimentally, one finds that if T is large—say, $T = 20$—the "chain store" can convince entrants early on that it will fight. (In fact, most "data" of this sort involves repeated play of a "cooperative" game, to be discussed in Section 22.3.) The paradox is that behavior *in theory* is very different when $T = \infty$ (or when there is always probability γ of at least one more round sufficiently close to 1) from when T is bounded above for sure by, say, 10,000 periods. But this isn't what one observes in experimental settings.

The incomplete-information resolution of the paradox

Selten resolves the paradox by supposing that, in real-life encounters, actors act "behaviorally" and not hyper-rationally. This is an excellent story, but one that fits in Volume III.[27]

---

[26] Please note that this argument is phrased in terms of subgame-perfect equilibria. There is, of course, a Nash equilibrium in which the entrants never enter, because the monopolist's strategy is to fight. Since the threat keeps entrants out, the threat never needs to be carried out, and so it doesn't hurt the chain store's ex ante payoff. For more on the distinction between Nash and subgame-perfect Nash equilibria, in the context of quantity competition between duopolists, see Problem 22.5.

[27] So if you are curious and don't want to wait, consult the original article: Selten (1978).

Here is a different resolution, which involves a "behavioral" actor, but one who is behavioral with relatively small probability. Suppose that the situation is one of incomplete information about the behavior of the chain store: With probability η (which is meant to be small but strictly positive), the chain store is an "angry" type, which fights any challenge, regardless of the financial cost of doing so. Alternatively—that is, with probability $1 - \eta$—the chain store is "rational," behaving in a way that maximizes the sum of its payoffs in each stage game.[28] Then there is a finite interger M such that, in a $(T + 1)$-region version of the chain-store game, for $T + 1 > M$, "the" sequential equilibrium of the game has the rational chain store fighting any entry in the first $T + 1 - M$ regions; hence the first $T + 1 - M$ prospective entrants do not challenge the chain store. (In the final M regions/time periods, the rational chain store and the corresponding entrants undertake a delicate dance of mixed strategies.)

How large is M? To answer this question, first answer another one: If an entrant assesses probability π that, if it enters, the chain store will fight, how large must π be so that the entrant is deterred from entering? Not entering nets a payoff of 0, while entering with probability π of being fought nets an expected payoff of $\pi a + (1 - \pi)d'$, and it is simple algebra to compute that, if $\pi > d'/(d' - a)$, the entrant is better off not entering. So, let ρ be the critical probability $\rho := d'/(d' - a)$. Then M is $\lfloor \ln(\eta)/ \ln(\rho) \rfloor$, where $\lfloor x \rfloor$ denotes the greatest integer less than or equal to x. Hence, if $-a = d'$, so that $\rho = 1/2$, and if $\eta = 0.001$—there is a one-in-a-thousand chance that the chain store is angry (and probability 0.999 that it is rational)—we have $N = \lfloor \ln(0.001)/ \ln(0.5) \rfloor = \lfloor (-6.90778)/(-0.69315) \rfloor = 9$. For all but the final 9 periods, the entrant is deterred from entry and, should it mistakenly enter, the rational chain store will fight.

This result is shown in Kreps and Wilson (1982a) and Milgrom and Roberts (1982b). In both papers, it is shown that, for this specific model, this is the unique sequential equilibrium (up to some knife-edge situations). The first few steps in their proof is provided in Appendix 15 in the context of the threat game.[29] But it is natural to wonder how general this phenomenon is. Will it work if there are other behavioral types? Will it work in a similar fashion for other games, and if so, for which games? Fudenberg and Levine (1989, 1992) provide a "proof technology" that generalizes the argument. Specializing their general result to this specific context, they show the following.

Proposition 22.1. *Suppose the chain store plays the game shown in Figure 22.2 against a sequence of short-run entrants at a finite number of times, $t = 0, 1, \ldots, T$, with each entrant playing once and once only. Assume that, at the outset, the entrants assess probability $\eta > 0$ that the chain store is the angry type; that is, it will fight any entry. There may be other behavioral types of chain store, but there is positive probability that the chain store is the*

---

[28]   Since there is a fixed, finite number of periods, it is unnecessary to discount the chain store's stage-game payoffs. It doesn't change matters much to include a discount factor, but it makes the statement of results a bit more opaque.

[29]   See pages 710–14. To simplify the exposition, it is assumed that $m > 3d$.

rational type; it seeks to maximize the expectation of its overall payoff. Finally, each entrant observes the history of play up to the time when it must decide whether to enter.

*Then, **in any Nash equilibrium of this game**, the rational chain store's payoff is bounded below $(T + 1 - M)m$, where $M = \lfloor \ln(\eta)/\ln(\rho) \rfloor$. Hence, as $T \to \infty$, the chain store's average payoff per period converges to m, its best possible outcome in the stage game.*

This result is discussed in Appendix 15; a version is given as Proposition A15.8 (page 715). A more detailed look at the proof is provided there, but since the idea is relatively simple in this context, I sketch the proof here.

The rational chain store's payoff in any Nash equilibrium is its payoff from its optimal strategy. This is necessarily greater than or equal to its payoff if it plays the particular strategy of always acting as if it were angry; that is, in all cases that it is challenged with entry, it fights. And in any Nash equilibrium, along any path of play in which every challenge is met by a fight, there cannot be more than M times that an entrant challenges the chain store.

Why this upper bound? Fix an equilibrium, a path of play, and a time t. The current entrant will challenge the chain store with entry *only if* it believes that the probability that it will be fought is no larger than ρ. Now, the probability that it will be fought is *at least* the probability it assesses that the chain store is the angry type; call this p_t. And let π_t be the probability that the current entrant thinks that it will be fought. Then, if it is fought, all future entrants apply Bayes rule: The posterior probability that the chain store is the angry type is

$$p_{t+1} = \frac{\text{Probability that the chain store is angry and will fight}}{\text{Probability that the chain store will fight}} = \frac{p_t}{\pi_t}.$$

And since $\pi_t < \rho$, this application of Bayes' rule implies that, every time the chain store is challenged and fights, the probability that it is the angry chain store must increase by at least the multiplicative factor $1/\rho$. Starting from the initial value η, with M such increases, the posterior probability exceeds η/ρ^M. Take the log of this probability:

$$\ln(\eta/\rho^M) = \ln(\eta) - M\ln(\rho) \geq \ln(\eta) - \left(\frac{\ln(\eta)}{\ln(\rho)} - 1\right)\ln(\rho) = \ln(\rho),$$

because $M > \ln(\eta)/\ln(\rho) - 1$, and the sign of $-\ln(\rho)$ is positive. Hence, $\eta/\rho^M > \rho$. Therefore, after M entrants challenge the chain store *and the chain store fights each of these challenges*, subsequent entrants assess probability greater than ρ that the chain store is the angry type of chain store. This means no more challenges.

It is worth observing that the same logic applies if we have an infinite-horizon model; that is, a single chain store faces an infinite sequence of short-lived entrants. With complete information about the chain-store's preferences, the infinite-horizon model admits a subgame-perfect equilibrium in which entrants alway avoid challenging the chain store *and another* equilibrium in which every entrant challenges the chain store. This result shows that, with a bit of incomplete information about the chain store's preferences—specifically, if there is a small probability that it is an angry chain store—in any Nash equilibrium of the infinite-horizon version of the repeated game, the chain store will be challenged at most a fixed and finite number M of times, as long as it fights every entry. Which then implies that the rational chain store's Nash equilibrium payoff is no worse than $m\delta^M/(1-\delta)$, and this lower bound is based on the pessimistic estimate that the M challenges come at times $t = 0, \ldots, M - 1$.

In other words, this little bit of incomplete information "kills" the wimpy-chain-store equilibrium, in which the chain store always gives in.

This construction depends on an initial prior by the entrants attaching an atom of probability on the angry type, which fights any entry. With all the possibilities for "behavioral types," why single out that one? The (informal) logic behind this assumption involves two steps. First, the idea that the chain store is with probability 1 motivated only by its desire to maximize its (discounted or not) expected profits is unrealistic. The prospective entrants can't be that sure. And, among all the behavioral types one can imagine, I would argue that "simple behavior" is more likely than something complex. Perhaps the most likely behavioral type is a wimpy (or naive) chain store that doesn't recognize the possibilities of fighting and so behaviorally just accommodates entry. But after that, always-fight is a type that ought to attract a nonzero assessment. And then it is only a question of how big T is relative to M.

The reader is entitled to ask: If it is reasonable to argue that the prospective entrants surely must entertain some doubts about the motivations of the chain store, doesn't it follow with equal force that the chain store should entertain some doubts about the motivations of the prospective entrants? And, if so, (how) does that change the story? In particular, what if, a priori, the chain store believes that prospective entrants may be a "type" that prefers entry to staying out, *even if* it is certain that the chain store will fight? See Problems 22.10 and 22.11.

One prospective entrant and wars of attrition

This last consideration—that the prospective entrant(s) may be a type that will enter no matter what the chain store will do—begs a further question: What if only one prospective entrant is prepared to challenge (or not) an incumbent firm in all its $T + 1$ markets, one at a time, at times $t = 0, 1, 2, \ldots, T$?[30] The distinction between $T+1$ distinct prospective entrants and only one is this: With a different prospective entrant in each encounter, each entrant is only concerned with what the chain store will do in its one encounter, based on its reading of history and the strategy of the chain store. It has no stake in the future or, in particular, on how its own choice to enter or not will affect the behavior of the chain store in the future. But, with a single prospective entrant, the chain store (or, in this variation, the incumbent firm)

---

[30] Or you can interpret this as the one entrant challenging the incumbent firm in a single market, where it can mount its challenge in each of $T + 1$ periods, where the stage-game payoffs in Figure 22.2 are the payoffs to the incumbent (chain store) and the entrant in each time period t.

and the entrant are more or less on an "equal footing" in terms of their concern for how each encounter affects the future behavior of its rival.

Please note: The incumbent and the entrant are not entirely on an equal footing, because in each period the entrant first decides whether to (continue to) challenge the incumbent, and then the incumbent decides whether to fight or not. A fully symmetric story would be where the two firms, in each period, simultaneously decide whether to continue the fight or give in.

Specifically, suppose the (now) single prospective entrant assesses probability η at the outset that the incumbent is an angry type that will fight in every period that the entrant mounts a challenge. And suppose the incumbent initially assesses probability η' at the outset that the (single) prospective entrant is a "truculent" type, meaning that it will mount a challenge in each period, no matter what it expects the incumbent to do. And with complementary probabilities $1 - \eta$ and $1 - \eta'$, each is the "rational" type, playing to maximize its expected net present value of per-period payoffs over the $T + 1$ encounters.

If we had $T = \infty$ (an infinite sequence of encounters), discounting, and no behavioral types, the folk theorems apply, stating that all sorts of outcomes are possible for discount factors close enough to one.

For finite T but again without the behavioral types, the logic of the chain-store paradox tells the game-theoretic tale: In the final round, the chain store is bound to accommodate a challenge, so the entrant challenges. And so forth. (And again, please note: This happens because, in each stage, the "last move" belongs to the incumbent. Faced with a challenge from the entrant in the final round, subgame perfection implies accommodation by the entrant. The story would reverse entirely if we supposed that, in each round, the incumbent could face the entrant with a fait accompli. What, then, would happen, without behavioral types, over a finite horizon, if they moved simultaneously? See Section A15.5 for the relevant theory.)

However, with finite or infinite T and both behavioral types, one intuitively expects a war of attrition: The rational entrant, wishing to convince the incumbent that it is truculent (so the rational incumbent might as well accommodate entry), starts at $t = 0$ by challenging the incumbent. The rational incumbent, wishing to convince the rational entrant that it the angry type, fights in response. Both sides lose relative to what might have happened in the short run. And at $t = 1$, this pattern recurs, until one side or the other gives in: If the incumbent gives in first by accommodating the challenge, it confirms that it is not the angry incumbent, and the logic of the chain-store paradox implies that there will be entry and accommodation for the rest of time. If the entrant gives in by not choosing not to challenge in period t, it confirms that it is not a truculent entrant, and (we expect) that, for most of the remaining periods, the entrant fails to challenge the incumbent, because the incumbent stands ready to fight any challenge. (Following the equilibrium construction in Appendix 15, we expect a complex dance over the final few periods.)

Formal equilibrium models of wars of attrition can be found in the literature. I won't present the analysis of one here, because they come up very naturally Chapter 16, where the subject is bilateral bargaining. (Think of a labor union on strike against a company.) But if you can't wait, Kreps and Wilson (1982a) provide an analysis of this sort of model (albeit in continuous time).

22.3. Relational Contracting

The applications discussed in Sections 22.1 and 22.2 involve practices that antitrust authorities frown upon, because those practices usually hurt the general public. So, at this point, it may seem that credibility based on reciprocity and reputation is used only in ways that are detrimental to the general welfare. However, in this section, we discuss models of contextual applications that are, in general, efficiency promoting. And, if I may editorialize, these contexts far outweigh the contexts of the previous two sections in terms of their prevalence, economic significance, and impact on social welfare.[31]

The basic idea is that two economic agents—it could be two firms, or a firm and an employee, or two individuals—are engaged in a long-term relationship in which each can take actions that, while personally costly, provide benefits to their partner greater than the cost to themselves; that is, each benefits if they reciprocate when the opportunity presents itself to do a "favor" for each other. Various terms are used to describe this sort of positive relationship between agents; I've chosen *relational contracting* for the activity as perhaps the most common term, but see also footnote 34.

For instance, a bottler wishes a bottle manufacturer to invest in a plant adjacent to the bottler's plant, to save on the transportation costs of empty bottles. This requires the bottle manufacturer to make a sunk-cost investment in the plant. To convince the bottle manufacturer to make this investment, the bottler "promises" a steady business and, stretching into the future, that it (the bottler) will not suddenly drop the supplier for another, slightly less expensive supplier. Moreover, the bottler promises that it will agree to per-empty-bottle prices that cover the variable costs of the bottle manufacturer with enough left over to amortize the cost of the sunk-cost investment. This is a *bilateral* relational contract between two long-lived entities.

In some cases, the relational contract "works," because one party (or both) is engaged in many similar relationships, perhaps relatively short-lived relationships, and each party can trust the other because of reputational concerns. Consider, for instance, a small college that asks a new PhD to accept a job as assistant professor. Accepting this offer requires the PhD to move her family to the small town in which the college is located, putting her children into local schools and otherwise making "investments," both in terms of locating in the small college town and learning the "do's and don't's" of working at the college, such as preparing to teach the courses assigned. In return, and if the now-faculty member performs up to standard, the college promises a reasonable teaching schedule with not-too-many new preparations, generous research support, and a fair shot at tenure. In this case, the former student, now a new faculty member, is willing to make the required personal in-

---

[31] So why put these applications at the end of the chapter? Only because, the collusion and entry-deterrence stories appear first in the literature.

vestments, because she judges that the college's promises are credible: While the college's short-term interests may be to exploit their new assistant professor, doing so will compromise the college's ongoing ability to hire future assistant professors.

The use of the term "favor" may mislead. In common parlance, one might not say that A has done B a favor by *not* taking an available action that harms B (and enhances the welfare of A). But this interpretation is meant to be included here. In terms of the introduction to this chapter, forgoing the opportunity to "hold up" a trading partner who earlier made sunk cost investments in the relationship is coded as a "favor"; a part of this story.

Relational contracts—long-run and generally positive relationships between economic agents, held together by a mix of self-interested reciprocity and reputation preservation—are very widespread in economic contexts. Correspondingly, the literature that analyzes specific examples and contexts is very broad. To give two early examples: Simon (1951) models employment as a hierarchical arrangement in which, after the employee takes a job, he is told what to do by the boss. Similar to the new assistent professor discussed earlier in this section, the employee must make sunk-cost investments when taking the job and then is at risk of being exploited by the boss, who could ask for overly onerous tasks, threatening the employee with discharge. In an analysis that anticipates both subgame perfection and the power of repeated play—Simon wrote before the relevant ideas in game theory had been invented—Simon explains, in terms that are identical to those a game theorist would use, how the boss resists the temptation to exploit the employee. And Lazear (1979) explains mandatory retirement (when it was legal) as resulting from a relational contract in which employers pay employees less than their worth early in the careers, with a (fulfilled) promise to pay them more than their worth later. This arrangement is to the benefit of the employer insofar as it leads to lower voluntary turnover—the employee is unwilling to give up the premium he will earn if he sticks to his current employer—but this is predicated on the credibility of the employer's promise to "overpay" late in an employee's career.

The obvious question is: At the outset of their relationship, why not draft and sign a formal contract that specifies that they will take all such appropriate actions? In real life—and in Volume III—one answer relies on bounded rationality on the part of the participants and, in particular, an inability to foresee all the contingencies that will arise over the life of the relationship. Or, at least, that it would be too costly to think through all future contingencies and negotiate how to proceed when and if they occur. In this volume, though, where bounded rationality is not allowed, while we could (and some analyses do) try to model the cost of negotiations, the tendency will be to rely on a third reason (that does apply in real life, along with the aforementioned two): It would be impossible to enforce (in the courts or through third-party arbitration) a "contract" that depends on certain contingencies. An example involves the tenure decision. Imagine a contract that specifies that tenure will be granted if teaching is at an *acceptable* level and the candidate has produced *enough* papers that are *clearly outstanding*, in the sense that they have had a real *impact* on the profession, *changing* how scholars in the profession think.[32] Who can credibly judge all those nebulous terms? This is not to say that there isn't an in-place process that tries to administer such criteria equitably. Faculty members denied tenure have rights of appeal, usually, to deans and provosts.[33] Of course, there are cases in which counting papers (and where they are published) is largely the criterion applied. And (for reasons to be discussed), when that is the criterion applied, it may be in response to the subjectivity of a criterion based on the subjectively judged quality of the papers. But when feasible in equilibrium, the subjective criterion could be seen as superior. And, if subjectivity is to be employed, a third-party-enforceable contract specifying this is out the window; we rely on *self-enforcement*, based on the individual interests of the institution.[34]

Hence, when we discuss relational contracting according to the rules of discourse of Volume II—a game is being played and an equilibrium is how it is played—we are a bit hamstrung. While we can (and do) tell stories about unenforceable contingent provisions in the relationship in the analytic style of this volume, the participants understand all possible contingencies and what will transpire in each of them, including those that are off path. These rules of modeling and analysis are consistent with credible dynamic self-enforcement; that's what things like subgame perfection and sequential rationality are about. But, in my opinion, this is less than entirely satisfactory, if our objective is to get into many of the real issues in and nuances of relational contracting. This, prospectively, is one of the major themes of Volume III.[35]

The trust game

One caricature model of relational contracting is the trust game, discussed in Appendix 15 and depicted here in Figure 22.3. At each time $t = 0, 1, \ldots$, Bob must decide whether to trust Alice. If he does not, both receive a payoff of 0. If he trusts Alice, she chooses between being nice, with payoffs of 1 for each, or to take advantage of Bob, with payoffs -1 for Bob and 2 for Alice.

In what sense is this a model of relational contracting? Bob is putting himself at risk if he trusts Alice. But doing so can be profitable for both, if Alice can be trusted to be nice, so Bob trusting Alice is doing her a favor. And being nice is a costly favor Alice does for Bob in the short run. But being nice can be a good idea in the longer

---

[32] This is roughly the tenure standard, subjectively applied, that my home institution proclaims.

[33] But at least in some cases, one role of deans and provosts is to make certain that departments are sufficiently stringent in their tenure judgments; the concern of these deans and provosts is that, owing to personal ties, departments will grant tenure too freely.

[34] In view of this paragraph, the term "relational contracting" is misleading if "contract" is taken to imply the existence of a formal legal contract: It is precisely the inability to have such a thing that motivates the discussion. The cleanest language, in my opinion, is that we are describing efficiency-promoting long-term exchange relationships, governed not by a formal legal contract but instead by the ongoing self-interest of the parties involved. Except that, in Volume III, when the notion that parties in such relationships often increasingly internalize the welfare of their trading partners, "self-interest" will have a very broad meaning. But this "clean" definition of the topic of this section and the next doesn't fit in a section title, so I use the imperfect name "relational contracting."

[35] If I ever write it.

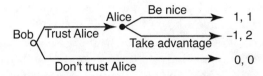

Figure 22.3. The trust game. (Bob's payoffs are listed first.)

run, if it induces Bob to trust her going forward. Appendix 15 discusses repeated versions of trust game at length: Here is a summary:

- If Bob and Alice play this game infinitely often, at times $t = 0, 1, 2, \ldots$, discounting their payoffs at rate δ, the following strategy profile is a subgame-perfect equilibrium, if δ is close enough to 1 (for these numbers, if $\delta \geq 1/2$): Bob trusts Alice as long as she has never taken advantage of him, but never trusts her again if she earlier ever did take advantage. Alice is nice to Bob when he trusts her, as long as she has always been nice in the past. But if she earlier took advantage (which she won't, according to this strategy), she will take advantage at every subsequent opportunity (of which, there will be none, according to Bob's strategy).

- But for long-lived Bob and Alice, there are many other equilibria, including the strategy profile where Bob never trusts Alice, and Alice, given the opportunity, always takes advantage.

- If Alice and Bob are both long-lived and play this game a fixed and finite number of times, things unravel from the back. In the final period, if trusted, Alice will take advantage of Bob. So, in the final period, Bob will not trust Alice. But then, in the penultimate period, Alice will take advantage of Bob if she is trusted, so he doesn't trust her then. And so forth. The only subgame-perfect Nash equilibrium outcome is no trust.[36]

- This "problem" with a finite-horizon can be fixed with a little bit of incomplete information about Alice's type, as in the case of the chain-store paradox. Specifically, if long-lived Bob initially assesses a small but strictly positive probability that Alice may be a "nice type," who would never, ever take advantage of him, then (in equilibrium), rational Alice will be nice to Bob for "most" periods, so Bob will trust Alice for most periods.[37]

The trust game could alternatively be played by long-lived Alice facing a sequence of short-lived Bobs. (This is the caricature that may best fit the situation facing the newly minted PhD student, taking a job at a small rural college.) Per the discussion in Appendix 15:

---

[36] In fact, this is the only Nash equilibrium outcome, because both Alice's and Bob's minmax values are the outcome of the unique Nash equilibrium of the subgame. See Proposition A15.5.

[37] But if Bob is long-lived, what about incomplete information about his type? Ponder the following: Suppose there is a small probability ν that Bob is someone who will trust Alice and continue to trust her, no matter how many times she takes advantage of him. What happens then?

- With complete information (specifically, about Alice being Rational Alice) and an infinite horizon, we have a host of "reputational equilibria." In one, Alice carries a reputation for being nice to Bobs who trust her, unless and until she fractures that equilibrium, as long as δ is close enough to 1. In another, no Bob ever trusts Alice, and Alice would take advantage of any Bob foolish enough to trust her.

- But with complete information and a finite horizon, things unravel from the final period: Bobs never trust Alice, and Alice takes advantage of any Bob who does trust her.

- If we add in a small positive probability that Alice is Nice Alice: It remains a *Nash* equilibrium for no Bob to trust Alice and for Rational Alice to stand ready to take advantage of any Bob who trusts her. (This is true for both finite- and infinite-horizon models). Since Alice is never trusted, her behavior is off path (and off path not because of her own actions), so her behavior is unconstrained by the requirement of being a Nash equilibrium.[38]

- But Rational Alice's behavior in this Nash equilibrium is not sequentially rational. In Appendix 15 (pages 718–22), it is argued that the (more or less) unique sequential equilibrium for the specific finite-horizon model where Alice is either Rational Alice or Nice Alice has the Bobs trusting her and Rational Alice being nice for all but the final "few" periods of the game.

Details are given in Appendix 15.

Trading favors

A richer and more symmetrical caricature model of a bilateral relational contract is the *Trading Favors* game. There are two parties, Alice and Bob, who interact over an infinite horizon, $t = 0, 1, 2, \ldots$ At each time t, an opportunity arises for one of the two parties to do a favor for the other party. This opportunity is encoded by a "state of the world at time t," θ_t, where θ_t takes the form (X_t, a_t, b_t); $X_t = A$ or B, and both a_t and b_t are real numbers. If $X_t = A$, then Alice must choose whether to do a favor for Bob (Bob is passive); if she does the favor, her immediate payoff will be $a_t < 0$, while Bob's immediate payoff witll be $b_t > 0$. If $X_t = B$, Bob must decide whether to do a favor for Alice; if he does so, his immediate payoff will be $b_t < 0$, while Alice gets $a_t > 0$. If the time-t favor is not done, both parties get immediate rewards of 0. At each time, the decision whether to do the favor is a simple "yes" or "no"; write $z_t = 1$ if the favor giver at time t chooses to do the favor and $z_t = 0$ if not. Of course, the choice of z_t is Alice's to make if $X_t = A$ and Bob's to make if $X_t = B$. Both Alice and Bob seek to maximize through their choices the expected discounted sum of their payoffs, $\sum_{t=1}^{\infty} \delta^t z_t a_t$ for Alice and $\sum_{t=1}^{\infty} \delta^t z_t b_t$ for Bob, for some discount factor $\delta < 1$. Assume that the sequence $\{\theta_t; t = 0, 1, \ldots\}$ is i.i.d. Assume for now that at each time t, and before the decision whether to do

---

[38] Compare with Proposition 22.1: Fudenberg and Levine (1989, 1992) show that the chain store faces no entry in most periods, in any *Nash* equilibrium. Their technology doesn't work for the trust game; see Appendix 15 for the reason.

the time-t favor must be made, both Alice and Bob observe all of θ_t.[39]

The all-favors (grim) strategy profile

For the base-model formulation (not the two instant variations), the all-favors (grim) strategy profile is defined as: $z_t = 1$ for every t and θ_t, as long as, at earlier times $t' < t$, $z_{t'} = 1$. But if at any time t and history of previous play, there is a t' when a favor wasn't done, $z_t = 0$. In other words, all favors are done as long as all favors were done in the past. But if a favor fails to be done, no more favors, forever.

Is it an equilibrium? Yes, under certain conditions.

Proposition 22.2. Suppose that

a. *The supports of the random variables a_t and b_t are bounded below, and*

b. *Writing a^e for the expectation of a_t and b^e for the expectation of b_t (which are well defined given the previous assumption, although they may be $+\infty$), a^e and b^e are both strictly positive. (That is, on average, both Alice and Bob get more from favors done for them than it costs them to do favors for the other.)*

Then the all-favors strategy profile is a subgame-perfect equilibrium for all δ close enough to 1.

Proof. There is very little to the proof. At any time t, if at a previous time a favor was not done, the party called on to do the favor this time is better off not doing the favor: It will be personally costly, and there will be no future compensation for doing the favor. But if, in the past, all favors were done, and if (say) $X_t = A$, Alice's choices are to do the favor, for an immediate cost of a_t and a discounted continuation value $\delta a^e/(1 - \delta)$, or not to do the favor, for 0 immediately and 0 in the future. That is, doing the favor is unimprovable, hence optimal, as long as

$$a_t + \delta \frac{a^e}{1 - \delta} \geq 0.$$

Since $a^e > 0$ and the support of a_t is bounded below, this clearly holds if δ is close enough to 1 (and similarly for Bob when $X_t = B$). ∎

A couple of remarks are in order:

---

[39] Two instant variations on this formulation are: (1) The opportunities to do favors alternate. That is, $\{\theta_t, t = 0, 2, \ldots, \}$ and $\{\theta_t, t = 1, 3, \ldots\}$ are two different i.i.d. sequences (with the full sequence independent), where $X_t = A$ for even numbered t and $X_t = B$ for odd numbered t. (2) Both Alice and Bob have an opportunity to do a favor for the other at each time t. In this formulation, θ_t would take the form $(\hat{a}_t, \hat{b}_t, \check{a}_t, \check{b}_t)$, where $\hat{a}_t$ and $\check{b}_t$ are both strictly negative and $\hat{b}_t$ and $\check{a}_t$ are both strictly positive. The interpretation is that, at time t, Alice can do a favor for Bob (or not) that will cost her $\hat{a}_t$ and provide him with benefits $\hat{b}_t$; and Bob can do a favor for Alice that benefits her $\check{a}_t$ and costs him $\check{b}_t$. Assume that, at each time t, they observe all of θ_t and then must decide simultaneously and independently whether to do the favor for the other party. This game, then, is a fancied-up version of the prisoners' dilemma, fancied up by the fact that the costs and benefits from cooperation and betrayal change in i.i.d. fashion from period to period.

- First, unimprovability implies that optimality holds as long as the decision-maker's problem is lower convergent. Discounting with a discount favor $\delta < 1$ and with a lower bound on per-period payoffs ensures lower convergence. (And if this makes no sense, either ignore this remark and assume the supports of a_t and b_t are bounded on both sides, or review Appendix 6 from Volume I.)

- If we hadn't assumed that the supports of a_t and b_t were bounded below, we'd have problems: For one thing, it wouldn't be clear that a_t and b_t are integrable. For another, we couldn't assume that unimprovability implies optimality. And, even if we assumed directly that a_t and b_t are integrable and that their expectations a^e and b^e are finite (and strictly positive), then for every $\delta < 1$, there would be a_t and b_t so large negative that unimprovability would fail.

Less than "all favors"

Even if we insist on lower-bounded supports for a_t and b_t, it is possible that one (or both) of a^e or b^e is negative. And even if both a^e and b^e are strictly positive and the supports of a_t and b_t are bounded below, for a given $\delta < 1$, there may be values or a_t or b_t so large negative that "all favors" fails to be an equilibrium. And even if "all favors" is an equilibrium, the parties may be better off if they agree that some favors are simply too expensive or generate too little benefit relative to their cost to be done.

A general structure for a strategy profile that has fewer than all favors done is constructed as follows. Begin with a (measurable) subset Λ of all possible values of the θ_t. For instance:

- Let $\hat{a}$ and $\hat{b}$ be negative numbers. And let

$$\Lambda := \big\{ \theta_t = (X_t, a_t, b_t) : a_t \geq \hat{a} \text{ and } b_t \geq \hat{b} \big\}.$$

In words, this specification of Λ includes only favors by Alice for Bob for which Alice's (negative) payoff is no smaller than $\hat{a}$, and symmetrically for Bob.

- Let

$$\Lambda := \big\{ \theta_t = (X_t, a_t, b_t) : a_t + b_t > 0 \big\}.$$

In words, this specification of Λ includes only favors by one or the other party whose cost is strictly less than the benefit it provides for their partner.

In general (that is, for a general Λ), define the Λ-strategy profile as the profile in which, if $\theta_t = (X_t, a_t, b_t) \in \Lambda$, player X_t does the favor; but if $\theta_t \notin \Lambda$, then X_t does not do the favor, both as long as all such favors have been done in the past. And, if ever a Λ-constrained favor is not done, Alice and Bob grimly refuse to do any favors for one another, forever.

To see whether this strategy profile is an equilibrium, apply the usual test: First, we compute the (before θ_t is realized) expected one-period payoff for the players:

$$a^e(\Lambda) := \mathbf{E}\big[a_t \cdot 1_\Lambda(\theta_t)\big] \quad \text{and} \quad b^e(\Lambda) := \mathbf{E}\big[b_t \cdot 1_\Lambda(\theta_t)\big],$$

where the expectations are taken over all values of $\theta_t = (X_t, a_t, b_t)$, and 1_Λ is the indicator function of the event Λ; that is, $1_\Lambda(\theta_t) = 1$ if $\theta_t \in \Lambda$ and $= 0$ if not. Let $\underline{a}(\Lambda)$ be the lower bound on the support of $a_t \cdot 1_\Lambda(\theta_t)$—that is, the lowest possible cost to Alice of a favor she does for Bob if favors are restricted to $\theta_t \in \Lambda$, and similarly for $\underline{b}(\Lambda)$. Then the Λ-favors strategy profile is an equilibrium for given δ if and only if

$$\underline{a}(\Lambda) + \delta \frac{a^e(\Lambda)}{1 - \delta} \geq 0 \quad \text{and} \quad \underline{b}(\Lambda) + \delta \frac{b^e(\Lambda)}{1 - \delta} \geq 0.$$

Is there a "best" specification of Λ? One obvious criterion is: Is the corresponding strategy profile an equilibrium?[40] Beyond this, the obvious criterion is efficiency: If, for a given Λ', there is some Λ'', both equilibrium Λs, such that the a priori equilibrium payoffs for Λ'' are as good as those from Λ' for both Alice and Bob and are strictly better for one or the other, then we should dismiss Λ' from consideration. Perhaps you can guess the characterization of efficient Λ, but if not, see Problem 21.14.

Asking for favors

Consider a variation in which we relax the assumption that Alice and Bob both observe θ_t in each period. For this variation, we first must change the basic model a bit. Instead of having $X_t = A$ or B—that is, at each time t, either Alice can do a favor for Bob or Bob can do one for Alice—suppose that for some t, neither has a favor to do. Formally, allow X_t to also equal 0, which means "no favor this time," and assume that, conditional on $X_t = 0$, $a_t = b_t = 0$ with probability one. This has no impact on the characterizations of all-favors and Λ-favors models, although if $a_t = b_t = 0$ with the positive probability that $X_t = 0$, this lowers $a^e(\Lambda)$ and $b^e(\Lambda)$ in general, making it more difficult to have an equilibrium. In essence, if X_t can equal 0, it lengthens the time between favors; if $X_t = A$, Alice has to compute the immediate cost with prospective future gains, and the longer she must wait for some reciprocal favor, the less likely it is that she'll be willing to do the favor.[41]

And now suppose that, when $X_t = A$, only Bob is told this, and he is told b_t. That is, when there is a favor that Alice can do for him, he recognizes this, but Alice does not. Bob must then ask Alice for the favor, describing what it is he wants ("Alice, could you drive me to the airport today?"), at which point she understands

---

[40] You might wonder whether a specification of Λ that fails the unimprovability test for some values of a_t or b_t—which means favors are done at least for a while—perhaps combined with a less drastic "punishment" than grim refusal to grant any more favors—so that "reciprocity" can be restored—might be worthy of consideration. The answer is No. See Problem 22.13.

[41] If one thinks of time intervals occuring very rapidly in "real time," say, each time interval t to $t+1$ lasts h units of real time, then one can think of the discount factor δ as being e^{-rh} for real-time interest rate r. And, then, if one takes $h \to 0$ and adjusts the probability that $X_t = 0$ to be $1 - kh$ for some constant k, but preserves the conditional distributions of θ_t conditional on $X_t \neq 0$, one gets in the limit a continuous-time model in which favor opportunities arise according to a Poisson process; that is, each (random) time between favors is exponentially distributed. You may encounter this continuous-time version of exchanging favors in the literature.

that there is a favor she can do for Bob. And, if he asks for the favor, she learns a_t, but he does not. However, she doesn't see b_t, although she may be able to infer something about b_t from a_t. Based on having been asked for the favor, knowing a_t, and inferring what she can about b_t, she then must decide whether to grant the favor or not.

And, when $X_t = B$, symmetrical conditions apply.

What happens to the "all favors" equilibrium? What about Λ-equilibria where Λ is less than all favors? And, taking your cue from the discussion of "chips" back on pages 229–30, can you provide a chips-based equilibrium concept in this setting? Answering these three questions constitutes Problem 22.16.

Long but finite horizon, plus long-lived Alice and long-lived Bob

Suppose long-lived Alice plays the trading-favors game against long-lived Bob a fixed and finite number of times. Then, both in the base model and in the variation just described, things fall apart. In the last period, whoever is meant to do the favor will not do it—there is no more time in which to be "paid back"—and then the same is true in the penultimate period, since in the last period no favors will be done, and the trading of favors unravels all the way to the start.[42] Suppose we have identified a subset Λ of all possible favors such that $a^e(\Lambda)$ and $b^e(\Lambda)$ are both strictly positive, and there is a finite lower bound on both a_t and b_t, over all $\theta_t \in \Lambda_t$. With lots of periods to go (and either no discounting or δ close to 1), it is in the interests of both parties to "get past" this unraveling, and the right sort of incomplete information about Alice or Bob (or both) accomplishes this. For instance, suppose there is a type of Alice with small but strictly positive prior probability who will do all favors she is called on to do for Bob and that arise from $\theta_t \in \Lambda$, but only as long as Bob has reciprocated. If Bob ever fails to undertake a favor in Λ that he is meant to do, this type of Alice does no more favors for Bob. A small probability of this type of Alice is enough to undo the unraveling.

Because of the general nature of the underlying model, the proof of this assertion is complex. But it follows the basic logic of a similar proof for the finitely repeated trust game with two long-lived players provided in Appendix 15. A sketch runs as follows: Let η be the probability that Alice is this behavioral type and, for simplicity, assume that Alice is rational with probability $1 - \eta$. With enough periods left to go, and assuming Bob assesses probability η or more that Alice is this behavioral type, Bob can choose to stop doing favors (called for by Λ) for Alice, in which case, both the behavioral and rational types will stop doing Λ-favors for him. (Either Rational Alice mimics the behavioral type or not; not mimicking the behavior type in this situation means doing a later favor for Bob. But to do a favor for Bob later confirms that she is Rational Alice, and the unraveling argument implies that Bob will do no favors for her, so she is better off not doing any favors for him.) Or Bob can continue to do Λ-favors for Alice, until she reveals that she is Rational Alice by not doing a favor for him. The probability η that she is the behavioral type gives

---

[42]   This is true in terms of subgame-perfect equilibria; is it true in terms of Nash equilibria? It is, and the real question is: Why?

Bob an expected gain that rises linearly in the number of periods left; he has at risk an expected amount that is bounded above in expectation (computing this bound is where the proof becomes a bit complex). So with enough periods left to go, Bob will carry out any favors called for by Λ for Alice, as long as she hasn't "burst the bubble" by having failed to do a called-for favor for him. And, so, with enough periods left to go, Rational Alice, who benefits from an "unburst bubble," will do all called-for favors for Bob.

All that said, it is worth observing here that, as the specification of Λ becomes more complicated, it is harder to put faith in a behavioral type of the sort described. But relatively simple specifications of Λ, like the two highlighted in the previous subsection, do not seem unreasonable.

Long-lived Alice, short- and intermediate-lived Bob

Suppose Alice plays trading favors against a sequence of Bobs, each of whom lives for only one period. Whether the formulation is infinite horizon or finite horizon, the only equilibrium is no favors: No Bob will do a favor for Alice in his one period of play, and so there is no return to Alice of doing favors for any Bob.[43] Adding a small probability of a do-all-favors type of Alice doesn't help. Any Bob, if called on to do a favor in his one period of life, won't do so, so rational Alice gets no return from trying to appear like the do-all-favors type. And, it doesn't help to add a small probability that the Bobs will do all favors, *even if there is perfect correlation in this type*—that is, if one Bob is of this type, all Bobs are of this type—because a rational Bob, if called uon to do a favor in his one period, won't do it, not even if he expected Alice to do a simultaneous favor for him, and even if doing so preserves in Alice's mind the possibility that he and all his fellow Bobs are the generous type.[44]

Suppose instead that Alice faces a sequence of *intermediate*-lived Bobs, meaning that each Bob lasts for some fixed number of periods N, before giving way to a new Bob. Assume for the moment that the sequence is infinite, and there are only rational Alice and rational Bobs.

Then, depending on the underlying data (the distributions of the θ_t), some favors could get done in a subgame-perfect equilibrium. The key is Alice's strategy: Suppose, every time a new Bob appears, she stands ready to do favors for him unless and until he doesn't do a favor for her. If he doesn't do a favor for her, then she stops doing favors for him for the duration of *his* lifetime. But, even if the nth Bob fails to do a favor for her, so she stops doing favors for him, when the $(n+1)$st Bob comes along, her strategy is to begin doing favors for him. And, if she ever fails to do a favor for a Bob *before* he has failed to do any favor for her, she no longer does any favors. That is, along the path of play, she carries an instrumental reputation of being generous to each and every Bob she meets, but her generosity is limited to Bobs who, so far, have been generous in return.

---

[43] Suppose long-lived Alice plays the prisoners' dilemma against an infinite sequence of Bobs, each of whom plays only once. What happens?

[44] The only salvation for favors here is if the Bobs all put significant weight on the welfare of Alice or of future Bobs. This is not impossible, but it takes us to Volume III ideas.

Note that, with this strategy, if it is the last period of the current Bob's lifetime, if he has done all favors for her that came alone, and if this last period is an opportunity for her to do a favor for him, she does it. If she failed to do so, she would lose her reputation for being *generous within bounds*, and so going forward no Bob will do any favors for her.

Will intermediate-lived Bobs do any favors for Alice? No Bob will do a favor for Alice in the last period of his life. But what about in the penultimate period of his life? If he has so far done all called-for favors for Alice, and if the cost of the favor he is asked to do is small enough, he may do this penultimate-period favor, since she will then reciprocate if she gets the call in his last period. And even if no favor he is asked to do in the next-to-last period costs him so little that he'll do it, with two periods left to go, there is some prospect that Alice will be called on to do favors for him in both the next-to-last and last periods of his life, which may justify doing a favor for her with two periods left to go. And so forth.

Why not have Alice do favors for each Bob, without regard to his behavior? Because a Bob's best response to this is not to do any favors for Alice. He must face some "penalty" for refusing to do favors for her.

This construction depends crucially on the data: the distribution of the θ_t and the discount factor δ (if Bob does discount his period-by-period payoffs). Problem 22.17 provides specific data for which you are asked to compute this sort of equilibrium (or show that it can't be bootstrapped).

Four remarks are relevant concerning this construction:

- Suppose the economics department of a small liberal arts college deals with one young assistant professor at a time. At various points in time, the department can do favors for the assistant professor; at other times, the assistant professor can do favors for the department. Even if, near the end of his appointment, the young AP knows that tenure is not going to happen, so he stops doing favors for the department, the department may do favors for him as long as he hasn't signaled by his behavior (he stopped doing favors for the department) that his interests lie elsewhere, so that future prospective APs find this department an attractive place to take a job.

  Of course, the arrival of information about his tenure prospects complicates this story concerning his "stopping time" for doing favors for the department, and there is some signaling that he is doing for the benefit of future prospective employers about his nature. Finally, if his tenure prospects are reasonable, he has added incentive to keep the goodwill of his senior colleagues. So, this story is a good deal more complex than the simple one I've constructed. Still...

- One can think of this as a model of relational contracting in other employment contexts, where the employer goes on "forever," but employees last for limited lifetimes. And, in that case, an elaboration of the model has Alice dealing with multiple Bobs at different stages in their careers at the same time. If Alice's reputation as an employer stands or falls on her doing favors for each employee—that is, if she fails to do a favor for one employee who has so far reciprocated (behaved well on the job), she loses the cooperation of all employees, now and in the future—then this strengthens her reputation stake.

- Another elaboration, again with ties to employment but also to the sort of relational contracting that (for instance) Toyota has with its suppliers, would allow Alice/Toyota/the employer to discharge any Bob before his time is up if he fails to do a favor for her. And we can further enrich the model by adding in, for Alice/Toyota/the employer, a cost for finding a replacement for a discharged Bob, if Alice/Toyota/the employer chooses to discharge a current shorter-lived partner.

- This construction requires that Alice is infinitely-lived. If she faced a hard deadline, she loses the incentive to do a favor in the final period of *her* time, and the unraveling kicks in. But with a bit of incomplete information of the right sort—namely, a small initial probability that Alice is a type who is *generous within bounds*—this can be salvaged for most of the game, if the data are supportive.

Multilateral relational contracts

The construction of a relational contract between long-lived Alice and intermediate-lived Bob depends on Alice's interest in her constellation of relational contracts with multiple Bobs, whether in sequence (as in the construction sketched) or somewhat more simultaneously (as in the case of an employer). The same is true of the repeated trust game, with short-lived Bobs trusting long-lived Alice, because she will treat each Bob well in order to get future Bobs to trust her.

And, in the case of the trust game, Alice may deal with different Bobs simultaneously as well as sequentially. Consider, for instance, the small college, which hires more than one assistant professor at a time; perhaps one assistant professor is being reviewed for tenure at the same time as others are in their first couple of years of employment. If the tenure decision is unfairly administered for the current candidate, it not only affects the college's ability to hire afresh, but it may lead current early-term assistant professors to seek employment elsewhere or to spend less time and effort on tasks that are of benefit to their employer in order to spend more time and effort creating a CV that will make desirable employment elsewhere easier to obtain.

Consider as well the story from Problem 19.17(b), where Alice, the employer, motivates five employees, all named Bob, by promising to divide a fixed bonus pool among them, with the amount each receives depending on her subjective assessment of their performance. Since the bonus pool is fixed, as long as she distributes it (and assuming that there is no suspicion of favoritism, which in real life is a concern), she can get away with subjective assessment of performance, something that is harder to implement for a single employee who works for one period and who is promised a bonus that depends on the employer's subjective assessment of how the employee has performed.

The same consideration affects Toyota in its dealings with its different suppliers. Without going into full details (see references provided in the Bibliographic Notes), the nature of Toyota's relationship with each supplier provides Toyota with enormous leverage in each bilateral relationship. This grant of leverage by the suppliers requires them to trust that Toyota will not take advantage of its leverage and engage in a holdup. So, to provide suppliers with this assurance, Toyota goes out of its way to have all its suppliers meet with one another regularly. Then, if Toyota tried to hold up or otherwise take advantage of one supplier, the others would learn this, and for their own safety, demand that Toyota offer more (rigid) contractual guarantees. Since the flexibility of the arrangement is very valuable to it, Toyota will avoid taking advantage of any supplier. This is the assurance its suppliers need to trust Toyota.

In all these cases, Alice/the college/the employer/Toyota has a bilateral relational contract with each trading partner, but in a greater sense, it has a multilateral relational contract with all of them at once.

Community enforcement

Yet another (and important) variation on this theme concerns cases where a community of individuals have "favor-giving" interactions with one another, but no pair interacts frequently enough so that, on their own, this pair could construct an effective relational contract: If the expected time between interactions of a given specific pair is large, then the relevant discount factor—comparing the cost of doing an immediate favor with the discounted value from future favors that will be done—is too far from 1. But imagine that each individual in the group has much more frequent opportunities to give and to receive favors from different members in the group. Alice may one day have the opportunity to do a favor for Bob; a few periods later, she may be the potential recipient of a favor from Carol, who in turn may be the potential recipient of a favor from Daniel, and so forth. *If*, and it is a big *if*, this "community" is sufficiently closely knit so that, when one member fails to do a "called for" favor for another member, all observe this, then the potential exists to construct a symmetric multilateral relational contract, where if Carol doesn't do the favor for Alice, Daniel and all other members of the community will punish Carol for her transgression.[45]

You have all the tools to build a model of this sort of community-based relational contract, so I'll leave it to your imagination, except to insert the following throwaway: A real strength of family businesses is meant to derive from this sort of arrangement, although there is a Volume III trade-off to consider simultaneously.

Noise: The quality of performance and monitoring

Alice asks Bob to drive her to the airport. He says he will, but in the event, he shows up half an hour late, and Alice misses her flight. Bob pleads that traffic was very bad and, while he tried to be on time, circumstances prevented it. But Alice had asked to be picked up very early in the morning, and she suspects that Bob forgot to set his alarm clock or just decided to sleep a bit more and subject her to the risk of missing her flight. Does this count as a favor done or undone?

---

[45] But what members of the community see about pairwise interactions then becomes crucial. See, for instance, Bowen, Kreps, and Skrzypacz (2013).

Take the base model of trading favors and suppose that commission of the favor, encoded by the variable x_t, involves a quality-of-performance variable. That is, instead of being a 0 or 1 variable, x_t is drawn from the unit interval, where both the cost of doing the favor and its benefit to the receiver are increasing in x_t from 0 (but not necessarily linearly). Or, suppose the favor giver chooses to try to do the favor— back to $x_t = 0$ or 1—but the favor is actually accomplished, if $x_t = 1$, with some probability $\pi(\theta_t)$. (If the favor giver chooses $x_t = 0$, there is zero probability that the favor is done.) Suppose the favor giver knows whether she tried—she knows x_t—but the favor receiver only sees whether the favor was actually accomplished.

In a one-period setting, we have a standard principal–agent problem, where the principal (favor receiver) must provide the agent (favor giver) with sufficient incentive (through some financial payment) to undertake the favor. In this multi-period, ongoing game of trading favors—where Bob's incentives arise from the prospect of future favors done for him—some "adjustment" in the future must be made in the face of non- or poor performance. Again, you have all the tools needed to tackle these further elaborations. So I leave it up to you.

Social enforcement of norms of behavior

Which takes us, finally, to social norms and the notion that a social norm is a relational contract between an individual and his or her society.

Let me illustrate with my favorite example.[46] The MBA students at Stanford Graduate School of Business (GSB) have developed a social norm that each student, when discussing job prospects with potential employers, may not show her grades to the employer. This is a norm: It depends on "voluntary" compliance and, indeed, the relevant law on such matters in the United States, known as the Family Educational Rights and Privacy Act, or FERPA, gives each adult student an absolute right to control any information about his or her grades.

For some jobs with some employers sought by some students, it would be to the student's advantage to quietly reveal his or her grades. However, adherence to the norm is reputed to be nearly total. The question to be addressed is: Why would a student adhere to this norm, when it is to his or her immediate advantage to violate it in terms of getting a desirable job?

The story that fits in with this chapter is: If a student were to violate the norm, there is a nonnegligible probability that this would be discovered, and said student would be sent to social purgatory. Since students at the GSB view access to the network of classmates and alumni as the most important advantage that the program provides, this is a severe punishment, so severe that even a small probability of being discovered isn't worth the risk. Indeed, students tell tales of alumni who, acting jointly as recruiters and as the enforcement arm of society, try to get students to violate the norm, with the intention of "turning them in" if they don't resist.

There are other stories one can tell about adherence to social norms: The individual may value the specific norm; for instance, a student, seeing the logic behind

---

[46] This story is not as relevant today as it was in decades past, because Stanford MBAs nowadays are much more likely to join start-up ventures based on personal ties. But the story is a good illustration of my point, so I use it.

students not revealing their grades, values that specific practice enough that she won't violate the norm, even if there is no chance her behavior would be revealed. And the individual, while disagreeing with the specific norm, may still identify with the group; a student whose self-image is very tightly bound with being a Stanford MBA may think the norm of no grade disclosure is silly, but as it is a norm of her "tribe," she will not violate it, even if a violation could never be detected.

Only the first story fits in this chapter. But I mention the other two here as a teaser for Volume III, where such "noneconomic behavior" will be a central theme.

The bottom line on relational contracts

Relational contracts—based on reciprocity and reputation, as well as on other "forces" that will only come into the story in Volume III—are in many instances essential "glue" in holding efficient economic relationships together. Notwithstanding the "Principles of Economics" insistence that economics is first and foremost about supply-equals-demand in anonymous markets with many buyers and many sellers, the importance to economics of this glue and the relational contracts it fosters should not be underestimated.

Bibliographic Notes

References to purely game-theoretic tools applied in this chapter are provided at the end of Appendix 15 and (for the most part) are not repeated here. But I do repeat citations of papers here that employ those tools contextually.

Oligopolistic collusion

As noted in the chapter, the idea that oligopolists will collude to the detriment of their customers goes back to Adam Smith in *The Wealth of Nations* (Smith 1776). *The* classic (modern) paper on oligopolistic collusion is Stigler (1964).

The story of collusion between General Electric and Westinghouse generally, and, in particular, the story about how they, together with Allis–Chalmers, colluded using phases of the moon to coordinate their bids, is told in Sultan (1974). I fear this is long out of print, but as I write this, Amazon is advertising used copies, and perhaps academic libraries will have copies. The story of what happened after the phases-of-the-moon scheme was discovered and stopped is told in a series of Harvard Business School cases, Porter (1970a, b, c).

The seminal paper on oligopolistic collusion based on Nash (Cournot or Bertrand) punishment is Friedman (1971). The classic collusion-with-price-noise paper is Green and Porter (1984). Abreu, Pearce, and Stacchetti (1986) provides a deeper look into the Green–Porter problem.

Oligopolistic collusion where there is clarity about the winner but not about what the winner did to achieve its win is similar to bid rigging in auctions. See Skrzypacz and Hopenhayn (2004) and Harrington and Skrzypacz (2007, 2011).

Entry deterrence and the chain-store paradox

There is a rich literature on entry deterrence as a general topic in industrial organiza-tion, which can be divided into (at least) three parts: (1) Tangible steps a monopolist (or, more generally, members of an oligopoly) can take to make entry more diffi-cult for outsiders. This includes the example provided: Choosing technology so that, if there is entry, the monopolist is a more formidable opponent. (2) Behavior pre-entry that is meant to signal potential entrants that the monopolist will be too formidable a rival post-entry. See Problem 20.22 and Milgrom and Roberts (1982a). (3) Predation: Convincing prospective entrants that, post-entry, the monopoly firm will, even at significant cost to itself, make entry unprofitable, thereby forestalling entry. The parable of the chain store, its paradox, and the incomplete-information resolution fit in this third category.

Without trying in the least to provide full references to this rich literature, the specific references for the chain-store parable are: Selten (1978), Kreps and Wilson (1982a), and Milgrom and Roberts (1982b). The techniques employed in the latter two papers are generalized in two papers by Fudenberg and Levine (1989, 1992).

With two long-lived opponents playing the repeated threat game, and with the appropriate sort of incomplete information about both, a war of attrition will ensue. The first formal model of this (of which I know) is in Kreps and Wilson (1982a) (although, for analytical convenience, the model is in continuous time).

Relational contracting

Because, in my opinion, the full "story" of relational contracting requires concepts and ideas that belong to Volume III, I have a hard time giving a fair bibliography for this topic. But, for what it is worth, the first formal model of bilateral relational contracting of which I am aware is Simon (1951). This is, essentially, construction of the efficient repeated-trust-game equilibrium before most of the relevant ideas in game theory had been invented. And it wouldn't surprise me to find earlier formal models.

I don't know who first wrote down the trading-favors model (and if someone could supply me with this information, I'd be grateful). But I know this model has been used by many authors. Similarly, I don't know who first discussed com-munity enforcement of modes of behavior or the connection between community enforcement and social norms.

The chapter leads off with the story of the relationship between Toyota and its suppliers in the United States, and I mentioned there (in footnote 3) the case study that describes this system, Milgrom and Roberts (1993). A more analytical discussion of the system and issues connected to this form of relational contracting is provided in Kreps (2019, Chapter 5), albeit at an MBA-student level and involving considerations that will be a main focus of Volume III.

Problems

■ 22.1. Consider the prototypical two-firm, symmetric, infinitely repeated Cournot (quantities chosen) model. Inverse demand facing the two firms is $P(x) = 9 - x$.

Both firms have constant marginal cost of 1 (and no fixed costs). The discount factor is δ. Assume that each firm, after each round is over and done with, learns the quantity choice of its rival.

a. Suppose the two firms aim for the collusive scheme in which each firm produces half the monopoly quantity, backed by the threat to resort to grim play of the Cournot equilibrium. For which values of δ does this scheme give a subgame-perfect equilibrium?

On page 221, the possibility of non-Nash punishment was raised. We are interested, in particular, in punishment that targets a deviator. The general theory of such punishments can be difficult, but creating and studying specific forms of punishment can be easier. So this is what the rest of this problem does.

b. As an alternative scheme for achieving collusion with each of the two firms producing half the monopoly quantity, consider the following, which I'll call the *take-your-medicine strategy profile*. Both firms begin by producing half the monopoly quantity. They continue in this fashion unless and until the price deviates from the monopoly price of $10/2 = 5$. If both firms deviate from the monopoly quantities in any round, it is ignored. If one firm deviates and other does not, then, in the next round, the deviator produces 0 (must take its medicine) and the firm that didn't deviate produces the full monopoly quantity (which is 4). If, while being punished for one round, the deviator produces anything more than 0, it does not restore cooperation; it must submit 0 (take its medicine) in a round to do so. Finally, while one of the firms is being punished, the actions of the other firm carry no penalty.

For which δ does this give a subgame-perfect equilibrium?

c. Generalize the scheme in part b to the case of N symmetric firms. Assume that if two or more firms deviate, it is ignored, but if only one firm deviates, that firm is punished as in part b, where it is part of your job to interpret what punishment means in this context. (In particular, there are at least two natural ways to interpret what the other firms do while some deviator is being punished. The answer you get will depend on which interpretation you give.)

■ 22.2. At the start of Section 22.1, we take the simple formulation in which there are N identical firms, each with constant marginal cost of c, facing an inverse-demand function $P(X) = a - bX$, where $a > c$, where the firms compete in terms of quantities: In each round, each firm submits a quantity x_n, and price is $a - b(x_1 + \ldots + x_N)$.

Suppose instead that each firm posts a price p_n, and demand is evenly split among all firms that post the lowest price.

Construct a strategy profile for the firms that (for large enough δ) supports perpetual posting of the monopoly price $(a + c)/2$ by each firm, supported by the threat that, if any firm deviates, what follows is grim play of the Bertrand equilibrium.

What is the range of δ for which this is an equilibrium? What are you assuming about what each firm learns after each round ends, and how does that affect what sort of "equilibrium" you have produced?

■ 22.3. Continuing with the case of symmetric firms competing in prices (naming prices), suppose we continue to look for equilibria where, along the path of play, each firm names the price $(a + c)/2$ and gets $1/N$ share of the monopoly profit. In the spirit of Problem 22.1, would a take-your-medicine style strategy profile give an equilibrium for a wider range of δ than works for grim-Bertrand?

It will not. Why not?

■ 22.4. In Section 22.1, where the focus is on firms that engage in quantity competition, it is relatively easy to think of asymmetric equilibrium outcomes; simply have an equilibrium agreement where firms submit different quantities.

However, with firms that compete on the basis of prices, asymmetries (among the firms or, for symmetric firms, asymmetries in outcomes) can be problematic. This problem looks at a few of the problems for the following setting: There are two firms, call them A and B, who compete at times $t = 0, 1, \ldots.$ Demand in each period is given by $D(p) = 10 - p$. Suppose they discount profits earned with the discount factor $\delta = 0.9$.

a. Suppose firm A has constant marginal cost 3, and firm B has constant marginal cost 2. The efficient arrangement would be for firm B to do all the producing, with an equilibrium price of 6. But if firm B does all the producting and selling, firm A has zero profit and, of course, would want to undercut B's price. To fix this, suppose that firm A can, in each period, make a side-payment to firm B. What side-payment (per period) is required so that, in an equilibrium, firm A will not try to undercut firm B? (You will need some "punishment" regime if either firm deviates from the scheme, and the discontinuity inherent in price competition will cause technical problems. So you may suppose that prices must be quoted in integer multiplies of 0.0001.)

b. And, if direct side-payments are not allowed, but firm B can sell units to firm A, which firm A can resell, then [finish this sentence].

c. Now suppose that both firms have a constant marginal cost of 4, but for reasons that are beyond explanation, the two firms decide to implement a solution where the price is the monopoly price of 7 (so total profit is 9), and the two firms decide to distribute the profit asymmetrically, with firm A getting profit 6 per period and firm B getting 3. One way to do this would be for them both to name the price 7, so 1.5 units of demand show up at each firm. And then firm B shuts its doors after it has served 1 unit of demand, with the other 0.5 going across the street to buy for firm A. Assuming grim-Bertrand punishment if either firm deviates from this arrangement, for which values of δ (no longer necessarily 0.9) is this an equilibrium?

d. Continuing from part c, suppose that the rules are that the firms must serve all demand that shows up at their door. (Or, imagine that frustrated demand does not go "across the street" but instead goes home, disgruntled.) Suppose that firms A and B in part c decide to use a publicly observable random variable in each period to decide on what prices to quote. Let $\{u_t\}$ be an i.i.d. sequence of uniformly distributed random variables on the interval $[0,1]$, with u_t observed by the two firms just minutes before they must post their time-t price. Suppose that they somehow decide on the following strategy for time t: If $u_t \leq 1/3$, then firm B names the price 7, and firm A names 7.5. If $u_t > 1/3$, then firm A names the price 7, and B names 7.5. And, if either firm deviates from this, it is grim Bertrand. For which values of δ does this give an equilibrium?

e. Suppose that publicly observable random variables are not available. Suppose instead that the two firms behave as follows: In periods $0, 2, 3, 5, 6, 8, 9, \ldots$ (in other words, in periods t, when $t = 3k$ or $3k + 2$ for integer k), firm A charges 7 and firm B charges 7.5. In periods $1, 4, 7$, (i.e., t such that $t = 3k + 1$), firm A charges 7.5 and firm B charges 7. (And if either firm deviates from this pattern, they both grimly charge 4 for the rest of time.) For which values of δ does this give an equilibrium?

▪ 22.5. In Section 22.2, a fair amount of time is spent discussing the differences between infinite-horizon models and models with a fixed and finite time horizon. Since, in the text, this issue is not discussed in the context of oligopolistic collusion, here is a brief introduction.

Consider two firms, J and K, that compete at times $t = 0, 1, \ldots, T$ in a single market. They compete in quantities: At each time t, the two firms choose quantities x_{Jt} and x_{Kt} to bring to market. The market price is then $p_t = a - (x_{Jt} + x_{Kt})$, and the profit of each firm is $(p_t - c)x_{Zt}$ for $Z = J$ or K. (That is, inverse demand is linear with slope coefficient 1, and the firms have constant marginal cost c, with $a > c$.) Profits are discounted with discount factor $\delta < 1$ per period. You may suppose that both firms observe the quantity choices of their rival in each period (after choosing their own quantity).

a. What can you say about subgame-perfect Nash equilibria in this setting? Prove your assertions.

b. Are there any Nash equilibria that are not subgame perfect? If not, prove this. If so, show one. (Hint, if you need one: See Proposition A15.5(b).)

c. Suppose inverse demand is given by Figure 18.1 (page 16), and $c = 1$. How does this change your answer to part a?

d. And what if the firms competed on the basis of posted prices?

▪ 22.6. Suppose Firms A and B produce and sell differentiated goods that are substitutes. Specifically, $D_A(p_A, p_B) = 100 - 2p_A + p_B$, and $D_B(p_A, p_B) = 100 - 2p_B + p_A$. Both have constant marginal costs of 10.

a. What is the (one-period) Bertrand equilibrium for these firms?

b. What pair of prices maximizes the sum of their profits in a single period?

c. Suppose they compete repeatedly, at times $t = 0, 1, \ldots$, discounting profits by discount factor δ per period. For which values of δ can they sustain the (symmetric) collusive prices you found in part b, if the threat is that, for any defection from the scheme, they resort to grim play of the equilibrium prices you found in part a?

d. Suppose these two firms compete Cournot style. What are the corresponding answers to parts a, b, and c?

■ 22.7. *Even with Cournot competition and noisy price observations, perfect collusion is possible, I: An example.* Once again, we have two firms, A and B, attempting to collude. The two compete Cournot style, selecting quantities x_A and x_B simultaneously and independently in each period, and the market price in period t is then $\theta_t(12 - (x_A + x_B)/1000)$, where $\{\theta_t; t = 0, 1, \ldots\}$ is an i.i.d. sequence of random variables, each of which is uniform on $[0.95, 1.05]$. To keep the story simple, suppose they both have constant marginal cost of 0. Assume both firms are risk neutral.

a. If the two competed in a single period, what would be the Cournot (Nash) equilibrium quantities they would supply?

b. What total quantity X^* supplied by the two firms together maximizes the sum of their profits?

c. Now imagine that they compete in periods $0, 1, \ldots$, with profits discounted with discount factor δ per period. They seek the following equilibrium: Each firm begins supplying $X^*/2$ and continues to do so as long as price is always at least $\underline{P}^* := 0.95(12 - X^*/1000)$. But if price is ever strictly less than $\underline{P}^*$, they resort to grim play of Cournot equilibrium for the rest of time. For what values of δ (if any) is this a Nash equilibrium (in sequentially rational strategies)? In contrast with the discussion of the Green–Porter model in the text, here I am supposing that, if a price below the trigger price $\underline{P}^*$ is ever observed, collusion is never restored. Why is this supposition okay?

■ 22.8. *Even with Cournot competition and noisy price observations, perfect collusion is possible, II: A somewhat general result.* Problem 22.7 gives an example of the Green–Porter model in which, at least for large enough δ, monopoly quantities can be sustained forever, even though prices are noisy. That is, there is a threat of punishment, but punishment is never incurred along the path of play. This problem looks to generalize the example of Problem 22.7.

The setting is just as in Green–Porter: There are two firms, A and B, who compete in a repeated market for a single good at times $t = 0, 1, 2, \ldots$. In period t, the two firms supply quantities x_{At} and x_{Bt}, and price is then $\theta_t P(x_{At} + x_{Bt})$, where $\{\theta_t\}$ is an i.i.d. sequence of strictly positive, mean-one random variables. Let $\underline{\theta} := \inf\{\theta \geq$

$0 : \theta_t \geq \theta$ with probability 1}; that is, $\underline{\theta}$ is the lower endpoint of the support of θ_t. Let Φ be the distribution function of each θ_t.

The following assumptions about the basic data of the problem are made:

- $P(X)$ is nonnegative for all $X \in (0, \infty)$ and $X \to P(X)$ is continuous. More-over, $X \to P(X)$ is strictly decreasing and continuously differentiable with a strictly negative derivative, for all values of X such that $P(X) > 0$.

- There is some (finite) total quantity $X^* > 0$ that is maximizes total (industry) revenue. This joint-revenue-maximizing quantity is unique.

- The two firms have total cost identically equal to zero (easily generalized, but this makes the solution easier to parse).

- There is a single-period Cournot equilibrium, in which Firm A supplies x_A^C and Firm B supplies x_B^C. Let $U_A := x_A^C P(x_A^C + x_B^C)$; that is, U_A is the single-period Cournot equilibrium expected profit for Firm A. Define U_B similarly. (I don't necessarily assume that this is the only Cournot equilibrium; uniqueness is irrelevant to what follows.)

- In each period, players choose their quantities with no knowledge of the value of θ_t that will prevail this period (other than knowing its distribution). And in each period, they observe (only) their own choice of quantity and the price $\theta_t P(x_A + x_B)$.

We look for an equilibrium of the following character: The two firms choose quan-tities x_A^* and x_B^* in each period, with $x_A^* + x_B^* = X^*$, until the observed price is strictly less than some trigger price P^*, after which they resort to grim play of the Cournot equilibrium quantities x_A^C and x_B^C. And in the equilibrium, P^* is chosen so that there is zero probability of triggering, as long as the two firms are choosing x_A^* and x_B^*, respectively.

Let $V_A = x_A^* P(X^*)$; that is, V_A is the profit per period for Firm A along the alleged path of play. Define V_B similarly.

Assume that:

- Both firms have higher immediate profit if they choose x_A^* and x_B^* than at the one-period Cournot equilibrium; that is, $V_A > U_A$, and $V_B > U_B$.

- If (say) B is choosing x_B^*, A's gains from a small increase in x_A from x_A^* are first order in the increase; or, in symbols,

$$\frac{\mathrm{d}x_A P(x_A + x_B^*)}{\mathrm{d}x_A}\bigg|_{x_A = x_A^*} > 0,$$

and similarly with reversed roles.

Your assignment in this problem is to prove all the lettered assertions that follow. You may assume any assertions that are not lettered.

Because the alleged-equilibrium strategy profile entails grim play of the specified Cournot equilibrium once punishment is triggered, the only property that must be verified to show that we have a (sequentially rational strategy) equilibrium is that neither firm wishes to deviate from its assigned quantity, x_A^* and x_B^*, respectively, along the path of play.

a. If $\underline{\theta} = 0$, then an equilibrium as described is not possible, in that, for any trigger price P^*, either $P^* = 0$ (in which case the players will defect from choosing x_A^* and x_B^*) or $P^* > 0$ (in which case punishment will eventually be triggered with probability 1).

b. If $\underline{\theta} > 0$, then for the firms optimally to choose x_A^* and x_B^*, it cannot be that $P^* < \underline{\theta} P(x_A^*, x_B^*)$. However, if $P^* > \underline{\theta} P(x_A^*, x_B^*)$, then punishment will occur at some point with probability 1. Hence, to have an equilibrium of the character described, it must be that $P^* = \underline{\theta} P(x_A^*, x_B^*)$.

So, for the remainder of this problem, assume that $P^* = \underline{\theta} P(x_A^*, x_B^*)$.

c. Neither firm will wish to decrease its quantity. We need only consider the desirability of increases.

d. Suppose that the distribution of θ_t has an atom of probability at $\underline{\theta}$; that is, $\Phi(\underline{\theta}) > 0$. Then an equilibrium of the character described is possible for all δ close enough to 1. (This should be pretty easy.)

e. Consider one-period deviations by Firm A of the form $x^A \geq x_A^* + \epsilon$ for $\epsilon > 0$. That is, the deviations considered are increases in the quantity supplied, where the increase is *at least* ϵ for some ϵ. For all δ close enough to 1, no such deviation is worthwhile (i.e., none does better than following the alleged equilibrium strategies).

So, if there are going to be problems, they will be in cases where a firm contemplates a small increase in x_A from x_A^*. The key quantity, it turns out, is

$$\liminf_{\epsilon \downarrow 0} \Phi(\epsilon)/\epsilon.$$

f. If $\liminf_{\epsilon \downarrow 0} \Phi((\underline{\theta} + \epsilon)/\epsilon > 0$ (including $+\infty$), then there are values of δ close enough to 1 such that, for those δ, the strategies described do constitute an equilibrium.

g. But if $\liminf_{\epsilon \downarrow 0} \Phi(\underline{\theta} + \epsilon)/\epsilon = 0$, then for all $\delta < 1$, the alleged equilibrium doesn't work. In particular, for every $\delta < 1$, there is some "small" increase in x_A that (very slightly) is better for Firm A than is following the equilibrium strategies.

h. Finally, to tie back to Problem 22.7, if the distribution of the θ_t is described by a continuous density function ϕ, and if $\phi(\underline{\theta}) > 0$, then $\liminf_{\underline{\theta}+\epsilon\downarrow 0} \Phi(\epsilon)/\epsilon = \phi(\underline{\theta})$, so we are in the case of part e of this problem. But if instead $\phi(\theta) = 0$, then we are in the case of part f; for no δ is this an equilibrium.

■ 22.9. Two firms contemplate entering a market for a single good, which will exist for four periods in total, numbered $t = 1, 2, 3, 4$. Demand in each period is given by $D(p) = 12 - p$. Firm A has the opportunity to enter the market at time $t = 1$ (and then to be present in the remaining periods), while Firm B only has the opportunity to enter at time $t = 2$. In consequence, Firm A, if it enters, will be a monopoly in the first period. Whether it is a monopoly or a part of a duopoly in the second through fourth periods depends on whether Firm B enters. In case both firms are present in the second through fourth periods, they act as Cournot duopolists.

Each firm chooses its constant marginal cost, c_A for Firm A and c_B for Firm B. There are no per-period fixed costs, but there are sunk costs incurred upon entry. And the amounts of the sunk costs of entry depend on the marginal costs selected by the firms: The sunk cost of entry for Firm X, where X is A or B, is $60 - 40\ln(c_X)$, for $0 \le c_X \le 3$. That is, each firm can have a smaller marginal cost, although doing so raises its sunk cost of entry; it can lower its marginal cost to 0, but this raises its entry cost to $+\infty$; it can lower its sunk cost to a bit over 16, if it accepts a marginal cost of 3. (Think of this as a sunk cost of setting up a production process that is more or less labor intensive. The lower bound on c_X is natural; the upper bound is there to keep the sunk cost of entry strictly bounded away from zero.) Note that Firm A only pays the sunk cost if it enters in the first period; it does not have to pay the sunk cost again for subsequent periods. And note that neither firm needs to pay the sunk cost if it chooses not to enter.

a. If Firm A could be assured that Firm B will not enter—that is, if Firm A were going to be four-period monopoly—which marginal cost c_A would it choose? You may assume that Firm A acts to maximize the undiscounted sum of its profits in the four periods.

b. However, there is the threat of entry by Firm B. What should Firm A do? Besides assuming no discounting, assume that Firm B knows what choice of marginal cost Firm A made (assuming Firm A entered in the first period), and this is common knowledge between them before Firm B must decide whether to enter. And assume that, before choosing its quantity in the second period, Firm A knows whether Firm B has entered or not.

(Warning: The parametric assumptions made in this exercise make it possible to solve, although you may want to resort to numerical optimization for part b. But however you proceed, the numbers that emerge are *not* dramatic. The specific numbers in this example are cooked to get the desired result.)

■ 22.10. This problem concerns the classic chain-store parable, in which a chain store faces sequentially an infinite sequence of prospective entrants, each of which must decide whether to compete with the chain store in a market inhabited (only) by the chain store and the entrant, if the entrant enters. If prospective entrant t (for $t = 0, 1, \ldots$) does choose to compete, then the chain store must choose whether to accommodate the entrant or to fight entry. The outcomes in each period/market t are therefore: The entrant chooses not to enter, with (stage-game) payoffs m for the chain store and 0 for the entrant; the entrant enters and is accommodated, with payoffs d for the chain store and d' for the entrant; the entrant enters and the chain store responds by fighting, in which case the chain store has payoff 0 and the entrant a. These values are arranged: $m > d > 0$ and $d' > 0 > a$. Entrant t is only concerned with its expected stage-game payoff. The chain store's objective is to maximize the discounted sum of its expected payoffs in the various stages, using discount factor δ.

In the original story (page 234–36), both the chain store and all the entrants were "rational," meaning that they played to maximize their expected payoffs. And we constructed an equilibrium for this infinite-horizon model in which the chain store will fight every entrant who enters, as long as it has conformed to this pattern up to the current moment, but will accommodate entry if, at any time in the past, it accommodated an entry. And entrants do not enter if the chain store has always fought past entry, but they enter if the chain store ever accommmodates a previous entry. We showed that this is a (subgame-perfect) equilibrium if $\delta \geq d/m$.

Suppose we change the story to include incomplete information about the motivations of the entrants (but keep only one type, the rational type, of chain store). Specifically, suppose there are two types of entrant, "rational" and "heedless," where are rational type behaves according to its expected payoff for the parameters given, but a heedless type enters no matter what (in equilibrium) the response of the chain store will be. (Alternatively, for a heedless type, $0 < a < d'$.) Suppose the probability that any entrant is heedless is μ, with $0 < \mu < 1$, and where the types of disjoint sets of entrants are statistically independent. To be clear, the type of each entrant is private information to that entrant.·

Does the "instrumental reputation" equilibrium work if entrants come in these two types, as just described? If so, how and when?

■ 22.11. To continue from the previous problem: Now consider to the finite horizon model, where the chain store interacts with a different prospective entrant sequentially, at times $t = 0, 1, \ldots, T$. The "game" (or interaction) at each stage is as in the classic model (and in the previous problem) and, to be clear, what happens in each period t is public. The chain store is one of several types, where one type is the rational type, and another is the "angry" chain store, which will fight any entrant, regardless of cost. The probability that the chain store is the angry type is η, for $0 < \eta < 1$. And the probability that each entrant is heedless is μ, where the types of the entrants and the chain store are statistically independent.

As in the text (specifically, Proposition 22.1), assume that the rational chain store does not discount its period profits. It simply seeks to maximize the sum (over the $T + 1$ periods) of its period profits. Provide (with proof, of course) a generalization of Proposition 22.1, allowing for the possibility of heedless entrants.

■ 22.12. After some preliminary observations, Section 22.2 is a somewhat meandering path through a variety of models having to do with whether a threat of predation, even if costly to the incumbent firm, is credible. The point of this problem is to classify these models and then to consider some variations.

The starting point is the stage game, depicted in Figure 22.2 (page 235). An entrant chooses whether to enter and, if it does, the chain store chooses whether to fight or accommodate the entry. Concerning this stage game, please note the following:

- Played one time, the game has two (pure-strategy) Nash equilibria, enter–accommodate and don't enter–fight.

- But only one of these two equilibria, enter–accommodate, is subgame perfect. (And, correspondingly, in don't enter–fight, the chain store is playing a weakly dominated strategy.)

- This is *not* a sequential version of the Prisoners' Dilemma. We know this because there are two Nash equilibria; the Prisoners' Dilemma has only one.

This stage game is played "many times," with the following possible variations:

1. We could specify an infinite horizon, where the game is played at an infinite sequence of times $t = 0, 1, 2, \ldots$. Or we could have it played a finite number of times, $t = 0, 1, \ldots, T$.

2. Players could be long-lived, playing in all rounds of the game, or short-lived, playing in one and only one round.[47]

3. Finally, there is the dimension of "incomplete information." To keep things simple, restrict attention to cases of incomplete information, where, for both players, there is a "rational" type and an "aggressive" type, where the aggressive type is the angry type of chain store, and the aggressive type of entrant is the heedless entrant of Problems 22.9 and 22.10. For long-run players, the player is one type or the other for all periods; for short-run players, the types form an i.i.d. sequence. And in all cases of incomplete information, the probability of the aggressive type is meant to be small: The player is very likely to be rational, but her opponent(s) isn't (aren't) sure of this at the outset.

a. Classifying the models of Section 22.2 along these dimensions, which variations are examined in the section and in the previous two problems? That is, for each model discussed, where does the model fit in terms of these characteristics?

---

[47] One can imagine many further variations along this design dimension: We could have overlapping generations. We could imagine that the "winner" of each round "holds the court"; that is, gets to play again while her opponent is dismissed (this requires a definition of a "winner"). And so forth.

b. One sort of model we didn't examine is where the chain store is short lived and the entrant is long lived. Think of this with the following story: A giant corporation must decide (sequentially) whether to enter in each of a sequence of markets inhabited by different mom-and-pop style incumbents. If it does enter against one of these incumbents, the incumbent can be accommodating or can fight. Why are these variations essentially uninteresting?

■ 22.13. In the subsection "Less than 'all favors,'" and in particular in footnote 40, the question is asked: Should one consider strategy profiles and equilibria in which, for some low values of a_t and/or b_t, if the favor is not done and period of punishment ensues? The short answer, No, is then given. Explain. (You can restrict attention to pure-strategy equilibria.)

■ 22.14. Among Λ that give equilibria in the sense of the discussion at the top of page 249, which provide efficient a priori payoffs for Alice and Bob?

■ 22.15. In the basic trading-favors model discussed on page 246, the values of a_t and b_t are sign restricted: When $X_t = A$ (it is Alice who must choose whether to "take" the action of not), it is assumed that $a_t < 0$ and $b_t > 0$, and symmetrically when $X_t = B$. What happens if we remove those sign restrictions?

■ 22.16. Answer the three questions at the end of the "asking for favors" variation (top of page 250).

■ 22.17. Suppose Alice is long-lived and interacts with a Bob at times $t = 0, 1, \ldots$. But each Bob lives for only 10 periods: The first Bob interacts with Alice at times $t = 0, 1, \ldots, 9$, the second Bob at times $10, 11, \ldots, 19$, and so forth. In each period, $\theta_t = (X_t, a_t, b_t)$ takes on one of four values (only), $(A, -5, 10), (A, -1, 4), (B, 10, -5)$ or $(B, 4, -1)$, each with probability $1/4$. In words, in each period, there is a $1/2$ probability that Alice can perform a favor for Bob, and a $1/2$ probability that he can perform a favor for her. Half the time that $X_t = A$, Alice's favor for Bob is fairly expensive for her, but is very beneficial to Bob. And half the time that $X_t = A$, the favor is both inexpensive for Alice and of limited value for Bob. The favors distribution when $X_t = B$ is identical. To keep matters simple, assume that Alice discounts her payoffs with discount factor 0.99 per period (roughly 0.9 per Bob), while each Bob seeks to maximize the expectation of his undiscounted sum of payoffs.

Is it possible that, even though each Bob is intermediate-lived, that he does (some) favors for Alice and she reciprocates. What does "the" equilibrium look like, where I put "the" in scare quotes because I'm asking you to find an equilibrium of the type described in the subsection on intermediate-lived Bobs.

Chapter Twenty-Three

Bilateral Bargaining

The rest of Volume II: Mechanisms of exchange

In Volume I, prices are, for the most part, set by no one in particular. The "market," through a somewhat mysterious and unmodeled process, arrives at equilibrium prices, which both buyers and sellers take as given. In the classic theory of monopoly, and in the dynamic monopoly stories told in Chapter 20, the seller of a good sets the price, which buyers take as given. In both the classic theories of oligopoly (Chapter 18) and the dynamic versions in Chapter 22, sellers effectively set prices,[1] which buyers are modeled as taking as given.

A lot of economic exchange is conducted within a specific institutional framework. This includes bilateral bargaining between two (or more) parties, auctions, matching markets, and financial-market exchanges organized in one fashion or another. Each of these institutional frameworks has been the object of study on two levels: Given an institutional framework or *protocol* or *mechanism*, and given a *context* that specifies the participants, their preferences, and their endowments both of goods and of information, what are the possible equilibria that emerge? And, in analyses that go by the name *mechanism design*, given the context, which outcomes are feasible as equilibria for some institutional mechanism and, among those outcomes that are feasible as equilibria, which are optimal according to some given criterion?

The final four chapters of this book concern both levels of analysis. In the next three chapters, we examine in turn bilateral bargaining, auctions, and matching markets at the first level: Given a specific context and a specific exchange mechanism, which equilibria might emerge? Then in Chapter 26, the foundations and techniques of general mechanism design are presented and applied to the contexts of the previous three chapters.

Overview of this chapter

In a wide variety of economic transactions, two (or more) parties bargain over the "terms of trade." This includes a buyer and seller bargaining over the price the buyer will pay for a given object, but it also includes, for instance, cases in which partners in some venture bargain over how they will split the profit that will accrue to their venture. Fancy terms like *bilateral monopoly* or monopoly–monopsony are

---

[1] In Cournot-style models, sellers choose quantities, and prices adjust to clear markets, so sellers only set prices indirectly. Of course, in Bertrand-style models, sellers directly quote the prices at which they are willing to supply, so they collectively set the market price. But with differentiated goods and price competition, each seller sets her own price.

sometimes used, but it comes down to two (or more) parties making proposals and counterproposals, trying to find mutually agreeable terms.

The theoretical literature on bargaining comes to no firm conclusions. Instead, the literature is exemplifying theory: Various bargaining protocols are examined using tools of noncooperative game theory in a variety of contexts, leading to insights into which features of the context and protocols may be important in predicting outcomes. Most of this chapter samples from this literature and mimics the broader literature in coming to no firm conclusions.

And since, in more contextual fields of economics (e.g., Industrial Organization, Trade, Labor Economics), empirical work demands more definite results, an alternative mode of analysis—searching for a bargaining *solution* based on axiomatic properties that a solution "ought" to satisfy—is introduced. The chapter concludes with the *Nash bargaining solution*, which is by far the most commonly employed of the axiom-based "solutions."

The terms *protocols* and *contexts* may be clear to you, but just in case, let me define terms.

Insofar as we are using noncooperative game theory to analyze bargaining, we must set out a common-knowledge set of rules that describe how the bargaining takes place. This is the bargaining *protocol*. Some examples include:

- In *one-sided bargaining*, one of the two parties (assuming there are two parties) makes all the offers. It could be one offer, made on a take-it-or-leave-it basis. Or the party making the offers may be able to offer a menu of options. And it may be possible to make subsequent offers, if the first offer is not accepted.

- In the *two-sided demand game*, the two parties involved simultaneously and independently propose terms they are willing to accept. If their proposals are consistent, the deal is made (with some rules about compromise, if the proposed deal leaves money on the table). This could be a one-shot procedure, or it could be repeated. In continuous-time models, the parties continuously make demands until an acceptable deal is struck (or the parties give up).

- In *alternating-offer bargaining*, one side makes a proposal, which the other side accepts or rejects. And if rejected, the other side can propose a deal, and so forth. There may be a limit to the number of back-and-forth proposals; and proposals could be menus.

Of course, in many bargaining situations, the "rules" are not so formal or set in stone. One objective in the literature is to find contexts in which the protocols, within limits, have little influence on the bargaining outcome, which indicates that the outcome is robust to the protocol specification. Sometimes this objective is achieved; often it is not.

Context refers to such things as: the issue(s) being negotiated; the preferences of the bargainers; outside options the bargainers may have available; the impact of delay to agreement; and, very significantly in terms of theory, how much information each party has about the preferences and proclivities of his or her bargaining partner.

Two paradigmatic contexts are:

- The owner of an object is willing to sell it to a prospective buyer, if the terms offered (the price, primarily) are acceptable. (Or the provider of a service is willing to provide that service to a prospective client, if acceptable terms are found.) Perhaps the most significant details in this context are the "reservation price" of the buyer (the most the buyer is willing to pay—does the prospective seller know this?) and the minimum amount the seller is willing to accept (which may or may not be known to the buyer). In the paradigmatic specific example of a rug merchant negotiating with a prospective buyer, both sides are in the dark about the other side's valuation.

- Two parties can split a "pot" or "pie," but only if they agree on the split. In many analyses, the pot is one dimensional—say, some amount of money—and each party unambiguously prefers to get more of the pot. Variations that make the problem more interesting include: One or both parties might prefer no deal to a deal that gives too much of the pot to the other side; one or both parties have outside options, which are (perhaps) of unknown value to their trading partner; and the "pot" is multi-dimensional, and each side is uncertain what trade-offs the other party is willing to make in terms of the different dimensions.

Either of these two paradigmatic contexts can be translated into the other in some cases. For instance, the sale-of-an-object problem with each side uncertain of the valuation that the other side puts on the object is isomorphic to splitting a pot, where if no agreement is reached, each side can pursue an outside option, the value of which is unknown to the other side.

Combining a specification of protocol with a specification of each dimension of context gives a very wide variety of situations that we could investigate. Only a few of these are discussed in this chapter. The discussion drifts back and forth between the context of a buyer–seller interaction and the context of two parties splitting a pot. And this introductory chapter ignores entirely those situations with more than one dimension over which the parties are bargaining.

23.1. One-Sided Bargaining

In the case of one-sided bargaining, one party proposes the deal, which the other side then accepts or rejects.

Suppose that Alice and Bob can split $100 if they can agree on the split. Suppose the split must be in even multiples of $1, and the protocol is: Alice proposes a split, and Bob either accepts—in which case that is the outcome—or rejects, in which case both get nothing. Assume they are risk neutral. Then:

- There are only two subgame-perfect, pure-strategy equilibrium outcomes: Subgame perfection forces Bob to accept any offer from Alice that leaves him with $1 or more, so if Alice offers $x \leq 99$ for herself and y for Bob such that $x + y \leq 100$ and $y \geq 1$, Bob will accept. Alice's best response to this is no worse than $x = 99$

and $y = 1$. And, if Bob is being nice, $x = 100$ and $y = 0$ is also a subgame-perfect equilibrium outcome.[2]

- If Bob, faced with the proposal $x = 100, y = 0$, is willing to accept with probability 99/100, we also have a continuum of subgame-perfect mixed-strategy equilibria in which Alice randomizes arbitrarily between $(100, 0)$ and $(99, 1)$, Bob accepts $(99, 1)$, and he accepts $(100, 0)$ with probability 99/100.

- Any split is the outcome of a Nash equilibrium, if we don't insist on subgame perfection. For $x = 0, 1, \ldots, 100$, Alice proposes "x for me and $100 - x$ for you, Bob." Bob accepts this and only this proposal. Indeed, if we allow Alice to make proposals "x for me and y for you," where $x + y < 100$, those are Nash outcomes as well, if Bob's strategy is to accept this and only this proposal.

When this game (or elaborations on it) is played in the lab, one often sees the individual in Bob's position reject Alice's proposal of $(99, 1)$ and even $(90, 10)$. (See Ross 1995 and discussion of the "ultimatum game.") This behavior can be modeled with a simple incomplete-information formulation: There are 101 types of Bob, where Type-n Bob (for $n = 0, \ldots, 100$) has the utility function

$$u_n(y) = \begin{cases} -1, & \text{if Bob accepts } y < n, \\ y, & \text{if Bob accepts } y \geq n, \text{ and} \\ 0, & \text{if Bob rejects.} \end{cases}$$

That is, type-n Bob would rather reject an offer that leaves him with less than n than accept such an "unfair" offer. If Alice assesses probability p_n that Bob is type n, then her maximization problem (in a subgame-perfect Nash equilibrium) is

$$\text{Choose } Y \text{ to maximize } (100 - Y) \sum_{y \geq Y} p_y.$$

And she offers Bob the maximizing Y, taking $100 - Y$ for herself. It is easy to see that we can induce any efficient outcome—that is, x for Alice and $100 - x$ for Bob—as the outcome of a subgame-perfect Nash equilibrium, if we are allowed to have any distribution $(p_n; n = 0, \ldots, 100)$.[3]

Suppose instead that we imagine that Alice owns an object that Bob would like to purchase, if the price is right. Suppose the object is worth v to Alice and u to Bob; both Alice and Bob have utility that is quasi-linear in money; and u and v are measured in "dollars." Hence Alice is willing to sell if the price she can get is greater than v, and Bob is willing to buy if the price is less than u. Alice knows v and Bob knows u. Now suppose Alice also knows u (and $u > v$). If the protocol is

---

[2] By the usual argument, if Alice can offer any $y \in [0, 100]$ to Bob, the only subgame-perfect equilibrium outcome is 100 for Alice and 0 for Bob. Bob must accept any $\epsilon > 0$, so Alice must get at least $100 - \epsilon$. But since $\epsilon > 0$ is arbitrary, *in an equilibrium*, she must get 100. This is an argument we've met a number of times already: Requiring an equilibrium in this situation forces Bob to be nice to Alice when he is indifferent.

[3] And if $p_{100} = 1$, disagreement is also a subgame-perfect Nash equilibrium outcome.

that Alice names her price p and Bob either accepts or rejects (and if we maintain the assumption that Alice must name a price in even multiples of \$1) then, by the same logic as above:

- If u is not an integer, the unique subgame-perfect equilibrium outcome is that Alice names $p = \lfloor u \rfloor$, the integer part of u, and

- if u is an integer, there are two subgame-perfect, pure-strategy equilibrium outcomes, namely, $p = u - 1$, which Bob accepts (and he will reject $p = u$); and $p = u$, which Bob accepts.

If Alice doesn't know u but assesses instead some probability distribution over u, then she maximizes the integer price $p > v$ that maximizes

$$p \times \text{Probability}(u \geq p) + v \times (1 - \text{Probability}(u \geq p)) = v + (p - v) \times \text{Probability}(u \geq p)$$

(although a bit of care is needed about whether Bob will accept if $p = u$. If instead, Alice doesn't know u but assesses that $u = v + n$ with probability p_n for $n = 0, 1, \ldots, 101$, then she is in a fully analogous position to the Alice in the previous divide-\$100 game, with her named price p equaling $v + Y$ (although one must be careful about what Bob does if he is indifferent between buying and not buying).

In this version of things, Alice is like a monopolist (with constant marginal cost v) selling her good. Typically, we think of monopolists as selling goods to a large number of prospective buyers, all of whom take the price the monopolist names as given. But when it comes to naming one price for a single good, and assuming the monopolist facing multiple buyers has constant marginal cost (with no capacity constraint) equal to Alice's valuation v, the stories are the same.

And once it is clear that this is "just the same" as the problem of monopoly pricing, plenty of variations are suggested:

- Suppose the object for sale can be crafted in more than one fashion, and Bob's preferences depend on the design. The theories of market screening from Chapter 20 apply: Alice may be best off offering Bob a menu of different prices for different specifications, from which he can choose.

- Suppose Alice could sell different quantities of the good to Bob. Stories about second-degree price discrimination, which we haven't covered, come into play.

- Suppose we have one-sided bargaining on the other side: Bob names a price, and Alice either agrees or not. This gives us standard theories of monopsony, and, if there are multiple specifications of the good (or service) together with incomplete information about Bob's characteristics, market signaling as in Chapter 20 becomes relevant.

- And suppose Alice, if her first price is rejected, can name a second price (after some costly delay). Then developments discussed in Chapter 21 become relevant. Although in this case, the theory of the Coase conjecture (where Alice is selling to a host of customers) doesn't perfectly align with this story (where Alice is selling to a single prospective customer Bob), see "An Alice-and-Bob variation" on pages 183-4, Sobel and Takahashi (1983), Problems 21.1 and 21.3, and Problem 23.1 (which continues the story of Problem 21.3 and shows how the alignment between the problems can break down).

To sum up, a lot of the theory developed in earlier chapters can be recast as one-sided bargaining (although a bit of care is required if dynamic price setting is introduced).

23.2. The Two-Sided Demand Game

In the two-sided demand game, we imagine Alice and Bob negotiating over the division of $100 with the following protocol. Simultanously and independently, each names a demand. Let x be the amount demanded by Alice and y the amount demanded by Bob. (For expositional simplicity, I'll assume that demands are constrained to lie in $[0, 100]$.) If $x + y \leq \$100$, then Alice gets x and Bob gets y. If $x + y > 100$, then both get 0. [4]

Since the game (so far) has no dynamic structure whatsoever—there is only one round of (simultaneous) demands—we look for Nash equilibria.

Proposition 23.1. *Every division* $(x, 100 - x)$ *is the outcome of a (pure-strategy) Nash equilibrium in which Alice demands* x *and Bob demands* $100 - x$. *And every pure-strategy Nash equilibrium is of this form, except for the no-deal equilibrium in which Alice demands 100, Bob demands 100, and they both receive 0.*

The proof is probably obvious to you, but just in case, Problem 23.2 asks you to spell out the simple details.

What about mixed-strategy equilibria? They abound and are (must be) invariably inefficient (under the rules where, if $x + y < 100$, money is left on the table); see Problem 23.3.

Consider instead the context in which Alice might sell a good to Bob, where Alice knows what the good is worth to Bob, and Bob knows what the good is worth to Alice if she doesn't sell. The bargaining protocol is that Alice and Bob simultaneously name ask and bid amounts, respectively: Alice says what she is asking for the item, and Bob says what he is bidding. If he bids more than she asks, the deal is consummated, although if he bids strictly more than she asks, we must specify what happens to the excess: If, say, the difference between bid and ask, if it strictly positive, is "burned" or otherwise goes to some third party (in whom neither Alice nor Bob have any interest), then this situation is isomorphic to the the two-sided demand game as formulated above (as long as Bob's value exceeds Alice's). If, alternatively, they split the excess—that is, the deal is consummated at the average of the bid and the ask—we don't quite have the same game. However, (1) in any pure-strategy Nash equilibrium, assuming Bob's valuation for the good exceed's Alice's valuation if she retains it, the bid and ask will agree;[5] and (2) in the two-sided demand game, we could reformulate so that if $x + y < 100$, Alice

---

[4] Or, the rules could specify that, if $x + y < 100$, they split the difference, or $x + (100 - x - y)/2 = 50 + x/2 - y/2$ to Alice.

[5] Except for no-trade outcomes, in which Alice asks for more than Bob's valuation, and Bob bids less than Alice's valuation

gets $x/2 + 50 - y/2$, and Bob gets $y/2 + 50 - x/2$. Then this reformulated two-sided demand game is isomorphic to the Alice-sells-to-Bob game where, if the bid exceeds the ask, they compromise at the midpoint between them.

In the split $100 game, we can enrich the story by supposing that both sides have minimum amounts they are willing to accept, with Alice having a subjective assessment of what that amount is for Bob and vice versa. In the version where Alice is selling to Bob, we could suppose that Bob is unsure what value Alice attaches to retaining the object, while Alice is unsure what value Bob places on possessing the object. These incomplete-information formulations will be discussed in Sections 23.6 and 23.7.

Dynamic versions

Rather than ending the bargaining with no deal if the initial demands are incompatible, we could allow Alice and Bob to try again, and again, going on forever or perhaps with some fixed-in-advance deadline. To get some traction out of this, we impose a cost each time they fail to come to agreement. Two obvious ways to do this are:

1. Reduce the "pie" proportionally each time an agreement is not reached: They can split 100 if they agree at $t = 0$, but (for some $\delta \leq 1$) they only have 100δ to split at $t = 1$, and $100\delta^2$ at $t = 2$, and so forth. (An alternative interpretation is that they always have 100 to split, but they discount at rate δ per period each period it takes to reach agreement.)

2. Reduce the "pie" by a set amount for each period that they fail to reach agreement: They can split 100 if they agree at $t = 0$; 99 if they agree at $t = 1$; ...; and $100 - t$ if they agree at time t, for $t < 100$.

If $\delta < 1$ in the first variation, and also in the second variation, there are pure-strategy Nash equilibria that are inefficient in the sense that, there is agreement, but only at a time $t > 0$. I'll illustrate with the first variation (with the interpretation that the pie shrinks in each period, rather than that Alice and Bob discount their agreed-to split): Pick a time t and a split of $100\delta^t$, say, x to Alice and $100\delta^t - x$ to Bob. At time s, $s < t$, along the equilibrium path, Alice and Bob both demand the whole pie, $\delta^s 100$. If they follow these prescriptions until time t, at time t they agree on the split x for Alice and $100\delta^t - x$ for Bob. And, if at any point either Alice or Bob (or both) deviates from these prescriptions, then each demands the whole (remaining) pie for the rest of time.

Focal equilibria

Notwithstanding this multitude of possible pure-strategy equilibria, experiments of the simplest type, where the two parties agree to split $10 (scaled down so the experiment can be financed), suggests that the $5-for-each split is focal.[6] But what if the situation is not so obviously symmetric between the players?

---

[6]   See page 513 in Appendix 9 if you need reminding about the concept of a focal equilibrium.

Roth and Schoumaker (1983) provide a particularly interesting experimental study of this sort, in which two parties bargain over the division of 100 "chips." If, say, the two agree to split the chips 35 for A and 65 for B, then A has a 0.35 probability of winning a prize, and B has a 0.65 probability of winning a possibly different prize. In particular, they look at an experiment in which A's prize is $10 and B's prize is $40. Two candidates for a focal equilibrium are created: Split the chips 50-50, so each party has a 0.5 chance of winning a prize; split them 80 to A and 20 to B, so each has an expected prize of $8. Without going into details here—read the paper!—Roth and Schoumaker show that subjects can be "taught" that one or the other of these two focal equilibria is "the right thing to do" and, having learned that lesson, subjects conform to what they have been taught.[7]

23.3. Rubinstein's Alternating-Offer Game

For many years, the indeterminacy of equilibrium outcomes in the simultaneous de-mand game was taken as an indication that self-interest-driven equilibrium analysis alone would not be a fruitful approach to determining how individuals bargain; a mixture of experimental and empirical study seemed the best path to understanding which protocols and contexts give "bargaining strength" to one of the two parties.

Rubinstein (1982) rekindled hope that equilibrium analysis of self-interested behavior alone could solve or, at least, shed light on the problem. Rubinstein proposes the following model: Alice and Bob are bargaining over how to split a pie of size z. At $t = 0$, Alice can propose a split (x_0, y_0) such that $x_0 + y_0 \leq z$. Bob can immediately accept this split or, at time h, he can propose a split (x_h, y_h) subject to $x_h + y_h \leq z$. If things get that far—if Bob rejects Alice's immediate offer and counter offers (x_h, y_h), Alice can immediately agree to Bob's offer or, at time $t = 2h$, she can make a counter-counteroffer (x_{2h}, y_{2h}), which Bob can accept immediately or counter at time $3h$, and so on, forever.

The pie size z never decreases. But Alice and Bob are impatient, and they prefer to get their share of the pie sooner rather than later. Specifically, Alice's payoff is 0 if they never reach agreement. And if agreement is reached at time $t = nh$, and the agreement gives x to Alice, her payoff is $e^{-rnh}x$ for fixed parameter r, the per-unit-time discount rate. Letting $\delta = e^{-rh}$, we can abbreviate this payoff as $\delta^n x$. Bob's payoffs are similar: 0 if agreement is never reached; $\delta^n y$ if agreement is reached at time nh and provides him with y as his share.

Proposition 23.2. (Rubinstein 1982) *In the unique subgame-perfect equilibrium of this game, when it is a player's turn to make an offer (regardless of what has happened previously), the player proposes that her or his share should be $z/(1 + \delta)$ and that the other party should get $\delta z/(1 + \delta)$. All such offers (or any better offer for the party not making the current offer) are immediately accepted, while any worse offer for the party not making the current offer is rejected.*

Proof. We must prove that the strategies given constitute a subgame-perfect Nash equilibrium, and that it is the only one. The first part is relatively easy. Suppose

---

[7] Their experiment is somewhat more complex than I've described. See footnote 15 on page 515.

we reach a stage in the game at which it is Alice's turn to make an offer. She is supposed to offer $z/(1+\delta)$ for herself and $\delta z/(1+\delta)$ for Bob, and Bob is supposed to accept this. Since this will be accepted, as will anything more for Bob and less for herself (per Bob's strategy), there is no reason for her to offer Bob more. And if she offers Bob less, he is supposed to reject and come back with a symmetric offer next time, which she is meant to accept. Since she'll be offered less next time, and it will be discounted by one period, that isn't a worthwhile deviation.

The more interesting part of the proof is the unimprovability of Bob's strategy when Alice offers him $\delta z/(1+\delta)$, or more, or less. If he rejects her offer, the continuation gives him $z/(1+\delta)$ next period, worth $\delta z/(1+\delta)$ in the current period, so acceptance of $\delta z/(1+\delta)$ in the current period is weakly a best response (given the alleged equilibrium continuation), and acceptance of any better offer is strictly a best response. As for the case where she offers him less than $\delta z/(1+\delta)$, by rejecting, the alleged equilibrium continuation has a current value of $\delta z/(1+\delta)$, so accepting such an offer is suboptimal.

When Bob is making the offer, the arguments are symmetrical. Each proposed strategy is unimprovable (given the other party's strategy) and hence optimal.

The harder argument is that this is the unique subgame-perfect Nash equilibrium. I use a proof originally provided in Shaked and Sutton (1984).

Let ν be the supremum value that the player whose turn it is to make an offer can achieve in any subgame-perfect Nash equilibrium, and let η be the infimum value. We know from the first part of the proof that this sup and inf are taken over nonempty sets. Of course, $\nu \geq \eta$.

I assert that $\eta \geq z - \delta\nu$. Suppose instead that $\eta < z - \delta\nu$, so there is a subgame-perfect Nash equilibrium in which the first player gets less than $z - \delta\nu$. But if the first player offers $\delta\nu + \epsilon$ for any $\epsilon > 0$ to her rival, leaving $z - \delta\nu - \epsilon$ for herself, then the second player is bound to accept: By rejecting, the second player (now on the move) can do no better than ν starting next time, which has a present value (in the "first" round) of $\delta\nu$. Hence, by offering $\delta\nu + \epsilon$ to the second player, the first player is assured of a payoff for herself of $z - \delta\nu - \epsilon$. If $\eta < z - \delta\nu$, we can find an ϵ small enough to give a contradiction.

(Put an asterisk in the margin of the previous paragraph. I just invoked a critical assumption that, as yet, I have not stated explicitly. Do you see what it is?)

And I assert that $\nu \leq z - \delta\eta$. Suppose instead that $\nu > z - \delta\eta$. Then there is a subgame-perfect equilibrium in which the first player gets strictly more than $z - \delta\eta$. But if the second player rejects the initial offer of the first player, the worst she can do starting with her offer in the next period is η, which has first-period value $\delta\eta$. So, the first player can't leave the second player with less than $\delta\eta$, which means no more than $z - \delta\eta$ for herself.

Now rearrange these inequalities:

$$\eta + \delta\nu \geq z \geq \nu + \delta\eta \quad \text{or} \quad \eta(1-\delta) \geq \nu(1-\delta) \quad \text{or} \quad \eta \geq \nu,$$

and (since $\nu \geq \eta$ by definition) $\nu = \eta$. And we know from the first part of the proof that both are equal to $z/(1+\delta)$.

This part of the proof nails down the subgame-perfect Nash equilibrium payoffs; it remains to nail down the strategies. Suppose we have a subgame-perfect Nash equilibrium in which there is positive probability that Alice and Bob fail to reach agreement at time $t = 0$. Since they only have x to split and rewards are discounted, the sum of their expected equilibrium values would be less than x. But Alice must have an expected payoff of $z/(1 + \delta)$, and if Bob has less than $\delta z/(1 + \delta)$, he can refuse Alice's first offer, and be in a position where he has an expected payoff of $z/(1 + \delta)$ starting at time $t = h$, for a time $t = 0$ value of $\delta z/(1 + \delta)$. Hence their combined payoff must equal z, and there can be no chance that Alice's first offer is refused. She must offer $\delta z/(1 + \delta)$ to Bob, leaving $z/(1 + \delta)$ for herself. And Bob must accept. ∎

Note that as $\delta \to 1$, $1/(1 + \delta) \to 1/2$. In terms of our original definition of δ as e^{-rh}, where h is the time it takes for either Alice or Bob to make a counteroffer, this corresponds (for fixed r) to $h \to 0$. As the (counter)offers can be made more and more quickly, the equilibrium split converges to $z/2$ for both Alice and Bob.

Finite horizons: Rubinstein versus the Folk Theorem

(This subsection is a bit wonky and can be skipped without breaking the flow of the chapter.)

Suppose Alice and Bob play the Rubinstein alternating-offer game for a finite number of periods, where, if no agreement is reached after $N+1$ rounds of offer and counteroffer, the game ends with zero payoff for both. What happens as $N \to \infty$?[8]

The analysis depends on whether N is even or odd, so suppose it is odd: That is, Bob makes the final offer x_N for Alice and y_N for Bob, such that $x_N + y_N \leq z$, and if Alice rejects, the game is over, and both players walk away with payoff 0.

If that final period is reached—if there is no agreement earlier—in any subgame-perfect equilibrium, Bob offers $(x_N, y_N) = (0, z)$, and Alice accepts. Because if she didn't accept, Bob could offer $(\epsilon, z - \epsilon)$, which she must accept if $\epsilon > 0$, and since $\epsilon > 0$ can be arbitrarily small, in an equilibrium, she must accept 0 by the usual "ties go to the betterment of the other player" argument.

Now consider $t = N - 1$, when it is Alice's turn to make an offer. Bob knows he can get z in period N if he refuses Alice's offer, which is worth δz to him. So if Alice offers him $(x_{N-1}, y_{N-1}) = ((1 - \delta)z - \epsilon, \delta z + \epsilon)$, he is bound to accept. And so, by the usual argument, the unique subgame-perfect equilibrium has her offering $((1 - \delta)z, \delta z)$, which he accepts.

Move back to $t = N - 2$. Alice knows she can get $(1 - \delta)z$ if she refuses Bob's offer, which, at time $N - 2$, is worth $\delta(1 - \delta)z = (\delta - \delta^2)z$ to her. So—again we invoke the usual argument—Bob will offer $((\delta - \delta^2)z, z(1 - \delta + \delta^2))$, which Alice accepts. And at $t = N - 3$, Alice offers $(z(1 - \delta + \delta^2 - \delta^3), z(\delta - \delta^2 + \delta^3))$, which Bob accepts. The iteration is clear, back at time 0, Alice offers

$$\left(z(1 - \delta + \delta^2 - \ldots - \delta^N), z(\delta - \delta^2 + \delta^3 - \ldots + \delta^N)\right),$$

---

[8] The analysis of this problem predates Rubinstein; it is due to Stähl (1972).

which Bob accepts. But

$$1 - \delta + \delta^2 - \delta^3 + \ldots - \delta^N = \frac{1 - \delta^{N+1}}{1 + \delta}, \quad \text{hence,} \quad \lim_{N \to \infty} 1 - \delta + \ldots - \delta^N - \frac{1}{1 + \delta}.$$

Alice ends up with (approximately, for finite N, and exactly in the limit) what she gets in Rubinstein's unique subgame-perfect equilibrium.

And, if instead N is even, so Alice makes the last offer, the answer is that Alice ends with $z(1 + \delta^N)/(1 + \delta)$, slightly better than what she gets in Rubinstein's equilibrium, but vanishingly so as $N \to \infty$. (This argument can be turned into an alternate proof of the uniqueness of the Rubinstein equilibrium: Do you see how? See Problem 23.5.)

Hence, in the limit as $N \to \infty$, the unique subgame-perfect equilibrium in the N-horizon alternating-offer game converges to the unique subgame-perfect equilibrium in the infinite-horizon alternating-offer game.

Compare this with, say, the trading-favors game where (departing a bit from the formulation of Chapter 22) we suppose that in each even-numbered period, Alice has the opportunity to do a favor for Bob that costs her 1 and provides him with benefit 10, and in each odd-numbered period, he has the opportunity to do a favor for her, costing him 1 and benefiting her 10. In any finite-horizon version of this game, the player called on to do a favor in the final period will not do so, and by the usual argument, this "rolls back," so that no favors are done. No favors is, of course, a subgame-perfect Nash equilibrium for the infinite-horizon version of this game. However, if δ is close enough to 1, there are other subgame-perfect equilibria such as the all-favors equilibrium in which both Alice and Bob always do favors along the path of play. That is, the uniqueness of subgame-perfect equilibria for each finite-horizon game *does not* in this case stand as a proof of the uniqueness of subgame-perfect equilibria for the infinite-horizon game.

(Now for the wonky part.) This connects to the dynamic-programming procedure known as *value iteration*, discussed in Section A6.11 in Volume I. In that discussion, and in particular in Proposition A6.12, it is asserted that in sequential-decision problems meeting certain conditions, the optimal values of (truncated) finite-horizon problems converges to the optimal values of infinite-horizon problems. The main tool we've used to show that some strategy profile is a subgame-perfect (or, in more complex problems, a sequential) equilibrium is the dynamic-programming result that unimprovability implies optimality. That being so, how is it that, in the trading-favors game, there are infinite-horizon equilibria that aren't the limit of finite-horizon equilibria?

The answer is that value iteration works in *single*-person sequential decision problems. When we enlist the theory of single-person decision problems—specifically, unimprovability implies optimality—in verifying equilibria, we look to show that each player's strategy is unimprovable, hence optimal, *fixing the strategies of the other players*. It doesn't work—and in particular, the idea of value iteration doesn't work—when we have multiple players optimizing simultaneously, since changing what Alice does changes the single-person sequential decision problem facing Bob.

But it can be made to work, in the following sense. In Appendix 6 in Volume I, value iteration was done with a terminal value function of 0. Without going into details, one can show that value iteration works for other terminal valuation functions. And, in the trading-favors game, one can find a (state-dependent) terminal value function for finite-horizon games that, as the horizon goes to infinity, gives the all-favors equilibrium. Specifically, suppose that, in an N-period version of trading favors, the terminal valuation function is that, if the last player called upon to do a favor fails to do it, her terminal value is 0. If she does it, but someone failed to do a favor in the past, her terminal value is 0. But if she does it, and if all previous favors were done, she gets δ times the net present value that she gets in these circumstances in the infinite-horizon game with the equilibrium you are trying to induce less the 1 it costs to do the current favor.

What distinguishes the Rubinstein bargaining model is that, no matter which terminal value function you employ for finite-horizon problems (subject to reasonable limits), as the horizon goes to infinity, you get the same initial value function in the limit. For instance, we specified that, if no agreement is reached up to period N in N-period, finite-horizon version of Rubsintein, both players walk away empty handed. Suppose that, instead, we specified that, say, Alice gets the whole pie if no agreement is reached by the end. Or specify that Alice gets $3z/4$ and Bob gets $z/4$. Redo the recursive calculation of what this means as $N \to \infty$; you still get the Rubinstein solution in the limit. And that is another explanation for why, in Rubinstein's model, there is only one subgame-perfect equilibrium.

Variations

Variations on the basic Rubinstein model provide some interesting results. Here are six variations. For each, there is a unique subgame-perfect Nash equilibrium. What is your guess as to the how the outcome of that equilibrium changes with the changed conditions?

1. Suppose Bob has an outside option: Whenever Alice proposes a split, Bob can accept or reject. If he rejects, he can immediately take advantage of an outside option he has, which gives him αz for $\alpha < 1$ and leaves Alice with 0. Or, with the usual time delay, he can counterpropose some split. (He can still take his outside option, but if this is his plan, it would be better to take it without the delay.)

2. Suppose that Alice and Bob have different per-period discount rates. Alice's per-period discount rate is $e^{-r_A h}$, and Bob's is $e^{-r_B h}$, where $3r_A = r_B$.

3. Suppose Alice can make a counteroffer h units of time after rejecting an offer from Bob, but it takes Bob $3h$ units of time to make a counteroffer.

4. We have supposed that Bob (and Alice) can accept an offer from Alice (Bob) instantly, but there is a delay in making a counteroffer. Suppose, instead, that there is a delay in both the acceptance of an offer and in making a counteroffer. Specifically, after Alice makes an offer, Bob can either accept or counteroffer after $3h$ units of time have passed; after Bob makes an offer, Alice can either

accept or counteroffer after h units of time have elaspsed.

5. Suppose that instead of discounting, Alice and Bob negotiate over a "pie" that decreases in size as time passes. Specifically, at $t = 0$, there is $9.90 to be split, and Alice proposes how it will be split. Bob can accept Alice's proposal or reject it, but if he rejects it, $0.11 is subtracted, so Bob's proposal is a division of $9.79. If Alice rejects this proposal, she can propose a split of $9.69. Every time Bob rejects a proposal by Alice, $0.11 is subtracted; every time Alice rejects a proposal by Bob, $0.10 is subtracted.

6. No discounting again, and the amount to be split is initially $10 and remains $10. But Alice must pay $0.10 every time she makes an offer, and Bob must pay $0.11 every time he makes an offer.

Proposition 23.3. *In each of the variations listed above, there is a unique subgame-perfect Nash equilibrium in which Alice's initial offer is immediately accepted by Bob. Concerning these unique equilibria:*

a. *In Variation 1, if $\alpha z \leq \delta z/(1+\delta)$, Alice proposes that she take $z/(1-\delta)$ and Bob take $\delta z/(1+\delta)$ (and Bob accepts). And if $\alpha z > \delta z/(1+\delta)$, Alice proposes that she take $(1-\alpha)z$ and Bob take αz (and he accepts).*

b. *In Variation 2, fix h, and let $\delta = e^{-r_A h}$. In the unique equilibrium, if Alice has the offer, she offers Bob $\delta^3 z/(1+\delta+\delta^2+\delta^3)h$, keeping $(1+\delta+\delta)z/(1+\delta+\delta^2+\delta^3)$ for herself. If Bob is making the offer, he offers Alice $(\delta+\delta^2+\delta^3)z/(1+\delta+\delta^2+\delta^3)$, keeping $z/(1+\delta+\delta^2+\delta^3)$ for himself. In both cases, the other party accepts. Hence, as $h \to 0$, Alice's share approaches $3z/4$, and Bob's approaches $z/4$.*

c. *In Variation 3, as $h \to 0$, Alice's initial proposal approaches $3z/4$ for herself and $z/4$ for Bob.*

d. *In Variation 4, as $h \to 0$, Alice's initial proposal approaches $z/4$ for herself and $3z/4$ for Bob.*

e. *In Variation 5, Alice initially proposes that she take $5.20, leaving $4.70 for Bob. He accepts.*

f. *In Variation 6, Alice proposes that she take all $10. Bob accepts.*

Proof. I provide proofs of parts c, d, and f. Regarding part e, note that at $t = 47$, there is only $0.03 left, so whatever Alice proposes, Bob must accept. From this point, it is simple backward induction to come to the conclusion stated. Concerning parts a and b, Problem 23.6 asks you to verify that the alleged equilibrium strategies are equilibria; you can trust me on the uniqueness part.

For parts c, d, and f, I use a method that is close to the argument given in the "Finite horizons" subsection. Begin with Variation 3, and fix $h > 0$. Let $\delta := e^{-hr}$, so that $e^{-3hr} = \delta^3$. Now suppose we have a subgame-perfect equilibrium. It provides equilibrium expected payoffs for Alice and Bob starting from every node (where agreement was not reached earlier). We know (how?) that these equilibrium values can be no larger than x and no smaller than 0.

Pick a very large and even T.

- Since Bob's equilibrium payoff starting from any node at time $T+1$ is no larger than z, if Alice offers Bob $\delta^3 z + \epsilon$, for any $\epsilon > 0$, subgame-perfection forces Bob to accept. (If he refuses, the best he can do is z next time, but this is discounted to present-value units by δ^3.) Hence, at time T, Alice's payoff must exceed $z - \delta^3 z - \epsilon$ for all $\epsilon > 0$; it must be at least $z(1 - \delta^3)$.

- Therefore, at time $T - 1$, Alice's expected payoff must be at least $\delta z(1 - \delta^3) = z(\delta - \delta^4)$; she can always refuse Bob's offer and wait for next period. But since the sum of their payoffs cannot exceed z, this puts an upper bound on Bob's payoff of $z(1 - \delta + \delta^4)$.

- Which implies that at time $T - 2$, if Alice offers Bob $\delta^3 z(1 - \delta + \delta^4) + \epsilon$ for any positive ϵ, he must accept. Which gives a lower bound on her expected payoff of $z(1 - \delta^3 + \delta^4 - \delta^7)$.

And so forth. The impact of giving Bob "credit" for a payoff of z (or less) at time T vanishes as $T \to \infty$, and we get a lower bound on Alice's payoff of

$$z(1 - \delta^3 + \delta^4 - \delta^7 + \delta^8 - \delta^{11} + \ldots) = z(1 - \delta^3)(1 + \delta^4 + \delta^8 + \ldots) = \frac{z(1 - \delta^3)}{1 - \delta^4} = \frac{z(1 + \delta + \delta^2)}{1 + \delta + \delta^2 + \delta^3}.$$

Now repeat the argument for an odd T, giving Alice "cedit" for a payoff of at most z at time $T+1$, and you find that this is an upper bound on her equilibrium payoff. And for Bob, his lower bound (given by the argument just provided) and upper bound (starting with an odd T) is z minus Alice's payoff, or $\delta^3 z/(1 + \delta + \delta^2 + \delta^3)$. Since their payoffs sum to z, it must be that there is agreement at time 0, with Alice proposing the split $z(1 + \delta + \delta^2)/(1 + \delta + \delta^2 + \delta^3)$ for herself and $\delta^3 z/(1 + \delta + \delta^2 + \delta^3)$ for Bob, which he accepts.

We must check that this does indeed give us a subgame-perfect equilibrium, and to do that, we also must specify what Bob offers Alice when he is making the offer. The answer is: He offers her $(\delta + \delta^2 + \delta^3)z/(1 + \delta + \delta^2 + \delta^3)$, retaining $z/(1 + \delta + \delta^2 + \delta^3)$ for himself, and she accepts. Both accept any offer more generous than these equilibrium offers and reject anything less generous.

To save on space, I will write Δ for $1 + \delta + \delta^2 + \delta^3$ in what follows.

Suppose Alice offers Bob $z\delta^3/\Delta$. He is supposed to accept this. If he turns it down, his strategy calls for him to counteroffer z/Δ, which will be accepted. But it takes $3h$ time units for this to happen, so his (accepted) counteroffer is worth (only) $z\delta^3/\Delta$ to him, and so it does not improve his payoff. If Alice offers him more, he will surely take it; if she offers him less, he surely refuses.

As for Alice (if she makes the first offer), if she offers $z\delta^3/\Delta$ to Bob, he will accept, and she nets $z(1 + \delta + \delta^2)/\Delta$. If she deviates and offers him more, he'll accept, which is worse for her. And if she asks for more, he'll decline and come back with a counteroffer of z/Δ for himself and $z(\delta + \delta^2 + \delta^3)/\Delta$, which has a current value to her of $z(\delta^3)(\delta + \delta^2 + \delta^3)/\Delta$, less than what she gets in the supposed equilibrium.

Now suppose Bob is making the offer. He offers $z(\delta + \delta^2 + \delta^3)/\Delta$ to Alice, which she is meant to accept. If she turns this down, she will get $z(1 + \delta + \delta^2)/\Delta$ with a one-period delay, worth in current-value terms just what she gets by accepting. So rejecting Bob's offer is not an improvement. If Bob offers her more, she surely will take it; if he offers her less, she surely will turn it down. As for Bob, if he offers her $z(\delta + \delta^2 + \delta^3)/\Delta$, he leaves z/Δ for himself. If he offers her more, she will accept, meaning less for him; not an improvement. And if he asks for more, she will reject. And then next time, she offers him $z\delta^3/\Delta$, which he will accept, for a current value of $z\delta^4/\Delta$, which is worse for him than taking z/Δ now.

Hence, we have a subgame-perfect equilibrium. The limit result that is given as part c is immediate.

Part d is similar. What changes is when Alice makes a proposal, both Bob's acceptance and counteroffer cause the same delay. Thus the largest possible payoff is not z but δz if Bob is making the offer and $\delta^3 z$ if Alice is making the offer. So, take a large and even T. At $T + 1$, Bob's largest possible payoff is δz.

- At time T, if Bob turns down Alice's offer, he must wait $3h$ before countering, so the best he can do in time-T present-value units is $\delta^4 z$. To make sure he accepts her offer, Alice can offer him $\delta z + \epsilon$ for $\epsilon > 0$, which gives him (if he accepts) $\delta^3(\delta z + \epsilon)$; he must accept. Hence, since Bob will accept $\delta z + \epsilon$, leaving Alice with a split of $z - \delta z - \epsilon$ for a current value of $\delta^3(z - \delta z - \epsilon)$, her payoff at time T must be at least $\delta^3(z - \delta z)$.

- At time $T - 1$, if Alice rejects Bob's offer, she gets at least $\delta^3(z - \delta z)$ in payoff units next period, which in current value terms is worth $\delta^4(z - \delta z)$. And Bob in that case, Bob gets no more than $\delta^5 z$ in $T - 1$ present-value units. But if he offers her $\delta^3(z - \delta z) + \epsilon$ for $\epsilon > 0$, she will accept, which gives him $z - \delta^3 z + \delta^4 z - \epsilon$ as a share, worth (when Alice's acceptance takes effect) $\delta z - \delta^4 z + \delta^5 z$. So it is better for him to get her to accept, leaving him with no more than $z(\delta - \delta^4 + \delta^5)$ in time $T - 1$ present-value units.

And so forth. If you take this all argument the way back to $t = 0$ and then let $T \to \infty$, you get a lower bound on Alice's *payoff* at time $t = 0$ of

$$z\delta^3(1 - \delta + \delta^4 - \delta^5 + \delta^8 - \delta^9 + \ldots) = z\delta^3 \frac{1 - \delta}{1 - \delta^4} = z\delta^3 \frac{1}{\Delta}.$$

And, working back from an odd T, you get this as the limit of the lower bounds on Bob's payoff:

$$z\delta^3 \frac{\delta + \delta^2 + \delta^3}{\Delta}.$$

Note that the δ^3 that pre-multiplies these values are there because of the delay. In the equilibrium, if Alice has the offer, she offers Bob $z(\delta + \delta^2 + \delta^3)/\Delta$, which he accepts. If he has the offer to make, he offers her $z\delta^3/\Delta$, which she accepts.

I'll leave it to you to verify that these strategies do give a subgame-perfect equilibrium, which immediately gives the limit result stated in part d.

As for part f, I'll first verify that this is part of a subgame-perfect equilibrium, where the other part is what happens if Bob is making the offer: He proposes that he'll take $0.10, leaving $9.90 for her, and she accepts. Of course, both accept if their partner is more generous, and both reject if their bargaining partner is less generous (which is hard for Alice, since she is already offering Bob $0).

Note that if Bob is making the offer and makes this proposal, Alice is indifferent between accepting and following the equilibrium prescription of offering him $9.90, since to reject and counteroffer costs her $0.10. If he is more generous (demanding less than $0.10 for himself), she'll surely accept, which is worse for him. And if he tries to get more than $0.10 for himself, she will reject, and he'll be left with $0.

And if Alice is making the offer: Bob can accept her offer of $0, since to reject and counteroffer that he'll take $0.10 costs him more than he stands to gain. And she can't ask for more, at least according to the rules.

So this is a subgame-perfect equilibrium. Why is it the unique subgame-perfect equilibrium? Suppose, when Bob is making the offer, he can succeed with asking for more than $0.10 for himself. Suppose in particular that $\nu >$ $0.10 is the largest payoff he can get in any subgame-perfect equilibrium.[9] Fix this alleged equilibrium. At some point, he'll have to ask for ν and be accepted. But if, at that point, Alice rejects, she can counteroffer $\nu -$ $0.105 for him (or, if $\nu <$ $0.105, then $(\nu +$ $0.10)/2$). It pays for her to do this, if he will accept, since her payoff improves by $0.105, and it only cost her $0.10 to make this counteroffer. And he must accept: To reject and counteroffer costs him $0.11, and (by assumption) ν is the most he can get, so he can't (in equilibrium) recover the $0.11 it costs him to counteroffer. (If $\nu <$ $0.105, then she must counteroffer something like $(\nu +$ $0.10)/2$ so that he is left with something strictly positive. That's why he can extract $0.10 if he is making the initial offer.)   ∎

Proposition 23.3 should make you a bit squeamish concerning Rubinstein's results. The conclusion of the base Rubinstein model does not run counter to intuition. If by declining Alice's initial order, Bob imposes a cost (on both parties) that agreement must be delayed for a bit of time, it is not unreasonable that Alice should be able to exploit this and obtain a bargaining advantage. But as the time between offers h shrinks to zero and $\delta = e^{-rh} \to 1$, this cost decreases, and so Alice's ability to extract a bit extra for herself—$1/(1 + \delta)$ versus $\delta/(1 + \delta)$—goes to zero.

And if it takes Bob longer to formulate a counteroffer than it does Alice (Variation 3), then Bob, by declining, imposes a larger cost by declining than does Alice. It is not unreasonable, in this case, that Alice does better than she does if they impose

---

[9] When I was giving the Shaked and Sutton proof of the uniqueness of the original Rubinstein equilibrium, back on page 276, I was careful to call ν the supremum of all possible equilibrium values. Here, I'm being sloppy when I say that ν is the largest (i.e., the supremum is attained). How could I, if I were more fastidious, avoid this sloppiness?

equal costs. By the same logic, in Variation 4, when Alice makes an offer, the time cost of waiting for Bob to accept or counteroffer is set and done. But if Bob declines, he imposes a further time cost (namely the h units it will take for Alice to accept or counteroffer). In contrast, in this variation, if Alice declines, she imposes a time cost of $3h$ units. So it is not unreasonable that Bob has the advantage.

However, in both Variations 3 and 4, as $h \to 0$, the time costs imposed by rejection of an offer become very small. And yet the consequences are huge, with (in Variation 3) Alice getting three times as much as Bob, and the reverse in Variation 4.

In Variation 1, Bob's outside option generates no bargaining leverage for him if his outside option is less than what he would get if he had no outside option. And if his outside option is greater than or equal to what he would get if there were no outside option, his benefit is simply that he gets his outside option from Alice and no more.

Finally, in Variation 6, a very small difference in the cost of making an offer or counteroffer generates for Alice enormous bargaining leverage: If she is making the first offer, she demands everything, and Bob agrees. And this would work just as effectively, *in theory*, if it cost her $0.02 to make an offer or counteroffer and it cost Bob $0.025.

If this is not enough to make you squeamish, how about one final variation: Suppose the prize is not infinitely divisible.

Proposition 23.4. *Suppose that Alice and Bob are bargaining over the division of $100, following the Rubinstein protocol of alternating-offer bargaining, with an h time-units delay in making a counterproposal, and with the value of the agreement discounted at rate $\delta = e^{-rh}$ per round of delay for a given r. However, unlike the base Rubinstein model, proposals must be in multiples of $0.01. That is, Alice can propose a split of $65.67 for herself and $21.34 for Bob, but she cannot propose $65.676 for herself and $21.334 for Bob. Then there exists $h_0 > 0$ such that, for all $h < h_0$ (and $h > 0$), any efficient split of the $100 (that respects the $0.01 constraint) is the outcome of a subgame-perfect equilibrium for this h (and corresponding $\delta = e^{-rh}$). And there are subgame-perfect equilibria that are inefficient (that leave money on the table) and for which there is some delay to agreement.*

I leave the proof to you as Problem 23.7 with the following hint: Go back to the paragraph at which I suggested you put an asterisk in the margin. Or, if you prefer, see the paragraph in the middle of page 287 (in Section 23.4).

The issue is that Proposition 23.4 can be viewed as an example of a double limit, except in this case, we can go further and add a third limit: Take alternating bargaining à la Rubinstein, but suppose there are only N rounds of bargaining, the smallest monetary unit (in which offers can be framed) is m, and the time between successive offers is h. Proposition 23.2 takes $N = \infty$, $m = 0$, and $h > 0$; one can get the same limit by fixing $h > 0$ and taking $m \to 0$ and $N \to \infty$ (in either order). That is, calling Alice's equilibrium share $\alpha_A(N, m, h)$, we get

$$\lim_{h \to 0} \Big[\lim_{N \to \infty} \big[\lim_{m \to 0} \alpha_A(N, m, h) \big] \Big] = \lim_{h \to 0} \Big[\lim_{m \to 0} \big[\lim_{N \to \infty} \alpha_A(N, m, h) \big] \Big] = 1/2,$$

where what I've written makes sense because, for fixed $h > 0$ and small enough m and large enough N, there is a unique subgame-perfect equilibrium. (I haven't proved this; I'm asserting that it is true.) Proposition 23.4 fixes $m > 0$ and takes $N \to \infty$ and $h \to 0$, and it concludes that any split is the result of a subgame-perfect equilibrium. As long as N is large, subgame perfection is being applied "many" times; if we simultaneously take $m \to 0$ and $h \to 0$, it is the relative rates at which the two approach zero that determines whether we get Proposition 23.2-type or Proposition 23.4-type results.

Nice theory, but economic insight?

While the base Rubinstein model doesn't generate an unreasonable or unintuitive conclusion, the variations certainly do. In particular, seemingly large changes in what is possible (Bob's outside option) have very limited impact on the conclusion, while seemingly small changes in the bargaining protocol have huge impact.

If you read carefully Appendix 11, it should not come as a surprise that enforcing subgame perfection can sometimes give conclusions that defy intuition based on casual or formal empiricism; see, for instance, the discussion of the "Centipede Game" around page 536. Rubinstein's conclusions depend entirely on the force of many rounds of subgame perfection; this is perhaps most obvious if you look at the argument offered in the subsection "Finite horizons..." and the proof of Proposition 23.3. (For a large T, we are applying subgame perfection iteratively T times.)

Moreover, and again based on intuition supported by (at least) casual empiricism of what real-life bargaining "looks like," the Rubinstein conclusion that agreement is reached on the first offer (in the original model and all the variations on pages 279–80) seems unreasonable. In real life, bargaining takes time; there is often delay in reaching agreement.

And, if you have ever engaged in bargaining—say, buying a rug from a rug merchant—you know that the essence of bargaining—and the reason bargaining typically takes time—is that you are trying to discern what price the merchant will accept, while he is trying to discern what price you are willing to pay. Each party is uncertain about the "reservation price" of the other party; you try to convince the merchant that you won't pay too much, while he is trying to convince you that he won't accept too little.

So, my bottom line on Rubinstein (1982) is that it is beautiful theory. It stands as a seminal contribution, because it gave impetus to attempts to cut the Gordian knot of bilateral bargaining. But in my estimation, it doesn't extend our knowledge or intuition about real-life bilateral bargaining. To do this, we need models in which the driving force in the bargaining is uncertainty on both sides about the other side's "preferences" or "character."[10]

That is precisely the next step taken in the literature. Many papers subsequent

---

[10] Colleagues who have read this "bottom line" say I am too harsh. The Rubinstein model and analysis—indeed, the delicacy of the result—teaches us that incomplete information is where we must look, to understand bargaining. I accept this slight softening of my opinion.

to Rubinstein study models of bilateral bargaining in which one or both of the parties involved is uncertain about salient aspects of the other party.

23.4. Alice and Bob Negotiate Where to Eat Dinner

Before we tackle bargaining with incomplete information, one more model of bargaining (perhaps "negotiation" is a better term) with complete information is worth discussing.

Suppose Alice and Bob wish to go to dinner, but they must agree on a restaurant. Alice prefers a French restaurant; Bob wants an Italian restaurant. Their negotiations are conducted Rubinstein-style: Alice makes a proposal at time $t = 0$, which Bob can accept (instantly) or reject; if he rejects, he can counter propose after h time units have passed. If things get that far, Alice can accept his proposal, with immediate effect, or reject; she then makes a counterproposal at time $t = 2h$. And so forth.

If they agree on a French restaurant at time t, Alice's payoff is $10e^{-rt}$, and Bob's is $5e^{-rt}$. If they agree on an Italian restaurant, Alice's payoff is $7e^{-rt}$, and Bob's is $9e^{-rt}$. If they never agree, they both get payoff 0. If Alice goes to one restaurant and Bob goes to the other, they both get payoff 0. [11]

Here are two pure-strategy subgame-perfect equilibria for this game:

- Alice proposes at time 0 that they go to the French restaurant, and Bob accepts. Alice always (in all parts of the game tree) proposes French, and Bob accepts. Bob always proposes French, and Alice accepts. If Alice were ever to propose Italian, Bob would accept. If Bob ever proposes Italian, Alice rejects.

- Alice proposes at time 0 that they go to the Italian restaurant, and Bob accepts. Alice always (in all parts of the game tree) proposes Italian, and Bob accepts. Bob always proposes Italian, and Alice accepts. If Bob were ever to propose French, Alice would accept. If Alice ever were to propose French, Bob would reject.

I should say that these are subgame-perfect Nash equilibrium for small enough h:

- In the first equilibrium, it is evident that Alice is made worse off at any point by proposing Italian, since by following the equilibrium proposal of French, she gets French. For Alice, the key unimprovability inequality concerns her rejection of Italian by Bob (were Bob to make this proposal): If she accepts, she gets 7. If she rejects, what happens next is that she proposes French and he accepts, giving a current-value payoff of $10e^{-rh}$. So, if $e^{-rh} \geq 7/10$, her strategy is unimprovable. As for Bob, if Alice were (mistakenly) to propose Italian, of course he accepts; his key unimprovability inequalities involve the questions: Why does he accept French? And why doesn't he propose Italian? For the first of these, if he rejects Alice's proposal of French, he is (per the

---

[11] In less politically correct times, this game would have been called an alternating-proposal version of the Battle of the Sexes.

equilibrium strategies) bound to propose French in his next turn, which she accepts. He is only delaying the inevitable, and the additional discount e^{-rh} makes this suboptimal. For the second question, if he proposes Italian, she will reject, come back with French, and he will accept. It is clearly better to propose French (as he is meant to do) and save e^{-rh} additional discounting.

- The argument for the second equilibrium is similar, with the one key step (placing a restriction on h) concerning Bob's rejection of French, should Alice propose that. If Bob were to accept, he would get 5 immediately. If he rejects, he gets 9 next time (by proposing Italian, which Alice's strategy calls for her to accept), for a net current value $9e^{-rh}$. So unimprovability requires $e^{-rh} \geq 5/9$. You can check the other requirements of unimprovability for each party.

So, each strategy profile is a pure-strategy, subgame-perfect Nash equilibrium, as long as $e^{-rh} \geq 7/10$. For fixed r and small h, this certainly holds.

And note, this isn't a case in which Alice gets a slight advantage from going first, as in the Rubinstein base model. In the second equilibrium, Alice is proposing Bob's preferred option.

Why doesn't the Rubinstein argument go through? The easiest way to see why is to make a change in the formulation that does allow it to go through: Suppose the two are not limited to proposing either French or Italian, but probability mixtures of the two: Alice could propose, for instance, "Let's go French with probability 0.54 and Italian with probability 0.46." (Those are *not* the equilibrium probabilities.) Were this possible, then suppose we wish to kill the "Always Italian" equilibrium. In this equilibrium, Bob is getting a payoff of 9. And, if Alice were to deviate and Bob were to stick to the equilibrium, he would get $9e^{-rh}$. But suppose Alice proposes

"French with probability ϵ and Italian with probability $1 - \epsilon$,"

where she picks $\epsilon > 0$ small enough so that $5\epsilon + 9(1 - \epsilon) > 9e^{-rh}$. Subgame perfection would then require that Bob accept this, rather than rejecting in expectation of Italian after h time units, and Rubinstein's argument would begin to bite, eventually providing a single subgame-perfect equilibrium.[12]

It is of course true that choosing between one of two discrete choices is different from dividing a pile of money, unless lotteries of the two choices are permitted. But, if you haven't already constructed a proof of Proposition 23.4, now would be a good time. In particular, the issue here isn't that there are only two discrete choices; rather, the issue is that the choices are "more discrete" than the cost incurred because of any delay in bargaining.

An equilibrium "war of attrition"

This model admits a third equilibrium, in which, with positive probability, there can be a very substantial delay to agreement. (Probabilistic offers are not allowed.)

---

[12] But, if you look for an equilibrium, it is trickier than this first step of the argument makes it seem. See Problem 23.8, which gives more insight into Rubinstein-style analysis.

Let

$$\rho_B := \frac{7(1 - e^{-2rh})}{10e^{-rh} - 7e^{-2rh}}, \quad \text{and} \quad \rho_A = \frac{5(1 - e^{-2rh})}{9e^{-rh} - 5e^{-2rh}}.$$

Here is a third subgame-perfect equilibrium:

> At time $t = 0$, and every time it is her turn to make a proposal (that is, if an agreement has not already been reached), Alice demands that they go to the French restaurant. Bob accepts this demand with probability ρ_B and rejects with probability $1 - \rho_B$. (If Alice slips up and demands Italian, Bob accepts.) If it is Bob's turn to propose, he demands Italian, and Alice accepts with probability ρ_A. (If Bob slips up and proposes French, Alice immediately accepts.)[13]

Why do these strategies constitute an equilibrium? Suppose it is Alice's turn to propose, and she proposes French, as she is meant to do. Bob can accept or reject this proposal; in equilibrium, he is supposed to randomize between them, so (if this is an equilibrium), *they should give him the same expected payoff.* Acceptance, of course, gives him 5 immediately. Rejection gives him the opportunity to make a proposal after h time units, which will be accepted with probability ρ_A and rejected with probability $1 - \rho_A$. And, if it is rejected, he'll be back where this started, facing Alice's proposal that they go French. Hence, if V is Bob's expected payoff in this position, V must solve the equations $V = 5$ and $V = \rho_A(9e^{-rh}) + (1 - \rho_A)(Ve^{-2rh})$. The second of these implies that

$$V = \frac{9\rho_A e^{-rh}}{1 - (1 - \rho_A)e^{-2rh}}.$$

For this to equal 5, we have

$$5 = \frac{9\rho_A e^{-rh}}{1 - (1 - \rho_A)e^{-2rh}} \quad \text{or} \quad 5 - 5(1 - \rho_A)e^{-2rh} = 9\rho_A e^{-rh} \quad \text{or}$$

$$5(1 - e^{-2hr}) = \rho_A(9e^{-rh} + 5e^{-2rh}),$$

which matches the definition of ρ_A. A similar computation verifies that Alice, faced with a proposal by Bob of Italian, is indifferent between immediate acceptance and rejection.

---

[13] It may be obvious, but this is different from what would be the Rubinstein equilibrium, if we allowed randomized proposals, on two grounds. First, as will be shown, on average, this equilibrium involves significant delay to agreement. The Rubinstein equilibrium would end with immediate acceptance of a randomized choice of restaurant. And the Rubinstein-style equilibrium requires some randomizing device that is observable to both Alice and Bob. Alice will propose "French with probability π and Italian with probability $1 - \pi$ for the equilibrium value of π, which Bob will accept, but then they must be able credibly to conduct the randomization. The outcome here is also random, because of the mixed strategies being used. But the mixing is done "privately," as is typically the case in a mixed-strategy equilibrium.

Would Alice, given the opportunity to make a proposal, prefer to propose the Italian restaurant? Doing this gives an immediate payoff of 7, and so unimprovability requires that

$$7 \leq 10\rho_B + (1 - \rho_B)7e^{-rh}.$$

The first term on the right-hand side is the probability that Bob will agree to French, and the second term is the probability that he rejects, times Alice's current-value payoff once Bob proposes Italian; I can substitute 7 for this, because we're shown that, given ρ_B, Alice is indifferent between accepting Bob's proposal and rejecting it. Rewrite the required inequality as

$$\rho_B(10 - 7e^{-hr}) \geq 7(1 - e^{-rh}) \quad \text{or} \quad \rho_B \geq \frac{7(1 - e^{-rh})}{10 - 7e^{-rh}}.$$

Then we have that

$$\rho_B = \frac{7(1 - e^{-2rh})}{10e^{-rh} - 7e^{-2rh}} \geq \frac{7(e^{-rh} - e^{-2rh})}{10e^{-rh} - 7e^{-2rh}} = \frac{7(1 - e^{-rh})}{10 - 7e^{-rh}}.$$

To interpret this: Alice would rather propose French than accept Italian immediately, because Bob might accept French, which more (slightly so) than compensates her for having to wait h time units to settle on Italian.

And, by similar calculations, Bob's strategy of always proposing Italian is better for him than settling immediately for French. We do have a (subgame-perfect) equilibrium.

What is happening here is simple. When Alice proposes that they go to a French restaurant, Bob may agree. But if he disagrees and, after a short delay, proposes Italian, Alice may agree to that. The chance that Alice might agree to Italian in h time units is precisely the compensation Bob needs to risk a $2h$ time delay in accepting French. And the chance that she will agree to Italian in h time units or, if she doesn't, that she will then agree to Italian in $3h$ time units, is just the compensation Bob needs to delay accepting French until time $t = 4h$, and so forth; and symmetrically for Alice deciding whether to accept Bob's proposal of Italian.

To give you an idea of the magnitude of these numbers, suppose that $r = 10\%$ per year, and $h = 1$ minute. Then $\rho_B = 1.4798 \times 10^{-8}$, approximately, and $\rho_A = 7.9275 \times 10^{-9}$, approximately. And, although in this equilibrium, Alice and Bob will eventually come to an agreement, the time required isn't trivial: Every $2h$ time units there is probability 2.2754×10^{-8} that they come to some agreement; the time to agreement is very nearly exponential, with an average duration of approximately 2.79069768 years. Alice and Bob are likely to become very hungry before they settle this. And the "eventual" outcome is French with probability of around 0.65116 and Italian with probability 0.34884.

How do the two pure-strategy equilibria compare with this equilibrium? In terms of payoffs to Alice and Bob: In the first equilibrium, Alice gets 10 and Bob gets 5. In the second equilibrium, Alice gets 7 and Bob gets 9. And in this third equilibrium, Alice gets a bit more than 7, and Bob gets 5, with "a bit more" approaching 0 as $h \to 0$. Note that a 65% chance at French and a 35% chance at Italian, if implemented at time 0, would provide expected payoffs of approximately 9 for Alice and 6.4 for Bob; the two do much worse than this in the third equilibrium because of the delay to agreement.[14]

Continuous time

It is common in the economics literature to skip the alternating-offer, discrete-time formulation of this sort of negotiation and move directly to a continuous-time version. This can raise some technical issues about strategies for Bob and Alice, but in this simple two-choice formulation, these issues are not difficult to handle. Formally, we imagine that Alice and Bob simultaneously select "concession times" t_A and t_B from $[0, \infty]$. Given these choices, if $t_A < t_B$, they go to the Italian restaurant at time t_A, for payoffs $7e^{-rt_A}$ for Alice and $9e^{-rt_A}$ for Bob. If $t_B < t_A$, Alice gets $10e^{-rt_B}$, and Bob gets $5e^{-rt_B}$. If there is a tie at a finite time—which will have probability zero in any equilibrium—a coin is flipped to determine which restaurant they choose. If they both choose never to concede, both get 0.

What are equilibrium strategies? The two pure-strategy equilibrium outcomes remain. For the first (immediate French), Bob chooses $t_B = 0$, and Alice chooses $t_A = \infty$, they immediately go to the French restaurant.[15] And for the second, Alice chooses $t_A = 0$, and Bob chooses $t_B = \infty$.

Corresponding to Equilibrium #3 is where Alice chooses t_A randomly: t_A has exponential distribution with hazard rate $\rho_A = 5r/4$. And Bob chooses t_B with a mixed strategy that has an exponential distribution with hazard rate $\rho_B = 7r/3$.[16]

Why does this give an equilibrium? Note that this strategy for Bob means that the cumulative distribution function for t_B is $1 - e^{-7rt/3}$, and its density function is $7re^{-7rt/3}/3$. Suppose Alice decides on some specific value of t_A. Her expected payoff is

$$\int_0^{t_A} \left[10e^{-rt} \times \frac{7r}{3} e^{-7rt/3} \right] dt \; + \; e^{-7rt_A/3} \times 7e^{-rt_A}.$$

The first term represents the possibility that Bob concedes before time t_A: If he concedes at time $t < t_A$, Alice gets $10e^{-rt}$; and the integral "counts up" all times up to t_A weighted by the density function of t_B. And the second term is the

---

[14] You might also wish to compare these expected payoffs with the unique subgame-perfect equilibrium that arises if the two can make randomized proposals. See Problem 23.8.

[15] In the formal game of choosing concession times, the notion of a "proper subgame" doesn't exist. Technically, this is handled by having, for all $t \in [0, \infty)$ a strategy for each player being a concession time greater or equal to t, which is what the player does if there is no concession up to time t. My specification of $t_A = \infty$ is done to fit this; think of Equilibrium #1 described as: Bob always immediately concedes in any subgame; Alice never does. Or, don't worry about this technicality.

[16] These *hazard rates* can be derived from the discrete-time concession probabilities by allowing $h \to 0$, or they can be derived from first principles. See Problem 23.9, but you should probably wait until you absorb the next section before tackling that problem.

probability that Bob doesn't concede by time t_B times Alice's discounted payoff when she concedes: $7e^{-rt_A}$. The integral is

$$\frac{70r}{3} \int_0^{t_A} e^{-10rt/3} \mathrm{d}t = \frac{70r}{3} \times \frac{3}{10r} \times \left[1 - e^{-10rt_A/3}\right] = 7\left[1 - e^{-10rt_A/3}\right].$$

Add in the second term, and we have

$$7\left[1 - e^{-10rt_A/3}\right] + 7e^{-10rt_A/3=} = 7.$$

That is, Alice's expected payoff from planning to concede at time t_A, for any $t_A \in [0, \infty)$, unless Bob concedes first, is a constant 7. So she is happy to play any mixed strategy.

The derivation for Bob is symmetric; we have an equilibrium. And the idea is the same as in the alternating-proposal, discrete-time model. Bob's concession rate makes Alice indifferent between conceding now and at any later time; Alice's concession rate makes Bob indifferent. It is perhaps worth noting that for $r = 0.1$ (the rate in the numerical example in the previous subsection), the overall concession rate is $0.7/3 + 0.5/4 = 43/120$, and so the average time until a concession is $120/43 = 2.790697674$ years. The probability that Alice concedes first is, to seven significant digits, the same as in the discrete-time model, roughly 65%. But, in this case, the delay to agreement means that Alice's expected payoff is 7 and Bob's is 5.

Because Alice's expected payoff is 7 for t_A = any $t \in [0, \infty)$ and, in particular, for $t = 0$, this allows for other equilibria besides the three so far described. Suppose Alice adopts the following strategy. She'll concede at time $t = 0$ with probability 0.5 and, with probability 0.5, she implements the strategy in the war-of-attrition equilibrium. Against the strategy by Bob prescribed above, this is an equilibrium strategy for her: Bob is happy if he sees an immediate concession, and if not, the game is just as described above. There is nothing special about 0.5; she can concede at the outset with any probability between 0 and 1. And there are equilibria in which Bob concedes immediately. But it can't be that both of them concede with strictly positive probability at the outset: If Alice is conceding with strictly positive probability, Bob wants to wait to see whether she does, and vice versa.[17]

Is this equilibrium really a war of attrition?

Economists call this third equilibrium, whether the discrete-time or the continuous-time version, a "war of attrition." Is the term appropriate?

The term *war of attrition* has the following dictionary definition (from Oxford Languages): "a prolonged war or period of conflict during which each side seeks to gradually wear out the other by a series of small-scale actions." In economics,

---

[17] Do such "other" equilibria exist in the discrete-time formulation? Yes, they do. Can you see what they are?

perhaps a natural context for this definition is two firms fighting to become dominant in an industry by keeping the price of some good below marginal cost, where
each firm hopes that its stock of resources for continuing the battle is larger than
that of its rival.

In the context of evolutionary biology, the term refers to contests between organ-
isms for some prize. I know little about this, and I am loathe to offer commentary.
But the interested reader might wish to look at Riley (1980).

How these "wars of attrition" connect to the equilibria between Alice and Bob
in either the discrete-time, alternating-offer game or its continuous limit is, at best,
unclear to me. (Perhaps it is Alice's and Bob's stocks of patience or repective
abilities to withstand the pangs of hunger that run out.) Nonetheless, the term "a
war of attrition" is used by economists to describe this sort of equilibrium. And the
continuous-time version provides the basis for the following model of bargaining
with incomplete information.

23.5. Abreu and Gul (2000): A War of Attrition with Incomplete Information

We now turn to models of bargaining with incomplete information. There are many
such models; in this section, I discuss one due to Abreu and Gul, and then turn to
the "most natural" formulation in Section 23.6.

Abreu and Gul (2000) study the following model. Alice and Bob are bargaining
over how to divide a pot of money, say, $100. Until they come to agreement, neither
side gets anything. And delay is costly: Both discount their eventual share at rate r:
That is, if they agree at time t that Alice will get $60 (say) and Bob will get $40, then
Alice's payoff is $60e^{-rt}$ and Bob's is $40e^{-rt}$.[18] The complicating factor is that both
Alice and Bob come in a variety of "types." One type of each is the "rational" type:
someone who seeks to maximize her or his expected payoff (= expected discounted
share). Other types are "behavioral," where a behavioral type in their model is
someone who is fixated on getting a given fixed share of the $100, no matter how
long it takes; indeed, such a type perfers no deal at all to settling for less than the
type's must-have amount.

A type who is fixated on getting, say, $90 is denoted Alice-90. The rational type
of Alice is denoted Alice-R, and similarly for Bob.

They model the bargaining protocol as a continuous-time negotiation. To deal
with technical issues, assume that the strategy set for each player is a "demand
function of time": At each time $t \in [0, \infty)$, Alice and Bob independently demand
a share of the $100: Let $A(t)$ be Alice's demand at time t, and let $B(t)$ be Bob's de-
mand. Assume that demand functions must be nonincreasing—once Alice lowers
her demand to, say, $45, she cannot subsequently increase it—and right continuous.
Given demand functions $A(t)$ and $B(t)$, the outcome is determined as follows: Let
$\tau = \min\{t : A(t) + B(t) \leq 100\}$, where $\tau = \infty$ if $A(t) + B(t) > 100$ for all t. If $\tau = \infty$,

---

[18]   Abreu and Gul allow the discount rates to be different, but I'll work with the simple case where the
two parties have the same discount rate.

Alice and Bob each get 0. Otherwise, the payoff for the rational type of Alice is

$$
e^{-r\tau}\left[A(\tau) + \frac{100 - [A(\tau) + B(\tau)]}{2} \right] = e^{-r\tau}\left[\frac{A(\tau) + 100 - B(\tau)}{2} \right],
$$

with a symmetric formula for the payoff of the rational type of Bob. As for the behavioral types, to keep matters simple, we simply assume that each behavioral type invariably bids her (or his) must-have amount. So, for example, if there is positive probability that one type of Alice must have \$70, that type demands $A(t) \equiv$ \$70.

Open-loop versus closed-loop strategies

In general, Alice's demand is naturally thought of as being responsive to Bob's history of demands, and vice versa. That is, imagine that, up to time t, Alice has demanded \$80, while Bob demanded \$80 up to time $t/2$ and then \$70 from time $t/2$ to time t. How should Alice respond? How should she respond, if Bob demanded \$80 up to time $t/3$, then lowered his demand to \$60 from time $t/3$ to time $t/2$, and, from time $t/2$ to t, has gradually and continuously been lowering his demand from \$60 down to \$40? In the second case, especially with Bob recently lowering his demand continuously, he is showing weakness; moreover, his demands have passed through the focal level of \$50. So, perhaps Alice should keep holding out for \$80 in the second case, while she should make some concession in the first. At least, one can imagine that what she does from time t changes with this change in Bob's history of demands.

I've just described what is called, at least in some parts of the literature, a *closed-loop* strategy, as opposed to a *open-loop* strategy in which Alice, at time 0, specifies a deterministic path of demands that she will make, regardless of what Bob does (up to the moment of agreement). Alternative langugage might distinguish between a *responsive* strategy versus a *committed* strategy.

Formulating a model with closed-loop strategies in continuous time can pose formidable technical issues. In discrete time, with either alternating or simultaneous demands—indeed, in any model in which some minimum time over which demands cannot be changed (i.e., demands must be piecewise constant over intervals of some minimum length)—the technical issues are much easier to handle.

Abreu and Gul use a continuous-time formulation with limited amount of closed-loop character, by adopting the following protocol. At the very start, both Alice and Bob simultaneously declare an initial demand. Fixated types demand the amount on which they are fixated. And Alice-R and Bob-R must declare for one of their fixated types. If there are two fixated types of Alice, say, Alice-70 and Alice-90, then Alice-R in this first declaration chooses between the two, declaring either "I want \$70" or "I want \$90." If there is only one fixated type of Bob, say, Bob-80, then Bob-R must declare "I want \$80." [19]

---

[19] This first declaration is superfluous if there is one fixated type for Alice and one for Bob. But it is important if there are multiple fixated types for either player.

Then, having heard the declaration of their opponent, both Alice and Bob have the opportunity to condede immediately. If Alice has two fixated types and declares for Alice-70, Bob can immediately concede to that type. He can concede to that type, but refuse to concede immediately if Alice declares for Alice-90. Alice-R can concede to Bob initially as well, although in equilibrium only one of Alice-R and Bob-R will immediately concede, so we don't need to worry about simultaneous immediate concessions.

And if neither concedes initially, a war of attrition ensues. Both rational types prepare to concede at some random time: Let T_A be the random time at which Alice-R will concede, while T_B is the random time at which Bob-R concedes. *If $T_A < T_B$ (which, I hasten to add, is a stochastic event), then Alice's concession comes first and, in their model, in equilibrium, she concedes by agreeing to Bob's consistent demand that he get $80, leaving her with $20. If $T_B < T_A$, Bob concedes first, by agreeing to Alice's demand that she get $70 (or $90, whichever she initially demanded).* Until one or the other concedes, he or she must maintain the demand initially declared.

This is closed-loop, but only significantly at the very start. The initial decision of Alice-R whether to demand $70 or $90 (if those are her two fixated types) affects both Bob's immediate reaction whether to concede or to begin a war of attrition. And, if he decides not to concede immediately, Alice's original demand can affect the rate at which Bob-R concedes (and the rate at which Alice-R concedes). So Bob-R is reacting to Alice's initial demand. But, after that initial flurry of activity and until there is a concession, no more information is provided by one side to which the other could react.

The bottom line is: Abreu and Gul are assuming closed-loop strategies for Alice and Bob. For behavioral types, their behavior is fixed. And, in the equilibrium they construct, the nature of Alice-R's and Bob-R's equilibrium strategies removes the technical issues that can arise more generally in closed-loop games in continuous time.

Only one behavioral type per player

Suppose for now that there is only one behavioral type of Alice, whose must-have amount is $90, and one behavioral type of Bob, whose must-have amount is $70. Suppose that the probability initially assessed by Bob that Alice is Alice-90 is 0.2, and the probability initially assessed by Alice that Bob is Bob-70 is 0.1. Then, in the equilibrium constructed by Abreu and Gul, Bob-R initially demand $70 (he has no other choice), and Alice-R initially demands $90. Following this, Alice-R immediately randomizes between concession and starting the war of attrition. The probability that she initially concedes is 0.7065, approximately. (Bob-R does not concede immediately.) If Alice-R does concede at the outset, the game is over; Alice gets $30 and Bob gets $70. And if she does not concede, then a war of attrition between the two ensues, where Alice-R and Bob-R concede at increasing hazard rates $\hat{\rho}_A(t)$ and $\hat{\rho}_B(t)$, respectively, increasing enough so that, by some time T^*, if there has been no concession, it is clear that Alice is Alice-90 and Bob is Bob-70, and no deal is possible. In other words, by this time T^*, there is probability 1 that one or the other of Alice-R of Bob-R will have conceded. And prior to time T^*, if there has been no concession on either side, there is (still) positive probability that Alice is Alice-R and that Bob is Bob-R.

That's the form of the equilibrium. Now to explain and derive the crucial parameters:

1. We know what strategy Alice-90 employs, namely, always demanding 90. If Alice-R ever demands anything else in equilibrium, it will be apparent to Bob that she is Alice-R and, as long as there is positive probability that Bob is Bob-70, Alice-R concedes by naming 30. One can argue that this must be so, but since I'm only showing that we have an equilibrium: Once Alice-R demands anything other than 90, no matter how she conducts herself subsequently, Bob will believe that she is Alice-R. And, if Bob could be Bob-70, Bob-R's strategy, once Alice is known to be Alice-R, is to demand 70. Alice-R's best response, given this, is to concede immediately (to which Bob-R's strategy of always demanding 70 is best).[20]

   And, similarly, if Bob-R ever demands a quantity other than 70, Alice concludes that he is Bob-R, a belief that she never modifies. As long as there is positive probability that she is Alice-90, she'll demand 90, so Bob's best response is immediate concession, by settling for 10. That being so, if Bob-R ever demands a quantity other than 70 (before Alice concedes), he must go immediately to the concession demand, 10.

2. This strategy profile makes the situation analogous to Alice and Bob negotiating over a restaurant. Both rational types concede at rates that make the other rational-type party indifferent between concession and imitation of their respective behavioral types. Alice's *overall* concession rate must be $r/6$, while Bob's must be $r/2$. I've emphasized *overall* here, because each overall concession rate concerns both types of the other party: the rational type, who does concede at a rate to be computed; and the fixated type, who never concedes. (Keep reading; it will become clear.)

   Once we know what the two concessions rates are, proving formally that they are the right rates involves the sort of calculations on pages 290–1. But if you wonder how I found them, here is the back-of-the-envelope technique I used: Alice-R, say, must be indifferent between conceding at time t and, for small h, at time $t + h$, assuming neither side has conceded up to time t. Conceding at time t gives Alice-R a current-value payoff of 30. Conceding at time $t + h$ gives her a current value payoff of $e^{-rh}30 \approx 30(1 - rh + o(h))$, using Taylor's Theorem. However, the compensation that she derives by waiting is that Bob might concede between times t and $t + h$. If his (overall) concession rate is ρ_B, then the probability of him conceding between times t and $t + h$ is

---

[20] Suppose Alice-R reveals herself by demanding something other than 90, while there is positive probability that Bob is Bob-70. Why doesn't Bob-R demand more than 70? We've ruled this out by supposing that demands cannot be increased, but if we hadn't put in this restriction, we could still construct a continuation in which Bob-R cannot profit from demanding anything other than 70.

$\approx \rho_B h + o(h)$, and Alice-R will then get a current-value $90(1 - rO(h))$, where the $O(h)$ term reflects the fact that concession will take place at some point in the interval $[t, t + h]$ and must be discounted. Hence, for Alice-R to be indifferent between conceding at time t and time $t + h$ requires that

$$30 = 30(1 - rh + o(h))\big[1 - \rho_B h + o(h)\big] + \big[\rho_B h + o(h)\big]\big[90(1 - rO(h))\big].$$

Cancel the 30 on both sides, and ignore all terms that are $o(h)$, and you get as the equilibrium condition:

$$30rh - 30\rho_B h + 90\rho_B h = 0, \quad \text{which is} \quad \rho_B = \frac{r}{2}.$$

Of course, once you know "the answer," for a formal proof that it is the answer, you must go back to page 290.

3. When I say that Bob's overall concession rate must be $r/2$, this is the concession rate as perceived by Alice-R. Since Bob-70 is never going to concede, this means that, if Alice at time t assesses probability $q_B(t)$ that Bob is Bob-70 and $1 - q_B(t)$ that he is Bob-R, then Bob-R's concession rate $\hat{\rho}_B(t)$ must satisfy

$$q_B(t) \times 0 + (1 - q_B(t))\hat{\rho}_B(t) = r/2 \quad \text{or} \quad \hat{\rho}_B(t) = \frac{r}{2(1 - q_B(t))}.$$

And, similarly, Alice-R's concession rate $\hat{\rho}_A(t)$ must take into account Bob-R's assessment $q_A(t)$ that she is Alice-90: It must be that

$$\hat{\rho}_A(t) = \frac{r}{6(1 - q_A(t))}.$$

4. Alice's assessment that Bob is Bob-70 will of course increase as time passes and there is no concession, since Bob-R's strategy involves concession, and Bob-70's strategy does not. The longer there is no concession, the surer Alice becomes that she is facing Bob-70, and similarly for Bob's assessment that Alice is Alice-90.

    Let $q_A(t)$ denote Bob's assessment that Alice is Alice-90, given no concession by time t. We use Bayes rule to find $q_A(t)$. We need the joint probability that Alice is Alice-90 and hasn't conceded by time t and the marginal probability of no concession by time t. The former is $q_A(0)$, the prior probability that Alice is Alice-90, times the conditional probability that Alice-90 has not conceded by time t, which is 1. And the latter, since the overall concession rate by Alice is $r/6$, is $e^{-rt/6}$. Therefore, $q_A(t) = q_A(0)/e^{-rt/6} = q_A(0)e^{rt/6}$. Similarly, $q_B(t) = q_B(0)e^{rt/2}$. Hence,

$$\hat{\rho}_A(t) = \frac{r}{6(1 - q_A(0)e^{rt/6})}, \quad \text{and} \quad \hat{\rho}_B(t) = \frac{r}{2(1 - q_B(0)e^{rt/2})}.$$

5. Recall that, at the outset, Bob assesses probability $p_A = 0.2$ that Alice is Alice-90, and Alice assesses $p_B = 0.1$ that Bob is Bob-70. In the formulas just displayed, I have $q_A(0)$ and $q_B(0)$. Hence, you might guess that $q_A(0) = p_A$ and $q_B(0) = p_B$. But that isn't quite right:

Note that $q_A(t)$ and $q_B(t)$ reach 1 in finite time. Call those two times T_A and T_B. Simple algebra gives

$$T_A = -\frac{6\ln(q_A(0))}{r}, \quad \text{and} \quad T_B = -\frac{2\ln(q_B(0))}{r}.$$

I assert that for this to be an equilibrium, $q_A(0)$ and $q_B(0)$ must be set so that $T_A = T_B$. Suppose to the contrary that $T_A > T_B$. Then at time T_B, two things are true: Alice-R is certain that she faces Bob-70. She can delay no longer, she *must* concede and accept 30. (There is no longer a concession rate from Bob-R that makes her indifferent between immediate concession and waiting a bit.) And, there is still a strictly positive probability that Alice is Alice-R; $q_A(T_B) < 1$. Consider the strategy of Bob-R just before time T_B. If, instead of following the strategy given by $\hat{\rho}_B(t)$, he waits for time T_B, then Alice will concede to him with probability $1 - q_A(T_B)$. That gives him a payoff of

$$70(1 - q_A(T_B)) + 10q_A(T_B).$$

Of course, he has to wait for this. But as t approaches T_B, the cost of waiting goes to 0. This is certainly larger than what he gets by following the alleged equilibrium strategy, which is a current-value of 10, for t close enough to T_B. Hence, we wouldn't have an equilibrium. And, by a symmetric argument, we don't have an equilibrium if $T_B > T_A$.

6. But, this result implies that the war of attrition, to be an equilibrium, must begin with $q_A(0)^6 = q_B(0)^2$. In the data of the problem that I provided, $p_A = .2$ and $p_B = .1$, and $(p_A)^6 = 0.000064 < 0.01 = (p_B)^2$. So, to get things "in balance" for the war of attrition, we need Alice-R to randomize between immediate concession and initiating the war of attrition in a fashion that, if she starts the war of attrition, Bob is assessing $q_A(0) = ((0.1)^2)^{1/6} = 0.46415888$. If you do the math (Bayes' rule), you find that she must initiate the war of attrition with probability 0.2934826, approximately, which means immediate concession to Bob with probability 0.70652174. And this in turn means that, in the equilibrium, Alice's expected payoff is her payoff of immediate concession, 30, while Bob's is $(0.70652174)(0.8)(70) + (1 - (0.70652174)(0.8))10 = 43.9130435$, more or less.

Had the initial data been such that $(p_A)^6 > (p_B)^2$, then it would have been Bob-R who would have been forced to undertake an initial randomization, and it would have been Alice whose equilibrium payoff would have exceeded her concession payoff of 30. Please note: Unless $(p_A)^6 = (p_B)^2$, the "stronger" player does better than her or his concession payoff, but only because of the initial randomization. Once the war of attrition begins, both sides are running hard just to keep up with what they can get immediately.

More than one behavioral type

Abreu and Gul (2000) go on from this relatively simple model (relative to the rest of the paper) to do several things. One is to consider how the model works if Alice-R and/or Bob-R can choose to mimic more than one behavioral type, where each behavioral type is, as previously, a type who is fixated on getting some given share of the $100 and who, as a consequence, always demands that share. This becomes quite complex, and I'll illustrate with the simplest possible example, where Alice is either Alice-R or Alice-90, while Bob can be Bob-R, Bob-70, or Bob-80. The prior probabilities are that Alice is Alice-90 with probability 0.1 (as assessed by Bob-R), and Bob is Bob-70 with probability 0.15 and Bob-80 with probability 0.1, as assessed by Alice-R.

Following the protocol outlined on page 293, Alice-R initially demands "I want $90," while Bob-R randomizes between "I want $70" and "I want $80." With the numbers I've specified, Alice-R is weaker, so after hearing Bob's declaration, she concedes with positive probability, but with the probability of concession depending on Bob's initial declaration. And, if she doesn't concede, a battle of attrition ensues, with both Bob-R's and Alice-R's concession rates dependent on which demand Bob initially made. In particular:

- If Bob initially demands $70, and Alice doesn't immediately concede, the overall concession rates must be $\rho_A = r/6$ and $\rho_B = r/2$, just as in the previous subsection.

- If Bob initially demands $80, and Alice doesn't immediately concede, the subsequent overall concession rates must be $\rho_A = r/7$ and $\rho_B = 2r/7$. (You can trust me, or you can check my calculations using the "back-of-the-envelope" technique sketched on page 297.)

Suppose that Bob-R chooses (in his initial demand) to mimic Bob-70 with probability α and Bob-80 with probability $1 - \alpha$. If that is his equilibrium choice, when Alice-R sees Bob begin with a demand of 70, she will assess

$$q_{B70}(0) = \frac{0.15}{0.15 + 0.75\alpha} \, ,$$

and if she sees Bob begin with a demand of 80, she'll assess

$$q_{B80}(0) = \frac{0.1}{0.1 + 0.75(1 - \alpha)} \, .$$

Suppose she sees Bob start with a demand of 70. She must set $q_A(0)$ so that, in the war of attrition that ensues, the time at which it is certain that Bob is Bob-70 (if neither side concedes) must equal the time at which Bob is certain that she is Alice-90. This is the condition

$$T_A = -\frac{6\ln(q_A(0))}{r} = T_B = -\frac{2\ln(q_B(0))}{r}, \quad \text{or} \quad q_A(0)^3 = q_{B70}(0).$$

If we use β as the probability that Alice-R does not immediately concede to Bob if he initially demands 70, then $q_A(0) = 0.1/(0.1 + 0.9\beta)$, and so β must satisfy

$$q_{B70}(0) = \frac{0.15}{0.15 + 0.75\alpha} = \left(\frac{0.1}{0.1 + 0.9\beta}\right)^3 = q_A(0)^3,$$

which can be solved to tell us what β must be as a function of α. Applying the same calculations to the case where Bob-R chooses to mimic Bob-80, we first find that $-7\ln(q_A(0))/r$ must equal $-7\ln(q_{B70}(0))/(2r)$, which is $q_A(0)^2 = q_{B80}(0)$. Hence, if Alice, upon observing Bob demand 80 at the outset, chooses to demand 90 at the outset with probability γ, we get the condition

$$\frac{0.1}{0.1 + 0.75(1 - \alpha)} = \left(\frac{0.1}{0.1 + 0.9\gamma}\right)^2,$$

which allows us to solve for γ as a function of α. Saving you from the algebra, for a given α, the equilibrium values of β and γ are given by

$$\beta = \frac{(5\alpha + 1)^{1/3} - 1}{9}, \quad \text{and} \quad \gamma = \frac{(8.5 - 7.5\alpha)^{1/2} - 1}{9}.$$

These are equilibrium conditions for Alice, who, for this selection of parameters, must randomize between immediate concession or starting the war of attrition. The final equilibrium condition is that Bob-R, who is randomizing between imitating Bob-70 and Bob-80, must be indifferent between the two. Alice-R's concession probabilities provide Bob-R with the following expected payoffs: If he imitates Bob-70, he gets $70(1 - \beta) + 10\beta$. If he imitates Bob-80, he gets $80(1 - \gamma) + 10\gamma$.

Hence, substituting for β and γ their formulas as a function of α, we get the final equilibrium condition:

$$70\left[1 - \frac{(5\alpha + 1)^{1/3} - 1}{9}\right] + 10\left[\frac{(5\alpha + 1)^{1/3} - 1}{9}\right]$$
$$= 80\left[1 - \frac{(8.5 - 7.5\alpha)^{1/2} - 1}{9}\right] + 10\left[\frac{(8.5 - 7.5\alpha)^{1/2} - 1}{9}\right].$$

I don't think this can be solved analytically—at least, I can't—so I resorted to numerical calculations. (Hence, all the numbers that follow are approximations.)

- The equilibrium probability that Bob-R begins mimicking Bob-70 is 0.2597. Therefore, if Alice sees Bob beginning with a demand of 70, she assesses probability 0.4351 that he is Bob-70; if she sees him beginning with a demand of 80, she assesses probability 0.1526 that he is Bob-80.

- If Alice observes Bob beginning with a demand of 70, she concedes with probability 0.9645. This leads Bob to assess that she is Alice-90 with probability 0.7577. Just to check the calculations, $0.7577^3 = 0.4351$, just as it should be.

- If Alice observes Bob beginning with a demand of 80, she concedes with probability 0.8267. This leads Bob to assess that she is Alice-90 with probability 0.3907. And $0.390663^2 = 0.1526$

- Bob-R's expected payoff is 67.869, and Alice-R's expected payoff is approximately $23.48 = 30[0.15 + (0.75)(0.2597)] + 20[0.1 + (0.75)(0.7403)]$.

And this, I remind you, is the second-easiest case in Abreu and Gul.

The rest of Abreu and Gul (2000)

Abreu and Gul (2000) go far beyond the construction of these equilibria:

1. They prove the existence of an equilibrium for every multi-type formulation of the basic model, as long as there are finitely many types of the "fixated-on-one-split" sort.

2. They prove that the equilibrium outcomes for any given formulation is unique.

3. After defining what it means for a discrete-time bargaining protocol to "converge" to their continuous-time formulation—essentially, both Bob and Alice must have the opportunity to make a proposal every h time units, for $h \to 0$ (although proposals can be "alternating," simultaneous, or some combination of these)—they show that, for their basic context (in terms of the type structure), the equilibrium outcomes of a sequence of discrete-time formulations converges to their (unique) continuous-time equilibrium outcome, as long as the sequence of discrete-time formulations converges in their sense to their continuous-time formulation.

The third of these results is very powerful: Recall that the Rubinstein (1982) equilibria changes dramatically with "small" changes in the bargaining protocol. Abreu and Gul (2000) show that incomplete information—or at least incomplete information of their sort—is ultimately dispositive when it comes to determining what the (equilibrium) outcome is, as long as the protocol allows both sides to make proposals "rapidly."

23.6. The "Most Natural" Context with Private Information and Simultaneous Bid and Ask

While Abreu and Gul (2000) and many other models in the literature are certainly of interest, one bargaining context with private information stands out as most natural: Alice is considering the sale of some indivisible good—think of a rug—to Bob. Alice has a reservation value r below which she will not sell the rug. Her objective is either to retain the object, with a gross-of-any-bargaining-cost payoff to her of r or, if she can get Bob to buy the object for a price $p > r$, then her gross-of-bargaining-cost payoff is p.[21] Bob has a reservation value v for the object. He won't pay more than this, and if he doesn't buy the object, his payoff is 0; if he can purchase the object for $p < v$, his gross-of-bargaining-cost payoff is $v - p$. (Hence, r and v are measured in dollar terms, the two have utility functions that are quasi-linear in money, and they are risk neutral in money units.)

The standard starting assumptions are that Alice knows r and has a (common-knowledge) prior assessment ϕ on v, and Bob knows v and has a (common-knowledge) prior assessment ψ on r. Suppose that all types of Alice—that is, regardless of her reservation value r—hold the prior ϕ, and all types of Bob hold the prior ψ. In other words, the random variables r and v are independent.

I'll maintain this independence assumption momentarily, but it is worthwhile to think about why r and v might be statistically dependent.

- It can simply be a matter of correlation in private values: Before bargaining begins, Bob examines the rug to assess its quality. If he finds it to be of high quality, it is worth more to him to possess it; v is larger. But, at the same time, his assessment of the value of the rug to Alice, $\psi(\cdot|v)$, is increasing in v, since a high-quality rug is worth more to any party.

- A different story supposes that v is (only) Bob's estimate of what the rug is worth; he is purchasing the rug in part as an investment, and so his assessment of its eventual resale value makes up a part of v. And r is Alice's assessment of what she can get for the rug at some later date, if she doesn't sell it to Bob. Then from Bob's perspective, if r is high, it means that when he goes to sell the rug, it is likely to sell for a higher price than if r is small. At the same time, if Alice knows that v is large, then other buyers are likely to attach a higher value to the rug, which raises the (conditional on v) value r that she attaches to retaining the rug instead of selling it to Bob.

As already stated , I'm going to assume r and v are independent random variables. But it is perhaps worth noting that, in Chapter 24 on auctions, the story in the second bullet point presages some instances of so-called common-value auctions. This is something to which we will return.

Let supp(ψ) denote the support of ψ, and let supp(ϕ) denote the support of ϕ. Assume throughout that both supp(ψ) and supp(ϕ) are bounded subsets of $[0, \infty)$. Write $\bar{r}$ for the supremum of supp(ψ), $\underline{r}$ for the infimum of supp(ψ), $\underline{v}$ for the infimum of supp(ϕ), and $\bar{v}$ for the supremum of supp(ϕ). If $\bar{r} < \underline{v}$, say that ϕ

---

[21] I assume that Bob is the only prospective customer for the rug, but in a different interpretation, one can imagine that rug-merchant Alice sees a steady stream of customers, and r is her assessed "opportunity cost" of selling the rug to Bob. With this interpretation, the discount factor that applies to a delayed agreement might, at least in part, be based on Bob's worries that another customer will show up and outbid him and, at the same time, on Alice's concern that Bob, frustrated with the bargaining, will depart to see whether he can find a better deal elsewhere.

and ψ have a *gap*. If $\bar{r} > \underline{v}$, say that there is *no gap*.

Begin with one round of simultaneous bid-and-ask bargaining: Alice writes down her *asking price* a and, simultaneously and independently, Bob writes down his *bid* b. Then the values a and b are compared. If $a \leq b$, the good changes hands with the price set at $p = (a+b)/2$. If $a > b$, there is no deal and, with a single round of bargining, there is no opportunity to engage in actual back-and-forth bargaining.

Definition of equilibrium

For purposes of making formal definitions, suppose that both $\text{supp}(\psi)$ and $\text{supp}(\phi)$ are finite sets.

Definition 23.5. *A pure strategy for Bob in this setting is a function $\beta : \text{supp}(\psi) \to [0, \infty)$. A pure strategy for Alice is a function $\alpha : \text{supp}(\phi) \to [0, \infty)$. Mixed strategies are defined behaviorally: Reinterpret $\beta(v)$ as a probability distribution on $[0, \infty)$ for each $v \in \text{supp}(v)$, and reinterpret $\alpha(r)$ as a probability distribution on $[0, \infty)$ for each $r \in \text{supp}(r)$.*

Given a pair of pure strategy profiles, α and β, two realizations r and v, and a pair of nonnegative numbers a and b, define

$$U(b; v, \alpha) := \sum_{r \in \text{supp}(\psi) \,:\, \alpha(r) \leq b} \psi(r)\left[v - \frac{\alpha(r) + b}{2} \right] \quad \text{and}$$

$$W(a; r, \beta) := \sum_{v \in \text{supp}(\phi) \,:\, \beta(v) \geq a} \phi(v)\left[\frac{a + \beta(v)}{2} \right] + r\left[\sum_{v \in \text{supp}(v) \,:\, \beta(v) < a} \phi(v) \right].$$

These two functions have the following meaning: Suppose Alice is employing the pure strategy α. Suppose Bob values the object at v, and he chooses to bid b. Then $U(b; v, \alpha)$ is his expected payoff: Summing over all $r \in \text{supp}(\psi)$ such that $\alpha(r) \leq b$, his expected payoff is v less the price he pays $(\alpha(r)+b)/2$, weighted by the probability he assesses concerning r. Note that for r such that $\alpha(r) > b$, his payoff is zero; we don't need to account for those r in his expected payoff. Similarly, if Bob employs the strategy β, Alice's reservation value is r, and she asks a, then $W(a; r, \beta)$ is her expected payoff: For v such that $\beta(v) \geq a$, she sells the object at price $(a + \beta(r))/2$; for v such that $\beta(v) < a$, she retains the object, which is worth r to her.

If the set of types of Alice or Bob (or both) is, say, an interval in R (as will be the case in some examples), integrals would replace the summations (and some measurability restrictions would be placed on the spaces of strategies). To accommodate mixed strategies, one could speak of a behavior strategy as a joint distribution on type and selection of bid/ask such that the marginal distribution on type matches ψ or ϕ, as appropriate, and sums (or integrals) would be over the joint distribution.

But, for purposes of formal definitions, I'll stick to the pure-strategy, finite-type case:

Definition 23.6. *A pure-strategy (Nash) equilibrium is a pair of strategies α for Alice and β for Bob such that*

$$\text{for each } r \in \text{supp}(\psi), W(\alpha(r); r, \beta) = \sup_{a \in [0,\infty)} W(a; r, v), \quad \text{and}$$

$$\text{for each } v \in \text{supp}(\phi), U(\beta(v); v, \alpha) = \sup_{b \in [0,\infty)} U(b; v, \alpha).$$

Don't let the symbols confuse you; this is nothing more than the condition that Alice, as a function of her type r, is choosing the optimal ask for herself, given Bob's strategy, and that Bob is similarly optimizing.

Examples of equilibria

The existence of pure-strategy Nash equilibria in general is a non-issue. For instance:

- A trivial, no-trade equilibria is where Alice asks for $\bar{v}$, the largest v in the support of Bob's values, and Bob bids $\underline{r}$, the smallest r in the support of Alice's reservation values. Faced with this maximalist demand by the other individual, neither side has any incentive to put in a compromise bid.

- A less-trivial example involves any price $p \in [\underline{r}, \bar{v}]$: All types of Bob with $v \geq p$ bid p. All types of Bob with $v < p$ bid $\underline{r}$. All types of Alice with $r \leq p$ ask for p. All types of Alice with $r > p$ ask for $\bar{v}$.

- In particular, in the case with a gap (that is, $\bar{r} < \underline{v}$), any $p \in [\bar{r}, \underline{v}]$ is an equilibrium price at which all types of both Bob and Alice trade.

- In the examples just listed, all sales that are made (and in the first case, "all" equals "none") are made at a single price. There are, in addition, equilibria in which sales are made at a variety of prices. An example is provided by Chatterjee and Samuelson (1983). Suppose that both v and r are uniformly (and independently) distributed on $[0, 12]$. Then $\alpha(r) := 2r/3+3$ and $\beta(v) := 2v/3+1$ give an equilibrium in which the item is sold by Alice if her r is between 0 and 9 and is bought by Bob if his v is between 3 and 12. In other words, Alice will retain the item if $r > 9$, and Bob will fail to buy it if $v < 3$. Therefore, $\alpha(r)$ for $r \in (9, 12]$ and $\beta(v)$ for $v \in [0, 3)$ are not particularly pinned down by optimality for the player. But these precise strategies in these ranges are important for optimality of the other player's strategy. I leave it to you (Problem 23.14) to verify that these strategies do constitute an equilibrium.

Characterizing best responses

Uniqueness of equilibrium is clearly hopeless. But can anything be said about equilibria? A couple of characterizations of equilibrium strategies are available and, indeed, these two characterizations characterize "rationalizable" strategies, defined as: The bidding strategy α for Alice is "rationalizable" if it maximizes her expected payoff against some strategy β by Bob, and vice versa for strategies β of Bob.[22]

Proposition 23.7. *Suppose that β is a best response by Bob to some strategy α by Alice.*

a. *Without loss of generality, one can assume that, for each $v \in \mathrm{supp}(\phi)$, $\beta(v) \leq v$.*

b. *Without loss of generality, one can assume that, for v and v' both in $\mathrm{supp}(\phi)$ such that $v' > v$, the bids $\beta(v)$ and $\beta(v')$ satisfy $\beta(v') \geq \beta(v)$.*

And, symmetrically, if α is a best response to some β, then one can assume that $\alpha(r) \geq r$ and, if $r' > r$, then $\alpha(r') \geq \alpha(r)$.

The meaning of "without loss of generality" and "one can assume" in these assertions is that, restricting attention to strategies with these properties does not restrict Bob or Alice in their optimizations. Or, put differently, if β is a best response to some α, an equally good response is $\beta'(v) := \max\{\beta(v), v\}$, and so forth.

Proof. If Alice employs some strategy α, this strategy induces a probability distribution η on her ask a. This is true for every strategy α that Alice might employ, whether or not it is in any sense an optimal response to what Bob is doing, and whether or not α is pure or mixed. For purposes of this proof, I assume that the support of η is finite, so I can write sums instead of integrals; I leave to you the simple task of rewriting the proof with integrals. (I later assume you have done so, at least for part a.)

Fix a strategy α by Alice and the resulting η. Define a function

$$\hat{U}(b;v) := \sum_{\{a \in \mathrm{supp}(\eta)\,:\,a \leq b\}} \eta(a)\left[v - \frac{a+b}{2}\right].$$

This, of course, is Bob's expected payoff, if his value for the object is v and he bids b.

To prove part a, I show that if, fixing α (hence η) and also some $v \in \mathrm{supp}(\phi)$, bidding v is at least as good as bidding any $b > v$ (and it may well be better). That is, for all $b > v$, $\hat{U}(b;v) \leq \hat{U}(v;v)$. But this is clear: By lowering his bid from $b > v$ to v, for all $a \leq v$, Bob gets the object with either bid and pays less for it with v. And while he will buy the object with the higher bid but not with v for $v < a \leq b$, for precisely those a, $(a+b)/2 > b$, and so Bob pays more for the object than it is worth to him.

(How could it be that the $b > v$ and v give the same payoff? If every $a \in \mathrm{supp}(\eta)$ is greater than b, then both bids give the same payoff of 0.)

In the proof of part b provided here, I assume that the support of ϕ is finite and show that, if $v, v' \in \mathrm{supp}(\phi)$ are such that $v < v'$, if b is optimal for v and b' is optimal for v', and if $b' < b$, then b is equally optimal for v' and b' is equally

---

[22] I've put scare quotes around rationalizable, but is this necessary? Is this the standard definition of rationalizability? Is this equivalent to the standard definition from Appendix 9?

optimal for v. Once I show this, for any optimal β, one can "adjust" β as necessary so that part b holds. As long as $\text{supp}(\phi)$ is finite, only finitely many adjustments are required (there are only finitely many pairwise comparisons to make).

So once again, fix α (hence η) and v, v' in $\text{supp}(\phi)$ such that $v' > v$. Suppose b is an optimal bid for v, and b' is optimal for v'. (Because the defining inequality in the summation is weak, $b \to \hat{U}(b; v)$ is upper semi-continuous in b, and as long as $b \leq v$, which is implied by part a. So a standard continuity argument shows that there are optimal bids.) Without loss of generality from part a, we can assume that $b \leq v$ and $b' \leq v'$. And, finally, suppose that $b' < b$.

Evaluate

$$\big[\hat{U}(b; v) - \hat{U}(b', v)\big] + \big[\hat{U}(b', v') - \hat{U}(b, v')\big].$$

This quantity is nonnegative: The two terms inside the two sets of square brackets are each nonnegative, since b is (assumed to be) optimal for v, and b' is optimal for v'. Rearrange this quantity:

$$\big[\hat{U}(b; v) - \hat{U}(b', v)\big] + \big[\hat{U}(b', v') - \hat{U}(b, v')\big] = \big[\hat{U}(b; v) - \hat{U}(b; v')\big] + \big[\hat{U}(b'; v') - \hat{U}(b'; v)\big].$$

Taking each of the two terms on the right-hand side in turn:

$$\hat{U}(b; v) - \hat{U}(b; v') = \sum_{a \,:\, a \leq b} \eta(a)\left[v - \frac{a+b}{2}\right] - \sum_{a \,:\, a \leq b} \eta(a)\left[v' - \frac{a+b}{2}\right]$$

$$= \sum_{a \,:\, a \leq b} \eta(a)(v - v'),$$

and by a similar calculation,

$$\hat{U}(b'; v') - \hat{U}(b'; v) = \sum_{a \,:\, a \leq b'} \eta(a)(v' - v).$$

Since by assumption, $b' < b$, the set $\{a : a \leq b'\} \subseteq \{a : a \leq b\}$; hence the sum of these two terms is

$$\sum_{a \,:\, b' < a \leq b} \eta(a)(v - v').$$

Since $v' > v$, there are two possibilities:

1. The set $\{a : b' < a \leq b\}$ has positive probability under η. Then the last displayed sum is strictly negative, contradicting the earlier assumption that we can have $v' > v$ and $b' < b$.

2. The set $\{a : b' < a \leq b\}$ has zero probability under η. (Essentially, in this case of a finite $\text{supp}(\eta)$, this means that the set is empty.) Then the last displayed

term is zero, which means that $\hat{U}(b; v) = \hat{U}(b', v)$ and $U(b', v') = \hat{U}(b, v')$, and β can be "adjusted" by changing $\beta(v)$ from b to b'. Do this finitely many times as necessary, and you get part b.

If supp(ϕ) is infinite, then a further argument enlisting continuity is required: For each v, you adjust an assumed-to-be-optimal β by resetting $\beta(v)$ to be sup$\{\beta(v') : v' > v\}$; then, show that this "adjusted" β is just as good as the original β. I leave this part of the proof to you.

That takes care of Bob's response to some α by Alice. The proof for Alice's response to some β by Bob is similar, and I leave it to you as Problem 23.15 (with a written-out proof in the *Online Supplement*).   ∎

Efficient outcomes?

A final remark concerns the efficiency of these bargaining equilibria. An equilibrium strategy profile (α, β) is called *efficient* if the good changes hands whenever $r \leq v$; that is, whenever there are gains from trade. In the case of a gap (that is, $\underline{v} > \overline{r}$), there are both efficient and inefficient equilibria. Any equilibrium in which a price $p \in (\overline{r}, \underline{v})$ is chosen and $\beta(v) \equiv \alpha(r) \equiv p$ is obviously efficient. However, if $p < \overline{r}$ and Alice chooses to ask $\overline{v}$ whenever $r > p$, the outcome is obviously inefficient.

In the no-gap case, we've listed several equilibria, and not one of the ones we've listed is efficient. A simple picture shows this: Suppose that supp(ψ) = supp(ϕ) = [0, 12] (so this includes the Chatterjee and Samuelson example.) The two panels of Figure 23.1 depict all possible values of (r, v) and, in the lightly shaded region, all pairs (r, v) for which gains from trade are possible. In panel a, the more heavily shaded region shows the pairs (r, v) for which trade happens in the Chatterjee and Samuelson equilibrium. In panel b, the more heavily shaded region shows the pairs for which trade happens in the "one-price-p" type of equilibrium, for $p \in [0, 12]$. In both panels, since there is lightly shaded area that is not heavily shaded, efficiency is not achieved.

There are no-gap examples for which efficient bargaining equilibria are possible. Suppose the support of ψ consists of two disconnected sets, $[3, 4] \cup [11, 12]$, and the support of ϕ is $[0, 1] \cup [9, 10]$. Then the set of (r, v) pairs with positive probability is the union of the four very dark squares depicted in Figure 23.2. The only (r, v) with positive probability for which there are gains from trade (that lie in the lightly shaded triangle in Figure 23.1) are points in the square $\{(r, v) \in [3, 4] \times [9, 10]\}$. And so setting a "price" of $p = 6$—Alice asks for 6 if $r \in [3, 4]$ and asks for 12 otherwise, while Bob bids 6 if $v \in [9, 10]$ and bids 0 otherwise—implements the efficient outcome.

However, we have the following negative result.

Proposition 23.8. *Suppose that there is some closed interval $[x, y]$, $x < y$, such that $[x, y] \subseteq supp(\psi) \cap supp(\phi)$. Suppose that ψ and ϕ have strictly positive densities on $[x, y]$. Then no bargaining equilibrium can yield an efficient outcome.*

Proof. By way of contradiction, suppose that there were an efficient equilibrium

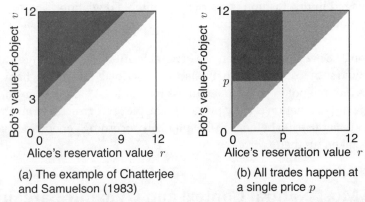

(a) The example of Chatterjee and Samuelson (1983)

(b) All trades happen at a single price p

Figure 23.1. Trades that take place. In both panels, the more lightly shaded region is the set of pairs (r, v) for which there are gains from trade. In panel a, the more heavily shaded region is the set of pairs (r, v) for which trade takes place in the Chatterjee–Samuelson example; in panel b, the more heavily shaded region is the set of pairs (r, v) for which trades occur in an equilibrium where all trades take place at a single price p.

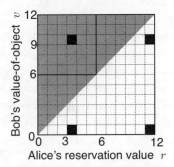

Figure 23.2. Efficiency is possible in the "gap" case. If the supports of ψ and ϕ are, respectively, $[3, 4] \cup [11, 12]$ and $[0, 1] \cup [9, 10]$, the points (r, v) for which trade is efficient consists (only) of the northwest square $[3, 4] \times [9, 10]$. Setting a "price" of 6 implements all these efficient trades.

with ask function α and bid function β. Then, on the interval (x, y), $\alpha(r) = r$ and $\beta(v) = v$ are required: We already know that we can restrict attention to $\alpha(r) \geq r$ and $\beta(v) \leq v$. So suppose, for instance, for some specific $v \in (x, y)$, $\beta(v) < v$. Since $\alpha(r) \geq r$, for $r \in (\beta(v), v)$, it follows that $\alpha(r) > \beta(v)$ for this pair (r, v), even though $r < v$. That is inconsistent with full efficiency. And a similar argument shows that $\alpha(r) = r$ over the interval.

Now pick some $v \in (x, y)$. Consider what the impact is on Bob's expected payoff if this v is his value, and he lowers his bid by small $\epsilon > 0$. For all $r \leq v - \epsilon$, he is able to purchase the item, but at a price that is decreased by $\epsilon/2$. Hence his gain from this variation for such r is $O(\epsilon)$. However, he loses the ability to purchase from Alice if her $r \in (v - \epsilon, v)$. His loss in value is no larger than $O(\epsilon)$, and the probability of this loss is $O(\epsilon)$, so his expected loss is $o(\epsilon)$. For small enough

ϵ, lowering his bid in this fashion is a strictly profitable deviation. The supposed equilibrium is not in fact an equilibrium.   ∎

Proposition 23.8 is a simple version of a general result by Myerson and Satterthwaite (1983), who show, under the circumstances described, that *no* mechanism (in which players are free not to participate unless they at least "break even" and for which each player's valuation is truly private to the player) can achieve an efficient outcome. This general result belongs to Chapter 26, concerning general mechanism design, and is taken up there.

23.7. The Most Natural Context and Dynamic Bargaining

A lot has been written about simultaneous bid-and-ask "bargaining," but the protocol of one-time, simultaneous bids and asks hardly meets the common notion of bargaining. Bargaining is commonly thought of as dynamic, with the two sides trading offers, either simultaneously or sequentially (or some combination of the two), trying to see to what the other side can and will agree. So it is natural to ask, What if we combine the "most natural" context with some form of dynamic bargaining?

This is not an easy question to answer for the following reason. In the framework of standard noncooperative game theory, when Alice, whose reservation value for the object r is private information, proposes that she will sell if Bob will pay p_1, Bob (whatever is his valuation v) must translate this into some revised beliefs about r. When he counterproposes p_2, it is Alice's turn to reassess her beliefs about Bob's v. The number of degrees of freedom in assessing the meaning of initial and perhaps nonserious bids and asks is enormous; and if beliefs aren't somehow pinned down, it is hard to see how equilibria might be.

Compare the situation with two models with incomplete information that we have already explored. The Abreu and Gul (2000) model involves a "behavioral type" (or several) together with a so-called "rational type" of both Alice and Bob. The beauty—if that's the right word—of a behavioral-type model is that the model specifies in advance exactly how the behavioral type or types will behave at each moment in time. The rational type, whose equilibrium behavior is the subject of analysis, either chooses to mimic that type (or one of those types) or let the other side definitively conclude that "this isn't me." Once the other side concludes that she or he is sure to be facing a behavioral type, we are in the setting of single-person optimization, and so rational types can figure out what they are *giving up* by failing to mimic a specific behavioral type. That is to say, in an equilibrium, if the rational type does not mimic a given behavioral type, behavior that conforms to the behavioral type meets a predictable response. And the rational type, in an alleged equilibrium in which she doesn't mimic that type, can therefore get that predictable response by deviating and mimicking the type. This provides powerful restrictions on what what an equilibrium payoff for the rational type must be.

The other sort of model with incomplete information consists of the simple models of one-sided incomplete information in Chapters 20 and 21. Suppose Alice is a single type, while Bob comes in two (or more) types. In these models, all types of Bob are "rational," not "behavioral"; in an equilibrium, we are concerned with finding optimal behavior for each type of Bob. And nominally, Alice is concerned with what Bob's behavior means in terms of her assessment of his type. But then:

- In Chapter 20, in the "screening" stories where Alice proposes a menu of options for Bob, the types of Bob individually optimize. Alice's subsequent beliefs don't enter, because Alice is done acting.

- Also in Chapter 20, in the "signaling" stories where Bob initially signals his type and Alice responds, Alice must indeed reassess her beliefs about Bob's type in light of his signal. And, as we saw in that chapter, Alice's off-path beliefs become crucial, leading (at least at the start of analysis) to a multiplicity of equilibria. But we are able (and, we *might* be willing) to cut back on the equilibrium set by imposing "reasonable" restrictions on off-path beliefs (e.g., with the intuitive criterion).

- And, moving on to Chapter 21 and true dynamics, Bob was (or, in Chapter 21, a continuum of Bobs were) were passive: Alice proposed a price at $t = 0$, then at $t = 1$, and so forth. Bob, in equilibrium, could anticipate the sequence of prices Alice would name and so, depending on his type, optimize. In this chapter, the one-sided bargaining model of Sobel and Takahashi (1983) has a similar structure: In equilibrium, Bob can anticipate what price Alice will ask for at each point in time (assuming he didn't buy earlier); in the face of these (correct) anticipations, he simply optimizes, depending on his type.

The situation here is more complex, and it is much harder to come to definitive conclusions.

Strategic delay in bargaining

Even so, the literature provides analyses refine our intuitive understanding of how particular bargaining strategies can credibly signal bargaining strength, leading the other side to compromise. Perhaps the best examples are models of strategic delay in bargaining: Alice (for instance) delays her response to Bob as a credible signal that she is in a strong position and, in an agreement, must be rewarded for being so.

Admati and Perry (1987) propose a model in which Alice may sell an object (worth 0 to herself) to Bob, whose valuation of the object is either $\underline{v}$ or $\overline{v}$, where $\overline{v} > \underline{v}$, and with $\phi \in (0, 1)$ being the probability that the object is worth $\underline{v}$ to Bob. Bargaining takes place over time: Alice makes an initial ask a_0 at time 0, to which Bob can respond with immediate acceptance or with rejection and a counteroffer at any time $t_1 \geq h$, for some strictly positive h.[23] Bob's counteroffer, if he makes one at t_1, is met by Alice's immediate acceptance or her counter-counteroffer at any time

---

[23] This isn't quite how Admati and Perry do things, but it aligns more closely with the treatment of the base Rubinstein model as described in Section 23.3.

$t_2 \geq t_1 + h$. In other words, we have the Rubinstein protocol with one modification: The response (acceptance or a counteroffer) by any player to a proposal by the other player at time t can be made after h time units have passed *or at any later time*, where the choice of when to respond is up to the player. *And the "other" player must sit passively until the first player chooses to respond.*

Payoffs are: If a deal is consummated at time t at an agreed-on price of p, Alice's payoff is $e^{-rt}p$, and Bob's is $e^{-rt}(v - p)$, where $v = \underline{v}$ or $\bar{v}$, depending on Bob's type.

Assume that money is infinitely divisible. Then, *if* Alice knew Bob's type, the Rubinstein analysis would imply that the unique subgame-perfect equilibrium is for Alice to ask Bob of type v that he pay $p = v/(1 + e^{-rh})$, to which he immediately agrees.

But Alice does not know Bob's type. Suppose, then, that she offers the compromise price of

$$p = \frac{\phi \underline{v} + (1 - \phi)\bar{v}}{1 + e^{-rh}}.$$

If Bob's type is $\bar{v}$, he is very happy about this relatively (for his type) low price, and he immediately accepts. But if Bob's type is $\underline{v}$, he is unhappy. He feels he should only pay $\underline{v}/(1 + e^{-rh})$. And so he rejects and comes back with a counteroffer: He is willing to pay $p = \underline{v}e^{-rh}/(1 + e^{-rh})$, which is the Rubinstein price when he is making the offer at time h.

If the $\bar{v}$ type of Bob were, in equilibrium, to accept Alice's initial offer, Alice would know that she is facing $\underline{v}$-Bob, and (per the logic of Rubinstein) she would accept this counteroffer. But, two problems with this story are:

1. Alice is charging $\bar{v}$-Bob the compromise price. Why not charge him the "correct" price for him, namely, $\bar{v}/(1 + e^{-rh})$ at the outset? Of course, this makes sense only if he'd accept this price.

2. Which brings up the second problem: If $\bar{v}$-Bob, by rejecting Alice's initial offer, convinces her to accept a counterproposal of $p = e^{-rh}\underline{v}/(1 + e^{-rh})$ in h time units, he may well be better off by "deviating" from immediate acceptance.

The parallels to the signaling models of Chapter 20 are evident: $\underline{v}$-Bob is "strong," and he needs to signal to Alice that he is strong. But his signal must be one that $\bar{v}$-Bob would not choose to send. The signal available to him is to delay his counteroffer sufficiently, so that $\bar{v}$-Bob would prefer to accept the appropriate price for him—namely, $\bar{v}/(1 + e^{-rh})$—to undergoing the delay that is satisfactory to $\underline{v}$-Bob. And, just as in the basic (Spence) model of job-market signaling, the problem of off-path beliefs appears; if Alice's beliefs given off-path actions by Bob are *optimistic*, meaning that she assesses probability 1 (or close to 1) that Bob's value is $\bar{v}$, this can be parlayed into all sorts of equilibria. As in Chapter 20, we need— and Admati and Perry (1987) use—a belief restriction in the spirit of the intuitive criterion to pin down the equilibrium.

Things are not so simple as the previous paragraph might suggest, because Alice does have the ability to make an initial offer, something that has no analogue in (say) the Spence job-market signaling game. If Alice anticipates that a substantial delay to agreement is likely—if ϕ, the probability that Bob's type is $\underline{v}$—then she will make an initial offer attractive enough so that both types of Bob agree immediately. Hence, there are three cases:

1. If ϕ lies in an interval $(\phi^*, 1]$, in the unique equilibrium that meets the assumptions made, Alice asks for an attractively low price that is immediately accepted by both types of Bob.

2. If ϕ lies in the interval $[0, 1 - \underline{v}/\overline{v})$, the unique equilibrium has Alice asking $\overline{v}/(1 + e^{-rh})$, which is accepted by Bob if his value is $\overline{v}$ and rejected if his value is $\underline{v}$. And, in case of rejection, after a sufficient amount of time has passed (so that this strategy is not attractive to $\overline{v}$-Bob), he counteroffers that he will pay $e^{-rh}\underline{v}/(1 + e^{-rh})$, which Alice accepts. [24]

3. For $\phi \in [1 - \underline{v}/\overline{v}, \phi^*]$, both the pooling and the separating equilibria "work." You can read the details in Admati and Perry (1987).

Admati and Perry have only one-sided incomplete information. Cramton (1992) picks up this story and, for a model with incomplete information on both sides, constructs a bargaining equilibrium in which both sides use delay to signal "strength." Cramton is explicit that his equilibrium is only one of a continuum of possible equilibria; to quote from his introduction (page 206), "rather than determining how rational traders *must* negotiate, the results here simply specify one form [that] rational behavior *may* take when bargainers are faced with two-sided undertainty." His equilibrium (and bargaining protocol) has the following features:

- At the start, either side can make the initial offer at any time. And, in equilibrium, neither side says anything for a length of time. This phase of "no offers" is a war of attrition between the two players, but with private information determining when one player or the other makes the first offer, based on their valuations, rather than randomization between continued silence and concession. The time of the first offer reveals the valuation of the first player to make an offer, following which there is one-sided incomplete information.

- After the initial offer (from either side), the protocol calls for the other party to respond. Response is delayed for (at least) a minimum amount of time, but it can be delayed further. For some valuations by the other side, the initial offer is accepted in minimum possible time. But, if it is not, the delay in making a counteroffer reveals the valuation of the other side.

---

[24] For ϕ in this interval, a moment after Bob doesn't accept Alice's initial offer, Alice knows that Bob is type $\underline{v}$. Why don't she and $\underline{v}$-Bob immediately (or, after h time units) come to agreement? Because the rules are that she is not allowed to make another offer; it is Bob's turn. And, if he made an offer too soon, her off-path beliefs..., well, you can finish this sentence. How fanciful is this story? In many cases of labor negotiations, a well known and often practiced tactic is for one side or the other walking away from the bargaining table, leaving the other side unable to make any new proposals.

- And, if the other side—the party that did not make the initial offer—counteroffers, since this reveals her or his type, this counteroffer, which conforms to the Rubinstein solution, is accepted, ending the negotiation.

Details are not provided here; consult the two papers.

Bilateral bargaining and economic theory: A (personal) bottom line

If you examined the "history" of how mainstream economists have regarded the theory of bilateral bargaining, I believe that the following is fair. (At least, this is how I perceive this bit of "history of thought." And, you will note, this is how this chapter unfolds.)

- Prior to Rubinstein (1982), and because of the multiplicity of equilibria in games like simultaneous demand, the consensus was that theory based on self-interested behavior alone would not provide a definitive answer.

- Rubinstein changed that opinion; it seemed that noncooperative game theory might in the end provide an ideal answer.

- However, the delicacy of the Rubinstein model to small changes in formulation dashed the hopes of a simple solution; if a solution was to be found, it would be based on incomplete information formulations, and the hunt for the bargaining version of the Holy Grail was on.

I've chosen to present Abreu and Gul (2000) in this volume in part because of the techniques that paper employs. At the same time, the "robustness" of their conclusions to small changes in protocol is precisely what is hoped for, in any true "answer." (Which is not to say that I showed their robustness results.) But one can criticize their formulation, with fixated types in addition to one rational type, as artificial; the "ultimate answer" should apply, and robustly so, to the most natural context. Strategic delay in making an offer, as a device to signal bargaining strength, is an idea that has a good deal of intuitive appeal as well as some empirical validity, but (as so far developed), it is very much exemplifying theory. So, perhaps—in my opinion, probably—the consensus opinion pre-Rubinstein is correct, after all.

Bilateral bargaining is an important part of real-life microeconomic practice , so it is natural that theorists have devoted effort and ink in trying to find the holy grail of this subject. I've only scratched the surface of the resulting literature. Linhart, Radner, and Satterthwaite (1992) collects twenty-one papers that search for the holy grail, stretching to over nearly 550 pages, and this omits (for instance) Cramton (1992) and Abreu and Gul (2000), as well as numerous subsequent papers.

This particular holy grail may one day be achieved. But—and, again, this is only my opinion—achievement, if it comes, will take an integration of psychological factors into the conditions of bargaining and the preconceptions of the bargainers. At this point, the theoretical literature is not where I'd go for practical advice about how to bargain effectively. Instead, for practical advice, I would turn to the experimental and empirical literature, in both the literatures of economics and psychology.

23.8. Axiomatic Approaches: The Nash Bargaining Solution

My bottom-line (personal) opinion just offered is not very helpful for economists who wish to study broader situations in which bilateral bargaining is a part of the story. Think, for instance, of a model of bargaining in supply chains, where downstream firms must conclude bargains with upstream suppliers. The deal may involve selecting a single upstream supplier, or it may involve striking deals simultaneously with a number of upstream suppliers. To model such situations, it is useful to have a "reasonable" solution to bilateral bargaining problems that the analyst can plug into the bigger model. For such purposes, and as a matter of general interest, several *bargaining solutions* have been advanced, based on the satisfaction of a specific set of axioms. To be clear, it is satisfaction of the axioms that defines "reasonable." A bargaining solution "ought" to satisfy certain "reasonable" properties and, ideally, if those reasonable properties nail down a single solution, ... well, ..., that single solution is reasonable to plug into a bigger model.

By far the most popular (and employed) of these bargaining solutions in applications is the *Nash bargaining solution*, axiomatized in Nash (1950a). So I'll present here the definitions and axioms that go with the Nash bargaining solution and then provide its derivation.

Definitions

The first step is define what one might mean by a bargaining solution and, to do that, we first define a bilateral bargaining problem: Roughly put, there is some abstract set C of "deals" that might be concluded between two parties—I'll call them Alice and Bob—and there is some outcome, also in C, that results if they do not come to an agreement. The parties involved have preferences concerning all the possible cs, which are represented by von Neumann–Morgenstern utilities for them; each $c \in C$ maps into a *utility imputation* $x = (x_A, x_B) = (u_A(c), u_A(c)) \in R^2$, where u_A is Alice's utility function, and u_B is Bob's. The disagreement outcome's utility imputation is denoted by $d = (d_A, d_B)$. Letting X be the set of utility imputations that arise from $c \in C$, we have the following formal definition.

*Definition 23.9 A **bilateral bargaining problem** consists of a **convex and compact** set $X \subseteq R^2$ of feasible utility imputations, and a distinguished point $d \in X$, called the **disagreement point**.[25] It is further assumed that there is some $x \in X$ that is strictly greater than d in both components. Denote by $\mathcal{X}$ the set of all bilateral bargaining problems.*

Compactness is assumed on technical grounds. If the set of possible deals is unbounded or open, there may be no solution. Convexity stems from the assumption

---

[25] In the literature, d is also known as the status-quo point or imputation, with the interpretation that, if no agreement is reached, this status-quo remains in force. And sometimes it is called the threat point, the bargainers' outside options, or their opporunity costs. The theory to follow assumes that this disagreement point is specified as part of the model; in applications, finding the right disagreement point is an important part of constructing the contextual model.

that utility imputations are measured in von Neumann–Morgenstern utilities—that is, Alice and Bob are both expected-utility maximizers—and the further assumption that they can agree on any simple lottery over elements of C, if they choose to, based on some publicly available randomizing device.

As for the assumption that the disagreement imputation is strictly dominated by some other $x \in X$ for every bargaining problem: Suppose this is not so. Then either Alice or Bob's utility is maximized at the disagreement point. Suppose it is Alice's that is maximized. Perhaps there is an x that is just as good for Alice as d and is superior for Bob; we assume that Alice would be willing to agree to this, as long as it doesn't harm her. And if d is Pareto efficient in X, then there is nothing worth bargaining over; Alice and Bob will naturally agree to disagree and move on. Hence, this assumption is there simply to guarantee that we have an interesting bargaining problem.

Definition 23.10. *A **bargaining solution** is a function $\phi : \mathcal{X} \to R^2$ such that, for each $(X, d) \in \mathcal{X}$, $\phi((X, d)) \in X$.*

As an analogy, think of Arrow's notion of a social decision rule, which, for any profile of ordinal preferences over social states, assigns a social ordering. Here, we are using cardinal preferences; there are only two consumers; and instead of an ordering, we are just picking out one point as "the bargain." This is asking a lot—perhaps too much—but we'll see where this leads us. Of course, existence of bargaining solutions is not an issue; one bargaining solution is the function $\phi((X, d)) = d$. But, as with Arrow's theorem, we want to impose "reasonable" axioms or properties that a bargaining solution ought to have.[26]

It is worth saying, though, that we could instead define this basic concept as a correspondence rather than a function, with the interpretation that if $\phi((X, d)) \subseteq X$, then given the bargaining problem (X, d), this sort of bargaining solution narrows down the *possible* agreements at which the bargaining parties might arrive.[27]

Axioms for a bargaining solution   •

The next step is to list some axioms that, one might argue, a bargaining solution ought to satisfy.

Axioms 23.11.

a. *A bargaining solution ϕ satisfies **efficiency** if, for every $(X, d) \in \mathcal{X}$, $\phi((X, d))$ is Pareto efficient in X.*

b. *A bargaining solution ϕ satisfies **symmetry** or **equal treatment** if, for every $(X, d) \in \mathcal{X}$ such that (i) $(x_1, x_2) \in X$ implies $(x_2, x_1) \in X$ and (ii) $d = (d_1, d_2)$ satisfies $d_1 = d_2$, then $\phi((X, d)) = \left(\phi_1((X, d)), \phi_2((X, d))\right)$ satisfies $\phi_1((X, d)) = \phi_2((X, d))$.*

---

[26] Having mentioned Arrow's social decision rule, let me foreshadow later developments in this volume: The problem of choosing a single social state in the Arrovian context is the topic of the Gibbard–Satterthwaite Theorem, the first topic of Chapter 26.

[27] And readers who are interested can chase down the von Neumann–Morgenstern Bargaining Set, which is a set-valued solution concept for games in coalitional form.

c. *A bargaining solution ϕ satisfies* **invariance (to rescaling of utilities)** *if, for every $(X, d) \in \mathcal{X}$ (where $d = (d_1, d_2)$,) and for every α_1 and α_2, both strictly positive scalars, and for every β_1 and β_2, both scalars, if we define the bargaining problem (X', d') by*

$$X' = \{(x', y') : x' = \alpha_1 x + \beta_1, y' = \alpha_2 y + \beta_2 \text{ for some } x \in X\} \quad \text{and}$$
$$d' = (\alpha_1 d_1 + \beta_1, \alpha_2 d_2 + \beta_2)$$

then $\phi\big((X', d')\big) = \big(\alpha_1 \phi_1((X, d)) + \beta_1, \alpha_2 \phi_2((X, d)) + \beta_2\big)$.

d. *A bargaining solution ϕ satisfies* **independence of irrelevant alternatives (IIA)** *if we have two bargaining problems (X, d) and (X', d) such that (i) $X' \subseteq X$ and (ii) $\phi\big((X, d)\big) \in X'$, then $\phi\big((X', d)\big) = \phi\big((X, d)\big)$.*

How reasonable are these axioms? That's a matter for you to decide for yourself, but to give you my opinions:

- *Invariance* seems entirely reasonable to me, given the setting. The cardinal utility functions used to represent Alice and Bob's preferences are imaginary constructs. A solution ought to depend only on their (cardinal) preferences, and not on the specific utility-function representations we choose. Now, saying that the bargaining solution depends on cardinal (von Neumann–Morgenstern expected-utility) preferences is another question. But, given that this is the setting here, I'm fine with invariance.[28]

- I'm okay with *symmetry*. There are differences in the bargaining strengths of real-life individuals, but for an axiomatic approach to bargaining, I find this property reasonable. And, if we know something about the relative bargaining abilities of Alice and Bob, enough to say how they'd (say) split $100, then we can accommodate that in our axiomatic theory.

- *Efficiency* strikes me as a bit of pie-in-the-sky, at least as an empirical proposition. But inefficiencies that we've seen have arisen from incomplete information, and the setting here makes no allowance for incomplete information. So, as long as we are dealing with a context without incomplete information, efficiency isn't totally unreasonable.

- *IIA* strikes me as the least palatable of these axioms. Consider two bargaining problems: (i) Alice and Bob can split $100 any way they wish. No agreement (the threat point) is $0 for both. Symmetry and efficiency immediately imply a $50 for each split. (ii) Alice and Bob can split $100 any way they wish, as long as Alice's share is at least as large as Bob's share. If they can't come to agreement, they both get $0. Impose IIA, and the result must be $50 apiece. It is true that the threat point ($0 for each) hasn't changed. But shouldn't Alice get something more than $50 in this situation? IIA (with symmetry and efficiency) says No.

---

[28] However, if you are ever engaged in modeling some situation in which bilateral bargaining is a part, and you decide to plug in the Nash solution based on, say, dollar outcomes, understand that you are assuming risk neutrality. This isn't a terrible thing. But it does matter. Also, what are the implications of invariance for the Roth and Schoumaker experiment described on page 276?

And, if you understand the example just given, you are on your way to understanding the proof of the big result.

The Nash bargaining solution

For a given problem $(X, d) \in \mathcal{X}$, define $f_{(X,d)} : X \to R_+$ by

$$f_{(X,d)}(x) := \max\{x_1 - d_1, 0\} \cdot \max\{x_2 - d_2, 0\} \quad \text{for } x = (x_1, x_2) \in X \text{ and } d = (d_1, d_2).$$

Definition 23.12. *The **Nash bargaining solution** $\phi_{\text{Nash}} : \mathcal{X} \to R^2$ is defined as*

$$\phi_{\text{Nash}}((X, d)) := \arg \max \{f_{(X,d)}(x) : x \in X\}.$$

If the notation "arg max" is new to you, this definition means the value of $x \in X$ that maximizes $f_{(X,d)}$ over all points $x \in X$.

The idea here is that, for the bargaining problem (X, d), we look at all points $x \in X$ that are strictly superior to d (that have $x_1 > d_1$ and $x_2 > d_2$) and, among those, we choose the point x that maximizes the product $(x_1 - d_1) \cdot (x_2 - d_2)$. The reason for the maxima in the definition is to restrict attention to points x that are strictly larger in both components than d; the function $f_{(X,d)}$ is just the desired product for those points and takes the value 0 for any $x \in X$ that is not strictly larger than d.

The Nash bargaining solution ϕ_{Nash} is well defined: For each (X, d), the function $f_{(X,d)}$ is continuous; since we are maximizing over X, which is compact, there are solutions to the maximization problem. Since, by assumption, there are points $x \in X$ that are strictly larger than d, the maxima lie among the points that are strictly larger than d. And since the function $f_{(X,d)}$ is strictly quasi-concave on points x strictly larger than d (draw the level sets if this isn't clear to you), and X is convex, there is necessarily a unique solution to the maximization problem.

Moreover, this Nash bargaining solution satisfies all four axioms listed in Axioms 23.11. Efficiency, symmetry, and even IIA should be clear to you (for IIA, if the maximum of a function taken over a set is contained in a subset of the set, it maximizes the function over that subset). As for invariance, if we translate the utility functions and the disagreement point, the additive scalar parts of the transformation cancel out in the differences $x_i - d_i$. And

$$(\alpha_1 x_1 - \alpha_1 d_1)(\alpha_2 x_2 - \alpha_2 d_2) = \alpha_1 \alpha_2 (x_1 - d_1)(x_2 - d_2).$$

As long as α_1 and α_2 are strictly positive, the maximizer (or arg max) is the same.

Proposition 23.13. *The unique bargaining solution ϕ that satisfies the four axioms given in Axioms 23.11 is the Nash bargaining solution.*

Proof. The proof is really quite simple. Start with a problem (X, d) and a bargaining solution ϕ that satisfies the four axioms. We will rescale the problem twice.

First, replace (X, e) with (X', e'), where

$$X' = \left\{(x_1', x_2') : (x_1', x_2') = (x_1 - d_1, x_2 - d_2) \text{ for some } (x_1, x_2) \in X\right\}, \quad \text{and} \quad e' = (0, 0).$$

Next, find $\phi_{\text{Nash}}((X', e'))$. Call this point (x_1^*, x_2^*). Replace $(X', e' = 0)$ with $(X'', 0)$, where

$$X' = \left\{(x_1'', x_2'') : (x_1'', x_2'') = \left(\frac{x_1'}{x_1^*}, \frac{x_2'}{x_2^*}\right) \text{ for some } (x_1', x_2') \in X'\right\}.$$

This is a legitimate rescaling of the utility functions, because x_1^* and x_2^* are strictly positive.

This second rescaling is such that $\phi_{\text{Nash}}(X'', 0) = (1, 1)$. And—the key step—I claim that for all $x'' \in X''$, $x_1'' + x_2'' \leq 2$. For if there were a point $x'' = (x_1'', x_2'') \in X''$ such that $x_1'' + x_2'' > 2$, then by looking at convex combinations of x'' with $(1, 1)$ (all of which are in X'', since it is convex), some convex combinations with weight close to but not quite equal to 1 on $(1, 1)$ would give a higher value of the product that defines $f_{(X'', 0)}$ than does $(1, 1)$. This would contradict $\phi_{\text{Nash}}(X'', 0) = (1, 1)$. This is true because the tangent to the iso-objective curve $f_{(X'', 0)}((1, 1))$ at $(1, 1)$ is the line $x_1'' + x_2'' = 1$; see Figure 23.3(a) if this isn't clear.

But then since X'' is compact, there is some $M < 0$ such that for all $x'' = (x_1'', x_2'') \in X''$, $x_1'' \geq M$ and $x_2'' \geq M$. Construct a third bargaining problem $(X^\sharp, 0)$ where

$$x^\sharp = (x_1^\sharp, x_2^\sharp) \in X^\sharp \text{ if } x_1^\sharp \geq M, x_2^\sharp \geq M, \text{ and } x_1^\sharp + x_2^\sharp \leq 2.$$

(See Figure 23.3(b).) This problem is symmetric with respect to its two components, so the combination of the symmetry and efficiency axioms implies that $\phi((X^\sharp, 0)) = (1, 1)$. And since $X'' \subseteq X^\sharp$ and contains $(1, 1)$, IIA implies that $\phi((X'', 0)) = (1, 1) = \phi_{\text{Nash}}((X'', 0))$. Undoing the first two transformations of (X, e) to $(X', 0)$ and then $(X', 0)$ to $(X'', 0)$, the invariance axiom tells us that $\phi((X, e)) = \phi_{\text{Nash}}((X, e))$. So ϕ is indeed ϕ_{Nash}. ∎

Rubinstein and Nash

The Nash bargaining solution and Rubinstein's subgame-perfect bargaining equilibrium have an interesting connection. To set this up, we generalize Rubinstein:

- Let $\mathcal{X}^0$ be the subset of bargaining problems $\mathcal{X}$ with the following additional characteristics: If $(X, e) \in \mathcal{X}^0$, then the disagreement point $e = (0, 0)$, and $X \subseteq R_+^2$.

- Consider the following extensive-form game between Alice and Bob.
  1. At time 0, Alice can propose as a deal any $x \in X$, where $x = (x_1, x_2)$, x_1 will be Alice's payoff, and x_2 will be Bob's payoff. Bob can agree to or reject this proposal.

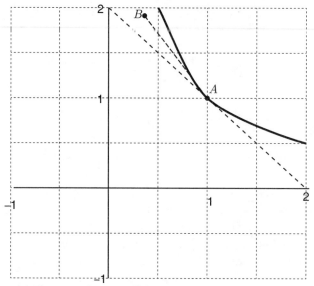

(a) There can be no points in X'' above the line $x_1 + x_2 > 2$

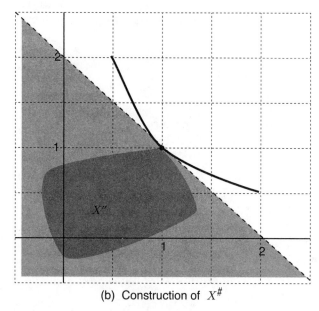

(b) Construction of $X^{\sharp}$

Figure 23.3. The proof of Proposition 23.12.   Panel a shows why X'' cannot contain a point such as B above the line $x_1 + x_2 = 2$, for if such a point existed, a convex combination of it and the point $A = (1,1)$—call the convex combination x^0— with most of the weight on $(1,1)$, would necessarily have $x_1^0 x_2^0 > 1$, contradicting the construction of $(1,1)$ being the point in X'' that maximizes this product. And, therefore, the set X''—the darker region in panel b—necessarily lies below (or on) this line. Since X'' is compact, it is bounded below, and we can therefore construct a symmetric set $X^{\sharp}$—the more lightly shaded set in panel b—that contains X''. From there, the proof consists of using the axioms to show that $(1,1)$ must be what ϕ chooses from $(X'', 0)$.

2. If Bob rejects, then, at time h, he can propose some other $x' \in X$, with $x' = (x_1', x_2')$, x_1' is Alice's current-value payoff, and x_2' is Bob's. Alice can accept this or reject it.

3. If Alice rejects, she can make a counter-counterproposal at time $2h$, and so on.

If an agreement is struck at time kh on the point $(x_1, x_2) \in X$, Alice's overall payoff is $e^{-rkh}x_1$, and Bob's is $e^{-rkh}x_2$, for some fixed discount rate r. If they never agree, their payoffs are each 0.

Definition 23.14. *For this game, a **generous proposal** by Alice is one such that, if she proposes $x^A = (x_1^A, x_2^A)$, then x_2^A maximizes x_2 over $\{(x_1, x_2) \in X : x_1 = x_1^A\}$. In words, given that she proposes x_1^A for herself, she is generous and proposes the largest x_2 consistent with this demand. A generous proposal by Bob is defined analogously.*

Proposition 23.15. *Fixing $X \in \mathcal{X}^0$ and $r > 0$:*

a. *For fixed h, there is a unique subgame-perfect equilibrium for the game in which Alice and Bob must make generous proposals. Without this restriction, there can by multiple subgame-perfect equilibria.*

b. *All subgame-perfect equilibria are characterized by a pair $x^A(h)$ and $x^B(h)$ such that*

   i. *When it is Alice's turn to make a proposal, she proposes $x^A(h)$, and Bob accepts.*

   ii. *When it is Bob's turn to make a proposal, he proposes $x^B(h)$, and Alice accepts.*

c. *If $x^* \in X$ is the Nash bargaining solution for X, and if, for each h, $\left(x^A(h), x^B(h)\right)$ is a subgame-perfect Nash equilibrium pair given h, then*

$$\lim_{h \to 0} x^A(h) = \lim_{h \to 0} x^B(h) = x^*.$$

I do not prove this result here, see, for instance, Osborne and Rubinstein (1990, chapter 15). But it is worthwhile to draw a couple of pictures, which illustrate the result.

Before drawing the pictures, let us characterize equilibrium pairs (x^A, x^B):

$$x_1^B \geq e^{-rh}x_1^A, \quad \text{and} \quad x_2^A \geq e^{-rh}x_2^B. \tag{23.1}$$

Take the first of these: Bob, when he is making a proposal, offers Alice x_1^B. Suppose Alice is certain that, should she reject his offer, he will accept her subsequent offer. Then if that offer gives her (current-value) x_1^A, and if $x_1^B < e^{-rh}x_1^A$, she would indeed reject his offer. To get her to accept his offer, the reverse inequality must hold. The other inequality is required for Bob to accept Alice's offer.

Now for pictures. They are easier to understand if we transform the problem. Map the set X into a corresponding set $Z \subseteq \left(R \cup \{-\infty\}\right)^2$, where $x = (x_1, x_2) \in X$ is mapped to $z = (z_1, z_2) = \left(\ln(x_1), \ln(x_2)\right)$. (This map is invertible if (x_1, x_2) is strictly positive.) The set Z is not compact. It is, however, bounded above and, for any $\underline{z} \in R^2$, the set $Z \cap \{z : z \geq \underline{z}\}$ is compact. In general, Z is not convex (see Problem 23.16). But the Pareto frontier of X maps into the Pareto frontier of Z, and that presents a "strictly concave function," due to the strict concavity of the natural log function. (To see what this means, see Problem 23.16.) The point of this mapping is:

- The Nash bargaining solution x^*, which maximizes $x_1 \times x_2$ for $x \in X$, also maximizes $\ln(x_1 \times x_2) = \ln(x_1) + \ln(x_2) = z_1 + z_2$. That is, x^* maps into the $z \in Z$ that maximizes $z_1 + z_2$.

- And, the inequalities (23.1) become

$$z_1^B \geq z_1^A - rh \quad \text{and} \quad z_2^A \geq z_2^B - rh.$$

Follow along on Figure 23.4.

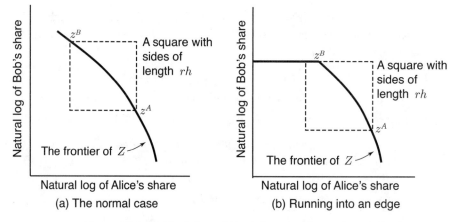

Figure 23.4. Rubinstein and Nash (see text for explanation)

Panel a depicts what might be called the "normal" case, where the two inequalities are equations. This mimics the classic Rubinstein equilibrium, where Bob is indifferent between accepting Alice's offer and waiting to make his equilibrium counterproposal, and vice versa. The square in panel a has sides of length rh, and we are looking (in Z-space) where the northwest and southeast vertices of a square lie along the the Pareto frontier. The strict concavity of the Pareto frontier ensures that there can be only one place where this happens; moreover, the point where $z_1 + z_2$ is maximized (over Z) is clearly to be found inside any such square.

However, there are cases, such as the case depicted in panel b, for which the northwest and southeast corners of the square never sit simultaneously on the strictly efficient frontier. When this happens, Bob can offer Alice any point along the intersection of the "flat" portion of the Pareto frontier and the square, and Alice will accept this offer (rather than wait to make her counterproposal). There are many subgame-perfect Nash equilibria. (Indeed, Bob's proposals can shift along this line segment, depending on, for instance, the time hk.) But a generous Bob will offer z^B; that pins down his half of the equilibrium. And, of course, it is still the case that the Nash bargaining solution lies along the Pareto frontier, inside the square.

Indeed, consider the case where, say, $X = \{(x_1, x_2) : x_1 \leq 1, x_2 \leq 1\}$. Alice and Bob can agree on 1 apiece. But, suppose in her turn, for a given h, Alice offers Bob $e^{-rh/2}$. In any subgame perfect-equilibrium, Bob must accept. If he delays, the very best he can conceivably get is 1 after a delay, which is worth only e^{-rh}. So, for this X, there are many subgame-perfect equilibria to the Rubinstein game, where Alice, or Bob, or both of them, are not generous.

Commentary

The Nash bargaining solution is the go-to reduced-form solution to bilateral bargaining in many contextual analyses of which bilateral bargaining is part. Indeed, empirical work in contexts in which parties are involved in many bilateral bargaining situations at once has has employed a solution concept called *Nash in Nash*: This is a full array of bilateral bargains in which each individual bargain is solved using the Nash bargaining solution, where the disagreement point for each individual bargaining problem is what the respective parties would get if all the other bargains were "solved" as per the rest of the array of solutions. Hence, "Nash" refers to both the use of the Nash Bargaining Solution and a sort-of Nash equilibrium in bargains: Each bargain is solved taking the other bargains (as solved) as fixed. (I'll leave it to you to judge this concept.)

There are other bargaining solutions. Perhaps the second most prominent is the Kalai–Smorodinsky solution, which is based on the idea that players should "split" gains over the disagreement point in proportion to their individually ideal bargains. Also, for multi-agent "bargaining problems," where a group of individuals each contribute to the joint pool that is to be split, the standard solution concept is the Shapley value. I won't go further into such things, although references are listed in the Bibliographic Notes.

Bibliographic Notes

The importance of the topic of this chapter—bilateral bargaining—to microeconomics is obvious. Combine this with (at least) my opinion that efforts by theorists so far have not "nailed" the topic, and you have a vast literature, and many talented theorists taking their shot. This has made construction of this chapter a difficult matter of choosing among the many models and papers that are out there. Rubinstein (1982) is the pivotal paper in this literature and must be included—I doubt anyone would quibble with this—but choosing among the rest has not been easy, and I make no claim that my selection is objectively ideal. So, with apologies, here are some references.

The analysis of one-sided bargaining and two-sided bargaining with complete information and simultaneous demands is, for the most part, folk wisdom. As noted, one-sided bargaining with incomplete information is, essentially, a topic covered in various guises in earlier chapters. For one-sided, multi-round bargaining (if Bob doesn't buy at the first price Alice names, she can try a lower price), I have relied on Sobel and Takahashi (1983).

The central paper in this literature—the paper that inspired attempts to use noncooperative game theory to solve bilateral bargaining—is Rubinstein (1982). The first proof I gave for the basic Rubinstein result is from Shaked and Sutton (1984). Stähl (1972) uses dynamic programming and a finite (but long) horizon, showing that as the number of periods approaches infinity, the (unique) equilibrium outcome converges, and what it converges to is the Rubinstein outcome. Rubinstein (1982) proves that this limit is the unique subgame-perfect equilibrium for the infinite-horizon model. Results concerning Rubinstein's dependence on perfectly divisible "money" are provided in Van Damme, Selten, Winter (1990).

The "war of attrition" equilibrium was, to the best of my knowledge, introduced to the economic literature in Kreps and Wilson (1982a). This model included two-sided incomplete information. Hendricks, Weiss, and Wilson (1988) sets out a very general treatment of these models in cases of complete information. The application to bargaining theory reported here is Abreu and Gul (2000). Riley (1980) provides an introduction to the use of "wars of attrition" in biology.

The linear equilibrium for the one-shot, simultaneous bid and ask model with two-sided incomplete information presented on pages 304-5 is taken from Chatterjee and Samuelson (1983). The papers described in the chapter in which strategic delay is used to signal type are Admati and Perry (1987) and Cramton (1992). An excellent collection of early papers concerning bargaining with incomplete information is Linhart, Radner, and Satterthwaite (1992).

The Nash bargaining solution is developed in Nash (1950a). The alternative bargaining solutions mentioned are by Kalai and Smorodinsky (1975) and, for n-player games, the Shapley Value (Shapley 1951; alternatively, see Hart 2016). The connection between the Nash bargaining solution and Rubinstein-style bargaining was originally noted by Ken Binmore. I provided a reference to the (free!) textbook by Osborne and Rubinstein (1990), but an earlier reference is Binmore, Rubinstein, and Wolinsky (1986).

Complementing the large literature of theoretical models of bargaining is a large literature on bargaining "experiments." In the chapter, I cited one paper, Roth and Schoumaker (1983). An excellent survey of the experimental literature is Roth (1995).

Problems

■ 23.1. Problem 21.3 pointed out a difference between the problem of a monopolist facing a (presumably large) collection of potential customers and Alice selling a good to Bob, when it comes to the distribution of "valuations" of the potential buyers (including Bob): If there is correlation in the valuations of buyers (emphasis on plural buyers), and if the monopolist sets prices more than once, with many buyers, she can learn from her sales level at an earlier price about the valuations of potential customers, informing the subsequent price she charges. Alice, facing a single Bob, either sells or doesn't, which is less information than the monopolist receives.

But suppose the monopolist faces a collection of potential customers, whose valuations are i.i.d.. Why does the "difference" pointed to by Problem 21.3 go away?

■ 23.2. Prove Proposition 23.1.

■ 23.3. Consider the basic model of the two-sided demand game, where Alice and Bob simultaneously and independently submit demands x and y, respectively, Alice's payoff is x if $x + y \leq 100$ and 0 otherwise; Bob's payoff is y if $x + y \leq 100$ and 0 otherwise; and both Alice and Bob seek to maximize what their expected payoff (that is, they don't care what the other person gets). (Note that if $x + y < 100$, the difference $100 - x - y$ is lost.) Is there a mixed-strategy equilibrium in which Bob randomizes between submitting $y = 30$ and $y = 60$, both with strictly positive probability? How about where Bob randomizes between submitting $y = 30, 50$, and 60, each with positive probability?

■ 23.4. In the basic model of the two-sided demand game, suppose there are 101 types of Alice, $n = 0, 1, \ldots, 100$, where the payoff to type-n Alice, if the demands are x and y, is -1 if $x < n$ and $x + y \leq 100$; x if $x \geq n$ and $x + y \leq 100$; and 0 if $x + y > 100$. Suppose (all types of) Bob assesses probability q_n that Alice is type n. And suppose there are 101 types m of Bob, where the payoff to type-m Bob, if the demands are x and y, is -1 if $y < m$ and $x + y \leq 100$; y if $y \geq m$ and $x + y \leq 100$; and 0 if $x + y > 100$. Suppose (all types of) Alice assesses probability p_m that Bob is type m. Suppose the types are (statistically) independent.

To interpret these preferences: Type-n Alice would rather there is no deal than that there is a deal in which she gets less than n, and similarly for Bob.

Under what conditions is the following a Nash equilibrium: For $k \in \{0, 1, \ldots, 100\}$ and $\ell = 100 - k$, all types n of Alice with $n \leq k$ demand k; all types of Bob with $m \leq \ell$ demand ℓ; all types n of Alice with $n > k$ demand n; all types of Bob with $m > \ell$ demand m.

What will happen if, say, both Alice and Bob are "greedy," meaning they are each likely to be types that want (say) 60 or more; if they get less than 60, they prefer no agreement? What will happen if, say, both are "reasonable," meaning that each is likely to be a type that is happy to reach agreement as long as they get 40 or more?

■ 23.5. On page 278, near the top, it is suggested that the derivation of subgame-perfect equilibria in the finite-horizon version of the Rubinstein alternating-offer bargaining game can be turned into a proof of Proposition 23.2, the uniqueness of the the Rubinstein subgame-perfect equilibrium for the infinite-horizon game. Provide the proof.

■ 23.6 Concerning parts a and b of Proposition 23.3:

a. Part a describes (for two cases) the outcomes, with Alice making the initial offer. Fill in full strategies, and prove that the strategies you create constitute a subgame-perfect equilibrium.

b. Part b describes, for fixed h, the strategies employed by both Alice and Bob Verify that these constitute a subgame-perfect equilibrium.

■ 23.7. Prove Proposition 23.4. Can you produce an equilibrium that involves some delay to agreement (and which, therefore, is inefficient)?

■ 23.8. In the Alice-and-Bob-negotiate-where-to-dine problem (Section 23.4), if Alice and Bob can propose randomized deals—Alice says, "We'll go French with probability π and Italian with probability $1 - \pi$—I claimed that there would be, Rubinstein style, a unique subgame-perfect Nash equilibrium. I won't ask you to prove uniqueness, but can you find one equilibrium, when $\delta = 0.95$? Note: This is not as straightforward as it may seem. And while you are at it, what would be the Rubinstein-style equilibrium if Alice valued French at 10 and Italian at 5, while Bob valued French at 5 and Italian at 10, again for $\delta = 0.95$? What happens as $\delta \to 1$?

■ 23.9. On page 290, concerning Alice and Bob negotiating over where to go for dinner and, specifically, concerning the third, war-of-attrition equilibrium set in continuous time, I told you that Alice's equilibrium strategy should be to concede at time t or earlier with probability $1 - e^{-5rt/4}$ and that Bob's equilibrium strategy should be to concede at time t or earlier with probability $1 - e^{-7rt/3}$. But how did I know this?

One method is to take the formulae for discrete-time concession probabilities, given on the top of page 288 (the derivation of which follows on pages 288–9), and pass to the limit as $h \to 0$. Do this.

And on pages 295–6 in the second paragraph under bullet point 2, I gave you a "back-of-the-envelope" method applied instead to the Abreu-Gul one-behavioral-type war of attrition. Adapt that argument to the restaurant negotiation.

You only need to demonstrate the technique for, say, Bob. And you should find that the two use essentially the same mathematics.

■ 23.10. For the model of Abreu and Gul (2000) with one behavioral type for Alice, Alice-90, and one behavioral type for Bob, Bob-70, where the probabilities of these behavioral types are 0.2 and 0.1, respectively, and with continuous-time bargaining, suppose Alice's discount rate is 10% per year and Bob's is 15%. (That is, if t is the time to agreement, measured in years, Alice's share of the \$100 is discounted by $e^{-0.1t}$ and Bob's by $e^{-0.15t}$.) What is the equilibrium?

■ 23.11 Suppose in the one-behavioral-type model of Abreu and Gul, Bob's behavioral type is Bob-70, but Alice's behavioral type is more complex: Called Alice-X, this type starts at time $t = 0$ with a demand of 90, but softens her demand as time passes: At time $t > 0$, this type demands $90 - 0.5t$, until time $t = 80$; for $t > 80$, Alice-X demands 50. The prior probability of Bob-70 is 0.1; the prior probability of Alice-X is 0.2, and both Alice-R and Bob-R apply a time discount of 10% per time unit. What happens?

And what happens if, instead of Alice-X demanding $90 - 0.5t$ at time t, she demands $90 - 5t$, up to time $t = 8$, after which she demands 50?

■ 23.12. For the model begun on page 298, where Bob has two behavioral types, Bob-70 and Bob-80, explain why it cannot be an equilibrium for Bob-R to only mimic Bob-70. Explain why, for the formulation given, it cannot be an equilibrium for Bob-R to mimic only Bob-80. But suppose that Bob's two behavior types are Bob-80 and, in place of Bob-70, Bob-60. Is it an equilibrium for Bob-R to only mimic Bob-80 in equilibrium?

■ 23.13. The one-behavioral-type model of Abreu and Gul (2000) is "close" to a war of attrition model found in Kreps and Wilson (1982a).[29] The actors in the Kreps–Wilson model are two firms, call them A and B, fighting for control of a market. There is only room for one of the firms in the market: As long as they are both there, Firm A loses money at a rate of 10 per unit time and Firm B loses money at a rate of 20 per unit time. If one firm or the other concedes, the firm that concedes has 0 profit, while the firm that does not concede is awarded a prize of 1000. (In this model, there is no time discounting of these profits. Note that the 10 figure is a flow loss; the 1000 is a stock.)

The complicating feature is that, for each firm, there is a chance that its CEO is crazy and will never concede. (Both firms have resources from other activites that allow each to sustain a per-time-unit loss in this market of 10 forever, which is what will happen if both CEOs are crazy.) Firm A's CEO is crazy with probability 0.1. Firm B's CEO is crazy with probability 0.2. With the complementary probabilities, each firm will act in a fashion that maximizes its expected net profit from this encounter.

What is the equilibrium?

■ 23.14. Verify that the bid and ask strategies presented on page 303 (attributed to Chatterjee and Samuelson 1983) do in fact constitute an equilibrium.

■ 23.15. Finish the proof of Proposition 23.7, showing that (without loss of generality), Alice's optimal ask strategy against any bid strategy β of Bob can be assumed to satisfy $\alpha(r) \geq r$ and, for $r' > r$, $\alpha(r) \geq \alpha(r')$. You may continue to assume that the support of Bob's possible bids is finite, as is the support of possible values of Alice's reservation values r.

■ 23.16. With regard to the Nash bargaining solution and its connection to Rubinstein's model of alternating-offer bargaining, Figure 23.5 gives three examples of sets in R_+^2, which, together with a disagreement point $(0, 0)$, gives three examples of bargaining problems from $\mathcal{X}^0$. (I've labeled them x, y, and z, to distinguish them from the three parts of the assignment.) For each one:

---

[29]   Noting my prejudice in making this claim, I believe this is the first example of an equilibrium war of attrition in the economics literature.

a. What is the Nash bargaining solution?

b. What is the shape of the corresponding Z set?

c. What can you say about subgame-perfect equilibria of the Rubinstein bargaining
    model, for discount factor e^{-rh}, for reasonably small h? In Definition 23.13,
    I introduced the concept of "generous" proposals. I am *not*, in this part of
    the problem, restricting you to subgame-perfect equilibria in strategies that
    are restricted to "generous" proposals. Hence, uniqueness of subgame-perfect
    equilibria is not guaranteed.

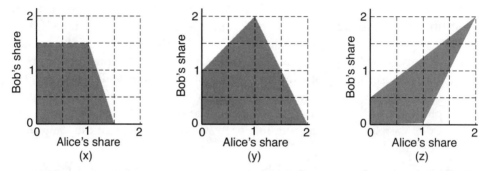

Figure 23.5. Three sets over which Alice and Bob bargain. (The sets are the shaded
regions.)

Chapter Twenty-Four

Auctions

Suppose that Alice has a single, indivisible item that she would like to sell, and she is blessed to have multiple prospective buyers. To encourage competition among the prospective buyers so as to get the best possible price, a common mechanism employed in such circumstances is an *auction*.

To a layperson, the term *auction* most likely conjures up the image of an *English* or *ascending-bid auction*: An auctioneer stands before the prospective buyers, offering for sale a single item, asking, "Is anyone willing to pay $\$X$?" If one of the prospective buyers indicates that he is willing (and $\$X$ is typically set low enough so that an initial bid is proffered with probability approaching one), the auctioneer asks "Do I hear $\$X+100$?" Assuming that a buyer indicates a willingness to pay this, the auctioneer tries $\$X + 200$, and so forth, until the price reaches a level where no buyer is willing to go higher than the last bid, at which time the auctioneer incants, "Going, going, gone! Sold to the gentleman in the pink hat" (or whomever).

But, beyond this layperson's image, auctions take on many forms, and in those forms, they are used in many real-world contexts, from the auction of classic automobiles and artwork (in which the ascending-bid-auction protocol is employed) to competitive bidding processes for the mineral rights on a tract of land (where sealed tenders are used), to multi-unit and share auctions (for instance, for Treasury bills (T-bills) and initial public offerings of equity shares in a corporation).

As a consequence, the theory of auctions and auction design is extensive. And this is a case in which economic theory is closely linked to practice; experts in the theory of auctions advise both governments and private corporations both on the design of auctions and on how to bid. In 2020, my colleagues Paul Milgrom and Robert Wilson were awarded the Nobel Prize in Economics for their contributions to auction theory *and also* its application to real-world auctions.

As has been the case in earlier chapters in this volume, I only present a few of the basics; in the Bibliographic Notes, I suggest three books that, while not comprehensive, can take you considerably beyond this chapter.

Furthermore, I think it is fair to say that the theoretical study of auctions brought the more general subject of *mechanism design* to the front burner of economic theory. In this chapter, I provide some preliminary mechanism-design theory; specifically, the revelation principle is introduced and used to prove revenue equivalence for a class of private-values auctions. But for the most part, mechanism design deserves and gets its own chapter, Chapter 26, and some questions concerning auction design—in particular, the design of optimal auctions—are left for that chapter.

While I an indebted to many colleagues listed in the Preface for advice concerning all chapters in this book, for this chapter, the assistance of Andrzej Skrzypacz was enormous.

24.1. A Typology: Context and Protocol

The wide variety of auction forms and models requires a typology. As in Chapter 25 concerning bargaining, I offer a (more or less) two-dimensional typology: the *context* of the auction and its *protocol*.

Context begins with a description of the nature of the item(s) being auctioned. The simplest cases involve a single indivisible item that will be awarded to at most one of the bidders. This item can be tangible—think of a bottle of vintage wine or a painting by Monet—or it can be a contract to fulfill a "service" for a client, where service here includes the construction of a building or the manufacture of a device, such as a large-turbine generator or an aircraft. (Competitive government procurement is, by itself, the subject of a fairly extensive literature.)

In other cases—think of a T-bill auction—there are from a few to many identical copies of the item up for auction. In so-called share auctions, the "item" at auction is assumed to be perfectly divisible, and bidders are bidding for shares of the item that, in the end, must add up to the whole; think, for instance, of an initial public offering of shares in a corporation. In still other cases, several similar but not identical items are being auctioned, either sequentially or simultaneously; the famous airwave-spectrum auctions are examples, as are mineral-rights auctions in which the government splits mineral rights to a large tract of land (or off-shore continental shelf) into smaller tracts, each of which is "for sale" separately.

Context continues with the bidders: Who are they? How many are there? What values do they attach to the item(s) being auctioned, and what information do they possess about those values? In *private-values contexts*, each bidder knows the dollar value that he attaches to the item, but, typically, is uncertain about how other bidders value the item. (In this chapter, bidders are he, and the seller is she.) In *common-value contexts*, the dollar value of the item is the same for all bidders, and they each have some, but generally incomplete, information about that common value. In many real-life cases, items at auction have both common-value and private-value components. For instance, if a house is being sold by auction, individual bidders look at the house both as a consumption good, for which individual tastes determine private values, and as an investment, which has much more of a common-value component. In mineral-rights auctions, the amount of crude oil or natural gas that can be extracted from a particular tract is largely common to all bidders, but the cost of extracting those resources from a particular tract may be different for different bidders, a component of private-values character.

The other dimension is the *auction protocol*. Begin with the auction of a single indivisible item. Among common protocols are:

- *Sealed-tender, first-price.* Prospective buyers write what they are willing to pay, place their bids in sealed envelopes, and submit them. The envelopes are opened, and the individual who bid the most gets the item for what he bid. Ties are resolved randomly. There may be a reserve price set by the seller,[1]

---

[1] I assume that the seller of the item sets the rules and administers the auction or, at least, I'll write things in this fashion. In real life, there is often an intermediary—an auctioneer—who negotiates with the

which may be known or unknown to the bidders; if the high bid is less than this reserve price, the item goes unsold.[2]

- *Sealed-tender, second-price, also known as a* **Vickrey** *auction.* Same as a sealed-tender, first-price auction, except that the high bidder pays the second highest bid. Or, if the highest bid exceeds a reserve price that has been set, while the second-highest bid is less than this reserve price, the high bidder pays the reserve price.[3]

In both sealed-tender forms, some provision is required in case of a tie for the high bid. We'll assume that, in the event of a tie, all high bidders have an equal probability of being the winner. In the second-price protocol, if there is a tie for the highest bid, the "second-highest bid" is the same as the high bid. Hence, in such circumstances, the winner pays what he bid.

- *Royalty auctions, both first- and second-"price."* Suppose the item at auction is the right to extract crude oil and/or natural gas from a defined tract of land. Rather than have bidders tender dollar bids—"I'll pay $100 million for the mineral rights"—they are asked to bid a royalty amount—"I'll pay 25% of the dollar (market) value of all crude/natural gas that I am able to extract (but I bear all the costs of exploration and extraction)"—and the bidder who offers the highest royalty wins, paying either what he bid (first-price) or the second highest royalty bid.

- *Dutch auction.* The auctioneer begins quoting a high price: "Is anyone willing to pay Z? If no one says they are willing, then "Is anyone willing to pay $Z - 1$?" And so forth, until someone steps up and volunteers to pay the current demand from the auctioneer, paying that amount. (In a fancy, electonic version of this—and in formal models—the demand price declines continuously, until some buyer pushes a button that signifies a willingness to pay the current demand.)

- *English auction,* also known as an *ascending-bid* or *open-outcry* auction. The image of a auctioneer taking bids from assembled bidders is a bit too unstructured for theory, so auction theory "mimics" the strategic nature of an English auction with a so-called *button auction*: Each bidder has a button that, if ever pressed, irrevocably signals that "I'm no longer interested." A "clock" continuously rises,

---

seller concerning the rules (including such things as a reserve price), administers the auction, and provides credibility that the rules will be followed. This credibility derives from the auctioneer's (or auction house's) desire to maintain a reputation for fair-dealing; Chapter 22 provides the theoretical framework.

[2] If the "item" at auction is a contract to fulfill some service, the low bid wins and is paid what it bid for performing the service. I won't mention this again; this chapter concerns the purchase of an item rather than the provision of a service. But all the theory to follow is easily adapted to the context of bidding for a contract.

[3] Reserve prices that are not public knowledge before the auction takes place raise interesting credibility issues. In a first-price auction, the ostensible purpose of a reserve price is to push bidders to bid closer to their value for the object but, after the fact, the seller might wish to represent that her (hidden) reserve price is something below the highest bid, in order to make the sale. In a second-price auction, however, if there is a gap between the highest and second-highest bids, then, after the fact, the seller wishes to represent that the reserve is just below the high bid.

denoting the "current price," and continues to rise until all bidders but one have pressed their button, at which point, the one bidder who has not given up gets the item for the price at which the next-to-last bidder gave up. There are several forms of button auction: Each bidder might see which of their rivals have given up and at which price they gave up. Alternatively, each bidder might see at each point in time how many bidders remain or, what is more to the point, the prices at which their (anonymous) rivals dropped out. Or, perhaps, all an active bidder knows is that at least one of his rivals is still active.

- *All-pay.* Same as the sealed-tender auction, except that everyone pays the amount they bid.

- *Pay-per-bid,* also known as a *bidding fee* or a *penny* auction. Same as an ascending-bid auction, except that every time someone improves on the previous high bid, they are charged some amount, which they are obligated to pay even if they don't win the auction. To keep track of who bids, this form of auction has found a home on the internet.

And then there are protocols for multi-item auctions. Let me give (only) four protocols, for the case of many identical items (T-bills, say) being sold:

- A *"first-price" protocol.* Each bidder provides a "demand" schedule that indicates how much the bidder is willing to pay for one T-bill, how much (on the margin) for the second, and so forth. From this, a market-demand function is computed, and where supply intersects demand, bids that exceed the market-clearing price are fulfilled, with winning bidders paying what they bid.

- A *"market-price" protocol.* Bids as in the first-price protocol are taken, the price at which supply equals demand is computed, but bidders who bid more than this market-clearing price get their "demand" and pay (only) the market-clearing price (say, the highest price bid for an unfulfilled order).

- *The Bourse tranche system.* At least for a while, the French Bourse arranged bids for new stock issues in bands or tranches. After the market-clearing price was determined (by a somewhat mysterious process), orders would be fulfilled based on how close to (but above) the market-clearing price were the bids: for instance, bids that were between the market-clearing price and 5% above that price were completely fulfilled, bids between 5% and 10% above were 80% fulfilled, those between 10% and 15% above were 50% fulfilled, and bids more than 15% above the market-clearing price went unfulfilled.

- A *share auction.* Bidders submit a single amount of money that each is willing to pay. Each bidder pays what he bid. The bids are summed up, and each bidder receives a share of the whole that equals his bid divided by the sum of all the bids.

My point in listing all these variations is to indicate the richness of "auctions." There is a lot of territory for theory to cover, much more than is possible to cover in a single chapter. So, with all this richness, what is covered in this chapter?

For the most part, only indivisible, single-item auctions are discussed; at the end, some simple observations about T-bill-style auctions are provided. Only pure private-values and pure common-value contexts will be studied in detail. Most of the developments concern contexts in which bidders are a priori symmetric. As for protocols, only first- and second-price and button auctions are discussed in detail, although a few remarks about Dutch auctions will be provided.

24.2. Private Values

Private-values contexts are the simplest, so they are discussed first.

Assumptions (and definitions) 24.1.

a. In the (basic) **independent private-values context**, there are N bidders. Bidder i ($i = 1, \ldots, N$) has a private value V_i for the (single) item at auction, which is private information to bidder i. Bidders $j \neq i$ have a common prior over V_i, given by the probability distribution function F_i; moreover, the collection of values $\{V_i; i = 1, \ldots, N\}$ is a fully independent collection of random variables, and is assessed as such by the bidders, so that bidder i, knowing V_i and conditioning on that, assesses the vector $(V_j)_{j \neq i}$ as having the joint distribution function $\prod_{j \neq i} F_j$. Each F_i has compact support that is contained in $[0, \infty)$. [4]

b. In the (basic) **symmetric (independent) private-values context**, the distribution functions F_i are identical; the index i on F is dropped.

c. In the **standard symmetric (independent) private-values context**, the following additional assumptions are maintained: The support of F is the compact subinterval $[\underline{v}, \overline{v}]$. The distribution function F is absolutely continuous, with a density function f that is strictly positive and continuous on $[\underline{v}, \overline{v}]$.

d. In any of the auction protocols discussed, bids must be nonnegative.

e. Bidders are risk neutral, with their values V_i measured in the monetary units used to formulate bids. So, bidder i, given his value V_i, seeks to maximize the probability that he wins the item, times V_i, less the expected amount of money he pays the seller.

The following notation is used:

- Random variables (such as the private values of bidders V_i and later the common value X and signals S_i) are denoted by upper-case letters. Lower-case letters are used for realizations of these random variables and other scalars.

- Bidding functions are denoted by the greek letter β. For the most part, we deal with pure-strategy bidding functions, so a bidding strategy for i is a function β_i from the support of V_i to $[0, \infty)$. Notation $\beta_i(V_i)$ and/or $\beta_i(v_i)$ is used.

---

[4] Assuming that the supports of the F_i are compact isn't necessary and, in fact, will be violated in some examples. But it makes for easier exposition later.

- For the collection of random variables (such as the private values $\{V_i : i = 1, \ldots, N\}$), order statistics are denoted by the calligraphic font. So, for instance, $\mathcal{V}^{(1)}$ denotes the *first order statistic* of the private values; that is,

$$\mathcal{V}^{(1)} := \max_{i=1,\ldots,N} V_i,$$

and $\mathcal{V}^{(2)}$ denotes the second order statistic; that is,

> if ι is an (arbitrarily chosen) index such that $\mathcal{V}^{(1)} = V_\iota$,
>
> then $\mathcal{V}^{(2)} := \max\{V_j : j \neq \iota\}$.

And, for any $i = 1, \ldots, N$, $\mathcal{V}_{\neg i}^{(1)}$ will denote the first order statistic of the "other" values; that is,

$$\mathcal{V}_{\neg i}^{(1)} := \max\{V_j; j = 1, \ldots, N, j \neq i\}.$$

This font is also used for order statistics of bids: $\mathcal{B}^{(1)}$ denotes the highest bid, $\mathcal{B}_{\neg i}^{(1)}$ denotes the highest bid by the bidders other than i, and so forth.

The second-price (or Vickrey) auction

The simplest format and context is the (sealed-tender) second-price auction in the context of private values.[5] It is simple, because there is an "obvious" bidding strategy to employ.

Proposition 24.2. In the private-values context and a second-price-auction protocol, bidding one's private value weakly dominates all other bids.

Proof. Let i be the bidder in question, and suppose his private value (known to him) is $V_i = v_i$ His payoff is determined by his own bid b_i and the largest bid from all other bidders, or $\mathcal{B}_{\neg i}^{(1)} = \max\{b_j; j \neq i\}$, where b_j is the bid of j, as follows:

$$i\text{'s payoff is } \begin{cases} v_i - \mathcal{B}_{\neg i}^{(1)}, & \text{if } \mathcal{B}_{\neg i}^{(1)} < b_i \\ 0, & \text{if } \mathcal{B}_{\neg i}^{(1)} \geq b_i. \end{cases}$$

(Note why this formula is correct for the case $\mathcal{B}_{\neg i}^{(1)} = b_i$.) So suppose i considers bidding some b different from v_i:

- If $b > v_i$, the two bids give the same outcome if $\mathcal{B}_{\neg i}^{(1)} \leq v_i$ or if $\mathcal{B}_{\neg i}^{(1)} \geq b$, but for $\mathcal{B}_{\neg i}^{(1)} \in (v_i, b)$, bidding v_i is strictly better: i's payoff is 0 if he bids v_i and is strictly negative if he bids b.[6]

- And if $b < v_i$, then bidding b_i does just as well as bidding b if $\mathcal{B}_{\neg i}^{(1)} \leq b$ or if $\mathcal{B}_{\neg i}^{(1)} \geq v_i$, while for $\mathcal{B}_{\neg i}^{(1)} \in (b, v_i)$, bidding v_i does strictly better: If $\mathcal{B}_{\neg i}^{(1)} \in (b, v_i)$,

---

[5] This form of auction is known as a *Vickrey* auction, following Vickrey (1961). But its use predates Vickrey's seminal article; Moldovanu and Tietzel (1998) report that it was used by Goethe in 1797 to sell a manuscript.

[6] In this case and the next, think your way through the case where $\mathcal{B}_{\neg i}^{(1)} = b$.

bidding v_i wins the auction and gives a strictly positive payoff, while bidding b gives zero payoff. ∎

Proposition 24.3. *With private values and the second-price protocol:*

a. *Each bidder bidding his private value is a Nash equilibrium in which (i) the item is won by (one of) the bidder(s) with the highest private value and (ii) the seller's revenue is the second-highest personal value, or $\mathcal{V}^{(2)}$.*

b. *In the symmetric private-values context, every (pure) symmetric equilibrium, in which each bidder bids $\beta(V_i)$ given his personal value V_i for some function β, has the property that the set $\{V_i : \beta(V_i) = V_i\}$ has F-probability one. That is, up to a set of values with prior probability 0, each bidder is bidding his private value.*

c. *There are many Nash equilibria, including (for each i) an equilibrium in which i's payoff is V_i and the payoffs for all the $j \neq i$ are zero.*

d. *In the spirit of trembling-hand perfection, call a Nash equilibrium **tremble-proof** if, for some strictly positive density function ϕ, for each player i, and for each personal value v_i in the support of his personal values, what he is bidding conditional on $V_i = v_i$ is a best response to the strategies of the other bidders **and also** is a best response to the following: For small $\epsilon > 0$, every other bidder j bids his equilibrium strategy with probability $1 - \epsilon$, and bids according to the distribution function given by ϕ with (independent) probability ϵ. In other words, i's bid must be a best response if every other bidder "trembles" a bit, where trembling means bidding according to ϕ (independently of other bidders j'). Then the only tremble-proof Nash equilibrium is for each bidder to bid his value; that is, the Nash equilibrium of part a. (Since this is only "in the spirit" of trembling-hand perfection, the made-up term **tremble-proof** is employed.)*

Part a is straightforward, given Proposition 24.2. I leave to you the proof of the rest of the proposition as Problem 24.1, or see its solution in the *Online Supplement*.

In view of these two propositions, is it reasonable to say that, in the second-price auction with private values, bidding one's own value is the obvious thing to do? For sophisticated bidders, it may be, but the experimental evidence on this point is somewhat mixed; see, for instance, the discussion in Li (2017).

The first-price auction: Preliminaries

The first-price auction is not nearly so simple.

Suppose Bob attaches private value V_{Bob} to the item at auction and bids b_{Bob}. If he wins the auction, his payoff will be $V_{\text{Bob}} - b_{\text{Bob}}$. But he only wins if $b_{\text{Bob}} > \mathcal{B}^{(1)}_{\neg\text{Bob}}$, where $\mathcal{B}^{(1)}_{\neg\text{Bob}}$ is the highest bid from other bidders. If he ties for the high bid, he gets $V_{\text{Bob}} - b_{\text{Bob}}$ with probability $1/(N^{(1)}_{\neg\text{Bob}}(b_{\text{Bob}}) + 1)$, where $N^{(1)}_{\neg\text{Bob}}(b_{\text{Bob}})$ is the number of bidders who match his (high) bid.[7] Therefore, from Bob's point of view, when computing his "optimal" bid (scare quotes to be explained momentarily), he

---

[7] The meaning of $N^{(1)}_{\neg\text{Bob}}(b_{\text{Bob}})$ is clear, but it is useful to explain the formalism here. The bidding strategies of Bob's bidding opponents are all fixed; think of them as given as part of an equilibrium analysis. Hence, from Bob's perspective, $\mathcal{B}^{(1)}_{\neg\text{Bob}}$ and $N^{(1)}_{\neg\text{Bob}}(b_{\text{Bob}})$ are random variables. This is

is concerned with the joint distribution of $(\mathcal{B}^{(1)}_{\neg\text{Bob}}, N^{(1)}_{\neg\text{Bob}}(b_{\text{Bob}}))$, where $\mathcal{B}^{(1)}_{\neg\text{Bob}}$ is the highest other bid, and $N^{(1)}_{\neg\text{Bob}}(b_{\text{Bob}})$ is the number of other bidders bidding b_{Bob}. Specifically, Bob's expected payoff if he bids b_{Bob} is the expectation of

$$(V_{\text{Bob}} - b_{\text{Bob}})\left[\mathbf{1}_{\{\mathcal{B}^{(1)}_{\neg\text{Bob}}=b_{\text{Bob}}\}}\frac{1}{N^{(1)}_{\neg\text{Bob}}(b_{\text{Bob}}) + 1} + \mathbf{1}_{\{\mathcal{B}^{(1)}_{\neg\text{Bob}}<b_{\text{Bob}}\}}\right],$$

where $\mathbf{1}_{\{\cdot\}}$ is the usual indicator function; that is, $\mathbf{1}_{\{\cdot\}} = 1$ if the event in the subscript is true and equals zero otherwise.

Why scare quotes around "optimal?" Suppose Bob's only bidding rival is Carol, $V_{\text{Bob}} = 10$, and Bob's assessment is that Carol is certain to bid 5. By bidding 5, Bob wins the prize half the time, for an expected payoff of 2.5. By bidding $5 + \epsilon$ for $\epsilon > 0$, Bob's expected payoff is $5 - \epsilon$. (Bidding less than 5 gives him payoff 0.) So Bob has no optimal bid.

The problem here is that Bob's outcome function is not continuous in his bid. If we assume that Bob will never bid more than his private value, then the set of bids he considers given V_{Bob} is the compact set $[0, V_{\text{Bob}}]$. If Bob's expected payoff function (with his bid b_{Bob} being the variable) were upper semi-continuous, this would ensure the existence of a solution to his problem (Proposition A2.26 in Appendix 2, Volume I). And if his outcome function were itself upper semi-continuous in b_{Bob}, then his expected payoff would also be upper semi-continuous. But because he only wins the prize with probability $1/(N^{(1)}_{\neg\text{Bob}}(b_{\text{Bob}}) + 1)$ if $b_{\text{Bob}} = \mathcal{B}^{(1)}_{\neg\text{Bob}}$, but he wins with probability 1 if $b_{\text{Bob}} > \mathcal{B}^{(1)}_{\neg\text{Bob}}$, the outcome function isn't upper semi-continuous.[8]

This example of nonexistence of an optimal bid begins with Bob holding a somewhat arbitrary assessment of how Carol bids. One might hope that the problem disappears if Bob (and other bidders) are holding *equilibrium* assessments. But such hopes are futile: This "wrong sort of discontinuity" can mean the nonexistence of a Nash equilibrium in first-price auctions. Examples are easy to find if we look only for pure-strategy equilibria or we use the fact that bids can't be negative. But general examples of nonexistence of equilibria are somewhat complex. See Problem 24.4 for more on this.

Are these serious problems? As a practical matter, I don't think so. If bids must be, say, in multiples of a penny, if valuations are as well, and if valuations are drawn from a finite set, then general existence results guarantee the existence of a Nash equilibrium. (What are the equilibria, if bids must be in multiples of a penny, in the case where Bob's and Carol's values are certain and unequal?)

---

straightforward for $\mathcal{B}^{(1)}_{\neg\text{Bob}}$, based on the independence assumption about the V_i and the assumption of independence of strategies that is implicit in a Nash-style analysis. (That is to say, neither V_{Bob} nor Bob's choice of b_{Bob} affects the probability distribution of $\mathcal{B}^{(1)}_{\neg\text{Bob}}$). But Bob's choice of b_{Bob} does change the random variable "the number of other bidders who tie Bob's bid b_{Bob}" Hence, when writing this random variable, it is formally necessary to acknowledge the dependence on b_{Bob}.

[8]　This issue didn't come up in Chapter 23, for instance, in the context of simultaneous ask/bid bargaining. Why not? See Problem 24.3.

Or, alternatively, one looks for sufficient conditions that guarantee the existence of equilibria. If valuations (and conditional distributions of others' valuations given one's own valuation) have absolutely continuous distribution functions (with well-behaved density functions), these problems disappear. I won't go into details but point you to the lovely paper by Reny and Zamir (2004). And even if the distribution functions have atoms, equilibria can be constructed in some cases (again, see Problem 24.4). This is the subject of work that is ongoing as I write this paragraph, so references may be out of date by the time you read it. However, if you are interested, see Reny (2021) and the references provided there.

The first-price auction in the standard symmetric, private-values auction context

Proposition 24.4. *In the standard symmetric, private-values context, define*

$$\beta^{\mathrm{PVF}}(v) := \mathbf{E}\big[\mathcal{V}_{\neg i}^{(1)}\big|\mathcal{V}_{\neg i}^{(1)} < V_i = v\big] \ \text{for } v \in (\underline{v}, \overline{v}], \tag{24.1}$$

where $\mathbf{E}[\cdot|\cdot]$ *denotes conditional expectation. It is a (symmetric) Nash equilibrium in the first-price auction for each bidder to bid according to* β^{PVF}. [9]

Proof. Note first that β^{PVF} is defined as a conditional expectation, conditioning on an event of positive probability. But it is not defined for $v = \underline{v}$; the conditioning event has prior probability zero. Since this event has prior probability zero, leaving $\beta^{\mathrm{PVF}}(v)$ undefined doesn't cause problems. But, because $\beta^{\mathrm{PVF}}(v)$ is the conditional expectation of $\mathcal{V}_{\neg i}^{(1)}$ on an event for which $\underline{v} \leq \mathcal{V}_{\neg i}^{(1)} < v$, and $\mathcal{V}_{\neg i}^{(1)} > \underline{v}$ with probability 1 (in the standard model), this conditional expectation satisfies $\underline{v} < \beta^{\mathrm{PVF}}(v) < v$, and therefore, $\lim_{v \searrow \underline{v}} \beta^{\mathrm{PVF}}(v) = \underline{v}$. So, to tie things down, simply define $\beta^{\mathrm{PVF}}(\underline{v}) = \underline{v}$.

As you probably know from your econometrics course, when the assumption is that a collection of random variables—in this case, the collection $\{V_i; i \in N\}$—is a collection of independent random variables, it means that any subset is independent of the complementary subset. Hence, any function of a subset is independent of any function of the complementary subset. And therefore, $\mathcal{V}_{\neg i}^{(1)}$ is independent of V_i. Moreover, we have that

$$G(v) := \mathbf{P}(\mathcal{V}_{\neg i}^{(1)} \leq v) = \prod_{j \neq i} \mathbf{P}(V_j \leq V_i = v) = F(v)^{N-1},$$

where $\mathbf{P}$ denotes Probability. Write $g(v)$ for the density function corresponding to G; that is, $g(v) = (N-1)F(v)^{N-2}f(v)$.

Therefore, for $v \in (\underline{v}, \overline{v}]$,

$$\beta^{\mathrm{PVF}}(v) = \mathbf{E}\big[\mathcal{V}_{\neg i}^{(1)}\big|\mathcal{V}_{\neg i}^{(1)} < V_i = v\big] = \frac{1}{G(v)}\int_{\underline{v}}^{v} ug(u)\mathrm{d}u = v - \int_{\underline{v}}^{v} \frac{G(u)}{G(v)}\mathrm{d}u < v, \tag{24.2}$$

---

[9] The superscript PVF is an abbreviation of *Private Values First-price.*

where the final equality uses integration by parts for $vG(v)$. (The use of integration by parts occurs frequently. Please verify my math at least one time.) From (24.2), or arguing based on first principles, it is clear that $v \to \beta^{\mathrm{PVF}}(v)$ is a continuous and strictly increasing function of $v \in (\underline{v}, \overline{v}]$, which extends (continuously) to $[\underline{v}, \overline{v}]$, once we set $\beta^{\mathrm{PVF}}(\underline{v}) = \underline{v}$. Write $\underline{b} := \beta^{\mathrm{PVF}}(\underline{v}) = \underline{v}$ and $\overline{b} := \beta^{\mathrm{PVF}}(\overline{v}) < \overline{v}$, and write γ^{PVF} for the inverse function of β^{PVF}, which is immediately strictly increasing and continuous on $[\underline{b}, \overline{b}]$.

For the remainder of the proof, maintain the assumption that all bidders except for i bid according to the function β^{PVF}. To show that everyone bidding according to β^{PVF} is a Nash equilibrium, it suffices to show that, fixing i's valuation of the item at v_i, i can do no better than to bid $\beta^{\mathrm{PVF}}(v_i)$.

First consider bidding less than or equal to $\underline{b}$. As long as all other bidders are using β^{PVF}, bidding $\underline{b}$ or less gives probability 0 of winning, for a payoff of 0. Since bidding $\beta^{\mathrm{PVF}}(v_i)$ means bidding less than $V_i = v_i$, this bid cannot do worse than a payoff of zero (and, in fact, if $V_i > \underline{v}$, it gives a positive probability of winning, since there is positive probability that $V_i = \mathcal{V}^{(1)}$). So bidding less or equal to $\underline{v}$ is not a profitable deviation. And bidding $\overline{b}$ is superior to any larger bid: Each guarantees that the bidder will win the auction; there is zero probability that $\mathcal{V}_{\neg i}^{(1)} = \overline{v}$, hence zero probability that the highest other bid is $\overline{b}$. But, higher bids mean paying more. So we can limit our attention to bids $\hat{b} \in (\underline{b}, \overline{b}]$. And, by the intermediate-value theorem and properties of β, for every such $\hat{b}$ there exists a $\hat{v}$ such that $\hat{b} = \beta^{\mathrm{PVF}}(\hat{v})$.

Fix $\hat{b} \neq \beta^{\mathrm{PVF}}(v_i)$, $\hat{b} \in (\underline{b}, \overline{b}]$, and let $\hat{v} = \gamma^{\mathrm{PVF}}(\hat{b})$. If i bids $\hat{b}$, i wins the item if $\hat{b} > \beta^{\mathrm{PVF}}(\mathcal{V}_{\neg i}^{(1)})$. This is the event $\{\hat{v} = \gamma^{\mathrm{PVF}}(\hat{b}) > \gamma^{\mathrm{PVF}}(\beta^{\mathrm{PVF}}(\mathcal{V}_{\neg i}^{(1)})) = \mathcal{V}_{\neg i}^{(1)}\}$, which has probability $G(\hat{v})$.[10] Hence, bidding $\hat{b}$ has expected value $(v_i - \hat{b})G(\hat{v})$. Similarly, bidding $\beta^{\mathrm{PVF}}(v_i)$ has expected value $(v_i - \beta^{\mathrm{PVF}}(v_i))G(v_i)$. Abbreviating $\beta^{\mathrm{PVF}}(v_i)$ as b_i, the difference in expected values is

$$
\begin{aligned}
(v_i - \hat{b})G(\hat{v}) - (v_i - b_i)G(v_i) &= v_i[G(\hat{v}) - G(v_i)] + b_i G(v_i) - \hat{b}G(\hat{v}) \\
&= v_i[G(\hat{v}) - G(v_i)] + \beta^{\mathrm{PVF}}(v_i)G(v_i) - \beta^{\mathrm{PVF}}(\hat{v})G(\hat{v}) \\
&= v_i[G(\hat{v}) - G(v_i)] + \left(v_i - \int_0^{v_i} \frac{G(u)}{G(v_i)}\mathrm{d}u\right)G(v_i) - \left(\hat{v} - \int_0^{\hat{v}} \frac{G(u)}{G(\hat{v})}\mathrm{d}u\right)G(\hat{v}) \\
&= v_i[G(\hat{v}) - G(v_i)] + v_i G(v_i) - \int_0^{v_i} G(u)\mathrm{d}u - \hat{v}G(\hat{v}) + \int_0^{\hat{v}} G(u)\mathrm{d}u \\
&= G(\hat{v})[v_i - \hat{v}] - \int_{\hat{v}}^{v_i} G(u)\mathrm{d}u \\
&= G(\hat{v})\int_{\hat{v}}^{v_i} 1\mathrm{d}u - \int_{\hat{v}}^{v_i} G(u)\mathrm{d}u = \int_{\hat{v}}^{v_i} \big[G(\hat{v}) - G(u)\big]\mathrm{d}u.
\end{aligned}
$$

If $v_i > \hat{v}$, the upper limit of the integral is larger than the lower limit, while the integrand is everywhere negative, so the integral is negative. And, if $v_i < \hat{v}$, the

---

[10]   There is zero probability of a tie; this is the last time I'll mention this.

integral is "backwards," with the upper limit less than the lower limit, while the integrand is everywhere positive. So, again, the integral is negative.

Bidding anything other than $\beta^{\mathrm{PVF}}(v_i)$ (when $V_i = v_i$) does worse in expectation than bidding $\beta^{\mathrm{PVF}}(v_i)$.   ∎

Revenue equivalence

The proof of Proposition 24.4 does not convey any intuition about why the bidding function $\beta^{\mathrm{PVF}}(v) = \mathbf{E}\big[\mathcal{V}_{\neg i}^{(1)} \,\big|\, \mathcal{V}_{\neg i}^{(1)} < V_i = v\big]$ works. It does, however, provide a fact that may at first seem a curiosity (and that provides some intuition, eventually): In the second-price auction, the expectation of the winning bid is $\mathbf{E}\big[\mathcal{V}^{(2)}\big]$. Think of breaking this integral into pieces:

- The events $\{\mathcal{V}^{(1)} = V_i\}$ for $i = 1, \dots, N$ nearly partition the full space of possibilities. I say "nearly," because there is overlap when more than one bidder's V_i is tied for highest. But the probability of that is zero, and so it is true that

$$\mathbf{E}\big[\mathcal{V}^{(2)}\big] = \sum_{i=1}^{N} \mathbf{E}\big[\mathcal{V}^{(2)} \,;\, V_i = \mathcal{V}^{(1)}\big],$$

where $\mathbf{E}[X; B]$ means the integral of X over the event B; we can express this alternatively as the expectation of $X \cdot \mathbf{1}_B$, where $\mathbf{1}_B$ is the indicator function of the event B, or as the conditional expectation of X given B multiplied by the probability of B.

- And, on the event $V_i = \mathcal{V}^{(1)}$, $\mathcal{V}^{(2)} = \mathcal{V}_{\neg i}^{(1)}$. Hence we can write

$$\mathbf{E}\big[\mathcal{V}^{(2)}\big] = \sum_{i=1}^{N} \mathbf{E}\big[\mathcal{V}_{\neg i}^{(1)} \,;\, V_i = \mathcal{V}^{(1)}\big].$$

- But from this starting point,

$$\mathbf{E}\big[\mathcal{V}^{(2)}\big] = \sum_{i=1}^{N} \mathbf{E}\big[\mathcal{V}_{\neg i}^{(1)} ; V_i = \mathcal{V}^{(1)}\big] = \sum_{i=1}^{N} \mathbf{E}\big[\mathcal{V}_{\neg i}^{(1)} \big| V_i > \mathcal{V}_{\neg i}^{(1)}\big] \mathbf{P}\big(\{V_i > \mathcal{V}_{\neg i}^{(1)}\}\big)$$

$$= \sum_{i=1}^{N} \beta^{\mathrm{PVF}}(V_i) \mathbf{P}\big(\{V_i > \mathcal{V}_{\neg i}^{(1)}\}\big) = \sum_{i=1}^{N} \beta^{\mathrm{PVF}}(V_i) \mathbf{P}\big(\{V_i = \mathcal{V}^{(1)}\}\big),$$

which, according to Proposition 24.4, is the overall expectation of the winning bid in the first-price auction. Moreover, suppose i's private value is V_i. In the second-price auction, i wins if $V_i = \mathcal{V}^{(1)}$ and pays $\mathcal{V}^{(2)}$ in that case. So i's expected payment is $\mathbf{E}\big[\mathcal{V}^{(2)} \,;\, V_i = \mathcal{V}^{(1)}\big]$, which is exactly his expected payment in the first-price-auction equilibrium. Restating this gives the following corollary.

Corollary 24.5. *In the standard symmetric, private-values context, the expectation of the winning bid—the revenue to the seller of the item—in the first- and second-price auctions are identical, as are the identity of the winner and the expected amount any bidder i pays to the seller conditional on V_i. (To be fastidious: This is so assuming that, in the first-price auction, bidders all use β^{PVF}, and in the second price auction, each bidder bids his private value, both of which are equilibrium bids in their respective auction protocols.)*

Corollary 24.5 is a "special case" of what is called *revenue equivalence*. For the general result, we require some definitions.

To set the stage, fix a standard symmetric, private-values context, with bidders $i \in I$, values V_i that are independently and identically distributed (i.i.d.) with distribution function F, and where each bidder knows his own value and nothing more.

Definitions 24.6.

a. *For this context, let Z be the set of **social outcomes** $\{1, \ldots, N\} \times R^N$, where $z = (i^*, p_1, \ldots, p_I) \in \{1, \ldots, N\} \times R^I$ has the interpretation: The item is given to bidder i^*, and bidder $i \in I$ pays p_i to the seller. Write $z = (z_0, (z_i)_{i \in I})$, that is, z_0 is the component of z that indicates which bidder gets the item, and z_i indicates how much i pays the seller.*

b. *A general **mechanism** in this context consists of:*
   i. *For each player i, a set of actions S_i from which i must choose; and*
   ii. *a social-outcome function $\xi : \prod_{i=1, \ldots, N} S_i \to Z$.*

This notion of a mechanism is a generalization of an auction protocol. We assemble the bidders and have each take an action, where i must choose from S_i; for instance, in both the first- and second-price auctions, s_i is a bid. Then the social-outcome function ξ maps the actions taken into a social outcome, determining which bidder gets the item and how much each bidder must pay the seller. So, for instance, in the first-price auction protocol/mechanism, the winner of the item is the high bidder, who pays his bid; the other bidders pay nothing.

If you combine a general mechanism with the other parts of the fixed context, you get a strategic-form game of incomplete information:

- So that the notation doesn't become overwhelming, write $\mathcal{N}$ for $\{1, \ldots, N\}$—that is, $\mathcal{N}$ is the set of the bidders—and write V for the vector of values $(V_i)_{i \in \mathcal{N}}$.

- The strategy space for bidder i is the set $\Sigma_i := S_i^{[\underline{v}, \overline{v}]}$. It may be clearer to write that a strategy σ_i for i is a function $\sigma_i : [\underline{v}, \overline{v}] \to S_i$, where $\sigma_i(v_i)$ is the action that i will take (in the mechanism) if his realized valuation for the item V_i is v_i.

- The expected payoff to j at the strategy profile $(\sigma_i)_{i \in \mathcal{N}}$ is computed as follows: Temporarily fix the strategy profile. For $j \in \mathcal{N}$, let

$$\Lambda_j = \mathbf{E}\big\{V_j; \big[\xi\big((\sigma_i(V_i))_{i \in \mathcal{N}}\big)\big]_0 = j\big\} \quad \text{and} \quad \Pi_j = \mathbf{E}\big[[\xi\big((\sigma_i(V_i))_{i \in \mathcal{N}}\big)]_j\big].$$

Then, i's expected payoff at $(\sigma_i)_{i \in \mathcal{N}}$ is $\Lambda_j - \Pi_j$.

- This last bullet point is clearer and, in terms of analysis, easier to comprehend, if we describe the decision problem facing a bidder i in "behavioral" terms. Suppose i has a hypothesis about the strategies of other players; write $\sigma_{\neg i}$ for the vector of these strategies. Write $\xi((s_i, \sigma_{\neg i}(V_{\neg i})))$ for the social outcome z that results if i takes action s_i, while the vector of actions taken by by the other bidders are given by their strategies $\sigma_{\neg i}$ evaluated at their respective values, given by $V_{\neg i}$. Then, player i, given that his value is V_i, wishes to choose his action s_i to maximize

$$V_i \times \mathbf{P}\left(\left[\xi((s_i, \sigma_{\neg i}(V_{\neg i})))\right]_0 = i \;\middle|\; V_i \right) - \mathbf{E}\left[\left[\xi((s_i, \sigma_{\neg i}(V_{\neg i})))\right]_i \;\middle|\; V_i \right].$$

This last expression is probably comprehensible but, to explain, just in case: The first term is the value i attaches to the item, V_i, times the probability that, if i chooses s_i, i is awarded the item, where the random element is the vector $V_{\neg i}$ of the other bidders' values. And the second term is the expected amount that i must pay, if he chooses s_i. Solving this for every V_i provides us with i's best strategic response to $\sigma_{\neg i}$.

Note that, for the term in the last display, I write both the probability and the expectation as conditional on V_i. This is more general than necessary in the current context, because it is assumed that the private values are independent. Hence, the distribution of the vector $V_{\neg i}$ is independent of the particular value of V_i.

The point here is that, for the fixed context, we are looking at a very general mechanism for deciding which bidder gets the item and how much each bidder pays the seller. And the punchline is the following proposition.

Proposition 24.7. Revenue equivalence. *For a fixed standard, symmetric private-values context, and for any mechanism at all, suppose that the strategy profile $(\sigma_i^*)_{i \in I}$ is a symmetric Nash equilibrium of the corresponding game of incomplete information. Suppose that this Nash equilibrium results in the item going to the bidder with the highest valuation. And suppose that the conditional Nash-equilibrium expected payoff to a bidder whose value $V_i = \underline{v}$ is 0.*[11] *Then, conditional on V_i, the conditional expected payoff for bidder i is*

$$\left(V_i - \mathbf{E}\left[\mathcal{V}_{\neg i}^{(1)} \middle| \mathcal{V}_{\neg i}^{(1)} < V_i\right]\right)\mathbf{P}\left(V_i > \mathcal{V}_{\neg i}^{(1)}\right),$$

bidder i's conditional expected payment to the seller of the item is

$$\mathbf{E}\left[\mathcal{V}_{\neg i}^{(1)} \middle| \mathcal{V}_{\neg i}^{(1)} < V_i\right]\mathbf{P}\left(V_i > \mathcal{V}_{\neg i}^{(1)}\right),$$

---

[11] I try to be careful to say "conditional (expected) payoff" when discussing the expected payoff for a bidder, conditional on various possible values of V_i. This "conditional payoff" or "conditional expected payoff" is distinguished from the bidder's overall expected payoff, which would be computed by integrating over all possible values of the bidder's own V_i, and the bidder's payoff, which is what happens for the bidder given a complete vector V of values. In other words, the conditional (expected) payoff integrates over the $V_{\neg i}$, for a fixed V_i.

and the (overall) expected revenue that the seller of the item receives is $E[\mathcal{V}^{(2)}]$.

This result generalizes Corollary 24.5. In the first-price auction with the symmetric equilibrium we found, and in the second-price auction in which the bidders all bid their values, both conditions hold: The item is won by the high-valuation bidder, and a bidder with $V_i = \underline{v}$ has no chance of winning the item but therefore can expect to pay nothing. So, for those two mechanisms—the first-price and second-price auction protocols being mechanisms—the corresponding games and (the specific) equilibria generate identical expected payments by each bidder, conditional on the bidder's own value, and these (specific) equilibria generate identical expected sales revenue for the seller.

But the proposition says more. Those are only two mechanisms. There are many others we could consider. For instance, there is the all-pay auction, in which each bidder submits a bid, the item goes to whichever bidder's bid is highest, and *every bidder pays his bid, whether he wins the item or not.* In a symmetric Nash equilibrium for this all-pay protocol in which bids are a strictly increasing function of the bidder's value, the item will go to the bidder with the high valuation. If, in addition, we have a symmetric equilibrium for this mechanism in which a bidder with $V_i = \underline{v}$ bids 0, the proposition applies; we know how much the conditional expected payment by each bidder is, conditional on his own value. Which, not to give too broad a hint, gives a very good candidate for an equilibrium in the all-pay auction; see Problem 24.5.

However, the proposition does not establish the existence of a suitable symmetric equilibrium. Proposition 24.7 doesn't replace Propositions 24.3(a) or 24.4. It (only) characterizes what the equilibrium must entail, if indeed it is an equilibrium.

That said, suppose you set out to find a mechanism and a symmetric equilibrium for the mechanism that (1) ensures the item goes to the high valuation bidder and (2) gives a conditional payoff of 0 to a bidder with $V_i = \underline{v}$, and that, at the same time, provides more sales revenue for the seller. Proposition 24.7 tells you not to bother. For any mechanism, no matter how cleverly designed, and any symmetric equilibrium of the corresponding game, conditions 1 and 2 lock down the seller's expected revenue, as well as the conditional payoffs and payments of the bidders.

Proving Proposition 24.7: The revelation principle and the envelope theorem

The proof of Proposition 24.7 requires two tools: the revelation principle and the envelope theorem or, more precisely, the Nash-equilibrium version of the revelation principle and the integrated form of the envelope theorem. These are discussed in detail in Appendices 16 and 17, respectively. I don't want to repeat the analysis provided in the two appendices, although some repetition is necessary for the exposition here. (I go pretty fast, so if this is new to you, consult the two Appendices.)

The starting point is that, for a general mechanism and a fixed standard, symmetric private-values context, we have a symmetric Nash equilibrium in which (1) the item goes to the high valuation bidder, and (2) gives a conditional payoff of 0 to a bidder with $V_i = \underline{v}$. Then there are three steps to the proof.

Step 1. Invoke the Nash-equilibrium revelation principle

From Appendix 16:

Proposition A16.5. *Fix a social-choice problem as per Definition A16.1. Fix an arbitrary mechanism* $(\{S_n; n \in \mathcal{N}\}, \xi)$. *For the associated game of incomplete information (created from the social-choice problem and the mechanism), we have the following.*

a. ***The Nash-equilibrium revelation principle.*** *Consider any pure-strategy profile* $\sigma^* = (\sigma_1^*, \ldots, \sigma_N^*)$ *that is a Nash equilibrium for the game of incomplete information created by this mechanism. There is a corresponding direct-revelation mechanism ϕ for which truth telling is a Nash equilibrium, which gives the same contingent outcome as obtains in the original Nash equilibrium.*

There is also a part b, but we don't need it here. But we must translate some of this into the current context:

- The "social-choice" problem at issue here is simply the problem of assigning the item to one of the bidders and collecting revenues for the seller of the object as we do so.

- A *direct-revelation mechanism* is a particular sort of general mechanism: The action sets S_i for the players are the ranges of their information, in this case the range $[\underline{v}, \overline{v}]$ of each V_i. The players each choose a message $\hat{v}_i$ to send to a central authority, which then decides on the basis of these reports $(\hat{v}_i)_{i \in I}$ which bidder gets the item and how much each bidder must pay.

- In the corresponding game of incomplete information, a strategy σ_i for player i is a contingent plan for sending a message $\hat{v}_i$ to the central authority, contingent on his true value V_i.

- And, the strategy under which $\hat{v}_i = V_i$—i tells the truth about his value V_i—is the truth-telling strategy.

What Proposition A16.5(a) is telling us, then, is that any outcome of a Nash equilibrium of a general mechanism can be achieved as a Nash-equilibrium outcome of an appropriately defined direct-revelation game and, moreover, the equilibrium of the direct-revelation game involves truth-telling. (This may seem magical, but in fact it is entirely straightforward. See Appendix 16.) Hence, there is some direct-revelation game and a symmetric equilibrium for that game for which truth telling is a Nash equilibrium, the outcome of which is identical to our initial symmetric Nash equilibrium, V vector by V vector. And, therefore, since (1) and (2) hold for the original equilibrium, they hold here as well.

This direct-revelation game has three parts: The first, already described, is the space of messages that players must send to the central authority. The second and third describe what the central authority does with the vector of messages $(\hat{v}_i)_{i \in I}$ that it receives: It must decide on which bidder gets the item, and it must decide how much each bidder pays to the seller.

The assignment-of-the-item decision is fixed by the constraint that in equilibrium, the high-value bidder gets the object. In equilibrium, the submission of bidder i is $\hat{v}_i = V_i$—this is truth telling—and so, given a vector of reports $(\hat{v}_i)_{i \in I}$ from the bidders, the item goes to the bidder who submitted the highest report.

The what-does-a-bidder-pay part of the mechanism is not (yet) nailed down. We do know that, if a bidder submits $\hat{v}_i = \underline{v}$, he can expect not to win the item, so (on average) he won't have to pay anything. But, otherwise, the role of the payment part of the mechanism is constrained by the general requirement that it induces truth telling. In other words, if we look at the decision problem facing bidder i, under the hypothesis that the other bidders are all telling the truth, we have the following:

- The probability that i wins the item if he submits $\hat{v}_i$ is the probability that $\hat{v}_i > \mathcal{V}_{\neg i}^{(1)}$, which is $G(\hat{v}_i)$. (Recall that G denotes the distribution function of $\mathcal{V}_{\neg i}^{(1)}$.)

- So, writing $\pi_i(\hat{v}_i)$ for the expected amount that i must pay under the mechanism, if he submits $\hat{v}_i$ and under the hypothesis that all the other bidders are telling the truth, his objective function, given V_i, is to pick $\hat{v}_i$ to maximize

$$V_i\, G(\hat{v}_i) - \pi_i(\hat{v}_i).$$

  It is worth pointing out here that I can write $\pi_i(\hat{v}_i)$ as unconditional on V_i because of the independence assumption on the components of V.

- And because truth telling is an equilibrium, we know that

$$V_i\, G(V_i) - \pi_i(V_i) = \sup_{\hat{v}_i} \left(V_i\, G(\hat{v}_i) - \pi_i(\hat{v}_i) \right).$$

This finishes the first step.

Step 2. Invoke the envelope theorem

The decision problem facing bidder i, if his value is V_i, is to maximize

$$V_i\, G(\hat{v}_i) - \pi_i(\hat{v}_i).$$

Think of this as a parametric optimization problem in which V_i is the parameter and $\hat{v}_i$ is the variable. Define

$$\mathcal{U}_i^*(V_i) := \sup_{\hat{v}_i} V_i\, G(\hat{v}_i) - \pi_i(\hat{v}_i).$$

We know, of course, that the sup is attained for each V_i by $\hat{v}_i = V_i$, which means that $\mathcal{U}_i^*(V_i) = V_i\, G(V_i) - \pi(V_i)$. Hold that bit of knowledge in reserve. Treating this just as "another" parametric optimization problem, we can show that:

- The function $V_i \to \mathcal{U}_i^*(V_i)$ is convex and continuous. Convexity is proved by an argument that should be familiar to you from Volume I. (See, for instance, the proof that the profit function from the theory of the competitive firm is convex in prices, or Proposition 9.3, on page 202, Volume I.) This implies continuity on the open interval $(\underline{v}, \overline{v})$, and upper semi-continuous on the endpoints of the interval. Truth-telling then gives us continuity on the endpoints; Problem 24.6 asks you to provide this argument as well as the proof of convexity.

- Being convex and continuous, the function $\mathcal{U}_i^*$ is differentiable for almost every V_i and is absolutely continuous, so

$$\mathcal{U}_i^*(V_i) - \mathcal{U}^*(\underline{v}) = \int_{\underline{v}}^{V_i} \left.\frac{d\mathcal{U}_i^*}{dV_i}\right|_v dv,$$

where the integrand for v where $\mathcal{U}_i^*$ is not differentiable can be assigned arbitrarily; it doesn't matter, because this is for a set of v that has Lebesgue measure zero.

- The envelope theorem (see, specifically, Proposition A17.2 on page 749) tells us that, if $\mathcal{U}_i^*$ is differentiable at V_i, then

$$\left.\frac{d\mathcal{U}_i^*}{dV_i}\right|_{V_i} = \frac{\partial\big(V_i G(\hat{v}_i^*) - \pi_i(\hat{v}_i^*)\big)}{\partial V_i} = G(\hat{v}_i^*)$$

for any maximizer $\hat{v}_i^*$ at V_i. Since V_i is a maximizer at V_i, we have

$$\left.\frac{d\mathcal{U}_i^*}{dV_i}\right|_{V_i} = G(V_i), \quad \text{and, therefore,} \quad \mathcal{U}_i^*(V_i) - \mathcal{U}^*(\underline{v}) = \int_{\underline{v}}^{V_i} G(v)dv.$$

Step 3. The grand finale
Condition 2 is that $\mathcal{U}_i^*(\underline{v}) = 0$, so we have that

$$\mathcal{U}_i^*(V_i) = \int_{\underline{v}}^{V_i} G(v)dv. \tag{24.3}$$

But, $\mathcal{U}_i^*(V_i)$ is the conditional (on V_i) expected payoff of i in this equilibrium. We conclude that, no matter what the mechanism is, if we have a symmetric Nash equilibrium that meets the conditions 1 and 2, the conditional payoffs to every type V_i of bidder i are fixed by equation (24.3). (Since i was chosen arbitrarily, this is so for every bidder.) This includes the payoffs from the first- and second-price auction: Any general mechanism and Nash equilibrium outcome for the associated game of incomplete information matches the (conditional) expected payoffs of the first- and second-price auctions, which (of course) must match each other. The rest of the proof is straightforward.   ■

I promised you that this would provide some intuition about why the first- and second-price auctions produce the same expected revenues for the seller and conditional expected payments by the bidders. With emphasis on *some*, this is it: We insist that the good is allocated to the bidder with the high valuation in equilibrium. We use the revelation principle to convert an equilibrium to a truth-telling equilibrium in a direct-revelation game. And then, the allocation rule plus the envelope theorem imply that, to induce truth-telling, the what-the-bidder-must-expect-to-pay part of the mechanism is fixed.

It may be helpful to say what would muck up this very nice picture. Suppose that the values $\{V_i\}$ were not independent. Then, in writing down i's decision problem, we would write something like

$$\text{Maximize } V_i G(\hat{v}_i | V_i) - \pi_i(\hat{v}_i | V_i).$$

That is, both the probability that i gets the object with a report of $\hat{v}_i$ and the expected amount he must pay depend on V_i, because V_i shifts the conditional distributions of the elements of $V_{\neg i}$. The envelope theorem still holds, but because the partial derivative of the objective function in the parameter is quite complex, the beautifully simple integral we get for $\mathcal{U}_i^*$ in the case of independent values is neither beautiful nor simple, and revenue equivalence in general fails. (More about this will be said subsequently.)

Reserve prices

Suppose the seller of the item attaches some positive (dollar-denominated) value u to its retention. She wouldn't want to sell for an amount less than u. To prevent this, she can modify the rules of the auction—whether a second-price or a first-price auction—so that a bid of less than u will not be accepted. This is known as setting a *reserve* price for the item, something quite common in auctions. But is setting a reserve price equal to the seller's value u optimal for the seller? Perhaps she should set a reserve price $r > u$.

To be clear, if the seller sets the reserve price at r:

- In a first-price auction, if the high bid is less than r, the item is not sold.

- In a second-price auction, if the high bid is less than r, the item is not sold; if the high bid is greater than r, the high bidder gets the item for the larger of r and the second-highest bid.

Do the bidders know r before submitting their bids? One can imagine cases where they do not. But, I'll assume that they do. [12]

How does this change in the rules affect the bidding strategies of the bidders? Obviously, there is no point in submitting a bid if one's value V_i is less than r. (But it doesn't hurt to do so, since in either protocol, a bid less than the reserve r cannot possibly win.) But what if one's value exceeds (or is equal to) r?

---

[12] As noted in Section 24.1, if bidders do not know r before bidding, credibility issues about its administration can arise.

Proposition 24.8. *In the private-values context, suppose the seller of the item sets a reserve price of r.*

a. *For a second-price auction, it remains weakly dominant for each bidder to submit his private value V_i. It is a Nash equilibrium for each bidder to follow this strategy.* [13]

b. *In the standard symmetric private-values context, in the first-price auction, a symmetric Nash equilibrium is for each bidder whose $V_i \geq r$ to use the bid function β_r^{PVF} given by*

$$\beta_r^{\mathrm{PVF}}(V_1) := \mathbf{E}\big[max\{\mathcal{V}_{\neg i}^{(1)}, r\}\big|\mathcal{V}_{\neg i}^{(1)} < V_1\big] = r\frac{G(r)}{G(V_1)} + \frac{1}{G(V_1)}\int_r^{V_1} vg(v)\mathrm{d}v.$$

(Bidders with $V_i < r$ can submit anything they wish, as long as their bid is strictly less than r.)

c. *In the standard symmetric private-values context, the second- and first-price equilibria described in parts a and b give the same expected outcome for the seller of the item. (Indeed, a "revenue-equivalence theorem"—really, a "payoff-equivalence theorem"— can be given, where the who-gets-the-item rule is that it goes to the bidder with the highest valuation, as long as that valuation is at least r, but it is retained by the seller otherwise.)*

I'm not going to provide a proof; it follows very closely the lines of proofs given previously for auctions with no reserve prices.

Which reserve price r should the seller set, to maximize her expected payoff? It is obvious that the seller who attaches value u to the item is no worse off—and may be better off—setting a reserve price of u rather than setting $r < u$. But is it better to set a reserve price r that exceeds u? In many cases, it definitely is. Recall the notation $\mathcal{V}^{(1)}$ for the first order statistic of the V_i's, and $\mathcal{V}^{(2)}$ for the second order statistic.

The next two propositions (Propositions 24.9 and 24.11) assume that the context is the standard symmetric private-values context, the auction protocol is second-price, and bidders are employing the bid-your-value strategies. In this context, the joint distribution of $(\mathcal{V}^{(1)}, \mathcal{V}^{(2)})$ has a continuous density function that is strictly positive as long as $\mathcal{V}^{(1)} > \mathcal{V}^{(2)} > \underline{v}$. This allows us to "estimate" in little-o, big-O terms, the probability of various intervals (for instance, the probability that $u \leq \mathcal{V}^{(2)} \leq u + h \leq \mathcal{V}^{(1)}$ is $o(h)$, as long as $u + h < \bar{u}$).

Proposition 24.9. *In the standard symmetric private-values context, and for the bid-your-value equilibrium in a second-price auction:*

a. *Suppose that $u \in [\underline{v}, \overline{v})$. Then for small $h > 0$, the reserve price $u + h$ produces a better expected payoff for the seller than does a reserve price of u.*

---

[13] And in the sense of Proposition 24.3(d) and the spirit of trembling-hand perfection, this is the only "tremble-proof" Nash equilibrium.

b. If $u < \underline{v}$, then it may be that the optimal reserve price to set is $\underline{v}$, and it may be better
    for the seller to set $r > \underline{v}$.

By revenue equivalence, the same is true for the first-price-auction protocol with the symmetric equilibrium.

Proof. I will prove part a here in the case that $u > \underline{u}$, leaving the case $u = \underline{u}$ and
part b as an exercise (Problem 24.7).

Compare the outcomes for the seller if she sets a reserve price of u versus a
reserve price of $u + h$, in a second-price auction when the bidders are all using the
bid-your-value strategy. The outcome depends on the relative positions of $\mathcal{V}^{(1)}$ and
$\mathcal{V}^{(2)}$, relative to u and $u + h$. In "theory," $\mathcal{V}^{(1)}$ and $\mathcal{V}^{(2)}$ can each lie to the left of u,
between u and $u + h$, or to the right of $u + h$. Since $\mathcal{V}^{(2)} \le \mathcal{V}^{(1)}$, three of the combined
possibilities are inconsistent. Figure 24.1 provides the comparisons for each of six
consistent possibilities.

	$\mathcal{V}^{(1)} < u$	$u + h > \mathcal{V}^{(1)} \ge u$	$\mathcal{V}^{(1)} \ge u + h$
$\mathcal{V}^{(2)} < u$	1. Same outcome	2. Same payoff (but different outcomes)	4. $u + h$ better
$u + h > \mathcal{V}^{(2)} \ge u$	Inconsistent	6. u better	5. $u + h$ better
$\mathcal{V}^{(2)} \ge u + h$	Inconsistent	Inconsistent	3. Same outcome

Figure 24.1. Comparing a reserve price of u with a reserve price of $u + h$, in terms
of the outcome for the seller. There are six possible "arrangements" of $\mathcal{V}^{(1)}$ and $\mathcal{V}^{(2)}$
relative to u and $u + h$. (Since $\mathcal{V}^{(1)} \ge \mathcal{V}^{(2)}$, three of the nine cells in the figure are
inconsistent.) In three of the six possibilities, the two reserve prices give the same
outcome for the seller. In two, the reserve price $u + h$ is better than u. And in one,
the cell in which $u \le \mathcal{V}^{(2)} \le \mathcal{V}^{(1)} < u + h$, the reserve price u is better for the seller.
And—as argued in the text—for small h, the improvement in the one cell where u
is better is $o(h)$, while the improvement of $u + h$ over u in cell 4, which is $\mathcal{V}^{(2)} < u$
and $u + h \le \mathcal{V}^{(1)}$, is $O(h)$. Hence, for small h, $u + h$ is better in expectation. (The
numbers in the cells match the numbers in the text.)

Taking the six one at a time (the numbers matching the numbers in the figure):

1. If $\mathcal{V}^{(2)} \le \mathcal{V}^{(1)} < u$, the two give the same result for the seller: The item remains
    with her, for a payoff of u.

2. If $\mathcal{V}^{(2)} < u \le \mathcal{V}^{(1)} < u + h$, the two give the same payoff u for the seller, but with
    different outcomes: If the reserve price is u, the item goes to the high bidder
    who pays the seller u. If the reserve price is $u + h$, the seller retains the item.

3. If $\mathcal{V}^{(1)} \ge \mathcal{V}^{(2)} \ge u + h$, the result for the seller is the same: The item goes to the
    high bidder, who pays the seller $\mathcal{V}^{(2)}$.

4. If $\mathcal{V}^{(2)} < u$ and $\mathcal{V}^{(1)} \ge u + h$, the reserve price of $u + h$ is better for the seller; she
    sells the item for $u + h$ if that is the reserve price, and (only) for u if that is the
    reserve price.

5. If $\mathcal{V}^{(1)} \geq u + h > \mathcal{V}^{(2)} \geq u$, the reserve price of $u + h$ is better: With a reserve price of u, the high bidder gets the item and pays $\mathcal{V}^{(2)}$, while this bidder pays $u + h$ if that is the reserve price.

6. If $u + h > \mathcal{V}^{(1)} \geq \mathcal{V}^{(2)} \geq u$, the reserve price of u is (weakly) better: With a reserve price of $u + h$, the item goes unsold, giving the seller a payoff of u, while for a reserve price of u, the item sells for $\mathcal{V}^{(2)} \geq u$.

So a comparison of the two reserve prices comes down to a comparison of the relative gains from cases 4 and 5 versus the loss from case 6. The probability of case 4 is strictly positive (since we are in the standard symmetric setting), and the improvement in payoff is h. Add in case 5, and the advantage of $u + h$ over u in these two cells combined is $O(h)$. In case 6, the improvement in payoff for the seller of u versus $u + h$ is at most h, while the probability of this case goes to zero as $h \searrow 0$ (again, because we are in the standard symmetric setting). So this contributes a term of $o(h)$ in favor of a reserve price of u.

Letting $h \searrow 0$, the $O(h)$ from cases 4 and 5 in favor of $u + h$ dominates the $o(h)$ in case 6 in favor of u: For small enough h, $u + h$ is better.   ■

Denote by $\mathcal{W}(r)$ the expected payoff to the seller who sets the reserve price r in the second-price auction format, where bidders use the bid-your-value strategies.

For the case $u > \underline{v}$, the proof of the proposition implies right-hand differentiability of $\mathcal{W}$ at $r = u$ and that this right-hand derivative is strictly positive. (Can you see why?) In the other two cases: If $u = \underline{v}$, it turns out that $\mathcal{W}$ is strictly increasing to the right of u, but with derivative 0. And if $u < \underline{v}$ (part c), the impact of a small increase in r starting from $\underline{v}$ is ambiguous. (See Problem 24.7 and its solution on these points.)

Three comments are in order:

- This result says that the seller may set auction rules such that the outcome is *not* efficient. By setting the reserve price at $r > u$, there is the possibility—the case $r > \mathcal{V}^{(1)} > u$—that the item is more valuable to a buyer than to the seller, but it is not sold to that buyer. [14]

- Since the seller can do better with a reserve price than without, the obvious question to ask is: Are there are changes that the seller can make in the auction format—or with some other general mechanism—to increase her expected payoff? This is a subject we take up in Chapter 26.

- Proposition 24.8 assumes the setting is the standard symmetric private-values

---

[14] If bidders whose values are less than r don't bid, the seller won't know that this case holds; she only knows that no bidder was willing to meet her reserve price. But suppose we change the protocol a bit. It is still a second-price protocol, and the seller commits in advance to a reserve price—that commitment is not a trivial thing—but bidders don't know the reserve price. In that case, bidders will still submit their private values as bids; doing so is weakly dominant, no matter what the unknown reserve price is. And, then, in the case $r > \mathcal{V}^{(1)} > u$, the seller will know ex post that the item is worth more to a bidder than to herself. Can we trust that the seller won't go to the high-value buyer with "Let's make a deal?" And, if this is predicted to happen, will buyers want to bid their true values?

case, which allows us to apply revenue equivalence and get the same results for first-price auctions with the symmetric equilibrium. But if we stick to second-price auctions and the bid-your-value equilibrium, the method of proof generalizes as long as the probability of case 4 is bounded away from zero and the probability of case 6 goes to zero as $h \searrow 0$.

Proposition 24.8 shows that when $u > \underline{v}$, the optimal reserve price for the seller to set exceeds her private valuation for the item. But can we tell what the optimal reserve price is? We can do so, in some cases. We need some general mathematical facts about order statistics.

Mathematical Facts 24.10. *Suppose $\{V_i; i = 1, \ldots, N\}$ is an i.i.d. set of N random variables, each of which is distributed according to the cumulative distribution function F. Using the notation $\mathcal{V}^{(2)}$ and $\mathcal{V}^{(1)}$ for the second- and first order statistics, respectively, the conditional distribution of $\mathcal{V}^{(1)}$ given $\mathcal{V}^{(2)}$ is*

$$\mathbf{P}\left(\mathcal{V}^{(1)} < x \mid \mathcal{V}^{(2)}\right) = \begin{cases} 0, & \text{if } \mathcal{V}^{(2)} > x, \text{ and} \\ \left[F(x) - F(\mathcal{V}^{(2)})\right] / \left[1 - F(\mathcal{V}^{(2)})\right], & \text{if } x \geq \mathcal{V}^{(2)}. \end{cases}$$

Also, if F is absolutely continuous, then the distribution of $\mathcal{V}^{(2)}$ is absolutely continuous.

See, for instance, David and Nagaraja (2003).

We know from Proposition 24.9 that $\mathcal{W}(r)$ is increasing starting from $r = u$ if $u \geq \underline{v}$. It is obvious that $\mathcal{W}(r) \to 0$ as $r \to \overline{v}$. Hence, assuming $u \geq \underline{v}$, the optimal r must lie in the open interval $(u, \overline{v})$. If we know that $\mathcal{W}$ is differentiable over this interval—which we will prove momentarily—then we know the solution will be found at a point where $\mathcal{W}'(r) = 0$.

Proposition 24.11. *Still in a standard symmetric private-values context, where bidders bid their private values: If $u \geq \underline{v}$, the function $r \to \mathcal{W}(r)$ is differentiable on the open interval $(u, \overline{v})$, with derivative*

$$\mathcal{W}'(r) = \left[\int_{\underline{v}}^{r} \frac{\phi(v)}{1 - F(v)} dv\right] \left[(u - r)f(r) + (1 - F(r))\right],$$

where ϕ is the density function of $\mathcal{V}^{(2)}$. Hence, $\mathcal{W}'(r) = 0$ at points r^* such that

$$\frac{f(r^*)}{1 - F(r^*)}(r^* - u) = 1.$$

Proof. Consider the difference in expected payoffs to the seller if she sets the reserve price at $r + h$ versus r, for small h. As in Figure 24.1, there are six "regimes" concerning how $\mathcal{V}^{(1)}$ and $\mathcal{V}^{(2)}$ lie relative to these two reserve prices.[15] Figure 24.2

---

[15]   Three of the nine cells in Figure 24.2 are inconsistent with $\mathcal{V}^{(1)} \geq \mathcal{V}^{(2)}$.

	$\mathcal{V}^{(1)}<r$	$r+h>\mathcal{V}^{(1)}\ge r$	$\mathcal{V}^{(1)}\ge r+h$
$\mathcal{V}^{(2)}<r$	1. u, u	2. r, u	4. $r, r+h$
$r+h>\mathcal{V}^{(2)}\ge r$	Inconsistent	6. $\mathcal{V}^{(2)}, u$	5. $\mathcal{V}^{(2)}, r+h$
$\mathcal{V}^{(2)}\ge r+h$	Inconsistent	Inconsistent	3. $\mathcal{V}^{(2)}, \mathcal{V}^{(2)}$

Figure 24.2. Comparing a reserve price of r with a reserve price of $r+h$, in terms of the outcome for the seller. In each of the six "consistent" cells, the payoff to the seller from a reserve price of r is provided first, and then his payoff if he sets a reserve price of $r+h$.

denotes the six regimes and, for each one, gives the payoff to the seller if the reserve price is r and then if it is $r+h$.

In cells 1 and 3 the results are the same, so the difference is zero. In the two consistent cells in which $r+h>\mathcal{V}^{(2)}\ge r$, cells 5 and 6, the difference in expected payoffs is $O(h^2)$: in cell 6, the difference in payoffs $\mathcal{V}^{(2)}-u$ is $O(1)$, but the probability of this cell is $O(h^2)$. In cell 5, the difference $r+h-\mathcal{V}^{(2)}$ is $O(h)$), and the probability of this cell is $O(h)$ (because of $r\le\mathcal{V}^{(2)}\le r+h$), hence the contribution of this cell to the difference is $O(h^2)=o(h)$.

This leaves cells 2 and 4. In cell 2, where $r+h>\mathcal{V}^{(1)}\ge r>\mathcal{V}^{(2)}$, the difference is $r-u$, and the probability (up to terms of order $O(h)$) is

$$\int_{\underline{v}}^{r}\left[\frac{f(r)h}{1-F(v)}\right]\phi(v)dv = f(r)h\int_{\underline{v}}^{r}\frac{\phi(v)}{1-F(v)}dv.$$

In cell 4, the difference is h, and the probability of this cell (again up to terms of $O(h)$) is

$$\int_{\underline{v}}^{r}\frac{1-F(r)}{1-F(v)}\phi(v)dv = (1-F(r))\int_{\underline{v}}^{r}\frac{\phi(v)}{1-F(v)}dv.$$

Hence the difference, up to terms of order $O(h)$, is

$$\mathcal{W}(r+h)-\mathcal{W}(h) = \left[r-u\right]\left[f(r)h\int_{\underline{v}}^{r}\frac{\phi(v)}{1-F(v)}dv\right] + h(1-F(r))\left[\int_{\underline{v}}^{r}\frac{\phi(v)}{1-F(v)}dv\right]$$

$$= \left[\int_{\underline{v}}^{r}\frac{\phi(v)}{1-F(v)}dv\right]\left[(r-u)f(r)h + h(1-F(r))\right].$$

Divide both sides by h, and the asserted result about $\mathcal{W}'$ is proved. (I've only covered the case where $h>0$. So, being very rigorous, I've only shown that $\mathcal{W}$ has right-hand derivatives and what those right-hand derivatives are. Yet, this is sufficient to show full differentiability. Why? And what if anything can you say about right-hand differentiability of W at $r = \underline{v}$, if $u < \underline{v}$?)

Since the term in the first set of square brackets is always strictly positive, the assertion about values of r for which $W'(r) = 0$ is immediate. ∎

Observe that the necessary first-order condition for the optimal reserve price (under the assumptions of Proposition 24.11) can be written as

$$\frac{1 - F(r^*)}{f(r^*)} = r^* - u.$$

As r increases, $r - u$ increases, so if $(1 - F(r))/f(r)$ decreases, there can be only one solution to the first-order condition. Observe that, in this case, or in any case where there is a unique solution to the first-order condition (and $u \geq \underline{v}$), the optimal r^* must be that unique solution. Moreover, this solution depends only on u and the distribution F (and its density f) of a single V_i; the number of bidders is irrelevant. Different "intuitive" explanations of this fact can be found in the literature; my best attempt at intuition is that, once $\mathcal{V}^{(2)}$ is determined, the conditional distribution of $\mathcal{V}^{(1)}$ is just F truncated below at $\mathcal{V}^{(2)}$ and renormalized. (It is further the case that, if there is more than one solution to the first-order condition, all solutions—which are the only candidates for the optimal reserve price—are independent of N. But I am not asserting that which of those candidates is the actual optimum is independent of N; the values of W' away from its zeros depend on N through the density function ϕ of $\mathcal{V}^{(2)}$.)

Dynamic auctions

What about dynamic auctions and, in particular, the ascending-bid or English auction? As noted at the start of this chapter, the "rules" of English auctions are too fuzzy for formal analysis. Hence, auction theorists think in terms of the four variations on the button auction mentioned in Section 24.1. To repeat, each bidder has a button that he can push at any time, irrevocably signifying that he is no longer interested in purchasing the good. An analog "clock" slowly and continuously increases the dollar value that it shows; all bidders watch the clock. The moment that all bidders but one have pushed their respective buttons, the remaining bidder wins the item, paying what the clock read when the next-to-last bidder gave up. The four variations are:

1. Each bidder sees, as time passes, who gave up at which prices.

2. Each bidder sees as time passes how many bidders remain. That is, a still-active bidder knows how many bidders are still "bidding" but doesn't know their identities. He does know the "prices" at which bidders dropped out earlier.

3. Each bidder (still active) knows that there is at least one other active bidder until no other active bidders remain, but he doesn't know how many, and he doesn't know at what prices others have dropped out.

4. Each bidder knows nothing. After all bidders have punched their buttons, the auctioneer/seller tells bidders what has transpired.

Variations three and four of this button auction are strategically isomorphic to the second-price auction in the private-values context: Bidder i's strategy is to choose the price b_i at which he will push his button and end his participation, and the individual whose strategy is to release at the highest price b_i wins the item at the second-highest "release price" $B_{-i}^{(1)}$. Hence the Nash equilibria of this "button auction" are the same as the Nash equilibria of the second-price auction.

For the first and second variations, bidders have more strategies. In the first variation, they can adjust when they plan to give up to information they gain about who gives in when (prior to they themselves giving in) or, in the second variation, they can adjust when they plan to give in if they see, say, three bidders drop when the price reaches $100, even though they don't know which three. In cases where bidders are asymmetric, the differences between variations 1 and 2 can matter. But we will not deal with asymmetric-bidder situations, and to fix terminology, I'll refer to the second variation specifically as the *information-rich English-button protocol*.

One can show that, although the information-rich English-button protocol opens up new strategic possibilities for bidders that are not available in sealed-tender protocols, *in the context of individual private values*, these extra strategies are irrelevant in the sense that every Nash equilibrium outcome of the second-price auction is a Nash equilibrium outcome of these information-rich English-button auctions. The reverse is not true: One can produce "extraneous" Nash equilibria that involve players using weakly dominated strategies. What remains true is that bid-your-own-value weakly dominates all other strategies, in the context of private values.[16]

The other (somewhat) common type of dynamic auction is the Dutch auction, in which the auctioneer starts with an (unreasonably) high price and lowers it as time passes, waiting for one of the bidders to signal that he or she is willing to buy at the current price. Since bidders don't speak until one of them accepts the current price, this is strategically equivalent to a first-price auction: Bidders decide at which price they are going to accept, based on their private values, and the bidder whose acceptance time is earliest, corresponding to the highest bid in a first-price protocol, wins the auction.

Collusion in first-price (and other) auctions with private values

In some contexts, the bidders are well known to one another, and it is natural for them to conspire against the seller, by colluding to keep winning bids low. With private values, the tension in such collusive schemes is that it is sensible for colluding bidders to arrange somehow for the winning bidder to be a bidder whose private valuation is highest or, at least, among the highest. But, insofar as the collusive scheme is effective, each bidder has a private interest in winning the

---

[16] In Appendix 14, on page 641, I briefly "debate" the Kohlberg and Mertens contention that a "good solution concept" for a game should depend (only) on the essential strategic structure of the game. In this context, I direct your attention the recent paper by Li (2017), who argues—and is supported by empirical evidence—that (at least when it comes to how real people behave), the button auction (or the English auction) is "more straightforward" to play than is the sealed-bid second-price auction.

item. So, if the private values are truly private information held by each individual bidder, each has a private interest in representing to the other bidders that his valuation is higher than is in fact true. We encountered this problem in Chapter 22, in the subsection titled "Noisy observables, II: Quantities observed" (pages 225-30); the reference to Skrypacz and Hopenhayn (2004) given there provides an analysis of this problem.

For private-values contexts, there is a lot more that can be and has been said. For further analysis, see Problems 24.8 and 24.9.

24.3. Common-Value Contexts: Preliminaries

We now turn to common-value contexts. Auctions for common-value situations are more complex than are private-value auctions, because bidders must estimate what the common value is, based on private information that they have, while knowing that other bidders will have other relevant information about the common value.

Because of the complexity, results are fewer and less transparent. And, I'll be less complete in giving results; in places, I'll state results and send you to other sources for proofs. However, common-value contexts are arguably more descriptive of important cases of auctions, so a familiarity with the complexities is important, even if you do not specialize in auctions and auction design.

I begin with a very general formulation that mixes private and common values. As before, there are N bidders who compete in an auction to win a single, indivisible item. The bidders are indexed by $i = 1, 2, \ldots, N$. Each bidder is risk neutral, seeking to maximize the expectation of the value of the item to himself, V_i, less the amount he pays to the seller of the item as a result of the auction.

Bidder i does not (necessarily) know V_i. However, he is endowed with information, represented by a signal S_i, that provides information about V_i, and also (in general) about the values V_j of the item to other bidders and about their signals S_j. This is modeled with a collection of $2N$ random variables $\{V_j, S_j; j = 1, \ldots, N\}$, that have a prior joint probability distribution that is common knowledge to all the bidders (and to the seller, when it comes to that). This is their commonly held prior; since (each) bidder i is endowed as well with knowledge of the value of S_i, bidder i uses this information and Bayes' rule to form a posterior assessment over the joint distribution of $(V_i, (V_j, S_j)_{j \neq i})$. (Bidder i doesn't really care about the V_j for $j \neq i$. But because it will affect how the other bidders will bid, he is concerned with the information S_j held by the other bidders.)

We specialize immediately to the *common-value* context, in which the value random variables V_i are identical; write V for the common value. And we specialize further to one of the following three specifications of how V relates stochastically to the array of private signals $\{S_i\}$:

The wallet-game context. In this specification, the signals S_i are i.i.d. nonnegative-valued random variables, with common distribution function F that is absolutely continuous. We write f for the density function of each S_i. And $V = S_1 + \ldots + S_N$.

For this context, visualize that seller/auctioneer Alice owns N wallets. Each contains an amount of money S_i; the random (to the bidders) $\{S_i; i = 1, \ldots, N\}$ i.i.d. Each of the N bidders is allowed to examine one of the wallets—bidder i is allowed to examine the contents of wallet i—so i knows S_i but is "in the dark" about the other $N - 1$ wallets. An auction (of some format) is conducted where the prize is the contents of all the wallets, $V = S_1 + \ldots + S_N$, with the proceeds from the auction (e.g., the winning bid in a first-price auction) going to the seller/auctioneer.

This is a pretty contrived situation: The seller, on average in a bidding equilibrium, sells the N wallets for less than they hold. Why not just take the contents of the wallets and depart? Perhaps the story should be: The government is auctioning off the timber rights to N tracts of land; for some reason, it will award the rights to all N tracts to a single bidder. Each bidder has been allowed to inventory one and only one of N tracts; the tracts are similar enough a priori so that bidders regard the value of timber in each tract as being i.i.d.; bidder i's inventory of tract i is sufficient for i to determine the value of timber rights on that one tract, without providing any information about other tracts.[17] This is still pretty contrived; a more reasonable model would be that the S_i are exchangeable (i.i.d. conditional on some unknown-to-the-bidders distribution), so that S_i provides information about the other S_j. (This, more or less, is the next model we pose.) However, despite its contrived nature, this context is useful as a "training exercise" for more complex common-value contexts.

Conditionally independent signals. In this specification, the value V is distributed randomly according to some given, absolutely continuous distribution function H on a compact subinterval of $[0, \infty)$. The support of V is denoted $[\underline{v}, \overline{v}]$, and the density function of V is denoted by h; we assume that h is strictly positive and continuous on its support.

And, then, the signals $\{S_i; i = 1, \ldots, N\}$ are *conditionally* i.i.d., conditional on the value of V. Each S_i has absolutely continuous conditional distribution function $F(\cdot | V = v)$, with continuous and strictly positive density $f(\cdot | V = v)$ on a closed subinterval $[\underline{s}, \overline{s}]$ of $[0, \infty)$, for each $v \in [\underline{v}, \overline{v}]$. Note that the conditional support of each S_i doesn't change with changes in V; this will allow us to avoid special cases. Of course, each S_i has an (unconditional) distribution function, given by

$$\mathbf{P}(S_i \leq s) = \int_{\underline{v}}^{\overline{v}} F(s|v)h(v)\mathrm{d}v;$$

the unconditional density function of each S_i is computed by the integral with $f(s|v)$ replacing $F(s|v)$. In general, the (unconditional) S_i's are not independent; insofar as S_i tells bidder i something about V, it indirectly tells him something about the signals the other bidders are observing.

---

[17]   As long as symmetry and risk neutrality are maintained, these inventories could leave some residual uncertainty in each bidder i's assessment of the value of rights on "his" tract i. And we could have $M > N$ tracts as the prize, if each of the N bidders has been allowed to inventory the timber on one (different) tract out of the M tracts.

Although it breaks the rules just set down in terms of the bounded supports, consider the following functional specification: V is Normally distributed with mean 100 and variance 10. (The use of Normal distributions opens the possibility that $V < 0$. But with a mean of 100 and a variance of 10, $V < 0$ is extremely unlikely. And Normal distributions allows for easy Bayesian inference.) The collection $\{S_i; i = 1, \ldots, N\}$ is a collection of conditionally independent random variables, conditional on V, with each S_i Normally distributed with mean V and variance 5. In other words, each $S_i = V + \epsilon_i$, for $\{\epsilon_i\}$ an i.i.d. family of mean 0, variance 5, Normally distributed random variables.

Consider bidder i in receipt of the signal S_i. What does he conclude about the distribution of V? Using standard formulas for this situation, his posterior assessment of V, given the signal $S_i = s$ is that it is Normally distributed with mean

$$\frac{2}{3}s + \frac{100}{3}$$

and variance $50/15 = 10/3$. From here, it is straightward to compute his conditional assessment of the collection $(S_j)_{j \neq i}$.

This conditionally independent signals context is advanced as an "ideal" version of a symmetric mineral-rights auction. In this story, the government is auctioning off the rights to whatever crude oil and/or natural gas can be extracted from a particular offshore tract. The bidders are companies that are in the business of developing and then extracting fossil-fuel deposits. This scenario is ideal in that each company is assumed to have its own estimate of the (unknown) size V of deposits; S_i is company i's privately gathered and closely held information concerning the value of V. In this ideal formulation, all N companies that are bidding are symmetrically informed, with signals that are conditionally independent, conditional on V. Of course, each would like to know what is the assessment of its rivals; the best assessment of V would be based on the full vector of signals.

In the context of conditionally independent signals, it will generally be the case that V, conditional on the full array of private signals $\{S_i\}$, will still have residual uncertainty. That is, we cannot write $V = v(S_1, \ldots, S_N)$ for some function v with domain $[\underline{s}, \overline{s}]^N$. But, because bidders are risk neutral, and because $(S_1, \ldots, S_N)$ is all the information that bidders (collectively) hold, from a strategic perspective, any auction in which they participate can be framed as competing for the common value

$$v(S_1, S_2, \ldots, S_N) = \mathbf{E}[V | S_1, \ldots, S_N].$$

In places in the analysis, we will frame the our analysis in this (strategically equivalent) fashion.

The drainage-tract context (also known as Maxco–Gambit). In the conditionally-independent-signals context, the bidders are symmetrically informed. But in some real-life contexts, one of the bidders may be better informed than are others concerning V. For instance, in a mineral-rights auction, suppose the auction is for the mineral rights on a tract of land (or offshore) that is adjacent to a tract that has already been explored by one of the bidders. That bidder will (presumably) have superior information to that possessed by any other bidders.

To model this, we imagine that there are two bidders, called Maxco and Gambit, after an ancient Harvard Business School Case Study (Hammond 1974). Gambit knows the value of V; Maxco assesses a probability distribution F for V (and this assessment is common knowledge). This situation is extreme in that Gambit, knowing the value of V, has strictly superior information to Maxco. Suppose instead that Maxco possesses a signal S_1 about V, while Gambit knows both S_1 and a further signal S_2 (and, again, all this is common knowledge). Then these assumptions reduces to the extreme formulation; for every possible realization of S_1, think of $V_{S_1}^o(S_2) = \mathbf{E}[V|S_1, S_2]$ as the common value known by Gambit, while Maxco, for the given S_1, only knows the distribution of the random (to it) $V_{S_1}^o$.

The winner's curse

The winner's curse refers to a phenomenon in which naive bidders in a common-value auction situation find that, if they win the auction, they have (most of the time) paid more than the item is ultimately worth. I'll illustrate with the mineral-rights context, with a common value V that is Normally distributed and with Normally distributed conditionally independent signals, using the numerical parameters provided above. (Problem 24.9 asks you to examine the winner's curse in the context of the wallet game.)

Suppose the auction format is a first-price auction. And suppose all the bidders, being somewhat naive (but risk neutral), decide to bid $1.50 below the mean of their posterior assessment. What happens? In particular, what is the difference between V and the winning bid $1.50 on average?

This depends on the number of bidders, N. If there are only two bidders, the average outcome for the winning bidder is that V is around $1.50 over the winning bid. If there are four bidders, the average winning bid is just about equal to V; the winning bidder gets an average payoff of around $0.15. If there are ten bidders, the average winning bid exceeds V by a bit more than $2.15. And if there are twenty bidders, the winning bidder loses $4.70 or so, on average.

The reason for the curse is that, if each bidder i bids $2S_i/3 + 100/3 - 1.5$, the winning bid comes from the bidder whose signal S_i is the largest of the two, four, ten, or twenty signals. And although the expected value of a signal, given V, is V, the signals are Normally distributed around V, so the largest signal will (usually) be greater than V, and more so the larger is N. Roughly put, the winning signal is a biased signal of the true value of V.[18] For twenty bidders, for instance, the largest signal is, on average, around $10 larger than V. If the winning bidder doesn't take

---

[18] More precisely, the conditional mean of V, conditional on the largest signal S_i, without taking into account that it is the largest signal in a set of conditionally independent signals, is a biased estimate of the mean of V.

into account that his signal is the largest, hence an "overestimate" of the true value of V, he can (for large N) wind up losing money, even though he has bid less than his expectation of V given (only) his signal.

Two remarks are in order:

- The winner's curse is different from *winner's* (or buyer's) *remorse*, which refers to situations in which the winning bidder learns that he could have won the auction with a smaller bid. (This applies to first-price auctions and other auction formats where the winning bidder pays an increasing function of his bid, of course. It does not apply, in particular, to a second-price auction.) Winner's remorse is possible in private-values contexts. But, as long as bidders don't bid more than their private value, the winner's curse is impossible with private values.

- Imagine that Bob is a naive buyer of Alice's used car, in the Akerlof context of Chapter 20: Alice's car's value to her is uniformly distributed between \$2000 and \$6000, and if it is worth q to Alice, it is worth $q + 200$ to Bob. Bob's naiveté leads him to offer Alice \$4000, this being the "average" value of the car to her. She sells him the car, and he is distressed to learn (most of the time) that the case is worth less than \$4000 to him; on average, it is worth only \$3200. This is *the* paradigmatic example of adverse selection with a naive buyer and, in a sense, the winner's curse is a different manifestation of the same phenomenon, albeit where the form of naivete that is involved is different.

24.4. Symmetric Equilibria in the Wallet-Game Context

Suppose there are N symmetric bidders in the wallet-game context. Suppose that F, the distribution function for amount of money S_i in each of the N wallets, has domain $[\underline{s}, \overline{s}]$ and is absolutely continuous with continuous and strictly positive density function f. (This implies that there is zero probability that any two S_i and S_j are equal, which is not a very realistic assumptions if we are thinking of real-life wallets, but this assumption does avoid ties, which is an expositional convenience.)

Begin with a second-price auction format. Each bidder, knowing his own wallet's content, enters a bid of b_i, and the winner is whoever submits the highest bid, paying the second-highest bid. In this format, asymmetric equilibria appear (as before for second-price auctions): Suppose bidder i submits a bid of $b = N\overline{s} + 1$, regardless of what is in his wallet. The best response to this by every other bidder is to submit a bid of 0; bidder i wins with probability 1 and pays nothing. In the context of private values, we ruled out this sort of equilibrium by appealing to weak dominance of bid-your-private value and a variation on trembling-hand perfection. In this context, because no bidding strategy is weakly dominant, the simple argument used before is unavailable. But, if the other bidders "tremble"—or if two bidders get the bright idea of bidding $N\overline{s} + 1$—bidder i's strategy of always bidding $N\overline{s} + 1$ could lead to disaster for him. And, in this very asymmetric equilibrium, bidder i does just as well against his rivals by bidding, say, $N\underline{s} + 0.01$. So, perhaps an argument can be constructed against bidding $N\bar{s} + 1$, in the spirit of trembling-hand perfection. Rather than chase this down, I'll confine attention to symmetric equilibria.

Define $\mathcal{S}_{-i}^{(1)} := \max\{S_j; j \neq i\}$; that is, the largest amount of money in any one of the wallets except for i's wallet. And let

$$\psi(s) := \mathbf{E}\left[\sum_{j \neq i} S_j \Big| \mathcal{S}_{-i}^{(1)} = s\right].$$

This is i's conditional expectation of the amount of money in all the other wallets, conditional on the largest of these holding s. If i knows that $\mathcal{S}_{-i}^{(1)} = s$ (and only that), then i's conditional assessment of the contents of each of the other $N - 2$ wallets contents is that they are i.i.d. with the distribution function F truncated at s.[19] Hence, if we define

$$\mu(s) := \left[\int_{\underline{s}}^{s} s' f(s') \mathrm{d}s'\right] \Big/ F(s),$$

then this is i's conditional expectation of the contents of each of the other wallets, and therefore,

$$\psi(s) = (N - 2)\mu(s) + s.$$

I'll state without proof the following mathematical facts.

Lemma 24.12. *Under the assumption that F has a strictly positive density on its support, $\mu(s)$ is strictly increasing and continuous (on the support of F), and so $\psi(s)$ is also strictly increasing and continuous. And $\mu(\underline{s}) = \underline{s}$, hence $\psi(\underline{s}) = (N - 1)\underline{s}$. Finally, $\mathcal{S}_{-i}^{(1)}$ has an absolutely continuous distribution function, which I'll denote G, and a strictly positive (except at $\underline{s}$, if $N > 2$) and continuous density g.[20]*

Proposition 24.13. *In the wallet-game context, under the assumption that F has a strictly positive density on its support, and in a second-price auction format, it is a symmetric equilibrium for each bidder i to bid $\psi(S_i) + S_i$ (where S_i is the contents of his own wallet.)*

Proof. Suppose all the bidders other than bidder i employ this strategy. Can i, when his wallet contains S_i, do better with some other bid?

First, rule out bids strictly less than $N\underline{s}$ and more than $\psi(\bar{s}) + \bar{s}$: A bidder j who is following the proposed equilibrium strategy is bidding $\psi(S_j) + S_j$. This function is strictly increasing in S_j, so the smallest bid any bidder will make is $\psi(\underline{s}) + \underline{s} = \underline{s}$, and the largest bid is $\psi(\bar{s}) + \bar{s}$. By bidding less than $\underline{s}$, bidder i is certain to lose the auction for a payoff of 0. So, if we show that his equilibrium payoff is nonnegative

---

[19] This is another mathematical fact about order statistics drawn from a collection of i.i.d. random variables.

[20] Indeed, $G(s) = [F(s)]^{N-1}$, and $g(s) = (N - 1)[F(s)]^{N-2} f(s)$.

(which we will do shortly), we can reject all such bids. And bidding strictly more than $\psi(\bar{s}) + \bar{s}$ is certain to win. But since there is zero probability that any other bidder has $S_j = \bar{s}$, bidding $\psi(\bar{s}) + \bar{s}$ also has probability 1 of winning, and so it does just as well. This shows that we can ignore all bids outside of $[\underline{s}, \psi(\bar{s}) + \bar{s}]$ (once we deliver on the promised result that following the equilibrium strategy gives a nonnegative expected payoff).

So consider any bid $b \in [\underline{s}, \psi(\bar{s}) + \bar{s}]$. By the intermediate-value theorem ($s \to \psi(s) + s$ is continuous), $b = \psi(s) + s$ for some $s \in [\underline{s}, \bar{s}]$. Because $s \to \psi(s) + s$ is strictly increasing, bidding b is the same as i "pretending" that his own wallet contains s instead of the true S_i. Does such a pretense ever pay off?

By pretending in this fashion, bidder i will win the auction if and only if $b > \psi(\mathcal{S}_{\neg i}^{(1)}) + \mathcal{S}_{\neg i}^{(1)}$, which is $\psi(s) + s > \psi(\mathcal{S}_{\neg i}^{(1)}) + \mathcal{S}_{\neg i}^{(1)}$, which is $s > \mathcal{S}_{\neg i}^{(1)}$ (ties being ignored). Hence, conditional on $\mathcal{S}_{\neg i}^{(1)}$ and S_i, his payoff is

$$\begin{cases} \psi(\mathcal{S}_{\neg i}^{(1)}) + S_i - \psi(\mathcal{S}_{\neg i}^{(1)}) - \mathcal{S}_{\neg i}^{(1)} = S_i - \mathcal{S}_{\neg i}^{(1)}, & \text{if } \mathcal{S}_{\neg i}^{(1)} < s, \text{ and} \\ 0, & \text{if } \mathcal{S}_{\neg i}^{(1)} > s. \end{cases} \tag{24.5}$$

The second line should be obvious: He loses and has payoff 0 if $\mathcal{S}_{\neg i}^{(1)} > s$. As for the first line, he wins the auction if $\mathcal{S}_{\neg i}^{(1)} < s$, he pays what the second-highest bidder has bid ($\psi(\mathcal{S}_{\neg i}^{(1)}) + \mathcal{S}_{\neg i}^{(1)}$), and he wins (in conditional expectation) $\psi(\mathcal{S}_{\neg i}^{(1)}) + S_i$. To calculate his expected payoff (given only that his own wallet holds S_i and he bids as if it held s), we must take the expectation of (24.5) with respect to the (unknown to him) $\mathcal{S}_{\neg i}^{(1)}$; this is

$$\int_{\underline{s}}^{s} (S_i - \mathcal{S}_{\neg i}^{(1)}) g(\mathcal{S}_{\neg i}^{(1)}) \, d\mathcal{S}_{\neg i}^{(1)}.$$

Because the integrand is positive when $S_i > \mathcal{S}_{\neg i}^{(1)}$ and is negative when $S_i < \mathcal{S}_{\neg i}^{(1)}$, the integral is largest (and is strictly positive, for $S_i > \underline{s}$) if the upper limit of the integral s is chosen to be $s = S_i$. Therefore, pretending that S_i is something other than its true value lowers his payoff; bidding "truthfully" the bid $\psi(S_i) + S_i$ is his best response. We have an equilibrium.   ∎

Revenue equivalence and the first-price auction

Suppose bidder i's wallet holds S_i. His expected payoff in this equilibrium is $\mathbf{E}[S_i - \mathcal{S}_{\neg i}^{(1)}; \mathcal{S}_{\neg i}^{(1)} < S_i]$. To be pedantic (since this is a bit ambiguous), i knows S_i, so that is fixed in this expectation. What he doesn't know is $\mathcal{S}_{\neg i}^{(1)}$; $\mathcal{S}_{\neg i}^{(1)}$ is random, with distribution function G and density g, so we can rewrite this a bit more precisely (if perhaps less transparently) as: If $S_i = s_i$, i's equilibrium expected payoff in this equilibrium, given his knowledge that $S_i = s_i$, is

$$\int_{\underline{s}}^{s_i} (s_i - \mathcal{S}_{\neg i}^{(1)}) g(\mathcal{S}_{\neg i}^{(1)}) d\mathcal{S}_{\neg i}^{(1)}.$$

This leads to the following result.

Proposition 24.14. *In the symmetric wallet-game context, maintaining the distributional assumptions of Proposition 24.13:*

a. *Revenue equivalence holds: Fix a wallet game (essentially, fix F, the distribution function for the contents of each wallet), where the assumptions of Proposition 24.13 hold. Suppose, for a general mechanism for deciding which bidder gets V and how much each bidder pays, in the associated game in incomplete information, there is a symmetric Nash equilibrium in which (i) the winner is whichever bidder's wallet contains the largest amount of money, and (ii) conditional on a wallet containing $S_i = \underline{s}$, the bidder holding this wallet has a (conditional) expected payoff of 0. Then, in this equilibrium, the conditional expected payoff to a bidder whose wallet holds S_i is $\mathbf{E}\left[S_i - \mathcal{S}_{-i}^{(1)}; \mathcal{S}_{-i}^{(1)} < S_i \middle| S_i\right]$, and the expected amount that bidder i will pay to the seller/auctioneer is $\mathbf{E}\left[\psi(\mathcal{S}_{-i}^{(1)}) + \mathcal{S}_{-i}^{(1)}; \mathcal{S}_{-i}^{(1)} < S_i \middle| S_i\right]$.[21]*

b. *In the first-price auction, it is a symmetric equilibrium for each bidder, given his S_i, to bid $\mathbf{E}\left[\psi(\mathcal{S}_{-i}^{(1)}) + \mathcal{S}_{-i}^{(1)} \middle| \mathcal{S}_{-i}^{(1)} < S_i\right]$.*

Note that the strategies in part b of the proposition give the expected payoffs and payments for bidder i that are listed in part a, as indeed they must, if revenue equivalence holds. Bidder i wins the first-price auction on the event $\{S_i > \mathcal{S}_{-i}^{(1)}\}$, his expected "prize" if he wins is the expectation of $S_i + \psi(\mathcal{S}_{-i}^{(1)})$ on that event, and he pays his bid if he wins. That is,

> his expected prize is $\mathbf{E}\left[S_i + \psi(\mathcal{S}_{-i}^{(1)}); S_i > \mathcal{S}_{-i}^{(1)}\right]$,
>
> and his expected payment is $\mathbf{E}\left[\psi(\mathcal{S}_{-i}^{(1)}) + \mathcal{S}_{-i}^{(1)} \middle| S_i > \mathcal{S}_{-i}^{(1)}\right]\mathbf{P}\left(\{S_i > \mathcal{S}_{-i}^{(1)}\}\right) =$
> $\mathbf{E}\left[\psi(\mathcal{S}_{-i}^{(1)}) + \mathcal{S}_{-i}^{(1)}; S_i > \mathcal{S}_{-i}^{(1)}\right]$
>
> for a net expected payoff of $\mathbf{E}\left[S_i - \mathcal{S}_{-i}^{(1)}; \mathcal{S}_{-i}^{(1)} < S_i\right]$.

I'll leave the proof of this proposition to you as Problem 24.11.

Equilibrium in the information-rich English-button protocol

Consider finally (for the wallet-game context) (ascending) button auction, where bidders get to see the price levels at which their peers drop out.

In the equilibrium, in the button (continuous-time) protocol, there is some period of time before anyone drops out. Call this the first "round" of the continuous-time auction. With probability one, only one bidder drops out at any given time, because under the assumptions made, there is zero probability that two or more bidders have the same S_i. (In this auction protocol, ties are not that hard to handle, but I won't bother). Call the period from when the first bidder drops out until the second bidder drops out the second "round." And so forth.

Construct a strategy for each and every bidder i as follows:

---

[21] These conditional expectations are over the distribution of the $(S_j)_{j \neq i}$, fixing S_i, and over the event where $\mathcal{S}_{-i}^{(1)} < S_i$.

- During the first round, i watches as the posted price increases. When and if the price reaches NS_i, he drops out. Since this drop-out rule is strictly increasing in S_i, if some other player j (who is playing the same strategy) drops out first, say when the price reaches p_1, all the remaining players, and player i in particular, know that $S_j = p_1/N$. Moreover, this $S_j = \mathcal{S}^{(N)}$.

- Assuming i survives this first drop, we enter the second round. Now bidder i sets his drop-out price at $\mathcal{S}^{(N)} + (N-1)S_i$. Since all the bidders do this, when the next drop out occurs by (say) k at price p_2, they all know that the drop out S_k, which is $\mathcal{S}^{(N-1)}$, is $[p_2 - \mathcal{S}^{(N)}]/(N-1)$. Note that p_2 is necessarily greater than p_1, since $p_1 = N\mathcal{S}^{(N)} < \mathcal{S}^{(N)} + (N-1)\mathcal{S}^{(N-1)}$.

  Also note that the remaining bidders may not know the identities of j or k, but that is immaterial. What they know is there were drop outs at p_1 and then p_2, implying that $\mathcal{S}^{(N)} = p_1/N$, and $\mathcal{S}^{(N-1)} = [p_2 - \mathcal{S}^{(N)}]/(N-1)$. (Since the bidding strategies are symmetric, it doesn't hurt if they know the identities of j and k. But neither does that knowledge help, in the strategies being constructed.)

- And so forth. In the third round, bidder i (assuming he is still around) sets his drop-out price at $\mathcal{S}^{(N)} + \mathcal{S}^{(N-1)} + (N-2)S_i$.

- And, in this fashion, bidders drop out, revealing their wallet sizes, until only two bidders are left. These two remaining bidders use drop-out prices $\mathcal{S}^{(N)} + \mathcal{S}^{(N-1)} + \ldots + \mathcal{S}^{(3)} + 2S_i$. Call the two remaining bidders i and ℓ, and suppose that $S_i > S_\ell$. Then ℓ drops out first, at the price

$$\mathcal{S}^{(N)} + \mathcal{S}^{(N-1)} + \ldots + \mathcal{S}^{(3)} + 2S_\ell = \mathcal{S}^{(N)} + \mathcal{S}^{(N-1)} + \ldots + \mathcal{S}^{(3)} + 2S^{(2)}.$$

This is what bidder i, who has the largest signal pays. And since $V = \sum_j S_j$, bidder i's payoff is $S_i - \mathcal{S}^{(2)}$, this assuming that i has the wallet with the largest amount of money.

Proposition 24.15. *It is a (symmetric) Nash equilibrium for the N bidders to employ the strategies just described.*

I won't provide a full proof, but I'll give the gist of the main argument in the form of a puzzle. Suppose, in the middle of round 1—no one has dropped out yet— bidder j finds that his drop-out price has been reached. At that moment, he knows that his signal S_j is the least. He knows that all the other wallets contain more— strictly more (with probability one) given no ties—than S_j. Hence, he knows that $V > NS_j$ with probability one. And, yet, his drop-out price has been reached. So, why would he ever drop out at this price?

The reason—and the reason more generally we have an equilibrium—is that his decision whether to drop out influences the behavior of the other bidders. Put it this way: If he follows his part of the equilibrium strategy profile and drops out, he nets zero. The only way he can get a payoff other than zero is to sit patiently and wait for every other bidder to drop out, so he "wins" the auction. Will this alterative strategy prove fruitful, given that the others continue to do what they are supposed to do?

Round 1 will end when the bidder with the second lowest S_k is reached, but all the other bidders will (mistakenly) infer that this S_k is $\mathcal{S}^{(N)}$. That's wrong; it is actually $\mathcal{S}^{(N-1)}$, but only the defecting bidder j knows this. And so forth: $\mathcal{S}^{(N-2)}$ will mistakenly be inferred to be $\mathcal{S}^{(N-1)}$ (at the end of round 2), and when it finally comes down to our defecting bidder j and the bidder with the true highest S_i—I'll assume i (she) is her label—bidder i will *believe* that she knows $\mathcal{S}^{(N)} + \ldots + \mathcal{S}^{(3)}$ and that her sole remaining competitor, bidder j in fact (although his identity is irrelevant), has either the first or second largest S (when, in fact, he has the least). His defecting strategy is to wait her out, and eventually she will drop out, at the price that she believes is $\mathcal{S}^{(N)}+\ldots+\mathcal{S}^{(3)}+2\mathcal{S}^{(2)}$ but that in fact is $\mathcal{S}^{(N-1)}+\ldots+\mathcal{S}^{(2)}+2\mathcal{S}^{(1)}$. And this "in-fact" amount is what the defecting bidder j will pay. But his prize is $\mathcal{S}^{(N)} + \ldots + \mathcal{S}^{(3)} + \mathcal{S}^{(2)} + \mathcal{S}^{(1)}$, and since $\mathcal{S}^{(1)} > \mathcal{S}^{(N)}$, by following this strategy, bidder i will lose $\mathcal{S}^{(1)} - \mathcal{S}^{(N)}$. [22]

That's the point: Even though j knows that, in a sense, he is quitting at an unrealistically low price—less than the prize is worth—if he doesn't drop out at his appointed time, he causes other bidders to misread the situation and drop out at higher prices than they should. And, in particular, the bidder who should have won, if j sticks around that long, will misread the situation and drop out at a price—which j must pay—that exceeds the value of the prize. This defecting strategy simply doesn't work. [23]

As a final note: In this equilibrium, the prize goes to the bidder with the largest S_i with probability one. And, since revenue equivalence holds in this context, we know what must be each bidder's overall expected payoff and the amount that each bidder expects to pay to the auctioneer/seller. You should have no difficulty seeing that the outcomes that this equilibrium produces are precisely what revenue equivalence says they should be.

However, this is not the only symmetric equilibrium for this context and protocol. See Problem 24.13.

24.5. The Drainage-Tract Context (a.k.a. Maxco–Gambit)

Recall the setting. There are two bidders, Maxco and Gambit. The item at auction has value V, which Gambit knows. Maxco's assessment of V is given by a distribution function F with continuous and strictly positive density f on the support $[0, \bar{v}]$.

The second-price auction is trivial. Gambit's weakly dominant strategy is to bid the true value V of the prize. The argument that this is weakly dominant is the same as in the private values case, since the argument only required that the bidder

---

[22] Suppose bidder j in fact has the nth largest S and, instead of dropping out when he should, he waits out the others to win the item. How much does he lose?

[23] Here's a harder question: Suppose bidder j has the nth largest S but, instead of dropping out according to the equilibrium strategy, delays dropping out. But, lucky for him, he comes to his senses and drops out before the auction ends. How does this affect the outcome of the auction?

knows the value to itself. And, in a second-price auction, if Gambit is bidding V, Maxco must bid 0. Any positive bid by Maxco will only win when Gambit bids less, which is when V is less than Gambit's bid. Moreover, unlike in the private-values case, we have no worries here about other Nash equilibria. Gambit know that, by bidding V, Maxco must rationally bid 0. So Gambit wins the prize V and pays nothing for it.

The first-price auction is more interesting.

Proposition 24.16. *The following pair of strategies is a Nash equilibrium: For $\tilde{V}$ a random variable independent of V and with identical distribution,*

- *Gambit, when it knows that the value of V is v, bids $\beta(v) = \mathbf{E}\left[V \mid \tilde{V} < V = v\right]$; that is,*

$$\beta(v) = \left[\int_0^v u f(u) \mathrm{d}u\right] \Big/ F(u).$$

- *Maxco's bidding strategy is mixed: it bids $\beta(v)$ with density $f(v)$. That is, the probability that Maxco's bid is $\leq \beta(v)$ is $F(v)$.*

At this equilibrium, Maxco's expected payoff is zero.

Proof. To prove that Gambit is choosing a best response against Maxco's strategy, reason as follows. Pretend that this is a symmetric private-value model in which both parties have (independent) private values of V_G for Gambit and V_M for Maxco, both distributed according to F. We know (Proposition 24.4) that a symmetric equilibrium in this make-believe situation is for each party to bid $\beta(v) = \mathbf{E}\left[V_{\text{Other}} \mid V_{\text{Other}} < V_{\text{Self}} = v\right]$. Gambit's bid function β is precisely this function β. And Maxco's bidding strategy is constructed to mimic probabilistically this strategy. Since Gambit only cares in optimizing about the stochastic nature of Maxco's bids, the proof of Proposition 24.4 immediately implies that Gambit is playing a best response to Maxco's strategy.

Maxco is randomizing over bids from 0 to $\beta(\overline{v})$ (which is the mean of V). So, to show that Maxco is choosing a best response, we must show that it has the same expected payoff for every bid level in $[0, \beta(\overline{v})]$. And since bidding 0 is a loser with probability 1, Maxco's expected payoff for every bid must be zero.

Suppose that Maxco bids some $b \in [0, \beta(\overline{v})]$. It wins the auction when V has a value that causes Gambit to bid b or less. That is, it wins the auction when $V \leq \beta^{-1}(b)$. Write v^o for $\beta^{-1}(b)$. Maxco's expected payoff is

$$\int_0^{v^o} (v - b) f(v) \mathrm{d}v = \int_0^{v^o} v f(v) \mathrm{d}v - b F(v^o).$$

Divide this by $F(v^o)$, and the result is

$$\left[\int_0^{v^o} v f(v) \mathrm{d}v\right] \Big/ F(v^o) - b.$$

But the first term, by definition, is $\beta(v^o)$, and since $v^o = \beta^{-1}(b)$, $\beta(v^o) = b$. Maxco's payoff for every bid from 0 to $\beta(\overline{v})$ is indeed 0.   ∎

It should be noted that, in the second-price auction in this context, the seller gets nothing, while in the first-price auction, the seller certainly makes an expected amount of money. (How much? The answer is in plain sight back in Section 24.2.) This, however, is *not* a violation of revenue equivalence. Revenue equivalence is about the expected revenues of the sellers (and expected payments by the bidders) for different auction protocols that give the same "outcome" concerning who wins the auction. In this context combined with the second-price protocol, Gambit wins the auction with probability one. But in this context with the first-price protocol, Gambit wins with probability 1/2, at least for the equilibrium produced here. (And how did I know that Gambit wins with probability 1/2 in the first-price equilibrium? Again, the answer is in plain sight back in Section 24.2.)

Because asymmetric information is often the case in the real world, there is a lot more that can and has been said about this context and related contexts. But this is enough of an introduction.

24.6. Conditionally Independent Signals

The third (and final) common-value context is when the signals S_i held by the bidders are conditionally i.i.d., conditional on the true value.

"Good news": Affiliation and the monotone-likelihood-ratio property

While there is some theory about contexts in which the signals S_i are multidimensional, most theory—and everything we do in this chapter—assumes that each S_i is one-dimensional. And most theory is based on the assumption that higher values of the signals are "good news" about the common value V. This notion of "good news" translates formally into statements of how $\mathbf{E}[V|S_i, S_j, S_k]$ changes with changes in the conditioning variables: Writing $\mathbf{E}[V|S_i, S_j, S_k] = \phi(S_i, S_j, S_k)$ temporarily, "good news" assumptions guarantee that ϕ is strictly increasing in each of its three arguments. And more besides: We would like, for instance, $\mathbf{E}[V|\mathcal{S}_{-i}^{(1)} = S_i = s, \mathcal{S}^{(N)}, \mathcal{S}^{(N-1)}]$ to be strictly increasing in its three arguments. Put it this way: In the English button auction, it is natural to suppose that, the longer it takes (as the price rises) for bidders to drop out, the more optimistic bidders should be about V; sticking around longer "ought" to mean that their information indicates a larger common value. In the wallet-game context, these properties fall out almost for free, because V is the sum of the S_i. But, in the more general context of conditionally independent signals (and contexts even more general than that), assumptions are necessary to ensure that bigger signals and order statistics of the signals constitute "good news."

A seemingly natural assumption that a signal S_i is "good news" about V is that the conditional distribution of S_i, conditional on V, is stochastically increasing in

V. That is, if $v > v'$, then S_i conditional on $V = v$ has a "bigger" distribution than does S_i conditional on $V = v'$. But this assumption is insufficient. Suppose V is uniformly distributed on $[0, 1]$, and for each v, the conditional density function of S_i given $V = v$ is as depicted in Figure 24.3: At least ϵ everywhere, but with an additional "isoceles triangle" of probability centered at $v/2$ and another centered at v, each with a small base of size ϵ, and an area of $(1 - \epsilon)/2$, which, given ϵ, would mean a height of $A = (1 - \epsilon)/\epsilon$. (Some adjustments will be needed for $v < \epsilon/2$ and $v > 1 - \epsilon/2$.) It should be clear that, in this construction, the conditional distribution of S_i does increase stochastically (in the sense of first-order stochastic dominance) as V increases. And, in fact, as $\epsilon \to 0$, V and S_i are very highly correlated.

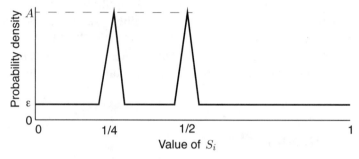

Figure 24.3. The shape of the density of S_i given $V = 1/2$ (not drawn completely accurately).

Now compare the inferences made when $S_i = 0.45$ versus $S_i = 0.6$. For small ϵ, the signal $S_i = 0.45$ leads to the inference that V is probably very close to either 0.45 or 0.9, with roughly equal probability. The signal $S_i = 0.6$ leads to the inference that V is very likely to be close to 0.6. Hence, the conditional expected value of V given $S_i = 0.45$ is greater than the conditional expected value of V given $S_i = 0.6$. This lower signal is "better news" about V—or, at least, about the expectation of V—than is the higher signal.

The problem is apparent: When conditioning on a particular value of S_i, what matters to the conditional distribution of V given S_i is the behavior of the conditional *density* of S_i given V for the different values of V. Recall that H is the marginal distribution function, h the density function of V, $F(\cdot | V = v)$ is the conditional distribution function, and $f(\cdot | v)$ the conditional density of S_i given $V = v$. Then, the conditional density of V given $S_i = s$ is given (by Bayes' rule) as

$$h(v | S_i = s) = \frac{h(v) f(s | v)}{\int_{\underline{v}}^{\overline{v}} h(u) f(s | u) du}.$$

Hence, in a context where we have all these absolutely continuous (conditional) distributions, assumptions on how the conditional densities change with changes in the conditioning variable are required.

Begin with a definition concerning the joint densities of a collection of random variables.

Definition 24.17. *For a finite collection of real-valued random variables $\{\zeta_k; k = 1, \ldots, K\}$ with a (joint-distribution) support that is the product of intervals in R^K and joint density function ϕ, the family of random variables satisfies **affiliation** (the random variables are **affiliated**) if, for every $z = (z_1, \ldots, z_K)$ and $z' = (z'_1, \ldots, z'_K)$ from this product of intervals, we define*

$$z \vee z' := \left(max\{z_1, z'_1\}, \ldots, max\{z_K, z'_K\} \right) \text{ and } z \wedge z' := \left(min\{z_1, z'_1\}, \ldots, min\{z_K, z'_K\} \right),$$

then

$$\phi(z \vee z') \times \phi(z \wedge z') \geq \phi(z) \times \phi(z'), \tag{24.5}$$

or, equivalently,

$$ln\left(\phi(z \vee z') + ln\left(\phi(z \wedge z')\right) \geq ln\left(\phi(z)\right) + ln\left(\phi(z')\right). \tag{24.5'}$$

Specialize this definition to the case of two random variables, V and S_i, where V's density function h is strictly positive on some subinterval of $[0, \infty)$ (and zero otherwise) and S_i's have, for each v in the support of V, a conditional density function $f(s|v)$ that is strictly positive on some subinterval of $[0, \infty)$ (and zero otherwise), where the conditional support of S_i given V is the same no matter what is the conditioning value of V. Their joint density is, of course, $\phi(v, s) = h(v)f(s|v)$. Take two values for V, $v > v'$, and two values for S_i, $s > s'$, and compare $\phi(v, s')\phi(v', s)$ with $\phi(v, s)\phi(v', s')$. This is

$$h(v)f(s'|v) \times h(v')f(s|v') \quad \text{versus} \quad h(v)f(s|v) \times h(v')f(s'|h').$$

And, therefore, V and S_i are affiliated if, for all such pairs of pairs,

$$\frac{f(s|v)}{f(s'|v)} \geq \frac{f(s|v')}{f(s'|v')}.$$

That is:

Definition 24.18. *For two random variables V and S whose supports are $[\underline{v}, \overline{v}]$ and $[\underline{s}, \overline{s}]$, respectively, where V has a strictly positive density function h on its support and, for each $v \in [\underline{v}, \overline{v}]$, S has a conditional density $f(s|v)$ that is strictly positive on $[\underline{s}, \overline{s}]$: The variable S satisfies the **monotone-likelihood-ratio property** (with respect to V) if, for $v > v'$ and $s > s'$,*

$$\frac{f(s|v)}{f(s'|v)} \geq \frac{f(s|v')}{f(s'|v')}. \tag{24.6}$$

In words, the ratio of the conditional density of the larger value of S to the smaller value of S increases (weakly) as the conditioning variable v increases.[24] Now, the general definition of affiliation — even more general than Definition 24.17 — works in cases where Definition 24.18 makes no sense; for instance, if V and S_i have discrete supports (that allow the taking of $\vee$ and $\wedge$). The monotone-likelihood-ratio property is an equivalent condition only when it applies (e.g., under the conditions imposed in Definition 24.18).

Proposition 24.19.

a. *In the context of Definition 24.18, V and S are affiliated if and only if they satisfy the monotone-likelihood-ratio property.*

b. *In the symmetric conditionally-independent-signals context — that is, the value V has a density function as in Definition 24.18, and the signals $\{S_i; i = 1, \ldots, N\}$ are conditionally i.i.d. with each S_i having conditional density functions as in Definition 24.18, the full complement of random variables $\{V, S_i; i = 1, \ldots, N\}$ satisfies affiliation if and only if each (and, hence, every) S_i has the monotone-likelihood-ratio property with respect to V.*

Proof. Part a is just a matter of comparing definitions. For part b, the log-version of the affiliation inequality (24.5′) is used. Fix two vectors of values for V and the N signals, $(v, s_1, \ldots, s_N)$ and $(v', s_1', \ldots, s_N')$. The joint density function $(V, S_1, \ldots, S_N)$ at the values $(v, s_1, \ldots, s_N)$ is

$$h(v) \times \prod_{i=1}^{N} f(s_i|v), \quad \text{hence, the log of this is} \quad \ln\big(h(v)\big) + \sum_{i=1}^{N} \ln\big(f(s_i|v)\big),$$

and similarly for $(v', s_1', \ldots, s_n')$. Assume, without loss of generality, that $v \geq v'$. For each component i, either $s_i \geq s_i'$, in which case, in the required inequality of the logs of the joint density function, the corresponding terms $\ln\big(f(s_i|x)\big)$ and $\ln\big(f(s_i'|x)\big)$ are the same on the two sides of the inequality, or $s_i < s_i'$. But, in the case $s_i < s_i'$, because each signal is affiliated with V, we have $\ln\big(f(s_i|v)\big) + \ln\big(f(s_i'|v')\big) \leq \ln\big(f(s_i'|v)\big) + \ln\big(f(s_i|v')\big)$. Adding all these terms, we get the required inequality. ∎

Affiliation of a finite collection of random variables $\{\zeta_k\}$ is a powerful property with many useful consequences, among which are the following.

Proposition 24.20.

a. *If $\{\zeta_k; k = 1, \ldots, K\}$ is an affiliated set of random variables, then every subset of this set is affiliated.*

b. *For a finite set of (real-valued) random variables $\{\zeta_k; k = 1, \ldots, K\}$, whose support is a product of intervals in R^K and that have a joint density function ϕ that is strictly*

---

[24] Compare this definition with Definition 19.10 on page 64.

positive on the support and twice continuously differentiable: The collection $\{\zeta_k; k = 1, \ldots, K\}$ is affiliated if and only if, for all j and k,

$$\frac{\partial^2 ln(f(z))}{\partial z_j \partial z_k} \geq 0.$$

c. *Every finite collection of independent random variables is affiliated.*

d. *If $\{\zeta_k; k = 1, \ldots, K\}$ is an affiliated set of random variables with support Σ in R^k, and if $\Psi : \Sigma \to R$ is a bounded and (weakly) increasing function, then $\mathbf{E}[\Psi(\zeta_1, \ldots, \zeta_K)|\zeta_1]$ is (weakly) increasing in ζ_1.*

e. *$\{\zeta_k; k = 1, \ldots, K\}$ is an affiliated set of random variations if and only if, for each pair k and k', $k \neq k'$, ζ_k is affiliated with $\zeta_{k'}$.*

f. *Suppose $\{\xi, \zeta_k; k = 1, \ldots, K\}$ is an affiliated set of random variables with joint density function ϕ that is symmetric in the K ζ_k components. Then if $\zeta^{(k)}$ are the k-th order statistics of the ζ_k, the set $\{\xi, \zeta^{(1)}, \ldots \zeta^{(K)}\}$ is affiliated.*

I'll prove none of these facts; any of the three books mentioned in the Bibliographic Notes or the classic paper by Milgrom and Weber (1982) should be consulted for details.

However, let me indicate how some of these properties relate to "good news." Suppose $\{V, S_i; i = 1, \ldots, N\}$ is an affiliated set. Then $\Psi(V, S_1, \ldots, S_N) = V$ is a (weakly) increasing function of the random variables and, under the assumption that V has bounded support, $\mathbf{E}[V|S_i]$ is a (weakly) increasing function of S_i, as per part d of Proposition 24.20. We'd like it to be strictly increasing but, except for this, we have that with affiliation, signals are good news about the value. And, in the symmetric case, if we combine part d with part f, we know that $\mathbf{E}[V|\mathcal{S}^{(1)}]$ is a nondecreasing function of $\mathcal{S}^{(1)}$, where $\mathcal{S}^{(1)}$ is the first order statistic of the $\{S_i\}$.

The symmetric second-price equilibrium

Define the function $\chi : [\underline{s}, \overline{s}] \times [\underline{s}, \overline{s}] \to R$ by

$$\chi(s, s') := \mathbf{E}\left[V \big| \mathcal{S}_{-i}^{(1)} = s, S_i = s'\right].$$

Assumption 24.21. *The function χ is jointly continuous and (weakly) increasing in both variables.*

Earlier assumptions about the marginal distribution of V and the conditional distributions of each S_i given V nearly give continuity of χ; we need to add that the conditional density functions $f(s|v)$ are jointly continuous in (s, v). That χ is (weakly) increasing follows, for instance, if the signals and V are affiliated, applying Proposition 24.19.

The symmetric equilibrium bears a striking resemblance to the equilibrium for the wallet-game context.

Proposition 24.22. *In the symmetric conditionally independent signals context, with Assumption 24.21 maintained, a symmetric Nash equilibrium for the second-price auction protocol is for bidder i to bid $\chi(s, s)$ when his signal is $S_i = s$. This results in the prize being won by the bidder whose signal is largest, with $\mathbf{E}\big[\chi(S^{(2)}, S^{(2)})\big]$ the expected revenue received by the seller.*

Proof. The proof is so similar to the proof of Proposition 24.13 that I go quickly. First, $\chi(\underline{s}, \underline{s})$ is the lowest bid that will be made by anyone in equilibrium, and $\chi(\overline{s}, \overline{s})$ is the largest, so there is no profit in choosing a bid outside the range $\big[\chi(\underline{s}, \underline{s}), \chi(\overline{s}, \overline{s})\big]$. By the properties of χ, any bid b within that interval corresponds to some $s \in [\underline{s}, \overline{s}]$, in the sense that $\chi(s, s) = b$. So the issue is: If all bidders except for bidder i bid according to the equilibrium strategies, and i's signal S_i is s_i, can i do better by pretending to have received signal s instead of the true signal s_i he received? By the law of iterated conditional expectations, if he bids $b = \chi(s, s)$, his expected payoff is

$$\mathbf{E}\big[V - \chi(S^{(1)}_{\neg i}, S^{(1)}_{\neg i}); s > S^{(1)}_{\neg i}\big] = \mathbf{E}\big[\mathbf{E}[V | S^{(1)}_{\neg i}, S_i] - \chi(S^{(1)}_{\neg i}, S^{(1)}_{\neg i}); s > S^{(1)}_{\neg i}\big]$$
$$= \mathbf{E}\big[\chi(S^{(1)}_{\neg i}, S_i) - \chi(S^{(1)}_{\neg i}, S^{(1)}_{\neg i}); s > S^{(1)}_{\neg i}\big],$$

where the expectation is over the possible values of $S^{(1)}_{\neg i}$. To explain, the first term in the integral is the expected prize he wins, if he wins, (and is calculated based on the true signal that he received), and the second term is the second-highest bid, which he pays; this is integrated over the event that he wins. (This is correct, even if his bid ties for largest. Why?) Expressing this in integral form, it is

$$\int_{\underline{s}}^{s} \big[\chi(S^{(1)}_{\neg i}, S_i) - \chi(S^{(1)}_{\neg i}, S^{(1)}_{\neg i})\big] g\big(S^{(1)}_{\neg i} | S_i\big) dS^{(1)}_{\neg i},$$

where $g(\cdot | S_i)$ denotes the conditional density function of $S^{(1)}_{\neg i}$ given S_i, and the upper limit of the integral captures the idea that we're integrating over possible values of $S^{(1)}_{\neg i}$ for which he wins if he "pretends" to have received signal s. By Assumption 24.21, the integrand is nonnegative for $s_i > S^{(1)}_{\neg i}$ and nonpositive for $S^{(1)}_{\neg i} > s$. So the integral is at its largest if it is cut off at $s = S_i$. (If χ is strictly increasing in its second argument, which holds in most examples, $s = S_i$ is the unique maximizing upper limit of the integral.) Pretending to have received some other signal is never going to be better than using the true S_i.

The rest of the proposition is just bookkeeping.   ∎

Compare this situation with that of the wallet-game context. Of course, χ is a more complex function than was ψ. And, in this context, the distribution of $S^{(1)}_{\neg i}$ will in general depend on the value of S_i that i has observed; in the wallet-game context, the independence of the S_i's implies that no conditioning on S_i is required. This, it turns out, has implications for revenue equivalence, which doesn't hold in general.

The symmetric equilibrium for the information-rich English-button auction

Next comes the button auction, run so that bidders see the prices at which their rivals drop out. Once again, the construction should look very familiar, following the analysis of the button auction in the wallet-game context.

To begin, define

$$\xi(s_1, s_2, \ldots, s_N) = \mathbf{E}[V | S^{(1)} = s_1, S^{(2)} = s_2, \ldots, S^{(N)} = s_N].$$

Assumption 24.23. The function ξ is jointly continuous and strictly increasing in all its arguments.

Continuity follows from continuity of the conditional densities in v. I believe that, if the conditional densities satisfy a *strict* version of the monotone-likelihood-ratio property, then we get strictly increasing functions. But I cannot find a source to verify this, so I just make this assumption.

Proposition 24.24. The following strategy, played by all N bidders, is a symmetric Nash equilibrium for the information-rich, English-button-auction protocol in the symmetric conditionally independent signals context, under Assumption 24.23.

- *At the start, bidder i computes $\xi(S_i, S_i, \ldots, S_i)$. If no other bidder drops out before the price reaches that level, bidder i drops out.*

- *If another bidder drops out at price p_0, i inverts $\xi(s, s, \ldots, s) = p_0$; this tells i (and all other bidders who did not drop out) the S_j of the bidder who did drop out, which is $S^{(N)}$.*

- *Bidder i, having made this inference, changes his drop-out price to $\xi(S_i, S_i, \ldots, S_i, S^{(N)})$.*

- *Supposing some other bidder drops out before this price is reached, he inverts $\xi(s, s, \ldots, s, S^{(N)})$ to discover $S^{(N-1)}$, and changes his drop-out price to $\xi(S_i, \ldots, S_i, S^{(N-1)}, S^{(N)})$.*

- *And so on.* .

The outcome of this equilibrium is that the bidder, call him i, whose signal S_i is highest (hence, $= S^{(1)}$), wins the auction when the bidder with the second-highest signal, $S^{(2)}$, drops out. The winning bidder pays $\xi(S^{(2)}, S^{(2)}, S^{(3)}, \ldots, S^{(N)})$, for an expected payoff of

$$\xi(S^{(1)}, S^{(2)}, S^{(3)}, \ldots, S^{(N)}) - \xi(S^{(2)}, S^{(2)}, S^{(3)}, \ldots, S^{(N)}).$$

I won't provide the proof, but the intuition (and the main part of a formal proof) is identical to the case of the wallet-game context.

The symmetric first-price equilibrium

It would be nice if revenue-equivalence held in this context, as we could then write down the bid function for the first-price protocol from Proposition 24.22 or

Proposition 24.24. But, unhappily, revenue equivalence doesn't necessarily hold. I'll state the result in the next subsection, but a fuller discussion of why revenue equivalence fails is not provided until Chapter 26. (You can see some hints of what goes wrong by examining the proof of Proposition 24.14(a), provided in the *Online Supplement*.)

Although it isn't a rigorous proof of anything, we can get an idea of what an equilibrium bidding function should look like by developing "first-order conditions." Assume that all bidders are employing a continuous and strictly increasing bidding function $\beta : [\underline{s}, \overline{s}]$ that satisfies $\beta(\underline{s}) = \underline{s}$. Let $G(\cdot|s_i)$ be the conditional distribution function of $\mathcal{S}_{\neg i}^{(1)}$ given $S_i = s_i$, that is,

$$G(s|s_i) := \mathbf{P}\big(\mathcal{S}_{\neg i}^{(1)} \le s|S_i = s_i\big).$$

Write $g(s|s_i)$ for the conditional density corresponding to G. Suppose bidder i has signal $S_i = s_i$ and thinks of bidding b from the interval $[\beta(\underline{s}), \beta(\overline{s})]$. Write s' for $\beta^{-1}(b)$. This will be a winning bid with probability $G(s'|s_i)$, and so it provides the expected payoff

$$\big(\mathbf{E}\big[V\big|\mathcal{S}_{\neg i}^{(1)} \le s', S_i = s_i\big] - \beta(s')\big)\mathbf{P}\big(\mathcal{S}_{\neg i}^{(1)} \le s'\big|S_i = s_i\big)$$
$$= \mathbf{E}\big[V \; ; \; \mathcal{S}_{\neg i}^{(1)} \le s', S_i = s_i\big] - \beta(s')G(s'|S_i = s_i).$$

Abbreviate $\mathbf{E}\big[V\big|\mathcal{S}_{\neg i}^{(1)} = s', S_i = s_i\big]$ as $\nu(s', s_i)$, and the expected payoff is

$$\left[\int_{\underline{s}}^{s'} \nu(s, s_i)g(s|s_i)\mathrm{d}s\right] - \beta(s')G(s').$$

The first-order condition for optimality in s' is that the derivative of this in s' should be zero, or

$$\nu(s', s_i)g(s'|s_i) - \beta'(s')G(s'|s_i) - \beta(s')G(s'|s_i) = 0.$$

For β to be an equilibrium bidding function, the optimizing s' should be s_i, giving the differential equation

$$\nu(s_i, s_i)g(s_i|s_i) - \beta'(s_i)G(s_i|s_i) - \beta(s_i)g(s_i|s_i) = 0$$

which gives

$$\beta'(s_i) = \Big[\nu(s_i, s_i) - \beta(s_i)\Big]\left[\frac{g(s_i|s_i)}{G(s_i|s_i)}\right].$$

So, if you know how to evaluate the functions ν, g, and G, even numerically, you can solve this differentiable equation numerically (by extending β small step by small step, using the corresponding difference equation).

Will you get an equilibrium bidding function? As long as the monotone-likelihood-ratio property holds, you will. Indeed, we can write down the solution in closed form and verify that it does give an equilibrium. But it isn't pleasant: First, for s' and s_i in the range of the signals, with $s' \leq s_i$, define

$$L(s'|s_i) := \exp\left[-\int_{s'}^{s_i} \frac{g(s|s)}{G(s|s)} \mathrm{d}s \right].$$

Then define

$$\beta(s_i) := \int_{\underline{s}}^{s_i} \nu(s, s) L(\mathrm{d}s|s_i).$$

Proposition 24.25. *The functions β produce a symmetric equilibrium for the first-price auction, in the context of conditionally independent signals, if all previous assumptions hold, including the monotone-likelihood-ratio property.*

I'm not going to produce the proof here; consult any of the three books given in the Bibliographic Notes. But I can outline how the proof goes, and it resembles how all previous "it-is-a-symmetric-equilibrium" proofs have gone: First, you show that L has the properties of a family of distribution functions. (This step is new to this context.) Then you show that the function β is continuous and strictly increasing. And, then, you ask: If bidder i, holding signal S_i, pretends instead to hold signal s and so bids $\beta(s)$, can he do better? Write down his expected payoff in terms of $S_{\neg i}^{(1)}$. Then integrate out $S_{\neg i}^{(1)}$, from $S_{\neg i}^{(1)} = \underline{s}$ up to s (the event on which i wins by pretending to have s). The integrand increases until $s = S_i$ and decreases thereafter, so $\beta(S_i)$ is the optimal bid when S_i is what i knows.

Revenue equivalence?

I've already told you that, in general, revenue equivalence doesn't hold in this case. In fact, one can prove that the seller's expected revenue is highest for the information-rich English (button) auction, second highest for the second-price auction, and least for the first-price auction, where "highest" and so forth are formally *weak* inequalities. This the consequence of results with the general name *linkage*; other consequences of linkage include, for instance, that if the auctioneer can commit in advance to supply (truthful) information that is affiliated with all the bidders' signals, doing so will increase expected revenues.

Intuition as to why revenue equivalence fails in general in this context will be provided in Chapter 26. If you wish to learn about linkage, consult one of the three books given in the Bibliographic Notes.

24.7. Multi-Item Auctions

So far, the story has been about a single indivisible item that is being auctioned. In many auctions—in most cases, in auctions where a lot of money is at stake—there are from several to many, many items being auctioned. Sometimes the items are identical; for example, when the government auctions T-bills or in an initial public offering of shares of equity in a corporation. In other cases, the items are similar; for example, when the government auctions mineral rights to a number of tracts in a given geographic region, or when the government auctions the rights to parts of the electromagnetic spectrum. In these cases, things are made more complex by the fact that possession of one of the items affects the valuation to the winner of the other, "adjacent" items. In some cases, the auction protocol has all the items auctioned for sale in one, grand, one-round of bidding. In some cases, everything is auctioned "at once," but in a multiround protocol. And, in other cases, some of the items are awarded before other items are offered for sale.

These auctions can be very complex and, to be clear, when it comes to, for instance, spectrum auctions, the design of the auction by specialists is a matter of "art informed by science." Paul Milgrom's *Putting Auction Theory to Work* and Paul Klemperer's *Auctions: Theory and Practice* (see Bibliographic Notes for this chapter) give excellent accounts of how theory ("science") blends with art in real-world contexts.

This section provides the barest beginnings of the "science" part of the story.[25] Imagine an auction of M identical items among $N > M$ bidders, where bidders want no more than one of the items, all bidders are risk neutral, and each bidder i ($i = 1, \ldots, N$) has his own private valuation V_i for his one item, should he win one, against which the price he pays is subtracted.

Suppose in this context that the auction protocol is the generalized Vickrey or "$M + 1$st"-price auction. Each bidder submits a dollar value he is willing to pay. These are ordered, highest to lowest, as $\mathcal{B}^{(1)}, \mathcal{B}^{(2)}, \ldots, \mathcal{B}^{(N)}$. And the M items are awarded, one apiece, to the bidders who submitted the highest M bids, with each winning bidder paying $\mathcal{B}^{(M+1)}$; that is, they all pay the highest bid that *does not* win an item. Ties—when the Mth highest bid is the same as the $M + 1$st highest—are handled by random assignment among bidders whose bids equal $\mathcal{B}^{(M+1)}$. It should not surprise you that, in this context, it is weakly dominant for the bidders to bid their private values; that is, bidder i submits the bid V_i.

Contrast this with the procedure in which bidders are allowed to submit a single real-valued bid, the items are awarded (one per bidder) to the bidders who submit the highest M bids, but each bidder must pay what he bid. Assuming the V_i; $i = 1, \ldots, N$ are i.i.d., with common distribution function F with all the standard properties, it is an equilibrium for bidder i to bid

$$\mathbf{E}\left[\mathcal{V}_{\neg i}^{(M+1)} \middle| V_i > \mathcal{V}_{\neg i}^{(M+1)}\right].$$

Again, I'll leave the proof to you. But note that (a) in the Vickrey auction and (b) in this pay-what-you-bid auction, the items are allocated to the M individuals' whose private valuations are highest—that is, efficiently—and revenue equivalence holds.

---

[25] But see also Chapter 25 where the problem is reframed as being one of matching items to bidders.

That's about all one can say concerning "simple" stuff. Still assuming that the items are identical, if there is a common-value element to the items at auction—think of an initial public offering—or, even more challenging, if bidders might wish to purchase more than one of the items, then the theory becomes much harder. To give a hint, suppose the auction protocol is the Vickrey auction—every bidder pays the highest non-winning bid—but bidders may submit multiple bids. Suppose, for instance, bidder i values the first item he might win at V_{i1}, the marginal value of the second item he might win at V_{i2}, and so forth. (That is, if he were to win two, his payoff would be $V_{i1} + V_{i2}$ less whatever he pays for the two.) Assume the items are *substitutes*, in the sense that $V_{i1} \geq V_{i2} \geq V_{i3}$, and so forth. Then it is weakly optimal for him to submit V_{i1} for his first bid. But, in general, he will wish to submit something less than V_{i2} for his second bid, on grounds that his second bid might prove to be "pivotal"; that is, it might be the highest non-winning bid, which then sets to price for all winning bids. Of course, if the number of items M is huge, and the number of bidders, while greater than M, is also huge (say, $2N = M$ for very large M), then—with some assumptions—it is unlikely that one of i's bids will be the highest non-winning bid. Hence, i won't discount his "multi-unit" bids by much. But "with some assumptions" must be made precise.

And, to add to the complications in real-life contexts, in some real-life situations, the auctioneer allows the submission of "at market" orders. These orders are filled at whatever is determined to be the market price; the hope is that there are enough bids submitted with amounts attached so that a "market" price can be determined. ("At market" orders may have to be allocated, so "at market" bidders have to decide how many of these bids to make.)

And all this is for the case in which multiple *identical* items are being auctioned. What if the items are different? We return to further exploration of multi-unit auctions in Chapter 26, where we'll have the tools of general mechanism design (and, in particular, the Vickrey–Clarke–Groves mechanism) to employ in this context.

24.8. Why Do We (Think We) Know More about Auctions Than about Bilateral Bargaining?

Superficially, the topics of this chapter, auctions, and last chapter, bilateral bargaining, have many similarities. For each, there are large literatures, summarized to greater or lesser extent in entire books. But I think it is safe to say, while economists generally believe that the literature on auctions and auction design has been successful, as both desciptive and normative theory,[26] it is also safe to say that the economics literature has far to go before a similar claim can be made concerning our understanding of bilateral bargaining. It is interesting to ask, Why the difference?

Auctions—excluding real-life English auctions—generally come with fixed and formal rules for what strategies are possible for bidders. And, when they do not—as in the real-life English auction—economists invent "versions," with buttons and

---

[26] The theory is normative both as a tool for determining how to bid and how to design an auction.

suchlike, to make formal analysis feasible. This might be seen as a difference between auctions and bargaining. Except that, while free-form bargaining lacks well-defined rules, economists have no problem inventing "versions" (such as Rubinstein's alternating offer model) that allow formal analysis. Indeed, in the literature on bargaining, "robustness" to the formal version is a matter of significant concern (noting that robustness fails miserably in Rubinstein protocol with complete information).

In my opinion, the real difference is in the "sophistication" of the participants. There are, of course, auctions with unsophisticated bidders. If you examine bidder behavior in pay-per-bid auctions on the internet, it is hard to come up with any rational-behavior explanation for what you see. However, in many contexts— mineral rights auctions, spectrum auctions, auctions of government bonds—the bidders are quite sophisticated and, while they may not act strictly in accordance with economic theories of how they "ought" to behave, the distance between theory and practice is not that great. (Of course, a substantial empirical and experimental literature exists concerning how large this "distance" is.) In contrast, in almost all real-life instances of bilateral bargaining, the psychology of the bargaining process and the bargainers equals or even swamps in importance economic considerations. This includes, for instance, bargaining between an employer and a union, or bargaining between nations.[27] Economics has a long way to go before (if ever) it can deal with this sort of psychology.

Bibliographic Notes

We have not completed our study of auctions; we'll return to this topic in Chapter 26. And, one can regard the economic problem of auctions—especially multi-item auctions—as a problem in matching items to bidders. So Chapter 25 will have some pertinent things to say. For now, the bibliographic notes are provisional, to be supplemented at the end of Chapter 26. But, in terms of what has been discussed in this chapter, some must-be-mentioned classics are Vickrey (1961), Cassady (1967) (which surveys the "real world" of auctions), A. Ortega-Reichart (1968), R. Wilson (1969), and Milgrom and Weber (1982).

If you wish to see more, I think the best way to approach the subject is by reading one of the excellent books on the topic. In preparing this chapter (on a subject about which I am very inexpert), I have relied on Klemperer (2004), Milgrom (2004), and Krishna (2010).[28]

---

[27] An important consideration in such contexts is that the bargainers have constituencies to which they report. I don't discount the possibility that the bargainers are being rational given the constraints on their actions imposed by somewhat irrational constituencies.

[28] And I reiterate here that, in this chapter, the assistance of my colleague Andrzej Skrzypacz was monumental.

Problems

■ 24.1. Prove parts b, c, and d of Proposition 24.3.

■ 24.2. Continuing with the private-values context, why aren't the nonexistence problems discussed in the subsection "The first-price auction: Preliminaries" a problem for the second-price format?

■ 24.3. Concerning the discontinuity discussed on page 334, which causes problems for the existence of an auction equilibrium, why didn't we encounter similar problems in Chapter 23? To give away the story: What did we assume would happen in the simple simultaneous submission of bids and asks in Chapter 23, if the bid exactly equaled the ask?

■ 24.4. This problem explores issues arising because the payoff function in a first-price auction is discontinuous in an unpleasant way.

a. Suppose Carol and Bob are the only two bidders, and Carol is known to value the item at $10, while Bob is known to value it at $15. Show that it is impossible that a pure-strategy Nash equilibrium exists in this context for the first-price auction format.

b. However, there are mixed strategy equilibria in this context, in which Bob is certain to win the item, his bid is $b \in [10, 15)$, and Carol randomizes to keep Bob "honest." Can you produce such an equilibrium?

c. Suppose Carol and Bob are the only two bidders. Carol is known to value the item at $0, while Bob values it at either $0 or $10, each equally likely (from Carol's perspective). In this context, prove that there is no Nash equilibrium for the first-price auction format, whether mixed or pure. (Remember, we don't allow negative bids.)

(In the solution in the *Online Supplement*, I direct you to nonexistence examples that don't depend so heavily as does part c on the special properties of the value = $0.)

■ 24.5. In an "all-pay" auction, each bidder submits a bid $b \geq 0$, which he pays regardless of whether he wins the item or not. The bidder who submits the largest bid wins the item. In the standard symmetric private-values context, what is the symmetric equilibrium in the all-pay auction?

■ 24.6. In step 2 of the proof of the revenue equivalence theorem, Proposition 24.7, I asserted that the function $\mathcal{U}_i^*(V_i) := \sup_{\hat{v}_i} V_i \, G(\hat{v}_i) - \pi(\hat{v}_i)$ is convex in V_i. I further asserted that the proof of this follows the lines of proof of the convexity of the profit function, in Chapter 9 of Volume I. In fact, the proof for the profit function is more complex that is needed here, because there we allowed that the supremum might be attained, and a surpremum value of $+\infty$ was not ruled out. That can't happen here: In the course of proving the revenue equivalence theorem, step 1 of the proof left us with the conclusion that the supremum is attained, and it is attained by $\hat{v}_i = V_i$.

Supply the proof required in this simpler setting. And, while you are at it, provide details about why $\mathcal{U}_i^*$ is continuous on the endpoints of the interval $[\underline{v}, \overline{v}]$.

■ 24.7. The point of this problem is to finish the proof of Proposition 24.9

a. In the standard symmetric private-values context, suppose that the distribution function of the private values, F, has support $[\underline{v}, \overline{v}]$, and the seller of the item values it at the amount $u = \underline{v}$. Show that, from the seller's perspective of maximizing her expected payoff, if she sets a reserve price r, then $r > \underline{v}$. (It suffices to show that for some $h > 0$, the reserve price $\underline{v} + h$ is superior to the reserve price $\underline{v}$. And, indeed, you should be able to show that this is so for all h in some nontrivial interval $(0, h^*)$.) And, if $r \to W(r)$ is the expected payoff function to the seller if she sets reserve price r, what can you say about the shape of W over a small interval $[\underline{v}, \underline{v} + h]$?

b. And what if $u < \underline{v}$?

■ 24.8. In the text, bidders are always assumed to be risk neutral. What happens if they are risk-averse expected-utility maximizers?

Suppose, in a private-values context, the bidders are risk-averse expected-utility maximizers. Bidder i, $i = 1, \ldots, N$, has a strictly increasing, concave utility function $U_i : [0, \infty) \to R$, normalized so that $U_i(0) = 0$. The domain of U_i may extend to negative values. However, in this private-values context, I'll assume that bidders never bid more than their value. And, because we'll only look at first- and second-price auctions, they only pay if they win, so negative arguments for U never enter the story. To be clear, if bidder i loses the auction (isn't the high bidder), his outcome is $U_i(0) = 0$. If he wins, his outcome is $U_i(V_i - \text{what he pays})$. Hence in either first- or second-price auctions, his (expected) payoff is

$$\mathbf{P}(\text{his bid is the high bid}) \times U_i(V_i - \text{what he pays}).$$

a. Argue that, in a second-price auction, it remains weakly dominant to bid one's true value. Then, assuming we are in a standard symmetric private-values context, where all bidders bid their own values, what is the expected revenue to the seller?

b. Now add the assumption that all bidders have the same utility function U, which, moreover, is continuously differentiable. Derive a differential equation for a symmetric equilibrium in the first-price-auction protocol, where the bidding function $\beta : [\underline{v}, \overline{v}] \to R$ should satisfy the boundary condition $\beta(\underline{v}) = \underline{v}$ and (you may assume) is strictly increasing and differentiable. As in the text, use $G(v)$ to denote $\mathbf{P}\left[V_{\neg i}^{(1)} \le v\right]$.

c. How do the seller's revenues in the equilibrium in part b compare with the seller's revenues in part a? Fill in the blank in the following sentence: Since in either auction protocol, in this format, the prize goes to the bidder with the highest private valuation, revenue equivalence ____ hold. [Hint: If U is strictly concave (and strictly increasing), and if $U(0) = 0$, what can you say about the sign of $U(x) - U'(x)x$ for $x > 0$?]

■ 24.9. Maxco and Gambit, independent (and risk-neutral) crude-oil extractors, are engaged in an auction for the mineral rights on an isolated tract of land. They share a common assessment concerning the value V of the oil that can be extracted. Neither has any further information about V beyond this assessment, which is given by the distribution function F. That is, the probability that the crude oil that can be extracted is less than v is $F(v)$. Both have private development costs, given by C_M for Maxco and C_G for Gambit. Each knows its own level of extraction costs, each assesses that the extraction costs of the other has a probability distribution given by the distribution function H, independent of its own extraction costs. The distribution function H has all the "standard" properties; its support is a compact subinterval of $[0, \infty)$, and it is absolutely continuous with a density function h that is strictly positive on the support. (When you get to part d, you may make the same assumptions about F.)

a. Suppose the owner of this tract of land conducts a second-price auction. That is, Maxco and Gambit submit bids, and whichever firm submits the higher bid gets the mineral rights for a payment of the other firm's bid. What happens?

b. And what happens if the auction is a first-price auction?

c. As a possible alternative auction protocol, the government consider a *royalty-based* bidding scheme. Rather than bidding a lump-sum amount of money, the two bidders bid a percentage. If, say, Maxco bids 24% and Gambit bids 20%, then Maxco wins the auction and pays 24% of the dollar-value of royalties back to the government. (This is if the royalty protocol is a first-price royalty protocol.) So, supposing the dollar value of crude oil is V, Maxco wins with a royalty bid of 24%, and Maxco's extraction costs are C_M, Maxco pays the government $0.24V$ and so has a net payoff of $0.76V - C_M$. Does this make a difference to the outcome of the auction? It doesn't, and it is your job in this part of the problem to explain why it doesn't.

d. Things aren't so easy if the bidders are risk-averse expected-utility maximizers. (You may wonder why Maxco and Gambit, if they are widely held stock corporations, would be risk averse. But that's a question for another day.) To keep things relatively simple, suppose we are looking only at second-price auctions and the two bidders have identical constant-absolute-risk-aversion utility functions, $U(x) = -\exp(-\lambda x)$. If the two are bidding lump-sum amounts, which they pay no matter how big the reserves are, what is the equilibrium? (Why is it helpful to assume that the bidders have constant absolute risk aversion (CARA) utility functions?)

e. The obvious next step is to look for an equilibrium if the two bidders are risk-averse expected-utility maximizers, and they bid in royalties. Unhappily, this is a very difficult problem. So consider the following alternative: The government sets a royalty rate r and asks the bidders to bid lump-sum payments in addition, with the bidder who bids the higher lump-sum getting the mineral rights for the other bidder's lump-sum bid, while still having to pay the royalty rate r. So, for instance, if Maxco offers the higher lump-sum bid and Gambit's lump-sum bid is b_G, Maxco's outcome in dollar terms is $(1-r)V$, what it retains after paying the government the royalties on what it extracts, less its costs C_M, less b_G. Maxco, therefore, values this outcome according to its expected utility, or

$$\mathbf{E}\big[U\big((1-r)V - C_m - b_G\big)\big].$$

Maxco and Gambit both have the (identical) CARA utility function provided in part d. Assume that V is distributed Normally with mean $\$10,000,000$ and variance $\$100,000$. (This specification allows $V < 0$, but don't worry about this.) If the government fixed r at 50%, what is the bidding equilibrium? (I remind you of the following fact from Chapter 19: If a random variable X is Normally distributed with mean μ and variance σ^2, then

$$\mathbf{E}[\exp(X)] = \exp\big(\mu + \sigma^2/2\big).$$

In this equilibrium, what is the (risk-neutral) government's expected total profit, including its royalties and the lump sum that it receives in the auction?

f. In terms of maximizing the government's expected total profit, what is the best royalty rate r for it to fix? (Think back to Chapter 19 or even Section 8.5 in Volume I.)

g. To make part f harder, suppose that the costs C_M and C_G come in two parts. Half of these amounts are "exploration costs." If, say, Maxco wins the auction, it spends $C_M/2$ to learn the value of V. And having learned the value of V, it chooses whether to expend a further $C_M/2$ to extract the resources. (To keep things relatively simple, Maxco either chooses to expend $C_M/2$ to extract all V, or it chooses not to extract anything at all.) Why does this change the answer to part f? (Now you definitely need to think back to Chapter 19.)

∎ 24.10. Illustrate the winner's curse (pages 355–56) with the wallet game. Suppose the distribution of (each) wallet i's contents, the variable x_i, is uniform on [\$0, \$100]. Suppose there are five bidders. Hence, if one of the bidders knows that the contents of his wallet is \$42, his expectation for the sum of the five wallets is $\$42 + 4 \times \$50 = \$242$. Suppose he, being a cautious fellow, bids half of this. Suppose his four fellow bidders do the same. What happens?

∎ 24.11. Prove Proposition 24.14. Don't look for any mysteries here. This is entirely straightforward. But it is a good exercise to lock in your understanding of how the revelation principle and envelope theorem are employed in such proofs.

∎ 24.12. Answer the question in footnotes 22 and 23 on page 361.

■ 24.13. In the context of the symmetric wallet-game, with the information-rich version of the button auction (page 359), suppose that, instead of the strategies described on pages 359–60, bidders in all "rounds" but the last bid set their drop-out prices as follows: In round n, when surviving bidder i, who (of course) knows S_i, has learned $\mathcal{S}^{(N)}, \mathcal{S}^{(N-1)}, \ldots, \mathcal{S}^{(N-n+2)}$ and is still unsure what the other $n-1$ values of S_j are, sets his drop-out price at $\mathcal{S}^{(N)} + \mathcal{S}^{(N-1)} + \ldots + \mathcal{S}^{(N-n+2)} + (N-n-2)\mathbf{E}\big[S_j \big| S_j \in [\mathcal{S}^{(N-n+2)}, S_i]\big] + 2S_i$. Please note that, given the independence assumptions, the conditional distribution of an S_j conditional on $S_j \in [\mathcal{S}^{(N-n+2)}, S_i]$ (where the values defining the interval are known constants) is just F truncated over that interval. That is,

$$\mathbf{E}\big[S_j \big| S_j \in [\mathcal{S}^{(N-n+2)}, S_i]\big] = \left[\int_{\mathcal{S}^{(N-n+2)}}^{S_i} s f(s) \mathrm{d}s\right] \Big/ \left[F(S_i) - F(\mathcal{S}^{(N-n+2)})\right].$$

Hence, in these strategies, bidder i's drop-out price is a good deal less than in the strategies in the text, except in the final round (in which the drop-out prices are precisely as in the strategies in the text).

How does this affect what happens?

■ 24.14. In the context of the symmetric wallet game, imagine the following auction protocol. Bidders are invited to submit sealed bids. The bids are examined by the auctioneer, and the lowest bid is announced publicly, together with the identity of the lowest bidder, who is then disqualified from further bidding. (If there is a tie for the low bid, the public announcement includes the amount of the lowest bid and the number and names of low bidders, all of whom are disqualified.) The remaining bidders are invited to resubmit bids, with the stipulation that they cannot bid less than the previous low bid. Again, the lowest bid and bidder are revealed, and that bidder is disqualified. Rounds continue in this fashion; in each round, bidders not disqualified from bidding get to revise their previous bids, but cannot bid less than the last low bid; the low bid and bidder in each round is announced, and the bidder is disqualified. When the process gets down to two bidders, the bidders follow this drill: The high bidder gets the item, paying the bid of his (final) opponent. (Ties are handled in the usual fashion.)

Describe a symmetric equilibrium for this multiround auction protocol.

Chapter Twenty-Five

Matching Markets

The term *matching markets*, as used in microeconomics, applies to a variety of assignment problems such as the following: matching students with schools; interns with hospitals; students with courses; firms with suppliers in the context of supply chains; and cadaver kidneys with patients in need of a kidney transplant.

The issues tackled in the theory of matching markets include:

- What makes for a "good" match? The key terms here are *stability* and *core compatibility*.

- Given the criterion for a good match, do any exist? If there are many, what can be said about how they compare?

- How and how well do various specific matching processes work, in theory, in different contexts?

- In a given context, if the participants' preferences are private knowledge, are there mechanisms that motivate participants to tell the truth about their preferences? Do truth-inducing mechanisms give "good" outcomes?

Since, except for very simple settings, answers to these questions tend to be either hard or negative, the broader literature moves on to practice. This is descriptive: In real-life settings with real-life matching processes, how and how well do those processes work? And it is prescriptive: Given what we can learn from the theory of matching markets, combined with what we see in practice, can processes be redesigned to produce better outcomes?[1] Economists, in the practice of what has become known as *economic engineering*, design formal matching processes that improve on the processes in place. (Economic engineering is also practiced by auction designers, as mentioned in Chapter 24.) The progression from theory to practical application is extremely interesting (and challenging). This text only covers the theory of matching markets; however, in the Bibliographic Notes, I recommend some accounts of economists who have brought the theory to practical applications.

The literature on matching markets—even just the theoretical literature—is enormous. So I remind you that coverage here—as everywhere in this volume—is a bare introduction; moreover, it is an introduction (for the most part) to the foun-

---

[1] Alvin Roth, one of the titans of this subject, was asked whether he could design a procedure for matching new MDs to internships that would send more US nationals to rural hospitals; the clients of rural hospitals are generally less accepting of "foreign" doctors than the clients of urban hospitals are. This led Roth to develop the Rural Hospital Theorem, reported here as Proposition 25.23. This is a case where a practical design question inspired a theoretical result, which in turn informed what could be accomplished.

dational ideas in this literature. For further reading, see the Bibliographic Notes.

25.1. Contexts

Among the contexts in which matching is a significant feature are the following.

- There are finite sets M and W. Write $\overline{M} := \{\overline{m}\} \cup M$ and $\overline{W} = \{\overline{w}\} \cup W$. A *match* is a pair of function (μ, ν), where $\mu : M \to \overline{W}$ and $\nu : W \to \overline{M}$ such that, if $\mu(m) = w \in W$ then $\nu(w) = m$.

  This is known in the early literature as the *marriage market*, where men ($m \in M$) and women ($w \in W$) pair off. The interpretation of $\mu(m) = \overline{w}$ is that man m remains single; similarly, if $\nu(w) = \overline{m}$, then woman w remains single. Of course, the constraint that, if $\mu(m) = w \in W$, then $\nu(w) = m$, means that if man m is married to woman w, then she is married to him.

- Imagine instead that there is a single population A out of which pairs must be formed. In the early literature, this problem is called the *roommate problem*: An even number $2N$ of individuals must pair off as roommates to fill N two-person dorm rooms. In this context, a *match* is a function $\mu : A \to \overline{A} = A \cup \{\overline{a}\}$; where $\mu(a) = a' \in A$ implies that $\mu(a') = a$, and $\mu(a) = \overline{a}$ is interpreted to mean that a gets a single room (if any are available) or is left roomless.

  In view of single-sex marriages, this model can be interpreted as the *modern marriage market*. To distinguish between the original marriage market and the modern marriage market, I'll use the term *the classic marriage market* for the original.

- The *market for new economics PhDs* involves a finite set A of newly minted economics PhDs and a finite set D of departments of economics and business schools. Let $\mathcal{A}$ denote the set of all subsets of A (including the empty set). A *match* in this context is a pair (μ, ν), where μ is a function from A to $\overline{D} = D \cup \{\overline{d}\}$, and ν is a function from $D \to \mathcal{A}$, satisfying the condition that, if $\mu(a) = d \in D$, then $a \in \nu(d)$. The interpretation is that $\nu(d)$ is the set of new PhDs hired by department d; the condition is that each new PhD can be hired by at most one department. (Joint appointments are excluded under this definition.) The interpretation of $\mu(a) = \overline{d}$ is that a fails to land an academic job. If $\nu(d) = \emptyset$, department d hires no one from A.

  Several variations on this basic structure are found in the literature. Suppose that each department faces a quota on how many members of a it can hire. That is, for each $d \in D$, there is an integer $q(d)$, and a further constraint on ν is that the cardinality of the set $\nu(d)$ must be less than or equal to $q(d)$. In the seminal article on this subject, Gale and Shapley (1962), this is called the *college-admissions* model, where members of A are applicants to college and members $d \in D$ are colleges. Alternatively, it is viewed as a *(high)-school-assignment* model, where (say) members $a \in A$ are students in some school district, and members $d \in D$ are schools in that district to which the students can be assigned; it is also a model of the *market for medical interns/residents*, where members of A are newly minted MDs and members $d \in D$ are hospitals with internships to fill.

- The so-called *job-assignment model* is like the college-admissions model in that prospective employees comprising a set A are to be matched with prospective employers from a set D. But, in this case, there is no upper bound on the number of employees that any one employer can hire, if it wishes. (Further differences involve the nature of preferences of the firms.)

- The *course-assignment problem* concerns matching a set of students with a set of courses that they take. In college admissions and job assignment, matches are many-to-one: Each applicant $a \in A$ is matched with only one institution $d \in \overline{D}$, although $d \in D$ is matched to a set of applicants. In course assignment, each student is matched with several courses, and each course is matched with several students. In the previous examples, it is natural to think that both "sides" of the market have preferences concerning their match or matches. In this case, it is more natural to imagine that although students have (complex) preferences over the set of courses with which they are matched, the courses don't care which students enroll in the them.[2]

- One can think of a multi-item auction as a matching problem, where the problem is to match items with bidders. If the items are identical, the issue is: How many copies of the item are matched with a given bidder? If the items are not identical, questions about which items are matched with which bidders arise; this is true whether each bidder is limited to one item or a bidder can be matched with several (now distinct) items.

In at least some of the applications mentioned so far, one can imagine that the terms of each match are fixed, but one can also imagine that one side or the other can, to effect a preferred match, offer better terms. Deans have been known to say to newly minted PhD students, "We pay all our new Assistant Professors the same nine-month salary," and then bargain over research support, summer money, and teaching load. Or, in the case of multi-item auctions, the essence of the problem is: How much will a bidder pay for a particularly desirable item?

In much of the theory, the conceit is that the matches are made at a single point in time. This is certainly neither natural nor realistic in the cases of the marriage market and the general job-assignment market, if firms are continuously hiring. In cases like the market for new PhDs and the market for medical interns, the models are more natural when applied to matching the current crop of graduates to departments/hospitals. However, at least in terms of the market for new PhDs, I can attest to the notion that, in some years, the decision is made not to hire, so as to preserve a slot for the future. The model can accommodate this, of course; "preserving a slot for the future" suggests that an institution d faces a quota $q(d)$, and the institution is allowed to hire to its quota, but it can hire less if it so chooses, with some shadow value attached to an empty slot.

---

[2]   Although, as sometime Senior Associate Dean of the Stanford Graduate School of Business, I know of instructors who have had significant preferences concerning which students take their courses.

In other matching markets, the ongoing nature of matches is the essence of the problem. Perhaps the leading example in the literature concerns matching cadaver kidneys with individuals who need a kidney transplant. There is an inventory of such individuals, some cases more urgent than others. As time passes, kidneys that are donated upon death—called cadaver kidneys—become available. The quality of a cadaver kidney deteriorates rapidly—it becomes useless in a matter of days—so a fresh cadaver kidney must be matched quickly with a recipient from the inventory of eligible recipients. And a prospective recipient, offered a cadaver kidney, must decide quickly whether to accept it or to await a "better" kidney.

In each of the examples provided, matches are bilateral. At least two real-life contexts involve more complex matches.

- The first concerns live-donor kidneys. Think of the participants as pairs of individuals, X1 and X2, where $X1$ needs a kidney transplant, while X2—a very good friend or relative of X1—is willing to donate one of his or her kidneys *if* X1 is offered a suitable kidney, donated by the donating half of another pair. Two pairs, say A and B, could be matched, with the A1 getting the kidney donated by B2, and vice versa. But, one can imagine a cycle of donations, where A2 gives her kidney to B1, B2 gives his kidney to C1, and so forth, with (say) F2 closing the cycle by donating her kidney to A1.

- And in the context of manufacturing supply chains, each firm involved in some part of the overall production process looks to join a team of firms. This, in turn, takes us to the general literature on *coalition formation*.

Preferences over matches

In these and other examples, participants in the matching market come with preferences over the match. The preferences may be relatively simple:

- In either marriage market, each individual has preferences over prospective matches, where it is certainly possible that a pariticpant prefers to remain unmatched rather than being matched with some of the possible alternatives.

- In the market for new economics PhDs, each newly minted PhD has preferences over the departments with which she might be matched, and each department has preferences over prospective hires. A feature of the classic model of college admissions is that the colleges have relatively simple preferences over the cohorts they select. In particular, and somewhat roughly speaking, the college values some applicants more than others—State U prefers Alice to Bob—but Bob is still a worthwhile candidate for admission. If this is so, and as long as State U has room in its class, it will admit Bob if he is available. That said, State U may find that Carol is "below its line": Even if Carol is available and State U has not filled its quota of students, it will not admit Carol.

- In the job-assignment model, employees also have relatively simple preferences: Alice would rather work for Firm X than for Firm Y. But the preferences of the firms over cohorts of employees are more complex than in the college-admissions model. Daniel may be a close substitute for Alice, so that if Firm X cannot get Alice, they would happily take Daniel. But, if they can hire Alice, they do not want to hire Daniel, even though there is no upper bound on how may employees they can take.

- The same issue of substitutes arises in the course-assignment problem. Bob might wish to attend a specific course in investments or, if he cannot enroll in that class, in a second-best (for him) course in investments. But he prefers not to be enrolled in both.

- And once we introduce the notion that one side can influence the other side by offering better terms, we must incorporate those terms into the preferences of both sides.

These assumptions are formalized in the models to be discussed. But moving beyond formal models, real-life applications present preferences that add complexity to preference relations:

- New PhD Alice is in a committed relationship with Pat. Alice has preferences over her own match, but also concerning Pat's match; Alice might prefer that she and Pat are hired by the same department or, if not, that they are hired by departments that are in close geographic proximity. However, she might be willing to sacrifice these considerations, if both she and Pat are matched with outstanding but geographically distant departments.

  And it might go beyond committed relationships: fellow graduate students Bob and Daniel might fancy a long-term research collaboration with each other and so might look for an overall match that lands them in the same department.

- In the job-assignment model, Firm A's preferences are permitted (in a manner to be formalized) to regard Alice and Daniel as substitutes: If the firm can hire Alice, it no longer wishes to hire Daniel. But, in real life, Alice and Daniel may be complementary: In the context of new PhDs and departments, it may be that hiring both Alice and Daniel is seen as a good idea, because the two work in complementary fashion on the same set of problems. It turns out that complementarities pose difficulties for the theory of matching markets. For the basic theory, complementarities are assumed away.

- "Society" may have preferences concerning the match, preferences that must be taken into account in evaluating matches. Social preferences are clearly germane when thinking about the matching cadaver kidneys to patients, for instance. Or, to take a more mundane example, professional sports organizations in the United States (and elsewhere) that are concerned with competitive balance conduct drafts of new athletes or have "financial fair play" rules about rich clubs buying up star players. The dean of a business school is concerned, in the allocation of courses to MBA students, that the allocation rules are perceived to be equitable.[3]

---

[3] However, the dean may also be concerned that the daughter of a wealthy alum is able to take a

The term *one-sided matching market* is sometimes used to distinguish between cases in which only one side has preferences—as in course assignment—from cases in which both sides to the match have preferences, so-called *two-sided matching markets*. Unhappily, the term *one-sided matching market* is also used in the literature to describe *single-population* matching markets such as the modern marriage market. This chapter almost entirely concerns models in which two distinct and separate populations are matched (single-population models present severe difficulties, for reasons to be explained on page 393), so no confusion should result here. But, please beware of this terminological inconsistency.

25.2. The Classic Marriage Market

The theory of matching markets begins with Gale and Shapley (1962).

The deferred-acceptance algorithm (Gale and Shapley 1962)

Consider the following algorithm for determining a match in the context of the classic marriage market. Recall that M is the set of men, W is the set of women, $\overline{M} := \{\overline{m}\} \cup M$ is the set of men together with the not-matched alternative for women, and $\overline{W} = \{\overline{w}\} \cup W$ is the set of women with the not-matched alternative for men.

Assume that each man $m \in M$ has complete, transitive, and antisymmetric weak preferences over $\overline{W}$. Antisymmetry means that m is not indifferent between two different alternatives in $\overline{W}$. Write $\succ_m$ for m's strict preferences and $\succeq_m$ for his weak preferences. Assume as well that each woman $w \in W$ has complete, transitive, and antisymmetric (weak) preferences over $\overline{M}$, with w's strict preferences denoted by $\succ_w$ and her weak preferences denoted by $\succeq_w$.[4]

Initiate the algorithm by defining $R^0(w) := \emptyset$ for $w \in W$. (In what follows, superscripts refer to rounds.)

Round 1. For each $w \in W$, let $m^1(w)$ be w's most preferred match from $\overline{M}$. For each $m \in M$, let $W^1(m) := \{w : m = m^1(w), w \in W\} \cup \{\overline{w}\}$, and let $w^1(m)$ be m's most preferred match out of $W^1(m)$. For each $w \in W$, define $R^1(w) := \{m^1(w)\}$ if $w^1(m) \neq w$.

The symbols make this less than transparent: Each women proposes a match with her favorite man (which may be $\overline{m}$). Each man chooses his favorite match from among those women who propose to him; he can choose $\overline{w}$ if he prefers $\overline{w}$ to all the "real" women who propose to him. If no woman proposes to m, then he is tentatively matched with $\overline{w}$. If man m is proposed to by woman w, and he rejects her proposal, m is added to w's "rejection set" $R^1(w)$. If w's proposal is tentatively accepted, her rejection set after one round, $R^1(w)$, remains $R^0(w) = \emptyset$. Then, iteratively:

---

course offered by the alum's former mentor.

[4] Antisymmetry of preferences is not assumed simply for convenience. See Problem 25.3.

Round n. For each $w \in W$, let $m^n(w)$ be w's most preferred match out of $\overline{M} \setminus R^{n-1}(w)$. For each $m \in M$, let $W^n(m) = \{w : m = m^n(w), w \in W\} \cup \{\overline{w}\}$, and let $w^n(m)$ be m's most preferred woman from $W^n(m)$. For each $w \in W$, if $m^n(w) \neq w^n(m)$, let $R^n(w) = R^{n-1}(w) \cup \{m^n(w)\}$; if $m^n(w) = w^n(m)$, let $R^n(w) = R^{n-1}(w)$.

In round n, each woman proposes to her most preferred match out of those men who have not previously rejected a proposal from her. Men consider any proposals they receive in this round, (tentatively) accepting their most preferred woman out of all current proposals, which (again) can be $\overline{w}$. This continues (iteratively) until, in some round, no woman's proposal is rejected.

This algorithm has the following properties:

1. In round 1, each woman proposes to her favorite match. She continues to make that proposal as long as the object of her affections accepts. When and if he accepts a different proposal, she moves on to her second favorite match, and so forth.

2. In any round n, if w is proposing to m, she has (previously) been rejected by all men that she prefers to m.

3. If, in any round n, w proposes to m and he (tentatively) accepts her proposal, she proposes to him again in the next round; he is (still) her favorite among all men who have not previously rejected her.

4. Suppose that w proposes to m in some round n, he accepts, and then in round $n+1$ he accepts the proposal of a different woman. According to the algorithm, he joins w's rejection set. Also, w is left without a match in round $n+1$, but she gains the possibility of being matched with another man (the man who is her next favorite after m) in round $n+2$.

5. The algorithm permits woman w in some round to propose to go unmatched: That is, $m^n(w) = \overline{m}$. This will happen if w has previously been rejected by all men whom she prefers to being unmatched. Such a "proposal" is deemed to be "accepted"; once a woman makes such a proposal, she will continue to propose being unmatched for as long as the algorithm continues. And termination of the algorithm—when every proposal by a woman is accepted—includes acceptance of any woman's proposal to remain unmatched.

6. From the perspective of man m, as the rounds proceed, his fortunes can only improve. If he is the favorite of no woman, in Round 1 he is matched with $\overline{w}$, and it is entirely possible that he remains matched in this sense for the entire algorithm. However, once a woman w who is acceptable to him (whom he prefers to $\overline{w}$) proposes to him, he accepts the best acceptable woman who proposes. That woman proposes to him in the next round and for as long as he accepts her proposal. And he only rejects her proposal if, in some later round, a proposal arrives from a women whom he prefers to his current match. Hence and *in particular*, if m in the algorithm accepts the proposal of a real woman

(that is, a $w \in W$), in every subsequent round he accepts the proposal of a real woman.

Therefore, the "fortunes" of a man can only improve from one round to the next. At the start, he may be unmatched and remain so for a while or even for the whole algorithm. But once a woman that he finds acceptable proposes to him, he only rejects that proposal if a woman he prefers proposes to him.

The fortunes of a woman can move in either direction from one round to the next. Suppose Alice's first choice is Bob, she proposes to him, and he accepts. Then, in a subsequent round, Carol, whom Bob prefers to Alice, proposes to Bob. He abandons Alice, and she is left (for this round, at least) without a partner. But, in the next round, if Daniel is Alice's second favorite, she proposes to him, and he may accept. There is a sense, though, in which each woman's "fortunes"—"optimistic aspirations" is a better term—can only decline: Each woman starts with the optimistic aspiration that her favorite man will accept her. If and when he rejects her, she moves to her second favorite, and so forth. At any point, she is optimistically proposing to her favorite among all men who have not yet rejected her. (And, because of the previous paragraph, she has no hope of successfully re-proposing to a man who has rejected her; he has moved on to someone he prefers.)

7. Since there are finitely many men, the algorithm must terminate, eventually. It terminates if every proposal by a woman is accepted. And if this isn't the case, some woman's rejection set grows by one. (More than one woman's rejection set can grow in a given round.) Hence, writing $\#M$ for the number of men and $\#W$ for the number of women, $\#M \times \#W$ is an upper bound on the number of rounds.

8. In the final round of the algorithm, some woman $w \in W$ proposes to a man $m \in \overline{M}$ for the first time. This is because, if every woman proposes in the final round to the same $m \in \overline{M}$ to whom she proposed in the penultimate round, then every proposal in the penultimate round must have been accepted, which would mean that the penultimate round was actually the final round.

9. And, if, in the final round, $w \in W$ proposes for the first time to man $m \in M$, then, in the penultimate round, that man must have been unmatched. This is because, if that man had been matched to a woman $w' \in W$ in the penulti- mate round, she (w') would have proposed to him in the final round and been rejected, which means that the final round was not final.

10. This procedure is called an algorithm, because there is no claim whatsoever that the behavior proposed for the men and the women is in their best interests. We return to this point in a later subsection.

Test your intuition before reading further: Men's fortunes improve as the rounds pass. A woman's fortunes (in terms of whether she is matched with a man) can improve or decline from round to round. So is the "outcome" of this algorithm good for men or for women? Put it this way: Consider the algorithm with the roles reversed: Men makes proposals, which women accept or reject. Will the result of this reversed algorithm be better for women or for men than is the women-propose algorithm? Proposition 25.4 provides answers.

Stable matches and the results of the deferred-acceptance algorithm

Definition 25.1. *In the context of the classic marriage matching market, a **match** (μ, ν) consists of a function $\mu : M \to \overline{W}$ and a function $\nu : W \to \overline{M}$ such that, if $\mu(m) = w \in W$, then $\nu(w) = m$, and if $\nu(w) = m \in M$, then $\mu(m) = w$.*

*The match (μ, ν) is **stable** if*

a. *For each $m \in M$, $\mu(m) \succeq_m \overline{w}$.*

b. *For each $w \in W$, $\nu(w) \succeq_w \overline{m}$.*

c. *There exists no pair of one man $m \in M$ and one woman $w \in W$ such that m strictly prefers w to $\mu(m)$ and w prefers m to $\nu(w)$.*

Part a can be paraphrased as: If m is matched with $w \in W$, he (strictly) prefers w to be unmatched. (Remember, weak preferences are antisymmetric.) Part b is similar for women. Part c says that there is no unmatched pair, each of whom (strictly) prefers the other member of the pair to their match.

For a particular population of men and women, with preferences, more than one match can be stable. For instance, suppose there are two women, Alice and Carol, and two men, Bob and Daniel. Alice prefers Bob to Daniel. Carol prefers Daniel to Bob. Bob prefers Carol to Alice, and Daniel prefers Alice to Carol. All prefer a real partner to going unmatched. Then the match Alice–Bob and Carol–Daniel is stable, but so is Alice–Daniel and Carol–Bob.

Proposition 25.2. *The results of the deferred-acceptance algorithm is a stable match.*

Proof. By "the results of the deferred-acceptance algorithm" is meant: In the final round, each w proposes to some $m \in \overline{M}$ and is accepted. Define $\nu^\sharp(w)$ to be that $m \in \overline{m}$. And, for each $m \in M$, define $\mu^\sharp(m)$ to be $\overline{w}$ if no woman proposes to him in the final round and to be that woman w who does propose to him in the final round, if some woman does so. This is well defined: It can't be that more than one woman proposes to m in the final round; m would then have to reject one of the two, so the round wouldn't have been final. This $(\mu^\sharp, \nu^\sharp)$ then defines a match: If $\nu^\sharp(w) = m \in M$, then m, $\mu^\sharp(m) = w$ by definition. And if $\mu^\sharp(m) = w \in W$, then w must have proposed to m in the final round, hence $\nu^\sharp(w) = m$.

To show that this match is stable: Parts a and b of the definition of stability obviously hold, since the algorithm permits a woman to "propose" to be single if she has run out of men she prefers to being single, and the algorithm permits a man to choose to be single if all proposals he receives are worse for him than being single.

As for part c, suppose there were a pair (m, w) such that w prefers m to her final match $\nu^\sharp(w)$. The only reason that w would not have proposed to m in the final round is that he rejected her in some earlier round. But if he rejected her in an earlier round, it was to accept the proposal of some other woman w' that he prefers to w. And, as men's fortunes can only get better as rounds of the algorithm pass, he must in the final round be matched with a woman he likes as much as w', who is strictly better for him than w. Hence, if (m, w) is an unmatched pair such that w strictly prefers m to $\nu^\sharp(w)$, then m must strictly prefer $\mu^\sharp(m)$ to w. The match is stable. ∎

Stable matches and the core

The contrapositive definition of stability is: A match (μ, ν) is unstable if any one man or one woman would prefer being unmatched to accepting the partner prescribed by (μ, ν), or if a pair of one man and one woman would prefer to be matched to each·other rather than accept their prescribed matches.

What about larger sets of men and women? A subset $M' \subseteq M$ and a subset $W' \subseteq W$ is said to *block* the match (μ, ν) if M' and W' can, among themselves, arrange a match (μ', ν') that every member of $M' \cup W'$ strictly prefers to their match under (μ, ν).[5] The match (μ, ν) is said to be in the *core* if it cannot be blocked by any set $M' \cup W'$. This definition is consistent with the use of the term *core* in cooperative game theory (and with its use in Volume I, Chapter 15).

Proposition 25.3. Every stable match is in the core.

Proof. The proof is nearly trivial. Suppose $M' \cup W'$ could block (μ, ν) with some match (μ', ν') that involves only members of $M' \cup W'$. Choose any man $m \in M'$. If, under (μ', ν'), m is unmatched (that is, $\mu'(m) = \overline{w}$), then it is immediate that m strictly prefers $\overline{w}$ to $\mu(m)$, hence (μ, ν) fails to be stable by virtue of part a of the definition of stability, a contradiction. A similar argument works if $\nu'(w) = \overline{m}$ for some $w \in W'$. And, if m is matched under μ' to some "real" woman w in W', she (of course) is matched to him under ν'. Since both are strictly better off, antisymmetry implies that $\mu(m) \neq w$ and $\nu(w) \neq m$, and condition c of stability is violated. ∎

The deferred-acceptance algorithm yields the best stable match for each woman individually

Proposition 25.4. The deferred-acceptance algorithm with women making the proposals is the best stable match for each woman. That is, writing $(\mu^\sharp, \nu^\sharp)$ for the stable match produced by the deferred-acceptance algorithm with women making the proposals, if (μ, ν) is any other stable match, then each woman w (weakly) prefers $\nu^\sharp(w)$ to $\nu(w)$.

---

[5] In this definition, the group $M' \cup W'$ is assumed to have the "stay single" option available for each of its members, in constructing the match (μ', ν'). That said, if this option is used for, say, $m \in M'$ — that is, $\mu'(m) = \overline{w}$ — this would mean that $\overline{w} \succ_m \mu(m)$, and m alone would block to original (μ, ν).

Note that we are insisting that every member of $M' \cup W'$ is strictly better off under (μ', ν') than under (μ, ν). An alternative definition of blocking is to allow some members of $M' \cup W'$ to be indifferent under (μ', ν') to their position in (μ, ν), as long as some member of $M' \cup W'$ is strictly better off. However, in the current context, this alternative adds nothing: Since preferences are antisymmetric, if (say) $\mu'(m) = w$ and $\mu(m) \sim_m \mu'(m) = w$, then $\mu(m) = w$. We can delete m from M' and w from W' (if $\mu'(m) \in W$) and still have a blocking group of men and women. While this alternative definition comes to nothing in this context, it is important later, when we consider many-to-one matches.

Proof.[6] Say that man m is *available* to woman w if there is some stable match (μ, ν) such that $\nu(w) = m$.

If m is the first choice of w, and if he turns her down in the first round of the deferred-acceptance algorithm, then he can't be available to her. Because, if m turns down w in the first round, he is the first choice of some other women w' whom he prefers to w. Therefore, any match in which m is paired with w is unstable: m prefers w' to w, and m is the first choice of w', so m and w' would block a match in which m is paired with w.

Hence, if m is available to w, he cannot turn down a proposal made by w in the first round.

Now assume inductively that no man m who is available to a woman w has turned down w in any round of the deferred-acceptance algorithm up to and including the nth round. Suppose that some man m who is available to some woman w turns down her proposal to him in round $n + 1$. If he is available to her—that is, if $\nu(w) = m$ for some stable (μ, ν)—then the woman w' whom m accepts instead in round $n+1$ must have a different partner in (μ, ν) (which may be $\overline{m}$). This woman w' has proposed to m because she has been rejected by all men she prefers to m and, by the induction hypothesis, none of those men are available to her. Hence, $\nu(w')$ must be someone worse for her than m. But then (μ, ν) cannot be stable: $\nu(w')$ is worse for w' than is m, and $\mu(m) = w$, while m prefers w' to w.

Hence, if m is available to w, m cannot turn down a proposal from w in any round of the deferred-acceptance algorithm. But then, in the deferred-acceptance algorithm, either w ends with someone she prefers to m, or she ends with m. In either case, she does at least as well in the deferred-acceptance algorithm as she does in any stable match, which proves the proposition.   ∎

Of course, since the situation is symmetric, the deferred-acceptance algorithm with men making the proposals leads to the best outcome for men among all stable matches. In what follows, the results of the deferred-acceptance algorithm with men making the proposals will be denoted by (μ^b, ν^b).

This answers the question asked at the bottom of page 387: Deferred acceptance with women proposing is better for women than is deferred acceptance with men proposing, and indeed, no stable match makes any woman better off than does deferred acceptance with women proposing. This raises two questions:

1. Could the women, acting as a "cartel" by coordinating their responses, do even better?

2. Is the behavior prescribed for the men by this algorithm in their own (individual or collective) best interests? Is it in the best interests of women?

Is the result of the deferred-acceptance algorithm with women proposing Pareto efficient (for women) among all matches?

The answer is: No. Here is an example, from Roth (1982). Suppose there are

---

[6] This clever proof by induction is from the seminal article, Gale and Shapley (1962).

three women, Alice, Carol, and Ellen, and three men, Bob, Daniel, and Fred. Every woman and every man wishes to be matched rather than remain single. And their preferences are:

- Alice prefers Daniel to Bob to Fred.
- Carol and Ellen both prefer Bob to Daniel to Fred.
- Bob and Fred both prefer Alice to Carol to Ellen.
- Daniel prefers Ellen to Alice to Carol.

The result of the deferred-acceptance algorithm is that Alice is matched with Bob, Carol is matched with Fred, and Ellen is matched with Daniel. (It is a good exercise for you to take the algorithm, step by step, to generate this result. This is Problem 25.1(a).)

Consider, however, the match Alice with Daniel, Carol with Fred, and Ellen with Bob. Carol has Fred in both these matches, so she is indifferent. Alice is paired with Daniel, her first choice, instead of Bob, her second choice. And Ellen is paired with Bob, her first choice, instead of Daniel, her second choice. Since Carol is indifferent and Alice and Ellen are strictly better off, this match Pareto dominates the result of the deferred-acceptance algorithm.

Of course, in view of Proposition 25.4, this alternative match is not stable. Why not? (Problem 25.1.b.)

Since Carol is indifferent, this raises the question: Is there a feasible match that is *strictly* Pareto-superior for the women to the match generated by the deferred-acceptance algorithm with women proposing? That is, can there be a feasible match (obviously not stable) that every woman strictly prefers to her match under $(\mu^\sharp, \nu^\sharp)$? This question is asked not simply of this example, but in general. The answer is that it is possible, but it is a cheat. And if you don't cheat, it is not possible.

First, the cheat: There is one woman, Alice, and two men, Bob and Daniel. Alice strictly prefers Bob to Daniel. But, Bob doesn't like Alice and would rather be unmatched than be matched to Alice. Daniel, in contrast, finds Alice acceptable. Hence, the algorithm proceeds: Alice proposes to Bob, who turns her down. She proposes to Daniel, who accepts. The result of the algorithm is that Alice is matched to Daniel. But another feasible match, which is strictly better for Alice, is for her to be matched with Bob.

This is a cheat because, while matching Alice to Bob is "feasible," it is not individually rational for Bob. We have the following result:

Proposition 25.5. *It is not possible to find a feasible and individually rational match (μ, ν) that is strictly Pareto superior for women to the match $(\mu^\sharp, \nu^\sharp)$ that results from the deferred acceptance algorithm with women making the proposals, where* **strict** *Pareto superiority means that for every women, $\nu(w) \succ_w \nu^\sharp(w)$, and* **individually rational** *means that no man is matched to a woman that is worse for him than being unmatched.*

This result is, to my knowledge, first proved in Roth (1982) under the special conditions that the numbers of men and women are equal, and all women are acceptable to all men (and vice versa). A proof for the general case can be found in Roth and

Sotomayor (1990). What follows is a somewhat more loquacious proof than the proof in Roth and Sotomayor; the extra words are included because they shed light on how the deferred-acceptance algorithm works.

Proof. By way of contradiction, suppose that (μ^*, ν^*) is a match that is individually rational (for the men) and that satisfies $\nu^*(w) \succ_w \nu^\sharp(w)$ for all $w \in W$.

For each woman w, since $(\mu^\sharp, \nu^\sharp)$ is stable, it must be that $\nu^\sharp(w) \succeq_w \overline{m}$. Then $\nu^*(w) \succ_w \nu^\sharp(w)$ implies that $\nu^*(w)$ must be a "real" man; that is, $\nu^*(w) \in M$. Write M^* for the set of men matched under ν^*.

For each woman w, $\nu^*(w) \succ_w \nu^\sharp(w)$, and in the final round of the deferred-acceptance algorithm, w didn't propose $\nu^*(w)$. It must be that $\nu^*(w)$ is in her rejection set. Since w is acceptable to $\nu^*(w)$ by individual rationality, it must be that, when $\nu^*(w)$ rejected w in the algorithm, it was for some other real woman. And once matched with a real woman by the algorithm, a man is matched with a real woman in all subsequent rounds. Hence, under $(\mu^\sharp, \nu^\sharp)$, if $m \in M^*$, then $\mu^\sharp(m) \in W$. That is, the set of men matched to women in (μ^*, ν^*), M^*, is identical to the set of men matched under $(\mu^\sharp, \nu^\sharp)$. Moreover, each $m \in M^*$ must be matched with a real women in the *penultimate* round of the algorithm. (What if the algorithm concludes in the first round? See Problem 25.2.)

But this presents a contradiction. In the last round of the algorithm, some woman, call her w^o, must match with $\nu^\sharp(w^o) \in M^*$ for the first time. But, $\nu^\sharp(w^o)$ is matched with a real woman in the penultimate round, so in the final round, he is proposed to by two women, which means the final round isn't final.   ∎

Is the behavior of men prescribed by the deferred-acceptance algorithm rational?

The deferred-acceptance algorithm presumes that, in each round, men and women behave in a particular fashion. Is it in their individual interests to do so (assuming all others behave as presumed)? That is, if we think of this procedure as a game, does the prescribed behavior constitute a Nash equilibrium?

It is easy to see that the answer is no for men. We use the two-women-and-two-men example from page 388. Alice prefers Bob to Daniel. Carol prefers Daniel to Bob. Bob prefers Carol to Alice, and Daniel prefers Alice to Carol. No one prefers to remain single over any real match.

In the deferred-acceptance algorithm with women making the proposals, in the first round, Alice proposes to Bob, and Carol proposes to Daniel. Both Bob and Daniel accept and, since both proposals were accepted, the algorithm ends with Alice and Bob as partners and Carol and Daniel as partners.

But suppose that, instead, Alice, Carol, and Daniel all behave as presumed, while Bob deviates in the first round: Then

- In the first round, Alice proposes to Bob, and Carol proposes to Daniel. Daniel accepts Carol's proposal, but Bob turns Alice down.

- Since Alice's proposal was rejected, we move to a second round. In the second round, Alice must propose to Daniel; Bob is in her rejection set. Carol repeats her proposal to Daniel. No one proposes to Bob.[7] Daniel, faced with proposals from both Alice and Carol, accepts Alice's proposal.

- Since Carol's second-round proposal was rejected, we move to a third round. In this round, Alice again proposes to Daniel and he accepts. And Carol proposes to Bob, who accepts.

That ends things, with Bob paired with Carol and Daniel with Alice, which is the man-best stable match. Of course, this deviation by Bob requires that he understand how matters will evolve. There is no hint of the participants being unsure of how things will proceed, and perhaps, with enough men and women and plenty of uncertainty, it is less risky for men to behave as in the algorithm. But, as this example shows, it is possible for a man to benefit by "manipulating" the process.

What about the behavior prescribed for the women? One answer is simple: If we look at any process that results in a stable match, since women-proposing provides women with their best stable-match outcome, deviating from deferred acceptance with women proposing cannot provide an improvement. The example on page 391 shows that, by acting in concert, the women can manipulate men who comply with the algoritm into an unstable match that the women (weakly) prefer. But can a woman unilaterally deviate from the behavior prescribed by the algorithm, assuming the other women and the men comply, and be better off? I'll return to this question in Section 25.6.

Is it obvious that stable matches always exist? Or is it amazing? The roommates problem

No matter what the preferences of women are concerning men and of men concerning women, as long as they are complete, transitive, and antistymmetric, a stable match exists. Some people, confronted with this fact, find it obvious. Others are amazed. I'm at least a bit amazed, and to explain why, consider for a moment the roommate problem (or, if you prefer, the modern marriage market). Suppose we have four participants, Alex, Blair, Charlie, and Danny. No one prefers a single room to having a roommate, even if singles are available. And:
- Alex (strictly) prefers Blair to Charlie to Danny.
- Blair (strictly) prefers Charlie to Alex to Danny.
- Charlie (strictly) prefers Alex to Blair to Danny.
- Danny's preferences are irrelevant.

The point is that, since everyone prefers a roommate to being single, in any individually rational match, someone is rooming with Danny. The situation is symmetric, so suppose that person is Blair. Blair would rather room with Alex than with Danny. And Blair is Alex's first choice. Whomever you put in a room with Danny, that person can propose a different arrangement to one of roommates in the other match that is preferable to both. There are no stable matches in this case.

---

[7] Since Bob is deviating, the "men's fortunes improve" rule doesn't hold. But Bob is more farsighted.

25.3. The Lattice Structure of Stable Matches

Definition 25.6. *For two matches* (μ, ν) *and* (μ', ν'):

$$
\text{Define } \nu \vee \nu' \quad \text{by} \quad [\nu \vee \nu'](w_j) := \begin{cases} \nu(w), & \text{if } w \text{ prefers } \nu(w) \text{ to } \nu'(w), \text{ and} \\ \nu'(w), & \text{otherwise.} \end{cases}
$$

$$
\text{Define } \nu \wedge \nu' \quad \text{by} \quad [\nu \wedge \nu'](w) := \begin{cases} \nu(w), & \text{if } w \text{ prefers } \nu'(w) \text{ to } \nu(w), \text{ and} \\ \nu'(w), & \text{otherwise.} \end{cases}
$$

$$
\text{Define } \mu \vee \mu' \quad \text{by} \quad [\mu \vee \mu'](m) := \begin{cases} \mu(m), & \text{if } m \text{ prefers } \mu(m) \text{ to } \mu'(m), \text{ and} \\ \mu'(m), & \text{otherwise.} \end{cases}
$$

$$
\text{Define } \mu \wedge \mu' \quad \text{by} \quad [\mu \wedge \mu'](m) := \begin{cases} \mu(m), & \text{if } m \text{ prefers } \mu'(m) \text{ to } \mu(m), \text{ and} \\ \mu'(m), & \text{otherwise.} \end{cases}
$$

In words, $\nu \vee \nu'$ gives each women w whichever of her match under ν or ν' she prefers; $\nu \wedge \nu'$ gives her whichever she likes less. (If $\nu(w) = \nu'(w)$, $[\nu \vee \nu'](w) = [\nu \wedge \nu'](w) = \nu(w) = \nu'(w)$.) And $\mu \vee \mu'$ and $\mu \wedge \mu'$ are similar, in terms of mens' preferences.

For two matches (μ, ν) and (μ', ν'), $\nu \vee \nu'$ is not always half of a match; it can be that $[\nu \vee \nu'](w) = [\nu \vee \nu'](w')$ for two different women. For example, suppose we have two women, Alice and Carol, and two men, Bob and Daniel, and both Alice and Carol like Bob more than Daniel. If (μ, ν) matches Alice with Bob and Carol with Daniel, while (μ', ν') matches Carol with Bob and Alice with Daniel, then $[\nu \vee \nu'](\text{Alice}) = [\nu \vee \nu'](\text{Carol}) = \text{Bob}$.

However, we have the following:

Proposition 25.7. *Suppose that* (μ, ν) *and* (μ', ν') *are both stable matches. Then* $\nu \vee \nu'$ *and* $\nu \wedge \nu'$ *are both "half" of a* **stable** *match, as are* $\mu \vee \mu'$ *and* $\mu \wedge \mu'$. *(That is, there is a* μ'' *such that* $(\mu'', \nu \vee \nu')$ *is a stable match, etc.) Moreover, the "other half" of* $\nu \vee \nu'$ *is* $\mu \wedge \mu'$, *and the other half of* $\nu \wedge \nu'$ *is* $\mu \vee \mu'$.

This proposition is stated in terms of the "other half" of the function $\nu \vee \nu' : W \to \overline{M}$. So the first thing to do is to establish what this means.

Lemma 25.8. *Suppose* $\nu : W \to \overline{M}$. *There is another "half" to* ν, *denote it by* μ, *such that* (μ, ν) *is a match, if and only if* $\nu(w) = m \in M$ *for some* w *implies that* $\nu(w') \neq m$ *for any* $w' \neq w$. *In words, either* $m \in M$ *is "matched" by one and only one woman* $w \in W$, *or no woman* w *has* $\nu(w) = m$. *And, if this condition is met, the other half of* ν *is uniquely defined as*

$$
\text{for } m \in M, \mu(m) = \begin{cases} \text{the unique } w \text{ such that } \nu(w) = m, & \text{if there is such a } w, \text{ and} \\ \overline{w}, & \text{if no } w \in W \text{ has } \nu(w) = m. \end{cases}
$$

The proof is not complicated. Given $\nu : W \to M$, if for some $m \in M$ and two different women w and w', we have $\nu(w) = \nu(w')$, then there is no way to pair ν with a μ that gives a match. The man m would have to be matched with both w and w', and that is illegitimate in a match. But, as long as this condition is met, μ as defined in the statement of the lemma obviously "completes" ν and is obviously uniquely defined from ν. The lemma then allows us to prove Proposition 25.7.

Proof of Proposition 25.7. I'll prove this for $\nu \vee \nu'$; the proof for $\nu \wedge \nu'$ (and, for that matter, for $\mu \vee \mu'$ and $\mu \wedge \mu'$) are similar. Suppose (μ, ν) and (μ', ν') are both stable.

We begin by showing that $\nu \vee \nu'$ is half a match. Per Lemma 25.8, this means showing that for every $m \in M$, at most one woman w has $[\nu \vee \nu'](w) = m$. By way of contradiction, suppose that there are two women, w and w', $w \neq w'$, such that $[\nu \vee \nu'](w) = [\nu \vee \nu'](w') = m$.

- It cannot be that $\nu(w) = \nu(w') = m$, since (μ, ν) is a match. It cannot be that $\nu'(w) = \nu'(w') = m$, since (μ', ν') is a match. So it must be that $\nu(w) = m$, and $\nu'(w') = m$, or that $\nu'(w') = \nu'(w) = m$. This is just a matter of labeling, so I'll assume it is the first.

- And if $\nu(w) = m$, $\nu'(w') = m$, and $[\nu \vee \nu'](w) = [\nu \vee \nu'](w') = m$, then it must be that $m \succ_w \nu'(w)$ and $m \succ_{w'} \nu(w')$. (Why can I assert that both these preferences are strict?) Now, m strictly prefers w, or he strictly prefers w'. And if he strictly prefers w, then (μ', ν') is not stable: m strictly prefers w to his match under (μ', ν'), namely w', and w strictly prefers m to her match $\nu'(w)$. However, if m strictly prefers w' to w, it is (μ, ν) that is not stable: m strictly prefers w' to w, and w' prefers m to her match $\nu(w')$ under (μ, ν). Either way, we have a contradiction.

So, $\nu \vee \nu'$ is half a match.

The next step is to show that the "other half" of $\nu \vee \nu'$ is $\mu \wedge \mu'$. Fix some woman w, and suppose $[\nu \vee \nu'](w) = m$. Then $\nu(w) = m$, or $\nu'(w) = m$, or both.

- If $\nu(w) = \nu'(w) = m$, then $\mu(m) = \mu'(m) = w$, and it is immediate that $[\mu \wedge \mu'](m) = w$.

- If $[\nu \vee \nu'](w) = m$ and $\nu(w) \neq \nu'(w)$, then one or the other is m; suppose it is $\nu(w)$, so that $m \succ_w \nu'(w)$. Consider $w = \mu(m)$ versus $\nu'(m)$. Since $\nu'(w) \neq m$, $\mu'(m) \neq w$. Suppose that $w \succ_m \mu'(m)$. Then (μ', ν') is not stable: m strictly prefers w to $\mu'(m)$, and w strictly prefers m to $\nu'(w)$. This is a contradiction; it must be that $\mu'(m) \succ_m w$, and this immediately implies that $[\mu \wedge \mu'](m) = w$.

And, finally, we show that $(\mu \wedge \mu', \nu \vee \nu')$ is stable. Suppose not. Suppose first of all that, for some m, $\overline{w} \succ_m [\mu \wedge \mu'](m)$. Since $[\mu \wedge \mu'](m)$ is either $\mu(m)$ or $\mu'(m)$, for whichever it is—without loss of generality, say $\mu(m)$—we have $\overline{w} \succ_m \mu(m)$, which contradicts (μ, ν) being stable. The argument that $[\nu \vee \nu'](w) \succeq_w \overline{m}$ is similar.[8]

---

[8] It is, of course, possible that $[\nu \vee \nu'](w) = \overline{m}$, but only if $\nu(w) = \nu'(w) = \overline{m}$ (why only?). This raises the following question: Suppose $\nu(w) \succ_w \nu'(w) = \overline{w}$, so $[\nu \vee \nu'](w) = \nu(w) = m \in M$. What does this say about $[\mu \wedge \mu'](m)$?

Now suppose that m and w are such that

$$[\mu \wedge \mu'](m) \neq w, \quad [\nu \vee \nu'](w) \neq m, \quad w \succ_m [\mu \wedge \mu'](m), \quad \text{and} \quad m \succ_w [\nu \vee \nu'](w)$$

We know that $[\nu \vee \nu'](w) = $ either $\nu(w)$ or $\nu'(w)$; without loss of generality, suppose $[\nu \vee \nu'](w) = \nu(w)$. Since this implies that $[\nu \vee \nu'](w) = \nu(w) \succeq_w \nu'(w)$, we know that m is strictly preferred by w to both $\nu(w)$ and $\nu'(w)$. Now, since $w \succ_m [\mu \wedge \mu'](m)$, one of $w \succ_m \mu(m)$ or $w \succ_m \mu'(m)$ (or both) must be true. And, whichever it is, that one, together with the corresponding (either) ν or ν', is unstable, a contradiction. ∎

Corollary 25.9. *The set of stable matchings forms a complete lattice.*

In case you need the definition, a lattice is a set of elements with a partial order such that every pair of elements has a least upper bound (or supremum or join) and a greatest lower bound (or infimum or meet). For the partial order on stable matchings (μ, ν), define $(\mu, \nu) \succeq (\mu', \nu')$ if, for every $w \in W$, w prefers (weakly) $\nu(w)$ to $\nu'(w)$. Then the join of (μ, ν) and (μ', ν') under this order is $(\mu \wedge \mu', \nu \vee \nu')$, and the meet is $(\mu \vee \mu', \nu \wedge \nu')$.[9]

The lattice is complete when the previous sentence holds where we substitute "every subset of elements" for "every pair of elements." Since the number of matchings is finite, the number of stable matchings is finite, and so the lattice is complete; every finite lattice is necessarily complete, because for a finite set $\{(\mu_1, \nu_1), (\mu_2, \nu_2), \ldots, (\mu_I, \nu_I)\}$, applying the join operator sequentially—that is, find $\nu_1 \vee \nu_2$, call it ν_{12}^*; then find $\nu_{12}^* \vee \nu_3 = \nu_{123}^*$, and so forth—produces the join of the set, and similarly for the meet.

Let $\mathcal{S}$ be the set of all stable matches (μ, ν), and then define

$$\overline{\nu}(w) := \text{woman } w\text{'s favorite match } \nu(w), \text{ ranging over all } (\mu, \nu) \in \mathcal{S},$$
$$\underline{\mu}(m) := \text{man } m\text{'s least favorite match } \mu(m), \text{ ranging over all } (\mu, \nu) \in \mathcal{S},$$
$$\overline{\mu}(m) := \text{man } m\text{'s favorite match } \mu(m), \text{ ranging over all } (\mu, \nu) \in \mathcal{S}, \text{ and}$$
$$\underline{\nu}(w) := \text{woman } w\text{'s least favorite match } \nu(w), \text{ ranging over all } (\mu, \nu) \in \mathcal{S}.$$

Since $\mathcal{S}$ is a complete lattice, $\overline{\nu}$ is the stable match that is the join of all stable matches (where women's interests define the partial order on the lattice). And, from the proof of Proposition 25.7, it is clear that the "other half" of $\overline{\nu}$ is $\underline{\mu}$. Moreover, from Proposition 25.4 (and the symmetric result for the deferred-acceptance algorithm with men making the proposals), we have:

Corollary 25.10. *The deferred-acceptance algorithm with women making the proposals produces the (stable) match $(\mu^\sharp, \nu^\sharp)$, which is $(\underline{\mu}, \overline{\nu})$. The deferred-acceptance algorithm with men making the proposals produces the (stable) match $(\mu^\flat, \nu^\flat)$, which is $(\overline{\mu}, \underline{\nu})$.*

---

[9] If this isn't obvious to you, go step-by-step to see why it is true.

Tarski's fixed-point theorem and the construction of Adachi (2000)

Tarski's fixed-point theorem was introduced in Volume I, Appendix 8. Here is a somewhat modified and more complete statement of the theorem.

Tarski's Fixed-Point Theorem, 1955. Let $(L, \leq)$ *be any complete lattice, and let* $\phi : L \to L$ *be an isotone (or monotone increasing) function on* L, *meaning that* $\ell_1 \leq \ell_2$ *implies* $\phi(\ell_1) \leq \phi(\ell_2)$. *Then* ϕ *has fixed points: points* ℓ *such that* $\phi(\ell) = \ell$. *And the set of fixed points of* ϕ *is a complete lattice with respect to* $\leq$.

Rather than slog through the proof of Proposition 25.7, perhaps we can employ Tarski's Fixed-Point Theorem. After all, the set of matches is a complete lattice; all we need to do is to find an isotone function on the set of matches for which the fixed points are stable matches.

This seems simple enough, but it takes some cleverness to push it through: In particular, instead of working on the lattice of matches, the standard procedure for enlisting Tarski in this setting is to expand to the set of so-called *pre-matches*. The construction originates in Adachi (2000), with important reformulations and extensions of the basic idea in Echenique and Oviedo (2004), Hatfield and Milgrom (2005), and Ostrovsky (2008). The presentation here is close to, but not identical to, Ostrovsky (2008). Please take your time with this; the notation is fearsome, but the idea, once you get it, is not.

Definition 25.11.

a. *For each* $m \in M$, *let* $\mathcal{W}(m)$ *be the set of all subsets of* $\overline{W}$ *of the form*

$$\{w : w \succeq_m w' \text{ for some } w' \in W\},$$

plus the empty set. Denote such sets by $\hat{\mu}(m)$. *For such a set, call* w' *the* **root** *of the set (unless* $\hat{\mu}(m) = \emptyset$). *For each* $w \in W$, *define* $\mathcal{M}(w)$ *analogously. Let* $\mathcal{W} = \prod_{m \in M} \mathcal{W}(m)$, *and let* $\mathcal{M} = \prod_{w \in W} \mathcal{M}(w)$.

b. *A* **pre-match** *is a point* $(\hat{\mu}, \hat{\nu}) \in \mathcal{P} := \mathcal{W} \times \mathcal{M}$. *To be clear here,* $\hat{\mu}(m)$ *for each man* m *is an element of* $\mathcal{W}$; *that is, a subset of* $\overline{W}$ *that contains a woman* w', *the root of* $\hat{\mu}(m)$, *and all women that* m *prefers to* w' *(or is empty). And* $\hat{\nu}(w)$ *is an element of* $\mathcal{M}(w)$, *a similarly constituted set of men.*

c. *Define a partial order* $\geq$ *on pair* $(\hat{\mu}, \hat{\nu})$ *as follows:* $(\hat{\mu}, \hat{\nu}) \geq (\hat{\mu}', \hat{\nu}')$ *if, for all* $m \in M$, $\hat{\mu}(m) \supseteq \hat{\mu}'(m)$ *and, for all* $w \in W$, $\hat{\nu}(w) \subseteq \hat{\nu}'(w)$.

d. *Define a mapping* $\Phi : \mathcal{P} \to \mathcal{P}$ *as follows. For* $(\hat{\mu}, \hat{\nu}) \in \mathcal{P}$, *temporarily abbreviate* $\Phi((\hat{\mu}, \hat{\nu}))$ *by* $(\hat{\mu}', \hat{\nu}')$. *Then:*

  i. *For* $m \in M$, *let* $W(\hat{\nu}) = \{w : m \in \hat{\nu}(w)\}$. *Let* $w^*(\hat{\nu})$ *be man* m'*s favorite woman in* $W(\hat{\nu}) \cup \{\overline{w}\}$. *Let* $\hat{\mu}'(m) = \{w' \in W : w' \succeq_m w^*(\hat{\nu})\}$.

  ii. *For* $w \in W$, *let* $M(\hat{\mu}) = \{m : w \in \hat{\mu}(m))\}$. *Let* $m^*(\hat{\mu})$ *be* w'*s favorite man in* $M(\hat{\mu}) \cup \{\overline{m}\}$. *Let* $\hat{\nu}'(w) = \{m' \in M : m' \succeq_w m^*(\hat{\mu})\}$.

Although you should not take this literally, it may help you to understand these definitions with the following "interpretation." In a pre-match, $(\hat{\mu}, \hat{\nu})$, each man and women is suggesting a set of "matches I am willing to consider." Take man m: $\hat{\mu}(m)$ is the set of women that he might be willing to be matched with. The restriction to sets of women in $\mathcal{W}(m)$ is then natural: If m is willing to consider a match to some woman w', he should be willing to consider matches to all women who are, in his view, better than w'. Indeed, it might be reasonable to restrict even further: The root of $\hat{\mu}(m)$ should never be worse than $\overline{w}$. But this isn't necessary for what comes next.

And then the map Φ has the following interpretation. Given a pre-match $(\hat{\mu}, \hat{\nu})$, woman w (say) looks over all the men who are willing to consider being matched with her, together with going unmatched. She picks out the best of those men (according to her preferences)—this is $m^*(\hat{\mu})$—and says that she is "now" willing to consider only men who are just as good as or better than $m^*(\hat{\mu})$ for her. Note that, after one application of Φ to any pre-match, the resulting pre-match satisfies the restriction that women no longer consider men who are worse for them than going unmatched, and vice versa.[10]

Every match (μ, ν) induces a pre-match in an obvious fashion: For man m, let $\hat{\mu}(m) = \{w' : w' \succeq_m \mu(m)\}$, and similarly for each woman. Going in the other direction is not so easy. Some pre-matches are consistent with many matches: Consider the pre-match in which $\hat{\mu}(m) = \{w' : w' \succeq_m \mu^\sharp(m)\}$, and $\hat{\nu}(w) = \{m' : m' \succeq_w \nu^\flat(w)\}$. This is consistent with any stable match (assuming there are more than one) in the sense that, if (μ, ν) is a stable match, then $\mu(m) \in \hat{\mu}(m)$ for each man and $\nu(w) \in \hat{\nu}(w)$ for each woman.

In contrast, there are pre-matches that are inconsistent with any match. Suppose there are two women, Alice and Carol, and two men, Bob and Daniel. Suppose that Alice and Carol both prefer Bob to Daniel (and both prefer Daniel to being unmatched). And suppose we look at the pre-match in which both Alice and Carol say, "I'm only willing to consider being matched to Bob."

This concept of a pre-match raises some interesting questions that I do not answer: Which pre-matches are consistent with at least one match? Which pre-matches are consistent with one and only one match?

And while this "interpretation" can be used to help understand parts a, b, and d of the definition, there is still the partial order defined in part c to untangle. Doing so is the subject of the following proposition.

Proposition 25.12. *Suppose (μ, ν) and (μ', ν') are two matches. Let $(\hat{\mu}, \hat{\nu})$ and $(\hat{\mu}', \hat{\nu}')$ be the two pre-matches that correspond to the two matches, respectively. (That is, $\hat{\mu}(m) = \{w : w \succeq_m \mu(m)\}$, and so forth.) Then, per the partial order $\geq$ defined in part c of*

---

[10] Check your understanding of this construction: If $m \notin \hat{\nu}(w)$ for any w—that is, no woman is willing to consider m, what is $\hat{\mu}'(m)$? If $\hat{\nu}(w) = \emptyset$ for every w, what is $\hat{\mu}'(m)$?

Definition 25.11,

$(\hat{\mu}, \hat{\nu}) \geq (\hat{\mu}', \hat{\nu}')$ *if and only if*
$\nu(w) \succeq_w \nu'(w)$ *for all* $w \in W$, *and* $\mu'(m) \succeq_m \mu(m)$ *for all* $m \in M$.

This is straightforward, so I leave the proof to you as Problem 25.3. This takes us to the payoff of all these definitions:

Proposition 25.13. *The map Φ is isotone (monotone increasing) on the space of pre-matches $\mathcal{P}$ under the partial order $\geq$. Hence, by Tarski's Theorem, the set of fixed points of Φ constitute a complete lattice. Every fixed point of Φ is uniquely consistent with a single stable match. And if (μ, ν) is a stable match, then the corresponding pre-match $(\hat{\mu}, \hat{\nu})$ is a fixed point of Φ. Hence, by Tarski's Theorem, the set of stable matches constitutes a complete lattice, under the "what's best for women" order.*

This proposition is a little less straightforward than Proposition 25.12, but I still leave the proof to you as Problem 25.4. (Of course, if you need help or merely wish to read the proof, it is provided in the *Online Supplement* as the solution to Problem 25.4.)

The technique of working with isotone maps on a lattice can make life simple. For instance, having this map Φ provides a relatively fast proof of Proposition 25.4—that the deferred-acceptance algorithm produces the best stable match for women—and, therefore, Corollary 25.9. This is done in three steps.

Let $(\hat{\mu}_0, \hat{\nu}_0)$ be the pre-match $\hat{\mu}_0(m) = W$ for all m and $\hat{\nu}_0(w) = \emptyset$ for all w. This is the "largest" pre-match under the order $\geq$. Hence, if we write $(\hat{\mu}_1, \hat{\nu}_1)$ for $\Phi((\hat{\mu}_0, \hat{\nu}_0))$, the fact that $(\hat{\mu}_0, \hat{\nu}_0)$ is maximal under $\geq$ ensures that $(\hat{\mu}_0, \hat{\nu}_0) \geq (\hat{\mu}_1, \hat{\nu}_1)$. And, since Φ is isotone, this implies that

$$(\hat{\mu}_1, \hat{\nu}_1) = \Phi((\hat{\mu}_0, \hat{\nu}_0)) \geq \Phi((\hat{\mu}_1, \hat{\nu}_1)) : \text{Denote } \Phi((\hat{\mu}_1, \hat{\nu}_1)) \text{ by } (\hat{\mu}_2, \hat{\nu}_2).$$

Proceed iteratively, denoting $\Phi((\hat{\mu}_k, \hat{\nu}_k))$ as $(\hat{\mu}_{k+1}, \hat{\nu}_{k+1})$. Because Φ is isotone, this defines a sequence

$$(\hat{\mu}_0, \hat{\mu}_1) \geq (\hat{\mu}_1, \hat{\mu}_2) \geq \ldots \geq (\hat{\mu}_k, \hat{\mu}_k) \geq (\hat{\mu}_{k+1}, \hat{\nu}_{k+1}) \geq \ldots .$$

The sequence "terminates" if and when we reach a step L for which $(\hat{\mu}_L, \hat{\nu}_L) = (\hat{\mu}_{L+1}, \hat{\nu}_{L+1})$, which is then a fixed point of Φ; corresponding to a stable match. And it is a matter of when, not if: Until we reach a fixed point, the sets $\hat{\mu}$ sets are (weakly) getting smaller, and the $\hat{\nu}$ sets are (weakly) getting larger, and one or the other must be changing, or we've reached a fixed point. Since the sets M and W are finite, a fixed point must be reached. Write (μ^*, ν^*) for the stable match that corresponds to this fixed point of Φ.

Next, take *any* stable match (μ, ν) and create the corresponding pre-match $(\hat{\mu}, \hat{\nu})$ in the obvious fashion. We know that $(\hat{\mu}_0, \hat{\nu}_0)$ is maximal under $\geq$, so $(\hat{\mu}_0, \hat{\nu}_0) \geq$

$(\hat{\mu}, \hat{\nu})$. Apply the isotone Φ to both sides, to conclude that $(\hat{\mu}_1, \hat{\nu}_1) \geq \Phi((\hat{\mu}, \hat{\nu})) = (\hat{\mu}, \hat{\nu})$, where the equality is because (μ, ν) is stable, and so $(\hat{\mu}, \hat{\nu})$ is a fixed point of Φ. Repeating this, we conclude that the $(\hat{\nu}_k, \hat{\mu}_k)$, the result of applying Φ k times to $(\hat{\mu}, \hat{\nu})$, satisfies $(\hat{\mu}_k, \hat{\nu}_k) \geq (\hat{\mu}, \hat{\nu})$. Hence, $(\hat{\mu}^*, \hat{\nu}^*) \geq (\hat{\mu}, \hat{\nu})$, and this, per Proposition 25.13, implies that $\nu^*(w) \succeq_w \nu(w)$ for all $w \in W$.

The last step is to show that (μ^*, ν^*) is the same match as is produced by the deferred-acceptance algorithm with women making offers. The argument is a little tricky, because the kth application of Φ to $(\hat{\mu}_0, \hat{\nu}_0)$ isn't the same as the results of round k in the algorithm. In particular:

- Since $\hat{\mu} \equiv W$, $\hat{\nu}_1(w)$ for each w is a singleton set, consisting of the man m whom w likes most.

- Therefore, $\hat{\mu}_2(m)$ consists of all women as good as or better than the best woman w who chose man m in the first application of Φ.

- Take a woman w, and suppose that her favorite man m is not so keen on her; he prefers some other woman w', who chose him in the first application of Φ. Then $w \notin \hat{\mu}_2(m)$ and so, in $\hat{\nu}_3(w)$, she must pick some other man as the root of her "I'll consider" set. But there could be several men who reject her in the second round. And although in the deferred-acceptance algorithm, the "rejection" sets of a woman grow by no more than one man per iteration, in the application of Φ (on every other application), what is essentially the rejection set of a woman can grow by a more than one man in a single pair of iterations.

However, successive applications of Φ to $(\hat{\mu}_0, \hat{\nu}_0)$ must wind up at the stable match that is the end point of the deferred-acceptance algorithm. We know this is true, because both stable matches are maximal, and there can be only one supremum for the complete lattice of stable matches. But, if you think it through (and focus your attention on the shrinking sets $\hat{\mu}_k(m)$ for each man m), a direct argument is available.

A couple of comments about this argument and about the general idea of iterating Φ to find a fixed point are worth making:

- In the deferred-acceptance algorithm, each man m sees his fortunes (weakly) improve, round by round. This is a key element of deferred acceptance: If m tentatively accepts an offer made to him in some round, he holds on to that offer until a better (for him) offer comes along. And yet repeated application of Φ (weakly) "shrinks" $\hat{\mu}(m)$. These two facts are, in fact, manifestations of the same basic phenomenon, if you interpret $\hat{\mu}(m)$ as the set of matches that m is willing to consider. As iterations of Φ are processed, the shrinking of $\hat{\mu}(m)$ reflects the notion that there were matches that m had been willing to consider but that he no longer does, because better prospects have come along, as more and more women are "willing to consider" him, which is the manifestation of the (weak) expansion of the sets $\hat{\nu}(w)$.

- I assume that many readers who are simultaneously taking a sequence in macroeconomics have encountered (in the theory of dynamic programming) the notion of a contraction operator, for which, under appropriate assumptions, repeated iteration on any starting point converges to a fixed point of the operator. What we have here isn't quite as powerful. If we had started with some pre-match $(\hat{\mu}, \hat{\nu})$ such that $\Phi((\hat{\mu}, \hat{\nu}))$ was neither $\geq$ nor $\leq (\hat{\mu}, \hat{\nu})$, convergence is not guaranteed. This is why we took $\hat{\mu}_0 = W$ and $\hat{\nu}_0 = \emptyset$ as the starting point $(\hat{\mu}_0, \hat{\nu}_0)$; because $(W, \emptyset)$ is the $\geq$-order-maximal pre-match, it ensures that $(\hat{\mu}_0, \hat{\nu}_0) \geq (\hat{\mu}_1, \hat{\nu}_1) = \Phi((\hat{\mu}_0, \hat{\nu}_0))$.

Put it this way: *If we had chosen some other starting pre-match $(\hat{\mu}, \hat{\nu})$ such that* we could argue from first principles that $\Phi((\hat{\mu}, \hat{\nu})) \leq (\hat{\mu}, \hat{\nu})$, then becasue Φ is isotone and there are only finitely many pre-matches, we know that a fixed point must result from applying Φ repeatedly (as long as $\geq$ is acyclic). Moreover, for any fixed point $(\hat{\mu}', \hat{\nu}')$ that we know from first principles satisfies $(\hat{\mu}, \hat{\nu}) \geq (\hat{\mu}', \hat{\nu}')$, the fixed point we reach by iterating on Φ starting from $(\hat{\mu}, \hat{\nu})$ (or, in more general situations of complete lattices, to which we *converge* rather than *reach*) must also be $\geq (\hat{\mu}', \hat{\nu}')$. This is a second excellent reason for starting in this problem with the $\geq$-order-maximal pre-match, $(\hat{\mu}_0, \hat{\nu}_0)$.

Indeed, you have probably noted that Φ is symmetric between men and women. If we chose a starting point such that $\Phi((\hat{\mu}, \hat{\nu})) \geq (\hat{\mu}, \hat{\nu})$, we'd be in business again, but with successive applications of Φ resulting in "larger" pre-matches, until a fixed point is reached. Which, if you think about it, is how (for the right starting point, which is what?) you use Φ to produce the men-make-the-offers deferred-acceptance-algorithm result.

Who gets matched? The Lonely Hearts Club Theorem

In a match (μ, ν), whether stable or not, some women and men are matched; others may not be. If there are more men than women, then obviously, some men will go unmatched; but even under those conditions, if some women are unacceptable to some men, some women may not be matched. Suppose, in a particular stable match (μ, ν), m is not matched. Can m hope that in a different stable match (μ', ν'), he finds a partner? The answer is no. *Any man or woman who is unmatched in some stable match is unmatched in every stable match* (fixing the preferences of the men and women). This result might be called the *Lonely Hearts Club Theorem*, and you are asked to prove it (with a lot of help) in Problem 25.6.

25.4. Many-to-One Matches: The College-Admissions and Job-Assignment Models

We turn next to many-to-one matches, where both sides have preferences. Typically, members of the "many" side are individual agents, while the "one" side consists of institutions. A distinction is made between cases where the institution is unlimited in the number of individual agents with which it can be matched and cases where the institution has a quota. (The true distinction between the two models comes from assumptions that are made about the preferences of the institution. I'll explain once the assumptions are laid out.) In the literature, as noted in Section 25.1, there are many specific contexts associated with these two cases. I'll use *college admissions*,[11] in which the agents are prospective students, limited to attending one college, and the institutions are colleges with a strict upper bound on the number of students they can enroll. And *job assignment* will refer to stories in which the agents are prospective employees, limited to one employer, and the institutions are firms, which (we assume) are unconstrained in the number of individuals each can hire.

Complex and simple preferences

By focusing on the marriage market, Section 25.2 avoids complications when it comes to preferences. Specifically, and in the context of marriage, if the women are Alice, Carol, and Evelyn, and the men are Bob, Daniel, and Fred, it is somewhat natural to assume—and we did assume—that all Alice cares about when evaluating a full match is her own bit of the match. If Alice compares the matches

Alice–Daniel, Evelyn–Bob, Carol–Fred

with

Alice–Daniel, Evelyn–Fred, Carol–Bob

she professes indifference, since she is matched with Daniel in both cases. It is not beyond imagining that she might care about Carol's match—perhaps Carol is her sister—but in Section 25.2, we implicitly assumed that no man and no woman has any such concerns.

In many-to-one matches, things are naturally more complex. The institution side of the market—that is, the college or the employer—is naturally concerned with the full roster of individuals with whom it is matched. Take the case of college admissions, and suppose the applicants are Alice, Bob, Carol, and Daniel. Suppose that a college on the other side of this market can admit up to two students and, in terms of individual students, it believes that Alice is most desirable, Carol is second, Bob is third, and Daniel is fourth. But the college wishes to maintain gender balance, and so it ranks { Alice, Bob } as better than { Alice, Carol }. Indeed, and taking other aspects of the four into consideration, it might feel that { Bob, Carol } makes a better cohort than { Alice, Bob }, even though it feels that Alice is the best single choice it can have.

And, when thinking of firms hiring employees, it is natural to think that firm A cares about the composition of its "team." Indeed, firm A might care about firm B's roster of employees, if firm B is a direct competitor. If firm C is not a competitor of firm A, then firm A might be happy to hire Alice and Bob and not Daniel, who provides little discernible value to firm A if it (also) employs Alice and Bob, as long as Daniel goes to firm C. But it would prefer to hire all three, if omitting Daniel means that he takes a job with firm A's competitor, firm B.[12]

---

[11]   The titular subject of Gale and Shapley (1962).

[12]   This scenario is common when it comes to sports teams. Manchester United Football Club might be willing to keep a striker on the payroll at great expense, even if this striker rarely gets to play, if this keeps the striker from playing for Manchester City. But Man U might be happy to loan the striker to, say, Juventus or even some lesser rival in the Premier League, if this allows it to avoid paying the striker's wages.

These considerations have analogs in standard consumer theory. The notion that a consumer has preferences over bundles of goods she consumes that are not additively separable—that various goods are complements or substitutes—is so commonplace as to be unremarkable in the theory of demand. And, although the idea that Alice cares about what Bob is consuming is not so commonplace, it is key when we discuss externalities.

Moreover, it is somewhat natural in many-to-one matches that agents on the "one" side care about their peers in the match. Alice may wish to attend the same college as Bob. Indeed, if we are talking about job assignments, such as in the market for new assistant professors, and if newly minted PhD students Alice and Pat are a couple, they may strongly prefer that they are hired by the same department or, at least, by departments that are geographically proximate.[13]

Responsive and substitutable preferences

All these considerations make the theory of many-to-one matching markets quite difficult, unless and until assumptions are made that simplify things. So, in the theory, such assumptions are made.

Denote the individual agents by $a \in A$ and the institutions by $c \in C$, for finite sets A and C. Let $\mathcal{A}$ denote the set of subsets of A; call elements $\beta \in \mathcal{A}$ *cohorts*.

In terms of applicants or prospective employees, "simple" preferences over colleges or firms are assumed: Students or employees have complete, transitive, and antisymmetric preferences over colleges or firms, just as in the marriage market. That is, they aren't concerned with other members of their cohort. We allow $a \in A$ to prefer not to attend college c or work for firm c; write $\overline{C}$ for $C \cup \{\overline{c}\}$, for some $\overline{c} \notin C$; the general assumption is that each a has complete, transitive, and antisymmetric preferences over $\overline{C}$, with $\succ_a$ denoting the strict portion of a's preferences.

And, when it comes to the "institution" sides' preferences, one of two assumptions is made in the foundational literature.[14]

Definition 25.14. *Institution c's preferences over $\mathcal{A}$ are **responsive** if there is a real-valued function $v_c : A \to R$ such that $v_c(a) = v_c(a')$ only if $a = a'$, and $v(a) \neq 0$ for any a, such that $\beta \succeq_c \beta'$ if and only if $\sum_{a \in \beta} v_c(a) \geq \sum_{a \in \beta'} v_c(a)$.*

Note that $v_c(a) < 0$ is possible for a c and a; this means that institution c does not want a on any terms. If A are college applicants and C are colleges, then $v_c(a) < 0$ means that college c regards student a as *unadmittable*. And the requirement that $v_c(a) \neq 0$ means that every student is, for each college, either desirable or undesirable; colleges are not indifferent about any student.

I won't bother stating the following observations as a formal proposition. (I continue to use the language of applicants and colleges.)

---

[13] And, while Manchester United may not want striker Alberto to play for Manchester City, if Man U has a better striker, Alberto may have a strong desire not to be employed by Man U, if this is going to limit his playing time.

[14] The origination of these two assumptions is complex; see the Bibliographic Notes at the end of the chapter.

- Suppose c faces a quota of $q(c)$ students; it cannot admit more than $q(c)$ students, but it can admit less if it so chooses. Suppose it is able to pick any cohort it wishes from some subset $A' \subset A$, subject to this constraint. Then, if A' has $q(c)$ or more members with $v_c(a) > 0$, it would choose to admit the $q(c)$ "best" students (as measured by v_c) from A'. If A' has fewer than $q(c)$ students with $v_c(a) > 0$, then c would choose to admit all the $a \in A'$ that it finds desirable; that is, that have $v_c(a) > 0$.

- In particular, suppose c compares two cohorts β and β', both of which meet its quota constraint, such that β consists of a together with γ, and β' consists of a' together with γ. That is, the two cohorts differ only in that a is in β but not β', and a' is in β' but not β. Then college c strictly prefers β to β' if and only if $v_c(a) > v_c(a')$.

- If cohort β has strictly fewer than $q(c)$ applicants, and $a \notin \beta$ satisfies $v_c(a) > 0$, then c strictly prefers $\beta \cup \{a\}$ to β.

- If cohort β includes a student a such that $v_c(a) < 0$, then c strictly prefers $\beta \setminus \{a\}$ to β.

The exact cardinal values assigned by the function v_c to $a \in A$ are, for all the properties listed, unimportant. What is important is the each college c strictly orders all applicants $a \in A$, with (possibly) some students in A falling "below the line of admittability" in the estimation of college c. If you consult the early literature (Gale and Shapley 1962; Roth 1982, 1985) that assumes substitutable preferences, these authors write in terms of each college having a complete, transitive, and antisymmetric preference order over students, which allows for the expression of "not admittable." (Therefore, when we get to the theory, all that matters is the ordinal ranking over students that is established by v_c. And, of course, taking a complete, transitive, and antisymmetric ranking over $\overline{A} = A \cup \{\overline{a}\}$ for finite A and creating a numerical representation of that ranking with the "utility" of $\overline{a}$ set at 0 is entirely without loss of generality.)

In contrast, we have the following definition.

Definition 25.15. *For $c \in C$, its preferences over cohorts drawn from $\mathcal{A}$ are **substitutable** if those preferences are complete, transitive, and antisymmetric, and in addition: For $A' \subseteq A$, denote c's $\succ_c$-maximal subset of A' by $\chi_c^*(A')$. Then, if $a, a' \in A'$ ($a \neq a'$), $a \in \chi_c^*(A')$ implies $a \in \chi_c^*(A' \setminus \{a'\})$.*

The property in addition to the usual properties (i.e., completeness, transitivity, and antisymmetry) is perhaps easier to understand in contrapositive form: If $a \in A'$ is not in $\chi_c^*(A')$—if c would not include a in its favorite cohort chosen out of some set A'—then adding $a' \neq a$ to A' doesn't make a a desirable choice. In effect, this rules out complementary employees: If employee a' complemented a, so that the ability to hire them both makes a desirable, preferences may not be substitutable.

How do these two assummptions on institutional preferences compare? Strictly speaking, neither one implies the other. But this is something of a cheat: Strictly speaking, responsive preferences need not be antisymmetric. If, by coincidence, cohorts β and β' had $\sum_{a \in \beta} v_c(a) = \sum_{a \in \beta'} v_c(a)$, then institution c would be indifferent between β and β'. But, except for this, we have the following result.

Proposition 25.16. *If responsive preferences over cohorts, created by some v_c, are antisymmetric, then they are substitutable.*[15]

The proof is nearly trivial. If c has responsive preferences and doesn't want $a \in A'$, then it is because c has $q(c)$ better choices than a out of A', or because $v_c(a) < 0$, or both. Adding a' to A' certainly changes neither condition.

But it is equally obvious (I hope) that substitutable preferences are not necessarily responsive. For instance, a firm may require three mechanics but not four. The fourth-best mechanic who is available may be very superior; the firm would hire her if it couldn't get its three favorites. But, if its three favorites are available and employed by the firm, it wouldn't want to hire her. (Can you think of an example in the context of college admissions? How about in the context of a Department of Economics hiring newly minted PhDs?)

The college-admissions model: Gale and Shapley (1962) and Roth (1982, 1985)

In the *college-admissions model*, the set A is a finite set of I *applicants*, enumerated a_1 to a_I, and the set C is a finite set of J *colleges*, enumerated c_1 to c_J. As above, $\mathcal{A}$ denotes the set of subsets (including the empty set) of A, with generic member β, called a cohort or admissions class. Each college $c \in C$ has a *quota*, the maximum number of students it can admit; the quota for college c is an integer greater than or equal to 1, denoted $q(c)$. Let $\mathcal{A}_q$ denote all subsets of A of cardinality q or less. In this setting:

Definition 25.17. *A* **match** *is a pair of functions (μ, ν) where $\mu : A \to \overline{C}$ and $\nu : C \to \mathcal{A}$ such that*

a. *for $i = 1, \dots, I$ and $c = 1, \dots, J$, $\mu(a_i) = c_j$ if and only if $a_i \in \nu(c_j)$; and*

b. *for $j = 1, \dots, J$, the cardinality of $\nu(c_j)$ is less than or equal to $q(c_j)$; that is, $\nu(c_j) \in \mathcal{A}_{q(c_j)}$.*

Assumptions 25.18. *Applicants have preferences about colleges, and colleges have preferences over the cohort of applicants that they enroll:*

a. *The preferences of student a_i are given by a complete, transitive, and antisymmetric preference relation on the set $\overline{C}$, the strict portion of which is denoted $\succ_i$. If $\overline{c} \succ_i c_j$ for some college c_j, the interpretation is that a_i would rather not go to college than attend college c_j.*

---

[15] As already noted, the cardinal values given to each a by v_c have no impact on c's evaluation of cohorts. What is important are the relative (ordinal) values of $v_c(a)$ for different a, with $v_c(\overline{a}) = 0$. And—the reason for this footnote—since A is finite, you can always assign order-preserving cardinal values $v_c(a)$ such that c is never indifferent between two distinct cohorts. (Don't worry if you don't see the point of this remark.)

b. *Colleges have responsive preferences over the cohort of students they enroll. (The notation v_j is used as in Definition 25.14 for the student-ranking function of college c_j.)*

Definition 25.19. *A match (μ, ν) is* **stable** *if:*

a. *for no applicant a_i is it the case that $\overline{c} \succ_i \mu(a_i)$;*

b. *for no college c_j is there some $a_i \in \nu(c_j)$ such that $v_j(a_i) < 0$; and*

c. *for no pair of a student a_i and college c_j is it the case that $c_j \succ_i \mu(a_i)$, and either*

    i. *$v_j(a_i) > 0$ and the cardinality of $\nu(c_j)$ is strictly less than $q(c_j)$, or*

    ii. *for some $a' \in \nu(c_j)$, $v_j(a_i) > v_j(a')$.*

This definition mimics the definition of stability in the marriage market. In this definition:

- Condition a is individual rationality for applicants. No applicant is matched with a college that she does *not* want to attend, even if it means not attending any college.

- Condition b is individual rationality for colleges. No college is admitting a student that it considers unadmittable by its standards.

- Condition c concerns rematches: There is no unmatched pair of a student and a college for which the student prefers the college to her assigned (matched) college and for which, either (i) the college regards the student as admittable and has room for her under its quota, or (ii) the college prefers this student to some student that is assigned to it under the match.

From the classic marriage market, recall that stable matches in that context are core matches; see Proposition 25.3. Without going into details here—see Problem 25.7 for details—a similar but weaker result holds here, which depends on Assumption 25.18(a). In general cooperative game theory, the core is the set of "outcomes" such that no group of players has the ability to rearrange things among themselves in a way that makes members of the group "better off" than at an outcome in the core. The question is: How much better off? Is it necessary that every member of the group be strictly better off? Or is it sufficient that every member of the group be at least as well off (as in the proposed outcome), and at least one member of the group be strictly better off? In Proposition 25.3, an unstable outcome is "blocked" (is not in the core), because both the man and the woman involved are strictly better off. But, in this context, when (say) college c_j drops student a' to admit a, the other students in c_j's cohort are involved. Assumption 25.18(a) says that the other students are indifferent. But they are indifferent, not strictly better off, and so the formal result is that a stable match in this context is in the so-called *strong* core. (For a more detailed and exact rendition, see Problem 25.7.)

Definition 25.20. *In the **deferred-acceptance algorithm with applicants leading**:*

a. *In the first round, each applicant applies to his/her favorite college. Colleges look at the set of applicants and choose their best cohort up to their quota, choosing from those who applied. They reject other applicants.*

b. *In subsequent rounds, students apply to their favorite college that has not previously rejected them. (If they were not rejected in the previous round, they reapply to that college.) Colleges look at the set of applicants and choose their favorite cohort up to their quota, from those who applied. They reject other applicants.*

c. *The algorithm terminates when, in a given round, no applicant is rejected.*

*In the **deferred-acceptance algorithm with colleges leading**:*

a'. *In the first round, each college mails admissions letters to the members of its favorite cohort, subject to its quota constraint. Applicants then tentatively accept the admissions offer from their favorite college among those colleges that admitted them, rejecting admissions at other colleges that admitted them. (Applicants who get no admissions letter are tentatively assigned to $\bar{c}$, the college of hard knocks. And if they prefer $\bar{c}$ to all colleges that admitted them, they reject all offers of admission.)*

b'. *In subsequent rounds, colleges readmit all applicants who tentatively accepted their offer of admission in the previous round and make up the rest of their cohort with applicants who have not previously rejected them, choosing the best cohort possible, subject to their quota constraints. Applicants then tentatively accept the admissions offer from their favorite college among those colleges that admitted them, rejecting admissions at other colleges that admitted them. (The same parenthetical provisos as in part a' apply.)*

c'. *The algorithm terminates when, in a given round, every admission is accepted.*

There is no ambiguity about an applicant's favorite college from any subset of colleges (including $\bar{c}$), because applicants have antisymmetric preferences. And while we didn't assume that college's preferences over cohorts are antisymmetric, the nature of responsive preferences (rankings of students are antisymmetric, and no student has $v_c(a) = 0$) is such that, out of any pool, a college has a (unique) favorite cohort.

Proposition 25.21. *If Assumptions 25.18 holds, then both versions of the deferred acceptance algorithm terminate after finitely many rounds. Both terminate with a stable match. The deferred-acceptance algorithm with applicants leading terminates with a (stable) match $(\mu^{\sharp}, \nu^{\sharp})$ that is better for applicants than any other stable match, and the deferred-acceptance algorithm with colleges leading terminates with a (stable) match $(\mu^{\flat}, \nu^{\flat})$ that is better for colleges than any other stable match.*

*The set of stable matches forms a complete lattice under the partial order **what's-best-for-applicants**.*

The proof is omitted. Termination of the algorithms is trivial, given the finiteness of the sets of applicants and colleges. That they terminate in stable matches is fairly straightforward. Proving that the two are *side-optimal*—that is, the applicant-leading algorithm produces the best stable match for applicants, and the college-leading algorithm produces the best stable match for colleges—requires the sort of induction argument used to prove similar results for the marriage market; this part of the proof does take a bit of care.

Which leaves, in Proposition 25.21, the proof that the set of stable matches forms a complete lattice. Problem 25.8 leads you to a cute proof of this part of the proposition by setting up a one-to-one, somewhat order-preserving correspondence between stable matches in this context and stable matches in a related marriage-market model.

Say that college c_j is *available* to applicant a_i if, for some stable match (μ, ν), $\mu(a_i) = c_j$. Denote by $C(a_i)$ the set of colleges available to applicant a_i, and denote by $c^*(a_i)$ the college $c_j \in C(a_i)$ that a_i most prefers. An immediate corollary of Proposition 25.21 is that $\mu^\sharp(a_i) = c^*(a_i)$.

In symmetric fashion, say that student a_i is *available* to college c_j if, in some stable match, $a_i \in \nu(c_j)$. Write $A(c_j)$ for the set of all students who are available to c_j, and write $\beta^*(c_j)$ for the cohort drawn from $A(c_j)$ that college c_j most prefers (subject to its quota constraint).

Proposition 25.22 *For the college-leading algorithm that terminates in $(\mu^\flat, \nu^\flat)$, $\nu^\flat(c_j) = \beta^*(c_j)$ for every college c_j.*

This is a proposition and not a corollary, because it doesn't immediately follow from Proposition 25.21. To see why, suppose that college c_j, with a quota of 2, is able to enroll its first and fourth favorite students (as per $\succ_j$) in one stable match; in some other stable match, it can enroll its second and third favorite students. Then all four students are available to it and, given its choice out of the four, it would select its first and second favorites. Proposition 25.21 only tells us that $\nu^\flat(c_j)$ is at least as good as the better (according to $\succeq_j$) of $\{a_1, a_4\}$ and $\{a_2, a_3\}$, where a_n is shorthand for c_j's nth favorite student. Nonetheless, the stronger conclusion of Proposition 25.22 is true, implied by the careful induction argument that I am omitting. (Or see Problem 25.8(e).)

Problem 25.9 asks you to prove the following result, which generalizes the Lonely Hearts Club Theorem, the subject of Problem 25.6.

Proposition 25.23. The Rural Hospital Theorem. *Suppose that for some stable match (μ, ν) and some college c, $\nu(c)$ contains fewer than $q(c)$ applicants. Then in **every** stable match (μ', ν'), $\nu'(c) = \nu(c)$.*

This is called the Rural Hospital Theorem, because in the many-to-one matching of new MDs to internships at hospitals, hospitals in rural locations often find that they are unable to fill their quotas of slots for interns. This is typically thought to be because rural hospitals are less attractive to new MDs. So the question arises: Can the mechanism that allocates new MDs to internships be somehow "fixed" so that rural hospitals get their "fair share" of interns? The theorem says that, *insofar as the mechanism results in a stable match,* the answer is no. And, perhaps even worse, in every stable match, a hospital that fails to meet its quota in any stable match gets exactly the same cohort of interns in every stable match. (Footnote 1 on page 380 provides the genesis of this theorem.)

Problems 25.10, 25.11, and 25.12 provide further exercises with the college-admissions model.

The job-assignment model

In particular, Problem 25.12 asks the question: Suppose colleges, with responsive preferences, didn't face quotas. Then there is a unique stable match: Each applicant a is matched with the college c that she most prefers, among all colleges for whom a is considered admittable (that is, such that $v_c(a) > 0$). The college-leading algorithm takes no more than two rounds to clear; the student-leading algorithm can take more rounds, but it gets to the same place.

We don't think of firms having quotas on the number of prospective employees it can hire. Instead, hiring is limited by the value an employee provides, relative to the salary she must be paid.[16] If firms have responsive preferences, then the "answer" is given in the previous paragraph; each prospective employee is matched with her favorite firm from the set of firms that think (independent of whomever else the firm hires) the employee is worth her wages.

This is not a very interesting outcome, so instead, we assume that firms have substitutable preferences: The "incremental value" of each prospective employee to the firm (weakly) declines as the firm hires more employees (and, of course, some prospective employees aren't worth the salaries they require, no matter how large or small the firm's entire workforce is).

Definition 25.24. *The job-assignment model is composed of:*

a. *a finite set of applicants (or prospective employees) A, where each $a \in A$ has complete, transitive, and antisymmetric preferences over $\overline{C} := C \cup \{\overline{c}\}$, where $\overline{c}$ represents being unemployed ($\succ_a$ denotes the strict preferences of a); and*

b. *a finite set of companies (or employers) $c \in C$, without any binding quota on the number of applicants they may hire, but with substitutable preferences $\succ_c$, as in Definition 25.14. (Recall that, for a subset $A' \subset A$, $\chi_c^*(A')$ is firm c's $\succ_c$-best cohort of employees, chosen from A'.)*

c. *A **match** is a pair (μ, ν), where $\mu : A \to \overline{C}$, and $\nu : C \to \mathcal{A}$, such that $\mu(a) = c \in C$ if and only if $a \in \nu(c)$.*

f. *A match (μ, ν) is **stable** if:*

   i. *for each $a \in A$, if $\mu(a) = c \in C$, then $c \succ_a \overline{c}$;*

   ii. *for each $c \in C$, $\chi_c^*(\nu(c)) = \nu(c)$; and*

   iii. *there is no pair (a, c) such that $c \succ_a \mu(a)$, and $\chi_c^*(\nu(c) \cup \{a\}) \succ_c \nu(c)$.*

---

[16] This talk about "salaries" immediately begs the question: What if a prospective employee and a company can negotiate over the employee's salary? Section 25.5 provides some answers to this question.

By now, the meaning of stability should be clear: (i) No employee works for a firm if she prefers unemployment to working for that firm. (ii) No firm can improve its cohort by firing some its assigned workers. (iii) There is no pair of an employee and firm such that the employee prefers the firm to her assigned firm, and the firm, given the opportunity to hire the worker, and perhaps fire some of its current workforce, is better off doing so.

Proposition 25.25. *For the job-assignment model as defined: The set of stable matches is nonempty. The deferred-acceptance algorithm with applicants applying to companies*[17] *for jobs produces a stable match that is best among all stable matches for applicants. The deferred-acceptance algorithm with companies proposing to applicants*[18] *produces a stable match that is best among all stable matches for the companies.*

For proofs, see Kelso and Crawford (1982) and Roth (1984b). Or try to prove this result on your own.   · · ·

25.5. Salaries and Other Terms and Conditions

In the job-assignment model, if job applicant a takes a job with company c, she presumably provides gross benefits to the company that may decrease as company c hires more (other) employees, but that, at least ideally, never become negative. So why would company c choose not to hire a? The obvious reason is that c pays a wages or a salary, and c is interested in the *net* benefits that a provides, net of the salary she is paid.

But, suppose a finds employment at c very desirable. Perhaps a and c could arrange employment at a low wage that is agreeable to both. Suppose a is a very valuable employee for firm c, but a is not keen on working for c. Perhaps a and c could arrange employment at a wage high enough to overcome a's distaste for working for c.

The idea that agreeable matches can be made through negotiation about the terms and conditions of the match applies to other contexts than employment. Economics department d, chasing a particularly desirable newly minted PhD, can offer not only a higher salary, but also greater research support and a lighter or more desirable teaching load. In the classic marriage market, in some societies, the woman brings a dowry; in others, the man pays the family of the bride a bride price. In college admissions, students pay tuition; and to attract specific students, colleges give scholarships.

These ideas are developed in a progression of papers, following the seminal article of Gale and Shapley. Here are some landmark contributions.

---

[17] Applicants apply to their favorite company. Company c tentatively hires $\chi_c^*(A_c^1)$, where A_c^1 is the set of applicants who applied to c. Then in a second round, applicants who were rejected by their first-choice company apply to their second-choice, and so forth.

[18] In the first round, company c proposes to $\chi_c^*(A)$; applicants choose their favorite company; then, in the second round, c proposes to $\chi_c^*(A \setminus R_c^1)$, where R_c^1 is the set of applicants who rejected c's offer of employment in the first round, and so forth.

Shapley and Shubik (1971): The bilateral assignment problems

Shapley and Shubik (1971) begins with the the problem of selling indivisible items to a set of buyers.

- A set A of indivisible items, each with a different owner, are available for purchase.

- Potential buyers, from a set C, are interested in purchasing one of the items, but no more than one.

- The owner of item a attaches dollar value $r_a \geq 0$ to her item. If, in the end, she remains in possession of the item, her payoff is r_a. If she sells it for p dollars, her payoff is p. She is indifferent to the identity of buyer of her item, if she sells it.

- Buyer c attaches dollar value v_{ac} to item a. He attaches incremental value 0 to a second item. If he purchases no item, his payoff is 0. If he purchases item a at the price p, his payoff is $v_{ac} - p$.

Definition 25.26. *A **price-mediated match** is a triple (μ, ν, p) where:*

a. *the function μ records the buyer of each item, $\mu : A \to C \cup \{\bar{c}\}$, where $\mu(a) = \bar{c}$ means that item a is retained by its original owner;*

b. *the function ν records the purchase of each consumer, $\nu : C \to A \cup \{\bar{a}\}$, where $\nu(c) = \bar{a}$ means that buyer c does not purchase an item; and*

c. *prices are given by $p : A \to R_+$;*

all such that:

d. *$\mu(a) = c \in C$ if and only if $\nu(c) = a \in A$;*

e. *for each $a \in A$, $\mu(a) = \bar{c}$ if $p(a) < r_a$, and $\mu(a) \neq \bar{c}$ if $p(a) > r_a$; and*

f. *for each $c \in C$, if $\nu(c) = \bar{a}$, then $v_{\nu(c)c} - p(\nu(c)) \leq 0$ for all $c \in C$, and if $\nu(c) \in A$, then $v_{\nu(c)c} - p(\nu(c)) \geq v_{ac} - p(a)$, for all $a \in A$, and $v_{\nu(c)c} - p(\nu(c)) \geq 0$.*

That is, each item has its own price. The owner of an item sells the item if the price exceeds her value of retaining the item, she holds the item if its price is less than her retention value. A buyer only buys if some item costs no more than his value for the item, and, if he buys an item, it is one that gives him the largest value minus price.

This definition already incorporates the individual rationality portions of stability for this context. This leaves the question: Given a price-mediated match, can subsets of A and C feasibly rearrange matters in a manner that makes themselves better off? The answer is that they cannot. First we define what is feasible for subsets of sellers and buyers. Then we show that no subsets can find a feasible rearrangement that all members like at least as much as a price-mediated match, and some members strictly prefer.

Definition 25.27. *For subsets $A' \subset A$ and $C' \subset C$, a **feasible match with (possible) sidepayments** for $A' \cup C'$ consists of matching functions $\mu' : A' \to C' \cup \{\bar{c}\}$, $\nu' : C' \to$*

$A \cup \{\bar{a}\}$, and a set of net monetary transfers $\pi : A' \cup C' \to R$, such that $\mu'(a) = c \in C'$ if and only if $\nu'(c) = a \in A'$, and $\sum_{a \in A'} \pi(a') + \sum_{c \in C'} \pi(c') = 0$.

If (μ', ν', π) is a feasible match with (possible) sidepayments for A' and C', the **outcome** of the match is:

$$\text{For } a \in A', \begin{cases} \pi(a) + r_a, & \text{if } \mu(a) = \bar{c}, \text{ or} \\ \pi(a), & \text{if } \mu(a) \in C, \end{cases} \quad \text{and for } c \in C', \begin{cases} \pi(c), & \text{if } \nu(c) = \bar{a}, \text{ or} \\ v_{\nu(c)c} + \pi(c), & \text{if } \nu(c) \in A. \end{cases}$$

That's a lot of symbols for a relatively straightforward and simple idea, more or less following developments in Section 15.3 of Volume I. What is (perhaps) a bit novel here is that financial transfers are added to the story; this is possible because the formulation assumes that preferences are all quasi-linear in money. Along these lines, note that in a price-mediated allocation, the transfer of money from $\mu(a)$ to the original owner of a is "bilateral" in the sense that the two are consummating a bilateral deal. All the money that comes to the seller of an item comes from the buyer of that item. But in the definition of a feasible match, cross-subsidization is allowed: To achieve a match, buyer c, who purchases a, can transfer funds to a (previous?) owner of some $a' \neq a$ or to some other buyer c', in order to "bribe" them to let him have a. But, compared to a price-mediated match, permitting such "bribes" doesn't help:

Proposition 25.28. *If (μ, ν, p) is a price-mediated match, there do not exist subsets $A' \subset A$ and $C' \subset C$ and a feasible match with (possible) sidepayments for A' and C' such that: (a) For each $a \in A'$ and $c \in C'$, the outcome of the feasible match is at least as good as the outcome in the price-mediated match. And (b) for at least one $a \in A'$ or $c \in C'$, the outcome of the feasible match is strictly better. In other words (and a bit loosely), a price-mediated match is in the strong core of the game in which subsets of buyers and sellers can "object" to a feasible match.*

Proof. Suppose $(A', C', \mu', \nu', \pi)$ presents an "objection" to the price-mediated match (μ, ν, p) in the sense that it is at least as good for a and c in $A' \cup C'$ and is strictly better for at least one a or c.

For expositional ease, let $v_{\bar{a}c} = p(\bar{a}) = 0$. Then, for each buyer $c \in C'$,

$$v_{\nu'(c)c} + \pi(c) \geq v_{\nu(c)c} - p(\nu(c)) \geq v_{\nu'(c)c} - p(\nu'(c)).$$

The first inequality expresses the hypothesis that $c \in C'$ is at least as well off under $(A', C', \mu', \nu', \pi)$; the second is that, at the price vector p, c prefers (weakly) to buy $\nu(c)$ over any alternative. Hence, for every $c \in C'$, $\pi(c) \geq -p(\nu'(c))$.

For sellers, consider separately sellers who retain their item under μ', and those who sell them. For those who retain their object, their payoff is $r_a + \pi(a)$. This must be greater than or equal to $\max\{r_a, p(a)\}$, as that is what a seller gets in a price-mediated equilibrium. And, if $r_a > p(a)$, this gives $\pi(a) \geq 0$, while if $p(a) \geq r_a$, it gives $r_a + \pi(a) \geq p(a)$, or $\pi(a) \geq p(a) - r_a \geq 0$.

Then we have sellers whose items are sold under μ'. Their outcome is $\pi(a)$, which must be greater or equal to $p(a)$.

Finally, one of these inequalities must be strict. So,

$$0 = \sum_{a \in A'} \pi(a) + \sum_{c \in C'} \pi(c) \; > \; \sum_{a \in A' : \mu'(a) = \overline{c}} \pi(a) \; + \sum_{a \in A' : \mu'(a) \in C'} p(a) - \sum_{c \in C'} p(\nu'(c)).$$

The second and third terms on the right-hand side cancel out, because every item a that is sold under μ' is bought under ν'; for these items, their price under p is present in both sums. And the first term on the right-hand side is, term by term, greater than or equal to 0. Therefore, the three terms on the right hand side sum to something greater than or equal to 0. This provides a contradiction. ∎

Corollary 25.29. *Any price-mediated match is socially efficient. Moreover, if (μ, ν, p) is a price-mediated match, and if (μ', ν') is some other match of items to buyers, then*

$$\sum_{\mu(a) \in C} v_{a\mu(a)} + \sum_{\mu(a) = \overline{C}} r_a \geq \sum_{\mu'(a) \in C} v_{a\mu'(a)} + \sum_{\mu'(a) = \overline{C}} r_a.$$

The first statement follows because the "coalition of the whole," $A' = A$ and $C' = C$, cannot feasibly "block" a price-mediated match. As for the second statement, note that the term on either side of the displayed inequality is the "surplus" generated by the match. If some match (μ', ν') generated strictly more of this surplus than a match (μ, ν), then, whatever the transfers of money implied by p in (μ, ν, p), we can find sidepayments of the surplus generated by (μ', ν') that make each seller and each buyer as well off as in (μ, ν, p) and have surplus left over to distribute and make everyone strictly better off.[19]

This is all very nice, if a price-mediated match in fact exists. And, in terms of existence, one might doubt existence because of the indivisibility of the items. Volume I's existence theorems for pure exchange economies do not apply to indivisible goods. Nonetheless, Shapley and Shubik prove the following:

Proposition 25.30. *Price-mediated matches exist. In fact, the set of price-mediated matches, in terms of the payoffs of the participants, form a complete lattice under the "what's good for buyers" order. In particular, there is a buyer-best price-mediated match and a seller-best price-mediated match.*

This is a special case of (soon to be stated and proved) Proposition 25.34, so the proof follows from the proof of that proposition.

---

[19] With dollar-denominated unilities and money transfers, this is what is called a *transferable-utility* (or TU) game. And the second part of the corollary is a special case of properties of core allocations in TU games.

Now consider the following generalization and reinterpretation. Instead of selling items, where owners of items in set A don't care to whom they sell, as long as they get the best price, suppose that the story is that members of A are women, and members of C are men; or that $a \in A$ are otherwise potential (business?) partners of members of C. We keep the assumption that only bilateral pairs, one member of A with one member of C, are considered. But now, we imagine that, just as each member of c attaches a dollar value v_{ac} to being matched with $a \in A$, each member $a \in A$ attaches a dollar value u_{ca} of being matched with c. This reformulation takes us back to the classic marriage market, but with the following amendment: Before, men had preferences $\succ_m$ over women, and women had preferences $\succ_w$ over men. Now, we are assuming the existence of numerical representations of those preferences. That isn't saying much; the sets over which each side has preferences are finite, and preferences are complete and transitive, so of course, we could have spoken in terms of numerical representations. What is added here is that preferences are quasi-linear in money, this representation of preferences is the dollar-denominated representation, and money can change hands between partners to a match.

Talking in terms of dowries and bride prices may be distasteful (not to mention the notion that men's and women's preferences over partners are quasi-linear in money). So, think of bilateral partnerships where, *if a and c form a partnership, that partnership is worth some amount w_{ac} in dollar terms to the two partners*; in terms of previous variables, $w_{ac} = u_{ca} + v_{ac}$. *And, as part of the terms of a partnership agreement,* the partners must specify how their "partnership value" w_{ac} will be split between them.

To allow for members of A who do not wish to partner with some $c \in C$, or who cannot find a willing partner from C, expand C to $\overline{C}$, where $\overline{C}$ is the union of C and a set $\{\overline{c}_a : a \in A\}$, where if a is matched to $\overline{c}_a$, the value of that partnership, $w_{a\overline{c}_a}$, is a's value in dollars of going it alone, while $w_{a\overline{c}_{a'}}$ for $a' \neq a$ is something less than this (so a would always chose $\overline{c}_a$, a match that will always be available). And, put in place for each c an "unmatched match" $\overline{a}_c$ with similar constructions for $w_{\overline{a}_c c}$ and $w_{\overline{a}_{c'} c}$.

Definition 25.31. *In the context of this model, a **bilateral match** consists of a function $\mu : A \to \overline{C}$, a function $\nu : C \to \overline{A}$, and match values $r : A \to R$ and $s : C \to R$, such that*

a. *if $\mu(a) \in C$, then $\nu(c) \in A$, and vice versa,*

b. *if $\mu(a) = c \in C$, then $r(a) + s(c) = w_{ac}$,*

c. *if $\mu(a) \notin C$, then $\mu(a) = \overline{c}_a$ and $r(a) = w_{a\overline{c}_a}$, and*

d. *if $\nu(c) \notin A$, then $\nu(c) = \overline{a}_c$, and $s(c) = w_{\overline{a}_c c}$.*

The adjective "bilateral" refers not only to the notion that one a pairs with no more than one c, and vice versa, but also that monetary transfers are conducted entirely bilaterally; that is, condition b holds.

Definition 25.32. *A bilateral match (in this context) (μ, ν, r, s) is **stable** if:*

a. *for every* $a \in A$, $r(a) \geq w_{a\bar{c}_a}$;

b. *for every* $c \in C$, $s(c) \geq w_{\bar{a}_c c}$; *and*

c. *there does not exist a pair* $a \in A$ *and* $c \in C$ *such that* $w_{ac} > r(a) + s(c)$.

This is the usual notion of stability, adapted to this context: No member of A and no member of C will do better by going it alone, and no (necessarily unmatched) pair can do better by pairing off.

Definition 25.33. *For subsets* $A' \subset A$ *and* $C' \subset C$, *a **match with sidepayments** is an array* (μ', ν', π), *where* $\mu' : A' \to C' \cup \overline{C}$, $\nu' : C' \to A' \cup \overline{A}$, *and a function* $\pi : A' \cup C' \to R$, *such that* $\mu'(a) = c \in C'$ *implies that* $\nu'(c) = a$ *and vice versa, and*

$$\sum_{a \in A'} \pi(a) + \sum_{c \in C'} \pi(c) = \sum_{a \in A' : \mu'(a) = c \in C'} w_{ac} + \sum_{a \in A' : \mu'(a) \notin C'} w_{a\bar{c}_a} + \sum_{c \in C' : \nu'(c) \notin A'} w_{\bar{a}_c c}. \quad (25.1)$$

As in the earlier developments in this section, while a *bilateral match* as defined in Definition 25.31 does not allow sidepayments—each partnership is on its own—Definition 25.33 allows members of A' and C' to subsidize or be subsidized by other members of $A' \cup C'$. And note the different use of the π function: Now it incorporates the full value to each participant, so the constraint expressed in (25.1) is that, given A', C', μ', and ν', the sum of these values to the participants must equal the amount of "value" that the match (μ', ν') creates.

Proposition 25.34. *If* (μ, ν, r, s) *is a stable bilateral match, then there are no subsets* $A' \subseteq A$ *and* $C' \subseteq C$ *and a match with sidepayments* (μ', ν', π) *for* A' *and* C' *such that every member of* $A' \cup C'$ *is at least as well off under the match with sidepayments as they are under the stable bilateral match, and some member of* $A' \cup C'$ *is strictly better off.*[20] *So, in particular, in any stable bilateral match,* $\sum_a r(a) + \sum_c s(c)$ *is the socially efficient amount that can be obtained by any match.*

Proof. The proof follows the lines of the proof of Proposition 25.27. but the notation is sufficiently different, so it is worth spelling out. Suppose that, for A' and C', there is a match with sidepayments that is as good as (μ, ν, r, s) for every member of A' and C' and strictly better for at least one member. That is,

$$\sum_{a \in A'} \pi(a) + \sum_{c \in C'} \pi(c) > \sum_{a \in A'} r(a) + \sum_{c \in C'} s(c). \quad (25.2)$$

Break the sum on the left-hand side into three groups: pairs (a, c) that are matched in the match with sidepayments, $a \in A'$ that are not matched with a $c \in C'$ in the match with sidepayments, and $c \in C'$ that are not matched with an $a \in A'$ in the match with sidepayments.

---

[20] That is, and somewhat loosely, stable matches exactly comprise strong core. This proposition establishes that stable matches are in the strong core. And, if a match is not stable, it can be blocked by either one a, one c, or a pair a and c, depending on the condition of stability that fails.

For the second group, per condition a of a stable match, $r(a) \geq w_{a\bar{c}_a}$. For the third group, per condition b, $s(c) \geq w_{\bar{a}_c c}$. And for each pair a and c such that $\mu'(a) = c \in C'$, $r(a) + s(a) \geq w_{ac}$. Hence

$$
\sum_{a \in A'} r(a) + \sum_{c \in C'} s(c) = \sum_{a \in A: \mu'(a) = c \in C'} (r(a) + s(c)) + \sum_{a \in A': \mu'(a) \notin C'} r(a) + \sum_{c \in C': \nu'(c) \notin A'} s(c)
$$

$$
\geq \sum_{a \in A: \mu'(a) = c \in C'} w_{ac} + \sum_{a \in A': \mu'(a) \notin C'} w_{a\bar{c}_a} + \sum_{c \in C': \nu'(c) \notin A'} w_{\bar{a}_c c}.
$$

$$(25.3)$$

The equation (25.1) and the inequalities (25.2) and (25.3) are contradictory.   ∎

This leaves the existence question. The answer is supplied by Shapley and Shubik (1971):

Proposition 25.35. *A stable match exists and, in fact, in payoff space, the set of stable matches forms a complete lattice. In particular, there are a best-for-the-as stable match and a best-for-the-cs stable match.*

Proof. Imagine that, instead of settling for a deterministic match, we allowed probabilistic matching. Let z_{ac} be the probability that a matches with c. Consider the linear programming problem of choosing variables $(z_{ac})_{a \in A, c \in C}$ to maximize

$$
\sum_{a \in A} \sum_{c \in C} z_{ac} w_{ac} + \sum_{a \in A} \left[\left(1 - \sum_{c \in C} z_{ac} \right) w_{a\bar{c}_a} \right] + \sum_{c \in C} \left[\left(1 - \sum_{a \in A} z_{ac} \right) w_{\bar{a}_c c} \right],
$$

subject to constraints $\sum_a z_{ac} \leq 1$ and $\sum_c z_{ac} \leq 1$, and $z_{ac} \geq 0$ for all a-c pairs. The objective function is the total expected surplus generated if z_{ac} is the probability that a is matched with c: The first term is the expected surplus from all such matches, the second term records the probability that a is unmatched, times the surplus a generates when unmatched, and the third term is similar for each c. Write

$$
\hat{w}_{ac} \text{ for } w_{ac} - \left(w_{a\bar{c}_a} + w_{\bar{a}_c c} \right);
$$

this is the value of an a and c partnership above the value of the two going it alone. ($\hat{w}_{ac} < 0$ is not ruled out.) Then the objective function can be rewritten

$$
\sum_{a \in A} \sum_{c \in C} z_{ac} \hat{w}_{ac} + \sum_{a \in A} w_{a\bar{c}_a} + \sum_{c \in C} w_{\bar{a}_c c}.
$$

The second two sums are constants, and so the optimization problem consists of the maximization of the first double summation, subject to the constraints.

It is clear that, if $\hat{w}_{ac} < 0$, then the optimal value of z_{ac} is 0; rather than form a partnership of a and c, it would be better for the two of them to go their separate ways or, perhaps, to form some other partnerships. But, beyond this obvious remark, the question is: What can be said about the optimal solution?

- From the theory of linear-programming problems and, in particular, the simplex method for solving such problems, we know that an integer solution to this problem exists; see, for instance, Dantzig (1963, section 15.1).[21]

- Suppose we treat this as a standard maximization problem (of a concave objective function) subject to inequality constraints, the sort of problem that is found throughout Volume I. At any integer-valued solution, the constraint qualification holds, and so the first-order/complementary-slackness conditions are necessary and sufficient for a solution. Let $\hat{r}(a)$ be the (nonnegative) multiplier on the constraint $\sum_c \dot{z}_{ac} \leq 1$ for each a, let $\hat{s}(c)$ be the multiplier on the constraint $\sum_a z_{ac} \leq 1$, and let λ_{ij} be the multiplier on the constraint $z_{ij} \geq 0$. Then the first-order conditions are

$$\sum_a \sum_c \hat{w}_{ac} = \hat{r}(a) + \hat{s}(c) - \lambda_{ij}$$

at the optimal solution. Moreover, if, at the solution, $\sum_c z_{ac} < 1$, then $\hat{r}(a) = 0$, and if $\sum_a z_{ac} < 1$, then $\hat{s}(c) = 0$.

Put these two statements together, let $r(a) = \hat{r}(a) + w_{a\bar{c}_a}$ and $s(c) = \hat{s}(c) + w_{\bar{a}_c c}$, and, if z^*_{ac} is an integer solution to the problem with the multipliers $\hat{r}(a)$ and $\hat{s}(c)$, then we can conclude the following:

- If $\sum_c z^*_{ac} = 0$—if, at the solution, a is not matched with a c, then $r(a) = w_{a\bar{c}_a}$, and, moreover, for every c, $w_{ac} \leq w_{a\bar{c}_a}$.

- Similarly, if $\sum_a z^*_{ac} = 0$, then $s(c) = w_{\bar{a}_c c}$, and for every a, $w_{ac} \leq w_{\bar{a}_c c}$.

- If $z^*_{ac} = 1$—if, at the solution, a and c are matched—then $w_{ac} = r(a) + s(c)$.

- If $z^*_{ac} = 0$, then $w_{ac} \leq r(a) + s(c)$.

(These four assertions are true, but you may need to dig a bit to see why they are true. So dig.)

This establishes the existence of a stable match.

As for the lattice structure part, I provide the argument for the "generic case." Assuming the data of the problem, which are the values of the various w_{ac} are chosen generically, there is a unique solution to the optimization problem. Moreover, for each matched pair a and c at that solution (such that $z^*_{ac} = 1$) $w_{ac} = r(a) + s(c)$, while $r(a) + s(c)$ is strictly greater than $w_{ac'}$, $w_{a'c}$, $w_{a\bar{c}_a}$, and $w_{\bar{a}_c c}$, for all $c' \neq c$ and $a' \neq a$. In words, the matched pair a and c is strictly essential to efficiency; any other match would give a strictly smaller total.

---

[21] Most textbooks on linear programming will discuss the so-called assignment program or, if not, the transportation problem, of which this is an example. Or, see Kuhn (1955) for the *Hungarian method* for solving this sort of problem.

But then the choice of $r(a)$ and $s(c)$ to satisfy $w_{ac} = r(a) + s(c)$ while solving all the other required inequalities for optimality provides some wiggle room. In words, how a matched pair a and c split the surplus w_{ac} that they generate provides wiggle room. This wiggle room isn't infinite: For every matched pair a and c, there is a least value of $r(a)$ that will satisfy all the inequalities, and a greatest value (which is the least value of $s(c)$). But if we have two sets of splits—one of which favors a in an a-c match while favoring c' in an a'-c' match, and another that favors c and a'—we can adopt the values of the first split for a and c and the values of the second split for a' and c'. The result will still satisfy all the required inequalities, and it favors a and a'. This is the lattice property.   ∎

Four comments wrap up this subsection.

- If you consult the original article, the authors cite the Strong Duality Theorem of linear programming. This is something to know about, and in the *Online Supplement*, a short section at the end of the material for this chapter provides the Strong Duality Theorem, its proof, and how it applies in this setting.

- Comparing the first part of this subsection (with a price-mediated match in the context of sales of items) and the second part, it may seem (to anyone with the instincts of an economist) that the lack of a "price" in the second half is unfortunate. But the premise that there are no prices in the second half is incorrect. In particular, for $a \in A$, her price is $r(a)$. She says to various potential partners, "If you can get me $r(a)$ on net (or more)—if you are willing to settle for $w_{ac} - r(a)$—then I'm willing to partner with you." And, symmetrically, c's insist on getting their price, $s(c)$. There is typically some slack in these "demands." If a and c are matched, and if $r'(a)$ is the best a can do with some partner other than c and $s'(c)$ is similarly defined, then $r'(a) + s'(c) < w_{ac}$. That's the "wiggle room." Even so, the interpretation of $r(a)$ as a's price makes some sense.

  Suppose we think of members of A as employees and members of C as firms. Go back to the formulation where an $a \in A$ attaches gross dollar value u_{ca} to work for c, where (perhaps) $u_{ca} < 0$; and v_{ac} is the gross dollar value that a will generate for c, if c is able to employ a. Then, for a to match with (that is, to be employed by) c, a requires a salary of $r(a) - u_{ca}$. Therefore, the dollar salary that a requires to partner with c depends on c. Suppose, for instance, $u_{c'a} < u_{ca} < 0$ for $c' < c$: employee a finds working for c' more intrinsically distasteful than working for c. Then c', to hire a, must pay her a bigger salary than is on offer from c. Of course, if $v_{ac'}$ is much larger than v_{ac}, c' may be more than willing to do so.

- This discussion began with the notion of multiple dimensions over which prospective partners, or employees and employer, may negotiate. But, even in bilateral-matching contexts, there may still be things beside salary or profit share to discuss. And, conceptually, if not practically, it is trivial to incorporate these. The key variables here are the w_{ac}, the dollar-denominated "value" that a partnership between a and c would generate, were it to come about. One might then imagine that, before getting down to a negotiation over how the dollars will be split, each a and c settle all other issue in whatever fashion maximizes w_{ac}. Of course, that's a very starry-eyed view of how such negotiations might proceed, which explains my use of the term "conceptually." But in a world where everything can be reduced to its dollar value, dollar transfers between partners are possible, and *if* bargaining is efficient, this isn't just about negotiating over money shares. However, I've italicized the *if* for a reason; see the final section of Chapter 26.

- All developments in this section have concerned matching between two populations. If the interpretation is that we are matching items for sale with buyers, this is natural. For, say, principals hiring single agents, it is somewhat natural. But, when the context is pairs forming partnerships, it is more natural to think that there is a single population out of which two-person partnerships are formed; this is alternatively the modern marriage market and the roommate problem, now with monetary transfers. We saw (page 393) that, without monetary transfers, preferences in the roommate problem can be such that there are no stable matches. But, you might hope, if preferences are represented by utilities quasi-linear in money, and monetary transfers are allowed, stability always follows. Unhappily, this is not true. Consider the case of four individuals, Alex, Blair, Charlie, and Danny, who can pair off into two-person partnerships. The Alex–Blair partnership yields $8 of surplus. Alex–Charlie yields $7. Blair–Charlie yields $6. Anyone paired with Danny yields $0.50. And suppose that going it alone yields each of the four $0. The surplus-maximizing match is Alex–Blair and Charlie–Danny. But if Alex partners with Blair, one of them is getting less than $4. Suppose it is Blair. The most that Charlie can take out of Charlie–Danny is $0.50, so Charlie can propose to Blair that she (Charlie) will take $1, leaving $5 for Blair in a Blair–Charlie match. And, if you think that, perhaps, Alex and Blair can bribe Charlie to stick with Danny, more for Charlie (taken from the $8 generated by Alex–Blair) means less for the two partners. I'll let you do the algebra, but even with the possibility of monetary transfers, there is no stable match here. (For much more on the roommates problem with monetary transfers, see Chiappori, Galichon, and Salanié (2019), from which the example was taken.)

Crawford and Knoer (1981)

The developments in Shapley and Shubik (1971) are out of step with the developments in the rest of this chapter on two grounds:

- The existence of a stable match is proved using the theory of linear programming, rather than from some sort of algorithm that provides, step by step, matches and rematches, culminating in a stable match. Because prices are continuous variables—which means among other things, that indifferences on both sides are inevitable—one might speculate that a merger between the methods from earlier in this chapter and continuous salaries, prices, and terms and conditions is unlikely to be feasible.

- Moreover, to be able to employ linear programming, Shapley and Shubik must reduce all preferences to the dollar value of things. In earlier developments in this chapter (even in the job-assignment problem), preferences were essentially ordinal.

Crawford and Knoer (1981) take the model of bilateral matching (where both sides care about the partner with whom they are matched), and by discretizing the price variable, provide a deferred-acceptance algorithm for "solving" for the side-optimal stable match, an algorithm that, moreover, resembles a multi-item, simultanous ascending auction.[22] And, they do so in a fashion that, in the end, eliminates the need for quasi-linear-in-money utility functions in proving the existence of a stable match.

I conform to the language employed by Crawford and Knoer, which involves prospective employees and firms, where each firm is only interested in hiring one employee. But other interpretations are certainly possible, including a number of prospective buyers who are considering the purchase of indivisible items.

The setting concerns

- a finite set A of prospective employees; and

- a finite set C of employers.

- Each employer is interested in hiring at most one employee. The gross value to employer c of employee a is v_{ac}.

- Each prospective employee has a gross utility of working for firm c of u_{ac}. (There is no sign restriction on u_{ac}; think of a case in which working for firm c is distasteful, so that $u_{ac} < 0$.)

- In a match between employee a and firm c, a wage $\sigma(a, c)$ is paid by the firm to the employee. The firm's net outcome in this match is $v_{ac} - \sigma(a, c)$. The employee's net outcome is $\sigma(a, c) + u_{ac}$. An unmatched firm has payoff 0. An unmatched employee has payoff 0.

- Wages must be in integer units of some smallest possible monetary unit h. It can be a dollar, or a penny, or a mil.[23]

It is assumed that, for every $(a, c) \in A \times C$, $u_{ac} + v_{ac} \geq h$. That is, each employee is worth more to each firm than is the distaste for that employee of working for the firm by at least h.

In the algorithm, at times $t = 0, 1, 2, \ldots$, a salary function $\sigma_t : A \times C$ is specified. It begins with $\sigma_0(a, c) = kh$ for the smallest k such that $kh + u_{ac} \geq 0$. That is, the salary that c thinks it must pay a at time 0 is just enough so that a would accept this salary rather than go without a job. And, by the assumption that $u_{ac} + v_{ac} \geq h$, firm c makes a positive net profit if it offers this salary and a accepts.[24]

---

[22] Because this "algorithm" involves price adjustment, it might be called a price-adjustment *process*. I'll continue to use the term algorithm, to emphasize the connection to the deferred-acceptance algorithm.

[23] This isn't quite how Crawford and Knoer do things, but I believe it won't affect the results.

[24] $u_{ac} + (k-1)h \leq 0$ implies $u_{ac} \leq h - kh$; hence, $u_{ac} + v_{ac} \geq h$ implies $v_{ac} - kh + h \geq h$ implies $v_{ac} - kh \geq 0$.

Round 0 offers and acceptances

At time 0, each firm c considers, for each a, $v_{ac} - \sigma_0(a, c)$. It chooses the a that maximizes this net profit, and makes an offer of employment to the maximizing a. If there is a tie for best, the firm breaks the tie in any way it wishes.

After firms make offers, workers who received offers of employment tentatively accept the offer that is best; that is, that maximizes $u_{ac} + \sigma_0(a, c)$ in c. If there is a tie for best, the worker breaks the tie in any way she wishes. If a worker receives no offers, that worker is (at least, temporarily) unemployed.

Determination of $\sigma_1(a, c)$

For each c, $\sigma_1(a, c) = \sigma_0(a, c)$ for all a, except for one case: If c made an offer of employment to a in round 0, and a rejected this offer, then $\sigma_1(a, c) = \sigma_0(a, c) + h$. In words, if a firm offers employment and is turned down, it raises by h the salary it might offer in the next round for that one employee.

And, then, in all subsequent rounds, until termination:

Things continue in this fashion. In round t, each firm makes an offer to whichever employee a maximizes $v_{ac} - \sigma_t(a, c)$. If this is negative for all a, firm c has been priced out of the labor market and goes unmatched. Note that, once priced out of the labor market, firm c remains priced out for all $t' > t$, since $\sigma_{t'}(\cdot, c)$ is, for as long as the algorithm continues, identical to $\sigma_t(\cdot, c)$.

Prospective employees consider any offers of employment, choosing the one that maximizes $u_{ac} + \sigma_t(a, c)$.

For each c, $\sigma_{t+1}(a, c) = \sigma_t(a, c)$ for all a, except in the case where c has made an offer to a in the current round and has been turned down. In that case, and only in that case, is $\sigma_{t+1}(a, c) = \sigma_t(a, c) + h$.

The algorithm terminates when every offer of employment is accepted.

And the algorithm must terminate in finitely many steps. The maximum value of v_{ac} is finite, and in any round before termination, the salary of at least one employee increases by a discrete amount. That can happen only so many times before all firms are priced out of the labor market (although, of course, the algorithm will terminate before that happens).

In this algorithm, as in the classic deferred-acceptance algorithm, there is no claim that any of the behavior posited is optimal for the various actors. That said, as rounds pass, the fortunes of any worker can only improve, while the fortunes of any firm can only get worse. Note in particular that once a worker receives an offer of employment, she continues to get at least one offer: She will accept one of the offers, and the firm that made that offer to her faces the same wage schedule in the next round, so it remakes its offer to her. If she turns it down, it is because she received a better offer from another firm, necessarily one that she turned down the round before.

Write (μ^*, ν^*, p^*) for the match entailed when the algorithm terminates. That is, $\mu^* : A \to C \cup \{\bar{c}\}$, $\nu^* : C \to A \cup \{\bar{a}\}$, and $p^* : A \times C \to R$, where $\mu^*(a) = c$

and $\nu^*(c) = a$ if, in the final round of the algorithm, c offers employment to to a and a accepts this offer of employment, $\mu^*(a) = \bar{c}$ if a never receives an offer of employment, $\nu^*(c) = \bar{a}$ if c has been priced out of the labor market, and $p^*(a, c)$ is the price function that "clears the market" in the final round of the algorithm.

Proposition 25.36. *The match (μ^*, ν^*, p^*) is h-stable: Each a and c has a payoff greater than or equal to 0, and no unmatched pair can come to an agreement in h-denominated wages that makes both as well off and one strictly better off. Moreover, of all h-stable matches, this is the employer-best outcome.*

This is a story that has been told enough times in this chapter, so I do not supply a proof. Instead, a few remarks are offered:

- The wage offered by firm c to employee a is specific to that firm. This may make it seem as though the labor market is not competitive. But in the algorithm, firms take the wage structure as given, which makes it seem that each firm behaves "competitively," given the wage structure. Both perspectives contain a measure of truth; but in my opinion, the second assertion is "more true." To explain, suppose there are only two firms, c and c'. Suppose that, for both firms, prospective employee Alice is particularly valuable as an employee, considerably more so than the two other members of A, Bob and Carol. And suppose that Alice has \$100 greater distaste for working for c' than for c. So, until Alice's salary at c' is \$100 more than her salary at c, she accepts c, and c' raises its offer to her, one h per round, until its offer becomes competitive. (I assume Alice's value to c' exceeds the value of Bob or Carol to c' by some amount considerably larger than \$100.) At some point, the offer to Alice by c' exceeds c's offer to her by a bit more than \$100, at which point she accepts c', leading c to raise its offer to her. Then, for many rounds, first c and then c' raise their offer to her, and she goes back and forth between the two. This continues until, at some point, her salary offers are so large that one of c or c' finds Bob or Carol a better choice, and the market clears. The point is that Alice's ultimate salary is set by competition between the two firms. However, the firm that "wins" Alice's services wins by just enough so that the "loser" turns to a different employee. This is why, when the algorithm (or process) terminates, it terminates with the firm-best outcome in terms of salaries.

- The classic-marriage model has both women-proposing and men-proposing versions of the deferred-acceptance algorithm. The story here has firms leading. We could tell the story instead with employees leading: See Roth (1984b).

- Crawford and Knoer (1981) observe that their algorithm is "ordinal"; it can be adopted to general ordinal preferences of firms for employee–wage packages and of employees for firm–wage packages. Shapley and Shubik (1971) prove the existence of a stable bilateral match using linear-programming methods; their proof depends on the cardinal (quasi-linear in money) representation. Crawford and Knoer prove the existence of a (continuous-wage) stable match by showing that an h-stable match exists for every $h > 0$—the one produced by their algorithm—and then showing that this would contradict the nonexistence of a (continuous-wage) stable match. Therefore, the methods of Crawford and Knoer extends the existence result to cases where preferences are merely ordinal.

Kelso and Crawford (1982)

While formal developments in Crawford and Knoer concern one-to-one matches, with salaries as the sole "equilibrating" device, they propose two straightforward extensions of their model. The first concerns other terms and conditions besides salary: As long as they can assume "that firms always make offers...that involve a Pareto efficient specification of whatever endogenous job characteristics there are," everything extends.[25]

The second extension concerns the case where firms can hire multiple employees; that is, moving from one-to-one matches to the sort of matches in the college-admissions model (assuming quotas on hiring and responsive preferences), but with salaries. While straightforward, this prompts Kelso and Crawford (1982) to look at many-to-one matches, but without (unnatural?) quotas on how many employees can be hired by a firm. For essentially the reasons outlined on page 409, if firms have responsive preferences and no quotas, then the labor market for each employee is simple: Each employee is paid the minimum wage required by some firm to lock out all other firms from demanding that employee's services.

Kelso and Crawford relax the assumption of responsive preferences (in this context, that the value of each employee to a firm is independent of the firm's cohort of other employees), and instead assume that, in terms of their value to a firm, workers satisfy a *gross substitutes* assumption. This assumption is akin to substitutable preferences, but with salaries, and is formulated as follows.

Suppose firm c is constrained to offer the salary $\sigma(a, c)$ to employee a. Write σ for the full salary schedule, and let

$$\beta^*(\sigma) \in \arg\max\Big\{\pi_c(\beta) - \sum_{a \in \beta} \sigma(a, c); \beta \in \mathcal{A}\Big\},$$

where $\pi_c(\beta)$ is c's gross profit (gross of the salaries it must pay) from the cohort of employees β. That is, $\beta^*(\sigma)$ is a solution to firm c's profit-maximization problem (concerning the cohort of employees to hire), if σ gives the schedule of wages it must pay. Let σ' be an alternative wage schedule, such that $\sigma'(a, c) \geq \sigma(a, c)$ for all a, and $\sigma'(a, c) = \sigma(a, c)$ for a subset $\gamma \in \mathcal{A}$. Then (finally, the assumption) there is a solution $\beta^*(\sigma')$ to the firm's profit-maximization problem such that $\beta^*(\sigma) \cap \gamma \subseteq \beta^*(\sigma')$.

That's fairly opaque, so to explain: Suppose firm a, facing salary schedule σ, finds it optimal to hire cohort $\beta^*(\sigma)$. And suppose the salaries of some, but not all employees, are increased. This increase in salaries does not cause firm a to want to let go from $\beta^*(\sigma)$ any employees whose salaries *did not* increase.[26]

---

[25] This is a somewhat heroic assumption; see the discussion of Myerson and Satterthwaite (1983) in Chapter 26.

[26] Specialized to the model without salaries, this gives substitutable preferences and, in fact, is the origin of what has come to be called substitutable preferences.

With this assumption, the the authors then adapt the Crawford–Knoer wage adjustment algorithm (or process) to this setting, showing that the result is the employer-best stable match (with discrete salary levels given by the parameter h). They use this result to show the existence of a stable match for many-to-one matches with their gross-substitutes assumption on the preferences of the institutions (the C side of the market) and with continuous wages. They also give examples of how, without their gross-substitutes assumption, there may be no stable matches in the labor market.

To give some intuition as to why gross substitutes is sufficient, think in terms of the algorithm. At some stage, firm c, facing a wage structure σ, hires a cohort of employees β. Then, in the next stage, competition from another firm causes $a \in \beta$ to reject c's offer. This does not lead c to "regret" paying $\sigma(a', c)$ to some other $a' \in \beta$ and wishing to lower what it is offering to a'; it would have this effect if, say, a and a' are complementary in c's production function, but the gross-substitutes assumption rules this out.

Finally, Kelso and Crawford show how their results imply the existence of stable formation of "multi-partner partnerships," where partners are drawn from a single population. This might seem at first to contradict the nonexistence of a stable allocation in the roommate problem with monetary transfers; see the counterexample on page 419. But, of course, Kelso and Crawford make assumptions that allow them to prove that there are stable partnerships. As a challenge (and to make you read their paper), how are their assumptions violated in the example on page 419? (I'll answer in the *Online Supplement*.)

Hatfield and Milgrom (2005)

Hatfield and Milgrom (2005) continue these developments, both refining the definition of substitutable preferences in a richer setting, with a very general model of terms and conditions or, as they call it, contracts between the as and the cs. They adapt this general problem to Adachi's methodology of pre-matches and isotone operators, which allows them to derive some very interesting results concerning, for instance, vacancy chains. Their very elegant and abstract setup and analysis is well worth reading.[27]

25.6. Strategic Considerations

Until this chapter, the general approach taken in this volume to find "solutions" or "outcomes" in economic settings has been to enlist *noncooperative* game theory; sometimes relying on dominance, more often relying on (possibly refined) Nash equilibrium: A noncooperative game is advanced as a caricature of the situation, and the question posed of a purported solution is: Is there an obvious way for the individual participants to behave in this situation? In some cases, the answer

---

[27] Hatfield and Milgrom do not make a blanket assumption that the sets that play the rule of A, C, and the set of feasible "contracts" between an a and a c are finite sets. The paper is easier to read and comprehend if you make this blanket assumption from the start.

has been yes. In others, the answer is maybe. But—how our analysis has been conducted for the most part until this chapter—if there is an obvious way to play the game, it must be an equilibrium—Nash, or some refinement of Nash—based on the principle that, if some participant could be strictly better off with a (reasonable) deviation, then the purported solution cannot be so obvious. Hence, until this chapter, our focus has been on single-participant deviations in some well-specified and understood "game." (The one notable exception to this is the discussion of the Nash bargaining solution in Chapter 23. And, even in that case, the connection of the Nash bargaining solution to Rubinstein alternating-offer-bargaining equilibria connects Nash's solution to equilibrium analysis.)

In this chapter, in which the search has been for stable matches, a different approach is taken. To upset a given match, it takes two participants, one on each side of the match. One might argue that, given that two-sided matches are ... two-sided, this is a natural extension of the general approach taken before. However, that argument doesn't work for me. In the context of a strategic-form or extensive-form game and a nonequilibrium strategy profile for the game, we "know" what options the individual player has and which option she will take within the rules of the game to upset the strategy profile. In this chapter, if a match isn't stable, we rely on some unspecified process or mechanism that will bring the objecting pair together.

Think back to a competitive-market equilibrium from Volume I. An equilibrium in prices that match supply and demand involves a leap of faith that, somehow, prices will be set appropriately. And, in fact, a literature—not covered in this volume—uses noncooperative-game-theoretic-style analysis to suggest how this might happen, at least to a reasonable degree of approximation. But the lack of a story that specifies in detail how prices find their way to the point where supplies (roughly) equal demands doesn't affect the economist's nearly religious belief in price equilibrium, at least in cases that share characteristics (commodity goods, many anonymous buyers and sellers, free and full information) with other cases for which, empirically, a competitive equilibrium was the outcome. So, perhaps the same is true here: In a matching market, we may not know how a stable match is reached (and how an unstable match is avoided), but—insofar as this is what we observe—we have faith in stability as a reduced-form "solution" criterion.

This approach begs the obvious question: In which contexts is this what we do observe? One turns to the empirical and experimental literature to get a sense of what and when. Although not fit topics for a textbook on the *theory* of matching markets, the literature on how some of the theoretical ideas play out (or don't) in real-world applications is an essential complement to the theory.

I do not mean to assert that the noncooperative-game-and-equilibrium approach taken through most of this volume is better. Using equilibrium-analysis for a specific noncooperative game begs different and equally difficult questions: Who set the rules that the theorist so casually specifies? When and how did a common understanding that this strategy profile is the "obvious way to play" come about? The noncooperative-game-theory approach that has dominated this volume isn't better than the (essentially) cooperative-game-theory style of analysis employed in this chapter. It is different, and it is just as dependent on some level of empirical challenge and testing, as we try to understand how the world works.

So, you are entitled to ask: Why is this volume dominated by the noncooperative-game-and-equilibrium style of analysis? The answer is that this is what has been fashionable in microeconomic theory (and in some branches of applied micro, such as structural Industrial Organization). Fashion notwithstanding, a free opinion (and worth every penny) is that more attention paid to applications of the tools of cooperative game theory would benefit economic analysis.

All that said, this chapter began—and in many respects is dominated by—a precisely formed "mechanism," the deferred-acceptance algorithm. That algorithm can be viewed as nothing more than a means for showing that, in theory, there are stable matches and, moreover, there are side-optimal stable matches. But, if one implemented the deferred-acceptance algorithm as an extensive-form game, would it "work?" Is it in the best interests of the parties involved to respond in the way that the algorithm prescribes?

The answer has already been given back on pages 392–3. In the women-proposing algorithm for the classic marriage market, it may be individually rational for a man to act "dishonestly"; that is, to refuse a match that he (otherwise) finds acceptable, to set into play a sequence of events that—if everyone else behaves "honestly," will land him with a match that he finds superior.

Beginning with Roth (1982), the strategic underpinnings of matching markets have been investigated. The standard set is whether "truth telling"—being forthright about one's preferences—is a dominant strategy in direct-revelation and other mechanisms for achieving a match. Suppose we restrict attention to "stable mechanisms," that is, mechanisms that must produce a stable match.

Proposition 25.37. *For the classic marrian\\e-market model:*

a. *no stable-matching mechanism exists for which truth telling is a dominant strategy for all members of M and W (Roth 1982);*

b. *for any stable mechanism, there are preference arrays such that at least one agent can profitably mispresent his or her preferences, assuming the others are truthful (Roth and Sotomayor 1990); and*

c. *for the direct-relevation mechanism that takes stated preferences and generates (based on stated preferences) the outcome $(\mu^{\sharp}, \nu^{\sharp})$ (the best-for-women stable outcome), it is a dominant strategy for each woman to state her true preferences (Roth 1982).*

Because they concern *any* mechanism that yields a stable outcome, parts a and b of this proposition may be read as a significant criticism of stability. And there are specific cases in which misrepresentation of preferences can lead to significant gains. For instance, in the context of employment, if Alice believes that she is likely to be particularly valuable to company c in a context where salaries are negotiated, she may risk overstating her distaste for working for company c, to sweeten the terms c offers her. (This is not an unknown tactic among professional athletes, entertainers, and the occasional star academic.) That said, subsequent work establishes conditions under which the expected potential gains from misrepresentation are small.

As a formal matter, the negative parts of the forgoing proposition lead to the question: Is there any mechanism—albeit one that can lead to an unstable outcome, at least in some cases—for which truth-telling is the dominant strategy? Here is one:

Proposition 25.38. *Consider the following game for the classic marriage market. The women are arbitrarily enumerated $w_1, w_2, \ldots, w_J$.*

Phase 1. *Woman w_1 is allowed to propose to the man of her choice. If he accepts, the two are matched, and we move to Phase 2. If he rejects her offer, he is removed from the game; he is never allowed to be matched. And woman w_1 is allowed to propose to another man, and so forth, until either (a) her proposal is accepted, the match is made, the two depart, and we move to Phase 2; or (b) she is rejected by all the men, which ends the game.*

Phase 2. *Woman w_2 is allowed to propose to the man of her choice, excluding the man who was paired with w_1 and all men who rejected proposals of w_1. The rest of Phase 2 plays out in the same manner as Phase 1, with w_2 allowed to keep proposing until she is accepted (or runs out of men). When and if she is accepted, we move to Phase 3, and so forth.*

In this mechanism, each participant has a dominant strategy: Each woman, if called upon to propose, should propose to her favorite remaining men in order; each man, if proposed to, should to accept the proposal if he prefers the woman who proposed to being unmatched.

I'll leave it to you to verify the truth of this proposition. Note that we could order all the participants, men and women, and run the same process. We can alternate men and women in the "proposing slot." We can run this process in the modern marriage market, where matches are made by pairs out of a single population. But adapting this to many-to-one markets (e.g., college admissions, job assignment) is not so simple. (See Problem 25.14.)

And, of course, the match that is made is, in general, very unstable. Woman w_1's favorite man might reject her proposal, while being the favorite (as well) of woman w_2, whose proposal he would be happy to accept. Removing him from consideration (because he rejects woman w_1's proposal) is severe in terms of efficiency of the match. But if you don't do this, then his incentive to be forthright, given a proposal from w_1, evaporates.

Bibliographic Notes

The seminal article on matching markets is Gale and Shapley (1962). I strongly recommend that you read this article, including their concluding remarks. Roth (1982) is another important reference that, among other things, deals with strategic issues connected to the deferred-acceptance algorithm and other mechanisms for achieving matching.

The use of Tarski's fixed-point theorem to characterize the structure of stable matches was pioneered in Adachi (2000). Subsequent developments of this technique are Echenique and Oviedo (2004), Hatfield and Milgrom (2005), and Ostrovsky (2008). Ostrovsky uses this technique to discuss matching in supply chains.

In Section 25.4, concerning many-to-one matches (without salaries or other terms and conditions), I highlighted the two assumptions—responsive and substitutable preferences—and their connections to models where each c from the institutional side faces an upper bound on how many individuals from A can be matched with c, versus models where institutions face no such upper bounds but are instead limited in effect by "diminishing returns" from adding to its cohort. Responsive preferences for the college-admissions model are implicit in Gale and Shapley (1962), and formally defined in Roth (1985). As noted in footnote 26 (page 423) substitutability (somewhat implicitly) originates in Kelso and Crawford (1982).

The section on matching with wages and other terms and conditions featured Shapley and Shubik (1971), Crawford and Knoer (1981), Kelso and Crawford (1982), and Hatfield and Milgrom (2005). To add to your reading list, I recommend Roth (1984b) and Demange, Gale, and Sotomayor (1986).

The rest of the literature is extensive, and I leave it to interested readers to dive in. An excellent survey of results and references through the 1980s is Roth and Sotomayor (1990). Roth and Sotomayor (1992) provides a briefer overview of the literature.

Beyond articles on the theory of matching markets are articles that provide details about the history of real-life matching markets and relate the history and practice to theory. The seminal article of this type, dealing with the market in medical internships and residencies, is Roth (1984a). Kidney exchange is discussed in Ashlagi and Roth (2021). School-choice mechanisms are discussed in Pathak (2017).

Problems

■ 25.1. Suppose there are three women (Alice, Carol, and Ellen), and three men (Bob, Daniel, and Fred). Suppose that each prefers to be matched with one of the other side, so remaining single is ruled out. Suppose the strict preferences are

- Alice prefers Daniel to Bob to Fred.

- Carol and Ellen both prefer Bob to Daniel to Fred.

- Bob and Fred both prefer Alice to Carol to Ellen.

- Daniel prefers Ellen to Alice to Carol.

a. Go round by round through the deferred-acceptance algorithm, with women making the offers. What is the progression of offers and acceptances/rejections? What is the final result?

b. You should find that the result is (weakly) Pareto inferior to the alternative match of Alice with Daniel, Carol with Fred, and Ellen with Bob. So this alternative match must be unstable. (Why?) Which pair(s) of one woman and one man render this alternative match unstable?

■ 25.2. The proof of Proposition 25.5 is deficient in one respect: It doesn't cover the case in which the deferred-acceptance algorithm terminates in the very first round. But the proposition is true in that special case. Give the argument for why it is true.

■ 25.3. In the discussion of the classic marriage market, it has been assumed that each man's preferences on $\overline{W}$ and each woman's preferences on $\overline{M}$ are complete, transitive, and antisymmetric. Suppose we eliminate antisymmetry; man m has a (weak) preference relation $\succeq_m$ over $\overline{W}$, and similarly for women.

One thing we might do, if we wished to employ the deferred-acceptance algorithms, is to artificially make the preference relations strict. Since there are only finitely many men and finitely many women, there is "space" to do this; if (say) man m is indifferent between w, w', and w'', arbitrarily order them and create an antisymmetric preference relation $\dot\succ_m$ that "respects" $\succ_m$ in the sense that $\hat{w} \succ_m \breve{w}$ implies that $\hat{w} \dot\succ_m w$. (This, of course, is always possible.) Then run the deferred-acceptance algorithm using the $\dot\succ$ preference orderings.

The question is, What happens? Focus on the case where women make the proposals, and let $(\mu^\sharp, \nu^\sharp)$ be the result. Is $(\mu^\sharp, \nu^\sharp)$ stable? Is it the woman-best stable match?

■ 25.4. Prove Proposition 25.12.

■ 25.5. Prove Proposition 25.13.

■ 25.6. Prove the Lonely Hearts Club Theorem (page 401): Fix a marriage-market model, where all the men and all the women have strict preferences. The following four assertions are all true. The first one is obvious, the second and third require a bit of proof, and the fourth may (perhaps) take a bit more proof. Give the proofs of the second, third, and fourth.

1. In any match, stable or not, the number of men matched with a real woman equals the number of (real) women matched with a real man.

2. If man m is matched to a real woman in any stable match (μ, ν), then he is matched to a real woman in the man-best stable match, $(\mu^\flat, \nu^\flat)$.

3. If woman w is matched to a real man in $(\mu^\flat, \nu^\flat)$, then she is matched to a real man in every stable match (μ, ν).

4. The set of men who are matched in a stable match (μ, ν) is identical to the set of men who are matched in any other stable match (μ', ν'), and the same is true for women. Any man who is unmatched in any stable match (μ, ν) is unmatched in every stable match, and the same is true for women.

■ 25.7. In the context of the college-admissions model: Say that a match (μ, ν) is in the weak core if there do not exist subsets $A' \subseteq A$ and colleges $C' \subseteq C$ such that applicants in A' can be matched to colleges in C' in legitimate fashion, in a match (μ', ν'), such that all a in A' weakly prefer $\mu'(a)$ to $\mu(a)$, all colleges $c \in C'$ weakly prefer $\nu'(c)$ to $\nu(c)$, and at least one student or one college from $A' \cup C'$ strictly prefers its match under (μ', ν') to its match under (μ, ν).

To be clear, for any subsets A' and C', the option to use $\bar{c}$ is always available. Also, Assumptions 25.15 (all the assumed properties of the preferences of students and colleges) are maintained.

What is the connection between matches (μ, ν) in the weak core, so defined, and stable matches?

■ 25.8. Fix a college-admissions model, with applicant set A and colleges C. Assume that applicants only care about the college to which they eventually are admitted, with antisymmetric preferences over colleges (including, no college) given by $\succ_a$ for applicant a. Assume that each college c, with quota $q(c)$, has responsive preferences over cohorts from $\mathcal{A}_{q(c)}$, responsive relative to some function $v_c : A \to R$ as in Definition 25.14. To facilitate comparisons with the marriage-market model, I change notation: Let $\succ_c$ be the strict order on $\overline{A}$ induced by v_c (that is, $a \succ_c a'$ if $v_c(a) > v_c(a')$, $a \succ_c \bar{a}$ if $v_c(a) > 0$, and $\bar{a} \succ_c a$ if $v_c(a) < 0$). Of course, the weak counterpart to $\succ_c$ is complete, transitive, and antisymmetric.

Construct a corresponding marriage market as follows: In place of college c, whose quota is $q(c)$, we create $q(c)$ "college c slots," denoted by $\{c_1, c_2, \ldots, c_{q(c)}\}$. Each slot can be matched with at most one applicant. Each slot c_n has preferences, denoted by $\hat{\succ}_{c_n}$, over the augmented set of applicants, $A \cup \{\bar{a}\}$, that are identical to $\succ_c$, college c's preferences $\succ_c$ over $A \cup \{\bar{a}\}$. The applicants $a \in A$ have preferences over these slots, denoted by $\hat{\succ}_a$ and given by

$$c_n \hat{\succ}_a c'_m \text{ if } \begin{cases} c \succ_a c', \text{ for } c \neq c', \text{ and} \\ n < m, \text{ for } c = c'. \end{cases}$$

That is, applicants have lexicographic preferences over college slots: Applicant a prefers any slot at c to any slot at c' if, in the original model, he preferred c to c'. And, in comparing two slots at the same college, he prefers the slot with the lower index.

This meets all the requirements of the marriage-market model, so all the results of Section 25.2 hold.

a. Let $(\hat{\mu}, \hat{\nu})$ be a match in this marriage-market model.[28] Suppose, in this match, that two applicants a and a' are both matched to slots at college c; a is matched to c_n and a' to c_m, for $n < m$. What does it take for this part of the match to

---

[28] Careful: The hats here are not referring to the pre-matches of Section 25.2; I'm reusing notation here with an entirely different meaning.

render the match unstable? What, then, is the necessary and sufficient condition for stability in this marriage-market model?

b. Suppose (μ, ν) is a stable match in the college-admissions model. Show that there is a unique stable match in the corresponding marriage market that corresponds "naturally" to (μ, ν) in the sense that, if $\mu(a) = c$, then $\hat{\mu}(a) = c_n$ for some $n = 1, \ldots, q(c)$. Show that this mapping from each stable match (μ, ν) to a unique stable match $(\hat{\mu}, \hat{\nu})$ can be inverted. Where in your argument does the (required) assumption of responsive preferences appear?

c. Suppose that (μ, ν) and (μ', ν') are two stable matches for the college-admissions model such that $\mu(a) \succeq_a \mu'(a)$ for all applicants a. How do the corresponding marriage-market matches, $(\hat{\mu}, \hat{\nu})$ and $(\hat{\mu}', \hat{\nu}')$, compare? How about going from stable matches in the corresponding marriage-market model back to the college-admissions model?

d. Use this construction to prove that, in the college-admissions model, the set of stable matches forms a lattice under the ranking "what the applicants prefer?" In particular, suppose that (μ, ν) and (μ', ν') are two stable matches for the college-admissions model, and we construct the map (μ'', ν'') in which each applicant a is matched to whichever college $\mu(a)$ or $\mu'(a)$ that he likes least. Why do we know that this is a stable match?

e. Continuing part d, prove that for any college c, $\nu''(c)$ is c's favorite cohort from the set of applicants $\nu(c) \cup \nu'(c)$.

■25.9. Prove Proposition 25.23, the Rural Hospital Theorem (page 408). (A relatively simple proof in two steps: Use the constructions of Problem 25.8 and Problem 25.6 to show that the number of applicants assigned to a given college is constant in any stable match. Then use part e of Problem 25.8 to prove the full proposition.)

■25.10. (Roth 1982, 1985) Proposition 25.5 says that, in the context of the marriage-market model, it is impossible to find a match, stable or not, that gives a strict improvement for each woman over the woman-best stable match, $(\mu^\sharp, \nu^\sharp)$. This proposition fails for the college-admissions model, when we look at the deferred-acceptance algorithm with colleges making offers.

Suppose there are four students, Alice, Bob, Carol, and Daniel. There are three colleges, East State, West State, and State U. Quotas are two students for East State and one apiece for West State and State U. No student ranks "no college" higher than one of the three colleges. Every student is acceptable to every college. The four students rank the colleges as follows:

- Alice prefers State U to East State to West State.

- Bob prefers West State to East State to State U.

- Carol prefers East State to State U to West State.

- Daniel prefers East State to West State to State U.

The three colleges have responsive preferences over cohorts, based on the following rankings of the individual students:

- Both East and West State prefer Alice to Bob to Carol to Daniel.

- State U prefers Carol to Alice to Bob to Daniel.

First, compute step-by-step what happens in the deferred-acceptance algorithm with colleges leading. Then find a match (not stable, of course), that each college prefers, and show that the "better" match is unstable. And, finally: Proposition 25.5 says that it is impossible to find a match in the classic-marriage-market model that makes every woman strictly better off than does $(\mu^\sharp, \nu^\sharp)$, the stable match that results from women proposing. Problem 25.8 sets up a "correspondence" between the college-admissions model and the classic-marriage-market model. So, why doesn't the answer to this problem constitute a counterexample to Proposition 25.5?

■ 25.11. In their seminal article, Gale and Shapley (1962, page 10) write "On the philosophy that the colleges exist for the students, rather than the other way around" and go on to say that "optimality" should be based on students' welfare. Hence, granting that unstable matches are…unstable, they conclude that the match produced by the students-leading deferred-acceptance algorithm is the optimal outcome.

But if we take them at their word, shouldn't optimality be based solely on the preferences of the students? This suggests the following definition:

The match (μ, ν) is suboptimal if two or more applicants wish to arrange a feasible trade of their assigned matches. If Alice prefers Bob's assignment, Bob prefers Carol's, and Carol prefers Alice's, then the assignment is not optimal: The three students should be allowed to trade places. Also, the match is suboptimal if any applicant a wishes to switch to a college c that has room (given its quota) to admit another applicant. The match is Pareto-optimal if it is not suboptimal.

This definition ignores the preferences of the colleges entirely, of course. For instance, what if Alice's assigned college is absolutely dead-set against admitting Carol? So perhaps it is best to amend the criterion just given:

The match (μ, ν) is suboptimal if two or more applicants wish to arrange a feasible trade of their assigned matches, and the trades are "acceptable" to the colleges involved. If Alice prefers Bob's assignment and is acceptable to Bob's assigned college, Bob prefers Carol's and is acceptable to her college, and Carol prefers Alice's and is acceptable to Alice's assigned college, then the assignment is not optimal: The three students should be allowed to trade places. Also, the match is suboptimal if any applicant a wishes to switch to a college c that has room (given its quota) to admit another applicant, as long as a is acceptable to this college. The match is Pareto-optimal if it is not suboptimal.

a. Prove that, per the modified criterion, a Pareto-optimal match of students to colleges always exists. (Hint: see Volume I, Chapter 8.)

b. Prove that a Pareto-optimal match may be unstable.

c. What can we conclude along this line from Problem 25.10?

■ 25.12. Suppose colleges, with responsive preferences, didn't face quotas. In the text, I described what happens on the bottom of page 409. Prove that my assertions are correct.

■ 25.13. Read Kelso and Crawford (1982). Why isn't the example of the roommate problem on page 419 a counterexample to their Theorem 3 (page 1493 of their article)?

■ 25.14. Consider the college-admissions problem. Can you design a mechanism in which "truth-telling" is a dominant strategy, where colleges lead? Can you do this for a mechanism in which applicants lead?

■ 25.15. A common problem in graduate schools of business concerns the allocation of seats to students in popular elective courses. A typical process is: Students are put into some order. Student #1 chooses his or her favorite elective. Student #2 then chooses, and so forth, up to the final student in line, student N. Then, the order is reversed: Student #N chooses his or her second elective, then #$N-1$, and so forth. The order "snakes" back and forth on alternate rounds. The constraint on students' choices is that, when an elective is filled to its capacity, it can no longer be selected. (Assume that a student's schedule is finalized when the student has selected, say, five electives, and the process continues until every student has either (1) has chosen five electives or (2) has indicated that no remaining-available elective is attractive.)

Assume that instructors have no preferences about which students turn up in their classes; using the terminology introduced at the start of the chapter and never subsequently used, this is a one-sided, many-to-many market. What notion of "stability" would you propose should be used in this context?

While common, this procedure is problematic, at least in theory. Why? (Your answer should have at least two parts, with the word "substitutable" important in connecting those two parts.)

Chapter Twenty-Six

Mechanism Design

A substantial portion of economic theory involves the theoretical analysis of economic "mechanisms" seen in real life, such as first-price auctions or repeated interactions among trading partners. In the theory of such things, rules are specified formally and the questions are: What happens as economic agents act and interact, given the rules as specified? What prorperties, such as efficiency, do outcomes possess?

Mechanism design turns this approach somewhat on its head, asking whether mechanisms—rules, procedures, protocols—can be created to support desirable outcomes. The emphasis at first is on what is and isn't possible as an outcome—where "outcomes" can mean equilibria or the selection of a social state—and then, given some objective function, the question is: Which possible outcome best accomplishes the specific objective?

For the most part, Chapters 23 and 24 concern the first sort of analysis. We specify "reasonable" bargaining or auction protocols and characterize (in various contexts) the nature of the equilibria that emerge. In a few places, however, we dabbled in mechanism design: In Chapter 23, Proposition 23.8 provides conditions under which efficient outcomes are impossible in a bid-and-ask bargaining protocol. In Chapter 24, Proposition 24.9 and the discussion that follows concerns the optimal reserve price for the seller to set in an auction; the discussion gives both a partial characterization of what reserve price is best for the seller and a proof that, if the seller optimizes (from her perspective) the reserve price, the outcome will not be efficient. Also in Chapter 24, the revenue-equivalence result (Proposition 24.7) establishes that, in the standard symmetric private-values context, all mechanisms that satisfy two conditions generate the same level of expected income for the seller (in a symmetric equilibrium); it is futile to search for a mechanism that provides the seller with more while satisfying those conditions. Chapter 25 is different, because we eschew equilibrium analysis; instead, stability of a match is the focus of attention. But Chapter 25 provides a hint of mechanism design: Proposition 25.37, which is stated but not proved, gives a negative mechanism-design result: Stability of a match in the classic marriage market is incompatible with dominant-strategy implementation.

In this chapter, we no longer dabble but confront directly foundational ideas concerning mechanism design. This comes with a warning: Most chapters in this volume start with a basic and relatively simple story and then move on to complications and elaborations. That's not the case in this chapter. It begins with very general ideas and then examines more specific applications, with a high "degree of difficulty" from the start. And, especially when it comes to applications, the chapter gives a very limited sample of the many places that mechanism-design ideas have appeared in the literature. I say more about this at the end of the chapter.

26.1. Social-Choice Contexts, Mechanisms, Truth Telling, and the Revelation Principle

This chapter concerns, at various levels of generality, mechanisms for making social choices in the presence of incomplete information about underlying state of nature. The following are the abstract pieces in this sort of story:

- a *social-choice setting* or *context*, with a finite set of individuals $\mathcal{N}$, a state space Ω with a commonly held prior P, individual private information about the state given by (measurable) functions a_i on Ω for each $i \in \mathcal{N}$, a set of socially feasible outcomes X, and state-contingent payoffs for each individual of the socially feasible outcomes given by functions $u_i : X \times \Omega \to R$;

- a *mechanism* for implementing a socially feasible outcome, given by sets of feasible actions S_i for each individual, and a map from vectors of actions chosen to a socially feasible outcome, $\xi : \prod_{i \in \mathcal{N}} S_i \to X$;

- the *(strategic-form) game of incomplete information* formed by putting the context together with the mechanism;

- the concept of a *direct-revelation mechanism*, in which individuals report to a central authority what they know, which then implements the social outcome based on the reports received according to a function that is common knowledge among the individuals;

- the concept of *truth telling* as a strategy in the game formed by the context and a direct-revelation game; and

- various *revelation principles* (one for Nash equilibrium, one for dominant-strategy outcomes), which show that any contingent social outcome achievable as the "solution" to the game formed by a general mechanism and the context can be achieved by truth telling in an appropriately designed direct-revelation mechanism joined to the context.

All these pieces, how they fit together, and (in particular) the proof of the revelation principles are provided in Appendix 16. If you are at all uncertain about this story, please carefully review Appendix 16 before proceeding in this chapter.[1]

---

[1]   As you may recall, my intention in separating material between the text and appendices was to put economics in the text and tools for doing economics—primarily, noncooperative game theory—in the appendices. In places, the lines blur, and this is probably the case of the most blurry line. An excellent case can be made that Appendix 16 is economics and belongs in the text. My weak counter to this is that there are cases of the revelation principle being employed in, at least, political science, which puts it in the category of a tool of analysis. But, if you feel I've gotten this wrong, please regard Appendix 16 as the opening few sections of this chapter.

26.2. The Gibbard–Satterthwaite Theorem

The Gibbard–Satterthwaite Theorem (Gibbard 1973; Satterthwaite 1975) sets the stage for mechanism design with a negative result that is closely connected to Arrow's (1951) (Im)Possibility Theorem (Proposition 8.3 in Volume I).

A finite set of three or more possible social outcomes X is given. A finite set $\mathcal{N}$ of $N \geq 2$ citizens is given. Each citizen $i \in \mathcal{N}$ has complete, transitive, and antisymmetric preferences $\succeq_i$ over X. Write $\mathcal{P}$ for the space of all complete, transitive, and antisymmetric preference relations over X, so that $\mathcal{P}^{\mathcal{N}}$ is the space of arrays of preferences, one for each citizen–agent. I'll denote elements of $\mathcal{P}^{\mathcal{N}}$ by $(\succ_i)_{i \in \mathcal{N}}$; that is, by the associated asymmetric and negatively transitive strict preferences.[2]

How does this fit into the general story outlined in Section 26.1? Think of the set of states of nature Ω as being $\mathcal{P}^{\mathcal{N}}$, the preferences of the various citizens. Each citizen knows (at least) her own preferences; we'll be looking for direct-revelation mechanisms for which truth telling is a dominant strategy for each citizen, so we don't need a probability distribution over $\Omega = \mathcal{P}^{\mathcal{N}}$, and we can be agnostic as to what i knows about the preferences of her fellow citizens, as long as i knows her own preferences.[3]

Consider some common (real-life) voting mechanisms for choosing an x from X:

- *First Past the Post.* Each citizen votes for one of the social outcomes. The alternative x that gets the most votes is implemented, with an arbitrary (but fixed-in-advance) provision for resolving ties.

- *Borda Counts.* Each citizen votes for four social outcomes, specifying her favorite, second favorite, third, and fourth. Every first-choice favorite by a citizen is awarded ten points; second favorites get five points, third favorites get two, and fourth favorites get one. (Ties are permitted in cast ballots: If Alice wishes to say that x_1, x_2, and x_3 are her joint most favorite, they are each awarded $(10+5+2)/3$ points.) The points awarded to each x are added up, and the winner is the option with the highest total (with some fixed-in-advance provision for resolving ties).

- *Preference Voting.* Each citizen submits a rank-ordering of all the social outcomes. If an outcome is ranked first on a (strict) majority of the ballots, it is implemented. If not, the outcome x that has the fewest first-place votes is eliminated, any citizen who put that (eliminated) option first is considered to have put her

---

[2] Recall from Chapter 1, Volume I, that complete and transitive weak preferences correspond to asymmetric and negatively transitive strict preferences. When we add that weak prefences $\succeq_i$ are also antisymmetric, to keep the correspondence, we need to add that the corresponding strict preferences have the *nearly complete* property that, if $x \neq x'$, then either $x \succ_i x'$ or $x' \succ_i x$.

[3] In the general story of Section 26.1, an individual's preferences were given by a cardinal state-dependent utility function $u_i : X \times \Omega \to R$. And a probability distribution on Ω is part of the setting. In this story, we (only) have a preference order $\succeq_i$, and there is no probability distribution. I'll explain why this "limited" set of primitives is adequate for current purposes in the subsection "Ordinal preferences? Probabilities on the space of states of nature?" in Section 26.3.

second-place option first, and again, if there is no majority winner, the option that has the fewest first-place votes is eliminated. This process continues until a majority winner is found, or only two options are left, and the winner between those two is implemented. (If a citizen ranks only four options and they are all eliminated, she is no longer counted. Provision is made in advance to resolve ties in the two-option, final count.)

- *Runoffs.* Each citizen votes for an x as in First Past the Post. If some outcome gets more than 50% of the votes, then that x is implemented. Otherwise, the top two vote-getting x's are put in a runoff election, and the winner of the runoff is implemented. (Ties are handled, somehow.)

In comparison with such "real-life" mechanisms, the Gibbard–Satterthwaite Theorem concerns an abstract *voting-rule function.*

Definition 26.1.

a. A **voting-rule function** is a function $\Phi : \mathcal{P}^{\mathcal{N}} \to X$. The idea is that the voting-rule function Φ selects a social outcome on the basis of the array of citizen–agents' preferences, $(\succ_i)_{i \in \mathcal{N}}$.

b. A voting-rule function Φ is **Pareto efficient** if, for a given x and $(\succ_i)_{i \in \mathcal{N}}$, there exists $x' \in X$ such that $x' \succ_i x$ for every i, then $\Phi\big((\succ_i)_{i \in \mathcal{N}}\big) \neq x$. In words, if there is some x' that every citizen–agent strictly prefers to x, then x is not chosen by the voting rule.

c. A voting-rule function Φ is **nonmanipulable** if, for every $j \in \mathcal{N}$ and every $(\succ_i)_{i \in \mathcal{N}} \in \mathcal{P}^{\mathcal{N}}$, if we write $[(\succ_i)_{i \neq j}, \succ'_j]$ for the array of preference where $i \neq j$ have preferences $\succ_i$, while j "expresses" $\succ'_j$, then

$$\Phi\big((\succ_i)_{i \in \mathcal{N}}\big) \succeq_j \Phi\big([(\succ_i)_{i \neq j}, \succ'_j]\big).$$

In words, if everyone except j "expresses" preferences $(\succ_i)_{i \neq j}$, while j, whose true preferences are $\succ_j$, "expresses" preferences $\succ'_j$, the result of the voting-rule function is not an outcome that j (strictly) prefers from the outcome that results if she "expresses" her true preferences.

d. A voting-rule function Φ is **dictatorial** if, for some distinguished $j^* \in \mathcal{N}$, Φ, evaluated at $(\succ_i)_{i \in \mathcal{N}}$, chooses whichever social outcome is most preferred by j^*.

In part *c* of this definition, the word *expresses* appears four times, each time in scare quotes. To explain: Think of the direct-revelation game in which each citizen–agent i, whose true preferences are given by $\succ_i$, provides a referee with a full set of preferences $\succ'_i$. The referee takes these *expressed* preferences, feeds them into Φ, and Φ spits out the social outcome that will be implemented. Part *c* of the definition—nonmanipulability—then means: For each $j \in N$, whatever the other i's are reporting to the referee, j cannot improve the outcome for herself by submitting (or expressing) to the referee something other than the truth about her own preferences.

This is a very powerful property. Citizen j is not presumed to know the preferences $(\succ_i)_{i \neq j}$ of the other citizens or, more to the point, what they are expressing to the referee. They could be telling the truth; they could be trying to manipulate the outcome; but if Φ is nonmanipulable, j doesn't care. Whatever they do—whatever $(\succ_i)_{i \neq j}$ is—j cannot profit from lying about her own preferences. Since lying may not hurt her, telling the truth isn't a strictly dominant strategy in the direct-relevation game. But, if Φ is nonmanipulable, telling the truth about one's own preferences (at least) is at least as good as is misrepresenting those preferences.[4] And now the punchline:

Proposition 26.2. The Gibbard–Satterthwaite Theorem. *If there are at least three social outcomes, and if Φ is both Pareto efficient and nonmanipulable, then Φ is dictatorial.*

This is *not* the Gibbard–Satterthwaite Theorem as originally stated and proved. I make two assumptions that simplify the proof: First, I assume that preferences are antisymmetric. And second, I have added the condition of Pareto efficiency. For more on these points, see Problem 26.3.

Comparisons with Arrow's Theorem are immediate. Arrow's theorem assumes that the social planner somehow knows the preferences of citizen agents concerning various social states and attempts to blend those preferences into a social ordering. Perhaps the story is that X is the set of all conceivable social states, and the social planner will use the blended social order to choose a social state from whichever subset of X constitutes the feasible social states.

Gibbard–Satterthwaite, in contrast, concerns a voting-rule function that produces a single social outcome from the citizen's "expressed" preferences. Here, X is already the set of feasible social states, one of which is chosen to be implemented. If the voting rule is nonmanipulable, citizens have an easy task; whatever the preferences of their peers are—the *expressed* preferences of their peers—it is (at least) weakly dominant for them to vote truthfully. If instead the voting rule is manipulable, when it comes to expressing their preferences through their vote, their task is potentially vastly more complicated; presumably, they must have some idea of how others will vote, based on others' sense of how best to manipulate the vote to their own benefit.

But, somehow, the two questions wind up with the same answer: In Arrow's Theorem, if we insist on universal domain, unanimity (very close to Pareto efficiency here), and independence of irrelevant alternatives (IIA), then the only coherent answer is dictatorship. Here, universal domain (which was assumed where?), Pareto efficiency, and nonmanipulability mean a dictatorship.

---

[4] I'd like to say that "telling the truth *weakly dominates* misrepresenting one's preferences." But weak domination of one strategy by another is defined in Appendix 9 as: One strategy weakly dominates a second if it is at least as good as the second against any other strategy profile by the other players *and* is strictly better for some strategy profile by the others. Suppose Φ simply ignores i's submission, which in fact happens for a dictatorial voting-rule function, if i is not the dictator. Then, technically, we don't meet the Appendix 9 definition of weak domination. Nonetheless, I use "weak domination" to mean "is at least as good as"—that is, a bit incorrectly—in what follows.

Tying this back to the examples of real-life voting systems

Of the four examples of real-life voting systems, three "fit" with the formal definition of a voting-rule function, while one, the runoff system, doesn't quite. The issue is whether, by learning the full preferences profile—I should say, the full *professed* preferences profile $(\succ'_i)_{i\in\mathcal{N}}$—the referee can use an outcome function to mimic results of the real-life system.

- There is no problem with First Past the Post. The outcome function Φ would pick off of each $\succ'_i$ its best social outcome (where the prime indicates that this is what i submits), talleys how many votes each outcome gets, and declares the winner.

- Nor are there any problems with Borda Counts and Preference Voting. Both systems are based on each citizen submitting her "ballot" in a one-time action, and a full submitted rank order $\succ'_i$ from i can be configured to tell the referee what are i's top four (in order) or her full ordering, from which the Borda Count and Preference Voting calculations can be made.

- Runoffs, however, are a bit tricky. A true runoff election happens in stages, and citizens learn the results of first round of voting before they cast their second vote (if a second vote is required). Unless we assume that, in the second round, i will invariably vote for whichever social outcome was initially ranked above the other between the two survivors, we require a more dynamic version of the direct revelation game and revelation principle.

What are the implications of the Gibbard–Satterthwaite Theorem for the first three voting-rules? Since none of them is dictatorial, and since each satisfies Pareto efficiency (although you must prove that), they must be manipulable. And, indeed, this isn't such a surprising observation.

Consider an election using First Past the Post among three candidates, one from the Liberal Party, one from Labour, and one from the Conservatives. (The social outcomes are: the Liberal candidate wins; the Labour candidate wins; the Conservative candidate wins.) A voter whose rank order is Liberal best, then Labour, then Conservative, does not have as weakly dominant to cast her vote for the Liberal Candidate. (I trust that this assertion appeals to your intuition, but Problem 26.1(a) asks you to show this formally.) Based on what she knows, this citizen may decide that voting for her first choice is the best thing for her to do. However, doing so is not a dominant strategy for her; in specific circumstances concerning the votes of her peers, she benefits from voting for the Labour candidate (Problem 26.1(b)). If there were only two candidates running, however, then voting for her favorite between the two is weakly dominant; the Gibbard-Satterthwaite Theorem requires at least three social outcomes (Problem 26.1(c)).

Proving Proposition 26.2

Many distinct proofs of the Gibbard–Satterthwaite Theorem have been offered. I provide one that was suggested to me by Faruk Gul, based on ideas from Geanako-plos (2005). This proof takes Arrow's Theorem as proved—and it was proved in Volume I—and works from there. A very nice alternative proof is provided in Reny (2001) that simultaneously proves both Gibbard–Satterthwaite and Arrow. While proof I give here indicates how nonmanipulability is tied to the IIA, Reny's proof provides further insight into how these two classic results are connected.

In the proof, I continue to assume that each citizen–agent's weak preference relation $\succeq_i$ is complete, transitive, and antisymmetric. This assumption raises an immediate issue: Arrow's Theorem, given as Proposition 8.3 in Volume I, assumes "universal domain" for (weak) preferences that are complete and transitive. I've restricted attention to (weak) preferences that are also antisymmetric, which violates the universal domain assumption. One must go back to the *proof* of Proposition 8.3 and check that it works just as well if individuals' preferences are not allowed to express indifference between different social states. It does.

There is a bonus to this. The conclusion of Arrow's Theorem is that universal do-main, unanimity, and IIA implies a dictatorship. But, this means (only) that, when the dictator has strict preferences between social outcomes, the social preference relation must conform to those preferences. If the dictator is indifferent between x and x', the social preference relation *need not* express indifference. See, for in-stance, Problem 8.1 in Volume I. But with the assumption that each citizen–agent has antisymmetric weak preferences, Arrow's dictator completely determines the social preference relation.

Assume that Φ is a voting-rule function that satisfies Pareto efficiency and nonmanipulability. We will use Φ to construct a social preference function Ψ that satisfies universal domain, unanimity, and IIA. Hence, by Arrow's Theorem, Ψ must be dictatorial. This implies, more or less immediately, that Φ is dictatorial, with the same dictator.

We first construct Ψ. Suppose that X contains M elements. Fix some prefer-ence profile $(\succ_i)_{i \in \mathcal{N}}$ in the domain of both Φ and Ψ.

1. Let $x_1 = \Phi\big((\succ_i)_{i \in \mathcal{N}}\big)$. Assign $V(x_1) = M$.

2. Create from $(\succ_i)_{i \in \mathcal{N}}$ a new preference profile $(\succ_i^2)_{i \in \mathcal{N}}$ as follows: Maintain the relative order of all x except for x_1 in each $\succ_i$; and put x_1 at the bottom of the order for each i. That is, for each i, $x' \succ_i^2 x_1$ for all $x' \neq x_1$, and (otherwise) $x' \succ_i^2 x''$ if $x' \succ_i x''$. Let $x_2 = \Phi\big((\succ_i^2)_{i \in \mathcal{N}}\big)$, and assign $V(x_2) = M - 1$. Note that, by Pareto efficiency, $x_2 \neq x_1$.

3. (and beyond): Create $(\succ_i^3)_{i \in \mathcal{N}}$ from $(\succ_i^2)_{i \in \mathcal{N}}$ by sliding x_2 to the very bottom of $\succ_i^3$ for each i, maintaining all other relative orders from each $\succ_i^2$. Let $x_3 = \Phi\big((\succ_i^3)_{i \in \mathcal{N}}\big)$, assign $V(x_3) = M - 2$, and continue in this fashion.

Pareto efficiency at each stage ensures that the successive selections $x_1, x_2, x_3, \ldots$ are distinct, since in $(\succ_i^m)_{i \in \mathcal{N}}$, x_1 through x_{m-1} are all at the bottom of every citizen's preferences, arranged in the order $x_1 \succ_i^m x_2 \succ_i^m \ldots \succ_i^m x_{m-1}$ for each i (although how these are ordered turns out to be unimportant). Hence, after M steps of this sort, we'll have a sequence x_1 through x_M, exhausting X, and a "value" function $V(x_1) = M, \ldots, V(x_n) = M - n + 1, \ldots, V(x_M) = 1$. Use this value function to create the strict social order $\Psi((\succ_i)_{i \in \mathcal{N}})$. Because this is based on a numerical value function, it is clearly complete, transitive, and even antisymmetric (no two different x_n and x_m are assigned the same value).

And unanimity is obvious, since if, under the original $(\succ_i)_{i \in \mathcal{N}}$, some x was the unanimous favorite, it must be chosen in the first step as x_1 by Pareto efficiency.

So, once we show that IIA holds, we know that Ψ must be dictatorial. Then, if i^* is the dictator for Ψ, she must also be the dictator for Φ; her favorite in any $(\succ_i)_{i \in \mathcal{N}}$ must be the first x chosen and, therefore, $\Phi((\succ_i)_{i \in \mathcal{N}})$.

All that remains is to show that IIA holds. Since the word "nonmanipulable" has so far made no appearance in this proof, it must be that nonmanipulability of Φ implies IIA for Ψ.

Two lemmas are required.

Lemma 26.3. *Suppose that* $\Phi((\succ_i)_{i \in \mathcal{N}}) = x$. *Choose any* $x' \neq x$ *and create a different set of preferences* $(\succ_i^{xx'})_{i \in \mathcal{N}}$ *as follows: For every* i, *if* $x \succ_i x'$, *then under* $\succ_i^{xx'}$, $x \succ_i^{xx'}$ $x' \succ_i^{xx'} y$ *for all other* $y \in X$.[5] *And if* $x' \succ_i x$, *then* $x' \succ_i^{xx'} x \succ_i^{xx'} y$ *for all other* $y \in X$. *Otherwise (for* $y, y' \in X$, *both different from* x *and* x'*),* $y \succ_i^{xx'} y'$ *if* $y \succ_i y'$. *Then* $\Phi((\succ_i^{xx'})_{i \in \mathcal{N}}) = x$.

In words, we start with a preference array $(\succ_i)_{i \in \mathcal{N}}$, for which Φ selects x. We take any other x', and we modify each i's preferences by sliding both x and x' to the very top, preserving their relative order under $(\succ_i)_{i \in \mathcal{N}}$. Otherwise, we preserve the relative rankings of all other pairs y and y'. The conclusion is that since Φ chose x under the original preference profile, it still chooses x at this modified preference array.

Of course, this has a very strong IIA flavor: If x is chosen by Φ instead of x', then the choice of x over x' is maintained if we bring x and x' to the top, regardless of (independent of) other y (irrelevant alternatives). We keep in $(\succ_i^{xx'})_{i \in \mathcal{N}}$ the relative ranking of x and x' for each i. And by bringing them to the top, we ensure (by Pareto efficiency) that one or the other will be chosen. So, to prove the lemma, we only need to rule out that x' is chosen from $(\succ_i^{xx'})_{i \in \mathcal{N}}$.

Do this as follows. First, enumerate (in arbitrary order) the citizens as i_1, i_2, $\ldots, i_N$, where N is the cardinality of the set $\mathcal{N}$. Temporarily, let $(\succ_i^{[0]})_{i \in \mathcal{N}}$ be $(\succ_i)_{i \in \mathcal{N}}$, and for $k = 1, 2, \ldots, L$, let $(\succ_i^{[k]})_{i \in \mathcal{N}}$ be the array of preferences where

$$\succ_{i_\ell}^{[k]} = \begin{cases} \succ_{i_\ell}^{xx'}, & \text{if } \ell \leq k, \text{ and} \\ \succ_{i_\ell}, & \text{if } \ell > k. \end{cases}$$

---

[5] My notation here is horrible. Previously, I used $\succ_i^m$, for an integer m, as the mth modification of $\succ_i$ in the construction of Ψ. Now I'm using the superscript xx' on $\succ_i$ to indicate a completely different sort of modification of $\succ_i$. To make matters worse, in a few paragraphs, I'll use the notation $\succ_i^{[k]}$ to mean yet another thing. And, in the final stages of the proof, the notation will be $\succ_i^{m,xx'}$. I apologize and ask that you keep careful track of all these variations.

In words, we move from $(\succ_i)_{i \in \mathcal{N}}$ to $(\succ_i^{xx'})_{i \in \mathcal{N}}$ one citizen at a time, changing that one citizen's preferences from $\succ_i$ to $\succ_i^{xx'}$. And, for each k, let

$$x^{[k]} = \Phi\big((\succ_i^{[k]})_{i \in \mathcal{N}}\big).$$

Of course, $x^{[0]} = x$; we want to show that $x^{[N]} = x$ (since $(\succ_i^{[N]})_{i \in \mathcal{N}} = (\succ_i^{xx'})_{i \in \mathcal{N}}$).

In fact, we will show that $x^{[k]} = x$ for all k. Suppose this is not so. Let k^* be the smallest index such that $x^{[k]} \neq x$. Then:

- If $x^{[k^*]} = y$ different from x and different from x': In the preference array $(\succ_i^{[k^*]})_{i \in \mathcal{N}}$, the citizen–agent k^* strictly prefers both x and x' to this y. Had she misrepresented her preferences as $\succ_{k^*}$, Φ would instead have chosen $\Phi\big((\succ_i^{[k^*-1]})_{i \in \mathcal{N}}\big) = x$, which she strictly prefers. This is inconsistent with Φ being nonmanipulable.
- This leaves $x^{[k^*]} = x'$. And, then, we ask whether i_{k^*} strictly prefers x' or x.
  - If she strictly prefers x, then at the preference array $(\succ_i^{[k^*]})_{i \in \mathcal{N}}$, had she misrepresented her preferences as being $\succ_{k^*}$, Φ would have chosen x, inconsistent with the nonmanipulability of Φ.
  - And if she strictly prefers x', then at the preference array $(\succ_i^{[k^*-1]})_{i \in \mathcal{N}}$, had she misrepresented her preferences as being $\succ_{k^*}^{xx'}$, Φ (at step $k^* - 1$) would have chosen x' instead of x, which is inconsistent with the nonmanipulability of Φ.

Hence, and assuming non-manipulability of Φ, $x^{[k]} = x$ for all k and, in particular, $\big((\succ_i^{[N]})_{i \in \mathcal{N}}\big) = \Phi\big((\succ_i^{xx'})_{i \in \mathcal{N}}\big) = x$, which proves the lemma.   ∎

Lemma 26.4. *Suppose that $\Phi\big((\succ_i)_{i \in \mathcal{N}}\big) = x$, and let $x' \neq x$ be another member of X. Suppose that $(\hat{\succ}_i)_{i \in \mathcal{N}}$ is another preference array in which $x \succ_i x'$ if and only if $x \hat{\succ}_i x'$ for all i. Then $\Phi\big((\hat{\succ}_i)_{i \in \mathcal{N}}\big) \neq x'$.*

This lemma also has a very strong flavor of IIA. I leave the proof of this lemma to you as Problem 26.2 with the following hints. Compare the profiles $(\succ_i^{xx'})_{i \in \mathcal{N}}$ and $(\hat{\succ}_i^{xx'})_{i \in \mathcal{N}}$. In particular, construct a sequence of preference arrays that move from $(\succ_i^{xx'})_{i \in \mathcal{N}}$ to $(\hat{\succ}_i^{xx'})_{i \in \mathcal{N}}$ one citizen at a time.

The proof that Ψ satisfies IIA follows quickly. Pick distinct x and x' from X, and choose two preference arrays, $(\succ_i)_{i \in \mathcal{N}}$ and $(\hat{\succ}_i)_{i \in \mathcal{N}}$, such that $x \succ_i x'$ if and only if $x \hat{\succ}_i x'$ for all $i \in N$. Let ℓ be the smallest index such that $\Phi\big((\succ_i^{\ell})_{i \in \mathcal{N}}\big)$ is either x or x', and let ℓ' be the smallest index such that $\Phi\big((\hat{\succ}_i^{\ell'})_{i \in \mathcal{N}}\big)$ is one of the two. The constructed social preference function Ψ will give the same answer at $(\succ_i^{\ell})_{i \in \mathcal{N}}$ and $(\hat{\succ}_i^{\ell'})_{i \in N}$—that is, will satisfy IIA—as long as $\Phi\big((\succ_i^{\ell})_{i \in \mathcal{N}}\big) = \Phi\big((\hat{\succ}_i^{\ell'})_{i \in \mathcal{N}}\big)$. So, suppose they are different. In particular, suppose that $\Phi\big((\succ_i^{\ell})_{i \in \mathcal{N}}\big) = x$ and $\Phi\big((\hat{\succ}_i^{\ell'})_{i \in \mathcal{N}}\big) = x'$.

(Now for the last and final abuse of notation:) Let $\succ_i^{k,xx'}$ denote the modification of $\succ_i$ (from the kth step in the construction of Ψ) that slides x and x' to the top without affecting their relative order or the relative order of any other (distinct) pair. If $\Phi((\succ_i^{\ell})_{i \in \mathcal{N}}) = x$, then by Lemma 26.3, $\Phi((\succ_i^{\ell,xx'})_{i \in \mathcal{N}}) = x$. And, similarly $\Phi((\hat{\succ}_i^{\ell',xx'})_{i \in \mathcal{N}}) = x'$. But, since ℓ and ℓ' are chosen as the smallest indices such that x or x' gets chosen, in constructing each of $\succ_i^{\ell}$ and $\hat{\succ}_i^{\ell'}$, the relative orders of x and x' from each $\succ_i$ and $\hat{\succ}_i$ have been preserved. (It is only at the next step that the "winner" is send to the bottom.) This—that is, $\Phi((\succ_i^{\ell,xx'})_{i \in \mathcal{N}}) = x \neq x' = \Phi((\hat{\succ}_i^{\ell',xx'})_{i \in \mathcal{N}})$—contradicts Lemma 26.4.

This proves that Ψ satisfies IIA, finishing the proof of the Gibbard–Satterthwaite Theorem. ∎

The Muller–Satterthwaite Theorem

Nonmanipulability of a voting-rule function may seem a very strong assumption, since it says that there is *no* submission of preferences by citizen–agents other than j such that j would profit from misrepresenting her preferences. Hence, it may not be surprising that nonmanipulability (and Pareto efficiency) imply that the voting-rule function is dictatorial. And, indeed, nonmanipulability is very strong. The Muller–Satterthwaite Theorem (Muller and Satterthwaite 1977) provides a different condition on voting-rule functions that may seem more reasonable but that is equivalent to non-manipulability.

Definition 26.5. *The voting-rule function Φ satisfies* **strong positive association** *if, for an array of preferences $(\succ_i)_{i \in \mathcal{N}}$ such that $\Phi((\succ_i)_{i \in \mathcal{N}}) = x$, if $(\hat{\succ}_i)_{i \in \mathcal{N}}$ is another array of preferences such that, for all $x' \neq x$,*

$$x \succ_i x' \text{ for } i \in \mathcal{N} \text{ implies that } x \hat{\succ}_i x',$$

then $\Phi((\hat{\succ}_i)_{i \in \mathcal{N}}) = x$.

In words, $(\hat{\succ}_i)_{i \in \mathcal{N}}$ is like $(\succ_i)_{i \in \mathcal{N}}$ insofar as the ranking of x and other x' are the same, except that, in $(\hat{\succ}_i)_{i \in \mathcal{N}}$, x may be ranked more highly versus another x' by some citizens than it is under $(\succ_i)_{i \in \mathcal{N}}$. Note that how the $\succ_i$ and $\hat{\succ}_i$ compare regarding a pair y and y', neither of which is x, doesn't enter the condition. The outcome x is distinguished by the fact that Φ selects it when the preference profile is $(\succ_i)_{i \in \mathcal{N}}$; improving (or leaving fixed) its relative position keeps it selected.

Proposition 26.6. The Muller–Satterthwaite Theorem. *The voting-rule function Φ satisfies strong positive association if and only if it satisfies nonmanipulability.*

Proving that nonmanipulability implies strong positive association is relatively straightforward; Problem 26.4 provides hints and then asks you to finish the proof. Proving that nonmanipulability implies strong positive association is a bit trickier; see the original article.

26.3. Nash Implementation: Monotonicity and Maskin's Theorem

One way to interpret the Gibbard–Satterthwaite Theorem is that asking simultaneously for implementation of a voting-rule function in (weakly) dominant strategies and for a universal domain of preferences is asking too much. It is natural to ask, therefore, what we can obtain along these lines if we relax our objective from dominant-strategy implementation to implementation in Nash equilibria and, perhaps, we restrict the domain of individual preferences. The foundational treatment of this question is Maskin (1999).[6]

The setting is as follows:

- There are a finite collection of citizens, $\mathcal{N}$, and an abstract set of social states, X. Each citizen i has complete and transitive preferences $\succeq_i$ over X. Indifference between distinct social outcomes is (in this story) allowed; $\succeq_i$ need not be antisymmetric. Let $\mathcal{R}$ denote the space of all complete and transitive preferences on X, so a preference array is an element of $\mathcal{R}^{\mathcal{N}}$.

- A *social planner* is uncertain what the array of citizen preferences is, but she knows that the full array lies in some set $\mathbf{R} \subseteq \mathcal{R}^{\mathcal{N}}$. This restriction of attention to a subset $\mathbf{R}$ of $\mathcal{R}^{\mathcal{N}}$ relaxes the universal-domain assumption in two ways. First, citizen i's range of possible preferences may be less than all of $\mathcal{R}$. And, second, if the social planner somehow learns that i's preferences are $\succeq_i$, that can give the planner information about the preferences $\succeq_{i'}$ of $i' \neq i$, even to the point of ruling out some otherwise possible preferences for i'.

- The social planner wishes to implement a social-choice correspondence $\Phi : \mathbf{R} \Rightarrow X$, in the sense that, given the array of preferences $(\succeq_i)_{i \in \mathcal{N}}$, the social planner wishes to put in place some $x \in \Phi\big((\succeq_i)_{i \in \mathcal{N}}\big)$. The idea that Φ is a correspondence captures the idea that, from the social planner's perspective, for a given $(\succeq_i)_{i \in \mathcal{N}}$, more than one social state is "acceptable."

- However, since the social planner doesn't know $(\succeq_i)_{i \in \mathcal{N}}$, she must devise a scheme for getting the required information. Her scheme, or mechanism, is an abstract strategic-game game form: It specifies, for each $i \in N$, a strategy set Σ_i and for each strategy profile $(\sigma_i)_{i \in \mathcal{N}} \in \prod_{i \in N} \Sigma_i$, a social outcome $\chi\big((\sigma_i)_{i \in I}\big) \in x$. Write Γ for such a game form or mechanism; that is, Γ specifies strategy sets Σ_i for each i together with an outcome function $\chi : \prod_{i \in N} \Sigma_i \to X$.

Definition 26.7. *The game form Γ **implements** the social-choice correspondence Φ **in Nash equilibria** if the set of pure-strategy Nash-equilibrium outcomes of Γ when the preferences profile is $(\succeq_i)_{i \in \mathcal{N}} \in \mathbf{R}$ is (precisely!) the set $\Phi\big((\succeq_i)_{i \in \mathcal{N}}\big)$, for every $(\succeq_i)_{i \in \mathcal{N}} \in \mathbf{R}$.*

I highlight with "(precisely!)" the requirement that the set of Nash-equilibrium

---

[6] Although only published in 1999, Maskin's treatment of these issues was widely circulated in working-paper form from 1977, which should be considered the date at which these ideas entered the literature.

outcomes of Γ at each $\in \mathbf{R}$ must be identical to the set $\Phi((\succeq_i)_{i \in \mathcal{N}})$. Because $\Phi((\succeq_i)_{i \in \mathcal{N}})$ is interpreted as the set of social outcomes that are acceptable to the social planner, one might ask for something less, namely, that the set of Nash-equilibrium outcomes is a *subset* of $\Phi((\succeq_i)_{i \in \mathcal{N}})$. However, that's not how the formal definition goes.

The definition is not ambiguous in a formal sense, but buried in the definition is an important implicit assumption. The story is that the social planner doesn't know $(\succeq_i)_{i \in \mathcal{N}}$; she only knows that $(\succeq_i)_{i \in \mathcal{N}}$ comes from the domain $\mathbf{R}$. This begs the question: If the social planner is unaware of the citizens' preferences, what does citizen i know about $\succeq_{i'}$ for $i' \neq i$? One assumes, of course, that each i knows her own preferences. But the definition speaks of Nash equilibria of the "game" that combines the pieces Γ with the preferences array $(\succeq_i)_{i \in \mathcal{N}}$. Is this a game of incomplete information, where i only knows her own preferences (and what that knowledge, combined with some prior assessment over $\mathbf{R}$, tells her about the preferences of others)? Or does i know all of $(\succeq_i)_{i \in \mathcal{N}}$? *In this setting, while the story is based on the idea that the social planner doesn't know $(\succeq_i)_{i \in \mathcal{N}}$, it is assumed that each i is knows all of $(\succeq_i)_{i \in \mathcal{N}}$.* Hence, the "game" formed from Γ and $(\succeq_i)_{i \in \mathcal{N}}$ is a game of complete information, which, if you read the definition carefully, is implicit.

Ordinal preferences? Probabilities on the space of states of nature?

An important model-construction point should be made here. Both in the context of the Gibbard–Satterthwaite Theorem and in this context, states of nature concern the array of preferences of the individual citizens. In fact, in all the contextual applications that follow in this chapter, aspects of the individuals' preferences make up the set of states of nature. But unlike the general "story" of Section 26.1 in which individuals' preferences are given by cardinal state-dependent utility functions, in both these specific contexts, preferences are utterly ordinal; indeed, no numerical representation is mentioned.

And, quoting the general description of a social-choice context, on page 436, we are meant to specify "a state space Ω *with a commonly held prior* P". But, in both the Gibbard–Satterthwaite context and in this section's context, no prior is specified.

The point to be made is: In these two contexts, both cardinal representations of preferences and a prior probability distribution are unnecessary, *but for two very different reasons*.

In the context of Gibbard–Satterthwaite, the objective is dominant-strategy implementation. Citizen i knows her preferences, and the objective is to figure out what must be true of a voting-rule function—a function that maps preference arrays into social outcomes—such that truth telling by citizen i is a (weakly, in the sense of footnote 4) dominant strategy. Does i know about the preferences of her fellow citizens? The story can afford to be agnostic on this point. If we require that truth telling by i is a dominant strategy, it must be a best response whatever the other citizens report. Hence, knowledge of the preferences of others is irrelevant to truth telling being dominant against *anything* they might do. And truth telling being dominant only depends on ordinal preferences.

The current context is different, because we are aiming at Nash-equilibrium implementation. If citizen i doesn't know what the preferences of her fellow citizens are, and if the choice of action of a fellow citizen in the social-planner-designed mechanism is contingent on that citizen's own preferences, i requires a probabilistic assessment over the preferences of others (and a Nash-equilibrium hypothesis of which contingent strategies the others use). Maskin, however, assumes that every i knows the preferences of every other i', so once the mechanism is in place, it, together with each preference array from $\mathbf{R}$, gives a game of complete information. And attention is (only) on pure-strategy Nash equilibria, so cardinal preferences are again superfluous.

Now, if the social planner knew the array of preferences, he or she could design a *contingent mechanism* for each element of $\mathbf{R}$. To give juice to this problem, Maskin asks the social planner to design a single mechanism that implements, as Nash equilibria of the complete-information game for each preference array from $\mathbf{R}$, precisely the outcomes in the social-choice correspondence evaluated at that preference array.

Or, to put it more directly, Maskin is asking: For which social-choice correspondences can such a general-purpose mechanism or game form be constructed?

Maskin's Theorem

Definition 26.8.

a. *In this setting, the social-choice correspondence Φ is **monotone** if, for any preference profiles $(\succeq_i)_{i \in \mathcal{N}}$ and $(\succeq'_i)_{i \in \mathcal{N}}$ from $\mathbf{R}$,*

   i. $x \in \Phi((\succeq_i)_{i \in \mathcal{N}})$, *and*

   ii. *for all x' and $i \in N$, if $x \succeq_i x'$, then $x \succeq'_i x'$,*

   then $x \in \Phi((\succeq'_i)_{i \in \mathcal{N}})$.

b. *The social-choice correspondence Φ satisfies **no-veto** if for every $i \in \mathcal{N}$ and $x \in X$, if the preference profile $(\succeq_i)_{i \in \mathcal{N}}$ is such that for all $i' \neq i$ and for all $x' \neq x$, $x \succeq_{i'} x'$, then $x \in \Phi((\succeq_i)_{i \in \mathcal{N}})$.*

The comparison of monotonicity with strong positive association is immediate. We're dealing with weak preference relations, and not necessarily all of them. And social-choice correspondences are correspondences. But if x is one of the socially acceptable options at $(\succeq_i)_{i \in \mathcal{N}}$, and if, in $(\succeq'_i)_{i \in \mathcal{N}}$, the relative positive of x relative to every other option x' either stays the same or improves, then it "ought" to be that x is one of the socially acceptable options at $(\succeq'_i)_{i \in \mathcal{N}}$.

However, the no-veto property presents an interesting contrast with the results of Gibbard–Satterthwaite. In Gibbard–Satterthwaite, the only voting-rule function that emerges (for implementation in dominant strategies, of course) is dictatorship, and dictatorship certainly doesn't satisfy the no-veto condition. Instead, no-veto says, quite explicitly, that there cannot be a dictator; for every citizen i who might be a dictator, i is "overruled" if everyone else puts some x at the top (or tied for the top) of their list.[7]

Proposition 26.9. Maskin's Theorem. *If Φ can be implemented in Nash equilibria, it is monotonic. If Φ is monotonic and satisfies the no-veto condition, and if $\mathcal{N}$ consists of at least three citizens, then Φ can be implemented in Nash equilibrium.*

Proving the first half of Maskin's Theorem is easy. Suppose that Φ can be implemented in Nash equilibria by the mechanism Γ. And suppose we have x, $(\succeq_i)_{i \in \mathcal{N}}$, and $(\succeq_i')_{i \in \mathcal{N}}$ such that $x \in \Phi((\succeq_i)_{i \in \mathcal{N}})$, and the position of x in $(\succeq_i')_{i \in \mathcal{N}}$ is at least as good for every citizen i as in $(\succeq_i)_{i \in \mathcal{N}}$. Because $x \in \Phi((\succeq_i)_{i \in \mathcal{N}})$ and Φ can be implemented in Nash equilibria, there is a strategy profile $(\sigma_i)_{i \in I}$ for the game form Γ such that $\chi((\sigma_i)_{i \in \mathcal{N}}) = x$ and $(\sigma_i)_{i \in \mathcal{N}}$ is a Nash equilibrium when preferences are $(\succeq_i)_{i \in \mathcal{N}}$. Being a Nash equilibrium means that, for each i, changing his strategy in Γ from σ_i to some σ_i' does not make him better off. But, then, this must be true as well if his preferences are σ_i', since the relative position of x only improves. Which means that $(\sigma_i)_{i \in \mathcal{N}}$ is still a Nash equilibrium for Γ combined with $(\succeq_i')_{i \in \mathcal{N}}$. Which, given how implementation in Nash equilibrium is defined, means that $x \in \Phi((\succeq_i')_{i \in \mathcal{N}})$. This proves monotonicity.

The converse half of the theorem is, for me, less...convincing. Proofs involve construction of the game forms Γ that are quite artificial. Without going into the details, the idea is that strategy spaces Σ_i involve each i' telling the social planner all of $(\succeq_i)_{i \in \mathcal{N}}$. That is, each i' tells the social planner what everyone's preferences are, including her own. Of course, this depends on each i' knowing all of $(\succeq_i)_{i \in \mathcal{N}}$. This is where the assumption of at least three citizens enters the story: Nash equilibria are characterized by "no unilateral deviations." Hence, if in the equilibrium, every citizen is supposed to tell the truth about $(\succeq_i)_{i \in \mathcal{N}}$, then if one player deviates in her report but the others do not, the social planner will know; all but one of the reports agree, and the one report that disagrees can be ignored. If there are only two citizen–agents and they disagree, it isn't clear which one deviated. With three or more reports and only one deviation, it is clear.

This, by itself, isn't enough. Another (and quite artificial) aspect of the constructed game form Γ deals with strategy-profile choices where there is a lot of "disagreement": If so, bad things happen. In one constructed proof, by Repullo (1987), which is perhaps the least complicated construction, if there is too much disagreement, then the outcome is determined by (essentially) whichever citizen–agent has named the largest integer, as part of her submission to the social planner. This rules out a Nash equilibria with lots of disagreement, because the "name-the-largest-integer-and-you-win" game has no Nash equilibrium; this "contingency" must be avoided in any Nash equilibrium (unless there is agreement about what should be done, so everyone else is content with whomever names the largest integer), which forces (in the set of Nash equilibria) the citizens to agree in essential ways.

Let me leave it at this: If you are so minded, consult Repullo (1987) for a relatively simple (but artificial) construction. I do not pursue the topic of Nash-

---

[7] See Problem 26.5 concerning this property.

implementation at this level of generality any further. A great deal of interesting theory has been developed; I recommend very strongly the survey Jackson (2001) for a "crash course" on the substantial literature that followed Maskin's foundational result. (Jackson also discusses the issue of mixed-strategy Nash equilibria, which Maskin's Theorem avoids.)

26.4. The Vickrey–Clarke–Groves (VCG) Mechanisms

Suppose that social planners in the government of the city of Metropolis are debating whether to build a second airport for their city. There are a variety of locations at which the airport could be sited and, at each site, several designs that could be adopted (concerning the number of runways, public transportation connections, fanciness of the terminal, and so forth). And there remains the option of *not* building a second airport, but continuing with the existing facility only.

Let X be the list of all the different options in terms of site and design. Each option x has an implementation cost $c(x)$. Suppose that the government plans to raise this implementation cost if x is adopted by some tax scheme imposed on the citizens $i \in \mathcal{N}$ of Metropolis. Part of the description of each x is the tax scheme that will be employed; citizens are well informed about all aspects of each option, including what will be their share of the tax.

In this story, the preferences of citizen i are given by a utility function that is quasi-linear in money transfers. Specifically, each i attaches to each of the options x a dollar-denominated value relative to the no-airport option, $V_i(x)$, where $V_i(x)$ includes the impact on i of the tax she pays to implement x, if x is adopted. In the course of deciding which x to implement, the government may transfer money to or from each citizen (in addition to the tax charged to implement the chosen option); if, as part of "mechanism for deciding" which x to implement, x is chosen and i faces a transfer (to i) of z_i dollars (where $z_i < 0$ is possible), then i's overall utility is $V_i(x) + z_i$. I reiterate that z_i is the transfer of funds to i incremental to i's share of the implementation tax. And because $V_i(x)$ is the value to i of option x relative to the no-airport option, each i's overall utility is $0 + z_i$ if the no-airport option is adopted together with a transfer of z_i.

Assume that each citizen i knows her dollar-denominated value $V_i(x)$ attached to each option x. In the terminology of Chapter 24, this is a "private-values" model (but without any particular assumption concerning i's knowledge about other citizens' valuations). One could alternatively imagine that i has an assessment of how valuable the airport will be to her for each possible configuration x, but she recognizes that i' may have information that, if i knew what i' knows, would change i's values. That sort of thing is not permitted in this simple setting.

The social planners, who will decide which option to adopt, are very civic minded, believing that the decision should be left to the citizens. Specifically, the social planners wish to choose whichever x maximizes

$$V(x) = \sum_{i \in \mathcal{N}} V_i(x),$$

the dollar-denominated social surplus generated by option x, net of its cost.[8] If $V(x) \leq 0$ for all the second-airport options, then the social planners wish to choose the no-second-airport option. However, these well-meaning social planners don't know the values of $V_i(x)$, ranging over all options x and all citizens i. So they look for a mechanism that will allow them to learn these values from the citizens. (What does citizen i know about $V_{i'}(x)$ for $i' \neq i$ and the various x? Read on.)

The Vickrey–Clark–Grove (VCG) mechanism does the trick. The social planners ask each citizen i to provide a vector $\hat{v}_i \in R^X$. The social planners then compute, for each x,

$$\hat{V}(x) = \sum_{i \in \mathcal{N}} \hat{v}_i(x).$$

If $\hat{V}(x) \leq 0$ for every x, then the airport is not built. If any $\hat{V}(x) > 0$, then the x that maximizes $\hat{V}(x)$ is the option chosen, with ties for the x values that maximize $\hat{V}(x)$ broken arbitrarily. This, of course, isn't the end of the story: The social planners look for a set of incremental transfers that will induce the citizens to tell the truth about their valuations.

While I continue with the airport story in the following discussion, note that, in general, this story generalizes to any social-state choice problem as follows.

- $\overline{X}$ is the set of all possible social states, and $X = \overline{X} \setminus \{x_0\}$ for some distinguished social state x_0.

- $\mathcal{N}$ is the set of citizens who will be affected by the social state that is chosen.

- $V_i(x)$, for $i \in \mathcal{N}$, is i's quasi-linear, gross-of-transfers, dollar-denominated, *relative-to-x_0* payoff, if $x \in X$ is implemented (including any taxes collected from i for implementing x). Quasi-linearity pins down the "interval scale" on which utilities are measured, but not the absolute levels. Pinning down the absolute levels is the job of the distinguished social state x_0: The values $V_i(x)$ are the dollar-denominated values on a scale where $V_i(x_0) = 0$. In other words, you can think of $U_i(x)$ as the dollar-denominated (absolute) payoff for i of implementing x, for a utility function U_i that is quasi-linear in money; then $V_i(x) = U_i(x) - U_i(x_0)$.

- The social planners wish to choose the x, including possibly x_0, that maximizes the utilitarian (sum of) relative values; they wish to choose an x that maximizes $\sum_i V_i(x)$, if that maximized sum-of-relative-values is positive, choosing x_0 if the maximized-sum-of-relative-values for social states $x \in X$ is ≤ 0.

The question whose answer is the key to the VCG mechanism is: How can the social planners give the citizens the incentive to tell the truth? Suppose that the request to i is phrased as follows:

---

[8] This objective function is "dollar-denominated, equal-weighted utilitarianism," which can be somewhat justified in this context, because we assume that monetary transfers are feasible.

Citizen i: Be so kind as to submit a vector of (relative) valuations $(\hat{v}_i(x))_{x \in X}$. We shall decide whether to build a second airport at all, and which option to take if we do decide to build a second airport, based on maximizing over the options the values $\hat{V}(x) = \sum_{j \in \mathcal{N}} \hat{v}_j(x)$, with no-airport the result if all the $\hat{V}(x) \leq 0$. If the decision is not to build a second airport, that's that. But if we do decide on option x^*, you, Citizen i, will receive a net transfer in the amount $\sum_{j \neq i} \hat{v}_j(x^*)$.

Note that, if x^* is the chosen option, the government cash expenditure in running this scheme is

$$\sum_{i \in \mathcal{N}} \left[\sum_{j \neq i} \hat{v}_j(x^*) \right] = [N - 1] \sum_{i \in \mathcal{N}} \hat{v}_i(x^*).$$

By rule, the government chooses option x^* only if $\sum_i \hat{v}_i(x^*) > 0$; indeed, the chosen x^*, by rule, maximizes $\sum_i \hat{v}_i(x^*)$. So this process is very far from free, especially if the number of citizens is large. However, insofar as the objective is to learn the true values of the various $V_i(x)$, the mechanism works in the following fairly strong sense.

Proposition 26.10. *For the mechanism described, it is a (weakly) dominant strategy for each citizen to submit her true valuations; that is, to submit $\hat{v}_i(x) = V_i(x)$ for all $x \in X$. And, as long as there is at least one $x \in X$ (one social state besides "no second airport") and at least two citizens, submitting the truth is the **only** weakly dominant strategy.*

Proof. The proof of the first assertion virtually writes itself. If the social planners choose the option x, the payoff for i will be

$$V_i(x) + \sum_{j \neq i} \hat{v}_j(x).$$

(If they choose the no-airport option, i's payoff is 0.) The first term in this expression, $V_i(x)$, is what the i gets in value from the chosen option in personal benefits, while the second term is the net monetary transfer to i. Hence, i wants to choose her submissions $\hat{v}_i(x)$ so that the social planners choose x to maximize this expression in x. (If this expression, maximized over x, is ≤ 0, she wants the social planners to choose no-airport.) Given the social planners' decision rule, submitting her true values accomplishes this, *regardless of what are the submissions $\hat{v}_j(x)$ of all the other citizens*. Which, of course, shows that submitting her true values is a dominant strategy for i.

Proving that truth telling is the unique (weakly) dominant strategy is left to you as Problem 26.7.   ∎

So, what are we assuming about i's knowledge concerning $V_{i'}(x)$ for $i' \neq i$ and the various x? As in the Gibbard–Satterthwaite context, we're agnostic about this. We are aiming for dominant-strategy implementation, so what i knows or doesn't know is irrelevant, as long as i knows her own relative valuations of the various options. And, for the same reason, we once again have no need for a probability over the possible states of nature, which are the (possible) full vectors of individual relative valuations, or $(V_i(x))_{i \in \mathcal{N}, x \in X}$.

Reducing the government deficit: The pivot form of VCG

Suppose that each citizen chooses to submit her true values. The result is that, in dollar terms, every citizen has the same payoff. If x^* is the option chosen, and $V(x^*) = \sum_i V_i(x^*)$, then each citizen i gets $V(x^*)$ as her payoff, $V_i(x^*)$ worth of value from the choice (and implementation) of x^*, plus a monetary transfer of $\sum_{j \neq i} V_j(x^*)$. This, of course, is how this mechanism works: It aligns each citizen's interests with those of those civic-minded social planners, who want to pick the x that maximizes V.

However, as already noted, with a large number of citizens and a project x^* for which $V(x^*)$ is even slightly bigger than zero, this looks like a budget-buster. The social planners can improve matters with an "add-on" term to the formula presented to each citizen. Some notation will help the exposition:

- For each $i \in \mathcal{N}$, write $\mathbf{V}_i$ for the vector $(v_i(x))_{x \in X}$, and write $\hat{\mathbf{v}}_i$ for the vector $(\hat{v}_i(x))_{x \in X}$.

- Write $\mathbf{V}$ for the vector $(\mathbf{V}_i)_{i \in \mathcal{N}}$, $\mathbf{V}_{\neg i}$ for the vector $(\mathbf{V}_j)_{j \neq i}$, $\hat{\mathbf{v}}$ for $(\hat{\mathbf{v}}_i)_{i \in \mathcal{N}}$, and write $\hat{\mathbf{v}}_{\neg i}$ for $(\hat{\mathbf{v}}_j)_{j \neq i}$.

That is (for instance), $\mathbf{V}$ is the full vector of all values, for all projects $x \in X$ and citizens $i \in \mathcal{N}$, and (the most important of these) $\hat{\mathbf{v}}_{\neg i}$ is the full vector of all reported values, for all projects $x \in X$ and all citizens j other than i.

Suppose that, for each i, we are given a real-valued function b_i whose domain is the space of all vectors $\hat{\mathbf{v}}_{\neg i} \in (R^X)^{\mathcal{N} \setminus \{i\}}$; that is $\hat{\mathbf{v}}_{\neg i} \to b_i(\hat{\mathbf{v}}_{\neg i}) \in R$. And suppose that, in place of the mechanism described in italics at the top of page 450, the social planners inform the citizens that the rules are:

*Citizen i: Be so kind as to submit a vector of (relative) valuations $(\hat{v}_i(x))_{x \in X}$. We will decide whether to build a second airport at all, and which option to take if we do decide to build a second airport, based on the decision rule of maximizing (over x) $\sum_j \hat{v}_j(x)$, with the no-airport option taken if this sum is nonpositive for every x. If we do decide on option x^*, you, citizen i, will receive a bill (which you must **pay**, under penalty of law) in the amount*

$$b_i(\hat{\mathbf{v}}_{\neg i}) - \sum_{j \neq i} \hat{v}_j(x^*),$$

in addition to your pro rata share of the cost of implementing option x^*. If we decide not to build an airport, you may still receive a bill that you must pay in the amount $b_i(\hat{\mathbf{v}}_{\neg i})$.

Imposing this bill on i means that her net payoff if x is the chosen option is

$$V_i(x) + \sum_{j \neq i} \hat{v}_j(x) - b_i(\hat{\mathbf{v}}_{-i}),$$

Since $b_i(\hat{\mathbf{v}}_{-i})$ is constant with regard to the values $(\hat{v}_i(x))_{x \in X}$ that i submits—including the impact her submission has on the chosen option—its inclusion in her net payoff doesn't change her incentives about what to submit. (Don't pass over this last assertion too quickly. Be sure you understand why it is true.) Hence, the submission of her true values is, as before, weakly dominant, no matter what her fellow citizens submit.

The question then becomes: What would be a good choice for these b_i functions? A very nice specific choice is

$$\beta_i(\hat{\mathbf{v}}_{-i}) := \max\left\{0, \max_{x \in X} \sum_{j \neq i} \hat{v}_j(x)\right\}.$$

These functions have a simple interpretation. The function $V(x) = \sum_{i \in \mathcal{N}} V_i(x)$ is the "social value" of option x, the quantity that the social planners wish to maximize through their choice of x. This particular $\beta_i(\hat{\mathbf{v}}_{-i})$ function, evaluated at the true values for the other citizens is $\max\left\{0, \max_{x \in X} \sum_{j \neq i} V_j(x)\right\}$, or the social value of the optimal choice of x (including the possibility of deciding not to build a second airport)—denote this optimal choice by $x_i^\sharp$—*if we remove i from the ranks of citizens and her valuations from the decision which x to choose.*

The possibility that $x_i^\sharp$ is "no airport" or that the optimal decision (based on the full vector of submissions $\hat{\mathbf{v}}$ is "no airport" makes for ugly exposition in what follows, so tweak the notation as follows. The social planners base their decision on the vector of submissions of relative-to-no-airport valuations $\hat{\mathbf{v}}$. Writing x_0 for the no-airport decision, define $V_i(x_0) = 0$ and $\hat{v}_i(x_0) = 0$ for all i; that is, the social planners don't ask citizens for their relative-to-x_0 valuations of option x_0; they know that the relative-to-x_0 valuations of x_0 are all 0 (a tautology, and if this confuses you, think harder about it).

Denote by x^* the choice of the social planners based on the submission $\hat{\mathbf{v}}$ of all the citizens, including the possibility that $x^* = x_0$. Continue to denote by $x_i^\sharp$ the choice of the social planners, based on the submission $\hat{\mathbf{v}}_{-i}$ of all citizens except i. Then, assuming that the citizens all do in fact submit their true relative values—that is, $\hat{\mathbf{v}} = \mathbf{V}$—each citizen i is being asked to pay

$$\sum_{j \neq i} V_j(x_i^\sharp) \;-\; \sum_{j \neq i} V_j(x^*),$$

where the convention that $V_j(x_0) = 0$ for all j is employed. *That is, with these β_i add-on terms, each citizen i is asked to pay the "externality" she imposes on her fellow citizens by her submission: what the net value of the implemented social state would be for* *everyone else if i is not counted, minus the net value of the actually implemented social state for everyone else, if i's preferences are into account in deciding which option to choose.*

In particular, if $x^* = x_i^\sharp$—if i's reported preferences aren't *pivotal* in determining which social state is implemented—then i's additional tax bill (in addition to what she pays to implement x^*) is zero. For this reason, the VCG mechanism with the particular set of "add-on functions" $(\beta_i)_{i \in I}$ is called the *pivot* form of VCG; some authors refer to it as *the VCG mechanism*.

What is the most that the imposition of these β_i functions cost citizen i? How much is i "likely" to be asked to pay? Fix i, and let $x^\sharp$ be the choice of x were it not for i's presence, as before. Assuming that i submits her true values (and making no assumptions about whether the other citizens do so in the determination of either x^* or $x^\sharp$), we know by the definition of x^* that

$$V_i(x^*) + \sum_{j \neq i} \hat{v}_j(x^*) \geq V_i(x_i^\sharp) + \sum_{j \neq i} \hat{v}_j(x_i^\sharp),$$

(where $x_i^\sharp$ depends implicitly on the submissions of the others). Rewrite this as

$$V_i(x^*) + \sum_{j \neq i} \hat{v}_j(x^*) - \sum_{j \neq i} \hat{v}_j(x_i^\sharp) \geq V_i(x_i^\sharp).$$

The left-hand side of the previous display is i's payoff from the scheme; she gets the benefit $V_i(x^*)$ from the implementation of option x^*, and the other terms are the net money transfer to her. Hence, i is no worse off in total (including the dollar value to her of the social choice) than $V_i(x^\sharp)$. It could be that i so hates option $x^\sharp$ that her value $V_i(x^\sharp) < 0$. Suppose, for instance, i lives in a house that will be on the landing glide path for aircraft if $x^\sharp$ is the chosen option. However, this does put a lower bound on how badly off a citizen can be.

Let me emphasize: If the chosen option is not to build a second airport, i may still get a bill in the amount $\beta_i(\hat{\mathbf{v}}_{-i})$. This happens if i is pivotal for deciding not to build the airport; that is, were it not for i, the airport would be built, with some option $x_i^\sharp \neq x_0$ chosen. However, for such a pivotal i, she is better off paying this bill than if $x_i^\sharp$ was chosen; that is (and what the previous paragraph shows), $-\beta_i(\hat{\mathbf{v}}_{-i}) \geq V_i(x_i^\sharp)$ if $x^* = x_0$.

Suppose that i is not alone in living on that glide path. Suppose we have a fairly large population of citizens, with large subgroups who share roughly similar preferences. Then it becomes unlikely that any *single* citizen is pivotal. The home-owners whose houses lie on the glide path may, as a group, be pivotal. But the odds of any one being pivotal are fairly low. And, in that case, if no single citizen is pivotal—if $x_i^\sharp = x^*$ for all i—then no citizen pays anything (beyond the tax collected to implement the chosen option). In such (vaguely specified) circumstances, getting honest information from each citizen is "free." (And in Problem 26.8, you are asked to remove the vagueness of this vague argument.)

26.5. The VCG Mechanism and Auctions

Consider the following special case of the model discussed in Section 26.4. There are N citizens—hereafter, I'll use *bidders*[9] instead of *citizens*—and N social states. In the social state x_j, bidder j takes possession of an indivisible item. and all $i \neq j$ get nothing. The value for each bidder i and state x_j is

$$V_i(x_j) = \begin{cases} U_i, & \text{if } i = j, \text{ and} \\ 0, & \text{if } i \neq j, \end{cases}$$

where $U_i > 0$ is i's private value for the item.

This "allocation-of-an-indivisible-item" problem is, of course, the sort of problem that is meant to be solved by auctioning off the item to the highest bidder. So, what happens if, instead of relying on an auction, the seller uses the pivot form of the VCG mechanism? If the bidders submit true values—which is weakly dominant—then $V(x_j) = \sum_i V_i(x_j) = V_j(x_j) = U_j$, so the implemented social state is that x_j such that U_j is largest.

Let j^* be that j. Bidder j^*'s overall payoff is

$$x_{j^*} + \sum_{i \neq j^*} V_i(x_{j^*}) - \max\left\{ \sum_{i \neq j^*} V_i(x_j); j \neq j^* \right\} = U_{j^*} - \max_{j \neq j^*} U_j;$$

the bidder j^* who values the item most highly gets the item, paying the second-highest value for the privilege.

For $i \neq j^*$, bidder i does not get the item, which provides 0 value; and his net money transfer is 0, because

$$\sum_{i' \neq i} V_{i'}(x_{j^*}) = U_{j^*}, \quad \text{and} \quad \max_{j=1,\ldots,I} \sum_{i' \neq i} V_{i'}(x_j) = U_{j^*};$$

in words, $i \neq j^*$ is not pivotal; only j^* is: Bidder j^* changes the social state from, say, the state in which the item goes to the bidder with the second largest U_i, to the state where he, j^*, gets the item.

This outcome—the bidder whose U_i is largest gets the item and pays the second highest value, and all other bidders get a net 0—is of course the outcome of the second-price auction. In other words, the second-price auction mechanism is a different mechanism that gives the same outcome as does the pivot form of the VCG mechanism (as long as all citizen-bidders choose their weakly dominant strategies). Since the second-price auction was first analyzed in Vickrey (1961), this explains the V in VCG.[10]

---

[9] Following conventions from Chapter 24, bidders are he and sellers are she.

[10] In this setting with all the $U_i > 0$, for both the set of all bidders and any nonempty subset, the item is awarded to someone. So the "status-quo" state x_0 doesn't enter. Challenge: Walk your way through the situation where the seller attaches some residual value $U_0 > 0$ to the item, and x_0 is the state where the seller retains the item. Questions you must ponder are: Should the seller be treated as a "citizen" when it comes to applying the VCG mechanism? How does the outcome compare with a second-price auction, where the seller is free to set her optimal reserve price?

A Vickrey auction with multiple items: The assignment problem

Suppose we have N bidders and K items. Each item x_k has a value $U_{ik} > 0$ to bidder i.[11] The rule is that no bidder can be assigned more than one of the items. Or think of the case where the value to bidder i of the *package* of items $\{x_{k_1}, \ldots, x_{k_L}\}$ is $\max_{\ell=1,\ldots,L} U_{ik_\ell}$; that is, no bidder gets any value out of a "second" item, if the first has the higher individual value.

Describe a match of items to citizens by a function $\mu : \{1, \ldots, K\} \to \{0, 1, \ldots, N\}$, subject to the constraint that if $k \neq k'$, and if $\mu(k) \geq 1$, then $\mu(k') \neq \mu(k)$. The meaning of the function μ is that item k is assigned to bidder $\mu(k)$; $\mu(k) = 0$ means that item k is not assigned to any bidder. The constraint is that no (real) bidder can be assigned more than one item; the "null" bidder 0 can be assigned multiple (otherwise unassigned) items. If, for a given i, there is no k such that $\mu(k) = i$, then i goes away empty-handed, which of course can happen; indeed, if $K < N$, this must happen.

For a given match μ, let ν be its inverse: That is, $\nu : \{1, \ldots, N\} \to \{0, \ldots, K\}$ in one-to-one fashion, where $\nu(i) = 0$ if there is no k such that $\mu(k) = i$, and $\nu(i) = \mu^{-1}(i)$ otherwise.

Suppose the central authority does not know the values U_{ik} but wishes to assign items in a way that maximizes the total value. That is, we look for a match (μ, ν) that maximizes

$$V\big((\mu, \nu)\big) = \sum_{i=1}^{N} U_{i\nu(i)} = \sum_{k=1}^{K} U_{\mu(k)k},$$

where, in the first sum, $U_{i0} := 0$, and in the second sum, $U_{0k} := 0$.

(I write here about "matches" instead of social outcomes. In social-outcome terminology, each match is a social outcome, and $V_i\big((\mu, \nu)\big) = U_{i\nu(i)}$.)

Proposition 26.11. *Suppose (μ^*, ν^*) is an **efficient** match, in the sense that $V\big((\mu^*, \nu^*)\big) \geq V\big((\mu, \nu)\big)$ for any other match (μ, ν). If $K \geq N$, then every i is matched with some item under (μ^*, ν^*). If $N \geq K$, then every item is matched with some bidder under (μ^*, ν^*). Moreover, in the case $N > K$, if i is left without an item under (μ^*, ν^*), then $\max_k U_{ik} \leq U_{j\nu^*(j)}$ for any j that is matched with an item.*

This proposition is entirely straightforward to prove—it is a consequence of the assumption that $V_{ik} > 0$ for all i and k—so it is left to you as Problem 26.9.

In theory, a mechanism for solving the central authority's problem is any VCG mechanism. Consider, specifically, the pivot form of VCG. The social outcomes are all the possible matches (μ, ν). In its search for efficient matches, the central authority can restrict attention to those matches that satisfy the conclusion of Proposition 26.11 (either all items are matched, or each bidder gets an item), of which there are

---

[11] This assumption that every item has strictly positive value to every bidder is not entirely necessary, but it makes for simpler exposition. An even simpler case is where the items are identical. See Problem 26.12 for this special case, but wait until you read the remainder of this section.

only $N!/(N-K)!$ or $K!/(K-N)!$, depending on whether $N \geq K$ or $K \geq N$. This explains why this is an "in theory" assertion; that's a lot of matches to evaluate. The bidders, if they understand how the VCG mechanism works, have the simple task of submitting their true values for every item. But the central authorities have a lot of work to do: They must not only find an efficient match; they must also solve N additional optimization problems, to find for each bidder i what would have been the optimal match were it not for i.

Happily, this task is relatively easy. Given the (true, one hopes) submissions of the citizens, the first step is to maximize over all matches (μ, ν) the quantity $\sum_{i=1}^{N} U_{i\nu_i}$. Since the items are indivisible, this is an integer programming problem, and (as you probably know), integer programming problems can be difficult to solve. However, in this case, we know that if we pose the problem by relaxing the integer constraints, looking for allocation weights z_{ik} that solve the problem

$$\text{maximize over nonnegative allocation weights } (z_{ik}) \text{ the sum } \sum_{i=1}^{N}\sum_{k=1}^{K} z_{ik}U_{ik},$$

$$\text{subject to the constraints } \sum_{i} z_{ik} \leq 1, \ \sum_{k} z_{ik} \leq 1, \text{ and } z_{ik} \geq 0,$$

then we know from Chapter 25 (and the theory of linear programming) that a solution exists in integer values. Indeed, for generic values of the U_{ik}, the solution will be unique and in integer values. So, the problem can be solved with the simplex method or a variant, such as the so-called Hungarian method (Kuhn 1955). And, while the authorities must solve an additional N such problems, these problems are all of this nature.

The following proposition is nearly trivial to prove (Problem 26.10):

Proposition 26.12. *If, in the implementation of this mechanism, bidder i winds up with no item, his net cash transfer is 0. If he winds up with an item, the item he gets is worth (weakly) more to him than he is forced to pay.*

Since "bidding" is voluntary, this result is important; it implies that the mechanism satisfies so-called participation constraints.

The assignment problem as a Shapley and Shubik (1971) and Crawford and Knoer (1981) matching problem

Recall Definition 25.26, adjusted here to fit the notation being employed. Since this is a bit of a special case of the slightly more general situation in Chapter 25, I give this definition a new number.

Definition 26.13. *A price-mediated match (in the current context) is a triple (μ, ν, p):*

a. *The function μ records the buyer of each item, $\mu : \{1, \ldots, K\} \to \{0, \ldots, N\}$, where $\mu(k) = 0$ means that item k goes unsold.*

b. *The function ν records the purchases of each consumer, $\nu : \{1, \ldots, N\} \to \{0, 1, \ldots, K\}$, where $\nu(i) = 0$ means that buyer i does not purchase an item.*

c. *Prices are given by $p : A \to R_+$.*

These pieces satisfy:

d. *$\mu(k) = i \geq 1$ if and only if $\nu(i) = k$;*

e. *for each $k \in \{1, \ldots, K\}$, if $\mu(k) = 0$ then $p(k) = 0$;, and*

f. *for each $i \in \{1, \ldots, N\}$, if $\nu(i) = 0$, then $U_{ik} \leq p(k)$ for all k, and if $\nu(i) \geq 1$, then $\nu(i)$ maximizes $U_{ik} - p(k)$ over $k \in \{1, \ldots, K\}$, and the maximized value is ≥ 0.*

We know from Chapter 25 that a price-mediated match exists, that any price-mediated match is socially efficient, and that a buyer–best price-mediated match exists. In Chapter 25, social efficiency meant Pareto efficiency, taking into account the buyers and the sellers. Because sellers are only concerned with the payments they receive, and because those payments come from buyers, in terms of overall efficiency, the payments net out to zero. So, it is equally true in this setting that "social efficiency" means maximizing the gross-of-payments sum of values of the buyers of objects under the match. (This is the second half of Corollary 25.29, adapted to this special setting.) That is, a price-mediated match produces an allocation of the goods that is the same as an allocation that would be obtained under any VCG mechanism and, in particular, the pivot form of VCG.

To avoid complications, suppose that there is a unique socially efficient match; this is true for a generic choice of the U_{ik}. Then the match part of the VCG mechanism, which by definition is socially efficient, is the same as the match part of any price-mediated match. So, a natural question to ask is: How do the "prices" paid by $i \in \{1, \ldots, N\}$ in the pivot-form VCG mechanism compare with the buyer-best price-mediated-match prices?

Let p^* be the buyer-best price vector in a price-mediated match. We know that, if item k is not allocated to a buyer, $p^*(k) = 0$. Since the allocation provided by the VCG process is identical to the match, k is not allocated in the VCG procedure, and by convention, we can declare that its "price" in the VCG process is also 0. Suppose that bidder i is not allocated an item in the efficient match. Bidder i then pays nothing under the pivot form of the VCG process, the same as what i pays in the price-mediated match. This leaves the case of the bidders who are allocated an item in the efficient match. For such a bidder i, let k be the item allocated to i, and let $\pi(k)$ be "price" she pays for item k; that is, $\pi(k)$ is efficient social surplus (gross of payments) generated for all the others if she doesn't participate, less the social surplus (gross of payments) generated for everyone except i by the overall efficient match.

Proposition 26.14. *For every k that is allocated to a bidder in the efficient match, $\pi(k) = p^*(k)$.*

This was originally proved in Leonard (1983). The following ingenious proof is by

Ostrovsky.[12]

Proof. Fix an item k that is allocated to bidder i.

Step 1. $p^*(k) \geq \pi(k)$. Suppose by way of contradiction that $p^*(k) < \pi(k)$. Of course, $U_{ik} \geq \pi(z)$. Imagine that i's values are, instead,

$$U'_{ik'} = \begin{cases} \big(\pi(k) + p^*(k)\big)/2, & \text{for } k' = k, \text{ and} \\ 0, & \text{for } k' \neq k. \end{cases}$$

All other bidders in this alternative world have the same valuations for items as before. I claim that the same allocation of goods as before is still a price-mediated equilibrium at the prices p^*: The prices haven't changed, so the other bidders are happy to choose as before. As for bidder i, she continues to get a bit of positive surplus from purchasing item k, and since her valuations of all other items are 0, purchasing item k would be her choice. But, according to VCG, $\pi(k)$ is the difference between the sum of utilities of all other bidders if they are allowed to distribute k among themselves, less what they get under the original, efficient allocation. That is, by taking item k from i, the net gain to everyone else is $\pi(k)$. And taking it away from i causes her (dollar-denominated) utility to drop by $\big(\pi(k) + p^*(k)\big)/2 < \pi(k)$, which means that the original allocation is no longer efficient, a contradiction.

Step 2. $p^*(k) \leq \pi(k)$. Suppose by way of contradiction that $p^*(k) > \pi(k)$. Let $\delta = U_{ik} - \big(p^*(k) + \pi(k)\big)/2$, and change i's values to $U'_{ik'} = \max\big\{0, U_{ik} - \delta\big\}$. All other bidders retain their original valuations. In this alternative situation, $U'_{ik} = \big(p^*(k) + \pi(k)\big)/2 > \pi(k)$. But, $\pi(k)$ is the total utility of all bidders except for i if they have access to all the items, less what they get in total if k is assigned to i. So, giving k to i and otherwise optimizing over the other bidders—which is what VCG does—generates more utility than giving i no item. Therefore, with these new valuations, it is efficient to give i some item. Moreover, that item must be item k, since the new situation reduces i's valuation for every item by the same amount (or takes that valuation to zero). That is, if it was efficient before to give k to i, it is efficient as well in this new situation.

But then, if we apply Shapley and Shubik (1971), there are prices p' that make this allocation into a price-mediated allocation. Bidder i is awarded k, so the price $p'(k)$ must be less than or equal to i's valuation; that is, $p'(k) \leq U'_{ik} = \big(p^*(k)\big) + \pi(k)\big)/2 < p^*(k)$.

And, I assert, these new prices p' provide a price-mediated equilibrium for the original valuations. For bidders other than i, this is obvious: Their valuations are all the same in the two sets of valuations, so if p' makes it optimal for them to make their original purchases when i's valuations have changed, nothing has changed for them. As for i, moving from $U'_{i.}$ back to $U_{i.}$ increases the value of each item by the same amount (or less, if $U'_{i.} = 0$), so if i wishes to buy k at the prices p' with $U'_{i.}$, he surely wishes to make the same purchase with $U_{i.}$.

---

[12]   Michael Ostrovsky, private communication 2022.

But the prices p^* were supposed to be the buyer-best prices in any stable match. And for bidder i, $p'(k) < p^*(k)$. This is a contradiction. ∎

Package auctions

Suppose now we allow bidders to purchase more than one item. There are finite sets of N bidders and K indivisible items. Let $\mathcal{K}$ be the set of all subsets of the K items, with typical element κ. Each bidder i attaches a value $U_{i\kappa}$ to the *bundle* or *package* κ; assume that $U_{i\emptyset} = 0$ and, if $\kappa \subseteq \kappa'$, then $U_{i\kappa} \leq U_{i\kappa'}$, which is (more or less) a free-disposal assumption. Start with the story that the items are held by some central authority. The central authority doesn't know the values $\{U_{i\kappa}; i = 1, \ldots, N, \kappa \in \mathcal{K}\}$. And the central authority wishes to distribute the items efficiently so as to

$$\text{Maximize } \sum_i U_{i\kappa_i}, \text{ over all partitions } \{\kappa_1, \ldots, \kappa_I\} \text{ of } K.$$

As before, in theory, the VCG mechanism is just the thing. Except that, unlike in the assignment problem, there are N^K possible partitions of the K items, and the "corresponding" divisible-goods linear-programming problem doesn't give a solution to the actual integer-programming problem that must be solved. Moreover, to implement VCG, it isn't one integer programming problem, but the main problem plus N subproblems, all of which are themselves difficult integer programming problems. With, say, $N = 3$ and $K = 3$, this can be done. But with N and K on the order of 10 each, good luck.

Both Shapley–Shubik and Crawford–Knoer are concerned with one-to-one matches, in terms of their formal developments. Because Shapley–Shubik rely on linear programs that admit integer-valued solutions, their methods are incapable of handling many-to-one matches. The many-to-one version of Crawford–Knoer is developed in Kelso and Crawford (1982) and extended in Hatfield and Milgrom (2005). These papers prove the existence of an appropriately defined extension of a many-to-one price-mediated equilibrium with continuous prices (and a lot more), as long as buyer preferences satisfy the appropriate general notion of substitutability.

Generically, in terms of buyer preferences (if we continue to assume that sellers care only about the prices they get), there is a unique efficient allocation of the items to buyers. So, it continues to be true that for generic data, VCG and generalizations of price-mediated equilibria give the same allocations of the items. However, the analogue to Proposition 26.14 is false. The "prices" are different, even for the same overall allocation of the items. Problem 26.12 asks you to explain why (in the special case where the items are identical).

Note that VCG works perfectly well without substitutability. But the results can be somewhat anomalous. The following example exhibits what could happen. Suppose there are two items and two bidders. Alice values a package of either item at \$10, and she values the package of both items at \$11. Bob values a package of one item at \$1, but (here is the nonsubstitutability) he values the package of both items at \$12. The efficient distribution of the items is to give them both to Bob; Alice gets neither, so her value at the social optimum is \$0. And if Bob is eliminated from consideration, we give both to Alice, for a total value of \$11. Hence, applying VCG, Alice gets neither item and pays \$0, while Bob gets both and pays \$11.

But suppose we add a third bidder, Carol, whose valuations are identical to Alice's. Now it is efficient to give one item to Alice and the other to Carol. And if either of them is eliminated from consideration, the social optimum is to to give both to Bob. The VCG mechanism, therefore, requires that Alice (and Carol) pay \$12 − \$10 = \$2, for a net payoff of \$8 apiece. The point is, by adding a bidder, the "price" of the two items goes down (from \$5.50 to \$2). And Alice, if she is competing with Bob alone, will do better by inviting Carol to be an additional "competitor." One might interpret this as: Alice wishes to find a shill bidder, Carol. This is true even if Carol, having claimed that one of the items is worth \$10 to her, throws it away, while Alice gives Carol \$2 to cover what Carol paid; this leaves Alice with a payoff of \$6. Indeed, Alice has plenty of room to compensate Carol for acting as a shill.

Is the VCG mechanism practical?

In theory, the VCG mechanism is a wonderful "all-purpose" way to elicit private values in a dominant-strategy mechanism. And this is a book on theoretical foundations, so, at least in some sense, the line has to be that it is indeed wonderful, in theory. But, in the real world, is it practical?

In some cases, yes. In others, no. For the case against, see Rothkopf (2007), which provides "Thirteen Reasons..." why it is not practical. And, in addition, see the INFORMS online commentaries by Healty, by Hoffman, and by Ledyard [13]

My nominee for the most important reason is that the VCG mechanism—applied to the sort of project-selection problem with which this section began—is very easy to manipulate in real life, in the following sense. The (weak) optimality for Alice of submitting her true values is based on the Nash hypothesis that she can't change what other folks submit. Suppose, however, that Alice, and only Alice, lives on the landing glide path of some version x^b for the second airport. But option x^b is otherwise a wonderful option, and Alice is worried that, if she truthfully reveals how much she dislikes x^b, she'll be outvoted by the other citizens for whom x^b is the best alternative. Of course, she can stop x^b from being chosen by submitting a hugely negative valuation for x^b. But this will make her pivotal, and the VCG mechanism means a very large sum will be demanded from her.

However, suppose that Alice's brother Bob, who loves her dearly, can be convinced by Alice to submit a second (false) hugely negative valuation for x^b. (If Bob really loves Alice dearly, he might attach a negative value to x^b out of honest concern for Alice's welfare. But imagine that even such an honest negative value from

---

[13]   Available at https://www.informs.org/Blogs/Operations-Research-Forum/Thirteen-Reasons-Why-the-Vickrey-Clarke-Groves-Process-is-Not-Practical.

both Alice and Bob won't stop x^b from being chosen. It takes a hugely negative value from one or the other or both.) The point is that, if both of them (falsely) submit a hugely negative value, so hugely negative that either one stops x^b, then neither is pivotal, and they jointly avoid both x^b and a huge VCG bill.

The VCG mechanism works, in theory, because a single individual who is trying to manipulate the outcome by lying about his or her valuations pays the price. But, at least in the project-selection context, coalitions as small as two, by coordinating their lies, can manipulate it at no cost to themselves. This is not very practical.

And that was widely considered as the "truth" of the matter until recently. However, in auction settings and, in particular, in auctions for advertisement placement on webpages and smartphone apps, the VCG mechanism has been widely and successfully employed. See, for instance, Metz (2015). These are far from trivial applications, in terms of the amount of money involved. So, for at least some (very signficant) applications, VCG has proved to be wonderful not only in theory.

26.6. Optimal Auctions: Myerson (1981)

Let us return to the basic auction context with independent and identically distributed (i.i.d.) private values, discussed at the start of Chapter 24. A seller possesses an item that she wishes to sell. A finite set $\mathcal{N}$ of prospective buyers wish to buy, if the price is right. Each buyer i attaches a private value V_i to the item; the buyers are risk neutral and have utility functions that are quasi-linear in money, so each seeks to maximize $V_i \mathbf{P}(\{i \text{ gets the item}\}) - \mathbf{E}[p_i]$, where p_i is what i pays for participating, $\mathbf{P}(\{\cdot\})$ is the probability of the event $\{\cdot\}$, and $\mathbf{E}[\cdot]$ denotes expectation. The $\{V_i; i \in \mathcal{N}\}$ are i.i.d., with cumulative distribution function F. Assume that F has support that is a compact interval $[0, \overline{v}]$ and is absolutely continuous with corresponding density function f that is continuous and strictly positive on this support.[14] Each bidder knows his own V_i, but has no knowledge about the other bidders' values beyond knowing that they are independent of his value and are i.i.d. according to F.[15]

A quick summary of what we saw in Chapter 24 is as follows:

- The first- and second-price auctions both "result" in an efficient placement of the item; that is, to the bidder who has the largest V_i. The reason for the scare quotes around "result" is: In the second-price auction, bidding one's own value is weakly dominant, and this result is predicated on bidders following this strategy. And, in the first-price auction, this is the "result" if each bidder follows the unique symmetric Nash-equilibrium strategy that was constructed in Chapter 24.

- The *Revenue Equivalence Theorem* (Proposition 24.7) shows that these two forms

---

[14] A small change from Chapter 24: We are setting $\underline{v} = 0$. Can you discover where I subsequently use this change?

[15] So, finally, we have a context in which there is a common prior on the space of states of nature. While we might get lucky and find a dominant-strategy mechanism, we'll generally be looking for Nash implementation for a game of incomplete information.

of auction (as well as the appropriate formalization of ascending- and descending-oral auctions) generate the same expected revenue for the seller, namely, $\mathbf{E}\left[\mathcal{V}^{[2]}\right]$, the expectation of the second-largest of the $\{V_i\}$.

- If the seller attaches a value V_0 to retaining the item, she won't want to sell for less than V_0, and she can guarantee this by running the auctions with a reserve price of V_0.

- But suppose the seller attaches a value V_0 to retaining the item, where $V_0 = 0$ is not ruled out. Then, to maximize her expected outcome (the expectation of her revenue if she sells the item or V_0 if she does not), she should set a reserve price in excess of V_0. This means the outcome may not be efficient; she may wind up keeping the item when the highest buyer valuation $\mathcal{V}^{[1]}$ lies in the interval between V_0 and the reserve price she sets.

The question to be addressed in this section is: Can she do even better? In the case of i.i.d. private values, does the optimal reserve-price auction maximize her expected payoff? What if the private values are independent but not identically distributed? What if they are not independent? What if they have common-value elements? (These are four good questions; in this section, only the first two will be answered.)

The title of this section is *Optimal Auctions*. *Optimal* refers to the interests of the seller and (perhaps) not society: If the optimal mechanism for the seller generates an inefficient placement of the item, so be it. As for the term *Auctions*: A more accurate title would be something like *Seller-Optimal Mechanisms for Placing an Indivisible Item under Certain Assumptions*. Never mind the tail end of that more accurate title; focus on *Mechanisms* versus *Actions*. The analysis in this section concerns direct revelation mechanisms designed so that truth telling is a Nash equilibrium. It takes a broad definition of the word *auction* to include this form of mechanism, unless and until we can translate the optimal direct-revelation game into a recognizable form of auction (which we will do before we are done).

Direct revelation, truth-telling, and the envelope theorem, with independent (but not necessarily identically distributed) private values

Assumptions 26.15.

a. *The seller of the item places zero value on its retention. Her objective is to design an auction that maximizes her expected revenue.*

b. *The value to bidder i of the item, V_i, is distributed according to cumulative distribution function F_i, which is absolutely continuous and (so) has density function f_i. This density function is strictly positive on an interval $[0, \overline{v}_i]$.*

c. *The values $\{V_i; i = 1, \ldots, N\}$ constitute a fully independent set of random variables.*

Let $\mathbf{V}_i := [0, \overline{v}_i]$, and let $\mathbf{V} := \prod_{i \in N} \mathbf{V}_i$. That is, $\mathbf{V}$ is the space of possible valuation *vectors* for the bidders in N. Let V denote a typical element of $\mathbf{V}$; that is, V is a vector of values $(V_i)_{i \in N}$.[16]

Definition 26.16. *In the current context, a **direct-revelation mechanism** is specified by two functions:*

a. *An **assignment** function $\mathcal{A} : \mathbf{V} \to [0,1]^N$, which satisfies $\sum_i \mathcal{A}_i(V) \leq 1$ for every $V \in \mathbf{V}$, where $\mathcal{A}_i$ is the ith component function of $\mathcal{A}$, and*

b. *A **payment-scheme** function $\mathcal{P} : \mathbf{V} \to R^N$.*

The interpretation is: Bidders simultaneously and independently give reports $\{\hat{v}_i\}$ of their private values (constrained to report $\hat{v}_i \in \mathbf{V}_i$). I write $\hat{v}_i$ and not V_i, because bidders are free to lie about their true values. Write $\hat{v} \in \mathbf{V}$ for the vector of reported values. The mechanism takes $\hat{v}$ and generates an outcome: i gets the item with probability $\mathcal{A}_i(\hat{v})$, and bidder j pays $\mathcal{P}_j(\hat{v})$. The constraint on the who-gets-the-item vector function $\mathcal{A}$ is simply a feasibility constraint: No more than one bidder can get the item (given the reports $\hat{v}$); it is conceivable that the item is randomly distributed, and it is conceivable that no bidder gets it (hence the sum of these probabilities is ≤ 1).

We seek to characterize direct-revelation mechanisms $(\mathcal{A}, \mathcal{P})$ for which truth telling—each bidder reports $\hat{v}_i = V_i$—is a Nash equilibrium, invoking the revelation principle to know that the outcome of *any* Nash equilibrium outcome of *any* general mechanism can be obtained as a truth-telling Nash equilibrium of some direct-revelation mechanism. Then, once we know this characterization, we can search over all such mechanisms to find one that maximizes the seller's expected revenue.

Because participation in this game may be voluntary, we must worry about participation constraints at some point. But for the time being, assume that all $i \in N$ have agreed to participate (or are compelled to do so).

Definition 26.17. *If $(\mathcal{A}, \mathcal{P})$ is a direct-relevation mechanism for which truth telling is a Nash equilibrium, define, for each i and $\hat{v}_i \in \mathbf{V}_i$*

$$\alpha_i(\hat{v}_i) = \mathbf{E}\big[\mathcal{A}_i(\hat{v}_i, V_{\neg i})\big] \quad and \quad \pi_i(\hat{v}_i) = \mathbf{E}\big[\mathcal{P}_i(\hat{v}_i, V_{\neg i})\big],$$

where the expectations are taken over truthful reports by all bidders except i, and i (possibly) misrepresents his value as $\hat{v}_i$.

That is, $\alpha_i(\hat{v}_i)$ is the marginal probability that i will win the item, if i submits $\hat{v}_i$, averaging over truthful reports by all the other bidders; $\pi_i(\hat{v}_i)$ is i's expectation of what he will pay.

The independence of the values $\{V_j\}_{j \in \mathcal{N}}$ is important in this definition. Bidder i will know V_i, and if knowledge of V_i affected i's assessment of the distribution of the V_j's for $j \neq i$, then we would need to write $\alpha_i(\hat{v}_i|V_i)$ and $\pi(\hat{v}|V_i)$ in what follows. Not having to do so makes life much simpler (an observation already made in Chapter 24).

---

[16] In Section 26.5, I used V to denote the sum of (reported) values. The notation is changing here!

Proposition 26.18. _Fix a direct-relevation mechanism $(\mathcal{A}, \mathcal{P})$. Define the functions α_i and π_i for all i as in Definition 26.17. Truth telling is a Nash equilibrium for this mechanism if and only if, for each i, $\hat{v}_i \to \alpha_i(\hat{v}_i)$ is nondecreasing, and_

$$\pi_i(V_i) = \pi_i(0) + V_i \alpha_i(V_i) - \int_0^{V_i} \alpha_i(v) dv, \quad \text{for all } V_i \in [0, \overline{v}_i]. \tag{26.1}$$

Proof. We first show that if truth telling is a Nash equilibrium, then $\hat{v}_i \to \alpha_i(\hat{v}_i)$ is nondecreasing, and equation (26.1) holds:

Fix a direct-revelation mechanism $(\mathcal{A}, \mathcal{P})$ and a bidder i. The objective function of bidder i, given his true value is V_i, is to choose $\hat{v}_i$ to maximize $V_i \alpha_i(\hat{v}_i) - \pi_i(\hat{v}_i)$. Write

$$\mathcal{U}_i^*(V_i) = \sup_{\hat{v}_i \in [0, \overline{v}_i]} V_i \alpha_i(\hat{v}_i) - \pi_i(\hat{v}_i).$$

The function $\mathcal{U}_i^*$ is convex and continuous in V_i—see the solution to Problem 24.6 for the proof—and so it is differentiable almost everywhere.[17] Therefore,

$$\mathcal{U}_i^*(v) - \mathcal{U}_i^*(0) = \int_0^v \frac{d\mathcal{U}_i^*(u)}{du} du,$$

where it is understood that the integrand is defined only where $\mathcal{U}_i^*$ is differentiable, which is almost everywhere. But, by the envelope theorem (precisely, Proposition A17.2), where $\mathcal{U}_i^*$ is differentiable, its derivative is

$$\frac{d\mathcal{U}_i^*(v)}{dv} = \frac{\partial \left[v\alpha_i(\hat{v}^*) - \pi_i(\hat{v}^*) \right]}{\partial v} = \alpha_i(\hat{v}^*),$$

where $\hat{v}^*$ is the maximizing $\hat{v}$ at v. And, if truth telling is optimal for i, the optimizing $\hat{v}_i^*$ at each V_i must be V_i; that is, for values V_i where $\mathcal{U}_i^*$ is differentiable, its derivative is $\alpha_i(V_i)$, which implies that

$$\left[V_i \alpha_i(V_i) - \pi(V_i) \right] - \left[0\alpha_i(0) - \pi_i(0) \right] = \int_0^{V_i} \alpha_i(v) dv,$$

from which we obtain $\pi_i(V_i) = \pi_0(0) + V_i \alpha_i(V_i) - \int_0^{V_i} \alpha_i(v) dv$.

Since $\mathcal{U}_i^*$ is convex, its derivative, α_i, is nondecreasing at every point where the derivative is defined. But the proposition says that α_i is nondecreasing _everywhere_. To show this requires two inequalities. Fix V_i and V_i' with $V_i > V_i'$:

$$V_i \, \alpha_1(V_i) - \pi_i(V_i) \geq V_i \, \alpha_i(V_i') - \pi_i(V_i'), \text{ and } V_i' \, \alpha_1(V_i') - \pi_i(V_i') \geq V_i' \, \alpha_i(V_i) - \pi_i(V_i),$$

---

[17] Continuity on the interior of the interval follows from convexity. Continuity at the endpoints requires a special argument, based on truth telling being optimal.

both of which are implications of truth telling. Add the two, cancel the common π_i terms, and you have

$$V_i\,\alpha_i(V_i) + V_i'\,\alpha_i(V_i') \geq V_i'\,\alpha_i(V_i) + V_i\,\alpha_i(V_i'), \text{ or } (V_i - V_i')(\alpha_i(V_i) - \alpha_i(V_i')) \geq 0.$$

That does it: Necessity is established.

For sufficiency: Suppose α_i is nondecreasing and that equation (26.1) holds. Choose some V_i and any $\hat{v}_i \in [0, \bar{v}_i]$. We must show that

$$V_i\alpha_i(V_i) - \pi_i(V_i) \geq V_i\alpha_i(\hat{v}_i) - \pi_i(\hat{v}_i).$$

Suppose this is not so. Rewrite the reverse inequality as

$$V_i(\alpha_i(V_i) - \alpha_i(\hat{v}_i)) < \pi_i(V_i) - \pi_i(\hat{v}_i)$$
$$= \left[V_i\alpha_i(V_i) - \int_0^{V_i} \alpha_i(v)\mathrm{d}v \right] - \left[\hat{v}_i\alpha_i(\hat{v}_i) - \int_0^{\hat{v}_i} \alpha_i(v)\mathrm{d}v \right],$$

which gives

$$(\hat{v}_i - V_i)\alpha_i(\hat{v}_i) < \int_{V_i}^{\hat{v}_i} \alpha_i(v)dv.$$

If $\hat{v}_i > V_i$, then (because α_i is nondecreasing), this is impossible, and likewise if $\hat{v}_i < V_i$. ∎

Proposition 26.18 can be stated as: The direct-revelation mechanism $(\mathcal{A}, \mathcal{P})$ has truth telling as a Nash equilibrium if and only if the associated α_i functions are nondecreasing, and the associated α_i and π_i functions are related according to Equation (26.1). Suppose that instead of starting with both $\mathcal{A}$ and $\mathcal{P}$, we start with an assignment function $\mathcal{A}$ only. We don't need $\mathcal{P}$ to construct from $\mathcal{A}$ the associated α_i functions; they are given (simply) by $\alpha_i(\hat{v}_i) = \mathbf{E}[\mathcal{A}_i((\hat{v}_i, V_{\neg i}))]$. In particular, suppose we look at an assignment-rule (vector) function with the following property:

> *If V and V' are two (full) vectors of values, such that, for some i,* $V_i > V_i'$, *and, for all $j \neq i$, $V_j = V_j'$, then* $\mathcal{A}_i(V) \geq \mathcal{A}_i(V')$. (26.2)

In words, the probability that i is assigned the item cannot decrease if i submits a larger value, holding the submissions of everyone else constant.

It is immediate that the α_i functions are nondecreasing. So, suppose we use Equation (26.1) to *define* functions π_i,[18] and then we define a payment function $\mathcal{P}$ by $\mathcal{P}_i(V) = \pi_i(V_i)$. That is, bidder i's payment as a function of the whole vector of

---

[18] I'm cheating here; see the next subsection.

values only depends on his own submitted value. In that case, we would have a mechanism $(\mathcal{A}, \mathcal{P})$ for which truth telling is a Nash equilibrium. This mechanism demands payments from bidders even in circumstances where they don't get the item, but (recalling discussion from Chapter 24) that is nothing new; recall the all-pay auction of Problem 24.5. (Mark the margin of this paragraph with an X.)

The point is, in our search for a revenue-maximizing direct-revelation-with-truth-telling mechanism, if we discover it is optimal to assign the item according to a scheme that satisfies the italicized property (26.2), we know that it can be implemented. Which is what is about to happen, under the appropriate conditions.

The participation constraint

Before getting there, a few words about participation constraints are in order. There are (at least) two ways to think about participation constraints, depending on what a bidder knows when he decides whether to participate. The *ex ante participation constraint* is that, prior to learning V_i, i is informed of the rules of the mechanism that will be employed, and he chooses to participate or not based on his expected net outcome, averaged over all his possible values of V_i. The "rule" here is, if he opts in, and he then learns that, say, V_i is very low, so that his conditional payoff is less than zero, he is still forced to participate, according to the rules of the mechanism.

In contrast, so-called *interim participation constraints* involve the bidder choosing whether to participate already knowing V_i, and the standard interim participation constraint is that, for every possible value of V_i, bidder i expects a payoff that makes him no worse off than if he demurs.

I employ interim participation constraints. And, I can now explain how I cheated a few paragraphs back. Given an α_i function, Equation (26.1) doesn't quite completely determine the corresponding π_i; there is the boundary condition $\pi_i(0)$ to be specified. But at least, imposing an interim participation constraint in this context nails down the sign of $\pi_i(0)$; it must be that $\pi_i(0) \leq 0$. To see why, note that for V_i close to 0, even if i is sure to get the item, his overall payoff is bounded above by V_i. So, if $\pi_i(0) > 0$, there is a neighborhood of 0 in which bidder i must lose on average.

And, as long as Equation (26.1) holds, if $\pi_i(0) \leq 0$, then i's interim participation constraint holds for *all* V_i in the truth-telling equilibrium: If his value is V_i, his expected net payoff is

$$
V_i \alpha_i(V_i) - \pi_i(V_i) = V_i \alpha_i(V_i) - \left[V_i \alpha_i(V_i) - \int_0^{V_i} \alpha_i(v) dv + \pi_i(0) \right]
$$

$$
= \int_0^{V_i} \alpha_i(v) dv - \pi_i(0) \geq 0.
$$

(Or you could come to the same conclusion by observing that truth telling is a best response, and misrepresenting his preferences by reporting $\hat{v}_i = 0$ gets him the payoff $V_i \alpha_i(0) - \pi_i(0) \geq 0$.)

Optimality with independent values

Now that we know what characterizes truth-telling equilibria, we can see which direct-revelation mechanism with truth telling gives the seller the maximum expected revenue. I remind that we are assuming that private values are independent but not necessarily identically distributed, with F_i the distribution function of V_i, with F_i absolutely continuous on a compact interval $\mathbf{V}_i = [0, \overline{v}_i]$ and with a density function that is strictly positive.

Definition and Assumption 26.19. *For each F_i and $v_i \in [0, \overline{v}_i]$, let*

$$\zeta_i(v_i) := v_i - \frac{1 - F_i(v_i)}{f_i(v_i)}.$$

*If i's true value is V_i, the value $\zeta_i(V_i)$ is called i's **virtual valuation**. Assume that, for each i, $v_i \to \zeta_i(v_i)$ is nondecreasing.*

This mysterious definition and assumption beg the questions: What is this *virtual valuation* function? How restrictive is the assumption that it is an increasing function? The best interpretation that I can offer for the function comes in a bit. As for the assumption, you may recognize $f_i(v)/(1 - F_i(v))$ as the *hazard-rate function* of the distribution function F_i. For ζ_i to be nondecreasing (and, even, strictly increasing), it suffices—but is not necessary—for the hazard-rate function of F_i to be nondecreasing.

Be that as it may, here is the punchline, derived in the classic paper Myerson (1981):

Proposition 26.20. Myerson's Theorem, Part 1. *Assuming that every bidder's virtual-valuation function is nondecreasing. Then the direct-mechanism assignment rule $\mathcal{A}$ that maximizes the seller's expected revenue (in a truth-telling Nash equilibrium) is:*

1. $\mathcal{A}_i(V) = 0$, *if $\zeta_i(V_i) < \max\{0, \zeta_j(V_j)\}$ for some $j \neq i$, and*

2. $\sum_i \mathcal{A}_i(V) = 1$, *if for some i, $\zeta_i(V_i) > 0$.*

Moreover, in the corresponding payment scheme $\mathcal{P}$, $\pi_i(0) = 0$ for all i.

This description of $\mathcal{A}$ may be less than clear, so let me restate it in words: The item is never allocated to any bidder whose virtual valuation is less than zero or is less than the virtual valuation of some other bidder. It can be allocated to bidders whose virtual valuations are maximal and are greater than or equal to zero, and it must be allocated to one of those maximal-virtual-valuation bidders, if their virtual valuation is strictly positive.

This is (only) Part 1, because it doesn't fully characterize the second part of the mechanism, $\mathcal{P}$. That happens in Part 2, after we prove Part 1.

Proof. Fix any direct-revelation mechanism $(\mathcal{A}, \mathcal{P})$ for which truth telling is a Nash equilibrium. For each i, let α_i and π_i be the associated marginal-probability-of-winning and expected-amount-to-pay functions, both as functions of i's submitted value, both assuming truth telling by all the other bidders. Then the overall expected amount paid by i to the seller is is found by averaging $\pi_i(V_i)$ for all possible values of V_i, weighted by the density function of V_i, which is f_i:

$$
\begin{aligned}
\mathbf{E}[\pi_i(V_i)] &= \int_0^{\overline{v}_i} \pi_i(v) f_i(v) dv \\
&= \int_0^{\overline{v}_i} \left[\pi_i(0) + v\alpha_i(v) - \int_0^v \alpha_i(u) du \right] f_i(v) dv \\
&= \pi_i(0) + \int_0^{\overline{v}_i} v\alpha_i(v) f_i(v) dv - \int_0^{\overline{v}_i} \left[\int_0^v \alpha_i(u) du \right] f_i(v) dv \\
&= \pi_i(0) + \int_0^{\overline{v}_i} v\alpha_i(v) f_i(v) dv - \int_0^{\overline{v}_i} \left[\int_u^{\overline{v}_i} f_i(v) dv \right] \alpha_i(u) du \\
&= \pi_i(0) + \int_0^{\overline{v}_i} v\alpha_i(v) f_i(v) dv - \int_0^{\overline{v}_i} (1 - F_i(u)) \alpha_i(u) du \\
&= \pi_i(0) + \int_0^{\overline{v}_i} \left(v - \frac{1 - F_i(v)}{f_i(v)} \right) \alpha_i(v) f_i(v) dv.
\end{aligned}
$$

The key steps are the second equality, which uses Equation (26.1) and the assumption that this is a truth-telling mechanism, and the fourth, which is a standard change in the order of integration.

Now take the first and last terms in the previous string of equalities and rewrite in terms of $\mathcal{A}$. For each bidder i,

$$
\begin{aligned}
\mathbf{E}\big[\pi_i(V_i)\big] &= \mathbf{E}\left[\pi_i(0) + \left(V_i - \frac{1 - F_i(V_i)}{f_i(V_i)} \right) \alpha_i(V_i) \right] \\
&= \mathbf{E}\left[\mathbf{E}^*\left[\pi_i(0) + \left(V_i - \frac{1 - F_i(V_i)}{f_i(V_i)} \right) \mathcal{A}_i(V) \Big| V_i \right] \right] \\
&= \mathbf{E}^*\left[\pi_i(0) + \left(V_i - \frac{1 - F_i(V_i)}{f_i(V_i)} \right) \mathcal{A}_i(V) \right],
\end{aligned}
$$

where the star in $\mathbf{E}^*$ indicates that this expectation is taken over the distribution of the full vector of values V, I'm using the definition of α_i for the second equality, and I'm using the law of iterated (conditional) expectations for the third equality.

The seller's expected revenue overall is therefore

$$
\begin{aligned}
\sum_i \mathbf{E}\big[\pi_i(V_i)\big] &= \sum_i \mathbf{E}^*\left[\pi_i(0) + \left(V_i - \frac{1 - F_i(V_i)}{f_i(V_i)} \right) \mathcal{A}_i(V) \right] \\
&= \left[\sum_i \pi_i(0) \right] + \mathbf{E}^*\left[\sum_i \left(V_i - \frac{1 - F_i(V_i)}{f_i(V_i)} \right) \mathcal{A}_i(V) \right] \\
&= \left[\sum_i \pi_i(0) \right] + \mathbf{E}^*\left[\sum_i \zeta_i(V_i) \mathcal{A}_i(V) \right].
\end{aligned}
$$

Since, to meet the participation constraint, we require each $\pi_i(0) \leq 0$, the seller certainly wishes to set $\pi_i(0) = 0$. And to maximize the second term, we maximize, V-by-V, the bidder to whom the item is best awarded. For a given V, if all the terms $\zeta_i(V_i)$ are strictly negative, then for that V, it is optimal not to award the item to any bidder. If at least one $\zeta_i(V_i)$ is strictly positive, it is optimal to give the item (at that V) to whichever i achieves the maximum value of $\zeta_i(V_i)$; if there is a tie for the largest value, the award can be done arbitrarily, including by random assignment, as long as the item is awarded with probability one. And if the largest $\zeta_i(V_i)$ is zero, the seller can keep the item or assign it (or a mixture of the two), as long as he only assigns it to a bidder for whom $\zeta_i(V_i) = 0$.

We still must show that this allocation rule $\mathcal{A}$ will result in a mechanism $(\mathcal{A}, \mathcal{P})$ for which truth telling is a Nash equilibrium. This requires that we show that the corresponding α_i are nondecreasing. But, they certainly are, because this $\mathcal{A}$ satisfies the condition (26.2) on page 465; this follows from how $\mathcal{A}$ is defined, together with the assumption that the virtual utilities are all nondecreasing in the bidder's value. (Why does (26.2) work if the seller/referee/auctioneer has discretion to whom to allocate the item, given the possibility of ties for the largest virtual valuation?)   ∎

This proof establishes what the maximized expected revenue of the seller will be:

$$\mathbf{E}^*\big[\max\{0, \, \zeta_i(V_i) \, ; \, i \in I\}\big].$$

But it doesn't tell us what payment rule $\mathcal{P}$ will work along with $\mathcal{A}$ to induce truth telling. One might hope that simply asking the winner of the item (if the item is awarded) to pay his virtual valuation would work; this certainly generates the right total expected revenue. But it is not compatible with truth telling; in just the way that, in a first-price auction, bidders bid less than their true value to trade off the probability that they win with the amount they must pay, so it would be here: A bidder with a very high V_1 and, more to the point, an assessment that he has excellent prospects for having the highest virtual utility, would see it in his interests to report a slightly smaller V_1. (It can go in the other direction for bidders who think they are very unlikely to have the highest virtual valuation.)

So, we need to finish Myerson's Theorem with a description of $\mathcal{P}$. As noted on page 466, in the paragraph you marked with an X, we can simply tell bidders that, if they submit the value $\hat{v}_i$, this submission must be accompanied by a nonrefundable payment in the amount

$$\mathcal{P}_i(\hat{v}_i) = \hat{v}_i \, \alpha_i(\hat{v}_i) - \int_0^{\hat{v}_i} \alpha_i(v)\mathrm{d}v.$$

That certainly works. But, suppose we want a payment scheme $\mathcal{P}$ where only the winner of the item must pay something. This is part 2 of Myerson's Theorem.

Proposition 26.21. Myerson's Theorem, Part 2. *For each* i *and* V *, define*

$$\gamma_i(V) := \inf\left\{v_i \; ; \; \zeta_i(v_i) > \max\{0, \zeta_j(V_j); j \neq i\}\right\}.$$

And establish the payment rule for i*: If you are awarded the item when the full set of reports is* V*, then you must pay* $\gamma_i(V)$*. This, together with the revenue-maximizing* $\mathcal{A}$*, will induce truth telling **as a weakly dominant strategy**, while providing the maximal expected revenue for the seller.*

Because submitting true values is weakly dominant (and not just a Nash equilibrium), that's a definite plus for this scheme. However, observe that, in comparison with the "nonrefundable payment with submission" scheme (that is, $\mathcal{P}_i(\hat{v}_i)$ defined above), this doubles the responsibility of the referee–auctioneer. With the nonrefundable payment scheme, bidders know going in (subsequent to learning their V_i) how much they must pay. They still must trust that the referee–auctioneer will award the item according to $\mathcal{A}$. But once the money is in, and as long as the seller has no interest in keeping the item, there is no definite conflict of interest (so long as no money is transfered under the table).[19] But, in this alternative scheme, along with the item is a bill that depends on all the other submissions. The referee–auctioneer, if she is anxious to please the seller, might misrepresent (upwards) what others submitted. This problem also arises with second-price auctions. But in this case, with a mix of distribution functions F_i, one wonders whether bidders might be a bit more skeptical about implementation.

Be that as it may, there is a proposition to prove: One could try to show that this payment scheme bears the correct relationship to the assigment rule $\mathcal{A}$, but an easier argument is available. If i tells the truth (and assuming everyone else does as well), he wins the item when his virtual valuation exceeds the next highest virtual valuation (I'll ignore ties) or zero, and he pays the smallest *value* for which this is true, $\gamma_i(V)$. Note that $\gamma_i(V)$ is independent of his value; to emphasize this, I write $\gamma_i(V_{\neg i})$. There are two cases:

1. His value V_i is less than $\gamma_i(V_{\neg i})$. Then, if he wins the item, he pays more than it is worth to him. He prefers not to win the item, and submitting his true value guarantees that he will not win.

2. His value V_i exceeds $\gamma_i(V_{\neg i})$. If he wins the item, he pays less than it is worth to him, and the amount he pays is independent of what he bids. He prefers to win the item, and submitting his true value guarantees that he will win.

So, submitting his true value is weakly dominant.

How do we know that this scheme produces the right (maximal) expected revenue for the seller? The answer is revenue equivalence. If the allocation rule stays the same (with independent values), and if the mechanism induces truth telling, which it does, then the envelope theorem tells us what the expected payment must be.

---

[19] Well, this is not quite true. Why not? See Problem 26.14.

The case of i.i.d. values

Suppose that the bidders' private values are identically distributed; that is, all the F_i are the same. Then the virtual-utility functions ζ_i are all the same. Maintaining the assumption that virtual valuation is nondecreasing, the outcome is that the item goes to the high-value bidder, *as long as that bidder's virtual valuation is greater than 0*. Writing r^* for $\zeta_i^{-1}(0)$—that is, the smallest value V_i whose virtual valuation is 0 or more, this optimal-revenue auction is simply a first- or second-price auction, with a seller's reserve price of r^*.

What is virtual valuation? Bulow and Roberts (1989)

Bulow and Roberts (1989) provide a "story" to explain the role that virtual valuation plays in this model, drawing an analogy to price discrimination by a monopolist. Their explanation is well worth reading in detail; here I will give a shorter (and less satisfactory) story that employs their basic insight.

Suppose the seller, Carol, faces a single buyer, Alice, whose value for the item, V_A, is distributed according to the distribution function F_A. Suppose the seller, unwilling to engage in extended bargaining, decides to make a take-it-or-leave-it offer to Alice. If Alice buys at the take-it-or-leave-it price, great. If not, Carol will live with the consequences. What take-it-or-leave-it price p should Carol name?

It helps to work with the complementary cumulative distribution function $G_A(V) = 1 - F_A(V)$, so that $g_A(V) = dG_A(V)/dV = -f_A(V)$. Then Carol's problem (if she attaches zero value to the item if she retains it) is to set her take-it-or-leave-it price r^* to maximize the product of the probability that the offer is taken times that price. At the price r^*, the probability that the offer is taken is the probability that $V_A \geq r^*$, which is just $G_A(r^*)$. So Carol's objective is to maximize $r^* G_A(r^*)$, the first-order condition for which is

$$G_A(r^*) + r^* g_A(r^*)) = 0.$$

Letting $V^* = r^*$ (so V^* is the cutoff value at which the sale will be made), the first-order condition can be rewritten

$$V^* + \frac{G_A(V^*)}{g_A(V^*)} = 0, \quad \text{which is} \quad V^* - \frac{1 - F_A(V^*)}{f_A(V^*)} = 0, \quad \text{or} \quad \zeta_A(V^*) = 0.$$

If Alice is the only buyer, then to maximize her revenue, Carol sets the "reserve price" r^* for Alice at the price at which Alice's virtual valuation (computed using F_A) is zero. Since there is no competition in a one-buyer auction, Alice buys if her value V_A is greater than the level V^* at which her virtual valuation is greater than zero, paying (of course) the reserve price that Carol set.

Bulow and Roberts suggest the sort of diagram shown in Figure 26.1, which comes straight out of the typical intermediate level course in microeconomics.

Use the y-axis for values V_A that Alice might have. The x-axis records probabilities, and the upper curve on the graph shows, for each probability r, the corresponding value V_A such that $G_A(V_A) = r$, or $V_A = G_A^{-1}(r)$. Thinking of the x-axis

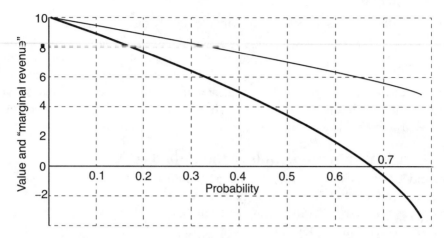

Figure 26.1. Virtual utility "is" marginal revenue. (See text for explanation.)

as quantities, the virtual-valuation function—the lower of the two curves—traces out the marginal-revenue function appropriate in this story: In intermediate micro, the marginal-revenue function is the derivative of total revenue in the quantity sold; this is relevant because the price-setting firm's decision variable is the quantity to sell. Here we can think of the probability of a sale as Alice's decision variable, so that the appropriate marginal-revenue function is the derivative of total revenue in the probability of a sale; that's what the lower function provides, and that—looking at the inverse of this marginal-revenue function—is the virtual-valuation function.

The analogy is clear: As we saw in earlier chapters, probabilities of making a transaction are, in many ways, analogous to quantities sold for risk-neutral parties. And, since Carol's marginal cost is zero, marginal cost equals this marginal revenue where the marginal-revenue function hits zero, which is the r^* we computed above, or $\zeta(V^*) = 0$.

For instance, suppose $F_A(v_A) = v_A^2/100$ for $v^A \in [0, 10]$. (That's precisely what the graph in Figure 26.1 shows.) The upper curve in Figure 26.1 is the corresponding $G_A(v_A)$; 0 at $v_A = 10$; approximately 0.5 at $v_A = 7.07$. And we compute

$$\zeta_A(V_A) = V_A - \frac{1 - V_A^2/100}{2V_A/100}, \quad \text{so that} \quad \zeta_A(V_A) = 0 \quad \text{at} \quad V_A = \frac{10}{\sqrt{3}},$$

which is (roughly) $V_A = 5.7735$. The corresponding cut off probability—the probability that Alice accepts Carol's offer—is $1 - (10/\sqrt{3})^2/100 = 2/3$; at Carol's optimal take-it-or-leave-it offer at the price $10/\sqrt{3}$, the probability of no sale is fully $1/3$.

All this is for a single buyer. What about auctions where there are buyers other than Alice? Here is a quick explanation, not as good as in Bulow and Roberts, but one that conveys the basic intuition. Suppose Carol, the seller, has gotten offers for her item, and the best offer received is p. Before accepting that offer, she has one last individual to whom she might sell the item, Alice, and she is prepared to make a take-it-or-leave-it offer to Alice. But because she has those other offers, her marginal cost of selling the item to Alice is no longer zero but p. So, her take-it-or-leave-it offer to Alice, which is designed to maximize the probability that Alice will buy times the take-it-or-leave-it price plus the probability that Alice says "no thanks" times p, is the price at which Alice's virtual valuation = Carol's "marginal-revenue in probability" = p. That's essentially what the revenue-maximizing auction, with the payment rule in Part 2 of Myerson's Theorem (Proposition 26.21), accomplishes.

Note that this can mean an inefficient assignment of the item, now for two reasons. As in Chapter 24 (and the take-it-or-leave-it story just provided), the seller sets the reservation price for a buyer at the level r_i where $\zeta_i(r_i) = 0$, which is greater than zero, even though the item is worth (only) zero to the seller. And, if bidders have differently shaped virtual utility functions, the item might be sold to a bidder who values it less than a bidder who goes away empty handed. (Problem 26.15 walks you through a specific example.)

What about . . . ?

This is where I leave the story about optimal (revenue-maximizing) auctions. The literature contains a large number of extensions and elaborations. Two particularly obvious questions are:

- *What if the virtual-valuation functions of one or more bidders are not monotonically decreasing?* This is dealt with by a procedure called *ironing*, first analyzed in Myerson (1981) and discussed in terms of a price-discriminating monopolist in Bulow and Roberts (1989).

- *What if the buyers have values V_i that are not statistically independent?* Crémer and McLean (1988) show that, if the values $\{V_i\}$ are not statistically independent, then (generically, in terms of their distribution) the seller can arrange an efficient mechanism (the item goes to the bidder who values it most highly), and every bidder has an expected payoff of zero. In other words, the seller extracts all the surplus available from the sale of the item. The construction comes down to a VCG mechanism with a particularly clever "add-on" term, and (especially when the correlation in values is slight) involves monetary transfers that (with positive probability) can be enormous.

    With all due respect for a brilliant piece of theory, I don't know that this tells us much about the economics of such situations. Instead, it illustrates that, in places, mechanism-design analyses can go too far. The monetary transfers in Crémer and McLean are very sensitive to the full probability law of the vector of values; slight changes in the probability law can mean large changes in the transfer rules. We should wish instead for mechanism designs that are robust to variations in the environment in which they are meant to operate. Some progress has been made on this topic; much more progress is needed.

26.7. Mechanism Design for Bilateral Bargaining: Myerson and Satterthwaite (1983)

Mechanism-design ideas have also been applied to bilateral bargaining, the subject of Chapter 23. The basic context is that Alice owns an item that Bob is interested in purchasing. The item, if retained by Alice, has value V_A for her (in units of money). If she doesn't sell it to Bob, this is her payoff. If she does sell it, her payoff is the price she gets. We'll allow for outcomes in which Bob gets the item with some probability p, and he may pay her even if he doesn't get the item; in general, her payoff is the probability that she retains the item times V_A plus the expected net transfer of money to her from Bob. Bob's value is V_B, and his payoff is the probability that he gets the item times V_B less the expected net tranfer of money from him to her. (So, both parties are risk neutral, with utility functions that are quasi-linear in money.)

Myerson and Satterthwaite (1983) address this general context with the following additional assumptions:

- Alice knows V_A but does not know V_B. Alice's hypothesis about V_B does not depend on V_A and is given by an absolutely continuous cumulative distribution function F_B on a compact interval $[\underline{v}_B, \overline{v}_B]$. We further assume that the density function corresponding to F_B, f_B, is continuous and strictly positive on the interval $[\underline{v}_B, \overline{v}_B]$.

- Bob's situation is symmetrical. He knows V_B but does not know V_A. His hypothesis about V_A does not depend on V_B and is given by an absolutely continuous cumulative distribution function F_A on a compact interval $[\underline{v}_A, \overline{v}_A]$. The density function corresponding to F_A, f_A, is continuous and strictly positive on the interval $[\underline{v}_A, \overline{v}_A]$.

That is, we have the "most natural" bargaining context from Chapter 23.

Recall what we said about this situation in Chapter 23. If there is a gap between the two supports—that is, if $\overline{v}_A < \underline{v}_B$—then an efficient equilibrium in the simultaneous bid-and-ask game is feasible, with Alice asking and Bob bidding any price in the interval $(\overline{v}_A, \underline{v}_B)$. However, if the supports overlap, an efficient equilibrium is impossible in the simultaneous bid-and-ask game (cf. Proposition 23.8). The question left open there is: Might a more complex mechanism lead to an efficient outcome as a *bilateral-bargaining* Nash equilibrium?

Proposition 26.22. (Myerson and Satterthwaite 1983) *Suppose that $\underline{v}_A < \underline{v}_B < \overline{v}_A < \overline{v}_B$. (That is, the supports overlap.) Then, the efficient outcome—Bob gets the item whenever $V_B > V_A$—cannot be produced in a bilateral-bargaining Nash equilibrium of any mechanism.*

The italicized *bilateral-bargaining*, as a modifier of *Nash equilibrium*, signifies that the search is for a Nash equilibrium of a mechanism that meets three conditions:

- Both Bob and Alice must meet *interim* participation constraints. Alice knows V_A as she contemplates whether to participate in the mechanism. If her expected payoff is less than her payoff from walking away, which is V_A, she won't participate. We insist that, for every value of V_A, she passes the "I'm willing to participate" constraint. And the same is true of Bob: Knowing V_B, he must be assured of an expected payoff of at least 0 for every value of V_B.

- It should be fairly obvious that, if any trade at all is to take place, money must change hands; on average, Bob must pay for the item if he has a chance of getting it. But, any money paid to Alice must come from Bob. No "extra money" can be brought into the deal.

- The mechanism must consummate the deal immediately. Delay until the exchange is made is inefficient.

Proof. Here is a simple mechanism that achieves efficient exchange and satisfies the interim participation constraints. Alice and Bob simultaneously declare (to, say, a neutral referee) their values, where for the moment, misrepresentation is not ruled out. Suppose that Alice declares $\hat{v}_A$ and Bob declares $\hat{v}_B$.

- If $\hat{v}_A > \hat{v}_B$, the item is not exchanged, and no money changes hands.
- If $\hat{v}_A \leq \hat{v}_B$, the item is exchanged. Alice is paid $\hat{v}_B$. Bob pays $\hat{v}_A$.

Alice's net payoff, given V_A, is

$$U_A(\hat{v}_A, \hat{v}_B) = \begin{cases} V_A, & \text{if } \hat{v}_A > \hat{v}_B, \text{ and} \\ \hat{v}_B, & \text{if } \hat{v}_A \leq \hat{v}_B. \end{cases}$$

Whatever Bob is doing, among Alice's optimal declarations is $\hat{v}_A = V_A$. And Bob's net payoff, given V_B, is

$$U_B(\hat{v}_A, \hat{v}_B) = \begin{cases} V_B - \hat{v}_A, & \text{if } \hat{v}_A \leq \hat{v}_B, \text{ and} \\ 0, & \text{if } \hat{v}_A > \hat{v}_B. \end{cases}$$

Whatever Alice does, submitting $\hat{v}_B = V_B$ is among Bob's optimal choices.

It is clear that the outcome of this simple mechanism induces truth telling, and it satisfies the interim participation constraints.[20] Unhappily, though, it fails the "no outside cash" constraint: Bob's expected payment to Alice is $\mathbf{E}[V_A; V_A \leq V_B]$, while Alice's expected payment from Bob is $\mathbf{E}[V_B; V_A \leq V_B]$. Alice on average is getting paid more—$\mathbf{E}[V_B - V_A; V_A \leq V_B] = \mathbf{E}[\max\{V_B - V_A, 0\}]$ more—than Bob is paying.

And, at this point, with a bit of a handwave (which can be justified!), I declare the proposition proved. Since the values are independent, payoff equivalence holds. Any mechanism that satisfies the interim participation constraints and produces the same allocation outcome necessarily involves the same payoffs and, therefore, the same expected flow of funds.

---

[20] Indeed, it is precisely the VCG mechanism. Problem 26.16 asks you to verify this, then to speak to the question of the VCG mechanism versus "interim participation."

But, since we haven't seen "payoff equivalence" with these sorts of interim participation constraints, let me take you through a more complete argument.

If it were possible to have a mechanism that achieved what Proposition 26.22 says cannot be done, it would have to be possible to do this in a truth-telling Nash equilibrium for a direct-revelation mechanism. (This, of course, is the revelation principle.) So examine direct-revelation mechanisms: Alice reports some $\hat{v}_A$, Bob reports some $\hat{v}_B$, and the referee affects an outcome, which, in this case, involves a probability $\mathcal{A}(\hat{v}_A, \hat{v}_B)$ that the item is transferred to Bob and a net payment $\mathcal{P}(\hat{v}_A, \hat{v}_B)$ from Bob to Alice.

And we immediately know what the assignment probability must be, if this is to produce an efficient outcome with truth telling:

$$\mathcal{A}(\hat{v}_A, \hat{v}_B) = \begin{cases} 1, & \text{if } \hat{v}_A < \hat{v}_B, \\ 0, & \text{if } \hat{v}_A > \hat{v}_B, \text{ and} \\ \text{something between 0 and 1}, & \text{if } \hat{v}_A = \hat{v}_B. \end{cases}$$

It may help to have a picture in your mind; see Figure 26.2.

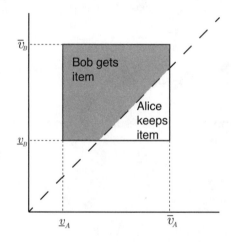

Figure 26.2. The efficient allocation of the item

Write

$$\alpha_A(\hat{v}_A) := \int_{\underline{v}_B}^{\overline{v}_B} \mathcal{A}(\hat{v}_A, v_B) f(v_B) dv_B \quad \text{and} \quad \pi_A(\hat{v}_A) := \int_{\underline{v}_B}^{\overline{v}_B} \mathcal{P}(\hat{v}_A, v_B) f(v_B) dv_B;$$

these are the probability that Alice transfers to item to Bob and the expected payment to her, respectively, if she reports $\hat{v}_A$, assuming he tells the truth about the value V_B. Define $\alpha_B(\hat{v}_B)$ and $\pi_B(\hat{v}_B)$ in similar fashion for Bob; please note that π_B records what Bob pays to Alice. And, since we know what $\mathcal{A}$ is, we can immediately write

$$\alpha_A(\hat{v}_A) = 1 - F_B(\hat{v}_A) \quad \text{and} \quad \alpha_B(\hat{v}_B) = F_A(\hat{v}_B).$$

Alice's expected payoff, given V_A, if she reports $\hat{v}_A$, is

$$V_A F_B(\hat{v}_A) + \pi_A(\hat{v}_A).$$

For truth telling to be optimal for her, the standard envelope-theorem argument tells us that her optimized payoff function, $\mathcal{U}_A^*(V_A)$, must satisfy the equation

$$\mathcal{U}_A^*(V_A) = \mathcal{U}_A^*(\underline{v}_A) + \int_{\underline{v}_A}^{V_A} F_B(u)\,du. \tag{26.3}$$

Now we can worry about the interim participation constraints: They are that $\mathcal{U}_A^*(V_A) \geq V_A$. Inspection of Equation (26.3) immediately tells us that $V_A \to \mathcal{U}_A^*(V_A)$ increases at no greater than rate 1, so the binding interim participation constraint will be at $V_A = \overline{v}_A$; if $\mathcal{U}_A^*(\overline{v}_A) \geq \overline{v}_A$, the interim participation constraints for all lesser values of V_A will immediately hold. So, first rewriting Equation (26.3) using the upper endpoint of integration to fix the integral and then substituting $\overline{v}_A$ for $\mathcal{U}_A^*(\overline{v}_A)$, we get

$$\mathcal{U}_A^*(V_A) = \mathcal{U}_A^*(\overline{v}_A) - \int_{V_A}^{\overline{v}_A} F_B(u)\,du = \overline{v}_A - \int_{V_A}^{\overline{v}_A} F_B(u)\,du. \tag{26.3'}$$

Why did I substitute $\overline{v}_A$ for $\mathcal{U}_A^*(\overline{v}_A)$? Why not leave the interim participation constraint at $V_A = \overline{V}_A$ slack? To answer that question, write $\mathcal{U}_A^*(V_A) = V_A F_B(V_A) + \pi_A(V_A)$. Combine this with (26.3'), and we have

$$\pi_A(V_A) = \mathcal{U}_A^*(V_A) - V_A F_B(V_A) = \overline{v}_A - \int_{V_A}^{\overline{v}_A} F_B(u)\,du - V_A F_B(V_A). \tag{26.4}$$

Just meeting the interim participation constraint at $\overline{v}_A$ makes the payment schedule that Alice must receive as small as possible, if truth telling is to be achieved. To get insight into the quantity $\pi_A(V_A)$, integrate by parts in (26.4):

$$\pi_A(V_A) = \overline{v}_A - \left[uF_B(u)\Big|_{V_A}^{\overline{v}_A} - \int_{V_A}^{\overline{v}_A} uf_B(u)\,du \right] - V_A F_B(V_A)$$

$$= \overline{v}_A - \overline{v}_A F_B(\overline{v}_A) + \int_{V_A}^{\overline{v}_A} uf_B(u)\,du \tag{26.4'}$$

$$= \overline{v}_A(1 - F_B(\overline{v}_A)) + \int_{V_A}^{\overline{v}_A} uf_B(u)\,du = \mathbf{E}\big[V_B; V_B \geq V_A | V_A\big],$$

where $\mathbf{E}\big[V_B; V_B \geq V_A | V_A\big]$ means the conditional expectation of V_B on the event where it is at least as large as V_A, conditional on V_A.

Bob's problem, given V_B, is to pick $\hat{v}_B$ to maximize $V_B \alpha_B(\hat{v}_B) - \pi_B(\hat{v}_B) = V_B F_A(\hat{v}_B) - \pi_B(\hat{v}_B)$, and for truth telling to be optimal for him, the standard envelope-theorem argument requires that

$$\mathcal{U}_B^*(v_B) = \mathcal{U}_B^*(\underline{v}_B) + \int_{\underline{v}_B}^{v_B} F_A(u)du, \tag{26.5}$$

where $\mathcal{U}_B^*(V_B)$ is his optimized value function from truth telling, if his value is V_B.

Bob's participation constraints are that $\mathcal{U}^*(v_B) \geq 0$, and it is clear from Equation (26.5) that if $\mathcal{U}_B^*(\underline{v}_B) \geq 0$, the constraint will be met for all larger v_B. It is furthermore clear that if we set $\mathcal{U}_B^*(\underline{v}_B) > 0$, the amount by which $\mathcal{U}_B^*(\underline{v}_B)$ exceeds zero will propagate on up the line. Now, if the $v_B \to \mathcal{U}_B^*(\underline{v}_B)$ schedule is higher, since Bob's payoff from possessing the item doesn't change, it must be that the amount he is paying Alice is decreasing. And, I want to set his payoff function so that he is paying as much as possible to Alice (again, stay tuned to see why). So, with this as my objective, I set $\mathcal{U}^*(\underline{v}_B) = 0$, and we get

$$\mathcal{U}_B^*(v_B) = \int_{\underline{v}_B}^{v_B} F_A(u)du. \tag{26.5'}$$

Combine this with $\mathcal{U}^*(v_B) = v_B F_A(v_B) - \pi_B(v_B)$, and we have

$$\pi_B(v_B) = v_B F_A(v_B) - \int_{\underline{v}_B}^{v_B} F_A(u)\,du.$$

Recast this using integration by parts, and we have

$$\pi_B(v_B) = v_B F_A(v_B) - \left[uF_A(u) \Big|_{\underline{v}_B}^{v_B} - \int_{\underline{v}_B}^{v_B} uf_A(u)\,du \right]$$

$$= \underline{v}_B F_A(\underline{v}_B) + \int_{\underline{v}_B}^{v_B} uf_A(u)\,du = \mathbf{E}\big[V_A \, ; V_A \leq V_B | V_B \big]. \tag{26.6}$$

If you believed my handwave about revenue equivalence, nothing since I announced that we had a proof is really necessary. And it certainly isn't surprising: These are the expected payments we computed for the VCG mechanism. But, if you were unhappy with the handwave, it is now justified: Given V_B, Bob is willing to pay Alice no more than $\mathbf{E}\big[V_A \, ; V_A \leq V_B | V_B \big]$ (and he'd pay her even less if we set $\mathcal{U}_B^*(\underline{v}_B)$ at greater than 0). Given V_A, Alice needs to be paid at least $\mathbf{E}\big[V_B \, ; V_A \leq V_B | V_A \big]$. Hence, the minimum total expected amount Alice requires (averaging over V_A) less the maximum total expected amount Bob is willing to pay (averaging over V_B) is

$$
\int_{\underline{v}_A}^{\overline{v}_A} \left[\int_{v_A}^{\overline{v}_B} v_B\, f_B(v_B)\, \mathrm{d}v_B \right] f_A(v_A)\, \mathrm{d}v_A - \int_{\underline{v}_B}^{\overline{v}_B} \left[\int_{\underline{v}_A}^{v_B} v_A\, f_A(v_A)\, \mathrm{d}v_A \right] f_B(v_B)\, \mathrm{d}v_B
$$

$$
= \int_{\underline{v}_A}^{\overline{v}_A} \int_{\underline{v}_B}^{\overline{v}_B} \max(v_B - v_A, 0) f_B(v_B) f_A(v_A)\, \mathrm{d}v_B \mathrm{d}v_A > 0,
$$

where the best way to understand how I got from the first line to the second is to go back to Figure 26.2 and carefully map out the areas and orders over which the integrals are being taken.   ∎

Other applications of mechanism design to bilateral bargaining

The paper Myerson and Satterthwaite (1983) does much more than to prove this result. Using the same methods that are used in Myerson (1981), it characterizes which outcomes can be obtained in a bilateral-bargaining equilibrium, it characterizes mechanisms that are second-best (in the sense that the mechanism maximizes the total expected gains from trade), it shows how much of a "subsidy" is required to effect efficient exchange, and it describes mechanisms that maximize a broker's expected profit (if Alice and Bob can find an honest broker who is willing to intercede). In so doing, the paper provides additional insight into the concept of virtual utility. So, here is another reading assignment for you, but with a warning: The authors sometimes skip steps, so be patient with their paper.

Samuelson (1984) uses mechanism design methods to "solve" the Akerlof problem from Chapter 20, where Alice contemplates selling her used car to Bob. In the basic context, we suppose that Alice knows the value to herself of retaining the car, which is denoted by V. Bob does not know V and, moreover, he is unsure how much the car would be worth to him, were he to purchase it from Alice. But he (and Alice) know that the value to Bob of the car is a deterministic (and continuous, increasing) function of V, $\psi(V)$. Bob has an assessment about V: It has an absolutely continuous distribution function F on a compact interval, with a density function that is strictly positive and continuous on that interval. (Going back to the start of Chapter 20, V is uniformly distributed on $[2000, 6000]$, and $\psi(V) = V + 200$.) All of this is common knowledge.

In this setting, Samuelson employs mechanism design methods to find the Bob-optimal bargaining equilibrium—it involves Bob making a take-it-or-leave-it offer to Alice—and the Alice-optimal bargaining equilibrium, which may involve a take-it-or-leave-it offer from Alice, but which may be more complex than that.

Between these two extremes are cases in which Alice knows V_A, Bob knows V_B, and the two are correlated. For this case, the paper by McAfee and Reny (1992) is recommended.

26.8. And What about . . . ? A Bottom Line on Mechanism Design

Mechanism design has been and continues to be a very active topic in both microeconomic theory and in applications. In terms of applications, this chapter has discussed applications to auctions and bilateral bargaining and has only given the bare beginnings of the literature on these topics. Applications to matching markets (school choice, kidney exchange) and to contract design can be found. And while the theory here is restricted to static mechanism design, applications often require that the analyst confront dynamic aspects of mechanism design. For instance (and this is only a sample):

- In the context of kidney exchange, patients desiring a kidney and cadaver kidneys both arrive through time.

- In the context of contracts, the possibility that parties to the contract will, following the receipt of information, seek to renegotiate the contract often looms large.

- In the context of auctions, resale of rights and information gained by winning an earlier auction that is useful in subsequent auctions affects the value that parties attach to winning the earlier auction, which sellers may wish to control through the design of both the earlier *and* the later auctions.

- An issue mentioned briefly here (and the focus of Chapter 21): The optimal static mechanism may provide parties with information that, in a dynamic world, they would want to exploit, which affects the incentives of parties to participate in the original mechanism.

- In this chapter, and in many applications of mechanism design, the information endowments of the agents (citizens/bidders/bargainers) are fixed. A lot of attention recently has been directed to the design of information, both statically and dynamically, as a part of mechanism design.

I provide a very limited sample of papers that delve into some of these issues in the Bibliographic Notes for this chapter.

As for my bottom line on mechanism design, I have two main criticisms or, better, cautions:

- Concerning Crémer and McLean (1988), I provided one bottom-line caution about mechanism design and, in particular, optimal mechanism design: Taken to an extreme, mechanisms can be designed that do wonderful things, but whether those wonderful things are achieved is very sensitive to the specific features of the environment that are put into the model.

- And, along with such "sins of commission" are possible "sins of omission": As in any theoretical model and analysis of real-life situations, real life presents complications and issues that the application of mechanism-design theory may miss, having been left out of the model. To give a prominent example: What if bidders collude in an otherwise theoretically well-designed mechanism? The discussion at the end of Section 26.5 about the frailties of pivot form of the VCG mechanism (for instance, when two citizens are brother and sister) serves as a cautionary tale.

Hence, I end with the frequently repeated caution: The theories in this chapter, and throughout this volume, can be very helpful in refining your understanding of real-world phenomena. But these theoretical constructions must be used with circumspection and caution, also known as common sense, and should ideally be subjected to empirical testing of a formal variety (or, lacking that, with casual empiricism, which can also be termed common sense).

This leads from the *theory of mechanism design* to the *applied pactice of market design*: Mechanism-design theory informs the analyst, but it is complemented by experimentation, computation, experience (field-based empirical evidence), and a healthy dose of common sense. I'm approaching the Bibliographic Notes, so let me begin by suggesting that you read Al Roth's 2002 paper on "The economist as engineer: Game theory, experimentation, and computation as tools for design economics."

Bibliographic Notes

The classic articles for each of the five topics covered are listed below, along with other papers referenced in the chapter. Beyond these references are entire books that, to some degree or other, use the ideas of mechanism design and are worth reading to advance beyond the basics covered here. The three books on auctions, by Paul Klemperer (2004), Vijay Krishna (2010), and Paul Milgrom (2004), that are referenced in Chapter 24, are all excellent sources for the theory and applications to auction design.

The original references for the Gibbard–Satterthwaite Theorem are Gibbard (1973) and Satterthwaite (1975). The Muller–Satterthwaite Theorem is in Muller and Satterthwaite (1977). The proof of the Gibbard–Satterthwaite Theorem that is provided here follows notes by Faruk Gul and, in turn, is based on ideas from Geanakoplos (2005). I recommend as well the proof provided in Reny (2001).

The seminal paper on Nash implementation is Maskin (1999). As already mentioned in the text, don't misled be by the publication year. This paper was in circulation among economists in 1977, which is its proper "publication" date. A clever proof of Maskin's Theorem is provided in Repullo (1987). Jackson (2001) provides a survey of subsequent work, including a lot of extensions and elaborations not covered here, and is highly recommended.

The history of the VCG mechanism is both nuanced and interesting. Groves' thesis contained the basic idea and caused a great stir among economists when circulated circa 1970–1. It appeared in Groves (1973), due to publication lags. Clarke's (1971) work was contemporaneous. It was only later that people recognized the basic idea of these mechanisms in second-price auctions, which were pioneered in Vickrey (1961). What complicates the story is that Groves' work was done in terms of a Nash equilibrium of a game of incomplete information (what was at the time called a Bayesian–Nash equilibrium), rather than a dominant-strategy mechanism of the sort discussed here. The "pivot" add-on is the invention of Green and Laffont (1979). These ideas were further developed by a number of authors; for those interested, Groves and Ledyard (1977, Section 5) provides a brief history.

The seminal article on optimal auctions (with independent private values) is Myerson (1981). Bulow and Roberts (1989) provide an in intuitive explanation, drawn from intermediate microeconomics, of virtual utility. Crémer and McLean (1988) provides the startling result that, with generic dependencies in the bidders valuations, the seller can devise an "auction" mechanism that extracts all the surplus.

Concerning bilateral bargaining, the classic reference is Myerson and Satterthwaite (1983). Samuelson (1984) analyzes the "Akerlof" problem, and McAfee and Reny (1992) to for bilateral bargaining (and other topics) what Crémer and McLean do for auctions.

A sample of other papers that take you beyond the topics covered in this chapter include: Bergemann and Välimäki (2010), for the pivot form of VCG in dynamic contexts; Maskin and Moore (1999), for renegotiation of contracts with subgame-perfect implementation; Segal (1999), for an example of mechanism design in the context of multi-agent principal-agent problems; and Watson (2007), for mechanism design meets optimal contracting.

Problems

■ 26.1. Page 439 describes a First-Past-the-Post election with three candidates, one each from the Liberal Party, the Labour Party, and the Conservative Party. In particular, we have a citizen who will vote in this election and whose preferences are that the Liberal candidate is best and then the Labour candidate, while the worst outcome for this citizen is for the Tory candidate to win.

a. Under what circumstances in terms of the "expressed preferences" (votes) of other citizens is it better for this citizen to misrepresent her preferences? (Hint: To answer this question, you must specify the tie-breaking rule in the election, and note that "flip a coin," while it may be used in real life, doesn't fit the framework of Gibbard–Satterthwaite. Your answer must deal with this.)

b. Suppose this citizen believes that each of her fellow citizens will vote statistically independently, with each other citizen voting for the Liberal candidate with probability 0.2, for the Labour candidate with probability 0.39, and for the Conservative candidate with probability 0.41. What is the best vote for this citizen to cast? (I haven't given you enough information to answer this question; you must supply some missing information, and part of the problem is to figure out what information is missing.)

c. Suppose there are only two candidates, one from the Labour party and one from the Tory party. Why is it (weakly) dominant for our citizen to vote for the Labour candidate?

■ 26.2. Prove Lemma 26.4.

■ 26.3. The version of the Gibbard–Satterthwaite Theorem supplied in the text, Proposition 26.2, is simplified in two ways. First, it is assumed that citizens' weak preferences are antisymmetric. In the "full" G–S Theorem, preferences are (only) complete and transitive. In view of this, let $\mathcal{R}$ be the space of complete and transitive (weak) preferences on X, let Φ have domain $\mathcal{R}^N$, and write $\Phi((\succeq_i)_{i\in N})$ for Φ evaluated at $(\succeq_i)_{i\in N}$.

And the condition that Φ satisfies Pareto efficiency has been added to nonmanipulability. Among other things, this ensures that every social outcome $x \in X$ is the outcome chosen by some preference array $(\succeq_i)_{i\in N}$. In the full theorem, Pareto efficiency is not assumed present. Instead, the assumption is that the image of Φ, defined as

$$\text{im}(\Phi) := \big\{ x \in X : x = \Phi((\succeq_i)_{i\in N}) \text{ for some } (\succeq_i)_{i\in N} \in \mathcal{P}^N \big\},$$

contains at least three social outcomes.

I will not ask you to prove the full theorem, but the two parts of this problem will get you started.

a. First, suppose there are ten social states, labeled $\{x_1, \ldots, x_{10}\}$. Suppose that N contains two or more citizens, with citizen 1 a distinguished elder of the community. Define a voting-rule function Φ by: If citizen 1 has a strict preference among x_1, x_2, and x_3, that is the chosen social state. If citizen 1's favorite among x_1, x_2, and x_3 is a tie, Φ chooses from among citizen 1's favorites (out of those three) whichever has the lowest index. Is this rule manipulable?

b. A weaker property than Pareto efficiency is *unanimity*, which holds that, at preference array $(\succeq_i)_{i\in N}$, if every citizen strictly prefers x^* to every other social outcome, then $\Phi((\succeq_i)_{i\in N}) = x^*$. Here is a variation of unanimity, which might be called *set unanimity*: Fix a set $\hat{X} \subseteq X$. Suppose that, at the preference array $(\succeq_i)_{i\in N}$, every citizen i strictly prefers each member of $\hat{X}$ to each member of $X \setminus \hat{X}$. Then, if $\hat{X} \cap \text{im}(\Phi)$ is nonempty, $\Phi((\succeq_i)_{i\in N}) \in \hat{X} \cap \text{im}(\Phi)$.

   Prove that nonmanipulability implies this property of *set unanimity*.

■ 26.4. Prove that nonmanipulability implies strong positive association. (Hint: If Φ doesn't satisfy strong positive association, there must exist preference profiles $(\succ_i)_{i\in N}$ and $(\hat{\succ}_i)_{i\in N}$ such that $\Phi((\succeq_i)_{i\in N}) = x$ and, for all y and i, $x \succ_i y$ implies $x \hat{\succ}_i y$, but $\Phi((\hat{\succ}_i)_{i\in N}) \neq x$. In the fashion used in Lemmas 26.3 and 26.4, create profiles $(\succ_i^n)_{i\in N}$ for $n = 0, 1, \ldots, N$, where n also enumerates the citizens and, in $(\succ_i^n)_{i\in N}$, $\succ_i^n = \succ_i$ for $i = 1, \ldots, n$ and $\succ_i^n = \hat{\succ}_i$ for $i = n+1, \ldots, N$. That is,

$(\succ_i^0)_{i\in\mathcal{N}} = (\succ_i)_{i\in\mathcal{N}}$, $(\succ_i^N)_{i\in\mathcal{N}} = (\hat{\succ}_i)_{i\in\mathcal{N}}$, and, along the sequence, we change one citizen's preferences from $\succ_i$ to $\hat{\succ}_i$. You take it from there.)

■ 26.5. Consider Maskin's Theorem (Proposition 26.9) and, in particular, the no-veto property. Suppose we have three citizens, Alice, Bob, and Carol. Suppose that among the states in X are x and y. Suppose that, in a particular set of preferences, Alice and Bob rank x and y as equally good and strictly better than any other social state; while Carol ranks y as strictly better than any other social state and, ranks x as the worst of all social states. If the social-choice correspondence Φ satisfies no-veto, what can you say about Φ evaluated at these preferences?

■ 26.6. Again consider Maskin's Theorem. Suppose there are three citizens: Alice, Bob, and Carol. Suppose there are three social states: Conservative wins, Labour wins, and Liberal wins. Restrict attention to antisymmetric preferences only.

a. Suppose the social-choice correspondence is: If a majority of the citizens strictly prefers one party to each of the other two, that party alone is acceptable. If a majority of the citizens places a party in third place, that party is not acceptable. Except for these two rules, parties are acceptable. Can this social-choice rule be implemented in the sense of Maskin?

b. Suppose the mechanism is First-Past-the-Post voting where, if there is a tie for outcome with the most votes that includes Conservative, then Conservative wins, and if there is a tie between Labour and Liberal (but not Conservative), then Labour wins. What social-choice correspondence Φ does this mechanism implement?

■ 26.7. Prove the second part of Proposition 26.10 (that truth telling is the only (weakly) dominant strategy for the VCG mechanism).

■ 26.8. On page 453 (at the bottom of the page), I ask you to remove the vagueness of my assertions. Do so. To give you a hint, here is how the solution in the *Online Supplement* approaches this problem. Fix a set of N citizens. Now consider what happens as we "replicate" those N citizens; in the Kth "replica" economy, there are KN citizens, K with the preferences over social states of the original citizen #1, K with the preferences of the original citizen #2, and so forth. If (fill in a condition here), then for all large enough K, the VCG mechanism will require no payment by any one of the KN citizens.

■ 26.9. Prove Proposition 26.11. What can be said about efficient matches, if we do not insist on $U_{ik} > 0$ for all i and k?

■ 26.10. Prove Proposition 26.12.

■ 26.11. The Kelso and Crawford algorithm, put in the context of the assignment problem of Section 26.5, assumes that sellers tentatively agree to sell their item to whichever buyer is offering the best price, with ties somehow resolved. Suppose instead that we allow sellers to refuse all offers. (This is entirely consistent with the Kelso and Crawford model if we assume that sellers, if they retain the item, get a (private-information) positive payoff from doing so.) Show that, in this case, behaving as postulated in the Kelso and Crawford algorithm may not be optimal for sellers.

■ 26.12. In the context of both the assignment-auction problem (each bidder wants/ gets at most one item) and the package-auction problem (bidders can get packages with more than one item), suppose that all the items are identical. In the context of the package-auction, substitutability implies that the value any bidder i attaches to a package of n items, which I'll write U_{in}, is such that $n \to U_{in}/n$ is nonincreasing.

What can you say about the pivot form of the VCG mechanism in these cases? Discuss this in general, and then discuss how Proposition 26.14 specializes (or doesn't) in these cases.

■ 26.13. In terms of participation constraints, what may seem like a third possibility is to allow bidders to opt in *only if* their expected payoff is positive (after they receive any private information); in an equilibrium, only a subset of types may choose to opt in, so the mechanism specifies outcomes if a subset of bidders choose "not participating." Why does optimizing with this sort of participation constraint give the same optimal auction design as does the interim participation constraint as defined in the text?

■ 26.14. With reference to footnote 19 on page 470, suppose that after the submission of V, every virtual valuation $\zeta_i(V_i) < 0$ but, inverting the ζ_i to find each V_i, it turns out that one or more $V_i > 0$. Why, in such circumstances, would the seller of the item want to "recontract?" Would this be a problem if the rules of the mechanism were changed to be: Bidder i should submit a valuation $\hat{v}_i$ if $\zeta_i(\hat{v}_i) \geq 0$, but if $\zeta_i(\hat{v}_i) < 0$, he is allowed to walk away. (Payment rules are as in Part 2 of Myerson's Theorem, Proposition 26.21.)

■ 26.15. Suppose Carol wishes to sell an indivisible item to either Alice or Bob. Suppose Carol has no interest in retaining the item; she attaches zero value to it. Suppose Alice and Bob have independent values for the item. Bob's value is distributed on the interval $[0, 10]$, with a uniform distribution. Alice's value has the same support, but the cumulative distribution function for her value is $F_A(v_A) = v_A^2/100$. What is Carol's expected revenue if she auctions off the item using a second-price auction with no reserve price? (Assume that Alice and Bob use their weakly dominant strategies.) What is Carol's expected revenue if she auctions off the item using a second-price auction with an optimal reserve price ≥ 0? (You must find the optimal reserve price.) What is Carol's expected revenue if she auctions off the item using Myerson's optimal auction under these circumstances? And, for Myerson's optimal auction, build a diagram that is a square, $[0, 10] \times [0, 10]$ for all possible valuations by Alice and by Bob, showing three regions: Where Carol retains the item; where she sells it to Alice; and where she sells it to Bob.

Feel free to resort to numerical methods to answer any or all parts of this question.

■ 26.16. On page 475, I describe a simple mechanism that arrives at an efficient outcome in the classic bilateral bargaining problem, that satisfies interim participation constraints on both side, but that (unhappily) requires an outside infusion of cash.

a. I describe this mechanism in footnote 20 (also page 475) as nothing more than the VCG mechanism. Explain why this description is accurate.

b. On the subject of the VCG mechanism and, in particular, the pivot form of the VCG mechanism, discuss how the general pivot VCG mechanism connects to the general concept of "interim participation constraints."

c. Suppose we looked at the Myerson–Sattherwaite context, but without assuming that V_A and V_B are independent, so that (for instance) Alice, conditional on V_A, has a conditional assessment about the distribution of V_B. In that context, what can you say about the mechanism described on page 475? Does it still give an efficient outcome? Does it still satisfy the interim participation constraints? Does it still require an infusion of outside cash? (The answer to the first two questions is yes. The answer to the third question is a qualified yes. Your job is to check that this is so and to give the qualification for the third question.) So, then, why can't I wave my hands and conclude that, per payoff equivalence, the extra cash required by this mechanism will be required by any mechanism that achieves efficiency and satisfies the interim participation constraints? (This is an easy question: A one-sentence answer will do.)

Appendix Nine

Strategic-Form Games

About the appendices

These appendices provide a sketch of those portions of noncooperative game theory that are employed in Volume II, together with a substantial amount of commentary about the use of noncooperative game theory in microeconomic theory. (The final two appendices discuss the revelation principle and the envelope theorem, tools that are used in the last few chapters of the volume and, in particular, in Chapter 26, concerning mechanism design.)

The appendices *are not* a substitute for a textbook in noncooperative game theory, in my opinion. Most importantly, they lack exercises for you to do. There are a number of excellent textbooks out there, and I urge you to consult one or more of these, if you are learning this material for the first time. These appendices are meant for review and to set terminology as it is used in the text; I also take the opportunity to offer my own opinions about some of the tools and concepts.

A9.1. Basic Definitions

A strategic-form game is specified by three elements:

1. A set $\mathcal{N}$ of *players*.

2. For each player $n \in \mathcal{N}$, a set S_n of feasible *strategies*. From these sets of feasible strategies, the set of *strategy profiles* $S := \prod_{n \in \mathcal{N}} S_n$ is constructed. We use s_n to denote a typical member of S_n and $s = (s_n)_{n \in \mathcal{N}}$ to denote a typical strategy profile.

3. For each strategy profile s and each $n \in \mathcal{N}$, a *payoff* $v_n(s)$ for player n if s is the profile played; formally, $v : S \to R^{\mathcal{N}}$.

In some applications, the set of players $\mathcal{N}$ can be infinite. But we will mostly be concerned with games with a finite number of players. Unless otherwise indicated, assume throughout that $\mathcal{N}$ is a finite set of N players. In formal statements, the players are ennumerated, so that $\mathcal{N} = \{1, \ldots, N\}$. (In examples, players are often given names.)

We do not restrict attention to games where each player has a finite set of feasible strategies. In particular, in many applications, the S_n are subsets of R^k for some finite k. But when we refer to a *finite strategic-form game*, we mean a game in which both $\mathcal{N}$ and all the S_n are finite.

In what follows, we often discuss how a player n's payoff changes as the player changes her strategy, holding fixed the strategies chosen by other players. The following notation and terminology are used:

- For a player n, let $S_{\neg n} := \prod_{n' \in \mathcal{N}, n' \neq n} S_{n'}$, with typical element $s_{\neg n}$; we refer to $S_{\neg n}$ as a *strategy profile for all players except* n.

- For $s_{\neg n} \in S_{\neg n}$ and $s_n \in S_n$, $(s_n, s_{\neg n})$ is used for the full strategy profile in which n chooses s_n and everyone except for n chooses according to $s_{\neg n}$.

- And $v_n(s_n, s_{\neg n})$ denotes the payoff to n under this full strategy profile.

In Chapter 14 of Volume I, on page 339, the concept of a *generalized game* is introduced. The adjective "generalized" refers to the notion that player n's choice of strategy may be constrained by the strategy choices of other players. In standard strategic-form games, this notion is not employed, although we could incorporate it surreptitiously by assuming that payoffs $v_n(s)$ are drawn from $[-\infty, \infty)$ and assigning $v_n(s) = -\infty$ if player n's strategy choice s_n is incompatible with the strategy choices $s_{\neg n}$.

When there are only two players and each player has a finite set of strategies, the game is represented in *bimatrix* form, as in Figure A9.1. In such figures, one player chooses a row, the second a column, and their payoffs are presented in the corresponding cell, with the row-choosing player's payoff always listed first. For instance, in Figure A9.1, the two players are Alice, who chooses as her strategy one of three rows (that is, $S_{\text{Alice}} = \{\text{Row 1, Row 2, Row 3}\}$), and Bob, who chooses as his strategy one of four columns. If Alice chooses the third row and Bob the fourth column, the payoffs are 3 for Alice and 5 for Bob.

		Bob's choice			
		Column 1	Column 2	Column 3	Column 4
	Row 1	5, 1	4, 2	6, 0	2, 3
Alice's choice	Row 2	4, 2	5, 5	8, 5	4, 6
	Row 3	3, 6	4, 3	7, 2	3, 5

Figure A9.1. A strategic-form game with two players in bimatrix form

While many of the games used to illustrate concepts in this appendix are two-player, finite-strategy games (as in Figure A9.1), we also discuss other, more complex games. One such game is the following takeoff on the Keynes *Beauty Contest*: For a finite number N of players, each player has as strategy set $S_n = [0, 100]$. For a strategy profile s, let $\gamma(s) = 0.7\left(\sum_{n=1,\ldots,N} s_n\right)/N$. That is, $\gamma(s)$ is 70% of the average of the strategies chosen in s. Payoffs are determined by computing

$$\beta_n(s) = |s_n - \gamma(s)|, \quad \beta^*(s) = \min_{n=1,\ldots,N} \beta_n(s), \quad \text{and}$$

$$v_n(s) = \begin{cases} 0, & \text{if } \beta_n(s) \neq \beta^*(s), \text{ and} \\ 1000/M(s), & \text{if } \beta_n(s) = \beta^*(s), \end{cases}$$

where $M(s)$ is the number of players for whom $\beta_n(s)$ is equal to $\beta^*(s)$. That is, each player chooses a number between 0 and 100, and the winner is whoever chooses a number closest to 70% of the average number chosen, with the prize (1000) split evenly in case of ties.

So much for the definition of a strategic-form game. It is to be understood that

- each player in the game selects a strategy from her set of feasible strategies "simultaneously and independently" (where the scare quotes will be explained below), and

- each player chooses a strategy with the objective of maximizing her (expected) payoff. (What about risk aversion? Payoffs in the game are meant to represent the utility to each player of the physical "outcomes" of the game, where each player is an expected-utility maximizer.)

We generally (which is to say, not always) imagine that each player n forms by some means a *hypothesis* as to the strategy choices $s_{\neg n}$ of her opponents, taking the form of a probability assessment over $S_{\neg n}$. Player n, having come up with that assessment, chooses from S_n a strategy that maximizes the expectation of her payoff. (Where the strategy sets are more than countably infinite, some technical restrictions on these probability assessments on $S_{\neg n}$, such as measurability, are likely to be required to ensure that the player's expected payoff makes sense. And if v_n is unbounded, [finite] integrability must be addressed.)

And having formulated a strategic-form game, we seek answers to the questions: Can we predict which strategies the players will choose? Can we at least predict which strategies will *not* be chosen? And, related to this: What sorts of restrictions on or properties of each player's assessment make sense?

Modeling considerations

Before taking up these questions, a word from our "sponsor," namely economics. It is simple to list the constituent parts of a strategic-form game: players; strategies; payoffs. But when one builds a strategic-form-game model of some economic context, choices must be made. Who are the players? How wide a net do you, as model creator, cast when determining the involved individuals? To give an example that will play a very important role in Volume III, suppose you are modeling an employer–employee relationship. This is the stuff of Chapter 19, where principal–agent models are discussed, and, in most of the models of Chapter 19, there is one principal and one agent. However, in real-life employer–employee relationships, how one employee is treated by his employer affects the relationship between the employer and other employees. This isn't entirely ignored in Chapter 19; near the end, we discuss incentive schemes based on comparative evaluation of performance. But, for the most part, the focus is on one employer and one employee.

When (and if) we get to such matters in Volume III, I will assert that this can be a terribly short-sighted way of thinking.

Similarly, in a model, the decision on how to model strategies available to the players can affect what is learned from the analysis. Examples of this influence are found throughout the chapters of this volume, so I leave this for now.

As for the selection of payoffs: In standard noncooperative game theory, the type employed in this volume, the assumption is that players seek to maximize their payoffs and, insofar as they aren't sure what will happen (say, because they aren't certain what the other players will do), they seek to maximize their *expected* payoffs. Payoffs, then, are in the units of some von Neumann–Morgenstern or Savage style utility function, with the assumption that expected-utility representations of the players' preferences are appropriate. Assuming that players are expected-utility maximizers is by itself a modeling choice. But, beyond this, what are the units of these "payoffs?" In most of the models in this volume, the models are based on "risk neutrality in monetary units." That is, payoffs are equated with money (or profits, or the net present value of a stream of net cash flows). In some models— most notably, in principal–agent models—risk aversion (for dollar rewards) plays an important and explicit role. And in many instances, payoffs are based on a (cardinal) utility function that is quasi-linear in money. For instance, in Chapter 24, concerning auctions, bidders are assumed to attach a dollar value to some item that they may purchase, and if they get the item, the payoff is that dollar value less whatever they pay.

These are not considerations in *game theory* per se. Payoffs in game theory are...payoffs. But when we apply game theory to study economic phenomena, modeling choices must be made that can be crucial to what emerges.

A9.2. Mixed Strategies: Simple and Otherwise

Fix a strategic-form game, and take a player n and her strategy set S_n. A *mixed strategy* for the player is a probability measure σ_n on S_n, with the interpretation that player n chooses her strategy in a fashion such that the probability that her choice comes from a set $\hat{S}_n \subseteq S_n$ is $\sigma_n(\hat{S}_n)$. You may encounter the term "randomized strategy" in your reading; it means the same thing. And a "pure strategy" means a probability-one choice of some s_n from S_n.

If S_n is a finite set or even countable, no mathematical difficulties intrude: We can identify a mixed strategy σ_n with the probabilities that it ascribes to each individual strategy, writing $\sigma_n(s_n)$ for the slightly more appropriate $\sigma_n(\{s_n\})$. But if S_n is uncountable—say, a subset of R^k for some integer k—we will need to worry about measurability of sets $\hat{S}_n$. And even if steps are taken so that measurability is not an issue, depending on the behavior of v_n, integrability can become an issue.

For our immediate purposes, we can avoid these difficulties by restricting play- ers to so-called *simple* mixed strategies: probability measures σ_n on S_n with finite support. This provides the convexification needed for later results, while avoiding mathematical difficulties. And, of course, for games in which strategy sets S_n are finite, it is not a restriction at all.

However, in Section A9.5, when we get to Glicksberg's existence theorem, and in a few places in the text itself, more complex notions of mixed strategies will be required. They will be explained depending on the context.

Mixed strategies play several roles. (1) As discussed in this appendix, they are used in discussing dominance of strategies. You'll see what this means in Section A9.3. (2) Mixed strategies are important in games where players do not wish to be predictable by their rivals. Most readers will know that, in the children's games *matching pennies* and *rock, paper, scissors*, as well as the more grown-up game *poker*, being predictable allows rivals to exploit you. (Poker is an "action, reaction" game, so it doesn't quite fit in this Appendix, but the point is the same.) Specific examples where mixed strategies are required to avoid being predictable in significant economic contexts exist; Problem 20.9 provides an example of random auditing of tax returns by the government. (3) Mixing plays a role in games of incomplete information (a type of game is described in Appendix 13), where one type of economic agent pretends to be a different type; see, for instance, the analysis of Abreu and Gul (2000) in Chapter 23.

The following notation is used: For any set X, $\mathbf{P}(X)$ is the set of simple probabilities on X. For a given game, $\Sigma_n := \mathbf{P}(S_n)$ denotes the set of (simple) mixed strategies for player n. Finally, extend v_n to the domain $\Sigma_n \times S_{\neg n}$ by

$$v_n(\sigma_n, s_{\neg n}) := \sum_{s_n \in \text{supp}(\sigma_n)} \sigma_n(s_n) v_n(s_n, s_{\neg n}), \text{ for } \sigma_n \in \Sigma_n \text{ and } s_{\neg n} \in A_{\neg n},$$

where $\text{supp}(\sigma_n)$ means the (finite) support of σ_n.

A9.3. Dominance: What (Probably?) Won't Happen

Definition A9.1. *For a player n and two strategies s_n and s'_n from S_n, s_n* **strictly dominates** *s'_n if, for every $s_{\neg n} \in S_{\neg n}$, $v_n(s_n, s_{\neg n}) > v_n(s'_n, s_{\neg n})$. Strategy s_n* **weakly dominates** *s'_n if $v_n(s_n, s_{\neg n}) \geq v_n(s'_n, s_{\neg n})$ for all $s_{\neg n} \in S_{\neg n}$, with a strict inequality for at least one $s_{\neg n}$.*

If s_n strictly dominates s'_n, then no matter what strategies $s_{\neg n}$ are chosen by players other than n, Player n does strictly better with s_n than she does with s'_n. So, the story goes, if Player n is at all rational, she will not choose s'_n. If s_n weakly dominates s'_n, the force of this logic is weaker; Player n might do just as well with s'_n as with s_n. But if Player n assesses positive probability that a strategy profile $s_{\neg n}$ for which there is a strict inequality will be chosen by others, then she is strictly better off in expectation with s_n than with s'_n, and so the choice s'_n "probably" won't happen.

Two qualifications to these assertions are required. The first is that Player n is rational, meaning here that she acts as an expected-payoff maximizer for some assessment as to what her rivals will do. As we'll see, this is just the start of "rationality" assumptions that are made.

The second qualification is that Player n believes her choice of strategy s_n has no impact on the strategy choices of other players. Or, more precisely, her assessment of what others will do is unaffected by her own choice of strategy. To see why this qualification must be made, go back to Figure A9.1. Note that Row 2 dominates Row 3. But suppose that, for some reason, Alice believes that if she chooses Row 2, Bob is very likely to choose Column 2, while if she chooses Row 3, he is very likely to choose Column 3. Then by choosing the dominating Row 2, she is very likely to accrue a payoff of 5, while if she chooses the dominated Row 3, she assesses that she is very likely to get payoff of 7. Why, then, would she choose the dominating Row 2?

This takes us back to the presumption in that each player chooses a strategy "simultaneously and independently." "Independence" here is taken to mean that what one player does cannot and does not influence the choices of other players. Alice's assessment of what others will do is independent of her own choice.

This assumption is worth a moment's thought, at least. Consider the two-player game depicted in Figure A9.2, the famous *Prisoners' Dilemma*. For both Alice and Bob, "Betray" dominates "Cooperate." However, my experience staging this game with a variety of audiences is that "Cooperate" is often selected. One reason given, and perhaps the most important reason, is that the two players have an ongoing relationship with each other and with others who are observing how the two play this game—think of two students in an MBA program who value their reputation with their peers—so that the benefits of winning a bit more money (the payoffs represent, say, dollars paid at the end of the game) are outweighed by the future cost of being known to classmates as "the person who chose to betray a classmate." But "Cooperate" is frequently chosen even when the game is staged in a way that hides the players' choices from public view. And one explanation students offer goes something like: "My opponent is someone just like me. So if I choose 'betray,' it means that people like me make that choice. If I choose 'cooperate,' then people like me make that choice. So I should choose 'cooperate'; we are both better off."

	Bob	
	Betray Alice	Cooperate with Alice
Alice — Betray Bob	0, 0	20, −10
Alice — Cooperate with Bob	−10, 20	10, 10

Figure A9.2. Alice and Bob play the Prisoners' Dilemma

When subjects give this argument, I chide them, saying that they are engaging in magical thinking; why would their personal choice "magically" change what others do?[1] And game theory—at least, standard game theory, the type used in

---

[1] If you have never encountered Newcomb's Paradox, I suggest you search for it on the web and do a bit of reading.

this volume—rejects this form of magical thinking, so we reject it as well, at least in the current volume.[2]

Strict domination by mixed strategies

Now consider the game depicted in Figure A9.3. Neither row strictly dominates the other, and no column dominates any other. However, suppose Bob, who is choosing the column, decides to mix between Columns 1 and 2, playing each with probability 0.5. If Alice plays Row 1, Bob's expected payoff is 5, which is strictly better than the 2 that Bob would get from Column 3. And if Alice plays Row 2, Bob's expected payoff is 5, strictly better than the 3 he would get from Column 3. So, if Bob considers playing mixed strategies, Column 3 is strictly dominated by this mixture (among others).

	Bob		
	Column 1	Column 2	Column 3
Row 1	5, 0	2, 10	1, 2
Row 2	0, 10	1, 0	7, 3

(Alice chooses the row)

Figure A9.3. Dominance with mixed strategies

With this example in mind, we can extend Definition A9.1.

Definition A9.1'. *For a player n, a mixed strategy $\sigma_n \in \Sigma_n$, and a pure strategy s'_n from S_n, σ_n **strictly dominates** s'_n if, for every $s_{\neg n} \in S_{\neg n}$, $v_n(\sigma_n, s_{\neg n}) > v_n(s'_n, s_{\neg n})$. Mixed strategy σ_n **weakly dominates** s'_n if $v_n(\sigma_n, s_{\neg n}) \geq v_n(s'_n, s_{\neg n})$ for all $s_{\neg n} \in S_{\neg n}$, with a strict inequality for at least one $s_{\neg n}$.*

It goes almost without saying that skepticism about the prediction that players avoid strictly dominated strategies can only intensify with this extended definition.

Iterated strict dominance—the theory

Go back to the two-person game in Figure A9.1. Row 2 strictly dominates Row 3, and Column 4 strictly dominates Columns 2 and 3. So Alice (who chooses a row) will not choose Row 2, and Bob will not choose either Column 2 or Column 3. Or so the theory says, and for now, just accept the theory. Then Bob, thinking about what Alice might do, "ought" to conclude that she won't choose Row 3. And if Row 3 is out of the question, in what remains, Column 4 strictly dominates Column 1. So Bob, anticipating that Alice will not choose Row 3, sees Column 4 as the obvious choice. And if Alice gives Bob credit for these thoughts, she "ought" to anticipate that he will choose Column 4, so she should to choose Row 2. This is *iterated strict dominance*. To proceed formally, we begin with the following definition.[3]

---

[2] Insofar as we want models that predict how real individuals behave, rejecting this way of thinking is a flaw, not a feature, which deserves re-examination and, perhaps, revision in applications that are more behaviorally grounded.

[3] The scare quotes around "ought" are explained in the next subsection.

Definition A9.2. *Fix a strategic-form game and, for each $n \in \mathcal{N}$, a subset $\hat{S}_n$ of S_n. Write $\hat{S}_{\neg n}$ for $\prod_{n' \neq n} \hat{S}_{n'}$. Say that $\sigma_n \in \mathbf{P}(\hat{S}_n)$ **strictly dominates** $s_n \in \hat{S}_n$ **relative to** $\hat{S}_{\neg n}$ if, for every $s_{\neg n} \in \hat{S}_{\neg n}$, $v_n(\sigma_n, s_{\neg n}) > v_n(s_n, s_{\neg n})$.*

Since $\mathbf{P}$(anything) is the set of simple probability distributions on the set "anything," this definition, and Definition A9.1', should properly talk about domination in *simple* mixed strategies. The definitions could be extended to more complex mixtures; in some games, doing so increases what is dominated. For instance, suppose Alice has (pure) strategies $\{a_0, a_1, \ldots\}$, Bob has strategies $\{b_1, b_2, \ldots\}$, if Alice chooses a_0 and Bob chooses b_j, Alice's payoff is $1/2^{j+1}$, and if Alice chooses a_i, $i \geq 1$, and Bob chooses b_j, Alice's payoff is 1 if $i = j$ and 0 otherwise. Then a_0 is not strictly dominated by any simple mixed strategy of Alice, but it is dominated by the mixed strategy where she chooses a_i, $i \geq 1$, with probability $1/2^i$.[4] That said, if Bob has only finitely many pure strategies, then Definition A9.2 is fully adequate; there is no need for more complicated mixtures. (Reason: Carathéodory; see Volume I, Proposition A3.5.)

Note that, in this definition, we speak of a *pure* strategy s_n being dominated by a *mixed* strategy σ_n (relative to some $\hat{S}_{\neg n}$). What about mixed (or pure) strategies dominating *mixed* strategies? Consider the game in Figure A9.4. None of Bob's three (pure) strategies is dominated by any of his mixed strategies (relative to all of Alice's strategies); this is easily seen by noting that Column 1 is a strict best response to Row 2, Column 2 is a strict best response to Row 1, and Column 3 is a strict best response to Row 3. But the mixed strategy for Bob in which he chooses Column 1 with probability $1/2$ and Column 2 with probability $1/2$ is strictly dominated by the choice of Column 3.

		Bob		
		Column 1	Column 2	Column 3
	Row 1	10, 0	0, 5	0, 3
Alice	Row 2	0, 5	0, 0	10, 3
	Row 3	0, 0	1,0	0, 3

Figure A9.4. Mixtures of strictly undominated strategies can be strictly dominated

Therefore, it strengthens the implications of Definition A9.2 to have mixed strategies dominated by other mixed strategies. But we won't need this strengthening for later purposes, so we stick with Definition A9.2.

Two questions arise in the context of Definition A9.2. First, is it possible that *every* pure strategy in a strategy set $\hat{S}_n$ is strictly dominated (relative to some $\hat{S}_{\neg n}$) by some mixed strategy $\sigma_n \in \mathbf{P}(\hat{S}_n)$? And second, is it possible that two pure

---

[4] Now you construct an example where both players have strategy sets $[0, 1]$ and Alice needs to mix over all strategies in $(0, 1]$ to dominate her 0 strategy.

strategies s_n and $s'_n \in \hat{S}_n$ are both strictly dominated, with s_n needed for a mixed strategy that dominates s'_n and vice versa? Certainly, the former is possible when the set $\hat{S}_n$ is infinite: Think of a one-player game in which $\hat{S}_n = \{1, 2, 3, \ldots\}$, and the player's payoff from choosing s_n is s_n. But neither of these unsavory possibilities can happen if $\hat{S}_n$ is finite.

Proposition A9.3. *Suppose that $\hat{S}_n$ is a finite set. Following the notation in Definition A9.2, and relative to an arbitrary set of pure strategy profiles $\hat{S}_{\neg n}$ for the other players, let $\hat{B}_n$ denote the set of pure strategies out of $\hat{S}_n$ that are strictly dominated (relative to $\hat{S}_{\neg n}$) by some mixed strategy for n, σ_n, from $\mathbf{P}(\hat{S}_n)$. Then $\hat{S}_n \setminus \hat{B}_n$ is nonempty, and every pure strategy $s'_n \in \hat{B}_n$ is strictly dominated by a mixed strategy σ_n whose support consists solely of strategies from $\hat{S}_n \setminus \hat{B}_n$.*

Proof. For the first assertion (nonemptiness of $\hat{S}_n \setminus \hat{B}_n$), take any $s_{\neg n} \in \hat{S}_{\neg n}$, and let s_n be a strategy that maximizes $v_n(s_n, s_{\neg n})$ over $s_n \in \hat{S}_n$. (The existence of such a maximizer is obvious, since $\hat{S}_n$ is assumed to be finite.) Then no mixed strategy $\sigma_n \in \hat{\Sigma}_n(\hat{S}_n)$ can strictly dominate s_n; that is, $s_n \in \hat{A}_n \setminus \hat{B}_n$.

The second assertion takes a bit more work. Suppose that $s_n \in \hat{B}_n$. Then some $\sigma_n \in \mathbf{P}(\hat{S}_n)$ strictly dominates s_n. I assert that some $\sigma'_n \in \mathbf{P}(\hat{S}_n)$ that assigns zero probability to s_n strictly dominates s_n: Construct σ'_n from σ_n by deleting s_n from the support of σ_n (if indeed s_n is in the support of σ_n), renormalizing the probabilities of s'_n to sum to one. The necessary strict inequalities follow trivially. And then, I assert that every $s^{\sharp}_n \in \hat{B}_n$ is strictly dominated by some $\sigma^{\sharp}_n$ that assigns zero probability to s_n; since $s^{\sharp}_n \in B_n$, there is a mixed strategy $\sigma^{\flat}_n \in \mathbf{P}(\hat{S}_n)$ that strictly dominates it; construct $\sigma^{\sharp}_n$ from $\sigma^{\flat}_n$ by replacing s_n, if it is in the support of $\sigma^{\flat}_n$, with σ'_n.

Now move on to the case where $s'_n \in \hat{B}_n$, $s'_n \neq s_n$, assuming that one such exists. We know that s'_n is strictly dominated by some mixed strategy that avoids s_n. Apply the first argument of the previous paragraph to show that s'_n is strictly dominated by a mixed strategy that avoids both s_n and s'_n, and then use the second argument to show that every $s^{\sharp}_n \in \hat{B}_n$ is strictly dominated by a mixed strategy that avoids both s_n and s'_n. Proceed inductively. Since $\hat{B}_n$ contains a finite number of pure strategies, the proposition follows. ∎

(Can anything positive be said about cases where $\hat{S}_n$ is not finite? As an exercise, you are invited to ponder what happens if, say, $\hat{S}_n$ is compact and v_n is continuous.)

Definition A9.2 and Proposition A9.3 are used as follows.

Definition A9.4.

  a. *The **maximal iterated strict dominance procedure** for a given strategic-form game begins by letting $S^0_n = S_n$, $S^0 = S$, and $S^0_{\neg n} = S_{\neg n}$. Then, for $k = 1, 2, \ldots,$*

recursively define

$$B_n^k := \left\{ s_n \in S_n^{k-1} : s_n \text{ is strictly dominated by some } \sigma_n \in \mathbf{P}(S_n^{k-1}) \text{ relative to } S_{\neg n}^{k-1} \right\},$$

$$S_n^k := S_n^{k-1} \setminus B_n^k, \text{ and } S_{\neg n}^k := \prod_{n' \in \mathcal{N}, n' \neq n} S_n^k.$$

b. *Strategy $s_n \in S_n$ is said to be **iteratively strictly dominated** if $s_n \in B_n^k$ for some $k = 1, \ldots$.*

c. *Define $S_n^* := \cap_{k=1}^{\infty} S_n^k$ for each $n \in \mathcal{N}$, then s_n is said to be **iteratively strictly undominated** if $s_n \in S_n^*$.*

d. *If, for a given game, each S_n^* is singleton, the game is said to be **solvable by iterative strict dominance**.*

This definition is less complicated than it may seem. Beginning with all the strategy profiles S^0, B_n^1 consists of all (pure) strategies for player n that are strictly dominated by some other (mixed) strategy for n. Therefore, S_n^1 is the set of strategies for player n that are not strictly dominated, and S^1 is the set of all profiles that consist of strategies that are not strictly dominated. Then, recursively, B_n^2 are all strategies for player n that were not "eliminated" in moving from S_n^0 to S_n^1 and that are strictly dominated, *if players other than n choose strategies from their sets S_m^1* (for $m \neq n$). And so on.

For instance, for the game in Figure A9.1, $B_{\text{Alice}}^1 = \{\text{Row 3}\}$, so $A_{\text{Alice}}^1 = \{\text{Row 1}, \text{Row 2}\}$, while $B_{\text{Bob}}^1 = \{\text{Column 2, Column 3}\}$ and (therefore) $S_{\text{Bob}}^1 = \{\text{Column 1}, \text{Column 4}\}$. That's the first stage; in the second, $B_{\text{Bob}}^2 = \{\text{Column 1}\}$ and so $S_{\text{Bob}}^2 = \{\text{Column 4}\}$, while in this second stage, Alice eliminates nothing: $S_{\text{Alice}}^2 = S_{\text{Alice}}^1 = \{\text{Row 1, Row 2}\}$. But in the third stage, Alice eliminates Row 1, so $S_{\text{Alice}}^3 = \{\text{Row 2}\}$, and nothing further happens at any subsequent stage.

From Proposition A9.3, we know that if each S_n is finite, this procedure never eliminates all strategies. And it is evident that, if each S_n is finite, then the procedure must terminate in finitely many steps.

Before discussing how well iterated strict dominance predicts behavior, one piece of theory is left to mention. Definition A9.2 gives a definite procedure for how to perform iterated strict dominance: On each round or stage, as many strategies as possible for each player are simultaneously deleted. In applying iterated strict dominance, however, an analyst may deviate from this specific procedure. For instance, the analyst might start by deleting all (pure) strategies strictly dominated by other pure strategies for one player, then (with those deletions) going on to do the same thing for a second player, and so forth, and only when that process stalls (in the sense that there are no more deletions of pure strategies by pure strategies) looking for strict domination by mixed strategies. The question is: Will such alternative procedures matter in the end?

For games in which players have finitely many strategies, alternative procedures must get to the same end point, as long as they follow one rule: They don't stop if there are still strictly dominated strategies (including strategies strictly dominated by mixed strategies) left to dominate. I won't subject you to a full-blown proof, but here is the idea: (1) If a strategy s_n is strictly dominated by σ_n relative to strategies by the other players $\hat{S}_{\neg n}$, then it is strictly dominated by σ_n relative to strategy sets $\check{S}_{\neg n}$, if $\check{S}_{\neg n}$ consists of an array of "other than n" pure strategies smaller than those in $\hat{S}_{\neg n}$. This is an obvious consequence of the "for all $S_{\neg n}$" part of the definition of strict dominance. (2) If some strategy or strategies are eliminated in any stage relative to some set of strategies for opponents, the second half of Proposition A9.3 shows that those strategies are strictly dominated by mixtures of strategies that remain after the deletion. (3) Hence, for any strict-elimination procedure that doesn't stop as long as there are more pure strategies that (relative to what is left) are strictly dominated, it must be that all the strategies in B_n^1 must be eliminated. They are strictly dominated relative to the original set of "other than player n" $S_{\neg n}$, so reducing the set of strategies available to "other than n" doesn't make them less susceptible to strict domination. And, for the mixed strategy σ_n formed by mixtures of strategies in S_n^1 that eliminated a strategy from $a_n \in B_n^1$, if some of its component parts are removed before getting to s_n, then (perhaps in several steps) those components can be replaced by strategies that were instrumental in removing the component parts. The full-blown proof is a bit messy, but fairly straightforward. And, once it is clear that all strategies from B_n^1, for all n, must go, the argument extends inductively to all strategies from B_n^2, for all n, and so forth.

Of course, no such result is feasible for games in which players have infinitely many strategies, since the countably many steps involved in a alternative procedure might be "used up" before some dominated strategies are ever reached.[5]

Iterated strict dominance—reality

The prediction that goes with all this theory is that no (rational) player will ever play a strategy that is iteratively strictly dominated, *as long as that player believes that all other players are equally "rational."* The scare quotes around "rational" signal that rationality as used here is a fairly deep concept. To take a new example, consider the game depicted in Figure A9.5.

| | | Bob | |
	Column 1	Column 2	Column 3
Row 1	7, 3	3, 1	0, 5
Row 2	5, 1	5, 3	2, 2

(Alice labels the rows; Bob labels the columns.)

Figure A9.5. Another game in which iterated strict dominance applies.

Column 3 strictly dominates Column 1, so (the story goes) Bob will never choose Column 1. Alice, giving Bob credit for being rational enough to come to this conclusion, then sees that, with Column 1 out of consideration, Row 2 strictly dominates

---

[5] If you love abstract theory, consider this question where, instead of countably many steps, you enlist a transfinite induction.

Row 1. And Bob, giving Alice credit for (1) giving Bob credit enough not to play Column 1 and, therefore, (2) realizing that she should choose Row 2, understands his choice comes down to getting 3 if he chooses Column 2 and 2 if he chooses Column 3, so he chooses Column 2. Note that this isn't just a matter of Bob giving Alice credit for being rational. He believes that she believes that he is rational (enough not to pick Column 1) and to derive the rational conclusion therefrom. In the literature of game theory, justification for iterated dominance in general (for any number of back-and-forth stages) takes so-called "common knowledge of rationality."[6]

This explains the scare quotes around the word "ought" twice, back on page 495. In the context of the game in Figure A9.5, Bob "ought" not choose Column 1; to do so is clearly irrational. But, can we say that Alice "ought" not choose Row 1? This conclusion requires that she believe that Bob will never do what he "ought" not do. And, that's debatable, at least.

How well does this reasoning do in real life? I asked a group of eighty students in a professional master's degree program how they would play this game, if paired against a fellow student, prior to our discussion of iterated dominance. The first-round prediction that no one would pick Column 1 was largely borne out; only 11% chose Column 1. The second-round prediction that no one would pick Row 1 also did fairly well; only 17% chose Row 1. But the third-round prediction that no one would pick Column 3 (hence everyone would pick Column 2) failed badly: 27% chose Column 2, while 62% chose Column 3.

Apologists for game theory (and, in this instance, for iterated strict dominance) offer at least two "excuses" for such behavior:

1. The stakes (2 = $2, etc.) are not high enough for subjects to take the questions seriously.

2. The subjects know that they are not playing a rational opponent. (That said, if a "rational" subject choosing a column correctly predicted that his rival would choose Row 1 with probability 0.17, the expected payoff from Column 3 is 2.51 versus an expected payoff of 2.66 from Column 2. So a column-chooser with "rational expectations" about what the row-chooser will do still ought to choose Column 2.)

The apologist would then go on to say:

3. "Game theory (only) predicts how fully rational players will interact."

4. And game theory provides more advanced techniques (discussed in Appendix 13) that deal with cases in which some opponents are less than "fully rational."

Both statements 3 and 4 are true (although the notion of "full rationality" requires a definition). But surely they should temper your confidence in prediction based on iterated strict dominance for real-life situations.

---

[6] *Common knowledge* as a formal concept is discussed in Appendix 13, although "common knowledge of rationality" as an "axiom" of so-called epistemic game theory is not. If you are interested, a fairly recent treatment of these issues—and the subject of rationalizability that will shortly be explored—is Dekel and Siniscalchi (2015).

And note that this example involves iterated strict domination of pure strategies by pure strategies. The theory involves domination of pure strategies by mixed strategies, which requires still more "rationality" on the part of real-life subjects, as well as the attribution of such "greater rationality" to one's opponents.

Iterative elimination of weakly dominated strategies

One can also think of iteratively applying weak domination. Unhappily, iterative elimination of weakly dominated strategies can be path dependent. Consider the game in Figure A9.6. Row 3 weakly dominates Rows 1 and 2, while neither column dominates the other, so if we eliminate everything we can (using weak dominance) in the first round, we are left with Row 3, both columns. Since Column 1 gives the same payoff as Column 2, that's the end.

	Column 1	Column 2
Row 1	0, 0	2, 4
Row 2	5, 3	0, 0
Row 3	5, 4	2, 4

Figure A9.6. A game in which iterated weak dominance is path dependent

But suppose we eliminate only Row 1 first. Then Column 1 weakly dominates Column 2. With Column 2 gone, Rows 2 and 3 are the same for the row-chooser, so we end with Rows 2 and 3 and Column 1.

And if we eliminate only Row 2 first, then Column 2 weakly dominates Column 1. Once Column 1 is gone, Rows 1 and 3 give the same payoff to the row-chooser, and we end with Rows 1 and 3 and Column 2.

The bottom line is that one needs to be careful with iterative elimination of weakly dominated strategies, when the game allows more than one path for eliminating strategies. Nonetheless, this process can be applied to solve games that are less made up than the game in Figure A9.6. Consider, for instance, the game in which players try to get as close as they can to 70% of the average of all players' submissions. Recall that each player has as strategy set $[0, 100]$. Clearly, the average of all submissions can be no larger than 100, and 70% of that is 70. Submitting 70, then, weakly dominates submitting anything larger than 70; whatever is 70% of the average submissions, 70 is closer than is anything above 70, so it gives no smaller chance of winning the prize and is actually a winner if there are a lot of other players, all of whom submit 100.

But then, if all strategies greater than 70 are eliminated for all players, the average submission can be no larger than 70, 70% of which is 49. So iterative weak dominance eliminates all strategies above 49. And then all strategies above 70% of 49, or 34.3, are eliminated, and so forth: The only strategy for each player that survives is 0.

It probably doesn't need saying that the objection to iterated strict dominance as a method for predicting the play of real-life subjects applies with at least as much force, and probably more, to iterated weak dominance. I have played the 70%-of-the-average game twice with the same 80 professional-degree-program students, where a prize of $50 was split among those who were closest to 70% of the average submission. The first time I played the game, the average submission was 28.2847, so the winning bid was whichever bid was closest to 19.799. (To be precise, I limited submissions to integer amounts from 0 and 100, which slightly affects the final stages of iterated weak dominance.) We discussed this result in class, and I had the students play it again, knowing how the first round of play had gone; in this second round, the average submission fell to 16.585, 70% of which is 11.61, so the winning submission (of which there were four) was 12. Only 12% of the students submitted either 0 or 1, the "rational-if-everyone-is-rational" submissions. But the hypothesis that "everyone is rational"—essential to this conclusion—is certainly not empirically borne out. In fact, in the first round of play, several students submitted more than 70, and even after discussing the first round of play, five out of the eighty students submitted more than 50.

A9.4. Rationalizability: A Seemingly Different Take on What Won't Happen

Dominance is based on the idea that a strategy for Player n won't happen, because there is some other (perhaps mixed) strategy that is bound to do better. Rationalizability approaches the question of what won't happen differently: Player n, assumed to be an expected-payoff maximizer, won't choose s_n because no "rational" beliefs justify that choice.

An issue to settle right away concerns the nature of beliefs. Each player n is choosing her strategy s_n to maximize her subjective expected payoff, given her beliefs over the strategy choices of her rivals. Her rivals are choosing some strategy profile $s_{\neg n} \in S_{\neg n}$, so it seems sensible, at the outset, to suppose that n's beliefs take the form of a probability distribution on $S_{\neg n}$.

There are two problems with this supposition, one technical and one conceptual. Taking the technical problem first, if the strategy sets $S_{n'}$ for $n' \neq n$ are more than countably infinite, care is required in defining probabilities over $S_{\neg n}$. We avoided such issues earlier in this chapter by assuming that players only contemplate simple (finite-support) mixtures of pure strategies. But it is hard to justify an assumption that players' assessments of what their opponents might do are limited to simple probability assessments. For the remainder of this section, we avoid all such issues by assuming that each $S_{n'}$ is finite.

The second, conceptual problem concerns the possibility of correlation in subjective assessments and rates an entire subsection.

The issue of correlation in subjective assessments

This problem arises when there are more than two players in the game, so suppose there are three. What sorts of beliefs can Player 1 have concerning the choices of Players 2 and 3? Specifically, can Player 1 believe that the choices of Players 2 and 3 are correlated?

For instance, suppose Alice, Bob, and Carol play the following game. Bob and Carol are engaged in a coordination game historically called the "Battle of the Sexes."[7] The game is as depicted in Figure A9.7(a). Bob and Carol are (physically independently and simultaneously) choosing whether to go to one of two locations. For each, going to the location that the other chooses is better than going to the unchosen location, but Bob otherwise prefers Location A and Carol prefers Location B. For simplicity, I'll assume that Alice's choice of action has no impact on the payoffs to Bob and Carol.

	Carol	
	Location A	Location B
Bob — Location A	10, 8	0, 2
Bob — Location B	2, 0	8, 10

(a) Bob and Carol don't care what Alice does

	Bob and Carol both at Location A	Bob and Carol both at Location B	Bob and Carol at different locations
Alice — Location A	10	0	0
Alice — Location B	0	10	0
Alice — Location C	7	7	0
Alice — Location D	6	6	6

(b) Alice's payoff depends on her choice and the choices of Bob and Carol

Figure A9.7. Is Alice's choice of Location C rationalizable? (See text)

But their choices, along with Alice's choice, affect Alice's payoff. Specifically, if she is pretty sure they are both going to either Location A or Location B, and if she assesses high probability to which they are going, she wishes to join them. If she is fairly sure that they will go to the same location, but she is relatively unsure which one it will be, then a third location is best for her. If she believes that their choices will not match, she strongly prefers a fourth location. See Figure A9.7(b); this table

---

[7] I think the value of linking this discussion to a sizeable historical literature outweighs the cost of transgressing against politically correct norms, and so, with apologies to those who are offended, I'll use the historical name.

gives the payoffs to Alice (only), as a function of the choices of Bob and Carol and her own choice.

Obviously, if Alice assesses probability 1 that both Bob and Carol will choose Location A, which is an assessment of statistically independent strategies for the two of them, then choosing Location A is optimal for her. Similarly, Alice's choice of Location B can be rationalized by an assessment (by her) that Bob and Carol are both choosing Location B, each with probability 1. And Alice's choice of Location D is rational if she assesses that both Bob and Carol are each (independently) randomizing between A and B with probability $1/2$ each, so each of the four possibilities (both at A, Bob at A and Carol at B, etc.) have probability $1/4$. In this case, Alice choosing Location A gives her $10/4$, Location B gives her $10/4$, and Location C gives her $7/2$, all less than the sure 6 she gets by choosing Location D. (Location D is also her best choice if she believes that Bob will go to Location A with probability 1 and Alice will go to Location B with probability 1.)

Can the choice of Location C for Alice be rationalized? It can be, for instance, if Alice assesses probability $1/2$ that Bob and Carol will both be at A and $1/2$ that they will both be at B. But if her assessments of their choices are statistically independent—if she assesses probability p that Bob will go to Location A and q that Carol will go to Location A, *and $p \times q$ that they will both go there*—then for no values p and q is the choice of Location C for Alice rational. (I leave it to you to carry out the algebra that shows this.) That is, if we insist that Alice's assessment of Bob's and Carol's strategies reflects statistical independence, we cannot rationalize a choice of Location C by Carol. If we allow correlated (non-independent) assessments, we can.

I previously argued that a player ought to believe that her own choice of strategy is independent of the choices of others. In other words, she should not condition her assessment of what others are doing on her own (allegedly free) choice. Recall in this context the discussion of the Prisoners' Dilemma and so-called magical thinking. By analogy, since the story is that players choose their strategies "simultaneously and (physically) independently," shouldn't her assessment of each rival's choice be statistically independent of what other rivals are doing?

In my opinion, the answer is that physical independence should not imply statistical independence in subjective assessments. By analogy, think of the flipping of a bent coin. Each consecutive flip may well be physically independent of previous flips, but unless and until one knows the bias of the coin, it is witless to suppose that one's subjective assessments reflect independence. If, for instance, I told you that on 1000 previous flips of the coin, it came up heads 657 times, your assessment of heads on the next flip would surely be different than if I had told you it came up heads 322 times. The same logic holds here. Alice, if she is unsure what Bob and Carol will do, could be unsure because she thinks they are randomizing. If that is the source of her uncertainty, and if she thinks they are randomizing independently, then an assessment that reflects that independence may be warranted. But if her uncertainty is because she isn't sure what people like Bob and Carol do, then dependence in her subjective assessment is entirely natural. Or so it seems to me.

Having said all this, I warn you that (otherwise) intelligent people hold the view that, when it comes to rationalizability, assessments by one player concerning the strategy choices of two or more opponents should reflect independence. If you consult the literature, watch out for this (I say, mistaken) view.

Rationalizability versus strict dominance

Proposition A9.5. *Fix a (finite player and strategy) strategic-form game with the usual notation. Strategy s_n is strictly undominated if and only if it is rationalizable in the sense that, for some probability distribution π on $S_{\neg n}$,*

$$\sum_{s_{\neg n} \in S_{\neg n}} \pi(s_{\neg n}) v_n(s_n, s_{\neg n}) \geq \sum_{s_{\neg n} \in S_{\neg n}} \pi(s_{\neg n}) v_n(\sigma_n, s_{\neg n}) \quad \textit{for all } \sigma_n \in \Sigma_n.$$

Proof. This is obvious in one direction. If s_n is strictly dominated by, say, the mixed strategy σ_n, then $v_n(\sigma_n, s_{\neg n}) > v_n(s_n, s_{\neg n})$ for all $s_{\neg n}$, and since probabilities are nonnegative and, for at least one $s_{\neg n}$, strictly positive, the strict inequality

$$\sum_{s_{\neg n} \in S_{\neg n}} \pi(s_{\neg n}) v_n(\sigma_n, s_{\neg n}) > \sum_{s_{\neg n} \in S_{\neg n}} \pi(s_{\neg n}) v_n(s_n, s_{\neg n})$$

must hold for every probability distribution π on $S_{\neg n}$.

In the other direction, fix player n, and consider the set

$$X = \left\{ x \in R^{S_{\neg n}} : x(s_{\neg n}) = v_n(\sigma_n, s_{\neg n}) \quad \text{for some } \sigma_n \in \Sigma_n \right\}.$$

This set is clearly convex (the mixture of two mixed strategies for n is a mixed strategy for n, and v_n is linear in the mixing probabilities in σ_n). Now suppose s_n is not strictly dominated by any mixed strategy. For this s_n, let

$$Y = \left\{ y \in R^{S_{\neg n}} : y(s_{\neg n}) > v_n(s_n, s_{\neg n}) \text{ for each } s_{\neg n} \in S_{\neg n} \right\}.$$

This set is obviously convex. And because s_n is not strictly dominated by any mixed strategy for n, $X \cap Y = \emptyset$. Apply the separating hyperplane theorem: for some nonzero vector π and scalar γ, $\pi \cdot x \leq \gamma$ for all $x \in X$ and $\pi \cdot y \geq \gamma$ for all $y \in Y$. Since $v_n(s_n, \cdot) + (\epsilon, \epsilon, \ldots, \epsilon) \in Y$, by letting ϵ go to zero, it must be that $\pi \cdot v_n(s_n, \cdot) = \gamma$. And π is nonnegative: If some component of π were negative—say, $\pi(\neg n) < 0$—then by looking at the vector in Y that is $v_n(s_n, \cdot) + z$, where $z(s_{\neg n}) = 1$ for $s_{\neg n} \neq \hat{s}_{\neg n}$ and $z(\hat{s}_{\neg n})$ is large and positive, by driving $z(\hat{s}_{\neg n})$ to infinity, $\pi \cdot z$ goes to $-\infty$, contradicting the fact that $\pi \cdot y \geq \gamma$ for all $y \in Y$. Renormalize the (nonnegative, nonzero) π so its components add to one, and it is a probability over $S_{\neg n}$ that rationalizes s_n. ∎

Now we iterate: Fix a (finite player and strategy) strategic-form game, and initiate in precisely the same fashion as in Definition A9.4. But define B_n^1 differently: Have it consist of all strategies for player n that cannot be rationalized by a probability distribution over $S_{\neg n}^0$. And then continue, where at each stage, you throw out strategies for each player that cannot be rationalized by probability assessments over the strategies that remain (after the last stage) for the other players. Proposition A9.5 immediately implies that, at each stage, each player is left with precisely what she had at the corresponding stage in Definition A9.4. So, *iterating rationalizability is just iterating strict dominance (by mixed strategies) by another name, but with a different story.*

Why would one iterate rationalizability? The same "my opponents are just as rational as me" as in iterated strict dominance is at work: A given player will never play a strategy that cannot be rationalized by some assessment over her rivals' actions. Her rivals give her credit for this, so they assess zero probability to any profile by their opponents that involve strategies that cannot be rationalized. This (potentially) removes more not-rationalizable strategies, since it reduces the set of assessments that can be used to rationalize one's own strategy. And, moving to the third round, each player gives her rivals credit for not playing strategies that cannot be rationalized with some assessment that avoids strategies that cannot be rationalized in the first stage. And so forth.

But one warning must be included: In Proposition A9.4 and the discussion that follows from it, rationalizability is defined relative to arbitrary (that is, not-necessarily-independent-across-rivals) assessments of rivals' strategy profiles.[8] If you insist that rationalizing assessments must reflect independence, things are not so neat, unless the number of players is two (so the issue doesn't arise). Since I believe assessments that reflect correlation are sensible, I'm not troubled by this issue. But game theory texts that you consult may make a big deal about this point.

A9.5. Nash Equilibrium

The following definition formalizes some terminology and notation set earlier. And then, it adds a new concept: Nash equilibrium.

Definition A9.6. For a given strategic-form game:

a. A *(simple) mixed-strategy profile* is an N-tuple of **simple** mixed strategies, one for each player. Let Σ denote the set of mixed-strategy profiles; that is, $\Sigma := \prod_{n \in \mathcal{N}} \Sigma_n$, with generic element denoted by $\sigma = (\sigma_1, \dots, \sigma_N)$. Write $\Sigma_{\neg n}$ for a profile of mixed strategies for all players except for n: $\Sigma_{\neg n} := \prod_{n' \in \mathcal{N}, n' \neq n} \Sigma_{n'}$, with generic element $\sigma_{\neg n}$.

b. For a mixed-strategy profile σ, write $\pi(\sigma)$ for the induced probability distribution or measure on S, and write $\pi(\sigma_{\neg n})$ for the induced probability measure on $S_{\neg n}$,

---

[8] The separating hyperplane π that is normalized to give the rationalizing assessment need not reflect independent choices by rivals.

both assuming statistical independence in the choices of different players. That is, for $s = (s_1, \ldots, s_n) \in S$, $\pi(\sigma)(s) = \sigma_1(s_1) \times \ldots \times \sigma_N(s_N)$, where it is understood that $\sigma_n(s_n) = 0$ if s_n is not in the (finite) support of σ_n. (And similarly, for $\pi(\sigma_{\neg n})$.)

c. *For a mixed-strategy profile σ, a player n, and a strategy s_n for player n, let*

$$v_n(s_n, \sigma_{\neg n}) = \sum_{s_{\neg n} \in S_{\neg n}} v_n(s_n, s_{\neg n}) \, \pi(\sigma_{\neg n})(s_{\neg n}),$$

where the sum is "really" only over the finitely many terms $s_{\neg n}$ for which each $s_{n'}$, $n' \neq n$, is in the support of $\sigma_{n'}$.

d. *A **Nash equilibrium** is a mixed strategy profile $(\sigma_n)_{n \in N}$ such that, for each n and for each s_n in the support of σ_n, $v_n(s_n, \sigma_{\neg n}) \geq v_n(s'_n, \sigma_{\neg n})$ for all $s'_n \in S_n$.*

Because we are limiting mixed strategies to *simple* mixed strategies—that is, where each player mixes over finitely many pure strategies, the definitions of $\pi(\sigma)$ and $\pi(\sigma_{\neg n})$ are reasonably straightforward. If we allowed more complex mixtures (which we will do in specific cases in the text), similar definitions would apply where $\pi(\sigma)$ and $\pi(\sigma_{\neg n})$ would be product measures built from the σ_n.

Of course, the set of probability measures $\{\pi \in \mathbf{P}(S) : \pi = \pi(\sigma)$ for some $\sigma \in \Sigma\}$ is (as long as $N \geq 2$) a strict subset of $\mathbf{P}(S)$, the space of simple probability measures on pure-strategy profiles S, because, for any σ, $\pi(\sigma)$ reflects statistical independence among mixing undertaken by different players. This probably didn't need saying, but it is safer to say it explicitly, to avoid any possible confusion.

Before discussing the "meaning" of Nash equilibrium, two observations are in order. First, some games have several Nash equilibria. If we ignore Alice in the game between Bob and Carol depicted in Figure A9.7, it is obvious that Location A for Bob combined with Location A for Carol is a Nash equilibrium: If Bob chooses Location A, Location A is Carol's best response, and vice versa. But Location B for each is a second Nash equilibrium.

And there is a third. Suppose Bob mixes between locations, going to Location A with probability 5/8 and to Location B with probability 3/8. Then if Alice chooses Location A, her expected payoff is $(5/8)(8) + (3/8)(0) = 5$. And if she chooses Location B, her expected payoff is $(5/8)(2) + (3/8)(10) = 10/8 + 30/8 = 40/8 = 5$. So Carol is indifferent between going to Location A and going to Location B, and she is indifferent between those pure strategies and any mixture of them. If she mixes between Location A with probability 3/8 and Location B with probability 5/8, Bob is indifferent among his two pure strategies and all mixtures of them. So the strategy profile where Bob and Carol each mix in precisely this fashion is a third, *mixed-strategy* equilibrium.

Mixed-strategy Nash equilibria in games like the game in Figure A9.7 (so-called *coordination games*) may seem silly as predictions of how people play such games, but in other contexts—for instance, matching pennies, rock-paper-scissors, or poker, in which players don't want to be predictable—they are entirely natural.

Nash equilibrium as necessary for "an obvious way to play"

Many papers in economics—indeed, many sections of chapters in this volume—invoke the concept of Nash equilibrium in more or less the following fashion. A stylized game-theoretic model of some real-life context of interest is created. (The models are typically more complex than simple strategic-form games, but that doesn't affect the immediate discussion.) A Nash equilibrium for the game is described, and properties of the equilibrium are pointed out as insightful of what we see in the real-life context being modeled. That the behavior described constitutes a Nash equilibrium is advanced as a virtue; indeed, the mere fact that the behavior is a Nash equilibrium is sometimes viewed as sufficient justification for considering the behavior as insightful concerning how real players would behave in a real-life context. To be fair to the use of Nash equilibrium in economics, it is usually the case that the equilibrium in the model is justified based on properties that go beyond simply being a Nash equilibrium, such as, it is a perfect Nash equilibrium; or off-path beliefs (whatever they are) satisfy some "reasonableness" criterion; or it is the unique equilibrium. Such so-called *refinements* of Nash equilibrium are discussed in Appendices 11, 12, and 14. The obvious question is: What is virtuous about being a Nash equilibrium? To answer this question, a small excursion is required.

Begin with a game, and suppose that every player, considering the game, believes that there is an obvious way for everyone to play, so obvious that each player believes that every other player comes to precisely the same conclusion. Such games do exist. For instance, consider the game depicted in Figure A9.8, where the payoffs are denominated in dollars or thousands of dollars. I expect that anyone in the role of Alice would choose Row 1, confident that the column-chooser will pick Column 2 in anticipation that the row-chooser is going to choose Row 1.

		Bob	
		Column 1	Column 2
	Row 1	1, 1	25, 30
Alice			
	Row 2	2, 2	1, 1

· Figure A9.8. A game with an obvious way to play

You would be right to argue that this is a fairly obvious "game," (1) one for which the formal mechanics of game theory are unnecessary to understand, and (2) in any case, one that is unlikely to be of much value in studying economic phenomena. But at least, it illustrates that the concept of a game with an obvious way to play is not vacuous.

And, if a game has an obvious way to play, one that is obvious to all players, and one for which it is obvious to all of them that it is obvious to all their rivals in the game, then this obvious way to play necessarily constitutes a Nash equilibrium.

Why? Because if it is obvious, then each player n anticipates what his or her rivals will do, and if her strategy s_n (or σ_n, if she is mixing) is not a best response to what she fully anticipates her rivals will do, then (if we assume she is trying to maximize her expected payoff, which is always maintained) she would defect and choose a better response. The definition of a Nash equilibrium is simply that each player is playing some best response to what the others are doing.

What about games without an obvious way to play? What is the relevance or virtue of Nash equilibrium in such cases? In this regard, consider the game depicted in Figure A9.9. Row 1–Column 1 is a Nash equilibrium, as is Row 2–Column 4. And there is a mixed-strategy Nash equilibrium in which Bob mixes between Column 1 and Column 2. But in *no* Nash equilibrium does Bob choose Column 3 with positive probability. And yet, based on evidence from staging this game with students (payoffs in dollars), I anticipate that most individuals—perhaps I should say, most Stanford MBA students—placed in the role of Bob, would choose Column 3. Unravel this by putting yourself in the place of Bob, who explains his choice of Column 3 as follows:

> The two candidates for an obvious way to play are the Row 1–Column 1 equilibrium and the Row 2–Column 4 equilibrium. The first is better for both of us than is the second, so maybe that is the obvious way to play. But I [Bob] am at great risk if I choose Column 1. Alice knows this, and so she may anticipate that I'll play the safe strategy Column 3, which induces her to choose Row 2. Indeed, Alice might think that I think that she may play Row 2 for the reason just given, in which case Row 2 is her better choice. So perhaps I should avoid the dangers of Columns 1 or 2. But then, it would seem that Alice should pick Row 2, which makes Column 4 better for me. But what if Alice compares Row 1–Column 1 with Row 2–Column 2 and concludes that, since the first is Pareto superior, it should be obvious that this is what we do? Then Column 4 is dangerous for me. So, not being sure what Alice is thinking, the safe choice of Column 3 is best for me.

		Bob		
	Column 1	Column 2	Column 3	Column 4
Alice Row 1	200, 6	3, 5	4, 3	0, –50
Row 2	0, –100	5, –50	6, 3	3, 5

Figure A9.9. A game where the most likely choice by Bob is the only strategy that is part of no Nash equilibrium

I might fairly be accused of turning Bob in a game-theoretic version of indecisive Hamlet in the foregoing paragraph. I can certainly be accused of rigging the example. But to supplement Bob's indecisive explanation, think in terms of rationalizability. Suppose Bob assesses probability p that Alice will choose Row 1. If you do the math, you'll find that for p between 0.0365 and 0.963, Bob's expected payoff is maximized with Column 3. Of course, my choice of large negative payoffs for Bob is how I rigged this. Even so, it should weaken your faith in any claim that *the play of strategies that are part of no Nash equilibrium can be ruled out.* So, to return to the question that opened this subsection: What is the virtue, within a game-theoretic model of some real-life phenomenon, of some pattern of behavior being a Nash equilibrium? I can propose two possible (positive) answers.

1. The proposed strategy profile/behavior is for some *other* reason "the obvious way to play" in the particular context. Then the fact that it is a Nash equilibrium is a check that this obvious way to play doesn't involve one of the players acting stupidly, by failing to maximize her expected payoff.[9] But in such cases, being a Nash equilibrium per se doesn't tell you that the profile is the obvious way to play. You need some other reason to think so, and any modeling exercise that asserts this ought to supply those other reasons. The next subsection provides some possibilities.

2. More speculatively, and in the spirit of exemplifying modeling (see Chapter 17), the proposed strategy profile/behavior is advanced as way that matters might possibly arrange themselves. To take an example from Appendix 15 and Chapter 22, the Folk Theorem tells us how and when oligopolists *might* collude, not that they will. In such exemplifying-modeling exercises, the claim is that (for reasons perhaps unstated) this might be the obvious (and, one hopes, interesting) way to play for the participants in the interaction. And, then, being a Nash equilibrium is a virtue, because once again, it means the behavior passes the first test that no player is acting stupidly.

Why (when) might there be an obvious way to play

A variety of reasons are sometimes given for why, in a particular game, some strategy profile is the obvious way to play. Some are structural; that is, they are free of the context that the game is intended to model and depend only on the strategic nature of the iterations. Others depend heavily on the specific context in which the game is played. In the list to follow, I move (more or less) from structural to contextual.

Dominance solvability

To the extent that you believe that iteratively dominated strategies will not be played, you must believe that, in a game that is dominance solvable (at least, by iterated strict domination), the strategy profile that remains is the obvious way to play the game; every other strategy profile is eliminated. We have the following proposition.

Proposition A9.7. *Suppose S_n is finite for each n. If the game is dominance solvable by iterated strict dominance, the single strategy profile that remains is a Nash equilibrium, and no other strategy profile is a Nash equilibrium.*

Proof. Suppose the game is dominance solvable, with $s^* = (s_1^*, \ldots, s_N^*)$ the one strategy profile that survives. Fix a player n, and suppose that s_n^* is not a best

---

[9] I apologize to behavioral economists who think in terms of satisficing or otherwise less-than-maximizing behavior. In this volume, we don't admit to such things, although when we get to games with incomplete information in Appendix 13, we'll sneak them in through the back door.

response to s^*_{-n}; let s^1_n be a better response. Since s^1_n did not survive iterated strict dominance, there was a stage at which some mixed strategy σ^1_n was strictly better than s^1_n against all remaining strategy profiles for $\neg n$. That mixed strategy can be assumed to be constructed from strategies that survive the round in which s^1_n was eliminated. And so by simple properties of convex combinations, some one of the pure strategies s^2_n that make up σ^1_n must be strictly better than s^1_n against s^*_{-n}, hence strictly better than s^*_n against s^*_{-n}. Repeat the argument for s^2_n. That is, we have a chain of strategies for n, $s^1_n, s^2_n, \ldots$, each of which is eliminated at a later stage than those that precede it, each of which is strictly better against s^*_{-n} than is s^*_n. But, for a finite game, this chain must stop, since strict iterated dominance stops at some finite time, which is a contradiction.

Now suppose s^* is the unique strategy profile that survives iterated strict dominance but that $s' = (s'_1, \ldots, s'_N)$ is another Nash equilibrium for the game. Since this is a different Nash equilibrium, for some n, $s'_n \neq s^*_n$. So in some round, for some player n, s'_n is eliminated by iterated strict dominance. Let $\hat{n}$ be the player for whom this happens earliest. That is, in the round that $s'_{\hat{n}}$ is eliminated, none of the component parts of s' were eliminated earlier. And if some mixed strategy strictly dominates $s'_{\hat{n}}$ against everything remaining from the previous period, it strictly dominates $s'_{\hat{n}}$ against $s'_{-\hat{n}}$, which means that s' is not a Nash equilibrium, a contradiction.   ∎

What if the S_n are not finite? The second half of the proof—if all strategy profiles except for a single s^* are eliminated by iterated strict dominance, then there can be no Nash equilibrium except for s^*—nowhere invokes the finiteness of the S_n. But the first half—that the sole surviving profile s^* is a Nash equilibrium—certainly does need finiteness of the S_n. The following example is dominance solvable, and the strategy that survives is *not* a Nash equilibrium. (The second half of the proposition holds even when the sets S_n are not finite, which means that, in the example, no strategy profile is a Nash equilibrium.)

The game involves two players, each of whom has strategy set $S_n = \{0, 1, 2, \ldots\}$. The payoff functions for the players are symmetric, and writing $v_1(n, m)$ for the payoff to the first player if she chooses n and he (her rival) chooses m, suppose

$$
v_1(n, m) := \begin{cases} 0, & \text{if } n = 0 \text{ and } m = 0, \\ 1, & \text{if } n = 0 \text{ and } m \neq 0, \\ n/(n+1), & \text{if } n > 0 \text{ and } m = 0 \text{ or } n > 0 \text{ and } m \geq n - 1, \text{ and} \\ 0, & \text{if } n \geq 0 \text{ and } 0 < m \leq n - 2. \end{cases}
$$

In case this format is incomprehensible, Figure A9.10 provides $v_1(n, m)$ in tabular form, where the rows are n and the columns are m.

Note that strategy 2 strictly dominates strategy 1, but there is no other strict domination. However, once strategy 1 is eliminated (for both players), strategy 3 strictly dominates strategy 2 for both. And so forth: Each strategy n is, in turn, iteratively strictly dominated by $n + 1$, leaving only strategy 0 for each player. But

Other player's strategy

		0	1	2	3	4	
	0	0	1	1	1	1	
This	1	1/2	1/2	1/2	1/2	1/2	
player's	2	2/3	2/3	2/3	2/3	2/3	etc.
strategy	3	3/4	0	3/4	3/4	3/4	
	4	4/5	0	0	4/5	4/5	
	5	5/6	0	0	0	5/6	

etc.

Figure A9.10. The payoff function for a somewhat strange game. For a symmetric game with two players, each of whom has strategy space $\{0, 1, 2, \ldots\}$, the figure provides the payoff to a player as a function of her choice (the rows) and her rival's choice (the columns). Iterated strict dominance leaves only the profile 0 against 0, which is *not* a Nash equilibrium.

0 versus 0 is *not* a Nash equilibrium; any other strategy by one player is better than 0 if the second player chooses 0.

This result does not mean that dominance solvability as a rationale for the obvious way to play the game is useless in games where strategy sets are infinite. If a game with infinite strategy sets is dominance solvable, and *if* the sole surviving strategy profile is a Nash equilibrium—see Chapter 18 and the analysis of the classic Cournot game—perhaps on grounds of dominance solvability, you can believe that this profile is the obvious way to play.

But I remind you of the discussion concerning iterated strict dominance versus real-world behavior on page 497. The more rounds of iteration that are required, the less confident you should be that this is a valid way to predict behavior.

And then there is iterated weak dominance. For finite-strategy games, if the application of iterated weak dominance leads to a single strategy profile, that profile will be a Nash equilibrium. The proof given above works with little modification. But you do not get uniqueness. (I will return to this in Appendix 11, which concerns credibility of promises and threats.)

Uniqueness

Uniqueness of a Nash equilibrium is sometimes offered as justification for that strategy profile as the obvious way to play the game. In practice, this rationale is more often applied to some refinement of Nash equilibrium, as in "this game has a unique perfect equilibrium" or "this game has a unique equilibrium with off-path beliefs that satisfy the intuitive criterion."[10]

This type of rationale is used frequently in the text; see Chapter 19 and also Appendix 11 for the simplest examples, based on the logic of fait accompli and ex post credibility. But, when it is used, it is the logic of the rationale that justifies its use, and not simply the uniqueness that it engenders. Uniqueness as an equilibrium in and of itself can be insufficient.

Although it is (as such examples must be) concocted, consider the following

---

[10]   These refinements of Nash equilibrium are discussed in Appendices 11, 12, and 14.

two-person game: Each player has the feasible strategy set $\{0\} \cup [1, 2)$. If both choose 0, both get \$10. If one chooses 0 and the other a number from $[1, 2)$, both get \$0. If both choose a number from $[1, 2)$, the person choosing the smaller number gets \$20 and the person choosing the larger number gets \$21. Clearly, both choosing 0 is a Nash equilibrium. Because the alternative to choosing 0 is a set that is open at 2, and choosing a larger number than your rival is better for you, there are no other Nash equilibria. Even so, I imagine—and I hope you agree—that most people will choose a number in $[1, 2)$.[11]

I reiterate: Uniqueness (as a Nash equilibrium plus more) is used frequently, and it will be used frequently in the text. But it is not uniqueness per se that is persuasive; instead, what is (or is not) persuasive are the qualities that make the strategy profile/behavior "unique."

Mutual interest versus safety

I suggested that the game in Figure A9.8 has an obvious way to play, and the reason is clear: For both Alice and Bob, the strategy profile Row 1 and Column 2 is in their mutual interest. For each, it gives them their largest possible payoff, and while Row 2–Column 1 is another Nash equilibrium, there is little risk and much to gain by trying for the Row 1–Column 2 equilibrium.

Mutual interest, when it exists, can be a powerful argument. But one shouldn't lose track of the risk–reward trade-offs involved in the particular game. See the game in Figure A9.9, for instance. Or consider the following game, played by, say, ten players. Each player has two possible strategies; each $S_n = \{\text{Risk, Safe}\}$. If all ten players choose Risk, each gets \$20. If any player chooses Safe, that player is guaranteed \$15. And if a player chooses Risk, while any other player chooses Safe, the player choosing Risk gets \$0. This game has two Nash equilibria: One is where everyone picks Risk and gets \$20; the second is where everyone picks Safe and gets \$15. If instead of ten players there were only two, it might be that the logic of mutual interest would lead each to choose the mutually better Risk. But, with ten, I'd bet (once again, based on informal experiments with students) that most would choose Safe. And note: Suppose, playing this game, you think it very likely that any individual rival will choose Risk. To make the scenario concrete, suppose you assess probability 0.95 that each of your nine rivals will choose Risk, and you assess independence in these choices. (This last part is not innocuous, of course.) Then the odds that all nine will choose Risk is around 0.63, so that choosing Safe gives you a higher expected value.[12]

Learned behavior and stability

Imagine that a large number M of individuals play some N-player game repeatedly, where M is much larger than N, and one's rivals in any repetition of the game is a random and anonymous selection of $N - 1$ from the $M - 1$ other players. Each player, in each repetition, chooses a strategy that maximizes her immediate ex-

---

[11] The uncountable nature of the strategy sets is not the issue. You can construct a similar example where each player's strategy set is $\{0, 1, 2, \ldots\}$.

[12] In case you encounter it in your reading, this example is based on a classic two-player game known as the *Stag Hunt*.

pected payoff given her assessment of how rivals play the game, where that assessment is informed by (and adapted to) the history of past play. *This assumption — that each player chooses in each repetition based on her short-run interest and given her updated assessment — is more or less justified by random and anonymous matching of players from a much larger population.* This is so because, while a player's choice in any round of play might have an effect on what others do in the future, these assumptions make that effect very small relative to immediate concerns.[13]

If individuals in this population converge in behavior to some fixed choice of strategies, and *if* their learning therefore leads them to assess that this fixed choice is how their rivals behave, then the fixed "limit" must be a Nash equilibrium. Moreover, for specified learning dynamics and some source of "perturbation" to membership in the larger population—say, some members leaving, being replaced by new arrivals—attention can be limited to equilibria that are dynamically stable.

A lot of assumptions and *if*s go into the story of the previous paragraphs; I do not go further into this learning-story justification for Nash equilibrium. If you wish to see it spelled out, a good source is Fudenberg and Levine (1998).

Social custom

Consider the problem of walking on a sidewalk and encountering someone walking in the other direction. Each individual has a choice of moving to the right or the left. Suppose payoffs are as in Figure A9.11. There are two "obvious" Nash equilibria: Both move to the left; and both move to the right. Neither is more obvious than the other, simply on structural (context-free) grounds. However, in a well-mannered society (which, unhappily, does not completely describe pedestrian traffic at Stanford University), one or the other might be the custom, which then makes it a custom that is in everyone's interest to obey. And this would make whichever custom takes hold "the obvious way to play."

	Move left	Move right
Move left	1, 1	0, 0
Move right	0, 0	1, 1

Figure A9.11. Two pedestrians approach one another on a sidewalk . . .

At Stanford University, the general custom is to move to the right. Not everyone you meet on the sidewalks of Stanford adheres to this custom (and people engaged with their cell phones have reduced adherence). But the percentage who do is high enough so that moving to the right is the best strategy to try. Compare, in this regard, walking up or down Fifth Avenue in New York when the sidewalks are

---

[13] Be careful here. It is not simply a matter of thinking that you are unlikely ever to meet your current rivals again or, assuming your payoffs are discounted from one round to the next, you won't meet any current rival again for a long, long time. It is possible that what you play today affects one of your current rivals' future play, and that affects someone that one of your current rivals meets in the very near future, whom you will then meet in the near future. Formal analyses of this sort of "contagion" or diffusion of behavior exist in the literature; for now, I'll simply say that the argument here requires that M is significantly larger than N.

full. It may be that I don't understand the custom, but if there is one, I have been unable to comprehend it. (The copyeditor suggests that the custom in New York City is "chicken.")

Custom can work in games with asymmetric equilibria, in which case they are not so arbitrary. Consider two vehicles encountering one another on a steep one-lane road. One vehicle must pull to the side (and come out worse than if the other vehicle deferred). So who defers? The availability of a shoulder on one side or the other might be dispositive. If there is sheer drop on one side or the other, that might do it. Everything else being equal, the vehicle going downhill is expected to defer (and, in fact, this custom is codified in law, at least in the state of California).

Other examples involve getting in or out of elevators, who holds the door for whom, whether one queues or "mobs." In some cases, the custom is fairly universal. In others, social custom is different depending on the specific society. These examples might seem too pedestrian (ouch!) to care about, but underlying issues of deference and privilege—who gives way to whom—can play an important role in efficient economic and social exchange.

Focal points

Alice and Bob have agreed to meet in New York City on May 1 at 5 p.m., after which they will go to dinner. But, unhappily, they forgot to say where they would meet. What should they do? This story typically concludes with the two independently deciding to go to the observation deck of the Empire State Building, with a happy ending ensuing. Why this location? Because it is both unique and prominent, which makes it a *focal point*.

I don't put a ton of faith in this story. What about the Meeting Spot at Grand Central Station? What about Battery Park (at the very southern tip of Manhattan)? While the story is somewhat fanciful, the notion of a focal point is not. Let me provide another example.

Here is a list of nine cities in the United States: Baltimore, Boston, Chicago, Denver, Los Angeles, New York, Philadelphia, San Francisco, and Seattle. Two business school students, both born and raised in the United States, one from Harvard Business School (HBS) and one from Stanford Graduate School of Business (GSB), must simultaneously and independently list a subset of these nine, where the HBS student *must* include Boston on her list, and the GSB student *must* include San Francisco. In strategic-form-game terms, each has a strategy set of size 2^8, all subsets of the "other" cities to add to their mandated choice. As for payoffs: For each city on one list and not on the other, the student listing the city gets $2. For any city on both lists, each student loses $4. And if their lists exactly partition the set of nine cities—if each city is on one but only one list—in addition to the prizes above, each gets an additional $25.

There are $2^7 = 128$ pure strategy equilibria in this game, corresponding to all divisions of the seven cities that are not already assigned. With that many ways to coordinate, it seems unlikely that the $25 prize will be won. However, when I've played this game with students, they get it "right" a surprising fraction (less than 50% of the time, but more than 25%), and the percentage of times that they coordinate to the more limited extent that there are no overlaps is well above 50%. How? The student who must include Boston chooses Baltimore, Boston (of course), Chicago, New York, and Philadelphia, or, at least, a subset of those five. And the student who must include San Francisco chooses Denver, Los Angeles, San Francisco, and Seattle, or a subset thereof. The focal point here is a east versus west division.

By changing the contextual details of the game, while preserving its essential (strategic) structure, I can increase or decrease the focality of the outcome. For one thing, with nine cities, a partition involves one student having more cities, hence a bigger payoff, than the other. Adding Phoenix to the list fixes this. More significantly, a second "focal" equilibrium uses alphabetical order to divide the cities, with Baltimore, Boston, Chicago, Denver, and (perhaps) Los Angeles on one list. (Because there are nine cities and alphabetical order doesn't specify who gets Los Angeles, adding a tenth city might on those grounds *increase* the focality of alphabetical order and, therefore, *decrease* the focality of geographic split.) But if I specify that the "east coast" role is a student from the Wharton School of Business, who must list Philadelphia, an alphabetical split becomes less focal and, therefore, the geographic split becomes more focal. Substituting, say, Minneapolis and New Orleans for Baltimore and Seattle makes the geographic split less focal. Finally, I specified that the two players were both born and raised in the United States. In staging this game, I sometimes chose players less familiar with United States geography, with the result that the use of geography was less prevalent. Indeed, in one variation, instead of cities, I chose nine soccer players, all from South America, five of whom play in La Liga (the Spanish league) and four from the Premier (English) League. Choosing as players two students from the United States makes this variation of the game this a lot harder for them than if I pick two students from Europe or South America.

So, following all this talk, you may fairly ask: What exactly is the formal definition of a focal point or a focal-point equilibrium? There is no formal answer. U.S. Supreme Court Justice Potter Stewart famously said about pornography, "I know it when I see it." That pretty much captures what can be said about focal points.

Learning, social custom, and focal points

Both social custom and focal points are, in a real sense, "learned" behaviors. In the case of social custom, what is learned is fairly specific, and indeed, instead of saying that the behavior is learned, it might be better to say that it is "taught": When walking with parents, children—at least some children—are taught to move to the right. With focal points, what exactly is "learned" is fairly ambiguous. But, still, one learns how others in one's society think about things in general and, for coordination purposes, one learns that adherence to this way of thinking is beneficial. Roth and Schoumaker (1983) demonstrate experimentally that this learning can happen fairly quickly:

Consider the following two-player game. Each player has as her set of strategies $\{0, 1, \ldots, 100\}$. Call their choices s_1 and s_2. If $s_1 + s_2 \leq 100$, then the first player (whose choice was s_1) has an $s_1\%$ chance of winning \$40, while the second player as an $s_2\%$ chance of winning \$10. If $s_1 + s_2 > 100$, each gets payoff 0. To formalize this game, write

$$v_n(s_n, s_{\neg n}) = \begin{cases} s_n, & \text{if } s_n + s_{\neg n} \leq 100, \text{ and} \\ 0, & \text{if } s_n + s_{\neg n} > 100; \end{cases}$$

the difference in monetary prizes plays no formal role: Because (we assume) players maximize their expected payoffs, and (if we further assume) the two players are expected-utility maximizers, for each we can normalize their utility of \$0 to 0 and their utility of their assigned dollar prize to 100. And, in this formal game, there are 102 pure-strategy Nash equilibria, where $(s_n, s_{\neg n})$ is a pure-strategy Nash equilibrium if $s_n + s_{\neg n} = 100$.[14]

But, of course, when real subjects play this game, the dollar prizes matter. If the dollar prizes were the same, and if the players were anonymous, the most prominent focal equilibrium would be a 50-50 split, on grounds of equity. This would (probably) persist if the players weren't told each other's dollar prize, and they had no means of communication. But suppose they do know each other's dollar prize. Consider the following two equilibria:

1. Split 50-50, so each has a 50% chance of winning.

2. Split 20-80, so they have equal expected monetary values of \$8 apiece.

If "equity" is a good basis for a focal equilibrium, both of these can make a claim of focality.

Roth and Schoumaker have experimental subjects play this game repeatedly,[15] being told that they are playing against randomly selected rivals. (Players were either the \$40-prize player or the \$10-prize player in all trials in which they participated.) But, in fact, subjects played in the first several rounds against a computer. Some subjects played against a computer that, roughly speaking, insisted on the first equilibrium. Other subjects played against a computer that insisted on the second equilibrium. And, as you might expect, after being "trained" that the "obvious way to play" was one or the other, when matched against real opponents, the training persisted.[16]

Experience with a specific rival

Finally, where players interact repeatedly with specific rivals, one story that is occasionally told is that they learn how their specific rivals behavior and optimize. This

---

[14] That gives 101 of the 102 pure-strategy equilibria. Can you find the last one? If not, see Chapter 23.

[15] In fact, players in their experiment played a two-stage game. If, in the first stage, the demands totaled 100 or less, the game ended with payoffs as above. But if the first-stage demands totaled more than 100, a second stage ensued, in which each player could either repeat her initial demand or accede to the other player. If neither acceded, both got 0. If one acceded and one stuck to her initial demand, the outcome was a split on the terms demanded by the player who didn't accede. If both acceded, n got $100 - s_{\neg n}$. I'm using a simpler version of the game so that it fits into this appendix; while I assert that experimental results using my simpler game would be similar to what they observe, this is just my assertion.

[16] This quick summary doesn't do justice to the original paper. It is only 11 pages long, so I strongly suggest you read it.

is similar to the *learned behavior and stability* story, although learning how "others" play in general is replaced by learning how specific rivals behave. You encounter this story in Chapter 18, in the context of Cournot equilibria, for instance.

Be careful about such rationales. This story can work if, in each interaction, the players act to maximize their short-run payoffs. But if they are at all far sighted, the fact that they interact repeatedly opens the doors to equilibrium behaviors that are not equilibria in today's interaction, but are equilibria over the long-term series of interactions. See, in particular, Appendix 15 and, for the idea in economic contexts, Chapter 22.

Theoretical issues with Nash equilibria

Several theoretical issues concerning Nash equilibria of strategic-form games are of interest. The first is existence.

Proposition A9.8.

a. *For a strategic-form game with finite strategy sets (and finitely many players), a Nash equilibrium exists.*

b. *For a strategic-form game, suppose the sets of (pure) strategies S_n are nonempty convex and compact subsets of finite-dimensionsal Euclidean space and, for each n, the payoff function v_n is continuous in (pure) strategy profiles s and is quasi-concave in s_n. Then the game has a pure-strategy Nash equilibrium.*

Part b is an immediate corollary of Proposition 14.8 from Volume I. That proposition concerned generalized games, in which the strategies available to a player could depend on the strategy profile $s_{\neg n}$ chosen by her rivals. Here we assume that there is no dependence, so the "constraint correspondence" C_n from that proposition is $C_n(s_{\neg n}) \equiv S_n$, which is obviously continuous, nonempty valued, and convex valued (as long as each S_n is nonempty, convex, and compact). As for part a, apply Proposition 14.8 where, *in that proposition*, the "strategy set" for player n is all mixtures of the player's finitely many pure strategies. It takes a bit of work to show that conditions a and b of Proposition 14.8 hold with this interpretation, but that work is straightforward.

Next is a result analogous to Proposition 14.14 from Volume I.

Proposition A9.9. *Fix a finite **strategic form**, consisting of a finite set of players $\mathcal{N}$ and, for each player $n \in \mathcal{N}$, a finite set of strategies S_n. The description of a strategic-form game for the given strategic form is provided by a point in $v \in R^{\mathcal{N} \times S}$, where for $n \in \mathcal{N}$ and $s \in s$, $v_n(s)$ is the payoff to player n if the strategy profile s is chosen. Consider the correspondence*

$$\mathbf{NE} : R^{\mathcal{N} \times S} \Rightarrow \prod_{n \in \mathcal{N}} \Sigma_n = \Sigma,$$

which associates to each payoff vector $v \in R^{N \times A}$ the mixed-strategy profiles $\sigma = (\sigma_1, \ldots, \sigma_N)$ that are Nash equilibria for the game (over the fixed strategic form) with payoff vector v. This correspondence is upper semi-continuous.

Proof. Suppose, for $k = 1, 2, \ldots$, $\sigma^k \in \mathbf{NE}(v^k)$, where each $v^k \in R^{N \times S}$. Suppose that $\lim_k v^k = v$, and $\lim_k \sigma^k = \sigma$. We must show that $\sigma \in \mathbf{NE}(v)$. Suppose it is not. Then for some player n and some strategy s_n for n that has strictly positive probability under σ_n, there is an alternative strategy s'_n such that

$$v_n(s'_n, \sigma_{\neg n}) > v_n(s_n, \sigma_{\neg n}).$$

We have all the continuity needed to show that

$$\lim_k v_n^k(s'_n, \sigma_{\neg n}^k) = v_n(s'_n, \sigma_{\neg n}^k) \quad \text{and} \quad \lim_k v_n^k(s_n, \sigma_{\neg n}^k) = v_n(s_n, \sigma_{\neg n}),$$

so the strict inequality two displays ago would imply that, for all sufficiently large k,

$$v_n^k(s'_n, \sigma_{\neg n}^k) > v_n^k(s_n, \sigma_{\neg n}^k).$$

But if s_n has strictly positive probability in $\sigma_n = \lim_k \sigma_n^k$, then for all sufficiently large k, s_n has strictly positive probability in σ_n^k. And this combined with the previous display implies that σ_n^k is not a best response to $\sigma_{\neg n}^k$, for sufficiently large k, contradicting the hypothesis that each σ^k is a Nash equilibrium. ∎

Three remarks are worthwhile here.

- This proposition shows that, for a fixed (finite-player-and-strategy) strategic-form game, the set of Nash equilibria for the game is a closed subset of Σ, the space of all mixed-strategy N-tuples.

- For games with infinite strategy spaces, similar results are possible. If a game is fixed in which the conditions of Proposition A9.8(b) are met, a similar argument shows that the set of pure-strategy Nash equilibria is closed. Extending to situations, as in Proposition A9.9, in which payoffs move "continuously" over a given strategic form is feasible; however, one must maintain quasi-concavity of each player's payoff as a function of her own action, which makes the statement of the result complicated.

For games with infinite strategy spaces but where a player's payoff is not a quasi-concave function of her own actions, results showing the existence of mixed-strategy Nash equilibria (followed by results analogous to Proposition A9.9) are certainly possible. One such result, which will be employed occasionally in the text, is due to Glicksberg (1952).

Proposition A9.10. *Every strategic-form game with finitely many players, where each strategy set S_n is a nonempty and compact subset of a metric space, and where the payoff functions $v_n : S \to R$ are continuous, has a Nash equilibrium, where for mixed strategies we allow Borel probability measures on S_n.*

A few notes concerning this result:

- A Borel measure is a measure defined on the sigma-field generated by the open sets in the space.

- Since the v_n are continuous and each S_n is compact, we know that the v_n are bounded, and so no issues of integrability arise.

- I will not take you through the proof, but a fast sketch is in order. For $\ell = 1, 2, \ldots$, we find finite subsets S_n^ℓ of each A_n such that, as $\ell \to \infty$, S_n^ℓ becomes appropriately "dense" in S_n. Proposition A9.8(a) produces, for each ℓ, a (possibly mixed-) strategy Nash equilibrium for the ℓth game; that is, for the game where player n's strategy set is S_n^ℓ. Compactness ensures that we can find, along some subsequence, a weak limit of the equilibrium strategy profiles, which gives a (mixed-) strategy profile on the full game, albeit where this limit involves Borel probabilities. And then, using the sort of argument that is used in Proposition A9.8, this limit profile is shown to be a Nash equilibrium.

Further existence results are provided in the literature, in particular, for cases where the payoff functions contain discontinuities of the "right" type. See, in particular, Maskin and Dasgupta (1986).

A9.6. Correlated Equilibria

Consider the game in Figure A9.12, which is taken from Aumann (1974).

Bob

		Column 1	Column 2
Alice	Row 1	4, 4	1, 5
	Row 2	5, 1	0, 0

Figure A9.12. Correlated Equilibrium

This game has two pure-strategy equilibria, Row 2–Column 1 and Row 1–Column 2, and it has a mixed-strategy equilibrium in which Alice and Bob both randomize with probabilities 1/2 between their two respective strategies. (This mixed-strategy equilibrium gives each an expected value of 2.5.) The pure-strategy equilibria favor one or the other of them strongly, and so, if they wish to be equitable about things without resorting to the mixed-strategy equilibrium, they could conceivably hire a neutral third party who will flip a fair coin and send them "directions": If the coin comes up heads, Alice will be told Row 1 and Bob, Column 2. If tails, Alice is told Row 2 and Bob, Column 1. This arrangement, if feasible, will give each an expected payoff of 3. And note that, given their instructions, and understanding the instructions that must be going to their rival, both will rationally follow those instructions.

But as long as they are engaging a neutral third party, suppose Alice and Bob instruct the third party as follows.

> Throw a fair die. If it comes up 1, 2, 3, or 4, tell Alice to choose Row 1. If it comes up 5 or 6, tell her to choose Row 2. If (on the same throw) it comes up 1 or 2, tell Bob to choose Column 2. If it comes up 3, 4, 5 or 6, tell him to choose Column 1.

If Alice and Bob follow these instructions, the outcome will be Row 1–Column 1 with probability 1/3 (if the die comes up 1 or 2), Row 1–Column 2 with probability 1/3 (die is 3 or 4), and Row 2-Column 1 with probability 1/3 (die is 5 or 6). The expected payoff to each player is $(4+1+5)/3 = 10/3$, better than if the neutral third part were to flip a coin. But will they follow these instructions?

Examine Alice's incentives. Suppose she is told to choose Row 1. If she knows the *mechanism* employed by the third party, and she is told to choose Row 1, she knows that the die was 1, 2, 3, or 4. Conditional on those four possible throws of the die, Bob is being told Column 1 with probability 1/2 (if the die was 3 or 4) and to choose Column 2 with probability 1/2. Therefore, choosing Row 1 gives Alice an expected payoff of $(4+1)/2 = 2.5$, and choosing Row 2 gives $(5+0)/2 = 2.5$. So she is content to follow instructions.[17] However, if she is told to choose Row 2, she knows the die came up 5 or 6, which means that Bob was told to choose Column 1; of course she is happy to choose Row 2 in this case. Bob is in a symmetric position.

1. Both of these examples—where the third party flips a fair coin, so Alice and Bob can achieve equity and an expected payoff of 3 apiece—and where the third party rolls a fair die, so Alice and Bob can achieve 10/3 apiece—are *correlated equilibria*. The concept of a correlated equilibrium was invented by Aumann (1974) and is connected in the literature to rationalizability. This notion—that play can be coordinated by some "external randomizing device" such as a neutral third party—will be encounted in the text, primarily along the lines of the first example, where the idea that players can proceed in dynamic games based on some "publicly observable randomization" will simplify the construction of equilibria.

2. And the notion of a neutral third party who "coordinates" the actions of individuals will play a very large role in developments in the book, where the neutral third party does more than just coordinate players' actions: The neutral third party gets reports from the players concerning private information they hold and, based on those reports, either directly implements a desirable outcome or, in other applications, instructs players what to do (where it is individually rational for the players to follow those instructions.)

---

[17] If it concerns you that Alice, in this instance, is indifferent, change the two payoffs of 1 to 1.1 and repeat the analysis.

The use of external randomizing devices is prominent in Chapter 22 and Appendix 15, concerning repeated play. A referee who collects private information and implements a desirable outcome is the basis for revelation principle in Chapter 26 and Appendix 16.

Bibliographic Notes

It is difficult to identify the formal origins of the concept of a strategic-form game, so I won't try. It should be noted, however, that the early literature refers to this formal concept as a *normal-form* game. It should also be noted that the early literature— here I will specify the classic book by von Neumann and Morgenstern (1944)—is largely concerned with *zero-sum* (or *constant-sum*) games. But in most contexts of interest to economists, things are not constant sum.

Likewise, it is difficult to identify the origins of the concepts of dominance, iterated dominance, and dominance solvability.

Rationalizability was first proposed and developed independently in Bernheim (1984) and Pearce (1984). A recent treatment of rationalizability is provided in Dekel and Siniscalchi (2015).

Nash equilibrium as a solution concept first appears formally in Nash (1950b), although the concept is evident in, for instance, Cournot (1838) and Bertrand (1883). Nash (1950b) provides the proof of existence of an equilibrium in mixed strategies for finite games, using fixed-point methods. (For constant-sum games, existence of an equilibrium is simpler, using minimax or separating-hyperplane arguments.)

Regarding focal points, the classic work is Schelling (1960). Roth and Schoumaker (1983) provide a lovely experiment concerning the "creation" of focal points; I mention this paper in Chapter 23, concerning bilateral bargaining, as well as here. Fudenberg and Levine (1998) provide a thorough examination of learning how to play games (based on repeated play).

Among other papers on the existence of equilibria, I mention Glicksberg (1952) and Maskin and Dasgupta (1986).

Aumann (1974) creates the concept of correlated equilibrium.

Appendix Ten

Extensive-Form Games

The second (game-theoretic) model or form used by economists to depict strategic interactions is an *extensive-form* game.[1] Here the emphasis is on the dynamic structure of the game; in particular, on the idea that players can choose actions with some knowledge of which actions other players have taken. This form also permits the analyst to model players who know different things when they have the opportunity to act.

The formal definition of an extensive-form game is, at its most general, quite complex. This volume is not concerned with anything like the most general definition, but what is required is still complex enough (expressed in general terms) to cause confusion. So I first work through the definition of a finite extensive-form game—which, when laid out formally, still obscures some relatively simple ideas—and then tackle the complications that we require.

A10.1. Definition of a Finite Extensive-Form Game

A finite extensive-form game (for purposes of this volume) is specified by seven elements: players; a game tree; assignment of players (or Nature) to each node in the game tree; actions; information sets; payoffs; and probabilities concerning where the game begins and what Nature does. If you have never read of heard about extensive-form games before, the formal definitions and conditions can be confusing; please be patient: After you've seen some concrete examples, it will all make sense.[2]

1. The first element is *a finite set $\mathcal{N}$ of players*, who are enumerated $\mathcal{N} = \{1, 2, \ldots, N\}$. In addition to these players, a natural force, called *Nature*, may participate.

2. Next is *a game tree* $(Z, \mathcal{Z})$. The game tree is formally a directed graph, consisting of a finite set Z of nodes—with typical element z—and directed arcs, or ordered pairs $(z, z') \in \mathcal{Z} \subset Z \times Z$. We say that z' is a *direct successor* to z if $(z, z') \in \mathcal{Z}$. The tree $(Z, \mathcal{Z})$ must satisfy two conditions:

---

[1] In the more formal literature of noncooperative game theory, a third "form"—*epistemic-form games*—is encountered. And in cooperative game theory, you will encounter *coalition-form* games. We use neither of these forms in this volume. That said, the *core*, which was discussed in Chapter 15 of Volume I and which appears in Chapter 25, comes from coalition-form game theory. And in Chapter 23, the Nash bargaining solution, which is somewhere between cooperative and noncooperative game theory, is discussed. Finally, Appendix 13 touches on some basic ideas from epistemic game theory.

[2] It may be easier to jump ahead to example presented in Section A10.2 then return to these formalities.

a. It is acyclic: Starting from some node z_1, there is no progression $z_1, z_2, \ldots, z_I$ with $(z_i, z_{i+1}) \in \mathcal{Z}$, such that $z_1 = z_I$.

b. For each $z \subset \mathcal{Z}$, there is *at most* one node $z' \subset \mathcal{Z}$ such that $(z', z) \subset \mathcal{Z}$. When z has such a node z', we call z' the *immediate predecessor* of z and write $p(z)$ for that node z'. If z has no immediate predecessor, we say that z is an *initial* node. *The set of initial nodes is denoted* Z_I.

Game trees are typically depicted as shown in Figure A10.1(a). The open and filled-in circles are the nodes, where a node is left open (not filled in) if it has no immediate predecessor; that is, if it is an initial node. Note that the tree in Figure A10.1(a) has two initial nodes. Arrows pointing from one node to others represent the arcs of the graph; if an arrow points from node z to node z', it means that $(z, z') \in \mathcal{Z}$. Condition a then rules out cycles, the sort of thing depicted in Figure A10.2(b). Condition b rules out "paths" through the tree that grow together, the sort of thing depicted in Figure A10.2(c). In other words, with conditions a and b holding, the picture looks like a grove of trees: Starting from each initial node, the arrows branch out in the fashion of a tree, never growing around in a circle or having two branches merge. (It may be easier to see this if you orient things so that if $(z, z') \in \mathcal{Z}$, then the picture has z below z'. So, for instance, the tree in panel a is redrawn in panel d to look like a grove of two trees, one for each of the two initial nodes.) Except for the fact that this definition allows for multiple initial nodes, a mathematician would call this structure an *arborescence*.

A ton of vocabulary goes with a game tree:

- For any node z, z' is a *predecessor* of z if there is a sequence $z' = z_1, z_2, \ldots, z_I = z$, where $(z_i, z_{i+1}) \in \mathcal{Z}$ or, equivalently, $z_i = p(z_{i+1})$ for $i = 1, \ldots, I - 1$. The set of all predecessors of z is denoted by $P(z)$.

- For any node z, z' is a *successor* of z if there is a sequence $z = z_1, z_2, \ldots z_I = z'$, where $(z_i, z_{i+1}) \in \mathcal{Z}$ or, equivalently, $z_i = p(z_{i+1})$ for $i = 1, \ldots, I - 1$. The set of successors of z is denoted by $S(z)$.

- Call z a *final (or terminal) node* if it has no successors. Denote the set of final nodes by Z_F.

- For any node z that is not final, let $S^1(z)$ be the set of all *immediate successors* of z; that is, $S^1(z) = \{z' \in S(z) : z = p(z')\}$ or, equivalently, $S^1(z) = \{z' \in Z : (z, z') \in \mathcal{Z}\}$.

- An ordered I-tuple $(z_1, z_2, \ldots, z_I)$ is called a *path* through the tree if $z_i = p(z_{i+1})$ for $i = 1, \ldots, I - 1$, z_1 is an initial node, and z_I is a final node. Call an ordered I-tuple $(z_1, z_2, \ldots, z_I)$ a *partial path* if $z_i = p(z_{i+1})$ for $i = 1, \ldots, I - 1$ and z_1 is an initial node, but z_I is not a final node.

- It is easy to see from conditions 2a and 2b that if you begin with a node z and "go backward" through the tree, finding the unique $p(z)$, then the unique $p(p(z))$, and so forth, you will never cycle, and since Z is finite, you will eventually reach an initial node. Reversing the process, construct the (perhaps partial)

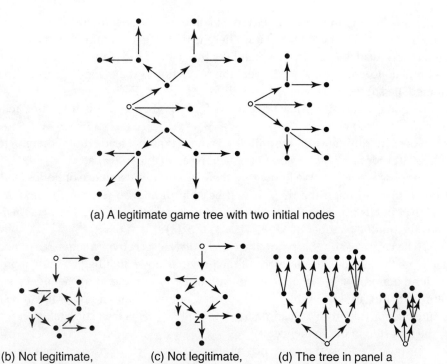

(a) A legitimate game tree with two initial nodes

(b) Not legitimate, because it has a cycle

(c) Not legitimate, because node z has two immediate predecessors

(d) The tree in panel a re-oriented to look more like a "grove" of (two) trees

Figure A10.1. Legitimate and illegitimate game trees

path from the initial node you reach back to z. (The path is partial if z is not a terminal node; if z is terminal, it is a (full) path.) Call this (perhaps partial) path the *history* up to z. It is clear from property 2b and a trivial induction argument that for each z, the history up to z is unique.

- And, because the game tree Z is finite and cycles are ruled out, it is clear that every (partial) path has finite length, being no longer than the number of nodes in Z. (When we get to infinite game trees, this will change.)

(To remind you where we are: there are seven elements that define a finite extensive-form game, and we've covered the first two, the set of players and the game tree $(Z, \mathcal{Z})$. Moving on...)

3. There is *an assignment of one of the players or Nature, to each nonfinal node.* We write $\iota(z)$ for this assignment, where $\iota : Z \setminus Z_F \to \mathcal{N} \cup \{\text{Nature}\}$. The interpretation is that, at nonfinal node z, it is $\iota(z)$'s turn to move. (We frequently say that at z, $\iota(z)$ is called on to take an action.)

4. There is *a (finite) set A of **actions** and, for each noninitial $z \in Z \setminus Z_I$, an element $a(z) \in A$, the **action** that leads from $p(z)$ to z, subject to the following condition:* If z

and z' are both immediate successors of some z'' (or, in symbols, $z, z' \in S^1(z'')$), then $a(z) \neq a(z')$. The interpretation here is that at each nonfinal node z'', there are actions available to $\iota(z'')$, which take the path of the game from z'' to one of its immediate successors. And, then, the restriction is that, from z'', each distinct immediate successor is reached by a different action. For any node z'' that is not a final node, write $A(z'')$ for $\{a(z) : z \in S^1(z'')\}$; then $A(z'')$ is the set of actions available to $\iota(z'')$ at node z''.

Note carefully: $a(z)$ for noninitial z is the action that leads (immediately) to z, while $A(z)$ for nonfinal z is the set of actions available to $\iota(z)$ at z.

Suppose $z \in P(z')$. We know that there is a unique sequence of nodes leading from z to z' through the tree. It will be helpful later to refer to the **first** action $a \in A(z)$ *in this sequence*; the notation is ugly, but write $a(z \rightarrow z') := a(z'')$, where z'' is the unique member of $\left(P(z') \cup \{z'\} \right) \cap S^1(z)$.

To be very clear on this point, the word *path* is reserved for a sequence of nodes, each one the immediate successor of the previous node, that begins with an initial node; the modifier *partial* attaches to *path* if the final node in the sequence is not terminal. But, in writing $a(z \rightarrow z')$, z need not be an initial node. It can be any sequence, starting from z, leading to z', and $a(z \rightarrow z')$ is the action taken at z that is the first step in the sequence.

Suppose we look at a sequence of nodes $z = z_1, z_2, \dots, z_I = z'$, such that $z_i = p(z_{i+1})$, for $i = 1, \dots, I - 1$. This is the unique sequence of nodes leading from z to z'. Alternatively, we can speak of the sequence of *actions* $a(z_2), a(z_3), \dots, a(z_I)$ that take us from z to z'. Since each noninitial node z'' has a unique action that leads to it, which is $a(z'')$, identifying the sequence by the starting point z and the sequence of subsequent nodes $z_2, \dots, z_I = z'$ *or* by the starting point z and the sequence of actions $a(z_2), \dots a(z_I)$ are equivalent. Both ways of expressing this idea are used.

5. *The set of nonfinal nodes $Z \setminus Z_F$ is partitioned into **information sets**, with the following two requirements for any pair of nodes z and z' that are in the same information set:*

a. $\iota(z) = \iota(z')$. *At any two nodes in one information set, the same player (or Nature) is assigned to move.*

b. $A(z) = A(z')$. *At any two nodes in the same information set, the sets of available actions are identical.*

The interpretation is that, at node z, player $\iota(z)$ is called on to move but, except for what this player infers based on her assessment of what other players have done, she does not know which node in the information set containing z is the game's current position. Condition 5a is the requirement that the player's identity doesn't reveal more information to the player. Condition 5b is that the set of available actions doesn't reveal more information to the player.

If we were modeling boundedly rational behavior, both of these conditions might be problematic: A player might think that she has the move at nodes where, in fact, she does not. And she might think that the options (actions) she has at some point in the game are not in fact the options she would have. (In other words, some options available to her might be unanticipated.) But in this volume, these things are not allowed (subject to some mild relaxation later, when we consider games of incomplete information in Appendix 13).

We use H to denote the set of information sets in an extensive-form game, with h a typical information set and $h(z)$ the information set that contains node z. Denote by H_n (for $n \in \mathcal{N}$) the set of information sets that "belong" to n; that is, $H_n = \{h \in H : \iota(z) = n \text{ for all } z \in h\}$. For $h \in H$, denote by $\iota(h)$ the player (or Nature) assigned to all nodes $z \in h$ and by $A(h)$ the set of actions a available to $\iota(h)$ at h; that is, $\iota(h) := \iota(z)$, and $A(h) := A(z)$ for any and all $z \in h$.

It is typical not to bundle nodes belonging to Nature into information sets; that is, any node belonging to Nature is an information set on its own. (But see point 7 below.)

6. *A **payoff** is assigned to each player at each final node.* That is, a function $u : Z_F \to R^{\mathcal{N}}$ is given, where $u_n(z)$ for $n \in \mathcal{N}$ and $z \in Z_F$ is the payoff to player n if, over the course of play, final node z is reached.

7. *A **probability distribution** ρ is given over the set of initial nodes and, for each nonterminal node z such that $\iota(z) = $ Nature, a probability distribution ρ_z is given over the set of available actions $A(z)$.* These probability distributions should be conditional on any previous "choices" by Nature in the tree; it is typically assumed that, whatever Nature does, her actions do not depend (are not probabilistically dependent) on choices made by players in the game. Also, in most applications, we will assume that all players share the same probability assessment over Nature's actions (and choice of initial node), and this assessment is part of the description of the game. (Neither of these two assumptions are necessary, however.)

While nodes of Nature are not typically bundled into information sets, it is often the case that several nodes belonging to Nature represent the "same" random event, in which case it is natural that the probabilities assigned to actions at those nodes are the same. (Figure A10.2 provides an example.)

A10.2. Diagraming Finite Extensive-Form Games

Rather than presenting examples with lists of these items, diagrams of finite extensive-form games are typically used. Consider, for instance, the game depicted in Figure A10.2. This game involves two players, called Firm A and Firm B, and Nature. There is one initial node, the open circle found a bit to the lower left of the center, which is labeled Firm A, meaning that, at this node, Firm A has the move. This node has two successors, and the arrows leading out of this node are labeled "do R&D" and "no R&D": At the start of the game, Firm A is choosing whether to do some research and development about the cost of a product it is contemplating introducing. (That this R&D is about the cost of the product will only become obvious further "up" the tree.) If Firm A chooses to do the R&D, we are at the node to the right of the initial node, labeled Nature. At this node, Nature "decides" whether the cost of manufacture will be high or low, with probability 0.3

of low cost, also labeled on the arrow. Following whichever cost structure Nature chooses, Firm A then decides whether to enter the market or not. Note that each successor node to Nature's move is labeled with Firm A, and the actions available to Firm A are "enter" and "don't enter." However, if Firm A initially chooses not to do R&D, we move from the initial node to the node to the left (and up a bit from) the initial node, where again Firm A must decide whether to enter or not.

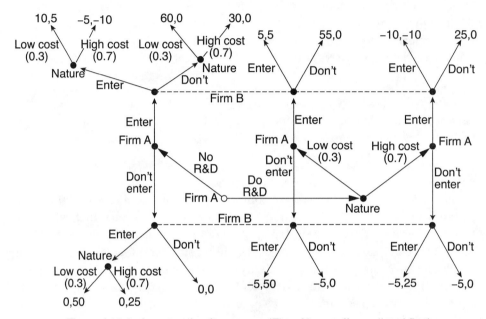

Figure A10.2. An extensive-form game (Firm A's payoffs are listed first)

Then we come to two information sets for Firm B. Each of these contains three nodes; the fact that each set of three nodes constitutes an information set is indicated by a dashed line joining the three; the fact that Firm B has the choice at the six nodes constituting these two information sets is indicated by labeling the *information sets* with "Firm B." At each of these information sets, Firm B's choice of action is to enter or not; note that these are two separate decisions, because there are two information sets.

What does it mean in terms of the game that there are two information sets at this point? Note that the first information set—the one in the upper half of the tree—all follow a decision by Firm A to enter. The second of these information sets, in the bottom half of the tree, all follow a decision by Firm A not to enter. So, when Firm B has the move, it does so knowing whether Firm A entered or not. But because the three nodes in the upper information set form an information set, that is all Firm B knows. In particular, Firm B, in this game, is presumed not to know whether Firm A chose to do R&D and, if Firm A did choose to do R&D, whether the costs of manufacture are high or low. And similarly for the bottom information set.

Back up a bit to the two nodes belonging to Firm A after a decision to do R&D, and following Nature's choice of high or low cost. These two nodes are not joined by a dashed line; they are information sets as singleton sets. Therefore, at either of these points, Firm A knows what has come "before": It knows (of course) that it chose to do R&D. And (not so "of course") it knows whether costs will be high or low; that is, doing the R&D definitively tells Firm A which cost structure prevails. However, the Firm A node that follows the choice not to do R&D, to the left, is also a single-node information set. In this position, Firm A knows (again, of course), that it didn't do the R&D. But, because Nature's "choice" of cost structure is not (yet) in the tree, Firm A, in this position, doesn't know whether costs are high or low.

Terminal nodes are depicted as pairs of numbers. As the caption indicates, the first number is the payoff to Firm A. So, for instance, if Firm A chooses to do R&D, if Nature determines that costs are low, if Firm A enters, and if Firm B enters, both firms get a payoff of 5.

On the left side of the figure, where Firm A chose not to do R&D, if either Firm A or B or both enter, there is one more node before we get to the payoffs: At these nodes, Nature chooses between high and low cost. We need this because, while in the right side, we have already put in a node for Nature's determination of the cost, on the left side, we need to know whether costs are high or low to determine payoffs (if either or both enter), and so we put this node in as convenient. We don't need this node if neither firm decides to enter, since (in the accounting for payoffs implicit in this model, which I do *not* explain here), if neither enters, and if Firm A chose not to do R&D, the payoffs for each firm are 0, regardless of whether the cost structure would have been high or low. When Nature is depicted as having a "move" in the game, the probabilities assigned to its choice are included (in parentheses) in the labels on the respective arrows.[3]

In general, you have flexibility in how to model a given "situation" as an extensive-form game. To build your understanding of this and of extensive-form game representations of a given situation, try the following exercise. The situation is precisely that depicted in Figure A10.2: Two firms, A and B, must decide whether to enter the market for a new product. The cost of manufacture of the new product will be high or low cost, with high cost having probability 0.7. (The cost is determined by Nature. It is not a choice of either firm.) Firm A decides whether to enter before Firm B makes its entry decision, and Firm B will know when making its decision whether Firm A entered or not. Before making its entry decision, Firm A can choose to do R&D about the cost; if it chooses to do R&D, it will learn the cost. Firm B, when it makes its entry decision, will not know whether Firm A chose to do R&D or, if Firm A did so, what Firm A learned. That's the situation or story. In Figure A10.2, I built an extensive-form representation of this with one initial node and four information sets for Firm A. Try to build an extensive-form representation

---

[3] And, referring back to the final comment in the previous subsection, the same probabilities 0.3 and 0.7 are assigned to Nature's actions at each of her nodes, because these all represent the same "natural" event.

of this story with *two* initial nodes, one where the cost will be high, the second where it will be low, and with three information sets for Firm A. (Hint: At Firm A's first information set, it has three options, namely, do R&D, don't do R&D and enter, don't do R&D and don't enter.) My rendering of this alternative extensive form will be provided in Section A10.9 as Figure A10.8.

Comments

Three comments about the basic definition and the mode of depicting extensive-form games are worth making:

1. The structure of the information sets in the game concerns who knows when. This can constrain the order in which you put nodes into the tree—that is, which nodes are predecessors of other nodes—but the order of nodes is otherwise not really constrained by the temporal order of actions taken. At its most basic, consider a game in which Alice and Bob choose actions independently, with Alice choosing, say, at 10 a.m. and Bob at 11 a.m. Of course, Alice, because she chooses before Bob does, won't know what Bob will choose. But if, in the same spirit, Bob doesn't know what Alice has chosen when it is his turn to choose, then you can either: (1) create an extensive-form depiction of this situation with Alice's choice node first, followed by choices for Bob (all joined in to a single information set); or (2) you can put Bob's choice in the tree first, followed by Alice's choice nodes (joined into a single information set). (And, of course, if Alice and Bob move independently and *simultaneously*, either representation is fine.) What constrains your construction is that, when Bob knows something that has happened before he has to make a choice, you must put the node for that earlier event before Bob's choice node(s).

2. You can depict situations in which the notion of temporal order of moves is ambiguous. Consider the game depicted in Figure A10.3.

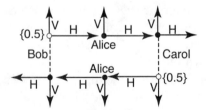

Figure A10.3. An extensive-form game with an ambiguous "order of moves" (payoffs omitted)

There are three players, Alice, Bob, and Carol. (It is the structure and not the payoffs that matters here, so I have not included payoffs. But, of course, for each terminal node, I need three payoffs, one for each of the three players.) Each player moves at most once, although both Bob and Carol have one information set, while Alice has two. At each opportunity to choose, each player's choice is either V (for vertical) or H (for horizontal). (Although it is by now probably obvious, observe that the names of actions can be used over and over again, as long as we don't use the same name twice at a single information set; and at each information set, the set of moves available at one node is identical to the moves available at another node in that information set.) There are two initial nodes. And—the point of this example—Bob may move first, or he may move third, and he doesn't know which it is if he is called on to move. The same is true about Carol. But if Alice is called on to move, because the first player to move chose H, she knows which of Bob and Carol made the first move. (What would it mean if Alice's two nodes were joined by a dashed line?)

3. In other texts and papers, the conventions for diagramming an extensive-form game can differ from those used here. In particular, it is often the case that diagrams have a single initial node; where I have multiple initial nodes, those diagrams will have an initial node assigned to Nature, with arrows pointing to the nodes that I depict as initial. Indeed, you may sometimes encounter the convention that *all* of Nature's moves are collected in a single initial node, although doing so will often require a complex structure of information sets. And, in many texts and papers, instead of connecting nodes in an information set by a dashed line (or curve), a "cloud" or "balloon" will encircle all the nodes in a given information set.

A10.3. Games with Perfect Recall

The two rules for information sets—that players know when they are asked to move and what actions they have available—are essentially derived from the idea that players have "reasonable" cognitive skills. But those rules do not preclude cognitive deficiencies of other sorts. In particular, they do not preclude models in which the players have memory problems: We can draw extensive forms in which Alice forgets that she earlier had moved, or in which she forgets what choices she made, or in which she forgets things that she knew previously. The panels in Figure A10.4 show, respectively, an extensive form (with payoffs suppressed) that depicts each of these memory lapses.

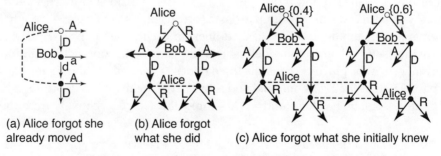

Figure A10.4. Alice has memory problems (payoffs are suppressed)

Is the model flexibility that such forms provide ever useful? People can forget what they knew or did earlier, especially if we think of them as having limited memory.[4] And, for those who know the rules of contract bridge, suppose we want to model this as a two-player game, with N-S and E-W as the two players. Then it is natural to suppose that, on alternate moves, N-S knows which cards N holds but not which S holds, and then knows S's holding but not N's. (Of course, we could alternatively model this as a four-person game, where each of the two members of each pair, N and S being one pair, and E and W being the other, have identical objectives.)

But notwithstanding the potential advantages of permitting such memory problems in models, ruling them out simplifies subsequent analysis considerably. So let us rule out such "pathologies."

To do so takes further restrictions on what we allow in the construction of information sets in an extensive-form game. The following definition is standard.

Definition A10.1. *An extensive-form game is a **game with perfect recall** if for any two nodes $\hat{z}$ and z such that $\hat{z}$ precedes z and $\iota(\hat{z}) = \iota(z)$, if $z' \in h(z)$, there is a node $\hat{z}'$ (which may be the same as $\hat{z}$) such that $\hat{z}' \in h(\hat{z}) \cap P(z')$, and the immediate action from $\hat{z}$ that leads to z is the same as the immediate action that leads from $\hat{z}'$ to z'.*[5]

Suppose we have a game with perfect recall and, for a player n, two information sets h and $\hat{h}$ that belong to n. Then *either h precedes $\hat{h}$ in the sense that for every $\hat{z} \in \hat{h}$, there is some $z \in h$ that precedes $\hat{z}$; or $\hat{z}$ precedes h; or they are completely "unordered," meaning that no pair $z \in h$ and $\hat{z} \in \hat{z}$ has one preceding the other.* Moreover, suppose $\hat{h}$ precedes h and z and z' are both in h. Let $\hat{z}$ and $\hat{z}'$ be the nodes in $\hat{h}$ that precede z and z', respectively. Then $a(\hat{z} \to z) = a(\hat{z}' \to z')$. (This is just restating the definition.)

Restating this a bit differently, if the game has perfect recall, take player n, $h \in H_n$, and $z, z' \in h$. Suppose the partial path leading to z is $(z_1, z_2, \ldots, z_I = z)$ (so z_1 is an initial node). And suppose that the partial path leading to z' is $(z'_1, \ldots, z'_{I'})$, where z'_1 is an initial node. Note, this does not preclude $z_1 = z'_1$. Then, if $h(z_i) \in H_n$ for any $i = 1, \ldots, I - 1$, there must be some $z'_{i'}$ such that $h(z'_{i'}) = h(z_i)$, and $a(z_i \to z_{i+1}) = a(z'_{i'} \to z'_{i'+1})$.

At the risk of confusing matters, a pair of pictures may help. Follow along on Figure A10.5. Panels a and b in Figure A10.5 depict portions of extensive-form games with perfect recall. In both panels, to focus is on a specific player n, whose information sets are depicted by dashed lines; in each panel, player n has three information sets. All other nodes belong to other players. In panel a, the rightmost information set for player n contains three nodes, z, z', and z''; the figure shows the partial paths leading from initial nodes to each of the three. As depicted, z has six predecessors, z' has four, and z'' has three, labeled consecutively from their

---

[4] There is a branch of the theoretical literature that models the behavior of the players as finite-state automata, with a given (limited) number of states. And there are papers that analyze situations in which, for instance, a somewhat inebriated driver knows that he must make one left turn to get home, but can't recall if he has already made it. We encounter neither of these "situations" in the text.

[5] Why does this definition rule out a node z and a predecessor $\hat{z}$ of z being in the same information set?

respective initial-node predecessors, as indicated. (That is, z'_n for $n = 1, 2, \ldots, 4$ is the nth node leading to $z' = z'_5$. Since the first initial node leads to both z and z', it is labeled $z_1 = z'_1$. Similarly, $z_2 = z'_2$ and $z_3 = z'_3$.) That is, as drawn, the partial paths leading to z and to z' are identical from their (joint) initial predecessor until $z_3 = z'_3$.

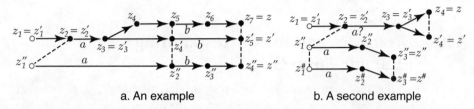

a. An example   b. A second example

Figure A10.5. The implications of perfect recall (see the text for explanation)

Along the path from z_1 to $z_7 = z$, two information sets of player n are encountered. Hence, per perfect recall, since z' and z'' are in the same information set as z, those two information sets must be encountered along the partial paths to z' and to z''. So, for instance, $z_2 = z'_2$ is in an information set with z''_1. And, also as per perfect recall, at the information set $\{z_2 = z'_2, z''_1\}$, the action taken at $z_2 = z'_2$ that leads to z (and z') must be the same as the action taken at z''_1 that leads to z''. The label a is used for this (identical) action. The same consideration implies that the actions taken at z_5, at z'_4, and at z''_2 that lead, respectively, to z, z', and z'', must be the same. Note that player n may have other actions at these two "early" information sets; the figure only depicts the partial paths leading to z, z', and z''.

Panel b is constructed similarly, but shows a case where player n has two "unordered" information sets, namely, $\{z, z'\}$ and $\{z'', z^\sharp\}$. The partial paths to these four nodes are shown. And, along these four partial paths, an "earlier" information set belonging to player n is encountered. As in panel a, since $\{z'', z^\sharp\}$ is a "successor" information set, the actions taken at z''_1 and at $z^\sharp_1$ that lead, respectively, to z'' and $z^\sharp$, must be the same; this action is labeled a. But, the action leading to $\{z, z'\}$ need not be the same, hence it is labeled $a?$. It could be that this action is different from a. This would explain why z and z' are in a different information set from z'' and $z^\sharp$: If player n takes a different action at her first information set, she must recall this. But, it could also be that she takes the same action a, and it happens that, per the rules of the game, she learns whether play passed through node z_2 before her next opportunity to act.

Panel b provides an important message about perfect recall: It works in one direction only. A player cannot forget what she knew or did previously. But she can certainly learn things she previously didn't know.

Although not germane to perfect recall per se, Figure A10.5(a) illustrates a few other features of extensive-form games that are worthy of note. First, note that z''_1 is an initial node, while $z_2 = z'_2$ is not. Yet they are all in an information set for player n. *A player, called on to move, may be unsure whether she is starting the game or is following someone else's move.* Second, note that node z''_2 immediately follows z''_1, while z_5 is three steps from z_2, and z_4' is one step from z_2'. Yet $z_2 = z_2'$ and z_1'' are all in an information set for n, as are z_2'', z_5, and z_4'. Player n, called on to move at her first information set and having chosen action a, may be called on to move again. If and when this happens, Player n only knows that she has been called on to move again; as depicted in the panel a, she doesn't know whether there were intervening moves by other players.

A10.4. Strategies and the Corresponding Strategic-Form Game

Fix a finite extensive-form game. For each player n, recall that $H_n \subseteq H$ is the set of information sets that belong to n. A *pure strategy* for player n is then a member of $\prod_{h \in H_n} A(h)$; that is, it assigns one available action for player n at each information set that belongs to player n. So, for instance, in the extensive-form game depicted in Figure A10.2, Firm A has four information sets, in each of which two actions are available. So Firm A has $2 \times 2 \times 2 \times 2 = 16$ strategies. Firm B has two information sets, with two actions available in each, so it has $2 \times 2 = 4$ strategies.

Definitions A10.2.

a. *Fixing a finite extensive-form game, the set of **strategies available to player** n, denoted S_n, is $\prod_{h \in H_n} A(h)$, with typical element denoted s_n.*

b. *A **strategy profile** is an $\mathcal{N}$-tuple of strategies, one for each player, or $s = (s_1, \ldots, s_N) \in \prod_{n \in \mathcal{N}} S_n$.*

c. *Each strategy profile s, together with probabilities assigned to initial nodes and actions emanating from nodes belonging to Nature, induces a probability distribution on final nodes, which we denote by $\pi(s)$ and call the **outcome** engendered by s, which is constructed as follows:*

> *Fix the strategy profile s. For each final node $z \in Z_F$, let $z_1, z_2, \ldots, z_K = z$ be the complete path leading to z from the unique initial-node predecessor z_1 of z. Write h_k for $h(z_k)$, that is, the information set that contains z_k. Write a_k for $a(z_{k+1})$, $k = 1, \ldots, K-1$. (Recall that $a(z_{k+1})$ is the action that leads from z_k to z_{k+1}.) If $\iota(z_k) \neq$ Nature and $s_{\iota(z_k)}(h_k) \neq a_k$ for any z_k along the path to z, then $\pi(s)(z) = 0$. Otherwise—in words, if along the path from z_1 to z, at every node that belongs to a player other than Nature, s calls for that player to take the action that continues along the path to z—then $\pi(z)$ equals $\rho(z_1)$ times the product of the probabilities that Nature takes the actions that continue the path to z at nodes that belong to Nature.*

d. *The **(expected) payoff to player** n **if strategy profile** s **is chosen** is $v_n(s) = \sum_{z \in Z_F} u_n(z) \pi(s)(z)$.*

e. *The strategic-form game with the same set of players, where player n has strategy set S_n, and where payoffs are given by $v_n(s)$, is the **strategic-form game corresponding to the given extensive-form game**.*

The notion is that players are "good strategic thinkers": When playing an extensive-form game, each player thinks at the outset about how she will act at each information set at which she may be called on to act, when and if that information set is reached. That is, at the outset, each player decides upon a strategy she will use and then carries out that strategy.[6]

To illustrate,take the game depicted in Figure A10.2, and consider the following strategy profile:

Firm A's strategy. At its initial information set, Firm A does not do R&D. At its information set where it has not done R&D, it enters. At its information set where it has done R&D and found that cost is low, it enters. And at its information set where it has done R&D and found that cost is high, it does not enter.[7]

Firm B's strategy. At its information set where Firm B has seen that Firm A has entered, it enters. At its information set where Firm B has seen that Firm A has not entered, it does not enter.

If the two firms adopt these strategies, respectively, the sequence of events is:

    1. Firm A does not do R&D.   2. Firm A enters.   3. Firm B enters.

This takes the game to the node marked Nature that is in the upper-left corner of all nonfinal nodes in Figure A10.2. Nature determines whether cost is low or high, so for this strategy profile, there is probability 0.3 of landing at the final node at which the two payoffs are 10 for A and 5 for B, in the extreme upper-left of the diagram, and probability 0.7 of landing at the final node with payoffs -5 and -10 that is second from the left in the top row of final nodes.

- For Firm A, its payoff is 10 with probability 0.3 and -5 with probability 0.7, for an expected payoff of -0.5.

- For Firm B, its payoff is 5 with probability 0.3 and -10 with probability 0.7, for an expected payoff of -5.5.

If you carry out these computations for each of the $16 \times 4 = 64$ strategy profiles and build a bimatrix representation of this strategic-form version of the extensive-form game in Figure A10.2, you get Figure A10.6. The sixteen rows are the sixteen strategies for Firm A, where I list each strategy in four columns: whether Firm A chooses to do R&D; if not, whether it enters or not; if it does, does it enter if it learns that costs are low; and if it does (do R&D), does it enter if it learns that costs are high. For Firm B, the four columns are its four strategies: Does it enter if it sees Firm A enter; and does it enter if it sees Firm A stay out. The strategies for each firm are numbered for expositional convenience; note that the strategy profile analyzed above is the combination of strategy 10 for Firm A and strategy 2 for Firm B.

---

[6] This is in line with the standard strategic approach to dynamic choice that is adopted in microeconomics; revisit Chapter 7 and, in particular, Section 7.1 from Volume I.

[7] Firm A has four information sets, each one a single node in the representation in Figure A10.2, so a strategy for Firm A specifies what it does in each of these four situations. If you observe that, having chosen not to do R&D, it becomes irrelevant what it *would have done* at the two information sets (nodes) subsequent to doing R&D, you are anticipating the next subsection.

Firm B's strategy

					1.	2.	3.	4.
		If firm A enters			enter	enter	don't	don't
		If firm A doesn't enter			enter	don't	enter	don't
	R&D?	If no R&D	If Low	If High				
1. yes	enter	enter	enter		−5.5, −5.5	−5.5, −5.5	34, 0	34, 0
2. yes	enter	enter	don't		−2, 19	−2, 1.5	13, 17.5	13, 0
3. yes	enter	don't	enter		−8.5, 8	−8.5, −7	16,15	16, 0
4. yes	enter	don't	don't		−5, 32.5	−5, 0	−5, 32.5	−5, 0
5. yes	don't	enter	enter		−5.5, −5.5	−5.5 , −5.5	34, 0	34, 0
6. yes	don't	enter	don't		−2, 19	−2, 1.5	13, 17.5	13, 0
7. yes	don't	don't	enter		−8.5, 8	−8.5, −7	16,15	16, 0
8. yes	don't	don't	don't		−5, 32.5	−5, 0	−5, 32.5	−5, 0
9. no	enter	enter	enter		−0.5, −5.5	−0.5, −5.5	39,0	39, 0
10. no	enter	enter	don't		−0.5, −5.5	−0.5, −5.5	39,0	39, 0
11. no	enter	don't	enter		−0.5, −5.5	−0.5, −5.5	39,0	39, 0
12. no	enter	don't	don't		−0.5, −5.5	−0.5, −5.5	39,0	39, 0
13. no	don't	enter	enter		0, 32.5	0, 0	0, 32.5	0, 0
14. no	don't	enter	don't		0, 32.5	0, 0	0, 32.5	0, 0
15. no	don't	don't	enter		0, 32.5	0, 0	0, 32.5	0, 0
16. no	don't	don't	don't		0, 32.5	0, 0	0, 32.5	0, 0

(Firm A's strategy — left margin label)

Figure A10.6. The strategic-form game corresponding to the extensive-form game in Figure A10.2.

Strategically equivalent strategies and the reduced strategic form

One feature of this strategic-form game that stands out is that many of the rows are identical: Rows 1 and 5, for instance, are identical, as are Rows 13, 14, 15, and 16. This feature "generalizes" as follows:

Definition A10.3. *Two strategies s_n and s'_n for player n are **strategically equivalent** (or, just **equivalent**) if, for all strategy profiles for players other than n, they induce the same outcome or probability distribution on final nodes.*

For games with perfect recall, this sort of thing happens when one information set h'_n for some player n follows an earlier information set h_n for that player. If the player takes an action a at h_n that precludes reaching h'_n (and, for a game with perfect recall, only one choice of action at h_n can lead to h'_n), then any strategy s_n that prescribes a at h_n means that h'_n will not be reached; two strategies s_n and s'_n that prescribe a at h_n and otherwise differ only on what they prescribe at h'_n will be strategically equivalent.

(Why have I put "generalizes" in scare quotes? Because Definition A10.3 is about probability distributions over endpoints of the original extensive-form game and not about equal payoffs. One might have two strategies for n that, for all strategy profiles of other players, give each player the same payoffs, simply by coincidence. Definition A10.3 doesn't apply to such "coincidental" equivalence.[8])

---

[8]   And readers with prior training in the finer points of extensive-form games will recognize that this definition applies to two strategies for a player in a single extensive-form representation of the game. In Appendix 14, where the topic is strategic stability, we'll speak of (different) strategically equivalent extensive-form representations of a "game," for which this definition is inadequate. (And ignore this footnote if it makes no sense to you at this point.)

Clearly, strategic equivalence of strategies for a player n is an equivalence relation (transitive, reflexive, symmetric), so we can group strategies in S_n into strategic-equivalence equivalence classes. Let $\hat{S}_n$ be the set of equivalence classes, with $\hat{s}_n$ denoting a typical element of $\hat{S}_n$; note that, formally, each $\hat{s}_n$ is a subset of S_n, and so writing $s_n \in \hat{s}_n$ is formally correct.

So, for instance, for Firm A in Figure A10.6, the formal definition of $\hat{S}_{\text{Firm A}}$ would be

$$\hat{S}_{\text{Firm A}} = \{\{\text{strategies } 1,5\}, \{2,6\}, \{3,7\}, \{4,8\}, \{9,10,11,12\}, \{13,14,15,16\}\}.$$

Informally, however, members of $\hat{S}_n$ are described by specifying the actions chosen by a player at every information set that is not ruled out by an earlier choice of the player. For instance, the equivalence class $\hat{s}_{\text{Firm A}} = \{2,6\}$ for Firm A is described as "Firm A chooses to do R&D, enters if it learns cost is low, and doesn't enter if cost is high."

And so, for the extensive-form game in Figure A10.2, while Figure A10.6 gives the corresponding strategic-form game where, for each player, a strategy is a complete description of what the player does at each of her information sets, we can (and do) talk of the corresponding *reduced strategic form* of the extensive-form game, which is depicted in Figure A10.7.

		Firm B's strategy			
		1.	**2.**	**3.**	**4.**
	If firm A enters:	enter	enter	don't	don't
	If firm A doesn't enter:	enter	don't	enter	don't
A.	Does R&D, enters regardless of what is learned (strategies 1 and 5)	–5.5, –5.5	–5.5, –5.5	34, 0	34, 0
B.	Does R&D, enters (only) if learns that cost is low (strategies 2 and 6)	–2, 19	–2, 1.5	13, 17.5	13, 0
C.	Does R&D, enters (only) if learns cost is high (strategies 3 and 7)	–8.5, 8	–8.5, –7	16,15	16, 0
D.	Does R&D but does not enter regardless of outcome (strategies 4 and 8)	–5, 32.5	–5, 0	–5, 32.5	–5, 0
E.	Does not do R&D and enters (strategies 9, 10, 11, & 12)	–0.5, –5.5	–0.5, –5.5	39,0	39, 0
F.	Does not do R&D and does not enter (strategies 13 through 16)	0, 32.5	0, 0	0, 32.5	0, 0

Firm A's (reduced) strategy

Figure A10.7. The reduced-strategic-form game corresponding to the extensive-form game in Figure A10.2

To distinguish between these two corresponding strategic forms, the adjectives *full* (as in "a full strategy for Firm A," "Firm A's full set of strategies," "a full-strategy profile," and "the full strategic form") and *reduced* (as in "a reduced strategy for Firm A," "Firm A's reduced strategy set," "a reduced strategy profile," and "the reduced strategic form") are used. Note in this figure that because Firm B's two information sets are unordered, Firm B's reduced strategy set consists of the same four strategies as in its full strategy set.

A10.5. Mixed Strategies, Behaviorally Mixed Strategies, and Kuhn's Theorem

The definition of a *mixed strategy* for a finite extensive-form game and a player n is just what it was for a finite strategic-form game: It is a probability distribution over n's (finite) set of pure full strategies S_n. We imagine, more or less, that the player—say, the Chief Operating Officer (COO) of Firm A in the game in Figure A10.2—considers at the outset her sixteen full strategies depicted in Figure A10.6 and declares, "We'll play strategy 1 with probability 0.2, strategy 2 with probability 0.25, etc."

Formally, Σ_n denotes the set of these mixed strategies. That is, Σ_n is the set of all probability distributions on S_n. And Σ denotes the product space of mixed (full) strategy profiles, or $\Sigma = \prod_{n \in \mathcal{N}} \Sigma_n$.

We can, and sometimes do, work instead with the reduced strategic form, in which case, a mixed strategy for player n is a probability distribution on $\hat{S}_n$: Imagine top management declaring "We'll play strategy A [in Figure A10.7] with probability 0.25, strategy B with probability 0.3, and so forth." The set of mixed reduced strategies is denoted by $\hat{\Sigma}_n$, and the space of mixed reduced-strategy profiles is denoted by $\hat{\Sigma}$.

For $\sigma_n \in \Sigma_n$, there is an obvious corresponding $\hat{\sigma}_n \in \hat{\Sigma}_n$, namely

$$\hat{\sigma}_n(\hat{s}_n) = \sum_{s_n \in \hat{s}_n} \sigma_n(s_n). \tag{A10.1}$$

Or, in words, $\hat{\sigma}_n$ evaluated at the reduced strategy $\hat{s}_n$ is simply the sum of $\sigma_n(s_n)$ over all s_n that are strategically equivalent in the equivalence class $\hat{s}_n$. Of course, if $\hat{s}_n$ contains more than one full strategy s_n—if there is real reducing going on—this is a many-to-one map: Many mixtures of full strategies for player n that give the same sums in equation (A10.1) are the same mixture over reduced strategies. But this is entirely natural: If Firm A in our ongoing example says that they will play strategy 2 with probability 0.1 and the (strategically equivalent) strategy 6 with probability 0.05, this is the same as saying that, with probability 0.15, they will do the R&D and then enter if the R&D reveals that cost is low and stay out if cost is high. The "distinction" between strategies 2 and 6 is in what the firm would do if they didn't do the R&D. But since they are doing the R&D, this is a distinction without any real difference.

Behaviorally mixed strategies

When it comes to players choosing what they do according to some probability distribution—that is, mixing—a different way to describe what they will do involves so-called *behaviorally mixed strategies*. Suppose, for instance, Firm A's management declares: "We'll do R&D with probability 0.4. If we don't do R&D, we'll enter with probability 0.2. If we do R&D and learn that cost is low, we'll enter with probability 0.9. And if we do R&D and learn that cost is high, we won't enter at all." Firm A's management, with this statement, is specifying how they will randomize among actions available at each information set $h \in H_n$, if and when h is reached in the course of play. This sort of object, which describes how a player will mix at each of her information sets, is called a *behaviorally mixed strategy* (in this case, for Firm A).

Formally, a behaviorally mixed strategy (for player n) is an element of $\prod_{h \in H_n} \mathbf{P}(A(h))$ (where, recall that $\mathbf{P}(A(h))$ means the set of probability distributions on $A(h)$.) Temporarily write a behaviorally mixed strategy for player n as ρ_n, where (for $h \in H_n$) $\rho_n(h)$ is a probability distribution over $A(h)$, and $\rho_n(h)(a)$ (for $h \in H_n$ and $a \in A(h)$) is the probability $\rho_n(h)$ assigns to action $a \in A(h)$.

Given a behaviorally mixed strategy ρ, it is easy to construct a corresponding mixed (full) strategy by assuming that the mixing done by the player at each of her information sets is independent of mixing done at another information set. Writing $\sigma_n(\rho_n)$ for the mixed strategy that corresponds to the behaviorally mixed strategy ρ_n, and writing $\sigma_n(\rho_n)(s_n)$ for this mixed (full) strategy evaluated at the (full) pure strategy s_n, the formula is

$$\sigma_n(\rho_n)(s_n) = \prod_{h \in H_n} \rho_n(h)(s_n(h)). \tag{A10.2}$$

And then equation (A10.1) can be used to construct an equivalent mixed reduced strategy.

Going in the other direction—constructing a behaviorally mixed strategy ρ_n that corresponds to a given mixed (full) strategy σ_n—is more complex. For what follows, assume that the game has perfect recall. We begin with some temporary notation.

Fix a player n and an information set h that belongs to n. Arbitrarily pick a node $z \in h$, and let $z_1, z_2, \ldots, z_K = z$ be the (unique) partial path from an initial node z_1 to z. Temporarily define

$$\mathcal{K} := \{k : \iota(h(x_k)) = n, k = 1, \ldots, K-1\};$$

that is, $\mathcal{K}$ is the set of indices of nodes along this partial path at which n has the move. And, for $a \in A(h)$, define

$$S_n(z, a) := \{s_n \in S_n : s_n(h(z_k)) = a(z_{k+1}) \text{ for all } k \in \mathcal{K}, \text{ and } s_n(h(z)) = a\},$$

that is, $S_n(z, a)$ is the set of strategies for n at which n makes choices that (1) lead to the node z, and (2) at z, equal a.

I assert that, as the game has perfect recall, the set of strategies $S_n(z, a)$ is the same as $S_n(z', a)$ if z' is another node in h. In words, the arbitrary choice of $z \in h$ doesn't affect the set of strategies for n identified by $S_n(z, a)$. Hence, I replace $S_n(z, a)$ with $S_n(h, a)$ in what follows. I won't give a detailed proof of this assertion, but if you stare at Figure A10.5, you should be able to convince yourself that it is true.

Now fix a mixed (full) strategy σ_n. In constructing the corresponding behavior strategy ρ_n and, in particular, in saying how n will mix at information set $h \in H_n$, there are two cases:

Case 1. If $\sum_{a' \in A(h)} \left[\sum_{s_n \in S_n(h,a')} \sigma_n(s_n) \right] = 0$, then under σ_n, player n is never choosing a strategy that causes information set h to be reached, even supposing that all other players do whatever they can to reach information set h. Accordingly, how n mixes (behaviorally) at h is strategically irrelevant, and you may define ρ_n at h however you wish.

Case 2. If $\sum_{a' \in A(h)} \left[\sum_{s_n \in S_n(h,a')} \sigma_n(s_n) \right] > 0$, define (for $a \in A(h)$)

$$\rho_n(h)(a) := \frac{\sum_{\{s_n \in S_n(z,a)\}} \sigma_n(s_n)}{\sum_{a' \in A(h)} \left[\sum_{\{s_n \in S_n(z,a')\}} \sigma_n(s_n) \right]}. \tag{A10.3}$$

In words, the effective probability that n takes action a at h (for $h \in H_n$ and $a \in A(h)$) is the sum of the probabilities that she chooses a strategy that will—if the others do their part—get her to h, and she then chooses a, divided by the sum of the probabilities that she chooses a strategy that will get her to h.

"If the others do their part": what does that mean? It means that the other players take actions that cause the information set h to be reached with positive probability. But, of course, there can be several different ways that h can be reached, based on the actions of others. And you may well ask: Does it matter what the others do, to cause h to be reached? It does not. Put it this way: Fix strategies of the others such that h is reached with positive probability. Based on those strategies together with the strategies of $\iota(h)$, we can compute the probability that each $z \in h$ is reached, and we can compute the probability of reaching the successor to z that involves the choice of a at h. I assert that the ratio of these two probabilities is identical for all $z \in h$: Since this is an information set of $\iota(h)$, her impact on the ratio of the two for each $z \in h$ is the same. And, while both the numerator and denominator in that ratio change with changes in what the others are doing, they change in identical multiplicative fashion, so in finding the ratio of the two, the effects of what others do cancel out. Hence, in the formula (A10.3), we simply ignore "what the others do" to ensure that h is reached.

Because of Case 1, there can be some indeterminacy concerning the ρ_n that corresponds to a given σ_n. (In case σ_n is fully mixed—that is, assigns positive probability to every $s_n \in S_n$—Case 1 never arises, so ρ_n is determined given σ_n.) However, you may ask whether two different values of σ_n's can give rise to the same ρ_n, for information sets where ρ_n is determined by equation (A10.3). This can happen: In general, a mixed (full) strategy can encode correlations in what a player does at two information sets that are unordered by precedence. If you start with such a mixed strategy σ_n, apply equation (A10.3), and then apply equation (A10.2) to get back to a mixed strategy, the mixed strategy to which you will "return" will wipe out that correlation, because equation (A10.2) is based on the idea that behavioral randomizations at different information sets are statistically independent. As long as the game has perfect recall, this issue won't arise between information sets ordered by precedence in the game tree. But, for two information sets belonging to a single player that are unordered, it can happen.

In case this remark is opaque, here is an example, which also illustrates how Case 1 information sets affect the round-trip from a mixed strategy to a behavior strategy and back to a mixed strategy. Suppose Firm A chooses to play a mixed strategy in which it chooses strategy 1 with probability $1/2$ and strategy 8 with probability $1/2$. In both of these full strategies, Firm A does R&D, so its behavioral strategy at its initial information set is to do the R&D with probability 1.

As a result, this mixed strategy precludes reaching the information set following no R&D, so this a Case-1 information set; you can make up any behavior strategy you wish there. For the sake of concreteness, suppose that we choose to have the firm enter at that information set with probability 0.6 and not enter with probability 0.4. Note that, when you apply equation (A10.2) to this arbitrary choice of behavior, because there is zero probability of choosing not to do R&D, the resulting mixed strategy will assign zero probability to all strategies from 9 to 16.

What is behavior (per equation (A10.3)) at the information set where the firm does R&D and cost is low? With probability $1/2$, Firm A (playing strategy 1) chooses to enter, and with probability $1/2$ it is playing strategy 8 and chooses not to enter. And if cost is high, it (behaviorally) mixes $1/2$ and $1/2$ between entry and not.

Now apply equation (A10.2) to this behavior strategy. For one thing, the arbitrary choice of probabilities at the *no R&D* information set matters. If you do the computations, you'll find that this means strategies 1 through 4 together must have probability 0.6, and 5 through 8 must have probability 0.4. If we had different probabilities assigned arbitrarily at the *no R&D* information set, those numbers would change.

However, that's not the important observation about what happens when you apply equation (A10.2) to the behavior strategy derived from applying equation (A10.3). Instead, if you go through the calculations, you'll find that the derived probabilities of strategies 1 and 5 together, of 2 and 6 together, of 3 and 7 together, and of 4 and 8 together, are each $1/4$. Specifically, strategies 1, 2, 3, and 4 each have probability 0.15, while 5, 6, 7, and 8 each have probability 0.1. In the original mixture of strategies 1 and 8, each with probability $1/2$, Firm A is either entering regardless of what the R&D tells them, or they are not entering. Do the roundtrip of applying equation (A10.3) and then equation (A10.2), and there is probability $1/4$ of the reduced strategy in which they do R&D and then enter if they learn the costs are low, but don't enter if costs are high.

But, this . . . seeming anomaly doesn't matter in the end.

Kuhn's Theorem

Proposition A10.4. Kuhn's Theorem (Kuhn 1953). *In a game with perfect recall, every mixed strategy σ_n for a player n is strategically equivalent to the corresponding behavior* strategy ρ_n defined by equation (A10.3) (and defined arbitrary for Case-1 information sets), and every behavior strategy ρ_n for player n is strategically equivalent to the corresponding mixed strategy defined by equation (A10.2).

I do not provide a proof of this fundamental result here. Roughly speaking, the result stems from the fact that, with perfect recall, if z and z' are two nodes in the same information set h for a player n, then what we denoted by $S_n(z, a)$ (for $a \in A(h)$) is identical to $S_n(z', a)$, which in turn is the basic message of Figure A10.5. But the proof from this starting point is still a fair amount of work.

There are two points worth making in this regard:

1. Return to the example given just prior to the statement of Kuhn's Theorem, in which Firm A mixes between full strategies 1 and 8 with probabilities 1/2 apiece. Kuhn's Theorem says that this mixed strategy is strategically equivalent to the behaviorally mixed strategy in which Firm A does R&D and then, based on the result of the R&D, enters or doesn't enter with probability 1/2 apiece and where (arbitrarily) at the *no R&D* information set it enters with probability 0.6. And, applying Kuhn's Theorem again, this behaviorally mixed strategy is strategically equivalent to the mixed strategy in which the firm chooses strategy 1 with probability 0.15, and so forth. Therefore, the first mixed strategy, which mixes between full strategies 1 and 8, and the second mixed strategy, which puts positive probability on full strategies 1, 2, ..., 8, must be strategically equivalent. Indeed they are, and you might want to try check that this is so by picking one of Firm B's strategies and checking that, with the strategy for Firm B that you choose, the two mixed strategies generate the same distibution over outcomes.[9]

   In the same vein, this discussion has been about the connections between mixed full strategies and behaviorally mixed strategies. What about the connections between mixed reduced strategies and behaviorally mixed strategies? A useful exercise is for you to translate the 50-50 mixture of full strategies 1 and 8 into the mixture of reduced strategies, and then to follow through the constructions in equations (A10.2) and (A10.3) with this as the example.

2. And it is instructive to see what happens for extensive-form games without perfect recall. For such games, mixed strategies allow for more "outcomes" than can be achieved with behaviorally mixed strategies.[10] A useful exercise to help build understanding is to take each of the three prototypes of imperfect recall—Alice forgets whether she has moved, or what she did, or what she knew previously—as depicted in Figure A10.4, and find a mixed strategy that cannot be "replicated" with a behaviorally mixed strategy. To get you started, consider

---

[9] If you like cryptic remarks, here is one: What is happening here is related to the "trick" employed by Anscombe and Aumann (cf. Volume I, page 105). But, here, it isn't a trick at all, since additive separability is natural in the current context.

[10] Here is a sketch of the proof: Given a game without perfect recall, you can, for each player, "break up" her information sets so that she suffers no memory lapses. This gives each player more information sets, hence more full strategies, and therefore more mixed strategies. But, at all the new information sets that previously were a single information set, she can adopt the same behavioral strategy.

panel a, where Alice forgets that she moved. Since she has a single information set, she has two pure strategies, A and D. Suppose she mixes 50-50 between these two pure strategies, and Bob plays d. What is the outcome? And why can't she replicate this outcome with a behaviorally mixed strategy?

The significance of Kuhn's Theorem is that, for games with perfect recall, whether we model and analyze an extensive-form game using mixed strategies (either for the full strategy set or the reduced strategy set) or using behaviorally mixed strategies, we'll get the same "basic" results.[11] Since, in this volume, we only work with games with perfect recall, we can therefore choose whichever way of modeling the use of mixed strategies is most convenient. In later appendices, and for most purposes, you'll see that behavior strategies are usually (but not always) easier to work with.

Recall Definition A10.2(c) (page 532), the definition of the outcome $\pi(s)$ engendered by a pure strategy s. If I wanted to define the outcome engendered by a (classically) mixed strategy $\sigma = (\sigma_1, \ldots, \sigma_N)$, it would be

$$\pi(\sigma)(z) := \sum_{s=(s_1,\ldots,s_N) \in S} \pi(s)(z) \left[\prod_{i \in \mathcal{N}} \sigma_i(s_i) \right],$$

for each terminal node z. That is, we take every pure-strategy profile s, compute the probability that z is reached under that profile, and multiply this by the probability that s is the profile played (under independent mixings by the players), and then sum over all the pure-strategy profiles.

This calculation is more straightforward if we are working with behaviorally mixed strategies. For noninitial nodes z, use $\rho(a(z))$ to denote the probability that, at the node $p(z)$, the action taken (whether by a player or by Nature) is the action that leads to z. Recall that, for initial nodes z, $\rho(z)$ is the notation used for the probability of starting at z. Then, for any final node z, let $(z_1, z_2, \ldots, z_K)$ be the (unique) complete path leading from an initial node $z_1 \in Z_I$ to $z_K = z$. Then

$$\pi(\rho)(z) = \rho(z_1) \times \prod_{i=2}^{I} \rho(a(z_i)).$$

That is, one simply multiplies along the path leading to z the probabilities of each "transition" entailed in moving from an initial node (including in the product the probability of that initial node), along the path that leads to z.

In view of Kuhn's theorem, I make the following notational shift. Henceforth, σ will be used for a mixed-strategy profile, whether behaviorally mixed or mixed in the strategic form. Which form of mixed strategy is being employed will be identified in context.

---

[11] This is a loose statement because of the scare quotes around "basic." For the time being, think of basic results as the identification of Nash equilibria or the application of (iterated) dominance.

A10.6. Dominance and Nash Equilibrium

Having formulated an extensive-form game, the next step is to analyze it. The two tools of analysis from Appendix 9, dominance and Nash equilibrium, are used just as they were in Appendix 9. That is, any strategy profile engenders a distribution on terminal nodes, which can be converted to a vector of expected payoffs for the players. One strategy for player n strictly dominates another strategy for n if the first gives n a higher expected payoff no matter what strategies the other players choose. And a strategy profile is a Nash equilibrium if the expected payoff it provides to each player is as great as the expected payoff the player would receive if she changed her strategy, all others maintaining their part of the original strategy profile.

In addition, all of the discussion about the interpretation and use of these tools of analysis (and, for that matter, rationalizability) from Appendix 9 apply in this context.

As a practical matter and at first blush, it may seem that the way to conduct analysis is to convert an extensive-form game into the corresponding strategic-form game and analyze the latter. Take the game in Figure A10.2; that is, the game in its extensive form. You can probably intuit the following:

- The (reduced) strategy for Firm A of doing R&D and then not entering, regardless of result of the R&D, is strictly dominated by just not entering: Why spend money on R&D, the results of which the firm will ignore?

- And the strategy for Firm A of doing R&D and then entering regardless of result is strictly dominated by just entering, by similar logic.

But it may be difficult, staring at Figure A10.2, to go any further with your analysis. Consider instead Figure A10.7. With this strategic-form representation of the game, we quickly verify that strategy D for Firm A is strictly dominated by strategy F, and strategy A is strictly dominated by strategy E, confirming our intuition. And, in addition:

- Strategy E for Firm A strictly dominates both strategies B and C.

- A 50-50 mixture of strategies 3 and 4 for Firm B strictly dominates strategy 2.

- Having eliminated strategy B for Firm A, strategy 3 for Firm B iteratively weakly dominates strategy 1.

- And if we can rule out Firm B using strategies 1 or 2, strategy E for Firm A iteratively strictly dominates strategy F.

So, having eliminated strategies A, B, C, D, and F for Firm A, we can confidently predict that it will enter without doing R&D, which makes entry an unprofitable venture for Firm B; Firm B will not enter.

This isn't to say that we couldn't, by staring hard at Figure A10.2, come to this conclusion. And, in fact, Figure A10.2 provides part of the answer we found: Firm B sees Firm A enter or not and then (in the style of a behavior strategy) decides whether to enter. If Firm A does not enter, by entering, Firm B nets a positive profit whether cost is high or low. So, of course, Firm B enters if it sees Firm A failing to do so.

The harder questions are: What will Firm A do? What will Firm B do if Firm A enters? Suppose Firm B hypothesizes that Firm A is doing R&D and then only enters when cost is low. Then Firm B would like to enter, if Firm A does. But if Firm B hypothesizes that Firm A will not do the R&D and will enter anyway, then Firm B's expected payoff from entry is $0.3 \times 5 + 0.7 \times (-10) = -5.5$; it should not enter. *The key is for Firm B to see that Firm A's reduced strategy E strictly dominates Firm A's reduced strategy B.* Maybe Firm B can see this, but it takes some pretty sharp eyesight, unless and until the reduced strategic-form game is constructed.[12]

My point is that *working with Figure A10.2 alone*, perhaps we (and, more importantly, Firm B) can reach the conclusion that Firm A will enter without doing the R&D, and Firm B will (in response) not enter. But having Figure A10.7 is certainly helpful.

All that said, as we will see in Appendix 11, presenting and analyzing a situation as an extensive-form game will give us tools of analysis and insights that are lacking if we look only at the corresponding strategic form. And, for more complex extensive-form games than the game in Figure A10.2, it is in any case nearly impossible to write out the corresponding strategic-form game.

Put it this way: The (reduced) strategy profile E-3 (strategy E for Firm A, strategy 3 for Firm B) is a Nash equilibrium of the strategic-form game in Figure A10.7, as is the profile E-4. But the strategy profile F-1 is also a Nash equilibrium, and we seem to have concluded that the "answer" is E-3. We might not be concerned with E-4 being another Nash equilibrium—E-3 and E-4 give the same overall outcome—but what is the logic that led us away from F-1 as a valid possibility? The next two appendices provide answers, answers based on extensive-form-game logic that strategic-form games do not provide.[13]

A10.7. Beyond Finite Extensive-Form Games

Everything so far in this appendix has concerned finite extensive-form games, where "finite" refers to the number of players and the number of nodes in the game. We might, in economic applications, have reason to think of extensive-form games with an infinite number of players, for instance, if we wanted to capture the notion of a perfectly competitive market as an extensive-form game. And we will certainly have occasion to look at games with a countable number of players, but in which only a finite number are "involved" at any point in time. But, what is far

---

[12] For Firm B to conclude that Firm A will not choose to do R&D, working only from Figure A10.2, Firm B must put itself in the shoes of Firm A and evaluate two scenarios: (1) if Firm A enters, Firm B will not enter; (2) Firm B will enter if Firm A enters. Do the computations for both scenarios, and you find that in both, not doing R&D is better for Firm A in terms of its expected payoff than is doing R&D and entering only if cost is low. But doing the required computations amounts to constructing those pieces of Figure A10.7 that tell us that Firm A's strategy E dominates its strategy B. You might as well construct Figure A10.7 and be done with it.

[13] Warning: My assertion that strategic-form games do not provide this logic is controversial; see the discussions in Appendices 12 and 14 of *proper* equilibria and *strategic stability*.

more prevalent, *and what we will do in the text with some frequency,* is look at games with an infinite number of nodes.

There are several ways in which this happens. Think, for instance, of duopolists choosing capacities for production and then, after those capacities become known, engaging in Bertrand-style competition. Suppose that, at the second stage of choosing prices, players know which capacity they chose (of course) and what capacity their rival chose (which is a modeling choice). If the first-stage range of possible capacities is a closed interval of nonnegative real numbers, this gives uncountably many second-stage information sets. Or, even more simply, think of a situation in which a finite number of players are engaged in a first-price auction for some object, where each individual knows what the object is worth to herself but doesn't know what it is worth to others. If "own-worth" is drawn from an interval of real numbers, and if a player knows the worth of the object to herself prior to submitting her bid, she has uncountably many information sets at which she must formulate a bid. Models with such features occur in many contexts. And, if we want to be able to model mixed strategies by the players—and we will—uncountably many information set means uncountably many strategies; this will raise technical issues.

A second and different category of important models involves extensive-form games where actions must be chosen by players at an infinite sequence of times. For instance, we'll look at games with a finite collection of players, each of whom must make a choice at times $t = 0, 1, 2, \ldots$. This sort of game presents (at least) two complications: First, the notion of a "final node" that provides payoffs needs fixing. It becomes more natural in such situations to formulate things so that there are no final nodes, and payoffs attach to complete (countable length) paths of play. And, when it comes to corresponding strategic forms, if a player has a choice of two or more actions at countably many information sets, she has uncountably many strategies, so mixed strategies for the strategic form are probability distributions on an uncountable set. In such cases, dealing with behaviorally mixed strategies—and analyzing the game in those terms—becomes essential.

Allowing infinitely many nodes in an extensive-form game raises other possibilities. For instance, because we dealt with finite extensive-form games in earlier sections, we know that, from any node, we can trace back (using the rule that each node has a unique immediate predecessor) to find an initial node that precedes the given node. With infinitely many nodes, this is not assured: Starting from a node in the game tree, we could work back immediate predecessor by immediate predecessor and never reach an initial node. Indeed, just as there need not be final nodes, there may be no initial nodes. Even worse, one can have models where the unique-immediate-precessor property fails: Games played "in continuous time" have this feature (and require delicate treatment of how "rapidly" players can adjust the actions they are choosing).

Advanced textbooks in game theory discuss in general the technical problems that can arise and how they can be handled. In this volume, I steer a middle path. When a particular context calls for a game with some of these complications, I call out the problems that arise and suggest sources that suggest cures. But I do not undertake detailed discussion of the cures.

One "cure" is worth mentioning here, concerning Kuhn's Theorem. Kuhn (1953) shows the equivalence of mixed and behaviorally mixed strategies for finite extensive-form games with perfect recall. When we encounter the two complications listed above, we'll typically be working with behaviorally mixed strategies, and you may be concerned as to whether Kuhn's Theorem holds for such games. As long as the game has perfect recall, and with the appropriate definition of what constitutes a strategy, Kuhn's Theorem does hold; see Aumann (1964).

A10.8. Existence of Nash Equilibria

The existence of at least one Nash equilibrium for finite extensive-form games is immediate: Since Nash equilibria for an extensive-form game are just Nash equilibria for the corresponding strategic-form games, since the corresponding strategic-form game to a finite extensive-form game is finite, and since we know that finite strategic-form games always possess a Nash equilibrium, that's it.

However, it is worth observing that the existence result depends on the (possible) use of mixed strategies. So, one can ask: Do finite extensive-form games without perfect recall necessarily have Nash equilibria when we restrict to behaviorally mixed strategies? Since we do not deal with games without perfect recall in this volume, the answer is not hugely interesting, except for readers who are curious about such things. (If you are not curious, skip the rest of this page.)

For the record, the answer is No. A counterexample is given as Exercise 7.40 in Jehle and Reny (2010): Alice must, at two consecutive information sets, choose either H or T. But she has forgotten at the second information set what she chose at the first. If she chooses differently at the two information sets, she receives payoff -1 and the game ends. (Bob, the second player, gets 0.) If she chooses the same thing at the two information sets, Bob (without knowing whether Alice chose HH or TT) must choose H or T. Bob gets 1 and Alice, -1, if Bob's choice matches Alice's two choices; Bob gets -1 and Alice 1 if Bob's choice does not match Alice's. So: Suppose Bob, if called on to act, chooses H with probability $p > 1/2$. Alice's best response to this is the pure (and behaviorally implementable) strategy TT, which leads Bob to defect to T with probability 1. Similarly, there cannot be a Nash equilibrium in which Bob chooses T (if called on to choose) with probability $q > 1/2$. The only possible equilibrium has Bob mixing between H and T with probability $1/2$ each. But then Alice's best response in behaviorally mixed strategies is HH for sure or TT for sure. And these lead Bob to defect from his supposed 50-50 strategy. Of course, the Nash equilibrium in mixed strategies is for Alice to mix between HH and TT, each with probability $1/2$. But she can't implement that strategy in behaviorally mixed strategies.

What about extensive-form games that are not finite? If the corresponding strategic-form game satisfies the conditions of Proposition A9.8(b) or A9.10, we get existence. But the application of A9.7(b) (strategy sets are nonempty, convex, and compact subsets of finite-dimensional Euclidean space) rarely hold for interesting not-finite extensive-form games, so to prove general existence results, A9.10 seems a more likely-to-succeed strategy. In any event, in applications found in the text, we'll generally be showing the existence of an equilibrium in the specific context of the application, which directly settles the existence question for the application.

A10.9. Strategically Equivalent Extensive Forms

On pages 527-8, I challenged you to redraw Figure A10.2 with two initial nodes and with three information sets for Firm A. Figure A10.8 is my rendering.

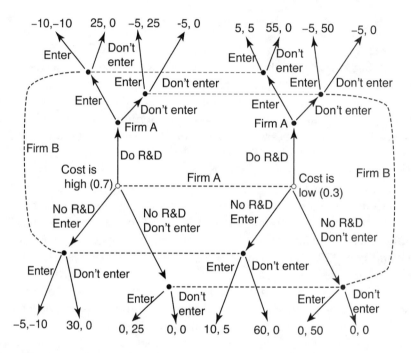

Figure A10.8. An alternate extensive-form game representation of Figure 10.2 (Firm A's payoff are listed first)

The two initial nodes split the tree into a lefthand side, where cost is hgh, and a righthand side, where it is low. The top half of the tree is where Firm A has chosen to do R&D; the bottom half is where it chose not to. Since Firm B doesn't know the cost or whether Firm A did R&D, its two information sets wind around the tree, with nodes in all four quadrants.

Because Firm A has three information sets in this figure, with three options at the first and two apiece at the other two, Firm A has $3 \times 2 \times 2 = 12$ full strategies, and not the 16 full strategies that it has if the extensive form is Figure A10.2. How is this possible, if the two extensive forms represent the same strategic situation? The answer is that the 12 full strategies for this extensive form "collapse" four pairs of full strategies into four full strategies. Look back at Figure A10.6 (page 534) and strategies 1 and 5 for Firm A. In the list of 12 full strategies for Figure A10.8, one of the 12 is: Do R&D (at Firm A's first information set), enter if cost is low (at the single-node information set where it has learned that cost is low), enter if it is high (at the cost-is-high information set). In Figure A10.6, this splits into full strategies 1 and 5, since the decision whether to enter or not if the firm doesn't do R&D is mooted in Figure A10.8: The first decision is to do R&D, or enter without doing R&D, or don't enter and don't do R&D. In Figure A10.8, therefore, there is no (irrelevant in terms of reduced strategies) information set at which Firm A decides whether to enter having chosen "no R&D" at its first (in Figure A9.2) information set. In other words, the 12 full strategies for Figure A10.8 have a somewhat reduced full strategy set, relative to the 16 full strategies for Figure A10.2.

This raises a technical question: For a given extensive form, which transformations can be made to the elements of the extensive form without altering the basic strategic structure being represented? There are more "strategically neutral" transformations than this example illustrates, and if you are interested, a full characterization of ways to transform an extensive form without changing the basic strategic structure is given by Dalkey (1953) and Thompson (1952). (These two papers, or rather, the point they make about strategically neutral transformations of an extensive form, will reappear in Appendix 14.)

Bibliographic Notes

The basic elements of an extensive-form game are developed in von Neumann and Morgenstern (1944), although in their development, the "order of moves" is fixed; they do not consider extensive forms in which, say, Alice might move first or third, and she won't know which it is if called on to move. (See, for instance, Figure 10 on page 78 of this classic work.)

The development of the basic elements and structure of extensive-form games as presented here is unclear to me, but it is clearly the case that, in the early 1950s, a number of fundamental contributions were made, including Kuhn (1953), Dalkey (1953), and Thompson (1952). Aumann (1964) must also be listed as a fundamental contribution, as it extends Kuhn's Theorem to non-finite games, providing foundations for a lot of the applications discussed in the text.

Appendix Eleven

Subgame Perfection (and Credibility)

Consider the extensive-form game in Figure A11.1(a) and its corresponding strategic-form representations in panel b. This game is called the *threat game*.

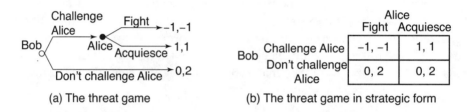

Figure A11.1. The threat game (Bob's payoff is listed first)

In this game, Bob must decide whether to challenge Alice. If challenged, Alice must decide whether to fight Bob or to acquiesce.[1] Bob reasons: If challenged, Alice's choice is between fighting, netting her a payoff of -1, or acquiescing, which nets her 1. Hence (he concludes), she will, if challenged, choose to acquiesce, and so he is safe in challenging her, which gives him 1 instead of 0 if he doesn't challenge her. And, indeed, if you examime panel b, Bob challenging Alice and Alice acquiescing is a Nash equilibrium of this game.

But, in this case, panel b provides a second Nash equilibrium, in which Alice fights and Bob does not challenge her. Alice can get away with "fighting" because, if Bob doesn't challenge her, she doesn't actually have to fight. One might imagine that this second equilibrium involves Alice *threatening* Bob, "If you challenge me, I'll fight." If Bob finds this credible, he doesn't challenge Alice, and the threat costs her nothing.

On technical grounds, we might dismiss this second Nash equilibrium because it involves Alice playing a weakly dominated strategy; that is, *Acquiesce* weakly dominates *Fight* for her. But, this doesn't disqualify *no challenge-fight* as a Nash equilibrium. A more convincing reason to dismiss the second equilibrium is that, if Bob challenges Alice, he has called her bluff, and put her to the test or on the spot, so to speak. She knows she has been challenged, her threat has failed, and there is nothing she can do about that. Surely, at this point, she realizes that acquiescing is the better choice for her.

---

[1]   The term "acquiesce" is used because of the connection of this game with the so-called chain-store paradox, which is discussed in Chapter 22 of the text.

The issue is one of credibility. In particular, is Alice's threat credible? Insofar as we judge that it is not, Nash equilibrium as a solution concept is inadequate. We need something stronger. Game theory suggests that we employ *subgame perfection*.

A11.1. Subgame Perfection

We restrict attention to games with perfect recall.

Definition A11.1. *A **proper subgame** of an extensive-form game is a set of nodes $\{z\} \cup S(z)$, together with all the accompanying parts of the original extensive-form game, such as the assignment of players to nodes, labels of actions, payoffs, and probabilities of Nature's actions (all restricted to $\{z\} \cup S(z)$), if the following additional property holds: For all $z' \in \{z\} \cup S(z)$, $h(z') \subseteq \{z\} \cup S(z)$. And if $\{z\} \cup S(z)$ is the game tree for a proper subgame, we say that z is the **root** of that subgame.*

This fairly opaque definition can be restated as follows: A proper subgame of an extensive-form game consists of some single node z and all of its successors, as long as every information set that contains z or any of its successors, is entirely contained in z and its successors (together with the other elements that make up an extensive-form game). Note that, by perfect recall, z must be an information set on its own, or $\{z\} \in H$. Because if some $z' \neq z$ was in the same information set as z, perfect recall implies that z' is not a successor of z, and so z and all its successors would fail the definition.

In essence, a proper subgame of an extensive-form game can be thought of as an extensive-form game in its own right. If we have a strategy profile for the original extensive-form game, that profile, restricted to nodes in a proper subgame, is a strategy profile for the subgame in its own right.

Two bits of care are called for here:

- When we say that a strategy profile for the whole game induces a strategy profile for a proper subgame, we necessarily mean a profile of full strategies for the players, not reduced strategies: Suppose that z^o is the root of a proper subgame. Suppose as well that for some information set h with $\iota(h) = n$, some $z \in h$ precedes z^o. And suppose that, in the proper subgame with root z^o, there is an information set h' with $\iota(h') = n$. Then if player n chooses an action at h that makes reaching h' impossible, a reduced strategy for n with this action gives no guidance as to what n would do in at the information set h' in the proper subgame.

- And, if we have a strategy profile that involves mixed strategies, the phrase "restricted to nodes in a proper subgame," requires that we take each pure strategy for the original game, restrict it to the nodes in the proper subgame, and sum up the probabilities in the mixed strategy for the full game that give the same restricted-to-the-subgame strategy. This is all a lot clearer if the mixed strategy is behaviorally mixed. Which calls for a remark (that you might want to prove): If an extensive-form game has perfect recall, then so do all of its proper subgames, viewed as games in their own right.

Definition A11.2. *A Nash equilibrium profile (whether in pure or mixed or behaviorally mixed strategies) for a given extensive-form game is **subgame perfect** if, for every proper subgame of the original game, the profile, restricted to the subgame, is a Nash equilibrium for the subgame.*

This definition is, essentially, a generalization of the logic employed above for the Threat Game. To explain, a further definition and a bit of a digression are useful.

Definition A11.3. *For a given extensive-form game and strategy profile, a node z is said to be **on-path** if there is positive probability (under the strategy profile) that the node z will be reached. An information set h is **on-path** if some node $z \in h$ is on-path. Nodes and information sets that are not on-path under a given strategy profile are said to be **off-path**.*[2]

To be a Nash equilibrium, a strategy profile requires that each player is playing (with positive probability) only pure strategies that are best responses to what other players are playing. At an information set $h \in H_n$ that is on-path, the actions of player n have real consequences for player n's overall payoff.[3] But, with one exception, if $h \in H_n$ is not on-path, then from the perspective of n playing a best response to what the other players are doing, n has a free choice of action; since there is zero probability of reaching the information set, there is zero probability of reaching any final node that follows nodes in the information set. As a result, in computing her expected payoff, n's payoffs for those final nodes all get zero weight. The one exception to this is if h is off-path solely because of earlier actions by n; in that case, if n changed her earlier actions, she might put h on-path, which would make her actions there consequential.

A couple of examples may help you through the previous paragraph. First, consider the actions of Alice in the Threat Game. In the strategy profile in which Bob chooses *no challenge* and Alice chooses *fight*, Alice's one-node information set is off-path; Bob choosing not to challenge Alice means that Alice will not have to act at this information set. And, so, in terms of her overall expected payoff, Alice can do whatever she wants. In particular, she can threaten to fight, since this threat has no impact on her expected payoff. But, in terms of being a Nash equilibrium, this threat is consequential for Bob's behavior. For Bob, not challenging Alice is a best response to her threatening to fight because, if instead he challenges her, against her bit of the strategy profile, he loses. (And, yes, this threat is not credible. But that's where we're headed. The point is that the criterion of being a Nash equilibrium doesn't get us there. Subgame perfection will do so, both in this particular game and more generally.)

---

[2] The terms *on-* and *off-path* are perhaps not standard in the literature, but they save on a lot of key strokes, so I use them. In the literature, synonyms for on-path include *along the path of play* or *in-equilibrium*; synonyms for off-path include *off the path of play* and, especially, *out of equilibrium*. I particularly dislike in and out of equilibrium, because the terms (should) apply to all strategy profiles and not only equilibrium profiles.

[3] Strictly speaking, this is not quite true. Suppose that all final nodes following nodes in $z \in h \in H_n$ that are along the path of play give player n the same payoff. Then, even if h is on-path, it doesn't matter to n what she does at that information set.

The one exception to "off-path behavior is unrestricted by Nash equilibrium" is illustrated by the game in Figure A11.2. Consider the strategy profile in which Alice plays D-α and Bob chooses a. Because Alice is choosing D, her second information set is off-path. And, accordingly, her choice of α has no impact on her overall payoff, *as long as she persists with D as her initial choice.* But Alice is not choosing separate actions; she is choosing a strategy. And if Bob is choosing a, Alice is better off with A-δ than with the strategy D-α. Of course, this kills the strategy profile D-α versus a as a Nash equilibrium: Can you reason your way to the conclusion that, in this game, the unique Nash-equilibrium outcome is A followed by d?[4]

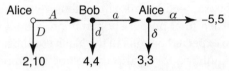

Figure A11.2. Alice threatens herself (Alice's payoffs are listed first)

Going back to the notions of proper subgames and subgame perfection: These two notions, working together, restrict the "free choices" of players at nodes off the path of play (that they themselves don't put off the path of play). Recall the basic philosophy of a Nash equilibrium. It is advanced as a necessary condition for the obvious way to play a given game, supposing that the game has such a way. The logic of subgame perfection then is: If a proper subgame is reached, every player will know that this is so, because whatever happens subsequently, since information sets don't cross to outside the successors of the root z, every player will know that play went through the node z. If some strategy profile is the obvious way to play the full game, then what the strategy profile prescribes "conditional on having gone through the node z" should involve each player playing a best response against what the other players are doing conditional on having gone through the node z. In other words, an obvious way to play should involve Nash behavior in at least every proper subgame.

And, going back to the Threat Game, this logic is, in simpler form, what led us to the conclusion that Bob should challenge Alice: Alice, if challenged, will know that she has been challenged. What remains is a trivial proper subgame, and she should be expected to choose a best response in that subgame, which is for her to acquiesce. This game has two Nash equilibria, but only *challenge-acquiesce* is subgame perfect.

Existence of subgame-perfect Nash equilibria

Proposition A11.4. *Every finite extensive-form game possesses at least one subgame-perfect Nash equilibrium.*

---

[4] Be careful here: I'm not asking you to show that A-δ versus d is the unique subgame-perfect equilibrium. That's easy. I want you to show that it is the unique *Nash*-equilibrium outcome. And I say "outcome" and not Nash equilibrium, because there are many Nash equilibria. (If Bob is playing d, what is true about Alice's second information set?) Can you characterize the full set of Nash equilibria?

Two proofs are available. The first anticipates Appendix 12. Among other things, in Appendix 12 we define *sequential equilibria*, assert that one exists for every finite extensive-form game (relying on a proof in Fudenberg and Tirole 1991b), and conclude that every sequential equilibrium is subgame perfect (Corollary A12.8). Alternatively, proceed as follows. First note that proper subgames of a given game are either disjoint or nested. That is, if nodes z and z' are (distinct) roots of two proper subgames of a given game, then one of $z' \in S(z)$ or $z \in S(z')$ or $[\{z\} \cup S(z)] \cap [\{z'\} \cup S(z')] = \emptyset$ must hold.[5] Hence, in any finite extensive-form game, we speak of "final" proper subgames—that is, proper subgames that contains no smaller proper subgames. Find a Nash equilibrium for every such final proper subgame—existence is guaranteed, because the extensive-form game is finite—and then turn the root z of each final proper subgame into a final node, with payoffs given by the equilibrium expected payoffs in the Nash equilibrium. Proceed in this fashion, finding Nash equilibria for final proper subgames and then substituting for them a final node (at the root of each proper subgame) whose payoffs are the Nash equilibrium payoffs; since the game is finite, this procedure ends at some point. Then paste together all the Nash equilibrium subgame strategies, and you have a subgame-perfect Nash equilibrium.

Of course, no such process works for infinite extensive-form games, especially those with paths of infinite length through the tree. Such games require (and, in Appendix A15 in particular, we develop) different arguments.

A small glich in these definitions

A small glich in how I've defined things should be noted: The game tree for a proper subgame consists of a single node z and all its successors. But a game tree, as defined here, can have several initial nodes. So it is possible, under my formal definitions, that an extensive-form game is, as a whole, not a proper subgame of itself. (Look back at Definition A11.2 to see how I finessed this issue.) If it bothers you, you can always take a game tree with several initial nodes and insert a single even-more-initial node that belongs to Nature, where Nature's actions lead to each of the original initial nodes, with probabilities given by the probability distribution originally provided for the initial nodes. Of course, then the root of a proper subgame z can be a move assigned to Nature. But nowhere in this section have I said otherwise.

A11.2. Games of Complete and Perfect Information

Definition A11.5. *An extensive-form game is said to have **complete and perfect information** if every information set consists of a single node.*

It is obvious that a extensive-form game of complete and perfect information has perfect recall and that every nonfinal node (or even final nodes, if you want to

---

[5]   Proof: Suppose $z'' \in [\{z\} \cup S(z)] \cap [\{z'\} \cup S(z')]$. Then both z and z' are in $P(z'')$. Tracing back the partial path leading from z'' back to an initial node, one of z or z' must be hit first, and whichever it hit first is a successor of the other.

stretch the point) in the game is the root of a proper subgame. Hence, the process
by which we just (informally) proved the existence of a subgame-perfect Nash
equilibrium for finite extensive-form games can be used with a vengeance in *finite*
extensive-form games with complete and perfect information. The process, which
goes by such names as *rollback* and *backward induction*, works as illustrated for the
game depicted in Figure A11.3(a). The game involves three players, Alice, Bob, and
Carol.

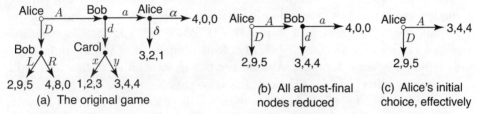

Figure A11.3. Rolling back a game of complete and perfect information (payoffs
are given in order Alice first, Bob second, and Carol third)

Suppose Alice chooses A and Bob chooses a. Then it is Alice's turn (again),
choosing between α and δ. If Alice chooses α, she gets 4. Choosing δ gets her
3. So, of course, she chooses α. Therefore, Bob knows that if he is given the move
after a choice of A by Alice and he chooses a, then Alice will choose α and his
payoff will be 0. (And in addition, Alice's eventual payoff will be 4, and Carol will
get 0.)

Similarly, if Alice chooses D, Bob will choose L. And if Alice chooses A and
Bob chooses d, Carol will choose y. We go to each almost-final node, ask whose
move it is, expecting that the person choosing will choose the action that gives him
or her the highest payoff. Hence, we can "reduce" the game to be, effectively, the
game in panel b. And in the game so reduced, if Bob gets to choose, we expect
him to choose d. Which reduces the game still further, to panel c and Alice's initial
choice, effectively: She will choose A, and now going back to previous steps, Bob
will choose d.

This procedure clearly generates a subgame-perfect equilibrium. Every node is
the root of a proper subgame, and from every node, this procedure is producing a
Nash equilibrium.

Each step of this procedure is "forced," unless and until we come up against a
node where the player making the choice has two or more options that give her the
same best payoff. In case of such a tie, the player who is choosing is free to choose
however she wishes (among those actions that are tied for best). However, if we
imagine that payoffs are chosen "generically," we'll never encounter any ties.[6]

---

[6] "Chosen 'generically'" means, chosen from a generic set in the space of payoffs, $R^{N \times Z_F}$. The term,
"generic set" has several definitions in mathematics; the one we will use is that the set is nongeneric if
it is the union of finitely many manifolds that have lower dimension than the host space (which in this
case is $R^{N \times Z_F}$), and a set is generic if its complement is nongeneric. Nongeneric sets have Lebesgue
measure zero in the host space, so for any probability distribution on the host space that is absolutely

Proposition A11.6. (Zermelo's Theorem) *A finite extensive-form game of complete and perfect information has a pure-strategy, subgame-perfect Nash equilibrium. If payoffs for the game are chosen generically, it has a **unique** (pure-strategy) subgame-perfect Nash equilibrium.*

Note that the uniqueness result concerns *subgame-perfect* equilibria. The Threat Game, a game of complete and perfect information, has two Nash equilibria, only one of which—the one that the rollback procedure generates—is subgame perfect.

This procedure corresponds to iterated weak dominance in the corresponding strategic-form game. Why weak dominance? Consider Alice's final choice on the right-hand side of the game in Figure A11.3(a). When we "eliminate" for her the choice of δ, we are in effect saying that her (full) strategy A-α weakly dominates A-δ. This is only weak domination because, if Bob chooses either d-L or d-R (and Carol chooses either x or y), Alice gets the same payoff whether she chooses A-δ or A-α. If is only where Bob chooses a that A-α is strictly superior to A-δ. But, in the spirit with which this appendix began—in which strategies by players are credible—Alice choosing A-δ lacks credibility. If put on the move at her right-hand node/information set and faced with choosing either a payoff of 4 for herself or 3, of course she will pick α to get the larger payoff 4.

"Of course?" Why this is less than clear

Consider the game depicted in Figure A11.4, which is a variation on the so-called centipede game.

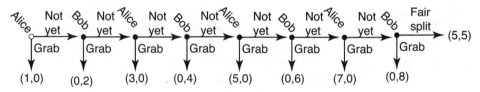

Figure A11.4. A centipede game (Alice's payoff is listed first)

A dollar is put on the table, and Alice is given the option of grabbing it or saying "not yet." If she grabs it, the game ends. If she doesn't, a second dollar is put on the table, and Bob can grab it or say "not yet." And so on, until $8 are on the table, and Bob has the final choice: At this final choice, he can grab $8 or say "fair split," in which case Alice and Bob get $5 each.

If you roll back this game of complete and perfect information, assuming that dollars = payoffs, you see that Bob will grab at the rightmost (nonterminal) node, so Alice should grab the node before that, and so forth. Eventually, you conclude that Alice should grab the $1 at the start. "Grab whenever you can" is the unique subgame-perfect Nash equilibrium for this game.

I've played variations of this game with different subject populations, and the prediction that Alice will grab the $1 at the start is rarely what happens. And it is

---

continuous with respect to Lebesgue measure, there is zero probability of choosing a point for which a tie is encountered.

easy to see why: Put yourself in Bob's shoes. If Alice starts by saying, "not yet," what is he to think? The great book of subgame perfection says that she should have grabbed the $1, but she didn't. Maybe she never read that book. Maybe she is too dumb to understand what it said. So, maybe, Bob reasons, if he says "not yet," there is a chance she'll say "not yet" again, and he'll be able to do better than grabbing the $2. In particular, he reasons, if he says "not yet," she'll entertain the same sort of doubts about him that he is entertaining about her.

But, he continues to think, if she anticipates that he will entertain these doubts and so say "not yet," she can grab $3. So maybe it is entirely sensible for her to start with "not yet" and lure him into this sort of logic. In which case, perhaps, he should expect her to grab $3 on the next stage, so he should just take his $2 and run.

I'm not asserting that there is a clear answer to this conundrum. But the "of course" with which the previous subsection ended is anything but obvious. To say more about this requires tools of game theory that arrive in Appendix 13.

Where "ties" have important consequences

Proposition A11.6 says that ties are unlikely with generically chosen payoffs for finite extensive-form games. But in many game-theoretic *models* of economic interest, ties are not only likely: They emerge in equilibrium analysis. You can see this at work in Chapter 19, but let me give a simple example here.

Alice wishes to hire Bob to perform a task for her. She will offer Bob a wage, and he will then either accept or say, "No thanks." If he takes the job, her payoff is 100 less the wage she offers (and pays). If he doesn't take the job, her payoff is zero. If he takes the job, his payoff is the wage less 10. If he turns down the job, his payoff (what we call his *reservation level of utility* or *reservation payoff*) is 35. So what wage should she offer?

The issue posed by this simple extensive-form game (of complete and perfect information) is that it is convenient to model Alice's choice of wage as being some number $w \in [0, 100]$. That is, she has a continuum of options at her (initial) node. So, this is not a finite extensive-form game.

First, dispose of imperfect equilibria. Suppose Bob adopts the strategy, "Unless Alice offers me a wage of $99 (or more), I'm saying no." Alice's best response to this strategy is to offer $99. And this, together with Bob's "I'm not working for less than $99" is a Nash equilibrium, because Bob's threat to refuse any wage less than $99 doesn't harm him; she's going to offer him $99, and he will accept.

But his threat to reject a wage of, say, $80, is not credible, at least not in terms of the game as we've described it. If she has the power to make a "take-it-or-leave-it" wage offer, which is implicit in the extensive-form model in which she offers a wage and he either accepts or declines, and if she offers $80, then his incentives given this fait accompli are to take the offer. In terms of the ideas in this appendix, the only credible strategies for Bob require him to take any wage offer strictly greater than $45.

What does this mean for subgame-perfect equilibria? The *only* subgame-perfect equilibrium is for Alice to offer precisely $45. Bob accepts, as part of the strategy of rejecting any offer strictly less than \$45 and accepting any offer of \$45 or more. This is the only subgame-perfect equilibrium, because in the proper subgames that start with Bob hearing an offer w from Alice, he must accept if $w > 45$ and reject if $w < 45$. By offering $w = 45 + \epsilon$ for $\epsilon > 0$ and small, Alice can get a payoff of $55 - \epsilon$. Since $\epsilon > 0$ is arbitrary, she must get \$45 or more in any subgame-perfect equilibrium (if she got less, she could defect to offering 45+ a small enough ϵ). And she can't do better than 55, given Bob's rejection of any wage offer strictly less than 45. So in a subgame-perfect equilibrium, if one exists (and we've already seen that one does exist), she must get 55 exactly. And the only way that can happen is if she offers $w = 45$ and Bob accepts.

We said earlier that, in finding subgame-perfect equilibria in games of complete and perfect information (of which this is one), a player who is indifferent has a free choice. But in this game, in the unique subgame-perfect equilibrium, Bob doesn't have a free choice when faced with the one offer that makes him indifferent.[7]

Suppose that, instead of allowing Alice to offer any wage $w \in [0, 100]$, she can only offer a wage that is an integer multiple of \$0.01. Then a second subgame-perfect equilibrium has Alice offer \$45.01, which Bob accepts; Bob will accept any offer greater or equal to \$45.01, and will turn down any offer of \$45.00 or less. And, for this model, you can construct any number of mixed-strategy equilibria. (Bob randomizes between accepting or rejecting an offer of \$45. His probability of acceptance can be such that Alice finds \$45 optimal, it can be such that she finds \$45.01 optimal, and it can make her indifferent, so she can randomize in what she offers.)

Allowing Alice to offer any wage $w \in [0, 100]$ is convenient when it comes to analysis ("there is a unique subgame-perfect equilibrium") and exposition (we avoid all those mixed-strategy equilibria). But this modeling convenience does raise the issue illustrated by this example and, as examples in Chapter 19 illustrate, this issue is not always so easily resolved as in this simple example.

Bottom line: The issue of what Bob does when he is indifferent appears frequently in the text, in many models. In terms of the insights provided by these models, the issue probably isn't significant. A real-life Alice, who probably isn't quite sure what real-life Bob's reservation level of utility is and who faces some serious losses if Bob says "no thanks," is likely to err on the side of caution and offer him, say, \$50. This is an issue where theoretical niceties should be addressed and must be tolerated, but not taken too seriously.[8]

A11.3. A Different Credibility Issue

Because the title of the appendix includes the term "credibility," I ought to mention another credibility issue that turns up in later appendices and in the text. It involves

---

[7] In general, things are not so simple as in this example. Chapter 19 will develop this idea further.

[8] That said, a seminal article in the theory of bilateral bargaining, Rubinstein (1982), comes to a dramatic conclusion that depends crucially on the ability to propose bargains drawn from a continuum of possibilities. This is discussed in Chapter 23.

subgame perfection in a different way. Consider the extensive-form game in Figure A11.5(a), and its strategic-form equivalent in panel b. In the literature, this is known as either the trust game or as the promise game.

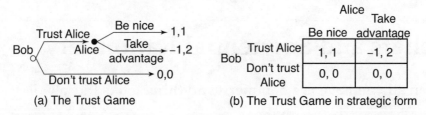

(a) The Trust Game (b) The Trust Game in strategic form

Figure A11.5. The trust (or promise) game (Bob's payoffs are given first)

This game has a single pure-strategy Nash equilibrium, which is that Bob doesn't trust Alice and Alice chooses *Take advantage*. Alice's information set is off-path, so she could choose *Be nice* without affecting her payoff. But, were she to choose *Be nice*, Bob's best response is to trust her, and if Bob trusts her, her best response to that is to take advantage of his trust, which leads him not to trust her. And, just to check, if he doesn't trust her, *Take advantage* is a best response for her.

The game does have mixed-strategy Nash equilibria as well: If Alice mixes between her two strategies, playing *Be nice* with probability $1/2$ or less and *Take advantage* with complementary probability, Bob's best response is not to trust her, which allows her to mix as a best response.

But (since this appendix is about subgame perfection), her one-node information set is the root of a trivial subgame at which taking advantage is her unique best response, so there is a unique subgame-perfect equilibrium; the mixed-strategy equilibria give the same outcome as the one subgame-perfect equilibrium, but they are not subgame perfect.

All that said, note that the unique Nash equilibrium *outcome* gives Bob and Alice payoffs of 0 apiece. Alice would like to promise Bob that she'll be nice. But, by the logic of that leads us to subgame perfection in the threat game—put "on the spot," she'll do what is best for herself—the promise to be nice isn't credible. We get back to this game in Appendix 15.[9]

Bibliographic Notes

The seminal paper related to this chapter is Selten (1965), in which the concept of subgame perfection first appears. Zermelo's Theorem originates in E. Zermelo (1913).

---

[9] And, when we do, remember how this game is different from the threat game, when we come to discussing the papers Fudenberg and Levine (1989, 1992).

Appendix Twelve

Beliefs and Sequential Rationality

When all you have is a hammer, everything looks like a nail

Assuming you read Chapter 17, you know my position that noncooperative game theory is *not* economics. It is, instead, a tool that economists use to study economic phenomena. And, since there are a lot of "tools" in the game-theory toolkit, let me rephrase: The different concepts and techniques of analysis that make up noncooperative game theory constitute a toolkit of concepts and techniques of analysis that economists use to study economic phenomena.

As with any sort of tool, different concepts and techniques from this toolkit work well in some cases but are wholly inappropriate in others. Insofar as you are using game-theoretic tools in your analysis of economic phenomena, it is up to you to judge when and whether a particular tool from the toolkit fits with what you are trying to explain or understand.

We saw the need for this sort of discretion in earlier appendices. Perhaps the most prominent and important example concerns the use of Nash equilibrium analysis; the message in Appendix 9 is that it makes sense when, for some reason outside the formal model, you think the individuals involved see, or at least might see, an *obvious way to act and interact*. And, on page 554, I suggest that, even in games with complete and perfect information, subgame perfection has its limits of applicability; this echoes a related comment about iterated dominance (pages 497–9).

This appendix concerns somewhat fashionable game-theoretic tools that are used to study complex extensive-form games: beliefs at information sets, sequential rationality from information sets, and various consistency criteria between a strategy profile and the players' beliefs. You may have encountered these tools already, with names such as *perfect Bayesian equilibrium* and *sequential equilibrium*.

These particular concepts and tools—and, more generally, this way of thinking about extensive-form games—are very dependent on the subgame-perfection principle that, if Alice, earlier in a game, does something that is not in her own "best interests," she is very unlikely to make that sort of mistake again. In the course of this appendix, as I describe these tools of analysis, I keep hammering on this general principle as it pertains to the tools being developed. I do so because it is not enough that you understand how the tool is used; you must also understand what the tool entails, so you know when it is (or is not) an appropriate tool to use. After developing this set of tools, my bottom line, stated in Section A12.5, is that one must be careful in their use; the implicit subgame-perfection principle is a strong assumption, and not every economic context is a nail to this particular hammer.

A12.1. Motivation for This Appendix

Consider the extensive-form game in Figure A12.1(a), whose corresponding strategic-form representation is in panel b. Panel b reveals two pure-strategy Nash equilibria: the first where Alice chooses A and Bob chooses x; the second where Alice chooses L and Bob chooses y. The extensive-form representation has no proper subgames, so both equilibria are subgame perfect.

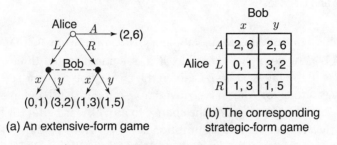

(a) An extensive-form game

(b) The corresponding strategic-form game

Figure A12.1. A motivating example (Alice's payoffs are given first)

Even though the A-x equilibrium is subgame perfect, it is based on a "threat" by Bob that costs him nothing if it works: Alice chooses A, because she fears x by Bob; if she chooses A, he needn't carry out his threat. But, in the *spirit* of subgame perfection, is Bob's threat credible? Given the opportunity to move, choosing y strictly dominates x for Bob whether he is at the left-hand node in his information set or the right-hand node: If Alice chose L—if Bob is at the left-hand node—then x will net him 1, while y nets him 2; and if Alice chose R, then x nets him 3 while y nets him 5. In the strategic-form representation of this game—that is, in panel b—y only weakly dominates x. But *conditional on being given the opportunity to move*, y strictly dominates x. The threat to choose x is not credible if Alice calls Bob's "bluff"; hence the L-y seems a much more reasonable prediction.

Think back to Appendix 9 and the connection between dominance and rationalizability. Rather than saying that y "conditionally strictly dominates" x for Bob, conditional on Bob being given the move, we can say: *If Bob is asked to move, for any beliefs he holds concerning which node in his information set he is at, x gives a lower expected payoff (given those beliefs) than does y.*

Figure A12.2 depicts a second and more complex motivating example.[1] Consider the Nash equilibrium in which Alice chooses D, Bob chooses a, and Carol chooses L. It is clear why Alice is choosing D: If she does so, and if Carol chooses L, Alice nets 4, versus 3 if she instead chooses A and Bob chooses a. As for Carol, if Alice is choosing D (and if this is clear to Carol), Carol, given the move, infers that she is at the left-hand node in her information set and so chooses L. As for Bob, as long as Alice is choosing D, Bob's one-node information set is off-path, so he has a free choice; his choice doesn't affect his expected payoff.

---

[1]   This example, known as Selten's Horse, is the example Selten used when first writing about these issues, in Selten (1975, Section 6). Selten's development is different from how I explain things here; I get to those differences later in this appendix.

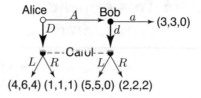

Figure A12.2. Another motivating example (payoffs are given in the order Alice first, then Bob, and Carol last)

And, as this game has no proper subgames, this equilibrium is subgame perfect.

But is Bob's choice of a is credible, *if* it is evident to the three players that the obvious way to play is D-a-L? Given the move, Bob is surprised—either his conjecture was wrong, or Alice has screwed up—but if he (still) believes that Carol will choose L, at this point (given the chance to move), d is better for him than a.

Please note a crucial planted assumption in the previous paragraph, *which dominates developments in this appendix*. Bob started with the firm belief that he would not be given the move; Alice was going to choose D and Carol would subsequently choose L. Hence, if he is surprised by being given the move, he understands that the part of his hypothesis that concerns Alice has gone awry. And yet—the argument continues—he still believes his original hypothesis that Carol will choose L. If instead he were to reason that, since Alice manifestly chose A, Carol may very well choose R if he chooses d, then he may well be justified in planning to choose a, and the argument that unravels D-a-L as an equilibrium itself unravels.

So what is the answer in this game? Another Nash equilibrium is A-a-R. In this equilibrium, since Carol is choosing R (or, rather, that she would choose R given the opportunity), it is evident why Alice and Bob are choosing A and a, respectively. And Carol's choice of R is a "free choice," since her information set is off-path. But in the spirit of our previous arguments, we must ask: Is Carol's contingent plan to choose R credible? If she is surprised by being given the move, when she expected A followed by a, can she rationalize her choice of R? She can, in the following sense: Since she expected Alice to choose A and Bob to choose a, it is evident (if she is asked to move) that she was wrong about one of them. And *if she decides that Bob was somewhat more likely than Alice to have done what she (Carol) didn't expect*—specifically, if given the move, Carol believes that she is at the right-hand node in her information set with probability 3/5 or more—then Carol's choice of R is sensible.

The issue in both these examples begins with the following observation for "equilibrium behavior" in an extensive-form game: What a player promises or threatens to do at a given information set does not affect that player's overall expected payoff if, per the equilibrium strategy profile, that information set is not reached with positive probability. Hence, behavior that is off-path is unconstrained by the requirement of being part of a Nash equilibrium.[2] This idea is not new; it was

---

[2]   This is subject to a caveat met in Appendix 11: The off-path information set cannot be off-path only because of prior actions by the same player.

in fact the subject of Appendix 11. But the formal cure for this problem offered in Appendix 11, subgame perfection, only works in proper subgames of the original game. This appendix extends the motivating idea of subgame perfection—the credibility of conjectured off-path play—to situations like the two sketched above, for which subgame perfection does not apply.

To do so requires that we complement the concept of a strategy profile with the concept of *beliefs* at every information set; then we extend the Nash equilibrium notion—that each player is playing a best response to what is (conjectured to be) her rivals' strategies—to the notion that this is true starting from every information set: so-called *sequential rationality*. And once this extension is put in place, we must go on to consider the question: Which beliefs for each player are consistent with the conjectured strategy profile?

A12.2. Beliefs and Sequential Rationality

To avoid complications, for the remainder of this appendix, assume that any extensive-form game under discussion has perfect recall.

In the developments to follow, I use $\sigma = (\sigma_n)_{n \in \mathcal{N}}$ to denote a general strategy profile, where the use of σ connotes that I am allowing for mixed strategies. For developments to follow, it is important that σ is in behavior-strategy form; that is, for each $h \in H$, $\sigma(a)(h)$ is the probability that $\iota(h)$ takes action $a \in A(h)$. (This is important later for two reasons, the first of which is given immediately following Definition A12.1.) To save on keystrokes, I assume that action names do not duplicate at different information sets; that is, $A(h) \cap A(h') = \emptyset$ for all $h \neq h'$. Hence, for a strategy profile σ and an action $a \in A(h)$ for $h \in H$, I can write $\sigma(a)$ in place of $\sigma(h)(a)$, because a "identifies" the information set. I also sometimes write $\sigma_n(a)$, where $n = \iota(h)$. (If $\iota(h) = $ Nature, and if $a \in A(h)$, then I'll abuse notation and write $\sigma(a)$ for the probability that Nature chooses a at h.) Recall that for any noninitial node z, $p(z)$ is the unique predecessor of z, and $a(z)$ is the action that leads from $p(z)$ to z. Hence, under strategy profile σ, the probability of reaching z from $p(z)$ is $\sigma(a(z))$.

Definitions A12.1. *Fix a finite extensive-form game (with perfect recall) and a strategy profile σ for the game.*

a. *For $h \in H$, **beliefs at information set** h are given by a probability distribution $\mu(\cdot|h)$ defined on $z \in h$. A **full set of beliefs for the game** specifies beliefs at every information set $h \in H$. (When the game is fixed, the phrase "a set of beliefs" and even just "beliefs" will usually mean a full set of beliefs.)*

b. *For $h \in H$, beliefs $\mu(\cdot|h)$, and the fixed strategy profile σ, the h-**conditional outcome** with respect to $\mu(\cdot|h)$ and σ is the probability distribution on final nodes that follow h, or $\cup_{z \in h} \left[S(z) \cap Z_f \right]$ induced by $\mu(\cdot|h)$ and σ, computed as follows: For each $z \in h$ and $z' \in \left[S(z) \cap Z_f \right]$, let $z = z_0, z_1, \ldots, z_J = z'$ be the unique sequence of nodes that* *lead from z to z'. Then the "conditional" probability of z' being reached from h is*

$$\mu(z|h) \times \prod_{j=1}^{J} \sigma(a(z_j)).$$

c. *The strategy σ_n for player $n \in \mathcal{N}$ is **sequentially rational against** $\sigma_{\neg n}$, **given (or, with respect to) beliefs** $\mu(\cdot|h)$ **at** $h \in H_n$, if the (conditional) expected payoff to n under the h-conditional outcome for those beliefs and $(\sigma_n, \sigma_{\neg n})$ is at least as large as the expected payoff to n under the h-conditional outcome for those beliefs and $(\sigma'_n, \sigma_{\neg n})$, for all alternative strategies σ'_n for n.*[3]

d. *The pair of a complete set of beliefs μ and a strategy profile σ are (together) **sequentially rational** if, for each $h \in H$, the strategy $\sigma_{\iota(h)}$ is sequentially rational against $\sigma_{\neg\iota(h)}$ for $\iota(h)$ given her beliefs $\mu(\cdot|h)$.*[4]

Two comments are in order concerning this fundamental definition:

*   The definition of sequential rationality provides the first reason that σ should be a strategy in behavioral form, or at least, not in the form of a reduced strategy profile. Consider the game depicted in Figure A12.3, and the *reduced* strategy profile in which Alice chooses X and Bob, u. If all we know is that Alice is using the reduced strategy X, we can't verify whether Bob's strategy is sequentially rational (starting from his sole, single-node information set), because we don't know what Alice would do at her second information set. Similarly, we can't tell whether Alice's strategy is sequentially rational starting from her two-node information set.)

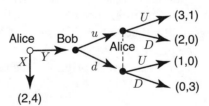

Figure A12.3. Why we must work with behavioral strategies, Part 1 (Alice's payoffs are given first)

---

[3] Compare this definition with Definition A9.6(d) on page 505. It would be more consistent with that definition to say that the conditional expected payoff to n under the h-conditional outcome for those beliefs and $(\sigma_n, \sigma_{\neg n})$ is at least as large as the expected payoff to n under the h-conditional outcome for those beliefs and $(a'_n, \sigma_{\neg n})$, for all (pure) strategies a'_n for n. And, to be fully consistent, we could compare the h-conditional outcome for those beliefs and $(a_n, \sigma_{\neg n})$ for all a_n that have positive probability under σ_n with the h-conditional outcome for those beliefs and $(a'_n, \sigma_{\neg n})$, for all strategies a'_n for n. But (you should convince yourself) these come to the same thing.

[4] Alternatively, μ and σ together are sequentially rational if, for every $n \in \mathcal{N}$ and $h \in H(n)$, σ_n is sequentially rational against $\sigma_{\neg n}$ given beliefs $\mu(\cdot|h)$. And we can and sometimes do say that player n's strategy is sequentially rational against $\sigma_{\neg n}$, given beliefs $\mu(\cdot|h)$, if σ_n is sequentially rational at every $h \in H(n)$.

- The scare quotes around "conditional" in part b are there because (so far) these conditional probabilities have nothing to do with Bayes' rule. The "conditional" probability of being at $z \in h$, "conditional" on being at h, is given by the beliefs $\mu(z|h)$, and from that starting point, σ is used to find the (independent, by assumption) probabilities of all subsequent transitions.

I hope that part c of these definitions is sufficiently clear, so that spelling it out precisely is unnecessary; the notation overload needed to spell it out isn't particularly illuminating or helpful. That said, an example may help clarify and identify an important (and controversial) part of this definition.

Consider the game depicted in Figure A12.4 and the strategy profile V-v-v'. (That is, every player at his or her information set chooses the vertical move.)

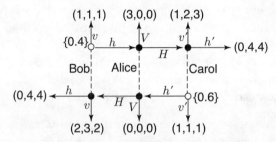

Figure A12.4. Interpreting sequential rationality (Alice's payoff are listed first, then Bob's, then Carol's)

- Bob may start the game—this happens with prior probability 0.4—or he could conceivably move last. But at the strategy profile V-v-v', if Carol starts the game, her choice of v' (and also Alice's contingent choice of V) means that the bottom node in Bob's information set is off-path. So, at this strategy profile, Bob *infers*, if he is given the move, that he is starting the game. It is natural for this reason to require that his beliefs at his information set, computed from Bayes' rule and σ, are that he is at the top node in his information set with probability 1. And, assuming his beliefs are given by this natural assignment, then choosing v gives him payoff 1, while choosing h would give the move to Alice, who will choose V, giving him 0. The choice of v is sequentially rational for Bob at his information set, given strategy profile V-v-v' and his "natural" beliefs for that strategy (viz., that given the opportunity to move, he is at the top node in his information set).

- Carol is completely symmetric with Bob (except that she is slightly more likely to be the first mover, which is irrelevant to this argument). She infers, given the move, that she must have started the game, and so it is natural for her beliefs at her information set to assign probability 1 to the bottom node. In this case, her choice of v' is sequentially rational.

- Alice's entire information set is off-path. Her beliefs are not provided by application of Bayes' rule. So, *suppose Alice believes that she is at the top node in her information set with probability 0.7.* (I've italicized this because I am just "supposing" here; these beliefs are not in any sense natural; they are simply my invention.) Then her choice of V is indeed sequentially rational (given these beliefs and the strategy profile V-v-v'). At this strategy profile, she knows that the only way she could have been given the move is if either Bob moved first and chose h, or Carol moved first and chose h'. So, she is surprised on being called upon to move. But conditional on her information set having been reached, and *for the beliefs I've posited,* she computes:

- "By choosing V, my expected payoff is $(0.7)(3) + (0.3)(0) = 2.1$."

- "By choosing H, if I am at the top node in my information set, *I anticiate that Carol will choose v'*, which gives me a payoff of 1. If I am at the bottom node in my information set and I choose H, *I anticipate that Bob will choose v*, which gives me a payoff of 2. So, if I choose H, my expected payoff (conditional on having reached my information set, given my beliefs there, and using the strategy profile V-v-v' for any subsequent actions), is $(0.7)(1) + (0.3)(2) = 1.3$. My choice of V is sequentially rational, with respect to *these particular beliefs* and *my (maintained) conjecture that, subsequent to my choosing H, my rivals will choose according to my initial hypothesis V-v-v'.*"

In the last paragraph, pay attention to the four italicized phrases. First, and pertaining to the third italicized phrase, *"these particular beliefs,"* you may well wonder how I assigned to Alice the belief that, if given the move, she is at the top node in her information set with probability 0.7. The beliefs assigned to Bob and Carol are not arbitrary; they are entirely natural, given the strategy profile. (Section A12.3 formalizes why they are natural.) But Alice's beliefs have come out of thin air, as it were.

Thin air or not, the philosophy here is that, if Alice is put on the spot and must decide whether to choose V or H, she will entertain some beliefs as to where in the information set she sits, which allows her to compute the consequences of choosing H versus choosing V. If her beliefs are that she is at the top node with probability 0.7 (or 0.8, or anything between 0.5 and 1), the choice of V makes sense; it is sequentially rational.[5]

Or, at least, the choice of V makes sense if, starting from this information set, with these beliefs, she maintains that "subsequent" play will conform to her initial hypothesis that Bob is choosing v and Carol is choosing v'. Because she is asked to move, she knows that either Bob or Carol didn't play according to the equilibrium

---

[5] If Alice's beliefs are, say, that she is at the top node in her information set with probability 0.4, then V gives her an expected payoff of 1.2, and H followed by either v' or v gives her an expected payoff of 1.6. Her beliefs matter as to which choice is sequentially rational for her.

So, you may well ask, where exactly did the 0.7 come from? In particular, since Carol has the first move with probability 0.6, isn't it more "natural" for Alice to believe she is at the upper node in her information set with probability 0.4?

In applications, the justification for specific beliefs is similar to the justification for strategies; they should represent "obvious" conclusions for players to make. (In Appendix 14, this assertion will be softened somewhat.) For now, the 0.7 is just an out-of-thin-air example. I'm not justifying it as something Alice should believe.

hypothesis. Notwithstanding this obvious flaw in her initial hypothesis as to how the game will be played, she continues to have faith that the "other" player—the one who did not start the game, has yet to have the opportunity to act, and whose identity is a mystery to her—can be counted upon to play as she (Alice) originally hypothesized. This is the import of the three other italicized phrases.

Objections to sequential rationality, 1: Is it necessary?

This argument raises what is probably the fundamental question about sequential rationality. Alice (and Bob and Carol, but the focus here is on Alice) begins thinking that play will evolve according the strategy profile V-v-v'. Hence, Alice begins thinking that she will not be asked to move. But by asking whether her portion of the strategy profile V is sequentially rational, we are asking: If given the move unexpectedly, does the choice of V make sense? And, to justify this choice, we suppose that, although surprised, Alice acts like a good expected-utility (payoff-) maximizing individual: She assigns "conditional" beliefs to where she is in her information set and computes her expected payoff from her various strategic options, *supposing that any subsequent actions by Bob or Carol will conform to their parts of* V-v-v'.

Why? Why would she think, having been surprised, that there is no (or, at least, negligible) chance of further surprises along the way? Although she doesn't know whether she was wrong about Bob or Carol, why wouldn't one clear flaw in her initial conjectures about Bob and Carol lead her to reevaluate her entire initial hypothesis? Since Bob and Carol are, in this game, different people, she might reason that, while one of them slipped up, the other is unlikely to do so. (This story is fleshed out in the Section A12.6, when we discuss *trembling-hand perfection*.) But suppose we are looking at a game in which Bob moves both before and after Alice, and Alice anticipates that Bob will act at his first opportunity in a way that means she won't be asked to move. Suppose she is asked to move, so she knows her theory about Bob's first move was wrong. Figure A12.5 provides an example.

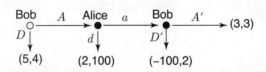

Figure A12.5. An extensive-form game (Alice's payoffs are given first)

Since all information sets are singleton, beliefs are trivial. And sequential rationality implies that Bob, at his right-hand information set, should choose A'; hence Alice should choose a; hence Bob, at his left-hand information set, should choose D. That is, DA'-a is the unique strategy profile that satisfies sequential rationality at every node; indeed, in this simple game, it is the unique subgame-perfect equilibrium.[6]

---

[6] A second Nash equilibrium—subgame imperfect—is AD'-d. In effect, Bob chooses A and "threat-

Following this logic, suppose that we—and, more to the point, Alice—decide that DA'-a is the obvious way to play the game. And then, Alice is surprised to see Bob choosing A. In light of this seemingly illogical choice by Bob, should Alice remain convinced that Bob will choose A' if she chooses a? Shouldn't she entertain some possibility that he will choose D' and, given the payoffs, play d to be safe? And then, shouldn't Bob be willing to try A? If the answers to these questions are Yes, then sequential rationality, as a principle of analysis, is challenged.

This is a story we met briefly in Appendix 11, on page 554. There, the chain of Alice-Bob alternating moves was longer; here, the payoffs they get—the 100 for Bob after A-d and the -100 for Alice after A-a-D'—have been enhanced to give a similar effect. But the point is the same. The principle of sequential rationality is: One deviation doesn't make another one "likely." Alice, seeing Bob start with A and believing in the powerful hold that the logic of sequential rationality has on Bob, should conclude: "Bob just made a silly mistake; he won't make another." And Bob, at the start, realizing that this is how Alice will reason, should choose D. At least, that's what the principle of sequential rationality would have you believe. In the case of Figure A12.5, do you?

If your answer is anything from "not a chance" to "maybe not," advocates for sequential rationality will respond by saying that it is not sequential rationality that is at fault here, but the model: Real-life Bob chooses A in the game in Figure A12.5 to play on uncertainty in Alice's mind about Bob's motivations. The simple model in Figure A12.5 makes no allowance for any uncertainty in Alice's mind. Advanced modeling techniques that are explored in Appendix 13 allow us to create and study models that incorporate the requisite sort of uncertainty; we need (advocates assert) not better principles—the principles are fine—but better models.[7]

The challenge these examples raise to sequential rationality reappear throughout this appendix and in particular when *consistency of beliefs* is discussed (Section A12.4). For now, I emphasize that sequential rationality requires that players maintain their initial hypotheses about what happens "after" one of their information sets has been reached, even if that information set was not supposed to be reached. This requirement, and the logic or (perhaps better, the spirit or the philosophy) that motivates it, colors a lot of what follows in this appendix, so please (if you are highlighting text) highlight this paragraph!

Objections to sequential rationality, 2: Certainly not sufficient

Note that I've inserted scare quotes in the previous paragraph around the word "after." To explain why, consider the two extensive-form games in Figure A12.6.

Look first at the game in panel a and, in particular, the strategy profile in which Alice chooses D, Bob chooses a, and Carol chooses d'. Alice and Bob have infor-

---

ens" that he will choose D', which makes d by Alice a best response, which makes AD' Bob's best response, because if Alice chooses d, Bob doesn't need to carry out his threat. Note that AA' is, for Bob, an equally good response to d by Alice. But if Bob's strategy is AA', Alice's best response is a, which pushes Bob to D.

[7] If Franklin Fisher's critique of game theory, discussed in Chapter 17, is faintly (or loudly) echoing in your mind, good for you!

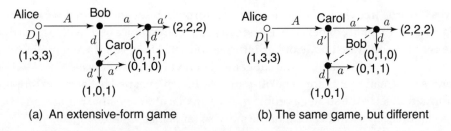

(a) An extensive-form game   (b) The same game, but different

Figure A12.6. Two extensive-form games (payoffs are Alice first, Bob second, Carol third)

mation sets with a single node, so their beliefs are trivially fixed, and you can easily compute that, given Carol's strategy choice of d', Bob's choice of a is sequentially rational, and given that Bob's strategy is a and Carol's is d', Alice's choice of D is sequentially rational. Carol's choice of d' is sequentially rational *if* her beliefs upon being given the move are that she is at the south-west node in her information set with probability exceeding 0.5.

Now consider panel b, labeled "The same game, but different." This label is appropriate, because from a strategic perspective, this is the same game as in panel a: In panel a, Carol chooses without knowing what Bob did (but knowing that Alice chose A): It is strategically equivalent to represent this as in panel b, where Carol's information set comes "before" Bob's, but Bob acts without knowing what Carol chose.

In terms of the implications of sequential rationality, it makes a difference whether we use the game tree in panel a or the tree in panel b. In panel b, Bob's information set is the only information set in which beliefs are nontrivial. But, for Bob's choice, his beliefs don't matter: a (conditionally) strictly dominates d. So, for any strategy profile for the game in panel b that is sequentially rational, Bob will be choosing a. Now, this reasoning is equally true for panel a. But since, in panel b, Bob's choice comes "after" Carol's, sequential rationality forces Carol to evaluate her choices anticipating that Bob will "subsequently" choose a. (I'm adding scare quotes here to emphasize that this chronology is an artifact of how the game has been formally depicted.) And this forces Carol to choose a', which in turn leads Alice to choose A.

Note that, going back to panel a, if we allow Carol the belief that she is at the southwest node in her information set with probability 0.5 or more, those beliefs (and the trivial beliefs for Alice and Bob) together with the strategy profile D-a-d' satisfy sequential rationality at every information set, but D-a-d' is not subgame perfect. Indeed, this provides an extreme (as in, extremely absurd) example: Imagine the game in Figure A12.6 but without Alice's participation: Bob chooses either a or d, and Carol, not knowing his choice, chooses a' or d'. If we allow Carol to have any beliefs—specifically, if we allow her to believe she is at her southwest node with probability 0.5 or more—relative to these beliefs, a-d' is a sequentially rational strategy profile. But a-d' isn't even a Nash equilibrium.

That is, in the game depicted in Figure A12.6(a) and with the strategy profile D-A-d', Carol's information set is off-path, because Alice is choosing D. This gives Carol a "free choice" of action at her information set and, even if we insist on sequential rationality of her choice, she can support the choice of d' with beliefs that she is at the southwest node of her information set. However, if we remove Alice from the game—if we look at the subgame that involves only Bob and Carol—then Carol's information set cannot be off-path. We haven't yet tied beliefs at an on-path information set to the strategy profile σ—we do that after one final paragraph—but this example surely indicates that the story so far is incomplete.

Sequential rationality, as defined above, has players computing h-conditional outcomes with (so far) complete freedom as to their beliefs concerning how h was reached, while at the same time adhering to the strategy profile σ concerning what happens "later." This complete freedom is certainly inadequate: Beliefs should, at least to some extent, be consistent with σ. Consistency of beliefs with a conjectured strategy profile is the subject of the next three sections.[8]

A12.3. On-Path Consistency and Nash Equilibrium

We begin with the simplest, most basic, and least controversial form of consistency: When, based on the strategy-profile conjecture σ, a player is not surprised to be given the move at one of her information sets, she forms her beliefs at that information set by applying Bayes' rule, using the conjectured strategy profile.

For instance, consider the simple two-player, simultaneous-move game depicted in Figure A12.7, which is the subgame between Bob and Carol from Figure A12.6(a).

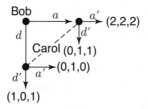

Figure A12.7. Carol's beliefs are fixed by Bob's strategy (Bob's payoff are given first)

We have already observed that Bob's beliefs are trivial and, whatever his conjecture about what Carol will do, a for Bob strictly dominates d. That is, sequential rationality for Bob, for any specification of Carol's strategy, involves Bob choosing a. Of course, Carol's information set will be reached with positive probability, so for any possible strategy profile σ in which Bob is choosing a, and in which Carol

---

[8]   There is a deeper issue here. We can (and will) fix this specific example with the consistency requirements set forth in the following sections. But even the strongest consistency requirements we develop in this appendix are inadequate to prevent examples in which the way the game tree is drawn—while maintaining the basic strategic situation—changes the "predictions" that can be made. This leads to the concept of *strategic stability*—that predictions of the theory should depend only on the underlying strategic situation and not on how it is represented as an extensive-form game—a concept and program that is discussed in Appendix 14.

anticipates this choice by Bob, Carol should employ simple Bayesian inference to infer that she is at the northeast node in her information set.

Don't be misled by the fact that a strictly dominates d for Bob. If, for some reason, Carol conjectures that Bob will choose d, then her "natural" beliefs at her information set, using her conjectures about Bob's strategy and Bayes' rule, would be that she is at the southwest node with probability 1.

This type of reasoning is formalized as follows. As always, assume the game has perfect recall. Recall from Appendix 10 that $\pi(\sigma)$ denotes the *outcome* if σ is played; that is, for a final node z', $\pi(\sigma)(z')$ is the probability that z' is reached, assuming that σ is played. Extend this definition to all nodes $z \in Z$, where $\pi(\sigma)(z)$ is defined as the probability that play reaches node z. That is, if $(z_1, \ldots, z_J)$ is the (possibly partial and always unique) path from some initial node z_1 to $z_J = z$,

$$\pi(\sigma)(z) := \rho(z_1) \times \prod_{j=2}^{J} \sigma(a(z_j)), \quad \text{which equals} \quad \sum_{z' \in Z_F \cap S(z)} \pi(\sigma)(z').$$

(You sould convince yourself that these two formulas give the same answer.) For each information set h, let $\pi(\sigma)(h) := \sum_{z \in h} \pi(\sigma)(z)$. Per Definition A11.3, we say that h is *on-path* if $\pi(\sigma)(h) > 0$.

Definition A12.2 *Fix a finite extensive-form game (with perfect recall) and a strategy profile σ for the game. The full set of beliefs $\mu(\cdot|\cdot)$ is **on-path consistent** with σ if, for every on-path information set h,*

$$\mu(z|h) := \frac{\pi(\sigma)(z)}{\pi(\sigma)(h)}.$$

Proposition A12.3. *The strategy profile σ is a Nash equilibrium if and only if, for each on-path $h \in H$ such that $\iota(h) = n$, σ_n is sequentially rational against $\sigma_{\neg n}$, given the on-path-consistent beliefs at h.*

Some students, seeing this proposition for the first time, think it is obvious. Others, probably fewer, think some sort of magic must be involved. My own vote is that it is nearly obvious, *but only if you understand the full implications of sequential rationality.*

To explain, consider Figure A12.8(a) and the strategy profile in which Alice chooses U, and Bob chooses Ry.

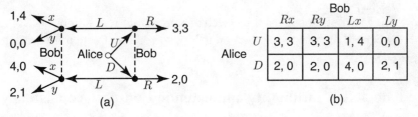

	Bob			
	Rx	Ry	Lx	Ly
U	3, 3	3, 3	1, 4	0, 0
D	2, 0	2, 0	4, 0	2, 1

(a)   (b)

Figure A12.8. (a) An extensive-form game and (b) the corresponding strategic-form game (Alice's payoffs are listed first)

- Alice has a single information set with a single node, so her beliefs are fixed. And if Bob is choosing Ry, U is the sequentially rational choice for Alice.

- Bob's left-hand information set is off-path, so on-path consistency does not restrict his beliefs. And, if he believes that he is at the lower of the two nodes with any probability greater than or equal to $4/5$, y is his sequentially rational choice at that information set.

Which leaves us to consider Bob's beliefs and behavior at his right-hand information set.

- Given that Alice is choosing U, this information set is on-path. So, if we insist that Bob's beliefs there are on-path consistent, he must believe that he is at the upper node with probability 1.

(And now, a *specious* argument:)

- And given that he is going to choose y if he chooses L, choosing R is better for him; it gives him 3, while L followed by y gives him 0.

- However, U against Ry is not a Nash equilibrium: The corresponding strategic-form game is depicted in Figure A12.8(b): Bob has four strategies, because he moves at both information sets with no information about how Alice chose, and at each information set, he has two options. And, from the strategic form, it is clear that if Alice chooses U, Bob does better with Lx than with Ry.

So, either Proposition A12.3 is wrong, or the argument just provided for the game in Figure A12.8 is flawed. And, no surprise here, the argument is flawed, not the proposition. Specifically, Bob's strategy Ry starting from his right-hand information set is *not* sequentially rational, given his on-path consistent beliefs there.

This is the key, so pay close attention: Sequential rationality is that a player's *strategy*, starting from any information set with given beliefs, is a best response to his or her rivals' strategies. At Bob's right-hand information set, given his on-path-consistent beliefs, the strategy Ry is beaten by the strategy Lx.

The flaw in the argument is that, in checking whether Bob's choice at his right-hand information set was sequentially rational, we only looked at changes in his *immediate choice of action*; the argument held fixed his subsequent action at his left-hand information set. Sequential rationality doesn't work that way; starting from an information set h, you compare what $\iota(h)$ is doing at h and at all subsequent information sets that belong to h with alternative choices at h *and at all subsequent information sets.*

(I owe you a proof, or at least the sketch of a proof, of Proposition A12.3. But to do that now would disrupt the expositional flow, so you must wait until the bottom of page 572.)

Immediate-action rationality and extended-on-path consistency

This example raises the following question. In Appendix 6 of Volume I, concerning dynamic programming, a fundamental result was that (certainly for finite-horizon problems and also for many infinite-horizon problems) an *unimprovable* strategy is necessarily optimal. Unimprovability means: What the decision maker does today is best, assuming she reverts tomorrow to her strategy. What Bob is doing at his right-hand information set is best, if he reverts to his subsequent choice of y (assuming he chooses L.) Does this mean that for game theory, the result that unimprovability implies optimality is no longer valid?

It does not. But let me add a second issue raised by the example. If Alice is hypothesized to be choosing U, it seems logical that Bob, asked to choose between L and R, believes that he is at the upper node in his right-hand information set with probability 1. That's just on-path consistency. Were he to choose L, then wouldn't it be just as logical for him, at his left-hand information set, to believe that he is at the upper node there with probability 1? While his left-hand information set is off-path, it is only off-path because he made it so. Why, then, would he believe that he is at the lower node with probability 4/5 or more, if he contemplates changing from R to L?

Two definitions and a proposition tie these considerations into a neat package.

Definition A12.4. *For a game with perfect recall:*

a. *A (behavior) strategy $\hat{\sigma}_n$ for player n is **strictly mixed** if, for every information set $h \in H(n)$ and action $a \in A(h)$, $\hat{\sigma}_n(a) > 0$.*

b. *For a fixed strategy profile σ, an information set $h \in H$ is **extended-on-path** if, for $\iota(h) = n$ and any strictly mixed (behavior) strategy $\hat{\sigma}_n$, $\pi\big((\hat{\sigma}_n, \sigma_{\neg n})\big)(h) := \sum_{z \in h} \pi\big((\hat{\sigma}_n, \sigma_{\neg n})\big)(z) > 0$.*

c. *Beliefs $\mu(\cdot|\cdot)$ are **extended-on-path consistent** with the strategy profile σ if, for every extended-on-path information set h, if $\iota(h) = n$ and $\hat{\sigma}_n$ is a strictly mixed (behavior) strategy for n, then*

$$\mu(z|h) = \frac{\pi\big((\hat{\sigma}_n, \sigma_{\neg n})\big)(z)}{\pi\big((\hat{\sigma}_n, \sigma_{\neg n})\big)(h)}.$$

In words, an information set h that is off-path is extended-on-path if the only reason that it is off-path is because the player n that chooses at h made it off-path by her earlier choices. (On-path information sets are automatically extended-on-path as well.) And, beliefs are extended-on-path consistent with σ if, at every extended-on-path information set h at which n has the move, n's beliefs at h are computed using Bayes' rule applied to $\sigma_{\neg n}$ and any strictly mixed strategy for n, $\hat{\sigma}_n$.

You may be concerned that the choice of the strictly mixed strategy $\hat{\sigma}_n$ affects the Bayes'-rule-computed beliefs at an extended-on-path information set $h \in H(n)$. But, because of perfect recall, it does not. The reason, essentially, is encapsulated in Figure A10.5 (page 531): Fix an information set $h \in H(n)$ and another information set $h' \in H(n)$ that precedes h. Perfect recall implies that if z and z' are both in h, then the action $a \in A(h')$ that is on the path to z is also on the path that leads to z'. So, in computing the Bayes' rule ratio, the assignment of $\hat{\sigma}_n$ to such an action

a cancels out in the numerator and in each term in the sum that makes up the denominator.

Definition A12.5. *For an extensive-form game with perfect recall: Fix a player n, a strategy profile σ for all the players, and beliefs μ_n for player n. (That is, μ_n gives beliefs for n at every information set $h \in H(n)$.) Player n's strategy σ_n is **immediate-action rational** against $\sigma_{\neg n}$, given beliefs μ_n, if, at every $h \in H(n)$, n's choice of **immediate action** at h, as given by σ_n, is optimal with respect to her beliefs at that information set and the hypothesis that all future actions, by her fellow players **as well as by herself**, are given by σ.*

Proposition A12.6. *For a fixed strategy profile σ and beliefs μ that are extended on-path consistent, if behavior at every information set h is immediate-action rational, then σ is a Nash-equilibrium profile. Conversely, σ is a Nash-equilibrium profile only if behavior at every information set h that is extended-on-path is immediate-action rational, for beliefs that are extended-on-path consistent.*

So, for example, in Figure A12.8, concerning the strategy profile U-Ry:

- Alice's choice at her information set is immediate-action rational, given her (only possible) beliefs and given the hypothesis that Bob is playing Ry.

- Bob's choice of R at his right-hand information set is immediate-action rational, given his on-path consistent beliefs, Alice's strategy (which is relevant only insofar as it provides his on-path beliefs), and Bob's subsequent choice of y.

- Bob's choice of y is immediate-action rational, if his beliefs at his left-hand information set are that he is at the lower of the two nodes with probability 4/5 or more.

- *However*, his left-hand information set is extended on-path, and extended-on-path-consistent beliefs at this information set, given Alice's strategy, are that he is at the upper node in his left-hand information set with probability 1. And, for those extended-on-path-consistent beliefs, his choice of y is *not* immediate-action rational.

Bottom line: The assertion that beliefs that are on-path consistent is, in the literature, literally uncontroversial, and with good reason. If σ is the obvious way to play the game, and if players are good Bayesians, on-path consistency makes perfect sense. And this extends, in my view, to extended-on-path consistency: If the only reason that an information set is off-path is because player n makes it so, she should understand that, if she deviated, and play reached that information set, Bayes' rule should determine her beliefs.

So, insofar as Nash equilibrium is the desired solution concept, sequential rationality at on-path information sets with on-path-consistent beliefs *and/or* immediate-action rationality with extended-on-path-consistent beliefs get you there.

About the proofs of Propositions A12.3 and A12.6

I'll only provide a sketch of the proofs.

Necessity in Proposition A12.3 derives from the fact that, fixing player n and information set $h \in H_n$, we can write the overall expected payoff of player n, playing σ_n against $\sigma_{\neg n}$, as the weighted sum of (i) her expected payoff conditional on play passing through each $z \in h$ times the probability that play passes through z and (ii) her expected payoff if play does not pass through h, times the probability of that. (This is just taking an expected value and conditioning and then unconditioning on a particular event.) If $h \in H_n$ is on-path, the probability that play passes through it is strictly positive. So if n's strategy σ_n were not sequentially rational at h against $\sigma_{\neg n}$, for beliefs at h derived from σ and Bayes' rule, changing her strategy at h and "afterward" (at all information sets that follow h) would provide her with a higher overall expected payoff, contradicting that σ_n is an overall best response by n to $\sigma_{\neg n}$.

For sufficiency in Proposition A12.3: Fix player n. Since the game has perfect recall, player n's information sets $h \in H_n$ form a tree structure. There are information sets for n that are "first-opportunity-for-n-to-choose," followed (perhaps) by "second opportunities," and so forth, where nth-opportunity-to-move information sets each have a unique $n-1$st-opportunity-to-move information set that precedes it.

Let H_n^1 be the subset of H_n consisting of first-opportunity-to-move information sets for n. Then n's overall expected payoff can be broken into the sum of her conditional payoffs from information sets $h \in H_n^1$ times the respective probabilities of reaching each $h \in H_n^1$, which (because these are first-opportunity-to-move information sets) depend only on $\sigma_{\neg n}$, plus a term that is constant in σ_n, namely, n's expected payoff if she never gets the chance to move. Sequential rationality applied at each $h \in H_n^1$ then immediately implies that n is playing an overall best response to $\sigma_{\neg n}$.

The proof of Proposition A12.6 is a bit different. Fix a player n. Using the tree structure of her opportunity sets, look at her "last-opportunity–to-move" information sets. Immediate-action optimality at those information sets is just sequential rationality. Move back one level, and use the conserving-implies-optimality logic from dynamic programming to show that immediate-action optimality at any such information set, given sequential rationality from the successor last-opportunity-to-move information sets, is sequential rationality from these next-to-last-opportunity information sets. Continue in this fashion, formally using induction on the length of the chain of n's information sets. (If you want a serious proof, consult Hendon, Jacobsen, and Sloth 1996.)

Personal decision trees "versus" game theory

(This lengthy subsection is very off-path from the main expositional line of this appendix. It can be skipped without loss, if you only want a "practical" education in consistent beliefs and sequential rationality. But to gain an appreciation for how game theory connects to single-person decision theory on a philosophical level, I suggest that you persevere.)

Every extensive-form game can be thought of as a collection of linked single-player decision problems, one for each player in the game. I can illustrate with the Firm A–Firm B example from Appendix 10. We start with the game tree for this extensive-form game, Figure A10.2, reproduced here.

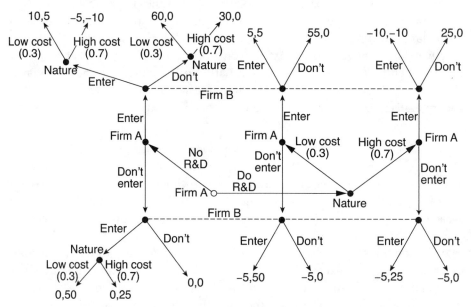

Figure A10.2. The Firm A–Firm B extensive-form game from Appendix 10 (Firm A's payoff is given first)

Consider the decision problem facing Firm A, following along with the decision tree depicted in Figure A12.9(a). Firm A begins with a decision on whether to do R&D or not. This is depicted by the box-shaped node, on the left-hand side of panel a. If the decision is to do R&D, A learns whether costs are high or low, depicted by the circle-shaped node that follows the arrow "Do R&D." I've put an N inside the circle, indicating that this is a "Nature node," and I've put the probabilities assessed by Firm A that costs are high or low on the branches. Then, in three places, Firm A must decide whether to enter or not—three more box-shaped nodes—and then A is done with decisions, but not with events it doesn't control: If it didn't do R&D but enters, it learns whether costs are high or low. And, after a decision to enter, Firm A learns what Firm B decides concerning entry. (Firm A probably sees whether Firm B chose to enter if it chooses not to enter, but that is irrelevant to Firm A's payoffs, so it is omitted from Firm A's decision tree.) All these so-called *chance nodes* are depicted by circle-shaped nodes. Finally, at the end of each sequence of choices by A and events that A doesn't control, I supply A's payoffs.

Panel b depicts B's decision tree: It first learns whether Firm A entered or not, following which it must make its own entry decision. If it enters, Firm B learns whether costs are high or low. And then we have Firm B's payoffs. Note that Firm A's decision whether to do R&D plays no role in Firm B's decision tree. This may be relevant to whether Firm A enters or not, but it has no impact on Firm B's

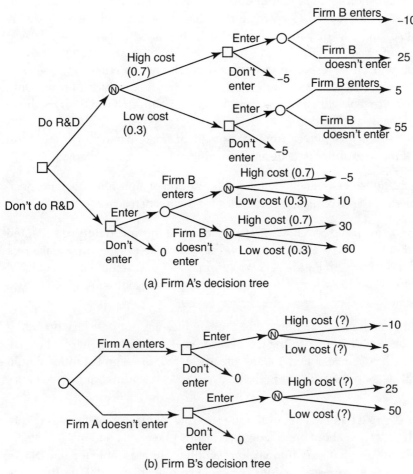

(a) Firm A's decision tree

(b) Firm B's decision tree

Figure A12.9. Decision trees for Firm A and Firm B

outcome, *once Firm B attaches probabilities to the cost-is-high/cost-is-low chance nodes in its decision tree.* And those probabilities are not immediately obvious, hence the question marks I've left on those branches.

The general rule about probabilities in decision trees is that probabilities on branches coming out of a chance node should be conditional on the path through the decision tree leading up to the chance node. So, in panel b, the probability on the topmost "High cost" branch should be conditional on Firm A entering. And this is where things become complicated. If Firm B hypothesizes that Firm A is going to do R&D and enter only if cost is low, then the probably of high cost conditional on the known fact that Firm A entered should be 0. But if Firm B hypothesizes that Firm A will not do the R&D, then observing that Firm A enters doesn't affect the (now marginal) probability of high cost, which is 0.7.

At least in the lower half of Firm B's tree, its optimal decision is clear. If Firm A is observed not to enter, it doesn't matter what are the probabilities of high and low cost. Firm B should enter. But to decide what to do if Firm A is observed to enter, Firm B must decide what strategy Firm A has chosen. Is it choosing to do the R&D and, if so, does its entry mean that cost is low?

And, moving back to Firm A's decision tree, it must assess probabilities for what Firm B will do in response to its decision whether to enter. Firm A, if it constructs Firm B's decision tree, understands that Firm B will enter if Firm A does not. But what Firm B will do if it sees Firm A enter depends on Firm B's hypothesis concerning what Firm A is doing.

And, with this, we've moved from the domain of single-person (or single-firm) decision making to multi-person decision making, which is game theory.

Having introduced (somewhat vaguely) the notion of a player's personal decision tree, here are the two fundamental rules for their construction:

- A chance node precedes a choice node if and only if the uncertainty represented by the chance node resolves for the player before the player must make that particular decision. In Figure A12.9(b), Firm B learns whether Firm A entered before it must decide whether to enter. So that chance node comes before Firm B's two choice nodes.

- To solve a decision tree requires that probabilities are put on every branch of every chance node, representing the decision maker's assessment of what will happen at that chance node. And, as already stated, these probabilities should be conditional on the path through the decision tree leading up to the chance node.

In general, game theory is about linking together single-person decision problems. Specifically, it is about analyzing the various players' situations simultaneously, to determine what (conditional) probabilities are reasonble for one player to assess about other players' actions, with every player undertaking the same exercise.

- If we are concerned (only) with dominance analysis or, more or less equivalently, rationalizability of some strategy for a given player, the single-person decision tree is all that is needed. For iterated dominance/rationalizability, however, we need decision trees for each player, and we must go back and forth between them.

  As we know from the analysis of the Firm A–Firm B problem in Appendix 10, iterated dominance does tell us the "answer." Here is how: In Firm A's decision tree, we need probabilities for how Firm B will act if it sees Firm A enter. (Looking at Firm B's decision tree, we know that it will enter if Firm A does not.) Since the only information that Firm B has is whether Firm A entered, it makes sense that, in Firm A's decision tree, the probability that Firm B enters (if it sees Firm A enter) should be the same at each of the three chance nodes for Firm B's decision. And, whatever probability you insert for Firm B entering if it sees Firm A entering, you will find that, in terms of A's expected payoff, not doing R&D and entering is better than doing R&D. (I'll let you do the calculations.) But once we rule out Firm A choosing to do R&D, we can supply the probabilities of high and low cost in Firm B's decision tree (they are 0.7 for high cost and 0.3 for low), and we conclude that if Firm A enters, Firm B's best action is not to enter. Put that back in Firm A's decision tree, and the conclusion is clear: Firm A should enter.[9]

- When we get to equilibrium analysis, the perspective that comes to the fore is that of solving N single-person decision problems simultaneously. Put it this way. Suppose we looking at some situation from Alice's perspective, and we construct a decision-tree model for her decision problem. Insofar as the only chance nodes in her decision tree belong to Nature, and insofar as (we believe that) Nature's actions are unaffected by what Alice decides to do, we can supply probabilities on all chance-node branches in Alice's decision tree and then find her optimal strategy.

  But if Alice's decision tree has chance nodes controlled by Bob or by Carol, we need Alice's assessments as to what Bob and/or Carol will do. And, perhaps Bob's and Carol's decisions depend on what they think Alice will decide to do. An equilibrium, viewed as an obvious way to play, seeks to find simultaneous and consistent solutions to all the players' decision problems. Now, if Alice infers that Bob has a dominant strategy, equilibrium analysis isn't required. And, if Alice assesses that Bob is going to act in a specific manner—if she thinks Bob is a dummy who doesn't understand how his behavior affects her, which ought to affect his choices—again we have no need for equilibrium analysis. But, in many cases of interest in economics, we must look for simultaneous and consistent solutions to the set of linked decision problems of the players; this sort of equilibrium analysis is the dominant methodology employed in the economics discussed in this volume.

All that said, it is important to bear in mind that we can think of an equilibrium in strategies for an extensive-form representation of the situation, or we can think of a consistent and simultaneous solution to the players' linked single-person decision problems. And, to build your understanding, it is often helpful to keep, at least in the back of your mind, both ways of thinking. Indeed, when we get to Appendix 15 on repeated play (and the application of repeated-play models in Chapter 22), the way we look for equilibria is to fix the strategies of all players except for one, cast that one player's problem as a single-person decision problem, and then apply the methods of dynamic programming.

To conclude this excursion into decision trees, let me connect it to what happened earlier in this section and what happens next.

If we work with decision trees—one per player—the challenge is to come up with assessments for the conditional probabilities at chance nodes controlled by other players (including Nature), and then to use simple backward induction in each decision tree, to see what is each player's best response to her conjectures about

---

[9] This is nothing new. It simply albeit clumsily replicates the dominance analysis we conducted in Appendix 10, based on Figure A10.7.

what the others are doing. An equilibrium is where each player's best response is consistent with what other players assess the first player is doing.

Information sets in the game tree for a given player correspond in one-to-one fashion with decision nodes in her personal decision tree. An information set for a given player with more than one node maps at some later point in the player's personal decision tree into a chance node that resolves her uncertainty.[10] If, per some strategy profile σ, an information set is on-path or even extended-on-path, Bayes' rule tells what the probabilities should be at the later-point chance nodes. However, if an information set is off-path (and not extended-on-path; that is, it is off-path even if the player tries to reach the information set), difficulties may arise concerning the assignment of probabilities in the player's decision tree.

I can illustrate with the simplest example of this sort. Consider the extensive-form game in Figure A12.10(a), with the strategy profile where Alice chooses X and Bob chooses y. Bob's information set is not extended on-path. So, at least as far as we've gone, any beliefs he holds there are consistent with this strategy profile. In particular, if he believes he is at the lower node in his information set, y is sequentially rational. And X is sequentially rational for Alice, against Bob's choice of y.

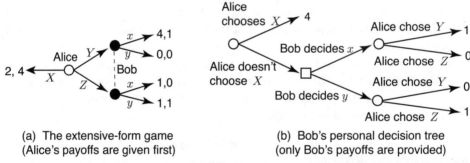

(a) The extensive-form game
(Alice's payoffs are given first)

(b) Bob's personal decision tree
(only Bob's payoffs are provided)

Figure A12.10. (a) An extensive-form game, and (b) Bob's personal decision tree

Now look at panel b, which provides Bob's personal decision tree for this game. If asked to choose, he knows that Alice didn't choose X. But he doesn't know if she chose Y or Z. And to evaluate his personal situation, he must assess probabilities for whether Alice chose Y or Z, given that she didn't choose X (and given his choice, although intuition suggests that his choice shouldn't affect these two conditional probabilities). The problem is that Alice's strategy of X provides no guidance. So, what to do?

---

[10] Combining multiple consecutive chance nodes into one can cloud this mapping. And some decisions by a player at her choice node make it unnecessary to resolve subsequently where she "was" in her information set. For instance, suppose we built the extensive-form game with Nature initially deciding whether cost will be low or high. If Firm A doesn't do R&D, its information set for deciding whether to enter will have two nodes; it isn't sure what Nature "did" initially. And, then, if it decides not to enter, in its decision tree, we don't need to resolve this uncertainty; Firm A doesn't care, because its payoff is 0 in either case. So, I'm being a bit sloppy in my assertions here.

This is where Bob's beliefs in the game tree come in. They correspond precisely to the probabilities he assesses at those two right-hand chance nodes. That is, they correspond to: She didn't choose X, so what did she do? Now, concerning this example:

- Bob's off-path beliefs matter, not to his payoff (since his information set won't be reached, even if he tries to make it so), but to what he would do, if somehow his information set were reached. That is, if he believes that he is at the lower node at his information set with probability greater than $1/2$—that is, he assesses that Alice, conditional on not choosing X, chose Z with probability greater than $1/2$—then he chooses y. And, *this* is why Alice chooses X. Had Bob instead believed that it was more likely that Alice chose Y, given that she didn't choose X, he would instead optimize with x, which would lead Alice to choose Y.

- And, for this specific example, one can argue that he should assess that, if she didn't choose X, Y is more likely, because Z is strictly dominated by X; Alice has no business choosing Z. This, though, is a very advanced sort of argument (in terms of the theory that justifies it); it is a simple example of so-called *forward induction*, which we consider in Appendix 14.

At this point, I abandon personal decision trees. In my biased opinion, thinking both in terms of the extensive-form game and in terms of a set of linked personal decision trees can help intuition. However, the literature doesn't deal with personal decision trees, at least not directly. So, to follow what is in the literature, we'll present ideas based solely in terms of strategy profiles and beliefs in a given extensive-form game.

For now, then, the question to be addressed is: What, if anything, can be said about off-path—truly off-path and not even extended-on-path—beliefs?

A12.4. Consistency of Off-Path Beliefs

In the literature, various analyses are based on the idea that any "reasonable" solution to a finite extensive-form game with perfect recall should have both a strategy profile and a full set of beliefs that together satisfy sequential rationality from *every* information set, not just those that are (extended-) on-path. Moreover, the beliefs should satisfy consistency-with-the-strategy criteria that go beyond (extended-) on-path consistency. Concepts such as *perfect Bayesian equilibrium* (abbreviated PBE) and *sequential equilibrium* formalize this general idea in the literature.

A rough overview is that sequential equilibrium [11] imposes a very strong consistency requirement on beliefs relative to a given strategy profile, a consistency requirement that can be difficult to verify in applications. To make verification of

---

[11] Sequential equilibrium came first and, indeed, initiated explicit discussion of equilibria in terms of strategies, beliefs, and sequential rationality. Note, however, as coauthor of the paper that started this, my rendition of the history of this approach to analyzing extensive-form games may be biased. In particular, a close connection exists between sequential equilibrium and trembling-hand perfection, a concept that came before sequential equilibrium and can fairly be said to have motivated sequential equilibrium. Section A12.6 discusses trembling-hand perfection.

consistency easier, the concept of a PBE is introduced, with weaker (and easier to verify) off-path consistency requirements. Unhappily, different accounts of PBE impose different formal off-path consistency requirements; I think (and I again note my prejudices in this regard) that PBE is a *family* of solution concepts rather than a single specific concept. Members of this family always insist on sequential rationality relative to beliefs that are extended on-path consistent, but they vary in their (other) off-path consistency requirements. This family includes sequential equilibrium as something of an extreme point (extreme in terms of the stringency of required off-path consistency).

At the other extreme is PBE defined so that no further off-path consistency requirements are imposed. This, as we already know from Figure A12.6(a), can result in PBE that are not even subgame perfect. This motivates the first and most obvious off-path consistency criterion.

Proper-subgame consistency

Definitions A12.7. *Fix a finite extensive-form game (with perfect recall). Suppose that node z_0 is the root of a proper subgame in this game.*

a. *If z is a node that is a successor to z_0, let $\pi(z|\sigma, z_0)$ denote the conditional probability of reaching z, starting from z_0, if players adopt the (behavior) strategy profile σ. That is, $\pi(z|\sigma, z_0)$ is the product of probabilities of the sequence of actions that lead from z_0 to z according to σ. If h is an information set that is a successor to z_0 (which, of course, is wholly contained in the subgame with root z_0), let $\pi(h|\sigma, z_0) = \sum_{z \in h} \pi(z|\sigma, z_0)$.*

b. *For a given strategy profile π and information set h that is contained in the proper subgame, say that h is **on-path within the subgame** under σ if $\pi(h|\sigma, z_0) > 0$. Say that beliefs μ are **subgame-on-path consistent with** σ if, for every information set h that is on-path within the subgame under σ, $\mu(z|h) = \pi(z|\sigma, z_0)/\pi(h|\sigma, z_0)$, for every proper subgame.*

c. *For a given strategy profile π and information set $h \in H_n$ that is contained in the proper subgame, say that h is **extended on-path within the subgame** under σ if $\pi(h|(\hat{\sigma}_n, \sigma_{\neg n}), z_0) > 0$ for (arbitrary) strictly mixed strategy $\hat{\sigma}_n$ for player n. Say that beliefs μ are **subgame-extended-on-path consistent with** σ if, for every information set h that is on-path within the subgame, $\mu(z|h) = \pi(z|(\hat{\sigma}_n, \sigma_{\neg n}), z_0)/\pi(h|(\hat{\sigma}_n, \sigma_{\neg n}), z_0)$, for every proper subgame.*

(For the reason given on page 571, the arbitrary choice of $\hat{\sigma}_n$ washes out when the ratio of $\pi(z|(\hat{\sigma}_n, \sigma_{\neg n}), z_0)$ to $\pi(h|(\hat{\sigma}_n, \sigma_{\neg n}), z_0)$ is taken, for $h \in H_n$.)

Corollary A12.8. *For a fixed finite extensive-form game and strategy profile σ, if σ is sequentially rational at every information set for a full set of beliefs $\mu(\cdot|\cdot)$ that are both on-path and subgame-on-path consistent with σ, then σ is a subgame-perfect Nash equilibrium. If σ is immediate-action rational at every information set for a full set of beliefs that are extended-on-path and subgame-extended-on-path consistent with σ, then σ is a subgame-perfect Nash equilibrium.*

Corollary A12.8 follows directly from Propositions A12.3 and A12.6. The idea here is simple. If z_0 is the root of a proper subgame, and play reaches an information set h contained within the subgame (which, since it is a proper subgame, means that all of h lies within the subgame), then $\iota(h)$ will know that play passed through z. Starting from that single node (for which beliefs are trivial), if h is subgame on-path within the subgame, then $\iota(h)$ can use σ and Bayes' rule to compute conditional beliefs, conditional on the known fact that play passed through z_0, and similarly for information sets that are extended-on-path within the subgame.[12] We are (simply) requiring that, upon reaching h, $\iota(h)$ uses these beliefs built from σ.

There is one point about which you might worry. Suppose information set h is contained in two proper subgames, with roots z_0 and z_0'. I assert that, in this case, either z_0 is a successor of z_0', or z_0' is a successor of z_0. This is so because, if you trace the (unique) sequence of immediate predecessors of any node in h, that sequence must pass through z_0', and it must pass through z_0. Whichever is hit first (as you move back through the tree) is a successor of the second. So, suppose that z_0 is a successor of z_0'. And suppose that h is (extended) subgame-on-path under σ in both subgames. The worry then is that the demands of (extended) subgame-on-path consistency of beliefs, applied for the two subgames, may give different answers. But this cannot happen. If h is reached under σ from z_0', then so is z_0, since every $z'' \in h$ lies on a sequence from z_0' to z'' that must pass through z_0. And, then, in applying Bayes' rule starting from z_0', all the relative probabilites in moving from z_0' to z_0 (to reach z'') cancel out, numerator and denominator.

And more: Consistency across Alice's consecutive information sets

Next come several "consistency" requirements of the form: What Alice believes at one information set should be consistent with what she believes at her subsequent information sets. In this regard, consider the piece of a game tree depicted in Figure A12.11(a). (In this figure, payoffs are omitted, as well as other features that are irrelevant to this discussion. For instance, in panel a, Alice's choices at her information sets #2 and #3 are not included—the focus is on her beliefs at those information sets.)

Start with panel a, and suppose we are looking at a strategy profile in which Bob chooses C. All of Alice's information sets are off-path, even extended-off-path. And there are no proper subgames. So none of the consistency requirements so far tell us anything. Alice's beliefs at the information set Alice #1 are a free choice, so suppose she believes that she is at the upper node in Alice #1 with probability 1/3. Then, I assert, she ought to assess in both Alice #2 and Alice #3 that she is at the upper node (in the respective information set) with probability 1/3. Why would she change her beliefs about what Bob did, after he didn't do the expected C, based on something she and she alone did? And this is true even if σ calls for her to choose u with probability 1.

Now consider panel b. Again suppose that Bob's strategy is to choose C, so

---

[12] The corollary also requires on-path or extended-on-path consistency, since the game as a whole may not be a proper subgame.

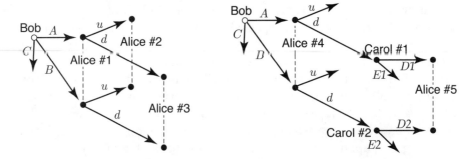

(a) Part of an extensive-form tree   (b) Another piece of an extensive-form tree

Figure A12.11. Consistency across Alice's information sets

all of Alice's information sets are extended-off-path. Suppose, that, at Alice #4, her beliefs are that she is at the upper of the two nodes with probability $2/3$. And suppose that σ calls for Carol, at Carol #1, to choose $D1$ with probability $1/2$ and to choose $D2$ at Carol #2 with probability 1. Then, I assert that, at Alice #5, Alice should reason as follows:

> Bob surprised me by not choosing C. But I assess that, given this surprise, he chose A with probability $2/3$. That explains my off-path beliefs at my #4 information set. If my #5 information set is reached, I know that I chose d. So, starting from my #4 information set and having reached #5, the joint probability of the upper node in #5 is $(2/3) \times 1 \times (1/2) = 1/3$; this is my belief that I'm starting at the upper node in #4, $2/3$, times the probability 1 that I choose d, times the probability $1/2$ that Carol chooses $D1$, according to σ. And, similarly, the joint probability of reaching the lower node in #5 is $(1/3) \times 1 \times 1 = 1/3$. So, at my #5 information set, Bayes' rule, applied starting from my #4 information set, dictates that I ought to believe that I am at the upper node of #5 with probability $(1/3)/(1/3 + 1/3) = 1/2$.

Indeed, by the "extended-on-path" logic, Alice should hold these beliefs at Alice #5, even if her strategy at Alice #4 is that she chooses u with probability 1.

How can we formalize these "ought to" considerations? The examples above are covered by the following general definition.

Definitions A12.9. *For an extensive-form game (of perfect recall):*

a. *For arbitrary strategy profile σ and a full set of beliefs μ, and for $h \in H$ and $z \in \cup_{z' \in h} S(z')$, let $\pi(z|\sigma, h) := \mu(z'|\sigma, h) \times \prod_{j=1}^{J} \sigma\big(a(z_j)\big)$ where $z' = z_0, z_1, \ldots, z_J = z$ is the (unique) sequence of nodes from $z' \in h$ to z. (That is, $\pi(z|\sigma, h)$ is the probability that z is reached conditional on passing through h, starting with $\iota(h)$'s beliefs at h and employing σ thereafter.)*

b. *Fix a player n and information sets h and h', both from H_n and such that h' precedes h. For a given strategy profile σ, say that h **is reached from** h' **according to** σ **and** n**'s beliefs at** h' if $\pi(h|\sigma, h') := \sum_{z \in h} \pi(z|h') > 0$.*

c. *Player n's beliefs $\{\mu(\cdot|h); h \in H_n\}$ are **own-previous-beliefs consistent with** σ if, for every pair of information sets $h, h' \in H_n$ such that h' precedes h and for $\hat{\sigma}_n$ an (arbitrary) strictly mixed behavior strategy for n,*

$$\mu(z|h') = \frac{\pi(z|(\hat{\sigma}^n, \sigma_{\neg n}), h')}{\pi(h|(\hat{\sigma}_n, \sigma_{\neg n}), h')} , \qquad (A12.2)$$

whenever the denominator in (A12.2) is strictly positive .

Roughly speaking, the import of part c is that player n is "using Bayes' rule whenever possible," where this means: any time Bayes' rule can be used, starting from one of her information sets to another that follows the first. Note that we are using the notion of "extended on-path" here; if, under σ, $h \in H_n$ is not reached from $h' \in H_n$ solely because of the actions of n, we assume that n nontheless applies Bayes' rule.

And even more: "Structural" considerations

Consider the piece of a game in Figure A12.12(a).

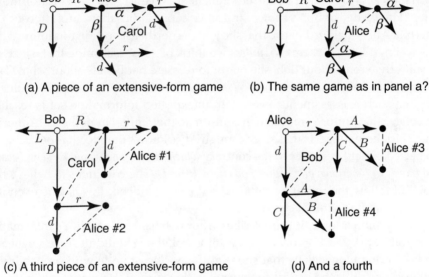

(a) A piece of an extensive-form game   (b) The same game as in panel a?

(c) A third piece of an extensive-form game   (d) And a fourth

Figure A12.12. "Structural" considerations for consistent beliefs

Suppose σ calls for Bob to choose D with probability 1 and for Carol to choose r with probability 1. Alice's information set is off-path, but since it has a single node, her off-path beliefs are both trivial and obvious: Given the move, she knows that Bob chose R. And then sequential rationality says that she should decide whether to choose α or β based on the expectation that Carol will choose r. Simple enough.

But now look at panel b, still assuming that σ specifies D for Bob. Alice's information set is off-path. And, if Bob chooses R instead of (the expected) D,

Alice's information set is reached. What should be her beliefs? Should the fact that Bob didn't act as expected lead her to conclude that, perhaps, Carol will deviate as well (which would allow her to have arbitrary beliefs at her information set). Or should she reason that, even though Bob manifestly deviated, Carol should still be expected to choose r, which means that Alice's beliefs are that she is at the upper node in her information set? Of course, the difference between panels a and b is that we've exchanged the order of simultaneous moves by Alice and Carol. So, if the spirit—indeed, more than the spirit, the clear rationale—of sequential rationality is "no further deviations," in that spirit, shouldn't Alice believe that Carol will/did not deviate, hence she is at the northeast of her two nodes with probability 1?

Note that this is a simple application of (proper) subgame consistency, since, in panel b, Carol's node is the root of a proper subgame. There is nothing new here, although I put the example here to make the point: Subgame consistency follows the general philosophy that a deviation from σ by one player does not (under subgame consistency) cause players to rethink those portions of σ that apply to the proper subgame.

Move on to panel c. Suppose that σ prescribes D for Bob and r for Carol. The information set Alice #2 is on-path, so on-path consistency tells us that, at this information set, she should believe that she is at the northeast node in her information set. But what about her beliefs at Alice #1? Because Carol moves without knowledge of Bob's choice, and since σ prescribes that Carol chooses r, it seems that Alice ought to believe that she is at the northeast node in this information set as well. At least, it seems so, *unless* we think of Alice reasoning that, since she is manifestly wrong about Bob, she ought to reassess her beliefs about what Carol is doing/did. But, again, the spirit of sequential rationality is that players do not engage in such reassessments; even if an unexpected information set is reached, they believe that "future" moves will conform to their initial hypothesis. Adhering to that spirit here suggests that, even though Alice knows that Bob has not behaved as expected, absent evidence to the contrary *which, in this case, is not present, because Carol moves in ignorance of whether Bob chose R or D*, she continues to believe that Carol will follow the initial hypothesis $\sigma_{\text{Carol}} = r$. Indeed, this is true even if σ prescribes that Bob's initial choice is D.

And, by similar logic, if σ prescribes L for Bob (so both of Alice's information sets are off-path), and if σ prescribes r for Carol, then shouldn't Alice's beliefs at both her information sets be that she is at the northeast node with probability 1? Or, at least, isn't this the logical conclusion in the spirit of sequential rationality?

Finally, consider panel d and σ that prescribes that Alice chooses r and Bob chooses C. If Alice's #3 information set is reached, suppose her beliefs are that she is at the upper node (the node after the path r and then A) with probability $1/3$. Then, because Bob chooses between A, B, and C without knowing what Alice did, it seems logical that, at Alice #4, Alice's beliefs should be that she is at the upper node in that information with the same probability $1/3$.

Two general principles are at work in these examples:

- Players, in forming beliefs at their various information sets, should expect that deviations from the hypothesized strategy profile σ conform to the structural (information) constraints faced by other players.

- Sequential rationality is based on the principle that even if a player knows there "have been" deviations from σ, no more deviations are expected. In that spirit, beliefs at an off-path information set should be based on as "few" deviations as is necessary to reach that information set, where here "few" means in a set-containment sense.

The second of these principles is pretty opaque, so let me illustrate the idea with two examples.

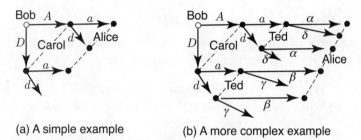

(a) A simple example   (b) A more complex example

Figure A12.13. Alice's off-path beliefs should be based on as "few" deviations as possible (see text for explanation)

Consider the piece of an extensive-form game depicted in Figure A12.13(a). Suppose that σ prescribes D for Bob and d for Carol. Then Alice's information set is off-path. Moving from southwest to northeast in her information set, the southwest node is reached if Carol (only) deviates to a. The middle node takes a deviation by Bob to A. And the northeast node requires both Bob and Carol to deviate. *Since the northeast node requires deviations by both Bob and Carol, and there are nodes in Alice's information set that require only one of those two deviations, the second principle requires that Alice's beliefs attach zero probability to her northeast node.* She can divide her beliefs in any fashion she desires between the southwest and central nodes—putting probability 1 on either, or splitting probability between them—but, in essence, either one is "vastly more likely" than the two deviations it takes to get to her northeast node.

Panel b presents a more complex example. Suppose σ prescribes D for Bob, d for Carol, and δ-γ for Ted. Going from southwest to northeast in Alice's five-node information set, the deviations needed are, respectively, $\{\beta\}$ for the most southwest, then (in order) $\{a, \beta\}$, $\{A, \alpha\}$, $\{A, a\}$, and finally $\{A, a, \alpha\}$ for the most northeast. Since $\{a, \beta\}$ is a strict superset of $\{\beta\}$ and $\{A, a, \alpha\}$ is a strict superset of both $\{A, \alpha\}$ and $\{A, a\}$ (although either one would be sufficient), the second principle, if adhered to, requires that Alice attach zero probability in her beliefs to the second and fifth of the five nodes; she can divide probability among the other three in any way she pleases and still adhere.

I do not assert that this second principle, as a general rule for off-path beliefs, must be accepted. But once again I cite the spirit of sequential rationality as its rationale: Evidence of deviation by one or more players does not "imply" deviations by other players. In this regard, for the example of panel b, note that the southeast-most node involves a single deviation (by Ted) and the second, third, and fourth require two deviations; one by Bob and one by Ted (at a different information set for Ted than his deviation from γ) in one case; and one each by Bob and Carol in the other. One might therefore argue that the southeast-most node requires the fewest (numerically) deviations, and so Alice ought to assess probability 1 that she is there. It could be argued that this follows logically from the spirit of sequential rationality. But, it turns out, this conclusion is not one that is required in "standard" theory.

Full consistency of each player's beliefs

This conclusion is not drawn because of how all these different consistency "requirements" are formally accomplished in one fell swoop:

Definition A12.10. *For a given strategy profile σ and a player n, beliefs $\mu(\cdot|h)$ for $h \in H_n$ are **fully consistent for player** n if there exists a sequence of fully mixed strategy profiles $\{\sigma^k; k = 1, 2, \ldots\}$ such that (i) $\lim_{k\to\infty}\sigma^k = \sigma$ and (ii) for each information set $h \in H^n$,*

$$\mu(z|h) = \lim_{k \to \infty} \frac{\pi(\sigma^k)(z)}{\pi(\sigma^k)(h)} .$$

The story—such as it is—that justifies this definition of consistency runs as follows. Think of player n making an assessment of what the other players are doing. The strategy profile $\sigma_{\neg n}$ is n's ideal assessment; she is pretty sure that this describes how each will play. But she isn't entirely certain, and so, for each player n', her real assessment is some $\sigma'_{n'}$ that is close to $\sigma_{n'}$ but still gives strictly positive probability to every action $a \in A(h)$ for $h \in H_{n'}$. If each $\sigma'_{n'}$ is strictly positive, then except for information sets that n herself excludes, every information set $h \in H_n$ is on-path, so Bayes' rule can be applied. And by the logic that gave us extended-on-path information sets, by choosing an arbitrary σ'_n for herself that is strictly positive, under σ', every information set is on-path. Of course, the arbitrary σ'_n that she chooses washes out as she computes beliefs at each $h \in H_n$ (because of perfect recall).

Definition A12.10 works in this fashion, except that it doesn't fix a single strictly positive $\sigma'_{n'}$ for each other player n'. Instead, it looks at a sequence of these assessments that approach $\sigma_{\neg n}$, computes beliefs at each $h \in H_n$, and then passes to a limit in those beliefs. So, it is an "asymptotic idealization" of what n's beliefs would be if slightly different from her "ideal" assessment $\sigma_{\neg n}$.

"Proposition" A12.11. *If player n's beliefs are fully consistent, then these beliefs pass all the consistency tests specified previously.*

Why the scare quotes around "Proposition?" Some of the consistency requirements stated previously—on-path and extended-on-path consistency, subgame-on-path consistency, and own-prior-beliefs consistency—were specified generally and formally. And it is fairly straightforward to verify that fully consistent beliefs for each player will satisfy those consistency requirements. However the "structural" considerations provided in the previous subsection were not given a general formalization; it is messy to do so, and in any case, in the literature, full consistency is where these ideas land.

To understand the all the implications of full consistency, I recommend Kohlberg and Reny (1997). They show the equivalence of consistency with a system of *relative probabilities*, which specifies for any two events belonging to a state space their relative probabilities, even if, relative to the whole state space, the events have relative probability zero. Hence, an information set may be off-path—have probability zero of being reached—but relative probabilities formalize the notion that nodes (or sets of nodes) in an off-path information set can be compared concerning how relatively likely they are. This formal concept, *together with axioms about the independence of certain events*, gives an interesting interpretation of a consistent system of beliefs.

Why did I italicize *together with axioms about the independence of certain events*? Go back to Definition A12.10. It is based on a sequence of fully mixed σ^k such that $\lim_k \sigma^k = \sigma$. That is to say, in computing player n's beliefs at $h \in H_n$, if there are two other players, call them m and ℓ, a σ^k is a triple $(\sigma_n^k, \sigma_m^k, \sigma_\ell^k)$. For reasons already given, the exact specification of σ_n^k is irrelevant. As long as it is fully mixed, it doesn't preclude h being reached, and in the computation of $\mu(\cdot|h)$, its exact specification washes out, numerator and denominator. It is instead σ_m^k and σ_ℓ^k that determine $\mu(\cdot|h)$ in the limit. And—here is the point—in computing any $\pi(\sigma^k)(z)$ for $z \in h$, it is (somewhat implicitly) assumed that m's and ℓ's randomizations in σ_m^k and σ_ℓ^k are conducted independently. This, if you think it through, is where the no-more-deviations-than-necessary property comes from.

Instead of pursuing this idea formally, I'll simply show, using the example in Figure A12.13(a), why full consistency leads to the conclusion that Alice's fully consistent beliefs cannot attach positive probability to her northeast node.

For Alice's beliefs at her information set in Figure A12.13 to be fully consistent with a σ that prescribes D for Bob and d for Carol, there must be a sequence $\{\sigma_{\neg\text{Alice}}^k; k = 1, 2 \ldots\}$ of fully mixed strategies for Bob and Carol, converging to $\sigma_{\neg\text{Alice}}$, such that Alice's Bayes'-rule determined beliefs at her information set for the profiles in the sequence converge to her beliefs. Let $\{\sigma^k\}$ be the sequence of fully mixed beliefs, and let σ_{Bob}^k attach probability ϵ_k to him choosing A and σ_{Carol}^k attach probability δ_k to her choosing a, where (of course) $0 < \epsilon_k < 1$, and $0 < \delta_k < 1$ (because σ^k must be fully mixed), and $\lim_n \epsilon_n = \lim_n \delta_n = 0$ (because $\sigma^n \to \sigma$). Then, at σ^k, the Bayes' rule (conditional) probabilities of Alice's three nodes in her information set, conditional on play reaching that information set, are (going from southwest to northeast)

$$\frac{(1 - \epsilon_k)\delta_k}{\epsilon_k + \delta_k - \epsilon_k\delta_k}, \quad \frac{(1 - \delta_k)\epsilon_k}{\epsilon_k + \delta_k - \epsilon_k\delta_k}, \quad \text{and} \quad \frac{\epsilon_k\delta_k}{\epsilon_k + \delta_k - \epsilon_k\delta_k}.$$

These three terms must converge to some values (per the definition of full consistency), and since both δ_k and ϵ_k have limit 0, it follows that $\epsilon_k \delta_k = o(\epsilon_k)$, and $\epsilon_k \delta_k = o(\delta_k)$. Hence, looking separately at the numerator and denominator of each of the three, the limits are the same as the limits of

$$\frac{\delta_k}{\epsilon_k + \delta_k}, \quad \frac{\epsilon_k}{\epsilon_k + \delta_k}, \quad \text{and} \quad \frac{o(\epsilon_k)}{\epsilon_k + \delta_k},$$

respectively. The last of these clearly must have limit 0, while the first and second (assuming they converge) must converge to numbers between 0 and 1 that sum to 1, and (moreover) can be set to converge to any division of probability 1 between the two.

And still more: Full cross-player consistency and sequential equilibrium

Consider the piece of an extensive-form game depicted in Figure A12.14a. Suppose that the strategy profile specifies X for Bob and d for Alice (at least, with positive probability). Suppose as well that Alice's beliefs at her off-path information set are that she is at the upper node with probability $1/3$.

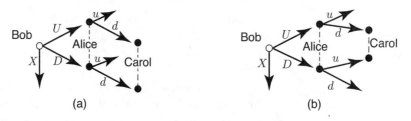

(a)   (b)

Figure A12.14. Cross-player considerations

Then Alice, surprised to be given the move, thinks it is twice as likely that Bob deviated to D as that he deviated to U. In this case, regardless of what Carol thinks is the likelihood of Alice choosing d—even if σ prescribes that Alice picks u with probability 1—shouldn't Carol adopt whatever "logic" led Alice to conjecture that Bob chose U with probability $1/3$ and so hold beliefs at her information set that she is at the upper node in her information set with probability $1/3$?

Panel b provides a variation. Suppose that σ prescribes X for Bob with probability 1 and u for Alice with probability $1/3$. And suppose that Alice's beliefs at her information set are that she is at the upper node in her information set with probability $2/3$. Shouldn't Carol then conclude that she is at the upper node in her information set with probability $[(1/3)(1/3)]/[(1/3)(1/3) + (2/3)(2/3)] = 1/5$? In other words, shouldn't Carol have the same off-path beliefs as does Alice about Bob and then use Bayes' rule to compute her (Carol's) beliefs at her information set?

As has been said many times, the spirit of equilibrium analysis is that it applies when the game has a "solution," a way to play that is obvious to all the players. But if the strategy profile is obvious, shouldn't off-path beliefs that sustain that strategy profile also be obvious? And, if so, shouldn't Alice and Carol share beliefs about what Bob has done, when he manifestly has deviated from what σ prescribes? In other words, shouldn't there be cross-player consistency in what each player assesses off-path (as well as on-path, but that's assured by on-path consistency and the fact that players share the strategy assessment σ).

One way to operationalize this notion leads to the final and most restrictive consistency requirement on beliefs (at least, most restrictive in this appendix):

Definition A12.12. *For a given strategy profile σ, beliefs $\mu(\cdot|\cdot)$ are **fully cross-player consistent** if there exists a sequence of fully mixed strategy profiles $\{\sigma^k; k = 1, 2, \ldots\}$ such that, (i) $\lim_{k\to\infty}\sigma^k = \sigma$, and (ii) for each information set $h \in H$,*

$$\mu(z|h) = \lim_{k\to\infty} \frac{\pi(\sigma^k)(z)}{\sum_{z'\in h} \pi(\sigma^k)(z')} \, .$$

*And if a given strategy profile σ and a full set of beliefs $\mu(\cdot|\cdot)$ are both sequentially rational and fully cross-player consistent, then the strategy profile and beliefs constitute a **sequential equilibrium.***

Being pendantic, what is added here to *full consistency, player by player*, is that in Definition A12.10, each player n is allowed her own sequence of fully mixed strategy profiles that generate (in the limit) her beliefs. Definition A12.12 says that one sequence of fully mixed strategy profiles serves for all the players.

In this definition, if we have three players, Alice, Bob, and Carol, the real force of the definition is that Alice's sequence of strictly positive assessments about Bob's strategy is the same as Carol's sequence for Bob, and so forth. The fact that, in the definition, Alice adopts Carol's and Bob's sequence of assessments about her own strategy when it comes to computing her (Alice's) beliefs at her information sets is of no consequence: As already noted several times, in games with perfect recall, when player n computes beliefs at her information set by Bayes' law, what she "conjectures" about her own strategy σ_n washes out in computing the Bayes'-rule ratios: Any strictly mixed strategy of her own—and the definition then uses the sequence assessed by Bob and Carol for notational convenience—will do.

A12.5. The Bottom Line on Consistency of Beliefs (and Sequential Rationality)

What is the appropriate level of consistency to require in an application? Of course, if a favored solution in a specific context meets all the requirements of sequential equilibrium, that's not a bad thing. And if the question is whether simply being a sequential equilibrium—sequentially rational behavior relative to fully cross-player-consistent beliefs—is *sufficient* for a strategy profile to be accepted as a solution, the answer is: Of course not. As is the case with the concept of (simple) Nash equilibrium, one must have a story or, at least, some intuition as to why the players—in the specific context—would conclude that the strategy profile is the obvious way to play, which will (presumably) involve an accompanying story about why players' beliefs are as specified.[13]

On the other hand is the question of *necessity*, which cuts two ways in applications:

- If some Nash equilibrium that you think is unreasonable cannot be supported by full cross-player consistency, is this adequate grounds to dismiss it as unreasonable?

- If you have an equilibrium that you believe is "the solution" (that is, is the obvious way to play a specific game), but either you are unable to verify that it can be supported by full cross-player consistency (or some lesser consistency criterion), or, worse, you can show that it *cannot* be supported by full cross-player consistency (or something less), is that grounds for doubting it is "the solution"?

My answer to both questions is: No, depending on the context of the application. And that No is for essentially the same reason that I expressed doubts about the necessity of sequential rationality, back on pages 565–6. Sequential rationality is based on the principle that, if Alice reaches an information set at which it is manifest that Bob has deviated from σ, she should nonetheless believe that Carol, subsequently, will adhere to σ. In roughly the same spirit, consistency of beliefs holds, in circumstances such as in Figure A12.13(a), that Alice can believe that either Bob has deviated, or Carol has deviated, and she can believe that the deviator might be either one. But she cannot assign positive probability to the event where they both deviated.

To see that these are two sides of the same coin, consider Figure A12.15: Bob and Carol are playing the stag-hunt game, which has two Nash equilibria, D-d and A-a. The first is Pareto superior for the two of them, the second is "safer" because, if either chooses A (or a), a payoff of at least 7 is guaranteed. Bob and Carol don't care what Alice does, but Alice cares about what they do. In panels b and c, we have two variations on this, where only Alice's payoffs are attached to terminal nodes; Bob and Carol's payoffs are as in panel a.

In panel b, Alice is aware of whether Bob chose A or D; in fact, Alice only has a choice to make if Bob chooses A. Suppose Alice is fairly certain that Bob and Carol will play D and d, respectively; she attaches probability 0.99 to this possibility as the obvious way for them to play, because (she believes) they are good friends who probably discussed this situation. But she assesses a 0.01 chance that this is a novel situation for them, in which case they are more likely than not to play the safer choices A and a. Hence, if she learns that Bob chose A, she reevaluates her assessment of what Carol will do, leading her to choose α. But

---

[13] In Appendix 14, attention will shift from a specific sequential equilibrium, or strategy profile and beliefs for the entire game, to sets of sequential equilibria, all of which give the same equilibrium *outcome*, that is, distribution of terminal nodes. This will be explained fully there; for now, I wish to signal that, for extensive-form game models of specific situations, interest is properly focused on "what will happen," which can and often does leave some freedom in specifying the off-path behavior and beliefs that support on-path behavior and beliefs.

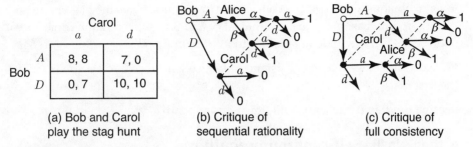

		Carol	
		a	d
Bob	A	8, 8	7, 0
	D	0, 7	10, 10

(a) Bob and Carol
play the stag hunt

(b) Critique of
sequential rationality

(c) Critique of
full consistency

Figure A12.15. The "same" critique for sequential rationality and consistency of beliefs

α is not sequentially rational if Alice initially assigns probability (close to) 1 that Bob and Carol are playing D-d. This is the critique made back on pages 565–6, although there it was made with respect to Figures A12.4 and A12.5.

Panel c depicts a situation in which Alice only has a choice to make if Bob and Carol didn't choose D-d. This is the game tree from Figure A12.13(a), and if Alice believes that D-d is the obvious way for Bob and Carol to play, her information set is off-path. As discussed previously, fully consistent beliefs by her requires (only) that she put zero probability on being at the northeast node in her information set, hence sequential rationality with fully consistent off-path beliefs means she must be choosing β. But if we adhere to the story that, while she believes that D-d is overwhelmingly likely, the next most likely pair of actions by Bob and Carol is A-a, then of course α is what she should do.

The point, one more time, is that both sequential rationality and full consistency (at the individual- or cross-player level) have roots in the same principle: One deviation should not imply that another deviation is likely. In specific applications, this may be an unreasonable principle on which to hang your hat.

That said, the rejoinder offered by advocates for sequential rationality mentioned on page 566—that it is not the principle of sequential rationality that is the problem, but rather an inadequate model—can be invoked for this example (that is, for the situation in panel c) as well.[14] That said, my opinion is that all these layered consistency requirements should be taken with several large grains of salt in applications. Especially when it comes to the final step—cross-player full consistency—the notion that players "share" off-path beliefs seems to me difficult to justify as a principle to which one should adhere. Whether it—or, for that matter, any of the tools developed in this appendix—makes sense for you to employ this notion in a specific economic context you are studying is a judgment that you alone—perhaps in conjunction with your referees—must make.

Which raises two questions:

- In any form of equilibrium that we've discussed, an equilibrium strategy profile

---

[14] One can think of full consistency as a reduced-form solution concept for more elaborate stories or theories of what causes deviations from the anticipated equilibrium strategy. A "better" model would explain the story that is at work. One such story is trembling-hand perfection; see Section A12.6. And, if you want to see stories that provide different reduced-form solution concepts, I can offer Kreps (1989b).

σ, as an obvious way to play, is conjectured in common by all the players. In applications, is it reasonable to insist that Alice and Bob hold common conjectures about what Carol will do at an off-path information set?

- Why was full cross-player consistency advanced in Kreps and Wilson (1982) in the first place?

Answering those two questions will finish this appendix.

Less than Nash: Self-confirming equilibria

Concerning the first of these questions, suppose that the rationale for assuming "common conjectures" among players is custom; players know what others will do and what is expected of them, because those behaviors are customary. It may make sense, in such circumstances, to weaken the requirement that the "obvious and customary way to play" constitutes a Nash equilibrium.

Imagine a situation in which Alice must choose between x and y. If she chooses x, Bob must choose between a and b; if she chooses y, Bob's option are c and d, following which Alice or others may have further moves to make. Suppose that, in the society in which Alice and Bob operate, it is customary in this sort of situation that Alice chooses x and Bob responds with a. Because this behavior is customary, we imagine that both Alice and Bob understand that it is expected of them and is what they expect of each other.

The choice of y by Alice, in contrast, takes play "off the customary path." Alice forbears from choosing y, because the response by Bob of d instead of c would be quite bad for her. [15] At the risk of introducing a controversial and fraught example, imagine that y is the use of tactical nuclear weapons in a local conflict involving one of the superpowers. The superpower forbears from y (x is "don't use such weapons"), because it is unsure how a rival superpower might respond, with some possible if perhaps unlikely responses spelling disaster. Because her choice of y is not customary, there is no settled and customary response by Bob on which she can rely. Still, her choice of x is based on a subjective assessment she has of how Bob will respond to y. She may be quite wrong in her assessment; Bob may be planning to choose c instead of d. But because y is not customary, she doesn't know this.

The point is: It may be obvious—due to custom—for Alice to choose x and for Bob to respond a. Both Alice and Bob understand that this is the "obvious way to play." Along-path behavior is obvious; off-path behavior is speculative.

In the literature, the concept of a *self-confirming equilibrium* formalizes this idea. In an extensive-form game, each player n entertains a hypothesis $\hat{\psi}^n$ of how rivals will behave, to which some σ_n is a best response. I'm using ψ here instead of $\sigma_{\neg n}$, because at this stage, I want to allow a player to hold an assessment about how her rivals will behave that reflects correlation in their behavior. (In this respect, I'm back to the philosophy of Appendix 9's rationalizability.) These best responses

---

[15] Although a bit outside the "standard" approach to single-person decision making, hence something that belongs in Volume III, Alice's aversion to y may reflect ambiguity in what might happen subsequently, combined with Alice's *ambiguity aversion*.

σ_n form a strategy profile σ, which determines behavior at all information sets and so determines which information sets are on-path and which are off-path. In a self-confirming equilibrium, we require that, at information sets $h \in H_{n'}$ that are on-path relative to σ, each player n's conjecture about what n' will do at h, given by $\hat{\psi}^n(h)$, must agree with $\sigma_{n'}(h)$. Players know (have learned?) what happens customarily. But there is no requirement that $\hat{\psi}^n$ agrees with $\sigma_n(h)$ at off-path information sets $h' \in H_{n'}$, $n' \neq n$. As for correlations of how others play in the ψ^n, any such correlations "wash out" at on-path information sets, but they can be present in off-path behavior.

Clearly, this will give us something less than Nash equilibrium, which is predicated on "accurate" assessments by all players for all information sets. Note that we get something less than a Nash equilibrium on at least two grounds:

- In a situation in which either Alice or Carol can unilaterally compel Bob to choose between c and d, Alice's and Carol's conjectures about what Bob will do may disagree. Alice forbears from choosing y because she fears d by Bob, while Carol forbears from y' because she fears c. Note that this story requires at least three players.

- But, even with two players, Nash equilibrium requires that what Alice believes that Bob will do off-path is what Bob plans to do. In a self-confirming equilibrium, this needn't be the case. Superpower A may refrain from using tactical nuclear weapons in a local conflict (not currently involving Superpower B) because it fears that, if it does, Superpower B will be compelled to intervene. Superpower B, in the event that A does use them, must decide whether to intervene based on its forecast of whether Superpower A will escalate their conflict; and B may in fact refrain from intervening based on a mistaken forecast of A's further response. But A may not correctly forecast this (non)response by B to the first action and so will not initiate the use of tactical nuclear weapons.[16]

In this context of such self-confirming equilibria, we still can speak of beliefs and sequential rationality and consistency criteria: Suppose $h \in H_{n'}$ is off-path. A player $n \neq n'$ has a hypothesis $\psi^n(h)$ as to how n' will behave there. And we might reasonably impose the requirement that this hypothesized behavior for n' is sequentially rational for some reasonably consistent beliefs by n'.

This line of thought takes us close to rationalizability. One can—and in the literature, some analyses do—discuss rationalizability in the context of extensive-form games. This topic is exotic enough (as is that of self-confirming equilibria) that I won't to chase down the details here. But to get you started (if you wish to chase down those details), consider the game in Figure A12.16.

If Bob is choosing Y in equilibrium, the interaction between Carol, Ted, and Alice is off-path. In a self-confirming equilibrium, Alice can conjecture that Carol and Ted will play r-R with probability close to $1/2$ and d-D with probability close

---

[16] Using techniques from Appendix 13, one can build a more refined and nuanced model of this situation as an equilibrium situation, by modeling the uncertainty in A's calculations about B's motivations and beliefs.

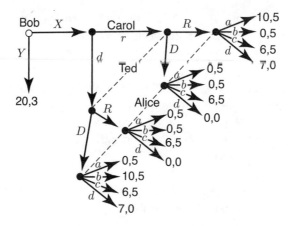

Figure A12.16. If Bob customarily chooses Y, can Alice hold an assessment about Carol and Ted that involves correlation in their actions?

to $1/2$. And with those off-path conjectures, d is her best choice, which makes Bob's choice of Y his own best response. Moreover, Bob can rationalize Alice's choice of d, if he believes that she might hold this assessment. But if he is forced to believe that Alice's conjectures about Carol and Ted reflect that they choose independently, then in this game, he must choose X.

A12.6. Trembling-Hand-Perfect and Proper Equilibria

To answer the question of why full cross-player consistency of beliefs was where this literature began, you must go back to the historical development of these ideas. As noted earlier (in footnote 11), sequential equilibrium originated the ideas of beliefs, sequential rationality, and consistency of beliefs with strategy profiles, around which this appendix has been built. But prior to the development of sequential equilibrium, Selten (1975) proposed the concept of a *trembling-hand perfect equilibrium* to deal with the problems that motivate this appendix.

Trembling-hand perfection in strategic-form games

Trembling-hand perfection can be thought of as an expression of the idea that no one should ever assess probability zero for some conceivable outcome of a random event. When a player says, for instance, "I believe my opponents will play this game according to the strategy profile $\sigma_{\neg n}$," where $\sigma_{\neg n}$ assigns zero probability to some strategy choice $s_{n'}$ by some other player n', we should think of n thinking that, "I suppose that n' *might* choose $s_{n'}$, but odds are so small that I can (for purposes of analysis) treat the odds as being zero." At least for finite games, or even games where there is a uniform bound on all the possible payoffs to each player, if σ_n is a best response to $\sigma_{\neg n}$, then playing σ_n will be *very close* to a best response against strategy profiles that are very close to $\sigma_{\neg n}$.

But σ_n may not an absolute best response. In a strategic-form game, a strategy σ_n for player n can both be weakly dominated by some other strategy *and* be part of a Nash equilibrium. Figure A12.1(b), reproduced here as Figure A12.17, provides an example: Although Bob's choice of x is weakly dominated by y, A-x is a Nash equilibrium, because (formally), at the A-x strategy profile, Bob is assessing that Alice will choose A with probability 1. *If instead, we believe that Bob can never be absolutely certain that Alice will choose A —if (at best) he thinks that Alice choosing A is only extremely likely—he would move to y.* And if Alice thinks that this is how Bob thinks, then she will switch to L, giving the Nash equilibrium L-y.

Bob

	x	y
A	2, 6	2, 6
L	0, 1	3, 2
R	1, 3	1, 5

Alice

Figure A12.17. Can Bob reasonably play a weakly dominated strategy?

To formalize this idea, we have the following definition and proposition.

Definition A12.13. *Fix a finite (player and action) strategic-form game, with player set $\mathcal{N}$, strategy sets $(S_n)_{n \in \mathcal{N}}$, corresponding mixed-strategy sets Σ_n and strategy-profile set $\Sigma = \prod_{n \in \mathcal{N}} \Sigma_n$, and (extended) expected-payoff functions $v_n : \Sigma \to R$.[17] A strategy profile σ is **trembling-hand perfect in the strategic form** if there exists a sequence of strategy profiles $\{\sigma^k ; k = 1, 2, \ldots\}$ such that:*

a.   *$\lim_{k \to \infty} \sigma^k = \sigma$.*

b.   *Each σ^k is completely mixed. That is, for each k and $n \in \mathcal{N}$, $\sigma_n^k(s_n) > 0$ for every $s_n \in S_n$.*

c.   *For each n and k, σ_n is a best response to $\sigma_{\neg n}^k$. That is, $v_n(\sigma_n, \sigma_{\neg n}^k) \geq v_n(s_n, \sigma_{\neg n}^k)$ for all $s_n \in S_n$.*

Proposition A12.14. *If σ is trembling-hand perfect in the strategic form, it is a Nash-equilibrium profile.*

The proof is simple. We have $v_n(\sigma_n, \sigma_{\neg n}^k) \geq v_n(s_n, \sigma_{\neg n}^k)$ for all $s_n \in S_n$; pass to the limit in k, noting that $v_n(\cdot, \sigma_{\neg n}^k)$ is continuous in its second argument.

For a two-player game, this definition captures the informal idea that both players cannot be absolutely sure what their rival will do; the choice of strategy by player n, σ_n, should be a best response to strategies $\sigma_{\neg n}^k$ (condition c) that are "very close" to $\sigma_{\neg n}$ (condition a) and that assign positive probability to every possible choice by the players other than n (condition b).

The definition is not limited to two-player games. However, it is worth noting that, when there are more than two players, this definition carries with it some hidden ideas: Suppose that there are three players, Alice, Bob, and Carol. Suppose that the equilibrium profile we are looking at has each player choosing a pure strategy; use the notation s_{Alice}, and so forth. Alice's choice of strategy s_{Alice} is

---

[17]   Since I'm assuming that $\mathcal{N}$ and each S_n are finite, no mathematical difficulties intrude.

not only a best response against (s_{Bob}, s_{Carol}), but also against fully mixed strategy profiles for Bob and Carol that are close to (s_{Bob}, s_{Carol}). And, similarly for Bob and for Carol. In this regard:

- Alice's "I can't be sure" hypotheses about what Bob and Carol may do has them playing independently. We're supposing that Alice believes that Bob is very likely to be playing s_{Bob}, and Carol is very likely to be playing s_{Carol}. But if she is wrong about this, does it make sense to rule out alternative hypotheses in which the "other" actions they might be choosing are correlated? Suppose Alice believes, as part of her reasoning, that it is very likely that Bob and Carol have not engaged in pre-play communication and coordination. (This is hardly a new story to this appendix; see the discussion around Figure A12.15.) But can she rule out, for sure, that they haven't coordinated their actions? If she cannot, then Definition A12.13 is inadequate.

- And Alice has small probability assessments about what Bob and Carol might be doing, if they aren't playing their parts of (s_{Bob}, s_{Carol}). Bob does as well. *And Alice and Bob not only agree that Carol is likely to be playing s_{Carol}. They also agree (more or less) on what Carol might be doing if she isn't playing s_{Carol}.* [18] It may well be that $(s_{Alice}, s_{Bob}, s_{Carol})$ is viewed by all three players as the obvious way to play this game, in the sense that each is virtually certain that this is how the others will play. But it goes a lot further to assume that their "what-if-I'm-wrong?" assessments about third parties coincide.

Nonetheless, this is how trembling-hand perfection in the strategic form is defined.

In fact, Definition A12.13 is not the original definition. Instead, Selten (1975) originally proposed:

Definition A12.13'. *Fix a strategic-form game (with the same notation as in Definition A12.13). Let Φ_n denote the set of functions $\phi_n : S_n \to (0, 1]$ such that $\sum_{s \in S_n} \phi_n(s) \le 1$, and let Φ denote the product $\prod_{n \in \mathcal{N}} \Phi_n$, with typical element ϕ. That is, ϕ assigns to each action at each information set a strictly positive number, such that the sum of the numbers assigned to the actions available for each player n is less than or equal to 1. Write $\phi(n, s_n)$ for the value of ϕ at n and $s_n \in S_n$. The strategy profile $\sigma \in \Sigma$ is **trembling-hand perfect in the strategic form** if there exist sequences $\{\phi^k; k = 1, 2, \ldots\} \subseteq \Phi$ and $\sigma^k, k = 1, 2, \ldots\} \subseteq \Sigma$ such that:*

a'. $\lim_{k \to \infty} \phi^k = 0$.

b'. For each k, $\sigma^k \ge \phi^k$.

c'. For each k and $n \in \mathcal{N}$, σ_n^k is a best response to σ_{-n}^k, if n is constrained to play each strategy $s_n \in S_n$ with probability at least $\phi(n, s_n)$.

d'. $\lim_{k \to \infty} \sigma^k = \sigma$.

The story that goes with this definition provides the adjective *trembling-hand:* The

---

[18]   This is a bit imprecise. The precise statement is that Alice's choice of s_{Alice} is a robust best response against her assessment concerning Bob and Bob's assessment concerning Carol, and so forth.

idea is that player n may want to play strategy σ_n, but if for some strategy $s_n \in S_n$, $\sigma_n(s_n) = 0$, player n cannot completely avoid this strategy. Think of "playing a strategy" as pushing the appropriate button; then as the player reaches to push the strategy that she wants, her hand may tremble, and instead she picks s_n. If we think of $\phi^k(n, s_n)$ for large k as the absolute minimum probability with which n chooses s_n—she can't reduce the probability of this any further—we have this definition, more or less.[19] Happily, the two definitions are equivalent.

Proposition A12.15. *A strategy profile σ is trembling-hand perfect in the strategic form according to either Definition A12.12 or A12.12' if and only if it is trembling-hand perfect according to the other definition.*

For a proof, see (for instance) Fudenberg and Tirole (1991a, Theorem 8.4).[20]

The agent-strategic form of the game and trembling-hand perfection in the extensive (agent-strategic) form

Selten's motivation for creating the notion of trembling-hand perfection was similar to the motivation offered here for the notions of beliefs and sequential rationality. He wanted to extend the notion of subgame perfection to encompass extensive-form games, such as the game in Figure A12.2.

Unhappily, trembling-hand perfection in the strategic form doesn't even imply subgame perfection. Consider the extensive-form game depicted in Figure A12.18a, and its reduced strategic form in panel b.

	Bob	
	α	δ
D	2, 0	2, 0
Alice Aa	3, 2	1, 1
Ad	0, 0	1, 1

(a) An extensive-form game (b) Its reduced strategic-form

Figure A12.18. Trembling-hand perfection in the strategic form does not imply subgame perfection

Subgame perfection implies that Alice will choose a at her second information set, if reached, hence Bob will choose α, hence Alice will choose A; that is, Aa-α is the unique subgame-perfect equilibrium. But suppose (looking at panel b) Bob assesses (for large integer k) that Alice is playing D with probability $1 - 1/k - 1/k^2$, Aa with probability $1/k^2$, and Ad with probability $1/k$. His expected payoff from α is $0(1 - 1/k - 1/k^2) + 2/k^2 + 0/k = 2/k^2$, and his expected payoff from δ is

---

[19] I say "more or less," because if I were formulating this concept from scratch, I'd prefer to say that if player n wishes to play σ_n, she actually plays a with probability $\phi^k(n, s_n) + [1 - \sum_{s'_n \in S_n} \phi^k(n, s'_n)]\sigma_n^k(s_n)$; that is, her involuntary trembles are given by $\phi^k(n, \cdot)$ for large k, and so $[1 - \sum_{a' \in A_n} \phi^k(n, a')]$ is the probability that her hand doesn't tremble at all. But this reformulation is equivalent to Selten's Definition A12.13'.

[20] Their Theorem 8.4 gives a third equivalent way to define trembling-hand perfection, to which we will come in a bit.

$1/k + 1/k^2$. For large enough k ($k \geq 2$ will do), his best reply to this completely mixed strategy by Alice is δ. And if Alice believes that Bob is choosing δ with probability $1 - 1/k$ and α with probability $1/k$, her best response for large enough k is D. So, D-δ, which is subgame imperfect, is trembling-hand perfect in the strategic form.

Selten, recognizing this, suggests that the issue is that, in the extensive form, Alice may have to "push buttons" twice. She certainly must choose between A and D, but if she chooses A and Bob chooses α, she must then choose between a and d. This, potentially, gives her two opportunities for her hand to tremble. And two trembles must be much less likely than either one of the two.

To formalize this, Selten (and we) define trembling-hand perfection in what is called the *agent-strategic form* of the game.[21] For an extensive-form game with perfect recall, the agent-strategic form is defined by creating, for each information set h in the game, an *agent h* of player $\iota(h)$, whose available strategies consist of the set of actions $A(h)$ available to $\iota(h)$ at h and whose payoff from the game, v_h, is identical to the payoff of the original player $\iota(h)$. The idea is that player n appoints agents to act on her behalf, one agent per information set. Since the game has perfect recall, agent $h \in H_n$ whose action follows the choice of agent $h' \in H_n$ knows that h' acted, knows what h' chose, and knows everything that h' knew when h' acted. And by assumption, all of n's agents (all $h \in H_n$) form a *team*, in the sense that they all share the same payoff. But, in the agent-strategic form, they act independently.

If the solution concept being employed is Nash equilibrium, this presents a problem. See Figure A12.19(a). In this one-player extensive-form game, the unique Nash equilibrium is Aa. But if we look at the agent-strategic form version of this game, where Alice has two agents, Left Alice and Right Alice, it is a Nash equilibrium for Left Alice to choose D and Right Alice to choose d. This happens because, if Left Alice chooses D, then Right Alice's (sole) information set is off-path, and simple Nash allows her to do anything she wishes. (Of course, subgame perfection will rule out this Nash equilibrium. But my assertion is only that Nash equilibria of the agent-strategic form may fail to be Nash in the original game.)

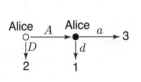

(a) A one-player game (there is only one payoff because Alice is the only player)

(b) Adding Bob, so it doesn't seem trivial

Figure A12.19. Nash equilibria for the agent-strategic form may not be Nash in the original game

[21] In the literature, you are more likely to encounter this idea as the *agent-normal form* of the game; recall from Appendix 9 that the terms strategic form and normal form are used interchangeably, with normal form being the original term and strategic form a more modern replacement.

(If it bothers you that this is a one-player game, panel b shows the same thing for a two-player game. Bob will choose α in any equilibrium, because α strictly dominates δ, and there is probability at least 0.5 that Bob's information set is on-path; he has no choice but to choose α. Hence, from Alice's perspective, knowing that Bob will pick α, this game "reduces" to the one-player game in panel a.)

This problem disappears if we look for strategy profiles that are trembling-hand perfect in the agent-strategic form, where Definitions A12.13 and A12.13′ are adapted from the strategic-form to the agent-strategic-form version of the game. This is so because, for strictly mixed strategies by every agent—essentially, for strictly mixed behavior strategies—every information set is reached, however small the probability. Hence, in games such as in Figure A12.19 (either panel), Left Alice *must* choose A with positive probability, which gives Right Alice the motivation to choose a.

And, returning to Figure A12.18, even if, in the limit, Left Alice is choosing D and Bob is choosing δ with probability 1, if Left Alice and Bob both tremble, however slightly, Right Alice's information set is be reached with strictly positive probability. So, to maximize the payoff of the Left-and-Right Alice-team, Right Alice must choose a.

This, then, is where Selten lands: Henceforth, the term *a trembling-hand perfect strategy profile* or *equilibrium* will, in the context of extensive-form games, mean ... *in the agent-strategic form*. We have the following proposition.

Proposition A12.16.

a. *Every finite extensive-form game with perfect recall has a trembling-hand perfect equilibrium. In fact, for any specification of the sequence of "tremble" probabilities $\{\phi^k\}$ from Definition A12.13′, there exists a trembling-hand perfect equilibrium for this sequence.* [22]

b. *Every trembling-hand perfect equilibrium for a finite extensive-form game with perfect recall is a sequential equilibrium of that extensive-form game.* [23]

c. *Conversely, fix a finite extensive-form with perfect recall; that is, an extensive-form game, except for the payoffs assigned to players at terminal nodes and probability assessments by the players concerning any moves by Nature/initial nodes. For generic specifications of payoffs and probability assessments (about Nature's move), every sequential equilibrium is a trembling-hand perfect equilibrium.*

I do not provide a detailed proof of a and b; see Fudenberg and Tirole (1991b), for instance. But the ideas for the proofs of these two parts are easily given. For part a, the proof of existence of a Nash equilibrium is employed for each k, but where players are constrained to play strategies that satisfy $\sigma_n(a) \geq \phi^k(n, a)$ for each

---

[22] To be clear here, each ϕ^k assigns strictly positive probability to every action a that is in $A(h)$ for every $h \in H$. In the agent-strategic form, every $a \in A(h)$ is a "strategy" for the agent of $\iota(h)$ who is assigned to decide what happens at h.

[23] As an instant corollary to a and b, every finite extensive-form game with perfect recall has at least one sequential equilibrium. This explains the first step of the proof of Proposition A11.4, pages 550-1.

$a \in A(h), h \in H_n$. Constraining players to such smaller feasible strategy sets makes for no difficulties, since the constraint sets are each compact subsets of the full space of behavioral strategies. This provides, for each k, a "constrained" equilibrium profile σ^k; looking along subsequences as necessary, find an accumulation point σ of the sequence $\{\sigma^k\}$, which immediately gives Definition A12.13′.

And for part b, in the same construction, looking along subsequences as is required, one can assume that the sequence of beliefs computed using Bayes' rule $\{\mu^k(a, h)\}$ converges to some beliefs at each information set. Full consistency is by construction; sequential rationality of the limit strategy for these limit beliefs is a simple exercise in continuity.

Part c of the proposition is, however, quite difficult. Kreps and Wilson (1982b) show that it is true for equilibrium *outcomes*; Blume and Zame (1994) provides the complete result.

This answers the question with which this section began: What is called *full cross-player consistency of beliefs* here (and *consistent beliefs* originally), used to define sequential equilibrium, was defined with this proposition in mind: Selten's trembling-hand perfection in agent-strategic form was the benchmark in the literature, and Wilson and I wanted a beliefs-based solution concept that "came close" to what, at the time, was the benchmark.

Proper equilibria

Myerson (1978) provides a third equivalent definition of trembling-hand perfection. I'll state it in terms of strategic-form games, although the same construction works for agent-strategic-form games.

Definition A12.17. *A strategy profile σ for a given (finite player and action) strategic-form game is an ϵ-**perfect equilibrium** if it is completely mixed and if, for any player n and strategies s_n and s'_n, both in S_n,*

$$v_n(s_n, \sigma_{\neg n}) < v_n(s'_n, \sigma_{\neg n}) \quad implies \quad \sigma_n(s_n) < \epsilon.$$

A perfect equilibrium is any strategy profile σ such that $\sigma = lim_{k \to \infty} \sigma^k$, where, for $k = 1, 2, \ldots,$ σ^k is an ϵ^k-perfect equilibrium for a sequence $\{\epsilon^k\}$ of strictly positive numbers with $lim_{k \to \infty} \epsilon^k = 0$.

Proposition A12.18. *A strategy profile σ is a trembling-hand-perfect profile (in the strategic form) if and only if it is a perfect equilibrium according to Definition A12.17.*

For a proof, see Fudenberg and Tirole (1991b).

Myerson goes on:

Definition A12.19. *A strategy profile σ for a given (finite player and action) strategic-form game is an ϵ-**proper equilibrium** if it is completely mixed and if, for any player n and strategies s_n and s'_n from S_n,*

$$v_n(s_n, \sigma_{\neg n}) < v_n(s'_n, \sigma_{\neg n}) \quad implies \quad \sigma_n(s_n) < \epsilon\sigma_n(s'_n).$$

A proper equilibrium is any strategy profile σ such that $\sigma = \lim_{k\to\infty} \sigma^k$, where for $k = 1, 2, \ldots$, σ^k is an ϵ^k-proper equilibrium for a sequence $\{\epsilon^k\}$ of strictly positive numbers with $\lim_{k\to\infty} \epsilon^k = 0$.

Proposition A12.20. *Every finite strategic-form game has at least one proper equilibrium.*

For a proof, see Myerson (1978) (or Fudenberg and Tirole 1991b).

The advantage of proper equilibria is that we don't need to bother with the agent-strategic form. For the intuition, consider again the extensive-form game and its reduced strategic form in Figure A12.18. D-δ is trembling-hand perfect in the (reduced) strategic form, because, if Alice is playing D with probability close to 1, we can "arrange" for her to tremble to Aa a lot less than she trembles to Ad, which then justifies Bob's choice of δ. But as long as we look at strategies for Bob that "mostly" are δ but with a small, strictly positive chance of α, Alice is slightly better off with Aa than with Ad. So, using the language of trembles, properness insists that she tremble much less toward Aa than toward Ad. And if this is so, Bob is not content with δ. Or put more abstractly, as long as every information set is hit, even if it is hit with probability that vanishes in the limit, players must put their behavioral-strategy chips at each information set on the actions that are best from that information set. We have the following proposition.

Proposition A12.21. *For a finite extensive-form game with perfect recall, a proper strategy profile σ for the reduced strategic-form of the game gives the same outcome as a trembling-hand perfect (in the agent-strategic form) equilibrium.*

But the converse is not true. Figure A12.20 depicts an extensive-form game (and its corresponding strategic form) for which L-δ is trembling-hand perfect but not proper. Because each player has a single information set, the agent-strategic form is the strategic form. Then: L-δ is trembling-hand perfect for trembles by Alice that, in the kth set of trembles in the sequence, give D probability $1/k$ and R probability $1/k^2$. But if Bob is choosing δ with probability close to 1, R is better for Alice than is D, and so she must "tremble" R much more than D, which causes Bob to switch to α.

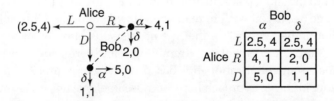

Figure A12.20. L-δ is trembling-hand perfect but not proper

So what is the proper equilibrium? Proposition A12.21 provides the answer, somewhat indirectly: Suppose that, instead of the extensive-form representation in Figure A12.19, we have Alice choose in two steps. First, she decides whether to choose L or *not L*. Then, if she chooses *not L*, she chooses between R and D.

This will make the subgame that begins with *not* L a proper subgame, and so in a subgame-perfect equilibrium, an equilibrium for the 2×2 simulatenous-move game between Alice and Bob that follows *not* L must be played. This requires a mixed-strategy equilibrium, with each of Bob and Alice choosing between their respective two moves with probability $1/2$. Note that this gives payoff 3 to Alice—more than the 2.5 that she gets from L—and 0.5 for Bob.

We know, then, that if we reformulated the extensive-form game in this fashion, Alice becomes two agents in the agent-strategic form: Starting-move Alice and If-not-L-Alice. And since every trembling-hand-perfect equilibrium for this agent-strategic-form game is sequential (hence subgame perfect in the extensive form), this means that the trembling-hand perfect equilibrium for this reformulated extensive form is *not* L followed by the randomized strategies by If-not-L-Alice and Bob.

But Proposition A12.20 says that every proper equilibrium—which is defined for the reduced strategic form—is trembling-hand-perfect in the agent-strategic form. *And this must be true for every agent-strategic form of every extensive-form representation that gives rise to the same reduced strategic-form game.* Hence, the unique proper equilibrium for the game in Figure A12.20 is L with probability 0, R with probability $1/2$, and D with probability $1/2$ for Alice; and α with probability $1/2$ and δ with probability $1/2$ for Bob.

This is a story to which we return Appendix 14.

Sequential rationality for consistent beliefs versus trembling-hand-perfect or proper equilibria

Trembling-hand perfection and properness on the one hand, and sequential rationality for consistent beliefs on the other hand, are two game-theoretic tools or approaches aimed at the same target: making sense of off-path—truly off-path and not extended-on-path—behavior in equilibrium analysis of extensive-form games. Such behavior is "free" from the perspective of the individual's payoff given the equilibrium strategies of others, but it can be hugely consequential in determining the on-path choices of other players. Proposition A12.16(c) indicates that these two approaches get to the same place; further results in Appendix 14 (see the italicized assertion on page 642 if you wish to read ahead) will strengthen this notion.

In my opinion, the "versus" in the title of this subsection is misleading. The two approaches are complementary. Trembling-hand perfection and properness are more formal; sequential rationality based on beliefs is more intuitive. I've favored the more intuitive approach here, because I believe it is more immediately useful when it comes to studying specific economic models. Speaking in terms of what players believe when confronted with something unexpected provides a more intuitive understanding of what is being assumed. In addition, the various consistency criteria give a graduated scale of criteria for what is reasonable for off-path beliefs. Speaking in these terms allows us to understand how the subgame-perfection priniciple, that one "mistake" doesn't portend others, works in specific games.

Hence, this appendix has been constructed with the (if you will) intuitionist approach first, and then the complementary formalist approach at the end. These two approaches—intuitionist versus formalist—reappear in Appendix 14, but in reverse order.

Bibliographic Notes

The three seminal papers for this appendix, in chronological order, are Selten (1975), Myerson (1978), and Kreps and Wilson (1982b).

Because full consistency can be difficult to verify, the search then commenced for weaker (and easier to verify) consistency criteria, giving birth to the family of perfect Bayesian equilibria. Important papers along these lines include: Fudenberg and Tirole (1991a); Battigalli (1996); Hendon, Jacobsen, and Sloth (1996); and Kohlberg and Reny (1997). Fudenberg and Tirole provides the first formalization of perfect Bayesian equilibrium (of which I am aware). Battigalli and Kohlberg and Reny are important as contributions to the formalization of PBE, as well for their development of relative (conditional) probability systems and their connection to full consistency. Hendon et al. explains the connection between extended on-path information sets, extended on-path consistency, one-step rationality, and sequential rationality.

The equivalence of sequential and trembling-hand-perfect equilibria (for generic extensive-form games) is established in Blume and Zame (1994).

For proofs of some of the results provided in this appendix, I recommend my go-to reference for game theory: Fudenberg and Tirole (1991b).

I briefly described self-confirming equilibria, for which, see Battigalli, Gilli, and Molinari (1992), and Fudenberg and Levine (1998).

All developments in this appendix are for finite extensive-form games. Extensions to countable-stage games with finite actions at each stage are relatively accessible, but when players have uncountably many actions available, things become difficult. See Myerson and Reny (2020).

Finally, a lot of "philosophical rants" in this appendix concern the general principle that one deviation should not (in the minds of players) make a second deviation likely, which underpins both sequential rationality and a number of consistency criteria. Concerning alternative approaches, the most prominent involve enriching the game-theoretic model to capture the idea that the observation of a deviation from what is expected to have happened raises doubts in the minds of players observing the deviation. The tools for such enriched models are the subject of Appendix 13. Those enriched models become complicated; an ad hoc approach to alternatives is discussed in Kreps (1989).[24]

---

[24] In the *Online Supplement*, I have posted a *Supplement to Appendices 12 and 13: More on Off-Path Beliefs*. This provides a brief and incomplete look at an alternative approach to off-path beliefs that permits correlation in off-path play, as well as discussion concerning how, using the ideas of Appendix 13, that alternative approach can be reconciled with the "standard" approach of this Appendix.

Appendix Thirteen

Common Knowledge and Games of Incomplete Information

Common knowlege is a term often encountered in the literature of game theory in various guises. Perhaps the most common occurence are statements such as *it is common knowlege (between Alice and Bob) that Alice is one of these two types*, or *Bob's assessment that Alice is the cooperative type is common knowledge (again, between Alice and Bob)*. And, in these two typical statements, we have the second topic of this appendix: When Alice comes in "types," the model is a game *of incomplete information*.

In general, we have that, *in (noncooperative) game theory, the rules of the game are assumed to be common knowledge among the players*. This means, somewhat informally, that (it is assumed that) every player knows the rules of the game, every player knows that every player knows the rules the game, every player knows that every player knows that every player knows the rules of the game, ad infinitum. And "the rules of the game" means the full form of the game, whether this is a strategic or extensive form, including all players' payoffs and probability assessments. In addition, and in the higher and more formal reaches of game theory, you may encounter such expressions as *common knowlege of rationality* and *common knowledge of the (equilibrium) strategies*.

To say that noncooperative game theory is predicated on the idea that the rules of the game are common knowledge among the players leads one to worry about using game-theoretic analysis to study real-life economic phenomena. In many real-life economic contexts, one agent—a player in the game-theoretic model—is uncertain about matters known to another agent. For instance, if Firms A and B compete, Firm A may not be certain about the cost structure of Firm B, and vice versa, even though the firms' payoffs—and therefore their choice of strategies—depend on those costs. One party may be unaware of options that the other party has available. One party may be unsure whether the other party knows that it (the other party) has a particular option it can exercise. And even if the parties to some interaction are pretty sure that each is aware of the rules, and each is aware that the others are aware, and so on, "pretty sure" doesn't mean "absolutely certain." To the extent that common knowledge = absolutely certain, we ought to worry whether the conclusions reached from a game-theoretic analysis are robust to "pretty sure" in place of "absolutely certain."

To deal with these matters and concerns, economists employ so-called *games of incomplete information*, a concept/modeling technique originated by John Harsanyi (references supplied in the Bibliographic Notes at the end of this appendix). By making creative use of this style of game, one can gain insight into the sorts of situations and questions posed in the previous paragraph.

For readers who expect (in the appendices, at least) a healthy dose of propositions and theorems, this appendix will be frustrating. The topics covered here are the subject of a good deal of higher-level theory. If your career objective is to be a game theorist (as opposed to an economist who uses game theory as a tool for modeling and analysis of economic phenomena), you should master this higher-level theory, which goes by the name *epistemic game theory* and connects to *epistemology*, a branch of philosophy that concerns the theory of knowledge. In Section A13.1, I provide the bare beginnings of this theory, concerning how the concept of common knowledge can be (and, in the main, is) formalized. This is included to give a taste of how this theory starts and to provide a springboard for discussing robustness of game-theoretic models and analysis to "almost common knowledge." Beyond this, when I come to a topic in the higher-level theory, I mention very briefly what is there and provide the interested reader with a place in the literature to begin.

If you are not particularly interested in this bit of cultural enrichment, skip ahead to Section A13.2, which gets to the main objective of this appendix: to show, largely by example, how games of incomplete information can be and, in the text, are used.

A13.1. Common Knowledge Formalized

Common knowledge concerns what individuals know and don't know about their situation, including what they know about what others know, and so forth. So we begin with a collection of individuals $\mathcal{N}$; a state-space Ω; and for each individual n, a partition $\mathcal{A}_n$ of Ω, representing n's (endowment of) information concerning the true state of nature $\omega \in \Omega$. The interpretation is that Nature selects some state $\omega \in \Omega$, and individual n is informed which cell $A_n(\omega) \in \mathcal{A}_n$ contains the true state of nature ω.

To keep things simple, assume that the collection of individuals $\mathcal{N}$ is finite; write $\mathcal{N} = \{1, 2, \ldots, N\}$. And since this is only meant as an introduction to the subject, assume as well that Ω is finite, so each $\mathcal{A}_n$ is a finite partition.[1]

This model of "knowledge," where each individual knows which cell in his or her partition contains the true state of nature, carries with it important limitations and implications. In particular, if $\omega' \notin A_n(\omega)$ and if ω is the true state of nature, individual n knows that ω' is *not* the state of nature. The model we have postulated then implies that if ω' is the state of nature, n knows that ω is not the state of nature. One could have a model where, in state ω, an individual knows that some other state ω' does not prevail, but in state ω', she cannot rule out ω. The formal model employed here precludes this possibility.

---

[1] The essential assumption here is that each $\mathcal{A}_n$ is a finite partition and not that Ω is finite. As long as each $\mathcal{A}_n$ is finite, with a finite collection of individuals, it wouldn't matter if Ω were infinite, since "total knowledge," or the join of all the individuals information, has finitely many elements.

Definitions A13.1.

a. *Individual* n **knows** *that the event* $E \subseteq \Omega$ *is true at state* $\omega \in \Omega$ *if* $E \supseteq A_n(\omega)$.

b. *The event* $K_n(E)$ *is defined by* $K_n(E) := \{\omega \in \Omega : E \supseteq A_n(\omega)\}$. *That is,* $K_n(E)$ **is the set of states (the event) in which** n **knows that** E **is true.**

For example, suppose that $\Omega = \{1, 2, \ldots, 12\}$ and that $\mathcal{N} = \{\text{Alice}, \text{Bob}\}$. Suppose that Alice's partition is $A_{\text{Alice}} = \{\{1, 2\}, \{3, 4\}, \{5, 6, 7, 8, 9, 10\}, \{11, 12\}\}$, and Bob's information partition is $\mathcal{A}_{\text{Bob}} = \{\{1, 2, 3, 4\}, \{5, 6, 7, 8\}, \{9, 10, 11, 12\}\}$.

Let E be the event $\{7, 8, 9, 10, 11, 12\}$, and suppose the state is $\omega = 9$. Alice's information is that the state is one of $\{5, 6, 7, 8, 9, 10\}$, so she cannot rule out the possibility that the state is 5, which is not in E; *Alice does not know that the event* E *is true in the state* $\omega = 9$. In contrast, Bob knows $\{9, 10, 11, 12\}$; that is, the true state is one of these four. Since $\{9, 10, 11, 12\} \subseteq E$, *Bob knows that* E *is true at the state* $\omega = 9$.

In which states does Alice that E is true? That is, what is $K_{\text{Alice}}(E)$? The answer is $K_{\text{Alice}}(E) = \{11, 12\}$. In those two states, she knows $\{11, 12\}$, and since $\{11, 12\} \subseteq E$, in those two states, she knows that E is true. But in the states 7, 8, 9, and 10, her information does not allow her to rule out 5 or 6, so she can't be sure that E is true. Of course, in states 1 through 6, Alice can't know that E is true, because E is false.[2] However, in each of $\omega = 9, 10, 11,$ or 12, Bob knows that the state is one of those four, hence he knows the truth of E. But if the state is either 7 or 8, he knows $\{5, 6, 7, 8\}$, and he doesn't know the truth of E. That is $K_{\text{Bob}}(E) = \{9, \ldots, 12\}$.

Just to give you one more example, suppose E' is the event $\{2, 5, 10\}$. Then $K_{\text{Alice}}(E') = K_{\text{Bob}}(E') = \emptyset$. There is no state in which either Alice or Bob knows that E' is true.

You should convince yourself that the example conforms to the definitions and that the formal definitions conform to the natural usage of the language.

Proposition A13.2.

a. *If* n *knows that* E *is true in state* ω *—that is, if* $\omega \in K_n(E)$ *—then* $\omega \in E$. *Hence it is immediately true that* $K_n(E) \subseteq E$.

b. *If* $\omega \in K_n(E)$, *and if* $\omega' \in A_n(\omega)$, *then* $\omega' \in K_n(E)$.

c. $K_n(K_n(E)) = K_n(E)$ *for all individuals* n *and events* E.

Proof. By definition, $\omega \in K_n(E)$ means that $A_n(\omega) \subseteq K_n(E)$; and since $\omega \in A_n(\omega)$, it follows that $\omega \in E$. And if $\omega' \in A_n(\omega)$, then $A_n(\omega) = A_n(\omega')$. Hence, $\omega \in K_n(E)$ implies $A_n(\omega) \subseteq E$ implies $A_n(\omega') \subseteq E$ implies $\omega' \in K_n(E)$. Finally, if $\omega \in K_n(E)$,

---

[2] Suppose we ask: In which states does Alice know *whether* E is true? This includes states in which Alice knows that E is false; that is, states where she knows E is true together with states where she knows that the complement of E, denoted E^C, is true. Of course, this is $K_{\text{Alice}}(E) \cup K_{\text{Alice}}(E^C)$, which in the example is $\{1, 2, 3, 4, 11, 12\}$.

then b implies that all of $A_n(\omega) \subseteq K_n(E)$, and so $\omega \in K_n(K_n(E))$. ∎

Part a of the proposition can be paraphrased as, If individual n knows that E is true, then (in this model) E is true. And part c of the proposition can be paraphrased as: If individual n knows E is true, she knows that she knows E is true.

We can now define the event on which n knows that m knows the event E is true: It is the event $K_n(K_m(E))$. And so forth: Moreover, for a given event E:

- The set of states in which every individual knows that E is true is $K(E) := \bigcap_{n \in \mathcal{N}} K_n(E)$.

- The set of states in which every individual knows that every individual knows that E is true is $K(K(E))$.

- The set of states in which every individual knows that every individual knows that every individuals knows that E is true is $K(K(K(E)))$.

And so forth. For an event E, write $K^0(E) = E$, $K^1(E) = K(K^0(E)) = K(E)$, and, iteratively, $K^{j+1}(E) = K(K^j(E))$ for $j = 2, 3, \ldots$.

From Proposition A13.2a, we know that $K(E) \subseteq E$. Hence for each integer j, $K^{j+1}(E) \subseteq K^j(E)$. And since we assumed at the outset that Ω is finite, each event E is finite, so either, for some (finite) integer j, we reach $K^j(E) = \emptyset$, or we reach a point at which $K^{j+1}(E) = K(K^j(E)) = K^j(E)$. Write $K^\infty(E)$ for this (set-inclusion) limit.

Definitions A13.3. *If $\omega \in K^\infty(E)$, then the truth of E is **common knowledge** among the individuals if the true state is ω. If $E = K^\infty(E)$, we say (a bit loosely) that E is **common knowledge** among the individuals.*

Why "a bit loosely?" The more proper statement would be that E is common knowledge among the individuals if, for every $\omega \in E$, E is common knowledge at ω. When we say an event E is common knowledge, it is understood that the phrase *in every state $\omega \in E$* is to be appended.

Going back to Alice and Bob, add a third individual, Carol, where $\mathcal{A}_{\text{Carol}} = \{\{1,2\}, \{3,4\}, \{5,6\}, \{7,8\}, \{9,10\}, \{11,12\}\}$. And let E' be the event $\{1, \ldots, 10\}$. Verify the following:

- $K_{\text{Alice}}(E') = K_{\text{Carol}}(E') = E'$, but $K_{\text{Bob}} = \{1,2,3,5,6,7,8\}$, and so $K^1(E') = \{1,2,3,5,6,7,8\}$

- $K_{\text{Alice}}(\{1,2,3,4,5,6,7,8\}) = \{1,2,3,4\}$,
  $K_{\text{Bob}}(\{1,2,3,4,5,6,7,8\}) = K_{\text{Carol}}(\{1,2,3,4,5,6,7,8\}) = \{1,2,3,4,5,6,7,8\}$, so $K^2(E') = K(K^1(E')) = \{1,2,3,4\}$.

- $K_{\text{Alice}}(\{1,2,3,4\}) = K_{\text{Bob}}(\{1,2,3,4\}) = K_{\text{Carol}}(\{1,2,3,4\}) = \{1,2,3,4\}$, and so $\{1,2,3,4\} = K^2(E') = K^j(E')$ for all $j \geq 2$. Hence, $\{1,2,3,4\} = K^\infty(E')$. The event E' is common knowledge among Alice, Bob, and Carol in states 1, 2, 3, and 4, and the event $\{1,2,3,4\}$ is common knowledge among them.

This example illustrates the following fundamental result.

Proposition A13.4. *An event E is common knowledge among a group of individuals $\mathcal{N}$ if and only if, for each $n \in \mathcal{N}$, E is the union of cells in the partitions $\mathcal{A}_n$. Or, put a bit more abstractly, E is common knowledge among the individuals if and only if E is in the* **meet** *of the information partitions $\{A_n; n \in \mathcal{N}\}$, defined as the finest common coarsening of the $\mathcal{A}_n$.*

Proof. First, suppose that the event E is, for each individual n, a union of cells in the information partition $\mathcal{A}_n$. Then for each $\omega \in E$, $K_n(\omega) \subseteq E$. So $K_n(E) = E$ for each n. Hence $\bigcap_n K_n(E) = K^1(E) = E$, and we're done.

Suppose, in contrast, that for some n, E is not the union of cells from $\mathcal{A}_n$. Then there are two states ω and ω' such that $\omega \in E$, $\omega' \notin E$, and $\omega' \in A_n(\omega)$. It is then immediate that at the state ω, n cannot tell if E is true; n considers ω' as possibly the true state, and $\omega' \notin E$. But then $K_n(E)$ is strictly smaller than E—ω is in E but not in $K_n(E)$—and so $K(E) \neq E$.   ∎

Please verify that, for Alice, Bob, and Carol, the three events that are common knowledge among them are $\{1, 2, 3, 4\}$, $\{5, \ldots, 12\}$, and $\Omega = \{1, \ldots, 12\}$, and only those three events. Note as well the following statement, which should be evident. In fact, it is trivially true. But, as we will see, it has profound implications for models of knowledge and common knowledge built on this framework:

> *The event Ω is always common knowledge among the individuals.*

Agreeing to disagree

In many economic applications, individuals will not know whether a particular event E is true or false. Instead, the individual n will assess a probability as to the truth of E. To model this, enrich the framework of the previous subsection by adding to it a prior (subjective) probability assessment P^n on the state space Ω for each $n \in \mathcal{N}$, the prior held by n. Hence, if the true state is ω, and if n is a Bayesian, then n, based on her information $A_n(\omega)$, assesses the conditional probability

$$P^n\big(E \big| A_n(\omega)\big) = \frac{P^n\big(E \cap A_n(\omega)\big)}{P^n\big(A_n(\omega)\big)}$$

that E is true.

Now consider two individuals, Alice and Bob, who are contemplating an event E. Suppose that Alice and Bob are endowed with (possibly different) information partitions $\mathcal{A}_{\text{Alice}}$ and $\mathcal{A}_{\text{Bob}}$ and with (possibly different) prior assessments P^{Alice} and P^{Bob}. Hence for a given event E and state ω, their conditional assessments of the event E,

$$P^{\text{Alice}}\big(E \big| A_{\text{Alice}}(\omega)\big) \quad \text{and} \quad P^{\text{Bob}}\big(E \big| A_{\text{Bob}}(\omega)\big),$$

can certainly differ. This could be because their priors are different. But even if they hold the same prior assessment over the state of nature, their information partitions may lead them to different posterior (conditional) assessments.

Now suppose Alice announces publicly: "My assessment of E is that it has probability 0.4." Suppose, in doing so, Alice makes it common knowledge between her and Bob that this is her assessment. Suppose Bob announces and, in so doing, makes it common knowledge between them, that his assessment is 0.5. *If Bob and Alice began with the same prior assessment, one or the other or both must, given the common-knowledge information, modify their assessment. The only way they can agree to disagree—which means hold different posteriors that are common knowledge between them—is if they began with different priors.*

Please note: I am assuming that, by making these public announcements, the truths of these events—the event $\{\omega : P^{\text{Alice}}(E|A_{\text{Alice}}(\omega)) = 0.4\}$ and the event $\{\omega : P^{\text{Bob}}(E|A_{\text{Bob}}(\omega)) = 0.5\}$—become common knowledge between the two. It is not enough that each knows the events; each knows that each knows the events, and so on. The public announcement of these things is meant to be sufficient to make these events common knowledge: When Alice announces her posterior, Bob knows that posterior. And because Bob knows that Alice knows that he heard her, he knows that she knows he knows this. And so on. (Imagine, if you will, how the theory might go if each believes that, in some states of nature, the other will be deceptive. We're not allowing this.)

This result is given in a classic paper by Robert Aumann (1976). In a slightly more general setting,[3] he proves (in the language of this section) the following proposition.

Proposition A13.5. *Suppose that Alice and Bob begin with the same prior. Suppose that, in a given state ω, it is common knowedge between Alice and Bob that $P^{\text{Alice}}(E|A_{\text{Alice}}(\omega)) = p_1$ and $P^{\text{Bob}}(E|A_{\text{Bob}}(\omega)) = p_2$ for two numbers p_1 and p_2. Then $p_1 = p_2$.*

Aumann introduces this result with the following remark: "We publish this observation with some diffidence, since once one has the appropriate framework, it is mathematically trivial." (And it is certainly that. I leave it to you to find the paper—it is readily available on the web—and read Aumann's proof. Or, challenge yourself and try to prove it on your own, using the characterization of common knowledge from the previous subsection.)

Aumann then continues, "Intuitively, though, it is not quite obvious; and it is of some interest in areas in which peoples' beliefs about each others' beliefs are of importance, such as game theory and the economics of information." (Both quotes are from Aumann 1976 page 1236.)

No-trade theorems

In financial markets, we see individuals trading securities; one person happily buys what another sells. It could be that sellers of a security sell for liquidity

---

[3] Aumann does not assume that Ω is finite, but he does assume that the meet of the information partitions of Alice and Bob contains only non-null events according to their (assumed) common prior.

purposes; they need cash to finance immediate consumption, while buyers buy to store wealth for later. And it could be that sellers and buyers hedge other risks they face. Someone who takes a job with General Motors, say, and whose future income prospects are therefore tied to the fortunes of GM, will sell shares of GM, since the risk of GM's share price compounds the employment risks that the individual faces.[4] But I think it reasonable to say that a lot of buying and selling is based on differences of opinion about where the market in general or a particular security is headed in terms of subsequent price and the dividends the security may pay.

So-called "no-trade theorems" take Aumann's result and show that, if investor expectations are "rational" and if differences of opinion are based solely on differences in information, then trading based on those differences of opinion should not take place. (See the Bibliographic Notes for references.) Or, at least, this is true if everyone starts with the same prior (see the discussion of the Harsanyi doctrine in Section 5.4 of Volume I). However, if one accepts that individuals trade based on differences of opinion, which in turn derive from differences in "prior assessments," this opens up many interesting possibilities concerning the nature of speculative trading in financial securities.

A13.2. Games of Incomplete Information

The previous section is meant to give you a quick introduction to the basic formal theory associated with common knowledge and epistemic game theory. This introduction is largely for purposes of "cultural enrichment," at least as concerns the text, which is to say: If what happened in the previous section is something of a blur, don't worry. It won't come back to bite you anywhere in this volume.

The main purpose of this appendix—and what is used in the text—is to introduce games of incomplete information as a tool for modeling and analyzing situations in which there is *not* common knowledge among the participants about certain aspects of the situation.

Figure A13.1 provides a concrete example. It involves Alice and Bob playing the depicted game, with Alice's payoffs listed first at each terminal node. The unique subgame-perfect equilibrium of this game is $a\text{-}DA'$, resulting in payoffs 5 for Alice and 4 for Bob. A second Nash equilibrium is $d\text{-}AD'$, but in the spirit of previous appendices, the choice of D' is not credible; Alice, aware of this, will choose a given the opportunity, and Bob, reasoning that this is so, chooses D.

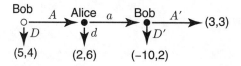

Figure A13.1. An extensive-form game (Alice's payoffs are listed first)

---

[4] This is what economic theory says that the new GM employee should do. Whether this theoretical prescription is valid is another matter. And Volume III will propose reasons for why GM might encourage its new employee to load up on GM stock, instead.

This analysis depends on Alice knowing Bob's payoffs following A' and D' or, at least, knowing that, if put in the position of having to choose at his right-hand information set, his payoffs will lead him to choose A'. *If the game is common knowledge between the two, and if the maintained hypothesis that players choose to maximize their (conditional) payoffs in the game given their beliefs—that is, they are sequentially rational—is* (loosely speaking) also common knowledge, then the analysis follows. But what if these assumptions are violated?

In particular, suppose Alice is uncertain about Bob's payoffs. Suppose that she knows his payoff if he chooses D is 4, she knows that his payoff if he chooses A and she chooses d is 6, and she knows that his two payoffs after A-a are both less than 4. But she is uncertain whether A' or D' is (conditionally) better for him. And suppose all of this is common knowledge between the two of them. If Bob chooses A, then Alice, reasoning about what is going on given her incomplete information, may reason as follows:

- "If Bob believes that I will choose a, the rational thing for him to have done would be to have chosen D."

- "So he must believe that I will choose d, at least with sufficient probability."

- "I am better off choosing d if I think there is sufficiently high probability that he will choose D'." (How high? If Alice believes that Bob will, given the opportunity, choose D' with probability q, then d is a better choice for her if $-10q + 3(1-q) = -13q + 3 < 2$, which is $q > 1/13$.)

- "Does Bob know that I don't know his payoffs after A-a? Is that why he chose D?"

Or suppose Alice *knows* Bob's payoffs—in particular, suppose she knows that, following A-a, he will choose A', but her knowledge of his payoffs isn't common knowledge. If Bob doesn't know that Alice knows his payoffs, he may think it possible that, given the choice, she will choose d. He is better off "trying his luck" with A, if his assessment p that she will choose d satisfies $4 < 6p + 3(1-p)$, which is $p > 1/3$. If Bob thinks that Alice may be unsure about his payoffs, unsure enough to choose d with high enough probability, then he'll choose A, and the outcome in this scenario will be A-a-A'; Bob will be disappointed to learn that Alice was sure enough about his payoffs to venture the choice a. But, since fortune favors the bold, putting Alice to the test by choosing A was worth trying.

The question is: Can we fruitfully model and analyze either or both of these scenarios? This is where the concept of *games of incomplete information* enters. In the next two subsections, I provide examples of game models that fit the two verbal stories just given. Then I will provide some general remarks. You may be tempted to skip the examples and go to the general remarks, but my strong suggestion is to persevere with the examples. Dealing with games of incomplete information is more art than science, and working through these examples is very instructive.

Model #1: Alice is unsure of Bob's payoffs (and Alice's assessment is common knowledge)

Consider the extensive-form game depicted in Figure A13.2. We imagine that, in the beginning, one of two possible states, ω_1 or ω_2, is chosen, with the probability of ω_1 being 0.4. Bob is told which state is chosen; Alice is not. In state ω_1, Bob's payoffs are as in Figure A13.1. In state ω_2, Bob's payoffs for A-a-A' and A-a-D' are reversed from what they are in state ω_1.

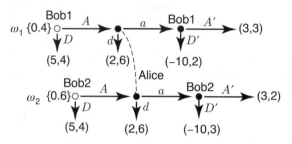

Figure A13.2. Alice doesn't know Bob's payoffs, and her assessment is common knowledge (Alice's payoffs are listed first)

This represents the following very specific version of a "world" in which Alice is unsure of Bob's payoffs, has a (very specific) subjective assessment of what they might be, and that assessment is common knowledge: Bob knows that Alice is uncertain, knows that she has a subjective assessment, knows what that assessment is, Alice knows all this, and so on.

In language often used in economic applications, Bob has two *types*, labeled in the game as Bob1 and Bob2, where in this instance a type of Bob is a specific set of payoffs for him.

Going back to the verbal story we are trying to model, state ω_1, in which Bob's type is Bob1, is the true state of nature. If we (as the analyst modeling the situation) know that this is the truth, then we are interested in the prediction of how Bob and Alice will behave in this state. But to make an informed prediction of how Bob and Alice will behave at ω_1, we must consider how Alice will behave given her state of information, which is the event $\{\omega_1, \omega_2\}$, and this in turn depends on how Bob would behave at his second information sets (the two information sets following A-a), since Alice's assessments of what Bob would do informs her choice of what she ought to do. In other words, to analyze Alice's behavior, we must be concerned with how Bob behaves in states of nature that, we know, do not pertain, because Alice's behavior depends on that hypothetical behavior. And since Bob's left-hand-information-sets behavior depends on how Alice will/would behave, what happens in the hypothetical state ω_2 may be informative for *all* our predictions concerning behavior in state ω_1.

The analysis is not entirely simple: Bob's behavior at his two information sets following A-a is simple (assuming sequential rationality): Bob1 will choose A', and Bob2 will choose D'. But Alice's decision at her information set depends on her beliefs: Let q be the probability she assesses, given the move, that Bob is Bob2 (that is, she is at the lower of the two nodes in her information set). Then d nets her 2 for sure, while a nets her $-10q + 3(1 - q)$. We already did this calculation; she will choose a if $q < 1/13$, d if $q > 1/13$, and she is indifferent if $q = 1/13$. As for the first choices of the two types of Bob, these depend (identically, given the numbers we chose for the model) on the probability r with which Alice chooses d. Hence we have the following two varieties of *pure-strategy* sequential equilibria:

1. Bob1 and Bob2 both choose A. This puts Alice's information set on-path, and (for on-path-consistent beliefs) she assesses $q = 0.6 > 1/13$ and chooses d (which justifies the choice of A by both types of Bob).

2. Bob1 and Bob2 both choose D. This puts Alice's information set off-path, and even full consistency imposes no restrictions on her beliefs. For the two Bobs to choose D, Alice must be choosing a (in a pure-strategy equilibrium), which means that her beliefs must have $q \leq 1/13$.

Note that I said that these are two *varieties* of sequential equilibria. The first possibility is a specific sequential equilibrium; all behavior (strategies) and beliefs are fixed. But in the second possibility, there is a variety of beliefs that Alice could hold; any q in $[0, 1/13]$ will do to render her choice of a sequentially rational. All these beliefs, though, if they lead Alice to choose a, give the same outcome (where an outcome = a distibution on final nodes): Both Bobs choose D, so the outcome is ω_1-D with probability 0.4 and ω_2-D with probability 0.6.

And there are other sequential equilibria in which Alice plays a mixed strategy, and the Bobs may do so. One sort is where the Bobs play D for sure, Alice has beliefs with $q = 1/13$ exactly, and she randomizes between d and a, playing d with probability r such that $6r + 3(1 - r) = 3r + 3 \leq 4$ or $r \leq 1/3$, which is necessary so that the Bobs choose D. Note that these equilibria give the same outcome as the second variety above: The Bobs' choice of D determines the outcome.

For the numbers in Figure A13.2, there is in addition a further family of mixed-strategy equilibria: Alice, holding the beliefs $q = 1/13$, mixes between a and d, choosing a with probability $r = 1/3$. This choice makes both Bob1 and Bob2 indifferent between D and A; note that we can make both types of Bob indifferent simultaneously because of the specific numbers in the model; this will not generally hold. Since this strategy by Alice makes the Bobs indifferent, they can mix between A and D, and we suppose that they pick (different!; what are some possibilities?) mixing probabilities, so that Alice's Bayes'-rule-determined beliefs give $q = 1/13$.[5]

Can we pick between the first sequential equilibrium, where the Bobs choose A and Alice chooses d, and the second type, in which the Bobs both choose D? The answer comes down to the question: Is there some criterion we can enlist that tells

---

[5] If you are tracking everything that is going on, here are three challenges. (1) What are the possible outcomes—that is, distributions of final endpoints—for this sort of equilibrium? (2) Change the payoff to Bob1 if A-a-A' to 3.5 instead of 3, keeping everything else the same. What happens to this sort of mixed-strategy equilibrium? (3) Now keep Bob1's payoffs as in the figure, but change Bob2's payoff after A-a-D' to 3.5 from 3. What happens?

us that Alice holding beliefs $q \leq 1/13$ are somehow "unreasonable?" Appendix 14 discusses answers to this question.

The point for now is that Figure A13.2 provides a game-theoretic model—again I stress, a very specific model—in which Alice is uncertain about Bob's payoffs and Alice's uncertainty is common knowledge. And, equally, the point is that even if we know which state of nature prevails, both we and Bob must consider what Alice would do in a state we (and Bob) know to be hypothetical, because Alice doesn't know the true state.

Model #2. Alice knows Bob's payoffs, but Bob doesn't know that Alice knows this (and Bob's lack of knowledge about this is common knowledge)

What if Alice knows Bob's payoffs, but Bob doesn't know this? What if, instead, Bob thinks that Alice may be uncertain about Bob's payoffs? Consider the extensive-form game depicted in Figure A13.3.

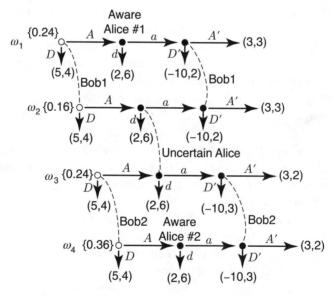

Figure A13.3. Alice may be aware of Bob's payoffs

This model has four states. In state ω_1, Bob has the payoffs that make A' conditionally dominant (that is, the original payoffs), and Alice is aware of this. (In the story, this is the objectively true state of nature.) In state ω_2, Bob has those payoffs, and Alice is uncertain what are his payoffs. In state ω_3, Bob has the "other" payoffs, and Alice is uncertain about those payoffs. And in state ω_4, Bob is type Bob2, and Alice is aware of this. The probabilities assigned to the four states are such that Bob is type 1 with probability 0.4, and Alice is aware of his type with probability 0.6, independent of his type. Bob knows his type, and Alice knows if she is Aware or not.

Note that this gives us *three* types of Alice: Aware Alice #1, who is aware she faces Bob1; Uncertain Alice; and Aware Alice #2, who is aware that she faces Bob2. Put in terms of the $\left(\Omega, (A_n)_{n \in \mathcal{N}}\right)$ formalisms of Section A13.1, $\mathcal{A}_{\text{Alice}} = \left\{\{\omega_1\}, \{\omega_2, \omega_3\}, \{\omega_4\}\right\}$, while $\mathcal{A}_{\text{Bob}} = \left\{\{\omega_1, \omega_2\}, \{\omega_3, \omega_4\}\right\}$.[6]

We proceed to analysis of this specific model. The sequentially rational choices of Bob1 and Bob2 at each one's information set after A-a are clear: Bob1 chooses A', and Bob2 chooses D'. We don't need to worry about their beliefs at their respective information sets (concerning whether Alice is aware or uncertain), because these choices are (conditionally) dominant.

The two Aware Alices' choices are therefore also clear. Aware Alice #1, at information set $\{\omega_1$-$A\}$, knows that she faces Bob1, hence a means a payoff of 3 for her, hence she chooses a. And Aware Alice #2, at information set $\{\omega_4$-$A\}$, chooses d.

The choice of Uncertain Alice at her (only) information set depends on her beliefs. If she assesses probability q that she is at the bottom node in that information set—that is, at the node that follows ω_3—and if $q > 1/13$, she chooses d. If $q < 1/13$, she chooses a.

And *in this formulation*, $q > 1/13$. To see why, consider the decision of Bob2 at his initial information set. His beliefs are forced: He believes he faces Aware Alice #2 (is at the node ω_4) with probability $0.36/(0.24 + 0.36) = 0.6$. Hence, he believes that, if he chooses A, the response from Alice will be d with probability 0.6 or more. It could be more if Uncertain Alice chooses d with positive probability. But even if Uncertain Alice chooses a with probability 1, the choice of Aware Alice at her information set $\{\omega_4$-A $\}$ is d, so Bob2 gets the payoff 6 with probability 0.6. It can't be less, and it could be more. Which is more than enough to make A a better initial choice for him than D. (A means at least $6 \times 0.6 + 3 \times 0.4 = 4.8$.)

Therefore, Uncertain Alice's information set is along the path of play. Even if Bob1 plays A with probability 1, the probability assessed by Uncertain Alice (using Bayes' rule) that she is at node ω_3-A is at least $0.36/(0.36 + 0.16) = 0.69\ldots$, more than the $1/13$ required to lead Uncertain Alice to choose d.

And if Uncertain Alice is choosing d, then Bob1, by choosing A, gets the payoff of 6 with probability (precisely, in this case) $0.16/(0.16 + 0.24) = 0.4$, which gives a payoff of $0.4 \times 6 + 0.6 \times 3 = 4.2$ from choosing A, making A a better choice than D.

At the risk of making an already difficult discussion more difficult, consider the model in Figure A13.4 as an alternative to the model in Figure A13.3.

The difference is that, in this model, if Bob is Bob2, there is no chance that Alice is aware of this. And, at least formally, it does make a difference. I assert that, in this formulation, we get back the second sort of equilibrium that we had with Figure A13.2. We still have the equilibrium in which Uncertain Alice chooses d with probability 1, hence both Bob1 and Bob2 choose A, hence Uncertain Alice's (on-

---

[6] Why three types of Aware Alice? Because the general rule is that a type of a player changes with changes in the player's information endowment. In this formulation, Alice's information partition of Ω has three cells, and so there are three types of Alice.

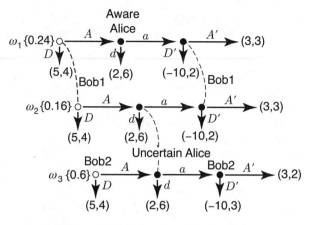

Figure A13.4. An alternative model

path-consistent) beliefs are that she is at the node $\omega_3 \text{-} A$ with probability $0.6/(0.6 + 0.16) = 0.79\ldots$, much more than the $1/13$ needed to make d the right choice for her. Which, in turn, justifies both types of Bob choosing A. (Aware Alice, in this game, always will choose a. She knows that Bob is Bob1, so she knows he will choose A'.)

But, in addition, there are sequential equilibria in which both types of Bob choose D with probability 1, which puts Uncertain Alice's information set off-path and allows her the freedom to hold beliefs that support the choice of a, which in turn supports Bob1's and Bob2's choice of D.

Beyond the two examples

These examples provide an introduction to how games with incomplete information can be used to create models of various situations. In the two examples, the uncertainty concerns payoffs, but much more is possible. With games of incomplete information, you can model situations in which players may be unaware of strategic options they or their rivals possess. Games of incomplete information can be used to model situations in which one player isn't certain whether a rival knows about a strategic option the first player possesses. In the literature, these games are used to model so-called behavioral or crazy types, players who, nothwithstanding the objective consequences of their actions for themselves, behave in ways that an objective observer would label as crazy.

Figure A13.5 provides some examples of such games of incomplete information. Suppose that, "objectively," Alice and Bob face the situation depicted in panel a: Alice chooses between L and R; if she chooses R, Bob has three possible responses. Panel b depicts a situation in which Alice assesses probability 0.4 that Bob is unaware of his third option. And panels c and d depict two ways to model a behavioral type of Bob, a type who will always choose option u. In panel c, the model forces Behavioral Bob to choose u by removing from the model other options for him. In panel d, the other two options remain, but Behavioral Bob's payoffs are chosen so that u is strictly dominant.

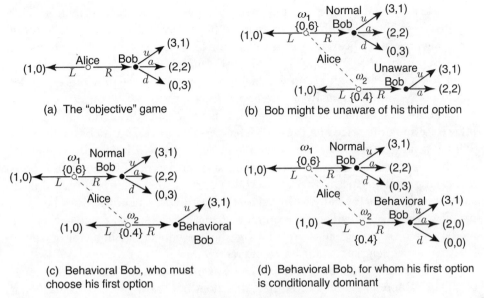

Figure A13.5. Modeling unaware and behavioral types

The second method for modeling Behavioral Bob can provide more flexibility: Suppose that, in the games in Figure A13.5, instead of Bob's choice ending the game, Alice learns what Bob has chosen, responds, and then Bob responds again. Suppose that, in some strategy profile, Behavioral Bob chooses u while Normal Bob chooses d, so that Alice's information set following a choice of a is off-path. If you model the situation as in panel c, Alice must "believe" that she faces Normal Bob at this off-path information set, because Behaviorial Bob doesn't have a as an option, and so there is no node in Alice's information set representing the choice of a by Behavioral Bob. In the second method, where Behavioral Bob has this option but choosing it is strictly dominated, the node following a by Behavioral Bob will be in Alice's information set, and her off-path beliefs could assign positive probability to that node. Which modeling method is better depends on whether you believe that Alice, having observed an unexpected choice by Bob, would assign positive probability to it having been chosen by a behavioral type who, it is assumed, never chooses that action.

As you proceed through the text—and, even more, through the literature of microeconomics in which players are differentially informed about their environment—you'll see more creative uses of the concept.

The general structure is as in these examples. In the formal model, there is a state space Ω, and for each agent/player/individual, both an initial information endowment (partition of Ω) and a prior probability assessment over Ω, leading via Bayes' rule to an initial posterior that is based on the individual's initial information endowment.

The language of "types" of an individual is typically used, where each cell in the individual's initial information endowment is a type of that individual. Perhaps most often in the literature, models identify types of players with their specific payoffs, as in Model #1. In that model, we have "one-sided uncertainty" about type, meaning that Alice's payoffs are common knowledge; only Bob's payoffs are uncertain (from Alice's perspective). Other examples in the literature have "two-sided" or "multi-sided uncertainty"; imagine a variation in the previous examples where Bob is simultaneously unsure about Alice's payoffs. A concrete example arises in bilateral bargaining (Chapter 23): Rug merchant Alice is bargaining with Bob concerning the price of a rug. Alice has a reservation price, below which she will not sell the rug; Bob has a reservation price, above which he will not buy the rug; both of these are private information, and the essence of the negotiation is that each party is trying to discover the other party's "this is the best I can do." In such examples, it is typically assumed that each individual knows his or her own payoffs. There is, however, no requirement that this is so, as, for instance, in a model where an individual is unsure what the consequences will be for herself of a particular sequence of actions in an interaction.[7]

As Model #2 indicates, modeling more complex incomplete information is feasible. In Model #1, Bob knows that Alice does not know his payoffs and what the nature of Alice's subjective assessment is (and these things are common knowledge). But in Model #2, Bob is uncertain about what Alice knows about his type; this is called "second-level uncertainty." In a third-level uncertainty model, Alice knows Bob's payoffs, Bob knows that Alice knows his payoffs, but Alice is uncertain whether Bob knows that she knows his payoffs. Most examples in the literature involve first-level uncertainty (although it is frequently multi-sided); second-order uncertainty is rare; and analyses of models with third- and higher-order uncertainty are virtually (but not entirely) nonexistent.

There is a theoretical question here: Is it mathematically coherent to have a model in which all higher orders of uncertainty are present? Can one formulate in coherent mathematical terms a state space Ω of that sort? The high-theory literature on universal type spaces answers this question in the affirmative; if you aspire to be a high-theory expert in game theory, this is a literature for you to study.[8]

When it comes to the analysis of models of this sort, the crucial (and, after-the-fact, obvious) insight is that, to understand what a player with incomplete information will do in a particular scenario (modeled as a state of nature), one must understand the world as that player sees it. Thus the analysis of all states of nature must be done simultaneously, even if some states are wholly hypothetical, as long as some player regards them as possible and germane to that player's decision. To reiterate from the analysis of the two examples, in Figure A13.2, Bob (and/or the analyst) may know that he is Bob1, but if Alice doesn't know this and entertains the

---

[7] Or, to give another example, in *the* seminal paper in the economics of private information, Akerlof (1970), we imagine (roughly) that Alice is selling her car to Bob. She knows the value of the car to herself, and the value of the car to Bob is that much plus a bit more. That is, she knows whether the car is a peach or a lemon; Bob doesn't. But Bob's payoff depends on whether the car is a peach or a lemon. In fact, Akerlof (1970) does not use game-theoretic terms. But, this is how a game-theoretic model of his problem would go. See Chapter 20.

[8] The seminal paper is Mertens and Zamir (1985).

possibility that he is Bob2. As a result, Bob1 (and/or the analyst) must analyze what Bob2 would do, at least insofar as the hypothetical behavior of Bob2 has an impact on Alice's behavior. And, more than that, Bob2's hypothetical behavior affects the behavior of Alice, and that in turn has an impact on the not-at-all-hypothetical behavior of Bob1.

Two comments are germane before turning to deficiencies of this form of analysis:

1. In the examples, I used the notion of a true state of nature (in all cases, state ω_1) to emphasize that analyzing behavior in the "true" state of nature requires analysis of behavior in all states, including entirely hypothetical states, simultaneously. In many applications, more of an ex ante perspective is taken; the different states of nature are all possible ex ante, and ultimate interest is in no one state in particular but in all of them and in how the different contingent behaviors interact. For instance, in the literature on auctions (Chapter 24), each bidder has his own valuation for the good being auctioned, other bidders and the seller are in the dark about this, and the seller wishes to set to rules of the auction to maximize her expected selling price, averaging over all states of nature. As a matter of semantics, one might want to distinguish between these two perspectives—I would call the first a case of *incomplete information* and the second *imperfect information*—but economists are not very good at semantics, so the distinction, if in fact there is one, is generally ignored.

2. And, also regarding semantics, an equilibrium (Nash, perfect, sequential, whatever) of a game of incomplete information is sometimes referred to as a *Bayesian* Nash, or *Bayesian* perfect, or *Bayesian* sequential equilibrium, with the adjective meaning that it is an equilibrium for a game of incomplete information. As far as I can tell, the adjective *Bayesian* has no further meaning—a *non-Bayesian* equilibrium is not a thing, except perhaps at the conjunction of game theory and behavioral economics—hence, I do not use this terminology. These are just Nash, or perfect, or whatever equilibria of the game in question.[9]

This paints a very nice and rosy picture of "things a creative game theorist can model and then analyze." But the use of this technology for modeling and analysis comes with some limitations.

For one thing, the very specific parameterizations in Figures A13.2–A13.4 hardly do full justice to the verbal and general stories about Alice and Bob that motivates them. The verbal story is that Alice is unsure of Bob's payoffs out on the right-hand side of the game tree; I arbitrarily chose a two-element-support probability distribution to model this uncertainty, while Alice's assessment is probably a good deal more diffuse than that. And I chose the same payoff value (3) for the two Bobs from their dominant choices, which allows for the possibility that Alice can randomize in a fashion that simultaneously makes both Bob's indifferent between

---

[9] (1) This is as opposed to a perfect Bayesian equilibrium (PBE) from Appendix 12, where "Bayesian" refers to the use of Bayes' rule in the specification of consistent off-path beliefs. (2) This terminology is found primarily in the early literature. Thankfully, it seems to have died out.

A and D, which in turn allows them to randomize in a fashion that provides her with beliefs that allow her to randomize.[10] The point is, specific parameterizatons can matter and matter in significant ways. Be aware of this and be alive to the possibility that a conclusion drawn from a specific parameterization is primarily (even only) a matter of that specific parameterization.

The second limitation—perhaps "complication" is a better word—rates a subsection all its own.

The game (you model) is common knowledge among the players, which can pose problems

Recall the italicized remark on page 608:

> *The event Ω is always common knowledge among the individuals.*

In the context of games of incomplete information, this remark means that, while your game-theoretic model may model the possibility of one or another player having incomplete information in some state of nature, in a broader sense the player is aware of this. In Figure A13.2, Bob1 knows that he is Bob1, but he knows (and, moreover, it is common knowledge) that he could have been Bob2. In Figure A13.3, Uncertain Alice knows that there was a chance that she would have known Bob's payoffs. In most applications, this assumption of common knowledge may seemed strained—perhaps a better (philosophical?) position to take is that players in games of incomplete information know only what they are "born" knowing—but in most applications, it doesn't present a challenge to the analysis.

However, if and when you wish to model a player who is "unaware" of certain aspects of the game, problems can arise.

Consider the game depicted in Figure A13.6(a). Alice chooses between U and D and then Bob, not knowing what she has chosen, chooses between u, a, and d. The payoffs (with Alice's payoffs first, as always) give an easy answer: Bob's choice of d dominates his other two choices, and Alice, aware of this, chooses D.

In this context, suppose I want to model the interaction between Alice and Bob where there is a 40% chance that Bob is unaware that he has option d. Following the discussion of Figure 13.5(b), we might try the game of incomplete information depicted in Figure 13.6(b). But now the requirement that Ω is common knowledge

---

[10] If you didn't take up the three challenges in footnote 5, or if you tried it and got stuck, here is a push. For Alice to be willing to randomize, her beliefs must be that she faces Bob2 with precisely probability $1/13$. Suppose we consider the variation where we change Bob2's payoff after $A\text{-}a\text{-}D'$ from 3 to 3.5, while leaving Bob1's payoff after $A\text{-}a\text{-}A'$ at 3. Then whatever Alice does, if Bob1 is willing to try A, then Bob2 definitely wants to do so. So either Bob1 plays A with probability 0, or Bob2 plays A with probability 1, or both. And if Bob2 plays A with probability 1, then Bayes' rule forces Alice to assess probability at least 0.6 that she is at the Bob2 node at her information set, which means she will play d, which means both Bobs will chose A, which is the first type of equilibrium outcome. Alternatively, if Bob1 plays A with probability 0 and Bob2 plays A with positive probability, Alice must believe that she is facing Bob2 with probability 1, she chooses d, and we once again wind up at the both-Bobs-play-A-and-Alice-plays-d equilibrium. The final possibility is that both Bob1 and Bob2 play D with probability 1, which is the second type of equilibrium. In other words, with this sort of change in the payoff structure, the possibility of a mixed-strategy equilibrium outcome disappears. But if, instead, we increase Bob1's $A\text{-}a\text{-}A'$ payoff..., well, that's enough of a hint.

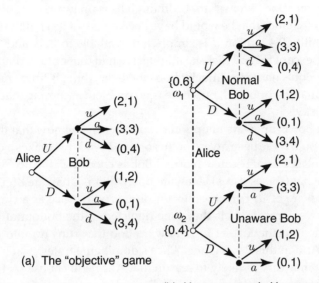

(a) The "objective" game

(b) How unaware is Unaware Bob?

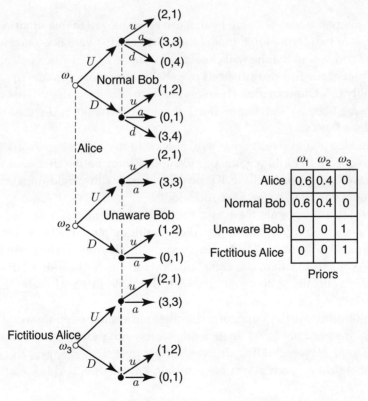

(c) A model that works, with diverse priors over Ω

Figure A13.6. Unawareness and the common knowledge of Ω

implies that Unaware Bob "knows" that, although he is unaware of option d, there was an apriori 60% chance that he would have been aware of it. Had the story been that, with probability 0.4, option d is simply not available to Bob, and "Unaware Bob" knows that, except for bad luck, he might have had that option, then we could change Unaware Bob's name to Unlucky Bob, and everything is fine. Unlucky Bob is unlucky in not having option d, but there is no problem assuming that he knows he has been unlucky.

But Unaware Bob is unaware of option d, so how can he know that there was a 60% chance he would have been aware of this option? And this makes a difference: With the numbers as given, because Normal Bob is choosing d, Alice will choose D regardless of what (she assesses) Unaware Bob will do. Unaware Bob, however, if he is truly unaware of d, perceives his encounter with Alice as a simple 2×2 simultaneous move game. This is the game depicted at the bottom of panel c, if you disregard the information set for Unaware Bob that runs up into the upper part of the tree. And in this 2×2 game, Alice's dominant strategy is U. Unaware Bob, if he is truly unaware, is likely to reason that Alice will choose U, to which a is his best response. But as already noted, Alice, whose attention is drawn by the 60% chance that Bob will choose d, is choosing D, to which Unaware Bob should choose u.

One modeling-and-analysis strategy that can be employed in this situation is to do the analysis in two steps. First, model the world as Unaware Bob perceives it, leading to the conclusion that he will choose d in the belief that Alice will choose U. Then, to model the full story, instead of panel b, we create a model in which, with probability 0.4, Unaware Bob chooses d as a dominant strategy. That is, we model "Unaware Bob" as "Behavioral Bob," where his behavior is dictated by the first step of the analysis.

This multi-step analysis technique will, at least in my experience, work fairly well. But if we want to build a game of incomplete information that, as a single game, matches the story we're telling, it is possible, albeit with an additional feature that none of our examples, so far, have included.

See panel c. In this game, there is a third state of nature ω_3. In this state, Alice takes on the identity of Fictitious Alice (fictitious objectively—she is very real in Unaware Bob's mind). And—here comes the the new feature—the four characters—Alice, Normal Bob, Unaware Bob, and Fictitious Alice—have different prior assessments on the state of nature, with the table in panel c giving each character's prior.

In most applications using games of incomplete information, common priors are assumed. But this need not be so. In general, games with incomplete information can have different players holding different priors over Ω, as long as the (non-common) priors held by each player are common knowledge.[11] This violation of

---

[11] Be careful here: Even when the model assumes common priors; the players' initial *posteriors*, which in the literature are sometimes called their *interim* beliefs, need not be common knowledge; indeed, this is often the point of the model. For instance, Figure A13.3 shows a situation in which, according to the model, the two types of Alice and the two types of Bob share a (common knowledge) common prior

the so-called Harsanyi doctrine or common prior assumption may be unusual in applications—indeed, referees of papers with this feature have been known to object that incorporating diverse priors in a model is "cheating"—but it is, technically, something the methodolgy can tolerate. Here, however, we are pushing very far from common priors: Alice and Normal Bob assign zero probability to the event $\{\omega_3\}$, which Unaware Bob and Fictitious Alice assess has probability 1.

Being pedantic about this point, it is still common knowledge that Bob may have at his disposal option d; Unaware Bob is aware that a state ω_1 in which he has a third option is, in theory, possible, (just as he is aware that states in which, say, he has ten options, are possible *in theory*). But his prior assessment is that this state has no chance of being true, and he dismisses any implications that might arise from its existence. Unaware Bob is aware of a character Alice whose assesses probability 0.4 that he is unaware. But he assesses probability zero that this type of Alice exists. One might want to make a distinction between states that are "impossible" and those that are "possible but have probability zero," but the standard way of doing business in economics doesn't allow for that distinction.

So what's the bottom line? For practical applications, the formal requirement that Ω must be common knowledge is rarely a problem. But, it is formally there, and in particular, when you want to model players who are unaware or ignorant, it can make you life as modeler more difficult. To reiterate, in practice, a common "trick" when dealing with unaware or ignorant individuals is to analyze the world as they see it, decide what behavior they will chose, and incorporate them in a broader model as "behavioral." Uglifications like Figure A13.6(c) are rarely if ever seen in practical applications. But—and again here is a topic for those who wish to become high-theory experts in the subject—a literature on unawareness in games, leading to so-called subjective epistemics, takes on the challenge of studying formally considerations of this type. A starting reference is provided in the Bibliographic Notes, if you wish to chase this down.

A13.3. (Non)Robustness to Lack of Common Knowledge

If game-theoretic analysis is premised on the notion that the rules of the game are common knowledge, and if (as seems evident) common knowledge is a theoretical ideal that never holds completely in real life, does this mean that game-theoretic analysis is incapable of helping us understand real-life phenomena?

And, when in an analysis you assert that some strategy profile is "the obvious way to play the game" (OWTP)—obvious to you *and* to all the participating players—how sensitive is such an assertion to the further notion that you—or the players in the game—can't be absolutely certain that this strategy profile is obvious to all participants, especially when there is some probability (albeit a small probability) that some players may think they are playing some very different game?

Of course, any model of a real-life situation is a simplification and caricature of

---

over the four states of nature. But once each player is endowed with his or her initial information, their posteriors are not common knowledge.

the real-life situation being modeled. So this question is a small part of the broader question: Do the sorts of models that populate economics texts and papers really provide insight into the real-life phenomena that the models caricature? Having gotten this deeply into the study of economics, I hope you believe that the answer is Yes. But, ultimately, the answer to this broad question is a matter of subjective judgment. Philosophers may debate the issue,[12] but I take it as virtually tautological that a formal "proof" of the proposition is impossible.

Coming back down to earth and the question as it relates to common knowledge, a substantial literature provides a variety of formal results concerning this question. Rather than provide any of these formal results (which generally require a great deal of technical setup), I point the interested reader to the discussion of these issues in Fudenberg and Tirole (1991b, Section 12.1.2 and, especially, Section 14.4). One reason that I forbear from tackling the formal literature is that, in evaluating how robust a specific conclusion is in a specific context, the formal results are not of much help. (I say this as someone who, in a minor way, contributed to this literature.) Let me illustrate with an example, a version of which was discussed in Appendix 9, in the context of "an obvious way to play the game."

This simple strategic-form game has $N > 1$ players, each of whom has the strategy set {Safe, Risky}. If every one of the players chooses Risky, then every player gets a payoff of 10. If player n chooses Risky and any other player chooses Safe, then player n's payoff is 0. And if player n chooses Safe, n's payoff is 5, regardless of the strategy choices of the other players.

This game—a variation on a game called *the stag hunt*—has two pure-strategy Nash equilibria: Every player chooses Safe, and every player chooses Risky.[13] Both Nash equilibria are strict, meaning that if all but player n adhere to their parts of the Nash equilibrium, then player n does strictly better adhering to her portion than if she does not. And, according to the formal theory, in a strategic-form game, if a Nash equilibrium is strict, it is "robust" to sufficiently small deviations from "common knowledge" that it is how people play the game. Put it this way: If it is common knowledge that each player does his or her part of a Nash equilibrium,[14]

---

[12]   And, to offer some casual empirical data: I've spent over forty years teaching an "intuitionist" version of microeconomics to skeptical MBA students and practitioners in executive education programs. And my impression is that a sizeable majority come away thinking that they've learned something about the real world that will be useful to them in their professional lives.

[13]   This game also has a mixed-strategy equilibrium. Can you find it?

[14]   This sentence introduces a so-far novel idea; namely, that the strategic choices of players can be common knowledge. As discussed so far, elements such as the rules of the game, players' payoffs, their probability assessments a priori, what they know about the payoffs and assessments of other players are specified as depending on the state of nature in a game of incomplete information. Hence these are the things about which the statement "X is common knowledge" makes formal sense. What players do, however, is derived from analysis. The choices the players make are not (up to now) a function of the state ω. In some higher-theory literature, which is intended to give foundations for such concepts as Nash and correlated equilibria or rationalizability, the state of nature ω is assumed to specify strategic choices of players. (The seminal reference in this literature is Aumann (1987), which is a good place to start if you are so minded.) If we formulated states ω in this fashion, as specifying strategic choices, then a statement such as "it is common knowledge that player n is choosing X" would make formal sense. But for this discussion, I will be content to speak informally about strategic choices being common

and if the Nash equilibrium is strict, then of course each player's private interest is (uniquely) to adhere to the equilibrium. Indeed, if the equilibrium is strict, then there is some $\epsilon > 0$ such that, if each player assesses probability at least $1 - \epsilon$ that her rivals will play their portions, it is strictly in the interests of the player to play her part of the (strict) equilibrium. One might say, then, that if a Nash equilibrium is strict and if it is "almost common knowledge" that each player will play according to that equilibrium, playing in that fashion is the right thing to do for every player.

Or, put in terms of an OWTP, if some strategy profile is an OWTP and, in addition, is a strict Nash equilibrium, we don't need that it is fully common knowledge that it is the OWTP, but (instead) that it is "almost common knowledge" that this is so.

Applied to the "everyone chooses Risky" equilibrium, which is a strict Nash equilibrium, this observation implies that if it is almost common knowledge that everyone is choosing Risky, then this is what everyone should do. The "everyone plays Risky" equilibrium is, formally, robust to slight deviations from common knowledge that this is how everyone plays.

The problem, if I may use that term, is that the formal result doesn't say how small ϵ must be, or, if you will, how large the neighborhood is of more complex games surrounding this simple game for which "everyone plays risky" is a strict equilibrium. In the context of this game, it is somewhat natural to assess that the act of an opponent choosing to defect to Safe is probably independent of whether other opponents defect.[15] And, moreover, that (marginal) assessed probability is probably *increasing* in N, as the larger is N, without complete common knowledge that everyone is playing Risky, the more risk any single player takes by choosing Risky. Letting $\epsilon(N)$ stand informally for the probability that a player assesses that any rival will defect to Safe as a function of N, then we can compute that the choice of Risky provides a payoff of $10(1 - \epsilon(N))^N$. It is, I think, somewhat cold comfort, for large N, to know that if $(1 - \epsilon(N))^N$ is sufficiently high (in this context, is > 0.5), then each player ought to choose Risky: If playing this game for real, I doubt that anyone would consider Risky as the OWTP as N gets large, notwithstanding that "all play Risky" is a strict Nash equilibrium in the game as originally specified.

What the formal literature does tell us is that, for extensive-form games and strategy profiles that leave some information sets off the path of play, specific equilibria can be even less robust in this regard. Consider the game depicted in Figure A13.7, a variation on the game in Figure A13.1, which (you may recall) was the topic of discussion in Appendix 12 (where it was Figure A12.5).

As in the game in Figure A13.1, the unique subgame-perfect equilibrium in this game is the profile a-DA'. But because of the payoff of 100 for Bob after A-d and the payoff of -100 for Alice after A-a-D', I assert that the strategy profile d-AA' is the obvious way to play this game, in the sense that I expect real-life players— say, Stanford MBA students—to behave in this way. And I expect that they would

---

knowledge or almost common knowledge.

[15] In fact, I would assert that it is more natural to assume positive correlation in defection, which in this context increases the size of the "neighborhood." But for discussion purposes, I'll assume independence.

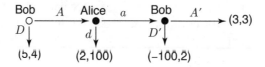

Figure A13.7. Another Alice and Bob game (Alice's payoffs are listed first)

expect each other to play in this way—both statements, with probability *close to* 1. And I assert this *even though A-d-A' is not a Nash equilibrium.*[16]

This assertion stands in direct contradiction to the assertion in Appendix 9, on page 506, that *if a game has an obvious way to play, one that is obvious to all players, and one for which it is obvious to all of them that it is obvious to all their rivals in the game, then this obvious way to play necessarily constitutes a Nash equilibrium.* Some explanation of these two contradictory assertions is certainly needed.

The explanation revolves around the answer to the question: What will Alice think if Bob chooses A, and how will she respond? If she chooses a and Bob then chooses A', she gets 3. By choosing d, she gets 2. So in the best possible scenario for her, choosing a gets her one extra unit of payoff. But if she chooses a and Bob responds with D', her payoff is -100. Let p be the probability she assesses that Bob, contrary to what seems to be in his best interests, will choose D' instead of A'. For her to persevere with a, it must be that $-100p + 3(1 - p) \geq 2$, or $p < 1/103$. If she assesses one chance in 100 that her hypothesis that Bob will choose A' is wrong, she is better off with d.

And then, for Bob, if he assesses q that Alice will choose d given the chance instead of a, even if he plans to choose A' if things get that far, choosing A is better for him than D if $100q + 3(1 - q) > 4$, or $q > 1/97$.

To model what Alice *might* be thinking when and if Bob chooses D, consider the game of incomplete information in Figure A13.8. This model has two types of Bob, Regular Bob, who has the same payoffs as in Figure A13.7, and Vindictive Bob, who seeks to maximize the difference between his payoff and that of Alice. Alice is unsure which Bob she faces, and she assesses probability π that Bob is vindictive.

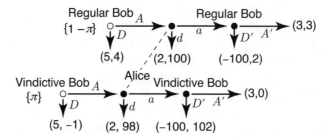

Figure A13.8. Bob might be vindictive (Alice's payoffs are listed first)

---

[16] Compare with the example from Figure A9.9, on page 507. "Extreme" payoffs in that example also gave a prediction that most players would choose a non-Nash strategy. What makes the current example even more compelling, in my opinion, is that Bob, by choosing A, puts Alice to the test.

For Vindictive Bob, it is both strictly dominant and conditionally (conditional on reaching his second information set) strictly dominant for him to choose A and then D'. The precise payoffs I have assigned to this second type of Bob are not essential; what matters is that there are types of Bob that Alice imagines she faces, for whom A and D' are strictly dominant and conditionally strictly dominant. And Alice assesses probability π that she faces such a Bob. Then, at her information set following A from Bob—which is now necessarily along the path of play—Bayes' rule leads her to assess probability π or greater that Bob is of this type. (Her assessment is π if she believes that all types of Bob will choose A. If, say, Regular Bob chooses D with positive probability, her beliefs at her [on-path] information set that she faces this sort of Bob will be greater than π.) So, if $\pi > 1/103$, her best choice is d. This (probability 1) choice is, of course, in excess of the $1/97$ probability it takes for Regular Bob to choose A, so that is what he will do. And if, having chosen A, Regular Bob finds that Alice responds with d, then he will choose A', regretting that things didn't work out for him.

That is why I think, for this game, d-AA' is the OWTP, where the O in this instance stands for "obvious, given reasonable caution on the part of Alice, and Bob's pretty good prospects from trying A." For a-DA'—the unique subgame-perfect Nash equilibrium in Figure A13.7—to be the OWTP, it takes a great deal of certainty on the part of Alice that Bob, given the choice, will choose A'. Being pretty sure is, because of that -100 payoff, not good enough.

But what if Alice is very, very sure? This corresponds to π in Figure A13.8 being very, very small; say, $\pi = 0.001$. As long as $\pi > 0$, it cannot be that Regular Bob chooses D with certainty, for if he did, no matter how small π is, Bayes' rule would force Alice, if called on to move, to conclude that she must be facing Vindictive Bob (or a Bob of this general variety), leading her to choose d, which would lead Regular Bob to choose A. Instead, Alice must randomize between a and d in a fashion that makes Regular Bob indifferent between A and D, and Regular Bob must randomize between A and D in a manner that makes Alice willing to randomize. Here are the calculations for $\pi = 0.001$: If Alice plays d with probability ρ, Regular Bob gets 4 for sure from D, and $100\rho + 3(1 - \rho) = 97\rho + 3$ from A. For Regular Bob to be indifferent between A and D, we require

$$4 = 97\rho + 3 \quad \text{which is} \quad \rho = 1/97.$$

And we know already that Alice will be indifferent between a and d if her belief p at her information set that she faces Vindictive Bob is precisely $1/103$. So if Regular Bob plays A with probability ϕ, Bayes's rule gives Alice the belief $0.001/(0.001 + 0.999\phi)$ that she faces Vindictive Bob, and the equilibrium condition is

$$\frac{0.001}{0.001 + 0.999\phi} = \frac{1}{103,} \quad \text{or} \quad 0.103 = 0.001 + 0.999\phi, \quad \text{or} \quad \phi = \frac{0.102}{0.999}.$$

For general $\pi < 1/103$, we get $\phi = 102\pi/(1 - \pi)$, which, as $\pi \to 0$, approaches 0. That is, if we think of Alice as being really, really [repeat many times], really sure that she faces Regular Bob, the "equilibrium outcome" is that, with probability approaching 1, we'll see Bob choose D. The equilibrium outcome does indeed converge to the outcome of the original, subgame-perfect equilibrium. But note that, in these equilibria for small π, no matter how small π is, Alice, if called on to move (which happens with probability approaching 0), randomizes, playing d with probability $1/97$ *no matter how small π is.*[17]

Of course, Figure A13.8 gives only one "incomplete information elaboration" of the game in Figure A13.7. You might wonder: What if Alice has positive probability of being absolutely certain that Bob is Regular Bob and so will choose A', but Bob is unsure if she has that knowledge? What if Bob doesn't know what probability Alice assesses that Bob is Vindictive Bob, but has a (common knowledge) prior over Alice's prior? And, in this second story, what if Bob believes Alice might be assessing $\pi > 1/103$ with positive probability, but she is also assessesing $\pi < 1/103$ with positive probability? Figure A13.9 provides some specific incomplete information formulations of these two stories; see if you can work out what happens in each. (Analysis of these two games of incomplete information is provided following the Bibliographic Notes. But, don't cheat and look ahead. They are not that hard.)

(My) Bottom line about robustness and the lack of complete common knowledge

Almost common knowledge is, in some instances, well modeled by assumptions of (complete or true) common knowledge, while in other instances it is not. Among the situations where assuming common knowledge *may* lead you astray are:

- games with many players, in which any single player can "undo" a particular equilibrium;

- games in which payoffs for some outcomes can be relatively extreme, which motivates behavior (either avoidance or attraction) even if the probabilities involved are small; and

- extensive-form games with off-path information sets, because "states" with small prior probability can loom quite large ex post, conditional on reaching such an otherwise off-path information set.

The examples described in this section give you examples where these features produce "unrobust" equilibrium predictions. In addition are

- extensive-form games in which players act and interact repeatedly.

For an example of this sort, read about the Chain-Store Paradox in Chapter 22 of the text, or see Section A15.7 in Appendix 15 and especially Section A15.8, on "Enduring Private (Incomplete) Information."

As discussed at the start of this section, a substantial literature explores this topic formally. Indeed, one of the most important parts of this literature concerns specifically the point about extensive-form games and off-path information sets

---

[17] And if you think that $1/97$ is pretty small, redo this analysis, but with Regular Bob's payoff from A-d equal to, say, 6, instead of 100.

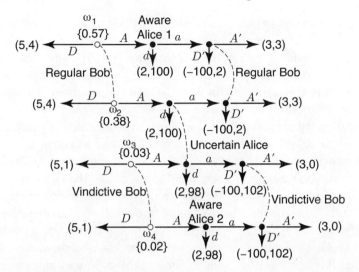

(a) Bob is vindictive with prior probability 0.05. Alice knows whether Bob is vindictive or not with probability 0.6 (independent of Bob's type). Bob doesn't know whether Alice knows his type or not. So there are two types of Bob and three types of Alice: Aware Alice 1, who knows that Bob is Regular Bob, Aware Alice 2, who knows that Bob is vindictive, and Uncertain Alice, who doesn't know Bob's type.

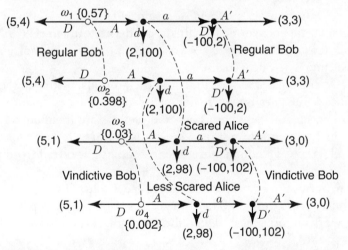

(b) Bob is Regular Bob or Vindictive, and Alice is Scared Alice or Less Scared Alice. Scared Alice assesses probability 0.05 that Bob is vindictive, while Less Scared Alice assesses probability 0.005 that Bob is vindictive. Bob assesses probability 0.6 that Alice is scared, and 0.4 that she is less scared (and the types of Bob and Alice are independent).

Figure A13.9. Two more complex incomplete-information elaborations of Figure A13.7.

(and the related phenomena of equilibria that are not strict or, at least, don't involve "strict sequential rationality"). Much of this formal literature—at least the positive results about robustness—involves results of the form: "For all sufficiently small

$\epsilon > 0$ in terms of the extent of lack of common knowledge, this or that category of equilibrium is robust." (Such results are sometimes camoflaged by highfalutin terms about lower semi-continuity.) In my (perhaps controversial) opinion, such results are not all that useful for practical application, because they don't indicate how large or small the magic ϵ is; this takes us to the first two bullet points above. However, the negative results—results that show when robustness to almost common knowledge will fail—usefully warn against trusting too much in some types of analysis.

That said, for practical application, I suggest first and foremost that you (as analyst or consumer of analysis) impose common sense, guided by the analysis of variations, for variations that involve small but "reasonable" deviations from common knowledge, where by "small" I mean small prior probability of significant deviations from the base model. This sort of ad hoc check of robustness is not the primary use of games of incomplete information, which instead is the examination of situations in which incomplete information is a central and prominent feature of the situation. But analysis of models of games with a "small" amount of such incomplete information, together with common sense, is an excellent tool for examining how robust a model analysis is to violations of the implicit assumption that the game as modeled is common knowledge.

Bibliographic Notes

Games of incomplete information and their use originated in Harsanyi (1967–68). Three other foundational papers referred to in this appendix are Aumann (1976), Aumann (1987), and Mertens and Zamir (1985). A very good introduction to epistemic game theory is Dekel and Siniscalchi (2015).

No-trade theorems are economics and, on those grounds, belong in the text, not these appendices. But, because I have not included a chapter on financial markets (and rational-expectations equilibria), no-trade results are mentioned here. The standard seminal reference to no-trade theorems is Milgrom and Stokey (1982). With a bit of reluctance, I mention that a prior example of a no-trade result is found in Kreps (1977).

I hope that, by now, references to Fudenberg and Tirole's (1991b) textbook *Game Theory* are unnecessary. Among other things, this book provides primary-source references to work on robustness of equilibria to "almost common knowledge."

Analysis of the two games in Figure A13.9

Begin with the game in panel b. Vindictive Bob will play A-D' as his dominant strategy. So, for Scared Alice, the probability that she faces Vindictive Bob, if she is given the move, is at least her prior, 0.05, and it could be more. Since this exceeds $1/103$, Scared Alice will certainly choose d. Hence, since Regular Bob assesses probability $0.6 > 1/97$ that he faces Scared Alice, regardless of what he thinks Less Scared Alice will do, he chooses A. And, therefore, Less Scared Alice, put on the move for sure, assesses probability 0.005 that she faces Vindictive Bob. Since this is less than $1/107$, she plays a.

Now for panel a: Clearly, Aware Alice 1 chooses a, and Aware Alice 2 chooses d. As always (given how these games are set up), Vindictive Bob will play A-D' as his dominant strategy. Hence regardless of what Regular Bob does, Uncertain Alice assesses probability at least $0.03/(0.03 + 0.38) = 3/41 = 0.0731\ldots > 1/107$ that she faces Vindictive Bob, and she chooses d. Hence Regular Bob knows that with probability $0.57/(0.57 + 0.38) = 0.6$, he faces Aware Alice 1, who will play a, and with probability $0.4 > 1/97$, he faces Uncertain Alice, who will play d. Hence, A is a better choice for him. (Which implies that Uncertain Alice assesses precisely $3/41$ that she faces Vindictive Bob.)

It is interesting to note that these two futher and more complex elaborations on the basic game *simplify* the analysis. This is because, while Alice's fears of the -100 payoff destabilize the analysis of the basic game in Figure A13.7, Bob's prospects of the big prize 100 acts to stabilize the overall conclusion that he'll "gamble" with A; it takes rather a lot to get him to forbear from this very attractive prospect, once he faces an (even possibly) worried Alice.

Forward Induction, Strategic Stability, and Beliefs-Based Refinements

In this appendix, we continue the story begun in Appendix 12, concerning refinements of the concept of Nash equilibrium. Recall that, in Appendix 12, we began with an approach—concerning beliefs, sequential rationality, and consistency of beliefs—that is rooted in answers to the question: Given the unanticipated opportunity to act (at an off-path information set), what would a player believe and how, in consequence, would she act subsequently? The approach to understanding off-path play was advanced as "intuition based." Then we looked at a more "axiomatic" or "formal" approach, with trembling-hand perfection and properness, concluding by asserting that the two approaches end in much the same place (cf. Proposition A12.16). This appendix follows a similar two-track approach, but in reverse order. The axiomatic approach involves *strategic stability*, looking for a solution concept that refines the concept of Nash equilibrium and that satisfies a list of axiomatic desiderata for equilibria, the most important of which is that two strategically equivalent extensive-form games should give the same "answers." *Beliefs-based refinements*, in contrast, continue the program of beliefs and sequential rationality, seeking criteria for "intuitively reasonable" beliefs that go beyond consistency, based on answers to questions of the form: What might a player reasonably believe at an off-path information set? Given that a defection from the equilibrium strategy profile has occured, which defections are unlikely? And we see that these two seemingly different perspectives for how to refine the concept of (Nash) equilibrium, come to quite similar conclusions, both falling under the general rubric of *forward induction*.

(If this appendix continues the story of Appendix 12, it is fair to ask: Why was Appendix 13 inserted between the two? The reason is that, for the more intuitive part of the program, concerning belief-based refinements, the prototypical applications are to games of incomplete information, where [say] Alice, faced with an off-path action by Bob, must form beliefs about the *type* of Bob that she is facing. For instance...)

A14.1. Motivation

... Suppose that Alice and Bob are involved in the encounter depicted in Figure A14.1.[1] In this figure, "descriptive" names are provided for the actions, and only

---

[1] Compare with Figure A11.1(a). This time it is Alice who must choose whether or not to challenge Bob.

Alice's payoffs are provided. (Think of this figure as Alice's initial thoughts about the encounter.)

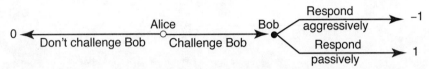

Figure A14.1. Should Alice challenge Bob? (Only Alice's payoffs are given)

It is clear that Alice's decision on whether to challenge Bob turns on her assessment of what he will do if challenged. And this, in turn, depends on her assessment of Bob's payoffs. She isn't certain what are his payoffs (nor are we, as analysts), and so she formulates the situation as a game of incomplete information, as depicted in Figure A14.2.

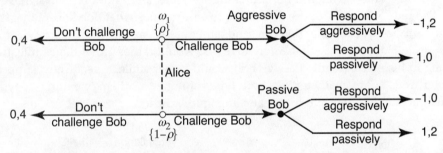

Figure A14.2. Should Alice challenge Bob?, continued (Alice's payoffs are given first)

There are a few things to note about this extensive-form game:

- The specific formulation of Bob's payoffs and, indeed, the formulation of there being only two states of nature, are irrelevant. All that matters (so far) is Alice's assessment that Bob, if challenged, will respond aggressively versus passively.

- As always, the full formulation is formally common knowledge to both Alice and Bob. But it is (again, so far) irrelevant what Bob knows or doesn't know about this formulation. Alice is going to decide whether to challenge Bob or not, and Bob will respond in a sequentially rational fashion. His understanding of the game simply doesn't matter, *so far.*

- However, note that the model assumes that Bob of either type would prefer not to be challenged. Even Aggressive Bob prefers not to be required to fight, although, if challenged, he will fight.

- The probability that Alice assesses that she faces an aggressive Bob is recorded as ρ. From Alice's payoffs, it is clear that she'll challenge Bob if $\rho < 0.5$, she won't do so if $\rho > 0.5$, and she is indifferent if $\rho = 0.5$.

Because in Figure A14.2, Bob's choice of action is determined by simple sequential rationality (in other words, conditional or ex post dominance), we can simplify the picture, replacing Figure A14.2 with A14.3. The reason for this (trivial) simplification comes next, when we give the Bobs a serious strategic role.

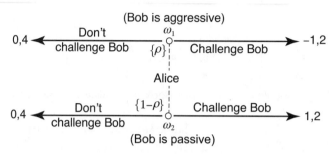

Figure A14.3. Figure A14.2, simplified (Alice's payoffs are given first)

Now for the point of this example. When trying to decide whether to challenge Bob or not, Alice looks at Bob, searching for clues as to how he will behave if challenged. At least, suppose that this is so, and suppose that Bob knows that this is so. Suppose further that Bob can send either of two signals: He can growl, or he can smile. And suppose that Aggressive Bob would rather growl than smile, that being in his nature, while Passive Bob would rather smile. Specifically, suppose that acting "out of character" for both types of Bob costs them one unit of payoff. This leads to the extensive-form game in Figure A14.4.[2]

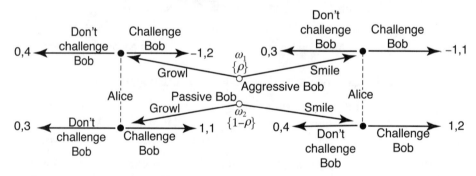

Figure A14.4. Before Alice chooses, she observes Bob's demeanor (Alice's payoffs are given first)

As already noted, both types of Bob would rather not be challenged. And, while each would rather act according to his nature (growl if aggressive, smile if passive), for each type, avoiding a challenge is so much better than being challenged that each would act against his nature if that prevents being challenged.

Therefore, it cannot be (in equilibrium) that both types of Bob act true-to-nature; that is, Aggressive Bob growls and Passive Bob smiles. For if that were true, then

---

[2]   In the literature of game theory applied to economics, this game is called "the beer–quiche game," because in the original version, growling was having beer for breakfast and smiling was having quiche. But the gods of political correctness demand a change from the original terminology. It may be, though, that this rephrasing is still un-PC; if so, I apologize.

each of Alice's two information sets would be on-path, and Bayes' rule leads her to believe that she faces Aggressive Bob after a growl and Passive Bob after a smile. Then, she would optimally choose not to challenge after a growl and to challenge after a smile. Given these payoffs and, in particular, the fact that Passive Bob would rather act against his nature if it means no challenge, this would lead Passive Bob to growl.

Is it an equilibrium for both types of Bob to growl? That depends on the value of ρ, Alice's prior assessment that she faces Aggressive Bob. Both types of Bob growling is *part of* an equilibrium if $\rho > 0.5$:

1. If both types of Bob growl, Alice's information set following growl is on-path, and her beliefs are that she faces Aggressive Bob with her prior probability ρ by Bayes' rule. With these beliefs, and as long as $\rho > 0.5$, Alice will choose not to challenge Bob.

2. If both types of Bob growl, Alice's information set following smile is off-path, and none of the restrictions on beliefs from Appendix 12 apply. If she believes that she faces Aggressive Bob with probability less than 0.5, her unique sequentially rational response is to challenge Bob; if she believes that she faces Aggressive Bob with probability exactly 0.5, she is indifferent.

3. So specify beliefs for her such that, if she sees Bob smiling, she believes that she faces Aggressive Bob with probability 0.5 or less, and specify that she chooses to challenge him if he smiles.

4. And, with that strategy choice by Alice—no challenge after growl, challenge after smile—both types of Bob choose to growl.

But if $\rho > 0.5$, it is also (part of) a sequential equilibrium for both types of Bob to smile:

1'. If both types of Bob smile, Alice's information set following smile is on-path, and her beliefs are that she faces Aggressive Bob with her prior probability ρ by Bayes' rule. With these beliefs, she chooses not to challenge Bob.

2'. If both types of Bob smile, Alice's information set following growl is off-path, and none of the restrictions on beliefs from Appendix 12 apply. If she believes that she faces Aggressive Bob with probability less than 0.5, her unique sequentially rational response is to challenge Bob; if she believes are that she faces Aggressive Bob with probability exactly 0.5, she is indifferent.

3'. So specify beliefs for her such that, if she sees Bob growling, she believes that she faces Aggressive Bob with probability 0.5 or less, and specify that she chooses to challenge him if he growls.

4'. And, with that strategy choice by Alice—no challenge after smile, challenge after growl—both types of Bob choose to smile.

So, it would seem, we can make no prediction about what the two types of Bob will do, at least based on what is (and is not) a sequential equilibrium. The two types could both growl, or they could both smile.

This appendix asserts that, considering these two equilibria, the *both-Bobs-smile* equilibrium can in fact be ruled out on "intuitive" grounds. The argument runs as follows: Thinking of an equilibrium as an obvious way to play, in the second *both-smile* equilibrium, Passive Bob, by following the equilibrium, has a payoff of 4. The best he can do by growling is a payoff of 3. So Passive Bob—*in that equilibrium*—has no business growling. Aggressive Bob, however, reasons that if growling will convince Alice that he is aggressive, then he can increase his payoff from 3 to 4. So, the argument goes, Alice should view a growl *in that equilibrium* as being an attempt by Aggressive Bob to signal to her that he is aggressive—it can't be coming from Passive Bob—and so her off-paths beliefs should be that Bob is aggressive, hence she should not challenge after a growl. This, of course, upsets the equilibrium.

In contrast, in the *both-growl* equilibrium, only Passive Bob stands any chance of gaining, relative to the equilibrium payoffs, by smiling. So Alice, seeing a smile, must conclude "it can't be Aggressive Bob." And, so concluding, she challenges Bob following a smile, hence Passive Bob doesn't try to signal his type; he wants instead to *hide* his type to the extent that he can do so.

The agenda for this appendix is to formalize and extend the allegedly intuitive argument just made.[3, 4] The terms *forward induction*, *strategic stability*, and *belief-based refinements* are used to describe various aspects and portions of this agenda:

- *Forward induction* is (in my opinion) a somewhat vague phrase that describes the nature of this general program. Recall from Volume I that, in *backward induction*, the idea is that what is optimal today can be determined by knowing what will be optimal starting tomorrow and optimizing today with that optimal continuation in mind. (Formally, this is the *conserving* criterion for optimality found in Appendix 6 of Volume I.) Hence, at least in a dynamic optimization problem with a "final date," one optimizes from the last decision date backward to the first. Here, in contrast, as we discuss equilibria, we reason about how actions taken today might affect beliefs that are held tomorrow, hence what will be done tomorrow. (At least, that's how I understand the term *forward induction*. I'm not a fan of this terminology, and I leave it to others to provide a better explanation for why this terminology is appropriate.)

- *Strategic stability* describes a formal program initiated by Kohlberg and Mertens

---

[3]   Another argument, which may have even more intuitive appeal, runs as follows. In the both-smile equilibrium, Alice's off-path beliefs—what she believes if, unexpectedly, she observes Bob growling—*decreases* the probability that she faces Aggressive Bob from her prior $\rho > 0.5$ to something less than or equal to 0.5. But growling is in the nature of Aggressive Bob and not in the nature of Passive Bob. Surely then, the alledgedly intuitive argument goes, if she sees Bob growl, she ought to *increase* the probability that she faces Aggressive Bob, or at least keep it at the value of her prior, which (of course) upsets the equilibrium: If she doesn't decrease the probability that she faces Aggressive Bob after observing him growling, she'll choose not to challenge Bob. And Aggressive Bob, anticipating this response from growling, happily chooses to be true to his nature and growl. If you find this argument convincing, well and good. But it is the argument in the text that will be formalized in this appendix.

[4]   And what if $\rho < 0.5$? See if you can work it out on your own, or see Section A14.2.

(1986), with subsequent contributions by these authors and others (see the Bibliographic Notes), which applies to this example. Roughly put, this program poses axiomatic properties that an (equilibrium-based) solution concept *ought* to have and then proposes a solution concept that has those properties, a concept that rules out the *both-smile* equilibrium outcome.

- *Belief-based refinements* describes a family of refinements that (1) are implied by strategic stability, but (2) are motivated by more direct (and, perhaps, more directly intuitive) stories concerning which off-path beliefs are "reasonable" and which are "unreasonable," in the spirit of the example just given. Three members of this family that will be discussed are the *intuitive criterion*, *divinity*, and *universal divinity*.

A14.2. Equilibrium Outcomes Instead of Equilibria

In this appendix, a "solution" is not an individual equilibrium, but instead the *outcome* generated by a set of equilibria. (Recall that the *outcome* of a strategy profile is the probability distribution that the strategy profile induces on terminal nodes.) We will be in the business of discarding as "unreasonable" whole sets of equilibria that lead to a single outcome, while keeping other sets of equilibria, where all equilibria in a set lead to a single outcome (in most cases), and where different sets lead to different outcomes. We do this, because when it comes to off-path behavior and beliefs, we often have a good deal of freedom in terms of what will support particular on-path behavior (therefore, the outcome). We may not be able to say for sure what will happen (or what are beliefs) off-path, but we are able—by criteria to be discussed—to identify *outcomes* that are and are not "reasonable."

The game depicted in Figure A14.4, for the case $\rho > 0.5$, is typical in this regard. We described two outcomes that arise in different sorts of equilibria.

Outcome G.   Both types of Bob growl, and Alice doesn't challenge Bob.

Outcome S.   Both types of Bob smile, and Alice doesn't challenge Bob.

Neither outcome is a full description of a Nash equilibrium strategy profile—a full specification of a Nash equilibrium must say what Alice does at her off-path information set—and, if we are looking for, say, sequential equilibria, while the Bobs' strategies tell us Alice's beliefs at her on-path informations set, they don't specify her off-path beliefs. But it isn't hard to fill in what is missing.

In a fully specified outcome-G Nash equilibrium, it doesn't matter to Aggressive Bob what Alice does at her off-path information set; if she doesn't challenge after a growl, he is sticking with growling. But for Passive Bob to be willing to growl, Alice, after a smile, must challenge with probability at least 0.5. So outcome-G Nash equilibria require Alice, in the event she sees a smile, to challenge with probability 0.5 or more. To support this behavior, we have two cases: If she challenges with probability one, she can hold any off-path beliefs that she faces Aggressive Bob with probability 0.5 or less, while if she randomizes, her beliefs must be that she faces Aggressive Bob with probability 0.5 exactly.

Filling out the outcome-S sort of equilibrium with off-path behavior and beliefs by Alice is similar.

So, in this instance, each of the two equilibrium outcomes is generated by a family of equilibria. And, in this case, these are the only two equilibrium outcomes. Reason as follows: We know that one or the other or both of Alice's information sets must be on-path. The two equilibria types already described are precisely where one or the other but not both is on-path; the only possibility left is that both her information sets are on-path. But if both are on-path, at one or the other, her belief that Bob is Aggressive must be ρ or more, since (by Bayes' rule, assuming both information sets are on-path) her beliefs at the two sets must average to her prior. Hence, at one or the other of her information sets, she must be responding *no challenge* with probability 1.

Suppose she responds *no challenge* with probability 1 following a growl. Then Aggressive Bob will optimally growl with probability 1. If there is positive probability that Alice's *smile* information set is reached, it can only come from Passive Bob. But then Alice will know at this information set that she faces Passive Bob and she will enter. Passive Bob, therefore, will certainly growl.

Suppose she responds *no challenge* with probability 1 following a smile. Then Passive Bob will, with probability 1, optimally smile. If her *growl* information set is reached with positive probability, it must come from Aggressive Bob, and Alice, knowing (by Bayes' rule) that growl means Bob is aggressive, will respond with no challenge. Thus Aggressive Bob will growl with probability 1, and so Alice must know, following a smile, that she faces Passive Bob, a contradiction.

To summarize, in this game (with $\rho > 0.5$), the full set of Nash (and sequential) equilibria consists of two sets of "connected components" (in the space of behavior strategy profiles and beliefs): All the equilibria in the first component give the G outcome; all the equilbria in the second component give the S outcome.

This is the "typical" situation:

Proposition A14.1. *Fix a finite extensive-form tree structure (including information sets) in which players have perfect recall. For generic specifications of the payoffs and probability assessments of Nature's moves, the sets of Nash equilibria (and of sequential equilibria) consist of a finite number of disjoint connected sets, such that each of the connected sets of equilibria gives a single equilibrium outcome to the game.*

This proposition is proved for Nash equilibria in Kohlberg and Mertens (1986).[5]

Note what this says: For generic specifications of payoffs and probability assessments concerning Nature, each connected set of equilibria can offer many degrees of freedom in off-path behavior and beliefs. But there are no degrees of freedom when it comes to the on-path behavior (and, by Bayes' rule, beliefs) within each of these finitely-many connected sets.

---

[5] They attribute the result to Kreps and Wilson (1982b), but I believe Kreps and Wilson only provide the result for the set of sequential equilibria. Happily, Kohlberg and Mertens offer an alternative proof for all Nash equilibria.

Hence, a program that proposes criteria for discarding some equilibrium outcomes while keeping others makes sense.

(The remainder of this section provides practice on analyzing extensive-form games. But it doesn't play a role in the rest of this appendix, and you are free to skip ahead if you wish.)

What if $\rho < 0.5$ for the game in Figure A14.4? It cannot be that both types of Bob growl with probability 1, and it cannot be that both smile: If either of these were the strategies of the Bobs, Alice, faced with the on-path signal, would enter, and the type of Bob who is acting out of character would wish to "defect" to his in-character signal. Hence it must be that both of Alice's information sets are on-path.

And it cannot be that each sends his in-character signal—that is, Aggressive Bob growls and Passive Bob smiles—because then Alice would respond to growling with no challenge and smiling with challenge, and Passive Bob would want to defect to growling. Nor can it be that both types of Bob act out of character— Aggressive Bob smiles and Passive Bob growls—since then Alice would respond to smiling with no challenge, and Passive Bob would defect. One or the other type of Bob, or perhaps both, must randomize.

So what does this leave? It cannot be that Alice randomizes at both her information sets; at one or the other, she must hold beliefs that she faces Aggressive Bob with probability ρ or less, because her "average" beliefs at the two information sets, averaged according to the probabilities that she reaches those information sets, must equal her prior. Thus she will certainly challenge Bob at that information set. Could it be that she definitely challenges Bob facing a growl? If she does, Passive Bob will certainly smile. And if Passive Bob certainly smiles, then her beliefs at the information set after seeing a smile must have beliefs that she faces Passive Bob with probability $1 - \rho > 0.5$ or more, which would mean she challenges Bob after seeing a smile, which means that Aggressive Bob will certainly growl, and the whole construction (based on the assumption that she definitely challenges Bob after a growl) unravels.

The remaining possibility is that both of Alice's information sets are on-path, and she must challenge Bob after observing a smile. Therefore, Aggressive Bob will certainly growl. So, to have both information sets reached, we need that Passive Bob must smile with positive probability. But we already know that this can't be probability one. So Passive Bob must randomize. And Passive Bob will only randomize if Alice, after a growl, randomizes 50-50 between challenging and not challenging. For Alice to randomize after a growl, she must assess probability 0.5 exactly that she faces Aggressive Bob. So, to get those beliefs after a growl, Passive Bob must growl with probability $\rho/(1 - \rho)$. That fixes everything.

To summarize: If $\rho < 0.5$, there is a unique Nash equilibrium in which both of Alice's information sets are on-path: Aggressive Bob growls. Passive Bob growls with probability $\rho/(1 - \rho)$. Alice challenges Bob if she sees a smile, and she randomizes 50-50 if she hears a growl. (Since both information sets are on-path, beliefs are fixed by Bayes' rule.) There is a single Nash equilibrium, hence a single Nash-equilibrium outcome.

A14.3. Strategic Stability: An Overview

The program of finding a "strategically stable" equilibrium criterion is initiated in Kohlberg and Mertens (1986) and has been the subject of a number of papers that modify in one way or another the basic criterion advanced. In this section, I stick to the original paper, covering what the authors were aiming at, the examples that motivated them, and the formal criterion at which they arrived. Readers with a deep interest in this topic should see the Bibliographic Notes at the end of the appendix for further reading.[6]

The objective is to have a criterion that satisfies a list of desirable features:

- *Existence.* Every game has at least one strategically stable set of equilibria.

- *Connectedness.* Every strategically stable set is connected. (Thus, at least for generic payoffs, every strategically stable set provides a single outcome.)

- *Backward induction.* A strategically stable set contains a perfect (or sequential) equilibrium of the game.

- *Admissibility.* The player's strategies are undominated at any point in a solution.

- *Iterated dominance.* A strategically stable set of a game G contains a strategically stable set of any game G' obtained from G by deletion of a dominated strategy.

Most importantly, and the reason for the term *strategic stability*,

- *Invariance.* A strategically stable set of equilibria should depend only on the reduced strategic form of the game. Put differently, two extensive-form games with the same reduced strategic form should provide the same "answers."

It is important to note that Kohlberg and Mertens use a broader concept of the reduced strategic form than the concept as defined in Appendix 10. In the definition of Appendix 10, the reduced strategic form is based on an equivalence relation of full strategies, where (recall) two full strategies, which specify the actions a player will take at every information set, are equivalent if for any strategy profile by the other players, the two give the same probability distribution over terminal nodes. It is implicit in this definition that the equivalence relation is defined for pairs of full strategies relative to a fixed extensive form.

Kohlberg and Mertens go further than this, saying that two strategies from different extensive forms can be treated as equivalent if they give the same probability distributions on payoffs. Consider, for instance, the three extensive-form games in Figure A14.5. Comparing panel a with panel b, the difference is that Alice's decision whether to choose D, a, or d is broken into two, whether to choose D or not, and then, if not, whether to choose a or d. And in panel c, a fourth move is added for Alice, namely, to flip a fair coin and play D if it comes up heads and a if tails. (In fact, Kohlberg and Mertens would have us insert a move by Nature into the extensive form, so that the random flip of the coin is explicitly depicted.)

---

[6] In Kohlberg and Mertens, as in many other papers in the literature, the term "normal form" is used instead of "strategic form." I will edit their specific contributions, using "strategic" in place of "normal" to avoid confusion.

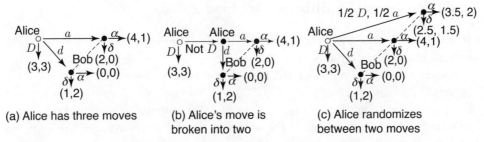

(a) Alice has three moves

(b) Alice's move is broken into two

(c) Alice randomizes between two moves

Figure A14.5. Extending strategic equivalence

The point is that, in their developments, all three of these games are considered to have the same reduced strategic form, and (hence) by invariance, they should give the same strategically stable sets of equilibria.

In general, when saying that two extensive-form games have the same reduced strategic form, Kohlberg and Mertens allow for "strategically inessential modifications of the extensive form," as set forth in classic papers by Thompson (1952) and Dalkey (1953). And going even further, they allow for deletion of "rows" that are convex combinations of other "rows"; this accounts for willful randomizations among strategies as in the transformation from panel a to panel c.[7] When they insist on invariance as a desirable feature, they are saying that none of these transformations affects the basic strategic nature of the interaction, and so they should not affect a good solution concept for the play of games.

Kohlberg and Mertens are vehement on this point. I strongly encourage you to read their original argument, because I do not agree. The root of my disagreement comes down to what one means by a *good* solution concept. It will not surprise you by now to read that when it comes to a *good* solution concept—and more broadly to *good* game-theoretic methods—my philosophy is that *good* equals *useful* for modeling, analyzing, and ultimately understanding economic phenomena. I believe that how a competitive situation is framed can affect behavior. For one thing, reframing a situation may make it easier for the parties to see an obvious way to play: Think, for instance, of unpacking a complex multi-option decision into a sequence of simpler choices. And, in some cases, how the situation is framed can affect the psychology of the players regarding their strategic choices: It is a topic that is best reserved for Volume III, but interested readers may wish to access to literature on *psychological games*. My bottom line is that a good = useful game theory should be capable of dealing with how presentation and perception of strategically equivalent situations affects behavior. But, for now, let us stipulate to their perspective: Where does it lead?

---

[7] As a technical aside, note that their way of doing business involves comparing strategies for one player in terms of those strategies' impact on payoffs for all players and for all strategy profiles of the other players. But as the extensive form changes, so does the space of strategy profiles of the other players. So their program requires that we "reduce" the strategic form one player at a time.

Why sequential equilibrium, trembling-hand perfection, and even proper equilibrium are inadequate

If we grant for now the force of their argument, we can see by example why the equilibrium concepts that have so far been covered are inadequate.

Begin with the game depicted in Figure A14.5(a). The strategy profile D-δ is trembling-hand perfect (and so, of course, sequential). Suppose the tremble constraints for a and d are ϵ, for very small $\epsilon > 0$. Alice won't willingly choose a or d (as long as Bob's strategy is D), so (for given ϵ) Bob's beliefs are 50-50, and he chooses δ.

But now consider the strategically equivalent game in panel b. Alice's right-hand node/information set is the root of a proper subgame. And in the subgame, a strictly dominates d. So in any subgame-perfect equilibrium, which includes all sequential and trembling-hand-perfect equilibria, she must (in the subgame) be playing a. Hence, given the move, Bob's subgame-consistent beliefs attach probability 1 to the uppermost node at his information set, leading him to choose α. And if Bob chooses α, Alice will change to *Not D* and then a. The unique subgame-perfect, hence sequential and trembling-hand-perfect equilibrium of the game as depicted in panel b, is *Not D–a* for Alice and α for Bob.

Hence, from the perspective of Kohlberg and Mertens, the sequential equilibrium and trembling-hand perfection criteria are inadequate: The strategically equivalent representation of Figure A14.5(a) given in Figure A14.5(b) changes the sets of equilibria (and equilibrium outcomes) that "qualify."

What about properness? As Kohlberg and Mertens observe, D-δ for the game in panel a is *not* proper. If Bob is choosing δ, Alice's payoff from a is 2, versus 1 if she picks d. So she must "tremble" in the direction of a asymptotically much more than in the direction of d (assuming that she wants D), which forces Bob's off-path beliefs asymptotically to be that he is at the *after-a-by-Alice* node in his information set, and he chooses α, which destroys D-δ. In fact, Kohlberg and Mertens state the following result as their Proposition 0:

> *A proper equilibrium of a strategic-form game is sequential in any extensive-form game with that strategic form.*

Since panels a and b in Figure A14.5 give the same strategic-form game, this result shows that the D-δ sequential equilibrium of panel a cannot be proper, because it does not correspond to a sequential equilibrium of the strategically equivalent game in panel b. So far, so good, for properness.

But now consider the variation on Figure A14.5(a) depicted in Figure A14.6(a). The change is that Alice's payoffs following a-δ and d-α are exchanged. Now a no longer "dominates" d for Alice, and in fact, because d-δ gives Alice a payoff of 1 while a-δ gives her 0, D-δ must be a proper equilibrium.

But the D-δ equilibrium (and equilibrium outcome) fails the *iterated dominance* test: Strategy D guarantees Alice 3, while d gives her a maximum payoff of 2; that is, D dominates d. And, in the game with strategy d removed, as depicted in panel b, Bob will know, given the move, that α is his sequentially rational option.

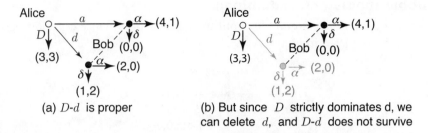

(a) D-d is proper
(b) But since D strictly dominates d, we
can delete d, and D-d does not survive

Figure A14.6. Alice's option d is dominated by her option D, so it should play no role

And if Bob chooses α, Alice will choose a.

So, while Myerson's proper equilibrium has some very desirable properties, it isn't good enough.

Strategic stability, version 1.0

In its place, Kohlberg and Mertens "settle" on the following formal definition:

Definition A14.2 (Kohlberg and Mertens 1986).

a. *A closed set of Nash equilibria of an agent-strategic-form game satisfies **Property S** if, for every $\epsilon > 0$, there exists some $\delta_0 > 0$ such that for any completely mixed-strategy profile $\sigma = (\sigma_1, \ldots, \sigma_H)$ and for any $(\delta_1, \ldots, \delta_H)$ such that $0 < \delta_h < \delta_0$, the perturbed game where every strategy $a \in A(h)$ of player h is replaced by $(1 - \delta_h)a + \delta_h\sigma_h$ has an equilibrium ϵ-close to S.*[8]

b. *A set of equilibria is **stable** in a given game if it is a minimal set (in terms of set inclusion) satisfying Property S.*

Note the scare quotes around "settle." This choice of verb may strike you as odd, but it describes the situation: Kohlberg and Mertens provide three definitions of "stability"—hyperstability, full stability, and stability (the last being Definition A14.2)—because no one definition is completely satisfactory. In particular, stability according to Definition A14.2 satisfies existence, a version of connectedness, iterated dominance, and invariance, but not, for instance, backward induction. And, because none of the three versions of stability they provide in their 1986 paper is completely satisfactory, subsequent papers (see the Bibliographic Notes) have continued the search for a fully satisfactory definition.

Readers who wish to become high-theory experts in the subject should consult the original paper and its successors for further details, including proofs of my assertions of what Definition A14.2 accomplishes. Rather than chase down technical details (which become heavily mathematical almost immediately), I go to a different and, I think, more practical question: What is the connection between strategic stability and the sort of argument provided in the motivating example with which this appendix began?

---

[8] Remember that, in the agent-strategic form, each $h \in H$ is a different player.

A quibble about iterated dominance

Before moving on, I have a quibble about the iterated-dominance criterion. Consider the game depicted in Figure A14.7.

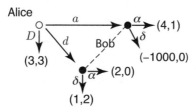

Figure A14.7. A variation on Figure A14.6 in which Alice risks a lot by choosing a

This game is the same as that in Figure A14.6(a), except that the payoff of 0 that Alice receives following the sequence a-δ has been changed to -1000. This change has no effect on the argument given previously for rejecting the D-outcome equilibria: D for Alice still strictly dominates d, so the iterated-dominance criterion says that we can "eliminate" the d option from the game, in which case, Bob, given the move, must "know" that he is at the upper node in his information set; hence he chooses α, and hence Alice should go with a. And of course, the outcome a-α is strategically stable, while the equilibrium outcome D is not.

However, *if* it is established in the community in which Bob and Alice live that D is the "right" choice for Alice, what goes through Bob's mind if he is given the move? (That is, what is the intuition that supports this formal conclusion?)

The story we've told is: Bob reasons that since d is dominated by D, the only reason for Alice to do other than choose D is to try to get the payoff 4 that follows a-α. Hence, Bob concludes that he is at the upper node, and he responds with α. And Alice, realizing that this is how Bob will reason if given the move, confidently chooses a.

But another story we can tell is: Bob expects Alice to choose D. If she doesn't, she has made an error. But which error, a or d, does Bob assess as more likely? By choosing d, Alice does no worse than a payoff of 1. But if she chose a, there is a chance that she will lose -1000. "She would," Bob reasons, "be very careful to avoid a, especially because, if she anticipates that this is how I'll reason, she will anticipate that I'll choose δ, which makes a-by-mistake catastrophic."

The first story supports the a-α outcome; the second supports the D outcome. I'm willing to grant that, if payoffs are as in the original Figure A14.6(a), the first story has a lot more force and appeal. And I'm not prepared to assert that with payoffs as in Figure A14.7, the second story wins. But I'm a lot less sure that I buy the first story—and the implications of iterated dominance and (therefore) strategic stability—as an analytic tool for predicting how the game will be played, when the payoffs resemble those in Figure A14.7.

Put it this way: The first argument—and to a certain (but limited) extent, strategic stability—is about what a player might hope to get by deviating from the equilibrium. This idea will be formalized in Section A14.4. But it ignores, at least to some extent, what a player *risks* by deviating. In real life, risks are surely something to be considered along with possible rewards.

A14.4. Disposing of Unstable Equilibrium Outcomes: The Never-a-Weak-Best-Response Test

Proposition A14.3. *Fix a generic extensive-form game (one for which the conclusion of Proposition A14.1 holds) and a particular sequential-equilibrium outcome. Fix an on-path information set* h *and an action* a *available to* $\iota(h)$ *at* h *that is not taken with positive probability in equilibrium. If there is no sequential equilibrium giving the fixed outcome such that action* a *at* h *does as well as the equilibrium actions at* h —*that is, **if* a *is never a weak best response for player-agent* h *in the agent-strategic form**—and if this equilibrium outcome cannot be sustained if the action* a *is removed from the game, then the equilibrium outcome is not strategically stable.*

Granting the truth of this proposition, it applies easily to show that the both-smile equilibrium outcome (for the game in Figure A14.4) is not strategically stable: Focus on Passive Bob and the action *growl*, which (in the both-smile equilibrium) is an action taken with zero probability at an on-path information set. In the equilibrium outcome, Passive Bob smiles and obtains payoff 4. If he growls, the best he can get is 3. So, at this equilibrium outcome, growling for Passive Bob is never a weak best response. And if we eliminate Passive Bob's option to growl, Alice must, on hearing a growl, know that she faces Aggressive Bob. She must, in consequence, respond to a growl with *no challenge*. But if Alice responds in this fashion, Aggressive Bob will growl, upsetting the equilibrium.

Rather than give a general proof of the proposition, I'll illustrate the proof in the specific context of the example.

The first step is to observe that, as ϵ goes to zero in the definition of strategic stability, δ_0 must do so as well. This is without loss of generality: For a given vector $(\delta_h)_{h \in H}$, we can replace δ_0 by $\max\{\delta_h ; h \in H\}$, and for the strategies $((1 - \delta_h)a + \delta_h \sigma_h)_{h \in H}$ to be "close" to σ, we will (generally) need that the δ_h are all small.

Now consider the connected set of sequential equilibria in which both types of Bob smile. Viewed as an agent-strategic-form game, this game has four player/agents, the two types of Bob and (oriented as in Figure A14.4) Left Alice and Right Alice. Suppose, in the notation of the definition, we have (small) δ_0 and set $\delta_{\text{Aggressive Bob}} = \delta_0$ and $\delta_{\text{Passive Bob}} = \delta_0^2$; that is, $\delta_{\text{Aggressive Bob}} \gg \delta_{\text{Passive Bob}}$. Fix the completely mixed strategy σ so that, at each information set, each player chooses between his or her two actions with equal probability 0.5.

Now for small ϵ, an equilibrium that is ϵ-close to a *both smile* equilibrium will have Passive Bob getting very close to his best payoff of 4. He will not wish to growl. Hence the probability that he growls in the perturbed game can be no larger than $\delta_{\text{Passive Bob}}/2 = \delta_0^2/2$, while the probability that Aggressive Bob growls in the perturbed game must be at least $\delta_{\text{Aggressive Bob}}/2 = \delta_0/2$. Since, by construction, $\delta_{\text{Aggressive Bob}} \gg \delta_{\text{Passive Bob}}$, Left Alice's beliefs must put weight approaching

1 on Bob being aggressive, which means she must not challenge, which causes Aggressive Bob to defect. The point is that for this set of perturbations, in which Aggressive Bob is "forced" to growl asymptotically much more than is Passive Bob, since growling is never a weak best response for Passive Bob, he will never prefer to growl here. To be strategically stable, the equilibrium outcome must be capable of sustaining itself in these circumstances, which amount to Alice assessing (with probability arbitrarily close to 1) that growl means Aggressive Bob. Which, of course, it cannot.

In contrast, the equilibrium outcome in which both Bobs growl is stable. If we are to "undo" this equilibrium outcome, Alice must conclude that a smile comes from Aggressive Bob, so she will choose *no challenge*, which will cause Passive Bob to defect. Accordingly, to give Alice beliefs of this sort, we "force" Aggressive Bob to smile more than Passive Bob does by setting $\delta_{\text{Passive Bob}} \ll \delta_{\text{Aggressive Bob}}$, just as before. Now at this equilibrium outcome, it is Aggressive Bob who is getting (nearly, in the perturbed games) a payoff of 4. So it is Aggressive Bob who will not voluntarily choose to smile; smiling is never a weak best response for him; he smiles no more than he is required to by the perturbation, which are three ways of saying the same thing. But *if* we can arrange things so that Right Alice randomizes between challenging and not challenging Bob with probabilities 0.5 apiece, Passive Bob becomes indifferent between growling and smiling. *That is, one specific sequential equilibrium in the set of sequential equilibria giving the both-growl outcome is where Alice holds beliefs that she is equally likely to be facing Passive and Aggressive Bob and randomizes 50-50 between challenging and not. And in this specific equilibrium, smiling is a weak best response for Passive Bob.* Hence, if we have Alice randomizing in this fashion, Passive Bob will be willing to do more smiling than he is forced to do, and we can (delicately) have him do enough to undo $\delta_{\text{Passive Bob}} \ll \delta_{\text{Aggressive Bob}}$, so that Alice is just indifferent between challenging or not challenging following a smile. The *both-growl* outcome is strategically stable.

Iterating on never a weak best response

Consider the game depicted in Figure A14.8.

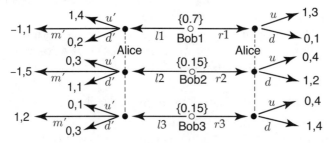

Figure A14.8. Iterating on never a weak best response (Alice's payoffs are given first)

Consider the equilibrium outcome in which all three Bobs choose their r option, so that Alice's right-hand information set is on-path. Her beliefs at that information set are her prior beliefs (by Bayes' rule), and so she chooses u.

It is clear Bob3 is going to select $r3$ instead of $l3$, since $r3$ is strictly dominant for him. Hence $l3$ is never a weak best response for him. But how about $l2$ for Bob2? Is this ever a weak best response? The reason for asking this question is that, if the answer is No, then Alice's off-path beliefs at her left-hand information set must put weight 1 on being at the topmost node in that information set, and then her response there must be u', which causes Bob1 to prefer $l1$ to $r1$, upsetting this equilibrium.

However, $l2$ is a weak best response for Bob2, if Alice's beliefs at her left-hand information set allows her to play m' with positive probability. And her beliefs, if they can attach positive probability at that information set to the possibility that she is facing Bob3—specifically, if her beliefs are that she is at the bottom node with probability $1/3$ and the middle node with probability $2/3$—then she is indifferent between m' and d', and by choosing m' with probability $3/4$ and d' with probability $1/4$, Bob2 gets an expected 4 if he chooses $l2$, making $l2$ a weak best response.

But—and here is the point—$l3$ is never a weak best response for Bob3. So how can Alice, at this equilibrium outcome, attach positive probability to the bottom node in her left-hand information set? And if her beliefs must be that she is at either the middle or the top node, m' is never a sequentially rational choice for her, and *then* $l2$ is never a weak best response for Bob2, in which case..., well, you can finish this sentence.

The point is: Never a weak best response rules out certain actions by certain players, and in so doing, it can be thought of as restricting the off-path beliefs of other players, which restricts their sequentially rational responses, which may make other actions never a weak best response. All of which is "implied by" strategic stability. Henceforth, "never a weak best response" will mean: Iterating on elimination of actions by this criterion, hence restricting off-path beliefs and sequentially rational responses, hence (possibly) increasing the power of never a weak best response. (I'll be more formal about this idea in the next section.)

A14.5. The Intuitive Criterion and Beyond: Intuitively Appealing Stories (Perhaps)

Weaker (in the sense of applying to fewer cases) restrictions on off-path beliefs that are implied by never a weak best response have been proposed in the literature. While weaker, the justification for these restrictions are that they are more "intuitive"; they go with stories about how players might reason at off-path information sets. I put scare quotes around "intuitive," because what is and isn't intuitive is largely subjective; it is your job to judge which of these restrictions appeals to your intuition and which do not.

And while I will not repeat the quibble I raised about iterated dominance at the end of Section A14.3, that quibble applies to every restriction that is discussed in this section.

Signaling games

These restrictions were initially posed in a simple class of extensive-form games called *signaling games*. They can be extended to other extensive-form games, but they are best explained in the context of signaling games, and so, in this section, we limit the discussion to such games. Here are the rules:

There are two players, whom we continue to call Alice and Bob. There is a state of nature ω, drawn from a finite set Ω. Alice's prior assessment concerning which ω prevails is given by a probability ρ on Ω, a prior that is common knowledge between Alice and Bob. Bob is informed at the outset which $\omega \in \Omega$ prevails and, based on that information, signals to Alice by sending her a message m, drawn from a finite set M. Alice hears the message and, contingent on what she hears, chooses an action a from a finite set of actions A. Alice's and Bob's payoffs depend on the action Alice takes, the state, and Bob's message; Alice's payoff is given by $v(a, \omega, m)$, and Bob's is given by $u(a, \omega, m)$.[9]

The game depicted in Figure A14.4 is a signaling game. The two states of nature determine whether Bob is aggressive or passive. The two messages that Bob (conditional on his type) can send are to growl or to smile. And Alice's two possible actions are to challenge Bob or not. Note that in this game, Alice's payoff depends directly only on the state (Bob's type) and her choice of action and not on the message Bob sends.

In the literature, as in the game of Figure A14.4, the language used is that the state of nature ω determines the *type* of Bob. This language is convenient for the developments in this section, so I will use it; henceforth, when the state is ω, I'll say "Bob is type ω" and refer to "type-ω Bob" or "ω-Bob."

Some useful notation concerning signaling games involves the range of possible responses by Alice to different messages m she might receive. Of course, her responses will depend on her beliefs concerning the type of Bob she faces given that message, regardless of whether those beliefs are determined by on-path consistency. So, for μ a probability distribution over Ω, define

$$\mathrm{BR}(\mu, m) := \arg\max\left\{ \sum_{\omega \in \Omega} \mu(\omega) v(a, \omega, m) : a \in A \right\};$$

this is the set of best responses to m by Alice if her beliefs are μ. And for any subset $\Omega' \subset \Omega$, define

$$\mathrm{BR}(\Omega', m) := \bigcup \left\{ \mathrm{BR}(\mu, m) : \mu \in \mathbf{P}(\Omega) \text{ such that the support of } \mu \text{ is } \Omega' \right\}.$$

In words, $\mathrm{BR}(\Omega', m)$ is the set of best responses by Alice if her beliefs after receiving the message m are concentrated on Ω'.

---

[9] In the literature, it is often assumed that Alice's payoff does not depend directly on Bob's message. (Of course, it will depend indirectly, insofar as Bob's message leads Alice to reassess the probability of different states ω.) But allowing m as an argument of Alice's payoff comes at virtually no cost.

Dominated messages and the test of dominated messages

Consider the signaling game depicted in Figure A14.9. One sequential equilibrium outcome of this game has both types of Bob sending the message m'. This puts Alice's left-hand information set on-path, her on-path beliefs are that the two nodes are equally likely, and so she chooses action b, which gives type-ω_1 Bob a payoff of 3 and type-ω_2 Bob a payoff of 1. There is no problem getting ω_1-Bob to send the signal m', since m' dominates m whatever Alice would do on receiving the message m and whatever she will do on receiving m'. But to get ω_2-Bob to send m' requires that, were Alice to receive message m, she would choose d with probability 0.5 or more. And for her to choose d on hearing m, her off-path beliefs at her right-hand information set must put probability 0.5 or more that the message m came from ω_1-Bob.

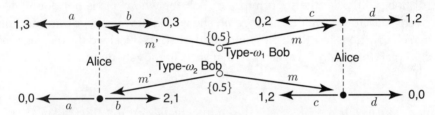

Figure A14.9. A dominated message (Alice's payoffs are given first)

However, this off-path assessment for Alice is "unintuitive," since m' dominates m for ω_1-Bob in the strong sense that

$$\max_{a \in A} u(a, m, \omega_1) < \min_{a \in A} u(a, m', \omega_1). \tag{A14.1}$$

Alice, on hearing m, should assess that this message must have come from ω_2-Bob, which implies that her "intuitive" choice, having heard ω_2, is c, which is inconsistent with any equilibrium that has ω_2-Bob sending m'. Hence, by what we might call *the test of dominated messages*, the equilibrium outcome where both types of Bob send message m' is "unintuitive."

The scare quotes around "unintuitive" and "intuitive" are there for the (I hope by now) obvious reason that intuition is subjective. You can decide if you find this argument compelling. But, whether you do or not, it should be clear that an equilibrium outcome that requires Alice, having received an off-path message m, to assign positive probability to types of Bob for whom m is a dominated message, cannot be strategically stable.

We can (and do) enhance the power of the test of dominated messages in two steps, corresponding to the "iteration" of last section.

First, as stated so far, for message m to be dominated by m' for type ω, inequality (A14.1) requires that $\min_{a \in A} u(a, \omega, m') > \max_{a \in A} u(a, \omega, m)$. But Alice can be counted on to avoid any response to m that is not a member of $\mathrm{BR}(\Omega, m)$. And she will avoid any response to m' not in $\mathrm{BR}(\Omega, m')$. Granting that she will avoid these responses (and that Bob understands this), we can (and do) say that m is dominated by m' for ω-Bob if

$$\max\left\{u(a,m,\omega): a \in \mathrm{BR}(\Omega,m)\right\} < \min\left\{u(a,m',\omega): a \in \mathrm{BR}(\Omega,m')\right\}. \quad \text{(A14.1')}$$

And then, for a given equilibrium outcome, we say that it fails the test of message domination if for some off-path message m, to sustain the equilibrium, Alice, having received the message m, must put positive probability on it coming from a type-ω Bob for whom m is dominated.

And, as a second enhancement, we can iterate on this criterion. Suppose that message m is dominated for some types of Bob—let Ω_m^1 be the set of types of Bob for whom m is not dominated—and/or suppose that m' is dominated for some types of Bob, with $\Omega_{m'}^1$ the set of types of Bob for whom m' is not dominated. Then, were Alice to receive the message m, she would (if we believe this intuition) limit herself to actions in $\mathrm{BR}(\Omega_m^1, m)$, and similarly if she received the message m'. Hence, in place of (A14.1'), we can say that m is iteratively dominated by m' for ω-Bob if

$$\max\left\{u(a,m,\omega): a \in \mathrm{BR}(\Omega_m^1,m)\right\} < \min\left\{u(a,m',\omega): a \in \mathrm{BR}(\Omega_{m'}^1,m')\right\}.$$
$$\text{(A14.1'')}$$

And if we want to go whole hog on such an enhancement, we could iterate again and again, creating Ω_m^j, the set of undominated types for message m after j iterations of the procedure. Since Ω is finite and these Ω_m^j sets are weakly nested as j increases, it is eventually the case that the process stops, albeit it may stop when all types ω have been eliminated for a given message m. In case that happens, Alice's beliefs at the off-path m are irrelevant: No type of Bob will send that message. [10]

Are these two enhancements intuitive? You must judge for yourself, in context. But it is worth observing that they correspond to extra rounds of iterated dominance. In the first enhancement (replacing (A14.1) with (A14.1')), Alice's conclusion that ω-Bob would not send the dominated message m is based on her belief that he believes she will not use a strategy that can't be rationalized. And each iteration in (A14.1'') involves two futher rounds of "iterated dominance" or, perhaps more in keeping with how things are formulated, iterated rationalizability: Alice believes that Bob believes that she believes that he won't use a message deleted on an earlier iteration, hence she believes that he believes that her rationalizable response sets are smaller, hence she believes that the set of messages he sees as dominated is (weakly) larger.

And, whether you find the enhancements intuitive or not, it is straightforward to see that the doubly enhanced test of dominated messages is implied by strategic stability; an equilibrium outcome that fails the test cannot be strategically stable.

---

[10]   Note that, as we iterate on (A14.1''), the sets of a on both sides of the inequality weakly decline, which decreases the max on the left and increases the min on the right. There is a slight issue to deal with if the set of qualifying a on the right becomes the empty set, but if it does, it is because some other message dominates it. And what are the implications of that?

Equilibrium-value domination and the intuitive criterion

Consider the game in Figure A14.4, for $\rho = 0.7$. Neither message (growling or smiling) is dominated by the other message for either type of Bob. So the test of dominated messages has no force. However, if we consider the equilibrium outcome where both types of Bob smile, at that outcome, Passive Bob is getting a payoff of 4, which is more than he can conceivably get by growling. Hence, according to the "intuitive" story told at the start of this appendix, Alice should conclude that, if she hears a growl, it must be Aggressive Bob.

Formalized, this is the test of *equilibrium-value domination*, giving rise to the so-called *intuitive criterion*. Unlike message domination, this criterion fixes a particular equilibrium outcome and uses the values that different types of Bob receive as the benchmark against which off-path messages are evaluated.

1. Fix a signaling game, and assume the specification of payoffs is generic in the sense that Proposition A14.1 holds. Fix an equilibrium outcome for this game in which the signals in $M^\sharp$ are on-path and those in $M^\flat = M \setminus M^\sharp$ are off-path. For each type ω of Bob, let $u^*(\omega)$ be ω-Bob's expected payoff at this outcome, conditional on the state being ω.

2. For each type ω of Bob and each off-path message $m \in M^\flat$, compare "the best" that ω-Bob can get from m with what he receives in equilibrium. There are, conceivably, two ways to formulate "the best": for any response by Alice, or for any rationalizable response by Alice. That is, we are comparing $u^*(\omega)$ with either

$$\max \left\{ u(a, m, \omega) : a \in A \right\} \quad \text{or} \quad \max \left\{ u(a, m, \omega) : a \in \mathrm{BR}(\Omega, m) \right\}.$$

And, whichever test we apply, we say that m is equilibrium-value dominated for type ω Bob if $u^*(\omega)$ strictly exceeds "the best" Bob can get.

And, if we choose the second sort of test, we can iterate on it: Initiate with $\Omega_m^0 = \Omega$ and then, recursively, define

$$\Omega_m^j = \left\{ \omega : u^*(\omega) > \max \left\{ u(a, m, \omega) : a \in \mathrm{BR}(\Omega_m^{j-1}, m) \right\} \right\}. \tag{A14.2}$$

The *intuitive criterion* as originally defined in the literature uses both sorts of enhancements applied to the equilibrium-value domination test. That is, for each off-path message $m \in M^\flat$, it finds the set of types $\Omega_m^* = \lim_j \Omega_m^j$ for whom m is not (iteratively) equilibrium-value dominated. If this limit set of types is empty, the equilibrium outcome passes the test for message m. If it is not empty, the equilibrium outcome fails the test if it cannot be sustained by off-path beliefs by Alice that, in the event she receives message m, give positive probability only to types in Ω_m^*. (It passes the test for m if it can be sustained for such beliefs.) And the equilibrium outcome satisfies the intuitive criterion if it passes the test for all $m \in M^\flat$.

Although it takes a bit of a proof, any message $m \in M^b$ for a type ω that is not in Ω_m^* is never a weak best response for that type of Bob. Hence, any equilibrium outcome that does not satisfy the intuitive criterion is not strategically stable.

But the point is not so much to find a test that is required by strategic stability as it is to find a criterion for Alice's off-path beliefs that appeals to your intuition. Of course, the sorts of objections to this line of thought set forth in the subsection "A quibble about iterated dominance": Alice, when deciding which types would *not* sent a particular message, looks only at what the type stands to gain (given a "reasonable" response by her) and not at what the type might lose.

But beyond these objections, there is the question whether the benchmark ω-Bob's equilibrium value is a valid benchmark. The allegedly intuitive story is that, for a given equilibrium outcome to be *the* outcome, each type of Bob should have faith that this is available if he complies with the equilibrium. Deviating to some off-path signal m only makes sense if it offers the prospect of a payoff greater than the guarantee. And, if an equilibrium outcome fails the intuitive criterion, then Alice, applying this logic and getting an off-path message m for which the test fails, must hold beliefs and take an action in consequence that makes it worthwhile for the deviating type(s) of Bob to defect from the equilibrium. That, at least, is the intuitive argument for applying the intuitive criterion.

Of course, the less one depends on Alice's conjectures about what Bob believes about her rationality (when she formulates her possible responses to a message $m \in M^b$), the more intuitive is the argument. To translate this difficult-to-parse assertion: If we only assume that Alice, on receiving the message $m \in M^b$, only rules out types ω for which $u^*(\omega) > \max \{u(a, m, \omega) : a \in A\}$, and still the equilibrium outcome fails—which is precisely the case in Figure A14.4—then the story is more believable than if, to disqualify the equilibrium, we have to iterate in the fashion of inequality (A14.2). But, to be clear, even in the case of Figure A14.4, Aggressive Bob, by deviating from the both-smile equilibrium outcome, is depending on Alice to draw the "right" conclusion if she hears a growl. The intuitive criterion says she will do so; you must decide whether you trust this "forward induction logic."

D1, D2, Divinity, and Universal Divinity

In the literature, tests of equilibrium outcomes stronger than equilibrium-value domination are posed, all of which are implied by strategic stability.

The D1 and D2 criteria fit the framework for message- and equilibrium-value domination. A benchmark is set that renders an off-path message "unsuitable" for types of Bob, and the question is: Can the equilibrium outcome be sustained with off-path beliefs that put zero probability on the unsuitable types?

Criterion D1 (with both enhancements) is defined in two steps: First, fix an equilibrium outcome with equilibrium values $v^*(\omega)$ for which Proposition A14.1 holds. For a message $m \in M^b$ and a set $\Omega' \subset \Omega$, say that type $\omega' \in \Omega'$ is *more suitable* for m than is $\omega \in \Omega'$ relative to Ω' if, for all simple probability distributions

π on $BR(\Omega', m))$ such that $\sum_a \pi(a)u(a, \omega, m) = u^*(\omega)$,

$$\sum_a \pi(a)u(a, \omega', m) > u^*(\omega').$$

And, then, in place of inequality (14.1″) or inequality (14.2), define

$$\Omega_m^j = \{\omega \in \Omega_m^{j-1} : \text{There is no } m' \in \Omega_m^{j-1}$$
$$\text{such that } \omega' \text{ is more suitable than } \omega \text{ for } m\}.$$

And then continue as before. In words, for a given type ω, ω' is more suitable for m if, for every possible response by Alice, if ω-Bob finds that response just as good as his equilibrium value, then ω'-Bob strictly prefers m to his equilibrium value. From here to "sending m is never a weak best response for ω-Bob" is fairly straightforward.

And for criterion D2, we don't insist on a single type ω' for whom every reasonable response by Alice that makes ω-Bob indifferent between m and the equilibrium would cause ω' to defect. Instead, we reverse quantifiers and insist that, for every reasonable response by Alice that makes ω-Bob as well or better off than at his equilibrium value, there is some other type of Bob who would strictly prefer that message and response to his equilibrium value. (I'll let you supply the formal definition, or see the original paper, Banks and Sobel 1987.)

Divinity is of a slightly different character, in that, so far, we have looked at criteria that, if satisfied, require Alice to try to sustain the equilibrium outcome with beliefs that put zero probability on certain messages coming from certain types. Divinity, using a criterion that is close to D1, only insists that Alice not increase the probability of a "disqualified" type. (Compare with the alternative argument given in footnote 3 on page 636.) University divinity, in contrast, is in line with the idea that probabilities of disqualified types should be set to zero.

I am not spelling out the details here because, while I am not prepared to assert definitively that the intuitive criterion is as intuitive as its name suggests, I'm utterly unconvinced that Alice would embrace D1 or D2 and yet not go all the way to using never a weak best response. And while the connection of never a weak best response to strategic stability is, I hope, clear, it is that connection that "justifies" it as a relatively easy test of strategic stability; not that it particularly appeals to my own intuition.

That said, if you are writing a paper that contains a model for which applying never a weak best response or one of the criteria in the title of this subsection would help you, it's a tool that many referees and editors will find legitimate. So, be my guest.

Bibliographic Notes

The prerequisites for the topics of this appendix are the papers on trembling-hand perfection, properness, and sequential equilibria: Selten (1975), Myerson (1978), and Kreps and Wilson (1982b), respectively.

The classic papers that define "strategically inessential modifications of the extensive form," are Thompson (1952) and Dalkey (1953).

The program of strategic stability begins with Kohlberg and Mertens (1986). Among the papers that undertake to "refine" and redefine strategic stability are Mertens (1989, 1991), Van Damme (1989), and Hillas (1990). Two more recent papers that attack forward induction from a decision-theoretic and an axiomatic approach are Govinden and Wilson (2009, 2012).

The intuitive criterion, D1, D2, and the two versions of divinity were developed roughly contemporaneously: Cho and Kreps (1987) for the intuitive criterion, and Banks and Sobel (1987) for divinity and universal divinity. (The preeminent application of these criteria is to market signaling; see Chapter 20 in the text.)

Appendix Fifteen

Repeated Play: Relationships, Reputation, and the Folk Theorem

In economic contexts, individuals can have encounters, in which they interact once (or briefly), and they can have relationships, in which they interact repeatedly. And even when an individual doesn't have long-term relationships with a small group of counterparties, she may carry reputations for how she behaves in short-term encounters, which affect how her brief encounters play out.

To model and study these things, game-theoretic models of repeated play are often employed. There are many variations on how these models are constructed, and the literature that fits this general category is huge. In this appendix, only a few of the basic themes are discussed, and I primarily present examples that illustrate the general results; some of the general results (such as the classic folk theorem) are stated and proved; a few more (e.g., subgame perfection in the classic folk theorem) are stated but not proved. But even for the limited number of variations touched here, I often refer to other sources for statements of the general results. (Other variations given short shrift here appear in specific contexts in the text.) For a comprehensive treatment, two excellent sources are Mailath and Samuelson (2006) and Fudenberg and Tirole (1991b, chapters 5 and 9).

Though this appendix discusses only basic themes, it is still the lengthiest appendix in this volume, running to a bit over 80 pages. Even readers for whom this appendix is a "refresher" might find reading it at one go is strenuous. If you wish to take it in chunks, I suggest Sections 15.1 and 15.2 as the first chunk, Sections 15.3 to 15.6 the second, and then Section 15.7 to the end as the third. And you may wish to break it down even further.

A15.1. The Base Model and Some Variations

We begin with a catalog of the base model and some of its many variations, to give a sense of how wide and varied the literature is. (Don't worry about the length of the list of variations. I reiterate that, while this appendix is long, it only skims the surface of the literature.)

In the base model, a game Γ is given, involving N players; this is called the *stage game*. The game may be in strategic form or in extensive form. As a result of the play of the game, each player gets a payoff, called the player's *stage-game payoff*.

The game is repeated multiple times, with play taking place in sequence. A discrete time parameter $t = 0, 1, \ldots$ marks the times at which the stage game is played.

The first set of variations concerns who plays in the various roles:

- In the base model, the same N players play in every round of play, with each player taking the same role in the stage game in each repetition.

- But in variations, the population of players is fixed, but players are randomly assigned to roles in each repetition of the game. For instance, the stage game Γ may have only two active roles, and on each repetition, two players out of the N are chosen to play. Or, for N an even number, the game Γ may consist of $N/2$ pairwise interactions, with random matching of all the players into interacting pairs on each repetition. The players may be divided a priori into subpopulations, with each subpopulation assigned to one "role" in the stage game and with random matching. And so forth. This appendix addresses none of these variations, but some examples are provided in Chapter 22, to illustrate the notion of community enforcement.

- In quite different variations, some subset of the roles in the stage game may be taken by players who play repeatedly—so-called long-lived players—while other roles are played by players who play only in a single round, so-called short-lived players. (Chapter 22 also discusses an intermediate case, with one long-lived player who faces, in sequence, short-run players who play the stage game a finite number of times and then depart, to be replaced by the next *intermediate-lived* player.)

- The population of players may change over time. One version of this has each player play for a fixed number of rounds, with departing players replaced by "new" players; this variation includes models with classic overlapping generations. In other versions, players have a probability of "death" after each round, with replacement by new players. In still other versions, the population shifts in composition toward players whose strategies are relatively more successful. (This variation is more related to evolutionary biology than to standard economics, but it also appears in behavioral economics, where players are modeled as adopting "more successful" strategies that they see others using.)

The second set of variations or modeling options concerns the number of times the game is played:

- It may be played countably many times. The term *an infinite-horizon (repeated) game* is used.

- It may be played a fixed, finite number of times, $T+1$, with time $t = T$ the final time the game is played, which is known to all players from the outset. This is called a *(fixed) finite-horizon game*.

- It may be played a finite but random number of times,. For instance, models sometimes specify that, after each round of play, an independent random event takes place, with some probability $1 - \gamma$ that the round just completed was the last round and probability γ that another round will take place, after which the same sort of random event determines whether there will be at least one more round of play. (A variation that is not so common has the random event taking place before the current round of play. That is, before the stage game is played at time t, the players are told either: "This is not the last round," or "This will be the last round."

- As a variation on the previous bullet point, the choices made by the players in a given round may determine, or at least affect, the chances that the current round is last.

- As a further variation, the actions taken by players in a given round may change the nature of further interactions by changing (say) the stage game that is played. (In the literature, such variations often go by the name *stochastic games*.)

- Rather than having the stage game played at a sequence of dates, play of numerous encounters may take place simultaneously. One player may play a number of counterparties simultaneously, in a "stage game" that takes some time (so that what happens in the player's encounter with one counterparty can affect the later-in-the-game behavior of other, simultaneous counterparties). Or play may mix simultaneity and sequentiality, where one party is engaged in an ongoing encounter with one counterparty while initiating a similar encounter with another. (Think of an academic department that deals with tenured faculty members, untenured faculty members, and new recruits, all at the same time.)

- Finally, while it is most common to have the stage game played at a discrete sequence of times—which is all that this appendix covers—in other applications, a continuous time parameter is employed. (Some relatively simple continuous-time games are analyzed in Chapter 23.) And, in some studies, the question of convergence from discrete and increasingly rapid play to continuous time is addressed.

Typically, the players' stage-game payoffs are discounted and summed. If we write $v_n(t)$ for player n's payoffs in stage t, the player's *overall payoff* is $V_n := \sum_{t=0}^{T} \delta^t v_n(t)$, where $T = \infty$ if the game is played countably many times, or T is the deterministic last time the game is played, or T is a random "stopping time" if one of the other variations is used.

Typically, $\delta < 1$ for infinite-horizon games, but δ often equals 1 in games with a finite horizon.[1] And in some cases with infinite horizons, an "average reward" criterion (typically, the limit infimum of the Cesàro sums) is employed; sharper criteria (such as, overtaking optimality with no discounting) are also found. Typically in the literature, the discount factor δ is common to all players; in variations, different players can have different discount factors, and this difference becomes central to the analysis.

When the stage game is played at times $t = 0, 1, \ldots$, and a discount factor $\delta < 1$ is

---

[1] In applications where, after each round of play, there is probability γ that the game is played at least once more and probability $1 - \gamma$ that the round just completed was the last one, we can take $\delta = 1$, in which case the analysis is the same as if the game were played countably many times with discount factor γ. In general, if a discount factor $\delta < 1$ is also employed, it is as if the game were played countably many times with discount factor $\gamma\delta$.

employed, we may be interested in what happens as $\delta \to 1$. If we imagine the game being played $T + 1$ times for some finite T, we may be interested in what happens as $T \to \infty$. To make valid comparisons about the players' overall payoffs (as $\delta \to 1$ or $T \to \infty$), the overall payoffs are "scaled," so they are measured on the same scale as are payoffs in the stage game. For infinite-horizon games with discounting, the *scaled player payoff* is $(1 - \delta) \sum_{t=0}^{\infty} \delta^t v_n(t)$. (Hence, if a player were to receive the same payoff v in every stage, her scaled payoff for the infinitely repeated game would be the same v.) For finite-horizon games without discounting, we simply compute the average per-period payoff that the player receives, or $\left(\sum_{t=0}^{T} v_n(t) \right)/(T + 1)$.

Nearly always, but not always, it is assumed that players know their own payoffs as they accrue. In the base case, it is typically assumed that, in addition, each player in the game knows which actions every other player took in the game.

- But, especially in games with "random matching," players may only learn what the actions were of those with whom they are matched in the current round (although, of course, they can remember what the outcomes were for themselves in the past, and perhaps the identity of their former counterparties).

- And players may see only noisy indications of what other players have done.

In the base case, all of this is common knowledge among all the players. But in an important family of variations, players may begin the sequence of encounters with private information not known to other players, information that affects the entire sequence of play. Perhaps most common in this regard is information about the own player's payoffs/motivation. That is, one player is one of several types, and the player may then have an incentive to reveal or to conceal from others what her type is. And she may have (or gain) other information that is relevant to how each stage game plays out, which she may wish to conceal or to reveal.

In all these variations and in others that I haven't listed, the analysis treats the entire sequence of encounters as a single grand game, where the objective in analyzing a given model is to apply domination and equilibrium concepts to the game.

A15.2. The Repeated Prisoners' Dilemma

I expect that many readers will have already seen examples of the base model and some variations. Those readers are free to skip this section and move on to the general results beginning with Section A15.3. However, the general results are more subtle than is generally believed—at least, I think so—and so a simple, concrete example is useful to have in mind.

The analysis, both in this section and in those following, requires that you understand the methods of dynamic programming as outlined in Appendix 6 of Volume I. In particular, if you feel shaky concerning the following statements, a review is called for before proceeding with this section.

- *In a problem with bounded rewards and a discount factor less than 1, every conserving strategy and every unimprovable strategy is optimal.*

- *To find an optimal strategy (and the optimal value function), a useful technique is to guess at a solution and check whether it is unimprovable.*

- *For a stationary infinite-horizon problem with a finite set of actions at each stage, some stationary strategy is optimal.*

Assuming that you are comfortable with these statements, we can proceed.

Consider the following example. The stage game Γ is the prisoners' dilemma game, depicted in Figure A15.1. Please note: I've changed the payoff to a player if she cooperates when the other party defects from the values used in Appendix 9 (Figure A9.2, page 492). You'll see why I did so in a bit.

There are two players, Alice and Bob. They play this game a countable number of times, at $t = 0, 1, \ldots$. Their stage-game payoffs are discounted and summed with discount factor $\delta < 1$. After each round of play, each player learns his or her payoff, which, for this simple game, together with the player's choice of stage-game action in the current round, reveals the other player's choice of action.

<table>
<tr><td></td><td></td><td colspan="2">Bob</td></tr>
<tr><td></td><td></td><td>Betray Alice</td><td>Cooperate with Alice</td></tr>
<tr><td rowspan="2">Alice</td><td>Betray Bob</td><td>0, 0</td><td>20, –15</td></tr>
<tr><td>Cooperate with Bob</td><td>–15, 20</td><td>10, 10</td></tr>
</table>

Figure A15.1. The prisoners' dilemma: a stage game

This is an extensive-form game but without a finite game tree. You might want to go back and reread Section A10.7, but to summarize:

- In this game, starting from any node in the game tree, there is a finite path back to the initial node.

- A complete history of play—that is, a complete path through the tree—is an infinite sequence of the form $h = ((X_0, Y_0), (X_1, Y_1), \ldots)$, where X_t is Alice's choice of action in round t and Y_t is Bob's choice; each X_t and Y_t is either *cooperate* or *betray*. Note that, as we have a countable number of items to specify, and each item has two possible values, the space of complete histories H is uncountable.

- There are no terminal nodes, so in the formal definition, payoffs for the two players are specified as a function from H to pairs of real numbers, one payoff for Alice and one for Bob. That function takes a particularly simple form: Letting $v(X, Y)$ denote the stage-game payoff for Alice if she plays X and Bob plays Y, where X and Y are both either *cooperate* or *betray*, Alice's payoff for the grand game, given a history $h = ((X_0, Y_0), (X_1, Y_1), \ldots)$ is $\sum_{t=0}^{\infty} \delta^t v(X_t, Y_t)$ for some $\delta < 1$. Bob's overall payoff is symmetrical, for the same discount factor δ.

- A partial history up to but not including time t is a finite sequence h_t of the form $((X_0, Y_0), (X_1, Y_1), \ldots, (X_{t-1}, Y_{t-1}))$. Let H_t denote the space of histories up to (but not including) time t, where (by convention) H_0 is $\{\emptyset\}$ (or any other convenient singleton set).

- In this extensive-form game, if we put Alice's choice in round t "first," then her choice nodes (one for each $h_t \in H_t$) are roots of proper subgames. And Bob's information sets will each have two nodes, those being the choice that Alice makes in the same round. (Of course, the order of these nodes could be reversed.)

- A (pure) strategy for either player is a sequence of functions $(s_0, s_1, \ldots)$, where $s_t : H_t \to \{\text{cooperate, betray}\}$. (When and if we deal with mixed strategies, we'll deal with behaviorally mixed strategies.)

To distinguish between what a player does in round t and her overall strategy, I'll refer to the former as the player's choice of *action* in round t. The player's *strategy* will always be her strategy for the grand game.

A subset of all the strategies for either player consists of so-called *nonreactive* strategies: strategies where what the player does in round t depends only on the date t; that is, each s_t is constant on H_t. Note that the number of nonreactive strategies is uncountable. And while the total set of strategies for a player has the same (uncountable) cardinality, nonreactive strategies are a "small" subset of all possible strategies.

That's a lot of strategies, and you may wonder how we will ever confirm that a pair of strategies constitutes a Nash equilibrium. This can be done, using dynamic programming methods, as long as we restrict attention to relatively simple strategies. For instance, here are five relatively simple strategies with names, two nonreactive and three reactive:

- **Sap**: *always choose to cooperate,* a nonreactive strategy.

- **Jerk:** *always choose to betray,* another nonreactive strategy.

- **Tit-for-tat:** *Begin with cooperation in round 0 and then, in each round $t > 0$, choose whichever action one's rival chose at time $t - 1$.* This strategy is famous, because it won a famous "repeated-prisoners'-dilemma tournament" (Axelrod 1984).

- **Grim:** *Begin with cooperate in round 0, and then play cooperate at any partial history for which both players have always played cooperate in the past. But after any partial history in which either player at any date chose to betray, choose to betray.*

- **Greedy grim.** *In even-numbered rounds, cooperate. In odd-numbered rounds, betray. Follow this pattern as long as the opponent never betrays and you don't deviate from this pattern. But if your opponent ever betrays, or you deviate from the pattern, then betray in all subsequent rounds.*

Which strategy profiles constitute a Nash equilibrium? Which constitute a subgame-perfect Nash equilibrium? Some results follow:

Jerk versus jerk is a subgame-perfect Nash equilibrium and is the only Nash equilibrium in nonreactive strategies

To see why, suppose Alice plays jerk. Bob's choice of strategy will have no impact on Alice's actions, so he may as well maximize his payoff in each round by betraying in each round, which means playing jerk. Moreover, whatever the history is at some point in the game (even a history where, say, Alice cooperated in the previous round, which is off-path if she is playing jerk), she will choose betray in every subsequent round, so Bob's best action choices are always to betray; that is, play jerk. Alice's position is symmetrical. Hence, jerk versus jerk is subgame perfect.

Suppose Alice and Bob are playing nonreactive strategies, at least one of which is not jerk. Suppose, for instance, it is Alice. Then at some date t, she will choose to cooperate. Bob's choices will not be affected if, instead, she plays betray at date t, and her overall payoff will increase. Hence, there is no other Nash equilibrium in nonreactive strategies.

What is Alice's optimal (stationary) response to Bob playing tit-for-tat?

Suppose Bob is playing tit-for-tat. What is Alice's best response as a function of δ? And why did I insert the parenthetical "(stationary)" in the title of this subsection?

From Alice's perspective, if Bob is playing tit-for-tat, she faces a (single-person) stationary (or time-homogeneous) sequential decision problem with two states, the two states being whether Alice cooperated in the previous period (denoted C) or she betrayed (denoted B).

These are the two states, in terms of Alice's decision problem, because at any point in time and given any history up to that time, Bob's future behavior if he is playing tit-for-tat-playing depends (in stationary fashion) only on what Alice did last time. Moreover, we can easily describe the dynamics of the problem facing Alice: *If the state is C*, Bob will cooperate. So if she cooperates, she nets an immediate reward of 10 and the state remains C; while if she chooses to betray, her immediate reward is 20 and the state transitions to B. *And if the state is B, so that Bob will betray*, betraying nets her an immediate 0 and the state stays as B, while cooperating nets her an immediate -15 and moves the state to C. These dynamics are illustrated in Figure A15.2.

Appendix 6 of Volume I applies. Stage payoffs are bounded, and $\delta < 1$. Alice's optimal value function at any time, given any history, going forward (that is, for the rest of the game) depends only on the state. Any conserving strategy is optimal, and since she has only two action choices, she has a stationary conserving, and therefore optimal, strategy. Thus one of her four stationary strategies must be a best response, those four being: choose to cooperate in both states; choose to betray in both states; choose to cooperate in C and betray in B; and choose to cooperate in B and betray in C. And we can check on optimality by applying the principle that an unimprovable (in one step) strategy is optimal.

So, we analyze each of the four stationary strategies in turn.

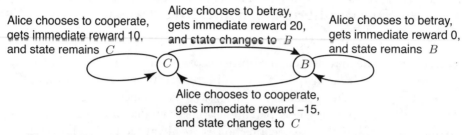

Alice chooses to cooperate, gets immediate reward 10, and state remains C

Alice chooses to betray, gets immediate reward 20, and state changes to B

Alice chooses to betray, gets immediate reward 0, and state remains B

Alice chooses to cooperate, gets immediate reward −15, and state changes to C

Figure A15.2. Alice's sequential-decision-problem structure, if Bob is playing tit-for-tat. There are two states, C (Alice cooperated last time) and B (she betrayed last time). In each state, she has two choices, to cooperate or betray, with state transitions and immediate rewards as shown.

1. *Cooperate in both states.* If Alice cooperates in both states, then starting from state C, she will accrue a payoff 10 in each period, for a net present value of $10/(1 - \delta)$. From the state B, she absorbs a loss of 15 in the first period but gets 10 in all subsequent periods, for a net of $-15 + 10\delta/(1 - \delta)$.

Is this strategy unimprovable? Or, rather, for which values of δ is this unimprovable? If, in state C, she betrays instead but then goes back to her "always cooperate" strategy, her net will be $20 - 15\delta + \delta^2 10/(1 - \delta)$. Comparing this with the $10/(1 - \delta)$ that she receives from the strategy, we see that the strategy is unimprovable in state C if

$$20 - 15\delta \leq 10 + 10\delta, \quad \text{or} \quad 10 \leq 25\delta, \quad \text{or} \quad \delta \geq 0.4.$$

And in state B, the comparison is between $-15 + 10\delta/(1 - \delta)$, which is what she gets by following the "always cooperate" strategy, and $0 - 15\delta + 10\delta^2/(1 - \delta)$, which is what she gets by playing betray in the current round and then reverting to the "always cooperate" strategy. The former is bigger than the latter as long as

$$-15 + 10\delta/(1 - \delta) \geq 0, \quad \text{or} \quad 10\delta \geq 15(1 - \delta), \quad \text{or} \quad 25\delta \geq 15, \quad \text{or} \quad \delta \geq 0.6.$$

The conclusion is that *cooperate in both states* is unimprovable, hence optimal, if (and only if) $\delta \geq 0.6$.

Let me remind you of an important lesson from Appendix 6. A strategy can be unimprovable from some positions (or states) but not others. If $\delta = 0.45$, say, Alice's strategy *cooperate in both states* is unimprovable when the state is C. *But this does not mean that this strategy is optimal, beginning from a position where the state is C.* The result that unimprovable implies optimal is valid *only* when the strategy is unimprovable from *all* positions (or states). (I won't make a big deal about it, but this is connected to the notions of extended-on-path information sets and immediate-action optimality, and in particular, the second sentence in Proposition A12.6.)

2. *Betray in both states.* This strategy nets 20 in state C and 0 in state B. It is unimprovable (hence optimal) if $20 \geq 10 + 20\delta$ for state C and $0 \geq -15 + 20\delta$ for state B. The first is $\delta \leq 1/2$ and the second is $\delta \leq 3/4$, so *betray in both states* is optimal when $\delta \leq 1/2$. (I'm going quickly here. You should be sure you understand why the two unimprovability inequalities are what they are.)

3. *Cooperate in state C and betray in state B.* In state C, this strategy against tit-for-tat nets 10 in each period, for a net present value of $10/(1 - \delta)$. In state B, it nets 0 in every period, for a net present value of 0. Hence, it is unimprovable (and so optimal) if

$$10/(1 - \delta) \geq 20 + 0, \quad \text{and} \quad 0 \geq -15 + 10\delta/(1 - \delta).$$

The first required inequality is $\delta \geq 1/2$, and the second is $\delta \leq 0.6$. So, *cooperate in state C and betray in state B* is optimal for δ in the range $0.5 \leq \delta \leq 0.6$.

We've covered all values of δ, but as a check, let's run the final (stationary) strategy:

4. *Betray in C and cooperate in B.* Against tit-for-tat, starting in state C, this leads to the outcome 20 in round 0, -15 in round 1, 20 in round 2, and so forth; starting in state B, it gives -15, then 20, then -15, and so forth. So the net present values are $(20 - 15\delta)/(1 - \delta^2)$ starting in state C and $(-15 + 20\delta)/(1 - \delta^2)$ in state B. The inequalities needed for unimprovability are

$$(20 - 15\delta)/(1 - \delta^2) \geq 10 + \delta(20 - 15\delta)/(1 - \delta^2) \quad \text{(for state } C \text{ unimprovability,)}$$
$$\text{and } (-15 + 20\delta)/(1 - \delta^2) \geq 0 + \delta(-15 + 20\delta)/(1 - \delta^2) \quad \text{(for state } D\text{).}$$

I will leave it to you to do the math, but the first inequality is $\delta \leq 0.4$, and the second is $\delta \geq 3/4$. There are no values of δ for which this strategy is optimal against tit-for-tat.

Table A15.1 summarizes the best stationary strategic responses to tit-for-tat, as well as the optimal value for Alice in either state, as a function of δ.

	Own last action was to cooperate	Own last action was betrayal
$\delta \geq 0.6$	Optimal response is to cooperate and optimal value is $10/(1-\delta)$	Optimal response is to cooperate and optimal value is $-15 + 10/(1-\delta)$
$0.5 \leq \delta \leq 0.6$	Optimal response is to cooperate and optimal value is $10/(1-\delta)$	Optimal response is betrayal and optimal value is 0
$0.5 \geq \delta$	Optimal response is betrayal and optimal value is 20	Optimal response is betrayal and optimal value is 0

Table A15.1. Optimal strategies and values against tit-for-tat

When is tit-for-tat versus tit-for-tat a Nash equilibrium?
When is it subgame perfect?

I've just performed an analysis in the spirit of Appendix 6: solving for Alice's optimal stationary strategy, playing against a tit-for-tat-playing Bob, as a function of her discount rate δ. But this is an appendix in game theory, so: How do we translate what just happened into answers to the two game-theory questions posed in the title of this subsection?

Not to be mysterious, the answers are: Tit-for-tat (hereafter, TfT) versus TfT is a Nash equilibrium if $\delta \geq 0.5$. It is *never* a subgame-perfect Nash equilibrium (at least, not for the stage game of Figure A15.1.).

The logic behind these assertions is as follows:

1. Table A15.1 and the analysis of the previous subsection that got us to that summary table tell us, as a function of δ, which stationary strategy for Alice is unimprovable and hence optimal. (We know that some stationary strategy is optimal by the general results from Appendix 6.)

2. So we have established the optimal values that Alice can accrue, from any point in the game, going forward. The second lines in the cells of Table A15.1 are not throwaways. They are important parts of what we have learned.

3. A pair of strategies constitutes a Nash equilibrium if, from the very start of the game, each player is playing a best (optimal) response to the other players' strategies. So, the question *Is TfT versus TFT a Nash equilibrium?* is answered affirmatively if Alice playing TfT is best response, starting from the beginning of the game, to Bob playing TfT. (Since Bob's situation is identical, answering this affirmatively means that both players would be playing best responses.)

4. At the start of the game, from Alice's perspective, the "state" of her sequential decision problem is C. And, if she plays TfT, she begins by cooperating. So, entering the second round, the state is still C. Both players cooperate again, the state remains C, and so on, forever. Alice gets 10 each period, for a payoff of $10/(1 - \delta)$. And, for $\delta \geq 0.5$, that's her optimal value, per Table A15.1. We have shown that TfT is a best response to TfT from the start of the game. We have a Nash equilibrium.[2]

As for subgame perfection:

5. Start at a proper subgame where, in the previous round, Alice betrayed and Bob cooperated. This makes the state (from Alice's decision-problem perspective) B, because her last action determines what Bob will do. If she is playing TfT, she is going to cooperate. And, per Table A15.1, that is a best immediate response by her only if $\delta \geq 0.6$. So, if $\delta < 0.6$, she is taking an action that is definitely suboptimal, because (in the language of Appendix 6) it is not conserving. Start

---

[2]   There are lots of strategies that Alice can play that are best responses to Bob, if Bob is playing TfT and $\delta \geq 0.5$. For instance, if Alice is playing Sap (always cooperate), that's a best response, because she'll net $10/(1 - \delta)$. But, even though Sap is a best response (from the start of the game) to TfT, for $\delta \geq 0.5$, TfT is not a best response to Sap. So, Sap versus TfT is not a Nash equilibrium.

at a proper subgame where, in the previous round, she cooperated and he betrayed, so the state is C. Playing TfT, she is going to betray. And that is optimal (only) if $\delta \leq 0.5$. That is, she is taking a suboptimal action is $\delta > 0.5$. So, for every value of δ, her playing TfT against TfT is suboptimal in one or the other sort of proper subgame. TfT versus TfT is not subgame perfect for any δ.

(Why did I change the -10 stage-game payoff for Alice if she cooperates and Bob betrays in Figure A9.2 to -15 in Figure A15.1? Suppose I had kept the -10. If you go back over the calculations that determine which (stationary) strategies are optimal for different values of δ, you will find that *cooperate in both states* is optimal for $\delta \geq 1/2$, *betray in both states* is optimal for $\delta \leq 1/2$, and the two other stationary strategies are optimal for $\delta = 1/2$ exactly. Hence, if $\delta = 1/2$, either action in either state is conserving. Which implies that for $\delta = 1/2$ exactly and the payoffs given by Figure A9.2, *every* strategy by Alice is optimal, starting in either state, against tit-for-tat by Bob. And so, in particular, tit-for-tat is versus tit-for-tat is subgame perfect.)

If $\delta \geq 1/2$, then grim versus grim is a subgame-perfect equilibrium

This may be obvious to you but, to be thorough, here are the details.

If Bob plays the grim strategy, Alice's decision problem is again a two-state sequential decision problem with two states C and B, but now C is the state following any history where both parties have so far always cooperated, and B is the state following any history in which one or the other party has betrayed. (Note: The states B and C have different definitions here than previously.) In state C, Bob cooperates; in state B, he betrays. And so the structure of Alice's sequential decision problem is as depicted in Figure A15.3.

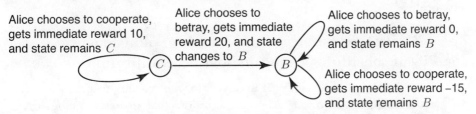

Figure A15.3. Alice's sequential decision problem, if Bob is playing grim

As before, a stationary strategy will be optimal for Alice, and we could evaluate all four and check for unimprovability, but I'll do the math for (only) the relevant two:

1. *Cooperate in state C and betray in state B.* In state C, if Bob is playing grim and Alice cooperates, she'll get 10 every round for a net present value of $10/(1 - \delta)$. In state B, if she betrays, she'll get 0 every round, for a net present value of 0. So, in state C, unimprovability holds if $10/(1 - \delta) \geq 20 + 0\delta$, which is $\delta \geq 1/2$. and, in state B, unimprovability holds if $0 \geq -15 + 0\delta$, which is true for all values of δ So this strategy is optimal when $\delta \geq 0.5$.

2. *Betray in both states.* In state C, against grim, this nets Alice an immediate 20 and nothing further, for a net present value of 20. In state B, it nets her 0. Checking for unimprovability: In state C, we need $20 \geq 10 + 20\delta$ which is $\delta \leq 1/2$. In state B, we need $0 \geq -15 + 0\delta$, which is true for all values of δ So this strategy is optimal when $\delta \leq 0.5$.

Hence, for $\delta \geq 0.5$, Alice's optimal (stationary) strategy against grim by Bob is precisely the grim strategy, not only from the start of the game but also from the start of every round, given the history up to that round. Grim versus grim is subgame perfect if (and only if) $\delta \geq 0.5$

Let me reiterate and emphasize what just happened. The Appendix 6 dynamic-programming solution produces an optimal solution starting from any state of the process. So:

1. Suppose that Alice is playing strategy σ against Bob's strategy σ', and Bob's σ' creates for Alice a stationary sequential decision problem with states, the sort of thing depicted in Figures A15.2 and A15.3.

2. And suppose that, if we use dynamic programming to find Alice's optimal stationary response in the sequential decision problem created for her by Bob's strategy σ', her optimal stationary strategy turns out to be σ.

3. Then she is playing a best response to σ' for every proper subgame.

4. If we turn this argument around and find that σ' is Bob's best stationary response to σ, then σ against σ' is a subgame-perfect Nash equilibrium. (And this works for more than two players, although all the examples I'll provide are for two players and, moreover, for cases where σ and σ' are identical.)

Here are two more examples: "two rounds of punishment"; and "one round of compensation."

If $\delta \geq (\sqrt{5} - 1)/2$, the strategy "two rounds of punishment" versus itself constitutes a subgame-perfect equilibrium

First, we must define this strategy. It involves, for any partial history h_t of play up to (but not including) round t, action prescriptions that are based on the *current state*, where h_t is assigned to be in one of three states, C, $P1$, or $P2$, as follows: For given h_t and $s < t$, let h_s be the partial history up to but not including round s that is part of h_t. Classify h_0 as being in state C. Then, inductively:

1. If h_{s-1} is state C and either player betrays in round $s - 1$, the state h_s is $P1$. If both players cooperated in round $t - 1$, the state stays as C.

2. If h_{s-1} is state $P1$, then h_s is state $P2$, regardless of what happens in round $s - 1$.

3. If h_{s-1} is state $P2$, then h_s is state C, regardless of what happens in round $s - 1$.

And once h_t is classified in this fashion, the strategy *two rounds of punishment* prescribes choosing cooperation in state C (if the state of h_t is C), and it prescribes betrayal in states $P1$ and $P2$.

To put this strategy profile in words: The two play C unless and until one or the other or both betray. Then, for two rounds, both betray. But, after two rounds of (mutual) punishment, regardless of what the two players do during those two rounds, cooperation is restored.

Suppose Bob is using this strategy. What is Alice's optimal response? The methodology should by now be clear: We look at the problem from Alice's perspective as a single-person sequential decision problem and see for which values of δ, if any, the prescribed strategy is unimprovable.

First compute (for each state) the value of following this strategy: In state C, if she follows the strategy, she'll get 10 every period, for a net present value of $10/(1 - \delta)$. In state $P1$, she gets 0, then 0, and then $10/(1 - \delta)$, for a net present value of $10\delta^2/(1 - \delta)$. And in state $P2$, good times are restored after one period of punishment, for a net present value of $10\delta/(1 - \delta)$.

Unimprovability in states $P1$ and $P2$ is trivial: The evolution to the next state is independent of what the players do, so Alice should definitely play her stage-game dominant strategy, which is to betray. The only real question is whether betraying in state C is or is not better than cooperation. If she does betray immediately and then goes back to the strategy posited, she gets 20 immediately and then, beginning next round, 0, then 0, and then 10 for the rest of time, for a net present value of 20 $+ 10\delta^3/(1 - \delta)$. Thus the test for unimprovability is

$$10/(1-\delta) \geq 20+10\delta^3/(1-\delta), \quad \text{or} \quad 10 \geq 20(1-\delta)+10\delta^3, \quad \text{or} \quad 0 \geq 10-20\delta+10\delta^3.$$

We can rewrite this inequality as $0 \geq 10(1-\delta) - 10\delta(1-\delta^2)$, and factoring out $1-\delta$, this is $0 \geq 10 - 10\delta(1 - \delta) = 10 - 10\delta + 10\delta^2$. Apply the quadratic formula to get the asserted result: The strategy is unimprovable as long as $\delta \geq (\sqrt{5} - 1)/2$.[3]

The strategy *two rounds of punishment* is like *grim*, in that if either player betrays in state C, sure punishment ensues. The length of the punishment period is shorter—two periods instead of "forever more"—but the nature of the punishment is the same: The players resort to betray–betray, which gives both 0. Because the punishment is less severe, it takes a larger δ for the punishment to be adequate to the task of keeping both cooperating; if we had formulated *three rounds of punishment* (with one state C and three punishment states), the required δ would be less than for *two rounds* but still greater than the 0.5 that works for *grim*.

But there is a possible problem with both *grim* and *N rounds of punishment*. They do give (for high enough δ) subgame perfect Nash equilibria. But, what if, in the middle of a punishment triggered, say, by Bob, Bob says to Alice, "This is

---

[3] Now that we have the result, here are two exercises for you to try: First, why is one round of punishment insufficient for any $\delta < 1$? And second, what if, in translating a history h_t into one of the three states, we changed the rules so that, from state C, if in the current round both players betray, the state remains C rather than transitioning to $P1$? (Answer: it makes no difference, and the real question is: Why not?)

silly. I regret what I did, but we are both better off if we forget this and restore cooperation."

If Alice falls for this line, she is (of course) setting herself up for more betrayal by Bob, followed by more tearful speeches about how it was all a mistake and he'll never do it again. But wouldn't it be better to arrange things so that, if Bob betrays Alice, Alice gets some compensation before cooperation can be restored. Here's one way this could be done:

When is "one round of compensation" versus itself subgame perfect?

We set this up with three states, C, PA, and PB. PA is a mnemonic for "punish Alice" and PB is "punish Bob." States evolve as follows (and these rules are used to determine the state after any history h_t, by applying the rules beginning in state C at h_0). From state C, if both players betray or both cooperate, the state stays C. If, in state C, Alice betrays and Bob cooperates, the state changes to PA, and symmetrically if Bob betrays and Alice cooperates. From, say, PA, if Alice cooperates, the next state is C, regardless of what Bob does. If Alice betrays in state PA, the state remains PA, again regardless of what Bob does. And similarly for PB.

In this context, the strategy *one round of compensation* for, say, Alice, is: In state C, cooperate. In state PA, cooperate. In state PB, betray. For Bob, the strategy is symmetrical: Cooperate in states C and PB, and betray in state PA. If Bob is playing this strategy, Alice's sequential decision problem has the structure shown in Figure A15.4. Note that this is predicated on Bob playing *one round of compensation*. In particular, the rule that from state C, if both sides choose to betray, the state remains C, does not apply in formulating Alice's problem, because Bob "never" chooses to betray in state C. However, this rule is needed to evaluate which of the three states prevails after some histories h_t.

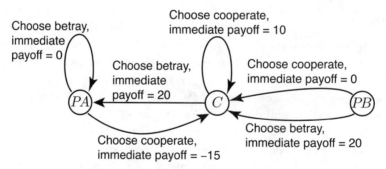

Figure A15.4. Alice's sequential decision problem if Bob plays the strategy *one round of compensation*

If, in this structure, Alice plays *one round of compensation*, her payoffs are: In state C, she plays C, gets an immediate 10, and it is 10s for all the rest of the game, for a net present value of $10/(1 - \delta)$. In state PA, she chooses to take her medicine and cooperate, for an immediate -15 and a continuation of $10/(1 - \delta)$, for a net present value of $-15 + 10\delta/(1 - \delta)$. And, in state PB, she betrays, for an immediate 20 and a continuation starting next period of $10/(1 - \delta)$, for a net $20 + 10\delta/(1 - \delta)$.

The three inequalities for unimprovability of this strategy (played against itself by Bob) are

For state A: $\quad 10/(1 - \delta) \geq 20 + \delta\left[-15 + 10\delta/(1 - \delta)\right],$

for state PA: $-15 + 10\delta/(1 - \delta) \geq 0 + \delta\left[-15 + 10\delta/(1 - \delta)\right]$, and

for state PB: $\quad 20 + 10\delta/(1 - \delta) \geq 0 + 10\delta/(1 - \delta).$

(Make sure you can derive each of these inequalities.) The first inequality holds if $\delta \geq 0.4$, the second if $\delta \geq 0.6$, and the third (obviously) holds for all δ. So the strategy is unimprovable for $\delta \geq 0.6$; the profile of this strategy played against itself is a subgame-perfect Nash equilibrium as long as $\delta \geq 0.6$.

Here are a few (somewhat obvious) remarks about this strategy profile. The two serious "unimprovability" inequalities represent the ideas that: (1) for Alice in state C, an immediate payoff of 20 isn't enough to initiate punishment against herself; and (2) Alice, in the state where she is supposed to be punished, is willing to accept her unhappy fate, in order to get back to state C. The third inequality—that Alice chooses to betray in state PB—which holds for all δ, is that Alice is willing and even eager to accept a "free" betrayal in compensation for Bob having betrayed at some earlier point. In other words, if a player betrays, he can only restore cooperation by cooperating while accepting betrayal. The critical inequality—the inequality for unimprovability in state PA—says that future cooperation is worth accepting this punishment.

What about two or more rounds of compensation and punishment? One could formulate such strategies, but in the context of this problem, with these specific numbers, it is unnecessary. The unimprovability inequality for state C says that one round of punishment (while compensating the other side) is sufficient to ensure continued cooperation. More rounds of punishment would only strengthen an inequality that is (for $\delta \geq 0.4$) already strong enough. And more rounds of punishment would make the unimprovability inequality for PA harder to achieve, in the sense that it would take a larger value of δ: More punishment increases the cost, hence decreases the willingness to accept punishment in order to restore cooperation.

Of course, in (say) state PA, Alice would like to convince Bob to let bygones be bygones and go immediately to restored cooperation. But, in this equilibrium, Bob would never agree: He is due to get a free 10 units of payoff over what he'd get by agreeing to Alice's proposal to restore cooperation immediately. Put it this way: The actions in, say, state PA do two things at once; they punish Player A *and also* compensate Player B. In terms of having a (subgame-perfect) Nash equilibrium, the punishment part is what matters: The threat of punishment keeps players honest in state C, and the relative value of restored cooperation (relative to the cost of submitting to punishment) provides an offending player with the incentive to "take her medicine." The value of the compensation provided doesn't enter into the on-path equilibrium computations. But the value of that compensation adds insurance that players will not be hoodwinked into letting their counterparties "off the hook."

However, the name is *one round of compensation* and not *one round of punishment*. While the two activities (punishing one player while compensating the other) are certainly tied, and while only one round of punishment is "scheduled" for a player who betrays, if the betraying player doesn't accept the punishment and compensate his or her rival, the punishment continues. Perhaps a better (but much longer) name for this is: *If you betray, you must show contrition for one round to restore cooperation.*

Summing up these examples

The first-order lesson is clear. Although betrayal is strictly dominant in the prisoners' dilemma game played once and once only, in repeated play of the prisoners' dilemma, cooperation can be sustained as a Nash and even as a subgame-perfect Nash equilibrium, as long as the discount factor δ is high enough. This requires the right sort of reactive strategy: Alice tells Bob that she will treat him well (cooperate) as long as he treats her well, but if he ever takes advantage of her good nature, she will punish him. For $\delta \geq 0.5$, tit-for-tat provides punishment sufficient to keep Bob "honest" along the path of play; to get cooperation along the path of play with subgame perfection requires one of the modifications sketched above.

Among these modifications, *one round of compensation* has the most appeal, because it compensates the offended party while punishing the offending party. Since, in equilibrium, there is never any offence, this might be viewed as an unnecessary feature. But: (1) In *grim* and *two rounds of punishment*, the punishment is dissipative; it hurts both the offender and the party offended. As noted previously, this raises the specter of the offended party forgiving the offender, to avoid the cost of the punishment. (2) When we introduce the possibility of noisy observation of the actions of the parties (in Section A15.6), equilibria that involve compensation linked to punishment will be more efficient than those that punish both parties in order to provide incentives to one.

And more variations

We could look at other variations. The equilibria constructed so far share two characteristics: The outcomes—measured in the expected payoffs of the two players—are efficient. And, in this symmetric game, the outcomes are symmetric.

Two examples of inefficient equilibria are:

1. Alice and Bob choose to cooperate in even-numbered rounds and to betray in odd-numbered rounds, as long as they both adhere to this pattern. But if either one ever chooses to betray in an even-numbered round, they both choose betray in all subsequent rounds.

2. Alice chooses to cooperate in even-numbered rounds and betray in odd-numbered rounds. Bob chooses to betray in even-numbered rounds and cooperate in odd-numbered rounds. Except that if Alice ever betrays in an even-numbered round

or Bob betrays in an odd-numbered round, they both choose betray in all subsequent rounds.

These examples are both subgame-perfect Nash equilibria as long as δ is close enough to 1. For the first equilibrium, δ must be greater or equal to $\sqrt{0.5}$, which is approximately 0.7071. The second requires $\delta \geq (\sqrt{7}-1)/2$, which is approximately 0.8229. (You should be able to reproduce my numbers.) Note that in each of these, I'm using the severity of "grim punishment" for any deviation from cooperation when called for.

These are both inefficient, and the second is somewhat asymmetric. (Alice has to cooperate first, so she is a bit disadvantaged relative to Bob.) This asymmetry can be seen by computing the equilibrium net present values at the initial node for, say, $\delta = 0.95$. For the efficient "always cooperate along the path of play" equilibria constructed previously, both players have on-path net present values of $10/(1 - \delta) = 200$. In the first of these two, at the start, each has net present value equal to (approximately) 102.5641. In the second, Alice's initial net present value (at $\delta = 0.95$) is approximately 41.0256, while Bob's is approximately 58.9844.

A point to note here is that, given a punishment regime, such as *grim for any deviation*, the lower is the player's value for sticking to the equilibrium, the higher δ must be to sustain the equilibrium, because keeping to the equilibrium is worth less relative to what might be gained by a defection from it. Somewhat roughly put, more efficient equilibria are easier to sustain than are less efficient equilibria.

It might be hard to imagine why players would settle on a less efficient equilibrium. But it is not so hard to imagine why one player or the other might have the "bargaining ability" required to insist on unequal treatment. For instance, in the second inefficient equilibrium just given, Alice and Bob have to bargain over who "goes first." More to the point, equilibria can be efficient but result in unequal treatment: Recall from earlier the strategy *greedy grim* that was suggested for Alice:

In even-numbered rounds, cooperate. In odd-numbered rounds, betray. Follow this pattern as long as the opponent never betrays and you don't deviate from this pattern. But if your opponent ever betrays, or you deviate from the pattern betray in all subsequent rounds.

Suppose Bob, in response to this strategy, plays *wimpy grim*:

In all rounds, cooperate, unless and until Alice betrays in an even-numbered round or you (Bob) betray. In either of those events, betray in all subsequent rounds.

This is never an equilibrium, because it asks Bob to alternate payoffs of -15 in odd-numbered rounds with 10 in even-numbered rounds. In the first odd-numbered round that comes along, he is bound to defect. And, knowing this, both he and Alice will defect in round 0 as well.

However, suppose we make Alice a little less greedy. She says she'll betray in periods $0, 3, 6, \ldots$, expecting Bob to always cooperate, and Bob is willing to go along. This means Bob's stream of payoffs, along the path of play, will be $-15, 10, 10, -15, 10, 10, \ldots$. The critical moment for his willingness to participate in this scheme comes in periods whose number is divisible by 3 and those of the form $3n + 2$; that is, in periods $0, 3, 6, \ldots$, his payoff from following the scheme is

$$-15 + 10\delta + 10\delta^7 - 15\delta^3 + \ldots = \frac{-15 + 10\delta + 10\delta^2}{1 - \delta^3},$$

which must be greater than or equal to zero for him to go along. And in periods $2, 5, 8,$, his payoff is

$$\frac{10 - 15\delta - 10\delta^2}{1 - \delta^3},$$

which must be no less than 20. The first necessary inequality is satisfied for δ greater or equal to (approximately) 0.8229, while the second requires $\delta \geq 0.9158$ (approximately). (For such values of δ, Alice clearly never wishes to betray when she is meant to cooperate.)

A15.3. The (Straightforward) Folk Theorem(s)

That's enough examples. Time for some theorems. The "straightforward" folk theorem[4] is actually a collection of results of the following general character: An N-player strategic-form game Γ is fixed; this is the stage game. This game is played by the N players repeatedly, at times $t = 0, 1, 2, \ldots$ After each round of play, players are informed about the action profile chosen in that round. Each player's overall payoff for the grand repeated game is the discounted sum of the player's stage-game payoffs using the (common) discount factor $\delta < 1$. In this setting, the question to be answered is: What is the set of (subgame-perfect) Nash equilibria (or payoffs resulting from Nash equilibria) as δ approaches 1?

The following notation will be used.

- Write A_n for the set of (pure) actions available to player n in the stage game,[5] A for the set of stage-game action profiles $a = (a_n)_{n \in \mathcal{N}}$, $v_n(a)$ for n's stage-game payoff at the stage-game action profile a, and $V := \{v(a) = (v_n(a))_{n \in \mathcal{N}} \in R^N\}$ for the set of "stage-game payoff profiles" feasible at different stage-game action profiles.

- Write $\mathcal{V}$ for the convex hull of V. Please note that $\mathcal{V}$ is, in general, larger than the space of stage-game payoff profiles that result from independent mixtures of (possibly mixed) strategies by the players. Since $V \subseteq R^N$ (where $\mathcal{N}$ is a finite set of cardinality N), Carathéodory's Theorem (Proposition A3.5 in Volume I)

---

[4] Results in this collection are known as "folk theorems" because the basic idea predates any formal theorizing, and no one is brazen enough to take credit for that basic idea. Which is not to say that the originators of formal, exact results and proofs of those results do not deserve credit for their ingenuity and insights.

[5] I continue the refer to "strategies" in the stage game Γ as *actions*, reserving *strategies* for strategies in the repeated game.

tells us that every point $v \in V$ can be written as a convex combination of no more than $N + 1$ points in V.

- Let $\mathcal{E}$ denote the set of stage-game Nash-equilibrium profiles $(\sigma_n)_{n \in \mathcal{N}}$; note that included here are mixed-action equilibria.[6] Write $V^{\mathcal{E}}$ for the space of Nash-equilibrium (expected-) payoff profiles.

A folk theorem based on grim Nash punishment

Proposition A15.1. *Suppose that V is bounded; specifically, there is some real number B such that, if $v = (v_1, \ldots, v_N) \in V$, then $B \geq |v_n|$ for $n \in \mathcal{N}$.[7] If there exists $e \in \mathcal{E}$, with $v(e) \in V^{\mathcal{E}}$, and $v \in V$, $v = v(a)$ for $a = (a_1, \ldots, a_N) \in A$, such that $v_n > v_n(e)$ for all $n \in \mathcal{N}$, then for all δ close enough to 1, there is a subgame-perfect Nash equilibrium in which each player repeatedly plays a_n along the path of play, and if any player deviates from this, all players (grimly) play the Nash equilibrium e.*

Proof. This proposition doesn't require much of a proof, given the analysis of the grim strategy perfect equilibrium for the repeated prisoners' dilemma. Player n, by deviating, will receive a payoff bounded above by $B + \delta v_n(e)/(1-\delta)$. By playing the equilibrium strategy, she gets $v_n/(1 - \delta)$. So (from any starting point along the path of play such that no one has deviated previously) sticking to the equilibrium is unimprovable, hence optimal, as long as

$$\frac{v_n}{1 - \delta} \geq B + \delta \frac{v_n(e)}{1 - \delta}, \quad \text{or} \quad B - v_n(e) \leq \delta \left(\frac{v_n - v_n(e)}{1 - \delta} \right).$$

Since $v_n > v_n(e)$, the limit of the right-hand side approaches infinity as $\delta \to 1$. Therefore, this inequality will hold for ϵ close enough to 1. (From the root of any subgame at which someone deviated previously, the strategies call for repeated play of the Nash equilibrium e, which is obviously a Nash equilibrium for the subgame.) ∎

Extending Proposition A15.1 to payoffs in $\mathcal{V}$

This result can easily be extended from payoffs in V to payoffs in $\mathcal{V}$, if we permit the players to access, at the start of each round, a *publicly observable randomizing device*. This modeling conceit supposes that, before play in round t, all the players observe the outcome of a random variable U_t, such that $\{U_t; t = 0, 1, 2, \ldots\}$ is an independent sequence of random variables, each of which is uniformly distributed on the interval $[0, 1]$, and such that none of the players has any information about

---

[6] I haven't said that the A_n are finite, and if they are uncountable, technical issues about the definition of mixed strategies can arise, with which I will not deal. It is fine to read this section under the assumption that each A_n is finite, although in some applications in the text, infinite A_n will be considered.

[7] If each A_n is finite, this condition is of course satisfied.

the value of U_t until after actions in round $t - 1$ are selected.[8] Then the following proposition holds.

Proposition A15.1′. *Suppose that V is bounded and that $v \in V$ is such that $v_n > v_n^e$ for $v^e = v(e)$ for some $e \in \mathcal{E}$. Use Carathéodory's Theorem to write $v = \sum_{j=1}^{N+1} \alpha^j v^j$, for $v^j = v(a^j) \in V$, $\alpha^j \geq 0$, and $\sum \alpha^j = 1$. Suppose each player behaves as follows:*

- *Each player chooses her action in round t according to the following rule, as long as no player has deviated before round t from this rule: For $j = 1, \ldots, N + 1$, let $\beta_j = \sum_{k=0}^{j-1} \alpha^k$. (By convention, $\beta_0 = 0$.) Then, if $U_t \in [\beta_j, \beta_{j+1})$, each player chooses her part of the strategy profile a^j that gives the payoffs v^j. (Use the closed interval $[\beta_{j-1}, 1]$ for $j = N$.) :*

- *If, in round t, any player has deviated from the previous rule in any earlier period, each player chooses her part of the Nash equilibrium e.*

Then for all δ sufficiently close to 1, these strategies constitute a subgame-perfect Nash equilibrium in which player n's expected payoff is $v_n/(1 - \delta)$.

The proof is virtually the same as before. Because $v_n > v_n^e$ for all n and V is bounded, a one-time deviation followed by v_n^e in all future rounds can't compensate for following the equilibrium, for δ close enough to 1. A bit of care, though, is required: For each player n, it must be that playing her part of each a^j is better than defecting. Since we have an upper bound on the value of defecting and a lower bound on how bad any individual equilibrium payoff can be, there is a δ sufficiently close to 1 so that sticking to the rule is better than defecting.

Because the publicly observable randomizing device is an artificial construct,[9] it is interesting to know whether it is necessary for this result. By switching among the $N + 1$ pure-action stage-game profiles that make up the convex combination v, can this result be obtained without this artificial device? It can be; see Sorin (1986). And if you are willing to settle for a partial result, it is relatively straightforward to show that the set of expected payoffs obtainable as $\delta \to 1$ is dense in V: Take a point $v \in V$, which is $v = \sum_{j=1}^{N+1} \alpha_j v^j$ for $v^j \in V$. For very large M, we can approximate this convex combination by a convex combination of the form $\sum_{j=1}^{N+1} \gamma_j v^j$, where each γ_j is a rational number of the form ℓ/M. Then create a rule where the players play the various a^j (the profiles that give the v^j) in blocks of size M. And then let δ be so close to 1 that in each block, the payoffs to the players approximate $\sum_{j=1}^{N+1} \gamma_j v^j$ and such that no player wishes to defect. (I leave the ϵ's and δ's that give this result to you.)

---

[8]   The assumption here is that the value of each U_t is observable by all the players. Compare with the construction of a correlated equilibrium in Appendix 9, where a randomizing device is used by an "neutral third party" to induce correlation in the choices made by players. In that construction, it is important that the players receive only partial information about the outcome of the randomizing device.

[9]   And if the players are oligopolists, it would certainly seem to run afoul of antitrust law.

Minmax payoffs

Suppose that Γ, the stage game, is the two-player game depicted in Figure A15.5. This is the prisoners' dilemma game, with a third action added for Alice. This is not a very attractive action for Alice—it is strictly dominated by betrayal—and so it doesn't change the set of Nash equilibria for the stage game and therefore has no impact on the conclusion of Propositions A15.1 or A15.1'.

| | | Bob | |
		Betray Alice	Cooperate with Alice
	Betray Bob	0, 0	20, –15
Alice	Cooperate with Bob	–15, 20	10, 10
	Confess to stuff neither did	–10, –10	–10, –5

Figure A15.5. A stage game where Alice has an additional (crazy) action.

Specifically in Figure A15.6(a), the lightly and heavily shaded areas together constitute the "per-period" set $\mathcal{V}$ for Alice and Bob in the original prisoners' dilemma game. (A "per-period payoff" is a payoff available in the stage game, which is (then) a payoff available for the repeated game pre-multiplied by $1 - \delta$. The point $(10, 10)$ in the graph means, for a given δ, the payoffs $10/(1 - \delta)$ for both Alice and Bob in the full repeated game.) The unique Nash equilibrium for the game is the point $(0, 0)$, so the more darkly shaded regions are the per-period payoff pairs that, per Proposition A15.1', can be sustained as subgame-perfect Nash-equilibrium payoffs. (The bottom and left borders of this region are *not* included. Proposition A15.1' requires a strict inequality between the payoffs to be attained and the Nash-equilibrium payoffs.)

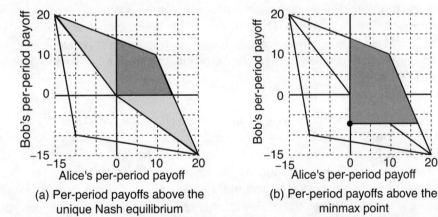

(a) Per-period payoffs above the
unique Nash equilibrium

(b) Per-period payoffs above the
minmax point

Figure A15.6. Using minmax threats. Panel a shows the (two-tone shaded) region $\mathcal{V}$ for the original prisoners' dilemma and (more darkly shaded) the region of per-period payoffs that can be sustained as subgame-perfect equilibria as per Proposition A15.1' for δ sufficiently close to 1. (The borders of the shaded area to the west and south are *not* sustainable.) Panel b shows the expanded set of per-period payoff pairs that are attainable as Nash equilibria, when the third row in Figure A15.5 is added, as this changes Bob's minmax value to -7.5.

Adding the third row expands the set $\mathcal{V}$—the new boundary is formed by the line segments joining $(-10, -10)$ to $(-15, 20)$ and $(20, -15)$, as shown—but doesn't change what Proposition A15.1' says can be attained in an equilibrium.

However, the addition of the third row allows Alice to "threaten" Bob more than before. Suppose she makes the following declaration to Bob:

> Bob, I want to use the public randomizing device as follows: If, in any period, $U_t \leq 0.56$, then I betray you, and you cooperate. If $U_t > 0.56$, then we both cooperate. This will give me a payoff per round of $0.56 \times 20 + 0.44 \times 10 = 15.6$, while your expected payoff will be $-15 \times 0.56 + 10 \times 0.44 = -4$. And if you ever deviate from these instructions, I will play my third option forever after, which means a per-period payoff of -5 for you.

If Bob finds this credible, compliance with this unfair scheme is his best response (for δ sufficiently close to 1). Bob may try to negotiate a more equitable arrangement, of course. But the point is, this makes the per-period payoff vector $(15.6, -4)$ the outcome of a *Nash*—but not necessarily a subgame-perfect—equilibrium. Subgame perfection comes in a bit. Start with a definition:

Definition A15.2. *For a strategic-form game Γ with player set $\mathcal{N}$, the **minmax value** for player $n \in \mathcal{N}$ is the value*

$$\underline{v}_n = \min_{\sigma_{\neg n}} \left[\max_{a_n} v_n(a_n, \sigma_{\neg n}) \right].$$

In this definition, we are asking: What is the worst that all the players except n can do to n in a single play of the game Γ, if n anticipates what they will do and optimizes accordingly? The players other than n choose a strategy profile, *which may be mixed*; hence $\sigma_{\neg n}$, against which n chooses her best response a_n. And all the players except for n, taking into account that n will play her best response against their mixed-strategy profile $\sigma_{\neg n}$, choose the profile that minimizes what player n can get.

Two qualifications are in order.

1. This definition is perfectly sensible mathematically if the action sets A_n are all finite, as long as we understand that $v_n(a_n, \sigma_{\neg n})$ means n's expected payoff if she chooses a_n and her opponents choose the mixed profile $\sigma_{\neg n}$. But if the A_n are infinite, the usual qualifications arise about defining mixtures of more than countably many actions and computing expectations, as well as new issues about whether we need to speak in terms of "infsup" instead of "minmax." Having raised these issues, I will not deal with them; you can assume that the A_n are all finite, or when you encounter a context where this doesn't hold, deal with these issues in that specific context.

2. In the definition, if there are more than three players, and if we are computing the minmax value for player 1, the definition assumes that players 2 and 3, if they mix at all, mix independently. If they could correlate their actions—say,

through the use of a randomizing device that they observe and player 1 does not, they may be able to inflict even worse punishment on player 1.[10]

Going back to the game in Figure A15.5, betraying Bob is a strictly dominant action for Alice and so, whatever Bob chooses, Alice's best response to Bob's choice in terms of her own (expected) payoff is betrayal. Hence, the worst punishment Bob can inflict on Alice is to betray her: Alice's minmax value is 0.

Computing Bob's minmax value is not so easy. Alice, seeking to hurt Bob as much as possible, will certainly avoid cooperating with him. If she betrays him, his best response is to betray her, giving him a payoff of 0. If she plays the third strategy (which I'll call *confess*, although the numbers don't quite match this story), his best response is cooperation, which gives him -5. However, by mixing, she can make him suffer even more. Suppose she mixes between betrayal and confession, with probability p on betrayal; then his two responses give him payoffs of

$$-15p - 5(1-p) = -10p - 5 \text{ if he cooperates, and } -10(1-p) \text{ if he betrays.}$$

If Alices chooses betrayal with probability $1/4$ and confession with probability $3/4$, Bob's best response is either, and both give him a payoff of -7.5. You should convince yourself that this is his minmax payoff.[11]

Write $\underline{v}$ for the vector of minmax values; that is, $\underline{v} := (\underline{v}_1, \ldots, \underline{v}_N)$. It is worth noting that, while $\underline{v} \in \mathcal{V}$ for both the simple prisoners' dilemma game and for the game in Figure A15.5, there are cases in which $\underline{v} \notin \mathcal{V}$. A simple example is the following three-player game.

Alice, Bob, and Carol are the players. Alice's action set is {*name Bob, name Carol*}, with Bob and Carol having symmetric action sets. If Alice *names Bob* and Bob *names Alice*, then Alice and Bob each get a payoff of 1, and Carol gets 0, regardless of whether Carol *names Alice* or *Bob*. Similar rules apply if Alice *names Carol* and Carol *names Alice*, and if Bob *names Carol* and Carol *names Bob*. And if no pair out of the three name each other, then each gets a payoff of $1/10$. It is evident that the minmax value for each player is 0; if Alice and Bob wish to minmax Carol, they simply name each other. But in every outcome (for every $v \in V$), the sum of the payoffs is either 2 or $3/10$. Hence for every point in $\mathcal{V}$, the sum of the payoffs is between 2 and $3/10$. Which means that $\underline{v} = (0,0,0) \notin \mathcal{V}$. Moreover, note that since $(1,1,0)$, $(1,0,1)$, and $(0,0,1)$ are all members of V, $(2/3, 2/3, 2/3)$ is in $\mathcal{V}$. Since $(1/10, 1/10, 1/10) \in V \subset \mathcal{V}$, this implies that $\mathcal{V}$ is *solid*, meaning that it contains an open set in R^3. (You'll see why this property is important in a moment.)

---

[10] Here's an example: Each player has two actions, $\{x_n, y_n\}$, for $n = 1, 2, 3$. If players 2 and 3 both choose their x option or both choose their y option, and if player 1 matches their choice, player 1 gets 1; if they choose the same option (both x_2 and x_3, or y_2 and y_3), and player 1 doesn't match their choice, player 1 gets 0. If players 2 and 3 choose different actions—say, 2 chooses x_2 and 3 chooses y_3—then player 1 gets 1 regardless of what she chooses. What is 1's minmax if players 2 and 3 cannot correlate their actions? What would be player 1's minmax if they could correlate their actions? (Answers: $3/4$ and $1/2$.)

[11] For two-player games, finding the minmax for each player involves a relatively simple linear-programming problem. For more than two players, the requirement that the players other than player n must independently mix, finding minmax values is more complex.

What is going on here is clear: Two players minmax the third player by ganging up on the third. And it is impossible, per the rules of the game, that every two-player set simultaneously gangs up on the third player.

This may suggest that, perhaps, $\underline{v} \in V$ if the game is a two-player game. But that is not true. I leave it to you to show that in the two-player, 3×3 game depicted in Figure A15.7(a), the minmax values for both players is 0. And V, which is the shaded polygon depicted in Figure 15.7(b), does not include $(0, 0)$.

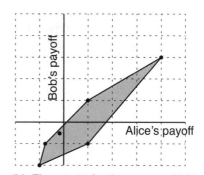

	Bob		
	-1/10, -1/2	-3/4, -1	1, 1
Alice	-1, -2	1, 1	1, -1
	1, 1	-1, -2	4, 3

(a) A 3 x 3 game in which both players have minmax values of 0

(b) The set V for the game, which excludes the vector of minmax values

Figure A15.7. A two-player game in which $\underline{v} \notin V$

The classic folk theorem

Proposition A15.3. The classic folk theorem. *Allowing players to access a publicly observable randomizing device, and assuming a bound on the set of payoffs in the stage game, any per-period payoff vector $v \in V$ such that, for each n, $v_n > \underline{v}_n$, can be realized as per-period payoffs in a Nash equilibrium, for all δ sufficiently close to 1.*

Hence, adding the third row expands the range of per-period Nash-equilibrium payoffs for Alice and Bob to the shaded region in Figure A15.7(b), again excluding the bottom and left boundaries.

The proof is probably apparent and, in any case, is simple. Players follow the on-path rules: Based on the public randomization, players do their assigned part in supporting the per-period expected payoffs of v. If two or more players deviate, it is ignored (just to have some definite strategies for the grand repeated game). If one player deviates, then for all future periods, that player is minmaxed by the others. Because of the bound on value of deviating and the "distance" between v_n and $\underline{v}_n$ for each player, there is a δ close enough to 1 such that deviating is not worthwhile. Hence players will follow the prescribed strategies along the path of play.

(If a publicly observable randomizing device is not available, the comments offered after Proposition A15.1' apply. But, certainly, any point $v = v(a) \in V$ that lies strictly above the minmax value vector can be implemented in a Nash equilibrium.)

The classic folk theorem with subgame perfection

Of course, these strategies prescribe a Nash equilibrium and not (necessarily) a subgame-perfect equilibrium. One worries, therefore, that faced with a defection, players will not carry out the task of minmaxing the defector. Hence, the threat of minmax punishment may fail to be credible, and players may defect.

Aumann and Shapley (1976) show how to implement the Folk Theorem with subgame perfection added in, in the context of games in which players don't discount payoffs but instead evaluate an infinite sequence of payoffs by the limit infimum of the Cesàro average sums of their payoffs. Roughly speaking, a deviator is punished for a finite length of time, long enough so that the gains from deviating are wiped out by the punishment. Then play returns to "cooperation." Players are willing to participate in the punishment, because it lasts only a finite amount of time, and so it doesn't affect their long-run average payoffs. Maximizing long-run average payoffs is, however, a fairly forgiving decision criterion, and one might hope for something stronger. Rubinstein (1979) uses instead an "overtaking optimality" criterion (where a player who refuses to participate in punishing a deviator is herself punished). [12] The interested reader should consult the original papers.

Concerning subgame-perfect implementation of the Classic Folk Theorem in a context with discounting, as the discount factor goes to 1, the seminal reference is Fudenberg and Maskin (1986). Here is a statement of their result:

Proposition A15.4. *Assume that V is bounded and solid (contains an open set in R^n). Then for any $v \in V$ such that $v_n > \underline{v}_n$ for all n, there exists a discount factor $\delta < 1$ such that, for all $\delta' \in (\delta, 1)$, the per-period payoffs v can be implemented as payoffs in a subgame-perfect Nash equilibrium in the repeated game with discount factor δ'.*

The proof in full detail is quite complex, and even advanced textbooks (in particular, Fudenberg and Tirole's (1991b) *Game Theory*) only provide the proof under simplifying assumptions. While I leave it to interested readers to chase down details, it is worthwhile to indicate how the construction goes and where difficulties arise.

Also, the proof given in the paper and repeated in Fudenberg and Tirole's textbook contains a minor glitch; it assumes that $\underline{v} \in V$. To circumvent the glitch, [13] my presentation proceeds in a slightly different order than does theirs.

Begin with the additional assumption that v is in the interior of V. Then, for some sufficiently small $\epsilon > 0$, we can find N points in V such that the nth of these points, v^n, has the form

$$v^n = (v_1 + \epsilon, v_2 + \epsilon, \ldots, v_{n-1} + \epsilon, v_n, v_{n+1} + \epsilon, \ldots, v_N + \epsilon)$$

for some $\epsilon > 0$.

---

[12] This treatment does raise questions about players knowing when another player is failing to participate in a mixed-strategy punishment regime.

[13] I use a fix suggested by Eric Maskin.

The equilibrium is constructed as follows: Play begins with all players doing what it takes to implement the payoff vector v, which continues unless and until some player deviates from her assigned role.

Difficulty #1: If v is a convex combination of several (no more than $N + 1$, of course) $v(a)$, either a publicly observable randomizing device is needed, or one must really get down in the weeds of how v is implemented. Things are easiest if $v = v(a)$ for some strategy profile a, and this is often one simplifying assumption that is made.

Deviations from the pattern of play that implements v by two or more players are ignored. But if one player deviates, then a phase of play begins in which all players other than the deviator play their joint minmax strategy against the deviator, for a number T of rounds that is chosen so that deviating from the first phase of play (of v) is not worthwhile. If two or more of the players deviate simultanously in this punishment phase, it is ignored; if one player deviates—and the concern here is that a player may receive very poor payoffs while participating in the punishment of another player by minmaxing that other player, and so will want to deviate—we go immediately (without finishing the punishment of the original deviator) to a phase in which the deviator from punishment is herself minmaxed for T periods. (To be a bit pedantic here, the logic of Nash equilibrium is that player n, contemplating a deviation from the play of v, must assume that she will undergo a full T periods of minmax punishment, as long as matters are arranged so that all players n' have no positive incentive to deviate from the punishment of n.)

Difficulty #2: In general, minmaxing another player involves playing a randomized strategy. And the player being minmaxed cannot be allowed to know what the randomizing players are going to do, so publicly observable random variables are of no help. In the original paper, Fudenberg and Maskin surmount this difficulty by assuming that in the next phase (see the next paragraph), matters are adjusted so that in this minmaxing phase, every player who is participating in punishing some other player is "compensated" later on for taking actions that, in the minmax phase, are personally more costly.[14]

And if play makes it through T rounds of punishment without incident: Suppose it was player n who was (last) successfully minmaxed for T periods. Players then implement the play of v^n. And if any one player deviates from their assigned tasks in this phase (as before, simultaneous deviations are ignored), that player is minmaxed for T periods, and so forth. Roughly, the idea is that a nondeviating player, say player ℓ, is rewarded with $v_\ell + \epsilon$, which is the "reward" for having minmaxed the miscreant in the previous stage.

Difficulty #1 again: Typically, the v^n will be convex combinations of $v(a)$, so it really helps to have the publicly observable randomizing device. Although, also again, many treatments of this construction, to keep things simple, make the

---

[14] This wouldn't be necessary if each player had access in each period to an ex ante privately observable, ex post verifiable randomizing device, so that each could choose her action based on the private signal she sees, and after the round is over, verify to the others that she "did the right thing." But this is probably carrying the use of such randomizing devices too far.

simplifying assumption that each $v^n = v(a^n)$ for some strategy profile a^n. This is not so bad an assumption as may seem, if you think of a stage game in which the A_ns are compact intervals of real numbers (or something topologically equivalent), and the v_n are continuous functions of the action choices of the players.

Having set up the basic scheme, to make it into an equilibrium, three parameters are adjusted. The first is ϵ, which is determined by the size of the open set around v. Next is T, which is set long enough so that no player, fearing being minmaxed, would defect either in the initial phase (the play of v) or the third phase (the play of v^n). And finally is δ, which in particular is essential for getting players to be willing to minmax miscreant fellows for T periods, with the reward being the return to v^n. Of course, the larger T must be to ensure that no deviations are profitable, the closer δ must be to 1, so that players, in off-path subgames where a player is meant to be minmaxed, will play their part.

This construction does not necessarily work if v is not in the interior of $\mathcal{V}$. In this case, proceed as follows. For each n, let $\hat{v}^n \in \mathcal{V}$ be the utility imputation for the players if all the players except for n take their minmax (possibly mixed) actions against n, and n plays her best response. Of course, $\hat{v}_n^n = \underline{v}_n$. Look at convex combinations of $\hat{v}^n$ and the originally specified v. For some α sufficiently close to 1, $\check{v}^n = \alpha v + (1 - \alpha)\hat{v}^n$ strictly exceeds $\underline{v}$ in all components (this is the part that requires α to be close to 1), and $\check{v}_n^n < v_n$. If $\check{v}^n$ is in the interior of $\mathcal{V}$, proceed to the next paragraph. If not, because $\mathcal{V}$ is both solid and convex, a payoff vector that is interior to $\mathcal{V}$ can be found that satisfies the inequalities of $\check{v}^n$. Replace $\check{v}^n$ with this interior point.

Hence, for each n, we have a vector $\check{v}^n$ in the interior of $\mathcal{V}$ such that $\check{v}_n^n < v_n$ and, for all n' (including n), $\check{v}_{n'}^n > \underline{v}_{n'}$. For each of these $\check{v}^n$, carry out the task of finding (a single) $\epsilon > 0$ sufficiently small so that, if we add ϵ to all components of $\check{v}^n$ except the nth component, we are still in $\mathcal{V}$.

Construct the equilibrium as before with one amendment. Play begins with the players implementing the original v. Ignore defections by two or more players. But if a single player, say m, deviates, then start minmaxing player m for T periods, *noting carefully that it was m who first defected*. And then, when and if T periods of minmaxing player n (which may be someone other than m, if players deviate in the minmax phase and so cause play to shift to minmaxing the deviator) are successfully completed, proceed as before, but implementing v^{mn}, where n is the player who was successfully minmaxed, and $v_{n'}^{mn} = \check{v}_{n'}^m + \epsilon$, if $n' \neq n$ and $= \check{v}_{n'}^m$ if $n' = n$. Finding the points $\check{v}^n$ first, then ϵ, then T, and finally δ, parameter values can be found—and in particular, δ close to 1 may be found—so this construction is a subgame-perfect Nash equilibrium.   ∎

My inclusion of an endproof mark is not serious, as I've only sketched a very clever and difficult proof.

Subsequent papers (for instance Abreu, Dutta, and Smith 1994) provide proofs of the basic result with weaker assumptions on $\mathcal{V}$ than that it is solid.

What does it all mean?

Roughly speaking, folk theorems say that, with repeated play, many feasible outcomes and patterns of outcomes can be implemented as Nash equilibria, if three conditions are met:

1. The future matters enough so that the temptations of the present are outweighed by the prospect of future punishment. Or, formally, δ must be close to 1.

2. (Repeating myself to make a different point), the future matters enough so that the temptations of the present are outweighed .... Here I refer to the formal assumption that the game is infinitely repeated. If, say, the stage game is repeated only, say, 10,000 times, one can wonder whether the lack of a restraining future in round 10,000 will "infect" earlier rounds.

3. Players who deviate for short-term personal gain can be detected and punished for their misdeeds. The formal assumption is that play in each round is observable to all players, and when convenient, a publicly observable randomizing device is available to allow V to be convexified in a manner that doesn't interfere with observability (and, in fact, allows for any mixture of pure-action profiles).[15]

Each of these conditions is the subject of a great deal of further research, some of which will be sketched in subsequent sections.

But the bigger picture here is that, when these conditions are met, one finds that many outcomes are Nash and even subgame-perfect outcomes. Which is very bad news for any analyst who wishes an answer to the question: "What will happen?" and relies solely on the criterion, "It's a subgame-perfect Nash equilibrium."

Recall from Chapter 17 the discussion of Fisher's "Games Economists Play" and his category of *exemplifying theory*. Fisher's objections to the rise of noncooperative analysis in the context of Industrial Organization was not limited to or even necessarily focused on the Folk Theorem.[16] But, certainly, the folk theorem is a poster child for exemplifying theory. Lots of outcomes are possible or, at least, satisfy the test of being an equilibrium. But "lots" is so many that it is reasonable to wonder whether this is progress or regress.

I think these results do help us to understand what might be the basic mechanics of sustainable collusion, in which competitors (or trading partners in a vertical relationship) can achieve outcomes in their relationships that, viewed as a static interaction, do not pass the Nash-equilibrium test. Namely, it takes a good balance of "good manners" backed up by "adequate threats" in the event that the good manners are not reciprocated.

But one shouldn't take seriously the elaborate dance among players that an exact subgame-perfect equilibrium requires. Put it this way: If, to sustain collusion,

---

[15] "Convenient" and not "required," because as already noted, one can mix pure-action profiles through time to achieve the same overall outcome for each player.

[16] In the Industrial Organization context, folk theorems are enlisted in the first instance concerning implicit collusion among oligopolists. (See Chapter 22.) But variations on the folk theorem also play an important role in the theories of output quality and vertical relations and supply chains.

real-life oligopolists must adhere to the very delicate equilibrium construction of Fudenberg and Maskin, then I doubt any real-life parties could get there. Where simple equilibria are possible—see the examples in Chapter 22 that are grounded in closer-to-real-life contexts—perhaps these are close to what we see in real life. While one certainly must admire the technical ingenuity of equilibrium constructions of the sort in Fudenberg and Maskin (and in the subsequent literature), the takeaways for economic analysis are much simpler and more direct.

In particular, the straightforward folk theorems of this section are supported by off-path behavior that, because those behaviors are effective, remain off-path. If these theories work as described in this section, we'd never see the elaborate dance of off-path punishment and reward, because (by definition) this dance is off-path. I have a lot more faith in what one learns from this variety of analysis for situations that are at least one level closer to reality, in that the situation provides for observation of what in this section is off the path of play. It is to those elaborations and extensions that we turn in Section A15.6.

A15.4. Discount Factors Bounded away from 1

The folk theorems of the previous section are all stated in terms of what can be achieved as $\delta \to 1$. In applications, there may be more interest in what can be achieved for a fixed $\delta < 1$.

1. In general, the "farther" is the payoff vector v that one is trying to achieve from the threatened punishment in the event of deviation, the greater will be the range of δ for which v can be achieved. This observation is a simple consequence of the fact that, the more one has to lose in the future by taking a short-run gain, the less the future in general must matter for the prospective loss to outweigh the prospective immediate gain. In this respect, note that payoff vectors v that are very far from the threatened punishment for some players but very close for others are "delicate" (require δ close to one), because every player needs to be on board, and, to use a somewhat trite adage, it is the weakest link that determines the strength of the chain.[17]

2. Given a vector $v \in \mathcal{V}$ above a Nash equilibrium outcome v^e for a stage-game Nash equilibrium e, it is straightforward to compute the range of δ that will allow v to be sustained as a subgame-perfect Nash equilibrium, if the equilibrium is based on grim punishment involving the play (forever after) of the equilibrium e. Indeed, if we have (say) two Nash equilibria, e and e', where e is better for some players than e', while the reverse is true for the rest, the range of δ for which v can be sustained with grim punishment may be made larger

---

[17] But, some delicacy here is required here: Often, the farther away the player is from the "threat point," the greater are the temptations of taking advantage in a single round. Or, put the other way, if the "on-path" behavior is close to the threat-point behavior, the gains from defection for a single round may be close to zero. See, for instance, the application of these ideas to repeated Cournot competition in Chapter 22 and, in particular, page 219.

if we choose the grim punishment regime of either e or e' forever after, based on who defects from the play that leads to v.

3. And if we are willing to give up subgame perfection, the range of δ for which v can be sustained is easily computed given the vector $\underline{v}$ of minmax values for each player, where the way that v is sustained is with the (imperfect) threat of minmaxing any (single) deviator forever.

But, if what is desired is the full range of discount factors δ for which v can be sustained with a subgame-perfect equilibrium, then matters get quite complex. It can be shown that, under conditions on the stage game, for each player n there is a least payoff that the player can receive in any subgame-perfect Nash equilibrium for each value of δ (see Fudenberg and Levine 1983 and Abreu 1988). If one could compute these least-payoff values, the computation of the range of δ that sustains a given payoff vector v would be relatively straightforward. To keep the exposition simple, suppose that $v = v(a)$ for some $a \in A$. For each player n, let $\bar{v}_n(a) = \max\{v(a'_n, a_{\neg n}); a'_n \in A_n\}$ (assuming the maximum exists, which is part of the conditions on the stage game). Finally, let $\underline{v}_n(\delta)$ be the value to player n of her "least value" subgame-perfect equilibrium. We can sustain v as a subgame-perfect Nash equilibrium most efficiently if the rule is: Everyone plays according to a as long as everyone has done so in the past. Deviations from a along the path of play by two or more players are ignored. And if n is the sole deviator along the path of play, the players implement whatever gives n her worst possible (subgame-perfect equilibrium) value $\underline{v}_n(\delta)$. This provides a subgame-perfect Nash equilibrium for discount factor δ as long as the unimprovability constraints

$$\bar{v}_n(a) + \delta \frac{\underline{v}_n(\delta)}{1 - \delta} \leq \frac{v_n(a)}{1 - \delta}, \quad \text{for all } n$$

are met. Unhappily, though, except in very special situations, computing the value of $\underline{v}_n(\delta)$ is not feasible.

For a detailed exposition on this point, see Fudenberg and Tirole (1991b, section 5.1.3).

A15.5. (So-Called) Finite Horizons

Suppose that, instead of playing the prisoners' dilemma game indefinitely, with payoffs in each round discounted and summed, Alice and Bob set out to play the game exactly 100 times. (Their payoffs can be added together without discounting or with discounting; it won't matter.)

Then, in any subgame-perfect equilibrium, whatever happened in rounds 1 to 99, both must necessarily betray the other in the 100th round, since that is the dominant strategy in the subgame. And, then, in round 99, they both must betray the other: Whatever they do has no effect on what they will do in the final round by the argument just given, so (to optimize), they certainly must take their short-run optimal action, which is betrayal. Which then implies that betrayal must be taken (in any subgame-perfect equilibrium) in round 98, and then 97, and so forth, all the way back to the very first round.

This, obviously, is quite different from what is possible in an infinitely repeated game. But how general is this result?

Before answering this question, let me explain the parenthetical "(So-Called)" in the title of this section. The issue is *not* that the stage game is played a finite number of times (with probability 1), but that there is a last period, and players know from the outset when that last period is. Suppose that the repeated prisoners' dilemma was played under the following rules: The stage game is played at time 0. Then, two dice are thrown, and if the throw comes up two sixes, Alice and Bob are told, "That was the last round of play." If any other throw comes up, they play again, after which the dice are thrown again. And so forth. And for their overall payoff from the grand game, we (and they) simply sum their payoffs from as many stage games as take place.

Assuming (as we do) that these dice are not so constructed that one or the other has zero probability of landing on six, there is probability 1 that eventually, a pair of sixes will be thrown, and the grand game will end. *With probability one, there will be finitely many rounds of play.* But because in any round they play, Alice and Bob are unsure whether this is the last round, their decision problems in terms of the total expected payoffs are identical with what would be their payoffs in the infinitely repeated game, with round-by-round payoffs discounted by $\delta = 35/36$ (the odds of a throw other than two sixes, if these are fair dice) and then summed.[18] The same strategies that are Nash or subgame-perfect Nash in the infinitely repeated version with discounting are Nash or subgame-perfect Nash here, with the proviso that, in this case, their strategies for how they'll play in round t based on the history h_t of play are contingent on round t being played.

"Played 100 times exactly" is different because, from the start, there is a definite looming horizon. Suppose the rules were that, prior to the play of each round, the dice are thrown, and if two sixes come up, players are told that "this round will be the last." You should convince yourself that, at least for the prisoners' dilemma stage game, this is equivalent to the dice being thrown after the play of each round, with a final, known-to-be-final round stuck on the end. In other words, strategically, this is more like the infinitely repeated game than it is the 100-round only version. And we can imagine other "end-of-times" disciplines. Suppose, for instance, the dice are thrown after each round. If the throw comes up anything other than two sixes, players are told: "Nothing is happening yet." But at the first throw of two sixes, they are told: "The end is near." And subsequent to that, after each round, the dice are thrown, and if the sum comes up 10, 11, or 12 (probability $1/6$), then that is the last round, except that in the 20th round after the first throw of two sixes, the game

---

[18] Clearly, the specific $\delta = 35/36$ comes from the specifics of how the final round is determined. With a publicly observable randomizing device that generates uniformly distributed variates, any δ can be "achieved." And if the players discount their round-by-round payoffs with some discount factor δ', while $1 - \delta$ is the round-by-round "after-the-round" probability that the round just played is the last one, this game is equivalent to the infinitely repeated game where the discount factor is $\delta\delta'$.

is over, regardless of how the dice are thrown. Convince yourself that, until the first throw of two sixes, this is like the infinitely repeated game but—for the stage game being the prisoners' dilemma—after the throw of two sixes, the logic of the second paragraph in this section applies, and Bob and Alice betray one another for as many rounds out of twenty that are left or, rather, the second paragraph shows that this is so for any subgame-perfect equilibrium.[19]

To avoid having to deal with all the variations of different "end-of-times" disciplines, the rules will be simple for the rest of this section: From the start, the players are told that the stage game will be played $T + 1$ times, at times $t = 0, 1, \ldots, T$, no more and no less. For expositional convenience, assume that the players evaluate how they do in the grand (finitely repeated) game according to their average stage-game payoff in the $T+1$ rounds. This is what, in the literature, is called the canonical *finitely repeated game*. And in this context, we look for both subgame-perfect and Nash equilibria of this finitely repeated game.

Suppose that, in this setting, the stage game is the prisoners' dilemma. The argument given earlier is that the only *subgame-perfect* Nash equilibrium is for both players always—that is, *everywhere* in the game, on-path and off—to betray her rival. What if we relaxed the criterion and looked for Nash equilibrium only? It turns out that players can, in a Nash equilibrium, have strategies that cooperate off-path. For instance, for Alice and Bob being the two players and for $T = 2$, Alice play the strategy: Betray at $t = 0$. Betray no matter what at $t = 1$. And if Bob chooses to cooperate in both of the first two rounds, then cooperate in the third round; but betray otherwise. In effect, Alice "promises" Bob a rosy final period if he will "pay her up front" in the first two rounds. But, of course, he will not do so, so this promise is a best response (for the three-period repetition as a whole) to, for instance, a strategy by Bob in which he always betrays.

That said, in any Nash equilibrium, betrayal must be each player's action along the path of play. Along the path of play of any Nash equilibrium, in the final stage, both sides must betray if the history up to the last stage has positive probability; to do otherwise would lower the player's overall expected payoff. So for any history h_{T-1} that has positive probability (is on-path), any action in stage $T - 1$ that has positive probability must be betrayal, because it leads to a history h_T that is on-path, and that means betrayal in the last stage. And so forth.

This logic holds if the stage game is the prisoners' dilemma. And this stage game is special for the following reason: The stage game has a unique Nash equilibrium, *and that unique Nash equilibrium involves each player minmaxing the other(s)*. More generally, we have the following three results.

---

[19]   I mention these alternatives, because there are economic contexts in which, for instance, firms in an industry interact repeatedly, with no specific horizon in mind, but in the knowledge that at some point, a disruption will take place that gives them only so many years left to interact. The fact that, eventually, they will know that the end is near, need *not* necessarily affect how they behave before they learn that this is so, although they do take into account the chances that they will learn that the end is near at some point. Hence collusion in a "mature and stable industry" may be feasible until participants recognize that their industry is "in decline."

Proposition A15.5.

a. *If the stage game Γ has a unique Nash equilibrium, then the unique **subgame-perfect** Nash equilibrium for the finitely repeated version of the stage game (of any length) is repeated play of that Nash equilibrium in every stage and after every history.*

b. *Suppose the stage game Γ is such that, for each player n, there is a Nash equilibrium profile (in the stage game) σ^n such that $v_n(\sigma^n) > \underline{v}_n$. Fix $\epsilon > 0$ and any $v \in \mathcal{V}$ that satisfies $v_n > \underline{v}_n$ for each n. There exists (large enough) T^* such that: In the finitely repeated game with $T + 1$ rounds or more, for $T \geq T^*$, there is a Nash equilibrium in which each player n gets an (average) payoff of at least $v_n - \epsilon$.*

c. *Suppose that the stage game Γ is such that, for each player n, there are Nash equilibria (in the stage game) σ^n and $\hat{\sigma}^n$ such that $v_n(\sigma^n) > v_n(\hat{\sigma}^n)$. Fix $\epsilon > 0$ and $v \in \mathcal{V}$ such that $v_n \geq \underline{v}_n$ for each n. There exists (large enough) T^* such that: In the finitely repeated game with $T + 1$ rounds or more, for $T \geq T^*$, there is a subgame-perfect Nash equilibrium in which each player n gets an (average) payoff of at least $v_n - \epsilon$.*

Part *a* of the proposition is folklore; or, if not folklore, it is probaby best attributed to Zermelo (1913). Parts *b* and *c* are due to Benoit and Krishna (1987 for part *b* and 1985 for part *c*).

The proof of part *a* follows the argument given at the start of this section for the case of the prisoners' dilemma. In the final round, given any history, subgame perfection mandates play of the unique Nash equilibrium. And so forth, moving back through the game tree.

To see how parts b and c are proved in general, please consult the cited papers. The main ideas of the proof, however, are easy to provide with a couple of simple examples.

For part b, suppose that the stage game is the prisoners' dilemma, augmented with one more strategy for each player. This extra strategy is called *devastation*; if either Alice or Bob choose *devastation* in any round, in that round, both players get -100. Note that this puts the stage game in the category of having a unique Nash equilibrium (both betray), but each player can minmax the other into a (much) worse payoff than the unique (stage-game) Nash payoff. And, with this amendment in the stage game, suppose that each player adopts the following strategy: In the final round ($t = T$), if both sides have always cooperated previously, betray. In any earlier round, if history has been cooperation by both sides, cooperate. But, following any history up to a time $t < T$ in which one side or the other has done anything other than cooperate, choose devastation. This strategy for Alice against the same strategy for Bob is a Nash equilibrium: Until the final period, both sides cooperate, so as not to trigger devastation. And both sides can (in a *Nash* equilibrium) threaten devastation, because it is never triggered. The final period is special—it involves betrayal along the path of play—and that is because a threat of devastation in the future won't work; there is no future.

For part c, imagine that the stage game involves two players, Alice and Bob, who play the 4×4 strategic-form game depicted in Figure A15.8. Note that there are three pure-strategy Nash equilibria in the stage game: A1-B1, A2-B2, and Ay-By.

Ax-Bx is *not* a Nash equilibrium, because if Bob is playing Bx, Alice will defect to Ay (and vice versa). And Ay-Bx is not a Nash equilibrium, because Bob will defect to By.

		Bob			
		B1	B2	Bx	By
	A1	60, 40	0, 0	0, 0	0, 0
Alice	A2	0, 0	40, 60	0, 0	0, 0
	Ax	0, 0	0, 0	75, 75	0, 100
	Ay	0, 0	0, 0	100, 0	5, 5

Figure A15.8. A strategic-form stage game to illustrate Proposition A15.5(c)

Nonetheless, for large enough T (in a $T + 1$ repetition of this stage game), we can get, as a subgame-perfect equilibrium outcome, play of Ax-Bx, for all but the last four periods:

- The on-path behavior is: Alice plays Ax and Bob plays Bx for all periods up to $t = T - 4$. In periods $T - 3$ and $T - 1$, Alice plays A1 and Bob plays B1. In periods $T - 2$ and T, Alice plays A2 and Bob plays B2.

- If, at any point in the repeated game, both players defect from this on-path pattern, it is ignored, and the on-path pattern continues.

- However, if, at any point, Alice and Alice alone defects, then, for whatever time remains, the two play A2-B2. (Any further defections are ignored.) And if, at any point, Bob and Bob alone defects, then the two play A1-B1 for the remaining periods.

You likely see why this produces a subgame-perfect equilibrium, but to give the explanation: Once the strategies call for play in each remaining period of a stage-game equilibrium, subgame perfection from that point on is assured. Defection can't help in the short run, and it has no impact on subsequent play. Hence, the final four periods of on-path play, and the "penalty phase," if it is ever triggered, present subgame-perfect behavior.

And the play of Ax-Bx up to period $T - 4$ constitutes a best response for the two players. As long as, say, Alice conforms, she gets 75 per period until period $T - 4$, and then she gets two periods of 60 and two periods of 40, a total of 200. If she defects prior to period $T - 4$, and in particular, she defects to Ay (the only defection that makes any sense at all), she gets 100 that period instead of 75, an immediate gain of 25, but in subsequent periods she gets (only) 40 per period. Even if she only defects in period $T - 4$ (so she stretches out those 75s for as long as possible), that means a total of 160 over the final four periods, which is 40 worse than what she would have gotten had she adhered to the equilibrium. So, along the path of play, she is playing a best response to Bob. The argument for Bob is nearly identical.

In other words, part b of Proposition A15.5 is based on the idea that Alice can threaten to blow up both parties if Bob doesn't adhere. This is a threat that, if a blow-up is severe enough, can be successfully employed until the penultimate period; otherwise, it may take a number of blow-up periods to deter defection. And, although not a credible threat in the subgame-perfection sense, the threat is legitimate in a Nash equilibrium because it is never carried out.

However, part c is based on a final few periods of alternating among stage-game equilibria, some of which are better for, say, Bob then others, as long as Bob complies. But if Bob defects, the subgame-perfect threat is, for the rest of time, "we'll move to the stage-game equilibrium that is worse for you."

Finally, concerning part a, it is worth observing that when (real-life) individuals play the repeated prisoners' dilemma for a set number of times, they often cooperate until near the final period (and, sometimes, even in the final period). A similar empirical phenomenon (not quite in the strict context of repeated games, but with a related game-theoretic "solution") is where players of the centipede game of Figure A11.4 forgo grabbing the money until the size of the pot has built up. Something else is going on in these games; we explore models of what that might be in Section A15.7.

A15.6. Imperfect Observability, Hidden Information, and Public Equilibria

As with the entirety of Section A15.2, this section begins with a lengthy discussion of a simple example, to set ideas. You may skip ahead to the next subsection if you feel this is a waste of your time. But I advise against doing so.

Suppose that Alice and Bob are playing the infinitely repeated prisoners' dilemma game, with discount factor δ, but with the following twist: In each round, Alice chooses between Betray and Cooperate as her *intention*. But, with a small probability p, what happens (her *actual* choice) is the opposite of what she intended to do. And similarly for Bob: He makes an intended choice, but what actually happens is the reverse of what he intends with the same probability p, independent of whether Alice's actual choice is what she intended. (And there is independence of these random events between rounds.) Alice and Bob know what they (each, individually) intended to do, and they know what they actually did, so they know whether their intentions were met or reversed. But each can only see what the other actually did and not what the other intended to do. If you prefer, the story is that they make their choices in remote locations, unable to communicate, but each sees her or his actual payoff, which is based on the actual choices and not on intentions.

I appreciate that this is a somewhat hokey story, but give me some time to develop this example before judging it too harshly.

This poses an immediate problem for the strategy profile *grim punishment*. To (re-)define grim punishment for this setting: Alice, say, begins in the first period intending to cooperate. And, as long as *neither* player has actually (not intendedly, but actually) betrayed the other, she intends to cooperate. But if, in an earlier period, either player actually betrayed the other, then Alice intends to betray. Bob's strategy is indentical.

Suppose in the first three rounds, Alice tries to cooperate and, in fact, this is what she actually does. And she perceives cooperation from Bob in those three rounds. (That is, her payoff is 10 in each round, which tells her (a) that she did in fact cooperate and (b) Bob did actually cooperate, although (c) she does not know for sure whether Bob intended cooperation and got what he intended or intended to betray and instead got cooperation.) Then, on the fourth round, she intends to cooperate, and her payoff comes back -15. This means that her "actual" choice was cooperation, and Bob's actual choice was betrayal.

Suppose she (and Bob) institute grim punishment, based on actual choices. Forever after, then, they both intend to betray. Assuming p is small, once the first betrayal is observed, there will be a smattering (probability p^2) of times where they both receive payoffs of 10, a larger number of times (probability $p(1-p)$) that Alice gets 20 and Bob -15 and, times (probability $(1-p)p$) when Alice gets -15 and Bob gets 20, and in "most" cases (probability $(1-p)^2$) each gets 0. This gives an average payoff per round of $0(1-p)^2 + 20(1-p)p - 15p(1-p) + 10p^2 = 5p + 5p^2$, which for small p is small. Thus in round t, if the history h_t includes a previous betrayal, their expected payoff for the rest of the game, discounted back to this round t, is $V_B := (5p + 5p^2)/(1 - \delta)$.

Computing the players' expected payoffs from round t on, when there has been no betrayal (yet), is more difficult. It is the solution to V_C in the recursive equation

$$V_C = (1-p)^2(10 + \delta V_C) + (1-p)p(-15 + \delta V_B) + p(1-p)(20 + \delta V_B) + p^2(0 + \delta V_B)$$
$$= (1-p)^2 \delta V_C + 10 - 15p + 5p^2 + (2p - p^2)\delta V_B.$$

To explain: both players are intending cooperation. So with probability $(1-p)^2$, that is what actually happens, in which case, both get an immediate 10 and, starting next round, V_C, which in present value terms is δV_C. With probabilities $(1-p)p$ one cooperates and the other actually betrays, giving the betrayer 20 and the cooperator -15 immediately, and a discounted continuation value V_B. And with probability p^2, both betray, which gives an immediate 0 to each and a discounted continuation value V_B.

Manipulating this recursive equation gives

$$V_C(1 - \delta(1-p)^2) = 10 - 15p + 5p^2 + (2p - p^2)\delta V_B, \quad \text{or}$$

$$V_C = \frac{10 - 15p + 5p^2 + 5\delta(2p - p^2)(p + p^2)/(1 - \delta)}{1 - \delta(1-p)^2}.$$

Do these strategies (grim betrayal against grim betrayal, where the grim punishment is based on any observation of actual betrayal) constitute a perfect Nash equilibrium? The usual test of *unimprovability* by either player is employed: We have discounted and bounded rewards, so unimprovability will imply optimality for each player in response to his or her rival playing this strategy.

But before I apply the test of unimprovability, I must say something about the meaning of the term *perfect Nash equilibrium*. I would dearly like to say *subgame perfect*, but I can't: At the start of the second round, in the grand extensive-form game tree, Alice has eight information sets, each of which contains two nodes. She knows what she intended, what was her actual action, and what was Bob's actual action; that $2 \times 2 \times 2$ array constitutes her eight information sets. And, in each one, there are nodes for "Bob intended to cooperate" and for "Bob intended to betray." Moreover, every one of her information sets is extended on-path (I'll let you puzzle that one out.) Since Bob's information sets are similar, subgame perfection has no role to play here.

However, I've described the strategies of the players in terms of a *publicly and commonly observed state*. In this case, the two states are: no observed betrayals yet; and there has been an observed betrayal. What each player does in the immediate period depends on the current state. And both players, based on what they have observed, know which state prevails. (Indeed, this knowledge is common between them.) So, when I refer loosely to a *perfect Nash equilibrium*, what I mean is: From either state (time plays no role in this instance, since their strategies depend on the state but not on calendar time), how Alice plays for the rest of the game is a best response (for the rest of the game) to Bob's strategy, and vice versa. I'll be more formal about this concept later in this section; I hope that, for now, it makes enough sense to proceed.

Unimprovability at points in the game where one or the other has actually betrayed is

$$V_B \geq (1-p)^2[-15 + \delta V_B] + (1-p)p[10 + \delta V_B] + p(1-p)[0 + \delta V_B] + p^2[20 + \delta V_B],$$

where the right-hand side of this inequality is what, say, Alice would get if she intends to cooperate while Bob intends to betray. Note that the continuation values are all V_B; the rules of these strategies are that once there has been a betrayal, the "state" stays betrayal. This inequality simplifies to

$$(1 - \delta)V_B \geq -15(1 - p)^2 + 10(1 - p)p + 20p^2, \quad \text{or} \quad 5p + 5p^2 \geq -15 + 40p - 5p^2,$$

which, after some algebra, holds if and only if $p \leq 1/2$. This has the following simple explanation: Alice knows that, whatever she intends and whatever she actually does, the "state" next period will be the state in which someone previously betrayed. So her choice today has no effect on her continuation value. And, whatever Bob does, her immediate payoff is better if she actually betrays than if she actually cooperates. So her intended choice should be whichever makes it more likely that her actual choice will be betrayal. If $p < 1/2$, intending to betray gives probability $1 - p > 1/2$ of actually betraying, while if $p > 1/2$, intending to cooperate gives probability $p > 1/2$ of betrayal. For this half of the test of unimprovability, we have that $p \leq 1/2$ is the necessary and sufficient condition. (At $p = 1/2$, it doesn't matter what she intends. And the same is true for Bob.)

The other unimprobability condition, for a position in which neither player has yet to have actually betrayed, is

$$V_C \geq (1-p)^2[20 + \delta V_B] + (1-p)p[0 + \delta V_B] + p(1-p)[10 + \delta V_C] + p^2[-15 + \delta V_B].$$

To explain the right-hand side: If Alice defects by intending to betray, with probability $(1-p)^2$, she actually betrays and Bob actually cooperates, which gives Alice an immediate 20 and moves her to a position where, since she betrayed, the continuation value is V_B. The second term represents the possibility that she actually betrays and Bob actually betrays (joint probability $(1-p)p$). The third is where, despite trying to betray, she cooperates, as does Bob—joint probability $p(1-p)$, which is the only outcome for which the continuation value is V_C. And the fourth term is where, despite her intentions, she actually cooperates, while Bob, despite his intentions to cooperate, actually betrays.

Because the formula for V_C is complex, trying to find the p values for which this inequality holds analytically seems fruitless. So I move to numerical calculations. See Table A15.2. For $\delta = 0.9$, the values of V_B, V_C, and the right-hand side of the second unimprovability constraint are computed for a variety of values of p, from $p = 0.01$ up to $p = 0.375$. (You'll see why I stopped at 0.375 in a bit.) A comparison of the third and fourth columns shows that this strategy profile passes the test of unimprovability for $p = 0.175$ but not for $p = 0.2$. Clearly (and one can prove this analytically), the unimprovability test is passed for an interval of values of p of the form $[0, p^*(\delta)]$; for $\delta = 0.9$, $p^*(0.9)$ is between 0.175 and 0.2. (It turns out that $p^*(0.9)$ is roughly 0.191.)

p	V_B	V_C	Test value
0.01	0.505	83.619	20.895
0.05	2.625	50.561	22.899
0.075	4.031	40.998	23.658
0.1	5.500	35.020	24.291
0.125	7.031	31.152	24.874
0.15	8.625	28.639	25.447
0.175	10.281	27.058	26.030
0.2	12.000	26.151	26.638
0.225	13.781	25.752	27.279
0.25	15.625	25.752	27.959
0.275	17.531	26.071	28.682
0.3	19.500	26.656	29.452
0.325	21.531	27.464	30.271
0.35	23.625	28.466	31.141
0.375	25.781	29.637	32.063

Table A15.2. The grim strategy values for $\delta = 0.9$ and various values of p.

(When I first looked at these values and saw that V_C is the same for $p = 0.225$ and 0.25, I thought I had made a mistake. But I hadn't. The explanation is that V_C declines with p for small values of p, but, past a certain point, which is between

$p = 0.225$ and 0.25, it begins to increase. The reason is that V_B is increasing with p, and this is because, in the grim phase of the game, bigger p means more instances where one player gets -15 but the other gets 20, as well as a smaller but still increasing probability that they both get 10. And this increase in V_B is what is driving the increase in V_C, which is most pronounced for larger p, because larger p means a transition to the grim stage more quickly.)

As an exercise, we can ask how these values—and in particular V_C, which is the expected payoff for Alice and Bob at the start of the game—change with changes in δ, holding p fixed. Table A15.3 gives some data. For different values of δ, it shows the corresponding values of V_C for different p values, up to the level of p at which the unimprovability test fails. That is what you see in panel a. Panel b shows the same data, but where I premultiply the values in the column for a given δ by $1-\delta$, to show the expected payoffs on a normalized, "per-round" basis.

	Value of δ				Value of δ			
Value of p	0.75	0.9	0.95	0.995	0.75	0.9	0.95	0.995
0.01	37.194	83.619	143.235	405.253	9.30	8.36	7.16	2.03
0.05	28.903	50.561	68.353	140.724	7.23	5.06	3.42	0.70
0.075	25.337	40.998	53.479	137.805	6.33	4.10	2.67	0.69
0.1	22.582	35.020	45.707	151.226	5.65	3.50	2.29	0.76
0.125	20.427	31.152	41.570	172.111	5.11	3.12	2.08	0.86
0.15		28.639	39.570	197.401		2.86	1.98	0.99
0.175		27.058	38.955	225.763		2.71	1.95	1.13
0.2			39.306	256.520			1.97	1.28
	(a) Unnormalized values of V_C				(b) Normalized values of V_C			

Table A15.3. The grim strategy initial payoffs for various p and δ (blank entries in the table are values of p for which, at the given δ, the unimprovability constraint is not satisfied, so the grim strategies do not form an equilibrium)

There are two things worth noting. First, as δ approaches 1, the range of p for which this gives an equilibrium increases. But, as $\delta \rightarrow 1$, the range of p for which we have an equilibrium has a limit. Although not shown in the table, I tried $p = 0.9999$ and found that the unimprovability constraint continues to fail for $p = 0.225$. And, second, if the values of V_C are normalized, larger δ for a given p (assuming the strategies constitute an equilibrium) gives a smaller normalized value. The reason is that, for fixed p, the probability distribution for the first (unintended) appearance of betrayal doesn't change with δ. But as δ increases, more and more of the "total value" to the players lies further and further out. Hence, in terms of total value, as δ increases, more of the total value will happen in rounds where the players are grimly intending to betray one another.

This points out the big disadvantage (for Alice and Bob) of grim strategies in a noisy environment: Eventually, intentionally or not, there is going to be a betrayal, and that is the end of cooperation. They might (as in, certainly will) do better if they include some mechanism for forgiving one another through compensation and resuming cooperation. In the spirit of the one-round-of-compensation strategies that go with Figure A15.4, I suggest the following strategy profile.

There will be three states, C, PA, and PB. The state of the game begins in state C, and evolves according to the *actual*—that is, not the *intended*—choices of Alice and Bob. From state C, if they both actually cooperate or both betray, the state remains C.[20] If Alice betrays and Bob cooperates, play moves to state PA. If Bob betrays and Alice cooperates, the state becomes PB. In state PA, the evolution depends only on what Alice does: If she betrays, the state stays PA. If she cooperates, the state moves back to C. Figure A15.9 depicts these state-evolution dynamics; note the similarity to Figure A15.4, but with an important distinction. Figure A15.4 depicts a situation in which Alice and Bob can *choose* the state-to-state transition. Here, because transitions are based on actual play and not intentions, they can only *influence* the likelihood of a transition.

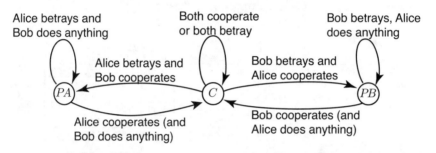

Figure A15.9. The state-evolution dynamics (dynamics are driven by what the players are observed to do, not what they intend to do)

The strategies employed by Alice and Bob depend on the current state. In state C, they both intend to cooperate. In state PA, Alice intends to cooperate and Bob intends to betray. In state PB, Bob intends to cooperate and Alice intends to betray. The general idea is much as in our analysis of at the end of Section A15.2. State PA is a punishment state for Alice, reached if, in the cooperative state C, she actually betrays Bob (and he doesn't simultaneously betray her). From PA, Alice restores cooperation by actually cooperating, while Bob is free to betray; in effect, in state PA, Alice is "paying Bob back" for the betrayal that put the two of them in state PA. But the transition is based on actuals, not intentions: State C is restored only when Alice actually cooperates. And so forth.

For a given p and δ, will these strategies—which I continue to call *one round of compensation*—constitute a perfect equilibrium? The methodology for checking is as before: We compute the expected payoffs in each state for, say, Alice, given that Bob is following the prescribed strategy. And then we see whether the strategy is unimprovable for Alice. (Since everything is symmetric, if Alice passes the test, so does Bob.)

There are three expected payoff values to compute for Alice: the value V_C that she gets starting in state C; the value V_A that she gets starting in state PA, and the

---

[20]   I won't always insert the adjective "actual" and the adverb "actually"; they apply throughout.

value V_B that she gets starting in state PC. To determine these values, we must solve the following trio of recursive equations:

$$V_C = (1 - p)^2(10 + \delta V_C) + p^2 \delta V_C + (1 - p)p(-15 + \delta V_B) + p(1 - p)(20 + \delta V_A);$$
$$V_B = (1 - p)^2(20 + \delta V_C) + (1 - p)p(0 + \delta V_B) + p(1 - p)(10 + \delta V_C) + p^2(-15 + \delta V_B); \text{ and}$$
$$V_A = (1 - p)^2(-15 + \delta V_C) + p(1 - p)(10 + \delta V_C) + (1 - p)p(0 + \delta V_A) + p^2(20 + \delta V_A).$$

I'll walk you through the equation for V_B; you should check the other two. In state PB, Bob intends to cooperate, and Alice intends to betray. With probability $(1-p)^2$, their intentions are realized, giving Alice an immediate 20 and, because this causes the state to transition to C, a continuation value V_C, which is discounted, since it begins next period. With probability $(1 - p)p$, Alice's intentions are realized, but Bob's are not—he betrays—which means an immediate 0 for Alice and a discounted continuation value δV_B, since Bob's betrayal keeps the state at PB. With probability $p(1 - p)$, Alice actually cooperates, as does Bob, for immediate 10 and a restoration of cooperation. And with probability p^2, Alice cooperates and Bob betrays, giving Alice an immediate -15 and a discounted continuation value δV_B.

These three entangled recursive equations are linear in the three unknowns, so, of course, they can be untangled. Because we assume the same probability p applies to Alice and Bob, the algebra is not so bad: The first of these recursive equations simplifies to

$$V_C = (1 - 2p + 2p^2)\delta V_C + (1 - p)p\delta(V_A + V_B) + 10 - 15p - 5p^2,$$

the point being that V_A and V_B enter only as their sum. So, if we add the second two equations, we have two recursive equations in $V_A + V_B$ and V_C. We can solve them for $V_A + V_B$ in terms of V_C, substitute the solution into the first equation, and then solve for V_C. I will spare you the algebra and just write the solutions for V_C, from which the solutions for V_A and V_B can be computed:

$$V_C = \frac{10 - 15p - 5p\delta + 20p^2\delta + 5p^2 - 25\delta p^3 + 10\delta p^4}{1 + p\delta - \delta - 2p^2\delta - p\delta^2 + 2p^2\delta^2},$$

$$V_A = \frac{(1 - p)\delta V_C - 15 + 40p - 5p^2}{1 - p\delta}, \quad \text{and} \quad V_B = \frac{(1 - p)\delta V_C + 20 - 30p - 5p^2}{1 - p\delta}.$$

And now that we have the three value functions (for Alice), we can check to see whether the proposed strategy for Alice is a best response to the proposed strategy for Bob, by checking whether it is unimprovable. There are three "unimprovability tests" to be passed:

$$V_C \geq (1 - p)^2(20 + \delta V_A) + (1 - p)p(0 + \delta V_C) + p(1 - p)(10 + \delta V_C) + p^2(-15 + V_B),$$
$$V_A \geq (1 - p)^2(0 + \delta V_A) + (1 - p)p(20 + \delta V_A) + p(1 - p)(-15 + \delta V_C) + p^2(10 + \delta V_C), \text{ and}$$
$$V_B \geq (1 - p)^2(10 + \delta V_C) + (1 - p)p(-15 + \delta V_B) + p(1 - p)(20 + \delta V_C) + p^2(0 + \delta V_B).$$

It is probably unnecessary at this stage, but let me go slowly through the first test. In state C, Alice and Bob are both meant to intend cooperation. So to test unimprovability for Alice, we compare what she will get, V_C, if she sticks with the equilibrium strategy, with her expected payoff if she intends to betray for one round and then goes back to the one-round-of-compensation strategy, which is the right-hand side of the first inequality: With probability $(1 - p)^2$, both will get their intentions, so she betrays and he cooperates, which gives her 20 and transfers the state to PA, where her continuation value is V_A. With probability $(1 - p)p$, she gets her intended betrayal, but Bob also betrays, which means Alice gets 0 and the state stays in C. With probability $p(1 - p)$, although she intends to betray, she cooperates, while Bob gets his intended cooperation, which gives her 10 and keeps the state in C. And with probability p^2, she actually cooperates and Bob actually betrays, giving her -15 and moving the state to PB.

In Table A15.4, I give numerically computed values for V_C, V_A, and V_B, as well as the expected payoffs to Alice if she contemplates a one-time deviation, all for $\delta = 0.9$. So, looking at the first two columns and the row for $p = 0.1$, we see that Alice's expected payoff V_C starting in state C (which is where the game begins), is 77.037, while a one-time deviation (to betrayal) in that state gives her an expected payoff of 71.351. So, when $p = 0.1$ and $\delta = 0.9$, the unimprovability test is passed for state C. Continuing across the same row, her expected payoff in state PA (where she is being punished) is 56.429, and a one-time deviation gives an expected payoff of 53.191, so again the unimprovability test is passed. And, in the last two columns, we see that her expected payoff starting in state PB is 87.198, and the unimprovability test is passed.

	V_C	V_C check	V_A	V_A check	V_B	V_B check
0.01	97.215	85.545	72.672	65.677	107.284	97.435
0.05	87.263	78.558	64.500	59.337	97.484	88.259
0.075	81.879	74.770	60.200	56.046	92.103	83.284
0.1	77.037	71.351	56.429	53.191	87.198	78.798
0.125	72.670	68.249	53.126	50.715	82.703	74.735
0.15	68.717	65.417	50.239	48.572	78.562	71.037
0.175	65.130	62.815	47.722	46.720	74.725	67.656
0.2	61.863	60.408	45.538	45.123	71.148	64.548
0.225	58.879	58.165	43.655	43.750	67.793	61.674
0.25	56.145	56.057	42.045	42.576	64.626	59.001
0.275	53.631	54.059	40.686	41.574	61.616	56.497
0.3	51.312	52.148	39.557	40.725	58.735	54.135
0.325	49.166	50.302	38.643	40.010	55.958	51.889
0.35	47.171	48.499	37.931	39.411	53.259	49.734
0.375	45.310	46.720	37.410	38.913	50.617	47.648

Value of p

Table A15.4. Expected payoffs for Alice starting in each of the three states, and expected payoffs from a one-step deviation, for the strategies described in the text and various values of p

Since, for $p = 0.1$, the unimprovability test is passed starting in each of the three states, Alice's proposed strategy is a best response (starting from any one of the three states) against Bob's; the same is true by symmetry of Bob against Alice, and so the proposed strategy profile is a perfect Nash equilibrium.

Moreover, this is true for the values of p up to $p = 0.2$, but at $p = 0.225$, Alice's strategy is no longer unimprovable in state PA, and we no longer have a perfect equilibrium. This is so even though we still pass the unimprovability test in states C and PB. Remember: The test must be passed in all three states.

In fact, one of the three unimprovability tests is quite simple, namely, the test for Alice in the state PB. When Bob is being punished—that is, in the state PB—Alice's actual action has no effect on the state dynamics; state C is restored only if Bob actually compensates Alice by cooperating (whether Alice actually betrays or cooperates). So, for Alice, all that matters in terms of her choice in that state is her immediate payoff. Hence, for $p < 0.5$, she does best to intend betrayal, while for $p > 0.5$, she does best to intend cooperation.

If you compare the values of V_C for this strategy profile with the expected payoffs for the two players if they use the grim punishment strategies, you'll see that this "forgiveness with compensation" strategy profile does significantly better. Fixing $\delta = 0.9$, even for $p = 0.01$, this strategy profile gives an expected payoff of 97.215, versus 83.619 for the grim punishment profile. For $p = 0.1$, the two expected payoffs are 77.037 versus 35.020; for $p = 0.175$, it is 65.120 versus 27.058; and while this strategy profile is an equilibrium for $p = 0.2$, that is not true for grim punishment. The same is true for other values of δ; in Table A15.5, I provide for different values of δ and p the unnormalized and normalized payoffs in state C, where blanks in the table indicate that, for that pair of p and δ, one of the unimprovability tests fails.[21]

	Value of δ				Value of δ			
Value of p	0.75	0.9	0.95	0.995	0.75	0.9	0.95	0.995
0.01	38.971	97.215	194.289	1941.610	9.74	9.72	9.71	9.71
0.05	35.251	87.263	173.955	1734.431	8.81	8.73	8.70	8.67
0.075	33.207	81.879	163.008	1623.379	8.30	8.19	8.15	8.12
0.1	31.347	77.037	153.201	1524.198	7.84	7.70	7.66	7.62
0.125	29.651	72.670	144.384	1435.318	7.41	7.27	7.22	7.18
0.15		68.717	136.434	1355.410		6.87	6.82	6.78
0.175		65.130	129.241	1283.341		6.51	6.46	6.42
0.2		61.863	122.715	1218.138		6.19	6.14	6.09
0.225			116.773	1158.965			5.84	5.79
0.25				1105.093				5.53
	(a) Unnormalized values of V_C				(b) Normalized values of V_C			

Table A15.5. Unnormalized and normalized expected payoffs from the one-round-of-compensation strategy profile in state C.

---

[21] For each value of p, the normalized values of V_C fall as δ increases. This is because, when computing the normalized value of V_C, we are looking at what happens starting in state C. This puts more weight on state C values, which we know (how?) are larger than the average of PA and PB values; it takes a while for Alice or Bob to betray unintentionally. As $\delta \to 1$, this effect is mitigated; we are getting closer to the long-run Cesàro-average payoff that is accrued.

Is this one-round-of-compensation strategy profile the "best," in the sense that it achieves the best symmetric payoff for Alice and Bob? No, it isn't. That this pair of strategies fails unimprovability for $p = 0.225$ in state PA while it still passes unimprovability for this value of p in state C means that we might want to decrease the amount of punishment a player absorbs / the amount of compensation she must give to restore the cooperative state. (How? One way might be to use a publicly observable randomizing device and, if one player or the other betrays, move to the appropriate punishment / compensation state with probability less than one. If you would like a challenge, see if you can work through this variation.)

What is this example meant to represent?
The issue of "imperfect observability"

In the classic folk theorem, deviations from the equilibrium strategies are instantly recognized and can be punished. In most real-life relationships, this is unlikely to hold. Partners in an ongoing relationship may, for a variety of reasons, be perceived by their counterparties as having *perhaps* stepped out of line for personal benefit. Here are some of those reasons.

1. Parties can only perceive a noisy indication of how their counterparties acted. This includes the paradigmatic model of oligopolists trying to collude in the face of demand shocks, which is described in detail in Chapter 22.

2. Parties' actual actions may not be what they intended, through no fault of their own (as in the hokey model just presented).

3. Partners may *intentionally* "step out of line" for good and substantial reasons, depending on circumstances that their counterparties cannot perceive. For instance, suppose that "cooperation" comes at a private cost to the individuals involved, where the private cost changes from period to period. Then, in a given round, if the private cost of cooperation to Alice is particularly high, she may face substantial motivation to "betray" Bob, even taking into account how Bob will react to this. If Bob could see Alice's private costs, he might give her a "pass." But if he is unable to do see that information, but only hear her assurances that "it was too costly for me to cooperate in this round," he may think that Alice is only making excuses.

4. And in a world where "deals" are not so cut and dried as in our toy models, it may be simply a matter of perception: The real world does not present partners to a relationship with a sequence of identical (repeated) encounters. Each "round" is unique in some way or another, and what the relationship calls for may be ambiguous. Alice, facing a somewhat novel set of circumstances, may decide that a particular action on her part is consistent with acceptable behavior in her relationship with Bob; Bob, observing what Alice did and even understanding the novel aspects of the situation, may interpret differently what is appropriate and worry that Alice's choice of action is motivated by her personal interests, rather than their joint (somehow agreed-to) interests.

And there are other stories one can tell. What is clear is that, in real life relationships, "cooperation" (generally interpreted) sometimes breaks down. And if Bob, seeing or perceiving a breakdown in cooperative efforts from Alice, does not (at some point) take action against her, this encourages Alice to take privately beneficial actions more often, blaming them on "circumstances beyond my control." Insofar as there are sometimes circumstances beyond Alice's control, Bob may (in a good relationship) understand that it wasn't Alice being greedy but, again, if he doesn't take some action but merely lets it go, he encourages Alice to be greedy.

In real life, there are several methods available to ameliorate such dilemmas. One is to find ways to strip out or at least diminish the noise that permeates the relationship. Getting rid of the "noise" is fully a Volume II method; examples are provided in Chapter 22. A second is to design the relationship so that transgressions can be efficiently dealt with: Think of liquidated-damage provisions in a long-term contractual relationship or, when and if legal, contracting with a neutral third party who will arbitrate disputes. A third is to arrange matters so that one party has more power to determine how the deal progresses but at the same time has more at stake through that party's general reputation with several counterparties. Transaction-cost economics, a topic to be dealt with in Volume III, concerns the economics of such arrangements. And a fourth, which is very much a topic for Volume III, is to trust in the idea that, in a healthy long-term relationship, at least among individuals, the counterparties may have preferences that evolve into increasingly internalizing the welfare of their counterparties.

Meanwhile, within the purview of this volume, models like the hokey model—where Alice intends to cooperate, but Nature sometimes changes her choice to betray—are the game theorist's attempt to gain insight into the impact of imperfect observability on long-term relationships and how that impact might be mitigated.

A second example: Hidden information

Given a specific real-life situation, different game-theoretic models can be employed. For instance, in an attempt to gain insight into scenario (number 3 in the previous subsection) where the issue isn't imperfect observation of what a player does or intends to do but instead *why* she acted as she did—consider the following caricature model.

In the context of the repeated play of the prisoners' dilemma, suppose that, in round t, the payoffs to each side of cooperation are $10 + \epsilon_t$ and $-15 + \epsilon_t$, for some independent and identically distributed sequence $\{\epsilon_t; t = 0, 1, \ldots\}$. To keep things very simple, suppose the distribution of each ϵ_t is

$$\epsilon_t = \begin{cases} 0, & \text{with probability 0.9, and} \\ -25, & \text{with probability 0.1,} \end{cases}$$

Suppose that there are separate and independent $\{\epsilon_t\}$ processes for Alice and Bob; denote the process for Alice by $\{\epsilon_t^A; t = 0, 1, \ldots\}$ and the process for Bob is $\{\epsilon_t^B; t = 0, 1, \ldots\}$. These values are private information to the two players: If in a particular round, cooperation is particularly expensive for Alice (her $\epsilon_t^A = -25$), she knows this, but Bob does not, and she cannot credibly prove to Bob that this is so. Also suppose that Alice learns the value of ϵ_t^A only at date t (but before she chooses whether to cooperate or betray in that period), with Bob's situation being the same. In this case, there is no "noise" between what a player intends to do and what she does. But, when $\epsilon_t^A = -25$, Alice may intend to and in fact betray.

In this setting, here are two symmetric strategy profiles that are worthy of analysis:

1. In the spirit of the one-round-of-compensation strategy profile, suppose that "state dynamics" are precisely as in Figure A15.4, but Alice's choice of action is: In state C, if she draws $\epsilon_t^A = -25$, she intentionally triggers her punishment state by betraying, and in state PA, she will not cooperate if she draws $\epsilon_t^A = -25$, hoping that next period she can restore state C at lower cost. (Bob acts in symmetrical fashion.)

2. Alternatively, we have what might be called the "suck-it-up" strategy profile. in which along the path of play, Alice always cooperates, even in the face of $\epsilon_t^A = -25$, and symmetrically for Bob, because if either player ever betrays the other, for the rest of time, both choose betrayal.

An analysis of these two strategy profiles—What values to they provide the players? For which values of δ do they constitute an equilibrium?—is easier than the example already analyzed; see if you can do it. A full analysis is provided at the end of this appendix (following the Bibliographic Notes).

And, to reiterate from the first paragraph of this subsection: The issue here isn't imperfect observability of what a player did, or even what she intended to do, but why she acted as she did. Any of these—and other, harder to model causes, such as a misunderstanding of what is "the deal"—can cause a breakdown of cooperation (or, in the case of the "suck-it-up" strategies, no breakdown in cooperation, but at a substantial cost to the participants).

Public signals, public-signal games, public-signal strategies, and perfect public-signal equilibria

The "general" theory in the literature that applies to the two previous examples begins with the following definitions.

Definitions A15.6.

a. *A **public-signal (repeated) game** is a repeated game where, in each period $t = 0, 1, \ldots$, each of a finite set $\mathcal{N}$ of players chooses an action $a_n(t)$ from an action set A_n. At time t, the action profile $a(t) = (a_n(t))_{n \in \mathcal{N}}$ and history of past public signals generates a random signal $y(t) \in Y$, the distribution of which is common knowledge, and which is independent of all other information possessed by any player. Each player observes in round t the public signal $y(t)$ and her payoff $v_n(t)$, which is a function of her action in that round and the public signal $y(t)$; we write $v_n : A_n \times Y \to R$ for this function. Player n's overall payoff from the grand repeated game is $\sum_{t=0}^{\infty} \delta^t v_n(a(t), y(t))$.*

b. *A **public-signal strategy** for player n in a public-signal game is a strategy in which her choice of action $a_n(t)$ depends **only** on the history of public signals $(y(0), \dots, y(t-1))$. (The player also knows the history of past actions that she took, and she may know more; the force of this definition is that her choice of action in round t does not depend in a meaningful way on this additional information.)*

c. *A **perfect public-signal equilibrium** for a public-signal game is a profile of public-signal strategies such that, beginning at every partial history $h(t) \in H(t)$, each player's choice of strategy is a best response to the strategy choices of all the other players.*

My use of partial histories $h(t) \in H(t)$ in part c needs explanation. A history up to (not including) time t is a full specification of all the action choices by all the players, all the public signals, and any other information that any player may possess. Each player, at time t, only knows part of $h(t)$: She knows which actions she took and the history of public signals $(y(0), \dots, y(t-1))$, and she may know more. But she may not know things that other players know, such as their past action choices.

In a public-signal strategy, her choice of action depends only on the history of past public signals. And, when I say in part c that her public-signal strategy is a best response to what the other players are doing, I mean that her choice is as good as any choice she could make, using *all* of the information she possesses.

It is obvious, I expect, how the first example—where players may intend one action but are "forced" by Nature into another—fits this framework. The actions chosen by the players are their intentions; the random signal $y(t)$ is the vector of their actual play; payoffs depend only on the actual actions; that is, on the $y(t)$. We posited two different public-signal strategies—the grim strategy and the one-round-of-compensation strategy—and then looked for conditions (on the discount factor δ) under which each strategy was a best response against the same strategy played by the other player.

The second example takes some cleverness to fit into this framework.[22] The problem is that the public signal—what is commonly observed by both players—is the action (cooperate or betray) taken by the players. But, at least for the one-round-of-compensation strategy, we want Alice to condition her choice of "action" in the stage game at date t on her private information ϵ_t^A. That's not allowed under the terms of the definition of a public-signal strategy.

The fix is to define the actions available to Alice as a contingent plan for what she will do as a function of the value of her cost of cooperation. That is, Alice's four actions are: (1) cooperate regardless of ϵ_t^A; (2) cooperate if $\epsilon_t^A = 0$ and betray if $\epsilon_t^A = -25$; (3) cooperate if $\epsilon_t^A = -25$ and betray if $\epsilon_t^A = 0$; and (4) betray regardless of the value of ϵ_t^A. The public signal is what each player actually did, and (of course) there is for each choice of one of these four, there is a probabilitic map from the choice to the public signal. But there remains one problem. Alice's payoff has to be a function of her choice and the public signal. If she chooses to cooperate regardless of ϵ_t^A, her half of the public signal will be that she cooperated. And that doesn't tell us what is her payoff. However, these two pieces of data do tell

---

[22]   I am grateful to Ennio Stachetti, who pointed me in the right direction for this example.

us her *expected* payoff, and that is adequate to make the formulation fit the general scheme. Bob is handled similarly.

For simplicity, add the assumption that, for each player n, the function v_n is bounded. Then we have the following proposition.

Proposition A15.7. *Suppose all players except for player n are using public-signal strategies.*

a. *If player n responds with a public-signal strategy, her (expected) payoff function beginning from round t, is a function of the history of public signals up to time t. That is, starting from two partial histories $h(t)$ and $h'(t)$ up to (but not including) time t that have the same record of public signals will provide her with the same expected payoffs for the remainder of the game. And her optimal value function—the supremum of her (expected payoff) over **all** strategies that she might employ, beginning from round t and partial history $h(t)$, depends only the record of past public signals that is part of $h(t)$.*

b. *Therefore, if we further assume that each A_n is finite, she has an optimal response to the strategy profile of her opponents, which is a public-signal strategy.*

Part a is proved by value interation. Her value function from using any strategy is the limit of her value functions for "truncated" problems, where we truncate at some time T, as $T \to \infty$, and where one assumes that, in the truncated problem, she receives her last payoff in round T (the continuation value is 0). One shows her value in round T in the truncated problem is a function of the history of past public signals, and then, inductively, it is a function of past public signals in round $n + k$ for $t < t + k \leq T$, then the same is true for round $t + k - 1$. The same works for her optimal-value function for each truncated problem. A technical note enters here: In Appendix 6, the notion that the decision maker has and might use information that is irrelevant to the future never entered the conversation. Here, it is the essence of the argument that, although Player n has additional information beyond the history of past public signals in round t, her optimal value doesn't involve the use of that information: This is shown using Bellman's equation.

And, part b is then a simple application of Bellman's equation and the conserving = optimal result.

In part b, the assumption that each A_n is finite is there for simplicity. With appropriate compactness assumptions on A_n and continuity assumptions on the reward functions v_n, and the "stochastic laws of motion" of the process, this part can be extended in relatively straightforward fashion.

And don't lose sight of the first half of part a. In applications, one follows the techniques we used in the example: One guesses at what might be the (public-signal) equilibrium strategies, computes the associated value functions, and verifies optimality—that is, that you have an equilibrium—using unimprovability = optimality.

From this starting point, a rich literature on public-signal games and equilibria has been developed, with important papers being Abreu, Pearce, and Stacchetti (1986, 1990), Fudenberg, Levine, and Maskin (1994), and Fudenberg and Levine (1994). The canonical application is to implicit collusion in an oligopoly with noisy observables; this application is discussed in Chapter 22; it should be noted that the seminal paper for this canonical application is Green and Porter (1984). Given the length of this appendix (with one more important topic still to go), I will not go into details; if you aspire to take the next step in this subject, the papers references should be high on your things to read.

And what if there is no public signal?
Or if public signals are not good enough?

Proposition A15.7 says, in effect, that when looking for her best response to counterparties who are playing public-signal strategies, Alice can ignore strategies for herself that are not based (solely) on the history of public signals. *As long as her counterparties are playing public-signal strategies, among her best strategic responses are public-signal strategies.* Hence, in a public-signal equilibrium, players have no positive individual incentive to move away from public-signal strategies. We are *not* restricting Alice's strategic options to public-signal strategies; she just doesn't need them.

Which is *not* to say that, in a world with few or poor public signals, an equilibrium profile where *all* players use strategies that are based on more than the available history of public signals wouldn't be a Pareto improvement on any public-signal equilibrium. Hence, there is good reason (in some contexts) to tackle the more general problem of finding equilibria in games with imperfect observability and/or private information. Such models are difficult to analyze, because one is (essentially) dealing with a dynamic decision problem with hidden state variables, a quite complex branch of dynamic programming. But "difficult" does not equal "impossible," and here is where you find the frontiers of this subject. There are even folk theorems for such models. See, for instance, Sugaya (2023).

A15.7. Instrumental Reputation

The repeated-game literature is game theory's attempt to shed light on relationships, in which two or more parties interact repeatedly. Variations on the classic repeated-game model are employed to explore the notion of *instrumental reputation*.

A dictionary definition of *reputation* is: "a widespread belief that someone or something has a particular habit or characteristic." For instance, "Pediatrician Dr. Browne has a reputation for chatting up the parents of his younger patients." Presumably, Dr. Browne acts in this fashion because he craves adult interaction; there is nothing more to it. Compare this with "District Attorney Black has a reputation for refusing to plead down the charges against accused offenders once their trial has begun." A possible explanation for this is that D.A. Black wishes to pressure the accused into taking a plea deal before they see the case against them; she is using their risk aversion about what might happen once the trial is underway to increase their motivation to take the deal she offers. Of course, this may not be the reason D.A. Black behaves in this manner. But insofar as this explanation is correct, this is an *instrumental reputation*, a reputation that the D.A. maintains for a particular and conscious purpose in terms of "transactions" she has with others. It is this sort of instrumental reputation that game theorists model and study.

Instrumental reputations are not free: In some percentage of cases, the D.A. may see substantial immediate benefits to working out a plea deal once the case goes to trial. Indeed, if the case goes to trial, it is manifest that, for this defendant, the pressure to take the offered plea deal before the trial didn't work. One could argue that in virtually all cases that reach the trial stage, D.A. Black might be better off for that case in isolation to come to a plea-bargain agreement. But, to maintain her reputation, and the impact it has on future defendants, D.A. Black must forgo any short-run advantage of settling today's case to maintain her reputation and the long-run benefits that accrue to it.

The canonical "stage games" connected to models of instrumental reputations are the trust and threat games, first discussed in Appendix 11, and reproduced in Figure A15.10, with a change in one of the payoffs for later expositional convenience. The figure supplies the games in extensive form only; while (to this point) stage games have been in strategic form, the literature generally discussess these issues in terms of the extensive-form stage games, and I follow that practice.

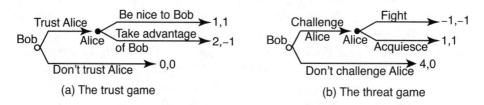

(a) The trust game   (b) The threat game

Figure A15.10. The trust and threat games (Alice's payoffs are listed first in both panels)

Recall what was said about these stage games in Appendix 11:

- The trust game has a unique (pure-strategy) Nash equilibrium in which Bob doesn't trust Alice, because she would take advantage of him (and a continuum of equilibria where Alice mixes at her off-path information set with probability 0.5 or more of taking advantage); only the pure-strategy equilibrium is subgame perfect. The issue is that both Bob and Alice would be better off if he could trust Alice and she was nice to him, and she'd like to promise good behavior. But such a promise is not credible.

- The threat game has two pure-strategy Nash equilibria: (1) Bob challenges Alice, and she acquiesces. (2) Bob doesn't challenge Alice, because she would fight. (There are also Nash equilibria in which Bob doesn't challenge Alice, and her strategy is a mixture of fighting and acquiescing, with probability 0.5 or more of fighting.) Only the challenge–acquiesce strategy profile is subgame perfect. Alice would like to threaten Bob that she will fight, but this threat is not credible.

Now imagine that Alice plays the trust game infinitely often, at dates $t = 0, 1, \ldots,$ against a different opponent in every round. Denote her date t opponent by Bob$t$. Alice is concerned with the discounted sum of her stage-game payoffs, discounted at rate δ. Bob$t$ is concerned only with his payoff in his one encounter. We say that Alice is a "long-lived" player, meeting a sequence of "short-lived" Bobs.[23]

What are the perfect Nash equilibria of this game? One Nash equilibrium, for all values of $\delta \in [0, 1)$, is for no Bob to trust Alice and for Alice to take advantage of any Bob foolish enough to trust her. Note that this is just a repetition of the one subgame-perfect equilibrium of the stage game.

But, in the general spirit of the Folk Theorem, consider the following strategy profile: Bob0 trusts Alice. Alice is nice to him. Subsequently, in round t, if Alice has been nice to all past Bobs who trusted her, Bob$t$ trusts her, and she treats him nicely. But Bob$t$ does not trust Alice if, in some earlier round $t' < t$, Bobt' trusted Alice and she took advantage of him. And if, in such circumstances, Bob$t$ is foolish enough to trust Alice (if he mistakenly trusts her), Alice takes advantage of him.

This is a subgame-perfect equilibrium as long as $\delta \geq 1/2$. For the Bobs, it is straightforward to see that, given Alice's strategy, they are all playing a best response. At Bob$t$'s one decision node, if Alice has never taken advantage of a previous Bob and he trusts her, she will respond by being nice, which nets him 1. He could alternatively not trust her, netting 0 for himself. So, for Bob$t$, at such a node, trust is optimal. But at another node belonging to Bob$t$—and each Bob$t$ has 3^t nodes, representing the 3^t possible previous histories of play—at which she did take advantage of an earlier Bob, if he trusts her, she is bound (by the proposed strategy profile) to take advantage of him, netting him -1. So no trust, for a payoff at this node of 0, is his best response.

And, concerning Alice: If the Bobs carry out this strategy profile (profile because there are many Bobs), and she does as well, she gets a payoff of 1 per period, for a net present value (NPV) of payoffs of $1/(1 - \delta)$. This is also her NPV from the start of her encounter with Bob$t$ if, previously, she never abused a Bobt' who trusted her. From the start of any encounter, if she did take advantage of some Bob in the past, she anticipates no further trust, which means an NPV of 0. And from the start of any proper subgame that begins with one of her nodes (which means this round's Bob trusted her) such that she took advantage of some Bob in the past, her NPV from following the strategy is 2; an immediate payoff of 2, followed by 0's forever after.

So, is her strategy—providing her with these NPVs—unimprovable? At any decision node for Alice where she hasn't taken advantage of a Bob in the past and the current Bob trusts her, her NPV is $1/(1 - \delta)$. If she instead takes advantage, she'll get an immediate 2, but 0s forever after. So we pass the unimprovability test at such a decision node as long as $1/(1 - \delta) \geq 2$, or $\delta \geq 1/2$. And at a decision node for Alice where, in the past, she did take advantage of an earlier Bob, and the current Bob has trusted her, her NPV is 2. Her alternative is to be nice to the

---

[23] In Appendix 9, I said that I'd limit discussion in these appendices to finite-player games unless otherwise indicated. Consider this the indication: This game has countably many Bobs.

current Bob, netting an immediate payoff of 1, but since she can't erase that past incident, all subsequent Bobs will not trust her, and she will still get 0s forever after. So she might as well take advantage of the (mistaken) opportunity given to her by the current Bob.

The previous three paragraphs are quite detailed in spelling out all the steps in showing this is a subgame-perfect equilibrium. I won't give quite so many details, but instead appeal to your good sense, from here on. And, in fact, I haven't quite covered every contingency for every proper subgame of the repeated game. Can you see what I've missed?[24]

The loose interpretation given to this equilibrium (when $\delta \geq 1/2$) is the game theorist's model of Alice having and preserving an instrumental reputation. The Bobs' strategies are paraphrased as, Alice begins with the reputation of being nice to Bobs, a reputation she preserves by always being nice to any Bob who trusts her. If she ever takes advantage of any Bob, her reputation is shattered, gone. Bob t will trust Alice if she has maintained the reputation for being nice; he won't trust her if she earlier shattered that reputation. And Alice, if she has the reputation, is nice in order to preserve it. But if ever she loses this reputation, she will take advantage of any Bob foolish enough to trust her.

This reputation is instrumental, because Alice, if she (still) has the reputation of being nice, is nice to the current Bob (assuming he trusts here). She could increase her immediate payoff from 1 to 2 by taking advantage of him. But this would shatter her reputation, and her reputation is worth more in the future (namely, $\delta/(1-\delta)$) than the extra one unit of payoff she could extract today. It isn't that she is nice because she is fundamentally a nice person. She is nice because this preserves her reputation, which will cause future Bobs to trust her. And a given Bob, facing Alice who has the reputation of being nice, can safely trust her, because he knows (as long as $\delta > 1/2$) that maintaining her reputation is worth more to her than would be taking advantage of him. Note the circularity in this argument: Alice's reputation is valuable because it induces Bobs to trust her. And the Bobs trust her (as long as she maintains her reputation), because her reputation is valuable, and they know (therefore) that she will maintain it.

About this:

- How did she get this reputation? In real life, individuals and organizations *build* reputations. That part of the real-life reputation story is not present here. The issue of reputation building will be discussed in the Section A15.9.

- Formally, Bob t learns of Alice's reputation by reviewing the entire history of her interactions with previous Bobs. In real life, of course, reputation doesn't work that way. Instead, Bob t might consult trusted friends ("Know a trustworthy car mechanic?" "Sure, Alice, the car mechanic, is one.") or, nowadays, read reviews

---

[24] Suppose we are at a position in which Bob t has not trusted Alice, even though Alice has been nice to all previous Bobs *who trusted her*. That ends the round, and the next move belongs to Bob $t + 1$. To cover such contingencies, it is important that I'm careful to say that Alice will treat a trusting Bob nicely *if she has never taken advantage any Bob previously* and not *if she has treated all previous Bob's nicely*, although it is also okay to describe her strategy as being nice *if she had treated nicely all previous Bob's who trusted her*.

on the internet. Especially when it comes to uncurated reviews on the internet, this raises a host of questions that have been explored in the literature.

- In the spirit of the folk theorem, and depending on δ, there are other equilibria that can be constructed. For instance, if $\delta \geq 1/\sqrt{2}$, things can be arranged so that Bob$t$ trusts Alice and is well treated for even numbered t, but he doesn't trust her and, were he to do so, she would take advantage of him, for odd numbered t. (But insofar as we are trying to model instrumental reputations in real life, simple reputations, based on clear and well-defined "rules" about how Alice behaves, seem a better prediction than more complex reputations, such as, She treats every other Bob well.)

- But there are limits to this sort of construction for one long-lived Alice facing a succession of short-lived Bobs. Put it this way: If we were back in the realm of the classic folk theorem, with one Alice facing one equally long-lived Bob, and for δ close enough to 1, we could get (as subgame perfect) the outcome where Alice is always trusted by Bob, treats him nicely for t divisible by 3 or divisible by 3 with remainder 1, but also gets to take advantage of him for t divisible by 3 with remainder 2. With short-lived Bobs, this doesn't work; each individual Bob will only trust Alice if he assesses probability $1/2$ or more that she will be nice to *him*. (If Alice and Bob, *after Bob trusts Alice but before she decides how to treat him*, could access a publicly observable randomizing device, then... [I'll let you finish this sentence.])

  And suppose we are in the world of one long-lived Alice facing a sequence of short-lived Bobs, and instead of the trust game, the stage game is the prisoners' dilemma, with simultaneous moves. Then one gets nowhere with reputation. Each short-lived Bob is going to play his strictly dominant strategy, betray. No reputation by Alice changes this. So Alice's only rational choice is to betray.

The other canonical case concerns long-lived Alice playing the threat game against a sequence of short-lived Bobs. Played once, the unique subgame-perfect equilibrium is that Bob challenges Alice and Alice acquiesces. So, it is an equilibrium in the "repeated" game for each Bob to challenge Alice and for Alice to acquiesce. But another subgame-perfect Nash equilibrium is: From the start, and as long as Alice has fought every previous Bob who challenged her, Bob$t$ does not challenge Alice. But if some Bob$t$ does challenge Alice, and she has fought every previous encounter with a challenger, she fights. However, if in some round t, Alice was previously challenged and acquiesced, Bob$t$ challenges Alice and she acquiesces. In effect, Alice begins with a reputation for being a fighter, a reputation she preserves (and, for δ large enough, is willing to preserve) by fighting any challenge. But she loses this reputation by acquiescing to any challenge, following which, all future Bobs challenge her, and she always acquiesces.

I'll leave it to you to check carefully that this gives a subgame-perfect equilibrium, but the key step (which identifies the range of δ for which this is true) is: If Alice has maintained her reputation and is challenged, she is meant to fight, giving her an immediate -1, but which preserves her reputation, for a discounted

NPV going forward of $\delta 4/(1 - \delta)$. Her alternative immediate action is to acquiesce, which means a payoff of 1 this round and in every subsequent round, for an NPV of $1/(1 - \delta)$. So for her to be willing to fight, we need

$$-1 + \delta \frac{4}{1 - \delta} \geq \frac{1}{1 - \delta}, \quad \text{which is} \quad \delta \geq 2/5.$$

Let me emphasize what just happened. In a single play of the threat game, there are two Nash equilibria. But, because the "threat" by Alice to fight is not credible, only the challenge–acquiesce strategy profile is subgame perfect. Repeat the game with Alice facing a sequence of short-run Bobs (or, for that matter, one long-lived Bob), and Alice's on-path threat becomes credible, and no-challenge in every round is the outcome of a *subgame-perfect* equilibrium. Credibility of the threat, and subgame perfection, results from Alice's desire to maintain a reputation as someone who carries out her threats. As long as she maintains that reputation, she faces no challenges. If she loses the reputation, she faces challenges without end (in the equilibrium constructed). This makes her reputation valuable. And, to protect that valuable reputation, she will fight if challenged.

Noise and the inability to monitor versus reputations

Continuing with the one long-lived versus a sequence of short-lived players, consider what happens if the short-lived players observe a noisy signal concerning what the long-lived player has done or, at the extreme, if they are unable to monitor what she does at all.

In the simple constructions just provided, Alice's reputation is completely shattered if she doesn't act as, in equilibrium, she is meant to act. This is akin to the grim punishment in the Folk Theorem. And, as we saw in the Folk Theorem with noisy observables, grim punishment strategies can be quite inefficient when there is noise. It is not hard to construct equilibria with less onerous punishments. Similar to the two-rounds-of-punishment, in the trust game, if Alice is perceived as taking advantage of Bob t, we might have the next several Bobs refuse to trust her, with a punishment period long enough so that Alice is effectively disciplined to try to be nice. And in the threat game, there may be a period of time in which Alice is challenged and must meekly acquiesce to the challenges before she can effectively reclaim the right to try to fight any challenge.

These constructions "work" as a matter of theory, but they are problematic in terms of their intuition: In the first, a Bob t is refusing to trust Alice because, if he did, she would abuse him. Hence, having abused one Bob, Alice is "punished" by telling her to abuse the next few Bobs who trust her, so that they won't trust her, which is her punishment. And, in the second construction, for the threat game, if challenged—and we need some story about why, along the equilibrium path, Alice faces the occasional challenge—and Alice appears to acquiesce, then to regain her reputation for fighting, she must *acquiesce* to several more challenges.)

Concerning the inability to monitor, the most obvious variation is where, in some rounds (randomly), the interaction between Alice and Bob t is not observed by the other Bobs. Here are three variations you can work through: (1) In each round t, there is small probability π that what happens is not observed by the other Bobs, and both Alice and Bob learn that this is one of those rounds before Bob has to act. (2) Same π, but Bob doesn't learn about this until after he acts (to trust Alice or to challenge her). But Alice, as she decides how to respond to Bob's trust/challenge (if he has done so), is aware that this is one of those rounds. (3) Same π, and Alice and Bob only learn that their interaction was unobserved after it is over.

Variations

Many variations on these basic models are examined in the literature.

- Suppose the "stage game" is an N-player game, where $M < N$ of the players are long-lived (discounting the sum of the rewards) and $N - M$ are short-lived, interested only in their payoff in the one round in which they participate. Folk theorems for this sort of situation have been developed; see Fudenberg and Tirole (1991b, Section 5.3.1) for the results and for citations to the original papers on the subject.

- Players may come and go, overlapping-generation style. See section 5.3.2 in Fudenberg and Tirole.

- A very substantial literature concerns "random matching" of players, going in two different directions: where each player only sees the history of her own interactions (although a variation on this allows for players to also carry reputations); and where the "community" observes the result of all interactions, leading to theories that are a game-theorist's attempt to model community norms and their enforcement.

- In Chapter 22, among the many models examined is one in which Alice is long-lived and the Bobs are short-lived, but short-lived means that each Bob plays Alice not once but (say) ten times, being replaced with a new Bob after his ten chances at the stage game.

A15.8. Enduring Private (Incomplete) Information

In this appendix so far, players have preferences that are common knowledge to their partners/rivals/counterparties in whatever interaction is being modeled and analyzed. And, for long-lived players, the trade offs that they face in the moment concern immediate rewards versus the consequences of their immediate actions on their counterparties' future actions and therefore on their future rewards.

A very different set of models, which nonetheless come to many of the same conclusions, marries repeated play with incomplete information, assuming that the prototypical Bob or Bobs are unsure of Alice's "nature" or, in the language of Appendix 13, her "type." The key here is that Alice's type endures across all her interactions with Bob or the Bobs (depending on the context), and how she behaves in early encounters may provide information about her type. That being so, a strategically aware Alice must be concerned in the moment with what she reveals about herself; put more positively from her perspective, she can take advantage and, under some conditions, "be the type of Alice that is most advantageous to her," even if she is not the type she pretends to be.

Long-lived Alice plays the threat game against finitely many short-lived Bobs

An example illustrates this:[25] Suppose Alice plays the threat game with a sequence of Bobs for a fixed finite number of rounds, indexed $t = 0, \ldots, T$, for a definite and finite T.[26] For simplicity, assume that Alice does not discount her round-by-round payoffs.

With nothing more added to the story, in any subgame-perfect equilibrium, Bob$T$ must anticipate that Alice will acquiesce if he challenges her—there is no future, hence no reason for her to cultivate any instrumental reputation—and so he challenges her without fear. Since this is so, Bob$T-1$ reasons that Alice will acquiesce if he challenges her—nothing she does will change round T—so he challenges her. And so forth. (Of course, it is a Nash equilibrium for none of the Bobs to challenge Alice, if her strategy is always to fight. She can get away with this threat in a Nash equilibrium, since if no Bobs challenge her, her actions are all off-path.)

But suppose that, in the minds of the Bobs, there is a slim possibility that Alice is a type who never backs down from any challenge. Formally, this type of Alice is provided with payoffs that make fighting in the event of a challenge a dominant strategy, regardless of future consequences.[27] Suppose, for instance, that the Bobs assess probability 0.001 that Alice is this type—call her "Fighting Alice"—and probability 0.999 that she is the regular type of Alice—call her "Rational Alice"—with payoffs as in the original model. Both types of Alice are fully knowledgeable that the Bobs entertain these doubts about her type. Formally, we create a game of incomplete information with two initial states of nature: One state, with prior probability 0.999, is that Alice is Rational Alice; the second state, with prior probability 0.001, is that she is Fighting Alice, inflexibly committed to fighting if challenged. "Inflexibly" here means just what it says: Fighting Alice makes no calculations to determine her optimal actions; she just fights whenever she is challenged.

We look for sequential equilibria of this game. All of Rational Alice's information sets are singleton, so her beliefs are trivial. It is the Bobs who have nontrivial information sets, as they don't know whether Alice is the rational or the fighting type. Use p_t for Bob$t$'s belief that Alice is Fighting Alice, prior to deciding whether to challenge her. And, to simplify the analysis, one restriction on the Bobs' beliefs is added: If, in any earlier round t', Bobt' believed that Alice is Rational Alice—if

---

[25]   This example is from Kreps and Wilson (1982a) and Milgrom and Roberts (1982b), the original papers that pursue this line of thought.

[26]   In the literature, the structure of this finitely repeated game is related to the story of the behavior of a chain store and goes by the rubric, the chain-store paradox. See Chapter 22.

[27]   Or, as discussed on pages 617–8, we could model things so that fighting is the only option available to this type of Alice. See, in particular, panel c in Figure A13.5. As you will see, doing this makes life of the modeler easier.

$p_{t'} = 0$—then $p_t = 0$. This assumption allows us to to assume that, once Alice acquiesces, for the rest of the game (from any information set belonging to a Bob) he will challenge her and she will acquiesce, using the logic from before.[28]

Now work from the back: What will Alice do in round T? Since this is the last round, if she is Rational Alice, she surely will acquiesce if challenged; there is no future to affect. Hence, if Bob$T$ assesses probability $p_T < 0.5$ that Alice is the fighting type, he will challenge her. If he assesses probability $p_T > 0.5$, he will not challenge her. And at the beliefs $p_T = 0.5$ exactly, he is indifferent. (We'll deal with Bob's behavior in the case $p_T = 1/2$ as we analyze round $T - 1$.)

Back up to round $T - 1$. Suppose Bob$T-1$ holds beliefs $p_{T-1} > 1/2$. Then, whatever he thinks is Rational Alice's behavior strategy in this round if challenged, there is probability *at least* p_{T-1} that he will face a fight, and he will not enter. And, since no challenge is forthcoming, no information about Alice's type is produced, and Bob$T$ will assess probability $p_T = p_{T-1}$ that Alice is the fighting type, so there will be no challenge in the final period.

But, what about starting from a position in which $p_{T-1} > 1/2$ and Bob$T-1$ mistakenly does challenge Alice? What should Rational Alice do?

- If she acquiesces, Bob$T$ will know that she is Rational Alice and challenge her. She will, of course, acquiesce again (in period T). Hence her payoffs will be 1 in each round, for a net 2. But, if she fights, whatever her equilibrium behavior is, Bob$T$ will assess probability *at least* p_{T-1} that she is Fighting Alice. (If Rational Alice's equilibrium strategy is to acquiesce with strictly positive probability, Bayes' rule leads to $p_T > p_{T-1}$.) Therefore, Bob$T$ will not challenge her. Thus, Rational Alice, by fighting in period $T-1$ if challenged, nets -1 in round $T-1$ and 4 in round T, for a net 3. Fighting is always the better response.

Therefore, if $p_{T-1} > 1/2$, both types of Alice will fight if challenged. Bob$T-1$ wasn't going to challenge her anyway, but his reasons not to challenge her have been enhanced; in equilibrium, he knows he will face a fight with probability 1. He doesn't challenge her, and p_T will equal p_{T-1}. In the last two rounds, starting from any information set of Bob$T-1$ where his beliefs are that Alice is Fighting Alice with probability $p_{T-1} > 1/2$, neither he nor Bob$T$ will challenge her, and Rational Alice has a net payoff of 8 from these final two payoffs.

What if $0 < p_{T-1} < 1/2$? The first step is to find out how Rational Alice will respond if she if she is challenged.

- If Rational Alice's equilibrium response is to fight with probability 1, then Bob$T$ will assess $p_T = p_{T-1} < 1/2$ and enter for sure, netting Alice -1 and then 1. A better response for her would be to acquiesce, netting 1 in this round and 1 in the next.

- If Rational Alice's equilibrium response is to acquiesce with probability 1, then

---

[28] With the alternative model mentioned in footnote 27, this assumption is unnecessary. If, in the model, Fighting Bob doesn't have the option of acquiescing, then, in any Bob's information sets after Alice is observed to have earlier acquiesced, there is a single node—Alice *must* be Rational Alice—and so the question of this and subsequent Bobs' beliefs is moot.

Bob T will assess $p_T = 0$ if he sees Alice acquiesce, hence challenge her. She gets 1 this round and 1 next. But, if acquiescing is Alice's equilibrium response, then fighting leads Bob T to conclude that she is Fighting Alice, and he won't challenge her. Hence, acquiescing with probability 1 can't be Rational Alice's equilibrium response: If it were, and if she deviated to fighting, she would get an immediate -1 and then 4.

- The only possibility left is for Rational Alice to randomize. For her to randomize, she must be indifferent between fighting and acquiescing. Acquiescing nets her 1 this round and 1 next, so fighting must also net her a total of 2, which, since fighting nets her -1 this round, means that she must be getting 3 in the next. But the only way she can get 3 in the final round is if Bob T randomizes between challenging her and not; specifically, he must challenge her with probability 1/3 and fail to challenge her with probability 2/3, so her expected payoff in the final round is $(1/3)(1) + (2/3)(4) = 9/3 = 3$. And for Bob T to randomize, his beliefs, on seeing Alice fight in round $T - 1$, must be $p_T = 1/2$.

  And that fixes the required randomization by Rational Alice in round $T-1$, assuming she is challenged. Suppose she fights with probability q_{T-1}. The posterior probability that she is Fighting Alice, by Bayes' rule, is

$$p_T = \frac{p_{T-1}}{p_{T-1} + q_{T-1}(1 - p_{T-1})}.$$

This must equal 1/2, which gives

$$q_{T-1} = \frac{p_{T-1}}{1 - p_{T-1}}.$$

- Finally, there is the case $p_{T-1} = 1/2$. If Rational Alice is challenged, and she acquiesces in equilibrium, she gets 2 for the last two rounds, versus the 3 she would get by deviating. If Rational Alice randomizes if challenged, then, if she fights, $p_T > p_{T-1} = 1/2$, and Bob T does not challenge her, which makes randomization less attractive than fighting for sure. So Rational Alice must fight if challenged, which leaves $p_T = p_{T-1} = 1/2$ and Bob T indifferent. This is a knife-edge case where there is some flexibility in the equilibrium: Bob T must challenge with probability 1/3 or less, so that Rational Alice is willing to fight in round $T - 1$. For simplicity, I'll assume that Bob T follows the rule that he must follow for $p_{T-1} < 1/2$, namely, challenge with probability $r_T = 1/3$.

We know, therefore, how Alice will respond in round $T - 1$ if challenged. Will Bob $T-1$, holding beliefs $p_{T-1} \leq 1/2$, challenge her? If he does, the calculations just completed show that will be fought with probabiity

$$p_{T-1} + (1 - p_{T-1})q_{T-1} = p_{T-1} + (1 - p_{T-1})\frac{p_T}{(1 - p_{T-1})} = 2p_{T-1}.$$

This is: Alice is Fighting Alice, who fights for sure, with probability p_{T-1}. And she is Rational Alice with probability $1 - p_{T-1}$, who fights with probability $p_T/(1 - p_{T-1})$, so the marginal probability that Bob $T - 1$ will be fought is the sum of these two: $2p_{T-1}$.

Clearly, Bob $T-1$ challenges Alice if $2p_{T-1} < 1/2$, or $p_{T-1} < 1/4$, and he doesn't challenge Alice if $2p_{T-1} > 1/2$, or $p_{T-1} > 1/4$. If $p_{T-1} = 1/4$, he is indifferent, and what he will do is randomize, so that Rational Alice in round $T - 2$ is indifferent between fighting or not. Just as what Bob T does in round T if he assesses $p_T = 1/2$ is devised to make Rational Alice indifferent between fighting or not in round $T-1$, so what Bob $T - 1$ does if $p_{T-1} = 1/4$ is devised so that, at time $T - 2$, Rational Alice (if challenged) is indifferent between fighting or not.

And now we move back to an analysis of round $T - 2$, and $T - 3$, and so forth. The pattern set described above continues:[29] In round $T - k$, if $p_{T-k} > 1/2^k$, Bob does not challenge Alice. If he were to challenge her, Rational Alice fights for sure; since to do otherwise is to reveal to later Bobs that she is Rational Alice, prompting all of them to challenge her. For $0 < p_{T-k} < 1/2^k$, it turns out that Rational Alice will randomize (if challenged) in a manner to get Bob $T-k+1$ to randomize; the randomization required of Rational Alice to do this is such that Bob $T-k$ does not challenge Alice if $p_{T-k} > 1/2^{k+1}$; he does challenge her if $p_{T-k} < 1/2^{k+1}$; and he randomizes if $p_{T-k} = 1/2^{k+1}$ in a manner that supports Rational Alice randomizing in round $T - k - 1$ when $p_{T-k-1} \leq 1/2^{k+1}$. (If $p_{T-k} = 1/2$, Rational Alice will fight for sure if challenged, just as above.)

The dance between Alice and the Bobs at the end of the game is complex. But for most of the game, things are simple: The current Bob doesn't enter and, if he did, Alice of either type will fight: Fighting Alice fights because that's who she is, and Rational Alice fights because she doesn't want to reveal herself as *not* a fighting type, which would get later Bobs to challenge her.

And how much is "most" of the game? We started with a prior probability of $1/1000$ that Alice was the fighting type. And $1/2^{10} < 1/1000$. So for all but the final 10 rounds, with both types of Alice ready to fight in the event of a challenge, Rational Alice goes happily unchallenged.

In essence, the Bobs are worried that Alice is the fighting type; if she is, they don't want to enter. Rational Alice, by fighting (for most of the game) "confirms" that she *might* be Fighting Alice, where I put "confirms" in in scare quotes, because Rational Alice is doing nothing of the sort. For all but the last ten rounds, she isn't challenged, so no information is produced that would cause the Bobs to change their assessment that she is Fighting Alice; it stays at 0.001. Indeed, even if, for $t < T - 9$, Bob t were mistakenly to challenge Alice, Rational Alice would fight, and the probability p_{t+1} assessed by Bob $t + 1$ that Alice is Fighting Alice would remain 0.0001. This changes in the last ten periods. But, for most of the game, while one can't say that Rational Alice isn't confirming that she is Fighting Alice,

---

[29] If you want further formal details, your options are: (1) See either Kreps and Wilson (1982a) or Milgrom and Roberts (1982b). (2) Look a few subsections ahead, where I provide full details for the case of long-lived Alice playing the trust game against a sequence of short-lived Bobs.

she would not, if challenged, reveal that she isn't. And that, it turns out, is enough.

Before moving on, I remind you that, at the outset of this section, I changed the payoff to Alice in the threat game if she is not challenged by Bob from 2 to 4. Now I can explain why. Suppose this payoff is 2.1.[30] And suppose, in round $T - 1$, p_{T-1} is quite high, say, 0.75. Then, if Alice is challenged and fights, $p_T \geq p_{T-1}$, and Bob$_T$ will not enter. If she is challenged and acquiesces, p_T will become 0, and Bob$_T$ will enter. Nonetheless, Alice will acquiesce, since fighting will mean payoffs of -1 and 2.1 (instead of -1 and 4), for a total of 1.1 (instead of 3), versus 1 and 1 for a total of 2. This doesn't kill the effect, but it does delay it: You must go back to $T - 2$: If $p_{T-2} = 0.75$, Alice is challenged, and she fights, Bob$_{T-1}$ will not enter, so her net will be $-1 + 2.1 + 2.1 = 3.2$, greater than the $1 + 1 + 1$ she gets if she acquiesces. It just takes longer for the reputation construction to get off the ground.

What's going on here? How general is it?
Fudenberg and Levine (1989, 1992)

This specific model was created to overcome the difficulties encountered by reputation stories in models with a fixed finite horizon. In particular, the original two papers explicitly present this model as a resolution of the so-called chain-store paradox, which is discussed in Chapter 22. But this leaves unanswered questions about the generality of the result. Are there other sequential equilibria with distinctly different overall outcomes? The derivation of the equilibrium seems to indicate that, at least for this specific model, the answer is no: At each step along the way, except for knife-edge cases, the next step in the derivation was always forced. But, if we grant that what is sketched is "the" sequential equilibrium—and it is certainly the case that sequential rationality was employed in the derivation—is this an artifact of a very specific model specification, or does this point to some general phenomenon?

Furthermore, compare with what we found in the infinite-horizon version of the repeated threat game. With no incomplete information, we do have an equilibrium where Alice can credibly and successfully threaten the Bobs. But we also have equilibria in which, perceived by the Bobs to be a wimp, Alice faces a challenge in each round and meekly acquiesces. If, somehow, the incomplete information in the finite-horizon game pins down the result that, at least in a sequential equilibrium, Rational Alice can avoid challenge, how does incomplete information of this sort affect results for the infinite-horizon model?

Two papers by Fudenberg and Levine (1989, 1992) provide answers. They show that a small amount of "right" kind of incomplete information about a long-lived player can be a very powerful tool for that player, if she is playing against a sequence of short-lived opponents. This works whether there is a long but finite horizon or an infinite horizon (with a discount factor close to 1). Their methods don't work for every stage game, but their methods do work for the threat game. Their general

---

[30] The case where it is 2 gives a knife-edge case that is expositionally messy.

analysis is complex, but their basic logic can be illustrated with the threat-game model.

Imagine Alice plays the threat game against a sequence of Bobs, where each Bob plays once and once only. The analysis covers both the case of an infinite-horizon model and a fixed-finite horizon model, so I won't fix one or the other. In the case of an infinite horizon, assume round-by-round payoffs are discounted by Alice with discount factor δ; in the case of a finite horizon, assume there is no discounting.

And assume that the Bobs are initially uncertain concerning Alice's nature: Rational Alice plays the game to maximize her expected overall payoff, but there can be other "behavioral" types who play according to a specific behavior and, in particular, there is probability $\eta > 0$ that Alice is the behavioral type Fighting Alice, who always fights any challenge by any Bob.

Proposition A15.8. *Let* $M := \lfloor ln(\eta)/ln(1/2) \rfloor$, *where* $\lfloor \cdot \rfloor$ *denotes the greatest integer less than the quantity inside the left and right delimiters. Then, in any **Nash** equilibrium of this game of incomplete information:*

a. *In the infinite-horizon version of the game, Rational Alice's expected payoff is at least*
$4\delta^M/(1-\delta) - (1 + \delta + \ldots + \delta^{M-1})$.

b. *In the T-horizon version of the game (with no discounting), Rational Alice's expected payoff is at least $4(T + 1 - M) - M = 4(T+1) - 5M$.*

Hence, in the infinite-horizon version of the game, Rational Alice's normalized payoff (multiplying her payoff by $(1 - \delta)$) approaches 4 as $\delta \to 1$. And in the finite horizon version of the game, her average payoff per period appoaches 4 as $T \to \infty$.

Proof. Fix a Nash equilibrium of the game. Rational Alice's expected payoff is the best she can do, so a lower bound on her expected payoff is what she would get if she followed the strategy of always fighting every entry; that is, if she pretends to be Fighting Alice.

Suppose she plays this strategy. Take any on-path path of play along which, every time Alice is challenged, she fights. If Alice pretends to be Fighting Alice, every path that matters in computing her expected payoff will be of this character.[31] Since we are looking at on-path paths of play, it follows that, in any Nash equilibrium, the Bobs must be employing Bayes' rule to update their beliefs that Alice is Fighting Alice.

And, I assert, along any such on-path path of play, at most M Bobs will challenge Alice. I'm not prepared to say if this will happen in the first M periods or the last or in between; the lower-bound estimate provided in part a of the proposition is premised on the pessimistic (from Rational Alice's perspective) hypothesis that all M are the first M periods. But once it is established that, along any such on-path path of play, there will be no more than M challenges by Bobs, the lower-bound estimates in parts a and b are immediate, and the assertions that follow at the end of the proposition are a matter of simple algebra.

---

[31] Conditional on her being Rational Alice, if she mimics Fighting Alice, the support of her "conditional outcome" will consist of a subset of such paths.

So, the job is to prove that this upper bound on the number of challenges that Alice (of any type) faces, along on-path paths of play where challenge is met by fighting, is valid.

The key is that, since the Bobs are short-lived, they only can enter with positive probability if they believe that the probability that Alice will fight is less than or equal to 1/2. Suppose, along the path, we are at such a contingency; that is, the time is t, Bob$t$ (along with all the other Bobs) assesses probability less or equal to 1/2 that Alice will fight, and so he enters. (If he assesses probability precisely equal to 1/2, he can randomize. In that case, I'm interested in a path where he does in fact enter.) Consider the joint probability table shown in Figure A15.11.

		Response to entry		
		Fight	Accommodate	
Alice's type	The "fighting" type	β	0	β
	Other behavioral types	$\gamma\zeta$	$\gamma(1-\zeta)$	γ
	The "rational" type	$\phi(1-\beta-\gamma)$	$(1-\phi)(1-\beta-\gamma)$	$1-\beta-\gamma$
		$\phi(1-\beta-\gamma)+\beta+\gamma\zeta$	$(1-\phi)(1-\beta-\gamma)+\gamma(1-\zeta)$	

Figure A15.11. A joint probability table (see text for explanation)

Suppose Bob$t$ challenges Alice when he assesses that she is Fighting Alice with probability β. The marginal the probability assessed by Bob$t$ that she will fight is the sum of (1) the marginal probability assessed (at the outset of this period) Alice is Fighting Alice, β, plus (2) the marginal probability that it is another behavioral type γ times the conditional probability that another behavioral type will fight in this circumstance ζ, for a joint probability $\gamma\zeta$, plus (3) the probability $1-\beta-\gamma$ that Alice is rational, times the probability ϕ that Rational Alice will fight in this circumstance. Hence, the marginal probability that Alice will fight is $\phi(1-\beta-\gamma)+\beta+\gamma\zeta$. Call this marginal probability ψ.

Suppose she does fight. What is the posterior probability assessed by all the Bobs (and, in particular, Bobs who follow Bob$t$ that Alice is Fighting Alice? Bayes' rule says that it is β/ψ.

But Bob$t$, being short-lived, will only challenge Alice if he assesses $\psi \leq 1/2$ (for the numbers in this example). Therefore, everytime a Bob challenges Alice and she does fight, the probability that she is Fighting Alice, $\beta/\psi \geq 2\beta$.

But how many times can this happen? Once the assessed probability that Alice is Fighting Alice exceeds 1/2, no Bob would ever contemplate challenging her, no matter what he assesses rational Alice and other behavioral types might be doing. And, starting from an initial prior η that Alice is Fighting Alice, after $\lfloor \ln(\eta)/\ln(1/2) \rfloor$ doubles, the posterior probability of Fighting Alice exceeds 1/2: Since both η and 1/2 are strictly less than 1, their logs are negative. Hence, another way to write the definition of M is that $M \ln(1/2) \geq \ln(\eta)$, and $(M+1)\ln(1/2) < \ln(\eta)$. Rewriting again, we have

$$\ln\left(0.5^M\right) \geq \ln(\eta) > \ln\left(0.5^{M+1}\right) \quad \text{or} \quad 0.5^M \geq \eta > 0.5^{M+1}, \quad \text{or} \quad 1 \geq \frac{\eta}{0.5^M} > \frac{1}{2}.$$

I reiterate that the lower-bound estimate on Rational Alice's payoff in the formulation with discounting is pessimistic, in that it assumes she is challenged in the first M periods. In the sequential equilibria constructed in the original papers, challenges only come in the final M periods. At least for finite-horizon models, I believe—but I'm not quite willing to assert—that challenges will only come at the end. But the nature of this proof doesn't allow me to claim that this is so.

Please note: The statement of Proposition A15.18 emphasizes that this is true of any *Nash* equilibrium. No perfection refinement is required to come to this conclusion.

If we allow incomplete information about Alice, shouldn't we allow for the possibility that she is a bit uncertain about the types of the Bobs? Suppose, for instance, each Bob comes in one of two types: Rational Bob, who plays to maximize his payoff in the one round of his life, and Fearless Bob, who will challenge Alice even if he is certain she will fight him. Suppose, for each Bob, there is probability μ that he is fearless. And suppose that the types of all the Bobs are independent of one another. (This last bit colors what follows, so be sure you understand it.)

Even if the Rational Bobs fail to challenge Alice, she is fairly certain to face a fearless type of Bob at some point, and then Rational Alice must decide whether mimicking Fighting Alice is worthwhile. If she decides to mimic Fighting Alice, at least for most of the game, her expected payoff in any round will be $4(1 - \mu) - \mu = 4 - 5\mu$. If she chooses to acquiesce on her first challenge, she nets 1 per period. (If her strategy is to acquiesce at the first challenge and if Bob0 is rational, he'll also challenge her: She can't tell the difference between rational and fearless types.) Suppose $4 - 5\mu > 1$, which is $\mu < 3/5$. Then, it turns out, Alice will wish to mimic Fighting Alice for most of the game. If $\mu > 3/5$, she acquiesces from the start. This is an implication of the general results of Fudenberg and Levine (1989).

And, to be very clear, in this case, Alice will face many more than M challenges. As she fights those challenges, the change in the probability that she is Fighting Alice may not change at all.[32] If Rational Alice's equilibrium strategy calls for her to fight any challenge for the first 10,000 periods, and if the prior probability that the she is either Rational Alice or Fighting Alice exceeds $1/2$, she will still be challenged $10,000\mu$ times on average, marking the challenger as a Fearless Bob. But she cannot adopt as behavior "I only fight Fearless Bobs" and save the cost of fighting them. Because, if her only indication that a Bob is fearless is that he challenged the odds of her fighting (per her equilibrium strategy), and if she says "Okay, I'm not fighting *you*," then all the Rational Bobs will mimic Fearless Bobs and challenge her. She must fight all those (roughly) $10,000\mu$ challenges, to keep from getting challenges from the other roughly $10,000(1 - \mu)$ Bobs.

Fudenberg and Levine (1992), however, gives her a tool for doing a bit better. Suppose there is a behavioral type of Alice, call her Ifilitm Alice (for "I fight if

---

[32] If there are other behavioral types of Alice who would acquiesce, the probability may change a bit.

I'm in the mood") who, when challenged, fights with (independent from round to round) probability a bit more than $1/2$. Suppose, initially, the Bobs assess positive probability that Alice is Ifilitm Alice. Fudenberg and Levine (1992) show that Alice can successfully imitate this type: Because this type fights with probability greater than $1/2$, Rational Bobs are deterred from challenging her for most rounds. And, when the occasional Fearless Bob comes along, Alice only needs to fight a bit more than half the time: instead of losing 1 to every Fearless Bob (to keep Rational Bobs at bay), against Fearless Bobs she loses 1 with probability a bit more than $1/2$ and gets 1 with probability a bit less.

At least, this ability to mimic Ifilitm Alice exists in theory, as long as the Bobs attach positive probability to Ifilitm Alice's existence a priori. As an intuitive outcome, I'm less convinced that the Bobs will comprehend that Alice might be Ifilitm Alice; the story with the rather simple behavioral type of Fighting Alice is a lot more plausible. But still, the power and elegance of the general results obtained by Fudenberg and Levine's two papers are very worthy of careful study.

Enduring private information in repeated play gives a variety of interesting results in other contexts. The next four subsections provide a selection of these results.

Long-lived Alice plays the trust game against a finite sequence of short-lived Bobs

Suppose long-lived Alice plays the trust game against a sequence of short-lived Bobs. For easy reference, I reproduce the trust game in Figure A15.12.

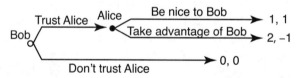

Figure A15.12. The trust game (Alice's payoffs are given first)

With a finite horizon and complete information about types, in the only subgame-perfect Nash equilibrium of this game, trust is never given, and Alice would take advantage of any Bob foolish enough to trust her. The usual unraveling-from-the-back argument applies. As discussed previously, an infinite horizon can fix this, where we construct an instrumental-reputation equilibrium in which Alice begins as trustworthy, unless and until she proves (by taking advantage of some Bob) that she is not. But, in the infinite-horizon repeated game, there is also a subgame-perfect equilibrium where Alice is never trusted, and as a consequence, she takes advantage of any Bob foolish enough to trust her.

In view of what we saw with the finitely repeated threat game, we might hope that, if (say) the Bobs initially assess a small probability η that Alice is "Nice Alice," who inflexibly responds to trust by being nice, then "Rational Alice"—Alice who seeks to maximize the (discounted) sum of her stage-game payoffs—will for much of the game mimic Nice Alice and in anticipation of this behavior, the Bobs for most of the game will trust her, to the benefit of both Alice and the Bobs, relative to the no-trust outcome.

Alas, it is not so simple. In particular, the general results of Fudenberg and Levine (1989, 1992) don't work for the repeated trust game.[33] This doesn't mean that a result of this sort cannot be crafted. But their general results don't provide the result.

Indeed, consider the conjecture (parallel to Proposition A15.8):

For every Nash equilibrium of the repeated game where the Bobs initially assess probability η that Alice is nice, in "most" periods, the Bob of that period will trust Alice, and Rational Alice will respond by being nice.

This conjecture is false by virtue of the quantifier *for every **Nash** equilibrium*. Consider the following strategy profile, for the case of only two types of Alice (Rational Alice and Nice Alice) and $\eta < 1/2$: No Bob trusts Alice, and Rational Alice takes advantage whenever she can (which, along the path of play, is never), as long as $\eta < 1/2$.

This is a Nash equilibrium, because if Rational Alice follows this strategy, it is certainly rational for each Bob not to trust her. And, if they never trust her, she never gets to play, and in a Nash equilibrium, she can do anything she wants at information sets that are unreached due to the choices of others.

Compare the situation here with repeated play of the threat game. If a Bob doesn't challenge Alice, Rational Alice gets the outcome she wants. If she is challenged, she gets to demonstrate that she's "just like" Fighting Alice. But in the trust game, if Rational Alice isn't trusted, she neither gets what she wants nor can she pretend to be good natured.

However, the Nash equilibrium strategy profile from two paragraphs ago involves behavior by Rational Alice that is *not* sequentially rational. Suppose that Bob t mistakenly trusts her. Per the equilibrium strategies, she is supposed to take advantage of him. But, if this is Rational Alice's equilibrium strategy and if Alice (of uncertain type to the Bobs) is nice, the Bobs infer that they are dealing with Nice Alice, and they will henceforth trust her. But if that's how they will behave and there are a lot of periods to go, Rational Alice should act nicely, misleading the Bobs into thinking that she is nice, thereafter pocketing a bunch of payoffs of 1, until the final period, when she reveals herself as Rational Alice.

Perhaps, if we changed "Nash equilibrium" in the italicized conjecture to "equi-

---

[33] For the reader who reads these two papers, let me point to why not. In these papers, the authors provide upper and lower bounds on what are possible equilibrium payoffs for the long-lived player. (They deal with an infinite-horizon, discounted formulation, and examine how those bounds work as the discount factor approaches 1, but the logic of their arguments extents easily to finite-but-long horizon formulations without [or, for that matter, with] discounting.) The key concept in regard to the assertion that their analysis doesn't help in this case is what they call an *identified* game; see page 572 of the 1992 paper. If the game is identified (and nondegenerate), the upper and lower bounds converge and give the sort of result aimed at here. Unfortunately, the trust game is not identified. (I'm grateful to Drew Fudenberg for clarifying discussions.)

librium in which Rational Alice plays a sequentially rational strategy," the conjecture would be true. I don't have that result. What I can do, instead, is to construct an exact sequential equilibrium of the sort in the original chain-store papers, for the following specification: There are (only) two types of Alice, Rational and Nice, with the prior probability of Nice Alice being $\eta > 0$. The stage game is played a large but finite number of times, $t = 0, 1, \ldots, T$, with a long-lived Alice facing short-lived Bob0, Bob1, ..., Bob$T$, in succession. In the sequential equilibrium I construct, Bob trusts Alice, and Alice of either type is nice to him, for all but the final few periods of the game. Because this model and equilibrium construction is not in the literature (so far as I know), I provide a full construction and proof.

Let p_t denote the probabilty assessed by the Bobs that Alice is nice at the outset of period t and let π_t be the equilibrium probability that Rational Alice, if trusted, will be nice. Then, Bob$t$, contemplating whether to trust Alice and being short-lived, responds as follows: If $p_t + \pi_t(1 - p_t) > 1/2$, he should trust her. If $p_t + \pi_t(1 - p_t) < 1/2$, he should not trust her. And if $p_t + \pi_t(1 - p_t) = 1/2$, he is free to do either and, in particular, to randomize between trusting her or not.

The equilibrium is constructed from the back: In period T, the final period, Rational Alice will certainly take advantage of Bob$T$'s trust, if he trusts her. That is, $\pi_T = 0$. Therefore, Bob$T$ trusts Alice if $p_T > 1/2$, doesn't do so if $p_T < 1/2$, and can randomize if $p_T = 1/2$. So that the equilibrium works, if $p_T = 1/2$, Bob$t$ trusts with probability $1/2$. Thus Rational Alice's payoff in the final period is 2 if $p_T > 1/2$; is 0 if $p_T < 1/2$; and, because she only gets Bob$T$'s trust with probability $1/2$, is 1 if $p_T = 1/2$.

With this start, I prove by induction on $n = 0, 1, \ldots$ that the following constitutes an equilibrium:

1. In period $T - n$, if $p_{T-n} \geq (1/2)^n$, and if Bob$T-n$ trusts Alice, Rational Alice is nice with probability 1. Therefore, Bob$T-n$ trusts her.

2. In period $T - n$, if $p_{T-n} < (1/2)^n$, and if Bob$T-n$ trusts Alice, Rational Alice is nice with probability $\pi = (2^n - 1)p_{T-n}/(1 - p_{T-n})$. Bob$T-n$ trusts her if $p_{T-n} > (1/2)^{n+1}$; he doesn't trust her if $p_{T-n} < (1/2)^{n+1}$; and he randomizes between trusting her and not, each with probability $1/2$, if $p_{T-n} = (1/2)^{n+1}$.

3. Let $V_{T-n}(p_{T-n})$ be Rational Alice's expected value of the sum of payoffs she receives in periods $T - n, \ldots, T$, from the start of period $T - n$ (anticipating equilibrium actions by Bob$T-n$ and all subsequent Bobs) until the end, if the period begins with Bob$T-n$ assessing probability p_{T-n} that Alice is nice. Then

$$V_{T-n}(p_{T-n}) = \begin{cases} 2 \text{ or more,} & \text{if } p_{T-n} \geq (1/2)^n, \\ 2, & \text{if } p_{T-n} \in ((1/2)^{n+1}, (1/2)^n), \\ 1, & \text{if } p_{T-n} = (1/2)^{n+1}, \text{ and} \\ 0, & \text{if } p_{T-n} < (1/2)^{n+1}. \end{cases}$$

Figure A15.13 presents the induction hypothesis graphically.

The first step in the induction is to verify these three assertions for $n = 0$. That's precisely what we did before giving the induction hypothesis.

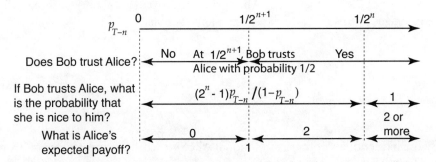

Figure A15.13. The induction hypothesis for long-lived Alice playing the trust game against a finite sequence of short-lived Bob

So, assume inductively that the induction hypothesis (statements 1, 2, and 3) holds for all n up to $N - 1$. In particular, it holds for $n = N - 1$. We must prove that it holds as well for $n = N$. (At this point, I remind you that the case $n = N$ means for periods $T - N$ to T.)

- Suppose $p_{T-N} \geq (1/2)^N$. Suppose Bob $T-N$ trusts Alice. If Rational Alice takes advantage of this trust, she nets 2 this period and 0s for the remainder of the game. If she is nice, netting 1 this period, p_{T-N+1} will be at least $(1/2)^N$, regardless of her equilibrium strategy, and so, starting from next period, Rational Alice's expected payoff will be at least 1. Being nice then gives her 2 or more. So it is a best response for her to be nice. Therefore, Bob $T-N$ will trust her, and her payoff starting from this period is 2 or more.

- Suppose $p_{T-N} < (1/2)^N$. The prescribed behavior for Rational Alice is that, if she is trusted, she is nice with probability $\pi = (2^N - 1)p_{T-N}/(1 - p_{T-N})$. If she behaves in this fashion, the probability that Bob $T-N$, if he trusts Alice (not knowing her type), is treated nicely is

$$p_{T-N} + (1 - p_{T-N})\pi = p_{T-N} + (2^N - 1)p_{T-N} = 2^N p_{T-N}.$$

Now,

$$2^N p_{T-N} \begin{cases} > 1/2, & \text{if } p_{T-N} > (1/2)^{N+1}, \\ = 1/2, & \text{if } p_{T-N} = (1/2)^{N+1}, \text{and} \\ < 1/2, & \text{if } p_{T-N} < (1/2)^{N+1}. \end{cases}$$

Therefore, Bob $T-N$ definitely trusts Alice if $p_{T-N} \in \left((1/2)^{N+1}, (1/2)^N\right)$, can randomize if $p_{T-N} = (1/2)^{N+1}$, and definitely will not trust Alice if $p_{T-N} < (1/2)^{N+1}$. The strategy specified in the induction hypothesis for Bob $T-N$ is a best response to Alice's alleged equilibrium strategy.

- Suppose Bob$T-N$ does trust Alice with $p_{T-N} < (1/2)^N$. Assuming Alice randomizes in this fashion, Bayes' rule tells us that

$$p_{T-N+1} = \frac{p_{T-N}}{2^N p_{T-N}} = \frac{1}{2^N}.$$

By the induction hypothesis, if Rational Alice is nice, her expected payoff starting from next period is 1. By being nice, she nets 1 today, so being nice today gives her a total value for the remainder of the game of 2. If she takes advantage, she gets an immediate 2 and zeros thereafter. So she is content to randomize; her strategy is a best response to what the Bobs are doing.

- The final step is to verify that the formula for $V_{T-n}(p_{T-n})$, given as part of the induction hypothesis, is correct for $T - N$. And, so it is: For $p_{T-N} \geq (1/2)^N$, Bob$T-N$ trusts Alice, and she responds by being nice. This gives her an immediate 1 and a continuation value of at least 1, hence 2 or more. For $p_{T-N} \in \big((1/2)^{N+1}, (1/2)^N\big)$, Bob$T-N$ definitely trusts her, and she randomizes. She gets 2, whether she is nice or takes advatnage. For $p_{T-N} = (1/2)^{N+1}$, Bob$T-N$ randomizes between trusting her or not. If he trusts her, she nets 2, if not, she gets 0 today and a continuation value of 0, for a net expected value of 1. And, for $p_{T-N} < (1/2)^{N+1}$, Bob$T-N$ doesn't trust her, so she gets 0 today and a continuation value of 0, for a net expected value of 0. The induction step is complete. We have an equilibrium with sequentially rational behavior.[34]

Note that the inequality $V_{T-n}(p_{T-n}) \geq 2$ for $p_{T-n} \geq (1/2)^n$ is, for most values of p_{T-n}, extremely loose. Rational Alice is accumulating payoffs of 1 in each period until the time $T - n$ such that $\eta > (1/2)^n$ or $n < \ln(\eta)/\ln(1/2)$. So, if $T \gg \ln(\eta)/\ln(1/2)$, Rational Alice's average per-period payoff will be approximately 1.

Is this the only sequential equilibrium for this finite-horizon game, with this specification of types of Alice (and all Bobs being short-lived and rational)? I believe so. Does this sort of incomplete information pin down the outcome in infinite-horizon games? I suspect so. But even if this turns out to be false, I'm not unduly concerned. This is a situation in which the interests of Alice and the Bobs align: She wants to be trusted, and they want to be able to trust her. For the finite-horizon game, the unraveling argument is unfortunate; the equilibrium just constructed shows how it might be avoided. And in the infinite-horizon game, the commonality of interests should, in any application, lead the parties to their jointly preferred overall outcome. Compare this with the threat game, where Alice's interests and those of the Bobs are directly opposed. And, to drive this point home, let us move on to finite-horizon versions, where both Alice and Bob are long-lived.

---

[34] In fact, it is a sequential equilibrium—full consistency holds—but I won't bother with the details.

Long-lived Alice plays the trust game finitely many times against long-lived Bob

Suppose long-lived Alice plays the trust game finitely many times against a single long-lived opponent, Bob. With complete information (both are rational), any chance of trust is gone by the usual unraveling-from-the-back argument.[35]

But, suppose there is a small probability η that Alice is Nice Alice. Let N be large enough so that $N\eta > 3$. If the game lasts for more than N periods and play reaches the point where there are N stages left to go and Alice has never yet taken advantage of Bob, it must be that Bob assesses probability at least η that Alice is nice. So, with N stages left to go, by trusting Alice unless and until she takes advantage of him, Bob's expected payoff from this point to the end must be at least $N\eta - 1 > 2$. This is because he loses -1 at most once—he'll stop trusting Alice once this happens—and if he faces Nice Alice, he'll get 1 for each of the N remaining periods. Given his assessment of η or greater that Alice is nice, this strategy gives him an expectation of at least $N\eta - 1$. This is not his necessarily his equilibrium strategy. But, in any sequential equilibrium, his continuation payoff from such a position must do at least this well. Thus, if this position is reached, in his equilibrium strategy, he must trust Alice at least twice, in expectation.

Now back up to when there are more than N periods left, and Alice so far has been nice. If Alice is trusted, she can take an immediate 2 and then get 0s for the rest of the game. Or she can be nice, getting an immediate 1, and continue to be nice in every period that she is trusted. This will net her at least an expectation of 2 more units of payoff, once we reach N stages left, for a total of 3. Hence, with more than N periods left, if trusted, she will definitely be nice. And, so, with more than N periods left, Bob can trust her. I won't write this down as a formal proposition—the argument is too simple for that—but for "most" of the game, if T is very large (relative to N, such that $N\eta > 3$), Bob trusts her and she is nice; both of them net a long-run average of 1 per period.

The logic here is that both Bob and Alice agree: Long-term trust and a nice response is in both their interests. As long as Bob has some incentive to explore Alice's type, to see whether Alice is indeed nice (which is where the $N\eta$ comes in), the two parties can bootstrap their way to the trust–nice outcome.

Because of this logic, the lower bounds provided above are very, very crude. With N periods left to go, it still makes sense for Rational Alice to string Bob along by being nice. In equilibrium, things work out with randomizations in the final few periods, Alice randomizing so that, in the very last period, Bob is indifferent between trusting or not, and Bob randomizes to support Alice's randomization. But, from the start and for most of time, Bob trusts, and Alice is nice.

---

[35] That is, there is no trust in the unique subgame-perfect equilibrium and no trust along the path of play in any Nash equilibrium.

Long-lived Alice plays the threat game finitely many times against long-lived Bob: A war of attrition

Contrast the previous scenario with the situation where a long-lived Alice plays the threat game finitely many times against a long-lived Bob. With complete information, since Alice has the misfortune of going last, she must acquiesce in the final round if challenged. So Bob challenges her in the final round, and the unraveling starts, ending with Bob always challenging Alice, who always acquiesces, in the unique subgame-perfect equilibrium.[36]

If we add incomplete information about Alice—specifically, we allow a small probability that she is Fighting Alice—then she wins for most of the game. The argument is harder than if the Bobs are short-lived, but it has been made.

However, if Bob entertains such uncertainty about Alice, it makes sense to suppose she entertains doubts about Bob. And, in this case of a long-lived Bob, these doubts can dramatically change matters. Rational Alice will, by fighting when challenged, try to convince Bob that she is Fighting Alice. But at the same time, Rational Bob from the start will try to convince Alice that he is Fearless Bob, a type of Bob who inflexibly challenges Alice. Since Bob is long-lived, he has a reputation stake, just as she does. An equilibrium analysis of this situation leads to a war of attrition, with (at the outset) Bob challenging Alice, and Alice fighting, which is costly to both rational types. In each round, there is a small probability that one side or the other will give in. And since they are randomizing, giving in must provide the same expected payoff as sticking it out, which carries a large chance of another round of pain balanced by a small chance of winning a sizeable prize, because the other party may be about to give in.

The first equilibrium model of this sort of war of attrition (of which I am aware) is in the second half of Kreps and Wilson (1982a), albeit done for analytical convenience in continuous time. I won't provide the details here; wars of attrition are particularly interesting in the context of bilateral bargaining (think of a labor union on strike against a corporation, with both parties losing from the strike, hoping that the other side will cave in). Models wars of attrition are presented in Chapter 23, in the context of bilateral bargaining.

Cooperation in the finitely repeated prisoners' dilemma?

Both the threat game and the trust game are asymmetric, in the sense that, in each round, Bob goes first and, if he chooses one of his two options, Alice must respond. So, for instance, in the case of the trust game, unless Bob (or a Bob) trusts her, she doesn't get to exhibit her trustworthiness. As we noted, this isn't a problem in the threat game: If Bob doesn't challenge Alice, Alice happily pockets the best possible payoff, and if he does challenge her, she gets to exhibit that she is ready and willing to fight.

A more symmetrical stage game is where this appendix began, with the pris-

---

[36] Among the Nash equilibria is one in which Bob never challenges her and, if challenged, she always fights; since never challenged, her less-than-credible threat to fight is allowed as part of a Nash equilibrium.

oners' dilemma. It's been quite a few pages since the game was depicted in Figure 15.1, so I reproduce that figure here.

Bob

	Betray Alice	Cooperate with Alice
Betray Bob	0, 0	20, −15
Cooperate with Bob	−15, 20	10, 10

Alice

Figure A15.1 (again) The prisoners' dilemma

We know quite a lot about the infinitely repeated prisoners' dilemma between two infinitely-lived players, but what about a finite-horizon version? And what if long-lived Alice plays against a sequence of short-lived Bobs, each of whom plays once and once only?

In these cases, and with complete information (both Alice and Bob or the Bobs are rational types), all that happens is Betray-Betray in every round. For a finite-horizon model, the unraveling argument is at work: In the final period, both Alice and Bob (or Bob T) will betray, no matter what came before; hence the same behavior happens at $t = T - 1$. (The distinction between outcomes of Nash equilibria and behavior in all parts of the tree in the unique subgame-perfect equilibrium applies.)

As already discussed, in the infinite-horizon model with complete information, long-run Alice versus long-run Bob gives a lot of possible equilibrium outcomes; this is the classic Folk Theorem. But short-lived Bobs, in their one shot at the game, will play betray whatever they think Alice is about to do. So long-lived Alice gains nothing by trying to cooperate. How about an intermediate case in which Alice is long-lived, playing infinitely often, and the Bobs are intermediate-lived: Each Bob plays Alice precisely ten times, and then is replaced by a new Bob? Then some cooperation is possible in equilibrium. See whether you can figure out how; I provide the answer in Chapter 22.

Does incomplete information help in the case of a fixed, finite horizon? With short-lived (one-period) Bobs, the answer is still no. They betray regardless of what they think Alice will do, and so Rational Alice has no incentive to do anything except betray. But a long-lived Bob and a long-lived Alice—together with a smidgen of the right sort of incomplete information about, say, Alice—offers some hope: This is the subject of Kreps, Milgrom, Roberts, and Wilson (1982).[37] If Bob, say, assesses small but strictly positive probability that Alice is "Tit-for-Tat Alice" (a type of Alice who begins by cooperating and then inflexibly always plays in round t whatever Bob played in round $t - 1$), then for most of the game, cooperation ensues. The paper provides a proof with fairly tight bounds on the meaning of "most of the game," but here is aother sketch of an argument in the spirit of long-lived Alice versus long-lived Bob in the trust game with a finite horizon and incomplete information.

Suppose Bob assesses a small but positive probability η that Alice is Grim-Punisher Alice, who will cooperate until the first time Bob betrays her and then

---

[37] If you hear an aged colleague referring to "the gang of four" paper, this is that paper.

will betray for the rest of the game. In this case, there is an N large enough so that, with N stages left to play, if Bob's assessment is that Alice is one of those two types is at least some η, it pays for him to find out by cooperating. His risk is at most 15 units (since if Alice does betray, he can betray for the rest of the game), and his potential expected gain is at least $10\eta N$. But then, prior to this time (when there are more than N periods to go), Rational Alice knows that, by precisely mimicking Grim-Punisher Alice, stage N will be reached with the prior probabilties (or more) attached to this behavioral type. Since her risk is at most 15, for large enough N, she is sure to make it up in the final N periods. And, in that case, Bob will respond optimally by always cooperating.

As in the two long-run players in the finitely repeated trust game, the logic is that both players would like to find a way to cooperate for most of the game. If a small seed of uncertainty about the type of one or the other allows them to get past the unraveling argument—and it does—they will embrace the opportunity.

A15.9. Building a Reputation?

As noted earlier (bottom of page 706), in these the simple, infinite-horizon models with complete information, reputation "arrives" fully formed: It is not built. With enduring incomplete information about a long-lived player's type, we are in somewhat better shape concerning the origins of reputation:

- The Fudenberg and Levine results show how, for situations similar to the threat game, Alice can be challenged only so many times by short-lived opponents before the probability that she is Fighting Alice rises to a level such that she will not be challenged again.

- If the context is two long-lived opponents playing something simiar to the threat game, war-of-attrition constructions (as in Kreps and Wilson 1982a) suggest something akin to reputation building. But see below.

- And in "cooperative" repeated-game situations, such as repeated play of the trust game or (with two long-lived players) the prisoners' dilemma, it is in the players' mutual interest to allow one or the other or both of them to have a reputation for being "nice."

But, in real life, it is commonly held that reputations must be earned through tangible actions; insofar as this commonsense holding is true, the models presented here are inadequate to this part of general story. We can regard these models as modeling the *maintenance* of a reputation, once it has been earned. But clearly, it is desirable to model the building through time of a reputation based on tangible actions..

For a game-theoretic, equilibrium model of building a reputation, it is manifest that there must be initial uncertainty in the minds of parties concerning the future behavior of their counterparties, who might build the reputation. We will need types of Alice, some of whom choose in equilibrium to do whatever it takes to build a particular reputation, and some of whom do not. The question then is: What distinguishes these types? Why would one "type" of Alice persevere in honoring Bob's or the Bobs' trust or in fighting his or their challenges, while another type would not? In a general sense, we probably will be looking at models of *signaling* in the sense that the term is used in Chapter 20. Many possibilities suggest themselves, depending on context. But if the model is driven by context, we move from theory per se into economic applications of theory. This is not a case in which one size fits all, when it comes to "reputation building."

- Recall Pediatrician Dr. Browne (Section A15.7), who has a reputation for always being behind schedule as he chats with the parents of his patients. Compare with Dr. Smith, who is "all business," only engaging parents when necessary and, in those cases, very much to the point. Presumably, the differences are rooted in their personal utility functions; they behave differently, because they desire different things, and their reputations arise without any strategic considerations on their part.

- Then we have District Attorney Black, who purposefully developed an instrumental reputation for never making plea deals once a case has gone to trial. D.A. Black compares with D.A. Jones, who is quite happy to make deals even when the jury is deliberating. Perhaps the difference results from the sorts of case loads they face; D.A. Black gets more "juice" from pressuring defendents to plea out prior to the trial, so the instrumental reputation she carries is more valuable to her. Perhaps they have different subjective assessments, based on experience, about how valuable such a reputation would be. Whatever story we might tell, as brand new D.A. Wilson takes office, his policy in this regard will be unknown to defense attorneys and their clients, and it will take a few refusals to entertain deals and an unwillingness to propose deals once the trial has begun for his reputation to emerge.

- In models of wars of attrition, one can say that, while holding out as the war proceeds, the parties are building their reputations. In the barebones models, such as in Kreps and Wilson (1982a), what actually happens is that, along the path of play, the posterior probabilities that each party is the "strong" behavioral type increase, because of the small probabilities in each round that the "rational" types give in. Whether this captures the notion of "building" a reputation is a matter for the eye of the beholder; my own opinion is that it gets us close to a desirable model, but in the end falls somewhat short. What is wanted are models in which there is a spectrum of rational types—some more able to sustain the war of attrition, some less—and the weaker types are those who give in. In such a model, the strong rational types, by lasting longer, are building a reputation. It isn't quite the same thing, but the models of bilateral bargaining in which delayed offers signal strength (Section 23.7) have this character.

- Without prejudicing the case against game-theoretic, equilibrium models of reputation acquisition, it is worth noting that somewhat boundedly rational learning models, such as reinforcement learning, may ultimately provide more insight about the real-life phenomena. But those are models for Volume III.

Bibliographic Notes

As I noted at the start of this appendix, this topic has engendered a huge literature, and I apologize for any seminal references that I may have missed.

Fudenberg and Tirole's *Game Theory* (1991b) provides, in chapters 5 and 9, an excellent survey of many of the most important developments, with many more technical details than have been provided here. And George Mailath and Larry Samuelson, *Repeated Games and Reputations: Long-run Relationships* (2006) gives a a very detailed survey of the topic. Both provide detailed bibliographies, and both are recommended. For readers interested in a deep technical dive, Jean-Francois Mertens, Sylvain Sorin, and Shmuel Zamir, *Repeated Games* (2015) is recommended.

Here, in addition, are a few of the seminal papers on the topics discussed in this appendix.

- To the best of my knowledge, the idea that, with repeated play, equilibrium outcomes over the course of play above Nash equilibrium outcomes are feasible, goes back to the early days of game theory, hence the name, "the folk theorem." That said, the earliest original exposition in economics of which I am aware of folk-theorem ideas is Friedman (1971). The seminal paper on the classic folk theorem is Aumann and Shapley (1976), which uses a long-term-average criterion to solve the issue of whether counterparties to a deviator will be willing to punish the deviator, even if it hurts themselves. Rubinstein (1979) sharpens these results with an overtaking-optimality criterion. Subgame perfection for the classic folk theorem with discounting first appears in Fudenberg and Maskin (1986). Abreu, Dutta, and Smith (1994) weakens the requirements used by Fudenberg and Maskin.

- Proposition A15.5, which gives folk-theorem-like results for finitely repeated games under certain conditions, is the work of Benoit and Krishna (1985, 1987).

- The formal literature on the problem of "noisy observables" and the folk theorem begins with the classic paper Green and Porter (1984). This paper is discussed at length in Chapter 22. Four seminal papers that develop the theory are Abreu, Pearce, and Stachetti (APS) (1986, 1990), Fudenberg and Levine (FL) (1994), and Fudenberg, Levine, and Maskin (FLM) (1994). APS (1986) sets out the basic dynamic-programming techniques in the specific context of cartel pricing. APS (1990) generalizes their techniques to general discounted repeated games with public signals. FLM (1994) uses similar dynamic-programming-based arguments to extend the work of APS and prove a folk theorem. FL (1994) does foundational work on these sorts of equilibria with the additional feature of a mix of long-run and short-run players. Work on folk theorems that go beyond public strategies and equilibria is the current frontier. See, for instance, Takuo Sugaya (2023).

- As with the basic idea of the folk theorem, the notion that folk-theorem-like ideas would work as well to generate instrumental reputations was, I think, well known for many years before the formal statements of exactly what is possible were published. So I am reluctant to cite any published work as being "first." Settings with multiple long-lived players as well as short-lived players are examined in Fudenberg, Kreps, and Maskin (1990) and Fudenberg and Levine (1994)

- The theory of reputation built from a small amount of incomplete information (the mimicking constructions) originated in two simultaneous papers, Kreps and Wilson (1982a) and Milgrom and Roberts (1982b). These four authors simultaneously published a short "comment" on their two longer papers, which has come to be known as "the gang of four" paper: Kreps, Milgrom, Roberts, and Wilson (1982). The two two-author papers are set in the context of repeated play of the threat game; the gang-of-four concerns repeated play of the prisoners' dilemma. Fudenberg and Levine (1989, 1992) generalize the specific equilibrium constructions in the two two-author papers, for long-run versus short-run players and for a broad class of games (but not, for instance, for the trust game).

  These papers concern cases in which encounters are sequential, with one long-lived and a sequence of short-lived players, or with two long-lived players (in the case of the four-author paper). A variation is where one individual Alice is simultaneously engaged in a finite number of encounters, and her counterparties are each engaged with Alice only. If there is a small amount of uncertainty about Alice's type, can she use that together with the fact that she is engaged in multiple encounters to her benefit? The answer is, Maybe: see Fudenberg and Kreps (1987).

- A branch of the literature on repeated games that I did not describe in the "catalog" at the start of this appendix concerns the play of such games where the players have various forms of cognitive limitations: They have bounded memory, or their strategies must be implementable with finite automata. For an introduction to this sort of analysis, in the context of games of common interest, see Aumann and Sorin (1989).

The model in which cooperation is sometimes very costly

This section provides analysis of the second model of imperfect observability. Recall the model. Alice and Bob play the repeated prisoners' dilemma with one amendment. In each round, the payoff from cooperation for each of them is random: If both sides cooperate, Alice's payoff in round t is $10 + \epsilon_t^A$, where ϵ_t^A is 0 with probability 0.9 and -25 with probability 0.1. If she cooperates and Bob betrays, she gets $-15 + \epsilon_t^A$. If she betrays Bob, her payoffs are 20 or 10, with no change. The situation with Bob is symmetric; but with random variables ϵ_t^B. Assume that the collection of random variables $\{\epsilon_t^A, \epsilon_t^B; t = 0, 1, \ldots\}$ is fully independent; conditional on the values of any subset of these random variables, the (conditional) distribution of any one of them not in the subset is the same as its unconditional distribution. As private information, Alice learns the value of ϵ_t^A prior to choosing her round t action but after round $t - 1$ has concluded; Bob learns as private information the value of ϵ_t^B at the same time. And there is no way for Alice, either before or after the time t choices are made, to verify to Bob what ϵ_t^A is, and vice versa.

We are interested in two symmetric strategy profiles:

- The "suck-it-up" profile, in which Alice and Bob always cooperate, no matter how costly it is for them. This is to be supported by grim punishment; since they are meant to suck it up and always cooperate, the extreme nature of grim punishment (always betraying in the event of an earlier betrayal by either player) is off-path. We need to be sure that δ is large enough so that sucking it up when the player's $\epsilon_t = -25$ is worthwhile. But other than checking on δ, this profile should be easy to analyze.

- The "modified one-round-of-compensation" strategy profile. This profile is based on the three-state dynamics of Figure A15.4, with one modification: In state C, if a player sees $\epsilon_t = -25$, the player willingly betrays, causing the state to transition the player's punishment state. And, in state PA, for instance, Alice betrays if $\epsilon_t^A = -25$, putting off the return to state C for at least one round.

A first-best benchmark

Suppose that Alice and Bob were able to observe each other's payoffs from cooperation in each round prior to making their choice. In this situation, we look for the first-best efficient arrangement, and in particular for the first-best symmetric arrangement, it is, in every round, to take whichever pair of actions maximizes the sum of their payoffs. This would be joint cooperation in rounds where $\epsilon_t^A = \epsilon_t^B = 0$, but joint betrayal if either ϵ_t^A or ϵ_t^B or both $= -25$. (The value -25 was chosen with this first-best efficient arrangement in mind.)

If the two can implement this first-best rule, each would get a payoff of 10 in any round with probability 0.81, and a payoff of 0 with probability 0.19, for an expected payoff per round of 8.1 and an expected payoff for their full interaction of $8.1/(1-\delta)$. Supposing they could form a binding agreement to behave in this fashion, this is the first-best symmetric outcome for all values of δ. But suppose, while each observes the other's perturbation term, round by round, they still choose their actions independently. How big does δ have to be to sustain this first-best outcome? In rounds where one or the other sees a perturbation of -25, both are meant to betray, and since betrayal is also short-run optimal, sustaining this choice is trivial.

But suppose both players observe that $\epsilon_t^A = \epsilon_t^B = 0$. For small enough δ, each might still want to betray and (if the other follows the strategy) grab an immediate payoff of 20. As for the future, if we want to make this betrayal as unattractive as possible, we would resort to grim punishment, but this time interpreted as: grimly betray in every round if, in any previous round $t' < t$, when $\epsilon_{t'}^A = \epsilon_{t'}^B = 0$, one or the other player betrayed. Then we have the "unimprovability" condition that

$$10 + \delta 8.1/(1-\delta) \geq 20,$$

because sticking to the equilibrium gives an immediate 10 and a continuation value of $8.1/(1-\delta)$, while betraying gives 20 immediately and zero forever after. This unimprovability condition holds as long as $\delta \geq 10/18.1 = 0.552$, approximately. This sets a first-best benchmark for the two strategy profiles we wish to investigate.

The "suck-it-up" strategy profile

In this profile, Alice and Bob always cooperate along the path of play. Hence, Alice's payoff in each round (along the path of play) is 10 with probability 0.9 and -15 with probability 0.1, for an expected payoff per round of 7.5, and an expected payoff over the course of the game of $7.5/(1-\delta)$. From any off-path node where someone has previously betrayed, the grim punishment strategy calls for constant betrayal, which means payoffs of 0 in every round and an expected payoff (beginning from such a position) of 0.

To check unimprovability, the only question is unimprovability along the path of play. (If your opponent is always betraying, then obviously your best response is always to betray). This means betrayal, hence a sure immediate payoff of 20 in the current period and 0 thereafter. But since Alice knows the value of ϵ_t^A before making her choice in round t, there are two unimprovability conditions, one if she knows that $\epsilon_t^A = 0$ and one if she knows that $\epsilon_t^A = -25$. The two inequalities to check are, respectively,

$$10 + \delta \frac{7.5}{1-\delta} \geq 20, \quad \text{and} \quad -15 + \delta \frac{7.5}{1-\delta} \geq 20.$$

Clearly, the binding unimprovability constraint is the second one; if we are asking Alice and Bob to "suck it up" when they get a bad draw of ϵ_t, that is when they are at the greatest danger of being unwilling to comply.

And solving for values of δ that satisfy the second inequality gives $\delta \geq 35/42.5 \approx 0.8235$.

That was easy.

The modified one-round-of-compensation strategy

The main difficulty in the analysis of this strategy profile (or rather the novel feature, because it isn't very difficult) is that each player gets private information prior to making a decision. Hence for, say, Alice, there is a expected payoff starting from any one of the three states, C, PA, and PB, when she knows that her current $\epsilon_t^A = 0$ and when it $= -25$. And, for analytical convenience, it helps to carry along an expected payoff function for her in any of three states but prior to receiving this private information. So, instead of three values for Alice, V_C, V_A, and V_B, I work with nine: those three, plus V_{C1} for her value in state C when she has learned that her current $\epsilon_t^A = 0$, $V_{C2} =$ her value in state C when she has learned that her current $\epsilon_t^A = -25$, $V_{A1} =$ her value in state PA when she has learned that her current $\epsilon_t^A = 0$, and so forth. Of course, we immediately have the following equations:

$$V_C = 0.9V_{C1} + 0.1V_{C2}, V_A = 0.9V_{A1} + 0.1V_{A2}, \text{ and } V_B = 0.9V_{B1} + 0.1V_{B2}.$$

(We really only need the six new value functions, but it saves on notation to have the old three around as well.)

The first step, as always, is to compute these expected payoffs if Alice and Bob follow the prescribed strategies. We have the following system of recursive equations, in addition to the three just provided:

$$V_{C1} = 0.9(10 + \delta V_C) + 0.1(-15 + \delta V_B),$$
$$V_{C2} = 0.9(20 + \delta V_A) + 0.1(0 + \delta V_C),$$
$$V_{A1} = -15 + \delta V_C, \quad \text{and} \quad V_{A2} = 0 + \delta V_A, \quad \text{and}$$
$$V_{B1} = V_{B2} = 0.9(20 + \delta V_C) + 0.1(0 + \delta V_B).$$

Let me explain a few of these equations:

- $V_{C1} = 0.9(10 + \delta V_C) + 0.1(-15 + \delta V_B)$: In state C, if $\epsilon_t^A = 0$, Alice is supposed to cooperate. The outcome for her depends on what Bob does, which depends on the value of ϵ_t^B. With probability 0.9, he sees $\epsilon_t^B = 0$ and cooperates, giving Alice 10 and leaving the state as C; hence her continuation expected payoff is V_C, discounted by δ. But if $\epsilon_t^B = -25$, Bob betrays: Alice gets an immediate -15 and a discounted continuation value of δV_B.

- $V_{A1} = -15 + \delta V_C$: In state PA, if $\epsilon_t^A = 0$, Alice is supposed to cooperate, to restore state C. The value of Bob's ϵ_t^B is irrelevant, because he is supposed to betray, and ϵ_t^B has no effect on this betrayal decision in state PA.

- $V_{B1} = V_{B2} = 0.9(20 + \delta V_C) + 0.1(0 + \delta V_B)$: In state PB, Alice betrays, regardless of the value of ϵ_t^A, which also has no impact on her immediate payoffs (since she is betraying), so $V_{B1} = V_{B2}$. But Bob's action does depend on the value of ϵ_t^B: With probability 0.9, he cooperates, giving Alice an immediate 20 and a discounted continuation value δV_C, and with probability 0.1, he sees $\epsilon_t^B = -25$ and so betrays, giving Alice an immediate 0 and keeping the state in PB.

Since $V_{B1} = V_{B2}$ and $V_B = 0.9V_{B1} + 0.1V_{B2}$,

$$V_B = 0.9(20 + \delta V_C) + 0.1\delta V_B, \quad \text{or} \quad V_{B1} = V_{B2} = V_B = \frac{18 + 0.9\delta V_C}{1 - 0.1\delta}.$$

And, $V_A = 0.9V_{A1} + 0.1V_{A2} = 0.9[-15 + \delta V_C] + 0.1[0 + \delta V_A]$, which solves (in terms of V_A) as $V_A = (-13.5 + 0.9\delta V_C)/(1 - 0.1\delta)$. Hence,

$$V_A + V_B = \frac{4.5 + 1.8\delta V_C}{1 - 0.1\delta}.$$

Next,

$$\begin{aligned}
V_C &= 0.9V_{C1} + 0.1V_{C2} \\
&= 0.9\left[0.9(10 + \delta V_C) + 0.1(-15 + \delta V_B)\right] + 0.1\left[0.9(20 + \delta V_A) + 0.1\delta V_C\right] \\
&= 8.1 + 0.81\delta V_C - 1.35 + 1.8 + 0.01\delta V_C + 0.09\delta(V_A + V_B) \\
&= 8.55 + 0.82\delta V_C + 0.09\delta(V_A + V_B) \\
&= 8.55 + 0.82\delta V_C + 0.09\delta(4.5 + 1.8\delta V_C)/(1 - 0.01\delta).
\end{aligned}$$

Solve for V_C, and you get

$$V_C = \frac{8.55 + 0.405\delta/(1 - 0.1\delta)}{1 - 0.82\delta - 0.162\delta^2/(1 - 0.1\delta),}$$

from which all the other values can be computed.

Now to check unimprovability. There is no serious unimprovability issue for Alice in state PB; she has no impact on the state dynamics, and she is supposed to betray, which strictly dominates cooperation. (In this case, there is no $p \geq 0.5$ condition, because there is no p in this model.)

But for states C and PA, we have an option: We could check unimprovability using V_C and V_A, but at that level, there are three one-step deviations from the strategy that we would need to check. For instance, in state C, Alice is supposed to apply the rule "cooperate if $\epsilon_t^A = 0$, and betray if $\epsilon_t^A = -25$." The three one-step deviations are: "cooperate regardless of the value of ϵ_t^A," "betray regardless," and "cooperate if $\epsilon_t^A = -25$ and betray if $\epsilon_t^A = 0$." I'm willing to reject the third of these out of hand as crazy, leaving only the first two.

But the algebra is a bit simpler if we test the one possible deviation from the substates C and $\epsilon_t^A = 0$, C and $\epsilon_t^A = -25$, and so forth. These four are

$$\begin{aligned}
V_{C1} &\geq 0.9(20 + \delta V_A) + 0.1(0 + \delta V_C), \\
V_{C2} &\geq 0.9(-15 + \delta V_C) + 0.1(-40 + \delta V_B), \\
V_{A1} &\geq 0 + \delta V_A, \quad \text{and} \quad V_{A2} \geq -40 + \delta V_C.
\end{aligned}$$

For instance, in state C with $\epsilon_t^A = -25$, Alice is supposed to betray, which nets her a current value of V_{C2}. If she deviates to cooperation, then with probability 0.9, Bob will cooperate, leaving her with an immediate $10 - 25 = -15$ and a discounted continuation value of δV_C, and with probability 0.1, Bob will betray, giving Alice an immediate $-15 - 25 = -40$ and a discounted continuation value of δV_B. This is the second inequality in the display just above. (There is no need to "average" across the two possible values of ϵ_t^B in state PA, because in that state, Bob will betray, regardless of wheher $\epsilon_t^B = 0$ or -25.)

Table A15.6 provides results for the unimprovability checks, for values of δ between 0.99 and 0.45. In each two-column block, the first column gives the value from following the prescribed strategy in the given substate; the second column gives the value from deviating. As you can see by inspection, for the substate $C1$— that is, state C when $\epsilon_t^A = 0$, the test is passed for $\delta = 0.5$ but not for 0.45. For substate $C2$, the test is passed at all values of δ in the table. For substate $A1$, the test is passed for $\delta \geq 0.675$ but not for $\delta \leq 0.65$; and for substate $A2$, it always passes.

Hence this modified one-round-of-compensation profile is subgame perfect to $\delta \geq 0.675$—the exact lower bound on δ for which it works turns out to be approximately 0.6566. It is noteworthy that this happens at the point where $V_{A1} = 0$; you can check the algebra to see why this is so.

δ	V_{C1}	Alternative action value	V_{C2}	Alternative action value	V_{A1}	Alternative action value	V_{A2}	Alternative action value
0.99	752.116	740.687	740.687	727.116	728.463	720.378	720.378	703.463
0.975	302.081	291.008	291.008	277.081	278.450	270.736	270.736	253.450
0.95	152.024	141.541	141.541	127.024	128.427	121.332	121.332	103.427
0.925	101.967	92.073	92.073	76.967	78.404	71.925	71.925	53.404
0.9	76.910	67.602	67.602	51.910	53.382	47.515	47.515	28.382
0.875	61.854	53.129	53.129	36.854	38.359	33.104	33.104	13.359
0.85	51.797	43.655	43.655	26.797	28.336	23.690	23.690	3.336
0.825	44.598	37.036	37.036	19.598	21.170	17.132	17.132	-3.830
0.8	39.185	32.200	32.200	14.185	15.789	12.357	12.357	-9.211
0.775	34.963	28.553	28.553	9.963	11.600	8.770	8.770	-13.400
0.75	31.574	25.738	25.738	6.574	8.243	6.015	6.015	-16.757
0.725	28.792	23.527	23.527	3.792	5.492	3.864	3.864	-19.508
0.7	26.464	21.768	21.768	1.464	3.196	2.165	2.165	-21.804
0.675	24.486	20.357	20.357	-0.514	1.249	0.814	0.814	-23.751
0.65	22.783	19.220	19.220	-2.217	-0.423	-0.264	-0.264	-25.423
0.625	21.300	18.300	18.300	-3.700	-1.875	-1.125	-1.125	-26.875
0.6	19.996	17.557	17.557	-5.004	-3.149	-1.809	-1.809	-28.149
0.575	18.839	16.960	16.960	-6.161	-4.276	-2.348	-2.348	-29.276
0.55	17.805	16.483	16.483	-7.195	-5.280	-2.766	-2.766	-30.280
0.525	16.874	16.108	16.108	-8.126	-6.181	-3.083	-3.083	-31.181
0.5	16.031	15.818	15.818	-8.969	-6.995	-3.314	-3.314	-31.995
0.475	15.263	15.603	15.603	-9.737	-7.734	-3.471	-3.471	-32.734
0.45	14.561	15.450	15.450	-10.439	-8.408	-3.566	-3.566	-33.408

Table A15.6. Checking for when the modified one-round-of-compensation profile is a (subgame-perfect) equilibrium.

And in Table A15.7, the values $V_C, V_A,$ and $V_B,$ along with the benchmark value of the first-best symmetric solution and the value function for the suck-it-up strategy profile are provided for a variety of values of δ. Both unnormalized and normalized, "per period" payoffs are shown. Empty cells indicate that, for those values of δ, the strategy profile fails to pass the test of being an equilibrium.

Note that the suck-it-up equilibrium always does worse than the modified one-round-of-compensation equilibrium, although the differences in values are slight in all cases. The real strength of the modified one-round-of-compensation strategy profile relative to suck-it-up is that it forms a subgame-perfect equilibrium for a much wider range of discount factors δ.

It may perhaps surprise you that, on a per-period basis, the payoffs in state C rise as δ falls for the one-round-of-compensation equilibrium. This phenomenon

		Unnormalized payoffs					Payoffs normalized by $1-\delta$			
δ	V_C	First-best benchmark	$V_{\text{suck-it-up}}$	V_A	V_B	V_C	First-best benchmark	$V_{\text{suck-it-up}}$	V_A	V_B
0.99	750.973	810	750	727.655	762.616	7.51	8.1	7.5	7.28	7.63
0.975	300.974	324	300	277.678	312.581	7.52	8.1	7.5	6.94	7.81
0.95	150.976	162	150	127.718	162.524	7.55	8.1	7.5	6.39	8.13
0.925	100.978	108	100	77.756	112.467	7.57	8.1	7.5	5.83	8.44
0.9	75.979	81	75	52.795	87.410	7.60	8.1	7.5	5.28	8.74
0.875	60.981	65	60	37.833	72.354	7.62	8.1	7.5	4.73	9.04
0.85	50.983	54	50	27.871	62.297	7.65	8.1	7.5	4.18	9.34
0.825	43.842	46.286	42.9	20.766	55.098	7.67	8.1	7.5	3.63	9.64
0.8	38.487	40.5		15.446	49.685	7.70	8.1		3.09	9.94
0.775	34.322	36		11.317	45.463	7.72	8.1		2.55	10.23
0.75	30.991	32.4		8.020	42.074	7.75	8.1		2.01	10.52
0.725	28.265	29.455		5.329	39.292	7.77	8.1		1.47	10.81
0.7	25.994	27		3.093	36.964	7.80	8.1		0.93	11.09
0.675	24.073	24.923		1.206	34.986	7.82	8.1		0.39	11.37

Table A15.7. The values of V_C, V_A, and V_B, compared to the values of the first-best benchmark and the suck-it-up equilibrium, for values of δ for which the unimprovability tests are passed.

has the following explanation. The stationary probability distribution for the state under this equilibrium is $5/6$ of the time in state C, and $1/12$ of the time in each of states PA and PB. But, starting in state C, for a while, more time is spent on average in state C. That is, if we look at the average (expected) amount of time in state C in the first t rounds, this falls toward $5/6$ as t grows. For smaller δ, more weight in the discounted net present value is put on earlier rounds. And the average of a player's payoff in the state in which she is being punished and the state in which she is being compensated is always worse than her payoff in state C. Hence, weighted by the discount factors, the more time that is spent in state C, the better is the overall payoff.

If you would like more practice with this sort of model, try analyzing the following: In each block of ten rounds, Alice and Bob are each given one free betrayal. But if they betray twice in a block of ten, grim punishment results.

Appendix Sixteen

The Revelation Principle

The revelation principle—more precisely, the revelation principles—concern "straightforward" ways to implement contingent social-choice outcomes, in lieu of employing possibly complex games. The chief use of the revelation principles in economics is in mechanism design, which is the topic of Chapter 26, although the principle is encountered for the first time in Chapter 24.

A16.1. The Problem

Definition A16.1. *An abstract **social-choice context** or problem consists of:*

a. *a finite set $\mathcal{N}$ of N individuals, indexed $i = 1, \ldots, N$, the **players** or **participants** or **citizens**;*

b. *a **state space** Ω with **probability distribution** (or measure) P;*

c. *for each $i \in \mathcal{N}$, an **information partition** $\mathcal{A}_i$ of Ω, where $\mathcal{A}_i$ represent's n's **(initial) information endowment**;*

d. *a set of **socially feasible outcomes** X; and,*

e. *for each individual i and state ω, a **state-contingent payoff function** $u_i(\cdot, \omega)$; that is, $u_i(x, \omega)$ is i's utility if the social outcome is x and the state is ω.*

For our purposes, it suffices to assume that each $\mathcal{A}_i$ is generated by a (measurable) function a_i with domain Ω and some (arbitrary) range A_i. That is, in state ω, player i is told the value $a_i(\omega)$. If A_i is finite, then $\mathcal{A}_i$ is generated by finitely many cells in Ω. In other applications, A_i is an interval of real numbers.

An auction problem

A paradigmatic example involves the auction of an indivisible item.

- One of the participants, say $i = 1$, has an indivisible item she wishes to sell to one of the other individuals, if the price is right.

- The state of nature ω takes the form of a *valuation vector* $\omega = (\omega_1, \ldots, \omega_N) \in R_+^N$, where ω_i is the value that i attaches to the object. This includes the incumbent owner, $i = 1$.

- The information partition $\mathcal{A}_i$ for each player i identifies ω_i only. That is, the function $a_i(\omega) = \omega_i$.

- The probability distribution P on Ω is a product measure,

$$P(\omega \leq w) := \prod_{i=1}^{N} F_i(w_i) \quad \text{where} \quad w = (w_1, \ldots, w_N) \in R_+^N,$$

and F_i is the cumulative distribution function for ω_i.[1]

- The set of social outcomes is $X \subseteq \mathcal{N} \times R^{N-1}$ with typical element $(i^*, x_2, \ldots, x_{N-1})$. The outcome $(i^*, x_2, \ldots, x_n)$ represents the situation in which, at the end of auction or encounter, individual i^* has possession of the item (not ruling out $i^* = 1$) and, for $i = 2, \ldots, N$, player i has made a net payment of x_i to player 1.

- The payoff functions u_i are given by

$$u_i((i^*, x), \omega) = \begin{cases} \omega_i \mathbf{1}_{i^*}(1) + x_2 + \ldots + x_N, & \text{if } i = 1, \text{ and} \\ \omega_i \mathbf{1}_{i^*}(i) - x_i, & \text{if } i > 1, \end{cases}$$

where $\mathbf{1}_{i^*}(i)$ is the indicator function of whether $i^* = i$; that is, $\mathbf{1}_{i^*}(i) = 1$ if $i = i^*$ and $= 0$ if $i^* \neq i$.

These symbols obscure a simple story. The variable i^* records who has possession of the item in the end. The variable x_i for $i \geq 2$ is the net payment made by i. Note that, in this formulation, it is possible that a prospective buyer i for $i \geq 2$ pays some amount of money even if i does not take possession of the item. Since the sign of x_i is (as yet) unrestricted, a "net payment" can be negative; indeed, in a "game" with these outcomes, prospective buyers can make side-payments to one another, as long as x_i represents the net *loss of cash* (which, again, could be negative) of prospective buyer i. But note that, in this formulation, the net of all payments and receipts is zero; the seller, $i = 1$, gets on net the sum of what the bidders lose. If one wished to limit attention to auctions in which buyers only pay to the seller and, then, only if they win the item, one simply adds constraints to the set of feasible outcomes.

Contingent outcomes and the questions asked

For the general formulation, call a function $\zeta : \Omega \to X$ a *contingent-outcome map*. That is, ζ maps the state of nature into an outcome.

For instance, one such ζ in the auction context would be: $\zeta(\omega)$ allocates the object to the bidder i who values the object most highly, with that individual (if it is someone other than $i = 1$) paying precisely her value to player 1, and with no one else paying anything.[2]

The questions to which we seek answers are:

---

[1] The assumptions that (a) the valuations are independent and (b) each bidder knows her own value and nothing more is called the case of *independent private values*.

[2] Please highlight this contingent-outcome map; I refer to it in a few paragraphs.

1. Which contingent-outcome maps ζ can be attained in some (strategic-form) game among the players as a Nash equilibrium of that game or as a (weakly) dominant-strategy equilibrium of the game?

2. Among all such "feasible" contingent-outcome maps, which one(s) is (or are) best according to some criterion? The criterion might be "social" in nature—we want to find the Pareto-efficient contingent-outcome maps—and they might be "private" in nature, such as feasible contingent-outcome maps that maximize the expected payoff for the seller of the object.

Mechanisms and the associated game of incomplete information

The problem with these questions is that the space of "games" is both very large and ill-defined. The lack of a formal definition of a "game" is fixed with the following definition.

*Definition A16.2. For a (finite) set of players $\mathcal{N} = \{1, \dots, N\}$ and a space of outcomes X, a **mechanism** consists of a **set of actions** S_i for each player i and an **outcome function** $\xi : S_1 \times \dots \times S_N \to X$.*

For instance, in the auction context, we might define $S_i = R_+$ for all i, interpreting s_i as i's bid; and, given $\xi(s_1, \dots, s_N)$, ξ awards the object to the high "bid," with the bidder paying what she bid (unless the high bid comes from $i = 1$), making some rules about what happens if there is a tie for the high bid).[3,4]

Given a mechanism $(\{S_i; i \in \mathcal{N}\}, \xi)$—which means we are already given the set of players $\mathcal{N}$ and the outcome space X—and given states of nature Ω, the probability P, information partitions $\{\mathcal{A}_i; i \in \mathcal{N}\}$, and payoff functions $\{u_i; i \in \mathcal{N}\}$, we marry the mechanism to the other elements of a context to create a strategic-form game of incomplete information:

- Player i's strategy set for this game of incomplete information is $\Sigma_i = S_i^{\mathcal{A}_i}$; that is, given her information $a_i(\omega)$, i chooses the action $\sigma_i(a_i(\omega))$, for $\sigma_i \in \Sigma_i$.[5]

- Player i's payoff function for this game is

$$v_i((\sigma_1, \dots, \sigma_N)) := \mathbf{E}\big[u_i\big(\xi(\sigma_1(\omega), \dots, \sigma_N(\omega)), \omega\big)\big],$$

where the expectation is taken with respect to P over Ω.

---

[3] This mechanism sounds like the contingent-outcome map that I asked you to highlight, but they are different animals. The contingent outcome works with the data in ω. The mechanism determines the outcome based on the bids of the players.

[4] In Chapter 23, concerning bilateral bargaining, and in Chapter 24, concerning auctions, the term *protocol* is used as a synonym for mechanism.

[5] In other parts of this volume, σ_i represented a mixed strategy. Not here: In this formulation, a σ_i is a pure strategy that specifies what action i takes as a function of i's information.

- We often look at this game of incomplete information in terms of each player's behavior strategy. Given $a_i(\omega)$, player i's conditional payoff is

$$v_i\big(s_i, (\sigma_j)_{j \neq i} | a_i\big) := \mathbf{E}\big[u_i\big(\xi(\sigma_1(\omega), \ldots, \sigma_{i-1}(\omega), s_i, \sigma_{i+1}(\omega), \ldots, \sigma_N(\omega)), \omega\big) | a_i\big].$$

That is, players consult their information, choose a (contingent-on-their-information) action from the set of actions presented to them by the mechanism, get an outcome, and evaluate things using the expected payoff of the outcome prescribed by the mechanism, given the array of strategy choices by all the (other) players.

So, questions like 1 and 2 in the previous subsection are to be answered, searching over the space of all mechanisms. The ambiguity is removed, but the space of mechanisms is still very, very large.

A16.2. Direct Revelation and Truth Telling

To make the problem manageable, suppose we retrict attention to a very specific sort of mechanism and, for the associated game of incomplete information, a very specific type of equilibrium:

Definition A16.3. *Given a set of players $\mathcal{N}$ and information partitions $\{\mathcal{A}_i; i \in \mathcal{N}\}$ given by functions $a_i : \Omega \to A_i$, a* **direct-revelation mechanism** *specifies $S_i = A_i$.*

This specification is only part of a direct-revelation mechanism. The other part is some function ϕ that takes the vector of reports $(\hat{a}_1, \ldots, \hat{a}_N)$ and turns it into an outcome $\phi(\hat{a}_1, \ldots, \hat{a}_N)$. I put hats on the reports = actions, because there is no guarantee at this point that players choose to "play" what they really do know. The story is the following.

Imagine that there is a neutral and independent referee who has the power to effect any feasible outcome $x \in X$ that she chooses. She proposes to each individual $i \in \mathcal{N}$, "Tell me what you know." This referee gathers up all the information supplied to her—write $\hat{a}_i$ for what she is told by i, which may or may not be the truth— and she causes $\phi(\hat{a}_1, \ldots, \hat{a}_N)$ to be the outcome. Her rule ϕ for translating message N-tuples into social outcomes is common knowledge among the players; there are no surprises about what she will do with their messages, although i, not (necessarily) knowing what i' knows, is unsure which message i' will send the referee. Hence, i knows the rule ϕ but is uncertain about the outcome.

Restricting attention to direct-revelation mechanisms, therefore, greatly reduces the space over which we must search, to answer questions 1 and 2. The strategy spaces are fixed, and while there are still, presumably, lots of functions ϕ that translate message vectors into outcomes that must be considered, the problem begins to seem manageable.

And, to make it even more manageable:

Definition A16.4. *Given all the contextual structure with which this appendix began, and given a direct-revelation mechanism specified by some ϕ,* **truth telling** *is a Nash equilibrium* *of the associated game of incomplete information if, for each* i*, reporting truthfully her information is a best response to truth telling by the other players. Truth telling is a (weakly) dominant equilibrium if, for each* i*, telling the truth about what she knows is as good any other possible reporting strategy, no matter what the other players are doing.*

The use of "weak domination" here clashes a bit with how the term is defined in Appendix 9. In Appendix 9, for one strategy to weakly dominate another, it is required that the first strategy is at least as good as the second no matter what the other players do, and the first is strictly better than the second for at least one strategy profile by the others. Here, I insist that truth telling does at least as well as any other strategy for i, no matter what the other players report, but not that, in a pairwise comparison of truth telling and some other strategy, there are submissions by the other players for which truth telling is strictly better. So, for instance, if the central authorities simply ignore what i reports—that is, if ϕ is constant in $\hat{a}_i$—this definition says that truth telling by i is "weakly dominant." I use the (sloppy) terminology that "truth telling is weakly dominant" in what follows; please be aware of the sloppiness. In applications, if I want to make the further claim that truth telling is truly weakly dominant, I must say so (and, presumably, prove so).

A16.3. The Revelation Principles

We come at last to the point of this appendix. *In terms of answering questions 1 and 2, it is without loss of generality to restrict attention to truth telling as an equilibrium in an appropriately defined direct-revelation mechanism.*

Proposition A16.5. *Fix a social-choice problem as per Definition A16.1. Fix an arbitrary mechanism* $(\{S_i; i \in \mathcal{N}\}, \xi)$*. For the associated game of incomplete information (created from the social-choice problem and the mechanism), we have the following:*

a. *The Nash-equilibrium revelation principle. Consider any pure-strategy profile* $\sigma^* = (\sigma_1^*, \ldots, \sigma_N^*)$ *that is a Nash equilibrium for the game of incomplete information created by this mechanism. There is a corresponding direct-revelation mechanism* ϕ *for which truth telling is a Nash equilibrium, which gives the same contingent outcome as obtains in the original Nash equilibrium.*

b. *The weak-dominance revelation principle. Consider any pure-strategy profile* $\sigma^* = (\sigma_1^*, \ldots, \sigma_N^*)$ *for the game of incomplete information created by this mechanism, such that each* σ_i^* *is (weakly) dominant for* i*. There is a corresponding direct-revelation mechanism* ϕ *for which truth telling is weakly dominant for each player* i*, which gives the same contingent outcome as obtains from each players choosing her (weakly) dominant strategy* σ_i^**.*

Proof. The idea is deep, but the proof, once you understand it, is almost trivial: The referee collects all the information and "plays the game" on behalf of the N players.

The first step is to create the (obvious) corresponding direct-revelation game:

$$\phi(\hat{a}_1, \ldots, \hat{a}_N) := \xi(\sigma_1^*(\hat{a}_1), \ldots, \sigma_N^*(\hat{a}_N)), \quad \text{for every } (\hat{a}_1, \ldots, \hat{a}_N) \in \mathcal{A}_1 \times \ldots \times \mathcal{A}_N.$$

Note that, in general, a vector of reports to the referee $(\hat{a}_1, \ldots, \hat{a}_N)$ may be inconsistent with any state ω.[6] The definition of the direct revelation game just given has the referee ignore this; she is "simulating" the play of the Nash strategies $(\sigma_i^*)_{i \in \mathcal{N}}$, it is assumed that ξ is defined on all of $S_1 \times \ldots \times S_N$, and σ_i^* has as its domain all of S_i. Hence, there is a rule the referee can employ.

And then, for part a of the proposition: To show that truth telling is a Nash equilibrium, simply observe that in each state ω, player n, observing $a_i(\omega)$, will have a probability distribution over what the others are seeing, hence what they are playing, in the original abstract game. In that original game, because $\sigma_i^*(a_i(\omega))$ is i's best response to what the others are playing, for i to "pretend" that he saw $\hat{a}_i' \neq a_i(\omega)$ and so choose $\sigma_i^*(\hat{a}_i')$ instead of $\sigma_i^*(a_i(\omega))$ will not benefit him; this is just the Nash condition. But, then, sending the report $\hat{a}_i'$ to the referee can't benefit him. Telling the truth is (among) i's best responses.

The argument for part b is similar.   ∎

I've given this result for pure contingent strategies σ_i^* only; the extension to mixed contingent strategies is not very difficult, but it involves some technical issues when the A_i are uncountable.

A16.4. Can You Find a Referee? Practical Implementation of a Contingent Outcome

The point of the revelation principle is *not* that it provides an effective way to implement a feasible contingent outcome. Instead, it is a tool of analysis that allows you to determine which contingent outcomes are (in theory) feasible. After you check on feasibility and settle on the contingent outcome that you find desirable—for instance, among all theoretically feasible contingent outcomes for the auction problem, you find one that maximizes the seller's expected payoff—you must find a practical mechanism for implementing the outcome. And it is unlikely that employing a referee who can run a direct-revelation game is practical. For one thing, the premise in the revelation-principle construction is that the referee has the authority to implement any social outcome $x \in X$ that she wishes. In the real world, the individuals involved may have certain "rights"; Alice, say, may have the right to veto the implementation of some social outcome. If this right cannot be alienated, it must somehow be incorporated into the revelation principle.

One important right that arises in many application is the right not to participate. Think of the auction context. Bob, who is one of the prospective bidders, always has the right to walk away without submitting a bid, if his expected payoff

---

[6] For instance, suppose that players 1 and 2 see the same information: $a_1 \equiv a_2$. And suppose they report different things, so different that there is no ω such that $a_1(\omega) = \hat{a}_1$ and, simultaneously, $a_2(\omega) = \hat{a}_2$.

leaves him worse off than if he refuses to play. In the application of the revelation principle—for instance, in Chapter 26—the question of participation constraints, in addition to truth-telling constraints, is made part of the analysis. (I leave this topic for that chapter; it is easier to develop in a specific context.)

Another problem with the revelation principle, at least as stated here for Nash equilibria, is that Nash equilibria as a solution criterion is fairly weak. An example illustrates this weakness (although the example is rather contrived): The two individuals are Alice and Bob. There are four states of nature, $\Omega = \{ac, bc, ad, bd\}$. Alice is privately informed about the first component of ω; Bob is informed about the second component. There are four social outcomes $X = \{w, x, y, z\}$. And preferences are given in Table A16.1, where a higher social outcome is more preferred.

<table>
<tr><td colspan="4" align="center">Alice's preferences</td><td colspan="4" align="center">Bob's preferences</td></tr>
<tr><td align="center">ac</td><td align="center">bc</td><td align="center">ad</td><td align="center">bd</td><td align="center">ac</td><td align="center">bc</td><td align="center">ad</td><td align="center">bd</td></tr>
<tr><td align="center">$w\ \ y$</td><td align="center">$w\ \ y$</td><td align="center">$x\ \ z$</td><td align="center">$x\ \ z$</td><td align="center">z</td><td align="center">x</td><td align="center">y</td><td align="center">w</td></tr>
<tr><td align="center">z</td><td align="center">x</td><td align="center">y</td><td align="center">w</td><td align="center">y</td><td align="center">w</td><td align="center">z</td><td align="center">x</td></tr>
<tr><td align="center">x</td><td align="center">z</td><td align="center">w</td><td align="center">y</td><td align="center">$w\ \ x$</td><td align="center">$y\ \ z$</td><td align="center">$w\ \ x$</td><td align="center">$y\ \ z$</td></tr>
</table>

Table A16.1. Preferences for Alice and Bob. The table gives the state-dependent preferences over social outcomes for Alice and Bob. For instance, the leftmost column gives Alice's preferences over the social outcomes if the state is ac: She is indifferent between w and y, strictly prefers both to z, and she strictly prefers z to x. For the point being made, ordinal preferences suffice.

Per the revelation principle, we can implement (as a truth-telling Nash equilibrium) the contingent outcome where w is the outcome in state ac, x is the outcome in state ad, y is the outcome in bc, and z is the outcome in bd. Here is the first step in the verification:

In state ac, Alice is meant to report a, and Bob should report c, which leads to w. If Alice instead reports b, the referee will (mistakenly) think the state is bc and implement y. But in state ac, Alice is indifferent between w and y, so truth telling is a best response for her, if Bob tells the truth. And if Alice tells the truth and Bob, instead of c, reports d, the referee thinks the state is ad and implements x. Since Bob is indifferent between w and x, truth telling is a best response for him (if Alice tells the truth). The same conclusions emerge for the other three states.

However, since (say) Alice is indifferent in state ac between w and y, and since lying would give y instead of w, what would be the consequences of lying if Bob "mistakenly" reports d? Then the outcome is z instead of x, which Alice prefers. That is, and assuming the referee flawlessly implements the rule stated and the basis of the reports, in state ac, Alice lying weakly dominates her telling the truth. And, indeed, this in this example, in all four states and for both Alice and Bob, lying weakly dominates telling the truth. (It is worth pointing out that, if both parties lie, the outcome is z in state ac, x in state bc, y in state ad, and w in state bd, which happens to give Bob his most favored outcome in each state.)

I reiterate that this example is completely contrived. However, it points out that, when it comes to practical applications of the revelation principle, you should watch for contingent outcomes that involve weakly dominant strategies. And, while truth telling may be a Nash equilibrium in the constructed direct-revelation game, there may be other Nash equilibria that involve lying about what players know.

I offer two final caveats about what has been done in this appendix:

- One can imagine contexts in which not all information is available at the outset. It can be that a player, after some time passes, gets new and valuable information. It can be (for a specific mechanism) that Alice, by taking a particular action, causes Bob to get new and valuable information, information that he would not get if she took another action. Insofar as the revelation principle is meant to say that "any contingent outcome that can be accomplished by a general mechanism can be achieved by truth telling in the direct-revelation mechanism," what has been presented here is inadequate to the task. To accommodate such possibilities, it is necessary to develop *dynamic* versions of the revelation principle. Such developments can be found in the literature.

- And in terms of what is possible, the revelation principle as presented here takes as fixed the information endowments of the players. But consider the possibility of designing the information endowments, to render feasible otherwise infeasible contingent outcomes. Chapter 26 concerns *mechanism design*. A relatively recent area of research extends these ideas to *information design*, a small taste of which, known as *Bayesian persuasion*, is presented in Problem 20.23.

A16.5. Variations

Not every application of the revelation principle follows the format sketched in this appendix. For instance, in Chapter 26, concerning mechanism design, the first two applications are the Gibbard–Satterthwaite Theorem (Gibbard 1973, Satterthwaite 1975) and Maskin's Theorem (Maskin 1999). In both those applications, rather than a cardinal utility function $u_i : X \times \Omega \to R$ for each individual, (only) an (ordinal) preference relation $\succeq_i$ is given. And the probability distribution P on the state space Ω is never specified. I won't go into details here about how the three authors can "get away" without cardinal utility or a probability distribution on Ω; explanations are found in the subsection "Ordinal preferences? Probabilities on states of nature?," on pages 445–6.

Bibliographic Notes

Various forms of the revelation principle are developed in Gibbard (1973), Das-Gupta, Hammond, and Maskin (1979), Myerson (1979, 1981), and Harris and Townsend (1981).

Appendix Seventeen

Envelope Theorems

Envelope theorems are results concerning the following basic problem. A parametric optimization problem is given:

For each $\theta \in \Theta$, maximize (or minimize) $F(x, \theta)$ over $x \in X(\theta)$.

Here, θ is a parameter, and x is a variable to be maximized. For now, assume that Θ is an open interval in R^m, and the correspondence $\theta \Rightarrow X(\theta)$ is a continuous, compact, and locally bounded correspondence with range R^n. For each $\theta \in \Theta$, write

$$f(\theta) = \sup\{F(x, \theta) : x \in X(\theta)\},$$

and in cases where the supremum is attained, write $X^*(\theta)$ for the set of maximizers; that is,

$$X^*(\theta) = \{x \in X(\theta) : F(x, \theta) = f(\theta)\}.$$

The term "envelope" in "envelope theorem" refers to the function f, which is the "upper envelope" (or lower envelope if the problem is one of minimizing F) of the functions $\theta \to F(x, \theta)$ for the collection of xs. (For a picture, see Figure A17.1.)

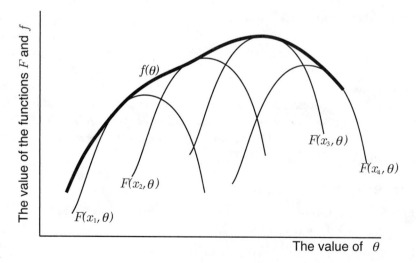

Figure A17.1. What does the word "envelope" in "Envelope theorem" mean? The function f is the upper envelope of the functions $\theta \to F(x, \theta)$ for the different $x \in X$.

Classically, envelope theorems concern the (partial) derivatives of f in the different θ_i and their connection to the partial derivatives of F in the same variables, evaluated at a point θ for f and $(x^*(\theta), \theta)$ for F, where $x^*(\theta) \in X^*(\theta)$. In mechanism-design applications, concern is with integrals of these partial derivatives.

In this appendix, I provide a "classical" version of an envelope theory and then report on a paper by Milgrom and Segal that allows us to use an "integrated envelope theorem" in wide applications to mechanism design.

A17.1. A Classical Envelope Theorem and an Extension

Proposition A17.1. Consider the problem

$$\text{Maximize } F(x, \theta) \text{ over } x \in X, \text{ for } \theta \in \Theta,$$

where X is a compact set in R^n, Θ is an open set in R^M, and F is jointly continuous in (x, θ) and continuously differentiable in θ for each $x \in X$. Assume further that the gradient of F with respect to θ is jointly continuous in (x, θ).

Let $f(\theta) = \max_{x \in X} F(x, \theta)$. If, for a given $\theta^0 \in \Theta$, there is a unique solution x^0 to the maximization problem, then f is differentiable at θ^0, and

$$\left.\frac{\partial f}{\partial \theta_i}\right|_{\theta_0} = \left.\frac{\partial F}{\partial \theta_i}\right|_{(x^0, \theta^0)} \text{ for } i = 1, \ldots, m.$$

Before giving the proof, note the following:

- The proposition establishes both that f is differentiable and that the partial derivatives of f at θ^0 are those of F at (x^0, θ^0). The key condition is that the maximization problem for θ^0 has a unique solution.

- Conditions for uniqueness of solutions for every θ^0 are standard: X is convex, and F is strictly quasi-concave in x for each θ

- In this proposition, unlike at the start of this appendix, the "constraint set" $X(\theta)$ is a constant compact set X. I'll comment further on this assumption after the proof.

- You may recall two classic results from Volume I that are nearly special cases of this general result: Proposition 9.22 (differentiability of the profit function in prices) and Proposition 10.6 (differentiability of the expenditure function in prices). Why only "nearly?" Because for those applications, the set Θ is the set of strictly positive prices, which is indeed an open set in some R^m (m being the number of commodities). But if we take $\Theta = R^m_+$, then X is the production possibility set for Proposition 9.22, and X is the set of consumption bundles giving utility greater than or equal to some fixed u in Proposition 10.6, neither of which is necessarily compact. However, the result is "local," meaning that it concerns the behavior of f in θ over open neighborhoods of θ, and in both applications, given a θ^0 of interest (a vector of strictly positive prices), we can find compact subsets of well-behaved production possibility sets in the first application and consumption bundles in the second application such that, for θ in an open neighborhood of θ^0, solutions are found (only) in the compact subset.

- And if you recall those applications, you may also recall Proposition 11.1, concerning the differentiability of the indirect utility function. This is a case where the constraint set $X(\theta)$ changes with θ; recall how that made things considerably more complex. This sort of extension will be discussed after the proof.

Proof. We begin with Berge's Theorem (Proposition A4.7 in Volume I). This is a parametric optimization problem in which the objective function is jointly continuous and the constraint set is compact and constant, hence it defines a locally compact and continuous correspondence. Berge's Theorem applies: There is a solution for every θ (and, of course, possibly more than one), so solution correspondence is upper semi-continuous, and the optimal value function f is continuous.

And the upper semi-continuity of the solution correspondence implies that if $\{\theta^n; n = 1, 2, \ldots\}$ is any sequence approaching θ^0 and, for each n, x^n is a solution—any solution—at θ^n, then $\lim_n x^n = x^0$, the unique solution at θ^0.

Now examine what we want to show: If $\{\theta^n\}$ is a sequence with limit θ^0, we wish to show that

$$\lim_{n \to \infty} \frac{f(\theta^n) - f(\theta^0) - \nabla_\theta F(x^0, \theta^0) \cdot (\theta^n - \theta^0)}{\|\theta^n - \theta^0\|} = 0,$$

where $\nabla_\theta F(x^0, \theta^0)$ is the gradient vector of F in θ evaluated at (x^0, θ^0).

Let x^n be any solution at θ^n. We know that

$$f(\theta^n) = F(x^n, \theta^n) \geq F(x^0, \theta^n), \quad \text{and} \quad f(\theta^0) = F(x^0, \theta^0) \geq F(x^n, \theta^0). \tag{A17.1}$$

Therefore, for each n,

$$f(\theta^n) - f(\theta^0) - \nabla_\theta F(x^0, \theta^0) \cdot (\theta^n - \theta^0) = F(x^n, \theta^n) - F(x^0, \theta^0) - \nabla_\theta F(x^0, \theta^0) \cdot (\theta^n - \theta^0),$$

and therefore

$$F(x^n, \theta^n) - F(x^n, \theta^0) - \nabla_\theta F(x^0, \theta^0) \cdot (\theta^n - \theta^0) \geq$$
$$f(\theta^n) - f(\theta^0) - \nabla_\theta F(x^0, \theta^0) \cdot (\theta^n - \theta^0) \geq$$
$$F(x^0, \theta^n) - F(x^0, \theta^0) - \nabla_\theta F(x^0, \theta^0) \cdot (\theta^n - \theta^0).$$

So we have the desired result if we can show that the limit of the terms on the left- and right-hand sides of the string of inequalities just given, when divided by $\|\theta^n - \theta^0\|$, are both zero.

Take the left-hand side first. By the exact form of Taylor's theorem (which is just the mean-value theorem),

$$F(x^n, \theta^n) - F(x^n, \theta^0) = \nabla_\theta F(x^n, \hat{\theta}^n) \cdot (\theta^n - \theta^0),$$

where $\hat{\theta}^n$ is some convex combination of θ^n and θ^0. Hence,

$$F(x^n, \theta^n) - F(x^n, \theta^n) - \nabla_\theta F(x^0, \theta^0) \cdot (\theta^n - \theta^0) = \left[\nabla_\theta F(x^n, \hat{\theta}^n) - \nabla_\theta F(x^0, \theta^0) \right] \cdot (\theta^n - \theta^0).$$

Of course,

$$\left| \left[\nabla_\theta F(x^n, \hat{\theta}^n) - \nabla_\theta F(x^0, \theta^0) \right] \cdot (\theta^n - \theta^0) \right| \leq \left\| \nabla_\theta F(x^n, \hat{\theta}^n) - \nabla_\theta F(x^0, \theta^0) \right\| \times \left\| \theta^n - \theta^0 \right\|.$$

Hence

$$\lim_{n \to \infty} \left| \frac{F(x^n, \theta^n) - F(x^n, \theta^0) - \nabla_\theta F(x^0, \theta^0) \cdot (\theta^n - \theta^0)}{\|\theta^n - \theta^0\|} \right| \leq$$

$$\lim_{n \to \infty} \left| \frac{\left\| \nabla_\theta F(x^n, \hat{\theta}^n) - \nabla_\theta F(x^0, \theta^0) \right\| \times \left\| \theta^n - \theta^0 \right\|}{\|\theta^n - \theta^0\|} \right| = \lim_{n \to \infty} \left\| \nabla_\theta F(x^n, \hat{\theta}^n) - \nabla_\theta F(x^0, \theta^0) \right\|.$$

But the last limit is zero, since $(x^n, \hat{\theta}^n) \to (x^0, \theta^0)$, and the gradient of F in θ is (by assumption) jointly continuous in x and θ. The other side is handled in an entirely similar fashion, completing the proof.   ∎

It is worth noting that the proposition assumes that X is a compact subset of R^n for some n. This obviously includes the case where X is an arbitrary finite subset, since then "continuity" in x is not an issue. That is, Berge's Theorem tells us that, in case X is finite, if x^0 is the unique solution to the problem at θ^0, then x^0 is the unique solution to the problem for all θ in some open neighborhood of θ^0. Of course, this makes the proposition, which *assumes* the uniqueness of the solution at θ^0, utterly trivial. (And in this case, the added assumption that X is a subset of R^n is purely superfluous.)

More generally, while it takes some work (you'll need to go back and redo the proof of Berge's theorem), the restriction to compact subsets of R^n is unnecessary. What one needs, after re-proving Berge's theorem, is that X is a compact subset of some normed linear space.

Moving constraint sets

Another generalization of this result concerns the case where the set of x over which $F(x, \theta)$ is maximized changes with θ. Think here of Proposition 11.1, where Θ is the space of strictly positive prices, some income level y is fixed and, given prices θ, the relevant set over which the consumer maximizes is all consumption bundles x whose cost at prices θ is less than or equal to y. (Proposition 11.1 also treats the income level y as a parameter, looking to prove the differentiability of the indirect utility function in y and to identify that derivative but, for purposes of this discussion, I'll assume that we are only worried about how the indirect utility function changes with prices, income fixed.)

If you recall this proposition, you will recall that the result was more complex. (If you have Volume I handy, turn to page 262.) The reason is that the heart of the proof provided above—and the heart of nearly every proof of an envelope theorem—is the pair of inequalities in display (A17.1). We are looking at a sequence of parameter values $\{\theta_n; n = 1, 2, \ldots\}$ approaching θ^0, and the two inequalities are that a solution x^n at θ^n does at least as well at θ^n as does x^0, the solution at θ^0, and vice versa.

But if the set of available xs at θ^0 is different from what's feasible at θ^n, these inequalities don't hold, because x^0 may be infeasible at θ^n and/or x^n may be infeasible at θ^0. We "fixed" this in the proof of Proposition 11.1 by "adjusting" x^0 in its first component so that the adjusted x^0 is feasible at prices θ^n and, simultaneously, adjusting x^n is its first component so that the adjusted x^n is feasible at prices θ^0. Not only that, these adjustments were constructed so that the budget constraint held for the adjusted consumption bundles with equality—giving a pair of inequalities similar to display (A17.1), from which the proof was constructed. About this:

- In the proof of Proposition 9.22, you'll find the two inequalities about four-fifths of the way down page 220 in Volume I. (Concerning Proposition 10.6, I tell you to construct the proof, so I can't point to where you enlisted the two inequalities.) And, once we had the two inequalities, the proof took less than half a page. In contrast, the proof of Proposition 11.1 more than four pages. But, if you reread the discussion following the proof of Proposition 11.1, on page 268 in Volume I, you'll see in those specific contexts how the two proof techniques are related.

- And then the proof of Proposition 11.1 points to how to get a "general" envelope theorem for the case where the set of feasible x's changes with θ: The manner of how the set of feasible x's changes must be structured enough so that we know how to adjust an x that is feasible for one θ so that it is feasible for a different θ. I won't provide such a general result here; be my guest.

A17.2. The Integrated Envelope Theorem

In this section, I assume that $m = 1$; that is, Θ is an interval in R. This is for expositional ease; extensions to $m > 1$ are not difficult. The following assumptions are also maintained throughout:

- X is a compact subset of some normed linear space.

- F is jointly continuous in (x, θ) and, for each x, continuously differentiable in θ. Fixing x, the partial derivative of F in θ will be denoted F_θ.

In view of these assumptions, the supremum in $f(\theta) = \sup\{F(x, \theta) : x \in X\}$ is attained. Write $X^*(\theta)$ for the (nonempty) set of maximizers at θ.

Suppose that, in the context of Proposition A17.1, we have sufficient assumptions to ensure that there is a unique solution $x^*(\theta)$ for every $\theta \in \Theta$; that is, each $X^*(\theta)$ is singleton. As already observed, assuming that X is convex and F is strictly quasi-concave in x for every θ is sufficient for this. Then we know that f is differentiable in θ for every θ and, in particular, $f'(\theta) = F_\theta(x^*(\theta), \theta)$, where f' denotes the derivative of f in θ. Therefore, for any pair θ^1 and θ^0 in Θ,

$$f(\theta^1) - f(\theta^0) = \int_{\theta^0}^{\theta^1} f'(\theta)\mathrm{d}\theta = \int_{\theta^0}^{\theta^1} F_\theta(x(\theta), \theta)\mathrm{d}\theta. \tag{A17.2}$$

This integrated version of the envelope theorem is convenient for purposes of mechanism design. And what makes it convenient is that it is not necessary that each θ admits a unique solution. It is only necessary that enough of them do.

Suppose, for instance, that X is a finite set and that we somehow know that, for any pair x^1 and x^2 from X, the set

$$\{\theta : F(x^1, \theta) = F(x^2, \theta)\}$$

is finite. Then we know (convince yourself if it isn't obvious) that f is differentiable with the derivative given by Proposition A17.1 for all but finitely many θs. And, then, it is clear that equation (A17.2) holds; when integrating in θ, there are only finitely many points—a set of Lebesgue measure 0—where the integrand fails to be correct.

More generally, if we know that f is absolutely continuous, we know that it is differentiable except for a set of Lebesgue measure 0, so the first (left-hand) equation in A17.2. holds. (See, for instance, Royden 1988.)[1] And the following simple proposition shows that wherever f is differentiable, its derivative is the partial derivative (in θ) evaluated at (x^*, θ) for any $x^* \in X^*(\theta)$. Therefore, the second equation also holds.

Proposition A17.2. *If f is differentiable at θ, then for any $x^* \in X^*(\theta)$,*

$$f'(\theta) = F_\theta(x^*, \theta).$$

---

[1] There are many editions of Royden's classic text; look for "absolute continuity" in its index.

Proof. Fix θ, and let $\{\theta^n; n = 1, 2, \ldots\}$ be a sequence in Θ that approaches θ from above. We know that

$$\lim_n \frac{f(\theta^n) - f(\theta)}{\theta^n - \theta} = f'(\theta), \quad \text{and} \quad \lim_n \frac{F(x^*, \theta^n) - F(x^*, \theta)}{\theta^n - \theta} = F_\theta(x^*, \theta).$$

We also know that $f(\theta^n) \geq F(x^*, \theta^n)$, $f(\theta) = F(x^*, \theta)$, and $\theta^n - \theta > 0$; hence, term by term, we have

$$\frac{f(\theta^n) - f(\theta)}{\theta^n - \theta} \geq \frac{F(x^*, \theta^n) - F(x^*, \theta)}{\theta^n - \theta},$$

which implies that $f'(\theta) \geq F_\theta(x^*, \theta)$. Now repeat this argument but with $\{\theta^n\}$ approaching θ from below. Term by term, $f(\theta^n) - f(\theta) \geq F(x^*, \theta^n) - F(x^*, \theta)$, but the common denominator $\theta^n - \theta$ is always less than zero, so the inequality reverses (term by term), and we get $f'(\theta) \leq F_\theta(x^*, \theta)$. Combine the two, and we have the result.[2]   ∎

Therefore, to derive equation (A17.2), where $x^*(\theta)$ is any selection from $X^*(\theta)$ for each θ, it suffices to give conditions that ensure that f is absolutely continuous. In the applications in the text, one can prove from first principles that f is convex and continuous. That suffices. We also have the following very nice result.

Proposition A17.3 (Milgrom and Segal 2002). *If*

a. $\theta \rightarrow F(x, \theta)$ *is absolutely continuous in θ for each $x \in X$, and*

b. *for some (finitely) integrable function $\alpha : \Theta \rightarrow [0, \infty)$, $|F_\theta(x, \theta)| \leq \alpha(\theta)$ for all $x \in X$,*

then f is absolutely continuous, and so equation (A17.2) holds.

Proof. Recall the definition of absolute continuity: The function f is absolutely continuous if, for every $\epsilon > 0$, there exists δ such that, if $\{[\underline{\theta}^i, \overline{\theta}^i]; i = 1, 2, \ldots, I\}$ is a finite collection of nonoverlapping closed intervals in Θ such that if $\sum_i \overline{\theta}^i - \underline{\theta}^i < \delta$, then $\sum_i |f(\overline{\theta}^i) - f(\underline{\theta}^i)| < \epsilon$.

Fix ϵ. Because α is finitely integrable, there exists $\delta > 0$ such that, $\{[\underline{\theta}^i, \overline{\theta}^i]; i = 1, 2, \ldots, I\}$ is a finite collection of non-overlapping closed intervals in Θ such that $\sum_i \overline{\theta}^i - \underline{\theta}^i < \delta$, then

$$\sum_i \int_{\underline{\theta}^i}^{\overline{\theta}^i} \alpha(\theta) d\theta < \epsilon.$$

---

[2] If this seems magical to you, think in terms of left- and right-hand derivatives at θ and (x^*, θ), which must be the same, because we've assumed differentiability, and it should become obvious.

So, fixing ϵ and the corresponding δ, take any finite collection of nonoverlapping closed intervals $\{[\underline{\theta}^i, \overline{\theta}^i]; i = 1, 2, \ldots, I\}$. Take one of the closed intervals, $[\underline{\theta}^i, \overline{\theta}^i]$. Suppose that $f(\underline{\theta}^i) \geq f(\overline{\theta}^i)$. Select some x^* from $X^*(\underline{\theta}^i)$. Then $f(\underline{\theta}^i) = F(x^*, \underline{\theta}^i)$, while $f(\overline{\theta}^i) \geq F(x^*, \overline{\theta}^i)$, and so

$$0 \leq f(\underline{\theta}^i) - f(\overline{\theta}^i) \leq F(x^*, \underline{\theta}^i) - F(x^*, \overline{\theta}^i) = \int_{\overline{\theta}^i}^{\underline{\theta}^i} F_\theta(x^*, \theta) d\theta \leq \int_{\underline{\theta}^i}^{\overline{\theta}^i} |F_\theta(x^*, \theta)| d\theta.$$

If, instead, $f(\overline{\theta}^i) \geq f(\underline{\theta}^i)$, choose x^* from $X^*(\overline{\theta}^i)$, and we can conclude by a similar argument that

$$0 \leq f(\overline{\theta}^i) - f(\underline{\theta}^i) \leq \int_{\underline{\theta}^i}^{\overline{\theta}^i} |F_\theta(x^*, \theta)| d\theta.$$

So, combining the two cases,

$$|f(\overline{\theta}^i) - f(\underline{\theta}^i)| \leq \int_{\underline{\theta}^i}^{\overline{\theta}^i} |F_\theta(x^*, \theta)| d\theta \leq \int_{\underline{\theta}^i}^{\overline{\theta}^i} \alpha(\theta) d\theta,$$

where the choice of x^* in the middle term depends on which of the two cases prevails.

But, then, this is true for every one of the closed intervals, so

$$\sum_i |f(\overline{\theta}^i) - f(\underline{\theta}^i)| \leq \sum_i \int_{\underline{\theta}^i}^{\overline{\theta}^i} \alpha(\theta) d\theta < \delta.$$

∎

References

In addition to the references cited in this volume, this list includes papers that are cited in the *Online Supplement* for this volume.

Abreu, Dilip (1988). "On the Theory of Infinitely Repeated Games with Discounting." *Econometrica* **56**, 383–96.

Abreu, Dilip, Prajit K. Dutta, and Lones Smith (1994). "A Folk Theorem for Repeated Games: A Neu Condition." *Econometrica* **62**, 929–48.

Abreu, Dilip, and Faruk Gul (2000). "Bargaining and Reputation." *Econometrica* **68**, 85–117

Abreu, Dilip, David Pearce, and Ennio Stacchetti (1986). "Optimal Cartel Equilibrium with Imperfect Monitoring." *Journal of Economic Theory* **39**, 251–69.

Abreu, Dilip, David Pearce, and Ennio Stacchetti (1990). "Toward a Theory of Discounted Repeated Games with Imperfect Monitoring." *Econometrica* **58**, 1041–64.

Adachi, Hiroyuki (2000). "On a Characterization of Stable Matchings." *Economic Letters* **68**, 43–9.

Admati, Anat R., and Motty Perry (1987). "Strategic Delay in Bargaining." *Review of Economic Studies* **54**, 345–64,

Akerlof, George (1970). "The Market for 'Lemons': Quality Uncertainty and the Market Mechanism." *Quarterly Journal of Economics* **84**, 488–500.

Arrow, Kenneth J. (1951). *Social Choice and Individual Values*. New Haven: Yale University Press.

Ashlagi, Itai, and Alvin E. Roth (2021). "Kidney Exchange: An Operations Perspective." *Management Science* **67**, 5455–78.

Aumann, Robert J. (1964). "Mixed and Behavior Strategies in Infinite Extensive Games." in M. Dresher, L. S. Shapley, and A. W. Tucker (eds.), *Advances in Game Theory*. Princeton: Princeton University Press, 627–50.

Aumann, Robert J. (1974). "Subjectivity and Correlation in Randomized Strategies." *Journal of Mathematical Economics* **55**, 1–18.

Aumann, Robert J. (1976). "Agreeing to Disagree." *The Annals of Statistics* **4**, 1236–9.

Aumann, Robert J. (1987). "Correlated Equilibrium as an Expression of Bayesian Rationality." *Econometrica* **55**, 1–18.

Aumann, Robert J., and Lloyd S. Shapley (1976). "Long-Term Competition—A Game Theoretic Analysis." Mimeo. Available at econ.ucla.edu/workingpapers/wp676.pdf.

Aumann, Robert J., and Sylvain Sorin (1989). "Cooperation and Bounded Recall." *Games and Economic Behavior* **1**, 5–39.

Axelrod, Robert (1984). *The Evolution of Cooperation*. New York: Basic Books.

Bacon, Nathaniel T. (1897). *Researches into the Mathematical Principles of the Theory of Wealth*. New York: Macmillan.

Baiman, Stanley, and Joel S. Demski (1980), "Economically Optimal Performance evaluation and Control Systems." *Journal of Accounting Research* **18** Supplement, 184–220.

Banks, Jeffrey S., and Joel Sobel (1987). "Equilibrium Selection in Signaling Games," *Econometrica* **55**, 647–661.

Battigalli, Pierpalo (1996). "Strategic Independence and Perfect Bayesian Equilibria." *Journal of Economic Theory* **70**, 301–34.

Battigalli, Pierpalo, Mario Gilli, and Cristina Molinari (1992). 'Learning and Convergence to Equilibrium in Repeated Interaction." *Richerche Economiche* **46**, 335–78.

Benoit, Jean-Pierre, and Vijay Krishna (1985). "Finitely Repeated Games." *Econometrica* **53**, 890–904.

Benoit, Jean-Pierre, and Vijay Krishna (1987). "Nash Equilibria of Finitely Repeated Games." *International Journal of Game Theory* **16**, 197–204.

Bergemann, Dirk, and Juuso Välimäki (2010). "The Dynamic Pivot Mechanism." *Econometrica* **78**, 771–89.

Bernheim, B. Douglas (1984). "Rationalizable Strategic Behavior." *Econometrica* **52**, 1007–28.

Bertrand, Joseph Louis Francois (1883). "Review of Cournot." *Journal de Savants* **67**, 499–508.

Binmore, Ken, Ariel Rubinstein, and Asher Wolinsky (1986). The Nash Bargaining Solution in Economic Modelling." *RAND Journal of Economics* **17**, 176–88.

Blume, Lawrence E., and William R. Zame (1994). "The Algebraic Geometry of Perfect and Sequential Equilibrium." *Econometrica* **62**, 783–94.

Bowen, T. Renee, David M. Kreps, and Andrzej Skrzypacz (2013). "Rules with Discretion and Local Information." *Quarterly Journal of Economics* **128**, 1273–320.

Bulow, Jeremy I. (1982). "Durable-Goods Monopolists." *Journal of Political Economy* **90**, 314–32.

Bulow, Jeremy I., John Geanakoplos, and Paul Klemperer (1985). "Multimarket Oligopoly: Strategic Substitutes and Strategic Complements." *Journal of Political Economy* **103**, 441–63.

Bulow, Jeremy I., and D. John Roberts (1989). "The Simple Economics of Optimal Auctions." *Journal of Political Economy* **97**, 1060–90.

Carroll, Gabriel (2015). "Robustness and Linear Contracts." *American Economic Review* **105**, 536–63.

Cassady, Ralph (1967). *Auctions and Auctioneering.* Berkeley: University of California Press (republished in 2021).

Chatterjee, Kaylon, and William Sanuelson (1983). "Bargaining under Incomplete Information." *Operations Research* **31**, 835–51

Chiappori, Pierre-André, Alfred Galichon, and Bernard Salanié (2019). "On Human Capital and Team Stability." *Journal of Human Capital* **13**, 236–59.

Cho, In-koo, and David M. Kreps (1987). "Signaling Games and Stable Equilibria." *Quarterly Journal of Economics* **102**, 179–221.

Clarke, Edward H. (1971). "Multipart Pricing of Public Goods." *Public Choice* **8**, 19–33.

Coase, Ronald H. (1972). "Durability and Monopoly." *Journal of Law and Economics* **15**, 143–49.

Cournot, Antoine-Augustin (1838). *Recherches sur les Principes Mathématiques de la Th'eorie des Rechesses.* Translation by Nathaniel T. Bacon, *Researches into the Mathematical Principles of the Theory of Wealth.* New York: Macmillan, 1897 (available on the web).

Cramton, Peter C. (1992). "Strategic Delay in Bargaining with Two-sided Uncertainty." *Review of Economic Studies* **59a**, 205–25.

Crawford, Vincent P., and Elsie Marie Knoer (1981). "Job Matching with Heterogeneous Firms and Workers." *Econometrica* **49**, 437–50.

Crawford, Vincent P., and Joel Sobel (1982). "Strategic Information Transmission." *Econometrica* **50**, 1431–51.

Crémer, Jacques, and Richard McLean (1988). "Full Extraction of the Surplus in Bayesian and Dominant Strategy Auctions." *Econometrica* **56**, 1247–57.

Dalkey, N. (1953). "Equivalence of Information Patterns and Essentially Determinate Games." in H. Kuhn and A. Tucker (eds.), *Contributions to the Theory of Games*, Vol. II. Princeton: Princeton University Press.

Dantzig, George B. (1963). *Linear Programming and Extensions*. Princeton: Princeton University Press.

Dasgupta, Partha, Peter Hammand, and Eric Maskin (1979). "The Implementation of Social Choice Rules: Some General Results on Incentive Compatibility." *Review of Economic Studies* **46**, 181–216.

David, H. A., and H. N. Nagaraja (2003). *Order Statistics*, 3rd edition. New York: John Wiley & Sons. (Free download at the Wiley Online Library.)

Dekel, Eddie, and Marciano Siniscalchi (2015). "Epistemic Game Theory." Chapter 12 in P. Young and S. Zamir (eds.), *Handbook of Game Theory with Economic Applications*, Vol. 4. Amsterdam: North-Holland, 619–702.

Demange, Gabrielle, David Gale, and Marilda Sotomayer (1986). "Multi-Unit Auctions." *Journal of Political Economy* **94**, 863–71.

Demski, Joel, and David Sappington (1984). "Optimal Incentive Contracts with Multiple Agents." *Journal of Economic Theory* **33**, 152–71.

Dr. Seuss (1961). *The Sneetches and Other Stories*. New York: Random House.

Dye, Ronald (1998). "Investor Sophistication and Voluntary Disclosure." *Review of Accounting Studies* **3**, 261–87.

Echenique, Frederico, and Jorge Oviedo (2004). "Core Many-to-One Matchings by Fixed-Point Methods." *Journal of Economic Theory* **115**, 358–76.

Edgeworth, Francis Ysidro (1889). "The pure theory of monopoly." Available in *Collected Papers Relating to Political Economy*, Vol. 1. London: Macmillan, 1925.

Fisher, Franklin (1989). "Games Economists Play: A Noncooperative View." *RAND Journal of Economics* **20**, 113–24.

Friedman, James (1971), "A Noncooperative Equilibrium for Supergames." *Review of Economic Studies* **28**, 1–12.

Fuchs, William, and Andrzej Skrzypacz (2013). "Bargaining with Deadlines and Private Information." *AEJ: Microeconomics* **5**, 219–43.

Fuchs, William, and and Andrzej Skrzypacz (2015). "Government Interventions in a Dynamic Market with Adverse Selection." *Journal of Economic Theory* **158**, 371–406.

Fudenberg, drew, and David K. Levine (1983). "Subgame-Perfect Equilibria of Finite- and Infinite-Horizon Games." *Journal of Economic Theory* **31**, 251–68.

Fudenberg, Drew, and David K. Levine (1989). "Reputation and Equilibrium Selection in Games with a Patient Player." *Econometrica* **57**, 759–78.

Fudenberg, Drew, and David K. Levine (1992). "Maintaining a Reputation When Strategies are Imperfectly Observed." *Review of Economic Studies* **59**, 561–79.

Fudenberg, Drew, and David K. Levine (1994). "Efficiency and Observability in Games with Long-Run and Short-Run Players." *Journal of Economic Theory* **62**, 103–35.

Fudenberg, Drew, and David K. Levine (1998). *The Theory of Learning in Games*. Cambridge, MA: MIT Press.

Fudenberg, Drew, David K. Levine, and Eric Maskin (1994). "The Folk Theorem with Imperfect Private Information." *Econometrica* **62**, 26–47.

Fudenberg, Drew, and David M. Kreps (1987). ""Reputation in the Simultaneous Play of Multiple Opponents." Review of Economic Studies **54**, 541–68.

Fudenberg, Drew, David M. Kreps, and Eric Maskin (1990). "Repeated Games with Long-Run and Short-Run Players." *Review of Economic Studies* **57**, 555–573.

Fudenberg, Drew, and Eric Maskin (1986). "The Folk Theorem in Repeated Games with Discounting or with Incomplete Information." *Econometrica* **54**, 533–56.

Fudenberg, Drew, and Jean Tirole (1991a). "Perfect Bayesian Equilibrium and Sequential Equilibrium." *Journal of Economic Theory* **53**, 236–60.

Fudenberg, Drew, and Jean Tirole (1991b). *Game Theory*. Cambridge, MA: MIT Press

Gale, David, and Lloyd Shapley (1962). "College Admissions and the Stability of Marriage." *The American Mathematical Monthly* **69**, 9–15.

Geanokoplos, John (2005). "Three Brief Proofs of Arrow's Impossibility Theorem." *Economic Theory* **26**, 211–15.

Gibbard, Alan (1973). "Manipulation of Voting Schemes: A General Result." *Econometrica* **41**, 587–602.

Glicksberg, I. L. (1952). "A Further Generalization of the Kakutani Fixed Point Theorem with Applications to Nash Equilibrium Points." *Proceedings of the American Mathematics Society* **3**, 170–74.

Govinden, Srihari, and Robert B. Wilson (2009). "On Forward Induction." *Econometrica* **77**, 1–28.

Govinden, Srihari, and Robert B. Wilson (2012). "Axiomatic Equilibrium Selection for Generic Two-Player Games." *Econometrica* **80**, 1639–99.

Green, Edward J., and Robert H. Porter (1984). "Noncooperative Collusion under Imperfect Price Information." *Econometrica* **52**, 87–100.

Green, Jerry R., and Jean-Jacques Laffont (1979). *Incentives in Public Decision Making*. Amsterdam: North-Holland.

Green, Jerry R., and Nancy L. Stokey (1983). "A Comparison of Tournaments and Contracts." *Journal of Political Economy* **91**, 349–64.

Green, Jerry R., and Nancy L. Stokey (2007). "A Two-Person Game of Information Transmission." *Journal of Economic Theory* **135**, 90–104. (Although first published in 2007, this paper was written and circulated in working-paper form in the early 1980s.)

Grossman, Sanford, and Oliver Hart (1983). "An Analysis of the Principal–Agent Problem." *Econometrica* **51**, 7–45.

Groves, Theodore (1973). "Incentives in Teams." *Econometrica* **41**, 617–31.

Groves, Theodore, and John Ledyard (1977). "Optimal Allocation of Public Goods: A Solution to the 'Free Rider' Problem." *Econometrica* **45**, 783–809.

Gul, Faruk, Hugo Sonnenschein, and Robert Wilson (1986). "Foundations of Dynamic Mnopoly and the Coase Conjecture." *Journal of Economic Theory* **39**, 155–90.

Hammond, John S. (1974). "Maxco, Inc. and the Gambit Co." Harvard Business School Case 174-091.

Harrington, Joseph E., and Andrzej Skrzypacz (2007). "Collusion Under Monitoring of sales." *RAND Journal of Economics* **38**, 314–31.

Harrington, Joseph E., and Andrzej Skrzypacz (2011). "Private Monitoring and Communication in Cartels: Explaining Recent Collusive Practices." *American Economic Review* **101**, 2425–49.

Harris, Milton, and Robert M. Townsend (1981). "Resource Allocation under Asymmetric Information." *Econometrica* **49**, 33–64.

Harsanyi, John (1967-68). "Games with Incomplete Information Played by Bayesian Players, I, II, and III." *Management Sciences* **14**, 159–82, 320–34, and 486–503.

Hart, Sergiu (2016). "Shapley Value." in J. Eatwell, M. Milgate, and P. Newman (eds.), *The New Palgrave: Game Theory*. New York: W. W. Norton, 210–16.

Hatfield, John W. and Paul Milgrom (2005). "Matching with Contracts." *American Economic Review* **95**, 913–35.

Hendon, Ebbe, Hans Jorgen Jacobsen, and Birgitte Sloth (1996). "The One-Shot-Deviation Principle for Sequential Rationality." *Games and Economic Behavior* **12**, 274–82.

Hendricks, Ken, Andrew Weiss, and Charles Wilson (1988). "The War of Attrition in Continuous Time with Complete Information." *International Economic Review* **29**, 663–80

Hillas, Jon (1990). "On the Definition of the Strategic Stability of Equilibria." *Econometrica* **58**, 1365–90.

Holmstrom, Bengt (1979). "Moral Hazard and Observability." *Bell Journal of Economics* **10**, 74–91.

Holmstrom, Bengt (1982a). "Managerial Incentive Problems—A Dynamic Perspective." in *Essays in Economics and Management in Honor of Lars Wahlbeck*. Helsinki: Swedish School of Economics, 1982 (reprinted in the *Review of Economic Studies* **66**, 1999, 169–82).

Holmstrom, Bengt (1982b). "Moral Hazard in Teams," *The Bell Journal of Economics* **13**, 324–40.

Holmstrom, Bengt, and Paul Milgrom (1987). "Aggregation and Linearity in the Provision of Intertemporal Incentives." *Econometrica* **55**, 303–28.

Holmstrom, Bengt, and Paul Milgrom (1991). "Multitask Principal-Agent Analyses: Incentive Contracts, Asset Ownership, and Job Design." *Journal of Law, Economics, and Organization* **7**, 24–52.

Jackson, Matthew O. (2001). "A Crash Course in Implementation Theory." *Social Choice and Welfare* **18**, 655–708.

Jehle, Geoffrey A., and Philip J. Reny (2010). *Advanced Microeconomic Theory*, 3rd edition. Harlow, UK: Pearson.

Jewitt, Ian (1988). "Justifying the First-Order Approach to Principal-Agent Problems." *Econometrica* **56**, 1177–90.

Kahn, Charles (1986). "The Durable Goods Monopolist and Consistency with Increasing Costs." *Econometrica* **54**, 275–94.

Kalai, Ehud, and Meir Smorodinsky (1975). "Other Solutions to Nash's Bargaining Problem." *Econometrica* **43**, 513–18.

Kamenica, Emir, and Matthew Gentzkow (2011). "Bayesian Persuasion." *American Economic Review* **101**, 2590–615.

Kelso, Alexander, and Vincent P. Crawford (1982). 'Job Matching, Coalition Formation, and Gross Substitutes." *Econometrica* **50**, 1483–1504.

Klemperer, Paul (2004). *Auctions: Theory and Practice*. Princeton: Princeton University Press.

Kohlberg, Elon, and Jean-Francois Mertens (1986). "Strategic Stability." *Econometrica* **54**, 1003–37.

Kohlberg, Elon, and Phillip J. Reny (1997). "Independence on Relative Probability Spaces and Consistent Assessments in Game Trees." *Journal of Economic Theory* **75**, 280–313.

Kreps, David M. (1977). "A Note on 'Fulfilled Expectations' Equilibria." *Journal of Economic Theory*, **14**, 32–43.

Kreps, David M. (1989). "Out of Equilibrium Beliefs and Out of equilibrium Behavior." in F. H. Hahn (ed.), *The Economics of Information, Missing Markets, and Games.* Oxford: Oxford University Press, 7–45.

Kreps, David M. (1990a). *A Course in Microeconomic Theory.* Princeton: Princeton University Press.

Kreps, David M. (1990b). *Game Theory and Economic Modelling.* Oxford: Oxford University Press.

Kreps, David M. (2013). *Microeconomic Foundations I: Choice and Competitive Markets.* Princeton, Princeton University Press.

Kreps, David M. (2018). *The Motivation Toolkit.* New York: W. W. Norton.

Kreps, David M. (2019). *Microeconomics for Managers,* 2nd edition. Princeton: Princeton University Press.

Kreps, David M., Paul R. Milgrom, D. John Roberts, and Robert Wilson (1982). "Rational Cooperation in the Finitely Repeated Prisoners' Dilemma." *Journal of Economic Theory* **27**, 245–52.

Kreps, David M., and Robert Wilson (1982a). "Reputation and Imperfect Information." *Journal of Economic Theory* **27**, 253–79.

Kreps, David M., and Robert Wilson (1982b). "Sequential equilibrium." *Econometrica* **50**, 863–94.

Krishna, Vijay (2010). *Auction Theory,* 2nd edition. Amsterdam: Academic Press.

Kuhn, Harold W. (1953). "Extensive Games and Problem of Information." in H. W. Kuhn and A. W. Tucker (eds.), *Contributions to the Theory of Games,* Vol. 2. Princeton: Princeton University Press, 193–216.

Kuhn, Harold W. (1955). "The Hungarian method for the assignment problem." *Naval Research Logistics Quarterly* **2**, 83–97.

Laffont, Jean-Jacques, and Jean Tirole (1988). "The Dynamics of Incentive Contracts." *Econometrica* **56**, 1153–75.

Lazear, Edward P. (1979). "Why Is There Mandatory Retirement." *Journal of Political Economy* **87**, 1261–84.

Lazear, Edward P., and Sherwin Rosen (1981). "Rank-Order Tournaments as Optimum Labor Contracts." *Journal of Political Economy* **89**, 841–64.

Leonard, Herman B. (1983). "Elicitation of Honest Preferences for the Assignment of Individuals to Positions." *Journal of Political Economy* **91**, 461–79.

Levin, Jonathan (2003). "Relational Incentive Contracts." *American Economic Review* **93**, 835–57.

Li, Shengwu (2017). "Obviously Strategy-Proof Mechanisms." *American Economic Review* **107**, 3257–87.

Linhart, Peter B., Roy Radner, and Mark Satterthwaite (1992). *Bargaining with Incomplete Information*. New York: Academic Press, Inc.

MacLeod, W. Bentley (2003). "Optimal Contracting with Subjective Evaluation." *American Economic Review* **93**, 216–40.

Mailath, George, and Larry Samuelson (2006). *Repeated Games and Repuations: Long-run Relationships*. Oxford: Oxford University Press.

Maskin, Eric (1999). "Nash Equilibrium and Welfare Optimality." *Review of Economic Studies* **66**, 23–38.

Maskin, Eric, and Partha Dasgupta (1986). "The Existence of Equilibrium in Discontinuous Economic Games, Part I (Theory)." *Review of Economic Studies* **53**, 1–26.

Maskin, Eric, and John Moore (1999). "Implementation and Renegotiation." *Review of Economic Studies* **66**, 39–56.

McAfee, R. Preston, and Philip J. Reny (1992). "Correlated Information and Mchanism Design." *Econometrica* **60**, 395–421.

Mertens, Jean-Francois (1989). "Stable Equilibria—A Reformulation. I. Definitions and Basic Properties." *Mathematics of Operations Research* **14**, 575–624.

Mertens, Jean-Francois (1991). "Stable Equilibria–A Reformulation. II. Discussion of the Definition, and Further Results." *Mathematics of Operations Research* **16**, 694–753.

Mertens, Jean-Francois, Sylvain Sorin, and Shmuel Zamir (2015). *Repeated Games*. Cambridge, U.K.: Cambridge University Press.

Mertens, Jean-Francois, and Shmuel Zamir (1985). "Formulation of Bayesian Analysis for Games with Incomplete Information." *International Journal of Game Theory* **14**, 1–29.

Metz, Cade (2015). "Facebook Doesn't Make as Much Money as It Could—on Purpose." *Wired*, September 21, 2015.

Milgrom, Paul R. (1981). "Good News and Bad News: Representation Theorems and Applications." *Bell Journal of Economics* **12**, 380–91.

Milgrom, Paul R. (2004). *Putting Auction Theory to Work*. Cambridge, England: Cambridge University Press.

Milgrom, Paul R., and D. John Roberts (1982a). "Limit Pricing and Entry under Incomplete Information: An equilibrium analysis." *Econometrica* **50**, 443–59

Milgrom, Paul R., and D. John Roberts (1982b). "Predation, Reputation, and Entry Deterrence." *Journal of Economic Theory* **27**, 280–312.

Milgrom, Paul R., and D. John Roberts (1993). "Johnson Controls, Inc.—Automotive Systems Group. The Georgetown, Kentucky Plant." Stanford Graduate School of Business BE-9.

Milgrom, Paul R., and Ilya Segal (2002). "Envelope Theorems for Arbitrary Choice Sets." *Econometrica* **70**, 583–601.

Milgrom, Paul R., and Nancy Stokey (1982). "Information, Trade, and Common Knowledge." *Journal of Economic Theory* **26**, 17–27.

Milgrom, Paul R., and Robert Weber (1982). "The Theory of Auctions and Competitive Bidding." *Econometrica* **50**, 1089–122.

Milgrom, Paul R., and Robert Weber (1985). "Distributional Strategies for Games with Incomplete Information." *Mathematics of Operations Research* **10**, 619–32.

Mirrlees, James A. (1999). "The Theory of Moral Hazard and Unobservable Behavior: Part I." *Review of Economic Studies* **66**, 3–21. (This paper was completed in October, 1975.)

Moldovanu, Benny, and Manfred Tietzel (1998). "Goethe's Second-Price Auction." *Journal of Political Economy* **106**, 854–59.

Mookherjee, Dilip (1984). "Optimal incentive schemes with many agents." *Review of Economic Studies*, Vol. 51, 433–46.

Moore, John, Ching-to Ma, and Stephen Turnbull (1988). "Stopping Agents from 'Cheating'." *Journal of Economic Theory* **46**, 355–72.

Muller, Eitan, and Mark A. Satterthwaite (1977). "The Equivalence of Strong Positive Association and Strategy-Proofness." *Journal of Economic Theory* **14**, 412–18.

Myerson, Roger B. (1978). "Refinements of the Nash Equilibrium Concept." *International Journal of Game Theory* **7**, 73–80.

Myerson, Roger B. (1979). "Incentive Ccompatibility and the Bargaining Problem." *Econometrica* **47**, 61–73.

Myerson, Roger B. (1981). "Optimal Auction Design." *Mathematics of Operations Research* **6**, 58–72.

Myerson, Roger B., and Philip J. Reny (2020). "Perfect Conditional ϵ-Equilibria of Multi-Stage Games with Infinite Sets of Signals and Actions." *Econometrica* **88**, 495–531.

Myerson, Roger B., and Mark A. Satterthwaite (1983). "Efficient Mechanisms for Bilateral Trading." *Journal of Economic Theory* **29**, 265–81.

Nalebuff Barry, and Joseph Stiglitz (1983). "Prices and Incentives: Towards a General Theory of Compensation and Competition." *Bell Journal of Economics* **14**, 21–43.

Nash, John F. (1950a). "The Bargaining Problem." *Econometrica* **18**, 155–62.

Nash, John F. (1950b). "Equilibrium Points in n-Person Games." *Proceedings of the National Academy of Sciences* **36**, 48–49.

Nöldecke, George, and Eric Van Damme (1990). "Signalling in a Dynamic Labor Market." *Review of Economic Studies* **57**, 1–23.

Ortega-Reichart, A. (1968). *Models of Competitive Bidding Under Uncertainty.* Ph.D. dissertation, Stanford University.

Osborne, Martin J., and Ariel Rubinstein (1990). *Bargaining and Markets.* Bingley, England: Emerald Publishing Limited.

Ostrovsky, Michael (2008). "Stability in Supply Chain Networks." *American Economic Review* **98**, 897–923.

Pathak, Parag (2017). "What Really Matters in Designing School Choice Mechanisms." in B. Honore, A. Pakes, M. Piazessi, and W. Samuelson (eds.), *Advances in Economics and Econometrics: 11th World Congress of the Econometric Society.* Cambridge: Cambridge University Press, 176–214.

Pearce, David G. (1984). "Rationalizable Strategic Behavior and the Problem of Perfection. *Econometrica* **52**, 1029–50.

Porter, Michael (1980a, b, and c). "General Electric vs. Westinghouse in Large Turbine Generators (A), (B), and (C)." Harvard Business School Cases ##380128, 380129, and 380130.

Rabin, Matthew, and Richard Thaler (2001). "Anomalies: Risk Aversion." *Journal of Economic Perspectives* **15**, 219–32.

Reinganum, Jennifer F., and Louis L. Wilde (1986). "Equilibrium Verification and Reporting Policies in a Model of Tax Compliance." *International Economic Review* **27**, 739–60.

Reny, Philip J. (2001). "Arrow's Theorem and the Gibbard–Satterthwaite Theorem: A Unified Approach." *Economic Letters* **70**, 279–85.

Reny, Philip J. (2021). "Notes on Games with Ties." Unpublished manuscript, Department of Economics, University of Chicago.

Reny, Philip J., and Shmuel Zamir (2004). "On the Existence of Pure Strategy Monotone Equilibria in Asymmetric First-Price Auctions." *Econometrica* **72**, 1105–25.

Repullo, Rafael (1987). "A Simple Proof of Maskin's Theorem on Nash implementation." *Social Choice and Welfare* **4**, 39–41.

Riley, John G. (1979). 'Informational Equilibrium." *Econometrica* **47**, 331–59

Riley, John G. (1980). "Strong Evolutionary Equilibrium and the War of Attrition." *Journal of Theoretical Biology* **82**, 383–400.

Rogerson, William P. (1985). "The First-Order Approach to Principal-Agent Problems." *Econometrica* **53**, 1357–67.

Ross, Stephen A. (1973). "The Economic Theory of Agency: The Principal's Problem." *American Economic Review* **63**, 134–39.

Roth, Alvin E. (1982). "The Eonomics of Matching: Stability and Incentives." *Mathematics of Operations Research* **7**, 617–28.

Roth, Alvin E. (1984a). "The Evolution of the Labor Market for Medical Interns and Residents: A Case Study in Game Theory." *Journal of Political Economy* **92**, 991–1016.

Roth, Alvin E. (1984b). "Stability and Polarization of Interests in Job Matching." *Econometrica* **52**, 47–57.

Roth, Alvin E. (1985). "The College Admissions Problem is Not Equivalent to the Marriage Problem." *Journal of Economic Theory* **36**, 277–88.

Roth, Alvin E. (1995). "Bargaining Experiments." in J. Kagel and A. E. Roth (eds.), *Handbook of Experimental Economics*. Princeton NJ: Princeton University Press, 253–348.

Roth, Alvin E. (2002). "The Economist as Engineer: Game Theory, Experimentation, and Computation as Tools for Design Economics." *Econometrica* **70**, 1341–78.

Roth, Alvin E., and Francoise Schoumaker (1983). "Expectations and Reputations in Bargaining: An Experimental Study." *American Economic Review* **81**, 1068–95.

Roth, Alvin E., and Marilda A. Oliveira Sotomayor (1990). *Two-Sided Matching: A Study in Game-Theoretic Modeling and Analysis.* Cambridge: Cambridge University Press.

Roth, Alvin E., and Marilda A. Oliveira Sotomayor (1992). "Two-Sided Matching." Chapter 16 in R. J. Aumann and S. Hart (eds.), *The Handbook of Game Theory*, Vol. 1. Amsterdam: Elsevier Science Publishers, 485–541.

Rothkopf, Michael H. (2007). "Thirteen Reasons Why the Vickry–Clarke–Grove Process is Not Practical." *Operations Research* **55**, 191–97.

Rothschild, Michael, and Joseph Stiglitz (1976). "Equilibrium in Competitive Insurance Markets: An Essay on the Economics of Imperfect Information." *Quarterly Journal of Economics* **80**, 629–49.

Royden, Halsey L. (1988). *Real Analysis*, 3rd edition. Englewood Cliffs: Prentice-Hall.

Rubinstein, Ariel (1979). "Equilibrium in Supergames with the Overtaking Criterion." *Journal of Economic Theory* **21**, 1–9.

Rubinstein, Ariel (1982). "Perfect Equilibrium in a Bargaining Model." *Econometrica* **50**, 97–109.

Samuelson, William (1984). "Bargaining Under Asymmetric Information." *Econometrica* **54**, 995–1005.

Satterthwaite, Mark A. (1975). "Strategy-Proofness and Arrow's Conditions: Existence and Correspondence Theorems for Voting Procedures and Social Welfare Functions." *Journal of Economic Theory* **10**, 187–217.

Savage, L. J. (1954). *The Foundations of Statistics.* New York: John Wiley and Sons. Revised and enlarged edition published 1972, New York: Dover Publications.

Schelling, Thomas C. (1950). *The Strategy of Conflict.* Cambridge, MA: Harvard University Press.

Scholes, Myron S., Mark A. Wolfson, Merle M. Erickson, Michelle L. Hanlon, Edward L. Mayhew, and Terrence J. Shevlin (2014). *Taxes and Business Strategy*, (6th edition). Westmont, IL: Cambridge Business Publishers.

Segal, Ilya (1999). "Contracting with Externalities." *Quarterly Journal of Economics* **114**, 337–88.

Selten, Reinhard (1965). "Spieltheortische Behandlung eines Oligopolmodells mit Nachfrageträgheit." *Zeitschrift für die Gesamte Staatswissenschaft* **12**, 301–24.

Selten, Reinhard (1975). "Re-Examination of the Perfectness Concept for Equilibrium Points in Extensive Games." *International Journal of Game Theory* **4**, 25–55.

Selten, Reinhard (1978). "The Chain Store Paradox." *Theory and Decision* **9**, 127–59.

Shaked, Avner, and John Sutton (1984). "Involuntary Unemployment as a Perfect Equilibrium in a Bargaining Model." *Econometrica* **52**, 1351–64.

Shapley, Lloyd S. (1951). "Notes on the n-Person Game, II: The Value of an n-Person Game." Project RAND Research Memorandum #670. Santa Monica, CA: RAND Corporation. (Available as download onlline.)

Shapley, Lloyd S., and Martin Shubik (1971). "The Assignment Game I: The Core." *International Journal of Game Theory* **1**, 111–130.

Shavell, Steven (1979). "Risk Sharing and Incentives in the Principal and Agent Relationship." *Bell Journal of Economics* **10**, 55–73.

Simon, Herbert A. (1951). "A Formal Theory of the Employment Relationship." *Econometrica* **19**, 293–305.

Smith, Adam (1776). *The Wealth of Nations*. London: W. Strahan and T. Cadell. *The Wealth of Nations* is available from a number of publishers.

Skrzypacz, Andrzej, and Hugo Hopenhayn (2004). "Tacit Collusion in Repeated Auctions." *Journal of Economic Theory* **114**, 153–69.

Sobel, Joel, and Ichiro Takahashi (1983). "A Multi-Stage Model of Bargaining." *Review of Economic Studies* **50**, 1151–72.

Sorin, Sylvain (1986). "On Repeated Games with Complete Information." *Mathematics of Operations Research* **11**, 147–60.

Spence, A. Michael (1974). *Market Signaling*. Cambridge, MA: Harvard University Press.

Stähl, I. (1972). *Bargaining Theory*. Stockholm: Stockholm School of Economics.

Stigler, George (1964). "A Theory of Oligopoly." *Journal of Political Economy* **72**, 44–61.

Stiglitz, Joseph (1977). 'Monopoly, Non-Linear Pricing and Imperfect Information: The Insurace Market." *Review of Economic Studies* **44**, 407–30

Stiglitz, Joseph, and Andrew Weiss (1990). "Sorting Out the Differences Between Signalling and Screening Models." Chapter 4 in M. Bacharach, M. Dempster, and J. Enos (eds.), *Mathematical Models in Economics*. Oxford: Oxford University.

Stokey, Nancy L. (1981). "Rational Expectations and Durable Good Pricing." *Bell Journal of Economics* **12**, 112–28.

Sugaya, Takuo (2022). "Folk Theorem in Repeated Games with Private Monitoring." *Review of Economic Studies* **89**, 2201–56.

Sultan, Ralph (1974). *Pricing in the Electrical Oligopoly.* Cambridge, MA: Harvard Business School.

Swinkels, Jeroen M. (1999). "Education Signalling with Preemptive Offers." *Review of Economic Studies* **66**, 949–70.

Thompson, F. B. (1952). "Equivalence of Games in Extensive Form." Santa Monica CA: RAND Corporation Research Memorandum.

Van Damme, Eric (1989). "Stable Equilibria and Forward Induction." *Journal of Economic Theory* **48**, 476–96.

Van Damme, Eric, Reinhard Selten, and Eyal Winter (1990). "Alternating Bid Bargaining with a Smallest Money Unit." *Games and Economic Behavior* **2**, 188–201.

Vickrey, William (1961). "Counterspeculation, Auctions, and Competitive Sealed Tenders." *Journal of Finance* **16**, 8–37.

von Neumann, John, and Oskar Morgenstern (1943). *Theory of Games and Economic Behavior.* Princeton: Princeton University Press.

Von Stackelberg, Heinrich (1934). *Marktform und Gleichgewicht.* Vienna: Julius Springer.

Watson, Joel (2007). "Contracts, Mechanism Design, and Technological Details." *Econometrica* **75**, 55–81.

Weiss, Andrew (1983). "A Sorting-Cum-Learning Model of Education." *Journal of Political Economy* **91**, 420–42,

Wilson, Charles (1977). "A Model of Insurance Markets with Incomplete Information." *Journal of Economic Theory* **16**, 167–207.

Wilson, Robert (1969). "Competitive Bidding with Disparate Information." *Management Science* **15**, 446–48.

Zermelo, E. (1913). "Über eine Adwendung der Megnenlehre aur der Theorie des Schachspiels." in *Proceedings of the Fifth International Congress on Mathematians.* Cambridge UK: Cambridge University Press, 501–504.

Index